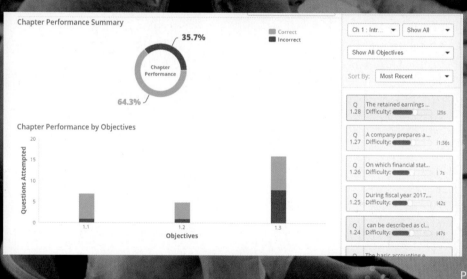

Business Statistics

Dedication

For Carolyn, Caycee, and Wendi

Business Statistics

For Contemporary Decision Making

Ninth Edition

KEN BLACK

University of Houston—Clear Lake

VICE PRESIDENT AND DIRECTOR	George Hoffman
EDITORIAL DIRECTOR	Veronica Visentin
EXECUTIVE EDITOR	Darren LaLonde
SPONSORING EDITOR	Jennifer Manias
EDITORIAL ASSISTANT	Ethan Lipson
PRODUCT DESIGN ASSOCIATE	Wendy Ashenberg
SENIOR CONTENT MANAGER	Dorothy Sinclair
SENIOR PRODUCTION EDITOR	Jane Lee Kaddu
EXECUTIVE MARKETING MANAGER	Christopher DeJohn
SENIOR DESIGNER	Wendy Lai
SENIOR PHOTO EDITOR	Billy Ray
COVER DESIGNER	Wendy Lai
PRODUCTION MANAGEMENT SERVICES	Aptara®
COVER IMAGE	shuoshu/iStockphoto

This book was set in 10/12 Stix by Aptara®, and printed and bound by RR Donnelley/Kendallville. The cover was printed by RR Donnelley/Kendallville.

This book is printed on acid free paper. ∞

Founded in 1807, John Wiley & Sons, Inc. has been a valued source of knowledge and understanding for more than 200 years, helping people around the world meet their needs and fulfill their aspirations. Our company is built on a foundation of principles that include responsibility to the communities we serve and where we live and work. In 2008, we launched a Corporate Citizenship Initiative, a global effort to address the environmental, social, economic, and ethical challenges we face in our business. Among the issues we are addressing are carbon impact, paper specifications and procurement, ethical conduct within our business and among our vendors, and community and charitable support. For more information, please visit our website: www.wiley.com/go/citizenship.

The inside back cover will contain printing identification and country of origin if omitted from this page. In addition, if the ISBN on the back cover differs from the ISBN on this page, the one on the back cover is correct.

ISBN-13: 978-1-119-32089-0

Printed in the United States of America.

10 9 8 7 6 5 4 3 2 1

The ninth edition of *Business Statistics for Contemporary Decision Making* continues the tradition of presenting and explaining the wonders of business statistics through the use of clear, complete, student-friendly pedagogy. The author and Wiley have vast ancillary resources available through WileyPLUS with which to complement the text in helping instructors effectively deliver this subject matter and in assisting students in their learning. With WileyPLUS instructors have far greater latitude in developing and delivering their course than ever before.

In the ninth edition, all the features of the eighth edition have been updated and changed as needed to reflect today's business world. Two new Decision Dilemmas located in Chapters 6 and 7 have been added to the ninth edition. Chapter 6, which introduces the student to continuous distributions including the normal curve, opens with a new Decision Dilemma titled "CSX Corporation," a leading rail transportation company in the U.S. Chapter 7 presents a new Decision Dilemma, "Toro" which discusses the Toro Company's 100 years of providing business solutions for the outdoor environment.

The ninth edition introduces five new cases. Chapter 2 contains the Southwest Airlines case. Chapter 6 presents a case on USAA, the United Services Automobile Association, which offers banking, investment, and insurance to people and families that serve, or served, in the United States military. Chapter 7 contains a new case on the 3M Company, best known for its adhesive products. Chapter 10 has a new case, Five Guys, a family hamburger restaurant chain with U.S. sales of $1.21 billion. Chapter 12 contains a new case on Caterpillar, Inc., the world's leading manufacturer of construction and mining equipment, diesel and natural gas engines, industrial gas turbines and diesel-electric locomotives.

All other cases in the ninth edition have been updated and edited for today's market. Three cases have been significantly revised. These include: "Statistics Describe the State of Business in India's Countryside" in Chapter 1, "Coca Cola Develops the African Market" in Chapter 3, and "Virginia Semiconductor" in Chapter 14.

Every chapter in the ninth edition contains one or two *Thinking Critically About Statistics in Business Today* features that give real-life examples of how the statistics presented in the chapter apply in the business world today. Each of these contains thought-provoking questions called *Things to Ponder* in which the objective is to effect critical thinking on behalf of the student and generate discussion involving critical thinking in the classroom. Some of these include: "Plastic Bags vs. Bringing Your Own in Japan," "Where Are Soft Drinks Sold?," "Recycling Statistics," "Probabilities in the Dry Cleaning Business," "Warehousing," and "Teleworking Facts."

This edition is designed and written for a two-semester introductory undergraduate business statistics course or an MBA-level introductory course. In addition, with 19 chapters, the ninth edition lends itself nicely to adaptation for a one-semester introductory business statistics course. The text is written with the assumption that the student has a college algebra mathematical background. No calculus is used in the presentation of material in the text.

An underlying philosophical approach to the text is that every statistical tool presented in the book has some business application. While the text contains statistical rigor, it is written so that the student can readily see that the proper application of statistics in the business world goes hand-in-hand with good decision making. In this edition, statistics are presented as a means for converting data into useful information that can be used to assist the business decision maker in making more thoughtful, information-based decisions. Thus, the text presents business statistics as "value-added" tools in the process of converting data into useful information.

Changes for the Ninth Edition

Chapters

In this edition, several changes have been made in an effort to improve the delivery and completeness of the text. The chapter organization is unchanged; however, the unit organization has been dropped. The text chapter organization allows for both one- and two-semester coverage. The first twelve chapters include the typical chapters covered in a one-semester course. The last seven chapters offer extended coverage allowing students to explore such topics as multiple regression, forecasting, analysis of categorical data, nonparametric statistics, statistical quality control, and decision analysis. For clarity and topic flow, some chapter topics have been combined and reduced in number. In Chapter 1, Statistics in Business has been included in the chapter introduction; and Variables and Data have been combined with Basic Statistical Concepts thereby reducing the number of chapter topics from four to two. In Chapter 4, Methods of Assigning Probabilities has been subsumed with Introduction to Probability.

Topical Changes

Sections and topics from the eighth edition remain virtually unchanged in the ninth edition with the exception that the former end of chapter feature, *Using the Computer*, has been removed from the text. Directions on how to use Excel and/or Minitab to compute statistics featured in the text are now housed exclusively in WileyPLUS.

In addition, in Chapter 14, the section on Logistic Regression has been significantly rewritten to reflect the changes in Minitab moving into version 17. Since much of the material on Logistic Regression is related to computer output, it was necessary to realign section 14.5 with current Minitab output for Logistic Regression. However, the conceptual explanations and the examples remain the same.

Decision Dilemma and the Decision Dilemma Solved

Each chapter of the ninth edition begins with a Decision Dilemma. Decision Dilemmas are real business vignettes that set the tone for each chapter by presenting a business dilemma and asking a number of managerial or statistical questions, the solutions to which require the use of techniques presented in the chapter. At the end of each chapter, a Decision Dilemma Solved feature discusses and answers the managerial and statistical questions posed in the Decision Dilemma using techniques from the chapter, thus bringing closure to the chapter. In the ninth edition, all decision dilemmas have been revised and updated. Solutions given in the Decision Dilemma Solved features have been revised for new data and for new versions of computer output.

In addition, two new Decision Dilemmas located in Chapters 6 and 7 have been added to the ninth edition. Chapter 6, which introduces the student to continuous distributions including the normal curve, opens with a new Decision Dilemma titled "CSX Corporation" This Decision Dilemma introduces the student to the CSX Corporation which is a leading rail transportation company in the U.S. Based in Jacksonville, Florida, the CSX Transportation network has 21,000 miles of track across the eastern half of the U.S. and two Canadian provinces. Analysis of this vignette focuses on average rail freight line-haul speed, terminal dwell time, and freight train arrival time. Students have to analyze data about these variables using probability distributions presented in Chapter 6.

Chapter 7, Sampling and Sampling Distributions, contains another new Decision Dilemma, "Toro", which discusses the Toro Company's 100 years of providing business solutions for the outdoor environment including turf, snow, and ground-engaging equipment along with irrigation and outdoor lighting solutions. The associated managerial and statistical questions tackle issues related to consumer and household spending on landscape services both in terms of dollars spent and population percentages.

Thinking Critically About Statistics in Business Today

Every chapter in the ninth edition contains at least one or two *Thinking Critically About Statistics in Business Today* features that give real-life examples of how the statistics presented in the chapter apply in the business world today. Each of these contains thought-provoking questions called Things to Ponder in which the objective is to effect critical thinking on behalf of the student and generate discussion involving critical thinking in the classroom. This approach to learning is in sync with various accreditation organizations and their current emphasis on developing critical thinking in our students. Some of these include: "Recycling Statistics," "Warehousing," "Canadian Grocery Shopping Statistics," "Beverage Consumption: America vs. Europe," "Are Facial Characteristics Correlated with CEO Traits?" "Assessing Property Values Using Multiple Regression," "Can Scrap Metal Prices Forecast the Economy?" "City Images of Cruise Destinations in the Taiwan Strait," and "Does an Iranian Auto Parts Manufacturer's Orientation Impact Innovation?" As an example, from "Beverage Consumption: America vs. Europe," Americans drink nearly five times as much soda as do Europeans and almost twice as much beer. On the other hand, Europeans drink more than twice as much tea (hot or cold), more than three times as much wine, and over four times as much tap water as Americans. Statistics show that the average American consumes forty-eight 12 oz. containers of carbonated soda per month compared to only 10 for Europeans. Europeans consume an average of sixteen 4 oz. containers of wine per month compared to an average of only five for Americans. One of the Things to Ponder questions is, "Can you think of some reasons why Americans consume more carbonated soda pop and beer than Europeans, but less wine, hot or iced tea, or tap water? Do you think that these outcomes may change in time?"

Cases

Every chapter in this text contains a unique business case. These business cases are more than just long problems; and in the discussion that follows the business scenario, several issues and questions are posed that can be addressed using techniques presented in the chapter. The ninth edition introduces five new, exciting cases. The Southwest Airlines case in chapter 2 discusses the company's rise from incorporation in 1967 to an operation with more than 3,600 flights a day, serving 94 destinations across the United States and six other countries. In Chapter 6, the reader is introduced to USAA, the United Services Automobile Association, which was founded in 1922 by 25 army officers who came together in San Antonio and decided to insure each other's automobiles. Offering banking, investment, and insurance to people and families that serve, or served, in the United States military, USAA currently has 10.7 million members, 42.6 million products, 26,300 employees and is ranked 57th in net worth ($25 billion) in Fortune 500 companies. Chapter 7 contains a new case on the 3M Company. Born as a small-scale mining company in 1902 and best known for its adhesive products, 3M is a global innovation company with over 100,000 patents, $31 billion in sales, and 90,000 employees. Five Guys, a hamburger restaurant chain whose philosophy is to serve fresh, hand-cooked burgers with "all the toppings you could stuff between fresh-baked buns" along with fresh-cut fries cooked in peanut oil, is the new case in Chapter 10. A family operation which opened its first restaurant in Arlington, Virginia in 1987 on $70,000 has grown to 1,163 U.S. restaurants with a U.S. system wide sales of $1.21 billion and units now existing in other countries. Chapter 12 contains a new case on Caterpillar, Inc. Caterpillar, headquartered in Peoria, Illinois, is an American corporation with a worldwide dealer network which sells machinery, engines, financial products and insurance. Caterpillar is the world's leading manufacturer of construction and mining equipment, diesel and natural gas engines, industrial gas turbines and diesel-electric locomotives.

All other cases in the ninth edition have been updated and edited for today's market. Three cases have been significantly revised. These include: "Statistics Describe the State of Business in India's Countryside" in Chapter 1, "Coca Cola Develops the African Market" in Chapter 3, and "Virginia Semiconductor" in Chapter 14. Here are some excerpts from one case, "The Container Store":

"In the late 1970s, Kip Tindell (chairman and CEO), Garrett Boone (Chairman Emeritus), and John Mullen (architect) drew up plans for a first-of-its-kind retail store specializing in storage solutions for both the home and the office. The vision that they created was realized when on July 1, 1978, the Container Store opened its doors in a small 1,600 square foot retail space in Dallas. The store was stocked with products that were devoted to simplifying people's lives, such as commercial parts bins, wire drawers, mailboxes, milk crates, wire leaf burners, and many others. Some critics even questioned that a store selling "empty boxes" could survive. However, the concept took off, and in the past 33 years, the company has expanded coast to coast in the United States with stores in 49 locations. Now headquartered in Coppell, Texas, the Container Store has 4,000 employees and annual revenues of over $650 million. Besides their innovative product mix, one of the keys to the success of the Container Store is the enthusiasm with which their employees work, the care that employees give to the customer, and employee knowledge of their products."

New Problems

There are 965 practice problems in the text. For ease of effort among adopters in moving from the eighth to the ninth edition, the number of problems and the problem numbers have remained the same. However, 105 of these problems have been updated to include the latest data and information available. Ten of the problems have been replaced with new problems.

Included in virtually every section of every chapter of the text is a demonstration problem which is an extra example containing both a problem and its solution and is used as an additional pedagogical tool to supplement explanations and examples in the chapters. Virtually all example and demonstration problems in the ninth edition are business oriented and contain the most current data available.

As with the previous edition, problems are located at the end of most sections in the chapters. A significant number of additional problems are provided at the end of each chapter in the Supplementary Problems. The Supplementary Problems are "scrambled"—problems using the various techniques in the chapter are mixed—so that students can test themselves on their ability to discriminate and differentiate ideas and concepts.

Databases

Available with the ninth edition are nine databases that provide additional opportunities for students to apply the statistics presented in this text. These nine databases represent a wide variety of business areas, such as agribusiness, consumer spending, energy, finance, healthcare, international labor, manufacturing, and the stock market. Altogether, these databases contain 61 variables and 7,722 observations. The data are gathered from such reliable sources as the U.S. government's Bureau of Labor, the U.S. Department of Agriculture, the American Hospital Association, the Energy Information Administration, *Moody's Handbook of Common Stocks,* and the U.S. Census Bureau. Five of the nine databases contain time-series data. The databases are 12-Year Gasoline Database, Consumer Food Database, Manufacturing Database, International Labor Database, Financial Database, Energy Database, U.S. and International Stock Market Database, Hospital Database, and Agribusiness Time-Series Database.

Video Tutorials by Ken Black

An exciting feature of the ninth edition package that will impact the effectiveness of student learning in business statistics and significantly enhance the presentation of course material is the series of videotape tutorials by Ken Black. With the advent of online business statistics courses, increasingly large class sizes, and the number of commuter students who have very limited access to educational resources on business statistics, it is often difficult for students to get the learning assistance they need to bridge the gap between theory and application on their own. There are now 21 videotaped tutorial sessions on key difficult topics in business statistics delivered by Ken Black and available for all adopters on WileyPLUS. In addition, these tutorials can easily be uploaded for classroom usage to augment lectures and enrich classroom presentations. Because there is at least one video for each of the first 12 chapters, the instructor has the option to include at least one video in the template of each chapter's plan for most, if not all, of the course. While the video tutorials vary in length, a typical video is about 10 minutes in length. The 21 video tutorials are:

1. Chapter 1: Levels of Data Measurement
2. Chapter 2: Stem-and-Leaf Plot
3. Chapter 3: Computing Variance and Standard Deviation
4. Chapter 3: Understanding and Using the Empirical Rule
5. Chapter 4: Constructing and Solving Probability Tables
6. Chapter 4: Solving Probability Word Problems
7. Chapter 5: Solving Binomial Distribution Problems, Part I
8. Chapter 5: Solving Binomial Distribution Problems, Part II
9. Chapter 6: Solving Problems Using the Normal Curve

Features and Benefits

Each chapter of the ninth edition contains sections called Learning Objectives, a Decision Dilemma, Demonstration Problems, Section Problems, Thinking Critically About Statistics in Business Today, Decision Dilemma Solved, Chapter Summary, Key Terms, Formulas, Ethical Considerations, Supplementary Problems, Analyzing the Databases, and Case.

- **Learning Objectives.** Each chapter begins with a statement of the chapter's main learning objectives. This statement gives the reader a list of key topics that will be discussed and the goals to be achieved from studying the chapter.

- **Decision Dilemma.** At the beginning of each chapter, a short case describes a real company or business situation in which managerial and statistical questions are raised. In most Decision Dilemmas, actual data are given and the student is asked to consider how the data can be analyzed to answer the questions.

- **Demonstration Problems.** Virtually every section of every chapter in the ninth edition contains demonstration problems. A demonstration problem contains both an example problem and its solution, and is used as an additional pedagogical tool to supplement explanations and examples.

- **Section Problems.** There are 965 problems in the text. Problems for practice are found at the end of almost every section of the text. Most problems utilize real data gathered from a plethora of sources. Included here are a few brief excerpts from some of the real-life problems in the text: "*The Wall Street Journal* reported that 40% of all workers say they would change jobs for 'slightly higher pay.' In addition, 88% of companies say that there is a shortage of qualified job candidates." "In a study by Peter D. Hart Research Associates for the Nasdaq Stock Market, it was determined that 20% of all stock investors are retired people. In addition, 40% of all U.S. adults have invested in mutual funds." "A survey conducted for the Northwestern National Life Insurance Company revealed that 70% of American workers say job stress caused frequent health problems." "According to Padgett Business Services, 20% of all small-business owners say the most important advice for starting a business is to prepare for long hours and hard work. "According to Nielsen Media Research, approximately 86% of all U.S. households have High-definition television (HDTV). In addition, 49% of all U.S. households own Digital Video Recorders (DVR)."

- **Thinking Critically About Statistics in Business Today.** Every chapter in the ninth edition contains at least one Thinking Critically About Statistics in Business Today feature. These focus boxes contain an interesting application of how techniques of that particular chapter are used in the business world today and ask probing questions of the student. They are usually based on real companies, surveys, or published research.

- **Decision Dilemma Solved.** Situated at the end of the chapter, the Decision Dilemma Solved feature addresses the managerial and statistical questions raised in the Decision Dilemma. Data given in the Decision Dilemma are analyzed computationally and by computer using techniques presented in the chapter. Answers to the managerial and statistical questions raised in the Decision Dilemma are arrived at by applying chapter concepts, thus bringing closure to the chapter.

- **Chapter Summary.** Each chapter concludes with a summary of the important concepts, ideas, and techniques of the chapter. This feature can serve as a preview of the chapter as well as a chapter review.

- **Key Terms.** Important terms are bolded and their definitions italicized throughout the text as they are discussed. At the end of the chapter, a list of the key terms from the chapter is presented. In addition, these terms appear with their definitions in the end-of-book glossary.

- **Formulas.** Important formulas in the text are highlighted to make it easy for a reader to locate them. At the end of the chapter, most of the chapter's formulas are listed together as a handy reference.

- **Ethical Considerations.** Each chapter contains an Ethical Considerations feature that is very timely, given the serious breach of ethics and lack of moral leadership of some business executives in recent years. With the abundance of statistical data and analysis, there is considerable potential for the misuse of statistics in business dealings. The important Ethical Considerations feature underscores this potential misuse by discussing such topics as lying with statistics, failing to meet statistical assumptions, and failing to include pertinent information for decision makers. Through this feature, instructors can begin to integrate the topic of ethics with applications of business statistics. Here are a few excerpts from Ethical Considerations features: "It is unprofessional and unethical to draw cause-and-effect conclusions just because two variables are correlated." "The business researcher needs to conduct the experiment in an environment such that as many concomitant variables are controlled as possible. To the extent that this is not done, the researcher has an ethical responsibility to report that fact in the findings." "The reader is warned that the value lambda is assumed to be constant in a Poisson distribution experiment. Business researchers may produce spurious results if the value of lambda is used throughout a study, but because the study is conducted during different time periods, the value of lambda is actually changing." "In describing a body of data to an audience, it is best to use whatever statistical measures it takes to present a 'full' picture of the data. By limiting the descriptive measures used, the business researcher may give the audience only part of the picture and skew the way the receiver understands the data."

- **Supplementary Problems.** At the end of each chapter is an extensive set of additional problems. The Supplementary Problems are divided into three groups: Calculating the Statistics, which are strictly computational problems; Testing Your Understanding, which are problems for application and understanding; and Interpreting the Output, which are problems that require the interpretation and analysis of software output.

- **Analyzing the Databases.** There are nine major databases located on the student companion Web site that accompanies the ninth edition and in WileyPLUS. The end-of-chapter Analyzing the Databases section contains several questions/problems that require the application of techniques from the chapter to data in the variables of the databases. It is assumed that most of these questions/problems will be solved using a computer.

- **Case.** Each chapter has an end-of-chapter case based on a real company. These cases give the student an opportunity to use statistical concepts and techniques presented in the chapter to solve a business dilemma. Some cases feature very large companies—such as Shell Oil, Coca-Cola, or Colgate Palmolive. Others pertain to smaller businesses—such as Virginia Semiconductor, The Clarkson Company, or DeBourgh—that have overcome obstacles to survive and thrive. Most cases include raw data for analysis and questions that encourage the student to use several of the techniques presented in the chapter. In many cases, the student must analyze software output in order to reach conclusions or make decisions.

WileyPLUS

WileyPLUS with ORION is a research-based, online environment for effective teaching and learning. *WileyPLUS* builds students' confidence because it takes the guesswork out of studying by providing students with a clear roadmap: what to do, how to do it, if they did it right. This interactive approach focuses on:

Design Research-based design is based on proven instructional methods. Content is organized into small, more accessible amounts of information, helping students build better time management skills.

Engagement Students can visually track their progress as they move through the material at a pace that is right for them. Engaging in individualized self-quizzes followed by immediate feedback helps to sustain their motivation to learn.

Outcomes Self-assessment lets students know the exact outcome of their effort at any time. Advanced reporting allows instructors to easily spot trends in the usage and performance data of their class in order to make more informed decisions.

With *WileyPLUS*, students will always know:

- What to do: Features, such as the course calendar, help students stay on track and manage their time more effectively.
- How to do it: Instant feedback and personalized learning plans are available 24/7.
- If they're doing it right: Self-evaluation tools take the guesswork out of studying and help students focus on the right materials.

WileyPLUS for *Business Statistics, Ninth Edition* includes numerous valuable resources, among them:

- **Ebook.** The complete text is available on WileyPLUS with learning links to various features and tools to assist students in their learning.
- **Videos.** There are 21 videos of the author explaining concepts and demonstrating how to work problems for some of the more difficult topics.
- **Applets.** Statistical applets are available, affording students the opportunity to learn concepts by iteratively experimenting with various values of statistics and parameters and observing the outcomes.
- **Learning Activities.** There are numerous learning activities to help the student better understand concepts and key terms. These activities have been developed to make learning fun, enjoyable, and challenging.
- **Data Sets.** Virtually all problems in the text along with the case problems and the databases are available to students in both Excel and Minitab format.
- **Animations.** To aid students in understanding complex interactions, selected figures from the text that involve dynamic activity have been animated. Students can download these animated figures and run them to improve their understanding of dynamic processes.
- **Flash Cards.** Key terms will be available to students in flash card format along with their definition.
- **Student Study Manual.** Complete solutions to all odd-numbered questions.
- **Demo Problems.** Step-by-step solved problems for each chapter.
- **ORION.** This adaptive, personalized learning experience delivers easy-to-use analytics so you can see exactly where your students excel and where they need help.
  - **Diagnose Early.** Simply by assigning ORION, you can diagnose the real-time proficiency of each student and see the areas that need reinforcement.

- **Facilitate Engagement.** With ORION's adaptive practice, students can interact with each other as they think more deeply about concepts at hand.
- **Measure Outcomes.** ORION helps you measure students' engagement and proficiency throughout the course so that you can easily assess how things are going at any point in time.

Ancillary Teaching and Learning Materials

www.wiley.com/college/black

Students' Companion Site

The student companion Web site contains:

- All databases in both Excel and Minitab formats for easy access and use.
- Excel and Minitab files of data from all text problems and all cases. Instructors and students now have the option of analyzing any of the data sets using the computer.
- A section on Advanced Exponential Smoothing Techniques (from Chapter 15) that offers the instructor an opportunity to delve deeper into exponential smoothing if so desired, and derivation of the slope and intercept formulas from Chapter 12.
- A tutorial on summation theory.

Instructor's Resource Kit

All instructor ancillaries are provided on the Instructor Resource Site. Included in this convenient format are:

- **Instructor's Manual.** Prepared by Ken Black, this manual contains the worked-out solutions to virtually all problems in the text. In addition, this manual contains chapter objectives, chapter outlines, chapter teaching strategies, and solutions to the cases.
- **PowerPoint Presentation Slides.** The presentation slides, contain graphics to help instructors create stimulating lectures. The PowerPoint slides may be adapted using PowerPoint software to facilitate classroom use.
- **Test Bank.** The Test Bank includes multiple-choice questions for each chapter. The Test Bank is provided in Microsoft Word format as well as in a Computerized Test Bank.

Acknowledgments

John Wiley & Sons and I would like to thank the reviewers and advisors who cared enough and took the time to provide us with their excellent insights and advice, which was used to reshape and mold the text into the ninth edition.

As always, I wish to recognize my colleagues at the University of Houston–Clear Lake for their continued interest and support of this project. In particular, I want to thank William Staples, president; Carl Stockton, provost; and Ted Cummings, dean of the School of Business for their personal interest in the book and their administrative support. A special thanks goes to Brent Goucher, my videographer, for his guidance, artistic direction, and patience in filming the videos.

There are several people within the John Wiley & Sons publishing group whom I would like to thank for their invaluable assistance on this project. These include: Lise Johnson, Darren LaLonde, Jennifer Manias, Wendy Ashenberg, Ethan Lipson, Jane Lee Kaddu, and Wendy Lai.

I want to express a special appreciation to my wife of 48 years, Carolyn, who is the love of my life and continues to provide both professional and personal support in my writing. Thanks also to my daughters, Wendi and Caycee, for their patience, love, and support.

—KEN BLACK

About the Author

KEN BLACK is currently professor of decision sciences in the School of Business at the University of Houston–Clear Lake. Born in Cambridge, Massachusetts, and raised in Missouri, he earned a bachelor's degree in mathematics from Graceland University, a master's degree in math education from the University of Texas at El Paso, a Ph.D. in business administration (management science), and a Ph.D. in educational research from the University of North Texas.

Since joining the faculty of UHCL in 1979, Professor Black has taught all levels of statistics courses, forecasting, management science, market research, and production/operations management. In 2005, he was awarded the President's Distinguished Teaching Award for the university. He has published over 20 journal articles and 20 professional papers, as well as two textbooks: *Business Statistics: An Introductory Course* and *Business Statistics for Contemporary Decision Making*. Black has consulted for many different companies, including Aetna, the city of Houston, NYLCare, AT&T, Johnson Space Center, Southwest Information Resources, UTMB, and Doctors Hospital at Renaissance. Black is active in the quality movement and is a certified Master Black Belt in Lean Six Sigma.

Ken Black and his wife, Carolyn, have two daughters, Caycee and Wendi. His hobbies include playing the guitar, reading, and traveling.

Brief Contents

CONTENTS

12 Simple Regression Analysis and Correlation   424

13 Multiple Regression Analysis   473

14 Building Multiple Regression Models   501

CHAPTER 1

Introduction to Statistics

LEARNING OBJECTIVES

The primary objective of Chapter 1 is to introduce you to the world of statistics, thereby enabling you to:

1. List quantitative and graphical examples of statistics within a business context.

2. Define important statistical terms, including population, sample, and parameter, as they relate to descriptive and inferential statistics.

3. Explain the difference between variables, measurement, and data.

4. Compare the four different levels of data: nominal, ordinal, interval, and ratio.

Decision Dilemma

Statistics Describe the State of Business in India's Countryside

India is the second largest country in the world with more than 1.25 billion people. More than 70% of the people live in rural areas scattered about the countryside in 650,000 villages. In fact, it can be said that one in every 10 people in the world live in rural India. While it has a per capita income of less than $1 (U.S.) per day, rural India, which has been described in the past as poor and semi-illiterate, now contributes to about one-half of the country's gross national product (GNP). However, rural India still has the most households in the world without electricity, over 300,000.

Despite its poverty and economic disadvantages, there are compelling reasons for companies to market their goods and services to rural India. The market of rural India has been growing at five times the rate of the urban India market. There is increasing agricultural productivity leading to growth in disposable income, and there is a reduction in the gap between the tastes of urban and rural customers. The literacy level is increasing, and people are becoming more conscious about their lifestyles and opportunities for a better life.

Around 60% of all middle-income households in India are in rural areas and more than one-third of all rural households in India now have a main source of income other than farming. Virtually every home has a radio, about one-third have a television, and more than one-half of rural households benefit from banking services. Forty-two percent of the people living in India's villages and small towns use toothpastes and that proportion is increasing as rural income rises and as there is greater awareness about oral hygiene.

© Hemis/Alamy Stock Photo

In rural India, consumers are gaining more disposable income due to the movement of manufacturing jobs to rural areas. It is estimated that nearly 75% of the factories that opened in India in the past decade were built in rural areas. Products that are doing well in sales to people in rural India include televisions, fans, bicycles, bath soap, two- or three-wheelers, cars, and many others. According to MART, a New Delhi-based research organization, rural India buys 46% of all soft drinks and 49% of motorcycles sold in India. Because of such factors, many U.S. and Indian firms such as Microsoft, General Electric, Kellogg's, Colgate-Palmolive, Idea Cellular, Hindustan Lever, Godrej, Nirma Chemical Works, Novartis, Dabur, Tata Motors, and Vodafone India have entered the rural Indian market with enthusiasm. Marketing to rural customers often involves persuading them to try and to adopt products that they may not have used before. Rural India is a huge, relatively untapped market for businesses. However, entering such a market is not without risks and obstacles. The dilemma facing companies is whether to enter this marketplace and, if so, to what extent and how.

MANAGERIAL AND STATISTICAL QUESTIONS

1. Are the statistics presented in this report exact figures or estimates?

2. How and where could researchers have gathered such data?

3. In measuring the potential of the rural India marketplace, what other statistics could have been gathered?

4. What levels of data measurement are represented by data on rural India?

5. How can managers use these and other statistics to make better decisions about entering this marketplace?

Source: Adapted from "Marketing to Rural India: Making the Ends Meet," March 8, 2007, in *India Knowledge@Wharton*, http://knowledge. wharton.upenn.edu/india/article.cfm?articleid=4172; "Rural Segment Quickly Catching Up", September 2015, IBEF (India Brand Equity Foundation) at: www.ibef.org/industry/indian-rural-market.aspx; "Unlocking the Wealth in Rural Markets", June 2014, *Harvard Business Review* at: https://hbr.org/2014/06/unlocking-the-wealth-in-rural-markets; "Much of Rural India Still Waits for Electricity", October 2013, University of Washington, at: artsci.washington.edu/news/2013-10/much-rural-india-still-waits-electricity

Every minute of the working day, decisions are made by businesses around the world that determine whether companies will be profitable and growing or whether they will stagnate and die. Most of these decisions are made with the assistance of information gathered about the marketplace, the economic and financial environment, the workforce, the competition, and other factors. Such information usually comes in the form of data or is accompanied by data. Business statistics provides the tool through which such data are collected, analyzed, summarized, and presented to facilitate the decision-making process, and business statistics plays an important role in the ongoing saga of decision making within the dynamic world of business.

Virtually every area of business uses statistics in decision making. Here are some recent examples:

- According to a national survey of independent business owners conducted by the Institute for Local Self-Reliance in partnership with the Advocates for Independent Business coalition, when asked "Which two public policy changes would most help your business?" (retailers only), 40% said "Pass the Marketplace Fairness Act" and 38% said "Cap Credit Card Swipe Fees".

- A survey of 1465 workers by Hotjobs reports that 55% of workers believe that the quality of their work is perceived the same when they work remotely as when they are physically in the office.

- A survey of 477 executives by the Association of Executive Search Consultants determined that 48% of men and 67% of women say they are more likely to negotiate for less business travel compared with five years ago.

- A global Family Business Survey of 2,378 respondents sponsored by PwC reported that 65% of family businesses reported growth in the last twelve months and 49% of respondents are apprehensive about their ability to recruit skilled staff in the next twelve months.

- A Deloitte Retail "Green" survey of 1080 adults revealed that 54% agreed that plastic, non-compostable shopping bags should be banned.

- A study of consumer electronics spending by a 2,500 member on-line panel of the NPD group showed that consumers expect to spend $555, on average, per person on new consumer electronics devices this year.

You can see from these few examples that there is a wide variety of uses and applications of statistics in business. Note that in most of these examples, business researchers have conducted a study and provided us rich and interesting information.

In this text we will examine several types of graphs for depicting data as we study ways to arrange or structure data into forms that are both meaningful and useful to decision makers. We will learn about techniques for sampling from a population that allow studies of the business world to be conducted more inexpensively and in a more timely manner. We will explore various ways to forecast future values and examine techniques for predicting trends. This text also includes many statistical tools for testing hypotheses and for estimating population values. These and many other exciting statistics and statistical techniques await us on this journey through business statistics. Let us begin.

1.1   Basic Statistical Concepts

Business statistics, like many areas of study, has its own language. It is important to begin our study with an introduction of some basic concepts in order to understand and communicate about the subject. We begin with a discussion of the word *statistics*. The word *statistics* has many different meanings in our culture. *Webster's Third New International Dictionary* gives a comprehensive definition of statistics as *a science dealing with the collection, analysis, interpretation, and presentation of numerical data*. Viewed from this perspective, statistics includes all the topics presented in this text. **Figure 1.1** graphically displays the key elements of statistics.

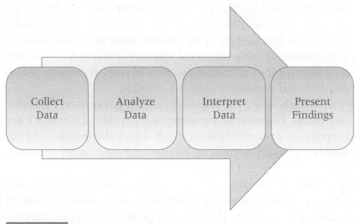

FIGURE 1.1   **The Key Elements of Statistics**

The study of statistics can be organized in a variety of ways. One of the main ways is to subdivide statistics into two branches: descriptive statistics and inferential statistics. To understand the difference between descriptive and inferential statistics, definitions of *population* and *sample* are helpful. *Webster's Third New International Dictionary* defines population as *a collection of persons, objects, or items of interest.* The population can be a widely defined category, such as "all automobiles," or it can be narrowly defined, such as "all Ford Mustang cars produced from 2014 to 2016." A population can be a group of people, such as "all workers presently employed by Microsoft," or it can be a set of objects, such as "all dishwashers produced on February 3, 2016, by the General Electric Company at the Louisville plant." The researcher defines the population to be whatever he or she is studying. When researchers *gather data from the whole population for a given measurement of interest,* they call it a census. Most people are familiar with the U.S. Census. Every 10 years, the government attempts to measure all persons living in this country.

A sample is *a portion of the whole* and, if properly taken, is representative of the whole. For various reasons (explained in Chapter 7), researchers often prefer to work with a sample of the population instead of the entire population. For example, in conducting quality-control experiments to determine the average life of lightbulbs, a lightbulb manufacturer might randomly sample only 75 lightbulbs during a production run. Because of time and money limitations, a human resources manager might take a random sample of 40 employees instead of using a census to measure company morale.

If a business analyst is *using data gathered on a group to describe or reach conclusions about that same group,* the statistics are called descriptive statistics. For example, if an instructor produces statistics to summarize a class's examination effort and uses those statistics to reach conclusions about that class only, the statistics are descriptive.

Many of the statistical data generated by businesses are descriptive. They might include number of employees on vacation during June, average salary at the Denver office, corporate sales for 2016, average managerial satisfaction score on a company-wide census of employee attitudes, and average return on investment for the Lofton Company for the years 1996 through 2016.

Another type of statistics is called inferential statistics. If a researcher *gathers data from a sample and uses the statistics generated to reach conclusions about the population from which the sample was taken,* the statistics are inferential statistics. The data gathered from the sample are used to infer something about a larger group. Inferential statistics are sometimes referred to as *inductive statistics.* The use and importance of inferential statistics continue to grow.

One application of inferential statistics is in pharmaceutical research. Some new drugs are expensive to produce, and therefore tests must be limited to small samples of patients. Utilizing inferential statistics, researchers can design experiments with small randomly selected samples of patients and attempt to reach conclusions and make inferences about the population.

Market researchers use inferential statistics to study the impact of advertising on various market segments. Suppose a soft drink company creates an advertisement depicting a dispensing machine that talks to the buyer, and market researchers want to measure the impact of the new advertisement on various age groups. The researcher could stratify the population into age categories ranging from young to old, randomly sample each stratum, and use inferential statistics to determine the effectiveness of the advertisement for the various age groups in the population. The advantage of using inferential statistics is that they enable the researcher to study effectively a wide range of phenomena without having to conduct a census. Most of the topics discussed in this text pertain to inferential statistics.

A *descriptive measure of the population* is called a parameter. Parameters are usually denoted by Greek letters. Examples of parameters are population mean (μ), population variance (σ^2), and population standard deviation (σ). A *descriptive measure of a sample* is called a statistic. Statistics are usually denoted by Roman letters. Examples of statistics are sample mean ($\overline{x}$), sample variance (s^2), and sample standard deviation (s).

Differentiation between the terms *parameter* and *statistic* is important only in the use of inferential statistics. A business researcher often wants to estimate the value of a parameter or conduct tests about the parameter. However, the calculation of parameters is usually either impossible or infeasible because of the amount of time and money required to take a census.

In such cases, the business researcher can take a random sample of the population, calculate a statistic on the sample, and infer by estimation the value of the parameter. The basis for inferential statistics, then, is the ability to make decisions about parameters without having to complete a census of the population.

For example, a manufacturer of washing machines would probably want to determine the average number of loads that a new machine can wash before it needs repairs. The parameter is the population mean or average number of washes per machine before repair. A company researcher takes a sample of machines, computes the number of washes before repair for each machine, averages the numbers, and estimates the population value or parameter by using the statistic, which in this case is the sample average. **Figure 1.2** demonstrates the inferential process.

Inferences about parameters are made under uncertainty. Unless parameters are computed directly from the population, the statistician never knows with certainty whether the estimates or inferences made from samples are true. In an effort to estimate the level of confidence in the result of the process, statisticians use probability statements. For this and other reasons, part of this text is devoted to probability (Chapter 4).

Business statistics is about measuring phenomena in the business world and organizing, analyzing, and presenting the resulting numerical information in such a way such that better, more informed business decisions can be made. Most business statistics studies contain variables, measurements, and data.

In business statistics, a **variable** is *a characteristic of any entity being studied that is capable of taking on different values*. Some examples of variables in business might include return on investment, advertising dollars, labor productivity, stock price, historical cost, total sales, market share, age of worker, earnings per share, miles driven to work, time spent in store shopping, and many, many others. In business statistics studies, most variables produce a measurement that can be used for analysis. A **measurement** is *when a standard process is used to assign numbers to particular attributes or characteristics of a variable*. Many measurements are obvious, such as time spent in a store shopping by a customer, age of the worker, or the number of miles driven to work. However, some measurements, such as labor productivity, customer satisfaction, and return on investment, have to be defined by the business researcher or by experts within the field. Once such measurements are recorded and stored, they can be denoted as "data." It can be said that **data** are *recorded measurements*. The processes of measuring and data gathering are basic to all that we do in business statistics. It is data that are analyzed by a business statistician in order to learn more about the variables being studied. Sometimes, sets of data are organized into databases as a way to store data or as a means for more conveniently analyzing data or comparing variables. Valid data

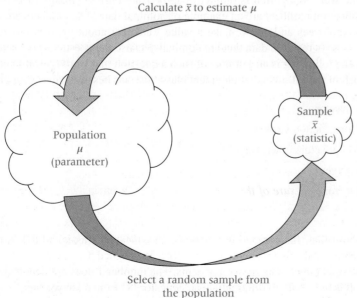

Calculate $\bar{x}$ to estimate μ

Population
μ
(parameter)

Sample
$\bar{x}$
(statistic)

Select a random sample from
the population

FIGURE 1.2   **The Inferential Process**

are the lifeblood of business statistics, and it is important that the business researcher give thoughtful attention to the creation of meaningful, valid data before embarking on analysis and reaching conclusions.

1.2 Data Measurement

Lecture Video

Millions of numerical data are gathered in businesses every day, representing myriad items. For example, numbers represent dollar costs of items produced, geographical locations of retail outlets, weights of shipments, and rankings of subordinates at yearly reviews. All such data should not be analyzed the same way statistically because the entities represented by the numbers are different. For this reason, the business researcher needs to know the *level of data measurement* represented by the numbers being analyzed.

The disparate use of numbers can be illustrated by the numbers 40 and 80, which could represent the weights of two objects being shipped, the ratings received on a consumer test by two different products, or football jersey numbers of a fullback and a wide receiver. Although 80 pounds is twice as much as 40 pounds, the wide receiver is probably not twice as big as the fullback! Averaging the two weights seems reasonable, but averaging the football jersey numbers makes no sense. The appropriateness of the data analysis depends on the level of measurement of the data gathered. The phenomenon represented by the numbers determines the level of data measurement. Four common levels of data measurement follow.

1. Nominal
2. Ordinal
3. Interval
4. Ratio

Nominal is the lowest level of data measurement followed by ordinal, interval, and ratio. Ratio is the highest level of data measurement, as shown in **Figure 1.3**.

Nominal Level

The *lowest level of data measurement* is the **nominal level**. Numbers representing nominal-level data (the word *level* often is omitted) can be *used only to classify or categorize*. Employee identification numbers are an example of nominal data. The numbers are used only to differentiate employees and not to make a value statement about them. Many demographic questions in surveys result in data that are nominal because the questions are used for classification only. The following is an example of such a question that would result in nominal data:

Which of the following employment classifications best describes your area of work?

Highest Level of Data Measurement

1. Educator
2. Construction worker
3. Manufacturing worker
4. Lawyer
5. Doctor
6. Other

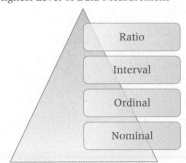

Lowest Level of Data Measurement

FIGURE 1.3 **Hierarchy of Levels of Data**

Suppose that, for computing purposes, an educator is assigned a 1, a construction worker is assigned a 2, a manufacturing worker is assigned a 3, and so on. These numbers should be used only to classify respondents. The number 1 does not denote the top classification. It is used only to differentiate an educator (1) from a lawyer (4).

Some other types of variables that often produce nominal-level data are sex, religion, ethnicity, geographic location, and place of birth. Social Security numbers, telephone numbers, employee ID numbers, and ZIP code numbers are further examples of nominal data. Statistical techniques that are appropriate for analyzing nominal data are limited. However, some of the more widely used statistics, such as the chi-square statistic, can be applied to nominal data, often producing useful information.

Ordinal Level

Ordinal-level data measurement is higher than the nominal level. In addition to the nominal-level capabilities, ordinal-level measurement can be used to rank or order people or objects. For example, using ordinal data, a supervisor can evaluate three employees by ranking their productivity with the numbers 1 through 3. The supervisor could identify one employee as the most productive, one as the least productive, and one as somewhere between by using ordinal data. However, the supervisor could not use ordinal data to establish that the intervals between the employees ranked 1 and 2 and between the employees ranked 2 and 3 are equal; that is, she could not say that the differences in the amount of productivity between workers ranked 1, 2, and 3 are necessarily the same. With ordinal data, the distances or spacing represented by consecutive numbers are not always equal.

Some questionnaire Likert-type scales are considered by many researchers to be ordinal in level. The following is an example of one such scale:

This computer tutorial is	___	___	___	___	___
	not helpful	somewhat helpful	moderately helpful	very helpful	extremely helpful
	1	2	3	4	5

When this survey question is coded for the computer, only the numbers 1 through 5 will remain, not the adjectives. Virtually everyone would agree that a 5 is higher than a 4 on this scale and that ranking responses is possible. However, most respondents would not consider the differences between not helpful, somewhat helpful, moderately helpful, very helpful, and extremely helpful to be equal.

Mutual funds as investments are sometimes rated in terms of risk by using measures of default risk, currency risk, and interest rate risk. These three measures are applied to investments by rating them as having high, medium, and low risk. Suppose high risk is assigned a 3, medium risk a 2, and low risk a 1. If a fund is awarded a 3 rather than a 2, it carries more risk, and so on. However, the differences in risk between categories 1, 2, and 3 are not necessarily equal. Thus, these measurements of risk are only ordinal-level measurements. Another example of the use of ordinal numbers in business is the ranking of the top 50 most admired companies in *Fortune* magazine. The numbers ranking the companies are only ordinal in measurement. Certain statistical techniques are specifically suited to ordinal data, but many other techniques are not appropriate for use on ordinal data. For example, it does not make sense to say that the average of "moderately helpful" and "very helpful" is "moderately helpful and a half."

Because nominal and ordinal data are often derived from imprecise measurements such as demographic questions, the categorization of people or objects, or the ranking of items, *nominal and ordinal data* are **nonmetric data** and are sometimes referred to as *qualitative data.*

Interval Level

Interval-level data measurement is the *next to the highest level of data in which the distances between consecutive numbers have meaning and the data are always numerical.* The distances represented by the differences between consecutive numbers are equal; that is, interval data have equal intervals. An example of interval measurement is Fahrenheit temperature. With Fahrenheit temperature numbers, the temperatures can be ranked, and the amounts of heat between consecutive readings, such as 20°, 21°, and 22°, are the same.

In addition, with interval-level data, the zero point is a matter of convention or convenience and not a natural or fixed zero point. Zero is just another point on the scale and does not mean the absence of the phenomenon. For example, zero degrees Fahrenheit is not the lowest possible temperature. Some other examples of interval-level data are the percentage change in employment, the percentage return on a stock, and the dollar change in stock price.

Ratio Level

Ratio-level data measurement is *the highest level of data measurement.* Ratio data *have the same properties as interval data,* but ratio data have an *absolute zero,* and *the ratio of two numbers is meaningful.* The notion of absolute zero means that zero is fixed, and *the zero value in the data represents the absence of the characteristic being studied.* The value of zero cannot be arbitrarily assigned because it represents a fixed point. This definition enables the statistician to create *ratios* with the data.

Examples of ratio data are height, weight, time, volume, and Kelvin temperature. With ratio data, a researcher can state that 180 pounds of weight is twice as much as 90 pounds or, in other words, make a ratio of 180 : 90. Many of the data measured by valves or gauges in industry are ratio data.

Other examples in the business world that are ratio level in measurement are production cycle time, work measurement time, passenger miles, number of trucks sold, complaints per 10,000 fliers, and number of employees.

Because interval- and ratio-level data are usually gathered by precise instruments often used in production and engineering processes, in national standardized testing, or in standardized accounting procedures, they are called **metric data** and are sometimes referred to as *quantitative* data.

Comparison of the Four Levels of Data

Figure 1.4 shows the relationships of the usage potential among the four levels of data measurement. The concentric squares denote that each higher level of data can be analyzed by any of the techniques used on lower levels of data but, in addition, can be used in other statistical techniques. Therefore, ratio data can be analyzed by any statistical technique applicable to the other three levels of data plus some others.

Nominal data are the most limited data in terms of the types of statistical analysis that can be used with them. Ordinal data allow the researcher to perform any analysis that can be done with nominal data and some additional analyses. With ratio data, a statistician can make ratio comparisons and appropriately do any analysis that can be performed on nominal, ordinal, or interval data. Some statistical techniques require ratio data and cannot be used to analyze other levels of data.

Statistical techniques can be separated into two categories: parametric statistics and nonparametric statistics. **Parametric statistics** require that data be interval or ratio. If the data are nominal or ordinal, **nonparametric statistics** must be used. Nonparametric statistics can also be used to analyze interval or ratio data. This text focuses largely on parametric statistics, with the exception of Chapter 16 and Chapter 17, which contain nonparametric techniques. Thus much of the material in this text requires that data be interval or ratio data.

Figure 1.5 contains a summary of metric data and nonmetric data.

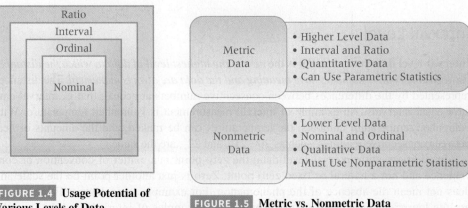

FIGURE 1.4 **Usage Potential of Various Levels of Data**

FIGURE 1.5 **Metric vs. Nonmetric Data**

DEMONSTRATION PROBLEM 1.1

Because of increased competition for patients among providers and the need to determine how providers can better serve their clientele, hospital administrators sometimes administer a quality satisfaction survey to their patients after the patient is released. The following types of questions are sometimes asked on such a survey. These questions will result in what level of data measurement?

1. How long ago were you released from the hospital?

2. Which type of unit were you in for most of your stay?

__Coronary care

__Intensive care

__Maternity care

__Medical unit

__Pediatric/children's unit

__Surgical unit

3. In choosing a hospital, how important was the hospital's location?

(circle one)

Very	Somewhat	Not Very	Not at All
Important	Important	Important	Important

4. What was your body temperature when you were admitted to the hospital?

5. Rate the skill of your doctor:

__Excellent   __Very Good   __Good   __Fair   __Poor

Solution: Question 1 is a time measurement with an absolute zero and is therefore ratio-level measurement. A person who has been out of the hospital for two weeks has been out twice as long as someone who has been out of the hospital for one week.

Question 2 yields nominal data because the patient is asked only to categorize the type of unit he or she was in. This question does not require a hierarchy or ranking of the type of unit. Questions 3 and 5 are likely to result in ordinal-level data. Suppose a number is assigned the descriptors in these two questions. For question 3, "very important" might be assigned a 4, "somewhat important" a 3, "not very important" a 2, and "not at all important" a 1. Certainly, the higher the number, the more important is the hospital's location. Thus, these responses can be ranked by selection. However, the increases in importance from 1 to 2 to 3 to 4 are not necessarily equal. This same logic applies to the numeric values assigned in question 5. In question 4, body temperature, if measured on a Fahrenheit or Celsius scale, is interval in measurement.

Statistical Analysis Using the Computer: Excel and Minitab

The advent of the modern computer opened many new opportunities for statistical analysis. The computer allows for storage, retrieval, and transfer of large data sets. Furthermore, computer software has been developed to analyze data by means of sophisticated statistical techniques. Some widely used statistical techniques, such as multiple regression, are so tedious and cumbersome to compute manually that they were of little practical use to researchers before computers were developed.

Business statisticians use many popular statistical software packages, including Minitab, SAS, and SPSS. Many computer spreadsheet software packages also have the capability of analyzing data statistically. In this text, the computer statistical output presented is from both the Minitab and the Microsoft Excel software.

Thinking Critically About Statistics in Business Today

Cellular Phone Use in Japan

The Communications and Information Network Association of Japan (CIAJ) conducts an annual study of cellular phone use in Japan. This past year a survey was taken of 1200 mobile phone users split evenly between men and women and almost equally over six age brackets of people residing in the larger Tokyo and Osaka metropolitan areas. The study produced several interesting findings. Of the respondents, 76.8% said that their main-use terminal was a smartphone while 23.2% said it was a feature phone. Of the smartphone users, 49.2% reported that their second device was a tablet (with a telecom subscription) compared to the previous year where 36.7% said that a tablet was their second device. Survey participants were asked what are the decisive factors in purchasing smart phone? The number one decisive factor was battery life, selected by over 70%, followed by manufacturer/brand selected by 67.5%. Survey participants who owned feature phones were asked the same question and the number one decisive factor was monthly payment cost (84.7%) followed by purchase price of handset (84.4%). In terms of usage of smart phone features and services, the number one most popular use was "searching the Internet" (90.2%) followed by "shooting still photos with camera" selected by 88.7%.

THINGS TO PONDER

1. In what way was this study an example of inferential statistics?
2. What is the population of this study?
3. What are some of the variables being studied?
4. How might a study such as this yield information that is useful to business decision makers?

Source: "CIAJ Releases Report on the Study of Mobile Phone Use", July 29, 2015 at http://www.ciaj.or.jp/en/news/news2015/2015/07/29/951/

Decision Dilemma Solved

Statistics Describe the State of Business in India's Countryside

Several statistics were reported in the Decision Dilemma about rural India. The authors of the sources from which the Decision Dilemma was drawn never stated whether the reported statistics were based on actual data drawn from a census of rural India households or on estimates taken from a sample of rural households. If the data came from a census, then the totals, averages, and percentages presented in the Decision Dilemma are parameters. If, on the other hand, the data were gathered from samples, then they are statistics. Although governments especially do conduct censuses and at least some of the reported numbers could be parameters, more often than not, such data are gathered from samples of people or items. For example, in rural India, the government, academicians, or business researchers could have taken random samples of households, gathering consumer statistics that are then used to estimate population parameters, such as percentage of households with televisions, and so forth.

In conducting research on a topic like consumer consumption in rural India, there is potential for a wide variety of statistics to be gathered that represent several levels of data. For example, ratio-level measurements on items such as income, number of children, age of household heads, number of livestock, and grams of toothpaste consumed per year might be obtained. On the other hand, if researchers use a Likert scale (1-to-5 measurements) to gather responses about the interests, likes, and preferences of rural India consumers, an ordinal-level measurement would be obtained, as would the ranking of products or brands in market research studies. Other variables, such as geographic location, sex, occupation, or religion, are usually measured with nominal data.

The decision to enter the rural India market is not just a marketing decision. It involves production capacity and schedule issues, transportation challenges, financial commitments, managerial growth or reassignment, accounting issues (accounting for rural India may differ from techniques used in traditional markets), information systems, and other related areas. With so much on the line, company decision makers need as much relevant information available as possible. In this Decision Dilemma, it is obvious to the decision maker that rural India is still quite poor and illiterate. Its capacity as a market is great. The statistics on the increasing sales of a few personal-care products look promising. What are the future forecasts for the earning power of people in rural India? Will major cultural issues block the adoption of the types of products that companies want to sell there? The answers to these and many other interesting and useful questions can be obtained by the appropriate use of statistics. The 800 million people living in rural India represent the second largest group of people in the world. It certainly is a market segment worth studying further.

Ethical Considerations

With the abundance and proliferation of statistical data, potential misuse of statistics in business dealings is a concern. It is, in effect, unethical business behavior to use statistics out of context. Unethical business people might use only selective data from studies to underscore their point, omitting statistics from the same studies that argue against their case. The results of statistical studies can be misstated or overstated to gain favor.

This chapter noted that if data are nominal or ordinal, then only nonparametric statistics are appropriate for analysis. The use of parametric statistics to analyze nominal and/or ordinal data is wrong and could be considered under some circumstances to be unethical.

In this text, each chapter contains a section on ethics that discusses how business people can misuse the techniques presented in the chapter in an unethical manner. As both users and producers, business students need to be aware of the potential ethical pitfalls that can occur with statistics.

Summary

Statistics is an important decision-making tool in business and is used in virtually every area of business. In this course, the word *statistics* is defined as the science of gathering, analyzing, interpreting, and presenting numerical data.

The study of statistics can be subdivided into two main areas: *descriptive statistics* and *inferential statistics*. Descriptive statistics result from gathering data from a body, group, or population and reaching conclusions only about that group. Inferential statistics are generated by gathering sample data from a group, body, or population and reaching conclusions about the larger group from which the sample was drawn.

Most business statistics studies contain variables, measurements, and data. A *variable* is a characteristic of any entity being studied that is capable of taking on different values. Examples of variables might include monthly household food spending, time between arrivals at a restaurant, and patient satisfaction rating. A *measurement* is when a standard process is used to assign numbers to particular attributes or characteristics of a variable. Measurements on monthly household food spending might be taken in dollars, time between arrivals might be measured in minutes, and patient satisfaction might be measured using a 5-point scale. *Data* are recorded measurements. It is data that are analyzed by business statisticians in order to learn more about the variables being studied.

The appropriate type of statistical analysis depends on the level of data measurement, which can be (1) *nominal,* (2) *ordinal,* (3) *interval,* or (4) *ratio.* Nominal is the lowest level, representing classification only of such data as geographic location, sex, or Social Security number. The next level is ordinal, which provides rank ordering measurements in which the intervals between consecutive numbers do not necessarily represent equal distances. Interval is the next to highest level of data measurement in which the distances represented by consecutive numbers are equal. The highest level of data measurement is ratio, which has all the qualities of interval measurement, but ratio data contain an absolute zero and ratios between numbers are meaningful. Interval and ratio data sometimes are called *metric* or *quantitative* data. Nominal and ordinal data sometimes are called *nonmetric* or *qualitative* data.

Two major types of inferential statistics are (1) *parametric statistics* and (2) *nonparametric statistics.* Use of parametric statistics requires interval or ratio data and certain assumptions about the distribution of the data. The techniques presented in this text are largely parametric. If data are only nominal or ordinal in level, nonparametric statistics must be used.

Key Terms

census	measurement	ordinal-level data	sample
data	metric data	parameter	statistic
descriptive statistics	nominal-level data	parametric statistics	statistics
inferential statistics	nonmetric data	population	variable
interval-level data	nonparametric statistics	ratio-level data	

Supplementary Problems

1.1. Give a specific example of data that might be gathered from each of the following business disciplines: accounting, finance, human resources, marketing, information systems, production, and management. An example in the marketing area might be "number of sales per month by each salesperson."

1.2 State examples of data that can be gathered for decision making purposes from each of the following industries: manufacturing, insurance, travel, retailing, communications, computing, agriculture, banking, and healthcare. An example in the travel industry might be the cost of business travel per day in various European cities.

1.3 Give an example of *descriptive* statistics in the recorded music industry. Give an example of how *inferential* statistics could be used in the recorded music industry. Compare the two examples. What makes them different?

1.4 Suppose you are an operations manager for a plant that manufactures batteries. Give an example of how you could use *descriptive* statistics to make better managerial decisions. Give an example of how you could use *inferential* statistics to make better managerial decisions.

1.5 There are many types of information that might help the manager of a large department store run the business more efficiently and better understand how to improve sales. Think about this in such areas as sales, customers, human resources, inventory, suppliers, etc., and list five variables that might produce information that could aid the manager in his or her job. Write a sentence or two describing each variable, and briefly discuss some numerical observations that might be generated for each variable.

1.6 Suppose you are the owner of a medium-sized restaurant in a small city. What are some variables associated with different aspects of the business that might be helpful to you in making business decisions about the restaurant? Name four of these variables, and for each variable, briefly describe a numerical observation that might be the result of measuring the variable.

1.7 Classify each of the following as nominal, ordinal, interval, or ratio data.

    a. The time required to produce each tire on an assembly line

    b. The number of quarts of milk a family drinks in a month

    c. The ranking of four machines in your plant after they have been designated as excellent, good, satisfactory, and poor

    d. The telephone area code of clients in the United States

    e. The age of each of your employees

    f. The dollar sales at the local pizza shop each month

    g. An employee's identification number

    h. The response time of an emergency unit

1.8 Classify each of the following as nominal, ordinal, interval, or ratio data.

    a. The ranking of a company in the *Fortune* 500

    b. The number of tickets sold at a movie theater on any given night

    c. The identification number on a questionnaire

    d. Per capita income

    e. The trade balance in dollars

    f. Profit/loss in dollars

    g. A company's tax identification

    h. The Standard & Poor's bond ratings of cities based on the following scales:

RATING	GRADE
Highest quality	AAA
High quality	AA
Upper medium quality	A
Medium quality	BBB
Somewhat speculative	BB
Low quality, speculative	B
Low grade, default possible	CCC
Low grade, partial recovery possible	CC
Default, recovery unlikely	C

1.9 The Rathburn Manufacturing Company makes electric wiring, which it sells to contractors in the construction industry. Approximately 900 electric contractors purchase wire from Rathburn annually. Rathburn's director of marketing wants to determine electric contractors' satisfaction with Rathburn's wire. He developed a questionnaire that yields a satisfaction score between 10 and 50 for participant responses. A random sample of 35 of the 900 contractors is asked to complete a satisfaction survey. The satisfaction scores for the 35 participants are averaged to produce a mean satisfaction score.

    a. What is the population for this study?

    b. What is the sample for this study?

    c. What is the statistic for this study?

    d. What would be a parameter for this study?

Analyzing the Databases

See **www.wiley.com/college/black**

Nine databases are available with this text, providing additional opportunities to apply the statistics presented in this course. These databases are located in WileyPLUS, and each is available in either Minitab or Excel format for your convenience. These nine databases represent a wide variety of business areas, such as agribusiness, consumer spending, energy, finance, healthcare, international labor, manufacturing, and the stock market. Altogether, these databases contain 61 variables and 7722 observations. The data are gathered from such reliable sources as the U.S. government's Bureau of Labor, the U.S. Department of Agriculture, the American Hospital Association, the Energy Information Administration, *Moody's Handbook of Common Stocks,* and the U.S. Census Bureau. Five of the nine databases contain time-series data. These databases are:

12-Year Gasoline Database

The 12-year time-series gasoline database contains monthly data for four variables: U.S. Gasoline Prices, OPEC Spot Price, U.S. Finished Motor Gasoline Production, and U.S. Natural Gas Wellhead Price. There are 137 data entries for each variable. U.S. Gasoline Prices are given in cents, the OPEC Spot Price is given in dollars per barrel, U.S. Finished Motor Gasoline Production is given in 1000 barrels per day, and U.S. Natural Gas Wellhead Price is given in dollars per 1000 cubic feet.

Consumer Food Database

The consumer food database contains five variables: Annual Food Spending per Household, Annual Household Income, Non-Mortgage Household Debt, Geographic Region of the U.S. of the Household, and Household Location. There are 200 entries for each variable in this database representing 200 different households from various regions and locations in the United States. Annual Food Spending per Household, Annual Household Income, and Non-Mortgage Household Debt are all given in dollars. The variable Region tells in which one of four regions the household resides. In this variable, the Northeast is coded as 1, the Midwest is coded 2, the South is coded as 3, and the West is coded as 4. The variable Location is coded as 1 if the household is in a metropolitan area and 2 if the household is outside a metro area. The data in this database were randomly derived and developed based on actual national norms.

Manufacturing Database

This database contains eight variables taken from 20 industries and 140 subindustries in the United States. Some of the industries are food products, textile mill products, furniture, chemicals, rubber products, primary metals, industrial machinery, and transportation equipment. The eight variables are Number of Employees, Number of Production

Workers, Value Added by Manufacture, Cost of Materials, Value of Industry Shipments, New Capital Expenditures, End-of-Year Inventories, and Industry Group. Two variables, Number of Employees and Number of Production Workers, are in units of 1000. Four variables, Value Added by Manufacture, Cost of Materials, New Capital Expenditures, and End-of-Year Inventories, are in million-dollar units. The Industry Group variable consists of numbers from 1 to 20 to denote the industry group to which the particular subindustry belongs. Value of Industry Shipments has been recoded to the following 1-to-4 scale.

1 = $0 to $4.9 billion
2 = $5 billion to $13.9 billion
3 = $14 billion to $28.9 billion
4 = $29 billion or more

International Labor Database

This time-series database contains the civilian unemployment rates in percent from seven countries presented yearly over a 40-year period. The data are published by the Bureau of Labor Statistics of the U.S. Department of Labor. The countries are the United States, Canada, Australia, Japan, France, Germany, and Italy.

Financial Database

The financial database contains observations on eight variables for 100 companies. The variables are Type of Industry, Total Revenues ($ millions), Total Assets ($ millions), Return on Equity (%), Earnings per Share ($), Average Yield (%), Dividends per Share ($), and Average Price per Earnings (P/E) ratio. The companies represent seven different types of industries. The variable Type displays a company's industry type as:

1 = apparel
2 = chemical
3 = electric power
4 = grocery
5 = healthcare products
6 = insurance
7 = petroleum

Energy Database

The time-series energy database consists of data on five energy variables over a period of 26 years. The five variables are U.S. Energy Consumption, World Crude Oil Production, U.S. Nuclear Electricity Generation, U.S. Coal Production, and U.S. Natural Dry Gas Production. U.S. Energy Consumption is given in quadrillion BTUs per year, World Crude Oil Production is given in million barrels per day, U.S. Nuclear Electricity Generation is given in billion kilowatt-hours, U.S. Coal Production is given in million short tons, and U.S. Natural Dry Gas Production is given in million cubic feet.

U.S. and International Stock Market Database

This database contains seven variables—three from the U.S. stock market and four from international stock markets—with data representing monthly averages of each over a period of five years resulting in 60 data points per variable. The U.S. stock market variables include the Dow Jones Industrial Average, the NASDAQ, and Standard & Poor's 500. The four international stock market variables of Nikkei 225, Hang Seng, FTSE 100, and IPC represent Japan, Hong Kong, United Kingdom, and Mexico.

Hospital Database

This database contains observations for 11 variables on U.S. hospitals. These variables include Geographic Region, Control, Service, Number of Beds, Number of Admissions, Census, Number of Outpatients, Number of Births, Total Expenditures, Payroll Expenditures, and Personnel.

The region variable is coded from 1 to 7, and the numbers represent the following regions:

1 = South
2 = Northeast
3 = Midwest
4 = Southwest
5 = Rocky Mountain
6 = California
7 = Northwest

Control is a type of ownership. Four categories of control are included in the database:

1 = government, nonfederal
2 = nongovernment, not-for-profit
3 = for-profit
4 = federal government

Service is the type of hospital. The two types of hospitals used in this database are:

1 = general medical
2 = psychiatric

The total expenditures and payroll variables are in units of $1000.

Agribusiness Time-Series Database

The agribusiness time-series database contains the monthly weight (in 1000 lbs.) of cold storage holdings for six different vegetables and for total frozen vegetables over a 14-year period. Each of the seven variables represents 168 months of data. The six vegetables are green beans, broccoli, carrots, sweet corn, onions, and green peas. The data are published by the National Agricultural Statistics Service of the U.S. Department of Agriculture.

Assignment

Use the databases to answer the following questions.

1. In the manufacturing database, what is the level of data for each of the following variables?

a. Number of Production Workers

b. Cost of Materials

c. Value of Industry Shipments

d. Industry Group

2. In the hospital database, what is the level of data for each of the following variables?

a. Region

b. Control

c. Number of Beds

d. Personnel

3. In the financial database, what is the level of data for each of the following variables?

a. Type of Industry

b. Total Assets

c. P/E Ratio

Case

Digiorno Pizza: Introducing a Frozen Pizza to Compete with Carry-Out

Kraft Foods successfully introduced DiGiorno Pizza into the marketplace in 1996, with first year sales of $120 million, followed by $200 million in sales in 1997. It was neither luck nor coincidence that DiGiorno Pizza was an instant success. Kraft conducted extensive research about the product and the marketplace before introducing this product to the public. Many questions had to be answered before Kraft began production. For example, why do people eat pizza? When do they eat pizza? Do consumers believe that carry-out pizza is always more tasty?

SMI-Alcott conducted a research study for Kraft in which they sent out 1000 surveys to pizza lovers. The results indicated that people ate pizza during fun social occasions or at home when no one wanted to cook. People used frozen pizza mostly for convenience but selected carry-out pizza for a variety of other reasons, including quality and the avoidance of cooking. The Loran Marketing Group conducted focus groups for Kraft with women aged 25 to 54. Their findings showed that consumers used frozen pizza for convenience but wanted carry-out pizza taste. Kraft researchers realized that if they were to launch a successful frozen pizza that could compete with carry-out pizza, they had to develop a frozen pizza that (a) had restaurant takeout quality, (b) possessed flavor variety, (c) was fast and easy to prepare, and (d) had the convenience of freezer storage. To satisfy these seemingly divergent goals, Kraft developed DiGiorno Pizza, which rises in the oven as it cooks. This impressed focus group members; and in a series of blind taste tests conducted by Product Dynamics, DiGiorno Pizza beat out all frozen pizzas and finished second overall behind one carry-out brand.

DiGiorno Pizza has continued to grow in sales and market share over the years. By 2005, sales had topped the $600 million mark, and DiGiorno Pizza held nearly a quarter of the market share of frozen pizza sales. In each of the last two quarters of 2009, DiGiorno sales increased 20%. On January 6, 2010, Kraft agreed to sell its North American frozen pizza business, including its DiGiorno products, to Nestlé for $3.7 billion. According to data reported by Statista, DiGiorno was by far the top frozen pizza brand in the United States in 2015 with over $957 million in sales when compared to the next brand which had sales of $463 million.

Discussion

Think about the market research that was conducted by Kraft and the fact that it used several companies.

1. What are some of the populations that Kraft might have been interested in measuring for these studies? Did Kraft actually attempt to contact entire populations? What samples were taken? In light of these two questions, how was the inferential process used by Kraft in their market research? Can you think of any descriptive statistics that might have been used by Kraft in their decision-making process?

2. In the various market research efforts made by Kraft for DiGiorno, some of the possible measurements appear in the following list. Categorize these by level of data. Think of some other measurements that Kraft researchers might have made to help them in this research effort, and categorize them by level of data.

  a. Number of pizzas consumed per week per household

  b. Age of pizza purchaser

  c. Zip code of the survey respondent

  d. Dollars spent per month on pizza per person

  e. Time in between purchases of pizza

  f. Rating of taste of a given pizza brand on a scale from 1 to 10, where 1 is very poor tasting and 10 is excellent taste

  g. Ranking of the taste of four pizza brands on a taste test

  h. Number representing the geographic location of the survey respondent

  i. Quality rating of a pizza brand as excellent, good, average, below average, poor

  j. Number representing the pizza brand being evaluated

  k. Sex of survey respondent

Source: Adapted from "Upper Crust," *American Demographics,* March 1999, p. 58; "Kraft Trading Pizza for Chocolate," *MarketWatch,* October 25, 1010, http://www.marketwatch.com/story/kraft-trading-pizza-for-chocolate-2010-01-05. "Sales of the leading 10 frozen pizza brands of the United States in 2015 (in million U.S. dollars)" at www.statista.com > Industries > Retail & Trade > Food & Beverage

CHAPTER 2

Charts and Graphs

LEARNING OBJECTIVES

The overall objective of Chapter 2 is for you to master several techniques for summarizing and depicting data, thereby enabling you to:

1. Construct a frequency distribution from a set of data.

2. Construct different types of quantitative data graphs, including histograms, frequency polygons, ogives, dot plots, and stem-and-leaf plots, in order to interpret the data being graphed.

3. Construct different types of qualitative data graphs, including pie charts, bar graphs, and Pareto charts, in order to interpret the data being graphed.

4. Construct a cross-tabulation table and recognize basic trends in two-variable scatter plots of numerical data.

Decision Dilemma

Container Shipping Companies

For decades, businesspeople in many countries around the world wrestled with the issue of how to store and ship goods via trucks, trains, and ships. Various sizes and shapes of containers were developed to ship goods even within a country. The lack of consistent containers created a lot of extra work, as products were relocated from one container to another. Fortunately, in 1955 a former trucking company executive teamed up with an engineer to develop a version of the modern intermodal container that is widely used today. Because it is a standard size, this container in various forms can be moved from trucks to trains to ships without being opened, thereby eliminating the work of loading and unloading its contents multiple times. The International Organization for Standardization (ISO) has set up standards for the modern-day container, and perhaps the most commonly used container is 20 feet long and 8 feet wide. The container capacity of a ship is often measured in the number of 20-foot equivalent units or TEUs that can be loaded or unloaded from the vessel. Containerization has revolutionized cargo shipping, and today approximately 90% of non-bulk cargo worldwide moves by containers stacked on transport ships.

Shown in the next column are TEU capacities available on board-operated ships for the top five companies in the world as of October 21, 2015. Also included in the data is the total number of ships operated by each company.

Alberto Biscaro/Masterfile

COMPANY	TOTAL TEU CAPACITY	NUMBER OF SHIPS
APM-Maersk	3,031,701	594
Mediterranean Shipping Co.	2,660,981	497
CMA CGM Group	1,821,328	467
Evergreen Line	949,525	199
Hapag-Lloyd	924,417	174

MANAGERIAL AND STATISTICAL QUESTIONS

Suppose you are a shipping container industry analyst, and you are asked to prepare a brief report showing the leading shipping companies both in TEU shipping capacity and in number of ships.

1. What is the best way to display this shipping container company information? Are the raw data enough? Can you effectively display the data graphically?

2. Because some of the data are close together in size, is there a preferred graphical technique for differentiating between two or more similar numbers?

Source: "Alphaliner—TOP 100 Operated fleets as per 21 October 2015" at www.alphaliner.com/top100/

In Chapters 2 and 3, many techniques are presented for reformatting or reducing data so that the data are more manageable and can assist decision makers more effectively. Some of the most effective mechanisms for presenting data in a form meaningful to decision makers are graphical depictions. This chapter focuses on graphical tools for summarizing and presenting data. Through graphs and charts, the decision maker can often get an overall picture of the data and reach some useful conclusions merely by studying the chart or graph. Key characteristics of graphs often suggest appropriate choices among potential numerical methods (discussed in later chapters) for analyzing data. Visual representations of data are often much more effective communication tools than tables of numbers in business meetings.

A first step in exploring and analyzing data is to reduce important and sometimes expensive data to a graphic picture that is clear, concise and consistent with the message of the original data. Converting data to graphics can be creative and artful. In this chapter, guidelines are provided for selecting appropriate graphical representations for data sets. Charts and graphs discussed in Chapter 2 include histograms, frequency polygons, ogives, dot plots, stem-and-leaf plots, bar charts, pie charts, and Pareto charts for one-variable data and both cross-tabulation tables and scatter plots for two-variable numerical data.

2.1 Frequency Distributions

Raw data, or data that have not been summarized in any way, are sometimes referred to as ungrouped data. As an example, Table 2.1 contains 60 years of raw data of the unemployment rates for Canada. *Data that have been organized into a frequency distribution* are called grouped data. Table 2.2 presents a frequency distribution for the data displayed in Table 2.1.

TABLE 2.1	60 Years of Canadian Unemployment Rates (ungrouped data)			
2.3	7.0	6.3	11.3	9.6
2.8	7.1	5.6	10.6	9.1
3.6	5.9	5.4	9.7	8.3
2.4	5.5	7.1	8.8	7.6
2.9	4.7	7.1	7.8	6.8
3.0	3.9	8.0	7.5	7.2
4.6	3.6	8.4	8.1	7.7
4.4	4.1	7.5	10.3	7.6
3.4	4.8	7.5	11.2	7.2
4.6	4.7	7.6	11.4	6.8
6.9	5.9	11.0	10.4	6.3
6.0	6.4	12.0	9.5	6.0

TABLE 2.2	Frequency Distribution of 60 Years of Unemployment Data for Canada (grouped data)
CLASS INTERVAL	**FREQUENCY**
1–under 3	4
3–under 5	12
5–under 7	13
7–under 9	19
9–under 11	7
11–under 13	5

The distinction between ungrouped and grouped data is important because the calculation of statistics differs between the two types of data. Several of the charts and graphs presented in this chapter are constructed from grouped data.

One particularly useful tool for grouping data is the **frequency distribution**, which is *a summary of data presented in the form of class intervals and frequencies.* How is a frequency distribution constructed from raw data? That is, how are frequency distributions like the one displayed in Table 2.2 constructed from raw data like those presented in Table 2.1? Frequency distributions are relatively easy to construct. Although some guidelines and rules of thumb help in their construction, frequency distributions vary in final shape and design, even when the original raw data are identical. In a sense, frequency distributions are constructed according to individual business researchers' taste.

When constructing a frequency distribution, the business researcher should first determine the range of the raw data. The **range** often is defined as *the difference between the largest and smallest numbers.* The range for the data in Table 2.1 is 9.7 (12.0–2.3).

The second step in constructing a frequency distribution is to determine how many classes it will contain. One rule of thumb is to select between *5 and 15 classes.* If the frequency distribution contains too few classes, the data summary may be too general to be useful. Too many classes may result in a frequency distribution that does not aggregate the data enough to be helpful. The final number of classes is arbitrary. The business researcher arrives at a number by examining the range and determining a number of classes that will span the range adequately and also be meaningful to the user. The data in Table 2.1 were grouped into six classes for Table 2.2.

After selecting the number of classes, the business researcher must determine the width of the class interval. An approximation of the class width can be calculated by dividing the range by the number of classes. For the data in Table 2.1, this approximation would be 9.7/6 = 1.62. Normally, the number is rounded up to the next whole number, which in this case is 2. The frequency distribution must start at a value equal to or lower than the lowest number of the ungrouped data and end at a value equal to or higher than the highest number. The lowest unemployment rate is 2.3 and the highest is 12.0, so the business researcher starts the frequency distribution at 1 and ends it at 13. Table 2.2 contains the completed frequency distribution for the data in Table 2.1. Class endpoints are selected so that no value of the data can fit into more than one class. The class interval expression "under" in the distribution of Table 2.2 avoids such a problem.

Class Midpoint

The *midpoint of each class interval* is called the **class midpoint** and is sometimes referred to as the **class mark**. It is *the value halfway across the class interval* and can be calculated as *the average of the two class endpoints.* For example, in the distribution of Table 2.2, the midpoint of the class interval 3–under 5 is 4, or (3 + 5)/2.

The class midpoint is important, because it becomes the representative value for each class in most group statistics calculations. (Chapter 3) The third column in **Table 2.3** contains the class midpoints for all classes of the data from Table 2.2.

TABLE 2.3	Class Midpoints, Relative Frequencies, and Cumulative Frequencies for Unemployment Data			
INTERVAL	FREQUENCY	CLASS MIDPOINT	RELATIVE FREQUENCY	CUMULATIVE FREQUENCY
1–under 3	4	2	.0667	4
3–under 5	12	4	.2000	16
5–under 7	13	6	.2167	29
7–under 9	19	8	.3167	48
9–under 11	7	10	.1167	55
11–under 13	5	12	.0833	60
Total	60			

Relative Frequency

Relative frequency is *the proportion of the total frequency that is in any given class interval in a frequency distribution*. Relative frequency is the individual class frequency divided by the total frequency. For example, from Table 2.3, the relative frequency for the class interval 5–under 7 is $13/60 = .2167$. Consideration of the relative frequency is preparatory to the study of probability in Chapter 4. Indeed, if values were selected randomly from the data in Table 2.1, the probability of drawing a number that is "5–under 7" would be .2167, the relative frequency for that class interval. The fourth column of Table 2.3 lists the relative frequencies for the frequency distribution of Table 2.2.

Cumulative Frequency

The cumulative frequency is *a running total of frequencies through the classes of a frequency distribution*. The cumulative frequency for each class interval is the frequency for that class interval added to the preceding cumulative total. In Table 2.3, the cumulative frequency for the first class is the same as the class frequency: 4. The cumulative frequency for the second class interval is the frequency of that interval (12) plus the frequency of the first interval (4), which yields a new cumulative frequency of 16. This process continues through the last interval, at which point the cumulative total equals the sum of the frequencies (60). The concept of cumulative frequency is used in many areas, including sales cumulated over a fiscal year, sports scores during a contest (cumulated points), years of service, points earned in a course, and costs of doing business over a period of time. Table 2.3 gives cumulative frequencies for the data in Table 2.2.

DEMONSTRATION PROBLEM 2.1

The following data from the Federal Home Loan Mortgage Corporation are the average monthly 30-year fixed rate mortgage interest rates for a recent 40-month period.

5.06	4.89	4.75	4.11	3.81
4.95	4.74	4.95	4.07	3.69
4.88	4.56	4.83	3.99	3.55
4.88	4.43	4.84	3.95	3.60
5.05	4.35	4.64	3.92	3.50
4.99	4.24	4.51	3.89	3.38
4.97	4.30	4.54	3.95	3.35
5.10	4.71	4.27	3.91	3.34

Construct a frequency distribution for these data. Calculate and display the class midpoints, relative frequencies, and cumulative frequencies for this frequency distribution.

Solution: How many classes should this frequency distribution contain? The range of the data is 1.76 (5.10 – 3.34). If 8 classes are used, each class width is approximately:

$$\text{Class Width} = \frac{\text{Range}}{\text{Number of Classes}} = \frac{1.76}{8} = 0.22$$

If a class width of .25 is used, a frequency distribution can be constructed with endpoints that are more uniform looking and allow for presentation of the information in categories more familiar to mortgage interest rate users.

The first endpoint must be 3.34 or lower to include the smallest value; the last endpoint must be 5.10 or higher to include the largest value. In this case, the frequency distribution begins at 3.25 and ends at 5.25. The resulting frequency distribution, class midpoints, relative frequencies, and cumulative frequencies are listed in the following table:

INTERVAL	FREQUENCY	CLASS MIDPOINT	RELATIVE FREQUENCY	CUMULATIVE FREQUENCY
3.25–under 3.50	3	3.375	.075	3
3.50–under 3.75	4	3.625	.100	7
3.75–under 4.00	7	3.875	.175	14
4.00–under 4.25	3	4.125	.075	17
4.25–under 4.50	4	4.375	.100	21
4.50–under 4.75	6	4.625	.150	27
4.75–under 5.00	10	4.875	.250	37
5.00–under 5.25	3	5.125	.075	40
Total	40			

The frequencies and relative frequencies of these data reveal the mortgage interest rate classes that are likely to occur during this period of time. Overall, the mortgage rates are distributed relatively evenly, with the 4.75–under 5.00 class interval containing the greatest frequency (10), followed by the 3.75–under 4.00 class interval (7), and the 4.50–under 4.75 interval (6).

2.1 Problems

2.1. The following data represent the afternoon high temperatures for 50 construction days during a year in St. Louis.

42	70	64	47	66	69	73	38	48	25
55	85	10	24	45	31	62	47	63	84
16	40	81	15	35	17	40	36	44	17
38	79	35	36	23	64	75	53	31	60
31	38	52	16	81	12	61	43	30	33

a. Construct a frequency distribution for the data using five class intervals.

b. Construct a frequency distribution for the data using 10 class intervals.

c. Examine the results of (a) and (b) and comment on the usefulness of the frequency distribution in terms of temperature summarization capability.

2.2. A packaging process is supposed to fill small boxes of raisins with approximately 50 raisins so that each box will weigh the same. However, the number of raisins in each box will vary. Suppose 100 boxes of raisins are randomly sampled, the raisins counted, and the following data are obtained.

57	51	53	52	50	60	51	51	52	52
44	53	45	57	39	53	58	47	51	48
49	49	44	54	46	52	55	54	47	53
49	52	49	54	57	52	52	53	49	47
51	48	55	53	55	47	53	43	48	46
54	46	51	48	53	56	48	47	49	57
55	53	50	47	57	49	43	58	52	44
46	59	57	47	61	60	49	53	41	48
59	53	45	45	56	40	46	49	50	57
47	52	48	50	45	56	47	47	48	46

a. Construct a frequency distribution for these data.

b. What does the frequency distribution reveal about the box fills?

2.3. The owner of a fast-food restaurant ascertains the ages of a sample of customers. From these data, the owner constructs the frequency distribution shown. For each class interval of the frequency distribution, determine the class midpoint, the relative frequency, and the cumulative frequency.

CLASS INTERVAL	FREQUENCY
0–under 5	6
5–under 10	8
10–under 15	17
15–under 20	23
20–under 25	18
25–under 30	10
30–under 35	4

What does the relative frequency tell the fast-food restaurant owner about customer ages?

2.4. The human resources manager for a large company commissions a study in which the employment records of 500 company employees are examined for absenteeism during the past year. The business researcher conducting the study organizes the data into a frequency distribution to assist the human resources manager in analyzing the data. The frequency distribution is shown. For each class of the frequency distribution, determine the class midpoint, the relative frequency, and the cumulative frequency.

CLASS INTERVAL	FREQUENCY
0–under 2	218
2–under 4	207
4–under 6	56
6–under 8	11
8–under 10	8

2.5. List three specific uses of cumulative frequencies in business.

2.2 | Quantitative Data Graphs

One of the most effective mechanisms for presenting data in a form meaningful to decision makers is graphical depiction. Through graphs and charts, the decision maker can often get an overall picture of the data and reach some useful conclusions merely by studying the chart or graph. Converting data to graphics can be creative and artful. Often the most difficult step in this process is to reduce data to a graphic picture that is both clear and concise and yet consistent with the message of the original data. One of the most important uses of graphical depiction in statistics is to help the researcher determine the shape of a distribution. Data graphs can generally be classified as quantitative or qualitative. Quantitative data graphs are plotted along a numerical scale, and qualitative graphs are plotted using non-numerical categories. In this section, we will examine five types of quantitative data graphs: (1) histogram, (2) frequency polygon, (3) ogive, (4) dot plot, and (5) stem-and-leaf plot.

Histograms

One of the more widely used types of graphs for quantitative data is the **histogram**. A histogram is a series of contiguous rectangles that represent the frequency of data in given class intervals. If the class intervals used along the horizontal axis are equal, then the heights of the rectangles represent the frequency of values in a given class interval. If the class intervals are unequal, then the areas of the rectangles can be used for relative comparisons of class frequencies. Construction of a histogram involves labeling the x-axis (abscissa) with the class endpoints and the y-axis (ordinate) with the frequencies, drawing a horizontal line segment from class endpoint to class endpoint at each frequency value, and connecting each line segment vertically from the frequency value to the x-axis to form a series of rectangles. **Figure 2.1** is a histogram of the frequency distribution in Table 2.2 produced by using the software package Minitab.

A histogram is a useful tool for differentiating the frequencies of class intervals. A quick glance at a histogram reveals which class intervals produce the highest frequency totals. Figure 2.1 clearly shows that the class interval 7–under 9 yields by far the highest frequency count (19). Examination of the histogram reveals where large increases or decreases occur between classes, such as from the 1–under 3 class to the 3–under 5 class, an increase of 8, and from the 7–under 9 class to the 9–under 11 class, a decrease of 12.

Note that the scales used along the x- and y-axes for the histogram in Figure 2.1 are almost identical. However, because ranges of meaningful numbers for the two variables being graphed often differ considerably, the graph may have different scales on the two

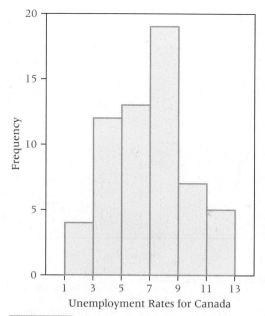

FIGURE 2.1 **Minitab Histogram of Canadian**
Unemployment Data

axes. **Figure 2.2** shows what the histogram of unemployment rates would look like if the scale on the *y*-axis were more compressed than that on the *x*-axis. Notice that with the compressed graph, Figure 2.2, there appears to be less difference between the lengths of the rectangles than those in Figure 2.1 implying that the differences in frequencies for the compressed graph are not as great as they are in Figure 2.1. It is important that the user of the graph clearly understands the scales used for the axes of a histogram. Otherwise, a graph's creator can "lie with statistics" by stretching or compressing a graph to make a point.*

Using Histograms to Get an Initial Overview of the Data   Because of the

widespread availability of computers and statistical software packages to business researchers and decision makers, the histogram continues to grow in importance in yielding information about the shape of the distribution of a large database, the variability of the data, the central location of the data, and outlier data. Although most of these concepts are presented in Chapter 3, the notion of histogram as an initial tool to access these data characteristics is presented here.

A business researcher measured the volume of stocks traded on Wall Street three times a month for nine years, resulting in a database of 324 observations. Suppose a financial decision maker wants to use these data to reach some conclusions about the stock market. **Figure 2.3**

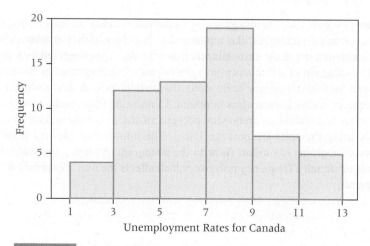

FIGURE 2.2   **Minitab Histogram of Canadian Unemployment Data**
(*y*-axis compressed)

*It should be pointed out that the software package Excel uses the term *histogram* to refer to a frequency distribution. However, by checking Chart Output in the Excel histogram dialog box, a graphical histogram is also created.

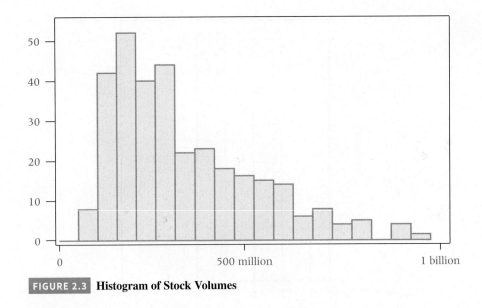

FIGURE 2.3 **Histogram of Stock Volumes**

shows a Minitab-produced histogram of these data. What can we learn from this histogram? Virtually all stock market volumes fall between zero and 1 billion shares. The distribution takes on a shape that is high on the left end and tapered to the right. In Chapter 3 we will learn that the shape of this distribution is skewed toward the right end. In statistics, it is often useful to determine whether data are approximately normally distributed (bell-shaped curve) as shown in **Figure 2.4**. We can see by examining the histogram in Figure 2.3 that the stock market volume data are not normally distributed. Although the center of the histogram is located near 500 million shares, a large portion of stock volume observations falls in the lower end of the data somewhere between 100 million and 400 million shares. In addition, the histogram shows some outliers in the upper end of the distribution. Outliers are data points that appear outside of the main body of observations and may represent phenomena that differ from those represented by other data points. By observing the histogram, we notice a few data observations near 1 billion. One could conclude that on a few stock market days an unusually large volume of shares is traded. These and other insights can be gleaned by examining the histogram and show that histograms play an important role in the initial analysis of data.

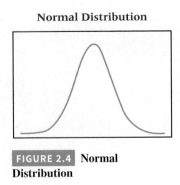

Normal Distribution

FIGURE 2.4 **Normal Distribution**

Frequency Polygons

A **frequency polygon**, like the histogram, is a graphical display of class frequencies. However, instead of using rectangles like a histogram, in a frequency polygon each class frequency is plotted as a dot at the class midpoint, and the dots are connected by a series of line segments. Construction of a frequency polygon begins by scaling class midpoints along the horizontal axis and the frequency scale along the vertical axis. A dot is plotted for the associated frequency value at each class midpoint. Connecting these midpoint dots completes the graph. **Figure 2.5** shows a frequency polygon of the distribution data from Table 2.2 produced by using the software package Excel. The information gleaned from frequency polygons and histograms is similar. As with the histogram, changing the scales of the axes can compress or stretch a frequency polygon, which affects the user's impression of what the graph represents.

Ogives

An **ogive** (o-jive) is *a cumulative frequency polygon*. Construction begins by labeling the *x*-axis with the class endpoints and the *y*-axis with the frequencies. However, the use of cumulative frequency values requires that the scale along the *y*-axis be great enough to include

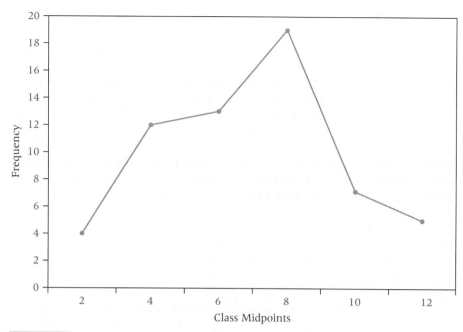

FIGURE 2.5 **Excel-Produced Frequency Polygon of the Unemployment Data**

the frequency total. A dot of zero frequency is plotted at the beginning of the first class, and construction proceeds by marking a dot at the *end* of each class interval for the cumulative value. Connecting the dots then completes the ogive. **Figure 2.6** presents an ogive produced by using Excel for the data in Table 2.2.

Ogives are most useful when the decision maker wants to see *running totals*. For example, if a comptroller is interested in controlling costs, an ogive could depict cumulative costs over a fiscal year.

Steep slopes in an ogive can be used to identify sharp increases in frequencies. In Figure 2.6, a particularly steep slope occurs in the 7–under 9 class, signifying a large jump in class frequency totals.

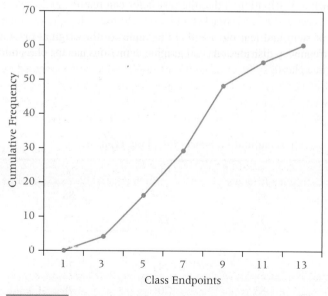

FIGURE 2.6 **Excel Ogive of the Unemployment Data**

Dot Plots

A relatively simple statistical chart that is generally used to display continuous, quantitative data is the **dot plot**. In a dot plot, each data value is plotted along the horizontal axis and is represented on the chart by a dot. If multiple data points have the same values, the dots will stack up vertically. If there are a large number of close points, it may not be possible to display all of the data values along the horizontal axis. Dot plots can be especially useful for observing the overall shape of the distribution of data points along with identifying data values or intervals for which there are groupings and gaps in the data. **Figure 2.7** displays a minitab-produced dot plot for the Canadian unemployment data shown in Table 2.1. Note that the distribution is relatively balanced with a peak near the center. There are a few gaps to note, such as from 4.9 to 5.3, from 9.9 to 10.2, and from 11.5 to 11.9. In addition, there are groupings around 6.0, 7.1, and 7.5.

Annual Unemployment Rates for Canada

FIGURE 2.7 **A Minitab-Produced Dot Plot of the Canadian Unemployment Data**

Stem-and-Leaf Plots

Another way to organize raw data into groups besides using a frequency distribution is a **stem-and-leaf plot**. This technique is simple and provides a unique view of the data. A stem-and-leaf plot is constructed by separating the digits for each number of the data into two groups, *a stem and a leaf*. The leftmost digits are the stem and consist of the higher valued digits. The rightmost digits are the leaves and contain the lower values. If a set of data has only two digits, the stem is the value on the left and the leaf is the value on the right. For example, if 34 is one of the numbers, the stem is 3 and the leaf is 4. For numbers with more than two digits, division of stem and leaf is a matter of researcher preference.

Table 2.4 contains scores from an examination on plant safety policy and rules given to a group of 35 job trainees. A stem-and-leaf plot of these data is displayed in Table 2.5. One advantage of such a distribution is that the instructor can readily see whether the scores are in the upper or lower end of each bracket and also determine the spread of the scores. A second advantage of stem-and-leaf plots is that the values of the original raw data are retained (whereas most frequency distributions and graphic depictions use the class midpoint to represent the values in a class).

TABLE 2.4 **Safety Examination Scores for Plant Trainees**

86	77	91	60	55
76	92	47	88	67
23	59	72	75	83
77	68	82	97	89
81	75	74	39	67
79	83	70	78	91
68	49	56	94	81

STEM	LEAF								
2	3								
3	9								
4	7	9							
5	5	6	9						
6	0	7	7	8	8				
7	0	2	4	5	5	6	7	7	8	9
8	1	1	2	3	3	6	8	9	
9	1	1	2	4	7				

TABLE 2.5 Stem-and-Leaf Plot for Plant Safety Examination Data

DEMONSTRATION PROBLEM 2.2

The following data represent the costs (in dollars) of a sample of 30 postal mailings by a company.

3.67	2.75	9.15	5.11	3.32	2.09
1.83	10.94	1.93	3.89	7.20	2.78
6.72	7.80	5.47	4.15	3.55	3.53
3.34	4.95	5.42	8.64	4.84	4.10
5.10	6.45	4.65	1.97	2.84	3.21

Using dollars as a stem and cents as a leaf, construct a stem-and-leaf plot of the data.

Solution:

STEM	LEAF						
1	83	93	97				
2	09	75	78	84			
3	21	32	34	53	55	67	89
4	10	15	65	84	95		
5	10	11	42	47			
6	45	72					
7	20	80					
8	64						
9	15						
10	94						

2.2 Problems

2.6. Assembly times for components must be understood in order to "level" the stages of a production process. Construct both a histogram and a frequency polygon for the following assembly time data and comment on the key characteristics of the distribution.

CLASS INTERVAL	FREQUENCY
30–under 32	5
32–under 34	7
34–under 36	15
36–under 38	21
38–under 40	34
40–under 42	24
42–under 44	17
44–under 46	8

2.7. A call center is trying to better understand staffing requirements. It investigates the number of calls received during the evening shift and obtains the information given below. Construct a histogram of the data and comment on the key characteristics of the distribution. Construct a frequency polygon and compare it to the histogram. Which do you prefer, and why?

CLASS INTERVAL	FREQUENCY
10–under 20	9
20–under 30	7
30–under 40	10
40–under 50	6
50–under 60	13
60–under 70	18
70–under 80	15

2.8. Construct an ogive for the following data.

CLASS INTERVAL	FREQUENCY
3–under 6	2
6–under 9	5
9–under 12	10
12–under 15	11
15–under 18	17
18–under 21	5

2.9. A real estate group is investigating the price a condominiums of a given size (sq ft). The following sales prices ($1,000) were obtained in one region of a city. Construct a stem-and-leaf plot for the following data using two digits for the stem. Comment on the key characteristics of the distribution. Construct a dot plot of the data and comment on how it differs from the stem-and-leaf plot in providing information about the data.

212	239	240	218	222	249	265	224
257	271	266	234	239	219	255	260
243	261	249	230	246	263	235	229
218	238	254	249	250	263	229	221
253	227	270	257	261	238	240	239
273	220	226	239	258	259	230	262
255	226						

2.10. The following data represent the number of passengers per flight in a sample of 50 flights from Wichita, Kansas, to Kansas City, Missouri.

23	46	66	67	13	58	19	17	65	17
25	20	47	28	16	38	44	29	48	29
69	34	35	60	37	52	80	59	51	33
48	46	23	38	52	50	17	57	41	77
45	47	49	19	32	64	27	61	70	19

a. Construct a dot plot for these data.

b. Construct a stem-and-leaf plot for these data. What does the stem-and-leaf plot tell you about the number of passengers per flight?

2.11. The Airports Council International—North America (ACI) publishes data on the busiest airports in the United States. Shown below is a Minitab-produced histogram constructed from ACI data on the number of passengers that enplaned and deplaned in 2014 in the United States. As an example, Atlanta's Hartsfield–Jackson International Airport was the busiest airport in the United States with 96,178,899 passengers. What are some observations that you can make from the graph? Describe the top 30 busiest airports in the United States using this histogram.

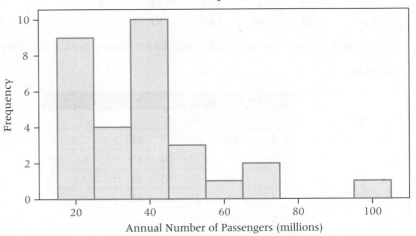

30 Busiest Airports in the U.S.

2.12. Study the Minitab-produced dot plot of the number of farms per state in the United States shown below. Comment on any observations that you make from the graph. What does this graph tell you about the number of farms per state? The average number of farms per state calculated from the raw data (not given here) and sourced from the U.S. Department of Agriculture is 44,060. Reconcile this number with the dot plot.

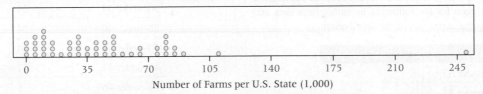

Dot Plot of Farms Per State in the U.S.

Number of Farms per U.S. State (1,000)

2.13. A full-service car wash has an automated exterior conveyor car wash system that does the initial cleaning in a few minutes. However, once the car is through the system, car wash workers hand clean the inside and the outside of the car for approximately 15 to 25 additional minutes. There are enough workers to handle four cars at once during this stage. On a busy day with good weather, the car wash can handle up to 150 cars in a 12-hour time period. However, on rainy days or on certain days of the year, business is slow. Suppose 50 days of work are randomly sampled from the car wash's records and the number of cars washed each day is recorded. A stem-and-leaf plot of this output is constructed and is given below. Study the plot and write a few sentences describing the number of cars washed per day over this period of work. Note that the stem-and-leaf display is from Minitab, the stems are in the middle column, each leaf is only one digit and is shown in the right column, and the numbers in the left column are cumulative frequencies up to the median and then decumulative thereafter.

Stem-and-Leaf Display: Cars Washed Per Day

Stem-and-leaf of Cars Washed Per Day N = 50 Leaf Unit = 1.0

	STEM	LEAF
3	2	599
9	3	344778
15	4	015689
18	5	378
21	6	223
24	7	457
(3)	8	112
23	9	05
21	10	1234578
14	11	466
11	12	01467
6	13	37
4	14	1457

2.14. A hundred or so boats go fishing every year for three or four weeks off of the Bering Strait for Alaskan king crabs. To catch these king crabs, large pots are baited and left on the sea bottom, often several hundred feet deep. Because of the investment in boats, equipment, personnel, and supplies, fishing for such crabs can be financially risky if not enough crabs are caught. Thus, as pots are pulled and emptied, there is great interest in how many legal king crabs (males of a certain size) there are in any given pot. Suppose the number of legal king crabs is reported for each pot during a season and recorded. In addition, suppose that 200 of these are randomly selected and the numbers per pot are used to create the ogive shown below. Study the ogive and comment on the number of legal king crabs per pot.

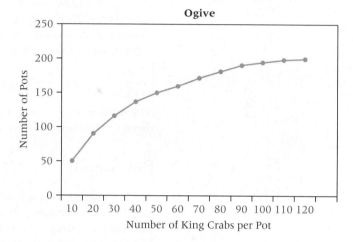

2.3 Qualitative Data Graphs

In contrast to quantitative data graphs that are plotted along a numerical scale, qualitative graphs are plotted using non-numerical categories. In this section, we will examine three types of qualitative data graphs: (1) pie charts, (2) bar charts, and (3) Pareto charts.

Pie Charts

A **pie chart** is *a circular depiction of data where the area of the whole pie represents 100% of the data and slices of the pie represent a percentage breakdown of the sublevels*. Pie charts show the relative magnitudes of the parts to the whole. They are widely used in business, particularly to depict such things as budget categories, market share, and time/resource allocations. However, the use of pie charts is minimized in the sciences and technology because pie charts can lead to less accurate judgments than are possible with other types of graphs.* Generally, it is more difficult for the viewer to interpret the relative size of angles in a pie chart than to judge the length of rectangles in a bar chart. In the feature Thinking Critically about Statistics in Business Today, "Where Are Soft Drinks Sold?" the percentage of sales by place are displayed by both a pie chart and a vertical bar chart.

Construction of the pie chart begins by determining the proportion of the subunit to the whole. Table 2.6 contains the refining capacity (1,000 barrels per day) of the

---

*William S. Cleveland, *The Elements of Graphing Data*. Monterey, CA: Wadsworth Advanced Books and Software, 1985.

TABLE 2.6	Top Five U.S. Petroleum Refining Companies in Capacity		
COMPANY	CAPACITY (1,000 BARRELS PER DAY)	PROPORTION	DEGREES
Exxon Mobil	5,589	.3693	132.95
Valero Energy	2,777	.1835	66.06
Chevron	2,540	.1678	60.41
ConocoPhillips	2,514	.1661	59.79
Marathon Oil	1,714	.1133	40.79
Totals	15,134	1.0000	360.00

top five petroleum refining companies in the United States in a recent year. To construct a pie chart from these data, first convert the raw capacity figures to proportions by dividing each capacity figure by the total capacity figure (15,134). This proportion is analogous to the relative frequency computed for frequency distributions. Because a circle contains 360°, each proportion is then multiplied by 360 to obtain the number of degrees to represent each company in the pie chart. For example, Exxon Mobil's capacity of 5,589 (1,000 barrels) represents a .3693 proportion of the total capacity for these five companies.

$\left(\dfrac{5,589}{15,134} = .3693 \right)$. Multiplying this value by 360° results in an angle of 132.95°. The pie chart is then constructed by determining each of the other angles and using a compass to lay out the slices. The pie chart in **Figure 2.8**, constructed by using Minitab, depicts the data from Table 2.6.

Bar Graphs

Another widely used qualitative data graphing technique is the **bar graph** or **bar chart**. A bar graph or chart contains two or more categories along one axis and a series of bars, one for each category, along the other axis. Typically, the length of the bar represents the magnitude of the measure (amount, frequency, money, percentage, etc.) for each category. The bar graph is qualitative because the categories are non-numerical, and it may be either horizontal or vertical. In Excel, horizontal bar graphs are referred to as **bar charts**, and vertical bar graphs are referred to as **column charts**. A bar graph is generally constructed from the same type of data that is used to produce a pie chart. However, an advantage of using a bar graph over a pie

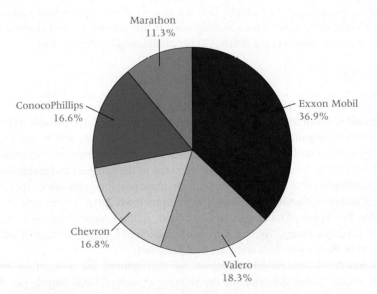

FIGURE 2.8 Minitab Pie Chart of the Petroleum Refining Capacity of the Top Five U.S. Companies

TABLE 2.7	How Much is Spent on Back-to-College Shopping by the Average Student
CATEGORY	AMOUNT SPENT ($ US)
Electronics	$211.89
Clothing and Accessories	134.40
Dorm Furnishings	90.90
School Supplies	68.47
Misc.	93.72

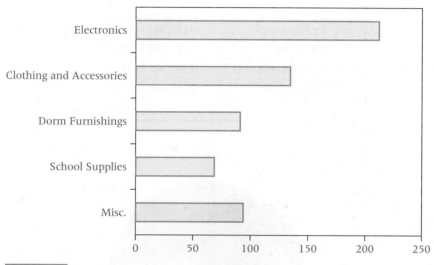

FIGURE 2.9 Bar Graph of Back-to-College Spending

chart for a given set of data is that for categories that are close in value, it is considered easier to see the difference in the bars of bar graph than discriminating between pie slices.

As an example, consider the data in Table 2.7 regarding how much the average college student spends on back-to-college spending. Constructing a bar graph from these data, the categories are Electronics, Clothing and Accessories, Dorm Furnishings, School Supplies, and Misc. Bars for each of these categories are made using the dollar figures given in the table. The resulting bar graph produced by Excel is shown in Figure 2.9.

DEMONSTRATION PROBLEM 2.3

According to the National Retail Federation and Center for Retailing Education at the University of Florida, the four main sources of inventory shrinkage are employee theft, shoplifting, administrative error, and vendor fraud. The estimated annual dollar amount in shrinkage ($ millions) associated with each of these sources follows:

Employee theft	$17,918.6
Shoplifting	15,191.9
Administrative error	7,617.6
Vendor fraud	2,553.6
Total	$43,281.7

Construct a pie chart and a bar chart to depict these data.

Solution: To produce a pie chart, convert each raw dollar amount to a proportion by dividing each individual amount by the total.

Employee theft	17,918.6/43,281.7 = .414
Shoplifting	15,191.9/43,281.7 = .351
Administrative error	7,617.6/43,281.7 = .176
Vendor fraud	2,553.6/43,281.7 = .059
Total	1.000

Convert each proportion to degrees by multiplying each proportion by 360°.

Employee theft	.414 · 360° = 149.0°
Shoplifting	.351 · 360° = 126.4°
Administrative error	.176 · 360° = 63.4°
Vendor fraud	.059 · 360° = 21.2°
Total	360.0°

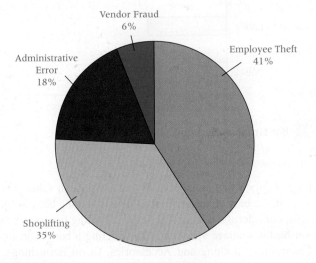

Using the raw data above, we can produce the following bar chart.

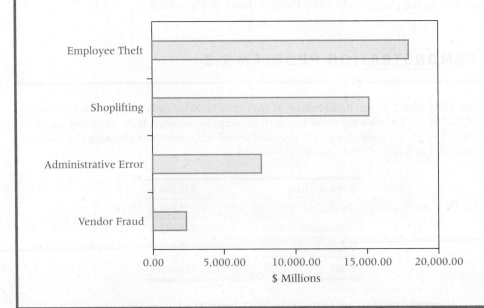

Pareto Charts

A third type of qualitative data graph is a Pareto chart, which can be viewed as a particular application of the bar graph. An important concept and movement in business is total quality management (see Chapter 18). One of the key aspects of total quality management is the constant search for causes of problems in products and processes. A graphical technique for displaying problem causes is Pareto analysis. Pareto analysis is a quantitative tallying of the number and types of defects that occur with a product or service. Analysts use this tally to produce *a vertical bar chart that displays the most common types of defects, ranked in order of occurrence from left to right*. The bar chart is called a **Pareto chart**.

Pareto charts were named after an Italian economist, Vilfredo Pareto, who observed more than 100 years ago that most of Italy's wealth was controlled by a few families who were the major drivers behind the Italian economy. Quality expert J. M. Juran applied this notion to the quality field by observing that poor quality can often be addressed by attacking a few major causes that result in most of the problems. A Pareto chart enables quality-management decision makers to separate the most important defects from trivial defects, which helps them to set priorities for needed quality improvement work.

Suppose the number of electric motors being rejected by inspectors for a company has been increasing. Company officials examine the records of several hundred of the motors in which at least one defect was found to determine which defects occurred more frequently. They find that 40% of the defects involved poor wiring, 30% involved a short in the coil, 25% involved a defective plug, and 5% involved cessation of bearings. **Figure 2.10** is a Pareto chart

---

Thinking Critically About Statistics in Business Today

Where Are Soft Drinks Sold?

The soft drink market is an extremely large and growing market in the United States and worldwide. In a recent year, 8.9 billion cases of soft drinks were sold in the United States alone. Where are soft drinks sold? The following data from Sanford C. Bernstein research indicate that the four leading places for soft drink sales are supermarkets, fountains, convenience/gas stores, and vending machines.

PLACE OF SALES	PERCENTAGE
Supermarket	44
Fountain	24
Convenience/gas stations	16
Vending	11
Mass merchandisers	3
Drugstores	2

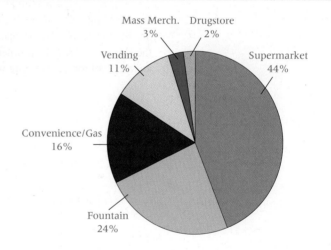

These data can be displayed graphically several ways. Displayed here are an Excel pie chart and a Minitab bar chart of the data. Some statisticians prefer the histogram or the bar chart over the pie chart because they believe it is easier to compare categories that are similar in size with the histogram or the bar chart rather than the pie chart.

THINGS TO PONDER

1. How might this information be useful to large soft drink companies?

2. How might the packaging of soft drinks differ according to the top four places where soft drinks are sold?

3. How might the distribution of soft drinks differ between the various places where soft drinks are sold?

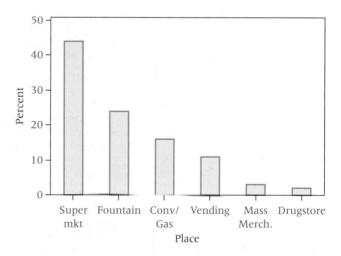

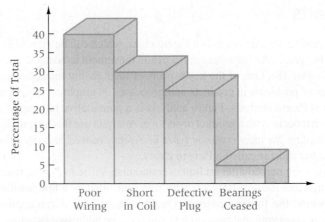

FIGURE 2.10 **Pareto Chart for Electric Motor Problems**

constructed from this information. It shows that the main three problems with defective motors—poor wiring, a short in the coil, and a defective plug—account for 95% of the problems. From the Pareto chart, decision makers can formulate a logical plan for reducing the number of defects.

Company officials and workers would probably begin to improve quality by examining the segments of the production process that involve the wiring. Next, they would study the construction of the coil, then examine the plugs used and the plug-supplier process.

Figure 2.11 is a Minitab rendering of this Pareto chart. In addition to the bar chart analysis, the Minitab Pareto analysis contains a cumulative percentage line graph. Observe the slopes on the line graph. The steepest slopes represent the more frequently occurring problems. As the slopes level off, the problems occur less frequently. The line graph gives the decision maker another tool for determining which problems to solve first.

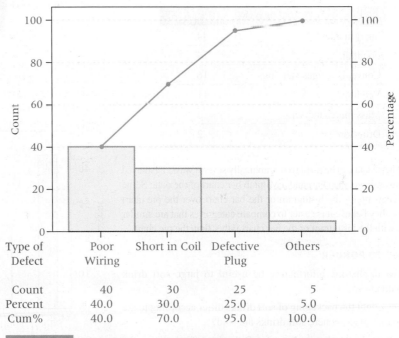

Type of Defect	Poor Wiring	Short in Coil	Defective Plug	Others
Count	40	30	25	5
Percent	40.0	30.0	25.0	5.0
Cum%	40.0	70.0	95.0	100.0

FIGURE 2.11 **Minitab Pareto Chart for Electric Motor Problems**

2.3 Problems

2.15. Shown here is a list published by Electronics Weekly.com of the top five semiconductor companies in the United States by revenue ($ millions).

FIRM	REVENUE ($ MILLION)
Intel Corp.	51,368
Qualcomm	19,100
Micro + Elpida	16,614
Texas Instruments	12,179
Broadcom	8,360

a. Construct a bar chart to display these data.

b. Construct a pie chart from these data and label the slices with the appropriate percentages.

c. Comment on the effectiveness of using a pie chart versus a bar chart to display the revenue of these five companies.

2.16. According to Bureau of Transportation statistics, the largest five U.S. airlines in scheduled system-wide (domestic and international) enplanements in 2013 (passenger numbers in millions) were: Delta with 120.4, Southwest with 115.3, United with 90.1, American with 86.8 and US Airways with 57.0. Construct a pie chart and a bar graph to depict this information.

2.17. The following list shows the top six pharmaceutical companies in the United States by revenue ($ billions) for a recent year as published by Contract Pharma. Use this information to construct a pie chart and a bar graph to represent these six companies and their revenue.

PHARMACEUTICAL COMPANY	SALES
Pfizer	51.2
Merck	40.6
Johnson & Johnson	25.4
Abbott Laboratories	23.1
Eli Lilly	20.6
Bristol-Myers Squibb	17.6

2.18. How do various currencies around the world stack up to the U.S. dollar? Shown below is a bar chart of the value of the currency of various countries in U.S. dollars as of April 2015. The currencies represented here are the Malaysia ringgit, United Arab Emirates dirham, New Zealand dollar, China yuan, Mexico peso, India rupee, Canada dollar, European euro, and U.S. dollar. Study the bar chart and discuss the various currencies as they relate to each other in value and as they compare to the U.S. dollar.

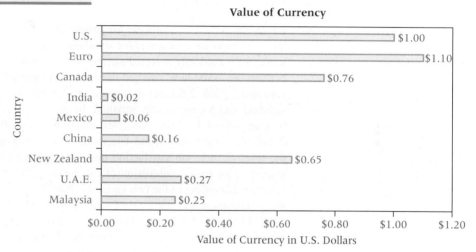

2.19. An airline company uses a central telephone bank and a semi-automated telephone process to take reservations. It has been receiving an unusually high number of customer complaints about its reservation system. The company conducted a survey of customers, asking them whether they had encountered any of the following problems in making reservations: busy signal, disconnection, poor connection, too long a wait to talk to someone, could not get through to an agent, connected with the wrong person. Suppose a survey of 744 complaining customers resulted in the following frequency tally.

NUMBER OF COMPLAINTS	COMPLAINT
184	Too long a wait
10	Transferred to the wrong person
85	Could not get through to an agent
37	Got disconnected
420	Busy signal
8	Poor connection

Construct a Pareto diagram from this information to display the various problems encountered in making reservations.

2.4 Charts and Graphs for Two Variables

It is very common in business statistics to want to analyze two variables simultaneously in an effort to gain insight into a possible relationship between them. For example, business researchers might be interested in the relationship between years of experience and amount of productivity in a manufacturing facility or in the relationship between a person's technology usage and their age. Business statistics has many techniques for exploring such relationships. Two of the more elementary tools for observing the relationships between two variables are cross tabulation and scatter plot.

Cross Tabulation

Cross tabulation is *a process for producing a two-dimensional table that displays the frequency counts for two variables simultaneously.* As an example, suppose a job satisfaction survey of a randomly selected sample of 177 bankers is taken in the banking industry. The bankers are asked how satisfied they are with their job using a 1 to 5 scale where 1 denotes very dissatisfied, 2 denotes dissatisfied, 3 denotes neither satisfied nor dissatisfied, 4 denotes satisfied, and 5 denotes very satisfied. In addition, each banker is asked to report his/her age by using one of the three categories: under 30 years, 30 to 50 years, and over 50 years. Table 2.8 displays how some of the data might look as they are gathered. Note that for each banker the level of their job satisfaction and their age are recorded. By tallying the frequency of responses for each combination of categories between the two variables, the data are cross tabulated according to the two variables. For instance, in this example, there is a tally of how many bankers rated their level of satisfaction as 1 and were under 30 years of age, there is a tally of how many bankers rated their level of satisfaction as 2 and were under 30 years of age, and so on until frequency tallies are determined for each possible combination of the two variables. Table 2.9 shows the completed cross-tabulation table for the banker survey. A cross-tabulation table is sometimes referred to as a contingency table, and Excel refers to such a table as a Pivot Table.

TABLE 2.8 Banker Data Observations by Job Satisfaction and Age

BANKER	LEVEL OF JOB SATISFACTION	AGE
1	4	53
2	3	37
3	1	24
4	2	28
5	4	46
6	5	62
7	3	41
8	3	32
9	4	29
·		
·		
·		
177	3	51

TABLE 2.9 Cross-Tabulation Table of Banker Data

		Age Category			
		Under 30	30–50	Over 50	**Total**
Level of Job Satisfaction	1	7	3	0	10
	2	19	14	3	36
	3	28	17	12	57
	4	11	22	16	49
	5	2	9	14	25
Total		67	65	45	177

TABLE 2.10 Value of New Construction Over a 35-Year Period

RESIDENTIAL	NONRESIDENTIAL	RESIDENTIAL	NONRESIDENTIAL
169635	96497	252745	169173
155113	115372	228943	167896
149410	96407	197526	135389
175822	129275	232134	120921
162706	140569	249757	122222
134605	145054	274956	127593
195028	131289	251937	139711
231396	155261	281229	153866
234955	178925	280748	166754
266481	163740	297886	177639
267063	160363	315757	175048
263385	164191		

Source: U.S. Census Bureau, *Current Construction Reports* (in millions of constant dollars).

Scatter Plot

A **scatter plot** is a *two-dimensional graph plot of pairs of points from two numerical variables*. The scatter plot is a graphical tool that is often used to examine possible relationships between two variables.

Observe the data in Table 2.10. Displayed are the values of new residential and new nonresidential buildings in the United States for various years over a 35-year period. Do these two numerical variables exhibit any relationship? It might seem logical when new construction booms that it would boom in both residential building and in nonresidential building at the same time. However, the Minitab scatter plot of these data displayed in Figure 2.12 shows somewhat mixed results. The apparent tendency is that more new residential building construction occurs when more new nonresidential building construction is also taking place and less new residential building construction when new nonresidential building construction is also at lower levels. The scatter plot also shows that in some years more new residential building and less new nonresidential building happened at the same time, and vice versa.

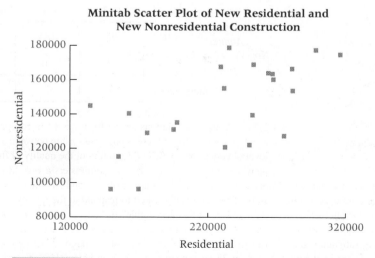

FIGURE 2.12 **Minitab Scatter Plot of New Residential and New Nonresidential Construction**

2.4 Problems

2.20. The U.S. National Oceanic and Atmospheric Administration, National Marine Fisheries Service, publishes data on the quantity and value of domestic fishing in the United States. The quantity (in millions of pounds) of fish caught and used for human food and for industrial products (oil, bait, animal food, etc.) over a decade follows. Is a relationship evident between the quantity used for human food and the quantity used for industrial products for a given year? Construct a scatter plot of the data. Examine the plot and discuss the strength of the relationship of the two variables.

HUMAN FOOD	INDUSTRIAL PRODUCT
3654	2828
3547	2430
3285	3082
3238	3201
3320	3118
3294	2964
3393	2638
3946	2950
4588	2604
6204	2259

2.21. Are the advertising dollars spent by a company related to total sales revenue? The following data represent the advertising dollars and the sales revenues for various companies in a given industry during a recent year. Construct a scatter plot of the data from the two variables and discuss the relationship between the two variables.

ADVERTISING (IN $ MILLIONS)	SALES (IN $ MILLIONS)
4.2	155.7
1.6	87.3
6.3	135.6
2.7	99.0
10.4	168.2
7.1	136.9
5.5	101.4
8.3	158.2

2.22. It seems logical that the number of days per year that an employee is tardy is at least somewhat related to the employee's job satisfaction. Suppose 10 employees are asked to record how satisfied they are with their job on a scale of 0 to 10, with 0 denoting completely unsatisfied and 10 denoting completely satisfied. Suppose also that through human resource records, it is determined how many days each of these employees was tardy last year. The scatter plot below graphs the job satisfaction scores of each employee against the number of days he/she was tardy. What information can you glean from the scatter plot? Does there appear to be any relationship between job satisfaction and tardiness? If so, how might they appear to be related?

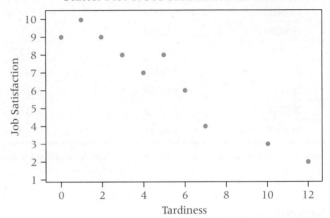

Scatter Plot of Job Satisfaction vs. Tardiness

2.23. The human resources manager of a large chemical plant was interested in determining what factors might be related to the number of non-vacation days that workers were absent during the past year. One of the factors that the manager considered was the distance that the person commutes to work, wondering if longer commutes resulting in such things as stress on the worker and/or increases in the likelihood of transportation failure might result in more worker absences. The manager studied company records, randomly selected 532 plant workers, and recorded the number of non-vacation days that the workers were absent last year and how far their place of residence is from the plant. The manager then recoded the raw data in categories and created the cross-tabulation table just shown. Study the table and comment on any relationship that may exist between distance to the plant and number of absences.

		One-Way Commute Distance (in miles)		
		0–3	4–10	More than 10
Number of Annual Non-Vacation-Day Absences	0–2	95	184	117
	3–5	21	40	53
more than 5		3	7	12

2.24. A customer relations expert for a retail tire company is interested in determining if there is any relationship between a customer's level of education and his or her rating of the quality of the tire company's service. The tire company administers a very brief survey to each customer who buys a pair of tires and has them installed at the store. The customer is asked to respond to the quality of the service rendered as either "acceptable" or "unacceptable." In addition, each respondent is asked the level of education attained from the categories of "high school only" or "college degree." These data are gathered on 25 customers and are given below. Use this information to construct a cross-tabulation table. Comment on any relationships that may exist in the table.

CUSTOMER	LEVEL OF EDUCATION	RATING OF SERVICE	CUSTOMER	LEVEL OF EDUCATION	RATING OF SERVICE
1	high school only	acceptable	14	high school only	acceptable
2	college degree	unacceptable	15	college degree	acceptable
3	college degree	acceptable	16	high school only	acceptable
4	high school only	acceptable	17	high school only	acceptable
5	college degree	unacceptable	18	high school only	unacceptable
6	high school only	acceptable	19	college degree	unacceptable
7	high school only	unacceptable	20	college degree	acceptable
8	college degree	acceptable	21	college degree	unacceptable
9	college degree	unacceptable	22	high school only	acceptable
10	college degree	unacceptable	23	college degree	acceptable
11	high school only	acceptable	24	high school only	acceptable
12	college degree	acceptable	25	college degree	unacceptable
13	college degree	unacceptable			

Decision Dilemma Solved

Container Shipping Companies

The raw values as shown in the table in the Decision Dilemma are relatively easy to read and interpret. However, these numbers could also be displayed graphically in different ways to create interest and discussion among readers and to allow for more ease of comparisons. For example, shown here is a Minitab pie chart displaying the TEU capacities for the five companies. In addition, there is an Excel-produced bar chart for the number of ships for these companies. Note that some of the slices in the pie chart are so close together in size that it is difficult to determine which company has the greater TEU capacity. Some statisticians prefer to use a bar chart in examining data that are similar in size and value because they believe that it is easier to differentiate between categories with close values when using a bar chart as compared to a pie chart. Since the number of ships is close together for two pairs of companies, determine for yourself if you prefer the bar chart to the pie chart in such instances.

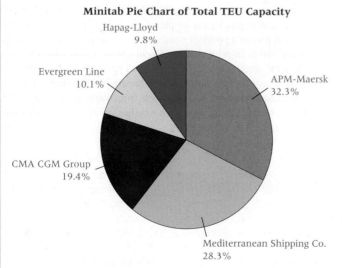

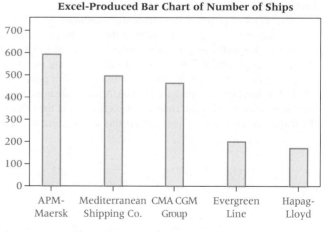

Ethical Considerations

Ethical considerations for techniques learned in Chapter 2 begin with the data chosen for representation. With the abundance of available data in business, the person constructing the data summary must be selective in choosing the reported variables. The potential is great for the analyst to select variables or even data within variables that are favorable to his or her own situation or that are perceived to be well received by the listener.

Section 2.1 noted that the number of classes and the size of the intervals in frequency distributions are usually selected by the researcher. The researcher should be careful to select values and sizes that will give an honest, accurate reflection of the situation and not a biased over- or understated case.

Sections 2.2, 2.3, and 2.4 discussed the construction of charts and graphs. It pointed out that in many instances, it makes sense to use unequal scales on the axes. However, doing so opens the possibility of "cheating with statistics" by stretching or compressing the axes to underscore the researcher's or analyst's point. It is imperative that frequency distributions and charts and graphs be constructed in a manner that most reflects actual data and not merely the researcher's own agenda.

Summary

The two types of data are grouped and ungrouped. Grouped data are data organized into a frequency distribution. Differentiating between grouped and ungrouped data is important, because statistical operations on the two types are computed differently.

Constructing a frequency distribution involves several steps. The first step is to determine the range of the data, which is the difference between the largest value and the smallest value. Next, the number of classes is determined, which is an arbitrary choice of the researcher. However, too few classes overaggregate the data into meaningless categories, and too many classes do not summarize the data enough to be useful. The third step in constructing the frequency distribution is to determine the width of the class interval. Dividing the range of values by the number of classes yields the approximate width of the class interval.

The class midpoint is the midpoint of a class interval. It is the average of the class endpoints and represents the halfway point of the class interval. Relative frequency is a value computed by dividing an individual frequency by the sum of the frequencies. Relative frequency represents the proportion of total values that is in a given class interval. The cumulative frequency is a running total frequency tally that starts with the first frequency value and adds each ensuing frequency to the total.

Two types of graphical depictions are quantitative data graphs and qualitative data graphs. Quantitative data graphs presented in this chapter are histogram, frequency polygon, ogive, dot plot, and stem-and-leaf plot. Qualitative data graphs presented are pie chart, bar chart, and Pareto chart. In addition, cross tabulation tables and two-dimensional scatter plots are presented. A histogram is a vertical chart in which a line segment connects class endpoints at the value of the frequency. Two vertical lines connect this line segment down to the x-axis, forming a rectangle. A frequency polygon is constructed by plotting a dot at the midpoint of each class interval for the value of each frequency and then connecting the dots. Ogives are cumulative frequency polygons. Points on an ogive are plotted at the class endpoints. A dot plot is a graph that displays frequency counts for various data points as dots graphed above the data point. Dot plots are especially useful for observing the overall shape of the distribution and determining both gaps in the data and high concentrations of data. Stem-and-leaf plots are another way to organize data. The numbers are divided into two parts, a stem and a leaf. The stems are the leftmost digits of the numbers and the leaves are the rightmost digits. The stems are listed individually, with all leaf values corresponding to each stem displayed beside that stem.

A pie chart is a circular depiction of data. The amount of each category is represented as a slice of the pie proportionate to the total. The researcher is cautioned in using pie charts because it is sometimes difficult to differentiate the relative sizes of the slices.

The bar chart or bar graph uses bars to represent the frequencies of various qualitative categories. The bar chart can be displayed horizontally or vertically.

A Pareto chart is a vertical bar chart that is used in total quality management to graphically display the causes of problems. The Pareto chart presents problem causes in descending order to assist the decision maker in prioritizing problem causes. Cross tabulation is a process for producing a two-dimensional table that displays the frequency counts for two variables simultaneously. The scatter plot is a two-dimensional plot of pairs of points from two numerical variables. It is used to graphically determine whether any apparent relationship exists between the two variables.

Key Terms

bar charts	cross tabulation	grouped data	range
bar graph	cumulative frequency	histogram	relative frequency
class mark	dot plot	ogive	scatter plot
class midpoint	frequency distribution	Pareto chart	stem-and-leaf plot
column charts	frequency polygon	pie chart	ungrouped data

Supplementary Problems

Calculating the Statistics

2.25. For the following data, construct a frequency distribution with six classes.

57	23	35	18	21
26	51	47	29	21
46	43	29	23	39
50	41	19	36	28
31	42	52	29	18
28	46	33	28	20

2.26. For each class interval of the frequency distribution given, determine the class midpoint, the relative frequency, and the cumulative frequency.

CLASS INTERVAL	FREQUENCY
20–under 25	17
25–under 30	20
30–under 35	16
35–under 40	15
40–under 45	8
45–under 50	6

2.27. Construct a histogram, a frequency polygon, and an ogive for the following frequency distribution.

CLASS INTERVAL	FREQUENCY
50–under 60	13
60–under 70	27
70–under 80	43
80–under 90	31
90–under 100	9

2.28. Construct a dot plot from the following data.

16	15	17	15	15
15	14	9	16	15
13	10	8	18	20
17	17	17	18	23
7	15	20	10	14

2.29. Construct a stem-and-leaf plot for the following data. Let the leaf contain one digit.

312	324	289	335	298
314	309	294	326	317
290	311	317	301	316
306	286	308	284	324

2.30. Construct a pie chart from the following data.

LABEL	VALUE
A	55
B	121
C	83
D	46

2.31. Construct a bar graph from the following data.

CATEGORY	FREQUENCY
A	7
B	12
C	14
D	5
E	19

2.32. An examination of rejects shows at least 7 problems. A frequency tally of the problems follows. Construct a Pareto chart for these data.

PROBLEM	FREQUENCY
1	673
2	29
3	108
4	202
5	73
6	564
7	402

2.33. Construct a scatter plot for the following two numerical variables.

x	y
12	5
17	3
9	10
6	15
10	8
14	9
8	8

Testing Your Understanding

2.34. The Whitcomb Company manufactures a metal ring for industrial engines that usually weighs about 50 ounces. A random sample of 50 of these metal rings produced the following weights (in ounces).

51	53	56	50	44	47
53	53	42	57	46	55
41	44	52	56	50	57
44	46	41	52	69	53
57	51	54	63	42	47
47	52	53	46	36	58
51	38	49	50	62	39
44	55	43	52	43	42
57	49				

a. Construct a dot plot for these data and comment on any observations you make about the data from the plot.

b. Construct a frequency distribution and histogram for these data using eight classes. What can you observe about the data from the histogram?

c. Construct a frequency polygon and an ogive from the frequency distribution created in part b above and note any information gleaned from these graphs.

2.35. A northwestern distribution company surveyed 53 of its midlevel managers. The survey obtained the ages of these managers, which later were organized into the frequency distribution shown. Determine the class midpoint, relative frequency, and cumulative frequency for these data.

CLASS INTERVAL	FREQUENCY
20–under 25	8
25–under 30	6
30–under 35	5
35–under 40	12
40–under 45	15
45–under 50	7

2.36. Suppose 1000 commuters in New York City submit their typical daily commute time to a transportation research company who then organizes the data into the histogram shown below. Study the histogram and comment on information gleaned from the graph. Describe commuter times in New York City based on what you see here.

2.37. The following data are shaped roughly like a normal distribution (discussed in Chapter 6).

61.4	27.3	26.4	37.4	30.4	47.5
63.9	46.8	67.9	19.1	81.6	47.9
73.4	54.6	65.1	53.3	71.6	58.6
57.3	87.8	71.1	74.1	48.9	60.2
54.8	60.5	32.5	61.7	55.1	48.2
56.8	60.1	52.9	60.5	55.6	38.1
76.4	46.8	19.9	27.3	77.4	58.1
32.1	54.9	32.7	40.1	52.7	32.5
35.3	39.1				

Construct a frequency distribution starting with 10 as the lowest class beginning point and use a class width of 10. Construct a histogram and a frequency polygon for this frequency distribution and observe the shape of a normal distribution. On the basis of your results from these graphs, what does a normal distribution look like?

2.38. In a medium-sized southern city, 86 houses are for sale, each having about 2000 square feet of floor space. The asking prices vary. The frequency distribution shown contains the price categories for the 86 houses. Construct a histogram, a frequency polygon, and an ogive from these data.

ASKING PRICE	FREQUENCY
$ 80,000–under $100,000	21
100,000–under 120,000	27
120,000–under 140,000	18
140,000–under 160,000	11
160,000–under 180,000	6
180,000–under 200,000	3

2.39. Shipping a 40-foot container by boat from Shanghai to Chicago via the port of Los Angeles takes, on average, 16 days. However, due to several possible mitigating circumstances, shipping times can vary. Suppose a transportation researcher randomly selects 20 different shipments over a yearly period and records the number of days that it takes for a container to travel

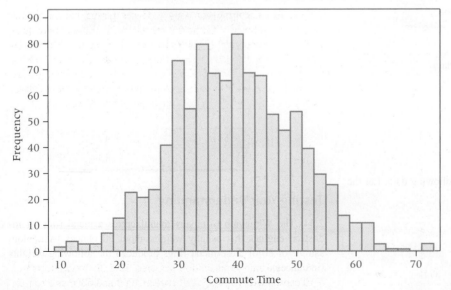

Commute Time for 1000 Workers in N.Y.C.

from Shanghai to Chicago. The resulting data in number of days is given below.

| 25 | 12 | 23 | 16 | 27 | 19 | 32 | 20 | 32 | 13 |
| 17 | 18 | 26 | 19 | 18 | 28 | 18 | 31 | 30 | 24 |

a. Construct a stem-and-leaf plot for the data.

b. Construct a dot plot for the data.

c. Comment on any observations that you glean from these two plots.

2.40. Good, relatively inexpensive prenatal care often can prevent a lifetime of expense owing to complications resulting from a baby's low birth weight. A survey of a random sample of 57 new mothers asked them to estimate how much they spent on prenatal care. The researcher tallied the results and presented them in the frequency distribution shown. Use these data to construct a histogram, a frequency polygon, and an ogive.

AMOUNT SPENT ON PRENATAL CARE	FREQUENCY OF NEW MOTHERS
$ 0–under $100	3
100–under 200	6
200–under 300	12
300–under 400	19
400–under 500	11
500–under 600	6

2.41. A consumer group surveyed food prices at 87 stores on the East Coast. Among the food prices being measured was that of sugar. From the data collected, the group constructed the frequency distribution of the prices of 4 pounds of Domino's sugar in the stores surveyed. Compute a histogram, a frequency polygon, and an ogive for the following data.

PRICE	FREQUENCY
$1.75–under $1.90	9
1.90–under 2.05	14
2.05–under 2.20	17
2.20–under 2.35	16
2.35–under 2.50	18
2.50–under 2.65	8
2.65–under 2.80	5

2.42. The top music genres for 2014 are Rock, R&B/ Hip Hop, Pop, and Country. These and other music genres along with the number of albums sold or downloaded in each category (in millions) are shown here.

GENRE	ALBUMS SOLD
Rock	138.2
R&B/ Hip Hop	82.0
Pop	71.0
Country	53.4
Dance/EDM	16.2
Christian/Gospel	14.8
Holiday/Seasonal	12.4
Latin	12.4

a. Construct a pie chart for these data displaying the percentage of the whole that each of these genres represents.

b. Construct a bar chart for these data.

c. Compare and contrast the displays of the pie chart and the bar chart.

2.43. The following figures for U.S. imports of agricultural products and manufactured goods were taken from selected years over a 30-year period (in $ billions). The source of the data is the U.S. International Trade Administration. Construct a scatter plot for these data and determine whether any relationship is apparent between the U.S. imports of agricultural products and the U.S. imports of manufactured goods during this time period.

AGRICULTURAL PRODUCTS	MANUFACTURED GOODS
5.8	27.3
9.5	54.0
17.4	133.0
19.5	257.5
22.3	388.8
29.3	629.7

2.44. Shown here is a list of the industries with the largest total toxic releases in a recent year according to the EPA. Construct both a bar chart and a pie chart to depict this information and comment on the advantages of each type of chart in depicting these data.

INDUSTRY	TOTAL RELEASES (BILLIONS POUNDS)
Metal Mining	1.970
Electric Utilities	0.539
Chemicals	0.505
Primary Metals	0.346
Paper	0.175
Hazardous Waste Mgmt.	0.146
Food/Beverages	0.134
All others	0.306

2.45. A manufacturing company produces plastic bottles for the dairy industry. Some of the bottles are rejected because of poor quality. Causes of poor-quality bottles include faulty plastic, incorrect labeling, discoloration, incorrect thickness, broken handle, and others. The following data for 500 plastic bottles that were rejected include the problems and the frequency of the problems. Use these data to construct a Pareto chart. Discuss the implications of the chart.

PROBLEM	NUMBER
Discoloration	32
Thickness	117
Broken handle	86
Fault in plastic	221
Labeling	44

2.46. A research organization selected 50 U.S. towns from the 2010 census with populations between 4000 and 6000 as a sample to represent small towns for survey purposes. The populations of these towns follow.

4420	5221	4299	5831	5750
5049	5556	4361	5737	4654
4653	5338	4512	4388	5923
4730	4963	5090	4822	4304
4758	5366	5431	5291	5254
4866	5858	4346	4734	5919
4216	4328	4459	5832	5873
5257	5048	4232	4878	5166
5366	4212	5669	4224	4440
4299	5263	4339	4834	5478

Construct a stem-and-leaf plot for the data, letting each leaf contain two digits.

Interpreting the Output

2.47. Suppose 150 shoppers at an upscale mall are interviewed and one of the questions asked is the household income. Study the Minitab histogram of the following data and discuss what can be learned about the shoppers.

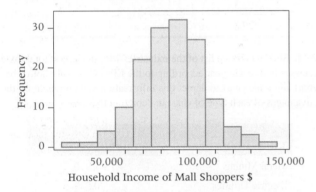

2.48. Study the following dot plot and comment on the general shape of the distribution. Discuss any gaps or heavy concentrations in the data.

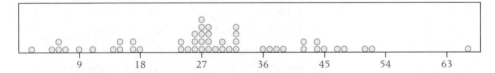

2.49. Shown here is an Excel-produced pie chart representing physician specialties. What does the chart tell you about the various specialties?

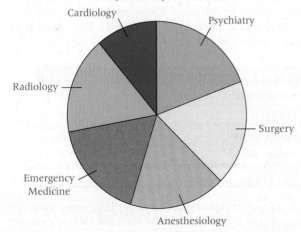

Physician Specialties

2.50. Suppose 100 CPA firms are surveyed to determine how many audits they perform over a certain time. The data are summarized using the Minitab stem-and-leaf plot shown in the next column. What can you learn about the number of audits being performed by these firms from this plot?

STEM-AND-LEAF DISPLAY: AUDITS		
Stem-and-leaf of Audits		N = 100
Leaf Unit = 1.0		
9	1	222333333
16	1	4445555
26	1	6666667777
35	1	888899999
39	2	0001
44	2	22333
49	2	55555
(9)	2	677777777
42	2	8888899
35	3	000111
29	3	223333
23	3	44455555
15	3	67777
10	3	889
7	4	0011
3	4	222

2.51. Shown here is a scatter plot of the NASDAQ-100 Index versus the Dow Jones Industrial Average on Friday closings over a period of one year (August 8, 2014 to August 7, 2015). What does the graph tell you about the relationship of the NASDAQ-100 Index to the Dow Jones Industrial Average? Explain what you observe in the graph and share any conclusions that you reach. The NASDAQ-100 data were obtained from the Federal Reserve Bank of St. Louis and the Dow Jones Industrial Averages were obtained from measuringworth.com.

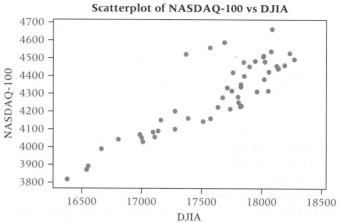

Analyzing the Databases

See www.wiley.com/college/black

1. Using the manufacturer database, construct a frequency distribution for the variable Number of Production Workers. What does the frequency distribution reveal about the number of production workers?

2. Using the Consumer Food database, construct a histogram for the variable Annual Food Spending. How is the histogram shaped? Is it high in the middle or high near one or both ends of the data? Is it relatively constant in size across the class (uniform), or does it appear to have no shape? Does it appear to be nearly "normally" distributed?

3. Construct an ogive for the variable Type in the financial database. The 100 companies in this database are each categorized into one of seven types of companies. These types are listed at the end of Chapter 1. Construct a pie chart of these types and discuss the output. For example, which type is most prevalent in the database and which is the least?

4. Using the international unemployment database, construct a stem-and-leaf plot for Italy. What does the plot show about unemployment for Italy over the past 40 years? What does the plot fail to show?

Case

Southwest Airlines

One night over dinner early in 1967 in San Antonio, Rollin King presented his idea for a new airline to Herb Kelleher by drawing a triangle on a napkin and labeling the three corners as Dallas, Houston, and San Antonio. King's idea was to offer reasonably priced nonstop service between the three cities; and as a result, Southwest Airlines was created. Out of this initial meeting, Southwest Airlines was incorporated in Texas on March 15, 1967. Commercial service commenced on June 18, 1971, with three Boeing 737 aircraft serving three Texas cities—Houston, Dallas, and San Antonio. Southwest Airlines grew rapidly; and on January of 1974, they carried their one-millionth customer. In the next couple of years, several new jets and destinations were added including five new cities in 1977 alone. By mid 1988, Southwest had expanded its service to offer almost 900 flights each day across its route system covering 27 cities in 13 states; and by 1989, revenue had exceeded the billion-dollar mark. Southwest won its first Triple Crown Award, based on Department of Transportation statistics for the year 1992 ranking first in fewest customer complaints, best on-time performance, and best baggage handling.

In 1993, Southwest was named one of the top ten best companies to work for in America—recognized for job security, opportunities, youngest companies, strongly unionized, and where fun is a way of life. In 1994, Southwest became the first major airline to offer ticketless travel; and in 1996, it became the first major airline to post a website with the launch of their "Home Gate" site. In 1997, the airline ranked first on Fortune magazine's "100 Best Companies to Work For in America" list.

Southwest topped the monthly domestic originating passenger rankings for the first time in May 2003. In 2011, AirTran Airways became a wholly owned subsidiary of Southwest Airlines.

In 2013, Southwest launched the first Southwest service to a destination outside the 48 contiguous states with service to San Juan, Puerto Rico. In July 2014, Southwest began its first international flights to Nassau, Bahamas; Montego Bay, Jamaica; and Aruba. Later in the year, Southwest continued its international launch with service to Mexico and the Dominican Republic. In 2015, Southwest's international service grew to seven countries with new service to San Jose, Costa Rica, Puerto Vallarta, Mexico, and Belize City, Belize.

Presently in its 44th year of service, Southwest Airlines (NYSE: LUV) continues to differentiate itself from other air carriers with exemplary customer service delivered by more than 47,000 employees to more than 100 million customers annually. Southwest operates more than 3,600 flights a day, serving 94 destinations across the United States and six additional countries. The mission of Southwest Airlines is "dedication to the highest quality of customer service delivered with a sense of warmth, friendliness, individual pride, and company spirit".

Discussion

1. Suppose you have been asked to write a report for Southwest Airlines discussing and displaying their share of the U.S. airline market. In your research, you are able to obtain from the Bureau of Transportation Statistics the following information on the Number of Passengers Carried in a recent year for the top seven U.S. airlines:

Southwest Airlines – 111,498,509
Delta Air Lines – 109,827,685
United Air Lines – 82,436,921
American Airlines – 80,113,333
US Airways – 52,955,303
ExpressJet Airlines – 30,576,553
JetBlue Airways – 27,836,405

Using at least two of the graphs and/or charts discussed in this chapter, present your findings on these seven airlines and briefly discuss the results.

2. Information gleaned from budgettravel.com and SITA (Specialist in Air Transport and IT Communications) indicates that there are at least five reasons that air passengers' luggage is lost. These include: 1.) The routing label is damaged or lost, 2.) Lost during transfer from one plane to another, 3.) The wrong destination code is typed at ticketing, 4.) The luggage is loaded into the wrong plane to begin with, and 5.) The passenger forgets to pick up their luggage at the destination. Suppose a study of 500 pieces of lost luggage is undertaken in which researchers are attempting to determine the main cause of luggage loss and it is determined that 98 of the pieces were lost due to a lost or damaged routing label, 255 were lost during transfer from one plane to another, 71 were lost due to the wrong destination code being typed at ticketing, 52 were lost because they were loaded into the wrong plane, and 24 were lost because the passenger failed to pick up their luggage at the destination. Use a Pareto Chart to analyze the results of this study. Based on your chart, what would you recommend as a way to attack the lost luggage problem?

3. Shown here are two scatter plots of data on U.S. airlines reported in a recent year by bga-aeroweb.com. The first scatter plot displays the number of passengers carried annually by the top nine airlines and the number of seats per aircraft for each airline. The second scatter plot displays the number of passengers carried and the number of flights by the top nine airlines in a recent year. Study the two scatter plots and comment on any insights you glean regarding the airline industry.

Sources: Adapted from: Southwest Airlines at swamedia.com/channels/Our-History/pages/our-history-sort-by/; Bureau of Transportation Statistics at www.transtats.bts.gov/

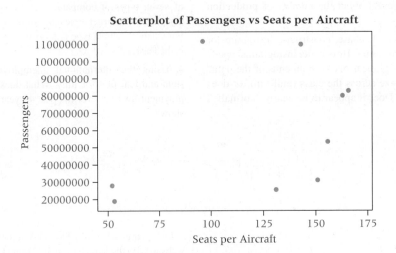

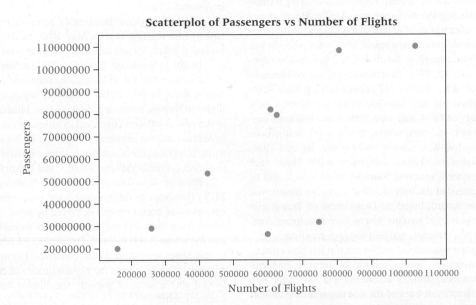

CHAPTER 3

Descriptive Statistics

LEARNING OBJECTIVES

The focus of Chapter 3 is the use of statistical techniques to describe data, thereby enabling you to:

1. Apply various measures of central tendency—including the mean, median, and mode—to a set of ungrouped data.

2. Apply various measures of variability—including the range, interquartile range, mean absolute deviation, variance, and standard deviation (using the empirical rule and Chebyshev's theorem)—to a set of ungrouped data.

3. Compute the mean, median, mode, standard deviation, and variance of grouped data.

4. Describe a data distribution statistically and graphically using skewness, kurtosis, and box-and-whisker plots.

5. Use computer packages to compute various measures of central tendency, variation, and shape on a set of data, as well as to describe the data distribution graphically.

Decision Dilemma

Laundry Statistics

A typical American family of four generates at least 300 loads of laundry annually. Considering that there are over 123 million households in the United States, somewhere near 37 billion loads of laundry are run in United States each year. Every second, more than 1,100 loads are started. Statistics show that one person in the United States generates a quarter of a ton of dirty clothing each year. The average U.S. resident spends 56 minutes per week doing laundry. Washing laundry accounts for between 15% and 40% of the overall water consumption of a typical American home. Prior to 2010, traditional clothes' washers in the United States used between 30 and 45 gallons of water per load. However, since then government standards have become more stringent, requiring washers to use less water and energy. More recently, washers using 26 gallons or more are considered poor in water usage, and there are efficient washing machines considered excellent in water usage that use only 13 gallons or less per load. Historically, the average washing machine in Europe

Keith Getter/Getty Images, Inc.

uses about 4 gallons of water. However, while the average wash cycle of an American wash is about 35 minutes, the average wash cycle in Europe is about 90 minutes. Americans have traditionally preferred top loading washing machines because they are less expensive, they have a longer life expectancy and the user does not have to bend over to load and unload. However, the percentage of Americans using front loaders is increasing and is now around 35%. Europeans, on the other hand, prefer front loaders because they use less water, they are stackable, and they use less space. Around 90% of Europeans still prefer front loaders.

MANAGERIAL AND STATISTICAL QUESTIONS

Virtually all of the statistics cited here are gleaned from studies or surveys.

1. Suppose a study of laundry usage is done in 50 U.S. households that contain washers and dryers. Water measurements are taken for the number of gallons of water used by each washing machine in completing a cycle. The following data are the number of gallons used by each washing machine during the washing cycle. Summarize the data so that study findings can be reported.

15	17	16	15	16	17	18	15	14	15
16	16	17	16	15	15	17	14	15	16
16	17	14	15	12	15	16	14	14	16
15	13	16	17	17	15	16	16	16	14
17	16	17	14	16	13	16	15	16	15

2. The average wash cycle for an American wash is 35 minutes. Suppose the standard deviation of a wash cycle for an American wash is 5 minutes. Within what range of time do most American wash cycles fall?

Source: Adapted from the following sources: www.greencontributor.com/index.php/human-foot-print.html; www.consumerreports.org › Home › Appliances; www.ibtimes.com/americans-spend-less-time-thinking-more-time-watching...; www.allianceforwaterefficiency.org › resource library

Chapter 2 presented graphical techniques for organizing and displaying data. Even though such graphical techniques allow the researcher to make some general observations about the shape and spread of the data, a more complete understanding of the data can be attained by summarizing the data using statistics. This chapter presents such statistical measures, including measures of central tendency, measures of variability, and measures of shape. The computation of these measures is different for ungrouped and grouped data. Hence we present some measures for ungrouped data and some measures for grouped data.

3.1 Measures of Central Tendency: Ungrouped Data

Interactive Applet

One type of measure that is used to describe a set of data is the **measure of central tendency**. Measures of central tendency *yield information about the center, or middle part, of a group of numbers.* Table 3.1 displays offer price for the 20 largest U.S. initial public offerings in a recent year according to Securities Data. For these data, measures of central tendency can yield such information as the average offer price, the middle offer price, and the most frequently occurring offer price. Measures of central tendency do not focus on the span of the data set or how far values are from the middle numbers. The measures of central tendency presented here for ungrouped data are the mode, the median, the mean, percentiles, and quartiles.

Mode

The **mode** is *the most frequently occurring value in a set of data.* For the data in Table 3.1 the mode is $19.00 because the offer price that recurred the most times (four) was $19.00. Organizing the data into an ordered array (an ordering of the numbers from smallest to largest) helps to locate the mode. The following is an ordered array of the values from Table 3.1.

TABLE 3.1	Offer Prices for the 20 Largest U.S. Initial Public Offerings in a Recent Year		
$14.25	$19.00	$11.00	$28.00
24.00	23.00	43.25	19.00
27.00	25.00	15.00	7.00
34.22	15.50	15.00	22.00
19.00	19.00	27.00	21.00

| 7.00 | 11.00 | 14.25 | 15.00 | 15.00 | 15.50 | 19.00 | 19.00 | 19.00 | 19.00 |
| 21.00 | 22.00 | 23.00 | 24.00 | 25.00 | 27.00 | 27.00 | 28.00 | 34.22 | 43.25 |

This grouping makes it easier to see that 19.00 is the most frequently occurring number.

In the case of a tie for the most frequently occurring value, two modes are listed. Then the data are said to be **bimodal**. If a set of data is not exactly bimodal but contains two values that are more dominant than others, some researchers take the liberty of referring to the data set as bimodal even without an exact tie for the mode. Data sets with more than two modes are referred to as **multimodal**.

In the world of business, the concept of mode is often used in determining sizes. As an example, manufacturers who produce cheap rubber flip-flops that are sold for as little as $1.00 around the world might only produce them in one size in order to save on machine setup costs. In determining the one size to produce, the manufacturer would most likely produce flip-flops in the modal size. The mode is an appropriate measure of central tendency for nominal-level data.

Median

The **median** is *the middle value in an ordered array of numbers.* For an array with an odd number of terms, the median is the middle number. For an array with an even number of terms, the median is the average of the two middle numbers. The following steps are used to determine the median.

Step 1   Arrange the observations in an ordered data array.

Step 2   For an odd number of terms, find the middle term of the ordered array. It is the median.

Step 3   For an even number of terms, find the average of the middle two terms. This average is the median.

Suppose a business researcher wants to determine the median for the following numbers.

15   11   14   3   21   17   22   16   19   16   5   7   19   8   9   20   4

The researcher arranges the numbers in an ordered array.

3   4   5   7   8   9   11   14   15   16   16   17   19   19   20   21   22

Because the array contains 17 terms (an odd number of terms), the median is the middle number, or 15.

If the number 22 is eliminated from the list, the array would contain only 16 terms.

3   4   5   7   8   9   11   14   15   16   16   17   19   19   20   21

Now, for an even number of terms, the statistician determines the median by averaging the two middle values, 14 and 15. The resulting median value is 14.5.

Another way to locate the median is by finding the $(n + 1)/2$ term in an ordered array. For example, if a data set contains 77 terms, the median is the 39th term. That is,

$$\frac{n+1}{2} = \frac{77+1}{2} = \frac{78}{2} = 39\text{th term}$$

This formula is helpful when a large number of terms must be manipulated.

Consider the offer price data in Table 3.1. Because this data set contains 20 values, or $n = 20$, the median for these data is located at the $(20 + 1)/2$ term, or the 10.5th term. This result indicates that the median is located halfway between the 10th and 11th terms or the average of 19.00 and 21.00. Thus, the median offer price for the largest 20 U.S. initial public offerings is $20.00.

The median is unaffected by the magnitude of extreme values. This characteristic is an advantage, because large and small values do not inordinately influence the median. For this reason, the median is often the best measure of location to use in the analysis of variables such as house costs, income, and age. Suppose, for example, that a real estate broker wants to determine the median selling price of 10 houses listed at the following prices.

$67,000	$105,000	$148,000	$5,250,000
91,000	116,000	167,000	
95,000	122,000	189,000	

The median is the average of the two middle terms, $116,000 and $122,000, or $119,000. This price is a reasonable representation of the prices of the 10 houses. Note that the house priced at $5,250,000 did not enter into the analysis other than to count as one of the 10 houses. If the price of the tenth house were $200,000, the results would be the same. However, if all the house prices were averaged, the resulting average price of the original 10 houses would be $635,000, higher than 9 of the 10 individual prices.

A disadvantage of the median is that not all the information from the numbers is used. For example, information about the specific asking price of the most expensive house does not really enter into the computation of the median. The level of data measurement must be at least ordinal for a median to be meaningful.

Mean

The **arithmetic mean** is *the average of a group of numbers* and is computed by summing all numbers and dividing by the number of numbers. Because the arithmetic mean is so widely used, most statisticians refer to it simply as the *mean*.

The population mean is represented by the Greek letter mu (μ). The sample mean is represented by $\bar{x}$. The formulas for computing the population mean and the sample mean are given in the boxes that follow.

Population Mean

$$\mu = \frac{\Sigma x_i}{N} = \frac{x_1 + x_2 + x_3 + \cdots + x_N}{N}$$

Sample Mean

$$\bar{x} = \frac{\Sigma x_i}{n} = \frac{x_1 + x_2 + x_3 + \cdots + x_n}{n}$$

The capital Greek letter sigma (Σ) is commonly used in mathematics to represent a summation of all the numbers in a grouping.* Also, N is the number of terms in the population, and n is the number of terms in the sample. The algorithm for computing a mean is to sum all the numbers in the population or sample and divide by the number of terms. It is inappropriate to use the mean to analyze data that are not at least interval level in measurement.

Suppose a company has five departments with 24, 13, 19, 26, and 11 workers each. The *population mean* number of workers in each department is 18.6 workers. The computations follow.

$$
\begin{array}{r}
24 \\
13 \\
19 \\
26 \\
\underline{11} \\
\Sigma x_i = \quad 93
\end{array}
$$

---

*The mathematics of summations is not discussed here. A more detailed explanation is given in WileyPLUS, Chapter 3.

and

$$\mu = \frac{\Sigma x_i}{N} = \frac{93}{5} = 18.6$$

The calculation of a sample mean uses the same algorithm as for a population mean and will produce the same answer if computed on the same data. However, it is inappropriate to compute a sample mean for a population or a population mean for a sample. Because both populations and samples are important in statistics, a separate symbol is necessary for the population mean and for the sample mean.

DEMONSTRATION PROBLEM 3.1

Shown below is a list of the top thirteen shopping centers in the United Kingdom by retail size in 1,000 square meters (m²). Calculate the mode, median, and mean for this data.

SHOPPING CENTRE	SIZE (1000 m²)
MetroCentre	190.0
Trafford Centre	180.9
Westfield Stratford City	175.0
Bluewater	155.7
Liverpool One	154.0
Westfield London	149.5
Intu Merry Hill	140.8
Manchester Arndale	139.4
Meadowhall	139.4
Lakeside	133.8
St. David's	130.1
Bullring	127.1
Eldon Square	125.4

https://en.wikipedia.org/wiki/List_of_UK_shopping_centres

Solution:

Mode: The mode for these data is 139.4. Two of the shopping centres, Manchester Arndale and Meadowhall, are 139.4 (1000 m²) in size.

Median: With 13 different shopping centres in this group, $N = 13$. The median is located at the $(13 + 1)/2 = 7$th position. Because the data are already ordered, the 7th term is 140.8 (1000 m²), which is the median. Thus, the median shopping centre of this group is Intu Merry Hill.

Mean: The total number (Σx) of square meters for this group of thirteen shopping centres is 1,941.1 (1000 m²). The mean is calculated as:

$$\mu = \frac{\Sigma x}{N} = \frac{1,941.1}{13} = 149.3$$

The mean is affected by each and every value, which is an advantage. The mean uses all the data, and each data item influences the mean. It is also a disadvantage because extremely large or small values can cause the mean to be pulled toward the extreme value. Recall the preceding discussion of the 10 house prices. If the mean is computed for the 10 houses, the mean price is higher than the prices of 9 of the houses because the $5,250,000 house is included in the calculation. The total price of the 10 houses is $6,350,000, and the mean price is $635,000.

The mean is the most commonly used measure of central tendency because it uses each data item in its computation, it is a familiar measure, and it has mathematical properties that make it attractive to use in inferential statistics analysis.

Percentiles

Percentiles are *measures of central tendency that divide a group of data into 100 parts*. There are 99 percentiles because it takes 99 dividers to separate a group of data into 100 parts. The *n*th percentile is the value such that at least *n* percent of the data are below that value and at most $(100 - n)$ percent are above that value. Specifically, the 87th percentile is a value such that at least 87% of the data are below the value and no more than 13% are above the value. Percentiles are "stair-step" values, as shown in **Figure 3.1**, because there is no percentile between the 87th percentile and the 88th percentile. If a plant operator takes a safety examination and 87.6% of the safety exam scores are below that person's score, he or she still scores at only the 87th percentile, even though more than 87% of the scores are lower.

Percentiles are widely used in reporting test results. Almost all college or university students have taken the SAT, ACT, GRE, or GMAT examination. In most cases, the results for these examinations are reported in percentile form and also as raw scores. Shown next is a summary of the steps used in determining the location of a percentile.

Steps in Determining the Location of a Percentile

1. Organize the numbers into an ascending-order array.

2. Calculate the percentile location (i) by:

$$i = \frac{P}{100}(N)$$

where

P = the percentile of interest
i = percentile location
N = number in the data set

3. Determine the location by either (a) or (b).

   a. If i is a whole number, the Pth percentile is the average of the value at the ith location and the value at the $(i + 1)^{st}$ location.

   b. If i is not a whole number, the Pth percentile value is located at the whole number part of $i + 1$.

For example, suppose you want to determine the 80th percentile of 1240 numbers. P is 80 and N is 1240. First, order the numbers from lowest to highest. Next, calculate the location of the 80th percentile.

$$i = \frac{80}{100}(1240) = 992$$

Because $i = 992$ is a whole number, follow the directions in step 3(a). The 80th percentile is the average of the 992nd number and the 993rd number.

$$P_{80} = \frac{(992\text{nd number} + 993\text{rd number})}{2}$$

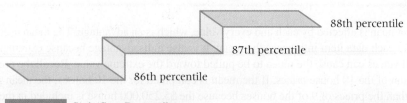

FIGURE 3.1 **Stair-Step Percentiles**

DEMONSTRATION PROBLEM 3.2

Determine the 30th percentile of the following eight numbers: 14, 12, 19, 23, 5, 13, 28, 17.

Solution: For these eight numbers, we want to find the value of the 30th percentile, so $N = 8$ and $P = 30$.

First, organize the data into an ascending-order array.

5	12	13	14	17	19	23	28

Next, compute the value of i.

$$i = \frac{30}{100}(8) = 2.4$$

Because i is not a whole number, step 3(b) is used. The value of $i + 1$ is $2.4 + 1$, or 3.4. The whole-number part of 3.4 is 3. The 30th percentile is located at the third value. The third value is 13, so 13 is the 30th percentile. Note that a percentile may or may not be one of the data values.

Quartiles

Quartiles are *measures of central tendency that divide a group of data into four subgroups or parts*. The three quartiles are denoted as Q_1, Q_2, and Q_3. The first quartile, Q_1, separates the first, or lowest, one-fourth of the data from the upper three-fourths and is equal to the 25th percentile. The second quartile, Q_2, separates the second quarter of the data from the third quarter. Q_2 is located at the 50th percentile and equals the median of the data. The third quartile, Q_3, divides the first three-quarters of the data from the last quarter and is equal to the value of the 75th percentile. These three quartiles are shown in **Figure 3.2**.

Suppose we want to determine the values of Q_1, Q_2, and Q_3 for the following numbers.

106	109	114	116	121	122	125	129

The value of Q_1 is found at the 25th percentile, P_{25}, by:

$$\text{For } N = 8, i = \frac{25}{100}(8) = 2$$

Because i is a whole number, P_{25} is found as the average of the second and third numbers.

$$P_{25} = \frac{(109 + 114)}{2} = 111.5$$

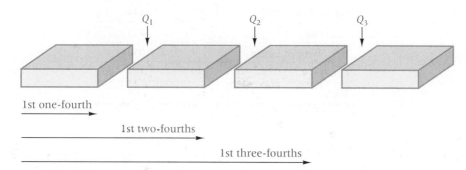

FIGURE 3.2 **Quartiles**

The value of Q_1 is $P_{25} = 111.5$. Notice that one-fourth, or two, of the values (106 and 109) are less than 111.5.

The value of Q_2 is equal to the median. Because the array contains an even number of terms, the median is the average of the two middle terms.

$$Q_2 = \text{median} = \frac{(116 + 121)}{2} = 118.5$$

Notice that exactly half of the terms are less than Q_2 and half are greater than Q_2.

The value of Q_3 is determined by P_{75} as follows.

$$i = \frac{75}{100}(8) = 6$$

Because i is a whole number, P_{75} is the average of the sixth and the seventh numbers.

$$P_{75} = \frac{(122 + 125)}{2} = 123.5$$

The value of Q_3 is $P_{75} = 123.5$. Notice that three-fourths, or six, of the values are less than 123.5 and two of the values are greater than 123.5.

DEMONSTRATION PROBLEM 3.3

The following shows the top 16 global marketing categories for advertising spending for a recent year according to *Advertising Age*. Spending is given in millions of U.S. dollars. Determine the first, the second, and the third quartiles for these data.

CATEGORY	AD SPENDING
Automotive	$22,195
Personal Care	19,526
Entertainment & Media	9,538
Food	7,793
Drugs	7,707
Electronics	4,023
Soft Drinks	3,916
Retail	3,576
Cleaners	3,571
Restaurants	3,553
Computers	3,247
Telephone	2,488
Financial	2,433
Beer, Wine & Liquor	2,050
Candy	1,137
Toys	699

Solution: For 16 marketing organizations, $N = 16$. $Q_1 = P_{25}$ is found by

$$i = \frac{25}{100}(16) = 4$$

Because i is a whole number, Q_1 is found to be the average of the fourth and fifth values from the bottom.

$$Q_1 = \frac{2433 + 2488}{2} = 2460.5$$

$Q_2 = P_{50}$ = median; with 16 terms, the median is the average of the eighth and ninth terms.

$$Q_2 = \frac{3571 + 3576}{2} = 3573.5$$

$Q_3 = P_{75}$ is solved by

$$i = \frac{75}{100}(16) = 12$$

Q_3 is found by averaging the 12th and 13th terms.

$$Q_3 = \frac{7707 + 7793}{2} = 7750$$

3.1 Problems

3.1. Determine the median and the mode for the following numbers.

2 4 8 4 6 2 7 8 4 3 8 9 4 3 5

3.2. Determine the median for the following numbers.

213 345 609 073 167 243 444 524 199 682

3.3. Compute the mean for the following numbers.

17.3 44.5 31.6 40.0 52.8 38.8 30.1 78.5

3.4. Compute the mean for the following numbers.

7 −2 5 9 0 −3 −6 −7 −4 −5 2 −8

3.5. Compute the 35th percentile, the 55th percentile, Q_1, Q_2, and Q_3 for the following data.

16 28 29 13 17 20 11 34 32 27 25 30 19 18 33

3.6. Compute P_{20}, P_{47}, P_{83}, Q_1, Q_2, and Q_3 for the following data.

120	138	97	118	172	144
138	107	94	119	139	145
162	127	112	150	143	80
105	116	142	128	116	171

3.7. On a certain day, the average closing price of a group of stocks on the New York Stock Exchange (to the nearest dollar) is shown.

21 21 21 22 23 25 28 29 33 35 38 56 61

What are the mean, the median, and the mode for these data?

3.8. The following list shows the 15 largest banks in the world by assets according to relbanks.com. Compute the median and the mean assets from this group. Which of these two measures do you think is most appropriate for summarizing these data and why? What is the value of Q_2 and Q_3? Determine the 63rd percentile for the data. Determine the 29th percentile for the data.

BANK	ASSETS ($ BILLIONS)
Industrial & Commercial Bank of China (ICBC)	3,452
China Construction Bank Corp.	2,819
Agricultural Bank of China	2,716
HSBC Holdings	2,670
JPMorgan Chase & Co.	2,600
Bank of China	2,584
BNP Paribas	2,527
Mitsubishi UFJ Financial Group	2,337
Credit Agricole Group	2,144
Barclays PLC	2,114
Bank of America	2,105
Deutsche Bank	2,078
Citigroup, Inc.	1,843
Japan Post Bank	1,736
Wells Fargo	1,687

3.9. A list of the top ten manufacturing companies in the United States according to Industry Week along with their total revenue in $billions follows. Compute the median, Q_3, P_{20}, P_{60}, P_{80}, and P_{93} on these data.

COMPANY	REVENUE ($ BILLION)
Exxon Mobil	398.6
Chevron	204.9
Apple	182.8
Phillips 66	161.6
General Motors	155.9
General Electric	148.6
Ford Motor	144.1
Valero Energy	130.8
Hewlett-Packard	111.5
Marathon Petroleum	97.9

3.10. The following lists the number of fatal accidents by scheduled commercial airlines over a 17-year period according to the Air Transport Association of America. Using these data, compute the mean, median, and mode. What is the value of the third quartile? Determine P_{11}, P_{35}, P_{58}, and P_{67}.

4	4	4	1	4	2	4	3	8	6	4	4
1	4	2	3	3							

3.2 Measures of Variability: Ungrouped Data

Measures of central tendency yield information about the center or middle part of a data set. However, business researchers can use another group of analytic tools, *measures of variability*, to *describe the spread or the dispersion of a set of data*. Using measures of variability in conjunction with measures of central tendency makes possible a more complete numerical description of the data.

For example, a company has 25 salespeople in the field, and the median annual sales figure for these people is $1.2 million. Are the salespeople being successful as a group or not? The median provides information about the sales of the person in the middle, but what about the other salespeople? Are all of them selling $1.2 million annually, or do the sales figures vary widely, with one person selling $5 million annually and another selling only $150,000 annually? Measures of variability provide the additional information necessary to answer that question.

Figure 3.3 shows three distributions in which the mean of each distribution is the same ($\mu = 50$) but the variabilities differ. Observation of these distributions shows that a measure of variability is necessary to complement the mean value in describing the data. Methods of computing measures of variability differ for ungrouped data and grouped data. This section focuses on seven measures of variability for ungrouped data: range, interquartile range, mean absolute deviation, variance, standard deviation, z scores, and coefficient of variation.

Range

The **range** is *the difference between the largest value of a data set and the smallest value of a set*. Although it is usually a single numeric value, some business researchers define the range of data as the ordered pair of smallest and largest numbers (smallest, largest). It is a crude measure of variability, describing the distance to the outer bounds of the data set. It reflects

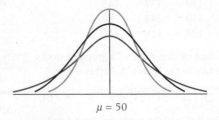

$\mu = 50$

FIGURE 3.3 **Three Distributions with the Same Mean but Different Dispersions**

those extreme values because it is constructed from them. An advantage of the range is its ease of computation. One important use of the range is in quality assurance, where the range is used to construct control charts. A disadvantage of the range is that, because it is computed with the values that are on the extremes of the data, it is affected by extreme values, and its application as a measure of variability is limited.

The data in Table 3.1 represent the offer prices for the 20 largest U.S. initial public offerings in a recent year. The lowest offer price was $7.00 and the highest price was $43.25. The range of the offer prices can be computed as the difference of the highest and lowest values:

$$\text{Range} = \text{Highest} - \text{Lowest} = \$43.25 - \$7.00 = \$36.25$$

Interquartile Range

Another measure of variability is the **interquartile range**. The interquartile range is *the range of values between the first and third quartile*. Essentially, it is the range of the middle 50% of the data and is determined by computing the value of $Q_3 - Q_1$. The interquartile range is especially useful in situations where data users are more interested in values toward the middle and less interested in extremes. In describing a real estate housing market, realtors might use the interquartile range as a measure of housing prices when describing the middle half of the market for buyers who are interested in houses in the midrange. In addition, the interquartile range is used in the construction of box-and-whisker plots.

Interquartile Range

$$Q_3 - Q_1$$

The following data indicate the top 15 trading partners of the United States in exports in 2014 according to the U.S Census Bureau.

COUNTRY	EXPORTS ($ BILLIONS)
Canada	312.4
Mexico	240.2
China	123.7
Japan	66.8
United Kingdom	53.8
Germany	49.4
South Korea	44.5
Netherlands	43.1
Brazil	42.4
Hong Kong	40.9
Belgium	34.8
France	31.3
Singapore	30.2
Taiwan	26.7
Switzerland	22.2

What is the interquartile range for these data? The process begins by computing the first and third quartiles as follows.

Solving for $Q_1 = P_{25}$ when $N = 15$:

$$i = \frac{25}{100}(15) = 3.75$$

Because i is not a whole number, P_{25} is found as the fourth term from the bottom.

$$Q_1 = P_{25} = 31.3$$

Solving for $Q_3 = P_{75}$:

$$i = \frac{75}{100}(15) = 11.25$$

Because i is not a whole number, P_{75} is found as the 12th term from the bottom.

$$Q_3 = P_{75} = 66.8$$

The interquartile range is:

$$Q_3 - Q_1 = 66.8 - 31.3 = 35.5$$

The middle 50% of the exports for the top 15 U.S. trading partners spans a range of 35.5 ($ billions).

Mean Absolute Deviation, Variance, and Standard Deviation

Three other measures of variability are the variance, the standard deviation, and the mean absolute deviation. They are obtained through similar processes and are, therefore, presented together. These measures are not meaningful unless the data are at least interval-level data. The variance and standard deviation are widely used in statistics. Although the standard deviation has some stand-alone potential, the importance of variance and standard deviation lies mainly in their role as tools used in conjunction with other statistical devices.

Suppose a small company started a production line to build computers. During the first five weeks of production, the output is 5, 9, 16, 17, and 18 computers, respectively. Which

---

Thinking Critically About Statistics in Business Today

Recycling Statistics

There are many interesting statistics with regard to recycling. Recycling one aluminum can saves enough energy, the equivalent of a half gallon of gasoline, to run a television for three hours. Because Americans have done such a good job of recycling aluminum cans, they account for less than 1% of the total U.S. waste stream. Recycling 1 pound of steel saves enough energy to run a 60-watt light bulb for over a day. On average, one American uses seven trees a year in paper, wood, and other products made from trees. In addition, Americans use 680 pounds of paper per year. Each ton of recycled paper saves about 17 trees, 380 gallons of oil, three cubic yards of landfill space, 4000 kilowatts of energy, and 7000 gallons of water. Americans use 2.5 million plastic bottles every hour and throw away 25 billion Styrofoam cups every year. The energy saved from recycling one glass bottle can run a 100-watt light bulb for four hours. Every year, each American throws out about 1200 pounds of organic garbage that could be composted. The U.S. is number one in the world in producing trash, with an average of 1609 pounds per person per year.

THINGS TO PONDER

1. The average person in the United States produces 1609 pounds of trash per year. What additional information could be gleaned by also knowing a measure of variability on these data (pounds of trash)?

2. On average, one American uses seven trees a year in products. What different information might a median yield on these data, and how might it help decision makers?

Sources: http://www.recycling-revolution.com/recycling-facts.html, National Recycling Coalition, the Environmental Protection Agency, Earth911.org.

descriptive statistics could the owner use to measure the early progress of production? In an attempt to summarize these figures, the owner could compute a mean.

$$x_i$$
$$5$$
$$9$$
$$16$$
$$17$$
$$18$$

$$\Sigma x_i = 65 \qquad \mu = \frac{\Sigma x_i}{N} = \frac{65}{5} = 13$$

What is the variability in these five weeks of data? One way for the owner to begin to look at the spread of the data is to subtract the mean from each data value. *Subtracting the mean from each value of data* yields the **deviation from the mean** $(x_i - \mu)$. Table 3.2 shows these deviations for the computer company production. Note that some deviations from the mean are positive and some are negative. Figure 3.4 shows that geometrically the negative deviations represent values that are below (to the left of) the mean and positive deviations represent values that are above (to the right of) the mean.

An examination of deviations from the mean can reveal information about the variability of data. However, the deviations are used mostly as a tool to compute other measures of variability. Note that in both Table 3.2 and Figure 3.4 these deviations total zero. This phenomenon applies to all cases. For a given set of data, the sum of all deviations from the arithmetic mean is always zero.

Sum of Deviations from the Arithmetic Mean is Always Zero

$$\Sigma(x_i - \mu) = 0$$

TABLE 3.2   **Deviations from the Mean for Computer Production**

NUMBER (x_i)	DEVIATIONS FROM THE MEAN $(x_i - \mu)$
5	$5 - 13 = -8$
9	$9 - 13 = -4$
16	$16 - 13 = +3$
17	$17 - 13 = +4$
18	$18 - 13 = +5$
$\Sigma x_i = 65$	$\Sigma(x_i - \mu) = 0$

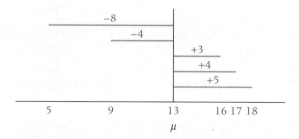

FIGURE 3.4   **Geometric Distances from the Mean (from Table 3.2)**

This property requires considering alternative ways to obtain measures of variability.

One obvious way to force the sum of deviations to have a nonzero total is to take the absolute value of each deviation around the mean. Utilizing the absolute value of the deviations about the mean makes solving for the mean absolute deviation possible.

Mean Absolute Deviation

The **mean absolute deviation (MAD)** is *the average of the absolute values of the deviations around the mean for a set of numbers.*

> **Mean Absolute Deviation**
>
> $$\text{MAD} = \frac{\Sigma|x_i - \mu|}{N}$$

Using the data from Table 3.2, the computer company owner can compute a mean absolute deviation by taking the absolute values of the deviations and averaging them, as shown in Table 3.3. The mean absolute deviation for the computer production data is 4.8.

Because it is computed by using absolute values, the mean absolute deviation is less useful in statistics than other measures of dispersion. However, in the field of forecasting, it is used occasionally as a measure of error.

Variance

Because absolute values are not conducive to easy manipulation, mathematicians developed an alternative mechanism for overcoming the zero-sum property of deviations from the mean. This approach utilizes the square of the deviations from the mean. The result is the variance, an important measure of variability.

The **variance** is *the average of the squared deviations about the arithmetic mean for a set of numbers.* The population variance is denoted by σ^2.

> **Population Variance**
>
> $$\sigma^2 = \frac{\Sigma(x_i - \mu)^2}{N}$$

TABLE 3.3   **MAD for Computer Production Data**

x_i	$x_i - \mu$	$|x_i - \mu|$
5	−8	+8
9	−4	+4
16	+3	+3
17	+4	+4
18	+5	+5
$\Sigma x_i = 65$	$\Sigma(x_i - \mu) = 0$	$\Sigma|x_i - \mu| = 24$

$$\text{MAD} = \frac{\Sigma|x_i - \mu|}{N} = \frac{24}{5} = 4.8$$

Table 3.4 shows the original production numbers for the computer company, the deviations from the mean, and the squared deviations from the mean.

The sum of the squared deviations about the mean of a set of values—called the **sum of squares of** x and sometimes abbreviated as SS_x—is used throughout statistics. For the computer company, this value is 130. Dividing it by the number of data values (5 weeks) yields the variance for computer production.

$$\sigma^2 = \frac{130}{5} = 26.0$$

Because the variance is computed from squared deviations, the final result is expressed in terms of squared units of measurement. Statistics measured in squared units are problematic to interpret. Consider, for example, Mattel Toys attempting to interpret production costs in terms of squared dollars or Troy-Bilt measuring production output variation in terms of squared lawn mowers. Therefore, when used as a descriptive measure, variance can be considered as an intermediate calculation in the process of obtaining the standard deviation.

Standard Deviation

The standard deviation is a popular measure of variability. It is used both as a separate entity and as a part of other analyses, such as computing confidence intervals and in hypothesis testing (see Chapters 8, 9, and 10).

Population Standard Deviation

$$\sigma = \sqrt{\frac{\Sigma(x_i - \mu)^2}{N}}$$

The **standard deviation** is *the square root of the variance*. The population standard deviation is denoted by σ.

	Computing a Variance and a Standard
TABLE 3.4	Deviation from the Computer Production Data

x_i	$x_i - \mu$	$(x_i - \mu)^2$
5	−8	64
9	−4	16
16	+3	9
17	+4	16
18	+5	25
$\Sigma x_i = 65$	$\Sigma(x_i - \mu) = 0$	$\Sigma(x_i - \mu)^2 = 130$

$$SS_x = \Sigma(x_i - \mu)^2 = 130$$

$$\text{Variance} = \sigma^2 = \frac{SS_x}{N} = \frac{\Sigma(x_i - \mu)^2}{N} = \frac{130}{5} = 26.0$$

$$\text{Standard Deviation} = \sigma = \sqrt{\frac{\Sigma(x_i - \mu)^2}{N}} = \sqrt{\frac{130}{5}} = 5.1$$

Like the variance, the standard deviation utilizes the sum of the squared deviations about the mean (SS_x). It is computed by averaging these squared deviations (SS_x/N) and taking the square root of that average. One feature of the standard deviation that distinguishes it from a variance is that the standard deviation is expressed in the same units as the raw data, whereas the variance is expressed in those units squared. Table 3.4 shows the standard deviation for the computer production company: $\sqrt{26}$, or 5.1.

What does a standard deviation of 5.1 mean? The meaning of standard deviation is more readily understood from its use, which is explored next. Although the standard deviation and the variance are closely related and can be computed from each other, differentiating between them is important, because both are widely used in statistics.

Meaning of Standard Deviation

What is a standard deviation? What does it do, and what does it mean? Insight into the concept of standard deviation can be gleaned by viewing the manner in which it is applied. Two ways of applying the standard deviation are the **empirical rule** and **Chebyshev's theorem**.

Empirical Rule The empirical rule is an important rule of thumb that *is used to state the approximate percentage of values that lie within a given number of standard deviations from the mean of a set of data if the data are normally distributed.*

The empirical rule is used only for three numbers of standard deviations: 1σ, 2σ, and 3σ. More detailed analysis of other numbers of σ values is presented in Chapter 6. Also discussed in further detail in Chapter 6 is the normal distribution, a unimodal, symmetrical distribution that is bell (or mound) shaped. The requirement that the data be normally distributed contains some tolerance, and the empirical rule generally applies as long as the data are approximately mound shaped.

Empirical Rule*

DISTANCE FROM THE MEAN	VALUES WITHIN DISTANCE
$\mu \pm 1\sigma$	68%
$\mu \pm 2\sigma$	95%
$\mu \pm 3\sigma$	99.7%

*Based on the assumption that the data are approximately normally distributed.

If a set of data is normally distributed, or bell shaped, approximately 68% of the data values are within one standard deviation of the mean, 95% are within two standard deviations, and almost 100% are within three standard deviations.

Suppose a recent report states that for California, the average statewide price of a gallon of regular gasoline is $4.12. Suppose regular gasoline prices vary across the state with a standard deviation of $0.08 and are normally distributed. According to the empirical rule, approximately 68% of the prices should fall within $\mu \pm 1\sigma$, or $4.12 \pm 1(\$0.08)$. Approximately 68% of the prices should be between $4.04 and $4.20, as shown in **Figure 3.5A**. Approximately 95% should fall within $\mu \pm 2\sigma$ or $4.12 \pm 2(\$0.08) = \$4.12 \pm \$0.16$, or between $3.96 and $4.28, as shown in **Figure 3.5B**. Nearly all regular gasoline prices (99.7%) should fall between $3.88 and $4.36($\mu \pm 3\sigma$).

Note that with 68% of the gasoline prices falling within one standard deviation of the mean, approximately 32% are outside this range. Because the normal distribution is symmetrical, the 32% can be split in half such that 16% lie in each tail of the distribution. Thus, approximately 16% of the gasoline prices should be less than $4.04 and approximately 16% of the prices should be greater than $4.20.

Many phenomena are distributed approximately in a bell shape, including most human characteristics such as height and weight; therefore the empirical rule applies in many situations and is widely used.

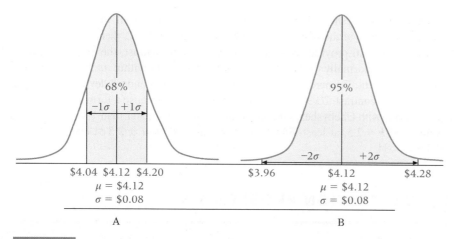

FIGURE 3.5   **Empirical Rule for One and Two Standard Deviations of Gasoline Prices**

DEMONSTRATION PROBLEM 3.4

A company produces a lightweight valve that is specified to weigh 1365 grams. Unfortunately, because of imperfections in the manufacturing process not all of the valves produced weigh exactly 1365 grams. In fact, the weights of the valves produced are normally distributed with a mean weight of 1365 grams and a standard deviation of 294 grams. Within what range of weights would approximately 95% of the valve weights fall? Approximately 16% of the weights would be more than what value? Approximately 0.15% of the weights would be less than what value?

Solution: Because the valve weights are normally distributed, the empirical rule applies. According to the empirical rule, approximately 95% of the weights should fall within $\mu \pm 2\sigma = 1365 \pm 2(294) = 1365 \pm 588$. Thus, approximately 95% should fall between 777 and 1953. Approximately 68% of the weights should fall within $\mu \pm 1\sigma$, and 32% should fall outside this interval. Because the normal distribution is symmetrical, approximately 16% should lie above $\mu + 1\sigma = 1365 + 294 = 1659$. Approximately 99.7% of the weights should fall within $\mu \pm 3\sigma$, and .3% should fall outside this interval. Half of these, or .15%, should lie below $\mu - 3\sigma = 1365 - 3(294) = 1365 - 882 = 483$.

Chebyshev's Theorem   The empirical rule applies only when data are known to be approximately normally distributed. What do researchers use when data are not normally distributed or when the shape of the distribution is unknown? Chebyshev's theorem applies to all distributions regardless of their shape and thus can be used whenever the data distribution shape is unknown or is nonnormal. Even though Chebyshev's theorem can in theory be applied to data that are normally distributed, the empirical rule is more widely known and is preferred whenever appropriate. Chebyshev's theorem is not a rule of thumb, as is the empirical rule, but rather it is presented in formula format and therefore can be more widely applied. Chebyshev's theorem states that *at least $1 - 1/k^2$ values will fall within $\pm k$ standard deviations of the mean regardless of the shape of the distribution.*

Chebyshev's Theorem

Within k standard deviations of the mean, $\mu \pm k\sigma$, lie at least

$$1 - \frac{1}{k^2}$$

proportion of the values.
Assumption: $k > 1$

Specifically, Chebyshev's theorem says that at least 75% of all values are within $\pm 2\sigma$ of the mean regardless of the shape of a distribution because if $k = 2$, then $1 - 1/k^2 = 1 - 1/2^2 = 3/4 = .75$. **Figure 3.6** provides a graphic illustration. In contrast, the empirical rule states that if the data are normally distributed 95% of all values are within $\mu \pm 2\sigma$. According to Chebyshev's theorem, the percentage of values within three standard deviations of the mean is at least 89%, in contrast to 99.7% for the empirical rule. Because a formula is used to compute proportions with Chebyshev's theorem, any value of k greater than $1(k > 1)$ can be used. For example, if $k = 2.5$, at least .84 of all values are within $\mu \pm 2.5\sigma$, because $1 - 1/k^2 = 1 - 1/(2.5)^2 = .84$.

DEMONSTRATION PROBLEM 3.5

In the computing industry the average age of professional employees tends to be younger than in many other business professions. Suppose the average age of a professional employed by a particular computer firm is 28 with a standard deviation of 6 years. A histogram of professional employee ages with this firm reveals that the data are not normally distributed but rather are amassed in the 20s and that few workers are over 40. Apply Chebyshev's theorem to determine within what range of ages at least 80% of the workers' ages would fall.

Solution: Because the ages are not normally distributed, it is not appropriate to apply the empirical rule; and therefore Chebyshev's theorem must be applied to answer the question.

Chebyshev's theorem states that at least $1 - 1/k^2$ proportion of the values are within $\mu \pm k\sigma$. Because 80% of the values are within this range, let

$$1 - \frac{1}{k^2} = .80$$

Solving for k yields

$$.20 = \frac{1}{k^2}$$
$$k^2 = 5.000$$
$$k = 2.24$$

Chebyshev's theorem says that at least .80 of the values are within ± 2.24 of the mean.

For $\mu = 28$ and $\sigma = 6$, at least .80, or 80%, of the values are within $28 \pm 2.24(6) = 28 \pm 13.4$ years of age or between 14.6 and 41.4 years old.

Population Versus Sample Variance and Standard Deviation The sample variance is denoted by s^2 and the sample standard deviation by s. The main use for sample variances and standard deviations is as estimators of population variances and standard deviations. Because of this, computation of the sample variance and standard deviation differs

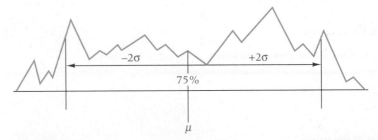

FIGURE 3.6 **Application of Chebyshev's Theorem for Two Standard Deviations**

slightly from computation of the population variance and standard deviation. Both the sample variance and sample standard deviation use $n - 1$ in the denominator instead of n because using n in the denominator of a sample variance results in a statistic that tends to underestimate the population variance. While discussion of the properties of *good estimators* is beyond the scope of this text, one of the properties of a good estimator is being *unbiased*. Whereas using n in the denominator of the sample variance makes it a *biased* estimator, using $n - 1$ allows it to be an *unbiased* estimator, which is a desirable property in inferential statistics.

Sample Variance

$$s^2 = \frac{\Sigma(x_i - \bar{x})^2}{n - 1}$$

Sample Standard Deviation

$$s = \sqrt{\frac{\Sigma(x_i - \bar{x})^2}{n - 1}}$$

Shown here is a sample of six of the largest accounting firms in the United States and the number of partners associated with each firm as reported by the *Public Accounting Report*.

FIRM	NUMBER OF PARTNERS
Deloitte & Touche	3030
Ernst & Young	2700
PricewaterhouseCoopers	2691
KPMG	1813
RSM McGladrey	644
Grant Thornton	529

The sample variance and sample standard deviation can be computed by:

x_i	$(x_i - \bar{x})^2$
3030	1,274,257.17
2700	638,129.37
2691	623,831.43
1813	7,773.95
644	1,580,476.41
529	1,882,850.51
$\Sigma x = 11{,}407$	$\Sigma(x_i - \bar{x})^2 = 6{,}007{,}318.84$

$$\bar{x} = \frac{11{,}407}{6} = 1901.17$$

$$s^2 = \frac{\Sigma(x_i - \bar{x})^2}{n - 1} = \frac{6{,}007{,}318.84}{5} - 1{,}201{,}463.77$$

$$s = \sqrt{\frac{\Sigma(x_i - \bar{x})^2}{n - 1}} = \sqrt{1{,}201{,}463.77} = 1096.11$$

The sample variance is 1,201,463.77, and the sample standard deviation is 1096.11

Computational Formulas for Variance and Standard Deviation An alternative method of computing variance and standard deviation, sometimes referred to as the computational method or shortcut method, is available. Algebraically,

$$\Sigma(x_i - \mu)^2 = \Sigma x_i^2 - \frac{(\Sigma x_i)^2}{N}$$

and

$$\Sigma(x_i - \bar{x})^2 = \Sigma x_i^2 - \frac{(\Sigma x_i)^2}{n}$$

Substituting these equivalent expressions into the original formulas for variance and standard deviation yields the following computational formulas.

Computational Formula for Population Variance and Standard Deviation

$$\sigma^2 = \frac{\Sigma x_i^2 - \frac{(\Sigma x_i)^2}{N}}{N}$$

$$\sigma = \sqrt{\sigma^2}$$

Computational Formula for Sample Variance and Standard Deviation

$$s^2 = \frac{\Sigma x_i^2 - \frac{(\Sigma x_i)^2}{n}}{n - 1}$$

$$s = \sqrt{s^2}$$

These computational formulas utilize the sum of the x values and the sum of the x^2 values instead of the difference between the mean and each value and computed deviations. In the precalculator/computer era, this method usually was faster and easier than using the original formulas.

For situations in which the mean is already computed or is given, alternative forms of these formulas are

$$\sigma^2 = \frac{\Sigma x_i^2 - N\mu^2}{N}$$

$$s^2 = \frac{\Sigma x_i^2 - n(\bar{x})^2}{n - 1}$$

Using the computational method, the owner of the start-up computer production company can compute a population variance and standard deviation for the production data, as shown in Table 3.5. (Compare these results with those in Table 3.4.)

TABLE 3.5	Computational Formula Calculations of Variance and Standard Deviation for Computer Production Data	
x_i		x_i^2
5		25
9		81
16		256
17		289
18		324
$\Sigma x_i = 65$		$\Sigma x_i^2 = 975$

$$\sigma^2 = \frac{975 - \frac{(65)^2}{5}}{5} = \frac{975 - 845}{5} = \frac{130}{5} = 26$$

$$\sigma = \sqrt{26} = 5.1$$

DEMONSTRATION PROBLEM 3.6

The effectiveness of district attorneys can be measured by several variables, including the number of convictions per month, the number of cases handled per month, and the total number of years of conviction per month. A researcher uses a sample of five district attorneys in a city and determines the total number of years of conviction that each attorney won against defendants during the past month, as reported in the first column in the following tabulations. Compute the mean absolute deviation, the variance, and the standard deviation for these figures.

Solution: The researcher computes the mean absolute deviation, the variance, and the standard deviation for these data in the following manner.

x_i	$|x_i - \bar{x}|$	$(x_i - \bar{x})^2$
55	41	1681
100	4	16
125	29	841
140	44	1936
60	36	1296
$\Sigma x_i = 480$	$\Sigma|x_i - \bar{x}| = 154$	$\Sigma(x_i - \bar{x})^2 = 5770$

$$\bar{x} = \frac{\Sigma x_i}{n} = \frac{480}{5} = 96$$

$$MAD = \frac{154}{5} = 30.8$$

$$s^2 = \frac{5770}{4} = 1442.5 \text{ and } s = \sqrt{s^2} = 37.98$$

She then uses computational formulas to solve for s^2 and s and compares the results.

x_i	x_i^2
55	3,025
100	10,000
125	15,625
140	19,600
60	3,600
$\Sigma x_i = 480$	$\Sigma x_i^2 = 51,850$

$$s^2 = \frac{51,850 - \dfrac{(480)^2}{5}}{4} = \frac{51,850 - 46,080}{4} = \frac{5,770}{4} = 1,442.5$$

$$s = \sqrt{1,442.5} = 37.98$$

The results are the same. The sample standard deviation obtained by both methods is 37.98, or 38, years.

z Scores

A *z score* represents the number of standard deviations a value (x) is above or below the mean of a set of numbers when the data are normally distributed. Using z scores allows translation of a value's raw distance from the mean into units of standard deviations.

z Score

$$z = \frac{x_i - \mu}{\sigma}$$

For samples,

$$z = \frac{x_i - \bar{x}}{s}$$

If a z score is negative, the raw value (x) is below the mean. If the z score is positive, the raw value (x) is above the mean.

For example, for a data set that is normally distributed with a mean of 50 and a standard deviation of 10, suppose a statistician wants to determine the z score for a value of 70. This value ($x = 70$) is 20 units above the mean, so the z value is

$$z = \frac{70 - 50}{10} = +2.00$$

This z score signifies that the raw score of 70 is two standard deviations above the mean. How is this z score interpreted? The empirical rule states that 95% of all values are within two standard deviations of the mean if the data are approximately normally distributed. Figure 3.7 shows that because the value of 70 is two standard deviations above the mean ($z = +2.00$), 95% of the values are between 70 and the value ($x = 30$), that is two standard deviations below the mean, or $z = (30 - 50)/10 = -2.00$. Because 5% of the values are outside the range of two standard deviations from the mean and the normal distribution is symmetrical, 2½% ($\frac{1}{2}$ of the 5%) are below the value of 30 and 2½% are above the value of 70. Because a z score is the number of standard deviations an individual data value is from the mean, the empirical rule can be restated in terms of z scores.

Between $z = -1.00$ and $z = +1.00$ are approximately 68% of the values.
Between $z = -2.00$ and $z = +2.00$ are approximately 95% of the values.
Between $z = -3.00$ and $z = +3.00$ are approximately 99.7% of the values.

The topic of z scores is discussed more extensively in Chapter 6.

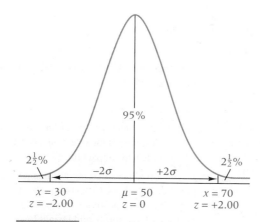

FIGURE 3.7 **Percentage Breakdown of Scores Two Standard Deviations from the Mean**

Coefficient of Variation

The **coefficient of variation** is a statistic that *is the ratio of the standard deviation to the mean expressed in percentage* and is denoted CV.

> **Coefficient of Variation**
>
> $$CV = \frac{\sigma}{\mu}(100)$$

The coefficient of variation essentially is a relative comparison of a standard deviation to its mean. The coefficient of variation can be useful in comparing standard deviations that have been computed from data with different means.

Suppose five weeks of average prices for stock A are 57, 68, 64, 71, and 62. To compute a coefficient of variation for these prices, first determine the mean and standard deviation: $\mu = 64.40$ and $\sigma = 4.84$. The coefficient of variation is:

$$CV_A = \frac{\sigma_A}{\mu_A}(100) = \frac{4.84}{64.40}(100) = .075 = 7.5\%$$

The standard deviation is 7.5% of the mean.

Sometimes financial investors use the coefficient of variation or the standard deviation or both as measures of risk. Imagine a stock with a price that never changes. An investor bears no risk of losing money from the price going down because no variability occurs in the price. Suppose, in contrast, that the price of the stock fluctuates wildly. An investor who buys at a low price and sells for a high price can make a nice profit. However, if the price drops below what the investor buys it for, the stock owner is subject to a potential loss. The greater the variability is, the more the potential for loss. Hence, investors use measures of variability such as standard deviation or coefficient of variation to determine the risk of a stock. What does the coefficient of variation tell us about the risk of a stock that the standard deviation does not?

Suppose the average prices for a second stock, B, over these same five weeks are 12, 17, 8, 15, and 13. The mean for stock B is 13.00 with a standard deviation of 3.03. The coefficient of variation can be computed for stock B as:

$$CV_B = \frac{\sigma_B}{\mu_B}(100) = \frac{3.03}{13}(100) = .233 = 23.3\%$$

The standard deviation for stock B is 23.3% of the mean.

Thinking Critically About Statistics in Business Today

Business Travel

Findings from the Bureau of Transportation Statistics' National Household Travel Survey revealed that more than 405 million long-distance business trips are taken each year in the United States. Over 80% of these business trips are taken by personal vehicle. Almost three out of four business trips are for less than 250 miles, and only about 7% are for more than 1000 miles. The mean one-way distance for a business trip in the United States is 123 miles. Air travel accounts for 16% of all business travel. The average per diem cost of business travel to New York City is about $450, to Beijing is about $282, to Moscow is about $376, and to Paris is about $305. Seventy-seven percent of all business travelers are men, and 55% of business trips are taken by people in the 30-to-49-year-old age bracket. Forty-five percent of

business trips are taken by people who have a household income of more than $75,000.

THINGS TO PONDER

1. In light of the fact that 7% of business trips are for more than 1000 miles, why is the mean distance 123 miles? How do the 1000+ mile trips impact the mean?

2. It is reported here that the average per diem cost of business travel to New York City is about $450. Would the median or even the mode be more representative here? How might a measure of variability add insight?

Sources: U.S. Department of Transportation site at http://www.dot.gov/affairs/bts2503.htm and Expansion Management.com site at http://www.expansionmanagement.com/cmd/articledetail/articleid/15602/default.asp.

With the standard deviation as the measure of risk, stock A is more risky over this period of time because it has a larger standard deviation. However, the average price of stock A is almost five times as much as that of stock B. Relative to the amount invested in stock A, the standard deviation of $4.84 may not represent as much risk as the standard deviation of $3.03 for stock B, which has an average price of only $13.00. The coefficient of variation reveals the risk of a stock in terms of the size of standard deviation relative to the size of the mean (in percentage). Stock B has a coefficient of variation that is nearly three times as much as the coefficient of variation for stock A. Using coefficient of variation as a measure of risk indicates that stock B is riskier.

The choice of whether to use a coefficient of variation or raw standard deviations to compare multiple standard deviations is a matter of preference. The coefficient of variation also provides an optional method of interpreting the value of a standard deviation.

3.2 Problems

3.11. A data set contains the following seven values.

6   2   4   9   1   3   5

a. Find the range.

b. Find the mean absolute deviation.

c. Find the population variance.

d. Find the population standard deviation.

e. Find the interquartile range.

f. Find the z score for each value.

3.12. A data set contains the following eight values.

4   3   0   5   2   9   4   5

a. Find the range.

b. Find the mean absolute deviation.

c. Find the sample variance.

d. Find the sample standard deviation.

e. Find the interquartile range.

3.13. A data set contains the following six values.

12   23   19   26   24   23

a. Find the population standard deviation using the formula containing the mean (the original formula).

b. Find the population standard deviation using the computational formula.

c. Compare the results. Which formula was faster to use? Which formula do you prefer? Why do you think the computational formula is sometimes referred to as the "shortcut" formula?

3.14. Use your calculator or computer to find the sample variance and sample standard deviation for the following data.

57	88	68	43	93
63	51	37	77	83
66	60	38	52	28
34	52	60	57	29
92	37	38	17	67

3.15. Use your calculator or computer to find the population variance and population standard deviation for the following data.

123	090	546	378
392	280	179	601
572	953	749	075
303	468	531	646

3.16. The following sample data represent the time (in minutes) required by business executives to complete an expense report. Determine the interquartile range on these data and comment on what it means.

44	18	39	40	59
46	59	37	15	73
23	19	90	58	35
82	14	38	27	24
71	25	39	84	70

3.17. According to Chebyshev's theorem, at least what proportion of the data will be within $\mu \pm k\sigma$ for each value of k?

a. $k = 2$

b. $k = 2.5$

c. $k = 1.6$

d. $k = 3.2$

3.18. Compare the variability of the following two sets of data by using both the population standard deviation and the population coefficient of variation.

DATA SET 1	DATA SET 2
49	159
82	121
77	138
54	152

3.19. A sample of 12 small accounting firms reveals the following numbers of professionals per office.

7	10	9	14	11	8
5	12	8	3	13	6

a. Determine the mean absolute deviation.

b. Determine the variance.

c. Determine the standard deviation.

d. Determine the interquartile range.

e. What is the z score for the firm that has six professionals?

f. What is the coefficient of variation for this sample?

3.20. Shown below are the top nine leading retailers in the United States in a recent year according to Statista.com

COMPANY	REVENUES ($ BILLIONS)
Walmart	343.62
The Kroger Co.	103.03
Costco	79.69
The Home Depot	74.20
Walgreen	72.67
Target	72.62
CVS Caremark	67.97
Lowe's Companies	54.81
Amazon. Com	49.38

Assume that the data represent a population.

a. Find the range.

b. Find the mean absolute deviation.

c. Find the population variance.

d. Find the population standard deviation.

e. Find the interquartile range.

f. Find the z score for Walgreens.

g. Find the coefficient of variation.

3.21. A distribution of numbers is approximately bell shaped. If the mean of the numbers is 125 and the standard deviation is 12, between what two numbers would approximately 68% of the values fall? Between what two numbers would 95% of the values fall? Between what two values would 99.7% of the values fall?

3.22. Some numbers are not normally distributed. If the mean of the numbers is 38 and the standard deviation is 6, what proportion of values would fall between 26 and 50? What proportion of values would fall between 14 and 62? Between what two values would 89% of the values fall?

3.23. According to Chebyshev's theorem, how many standard deviations from the mean would include at least 88% of the values?

3.24. The time needed to assemble a particular piece of furniture with experience is normally distributed with a mean time of 43 minutes. If 68% of the assembly times are between 40 and 46 minutes, what is the value of the standard deviation? Suppose 99.7% of the assembly times are between 35 and 51 minutes and the mean is still 43 minutes. What would the value of the standard deviation be now? Suppose the time needed to assemble another piece of furniture is not normally distributed and that the mean assembly time is 28 minutes. What is the value of the standard deviation if at least 77% of the assembly times are between 24 and 32 minutes?

3.25. Environmentalists are concerned about emissions of sulfur dioxide into the air. The average number of days per year in which sulfur dioxide levels exceed 150 milligrams per cubic meter in Milan, Italy, is 29. The number of days per year in which emission limits are exceeded is normally distributed with a standard deviation of 4.0 days. What percentage of the years would average between 21 and 37 days of excess emissions of sulfur dioxide? What percentage of the years would exceed 37 days? What percentage of the years would exceed 41 days? In what percentage of the years would there be fewer than 25 days with excess sulfur dioxide emissions?

3.26. Shown below are the per diem business travel expenses in 11 international cities selected from a study conducted for Business Travel News' 2015 Corporate Travel Index, which is an annual study showing the daily cost of business travel in cities across the Globe. The per diem rates include hotel, car, and food expenses. Use this list to calculate the z scores for Lagos, Riyadh, and Bangkok. Treat the list as a sample.

CITY	PER DIEM EXPENSE ($)
London	576
Mexico City	240
Tokyo	484
Bangalore	199
Bangkok	234
Riyadh	483
Lagos	506
Cape Town	230
Zurich	508
Paris	483
Guatemala City	213

Measures of Central Tendency and Variability: Grouped Data

Grouped data do not provide information about individual values. Hence, measures of central tendency and variability for grouped data must be computed differently from those for ungrouped or raw data.

Measures of Central Tendency

Three measures of central tendency are presented here for grouped data: the mean, the median, and the mode.

Mean   For ungrouped data, the mean is computed by summing the data values and dividing by the number of values. With grouped data, the specific values are unknown. What can be used to represent the data values? The midpoint of each class interval is used to represent all the values in a class interval. This midpoint is weighted by the frequency of values in that class interval. The mean for grouped data is then computed by summing the products of the class midpoint and the class frequency for each class and dividing that sum by the total number of frequencies. The formula for the mean of grouped data follows.

Mean of Grouped Data

$$\mu_{grouped} = \frac{\Sigma f_i M_i}{N} = \frac{\Sigma f_i M_i}{\Sigma f_i}$$

where

$$f_i = \text{class frequency}$$
$$N = \text{total frequencies}$$
$$M_i = \text{class midpoint}$$

Table 3.6 gives the frequency distribution of the unemployment rates of Canada from Table 2.2. To find the mean of these data, we need Σf_i and $\Sigma f_i M_i$. The value of Σf_i can be determined by summing the values in the frequency column. To calculate $\Sigma f_i M_i$, we must first determine the values of M, or the class midpoints. Next we multiply each of these class midpoints by the frequency in that class interval, f_i, resulting in $f_i M_i$. Summing these values of $f_i M_i$ yields the value of $\Sigma f_i M_i$.

Table 3.7 contains the calculations needed to determine the group mean. The group mean for the unemployment data is 6.93. Remember that because each class interval was represented by its class midpoint rather than by actual values, the group mean is only approximate.

Median   The median for ungrouped or raw data is the middle value of an ordered array of numbers. For grouped data, solving for the median is considerably more complicated. The calculation of the median for grouped data is done by using the following formula.

TABLE 3.6	Frequency Distribution of 60 Years of Unemployment Data for Canada (Grouped Data)	
CLASS INTERVAL	**FREQUENCY**	**CUMULATIVE FREQUENCY**
1–under 3	4	4
3–under 5	12	16
5–under 7	13	29
7–under 9	19	48
9–under 11	7	55
11–under 13	5	60

TABLE 3.7   Calculation of Grouped Mean

CLASS INTERVAL	FREQUENCY (f_i)	CLASS MIDPOINT (M_i)	$f_i M_i$
1–under 3	4	2	8
3–under 5	12	4	48
5–under 7	13	6	78
7–under 9	19	8	152
9–under 11	7	10	70
11–under 13	5	12	60
	$\Sigma f_i = N = 60$		$\Sigma f_i M_i = 416$

$$\mu = \frac{\Sigma f_i M_i}{\Sigma f_i} = \frac{416}{60} = 6.93$$

Median of Grouped Data

$$Median = L + \frac{\frac{N}{2} - cf_p}{f_{med}}(W)$$

where

L = the lower limit of the median class interval

cf_p = a cumulative total of the frequencies up to but not including the frequency of the median class

f_{med} = the frequency of the median class

W = the width of the median class interval

N = total number of frequencies

The first step in calculating a grouped median is to determine the value of $N/2$, which is the location of the median term. Suppose we want to calculate the median for the frequency distribution data in Table 3.6. Since there are 60 values (N), the value of $N/2$ is $60/2 = 30$. The median is the 30th term. The question to ask is: where does the 30th term fall? This can be answered by determining the cumulative frequencies for the data, as shown in Table 3.6.

An examination of these cumulative frequencies reveals that the 30th term falls in the fourth class interval because there are only 29 values in the first three class intervals. Thus, the median value is in the fourth class interval somewhere between 7 and 9. The class interval containing the median value is referred to as the *median class interval*.

Since the 30th value is between 7 and 9, the value of the median must be at least 7. How much more than 7 is the median? The difference between the location of the median value, $N/2 = 30$, and the cumulative frequencies up to but not including the median class interval, $cf_p = 29$, tells how many values into the median class interval lies the value of the median. This is determined by solving for $N/2 - cf_p = 30 - 29 = 1$. The median value is located one value into the median class interval. However, there are 19 values in the median interval (denoted in the formula as f_{med}). The median value is 1/19 of the way through this interval.

$$\frac{\frac{N}{2} - cf_p}{f_{med}} = \frac{30 - 29}{19} = \frac{1}{19}$$

Thus, the median value is at least 7, the value of L, and is 1/19 of the way across the median interval. How far is it across the median interval? Each class interval is 2 units wide (w). Taking 1/19 of this distance tells us how far the median value is into the class interval.

$$\frac{\frac{N}{2} - cf_p}{f_{med}}(W) = \frac{\frac{60}{2} - 29}{19}(2) = \frac{1}{19}(2) = .105$$

Adding this distance to the lower endpoint of the median class interval yields the value of the median.

$$\text{Median} = 7 + \frac{\frac{60}{2} - 29}{19}(2) = 7 + \frac{1}{19}(2) = 7 + .105 = 7.105$$

The median value of unemployment rates for Canada is 7.105. Keep in mind that like the grouped mean, this median value is merely approximate. The assumption made in these calculations is that the actual values fall uniformly across the median class interval—which may or may not be the case.

Mode   The *mode* for grouped data is *the class midpoint of the modal class. The modal class is the class interval with the greatest frequency.* Using the data from Table 3.7, the 7–under 9 class interval contains the greatest frequency, 19. Thus, the modal class is 7–under 9. The class midpoint of this modal class is 8. Therefore, the mode for the frequency distribution shown in Table 3.7 is 8. The modal unemployment rate is 8%.

Measures of Variability

Two measures of variability for grouped data are presented here: the variance and the standard deviation. Again, the standard deviation is the square root of the variance. Both measures have original and computational formulas.

Formulas for Population Variance and Standard Deviation of Grouped Data

ORIGINAL FORMULA	COMPUTATIONAL VERSION
$\sigma^2 = \dfrac{\Sigma f_i (M_i - \mu)^2}{N}$ $\sigma = \sqrt{\sigma^2}$	$\sigma^2 = \dfrac{\Sigma f_i M_i^2 - \dfrac{(\Sigma f_i M_i)^2}{N}}{N}$

where
f_i = frequency
M_i = class midpoint
$N = \Sigma f_i$, or total frequencies of the population
μ = grouped mean for the population

Formulas for Sample Variance and Standard Deviation of Grouped Data

ORIGINAL FORMULA	COMPUTATIONAL VERSION
$s^2 = \dfrac{\Sigma f_i (M_i - \bar{x})^2}{n - 1}$ $s = \sqrt{s^2}$	$s^2 = \dfrac{\Sigma f_i M_i^2 - \dfrac{(\Sigma f_i M_i)^2}{n}}{n - 1}$

where
f_i = frequency
M_i = class midpoint
$n = \Sigma f_i$, or total of the frequencies of the sample
$\bar{x}$ = grouped mean for the sample

For example, let us calculate the variance and standard deviation of the Canadian unemployment data grouped as a frequency distribution in Table 3.6. If the data are treated as a population, the computations are as follows.

For the original formula, the computations are given in Table 3.8. The method of determining σ^2 and σ by using the computational formula is shown in Table 3.9. In either case, the variance of the unemployment data is 7.129 (squared percent), and the standard deviation is 2.67%. As with the computation of the grouped mean, the class midpoint is used to represent all values in a class interval. This approach may or may not be appropriate, depending on whether the average value in a class is at the midpoint. If this situation does not occur, then the variance and the standard deviation are only approximations. Because grouped statistics are usually computed without knowledge of the actual data, the statistics computed potentially may be only approximations.

TABLE 3.8	Calculating Grouped Variance and Standard Deviation with the Original Formula					
CLASS INTERVAL	f_i	M_i	$f_i M_i$	$(M_i - \mu)$	$(M_i - \mu)^2$	$f_i(M_i - \mu)^2$
1–under 3	4	2	8	−4.93	24.305	97.220
3–under 5	12	4	48	−2.93	8.585	103.020
5–under 7	13	6	78	−0.93	0.865	11.245
7–under 9	19	8	152	1.07	1.145	21.755
9–under 11	7	10	70	3.07	9.425	65.975
11–under 13	5	12	60	5.07	25.705	128.525
	$\Sigma f_i = N = 60$		$\Sigma f_i M_i = 416$			$\Sigma f_i(M_i - \mu)^2 = 427.740$

$$\mu = \frac{\Sigma f_i M_i}{\Sigma f_i} = \frac{416}{60} = 6.93$$

$$\sigma^2 = \frac{\Sigma f_i(M_i - \mu)^2}{N} = \frac{427.74}{60} = 7.129$$

$$\sigma = \sqrt{7.129} = 2.670$$

TABLE 3.9	Calculating Grouped Variance and Standard Deviation with the Computational Formula			
CLASS INTERVAL	f_i	M_i	$f_i M_i$	$f_i M_i^2$
1–under 3	4	2	8	16
3–under 5	12	4	48	192
5–under 7	13	6	78	468
7–under 9	19	8	152	1216
9–under 11	7	10	70	700
11–under 13	5	12	60	720
	$\Sigma f_i = N = 60$		$\Sigma f_i M_i = 416$	$\Sigma f_i M_i^2 = 3312$

$$\sigma^2 = \frac{\Sigma f_i M_i^2 - \frac{(\Sigma f_i M_i)^2}{N}}{N} = \frac{3312 - \frac{416^2}{60}}{60} = \frac{3312 - 2884.27}{60} = \frac{427.73}{60} = 7.129$$

$$\sigma = \sqrt{7.129} = 2.670$$

DEMONSTRATION PROBLEM 3.7

Compute the mean, median, mode, variance, and standard deviation on the following sample data.

CLASS INTERVAL	FREQUENCY	CUMULATIVE FREQUENCY
10–under 15	6	6
15–under 20	22	28
20–under 25	35	63
25–under 30	29	92
30–under 35	16	108
35–under 40	8	116
40–under 45	4	120
45–under 50	2	122

Solution: The mean is computed as follows.

CLASS	f_i	M_i	$f_i M_i$
10–under 15	6	12.5	75.0
15–under 20	22	17.5	385.0
20–under 25	35	22.5	787.5
25–under 30	29	27.5	797.5
30–under 35	16	32.5	520.0
35–under 40	8	37.5	300.0
40–under 45	4	42.5	170.0
45–under 50	2	47.5	95.0
	$\Sigma f_i = n = 122$		$\Sigma f_i M_i = 3130.0$

$$\bar{x} = \frac{\Sigma f_i M_i}{\Sigma f_i} = \frac{3130}{122} = 25.66$$

The grouped mean is 25.66.

The grouped median is located at the 61st value (122/2). Observing the cumulative frequencies, the 61st value falls in the 20–under 25 class, making it the median class interval; thus, the grouped median is at least 20. Since there are 28 cumulative values before the median class interval, 33 more (61 − 28) are needed to reach the grouped median. However, there are 35 values in the median class. The grouped median is located 33/35 of the way across the class interval which has a width of 5. The grouped median is $20 + \frac{33}{35}(5) = 20 + 4.71 = 24.71$.

The grouped mode can be determined by finding the class midpoint of the class interval with the greatest frequency. The class with the greatest frequency is 20–under 25 with a frequency of 35. The midpoint of this class is 22.5, which is the grouped mode.

The variance and standard deviation can be found as shown next. First, use the original formula.

CLASS	f_i	M_i	$M_i - \bar{x}$	$(M_i - \bar{x})^2$	$f_i(M_i - \bar{x})^2$
10–under 15	6	12.5	−13.16	173.19	1039.14
15–under 20	22	17.5	−8.16	66.59	1464.98
20–under 25	35	22.5	−3.16	9.99	349.65
25–under 30	29	27.5	1.84	3.39	98.31
30–under 35	16	32.5	6.84	46.79	748.64
35–under 40	8	37.5	11.84	140.19	1121.52
40–under 45	4	42.5	16.84	283.59	1134.36
45–under 50	2	47.5	21.84	476.99	953.98
	$\Sigma f_i = n = 122$				$\Sigma f_i(M_i - \bar{x})^2 = 6910.58$

$$s^2 = \frac{\Sigma f_i (M_i - \bar{x})^2}{n-1} = \frac{6910.58}{121} = 57.11$$

$$s = \sqrt{57.11} = 7.56$$

Next, use the computational formula.

CLASS	f_i	M_i	$f_i M_i$	$f_i M_i^2$
10–under 15	6	12.5	75.0	937.50
15–under 20	22	17.5	385.0	6,737.50
20–under 25	35	22.5	787.5	17,718.75
25–under 30	29	27.5	797.5	21,931.25
30–under 35	16	32.5	520.0	16,900.00
35–under 40	8	37.5	300.0	11,250.00
40–under 45	4	42.5	170.0	7,225.00
45–under 50	2	47.5	95.0	4,512.50

$$\Sigma f_i = n = 122 \qquad \Sigma f_i M_i = 3,130.0 \qquad \Sigma f_i M_i^2 = 87,212.50$$

$$s^2 = \frac{\Sigma f_i M_i^2 - \frac{(\Sigma f_i M_i)^2}{n}}{n-1} = \frac{87,212.5 - \frac{(3,130)^2}{122}}{121} = \frac{6,910.04}{121} = 57.11$$

$$s = \sqrt{57.11} = 7.56$$

The sample variance is 57.11 and the standard deviation is 7.56.

3.3 Problems

3.27. Compute the mean, the median, and the mode for the following data.

CLASS	f
0–under 2	39
2–under 4	27
4–under 6	16
6–under 8	15
8–under 10	10
10–under 12	8
12–under 14	6

3.28. Compute the mean, the median, and the mode for the following data.

CLASS	f
1.2–under 1.6	220
1.6–under 2.0	150
2.0–under 2.4	90
2.4–under 2.8	110
2.8–under 3.2	280

3.29. Determine the population variance and standard deviation for the following data by using the original formula.

CLASS	f
20–under 30	7
30–under 40	11
40–under 50	18
50–under 60	13
60–under 70	6
70–under 80	4

3.30. Determine the sample variance and standard deviation for the following data by using the computational formula.

CLASS	f
5–under 9	20
9–under 13	18
13–under 17	8
17–under 21	6
21–under 25	2

3.31. A random sample of voters in Nashville, Tennessee, is classified by age group, as shown by the following data.

AGE GROUP	FREQUENCY
18–under 24	17
24–under 30	22
30–under 36	26
36–under 42	35
42–under 48	33
48–under 54	30
54–under 60	32
60–under 66	21
66–under 72	15

a. Calculate the mean of the data.

b. Calculate the mode.

c. Calculate the median.

d. Calculate the variance.

e. Calculate the standard deviation.

3.32. The following data represent the number of appointments made per 15-minute interval by telephone solicitation for a lawn-care company. Assume these are population data.

NUMBER OF APPOINTMENTS	FREQUENCY OF OCCURRENCE
0–under 1	31
1–under 2	57
2–under 3	26
3–under 4	14
4–under 5	6
5–under 6	3

a. Calculate the mean of the data.

b. Calculate the mode.

c. Calculate the median.

d. Calculate the variance.

e. Calculate the standard deviation.

3.33. The Air Transport Association of America publishes figures on the busiest airports in the United States. The following frequency distribution has been constructed from these figures for a recent year. Assume these are population data.

NUMBER OF PASSENGERS ARRIVING AND DEPARTING (MILLIONS)	NUMBER OF AIRPORTS
20–under 30	8
30–under 40	7
40–under 50	1
50–under 60	0
60–under 70	3
70–under 80	1

a. Calculate the mean of these data.

b. Calculate the mode.

c. Calculate the median.

d. Calculate the variance.

e. Calculate the standard deviation.

3.34. The frequency distribution shown represents the number of farms per state for the 50 United States, based on information from the U.S. Department of Agriculture. Determine the average number of farms per state from these data. The mean computed from the original ungrouped data was 41,796 and the standard deviation was 38,856. How do your answers for these grouped data compare? Why might they differ?

NUMBER OF FARMS PER STATE	f
0–under 20,000	16
20,000–under 40,000	11
40,000–under 60,000	11
60,000–under 80,000	6
80,000–under 100,000	4
100,000–under 120,000	2

3.4 | Measures of Shape

Measures of shape are *tools that can be used to describe the shape of a distribution of data.* In this section, we examine two measures of shape, skewness and kurtosis. We also look at box-and-whisker plots.

Skewness

A distribution of data in which the right half is a mirror image of the left half is said to be *symmetrical*. One example of a symmetrical distribution is the normal distribution, or bell curve, shown in Figure 3.8 and presented in more detail in Chapter 6.

Skewness is when *a distribution is asymmetrical or lacks symmetry.* The distribution in **Figure 3.8** has no skewness because it is symmetric. **Figure 3.9** shows a distribution that is

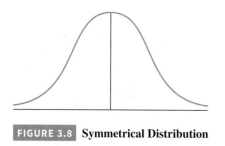

FIGURE 3.8 **Symmetrical Distribution**

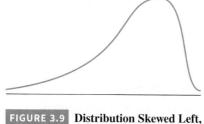

FIGURE 3.9 **Distribution Skewed Left, or Negatively Skewed**

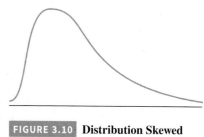

FIGURE 3.10 **Distribution Skewed Right, or Positively Skewed**

skewed left, or negatively skewed, and Figure 3.10 shows a distribution that is skewed right, or positively skewed.

The skewed portion is the long, thin part of the curve. Many researchers use a skewed distribution to denote that the data are sparse at one end of the distribution and piled up at the other end. Instructors sometimes refer to a grade distribution as skewed, meaning that few students scored at one end of the grading scale, and many students scored at the other end.

Skewness and the Relationship of the Mean, Median, and Mode   The concept of skewness helps to understand the relationship of the mean, median, and mode. In a unimodal distribution (distribution with a single peak or mode) that is skewed, the mode is the apex (high point) of the curve and the median is the middle value. The mean tends to be located toward the tail of the distribution, because the mean is particularly affected by the extreme values. A bell-shaped or normal distribution with the mean, median, and mode all at the center of the distribution has no skewness. Figure 3.11 displays the relationship of the mean, median, and mode for different types of skewness.

Kurtosis

Kurtosis *describes the amount of peakedness of a distribution.* Distributions that are high and thin are referred to as **leptokurtic** distributions. Distributions that are flat and spread out are referred to as **platykurtic** distributions. Between these two types are distributions that are more "normal" in shape, referred to as **mesokurtic** distributions. These three types of kurtosis are illustrated in Figure 3.12.

Box-and-Whisker Plots and Five-Number Summary

Another way to describe a distribution of data is by using a box and whisker plot. A **box-and-whisker plot**, sometimes called a *box plot*, is *a diagram that utilizes the upper and lower quartiles along with the median and the two most extreme values to depict a distribution graphically.* The plot is constructed by using a box to enclose the median. This *box* is extended outward from the median along a continuum to the lower and upper quartiles, enclosing not only the median but also the middle 50% of the data. From the lower and upper quartiles, lines referred to as *whiskers* are extended out from the box toward the outermost data values.

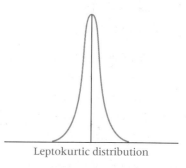

Leptokurtic distribution

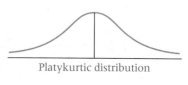

Platykurtic distribution

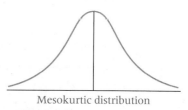

Mesokurtic distribution

FIGURE 3.12 **Types of Kurtosis**

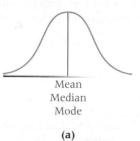

Mean
Median
Mode

(a)
Symmetric distribution (no skewness)

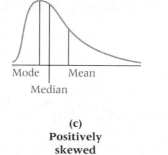

Mean | Mode
Median

(b)
Negatively skewed

Mode | Mean
Median

(c)
Positively skewed

FIGURE 3.11 **Relationship of Mean, Median, and Mode**

The box-and-whisker plot is determined from five specific numbers sometimes referred to as the **five-number summary**.

1. The median (Q_2)

2. The lower quartile (Q_1)

3. The upper quartile (Q_3)

4. The smallest value in the distribution

5. The largest value in the distribution

The box of the plot is determined by locating the median and the lower and upper quartiles on a continuum. A box is drawn around the median with the lower and upper quartiles $(Q_1$ and $Q_3)$ as the box endpoints. These box endpoints $(Q_1$ and $Q_3)$ are referred to as the *hinges* of the box.

Next the value of the interquartile range (IQR) is computed by $Q_3 - Q_1$. The interquartile range includes the middle 50% of the data and should equal the length of the box. However, here the interquartile range is used outside of the box also. At a distance of $1.5 \cdot$ IQR outward from the lower and upper quartiles are what are referred to as *inner fences*. A *whisker*, a line segment, is drawn from the lower hinge of the box outward to the smallest data value. A second whisker is drawn from the upper hinge of the box outward to the largest data value. The inner fences are established as follows.

$$Q_1 - 1.5 \cdot \text{IQR}$$
$$Q_3 + 1.5 \cdot \text{IQR}$$

If data fall beyond the inner fences, then *outer* fences can be constructed:

$$Q_1 - 3.0 \cdot \text{IQR}$$
$$Q_3 + 3.0 \cdot \text{IQR}$$

Figure 3.13 shows the features of a box-and-whisker plot.

Data values outside the mainstream of values in a distribution are viewed as *outliers*. Outliers can be merely the more extreme values of a data set. However, sometimes outliers occur due to measurement or recording errors. Other times they are values so unlike the other values that they should not be considered in the same analysis as the rest of the distribution. Values in the data distribution that are outside the inner fences but within the outer fences are referred to as *mild outliers*. Values that are outside the outer fences are called *extreme outliers*. Thus, one of the main uses of a box-and-whisker plot is to identify outliers. In some computer-produced box-and-whisker plots (such as in Minitab), the whiskers are drawn to the largest and smallest data values within the inner fences. An asterisk is then printed for each data value located between the inner and outer fences to indicate a mild outlier. Values outside the outer fences are indicated by a zero on the graph. These values are extreme outliers.

Another use of box-and-whisker plots is to determine whether a distribution is skewed. The location of the median in the box can relate information about the skewness of the middle 50% of the data. If the median is located on the right side of the box, then the middle 50% are skewed to the left. If the median is located on the left side of the box, then the middle 50% are skewed to the right. By examining the length of the whiskers on each side of the

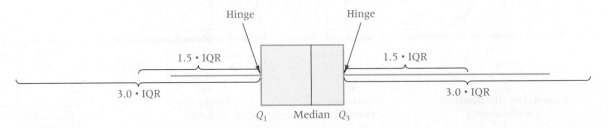

FIGURE 3.13   **Box-and-Whisker Plot**

TABLE 3.10	Data for Box-and-Whisker Plot						
71	87	82	64	72	75	81	69
76	79	65	68	80	73	85	71
70	79	63	62	81	84	77	73
82	74	74	73	84	72	81	65
74	62	64	68	73	82	69	71

TABLE 3.11	Data in Ordered Array with Quartiles and Median								
62	62	63	64	64	65	65	68	68	69
69	70	71	71	71	72	72	73	73	73
73	74	74	74	75	76	77	79	79	80
81	81	81	82	82	82	84	84	85	87

$$Q_1 = 69$$
$$Q_2 = \text{median} = 73$$
$$Q_3 = 80.5$$
$$\text{IQR} = Q_3 - Q_1 = 80.5 - 69 = 11.5$$

box, a business researcher can make a judgment about the skewness of the outer values. If the longest whisker is to the right of the box, then the outer data are skewed to the right and vice versa. We shall use the data given in Table 3.10 to construct a box-and-whisker plot.

After organizing the data into an ordered array, as shown in Table 3.11, it is relatively easy to determine the values of the lower quartile (Q_1), the median, and the upper quartile (Q_3). From these, the value of the interquartile range can be computed.

The hinges of the box are located at the lower and upper quartiles, 69 and 80.5. The median is located within the box at distances of 4 from the lower quartile and 7.5 from the upper quartile. The distribution of the middle 50% of the data is skewed right, because the median is nearer to the lower or left hinge. The inner fence is constructed by

$$Q_1 - 1.5 \cdot \text{IQR} = 69 - 1.5(11.5) = 69 - 17.25 = 51.75$$

and

$$Q_3 + 1.5 \cdot \text{IQR} = 80.5 + 1.5(11.5) = 80.5 + 17.25 = 97.75$$

The whiskers are constructed by drawing a line segment from the lower hinge outward to the smallest data value and a line segment from the upper hinge outward to the largest data value. An examination of the data reveals that no data values in this set of numbers are outside the inner fence. The whiskers are constructed outward to the lowest value, which is 62, and to the highest value, which is 87.

To construct an outer fence, we calculate $Q_1 - 3 \cdot \text{IQR}$ and $Q_3 + 3 \cdot \text{IQR}$, as follows.

$$Q_1 - 3 \cdot \text{IQR} = 69 - 3(11.5) = 69 - 34.5 = 34.5$$
$$Q_3 + 3 \cdot \text{IQR} = 80.5 + 3(11.5) = 80.5 + 34.5 = 115.0$$

Figure 3.14 is the Minitab computer printout for this box-and-whisker plot.

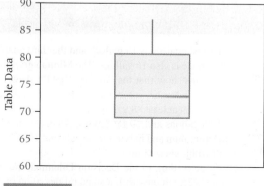

FIGURE 3.14   **Minitab Box-and-Whisker Plot**

3.4 Problems

3.35. On a certain day the average closing price of a group of stocks on the New York Stock Exchange is $35 (to the nearest dollar). If the median value is $33 and the mode is $21, is the distribution of these stock prices skewed? If so, how?

3.36. A local hotel offers ballroom dancing on Friday nights. A researcher observes the customers and estimates their ages. Discuss the skewness of the distribution of ages if the mean age is 51, the median age is 54, and the modal age is 59.

3.37. Construct a box-and-whisker plot on the following data. Do the data contain any outliers? Is the distribution of data skewed?

540 690 503 558 490 609

379 601 559 495 562 580

510 623 477 574 588 497

527 570 495 590 602 541

3.38. Suppose a consumer group asked 18 consumers to keep a yearly log of their shopping practices and that the following data represent the number of coupons used by each consumer over the yearly period. Use the data to construct a box-and-whisker plot. List the median, Q_1, Q_3, the endpoints for the inner fences, and the endpoints for the outer fences. Discuss the skewness of the distribution of these data and point out any outliers.

81 68 70 100 94 47 66 70 82

110 105 60 21 70 66 90 78 85

3.5 Descriptive Statistics on the Computer

Both Minitab and Excel yield extensive descriptive statistics. Even though each computer package can compute individual statistics such as a mean or a standard deviation, they can also produce multiple descriptive statistics at one time. Figure 3.15 displays a Minitab output for the descriptive statistics associated with the computer production data presented earlier in this section. The Minitab output contains, among other things, the mean, the median, the sample standard deviation, the minimum and maximum (which can then be used to compute the range), and Q_1 and Q_3 (from which the interquartile range can be computed). Excel's descriptive statistics output for the same computer production data is displayed in Figure 3.16. The Excel output contains the mean, the median, the mode, the sample standard deviation, the sample variance, and the range. The descriptive statistics feature on either of these computer packages yields a lot of useful information about a data set.

COMPUTER PRODUCTION DATA

Mean	13
Standard error	2.54951
Median	16
Mode	#N/A
Standard deviation	5.700877
Sample variance	32.5
Kurtosis	−1.71124
Skewness	−0.80959
Range	13
Minimum	5
Maximum	18
Sum	65
Count	5

FIGURE 3.16 Excel Output for the Computer Production Problem

DESCRIPTIVE STATISTICS

Variable	N	N*	Mean	SE Mean	StDev	Minimum	Q_1
Computers Produced	5	0	13.00	2.55	5.70	5.00	7.00

	Median	Q_3	Maximum				
	16.00	17.50	18.00				

FIGURE 3.15 Minitab Output for the Computer Production Problem

Decision Dilemma Solved

Laundry Statistics

The descriptive statistics presented in this chapter are excellent for summarizing and presenting data sets in more concise formats. For example, question 1 of the managerial and statistical questions in the Decision Dilemma reports water measurements for 50 U.S. households. Using Excel and/or Minitab, many of the descriptive statistics presented in this chapter can be applied to these data. The results are shown in Figures 3.17 and 3.18.

These computer outputs show that the average water usage is 15.48 gallons with a standard deviation of about 1.233 gallons. The median is 16 gallons with a range of 6 gallons (12 to 18).

The first quartile is 15 gallons and the third quartile is 16 gallons. The mode is also 16 gallons. The Minitab graph and the skewness measures show that the data are slightly skewed to the left. Applying Chebyshev's theorem to the mean and standard deviation shows that at least 88.9% of the measurements should fall between 11.78 gallons and 19.18 gallons. An examination of the data and the minimum and maximum reveals that 100% of the data actually fall within these limits.

According to the Decision Dilemma, the mean wash cycle time is 35 minutes with a standard deviation of 5 minutes. If the wash cycle times are approximately normally distributed, we can apply the empirical rule. According to the empirical rule, 68% of the times would fall within 30 and 40 minutes, 95% of the times would fall within 25 and 45 minutes, and 99.7% of the wash times would fall within 20 and 50 minutes. If the data are not normally distributed, Chebyshev's theorem reveals that at least 75% of the times should fall between 25 and 45 minutes and 88.9% should fall between 20 and 50 minutes.

GALLONS OF WATER

Mean	15.48
Standard error	0.174356
Median	16
Mode	16
Standard deviation	1.232883
Sample variance	1.52
Kurtosis	0.263785
Skewness	−0.53068
Range	6
Minimum	12
Maximum	18
Sum	774
Count	50

FIGURE 3.17 **Excel Descriptive Statistics**

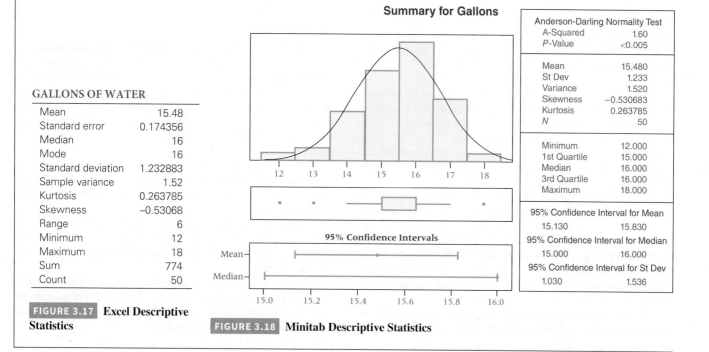

Summary for Gallons

Anderson-Darling Normality Test	
A-Squared	1.60
P-Value	<0.005
Mean	15.480
St Dev	1.233
Variance	1.520
Skewness	−0.530683
Kurtosis	0.263785
N	50
Minimum	12.000
1st Quartile	15.000
Median	16.000
3rd Quartile	16.000
Maximum	18.000

95% Confidence Interval for Mean	
15.130	15.830

95% Confidence Interval for Median	
15.000	16.000

95% Confidence Interval for St Dev	
1.030	1.536

FIGURE 3.18 **Minitab Descriptive Statistics**

Ethical Considerations

In describing a body of data to an audience, it is best to use whatever measures it takes to present a "full" picture of the data. By limiting the descriptive measures used, the business researcher may give the audience only part of the picture and can skew the way the receiver understands the data. For example, if a researcher presents only the mean, the audience will have no insight into the variability of the data; in addition, the mean might be inordinately large or small because of extreme values. Likewise, the choice of the median precludes a picture that includes the extreme values.

Using the mode can cause the receiver of the information to focus only on values that occur often.

At least one measure of variability is usually needed with at least one measure of central tendency for the audience to begin to understand what the data look like. Unethical researchers might be tempted to present only the descriptive measure that will convey the picture of the data that they want the audience to see. Ethical researchers will instead use any and all methods that will present the fullest, most informative picture possible from the data.

Summary

Statistical descriptive measures include measures of central tendency, measures of variability, and measures of shape. Measures of central tendency and measures of variability are computed differently for ungrouped and grouped data. Measures of central tendency are useful in describing data because they communicate information about the more central portions of the data. The most common measures of central tendency are the mode, median, and mean. In addition, percentiles and quartiles are measures of central tendency.

The mode is the most frequently occurring value in a set of data. Among other things, the mode is used in business for determining sizes.

The median is the middle term in an ordered array of numbers containing an odd number of terms. For an array with an even number of terms, the median is the average of the two middle terms. A median is unaffected by the magnitude of extreme values. This characteristic makes the median a most useful and appropriate measure of location in reporting such things as income, age, and prices of houses.

The arithmetic mean is widely used and is usually what researchers are referring to when they use the word *mean*. The arithmetic mean is the average. The population mean and the sample mean are computed in the same way but are denoted by different symbols. The arithmetic mean is affected by every value and can be inordinately influenced by extreme values.

Percentiles divide a set of data into 100 groups. There are 99 percentiles. Quartiles divide data into four groups. The three quartiles are Q_1, which is the lower quartile; Q_2, which is the middle quartile and equals the median; and Q_3, which is the upper quartile.

Measures of variability are statistical tools used in combination with measures of central tendency to describe data. Measures of variability provide information about the spread of the data values. These measures include the range, mean absolute deviation, variance, standard deviation, interquartile range, z scores, and coefficient of variation for ungrouped data.

One of the most elementary measures of variability is the range. It is the difference between the largest and smallest values. Although the range is easy to compute, it has limited usefulness. The interquartile range is the difference between the third and first quartile. It equals the range of the middle 50% of the data.

The mean absolute deviation (MAD) is computed by averaging the absolute values of the deviations from the mean. The mean absolute deviation has limited usage in statistics but is occasionally used in the field of forecasting as a measure of error.

Variance is widely used as a tool in statistics but is used little as a stand-alone measure of variability. The variance is the average of the squared deviations about the mean.

The square root of the variance is the standard deviation. It also is a widely used tool in statistics, but it is used more often than the variance as a stand-alone measure. The standard deviation is best understood by examining its applications in determining where data are in relation to the mean. The empirical rule and Chebyshev's theorem are statements about the proportions of data values that are within various numbers of standard deviations from the mean.

The empirical rule reveals the percentage of values that are within one, two, or three standard deviations of the mean for a set of data. The empirical rule applies only if the data are in a bell-shaped distribution.

Chebyshev's theorem also delineates the proportion of values that are within a given number of standard deviations from the mean. However, it applies to any distribution.

The z score represents the number of standard deviations a value is from the mean for normally distributed data.

The coefficient of variation is a ratio of a standard deviation to its mean, given as a percentage. It is especially useful in comparing standard deviations or variances that represent data with different means.

Some measures of central tendency and some measures of variability are presented for grouped data. These measures include mean, median, mode, variance, and standard deviation. Generally, these measures are only approximate for grouped data because the values of the actual raw data are unknown.

Two measures of shape are skewness and kurtosis. Skewness is the lack of symmetry in a distribution. If a distribution is skewed, it is stretched in one direction or the other. The skewed part of a graph is its long, thin portion.

Kurtosis is the degree of peakedness of a distribution. A tall, thin distribution is referred to as leptokurtic. A flat distribution is platykurtic, and a distribution with a more normal peakedness is said to be mesokurtic.

A box-and-whisker plot is a graphical depiction of a distribution. The plot is constructed by using the median, the lower quartile, the upper quartile, the smallest value, and the largest value. It can yield information about skewness and outliers.

Key Terms

arithmetic mean	five-number summary	measures of variability	quartiles
bimodal	interquartile range	median	range
box-and-whisker plot	kurtosis	mesokurtic	skewness
Chebyshev's theorem	leptokurtic	mode	standard deviation
coefficient of variation (CV)	mean absolute deviation (MAD)	multimodal	sum of squares of x
deviation from the mean	measures of central tendency	percentiles	variance
empirical rule	measures of shape	platykurtic	z score

Formulas

Population mean (ungrouped)

$$\mu = \frac{\Sigma x_i}{N}$$

Sample mean (ungrouped)

$$\bar{x} = \frac{\Sigma x_i}{n}$$

Mean absolute deviation

$$\text{MAD} = \frac{\Sigma |x_i - \mu|}{N}$$

Population variance (ungrouped)

$$\sigma^2 = \frac{\Sigma(x_i - \mu)^2}{N}$$

$$\sigma^2 = \frac{\Sigma x_i^2 - \frac{(\Sigma x_i)^2}{N}}{N}$$

$$\sigma^2 = \frac{\Sigma x_i^2 - N\mu^2}{N}$$

Population standard deviation (ungrouped)

$$\sigma = \sqrt{\sigma^2}$$

$$\sigma = \sqrt{\frac{\Sigma(x_i - \mu)^2}{N}}$$

$$\sigma = \sqrt{\frac{\Sigma x_i^2 - \frac{(\Sigma x_i)^2}{N}}{N}}$$

$$\sigma = \sqrt{\frac{\Sigma x_i^2 - N\mu^2}{N}}$$

Grouped mean

$$\mu_{grouped} = \frac{\Sigma f_i M_i}{N}$$

Grouped median

$$Median = L + \frac{\frac{N}{2} - cf_p}{f_{med}}(W)$$

Population variance (grouped)

$$\sigma^2 = \frac{\Sigma f_i (M_i - \mu)^2}{N} = \frac{\Sigma f_i M_i^2 - \frac{(\Sigma f_i M_i)^2}{N}}{N}$$

Population standard deviation (grouped)

$$\sigma = \sqrt{\frac{\Sigma f_i (M_i - \mu)^2}{N}} = \sqrt{\frac{\Sigma f_i M_i^2 - \frac{(\Sigma f_i M_i)^2}{N}}{N}}$$

Sample variance

$$s^2 = \frac{\Sigma(x_i - \bar{x})^2}{n - 1}$$

$$s^2 = \frac{\Sigma x_i^2 - \frac{(\Sigma x_i)^2}{n}}{n - 1}$$

$$s^2 = \frac{\Sigma x_i^2 - n(\bar{x})^2}{n - 1}$$

Sample standard deviation (ungrouped)

$$s = \sqrt{s^2}$$

$$s = \sqrt{\frac{\Sigma(x_i - \bar{x})^2}{n - 1}}$$

$$s = \sqrt{\frac{\Sigma x_i^2 - \frac{(\Sigma x_i)^2}{n}}{n - 1}}$$

$$s = \sqrt{\frac{\Sigma x_i^2 - n(\bar{x})^2}{n - 1}}$$

Chebyshev's theorem

$$1 - \frac{1}{k^2}$$

z score

$$z = \frac{x_i - \mu}{\sigma}$$

Coefficient of variation

$$CV = \frac{\sigma}{\mu}(100)$$

Interquartile range

$$IQR = Q_3 - Q_1$$

Sample variance (grouped)

$$s^2 = \frac{\Sigma f_i (M_i - \bar{x})^2}{n - 1} = \frac{\Sigma f_i M_i^2 - \frac{(\Sigma f_i M_i)^2}{n}}{n - 1}$$

Sample standard deviation (grouped)

$$s = \sqrt{\frac{\Sigma f_i (M_i - \bar{x})^2}{n - 1}} = \sqrt{\frac{\Sigma f_i M_i^2 - \frac{(\Sigma f_i M_i)^2}{n}}{n - 1}}$$

Supplementary Problems

Calculating the Statistics

3.39. The 2010 U.S. Census asked every household to report information on each person living there. Suppose for a sample of 30 households selected, the number of persons living in each was reported as follows.

```
2  3  1  2  6  4  2  1  5  3  2  3  1  2  2
1  3  1  2  2  4  2  1  2  8  3  2  1  1  3
```

Compute the mean, median, mode, range, lower and upper quartiles, and interquartile range for these data.

3.40. The 2010 U.S. Census also asked for each person's age. Suppose that a sample of 40 households taken from the census data showed the age of the first person recorded on the census form to be as follows.

42	29	31	38	55	27	28
33	49	70	25	21	38	47
63	22	38	52	50	41	19
22	29	81	52	26	35	38
29	31	48	26	33	42	58
40	32	24	34	25		

Compute P_{10}, P_{80}, Q_1, Q_3, the interquartile range, and the range for these data.

3.41. Shown below are the top 15 market research firms in the United States in 2014 according to the AMA Gold Top 50 Report. Compute the mean, median, P_{30}, P_{60}, P_{90}, Q_1, Q_3, range, and the interquartile range on these data.

COMPANY	SALES ($ MILLIONS)
Nielson Holdings N.V.	3194.3
Kantar	952.6
IMS Health Inc.	935.0
Ipsos	574.1
Westat, Inc.	563.7
Information Resources, Inc.	504.0
GfK USA	334.5
comScore Inc.	202.7
The NPD Group Inc.	202.3
Symphony Health Solutions	196.5
J.D. Power and Associates	172.9
ICF International Inc.	172.0
Abt SRBI Inc.	155.7
Maritz Research	138.9
dunnhumbyUSA LLC	121.5

3.42. Shown below are the top 10 contractors of the U.S. federal government by dollars according to the U.S. General Services Administration. Use this population data to compute a mean and a standard deviation for these data.

COMPANY	AMOUNT OF CONTRACTS ($ BILLIONS)
Lockheed Martin	44.1
Boeing	21.2
Raytheon	14.1
General Dynamics	13.1
Northrop Grumman	10.0
SAIC	6.3
Huntington Ingalls	6.2
L-3 Communications Holdings	5.8
United Technologies	5.7
BAE Systems PLC	4.8

3.43. Shown here are the top twelve biggest oil and gas companies in the world according to *Forbes*. Use these as population data and answer the questions that follow.

COMPANY	PRODUCTION VOLUME (MILLION BARRELS PER DAY)
Saudi Aramco (Saudi Arabia)	12.5
Gazprom (Russia)	9.7
NIOC (Iran)	6.4
ExxonMobil Corp. (USA)	5.3
PetroChina (China)	4.4
BP (UK)	4.1
Royal Dutch/Shell (NL/UK)	3.9
Pemex (Mexico)	3.6
Chevron Corp. (USA)	3.5
KPC (Kuwait)	3.2
ADNOC (UAE)	2.9
Sonatrach (Algeria)	2.7

a. What are the values of the mean and the median? Compare the answers and state which you prefer as a measure of location for these data and why.

b. What are the values of the range and interquartile range? How do they differ?

c. What are the values of variance and standard deviation for these data?

d. What is the z score for ADNOC? What is the z score for ExxonMobil? Interpret these z scores.

3.44. The U.S. Department of the Interior releases figures on mineral production. Following are the 15 leading states in nonfuel mineral production in the United States for 2014.

STATE	VALUE ($ BILLIONS)
Arizona	8.06
Nevada	7.49
Minnesota	4.71
Texas	4.24
Utah	4.18
California	3.51
Alaska	3.51
Florida	2.99
Missouri	2.48
Michigan	2.41
Wyoming	2.35
Colorado	2.32
New Mexico	1.87
Wisconsin	1.78
Georgia	1.60

a. Calculate the mean and median.

b. Calculate the range, interquartile range, mean absolute deviation, sample variance, and sample standard deviation.

c. Sketch a box-and-whisker plot.

3.45. The radio music listener market is diverse. Listener formats might include adult contemporary, album rock, top 40, oldies, rap, country and western, classical, and jazz. In targeting audiences, market researchers need to be concerned about the ages of the listeners attracted to particular formats. Suppose a market researcher surveyed a sample of 170 listeners of country music radio stations and obtained the following age distribution.

AGE	FREQUENCY
15–under 20	9
20–under 25	16
25–under 30	27
30–under 35	44
35–under 40	42
40–under 45	23
45–under 50	7
50–under 55	2

a. What are the mean and modal ages of country music listeners?

b. What are the variance and standard deviation of the ages of country music listeners?

3.46. A research agency administers a demographic survey to 90 telemarketing companies to determine the size of their operations. When asked to report how many employees now work in their telemarketing operation, the companies gave responses ranging from 1 to 100. The agency's analyst organizes the figures into a frequency distribution.

NUMBER OF EMPLOYEES WORKING IN TELEMARKETING	NUMBER OF COMPANIES
0–under 20	32
20–under 40	16
40–under 60	13
60–under 80	10
80–under 100	19

a. Compute the mean, median, and mode for this distribution.

b. Compute the sample standard deviation for these data.

Testing Your Understanding

3.47. Financial analysts like to use the standard deviation as a measure of risk for a stock. The greater the deviation in a stock price over time, the more risky it is to invest in the stock. However, the average prices of some stocks are considerably higher than the average price of others, allowing for the potential of a greater standard deviation of price. For example, a standard deviation of $5.00 on a $10.00 stock is considerably different from a $5.00 standard deviation on a $40.00 stock. In this situation, a coefficient of variation might provide insight into risk. Suppose stock X costs an average of $32.00 per share and showed a standard deviation of $3.45 for the past 60 days. Suppose stock Y costs an average of $84.00 per share and showed a standard deviation of $5.40 for the past 60 days. Use the coefficient of variation to determine the variability for each stock.

3.48. The Polk Company reported that the average age of a car on U.S. roads in a recent year was 7.5 years. Suppose the distribution of ages of cars on U.S. roads is approximately bellshaped. If 99.7% of the ages are between 1 year and 14 years, what is the standard deviation of car age? Suppose the standard deviation is 1.7 years and the mean is 7.5 years. Between what two values would 95% of the car ages fall?

3.49. According to a *Human Resources* report, a worker in the industrial countries spends on average 419 minutes a day on the job. Suppose the standard deviation of time spent on the job is 27 minutes.

a. If the distribution of time spent on the job is approximately bell shaped, between what two times would 68% of the figures be? 95%? 99.7%?

b. If the shape of the distribution of times is unknown, approximately what percentage of the times would be between 359 and 479 minutes?

c. Suppose a worker spent 400 minutes on the job. What would that worker's z score be, and what would it tell the researcher?

3.50. The following are per capita GDP figures for eight eastern European countries according to the World Bank. The monetary figures are in international dollars; and for comparison, the per capita GDP for the United States is 54,629.50 international dollars.

COUNTRY	PER CAPITA GDP (INT $)
Albania	10,428
Bosnia/Herzegovina	9,904
Bulgaria	16,323
Croatia	21,252
Czech Republic	30,444
Hungary	24,498
Poland	24,882
Romania	19,401

a. Compute the mean and standard deviation for Albania, Bosnia/Herzegovina, Bulgaria, and Croatia. Treat the data as population data.

b. Compute the mean and standard deviation for the Czech Republic, Hungary, Poland, and Romania. Treat the data as population data.

c. Compute a coefficient of variation for the countries in (a) and for the countries in (b). Compare the two coefficients of variation in light of each group's standard deviation.

3.51. According to the Bureau of Labor Statistics, the average annual salary of a worker in Detroit, Michigan, is $45,140. Suppose the median annual salary for a worker in this group is $41,369 and the mode is $39,500. Is the distribution of salaries for this group skewed? If so, how and why? Which of the measures of central tendency would you use to describe these data? Why?

3.52. According to the U.S. Army Corps of Engineers, the top 20 U.S. ports, ranked by total tonnage (in million tons), were as follows:

PORT	TOTAL TONNAGE
South Louisiana, LA	238.6
Houston, TX	229.2
New York/New Jersey	123.3
Beaumont, TX	94.4
Long Beach, CA	84.5

Hampton Roads, VA	78.7
New Orleans, LA	77.2
Corpus Christi, TX	76.2
Baton Rouge, LA	63.9
Los Angeles, CA	57.9
Plaquemines, LA	56.9
Lake Charles, LA	56.6
Mobile, AL	54.0
Texas City, TX	49.7
Huntington – Tristate	46.8
Baltimore, MD	36.6
Duluth-Superior, MN/WI	36.5
Port Arthur, TX	34.7
St. Louis, MO and IL	33.6
Pittsburgh, PA	32.7

a. Construct a box-and-whisker plot for these data.

b. Discuss the shape of the distribution from the plot.

c. Are there outliers? If so, what are they and why do you think that they are outliers?

3.53. *Business Travel News* reported that the average per diem total for a business traveler in Paris, France is $483. Suppose the shape of the distribution of the per diem costs of a business traveler to Paris is unknown, but that 53% of the per diem figures are between $451 and $515. What is the value of the standard deviation?

Interpreting the Output

3.54. U.S. Bank Locations compiled a list of over 6,000 banks in the United States in order of their total assets. Leading the list were JPMorgan Chase, Bank of America, and Wells Fargo Bank. Following is an Excel analysis of total assets ($ billions) for the top 100 of these banks using the descriptive statistics feature. Study the output and describe in your own words what you can learn about the assets of these top 100 U.S. banks.

TOP 100 BANKS IN U.S. ($ BILLIONS)	
Mean	128.0136
Standard Error	32.6032
Median	30.3950
Mode	#N/A
Standard Deviation	326.0321
Sample Variance	106296.9595
Kurtosis	21.7749
Skewness	4.6249
Range	2082.9820
Minimum	13.1320
Maximum	2096.1140
Sum	12801.3590
Count	100

3.55. happi.com published a list of the top 50 household and personal products companies in the United States. Topping the list was Procter & Gamble with $69.5 billion followed by Colgate-Palmolive with $15.2 billion and Estee Lauder with $10.1 billion. The data from these top 50 companies (excluding Procter & Gamble) were analyzed using Minitab's Graphical Summary. Study the output from this analysis and describe these companies using statistics. Data are given in $ billions.

Top Household and Personal Products Companies

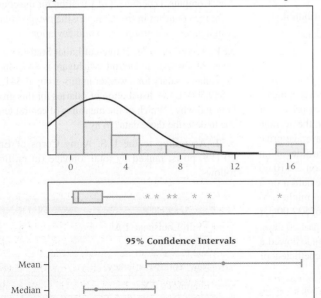

Anderson-Darling Normality Test	
A-Squared	6.61
P-Value	<0.005

Mean	2.0028
St Dev	3.1590
Variance	9.9794
Skewness	2.40268
Kurtosis	6.18162
N	49

Minimum	0.1170
1st Quartile	0.2170
Median	0.5100
3rd Quartile	2.3000
Maximum	15.2000

95% Confidence Interval for Mean	
1.0954	2.9101

95% Confidence Interval for Median	
0.3706	1.1928

95% Confidence Interval for St Dev	
2.6344	3.9466

95% Confidence Intervals

3.56. Excel was used to analyze the number of employees for the top 60 employers with headquarters around the world outside of the United States. The data was compiled by myglobalcareer.com, extracted from *My Global Career 500*, and was analyzed using Excel's descriptive statistics feature. Summarize what you have learned about the number of employees for these companies by studying the output.

TOP 60 EMPLOYERS OUTSIDE OF THE U.S.	
Mean	211942.9
Standard Error	12415.31
Median	175660
Mode	150000
Standard Deviation	96168.57
Sample Variance	9.25E+09
Kurtosis	1.090976
Skewness	1.356847
Range	387245
Minimum	115300
Maximum	502545
Sum	12716575
Count	60

3.57. The Nielsen Company compiled a list of the top 25 advertisers in African American media. Shown below are a Minitab descriptive statistics analysis of the annual advertising spending in $ million by these companies in African American media and a box plot of these data. Study this output and summarize the expenditures of these top 25 advertisers in your own words.

Variable	N	N*	Mean	SE Mean	StDev	Minimum	Q1
Advertisers	25	0	27.24	2.84	14.19	16.20	21.25

Variable	Median	Q3	Maximum
Advertisers	24.00	27.50	89.70

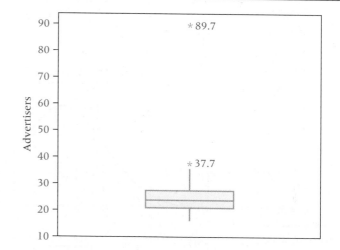

Analyzing the Databases

see **www.wiley.com/college/black**

1. What are the mean and the median amounts of new capital expenditures for industries in the Manufacturing database? Comparing the mean and the median for these data, what do these statistics tell you about the data?

2. Analyze U.S. finished motor gasoline production in the 12-Year Gasoline database using a descriptive statistics feature of either Excel or Minitab. By examining such statistics as the mean, median, mode, range, standard deviation, and a measure of skewness, describe U.S. motor gasoline production over this period of time.

3. Using measures of central tendency including the mean, median, and mode, describe annual food spending and annual household income for the 200 households in the Consumer Food database. Compare the two results by determining approximately what percent of annual household income is spent on food.

4. Using the Financial database, study earnings per share for Type 2 and Type 7 companies (chemical and petrochemical) using statistics. Compute a coefficient of variation for both Type 2 and Type 7. Compare the two coefficients and comment on them.

5. Using the Hospital database, construct a box-and-whisker plot for births. Thinking about hospitals and birthing facilities, comment on why the box-and-whisker plot looks like it does.

Case

COCA-COLA Develops the African Market

The Coca-Cola Company is the number-one seller of beverages in the world with more than 500 sparkling and still brands that include 17 billion-dollar brands such as Coca-Cola, Diet Coke, Fanta, Sprite, Coca-Cola Zero, Powerade, and Minute Maid. Every day an average of more than 1.9 billion servings of Coca-Cola's beverages are consumed worldwide. Such drinks are delivered via the world's largest beverage distribution system to more than 200 countries around the globe. Including its bottling partners, The Coca-Cola Company ranks among the world's top ten private employers with more than 700,000.

For a variety of reasons, sales in developed countries have been flat or slow growing. For example, in 1989, North Americans bought $2.6 billion worth of Coke; but twenty years later in 2009, the figure had only grown to $2.9 billion. Looking for attractive newer, growing markets, Coca-Cola turned its attention to Africa. According to forecasts by the United Nations, Africa's population will more than double by the year 2050 to 2.5 billion people; and after years of poverty, Africa's emerging middle class is now becoming a driver of growth with an expanding pool of consumers with increasing disposable income. Such factors along with a positive trade balance is attracting companies to Africa as a place in which to invest

While Coke has been in Africa since 1929, more recently it has made substantial efforts to significantly increase sales there. At present, Coke is Africa's largest private employer with 65,000 employees and 160 plants. Building on techniques learned in Latin America, Coke is trying to earn new customers in Africa by winning over small stores. Moving throughout villages and towns, Coca-Cola is distributing Coke signage and drink coolers to shop after shop. In an effort to distribute their products in areas with poor roads and to reach remote areas, Coca-Cola is establishing manual distribution centers such as they used in Vietnam and Thailand. Such centers currently employ more than 12,000 Africans and generate $500 million in annual revenue. In addition, Coca-Cola plans to invest $5 billion more in Africa for long-term sustainable growth increasing its total investment there to $17 billion over the decade ending in 2020. Such infusion of revenue is intended to fund new manufacturing lines, cooling and distribution equipment, more job opportunities, and sustainability initiatives focused on safe water access.

Minitab Output

Descriptive Statistics: Bottle Fills

Variable	Total Count	Mean	SE Mean	StDev	Variance	CoefVar	Minimum	Q_1
Bottle Fills	150	20.008	0.00828	0.101	0.0103	0.51	19.706	19.940

Variable	Median	Q_3	Maximum	Range	IQR
Bottle Fills	19.997	20.079	20.263	0.557	0.139

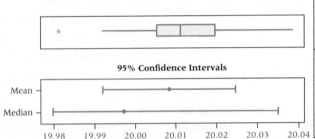

Summary for Bottle Fills

Anderson-Darling Normality Test	
A-Squared	0.32
P-Value	0.531
Mean	20.008
St Dev	0.101
Variance	0.010
Skewness	0.080479
Kurtosis	−0.116220
N	150
Minimum	19.706
1st Quartile	19.940
Median	19.997
3rd Quartile	20.079
Maximum	20.263

95% Confidence Interval for Mean
19.992   20.025
95% Confidence Interval for Median
19.980   20.035
95% Confidence Interval for St Dev
0.091   0.114

EXCEL OUTPUT BOTTLE FILLS	
Mean	20.00817
Standard error	0.008278
Median	19.99697
Mode	#N/A
Standard deviation	0.101388
Sample variance	0.010279
Kurtosis	−0.11422
Skewness	0.080425
Range	0.557666
Minimum	19.70555
Maximum	20.26322
Sum	3001.225
Count	150

Discussion

1. In several countries of Africa, a common size for a Coke can is 340 milliliters (mL). Because of the variability of bottling machinery, it is likely that every 340-mL bottle of Coca-Cola does not contain exactly 340 milliliters of fluid. Some bottles may contain more fluid and others less. Because of this variation, a production engineer wants to test some of the bottles from a production run to determine how close they are to the 340-mL specification. Suppose the following data are the fill measurements from a random sample of 50 cans. Use the techniques presented in this chapter to describe the sample. Consider measures of central tendency, variability, and skewness. Based on this analysis, how is the bottling process working on this production run?

340.1	339.9	340.2	340.2	340.0
340.1	340.9	340.1	340.3	340.5
339.7	340.4	340.3	339.8	339.3
340.1	339.4	339.6	339.2	340.2
340.4	339.8	339.9	340.2	339.6
339.6	340.4	340.4	340.6	340.6
340.1	340.8	339.9	340.0	339.9
340.3	340.5	339.9	341.1	339.7
340.2	340.5	340.2	339.7	340.9
340.2	339.5	340.6	340.3	339.8

2. Suppose that at another plant Coca-Cola is filling bottles with 20 ounces of fluid. A lab randomly samples 150 bottles and tests the bottles for fill volume. The descriptive statistics are given in both Minitab and Excel computer output. Write a brief report to supervisors summarizing what this output is saying about the process.

Sources: The Coca-Cola Company website at www.coca-colacompany. com; Pascal Fletcher, "Africa's Emerging Middle Class Drives Growth and Democracy," Reuters, May 10, 2013 at www.reuters.com/article/2013/05/10/ us-africa-investment-idUSBRE.

CHAPTER 4

Probability

LEARNING OBJECTIVES

The main objective of Chapter 4 is to help you understand the basic principles of probability, thereby enabling you to:

1. Describe what probability is and how to differentiate among the three methods of assigning probabilities.

2. Deconstruct the elements of probability by defining experiments, sample spaces, and events; classifying events as mutually exclusive, collectively exhaustive, complementary, or independent; and counting possibilities.

3. Compare marginal, union, joint, and conditional probabilities by defining each one.

4. Calculate probabilities using the general law of addition, along with a joint probability table, the complement of a union, or the special law of addition if necessary.

5. Calculate joint probabilities of both independent and dependent events using the general and special laws of multiplication.

6. Calculate conditional probabilities with various forms of the law of conditional probability, and use them to determine if two events are independent.

7. Calculate conditional probabilities using Bayes' rule.

Decision Dilemma

Equity of the Sexes in the Workplace

The Civil Rights Act was signed into law in the United States in 1964 by President Lyndon Johnson. This law, which was amended in 1972, resulted in several "titles" that addressed discrimination in American society at various levels. One is Title VII, which pertains specifically to employment discrimination. It applies to all employers with more than 15 employees, along with other institutions. One of the provisions of Title VII makes it illegal to refuse to hire a person on the basis of the person's sex.

Today, company hiring procedures must be within the perview and framework of the Equal Employment Opportunity Commission (EEOC) guidelines and Title VII. How does a company defend its hiring practices or know when they are within acceptable bounds? How can individuals or groups who feel they have been the victims of illegal hiring practices "prove" their case? How can a group demonstrate that they have been "adversely impacted" by a company's discriminatory hiring practices?

Image Source/Age Fotostock America, Inc.

Statistics are widely used in employment discrimination actions and by companies in attempting to meet EEOC guidelines. Substantial quantities of human resources data are logged and analyzed on a daily basis.

Assume that a small portion of the human resource data was gathered on a client company.

1. Suppose some legal concern has been expressed that a disproportionate number of managerial people at the client company are men. If a worker is randomly selected from the client company, what is the probability that the worker is a woman? If a managerial person is randomly selected, what is the probability that the person is a woman? What factors might enter into the apparent discrepancy between probabilities?

2. Suppose a special bonus is being given to one person in the technical area this year. If the bonus is randomly awarded, what is the probability that it will go to a woman, given that worker is in the technical area? Is this discrimination against male technical workers? What factors might enter into the awarding of the bonus other than random selection?

3. Suppose that at the annual holiday party the name of an employee of the client company will be drawn randomly to win a trip to Hawaii. What is the probability that a professional person will be the winner? What is the probability that the winner will be either a man or a clerical worker? What is the probability that the winner will be a woman and in management? Suppose the winner is a man. What is the probability that the winner is from the technical group, given that the winner is a man?

CLIENT COMPANY HUMAN RESOURCE DATA BY SEX			
	SEX		
TYPE OF POSITION	**MALE**	**FEMALE**	**TOTAL**
Managerial	8	3	11
Professional	31	13	44
Technical	52	17	69
Clerical	9	22	31
Total	100	55	155

Source: EEOC information adapted from "Title VII of the Civil Rights Act of 1964—EEOC" at www.eeoc.gov > Laws, Regulations & Guidance > Statutes

In business, most decision making involves uncertainty. For example, an operations manager does not know definitely whether a valve in the plant is going to malfunction or continue to function—or, if it continues, for how long. When should it be replaced? What is the chance that the valve will malfunction within the next week? In the banking industry, what are the new vice president's prospects for successfully turning a department around? The answers to these questions are uncertain.

In the case of a high-rise building, what are the chances that a fire-extinguishing system will work when needed if redundancies are built in? Business people must address these and thousands of similar questions daily. Because most such questions do not have definite answers, the decision making is based on uncertainty. In many of these situations, a probability can be assigned to the likelihood of an outcome. This chapter is about learning how to determine or assign probabilities.

4.1 Introduction to Probability

Chapter 1 discussed the difference between descriptive and inferential statistics. Much statistical analysis is inferential, and probability is the basis for inferential statistics. Recall that inferential statistics involves taking a sample from a population, computing a statistic on the sample, and inferring from the statistic the value of the corresponding parameter of the population. The reason for doing so is that the value of the parameter is unknown. Because it is unknown, the analyst conducts the inferential process under uncertainty. However, by applying rules and laws, the analyst can often assign a probability of obtaining the results. Figure 4.1 depicts this process.

Suppose a quality control analyst for a light bulb manufacturing company randomly selects a sample of 40 light bulbs from a population of brand X bulbs and burns each of them until they burn out. The number of hours of luminance for each bulb is recorded; from the data, the average bulb life is determined to be 1,000 hours. Using techniques presented later in this text, the analyst uses this figure as an estimate of the average number of hours of bulb life for the *population* of brand X bulbs. Because the light bulbs being analyzed are only a sample of the population, the average number of hours of luminance for the 40 bulbs may or may not accurately estimate the average for all bulbs in the population. The results are uncertain. By applying the laws presented in this chapter, the inspector can assign a value of probability to this estimate.

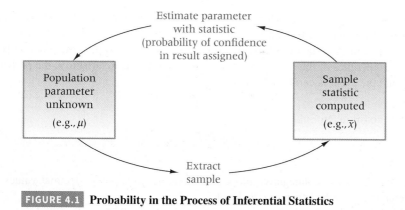

FIGURE 4.1 **Probability in the Process of Inferential Statistics**

In addition, probabilities are used directly in certain industries and industry applications. For example, the insurance industry uses probabilities in actuarial tables to determine the likelihood of certain outcomes in order to set specific rates and coverages. The gaming industry uses probability values to establish charges and payoffs. One way to determine whether a company's hiring practices meet the government's EEOC guidelines mentioned in the Decision Dilemma is to compare various proportional breakdowns of their employees (by ethnicity, gender, age, etc.) to the proportions in the general population from which the employees are hired. In comparing the company figures with those of the general population, the courts could study the probabilities of a company randomly hiring a certain profile of employees from a given population. In other industries, such as manufacturing and aerospace, it is important to know the life of a mechanized part and the probability that it will malfunction at any given length of time in order to protect the firm from major breakdowns.

The three general methods of assigning probabilities are (1) the classical method, (2) the relative frequency of occurrence method, and (3) subjective probabilities.

Classical Method of Assigning Probabilities

When probabilities are assigned based on laws and rules, the method is referred to as the **classical method of assigning probabilities**. This method involves an experiment, which is *a process that produces outcomes*, and an event, *which is an outcome of an experiment.*

When we assign probabilities using the classical method, the probability of an individual event occurring is determined as the ratio of the number of items in a population containing the event (n_e) to the total number of items in the population (N). That is, $P(E) = n_e/N$. For example, if a company has 200 workers and 70 are female, the probability of randomly selecting a female from this company is $70/200 = .35$.

Classical Method of Assigning Probabilities

$$P(E) = \frac{n_e}{N}$$

where

N = total possible number of outcomes of an experiment

n_e = the number of outcomes in which the event occurs out of N outcomes

---

Suppose, in a particular plant, three machines make a given product. Machine A always produces 40% of the total number of this product. Ten percent of the items produced by machine A are defective. If the finished products are well mixed with regard to which machine produced them and if one of these products is randomly selected, the classical method of assigning probabilities tells us that the probability that the part was produced by machine A and is defective is .04. This probability can be determined even before the part is sampled because with the classical method, the probabilities can be determined **a priori**; that is, *they can be determined prior to the experiment.*

Because n_e can never be greater than N (no more than N outcomes in the population could possibly have attribute e), the highest value of any probability is 1. If the probability of an outcome occurring is 1, the event is certain to occur. The smallest possible probability is 0. If none of the outcomes of the N possibilities has the desired characteristic, e, the probability is $0/N = 0$, and the event is certain not to occur.

> **Range of Possible Probabilities**
> $$0 \leq P(E) \leq 1$$

Thus, probabilities are nonnegative proper fractions or nonnegative decimal values greater than or equal to 0 and less or equal to 1.

Probability values can be converted to percentages by multiplying by 100. Meteorologists often report weather probabilities in percentage form. For example, when they forecast a 60% chance of rain for tomorrow, they are saying that the probability of rain tomorrow is .60.

Relative Frequency of Occurrence

The **relative frequency of occurrence method** of assigning probabilities is based on cumulated historical data. With this method, *the probability of an event occurring is equal to the number of times the event has occurred in the past divided by the total number of opportunities for the event to have occurred.*

> **Probability by Relative Frequency of Occurrence**
> $$\frac{\text{Number of times an event occurred}}{\text{Total number of opportunities for the event to have occurred}}$$

Relative frequency of occurrence is not based on rules or laws but on what has occurred in the past. For example, a company wants to determine the probability that its inspectors are going to reject the next batch of raw materials from a supplier. Data gathered from company record books show that the supplier sent the company 90 batches in the past, and inspectors rejected 10 of them. By the method of relative frequency of occurrence, the probability of the inspectors rejecting the next batch is 10/90, or .11. If the next batch is rejected, the relative frequency of occurrence probability for the subsequent shipment would change to 11/91 = .12.

Subjective Probability

The **subjective method** of *assigning probability is based on the feelings or insights of the person determining the probability.* Subjective probability comes from the person's intuition or reasoning. Although not a scientific approach to probability, the subjective method often is based on the accumulation of knowledge, understanding, and experience stored and processed in the human mind. At times it is merely a guess. At other times, subjective probability can potentially yield accurate probabilities. Subjective probability can be used to capitalize on the background of experienced workers and managers in decision making.

Suppose a director of transportation for an oil company is asked the probability of getting a shipment of oil out of Saudi Arabia to the United States within three weeks. A director who has scheduled many such shipments, has a knowledge of Saudi politics, and has an awareness of current climatological and economic conditions may be able to give an accurate probability that the shipment can be made on time.

Subjective probability also can be a potentially useful way of tapping a person's experience, knowledge, and insight and using them to forecast the occurrence of some event. An experienced airline mechanic can usually assign a meaningful probability that a particular plane will have a certain type of mechanical difficulty. Physicians sometimes assign subjective probabilities to the life expectancy of people who have cancer.

4.2 Structure of Probability

In the study of probability, developing a language of terms and symbols is helpful. The structure of probability provides a common framework within which the topics of probability can be explored.

Experiment

As previously stated, an **experiment** is *a process that produces outcomes*. Examples of business-oriented experiments with outcomes that can be statistically analyzed might include the following.

- Interviewing 20 randomly selected consumers and asking them which brand of appliance they prefer
- Sampling every 200th bottle of ketchup from an assembly line and weighing the contents
- Testing new pharmaceutical drugs on samples of cancer patients and measuring the patients' improvement
- Auditing every 10th account to detect any errors
- Recording the Dow Jones Industrial Average on the first Monday of every month for 10 years

Event

Because an **event** is *an outcome of an experiment*, the experiment defines the possibilities of the event. If the experiment is to sample five bottles coming off a production line, an event could be to get one defective and four good bottles. In an experiment to roll a die, one event could be to roll an even number and another event could be to roll a number greater than two. Events are denoted by uppercase letters; italic capital letters (e.g., A and E_1, E_2, . . .) represent the general or abstract case, and roman capital letters (e.g., H and T for heads and tails) denote specific things and people.

Elementary Events

Events that cannot be decomposed or broken down into other events are called **elementary events**. Elementary events are denoted by lowercase letters (e.g., e_1, e_2, e_3, . . .). Suppose the experiment is to roll a die. The elementary events for this experiment are to roll a 1 or roll a 2 or roll a 3, and so on. Rolling an even number is an event, but it is not an elementary event because the even number can be broken down further into events 2, 4, and 6.

In the experiment of rolling a die, there are six elementary events {1, 2, 3, 4, 5, 6}. Rolling a pair of dice results in 36 possible elementary events (outcomes). For each of the six elementary events possible on the roll of one die, there are six possible elementary events on the roll of the second die, as depicted in the tree diagram in **Figure 4.2**. **Table 4.1** contains a list of these 36 outcomes.

In the experiment of rolling a pair of dice, other events could include outcomes such as two even numbers, a sum of 10, a sum greater than five, and others. However, none of these events is an elementary event because each can be broken down into several of the elementary events displayed in Table 4.1.

Sample Space

A **sample space** is *a complete roster or listing of all elementary events for an experiment*. Table 4.1 is the sample space for the roll of a pair of dice. The sample space for the roll of a single die is {1, 2, 3, 4, 5, 6}.

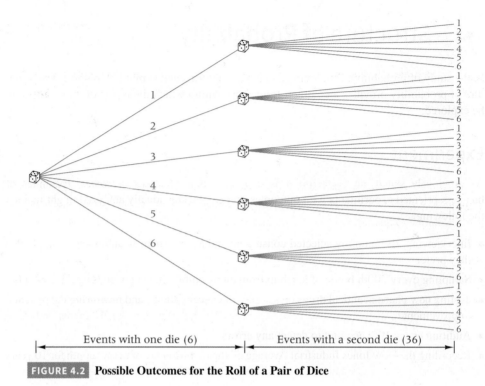

Events with one die (6)   Events with a second die (36)

FIGURE 4.2 **Possible Outcomes for the Roll of a Pair of Dice**

Sample space can aid in finding probabilities. Suppose an experiment is to roll a pair of dice. What is the probability that the dice will sum to 7? An examination of the sample space shown in Table 4.1 reveals that there are six outcomes in which the dice sum to 7—{(1,6), (2,5), (3,4), (4,3), (5,2), (6,1)}—in the total possible 36 elementary events in the sample space. Using this information, we can conclude that the probability of rolling a pair of dice that sum to 7 is 6/36, or .1667. However, using the sample space to determine probabilities is unwieldy and cumbersome when the sample space is large. Hence, business statisticians usually use other more effective methods of determining probability.

Unions and Intersections

Set notation, the use of braces to group numbers, is used as *a symbolic tool for unions and inter-sections* in this chapter. The **union** of X, Y is *formed by combining elements from each of the sets* and is denoted $X \cup Y$. An element qualifies for the union of X, Y if it is in either X or Y or in both X and Y. The union expression $X \cup Y$ can be translated to "X or Y." For example, if

$$A = \{1, 4, 7, 9\} \quad \text{and} \quad B = \{2, 3, 4, 5, 6\}$$
$$A \cup B = \{1, 2, 3, 4, 5, 6, 7, 9\}$$

TABLE 4.1 **All Possible Elementary Events in the Roll of a Pair of Dice (Sample Space)**

(1,1)	(2,1)	(3,1)	(4,1)	(5,1)	(6,1)
(1,2)	(2,2)	(3,2)	(4,2)	(5,2)	(6,2)
(1,3)	(2,3)	(3,3)	(4,3)	(5,3)	(6,3)
(1,4)	(2,4)	(3,4)	(4,4)	(5,4)	(6,4)
(1,5)	(2,5)	(3,5)	(4,5)	(5,5)	(6,5)
(1,6)	(2,6)	(3,6)	(4,6)	(5,6)	(6,6)

Note that all the values of A and all the values of B qualify for the union. However, none of the values is listed more than once in the union. In **Figure 4.3**, the shaded region of the Venn diagram denotes the union.

An intersection is denoted $X \cap Y$. To qualify for intersection, an element must be in both X and Y. The **intersection** *contains the elements common to both sets.* Thus, the intersection symbol, $\cap$, is often read as *and*. The intersection of X, Y is referred to as X and Y. For example, if

$$A = \{1, 4, 7, 9\} \qquad and \qquad B = \{2, 3, 4, 5, 6\}$$

$$A \cap B = \{4\}$$

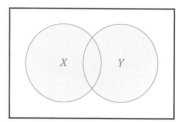

FIGURE 4.3   **A Union**

Note that only the value 4 is common to both sets A and B. The intersection is more exclusive than and hence equal to or (usually) smaller than the union. Elements must be characteristic of both X and Y to qualify. In **Figure 4.4**, the shaded region denotes the intersection.

Mutually Exclusive Events

Two or more events are **mutually exclusive events** if *the occurrence of one event precludes the occurrence of the other event(s).* This characteristic means that mutually exclusive events cannot occur simultaneously and therefore can have no intersection.

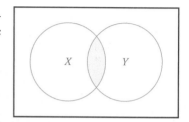

FIGURE 4.4   **An Intersection**

A manufactured part is either defective or okay: The part cannot be both okay and defective at the same time because "okay" and "defective" are mutually exclusive categories. In a sample of the manufactured products, the event of selecting a defective part is mutually exclusive with the event of selecting a nondefective part. Suppose an office building is for sale and two different potential buyers have placed bids on the building. It is not possible for both buyers to purchase the building; therefore, the event of buyer A purchasing the building is mutually exclusive with the event of buyer B purchasing the building. In the toss of a single coin, heads and tails are mutually exclusive events. The person tossing the coin gets either a head or a tail but never both.

The probability of two mutually exclusive events occurring at the same time is zero.

Mutually Exclusive Events X and Y

$$P(X \cap Y) = 0$$

Figure 4.5 shows a Venn diagram of mutually exclusive events.

Independent Events

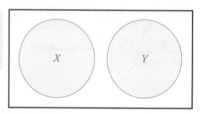

FIGURE 4.5   **A Venn Diagram of Mutually Exclusive Events** X and Y

Two or more events are **independent events** if *the occurrence or nonoccurrence of one of the events does not affect the occurrence or nonoccurrence of the other event(s).* Certain experiments, such as rolling dice, yield independent events; each die is independent of the other. Whether a 6 is rolled on the first die has no influence on whether a 6 is rolled on the second die. Coin tosses always are independent of each other. The event of getting a head on the first toss of a coin is independent of getting a head on the second toss. It is generally believed that certain human characteristics are independent of other events. For example, left-handedness is probably independent of the possession of a credit card. Whether a person wears glasses or not is probably independent of the brand of milk preferred.

Many experiments using random selection can produce either independent or non-independent events, depending on how the experiment is conducted. In these experiments, the outcomes are independent if sampling is done with replacement; that is, after each item is selected and the outcome is determined, the item is restored to the population and the population is shuffled. This way, each draw becomes independent of the previous draw. Suppose an inspector is randomly selecting bolts from a bin that contains 5% defects. If the inspector samples a defective bolt and returns it to the bin, on the second draw there are still 5% defects in the bin regardless of the fact that the first outcome was a defect. If the inspector does not replace the first draw, the second draw is not independent of the first; in this case, fewer than 5%

defects remain in the population. Thus, the probability of the second outcome is dependent on the first outcome.

If X and Y are independent, the following symbolic notation is used.

Independent Events X and Y

$$P(X|Y) = P(X) \quad \text{and} \quad P(Y|X) = P(Y)$$

$P(X|Y)$ denotes the probability of X occurring given that Y has occurred. If X and Y are independent, then the probability of X occurring given that Y has occurred is just the probability of X occurring. Knowledge that Y has occurred does not impact the probability of X occurring because X and Y are independent. For example, P (prefers Pepsi | person is right-handed) = P (prefers Pepsi) because a person's handedness is independent of brand preference.

Collectively Exhaustive Events

A list of **collectively exhaustive events** contains *all possible elementary events for an experiment*. Thus, all sample spaces are collectively exhaustive lists. The list of possible outcomes for the tossing of a pair of dice contained in Table 4.1 is a collectively exhaustive list. The sample space for an experiment can be described as a list of events that are mutually exclusive and collectively exhaustive. Sample space events do not overlap or intersect, and the list is complete.

Complementary Events

The **complement** of event X is denoted X', pronounced "not X." All *the elementary events of an experiment not in X comprise its complement*. For example, if in rolling one die, event X is getting an even number, the complement of X is getting an odd number. If event X is getting a 5 on the roll of a die, the complement of X is getting a 1, 2, 3, 4, or 6. The complement of event X contains whatever portion of the sample space that event X does not contain, as the Venn diagram in Figure 4.6 shows.

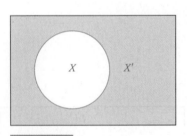

FIGURE 4.6 **The Complement of Event X**

Using the complement of an event sometimes can be helpful in solving for probabilities because of the following rule.

Probability of the Complement of X

$$P(X') = 1 - P(X)$$

Suppose 32% of the employees of a company have a college degree. If an employee is randomly selected from the company, the probability that the person does not have a college degree is $1 - .32 = .68$. Suppose 42% of all parts produced in a plant are molded by machine A and 31% are molded by machine B. If a part is randomly selected, the probability that it was molded by neither machine A nor machine B is $1 - .73 = .27$. (Assume that a part is only molded on one machine.)

Counting the Possibilities

In statistics, a collection of techniques and rules for counting the number of outcomes that can occur for a particular experiment can be used. Some of these rules and techniques can delineate the size of the sample space. Presented here are three of these counting methods.

The *mn* Counting Rule
Suppose a customer decides to buy a certain brand of new car. Options for the car include two different engines, five different paint colors, and three interior packages. If each of these options is available with each of the others, how many different cars could the customer choose from? To determine this number, we can use the *mn* **counting rule**.

The *mn* Counting Rule

For an operation that can be done *m* ways and a second operation that can be done *n* ways, the two operations then can occur, in order, in *mn* ways. This rule can be extended to cases with three or more operations.

Using the *mn* counting rule, we can determine that the automobile customer has $(2)(5)(3) = 30$ different car combinations of engines, paint colors, and interiors available.

Suppose a scientist wants to set up a research design to study the effects of sex (M, F), marital status (single never married, divorced, married), and economic class (lower, middle, and upper) on the frequency of airline ticket purchases per year. The researcher would set up a design in which 18 different samples are taken to represent all possible groups generated from these customer characteristics.

$$\text{Number of Groups} = \text{(Sex)(Marital Status)(Economic Class)}$$
$$= (2)(3)(3) = 18 \text{ Groups}$$

Sampling from a Population with Replacement   In the second counting method, sampling *n* items from a population of size *N with replacement* would provide

$$(N)^n \text{ possibilities}$$

where

N = population size
n = sample size

For example, each time a die, which has six sides, is rolled, the outcomes are independent (with replacement) of the previous roll. If a die is rolled three times in succession, how many different outcomes can occur? That is, what is the size of the sample space for this experiment? The size of the population, N, is 6, the six sides of the die. We are sampling three dice rolls, $n = 3$. The sample space is

$$(N)^n = (6)^3 = 216$$

Suppose in a lottery six numbers are drawn from the digits 0 through 9, with replacement (digits can be reused). How many different groupings of six numbers can be drawn? N is the population of 10 numbers (0 through 9) and n is the sample size, six numbers.

$$(N)^n = (10)^6 = 1,000,000$$

That is, a million six-digit numbers are available!

Combinations: Sampling from a Population Without Replacement
The third counting method uses **combinations**, sampling *n* items from a population of size *N without replacement* provides

$$_NC_n = \binom{N}{n} = \frac{N!}{n!(N-n)!}$$

possibilities.

For example, suppose a small law firm has 16 employees and 3 are to be selected randomly to represent the company at the annual meeting of the American Bar Association. How many different combinations of lawyers could be sent to the meeting? This situation does not allow sampling with replacement because three *different* lawyers will be selected to go. This problem is solved by using combinations. $N = 16$ and $n = 3$, so

$$_NC_n = {}_{16}C_3 = \frac{16!}{3!13!} = 560$$

A total of 560 combinations of three lawyers could be chosen to represent the firm.

4.2 Problems

4.1. A supplier shipped a lot of six parts to a company. The lot contained three defective parts. Suppose the customer decided to randomly select two parts and test them for defects. How large a sample space is the customer potentially working with? List the sample space. Using the sample space list, determine the probability that the customer will select a sample with exactly one defect.

4.2. Given A = {1, 3, 5, 7, 8, 9}, B = {2, 4, 7, 9}, and C = {1, 2, 3, 4, 7}, solve the following.

   a. $A \cup C =$ _____
   b. $A \cap B =$ _____
   c. $A \cap C =$ _____
   d. $A \cup B \cup C =$ _____
   e. $A \cap B \cap C =$ _____
   f. $(A \cup B) \cap C =$ _____
   g. $(B \cap C) \cup (A \cap B) =$ _____
   h. A or B = _____
   i. B and A = _____

4.3. If a population consists of the positive even numbers through 30 and if A = {2, 6, 12, 24}, what is A'?

4.4. A company's customer service 800 telephone system is set up so that the caller has six options. Each of these six options leads to a menu with four options. For each of these four options, three more options are available. For each of these three options, another three options are presented. If a person calls the 800 number for assistance, how many total options are possible?

4.5. A bin contains six parts. Two of the parts are defective and four are acceptable. If three of the six parts are selected from the bin, how large is the sample space? Which counting rule did you use, and why? For this sample space, what is the probability that exactly one of the three sampled parts is defective?

4.6. A company places a seven-digit serial number on each part that is made. Each digit of the serial number can be any number from 0 through 9. Digits can be repeated in the serial number. How many different serial numbers are possible?

4.7. A small company has 20 employees. Six of these employees will be selected randomly to be interviewed as part of an employee satisfaction program. How many different groups of six can be selected?

4.3 | Marginal, Union, Joint, and Conditional Probabilities

Four particular types of probability are presented in this chapter. The first type is **marginal probability**. Marginal probability is denoted $P(E)$, where E is some event. A marginal probability is usually *computed by dividing some subtotal by the whole*. An example of marginal probability is the probability that a person owns a Ford car. This probability is computed by dividing the number of Ford owners by the total number of car owners. The probability of a person wearing glasses is also a marginal probability. This probability is computed by dividing the number of people wearing glasses by the total number of people.

A second type of probability is the union of two events. **Union probability** is denoted $P(E_1 \cup E_2)$, where E_1 and E_2 are two events. $P(E_1 \cup E_2)$ is the probability that E_1 will occur or that E_2 will occur or that both E_1 and E_2 will occur. An example of union probability is the probability that a person owns a Ford or a Chevrolet. To qualify for the union, the person only has to have at least one of these cars. Another example is the probability of a person wearing glasses or having red hair. All people wearing glasses are included in the union, along with all redheads and all redheads who wear glasses. In a company, the probability that a person is male or a clerical worker is a union probability. A person qualifies for the union by being male or by being a clerical worker or by being both (a male clerical worker).

A third type of probability is the intersection of two events, or **joint probability**. The joint probability of events E_1 and E_2 occurring is denoted $P(E_1 \cap E_2)$. Sometimes $P(E_1 \cap E_2)$ is read as the probability of E_1 and E_2. To qualify for the intersection, both events must occur. An example of joint probability is the probability of a person owning both a Ford and a Chevrolet. Owning one type of car is not sufficient. A second example of joint probability is the probability that a person is a redhead and wears glasses.

The fourth type is conditional probability. **Conditional probability** is denoted $P(E_1|E_2)$. This expression is read: the probability that E_1 will occur given that E_2 is known to have occurred. Conditional probabilities involve knowledge of some prior information. The information that is known or given is written to the right of the vertical line in the probability statement. An example of conditional probability is the probability that a person owns a

Thinking Critically About Statistics in Business Today

Probabilities in the Dry-Cleaning Business

According to the International Fabricare Institute, about two-thirds or 67% of all dry-cleaning customers are female, and 65% are married. Thirty-seven percent of dry-cleaning customers use a cleaner that is within a mile of their home. Do dry-cleaning customers care about coupons? Fifty-one percent of dry-cleaning customers say that coupons or discounts are important; and in fact, 57% would try another cleaner if a discount were offered. Converting these percentages to proportions, each could be considered to be a marginal probability. For example, if a customer is randomly selected from the dry-cleaning industry, there is a .37 probability that he/she uses a dry cleaner within a mile of his/her home, $P(\leq 1 \text{ mile}) = .37$.

Suppose further analysis shows that 55% of dry-cleaning customers are female and married. Converting this figure to probability results in the joint probability: $P(F \cap M) = .55$. Subtracting this value from the .67 who are female, we can determine that 12% of dry-cleaning customers are female and not

married: $P(F \cap \text{not M}) = .12$. Suppose 90% of those who say that coupons or discounts are important would try another cleaner if a discount were offered. This can be restated as a conditional probability: $P(\text{try another} \mid \text{coupons important}) = .90$.

Each of the four types of probabilities discussed in this chapter can be applied to the data on consumers in the dry-cleaning industry. Further breakdowns of these statistics using probabilities can offer insights into how to better serve dry-cleaning customers and how to better market dry-cleaning services and products.

THINGS TO PONDER

1. Why do you think it is that two-thirds of all dry-cleaning customers are female? What are some of the factors? What could dry cleaners do to increase the number of male customers?

2. Sixty-five percent of customers at dry-cleaning establishments are married. Can you think of reasons why a smaller percentage of dry-cleaning customers are single? What could dry cleaners do to increase the number of single customers?

Chevrolet given that she owns a Ford. This conditional probability is only a measure of the proportion of Ford owners who have a Chevrolet—not the proportion of total car owners who own a Chevrolet. Conditional probabilities are computed by determining the number of items that have an outcome out of some subtotal of the population. In the car owner example, the possibilities are reduced to Ford owners, and then the number of Chevrolet owners out of those Ford owners is determined. Another example of a conditional probability is the probability that a worker in a company is a professional given that he is male. Of the four probability types, only conditional probability does not have the population total as its denominator. Conditional probabilities have a population subtotal in the denominator. Figure 4.7 summarizes these four types of probability.

Several tools are available for use in solving probability problems. These tools include sample space, tree diagrams, Venn diagrams, the laws of probability, joint probability tables, and insight. Because of the individuality and variety of probability problems, some techniques

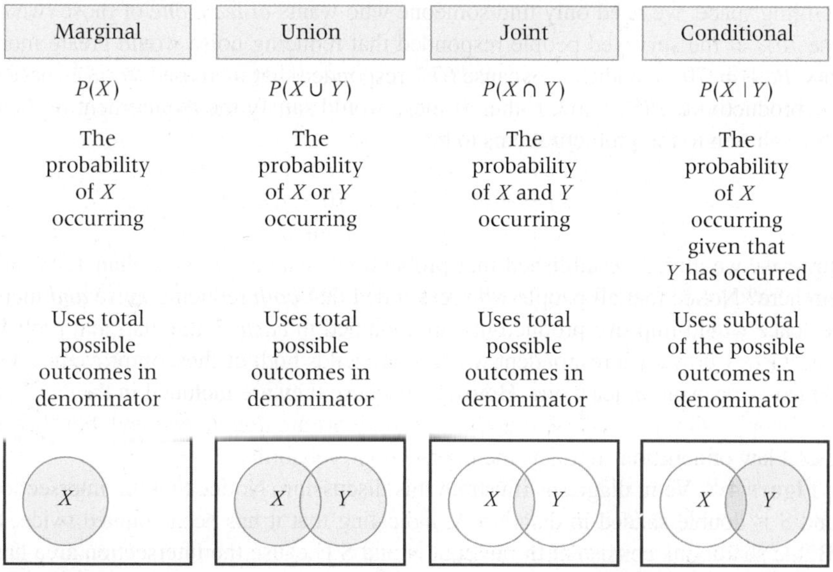

Marginal	Union	Joint	Conditional
$P(X)$	$P(X \cup Y)$	$P(X \cap Y)$	$P(X \mid Y)$
The probability of X occurring	The probability of X or Y occurring	The probability of X and Y occurring	The probability of X occurring given that Y has occurred
Uses total possible outcomes in denominator	Uses total possible outcomes in denominator	Uses total possible outcomes in denominator	Uses subtotal of the possible outcomes in denominator

FIGURE 4.7 Marginal, Union, Joint, and Conditional Probabilities

apply more readily in certain situations than in others. No best method is available for solving all probability problems. In some instances, the joint probability table lays out a problem in a readily solvable manner. In other cases, setting up the joint probability table is more difficult than solving the problem in another way. The probability laws almost always can be used to solve probability problems.

Four laws of probability are presented in this chapter: the addition laws, the multiplication laws, conditional probability, and Bayes' rule. The addition laws and the multiplication laws each have a general law and a special law.

4.4 | Addition Laws

The general law of addition is used to find the probability of the union of two events, $P(X \cup Y)$. The expression $P(X \cup Y)$ denotes the probability of X occurring or Y occurring or both X and Y occurring.

> **General Law of addition**
>
> $$P(X \cup Y) = P(X) + P(Y) - P(X \cap Y)$$
>
> where X, Y are events and $(X \cap Y)$ is the intersection of X and Y.

Yankelovich Partners conducted a survey for the American Society of Interior Designers in which workers were asked which changes in office design would increase productivity. Respondents were allowed to answer more than one type of design change. The number one change that 70% of the workers said would increase productivity was reducing noise. In second place was more storage/filing space, selected by 67%. If one of the survey respondents was randomly selected and asked what office design changes would increase worker productivity, what is the probability that this person would select reducing noise *or* more storage/filing space?

Let N represent the event "reducing noise." Let S represent the event "more storage/filing space." The probability of a person responding with N or S can be symbolized statistically as a union probability by using the law of addition.

$$P(N \cup S)$$

To successfully satisfy the search for a person who responds with reducing noise *or* more storage/filing space, we need only find someone who wants *at least one* of those two events. Because 70% of the surveyed people responded that reducing noise would create more productivity, $P(N) = .70$. In addition, because 67% responded that increased storage space would improve productivity, $P(S) = .67$. Either of these would satisfy the requirement of the union. Thus, the solution to the problem seems to be

$$P(N \cup S) = P(N) + P(S) = .70 + .67 = 1.37$$

However, we already established that probabilities cannot be more than 1. What is the problem here? Notice that all people who responded that *both* reducing noise *and* increasing storage space would improve productivity are included in *each* of the marginal probabilities $P(N)$ and $P(S)$. Certainly a respondent who recommends both of these improvements should be included as favoring at least one. However, because they are included in the $P(N)$ *and* the $P(S)$, the people who recommended both improvements are *double counted*. For that reason, the general law of addition subtracts the intersection probability, $P(N \cap S)$.

In **Figure 4.8**, Venn diagrams illustrate this discussion. Notice that the intersection area of N and S is double shaded in diagram A, indicating that it has been counted twice. In diagram B, the shading is consistent throughout N and S because the intersection area has been subtracted out once. Thus diagram B illustrates the proper application of the general law of addition.

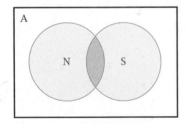

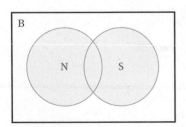

FIGURE 4.8   Solving for the Union in the Office Productivity Problem

So what is the answer to Yankelovich Partners' union probability question? Suppose 56% of all respondents to the survey had said that *both* noise reduction *and* increased storage/ filing space would improve productivity: $P(N \cap S) = .56$. We can use the general law of addition to solve for the probability that a person responds that *either* noise reduction *or* increased storage space would improve productivity as:

$$P(N \cup S) = P(N) + P(S) - P(N \cap S) = .70 + .67 - .56 = .81$$

Hence, 81% of the workers surveyed responded that *either* noise reduction *or* increased storage space would improve productivity.

Joint Probability Tables

In addition to the formulas, another useful tool in solving probability problems is using a joint probability table. A **joint probability table** *displays the intersection (joint) proba-bilities along with the marginal probabilities of a given problem.* Union probabilities or conditional probabilities are not directly displayed in a joint probability table but can be computed using values from the table. Generally, a joint probability table is constructed as a two-dimensional table with one variable on each side of the table. For example, in the office design problem, noise reduction would be on one side of the table and increased storage space on the other. In this problem, a Yes row and a No row would be created for one variable and a Yes column and a No column would be created for the other variable, as shown in Table 4.2.

Once the joint probability table is created, we can enter the marginal probabilities. $P(N) = .70$ is the marginal probability that a person responds yes to noise reduction. This value is placed in the "margin" in the row of Yes to noise reduction, as shown in Table 4.3. If $P(N) = .70$, then .30 of the people surveyed did not think that noise reduction would increase productivity, $P(\text{not } N) = 1 - .70 = .30$. This value, also a marginal probability, goes in the row indicated by No under noise reduction. In the column under Yes for increased storage space, the marginal probability $P(S) = .67$ is recorded. Finally, the marginal probability of No for increased storage space, $P(\text{not } S) = 1 - .67 = .33$, is placed in the No column. In this joint probability table, all four marginal probabilities are given or can be computed simply by using the probability of a complement rule, $P(\text{not } S) = 1 - P(S)$.

The intersection of noise reduction and increased storage space is given as $P(N \cap S) = .56$. This value is entered into the joint probability table in the cell under Yes Yes, as shown in Table 4.3. The rest of the table can be determined by subtracting the cell values from the marginal probabilities. For example, subtracting .56 from .70 and getting .14 yields the value for the cell under Yes for noise reduction and No for increased storage space. In other words, 14% of all respondents said that noise reduction would improve productivity and increased storage space would not. Filling out the rest of the table results in the probabilities shown in Table 4.3.

Now we can solve the union probability, $P(N \cup S)$, in at least two different ways using the joint probability table. The focus is on the Yes row for noise reduction and the Yes column for

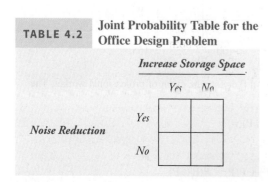

TABLE 4.2 Joint Probability Table for the Office Design Problem

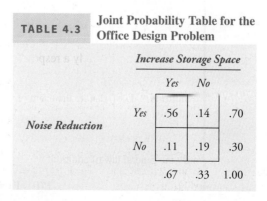

TABLE 4.3 Joint Probability Table for the Office Design Problem

TABLE 4.4	Yes Row and Yes Column for the Joint Probability Table of the Office Design Problem

	Increase Storage Space		
	Yes	*No*	
Noise Reduction *Yes*	.56	.14	.70
No	.11		
	.67		

increase storage space, as displayed in Table 4.4. The probability of a person suggesting noise reduction *or* increased storage space as a solution for improving productivity, $P(N \cup S)$, can be determined from the joint probability table by adding the marginal probabilities of Yes for noise reduction and Yes for increased storage space and then subtracting the Yes Yes cell, following the pattern of the general law of probabilities.

$$P(N \cup S) = .70(\text{from Yes row}) + .67 \text{ (from Yes column)}$$
$$- .56 \text{ (From Yes Yes cell)} = .81$$

Another way to solve for the union probability from the information displayed in the joint probability table is to sum all cells in any of the Yes rows or columns. Observe the following from Table 4.4.

$$P(N \cup S) = .56 \text{ (from Yes Yes cell)}$$
$$+ .14 \text{ (from Yes on noise reduction and No on increase storage space)}$$
$$+ .11 \text{ (from No on noise reduction and Yes on increase storage space)}$$
$$= .81$$

DEMONSTRATION PROBLEM 4.1

The client company data from the Decision Dilemma reveal that 155 employees worked one of four types of positions. Shown here again is the cross-tabulation table (also called a contingency table) with the frequency counts for each category and for subtotals and totals containing a breakdown of these employees by type of position and by sex. If an employee of the company is selected randomly, what is the probability that the employee is female or a professional worker?

COMPANY HUMAN RESOURCE DATA

		Sex		
		Male	*Female*	
	Managerial	8	3	11
Type	*Professional*	31	13	44
of *Position*	*Technical*	52	17	69
	Clerical	9	22	31
		100	55	155

Solution: Let F denote the event of female and P denote the event of professional worker. The question is

$$P(F \cup P) = ?$$

By the general law of addition,

$$P(F \cup P) = P(F) + P(P) - P(F \cap P)$$

Of the 155 employees, 55 are women. Therefore, $P(F) = 55/155 = .355$. The 155 employees include 44 professionals. Therefore, $P(P) = 44/155 = .284$. Because 13 employees are both female and professional, $P(F \cap P) = 13/155 = .084$. The union probability is solved as

$$P(F \cup P) = .355 + .284 - .084 = .555.$$

Suppose you want to solve this problem using a joint probability table. A joint probability table for this problem can be constructed from the contingency table by dividing all data by 155. The resulting table is:

		Sex		
		Male	Female	Total
	Managerial	.052	.019	.071
Type of Position	Professional	.200	.084	.284
	Technical	.335	.110	.445
	Clerical	.058	.142	.200
		.645	.355	1.000

Solving for the probability that the selected worker is female or a professional worker using a joint probability table is done by adding the values in the highlighted cells shown below:

$$.019 + .084 + .110 + .142 + .200 = .555$$

or by using the general law of multiplication from the table,

$$.355 + .284 - .084 = .555$$

		Sex		
		Male	Female	Total
	Managerial	.052	.019	.071
Type of Position	Professional	.200	.084	.284
	Technical	.335	.110	.445
	Clerical	.058	.142	.200
		.645	.355	1.000

DEMONSTRATION PROBLEM 4.2

Shown here are the cross-tabulation table and corresponding joint probability table for the results of a national survey of 200 executives who were asked to identify the geographic locale of their company and their company's industry type. The executives were only allowed to select one locale and one industry type.

CROSS-TABULATION TABLE

		Geographic Location				
		Northeast D	Southeast E	Midwest F	West G	
	Finance A	24	10	8	14	56
Industry Type	Manufacturing B	30	6	22	12	70
	Communications C	28	18	12	16	74
		82	34	42	42	200

By dividing every value of the cross-tabulation table by the total (200), the corresponding joint probability table can be constructed.

JOINT PROBABILITY TABLE

		Geographic Location				
		Northeast D	Southeast E	Midwest F	West G	
	Finance A	.12	.05	.04	.07	.28
Industry Type	Manufacturing B	.15	.03	.11	.06	.35
	Communications C	.14	.09	.06	.08	.37
		.41	.17	.21	.21	1.00

Suppose a respondent is selected randomly from these data.

a. What is the probability that the respondent is from the Midwest (F)?

b. What is the probability that the respondent is from the communications industry (C) or from the Northeast (D)?

c. What is the probability that the respondent is from the Southeast (E) or from the finance industry (A)?

Solution:

a. $P(\text{Midwest}) = P(F) = .21$

b. $P(C \cup D) = P(C) + P(D) - P(C \cap D) = .37 + .41 - .14 = .64$

c. $P(E \cup A) = P(E) + P(A) - P(E \cap A) = .17 + .28 - .05 = .40$

In computing the union by using the general law of addition, the intersection probability is subtracted because it is already included in both marginal probabilities. This adjusted probability leaves a union probability that properly includes both marginal values and the intersection value. If the intersection probability is subtracted out a *second* time, the intersection is removed, leaving the probability of X *or* Y but not *both*.

$$P(X \text{ or } Y \text{ but not both}) = P(X) + P(Y) - P(X \cap Y) - P(X \cap Y)$$

$$= P(X \cup Y) - P(X \cap Y)$$

Figure 4.9 is the Venn diagram for this probability.

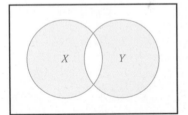

FIGURE 4.9 **The X or Y but Not Both Case**

Complement of a Union

The probability of the union of two events X and Y represents the probability that the outcome is *either X or it is Y or it is both X and Y*. The union includes everything except the possibility that it is neither (X or Y). Another way to state it is as *neither X nor Y*, which can symbolically be represented as $P(\text{not } X \cap \text{not } Y)$. Because it is the only possible case other than the union of X or Y, it is the **complement of a union**. Stated more formally,

$$P(\text{neither } X \text{ nor } Y) = P(\text{not } X \cap \text{not } Y) = 1 - P(X \cup Y).$$

Examine the Venn diagram in Figure 4.10. Note that the complement of the union of X, Y is the shaded area outside the circles. This area represents the neither X nor Y region.

In the survey about increasing worker productivity by changing the office design discussed earlier, the probability that a randomly selected worker would respond with noise reduction *or* increased storage space was determined to be

$$P(N \cup S) = P(N) + P(S) - P(N \cap S) = .70 + .67 - .56 = .81$$

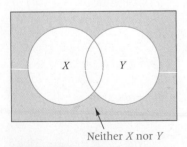

Neither X nor Y

FIGURE 4.10 **The Complement of a Union: The Neither/Nor Region**

The probability that a worker would respond with *neither* noise reduction *nor* increased storage space is calculated as the complement of this union.

$$P(\text{neither N nor S}) = P(\text{not N} \cap \text{not S}) = 1 - P(\text{N} \cup \text{S}) = 1 - .81 = .19$$

Thus, 19% of the workers selected neither noise reduction nor increased storage space as solutions to increasing productivity. In Table 4.3, this *neither/nor* probability is found in the No No cell of the table, .19.

Special Law of Addition

If two events are mutually exclusive, the probability of the union of the two events is the probability of the first event plus the probability of the second event. Because mutually exclusive events do not intersect, nothing has to be subtracted.

> **Special Law of Addition**
>
> If X, Y are mutually exclusive, $P(X \cup Y) = P(X) + P(Y)$.

The special law of addition is a special case of the general law of addition. In a sense, the general law fits all cases. However, when the events are mutually exclusive, a zero is inserted into the general law formula for the intersection, resulting in the special law formula.

Yankelovich Partners conducted a survey for William M. Mercer in which workers were asked what most hinders their productivity, and they were only allowed to choose from one of the following: Lack of direction, Lack of support, Too much work, Inefficient process, Not enough equipment/supplies, and Low pay/chance to advance.

Lack of direction was cited by the most workers (20%), followed by lack of support (18%), too much work (18%), inefficient process (8%), not enough equipment/supplies (7%), low pay/chance to advance (7%), and a variety of other factors added by respondents. If a worker who responded to this survey is selected and asked which of the given selections most hinders his or her productivity, what is the probability that the worker will respond that it is either too much work or inefficient process?

Let M denote the event "too much work" and I denote the event "inefficient process." The question is:

$$P(\text{M} \cup \text{I}) = ?$$

Because 18% of the survey respondents said "too much work,"

$$P(\text{M}) = .18$$

Because 8% of the survey respondents said "inefficient process,"

$$P(\text{I}) = .08$$

Because it was not possible to select more than one answer,

$$P(\text{M} \cap \text{I}) = .0000$$

Implementing the special law of addition gives

$$P(\text{M} \cup \text{I}) = P(\text{M}) + P(\text{I}) = .18 + .08 = .26$$

Twenty-six percent responded either "too much work" or "inefficient process."

DEMONSTRATION PROBLEM 4.3

If a worker is randomly selected from the company described in Demonstration Problem 4.1, what is the probability that the worker is either technical or clerical? What is the probability that the worker is either a professional or a clerical?

Solution: Examine the cross-tabulation table of the company's human resources data shown in Demonstration Problem 4.1. In many cross-tabulation tables like this one, the rows are nonoverlapping or mutually exclusive, as are the columns. In this matrix, a worker can be classified as being in only one type of position and as either male or female but not both. Thus, the categories of type of position are mutually exclusive, as are the categories of sex, and the special law of addition can be applied to the human resource data to determine the union probabilities.

Let T denote technical, C denote clerical, and P denote professional. The probability that a worker is either technical or clerical is

$$P(T \cup C) = P(T) + P(C) = \frac{69}{155} + \frac{31}{155} = \frac{100}{155} = .645$$

The probability that a worker is either professional or clerical is

$$P(P \cup C) = P(P) + P(C) = \frac{44}{155} + \frac{31}{155} = \frac{75}{155} = .484$$

4.4 Problems

4.8. Given $P(A) = .10$, $P(B) = .12$, $P(C) = .21$, $P(A \cap C) = .05$, and $P(B \cap C) = .03$, solve the following.

   a. $P(A \cup C) = $ _____

   b. $P(B \cup C) = $ _____

   c. If A and B are mutually exclusive, $P(A \cup B) = $ _____

4.9. Use the values in the cross-tabulation table to solve the equations given.

	D	E	F
A	5	8	12
B	10	6	4
C	8	2	5

   a. $P(A \cup D) = $ _____

   b. $P(E \cup B) = $ _____

   c. $P(D \cup E) = $ _____

   d. $P(C \cup F) = $ _____

4.10. Use the values in the joint probability table to solve the equations given.

	E	F
A	.10	.03
B	.04	.12
C	.27	.06
D	.31	.07

   a. $P(A \cup F) = $ _____

   b. $P(E \cup B) = $ _____

   c. $P(B \cup C) = $ _____

   d. $P(E \cup F) = $ _____

4.11. According to a survey conducted by Netpop Research, 65% of new car buyers use online search engines as part of their car-buying experience. Another study reported that 11% of new car buyers skip the test drive. Suppose 7% of new car buyers use online search engines as part of their car-buying experience and skip the test drive. If a new car buyer is randomly selected, what is the probability that:

   a. the buyer used an online search engine as part of the car-buying experience or skipped the test drive?

   b. the buyer did not use an online search engine as part of the car-buying experience or did skip the test drive?

   c. the buyer used an online search engine as part of the car-buying experience or did not skip the test drive?

4.12. According to the U.S. Bureau of Labor Statistics, 75% of the women 25 through 49 years of age participate in the labor force. Suppose 78% of the women in that age group are married. Suppose also that 61% of women 25 through 49 years of age are married and are participating in the labor force.

   a. What is the probability that a randomly selected woman in that age group is married or is participating in the labor force?

   b. What is the probability that a randomly selected woman in that age group is married or is participating in the labor force but not both?

   c. What is the probability that a randomly selected woman in that age group is neither married nor participating in the labor force?

4.13. According to Nielsen Media Research, approximately 86% of all U.S. households have High-definition television (HDTV). In addition, 49% of all U.S. households own Digital Video Recorders (DVR). Suppose 40% of all U.S. households have HDTV and have DVR. A U.S. household is randomly selected.

   a. What is the probability that the household has HDTV or has DVR?

   b. What is the probability that the household does not have HDTV or does have DVR?

   c. What is the probability that the household does have HDTV or does not have DVR?

   d. What is the probability that the household does not have HDTV or does not have DVR?

4.14. A survey conducted by the Northwestern University Lindquist-Endicott Report asked 320 companies about the procedures they use in hiring. Only 54% of the responding companies review the applicant's college transcript as part of the hiring process, and only 44% consider faculty references. Assume that these percentages are true for the population of companies in the United States and that 35% of all companies use both the applicant's college transcript and faculty references.

   a. What is the probability that a randomly selected company uses either faculty references or college transcript as part of the hiring process?

   b. What is the probability that a randomly selected company uses neither faculty references nor college transcript as part of the hiring process?

   c. What is the probability that a randomly selected company uses either faculty references or college transcript but not both as part of the hiring process?

   d. What is the probability that a randomly selected company does not use faculty references as part of the hiring process or does use college transcript as part of the hiring process?

4.5 | Multiplication Laws

General Law of Multiplication

As stated in Section 4.3, the probability of the intersection of two events $(X \cap Y)$ is called the joint probability. The general law of multiplication is used to find the joint probability.

> **General Law of Multiplication**
>
> $$P(X \cap Y) = P(X) \cdot P(Y|X) = P(Y) \cdot P(X|Y)$$

The notation $X \cap Y$ means that *both X and Y* must happen. The general law of multiplication gives the probability that *both* event X and event Y will occur at the same time.

A recent survey conducted for the National Restaurant Association revealed that 47% of adults said they would be likely to patronize a mobile food truck parked near their home. Suppose 70% of adults who would be likely to patronize such a mobile food truck earn less than $40,000 annually. If an adult is randomly selected, what is the probability that the adult would be likely to patronize a mobile food truck parked near their home and the adult earns less than $40,000 annually? This question is a joint (intersection) probability. Let M signify that an adult would be likely to patronize such a mobile food truck and let F signify that the adult earns less than $40,000 annually. In these terms, the probability question is:

$$P(M \cap F) = ?$$

What is given in this problem? The 47% of adults likely to patronize such a mobile food truck is a marginal percentage because it is a percentage of all adults. Thus, $P(M) = .47$. However, the 70% earning less than $40,000 annually is only of the adults likely to patronize a mobile food truck. This is a conditional percentage because the percentage is not of all adults but only of those who are likely to patronize a mobile food truck. Writing this as a conditional probability, $P(F|M) = .70$. With this information, the intersection or joint probability can be solved for as:

$$P(M \cap F) = P(M) \cdot P(F|M) = (.47) \cdot (.70) = .3290$$

Conceptually, what this means is that if 70% of adults who would patronize a mobile food truck earn less than $40,000 and if 47% of adults would patronize a mobile food truck, then 32.9% of adults would patronize a mobile food truck and earn less than $40,000. We are taking

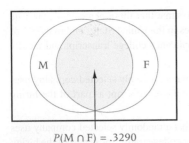

$P(M \cap F) = .3290$

FIGURE 4.11 **Joint Probability that an Adult Patronizes a Mobile Food Truck and Earns Less than $40,000**

TABLE 4.5 Joint Probability Table of Company Human Resource Data

		Sex		
		Male	*Female*	
Type of Position	*Managerial*	.052	.019	.071
	Professional	.200	.084	.284
	Technical	.335	.110	.445
	Clerical	.058	.142	.200
		.645	.355	1.000

70% of the 47% and hence multiplying the conditional by the marginal probabilities. The Venn diagram in Figure 4.11 shows these relationships and the joint probability.

Note that there is a second version of the general law of multiplication, which if, applied here, would be: $P(F) \cdot P(M|F)$ This expression could be used if we knew the probability that an adult earned less than $40,000 annually, $P(F)$, a marginal probability, and if we knew the proportion (or percentage) of adults earning less than $40,000 who would patronize a mobile food truck, $P(M|F)$, a conditional probability. Neither of these probabilities is given in this problem; therefore, this version of the general law of multiplication was not used in this problem.

Determining joint probabilities from joint probability tables is easy because every cell of these matrices is a joint probability, hence the name "joint probability table."

For example, suppose the cross-tabulation table of the client company data from Demonstration Problem 4.1 and the Decision Dilemma is converted to a joint probability table by dividing by the total number of employees ($N = 155$), resulting in Table 4.5. Each value in the cell of Table 4.5 is an intersection, and the table contains all possible intersections (joint probabilities) for the events of sex and type of position. For example, the probability that a randomly selected worker is male *and* a technical worker, $P(M \cap T)$ is .335. The probability that a randomly selected worker is female *and* a professional worker, $P(F \cap P)$ is .084. Once a joint probability table is constructed for a problem, usually the easiest way to solve for the joint probability is to find the appropriate cell in the table and select the answer. However, sometimes because of what is given in a problem, using the formula is easier than constructing the table.

DEMONSTRATION PROBLEM 4.4

A company has 140 employees, of which 30 are supervisors. Eighty of the employees are married, and 20% of the married employees are supervisors. If a company employee is randomly selected, what is the probability that the employee is married and is a supervisor?

Solution: Let M denote married and S denote supervisor. The question is:

$$P(M \cap S) = ?$$

First, calculate the marginal probability.

$$P(M) = \frac{80}{140} = .5714$$

Then, note that 20% of the married employees are supervisors, which is the conditional probability, $P(S|M) = 20$. Finally, applying the general law of multiplication gives

$$P(M \cap S) = P(M) \cdot P(S|M) = (.5714)(.20) = .1143$$

Hence, 11.43% of the 140 employees are married and are supervisors.

DEMONSTRATION PROBLEM 4.5

From the data obtained from the interviews of 200 executives in Demonstration Problem 4.2, find:

a. $P(B \cap E)$

b. $P(G \cap A)$

c. $P(B \cap C)$

JOINT PROBABILITY TABLE

		Geographic Location				
		Northeast D	Southeast E	Midwest F	West G	
Industry Type	Finance A	.12	.05	.04	.07	.28
	Manufacturing B	.15	.03	.11	.06	.35
	Communications C	.14	.09	.06	.08	.37
		.41	.17	.21	.21	1.00

Solution:

a. From the cell of the joint probability table, $P(B \cap E) = .03$. To solve by the formula, $P(B \cap E) = P(B) \cdot P(E|B)$, first find $P(B)$:

$$P(B) = .35$$

The probability of E occurring given that B has occurred, $P(E|B)$, can be determined from the joint probability table as $P(E|B) = .03/.35$ Therefore,

$$P(B \cap E) = P(B) \cdot P(E|B) = (.35)\left(\frac{.03}{.35}\right) = .03$$

Although the formula works, finding the joint probability in the cell of the joint probability table is faster than using the formula.

An alternative formula is $P(B \cap E) = P(E) \cdot P(B|E)$, but $P(E) = .17$. Then $P(B|E)$ means the probability of B if E is given. There are .17 Es in the probability matrix and .03 Bs in these Es. Hence,

$$P(B|E) = \frac{.03}{.17} \quad \text{and} \quad P(B \cap E) = P(E) \cdot P(B|E) = (.17)\left(\frac{.03}{.17}\right) = .03$$

b. To obtain $P(G \cap A)$, find the intersecting cell of G and A in the probability matrix, .07, or use one of the following formulas:

$$P(G \cap A) = P(G) \cdot P(A|G) = (.21)\left(\frac{.07}{.21}\right) = .07$$

or

$$P(G \cap A) = P(A) \cdot P(G|A) = (.28)\left(\frac{.07}{.28}\right) = .07$$

c. The probability $P(B \cap C)$ means that one respondent would have to work both in the manufacturing industry and the communications industry. The survey used to gather data from the 200 executives, however, requested that each respondent specify only one industry type for his or her company. The joint probability table shows no intersection for these two events. Thus B and C are mutually exclusive. None of the respondents is in both manufacturing and communications. Hence,

$$P(B \cap C) = .0$$

Special Law of Multiplication

If events X and Y are independent, a special law of multiplication can be used to find the intersection of X and Y. This special law utilizes the fact that when two events X, Y are independent, $P(X|Y) = P(X)$ and $P(Y|X) = P(Y)$. Thus, the general law of multiplication, $P(X \cap Y) = P(X) \cdot P(Y|X)$, becomes $P(X \cap Y) = P(X) \cdot P(Y)$ when X and Y are independent.

Special Law of Multiplication

If X, Y are independent, $P(X \cap Y) = P(X) \cdot P(Y)$

A study released by Bruskin-Goldring Research for SEIKO found that 28% of American adults believe that the automated teller has had a most significant impact on everyday life. Another study by David Michaelson & Associates for Dale Carnegie & Associates examined employee views on team spirit in the workplace and discovered that 71% of all employees believe that working as a part of a team lowers stress. Are people's views on automated tellers independent of their views on team spirit in the workplace? If they are independent, then the probability of a person being randomly selected who believes that the automated teller has had a most significant impact on everyday life *and* that working as part of a team lowers stress is found as follows. Let A denote automated teller and S denote teamwork lowers stress.

$$P(A) = .28$$
$$P(S) = .71$$
$$P(A \cap S) = P(A) \cdot P(S) = (.28)(.71) = .1988$$

Therefore, 19.88% of the population believes that the automated teller has had a most significant impact on everyday life *and* that working as part of a team lowers stress.

DEMONSTRATION PROBLEM 4.6

A manufacturing firm produces pads of bound paper. Three percent of all paper pads produced are improperly bound. An inspector randomly samples two pads of paper, one at a time. Because a large number of pads are being produced during the inspection, the sampling being done, in essence, is with replacement. What is the probability that the two pads selected are both improperly bound?

Solution: Let I denote improperly bound. The problem is to determine

$$P(I_1 \cap I_2) = ?$$

The probability of I = .03, or 3% are improperly bound. Because the sampling is done with replacement, the two events are independent. Hence,

$$P(I_1 \cap I_2) = P(I_1) \cdot P(I_2) = (.03)(.03) = .0009$$

TABLE 4.6

Cross-Tabulation Table of Data from Independent Events

	D	E	
A	8	12	20
B	20	30	50
C	6	9	15
	34	51	85

Most cross-tabulation tables contain variables that are not independent. If a cross-tabulation table contains independent events, the special law of multiplication can be applied. If not, the special law cannot be used. In Section 4.6 we explore a technique for determining whether events are independent. Table 4.6 contains data from independent events.

DEMONSTRATION PROBLEM 4.7

Use the data from Table 4.6 and the special law of multiplication to find $P(B \cap D)$.

Solution:

$$P(B \cap D) = P(B) \cdot P(D) = \frac{50}{85} \cdot \frac{34}{85} = .2353$$

This approach works *only* for cross-tabulation and joint probability tables in which the variable along one side of the table is *independent* of the variable along the other side of the table. Note that the answer obtained by using the formula is the same as the answer obtained by using the cell information from Table 4.6.

$$P(B \cap D) = \frac{20}{85} = .2353$$

4.5 Problems

4.15. Use the values in the cross-tabulation table to solve the equations given.

	C	D	E	F
A	5	11	16	8
B	2	3	5	7

a. $P(A \cap E) = $ _____

b. $P(D \cap B) = $ _____

c. $P(D \cap E) = $ _____

d. $P(A \cap B) = $ _____

4.16. Use the values in the joint probability table to solve the equations given.

	D	E	F
A	.12	.13	.08
B	.18	.09	.04
C	.06	.24	.06

a. $P(E \cap B) = $ _____

b. $P(C \cap F) = $ _____

c. $P(E \cap D) = $ _____

4.17. a. A batch of 50 parts contains six defects. If two parts are drawn randomly one at a time without replacement, what is the probability that both parts are defective?

b. If this experiment is repeated, with replacement, what is the probability that both parts are defective?

4.18. International Housewares Association (IHA) reported that 73% of all U.S. households have ceiling fans. In addition, 77% of all U.S. households have an outdoor grill. Suppose 60% of all U.S. households have both a ceiling fan and an outdoor grill. A U.S. household is randomly selected.

a. What is the probability that the household has a ceiling fan or an outdoor grill?

b. What is the probability that the household has neither a ceiling fan nor an outdoor grill?

c. What is the probability that the household does not have a ceiling fan and does have an outdoor grill?

d. What is the probability that the household does have a ceiling fan and does not have an outdoor grill?

4.19. A study by Peter D. Hart Research Associates for the Nasdaq Stock Market revealed that 43% of all American adults are stockholders. In addition, the study determined that 75% of all American adult stockholders have some college education. Suppose 37% of all American adults have some college education. An American adult is randomly selected.

a. What is the probability that the adult owns stock and has some college education?

b. What is the probability that the adult owns no stock and has some college education?

c. What is the probability that the adult owns stock and has no college education?

d. What is the probability that the adult neither owns stock nor has some college education?

4.20. According to a report released by the National Center for Health Statistics, 41% of U.S. households has only cell phones (no land line). According to the FCC, nearly 70% of the U.S. households have high-speed Internet. Suppose of the U.S. households having only cell phones, 80% have high-speed Internet. A U.S household is randomly selected.

a. What is the probability that the household has only cell phones and has high-speed Internet?

b. What is the probability that the household has only cell phones or has high-speed Internet?

c. What is the probability that the household has only cell phones and does not have high-speed Internet?

d. What is the probability that the household does not have only cell phones and does not have high-speed Internet?

e. What is the probability that the household does not have only cell phones and has high-speed Internet?

4.21. A study by Becker Associates, a San Diego travel consultant, found that 30% of the traveling public said that their flight selections are influenced by perceptions of airline safety. Thirty-nine percent of the traveling public wants to know the age of the aircraft. Suppose 87% of the traveling public who say that their flight selections are influenced by perceptions of airline safety wants to know the age of the aircraft.

a. What is the probability of randomly selecting a member of the traveling public and finding out that she says that flight selection is influenced by perceptions of airline safety and she does not want to know the age of the aircraft?

b. What is the probability of randomly selecting a member of the traveling public and finding out that she says that flight selection is neither influenced by perceptions of airline safety nor does she want to know the age of the aircraft?

c. What is the probability of randomly selecting a member of the traveling public and finding out that he says that flight selection is not influenced by perceptions of airline safety and he wants to know the age of the aircraft?

4.22. A nationwide CareerBuilder survey was conducted regarding the job hunting experience. From the survey, it was learned that 26% of workers have had a bad experience as a job applicant. Eighty-two

percent of workers expect to hear back from a company when they apply for a job. Suppose that 90% of workers who have had a bad experience as a job applicant expect to hear back from a company when they apply for a job. Based on these results, if a worker hunting for a job is randomly selected,

a. What is the probability that the worker expects to hear back from a company when they apply for a job and has had a bad experience as a job applicant?

b. What is the probability that the worker expects to hear back from a company when they apply for a job and has not had a bad experience as a job applicant?

c. What is the probability that the worker does not expect to hear back from a company when they apply for a job and has had a bad experience as a job applicant?

d. What is the probability that the worker does not expect to hear back from a company when they apply for a job and has not had a bad experience as a job applicant?

4.6 | Conditional Probability

Conditional probabilities are computed based on the prior knowledge that a business researcher has on one of the two events being studied. If X, Y are two events, the conditional probability of X occurring given that Y is known or has occurred is expressed as $P(X|Y)$ and is given in the *law of conditional probability*.

Law of Conditional Probability

$$P(X|Y) = \frac{P(X \cap Y)}{P(Y)} = \frac{P(X) \cdot P(Y|X)}{P(Y)}$$

The conditional probability of $(X|Y)$ is the probability that X will occur given Y. The formula for conditional probability can be derived by dividing both sides of the general law of multiplication by $P(Y)$.

In the study by Yankelovich Partners to determine what changes in office design would improve productivity, 70% of the respondents believed noise reduction would improve productivity and 67% said increased storage space would improve productivity. In addition, suppose 56% of the respondents believed both noise reduction and increased storage space would improve productivity. A worker is selected randomly and asked about changes in office design. This worker believes that noise reduction would improve productivity. What is the probability that this worker believes increased storage space would improve productivity? That is, what is the probability that a randomly selected person believes storage space would improve productivity *given that* he or she believes noise reduction improves productivity? In symbols, the question is

$$P(S|N) = ?$$

Note that the given part of the information is listed to the right of the vertical line in the conditional probability. The formula solution is

$$P(S|N) = \frac{P(S \cap N)}{P(N)}$$

but

$$P(N) = .70 \quad \text{and} \quad P(S \cap N) = .56$$

Therefore

$$P(S|N) = \frac{P(S \cap N)}{P(N)} = \frac{.56}{.70} = .80$$

Eighty percent of workers who believe noise reduction would improve productivity believe increased storage space would improve productivity.

Note in Figure 4.12 that the area for N in the Venn diagram is completely shaded because it is given that the worker believes noise reduction will improve productivity. Also notice that the intersection of N and S is more heavily shaded. This portion of noise reduction includes increased storage space. It is the only part of increased storage space that is in noise reduction, and because the person is known to favor noise reduction, it is the only area of interest that includes increased storage space.

Examine the joint probability table in Table 4.7 for the office design problem. None of the probabilities given in the table are conditional probabilities. To reiterate what has been previously stated, a joint probability table contains only two types of probabilities, marginal and joint. The cell values are all joint probabilities and the subtotals in the margins are marginal probabilities. How are conditional probabilities determined from a joint probability table? The law of conditional probabilities shows that a conditional probability is computed by dividing the joint probability by the marginal probability. Thus, the joint probability table has all the necessary information to solve for a conditional probability.

What is the probability that a randomly selected worker believes noise reduction would not improve productivity given that the worker does believe increased storage space would improve productivity? That is,

$$P(\text{not } N|S) = ?$$

The law of conditional probability states that

$$P(\text{not } N|S) = \frac{P(\text{not } N \cap S)}{P(S)}$$

Notice that because S is given, we are interested only in the column that is shaded in Table 4.7, which is the Yes column for increased storage space. The marginal probability, $P(S)$, is the total of this column and is found in the margin at the bottom of the table as .67. $P(\text{not } N \cap S)$ is found as the intersection of No for noise and Yes for storage. This value is .11. Hence, $P(\text{not } N \cap S)$ is .11. Therefore,

$$P(\text{not } N|S) = \frac{P(\text{not } N \cap S)}{P(S)} = \frac{.11}{.67} = .164$$

The second version of the conditional probability law formula is

$$P(X|Y) = \frac{P(X) \cdot P(Y|X)}{P(Y)}$$

This version is more complex than the first version, $P(X \cap Y)/P(Y)$. However, sometimes the second version must be used because of the information given in the problem—for example, when solving for $P(X|Y)$ but $P(Y|X)$ is given. The second version of the formula is obtained from the first version by substituting the formula for $P(X \cap Y) = P(X) \cdot P(Y|X)$ into the first version. In general, this second version of the law of conditional probabilities is likely to be used for solving $P(X|Y)$ when $P(X \cap Y)$ is unknown but $P(Y|X)$ is known.

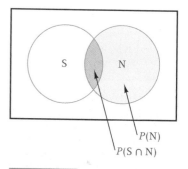

$P(N)$
$P(S \cap N)$

FIGURE 4.12 Conditional Probability of Increased Storage Space Given Noise Reduction

| TABLE 4.7 | Office Design Problem Joint Probability Table |

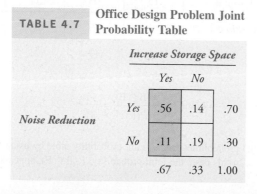

		Increase Storage Space		
		Yes	*No*	
Noise Reduction	*Yes*	.56	.14	.70
	No	.11	.19	.30
		.67	.33	1.00

DEMONSTRATION PROBLEM 4.8

A survey of web retailers published by *Internet Researcher* found that 55% of respondents had shipment tracking on their Web sites. In addition, 43% had a shipping costs calculator on their Web sites. Suppose that of the respondents who had shipment tracking on their Web sites, 60% had a shipping costs calculator on their Web sites. Based on this information, what is the probability that a randomly selected respondent said that it has shipping tracking on its Web sites given that it has a shipping costs calculator on its Web sites?

Solution: Let C = shipping costs calculator and T = shipment tracking. The question is to determine the probability that a respondent has shipping tracking on its Web sites given that it has a shipping costs calculator on its Web sites. This is a conditional probability that can be written as $P(T|C) = ??$.

In this problem, two marginal probabilities are given:

$$P(T) = .55 \text{ and } P(C) = .43$$

The third probability given in this problem is a conditional probability. The given condition is shipment tracking and the conditional probability is: $P(C|T) = .60$.

Note that we are solving for $P(T|C)$ but $P(C|T)$ is given. This is a candidate for solving for a conditional probability using the second form of the conditional probability law formula:

$$P(T|C) = \frac{P(T) \cdot P(C|T)}{P(C)} = \frac{(.55)(.60)}{.43} = .7674$$

Thus, 76.74% of those respondents who have a shipping costs calculator on their Web sites have shipment tracking on their Web sites.

DEMONSTRATION PROBLEM 4.9

The data from the executive interviews given in Demonstration Problem 4.2 are repeated here. Use these data to find:
a. $P(B|F)$
b. $P(G|C)$
c. $P(D|F)$

JOINT PROBABILITY TABLE

		Geographic Location				
		Northeast D	Southeast E	Midwest F	West G	
Industry Type	Finance A	.12	.05	.04	.07	.28
	Manufacturing B	.15	.03	.11	.06	.35
	Communications C	.14	.09	.06	.08	.37
		.41	.17	.21	.21	1.00

Solution:

a.
$$P(B|F) = \frac{P(B \cap F)}{P(F)} = \frac{.11}{.21} = .524$$

Determining conditional probabilities from a joint probability table by using the formula is a relatively painless process. In this case, the joint probability, $P(B \cap F)$, appears in a cell of the table

(.11); the marginal probability, $P(F)$, appears in a margin (.21). Bringing these two probabilities together by formula produces the answer, $.11/.21 = .524$. This answer means that 52.4% of the Midwest executives (the F values) are in manufacturing (the B values).

b.
$$P(G|C) = \frac{P(G \cap C)}{P(C)} = \frac{.08}{.37} = .216$$

This result means that 21.6% of the responding communications industry executives (C) are from the West (G).

c.
$$P(D|F) = \frac{P(D \cap F)}{P(F)} = \frac{.00}{.21} = .00$$

Because D and F are mutually exclusive, $P(D \cap F)$ is zero and so is $P(D|F)$. The rationale behind $P(D|F) = 0$ is that, if F is given (the respondent is known to be located in the Midwest), the respondent could not be located in D (the Northeast).

Independent Events

Independent Events X, Y

To test to determine if X and Y are independent events, the following must be true.

$$P(X|Y) = P(X) \quad and \quad P(Y|X) = P(Y)$$

In each equation, it does not matter that X or Y is given because X and Y are *independent*. When X and Y are independent, the conditional probability is solved as a marginal probability.

Sometimes, it is important to test a cross-tabulation table of raw data to determine whether events are independent. If *any* combination of two events from the different sides of the table fail the test, $P(X|Y) = P(X)$, the table does not contain independent events.

Thinking Critically About Statistics in Business Today

Newspaper Advertising Reading Habits of Canadians

A national survey by Ipsos Reid for the Canadian Newspaper Association reveals some interesting statistics about newspaper advertising reading habits of Canadians. Sixty-six percent of Canadians say that they enjoy reading the page advertising and the product inserts that come with a newspaper. The percentage is higher for women (70%) than men (62%), but 73% of households with children enjoy doing so. While the percentage of those over 55 years of age who enjoy reading such ads is 71%, the percentage is only 55% for those in the 18-to-34-year-old category. These percentages decrease with increases in education, as revealed by the fact that while 70% of those with a high school education enjoy reading such ads, only 55% of those having a university degree do so. Canadians living in the Atlantic region lead the country in this regard with 74%, in contrast to those living in British Columbia (63%) and Quebec (62%).

These facts can be converted to probabilities: The marginal probability that a Canadian enjoys reading such ads is .66. Many of the other statistics represent conditional probabilities. For example,

the probability that a Canadian enjoys such ads given that the Canadian is a woman is .70; and the probability that a Canadian enjoys such ads given that the Canadian has a college degree is .55. About 13% of the Canadian population resides in British Columbia. From this and from the conditional probability that a Canadian enjoys such ads given that they live in British Columbia (.63), one can compute the joint probability that a randomly selected Canadian enjoys such ads and lives in British Columbia (.13)(.63) = .0819. That is, 8.19% of all Canadians live in British Columbia and enjoy such ads.

THINGS TO PONDER

1. It is plain from the information given here that many Canadians enjoy reading newspaper ads. If you are a business in Canada, what implications might this have on your marketing plan?

2. What do you think might be some factors that contribute to fact that about 10% more of Canadians in the Atlantic region than in other regions of the country enjoy reading newspaper ads?

DEMONSTRATION PROBLEM 4.10

Test the cross-tabulation table for the 200 executive responses to determine whether industry type is independent of geographic location.

CROSS-TABULATION TABLE

		Geographic Location				
		Northeast D	Southeast E	Midwest F	West G	
Industry Type	Finance A	24	10	8	14	56
	Manufacturing B	30	6	22	12	70
	Communications C	28	18	12	16	74
		82	34	42	42	200

Solution: Select one industry and one geographic location (say, A—Finance and G—West). Does $P(A|G) = P(A)$?

$$P(A|G) = \frac{14}{42} \text{ and } P(A) = \frac{56}{200}$$

Does $14/42 = 56/200$? No, $.33 \neq .28$. Industry and geographic location are not independent because at least one exception to the test is present.

DEMONSTRATION PROBLEM 4.11

Determine whether the cross-tabulation table shown as Table 4.6 and repeated here contains independent events.

	D	E	
A	8	12	20
B	20	30	50
C	6	9	15
	34	51	85

Solution: Check the first cell in the table to find whether $P(A|D) = P(A)$.

$$P(A|D) = \frac{8}{34} = .2353$$

$$P(A) = \frac{20}{85} = .2353$$

The checking process must continue until all the events are determined to be independent. In this table, all the possibilities check out. Thus, Table 4.6 contains independent events.

▶ Lecture Video

4.6 Problems

4.23. Use the values in the cross-tabulation table to solve the equations given.

	E	F	G
A	15	12	8
B	11	17	19
C	21	32	27
D	18	13	12

a. $P(G|A) = $ _____

b. $P(B|F) = $ _____

c. $P(C|E) = $ _____

d. $P(E|G) = $ _____

4.24. Use the values in the joint probability table to solve the equations given.

	C	D
A	.36	.44
B	.11	.09

a. $P(C|A) = $ _____

b. $P(B|D) = $ _____

c. $P(A|B) = $ _____

4.25. The results of a survey asking, "Do you have a calculator and/or a computer in your home?" follow.

		Calculator		
		Yes	No	
Computer	Yes	46	3	49
	No	11	15	26
		57	18	75

Is the variable "calculator" independent of the variable "computer"? Why or why not?

4.26. In a recent year, business failures in the United States numbered 83,384, according to Dun & Bradstreet. The construction industry accounted for 10,867 of these business failures. The South Atlantic states accounted for 8,010 of the business failures. Suppose that 1,258 of all business failures were construction businesses located in the South Atlantic states. A failed business is randomly selected from this list of business failures.

a. What is the probability that the business is located in the South Atlantic states?

b. What is the probability that the business is in the construction industry or located in the South Atlantic states?

c. What is the probability that the business is in the construction industry if it is known that the business is located in the South Atlantic states?

d. What is the probability that the business is located in the South Atlantic states if it is known that the business is a construction business?

e. What is the probability that the business is not located in the South Atlantic states if it is known that the business is not a construction business?

f. Given that the business is a construction business, what is the probability that the business is not located in the South Atlantic states?

4.27. A national survey of small-business owners was conducted to determine the challenges for growth for their businesses. The top challenge, selected by 46% of the small-business owners, was the economy. A close second was finding qualified workers (37%). Suppose 15% of the small-business owners selected both the economy and finding qualified workers as challenges for growth. A small-business owner is randomly selected.

a. What is the probability that the owner believes the economy is a challenge for growth if the owner believes that finding qualified workers is a challenge for growth?

b. What is the probability that the owner believes that finding qualified workers is a challenge for growth if the owner believes that the economy is a challenge for growth?

c. Given that the owner does not select the economy as a challenge for growth, what is the probability that the owner believes that finding qualified workers is a challenge for growth?

d. What is the probability that the owner believes neither that the economy is a challenge for growth nor that finding qualified workers is a challenge for growth?

4.28. According to a survey published by ComPsych Corporation, 54% of all workers read e-mail while they are talking on the phone. Suppose that 20% of those who read e-mail while they are talking on the phone write personal "to-do" lists during meetings. Assuming that these figures are true for all workers, if a worker is randomly selected, determine the following probabilities:

a. The worker reads e-mail while talking on the phone and writes personal "to-do" lists during meetings.

b. The worker does not write personal "to-do" lists given that he reads e-mail while talking on the phone.

c. The worker does not write personal "to-do" lists and does read e-mail while talking on the phone.

4.29. According to a survey of restaurant owners in the U.S. by MustHaveMenus, 77% of restaurant owners believe that they need to use social media as a marketing tool. A different survey by the National Restaurant owners revealed that 80% of restaurant owners started their careers at entry-level positions. Suppose that 83% of restaurant owners who started their careers at entry-level positions believe that they need to use social media as a marketing tool. Assuming that these percentages apply to all restaurant owners, if a restaurant owner is randomly selected,

a. What is the probability that the owner does believe that he/she needs to use social media as a marketing tool and did start his/her career at an entry-level position?

b. What is the probability that an owner either believes that he/she needs to use social media as a marketing tool or he/she did start his/her career at an entry-level position?

c. What is the probability that the owner does not believe that he/she needs to use social media as a marketing tool given that he/she did start his/her career at an entry-level position?

d. What is the probability that the owner does believe that he/she needs to use social media as a marketing tool given that he/she did not start his/her career at an entry-level position?

e. What is the probability that the owner did not start his/her career at an entry-level position given that he/she does not believe he/she needs to use social media as a marketing tool?

4.30. In a study undertaken by Catalyst, 43% of women senior executives agreed or strongly agreed that a lack of role models was a barrier to their career development. In addition, 46% agreed or strongly agreed that gender-based stereotypes were barriers to their career advancement. Suppose 77% of those who agreed or strongly agreed that gender-based stereotypes were barriers to their career advancement agreed or strongly agreed that the lack of role models was a barrier to their career development. If one of these female senior executives is randomly selected, determine the following probabilities:

a. What is the probability that the senior executive does not agree or strongly agree that a lack of role models was a barrier to her career development given that she does agree or strongly agree that gender-based stereotypes were barriers to her career development?

b. What is the probability that the senior executive does not agree or strongly agree that gender-based stereotypes were barriers to her career development given that she does agree or strongly agree that the lack of role models was a barrier to her career development?

c. If it is known that the senior executive does not agree or strongly agree that gender-based stereotypes were barriers to her career development, what is the probability that she does not agree or strongly agree that the lack of role models was a barrier to her career development?

4.7 | Revision of Probabilities: Bayes' Rule

An extension to the conditional law of probabilities is Bayes' rule, which was developed by and named for Thomas Bayes (1702–1761). **Bayes' rule** is *a formula that extends the use of the law of conditional probabilities to allow revision of original probabilities with new information.*

Bayes' Rule

$$P(X_i|Y) = \frac{P(X_i) \cdot P(Y|X_i)}{P(X_1) \cdot P(Y|X_1) + P(X_2) \cdot P(Y|X_2) + \cdots + P(X_n) \cdot P(Y|X_n)}$$

Recall that the law of conditional probability for

$$P(X_i|Y)$$

is

$$P(X_i|Y) = \frac{P(X_i) \cdot P(Y|X_i)}{P(Y)}$$

Compare Bayes' rule to this law of conditional probability. The numerators of Bayes' rule and the law of conditional probability are the same—the intersection of X_i and Y shown in the form of the general rule of multiplication. The new feature that Bayes' rule uses is found in the denominator of the rule:

$$P(X_1) \cdot P(Y|X_1) + P(X_2) \cdot P(Y|X_2) + \cdots + P(X_n) \cdot P(Y|X_n)$$

The denominator of Bayes' rule includes a product expression (intersection) for every partition in the sample space, Y, including the event (X_i) itself. The denominator is thus a collectively exhaustive listing of mutually exclusive outcomes of Y. This denominator is sometimes referred to as the "total probability formula." It represents a weighted average of the conditional probabilities, with the weights being the prior probabilities of the corresponding event.

By expressing the law of conditional probabilities in this new way, Bayes' rule enables the statistician to make new and different applications using conditional probabilities. In particular, statisticians use Bayes' rule to "revise" probabilities in light of new information.

As an application of Bayes' rule, suppose the American Printer Company sells printer cartridges under its own brand name that are produced by two suppliers: Alamo and South Jersey. Of the printer cartridges sold by the American Printer Company, Alamo produces 65% and South Jersey produces 35%. All cartridges are made to the same specifications and are shipped to the American Printer Company, who puts their own label on the cartridges. Once the cartridges have the American Printer Company label on them, it is virtually impossible to determine from which supplier they came. If one of these cartridges is randomly selected, what is the probability that the cartridge was supplied by Alamo? Since Alamo produces 65% of the cartridges, the probability that an American Printer Company cartridge comes from Alamo, $P(A)$, is .65 where A denotes Alamo. The probability that the cartridges were produced by South Jersey is $P(SJ) = .35$ where SJ denotes South Jersey. These marginal probabilities are sometimes referred to as *prior* probabilities because they are determined before any new information is obtained. Suppose, however, the printer cartridge is tested and determined to be defective. How can this new information be used to change (or revise) the probability that the cartridge came from a particular supplier? Using Bayes' Rule, and some additional information, we are able to revise these original (marginal) probabilities in light of new information.

If both suppliers produced the same percentage of defects, knowing that the cartridge is defective would not change the marginal probabilities. However, suppose that 8% of Alamo cartridges are defective and 12% of South Jersey cartridges are defective. If it is determined that the randomly selected cartridge is defective, the probabilities that the printer cartridge came from a particular supplier will change because a higher percentage of South Jersey cartridges are defective than those produced by Alamo. Each of these defective probabilities by supplier is a conditional probability. That is, the probability that a cartridge is defective given that is comes from Alamo is .08. This can be written as $P(\text{defective}|\text{Alamo}) = .08$. For South Jersey, the conditional probability is $P(\text{defective}|\text{South Jersey}) = .12$.

Next, we solve for the joint probabilities that the cartridge is from a particular supplier and is defective. If 65% of the cartridges are produced by Alamo and if 8% of Alamo cartridges are defective, then $(.65)(.08) = .052$ or 5.2% of all cartridges used by the American Printer Company are Alamo cartridges *and* defective. We have determined the joint probability of a cartridge being from Alamo and defective by multiplying the marginal probability by the conditional probability:

$$P(\text{Alamo} \cap \text{defective}) = P(\text{Alamo}) \cdot P(\text{defective}|\text{Alamo}) = (.65)(.08) = .052$$

In a similar manner, we can solve for the joint probability for South Jersey:

$$P(\text{South Jersey} \cap \text{defective}) = P(\text{South Jersey}) \cdot P(\text{defective}|\text{South Jersey})$$
$$= (.35)(.12) = .042.$$

From these probabilities, we can build the Bayesian table shown in Table 4.8.

Because it was determined that the randomly selected cartridge is defective, we need not be concerned about good cartridges and can focus on defective cartridges only, as in Table 4.8. We know that 5.2% of all cartridges are from Alamo and are defective and 4.2% of all cartridges are from South Jersey and are defective. What percentage of all cartridges is defective? If we sum the two joint probabilities from both of the suppliers, $.052 + .042 = .094$, we

TABLE 4.8 Building the Bayesian Table: Calculating the Joint Probability

SUPPLIER	PRIOR PROBABILITY $P(S_i)$	CONDITIONAL PROBABILITY $P(d|S_i)$	JOINT PROBABILITY $P(d \cap S_i)$
Alamo	.65	.08	.052
South Jersey	.35	.12	.042

find that .094 or 9.4% of all cartridges are defective. That is, $P(\text{defective}) = .094$. Notice that until now, we only knew that probability of each supplier producing a defective cartridge, not the total.

Based on this information, we can now revise the original probabilities that the cartridge came from a particular supplier by following the rest of Bayes' rule. The probabilities are revised by dividing each supplier's joint probability by the total probability that a cartridge is defective (.094). For Alamo:

$$\text{Revised Probability} = \frac{P(\text{Alamo} \cap \text{Defective})}{P(\text{Defective})} = \frac{.052}{.094} = .553$$

Given that the cartridge is defective, the probability that a randomly selected cartridge is from Alamo is .553. Shown in Table 4.9 are the calculations for both revised probabilities.

Tree diagrams are another common way to solve Bayes' rule problems. Figure 4.13 shows the solution for the cartridge problem. Note that the tree diagram contains all possibilities, including both defective and acceptable cartridges. When new information is given, only the pertinent branches are selected and used. The joint probability values at the end of the appropriate branches are used to revise and compute the posterior probabilities. Using the total number of defective cartridges, $.052 + .042 = .094$, the calculation is as follows.

$$\text{Revised Probability: Alamo} = \frac{.052}{.094} = .553$$

$$\text{Revised Probability: South Jersey} = \frac{.042}{.094} = .447$$

TABLE 4.9 Revised Probabilities for the Printer Cartridge Problem

SUPPLIER	PRIOR PROBABILITY $P(S_i)$	CONDITIONAL PROBABILITY $P(d\mid S_i)$	JOINT PROBABILITY $P(S_i \cap d)$	REVISED OR POSTERIOR PROBABILITIES
Alamo	.65	.08	.052	$.052/.094 = .553$
South Jersey	.35	.12	.042	$.042/.094 = .447$
			$P(\text{defective}) = .094$	

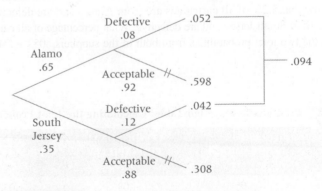

FIGURE 4.13 **Tree Diagram for Cartridge Problem Probabilities**

DEMONSTRATION PROBLEM 4.12

Machines A, B, and C all produce the same two parts, X and Y. Of all the parts produced, machine A produces 60%, machine B produces 30%, and machine C produces 10%. In addition,

40% of the parts made by machine A are part X.

50% of the parts made by machine B are part X.

70% of the parts made by machine C are part X.

A part produced by this company is randomly sampled and is determined to be an X part. With the knowledge that it is an X part, revise the probabilities that the part came from machine A, B, or C.

Solution: The prior probability of the part coming from machine A is .60, because machine A produces 60% of all parts. The prior probability is .30 that the part came from B and .10 that it came from C. These prior probabilities are more pertinent if nothing is known about the part. However, the part is known to be an X part. The conditional probabilities show that different machines produce different proportions of X parts. For example, .40 of the parts made by machine A are X parts, but .50 of the parts made by machine B and .70 of the parts made by machine C are X parts. It makes sense that the probability of the part coming from machine C would increase and that the probability that the part was made on machine A would decrease because the part is an X part.

The following table shows how the prior probabilities, conditional probabilities, joint probabilities, and marginal probability, $P(X)$, can be used to revise the prior probabilities to obtain posterior probabilities.

Event	Prior $P(E_i)$	Conditional $P(X\mid E_i)$	Joint $P(X \cap E_i)$	Posterior
A	.60	.40	$(.60)(.40) = .24$	$\dfrac{.24}{.46} = .52$
B	.30	.50	.15	$\dfrac{.15}{.46} = .33$
C	.10	.70	$\dfrac{.07}{P(X) = .46}$	$\dfrac{.07}{.46} = .15$

After the probabilities are revised, it is apparent that the probability of the part being made at machine A decreased and that the probabilities that the part was made at machines B and C increased. A tree diagram presents another view of this problem.

$$\text{Revised Probabilities: Machine A: } \frac{.24}{.46} = .52$$

$$\text{Machine B: } \frac{.15}{.46} = .33$$

$$\text{Machine C: } \frac{.07}{.46} = .15$$

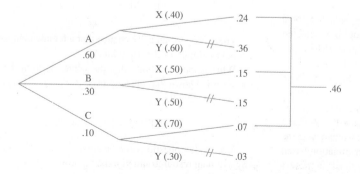

4.7 Problems

4.31. In a manufacturing plant, machine A produces 10% of a certain product, machine B produces 40% of this product, and machine C produces 50% of this product. Five percent of machine A products are defective, 12% of machine B products are defective, and 8% of machine C products are defective. The company inspector has just sampled a product from this plant and has found it to be defective. Determine the revised probabilities that the sampled product was produced by machine A, machine B, or machine C.

4.32. Alex, Alicia, and Juan fill orders in a fast-food restaurant. Alex incorrectly fills 20% of the orders he takes. Alicia incorrectly fills 12% of the orders she takes. Juan incorrectly fills 5% of the orders he takes. Alex fills 30% of all orders, Alicia fills 45% of all orders, and Juan fills 25% of all orders. An order has just been filled.

   a. What is the probability that Alicia filled the order?

   b. If the order was filled by Juan, what is the probability that it was filled correctly?

   c. Who filled the order is unknown, but the order was filled incorrectly. What are the revised probabilities that Alex, Alicia, or Juan filled the order?

   d. Who filled the order is unknown, but the order was filled correctly. What are the revised probabilities that Alex, Alicia, or Juan filled the order?

4.33. In a small town, two lawn companies fertilize lawns during the summer. Tri-State Lawn Service has 72% of the market. Thirty percent of the lawns fertilized by Tri-State could be rated as very healthy one month after service. Greenchem has the other 28% of the market. Twenty percent of the lawns fertilized by Greenchem could be rated as very healthy one month after service. A lawn that has been treated with fertilizer by one of these companies within the last month is selected randomly. If the lawn is rated as very healthy, what are the revised probabilities that Tri-State or Greenchem treated the lawn?

4.34. Suppose 70% of all companies are classified as small companies and the rest as large companies. Suppose further, 82% of large companies provide training to employees, but only 18% of small companies provide training. A company is randomly selected without knowing if it is a large or small company; however, it is determined that the company provides training to employees. What are the prior probabilities that the company is a large company or a small company? What are the revised probabilities that the company is large or small? Based on your analysis, what is the overall percentage of companies that offer training?

Decision Dilemma Solved

Equity of the Sexes in the Workplace

The client company data given in the Decision Dilemma are displayed in a cross-tabulation table. Using the techniques presented in this chapter, it is possible to answer the managerial questions statistically. If a worker is randomly selected from the 155 employees, the probability that the worker is a woman, $P(W)$, is 55/155, or .355. This marginal probability indicates that roughly 35.5% of all employees of the client company are women. Given that the employee has a managerial position, the probability that the employee is a woman, $P(W|M)$ is 3/11, or .273. The proportion of managers at the company who are women is lower than the proportion of all workers at the company who are women. Several factors might be related to this discrepancy; some of these may be defensible by the company—including experience, education, and prior history of success—and some may not.

Suppose a technical employee is randomly selected for a bonus. What is the probability that a female would be selected given that the worker is a technical employee? That is, $P(F|T) = ?$ Applying the law of conditional probabilities to the cross-tabulation table given in the Decision Dilemma, $P(F|T) = 17/69 = .246$. Using the concept of complementary events, the probability that a man is selected given that the employee is a technical person is $1 - .246 = .754$. It is more than three times as likely that a randomly selected technical person is a male. If a woman were the one chosen for the bonus, a man could argue discrimination based on the mere probabilities. However, the company decision makers could then present documentation of the choice criteria based on productivity, technical suggestions, quality measures, and others.

Suppose a client company employee is randomly chosen to win a trip to Hawaii. The marginal probability that the winner is a professional is $P(P) = 44/155 = .284$. The probability that the winner is either a male or is a clerical worker, a union probability, is:

$$P(M \cup C) = P(M) + P(C) - P(M \cap C)$$

$$= \frac{100}{155} + \frac{31}{155} - \frac{9}{155} = \frac{122}{155} = .787$$

The probability of a male or clerical employee at the client company winning the trip is .787. The probability that the winner is a woman *and* a manager, a joint probability, is

$$P(F \cap M) = 3/155 = .019$$

There is less than a 2% chance that a female manager will be selected randomly as the trip winner.

What is the probability that the winner is from the technical group if it is known that the employee is a male? This conditional probability is as follows:

$$P(T|M) = 52/100 = .52.$$

Many other questions can be answered about the client company's human resource situation using probabilities.

The probability approach to a human resource pool is a factual, numerical approach to people selection taken without regard to individual talents, skills, and worth to the company. Of course, in most instances, many other considerations go into the hiring, promoting, and rewarding of workers besides the random draw of their name. However, company management should be aware that attacks on hiring, promotion, and reward practices are sometimes made using statistical analyses such as those presented here. It is not being argued here that management should base decisions merely on the probabilities within particular categories. Nevertheless, being aware of the probabilities, management can proceed to undergird their decisions with documented evidence of worker productivity and worth to the organization.

Ethical Considerations

One of the potential misuses of probability occurs when subjective probabilities are used. Most subjective probabilities are based on a person's feelings, intuition, or experience. Almost everyone has an opinion on something and is willing to share it. Although such probabilities are not strictly unethical to report, they can be misleading and disastrous to other decision makers. In addition, subjective probabilities leave the door open for unscrupulous people to overemphasize their point of view by manipulating the probability.

The decision maker should remember that the laws and rules of probability are for the "long run." If a coin is tossed, even though the probability of getting a head is .5, the result will be either a head or a tail. It isn't possible to get a half head. The probability of getting a head (.5) will probably work out in the long run, but in the short run an experiment might produce 10 tails in a row.

Suppose the probability of striking oil on a geological formation is .10. This probability means that, in the long run, if the company drills enough holes on this type of formation, it should strike oil in about 10% of the holes. However, if the company has only enough money to drill one hole, it will either strike oil or have a dry hole. The probability figure of .10 may mean something different to the company that can afford to drill only one hole than to the company that can drill many hundreds. Classical probabilities could be used unethically to lure a company or client into a potential short-run investment with the expectation of getting at least something in return, when in actuality the investor will either win or lose. The oil company that drills only one hole will not get 10% back from the hole. It will either win or lose on the hole. Thus, classical probabilities open the door for unsubstantiated expectations, particularly in the short run.

Summary

The study of probability addresses ways of assigning probabilities, types of probabilities, and laws of probabilities. Probabilities support the notion of inferential statistics. Using sample data to estimate and test hypotheses about population parameters is done with uncertainty. If samples are taken at random, probabilities can be assigned to outcomes of the inferential process.

Three methods of assigning probabilities are (1) the classical method, (2) the relative frequency of occurrence method, and (3) subjective probabilities. The classical method can assign probabilities a priori, or before the experiment takes place. It relies on the laws and rules of probability. The relative frequency of occurrence method assigns probabilities based on historical data or empirically derived data. Subjective probabilities are based on the feelings, knowledge, and experience of the person determining the probability.

Certain special types of events necessitate amendments to some of the laws of probability: mutually exclusive events and independent events. Mutually exclusive events are events that cannot occur at the same time, so the probability of their intersection is zero. With independent events, the occurrence of one has no impact or influence on the occurrence of the other. Some experiments, such as those involving coins or dice, naturally produce independent events. Other experiments produce independent events when the experiment is conducted with replacement. If events are independent, the joint probability is computed by multiplying the marginal probabilities, which is a special case of the law of multiplication.

Three techniques for counting the possibilities in an experiment are the *mn* counting rule, the N^n possibilities, and combinations. The *mn* counting rule is used to determine how many total possible ways an experiment can occur in a series of sequential operations. The N^n formula is applied when sampling is being done with replacement or events are independent. Combinations are used to determine the possibilities when sampling is being done without replacement.

Four types of probability are marginal probability, conditional probability, joint probability, and union probability. The general law of addition is used to compute the probability of a union. The general law of multiplication is used to compute joint probabilities. The conditional law is used to compute conditional probabilities.

Bayes' rule is a method that can be used to revise probabilities when new information becomes available; it is a variation of the conditional law. Bayes' rule takes prior probabilities of events occurring and adjusts or revises those probabilities on the basis of information about what subsequently occurs.

Key Terms

a priori	complement	intersection	relative frequency of
Bayes' rule	conditional probability	joint probability	occurrence
classical method of assigning	cross-tabulation table	joint probability table	sample space
probabilities	elementary events	marginal probability	set notation
collectively exhaustive events	event	*mn* counting rule	subjective probability
combinations	experiment	mutually exclusive	union
complement of a union	independent events	events	union probability

Formulas

Counting rule

$$mn$$

Sampling with replacement

$$N^n$$

Sampling without replacement

$${}_N C_n$$

Combination formula

$${}_N C_n = \binom{N}{n} = \frac{N!}{n!(N-n)!}$$

General law of addition

$$P(X \cup Y) = P(X) + P(Y) - P(X \cap Y)$$

Special law of addition

$$P(X \cup Y) = P(X) + P(Y)$$

General law of multiplication

$$P(X \cap Y) = P(X) \cdot P(Y|X) = P(Y) \cdot P(X|Y)$$

Special law of multiplication

$$P(X \cap Y) = P(X) \cdot P(Y)$$

Law of conditional probability

$$P(X|Y) = \frac{P(X \cap Y)}{P(Y)} = \frac{P(X) \cdot P(Y|X)}{P(Y)}$$

Bayes' rule

$$P(X_i|Y) = \frac{P(X_i) \cdot P(Y|X_i)}{P(X_1) \cdot P(Y|X_1) + P(X_2) \cdot P(Y|X_2) + \cdots + P(X_n) \cdot P(Y|X_n)}$$

Supplementary Problems

Calculating the Statistics

4.35. Use the values in the cross-tabulation table to solve the equations given.

Variable 1

		D	E
	A	10	20
Variable 2	B	15	5
	C	30	15

a. $P(E) =$ _____

b. $P(B \cup D) =$ _____

c. $P(A \cap E) =$ _____

d. $P(B|E) =$ _____

e. $P(A \cup B) =$ _____

f. $P(B \cap C) =$ _____

g. $P(D|C) =$ _____

h. $P(A|B) =$ _____

i. Are variables 1 and 2 independent? Why or why not?

4.36. Use the values in the cross-tabulation table to solve the equations given.

		D	E	F	G
	A	3	9	7	12
	B	8	4	6	4
	C	10	5	3	7

a. $P(F \cap A) =$ _____

b. $P(A|B) =$ _____

c. $P(B) =$ _____

d. $P(E \cap F) = $ _____

e. $P(D|B) = $ _____

f. $P(B|D) = $ _____

g. $P(D \cup C) = $ _____

h. $P(F) = $ _____

4.37. The following joint probability table contains a breakdown on the age and gender of U.S. physicians in a recent year, as reported by the American Medical Association.

U.S. PHYSICIANS IN A RECENT YEAR

		<35	35–44	45–54	55–64	>65	
	Male	.11	.20	.19	.12	.16	.78
Gender	Female	.07	.08	.04	.02	.01	.22
		.18	.28	.23	.14	.17	1.00

Age (years)

a. What is the probability that one randomly selected physician is 35–44 years old?

b. What is the probability that one randomly selected physician is both a woman and 45–54 years old?

c. What is the probability that one randomly selected physician is a man or is 35–44 years old?

d. What is the probability that one randomly selected physician is less than 35 years old or 55–64 years old?

e. What is the probability that one randomly selected physician is a woman if she is 45–54 years old?

f. What is the probability that a randomly selected physician is neither a woman nor 55–64 years old?

Testing Your Understanding

4.38. Purchasing Survey asked purchasing professionals what sales traits impressed them most in a sales representative. Seventy-eight percent selected "thoroughness." Forty percent responded "knowledge of your own product." The purchasing professionals were allowed to list more than one trait. Suppose 27% of the purchasing professionals listed both "thoroughness" and "knowledge of your own product" as sales traits that impressed them most. A purchasing professional is randomly sampled.

a. What is the probability that the professional selected "thoroughness" or "knowledge of your own product"?

b. What is the probability that the professional selected neither "thoroughness" nor "knowledge of your own product"?

c. If it is known that the professional selected "thoroughness," what is the probability that the professional selected "knowledge of your own product"?

d. What is the probability that the professional did not select "thoroughness" and did select "knowledge of your own product"?

4.39. The U.S. Bureau of Labor Statistics publishes data on the benefits offered by small companies to their employees. Only 42% offer retirement plans while 61% offer life insurance. Suppose 33% offer both retirement plans and life insurance as benefits. If a small company is randomly selected, determine the following probabilties:

a. The company offers a retirement plan given that they offer life insurance.

b. The company offers life insurance given that they offer a retirement plan.

c. The company offers life insurance or a retirement plan.

d. The company offers a retirement plan and does not offer life insurance.

e. The company does not offer life insurance if it is known that they offer a retirement plan.

4.40. An Adweek Media/Harris Poll revealed that 44% of U.S. adults in the 18–34 years category think that "Made in America" ads boost sales. A different Harris Interactive poll showed that 78% of U.S. adults in the 18–34 years category use social media online. Suppose that 85% of U.S. adults in the 18–34 years category think that "Made in America" ads boost sales or use social media online. If a U.S. adult in the 18–34 years category is randomly selected,

a. What is the probability that the person thinks that "Made in America" ads boost sales and uses social media online?

b. What is the probability that the person neither thinks that "Made in America" ads boost sales nor uses social media online?

c. What is the probability that the person thinks that "Made in America" ads boost sales and does not use social media online?

d. What is the probability that the person thinks that "Made in America" ads boost sales given that the person does not use social media online?

e. What is the probability that the person either does not think that "Made in America" ads boost sales or does use social media online?

4.41. In a certain city, 30% of the families have a MasterCard, 20% have an American Express card, and 25% have a Visa card. Eight percent of the families have both a MasterCard and an American Express card. Twelve percent have both a Visa card and a MasterCard. Six percent have both an American Express card and a Visa card.

a. What is the probability of selecting a family that has either a Visa card or an American Express card?

b. If a family has a MasterCard, what is the probability that it has a Visa card?

c. If a family has a Visa card, what is the probability that it has a MasterCard?

d. Is possession of a Visa card independent of possession of a MasterCard? Why or why not?

e. Is possession of an American Express card mutually exclusive of possession of a Visa card?

4.42. A few years ago, a survey commissioned by *The World Almanac* and *Maturity News* Service reported that 51% of the respondents did not believe the Social Security system will be secure in 20 years. Of the respondents who were age 45 or older, 70% believed the system will be secure in 20 years. Of the people surveyed, 57% were under age 45. One respondent is selected randomly.

a. What is the probability that the person is age 45 or older?

b. What is the probability that the person is younger than age 45 and believes that the Social Security system will be secure in 20 years?

c. If the person selected believes the Social Security system will be secure in 20 years, what is the probability that the person is 45 years old or older?

d. What is the probability that the person is younger than age 45 or believes the Social Security system will not be secure in 20 years?

4.43. A telephone survey conducted by the Maritz Marketing Research company found that 43% of Americans expect to save more money next year than they saved last year. Forty-five percent of those surveyed plan to reduce debt next year. Of those who expect to save more money next year, 81% plan to reduce debt next year. An American is selected randomly.

a. What is the probability that this person expects to save more money next year and plans to reduce debt next year?

b. What is the probability that this person expects to save more money next year or plans to reduce debt next year?

c. What is the probability that this person expects to save more money next year and does not plan to reduce debt next year?

d. What is the probability that this person does not expect to save more money given that he/she does plan to reduce debt next year?

4.44. The Steelcase Workplace Index studied the types of work-related activities that Americans did while on vacation in the summer. Among other things, 40% read work-related material. Thirty-four percent checked in with the boss. Respondents to the study were allowed to select more than one activity. Suppose that of those who read work-related material, 78% checked in with the boss. One of these survey respondents is selected randomly.

a. What is the probability that while on vacation this respondent checked in with the boss and read work-related material?

b. What is the probability that while on vacation this respondent neither read work-related material nor checked in with the boss?

c. What is the probability that while on vacation this respondent read work-related material given that the respondent checked in with the boss?

d. What is the probability that while on vacation this respondent did not check in with the boss given that the respondent read work-related material?

e. What is the probability that while on vacation this respondent did not check in with the boss given that the respondent did not read work-related material?

f. Construct a joint probability table for this problem.

4.45. A study on ethics in the workplace by the Ethics Resource Center and Kronos, Inc., revealed that 35% of employees admit to keeping quiet when they see coworker misconduct. Suppose 75% of employees who admit to keeping quiet when they see coworker misconduct call in sick when they are well. In addition, suppose that 40% of the employees who call in sick when they are well admit to keeping quiet when they see coworker misconduct. If an employee is randomly selected, determine the following probabilities:

a. The employee calls in sick when well and admits to keeping quiet when seeing coworker misconduct.

b. The employee admits to keeping quiet when seeing coworker misconduct or calls in sick when well.

c. Given that the employee calls in sick when well, he or she does not keep quiet when seeing coworker misconduct.

d. The employee neither keeps quiet when seeing coworker misconduct nor calls in sick when well.

e. The employee admits to keeping quiet when seeing coworker misconduct and does not call in sick when well.

4.46. Health Rights Hotline published the results of a survey of 2,400 people in Northern California in which consumers were asked to share their complaints about managed care. The number one complaint was denial of care, with 17% of the participating consumers selecting it. Several other complaints were noted, including inappropriate care (14%), customer service (14%), payment disputes

(11%), specialty care (10%), delays in getting care (8%), and prescription drugs (7%). These complaint categories are mutually exclusive. Assume that the results of this survey can be inferred to all managed care consumers. If a managed care consumer is randomly selected, determine the following probabilities:

a. The consumer complains about payment disputes or specialty care.

b. The consumer complains about prescription drugs and customer service.

c. The consumer complains about inappropriate care given that the consumer complains about specialty care.

d. The consumer does not complain about delays in getting care nor does the consumer complain about payment disputes.

4.47. Companies use employee training for various reasons, including employee loyalty, certification, quality, and process improvement. In a national survey of companies, BI Learning Systems reported that 56% of the responding companies named employee retention as a top reason for training. Suppose 36% of the companies replied that they use training for process improvement and for employee retention. In addition, suppose that of the companies that use training for process improvement, 90% use training for employee retention. A company that uses training is randomly selected.

a. What is the probability that the company uses training for employee retention and not for process improvement?

b. If it is known that the company uses training for employee retention, what is the probability that it uses training for process improvement?

c. What is the probability that the company uses training for process improvement?

d. What is the probability that the company uses training for employee retention or process improvement?

e. What is the probability that the company neither uses training for employee retention nor uses training for process improvement?

f. Suppose it is known that the company does not use training for process improvement. What is the probability that the company does use training for employee retention?

4.48. Pitney Bowes surveyed 302 directors and vice presidents of marketing at large and midsized U.S. companies to determine what they believe is the best vehicle for educating decision makers on complex issues in selling products and services. The highest percentage of companies chose direct mail/catalogs, followed by direct sales/sales rep. Direct mail/catalogs was selected by 38% of the companies. None of the companies selected both direct mail/catalogs and direct sales/sales rep. Suppose also that 41% selected neither direct mail/catalogs nor direct sales/sales rep. If one of these companies is selected randomly and their top marketing person interviewed about this matter, determine the following probabilities:

a. The marketing person selected direct mail/catalogs and did not select direct sales/sales rep.

b. The marketing person selected direct sales/sales rep.

c. The marketing person selected direct sales/sales rep given that the person selected direct mail/catalogs.

d. The marketing person did not select direct mail/catalogs given that the person did not select direct sales/sales rep.

4.49. In a study of incentives used by companies to retain mature workers by The Conference Board, it was reported that 41% use flexible work arrangements. Suppose that of those companies that do not use flexible work arrangements, 10% give time off for volunteerism. In addition, suppose that of those companies that use flexible work arrangements, 60% give time off for volunteerism. If a company is randomly selected, determine the following probabilities:

a. The company uses flexible work arrangements or gives time off for volunteerism.

b. The company uses flexible work arrangements and does not give time off for volunteerism.

c. Given that the company does not give time off for volunteerism, the company uses flexible work arrangements.

d. The company does not use flexible work arrangements given that the company does give time off for volunteerism.

e. The company does not use flexible work arrangements or the company does not give time off for volunteerism.

4.50. A small independent physicians' practice has three doctors. Dr. Sarabia sees 41% of the patients, Dr. Tran sees 32%, and Dr. Jackson sees the rest. Dr. Sarabia requests blood tests on 5% of her patients, Dr. Tran requests blood tests on 8% of his patients, and Dr. Jackson requests blood tests on 6% of her patients. An auditor randomly selects a patient from the past week and discovers that the patient had a blood test as a result of the physician visit. Knowing this information, what is the probability that the patient saw Dr. Sarabia? For what percentage of all patients at this practice are blood tests requested?

4.51. A survey by the Arthur Andersen Enterprise Group/National Small Business United attempted to determine what the leading challenges are for the growth and survival of small businesses. Although the economy and finding qualified workers were the leading challenges, several others were listed in the results of the study, including regulations, listed by 30% of the companies, and the tax burden, listed by 35%. Suppose that 71% of the companies listing regulations as a challenge listed the tax burden as a challenge. Assume these percentages hold for all small businesses. If a small business is randomly selected, determine the following probabilities:

a. The small business lists both the tax burden and regulations as a challenge.

b. The small business lists either the tax burden or regulations as a challenge.

c. The small business lists either the tax burden or regulations but not both as a challenge.

d. The small business lists regulations as a challenge given that it lists the tax burden as a challenge.

e. The small business does not list regulations as a challenge given that it lists the tax burden as a challenge.

f. The small business does not list regulations as a challenge given that it does not list the tax burden as a challenge.

4.52. According to U.S. Census Bureau figures, 34.0% of all Americans are in the 0–24 age bracket, 13.3% are in the 25–34 age bracket, 13.3% are in the 35–44 age bracket, and 39.4% are in the 45 and older age bracket. A study by Jupiter Media Metrix determined that Americans use their leisure time in different ways according to age. For example, of those who are in the 45 and older age bracket, 39% read a book or a magazine more than 10 hours per week. Of those who are in the 0–24 age bracket, only 11% read a book or a magazine more than 10 hours per week. The percentage figures for reading a book or a magazine for more than 10 hours per week are 24% for the 25–34 age bracket and 27% the 35–44 age bracket. Suppose an American is randomly selected and it is determined that he or she reads a book or a magazine more than 10 hours per week. Revise the probabilities that he or she is in any given age category. Using these figures, what is the overall percentage of the U.S. population that reads a book or a magazine more than 10 hours per week?

4.53. A retail study by Deloitte revealed that 54% of adults surveyed believed that plastic, noncompostable shopping bags should be banned. Suppose 41% of adults regularly recycle aluminum cans and believe that plastic, noncompostable shopping bags should be banned. In addition, suppose that 60% of adults who do not believe that plastic, noncompostable shopping bags should be banned do recycle. If an adult is randomly selected,

a. What is the probability that the adult recycles and does not believe that plastic, noncompostable shopping bags should be banned?

b. What is the probability that the adult does recycle?

c. What is the probability that the adult does recycle or does believe that plastic, noncompostable shopping bags should be banned?

d. What is the probability that the adult does not recycle or does not believe that plastic, noncompostable shopping bags should be banned?

e. What is the probability that the adult does not believe that plastic, noncompostable shopping bags should be banned given that the adult does recycle?

Analyzing the Databases

See **www.wiley.com/college/black**

1. In the Manufacturing database, what is the probability that a randomly selected SIC Code industry is in industry group 13? What is the probability that a randomly selected SIC Code industry has a value of industry shipments of 4 (see Chapter 1 for coding)? What is the probability that a randomly selected SIC Code industry is in industry group 13 and has a value of industry shipments of 2? What is the probability that a randomly selected SIC Code industry is in industry group 13 or has a value of industry shipments of 2? What is the probability that a randomly selected SIC Code industry neither is in industry group 13 nor has a value of industry shipments of 2?

2. Use the Hospital database. Construct a cross-tabulation table for region and for type of control. You should have a 7 × 4 table. Using this table, answer the following questions. (Refer to Chapter 1 for category members.) What is the probability that a randomly selected hospital is in the Midwest if the hospital is known to be for-profit? If the hospital is known to be in the South, what is the probability that it is a government, nonfederal hospital? What is the probability that a hospital is in the Rocky Mountain region or a not-for-profit, nongovernment hospital? What is the probability that a hospital is a for-profit hospital located in California?

Case

Colgate-Palmolive Makes a "Total" Effort

In the mid-1990s, Colgate-Palmolive developed a new toothpaste for the U.S. market, Colgate Total, with an antibacterial ingredient that was already being successfully sold overseas. However, the word *antibacterial* was not allowed for such products by the Food and Drug Administration rules. So Colgate-Palmolive had to come up with another way of marketing this and other features of their new toothpaste to U.S. consumers. Market researchers told Colgate-Palmolive that consumers were weary of trying to discern among the different advantages of various toothpaste brands and wanted simplification in their shopping lives. In response, the name "Total" was given to the product in the United States: The one word would convey that the toothpaste is the "total" package of various benefits.

Young & Rubicam developed several commercials illustrating Total's benefits and tested the commercials with focus groups. One commercial touting Total's long-lasting benefits was particularly successful. Meanwhile, in 1997, Colgate-Palmolive received FDA approval for Total, five years after the company had applied for it. The product was launched in the United States in January of 1998 using commercials that were designed from the more successful ideas of the focus group tests. Total was introduced with a $100 million advertising campaign. Ten months later, 21% of all United States households had purchased Total for the first time. During this same time period, 43% of those who initially tried Total purchased it again. A year after its release, Total was the number one toothpaste in the United States. Total is advertised as not just a toothpaste but as a protective shield that protects you for a full range of oral health problems for up to 12 hours. Total is now offered in a variety of forms, including Colgate Total Advanced Whitening, Colgate Total Advanced Clean, Colgate Total Advanced Fresh Gel, Colgate Total Clean Mint Paste, Colgate Total Whitening Paste, Colgate Total Whitening Gel, Colgate Total Plus Whitening Liquid, and Colgate Total Mint Stripe Gel. In the United States, market share for Colgate Total toothpaste was 16.2% in a recent year, which was its highest quarterly share ever.

Discussion

1. What probabilities are given in this case? Use these probabilities and the probability laws to determine what percentage of U.S. households purchased Total at least twice in the first 10 months of its release.

2. Is age category independent of willingness to try new products? According to the U.S. Census Bureau, approximately 20% of all Americans are in the 45–64 age category. Suppose 24% of the consumers who purchased Total for the first time during the initial 10-month period were in the 45–64 age category. Use this information to determine whether age is independent of the initial purchase of Total during the introductory time period. Explain your answer.

3. Using the probabilities given in Question 2, calculate the probability that a randomly selected U.S. consumer is either in the 45–64 age category or purchased Total during the initial 10-month period. What is the probability that a randomly selected person purchased Total in the first 10 months given that the person is in the 45–64 age category?

4. Suppose 32% of all toothpaste consumers in the United States saw the Total commercials. Of those who saw the commercials, 40% purchased Total at least once in the first 10 months of its introduction. Of those who did not see the commercials, 12.06% purchased Total at least once in the first 10 months of its introduction. Suppose a toothpaste consumer is randomly selected and it is learned that they purchased Total during the first 10 months of its introduction. Revise the probability that this person saw the Total commercials and the probability that the person did not see the Total commercials.

Source: Colgate-Palmolive's home page at http://www.colgate.com/app/Colgate/US/HomePage.cvsp, Total's homepage at http://www.colgatetotal.com/home

CHAPTER 5

Discrete Distributions

LEARNING OBJECTIVES

The overall learning objective of Chapter 5 is to help you understand a category of probability distributions that produces only discrete outcomes, thereby enabling you to:

1. Define a random variable in order to differentiate between a discrete distribution and a continuous distribution.

2. Determine the mean, variance, and standard deviation of a discrete distribution.

3. Solve problems involving the binomial distribution using the binomial formula and the binomial table.

4. Solve problems involving the Poisson distribution using the Poisson formula and the Poisson table.

5. Solve problems involving the hypergeometric distribution using the hypergeometric formula.

Decision Dilemma

Life with a Cell Phone

As early as 1947, scientists understood the basic concept of a cell phone as a type of two-way radio. Seeing the potential of crude mobile car phones, researchers understood that by using a small range of service areas (cells) with frequency reuse, they could increase the capacity for mobile phone usage significantly even though the technology was not then available. During that same year, AT&T proposed the allocation of a large number of radio-spectrum frequencies by the FCC that would thereby make widespread mobile phone service feasible. At the same time, the FCC decided to limit the amount of frequency capacity available such that only 23 phone conversations could take place simultaneously. In 1968, the FCC reconsidered its position and freed the airwaves for more phones. About this time, AT&T and Bell Labs proposed to the FCC a system in which they would construct a series of many small, low-powered broadcast towers, each of which would broadcast to a "cell" covering a few miles. Taken as a whole, such "cells" could be used to pass phone calls from cell to cell, thereby reaching a large area.

The first company actually to produce a cell phone was Motorola, and Dr. Martin Cooper, then General Manager of Motorola and considered the inventor of the first modern portable handset, made his first call on the portable cell phone in 1973. By 1977, AT&T and Bell Labs had developed a prototype

© Cultura Creative/Alamy Stock Photo

cellular phone system that was tested in Chicago by 2,000 trial customers. After the first commercial cell phone system began operation in Japan in 1979, and Motorola and American Radio developed a second U.S. cell system in 1981, the FCC authorized commerical cellular service in the United States in 1982. By 1987, cell phone subscribers had exceeded 1 million customers in the United States, and as frequencies were getting crowded, the FCC authorized alternative cellular technologies, opening up new opportunities for development. Since that time, researchers have developed a number of advances that have increased capacity exponentially.

Today in the United States, nearly 44% of cell phone owners use only cellular phones; and the trend is rising. According to a Pew Research Center Internet Project Survey of $n = 1,006$ adults, 90% of American adults own a cell phone. In a survey conducted among 2,252 adults ages 18 and over, it was discovered that 29% of cell owners describe their cell phone as "something they can't imagine living without." In spite of American's growing dependence on their cell phones, not everyone is happy about their usage. Seventy-two percent of cell owners experience dropped calls at least occasionally, and 68% of cell phone owners receive unwanted sales/marketing calls at some point. Now there are multiple uses of the cell phone, including e-mail, maps and direction, texting, accessing the internet, and others. According to a study conducted by Princeton Survey Research Associates International from April 17 to May 19, 2013, texting was the predominant cell phone activity with 81% of the cell phone owners sending text messages using their cell phones. Nearly half (52%) of the owners used cell phones to send or receive e-mails and forty-nine percent used cell phones to look up directions and similar information related to their location.

MANAGERIAL AND STATISTICAL QUESTIONS

1. One study reports that nearly 44% of cell phone owners in the United States use only cellular phones (no land line). Suppose you randomly select 20 Americans. What is the probability that more than 12 of the sample use only cell phones?

2. A study reported that 90% of American adults own a cell phone. On the basis of this, if you were to randomly select 25 American adults, what is the probability that fewer than 20 own a cell phone?

3. Suppose the average person in the United States receives about 12 mobile phone calls per day (16 waking hours). This works out to about 1.5 calls per every 2 hours. If this figure is true, what is the probability that a mobile phone user receives no calls in a two-hour period? What is the probability that a cell phone user receives five or more calls in a two-hour period?

Sources: Mary Bellis, "Selling The Cell Phone—History Of Cellular Phones" at Inventorsinventors.about.com/library/weekly/aa070899.htm; http://www.pewinternet.org/fact-sheets/mobile-technology-fact-sheet/; http://www.pewinternet.org/2013/09/19/additional-demographic-analysis/; http://www.telecompetitor.com/report-44-of-u-s-adults-live-in-cellphone-only-households/.

TABLE 5.1

All Possible Outcomes for the Battery Experiment

$G_1 G_2 G_3$
$D_1 G_2 G_3$
$G_1 D_2 G_3$
$G_1 G_2 D_3$
$D_1 D_2 G_3$
$D_1 G_2 D_3$
$G_1 D_2 D_3$
$D_1 D_2 D_3$

In statistical experiments involving chance, outcomes occur randomly. As an example, a battery manufacturer randomly selects three batteries from a large batch of batteries to be tested for quality. Each selected battery is to be rated as good or defective. The batteries are numbered from 1 to 3, a defective battery is designated with a D, and a good battery is designated with a G. All possible outcomes are shown in Table 5.1. The expression $D_1 G_2 D_3$ denotes one particular outcome in which the first and third batteries are defective and the second battery is good. In this chapter, we examine the probabilities of events occurring in experiments that produce such discrete distributions. In particular, we will study the binomial distribution, the Poisson distribution, and the hypergeometric distribution.

5.1 Discrete Versus Continuous Distributions

A **random variable** is *a variable that contains the outcomes of a chance experiment.* For example, suppose an experiment is to measure the arrivals of automobiles at a turnpike tollbooth during a 30-second period. The possible outcomes are: 0 cars, 1 car, 2 cars, . . . , n cars. These numbers (0, 1, 2, . . . , n) are the values of a random variable. Suppose another experiment is to measure the time between the completion of two tasks in a production line. The values will range from 0 seconds to n seconds. These time measurements are the values of another random variable. The two categories of random variables are (1) discrete random variables and (2) continuous random variables.

A random variable is a **discrete random variable** *if the set of all possible values is at most a finite or a countably infinite number of possible values.* In most statistical situations, discrete random variables produce values that are nonnegative whole numbers. For example, if six people are randomly selected from a population and how many of the six are left-handed is to be determined, the random variable produced is discrete. The only possible numbers of left-handed people in the sample of six are 0, 1, 2, 3, 4, 5, and 6. There cannot be 2.75 left-handed people in a group of six people; obtaining nonwhole number values is impossible. Other examples of experiments that yield discrete random variables include the following:

1. Randomly selecting 25 people who consume soft drinks and determining how many people prefer diet soft drinks
2. Determining the number of defective items in a batch of 50 items
3. Counting the number of people who arrive at a store during a five-minute period
4. Sampling 100 registered voters and determining how many voted for the president in the last election

The battery experiment described at the beginning of the chapter produces a distribution that has discrete outcomes. Any one trial of the experiment will contain 0, 1, 2, or 3 defective batteries. It is not possible to get 1.58 defective batteries. It could be said that discrete random variables are usually generated from experiments in which things are "counted" not "measured."

Continuous random variables *take on values at every point over a given interval.* Thus continuous random variables have no gaps or unassumed values. It could be said that continuous random variables are generated from experiments in which things are "measured" not "counted." For example, if a person is assembling a product component, the time it takes to accomplish that feat could be any value within a reasonable range such as 3 minutes 36.4218 seconds or 5 minutes 17.5169 seconds. A list of measures for which continuous random variables might be generated would include time, height, weight, and volume. Examples of experiments that yield continuous random variables include the following:

1. Sampling the volume of liquid nitrogen in a storage tank
2. Measuring the time between customer arrivals at a retail outlet
3. Measuring the lengths of newly designed automobiles
4. Measuring the weight of grain in a grain elevator at different points of time

Once continuous data are measured and recorded, they become discrete data because the data are rounded off to a discrete number. Thus in actual practice, virtually all business data are discrete. However, for practical reasons, data analysis is facilitated greatly by using continuous distributions on data that were continuous originally.

The outcomes for random variables and their associated probabilities can be organized into distributions. The two types of distributions are **discrete distributions**, *constructed from discrete random variables,* and **continuous distributions**, *based on continuous random variables.*

In this text, three discrete distributions are presented:

1. binomial distribution
2. Poisson distribution
3. hypergeometric distribution

All three of these distributions are presented in this chapter.

In addition, six continuous distributions are discussed later in this text:

1. uniform distribution
2. normal distribution
3. exponential distribution
4. t distribution
5. chi-square distribution
6. F distribution

TABLE 5.2

Discrete Distribution of Occurrence of Daily Crises

NUMBER OF CRISES	PROBABILITY
0	.37
1	.31
2	.18
3	.09
4	.04
5	.01

5.2 | Describing a Discrete Distribution

How can we describe a discrete distribution? One way is to construct a graph of the distribution and study the graph. The histogram is probably the most common graphical way to depict a discrete distribution.

Observe the discrete distribution in Table 5.2. An executive is considering out-of-town business travel for a given Friday. She recognizes that at least one crisis could occur on the day that she is gone and she is concerned about that possibility. Table 5.2 shows a discrete distribution that contains the number of crises that could occur during the day that she is gone and the probability that each number will occur. For example, there is a .37 probability that no crisis will occur, a .31 probability of one crisis, and so on. The histogram in Figure 5.1 depicts the distribution given in Table 5.2. Notice that the x-axis of the histogram contains the possible outcomes of the experiment (number of crises that might occur) and that the y-axis contains the probabilities of these occurring.

It is readily apparent from studying the graph of Figure 5.1 that the most likely number of crises is 0 or 1. In addition, we can see that the distribution is discrete in that no probabilities are shown for values in between the whole-number crises.

Mean, Variance, and Standard Deviation of Discrete Distributions

What additional mechanisms can be used to describe discrete distributions besides depicting them graphically? The measures of central tendency and measures of variability discussed in Chapter 3 for grouped data can be applied to discrete distributions to compute a mean, a variance, and a standard deviation. Each of those three descriptive measures (mean, variance, and standard deviation) is computed on grouped data by using the class midpoint as the value to represent the data in the class interval. With discrete distributions, using the class midpoint is not necessary because the discrete value of an outcome (0, 1, 2, 3, . . .) is used to represent itself. Thus, instead of using the value of the class midpoint (M) in computing these descriptive measures for grouped data, the discrete experiment's outcomes (x) are used. In computing these descriptive measures on grouped data, the frequency of each class interval is used to weight the class midpoint. With discrete distribution analysis, the probability of each occurrence is used as the weight.

Mean or Expected Value The mean or expected value of a discrete distribution is *the long-run average of occurrences*. We must realize that any one trial using a discrete random variable yields only one outcome. However, if the process is repeated long enough, the average of the outcomes is most likely to approach a long-run average, expected value, or mean value. This mean, or expected, value is computed as follows.

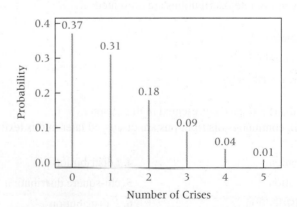

FIGURE 5.1 **Minitab Histogram of Discrete Distribution of Crises Data**

Mean or Expected Value of a Discrete Distribution

$$\mu = E(x) = \Sigma[x \cdot P(x)]$$

where

$E(x)$ = long-run average
x = an outcome
$P(x)$ = probability of that outcome

As an example, let's compute the mean or expected value of the distribution given in Table 5.2. See **Table 5.3** for the resulting values. In the long run, the mean or expected number of crises on a given Friday for this executive is 1.15 crises. Of course, the executive will never have 1.15 crises.

Variance and Standard Deviation of a Discrete Distribution

The variance and standard deviation of a discrete distribution are solved for by using the outcomes (x) and probabilities of outcomes [$P(x)$] in a manner similar to that of computing a mean. In addition, the computations for variance and standard deviations use the mean of the discrete distribution. The formula for computing the variance follows.

Variance of a Discrete Distribution

$$\sigma^2 = \Sigma[(x - \mu)^2 \cdot P(x)]$$

where

x = an outcome
$P(x)$ = probability of a given outcome
μ = mean of the distribution

The standard deviation is then computed by taking the square root of the variance.

Standard Deviation of a Discrete Distribution

$$\sigma = \sqrt{\Sigma[(x - \mu)^2 \cdot P(x)]}$$

The variance and standard deviation of the crisis data in Table 5.2 are calculated and shown in **Table 5.4**. The mean of the crisis data is 1.15 crises. The standard deviation is 1.19 crises, and the variance is 1.41.

TABLE 5.3

Computing the Mean of the Crises Data

x	$P(x)$	$x \cdot P(x)$
0	.37	.00
1	.31	.31
2	.18	.36
3	.09	.27
4	.04	.16
5	.01	.05
		$\Sigma[x \cdot P(x)] = 1.15$
	$\mu = 1.15$ crises	

TABLE 5.4 Calculation of Variance and Standard Deviation on Crises Data

x	$P(x)$	$(x - \mu)^2$	$(x - \mu)^2 \cdot P(x)$
0	.37	$(0 - 1.15)^2 = 1.32$	$(1.32)(.37) = .49$
1	.31	$(1 - 1.15)^2 = 0.02$	$(0.02)(.31) = .01$
2	.18	$(2 - 1.15)^2 = 0.72$	$(0.72)(.18) = .13$
3	.09	$(3 - 1.15)^2 = 3.42$	$(3.42)(.09) = .31$
4	.04	$(4 - 1.15)^2 = 8.12$	$(8.12)(.04) = .32$
5	.01	$(5 - 1.15)^2 = 14.82$	$(14.82)(.01) = .15$
			$\Sigma[(x - \mu)^2 \cdot P(x)] = 1.41$

The variance of $\sigma^2 = \Sigma[(x - \mu)^2 \cdot P(x)] = 1.41$

The standard deviation is $\sigma = \sqrt{1.41} = 1.19$ crises.

DEMONSTRATION PROBLEM 5.1

During one holiday season, the Texas lottery played a game called the Stocking Stuffer.

With this game, total instant winnings of $34.8 million were available in 70 million $1 tickets, with ticket prizes ranging from $1 to $1,000. Shown here are the various prizes and the probability of winning each prize. Use these data to compute the expected value of the game, the variance of the game, and the standard deviation of the game.

PRIZE (x)	PROBABILITY P(x)
$1,000	.00002
100	.00063
20	.00400
10	.00601
4	.02403
2	.08877
1	.10479
0	.77175

Solution: The mean is computed as follows.

PRIZE (x)	PROBABILITY P(x)	$x \cdot P(x)$
$1,000	.00002	.02000
100	.00063	.06300
20	.00400	.08000
10	.00601	.06010
4	.02403	.09612
2	.08877	.17754
1	.10479	.10479
0	.77175	.00000
		$\Sigma[x \cdot P(x)] = .60155$

$$\mu = E(x) = \Sigma[x \cdot P(x)] = .60155$$

The expected payoff for a $1 ticket in this game is 60.2 cents. If a person plays the game for a long time, he or she could expect to average about 60 cents in winnings. In the long run, the participant will lose about $1.00 - .602 = .398$, or about 40 cents a game. Of course, an individual will never win 60 cents in any one game.

Using this mean, $\mu = .60155$, the variance and standard deviation can be computed as follows.

x	P(x)	$(x - \mu)^2$	$(x - \mu)^2 \cdot P(x)$
$1,000	.00002	998797.26190	19.97595
100	.00063	9880.05186	6.22443
20	.00400	376.29986	1.50520
10	.00601	88.33086	0.53087
4	.02403	11.54946	0.27753
2	.08877	1.95566	0.17360
1	.10479	0.15876	0.01664
0	.77175	0.36186	0.27927
			$\Sigma[(x - \mu)^2 \cdot P(x)] = 28.98349$

$$\sigma^2 = \Sigma[(x - \mu^2) \cdot P(x)] = 28.98349$$

$$\sigma = \sqrt{\sigma^2} = \sqrt{\Sigma[(x - \mu)^2 \cdot P(x)]} = \sqrt{28.98349} = 5.38363$$

The variance is 28.98349 (dollars)^2 and the standard deviation is $5.38.

5.2 Problems

5.1. Determine the mean, the variance, and the standard deviation of the following discrete distribution.

x	P(x)
1	.238
2	.290
3	.177
4	.158
5	.137

5.2. Determine the mean, the variance, and the standard deviation of the following discrete distribution.

x	P(x)
0	.103
1	.118
2	.246
3	.229
4	.138
5	.094
6	.071
7	.001

5.3. The following data are the result of a historical study of the number of flaws found in a porcelain cup produced by a manufacturing firm. Use these data and the associated probabilities to compute the expected number of flaws and the standard deviation of flaws.

FLAWS	PROBABILITY
0	.461
1	.285
2	.129
3	.087
4	.038

5.4. Suppose 20% of the people in a city prefer Pepsi-Cola as their soft drink of choice. If a random sample of six people is chosen, the number of Pepsi drinkers could range from zero to six. Shown here are the possible numbers of Pepsi drinkers in a sample of six people and the probability of that number of Pepsi drinkers occurring in the sample. Use the data to determine the mean number of Pepsi drinkers in a sample of six people in the city, and compute the standard deviation.

NUMBER OF PEPSI DRINKERS	PROBABILITY
0	.262
1	.393
2	.246
3	.082
4	.015
5	.002
6	.000

5.3   Binomial Distribution

Perhaps the most widely known of all discrete distributions is the **binomial distribution**. The binomial distribution has been used for hundreds of years. Besides its historical significance, the binomial distribution is studied by business statistics students because it is the basis for other important statistical techniques. In studying various distributions, it is important to be able to differentiate among distributions and to know the unique characteristics and assumptions of each. To assist you in this undertaking, the assumptions of a binomial distribution are given here.

Assumptions of the Binomial Distribution

- The experiment involves n identical trials.
- Each trial has only two possible outcomes denoted as success or as failure.
- Each trial is independent of the previous trials.
- The terms p and q remain constant throughout the experiment, where the term p is the probability of getting a success on any one trial and the term $q = (1 - p)$ is the probability of getting a failure on any one trial.

As the word *binomial* indicates, any single trial of a binomial experiment contains only two possible outcomes. These two outcomes are labeled *success* or *failure*. Usually the outcome of interest to the researcher is labeled a success. For example, if a quality control analyst is looking for defective products, he would consider finding a defective product a success even though the company would not consider a defective product a success. If researchers are studying left-handedness, the outcome of getting a left-handed person in a trial of an experiment is a success. The other possible outcome of a trial in a binomial experiment is called a failure. The word *failure* is used only in opposition to success. In the preceding experiments, a failure could be to get an acceptable part (as opposed to a defective part) or to get a right-handed person (as opposed to a left-handed person). In a binomial distribution experiment, any one trial can have only two possible, mutually exclusive outcomes (right-handed/left-handed, defective/good, male/female, etc.).

The binomial distribution is a discrete distribution. In n trials, only x successes are possible, where x is a whole number between 0 and n inclusive. For example, if five parts are randomly selected from a batch of parts, only 0, 1, 2, 3, 4, or 5 defective parts are possible in that sample. In a sample of five parts, getting 2.714 defective parts is not possible, nor is getting eight defective parts possible.

In a binomial experiment, the trials must be independent. This constraint means that either the experiment is by nature one that produces independent trials (such as tossing coins or rolling dice) or the experiment is conducted with replacement. The effect of the independent trial requirement is that p, the probability of getting a success on one trial, remains constant from trial to trial. For example, suppose 5% of all parts in a bin are defective. The probability of drawing a defective part on the first draw is $p = .05$. If the first part drawn is not replaced, the second draw is not independent of the first, and the p value will change for the next draw. The binomial distribution does not allow for p to change from trial to trial within an experiment. However, if the population is large in comparison with the sample size, the effect of sampling without replacement is minimal, and the independence assumption essentially is met, that is, p remains relatively constant.

Generally, if the sample size, n, is less than 5% of the population, the independence assumption is not of great concern. Therefore the acceptable sample size for using the binomial distribution with samples taken *without* replacement is

$$n < 5\% \ N$$

where

n = sample size
N = population size

For example, suppose 10% of the population of the world is left-handed and that a sample of 20 people is selected randomly from the world's population. If the first person selected is left-handed—and the sampling is conducted without replacement—the value of $p = .10$ is virtually unaffected because the population of the world is so large. In addition, with many experiments the population is continually being replenished even as the sampling is being done. This condition often is the case with quality control sampling of products from large production runs.

There are many binomial distributions, each of which can be described or characterized by two parameters, n and p, where n is the size of the sample ($n > 1$) and p is the probability of getting a success on a single trial. For every different value of n or p, there is a different binomial distribution. With each binomial distribution, probability questions can be asked. Given here are three examples of business scenarios that produce a binomial probability question. In each one, try to determine the value of n and the value of p.

1. Data produced by the U.S. Bureau of Labor Statistics has shown that 34% of all new business establishments fail within the first two years. Suppose 25 business establishments that were newly established two years ago are randomly sampled. What is the probability that exactly three have failed?

2. Why do clients leave their vendors? According to Small Business Trends, 68% of small business clients who leave do so because they feel unappreciated, unimportant, and taken for granted. Suppose 20 business clients who have left a small business are randomly interviewed and asked why they left. What is the probability that 18 or more left because they felt unappreciated, unimportant, and taken for granted?

3. A study conducted by the Employment Benefit Research Institute showed that only 14% of workers feel "very confident" that they will have enough money to live comfortably in retirement. Suppose 16 workers are randomly selected. If the survey is accurate, what is the probability that exactly six feel "very confident" they will have enough money to live comfortably in retirement?

Solving a Binomial Problem

A survey of relocation administrators by Runzheimer International revealed several reasons why workers reject relocation offers. Included in the list were family considerations, financial reasons, and others. Four percent of the respondents said they rejected relocation offers because they received too little relocation help. Suppose five workers who just rejected relocation offers are randomly selected and interviewed. Assuming the 4% figure holds for all workers rejecting relocation, what is the probability that exactly one of the workers rejected the offer because of too little relocation help? Let's start by determining the probability that the *first* worker interviewed rejected the offer because of too little relocation help and the next four workers rejected the offer for other reasons.

Let T represent too little relocation help and R represent other reasons. The sequence of interviews for this problem is as follows:

$$T_1, R_2, R_3, R_4, R_5$$

The probability of getting this sequence of workers is calculated by using the special rule of multiplication for independent events (assuming the workers are independently selected from a large population of workers). If 4% of the workers rejecting relocation offers do so for too little relocation help, the probability of one person being randomly selected from workers rejecting relocation offers who does so for that reason is .04, which is the value of p. The other 96% of the workers who reject relocation offers do so for other reasons. Thus the probability of randomly selecting a worker from those who reject relocation offers who does so for other reasons is $1 - .04 = .96$, which is the value for q. The probability of obtaining this sequence of five workers who have rejected relocation offers is

$$P(T_1 \cap R_2 \cap R_3 \cap R_4 \cap R_5) = (.04)(.96)(.96)(.96)(.96) = .03397$$

Obviously, in the random selection of workers who rejected relocation offers, the worker who did so because of too little relocation help could have been the second worker or the third or the fourth or the fifth. All the possible sequences of getting one worker who rejected relocation because of too little help and four workers who did so for other reasons follow.

$$T_1, R_2, R_3, R_4, R_5$$
$$R_1, T_2, R_3, R_4, R_5$$
$$R_1, R_2, T_3, R_4, R_5$$
$$R_1, R_2, R_3, T_4, R_5$$
$$R_1, R_2, R_3, R_4, T_5$$

Thus, as you can see, there are five different ways to get exactly one worker who rejected relocation because of too little relocation help.

The probability of each of these sequences occurring is calculated as follows:

$$(.04)(.96)(.96)(.96)(.96) = .03397$$
$$(.96)(.04)(.96)(.96)(.96) = .03397$$
$$(.96)(.96)(.04)(.96)(.96) = .03397$$
$$(.96)(.96)(.96)(.04)(.96) = .03397$$
$$(.96)(.96)(.96)(.96)(.04) = .03397$$

Note that in each case the final probability is the same. Each of the five sequences contains the product of .04 and four .96s. The commutative property of multiplication allows for the reordering of the five individual probabilities in any one sequence. The probabilities in each of the five sequences may be reordered and summarized as $(.04)^1 (.96)^4$. Each sequence contains the same five probabilities, which makes recomputing the probability of each sequence unnecessary. What *is* important is to determine how many different ways the sequences can be formed and multiply that figure by the probability of one sequence occurring. For the five sequences of this problem, the total probability of getting exactly one worker who rejected relocation because of too little relocation help in a random sample of five workers who rejected relocation offers is

$$5(.04)^1(.96)^4 = .16987$$

An easier way to determine the number of sequences than by listing all possibilities is to use *combinations* to calculate them. (The concept of combinations was introduced in Chapter 4.) Five workers are being sampled, so $n = 5$, and the problem is to get one worker who rejected a relocation offer because of too little relocation help, $x = 1$. Hence $_nC_x$ will yield the number of possible ways to get x successes in n trials. For this problem, $_5C_1$ tells the number of sequences of possibilities.

$$_5C_1 = \frac{5!}{1!(5-1)!} = 5$$

Weighting the probability of one sequence with the combination yields

$$_5C_1(.04)^1(.96)^4 = .16987$$

Using combinations simplifies the determination of how many sequences are possible for a given value of x in a binomial distribution.

As another example, suppose 70% of all Americans believe cleaning up the environment is an important issue. What is the probability of randomly sampling four Americans and having exactly two of them say that they believe cleaning up the environment is an important issue? Let E represent the success of getting a person who believes cleaning up the environment is an important issue. For this example, $p = .70$. Let N represent the failure of not getting a person who believes cleaning up is an important issue (N denotes not important). The probability of getting one of these persons is $q = .30$.

The various sequences of getting two E's in a sample of four follow.

$$E_1, E_2, N_3, N_4$$
$$E_1, N_2, E_3, N_4$$
$$E_1, N_2, N_3, E_4$$
$$N_1, E_2, E_3, N_4$$
$$N_1, E_2, N_3, E_4$$
$$N_1, N_2, E_3, E_4$$

Two successes in a sample of four can occur six ways. Using combinations, the number of sequences is

$$_4C_2 = 6 \text{ ways}$$

The probability of selecting any individual sequence is

$$(.70)^2(.30)^2 = .0441$$

Thus the overall probability of getting exactly two people who believe cleaning up the environment is important out of four randomly selected people, when 70% of Americans believe cleaning up the environment is important, is

$$_4C_2(.70)^2(.30)^2 = .2646$$

Generalizing from these two examples yields the binomial formula, which can be used to solve binomial problems.

Binomial Formula

$$P(x) = {}_{n}C_{x} \cdot p^{x} \cdot q^{n-x} = \frac{n!}{x!(n-x)!} \cdot p^{x} \cdot q^{n-x}$$

where

n = the number of trials (or the number being sampled)
x = the number of successes desired
p = the probability of getting a success in one trial
$q = 1 - p$ = the probability of getting a failure in one trial

The binomial formula summarizes the steps presented so far to solve binomial problems. The formula allows the solution of these problems quickly and efficiently.

DEMONSTRATION PROBLEM 5.2

A Gallup survey found that 65% of all financial consumers were very satisfied with their primary financial institution. Suppose that 25 financial consumers are sampled. If the Gallup survey result still holds true today, what is the probability that exactly 19 are very satisfied with their primary financial institution?

Solution: The value of p is .65 (very satisfied), the value of $q = 1 - p = 1 - .65 = .35$ (not very satisfied), $n = 25$, and $x = 19$. The binomial formula yields the final answer.

$${}_{25}C_{19}(.65)^{19}(.35)^{6} = (177,100)(.00027884)(.00183827) = .0908$$

If 65% of all financial consumers are very satisfied, about 9.08% of the time the researcher would get exactly 19 out of 25 financial consumers who are very satisfied with their financial institution. How many very satisfied consumers would one expect to get in 25 randomly selected financial consumers? If 65% of the financial consumers are very satisfied with their primary financial institution, one would expect to get about 65% of 25 or $(.65)(25) = 16.25$ very satisfied financial consumers. While in any individual sample of 25 the number of financial consumers who are very satisfied cannot be 16.25, business researchers understand that x values near 16.25 are the most likely occurrences.

DEMONSTRATION PROBLEM 5.3

Recall early in this section that according to Small Business Trends, 68% of small business clients who leave do so because they feel unappreciated, unimportant, and taken for granted. Suppose 20 business clients who have left a small business are randomly interviewed and asked why they left. What is the probability that 18 or more left because they felt unappreciated, unimportant, and taken for granted?

Solution: This problem must be worked as the union of three probabilities: $x = 18$, $x = 19$, and $x = 20$. In each problem, $n = 20$, $p = .68$, and $q = .32$. The binomial formula gives the following result:

$x = 18$		$x = 19$		$x = 20$	
${}_{20}C_{18} \cdot (.68)^{18} \cdot (.32)^{2}$	+	${}_{20}C_{19} \cdot (.68)^{19} \cdot (.32)^{1}$	+	${}_{20}C_{20} \cdot (.68)^{20} \cdot (.32)^{0}$	=
.0188	+	.0042	+	.0004	= .0234

> If, indeed, 68% of small business clients leave because they feel unappreciated, unimportant, and taken for granted and 20 business clients who have left are randomly selected, the probability that 18 or more left because they felt unappreciated, unimportant, and taken for granted is .0234. Thus, this problem is the union of three probabilities. Whenever the binomial formula is used to solve for cumulative success (not an exact number), the probability of each x value must be solved and the probabilities summed.

Using the Binomial Table

Anyone who works enough binomial problems will begin to recognize that the probability of getting $x = 5$ successes from a sample size of $n = 18$ when $p = .10$ is the same no matter whether the five successes are left-handed people, defective parts, brand X purchasers, or any other variable. Whether the sample involves people, parts, or products does not matter in terms of the final probabilities. The essence of the problem is the same: $n = 18$, $x = 5$, and $p = .10$. Recognizing this fact, mathematicians constructed a set of binomial tables containing presolved probabilities.

Since two parameters, n and p, describe or characterize a binomial distribution, binomial distributions actually are a family of distributions. Every different value of n and/or every different value of p gives a different binomial distribution, and tables are available for various combinations of n and p values. Because of space limitations, the binomial tables presented in this text are limited. Table A.2 in Appendix A contains binomial tables. Each table is headed by a value of n. Nine values of p are presented in each table of size n. In the column below each value of p is the binomial distribution for that combination of n and p. Table 5.5 contains a segment of Table A.2 with the binomial probabilities for $n = 20$.

TABLE 5.5 Solution to the $x < 10$ Problem Using the Binomial Table

					$n = 20$				
					PROBABILITY				
x	.1	.2	.3	.4	.5	.6	.7	.8	.9
0	.122	.012	.001	.000	.000	.000	.000	.000	.000
1	.270	.058	.007	.000	.000	.000	.000	.000	.000
2	.285	.137	.028	.003	.000	.000	.000	.000	.000
3	.190	.205	.072	.012	.001	.000	.000	.000	.000
4	.090	.218	.130	.035	.005	.000	.000	.000	.000
5	.032	.175	.179	.075	.015	.001	.000	.000	.000
6	.009	.109	.192	.124	.037	.005	.000	.000	.000
7	.002	.055	.164	.166	.074	.015	.001	.000	.000
8	.000	.022	.114	.180	.120	.035	.004	.000	.000
9	.000	.007	.065	.160	.160	.071	.012	.000	.000
10	.000	.002	.031	.117	.176	.117	.031	.002	.000
11	.000	.000	.012	.071	.160	.160	.065	.007	.000
12	.000	.000	.004	.035	.120	.180	.114	.022	.000
13	.000	.000	.001	.015	.074	.166	.164	.055	.002
14	.000	.000	.000	.005	.037	.124	.192	.109	.009
15	.000	.000	.000	.001	.015	.075	.179	.175	.032
16	.000	.000	.000	.000	.005	.035	.130	.218	.090
17	.000	.000	.000	.000	.001	.012	.072	.205	.190
18	.000	.000	.000	.000	.000	.003	.028	.137	.285
19	.000	.000	.000	.000	.000	.000	.007	.058	.270
20	.000	.000	.000	.000	.000	.000	.001	.012	.122

DEMONSTRATION PROBLEM 5.4

One study by CNNMoney reported that 60% of workers have less than $25,000 in total savings and investments (excluding the value of their home). If this is true and if a random sample of 20 workers is selected, what is the probability that fewer than 10 have less than $25,000 in total savings and investments?

Solution: In this problem, $n = 20$, $p = .60$, and $x < 10$, making this a cumulative problem. To solve this problem using the binomial probability formula, one would have to solve for $x = 0, 1, 2, 3, 4, 5, 6, 7, 8$, and 9, a total of 10 different applications of the binomial formula, and then sum the individual answers to get the overall probability of $x < 10$. However, using binomial tables, this problem can easily be solved.

Note that Table 5.5 contains a binomial table for $n = 20$ and since the problem under consideration is for $n = 20$, we can use this binomial table to help us solve the problem. At the top of the binomial table, the word "probability" denotes the various values of p. In this problem, $p = .60$, so we peruse the top of the table until we find a column with .6. Down the left side of the binomial table are various values of x. At the intersection of p and each value of x lies the probability answer for that value of x. Looking at Table 5.5, we can see that the probabilities for $x = 0, 1, 2, 3, 4, 5, 6, 7, 8$, and 9 are .000, .000, .000, .000, .000, .001, .005, .015, .035, and .071, respectively. Summing these values results in an overall probability of .127 for $x < 10$. These probabilities are highlighted in Table 5.5.

Using the Computer to Produce a Binomial Distribution

Both Excel and Minitab can be used to produce the probabilities for virtually any binomial distribution. Such computer programs offer yet another option for solving binomial problems besides using the binomial formula or the binomial tables. Actually, the computer packages in effect print out what would be a column of the binomial table. The advantages of using statistical software packages for this purpose are convenience (if the binomial tables are not readily available and a computer is) and the potential for generating tables for many more values than those printed in the binomial tables.

For example, a study of bank customers stated that 64% of all financial consumers believe banks are more competitive today than they were five years ago. Suppose 23 financial consumers are selected randomly and we want to determine the probabilities of various x values occurring. Table A.2 in Appendix A could not be used because only nine different p values are included and $p = .64$ is not one of those values. In addition, $n = 23$ is not included in the table. Without the computer, we are left with the binomial formula as the only option for solving binomial problems for $n = 23$ and $p = .64$. Particularly if the cumulative probability questions are asked (for example, $x \leq 10$, the binomial formula can be a tedious way to solve the problem.

Shown in Table 5.6 is the Minitab output for the binomial distribution of $n = 23$ and $p = .64$. With this computer output, a researcher could obtain or calculate the probability of any occurrence within the binomial distribution of $n = 23$ and $p = .64$. Table 5.7 contains Minitab output for the particular binomial problem, $P(x \leq 10)$ when $n = 23$ and $p = .64$, solved by using Minitab's cumulative probability capability.

Recall from the beginning of this section that one study showed that 14% of workers feel "very confident" they will have enough money to live comfortably in retirement. Suppose 20 workers are randomly selected; the probability that more than five feel "very confident" that they will have enough money to live comfortably in retirement can be determined using Excel. The results are shown in Table 5.8.

TABLE 5.6

Minitab Output for the Binomial Distribution of $n = 23$, $p = .64$

PROBABILITY DENSITY FUNCTION	
Binomial with $n = 23$ and $p = 0.64$	
x	$P(X = x)$
0	0.000000
1	0.000000
2	0.000000
3	0.000001
4	0.000006
5	0.000037
6	0.000199
7	0.000858
8	0.003051
9	0.009040
10	0.022500
11	0.047273
12	0.084041
13	0.126420
14	0.160533
15	0.171236
16	0.152209
17	0.111421
18	0.066027
19	0.030890
20	0.010983
21	0.002789
22	0.000451
23	0.000035

TABLE 5.7	**Minitab Output for the Binomial Problem, $P(x \leq 10 \mid n = 23$ and $p = .64)$**

CUMULATIVE DISTRIBUTION FUNCTION	
Binomial with $n = 23$ and $p = 0.64$	
x $P(X \Leftarrow x)$	
10 0.0356916	

TABLE 5.8 Excel Output for Answer to Worker Confidence Problem

x	PROB(x)	
6	0.0353	
7	0.0115	
8	0.0030	
9	0.0007	
10	0.0001	The probability $x > 5$ when $n = 20$ and $p = .14$ is .0506
11	0.0000	
12	0.0000	
13	0.0000	
14	0.0000	
15	0.0000	
16	0.0000	
17	0.0000	
18	0.0000	
19	0.0000	
20	0.0000	
Total	0.0506	

Mean and Standard Deviation of a Binomial Distribution

A binomial distribution has an expected value or a long-run average, which is denoted by μ. The value of μ is determined by $n \cdot p$. For example, if $n = 10$ and $p = .4$, then $\mu = n \cdot p = (10)(.4) = 4$. The long-run average or expected value means that, if n items are sampled over and over for a long time and if p is the probability of getting a success on one trial, the average number of successes per sample is expected to be $n \cdot p$. If 40% of all graduate business students at a large university are women and if random samples of 10 graduate business students are selected many times, the expectation is that, on average, four of the 10 students would be women.

> **Mean and Standard Deviation of a Binomial Distribution**
>
> $$\mu = n \cdot p$$
> $$\sigma = \sqrt{n \cdot p \cdot q}$$

Examining the mean of a binomial distribution gives an intuitive feeling about the likelihood of a given outcome.

In the study previously mentioned where 14% of workers feel "very confident" that they will have enough money to live comfortably in retirement, if 20 workers are randomly selected, the expected number who feel "very confident" that they will have enough money to live comfortably in retirement is the mean of the binomial distribution $n = 20$ and $p = .14$:

$$\mu = n \cdot p = 20(.14) = 2.8$$

In the long run, if 20 workers are randomly selected over and over and if indeed 14% of workers feel "very confident" that they will have enough money to live comfortably in retirement, then the experiment should average 2.8 workers who feel "very confident" that they will have enough money to live comfortable in retirement. Notice that the probability values for $n = 20$ and $p = .14$ displayed in Table 5.8 are quite low because $x = 6, 7, 8, \ldots, 20$ are not near the mean or expected value. If the binomial probability were computed for $x = 3$, near the mean, the probability is .2409, which is relatively high.

The standard deviation of a binomial distribution is denoted as σ and is equal to $\sqrt{n \cdot p \cdot q}$. The standard deviation for the worker confidence problem discussed above is:

$$\sigma = \sqrt{n \cdot p \cdot q} = \sqrt{20(.14)(.86)} = 1.55$$

Chapter 6 shows that some binomial distributions are nearly bell shaped and can be approximated by using the normal curve. The mean and standard deviation of a binomial distribution are the tools used to convert these binomial problems to normal curve problems.

Graphing Binomial Distributions

The graph of a binomial distribution can be constructed by using all the possible x values of a distribution and their associated probabilities. The x values usually are graphed along the x-axis and the probabilities are graphed along the y-axis.

Table 5.9 lists the probabilities for three different binomial distributions: $n = 8$ and $p = .20$, $n = 8$ and $p = .50$, and $n = 8$ and $p = .80$. Figure 5.2 displays Excel graphs for each of these three binomial distributions. Observe how the shape of the distribution changes as the value of p increases. For $p = .50$, the distribution is symmetrical. For $p = .20$ the distribution is skewed right and for $p = .80$ the distribution is skewed left. This pattern makes sense because the mean of the binomial distribution $n = 8$ and $p = .50$ is 4, which is in the middle of the

TABLE 5.9

Probabilities for Three Binomial Distributions with $n = 8$

	PROBABILITIES FOR		
x	$p = .20$	$p = .50$	$p = .80$
0	.1678	.0039	.0000
1	.3355	.0312	.0001
2	.2936	.1094	.0011
3	.1468	.2187	.0092
4	.0459	.2734	.0459
5	.0092	.2187	.1468
6	.0011	.1094	.2936
7	.0001	.0312	.3355
8	.0000	.0039	.1678

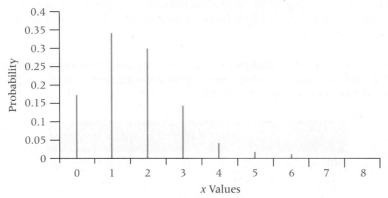

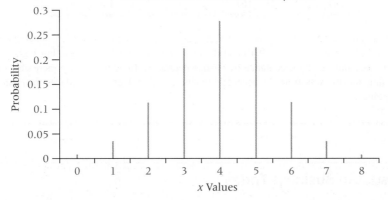

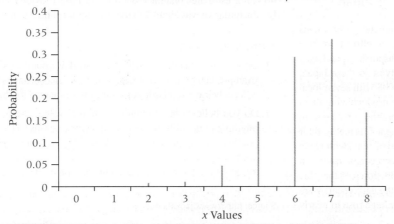

FIGURE 5.2 **Excel Graphs of Three Binomial Distributions with $n = 8$**

distribution. The mean of the distribution $n = 8$ and $p = .20$ is 1.6, which results in the highest probabilities being near $x = 2$ and $x = 1$. This graph peaks early and stretches toward the higher values of x. The mean of the distribution $n = 8$ and $p = .80$ is 6.4, which results in the highest probabilities being near $x = 6$ and $x = 7$. Thus the peak of the distribution is nearer to 8 than to 0 and the distribution stretches back toward $x = 0$.

In any binomial distribution the largest x value that can occur is n and the smallest value is zero. Thus the graph of any binomial distribution is constrained by zero and n. If the value of p for the distribution is not .50, this constraint will result in the graph "piling up" at one end and being skewed at the other end.

DEMONSTRATION PROBLEM 5.5

A manufacturing company produces 10,000 plastic mugs per week. This company supplies mugs to another company, which packages the mugs as part of picnic sets. The second company randomly samples 10 mugs sent from the supplier. If two or fewer of the sampled mugs are defective, the second company accepts the lot. What is the probability that the lot will be accepted if the mug manufacturing company actually is producing mugs that are 10% defective? 20% defective? 30% defective? 40% defective?

Solution: In this series of binomial problems, $n = 10$, $x \leq 2$, and p ranges from .10 to .40. From Table A.2—and cumulating the values—we have the following probability of $x \leq 2$ for each value of p and the expected value ($\mu = n \cdot p$).

p	LOT ACCEPTED $P(x \leq 2)$	EXPECTED NUMBER OF DEFECTS (μ)
.10	.930	1.0
.20	.677	2.0
.30	.382	3.0
.40	.167	4.0

These values indicate that if the manufacturing company is producing 10% defective mugs, the probability is relatively high (.930) that the lot will be accepted by chance. For higher values of p, the probability of lot acceptance by chance decreases. In addition, as p increases, the expected value moves away from the acceptable values, $x \leq 2$. This move reduces the chances of lot acceptance.

Thinking Critically About Statistics in Business Today

Plastic Bags vs. Bringing Your Own in Japan

In a move to protect and improve the environment, governments and companies around the world are making an effort to reduce the use of plastic bags by shoppers for transporting purchased food and goods. Specifically, in Yamagata City in northern Japan, the city concluded an agreement in May of 2008 with seven local food supermarket chains to reduce plastic bag use by having them agree to charge for the use of such bags. Before the agreement, in April of 2008, the average percentage of shoppers bringing their own shopping bags was about 35%. By the end of June, with some of the supermarket chains participating, the percentage had risen to almost 46%. However, by August, when 39 stores of the nine supermarket chains (two other chains joined the agreement) were charging for the use of plastic bags, the percentage rose to nearly 90%. It is estimated that the reduction of carbon dioxide emissions by this initiative was about 225 tons during July and August alone.

THINGS TO PONDER

1. Do you think that this strategy would work in your country? For example, in the United States, do you think that consumers would reduce their use of plastic bags if they were charged for them?

2. Do you believe that a country's cultural value systems have anything to do with the success of such programs? That is, do you believe that it is the extra money that consumers have to spend to purchase the plastic bags that drives the decrease in usage, or are there other factors in addition to the added cost?

Source: http://www.japanfs.org/en/.

5.3 Problems

5.5. Solve the following problems by using the binomial formula.

a. If $n = 4$ and $p = .10$, find $P(x = 3)$.

b. If $n = 7$ and $p = .80$, find $P(x = 4)$.

c. If $n = 10$ and $p = .60$, find $P(x \geq 7)$.

d. If $n = 12$ and $p = .45$, find $P(5 \leq x \leq 7)$.

5.6. Solve the following problems by using the binomial tables (Table A.2).

a. If $n = 20$ and $p = .50$, find $P(x = 12)$.

b. If $n = 20$ and $p = .30$, find $P(x > 8)$.

c. If $n = 20$ and $p = .70$, find $P(x < 12)$.

d. If $n = 20$ and $p = .90$, find $P(x \leq 16)$.

e. If $n = 15$ and $p = .40$, find $P(4 \leq x \leq 9)$.

f. If $n = 10$ and $p = .60$, find $P(x \geq 7)$.

5.7. Solve for the mean and standard deviation of the following binomial distributions.

a. $n = 20$ and $p = .70$

b. $n = 70$ and $p = .35$

c. $n = 100$ and $p = .50$

5.8. Use the probability tables in Table A.2 and sketch the graph of each of the following binomial distributions. Note on the graph where the mean of the distribution falls.

a. $n = 6$ and $p = .70$

b. $n = 20$ and $p = .50$

c. $n = 8$ and $p = .80$

5.9. Shown here is a graph of a binomial distribution for $n = 6$. Study the graph and from the graph, estimate what you think is the mean of this distribution. Approximately what do you think is the value of p and why?

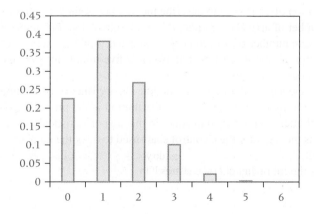

5.10. Shown here is a graph of a binomial distribution for $n = 12$. Study the graph and from the graph, estimate what you think is the mean of this distribution. Approximately what do you think is the value of p and why?

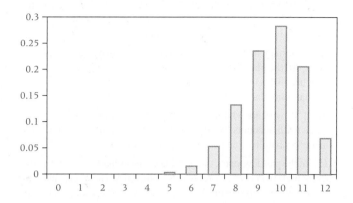

5.11. What is the first big change that American drivers made due to higher gas prices? According to an Access America survey, 30% said that it was cutting recreational driving. However, 27% said that it was consolidating or reducing errands. If these figures are true for all American drivers, and if 20 such drivers are randomly sampled and asked what is the first big change they made due to higher gas prices,

a. What is the probability that exactly 8 said that it was consolidating or reducing errands?

b. What is the probability that none of them said that it was cutting recreational driving?

c. What is the probability that more than 7 said that it was cutting recreational driving?

5.12. *The Wall Street Journal* reported some interesting statistics on the job market. One statistic is that 40% of all workers say they would change jobs for "slightly higher pay." In addition, 88% of companies say that there is a shortage of qualified job candidates. Suppose 16 workers are randomly selected and asked if they would change jobs for "slightly higher pay."

a. What is the probability that nine or more say yes?

b. What is the probability that three, four, five, or six say yes?

c. If 13 companies are contacted, what is the probability that exactly 10 say there is a shortage of qualified job candidates?

d. If 13 companies are contacted, what is the probability that all of the companies say there is a shortage of qualified job candidates?

e. If 13 companies are contacted, what is the expected number of companies that would say there is a shortage of qualified job candidates?

5.13. An increasing number of consumers believe they have to look out for themselves in the marketplace. According to a survey conducted by the Yankelovich Partners for *USA WEEKEND* magazine, 60% of all consumers have called an 800 or 900 telephone number for information about some product. Suppose a random sample of 25 consumers is contacted and interviewed about their buying habits.

a. What is the probability that 15 or more of these consumers have called an 800 or 900 telephone number for information about some product?

b. What is the probability that more than 20 of these consumers have called an 800 or 900 telephone number for information about some product?

c. What is the probability that fewer than 10 of these consumers have called an 800 or 900 telephone number for information about some product?

5.14. Studies have shown that about half of all workers who change jobs cash out their 401(k) plans rather than leaving the money in the account to grow. The percentage is much higher for workers with small 401(k) balances. In fact, 87% of workers with 401(k) accounts less than $5,000 opt to take their balance in cash rather than roll it over into individual retirement accounts when they change jobs.

a. Assuming that 50% of all workers who change jobs cash out their 401(k) plans, if 16 workers who have recently changed jobs that had 401(k) plans are randomly sampled, what is the probability that more than 10 of them cashed out their 401(k) plan?

b. If 10 workers who have recently changed jobs and had 401(k) plans with accounts less than $5,000 are randomly sampled, what is the probability that exactly 6 of them cashed out?

5.15. In the past few years, outsourcing overseas has become more frequently used than ever before by U.S. companies. However, outsourcing is not without problems. A recent survey by *Purchasing* indicates that 20% of the companies that outsource overseas use a consultant. Suppose 15 companies that outsource overseas are randomly selected.

a. What is the probability that exactly five companies that outsource overseas use a consultant?

b. What is the probability that more than nine companies that outsource overseas use a consultant?

c. What is the probability that none of the companies that outsource overseas use a consultant?

d. What is the probability that between four and seven (inclusive) companies that outsource overseas use a consultant?

e. Construct a graph for this binomial distribution. In light of the graph and the expected value, explain why the probability results from parts (a) through (d) were obtained.

5.16. According to Cerulli Associates of Boston, 30% of all CPA financial advisors have an average client size between $500,000 and $1 million. Thirty-four percent have an average client size between $1 million and $5 million. Suppose a complete list of all CPA financial advisors is available and 18 are randomly selected from that list.

a. What is the expected number of CPA financial advisors that have an average client size between $500,000 and $1 million? What is the expected number with an average client size between $1 million and $5 million?

b. What is the probability that at least eight CPA financial advisors have an average client size between $500,000 and $1 million?

c. What is the probability that two, three, or four CPA financial advisors have an average client size between $1 million and $5 million?

d. What is the probability that none of the CPA financial advisors have an average client size between $500,000 and $1 million? What is the probability that none have an average client size between $1 million and $5 million? Which probability is higher, and why?

5.4 | Poisson Distribution

A second discrete distribution is the **Poisson distribution**, seemingly different from the binomial distribution, but actually derived from the binomial distribution. Unlike the binomial distribution in which samples of size n are taken from a population with a proportion p, the Poisson distribution, named after Simeon-Denis Poisson (1781–1840), a French mathematician, focuses on the number of discrete occurrences over some interval or continuum.

The Poisson distribution describes the occurrence of *rare events*. In fact, the Poisson formula has been referred to as the *law of improbable events*. For example, serious accidents at a chemical plant are rare, and the number per month might be described by the Poisson distribution. The Poisson distribution often is used to describe the number of random arrivals per some time interval. If the number of arrivals per interval is too frequent, the time interval can be reduced enough so that a rare number of occurrences is expected. Another example of a Poisson distribution is the number of random customer arrivals per five-minute interval at a small boutique on weekday mornings.

In the field of management science, models used in queuing theory (theory of waiting lines) are usually based on the assumption that the Poisson distribution is the proper distribution to describe random arrival rates over a period of time. In the area of statistical quality control, the Poisson distribution is the basis for the c control chart used to track the number of nonconformances per item or unit.

The Poisson distribution has the following characteristics:

- It is a discrete distribution.
- It describes rare events.
- Each occurrence is independent of the other occurrences.
- It describes discrete occurrences over a continuum or interval.
- The occurrences in each interval can range from zero to infinity.
- The expected number of occurrences must hold constant throughout the experiment.

Examples of Poisson-type situations include the following:

1. Number of telephone calls per minute at a small business
2. Number of hazardous waste sites per county in the United States
3. Number of arrivals at a turnpike tollbooth per minute between 3 A.M. and 4 A.M. in January on the Kansas Turnpike
4. Number of sewing flaws per pair of jeans during production
5. Number of times a tire blows on a commercial airplane per week

Each of these examples represents a rare occurrence of events for some interval. Note that, although time is a more common interval for the Poisson distribution, intervals can range from a county in the United States to a pair of jeans. Some of the intervals in these examples might have zero occurrences. Moreover, the average occurrence per interval for many of these examples is probably in the single digits (1–9).

If a Poisson-distributed phenomenon is studied over a long period of time, a *long-run average* can be determined. This average is denoted **lambda** (λ). Each Poisson problem contains a lambda value from which the probabilities of particular occurrences are determined. Although n and p are required to describe a binomial distribution, a Poisson distribution can be described by λ alone. The Poisson formula is used to compute the probability of occurrences over an interval for a given lambda value.

Poisson Formula

$$P(x) = \frac{\lambda^x e^{-\lambda}}{x!}$$

where

$x = 0, 1, 2, 3, \ldots$
$\lambda = \text{long-run average}$
$e = 2.718282$

Here, x is the number of occurrences per interval for which the probability is being computed, λ is the long-run average, and $e = 2.718282$ is the base of natural logarithms.

A word of caution about using the Poisson distribution to study various phenomena is necessary. The λ value must hold constant throughout a Poisson experiment. The researcher must be careful not to apply a given lambda to intervals for which lambda changes. For example, the average number of customers arriving at a Macy's store during a one-minute interval will vary from hour to hour, day to day, and month to month. Different times of the day or week might produce different lambdas. The number of flaws per pair of jeans might vary from Monday to Friday. The researcher should be specific in describing the interval for which λ is being used.

Working Poisson Problems by Formula

Suppose bank customers arrive randomly on weekday afternoons at an average of 3.2 customers every 4 minutes. What is the probability of exactly 5 customers arriving in a 4-minute interval on a weekday afternoon? The lambda for this problem is 3.2 customers per 4 minutes. The value of x is 5 customers per 4 minutes. The probability of 5 customers randomly arriving during a 4-minute interval when the long-run average has been 3.2 customers per 4-minute interval is

$$\frac{(3.2)^5(e^{-3.2})}{5!} = \frac{(335.54)(.0408)}{120} = .1140$$

If a bank averages 3.2 customers every 4 minutes, the probability of 5 customers arriving during any one 4-minute interval is .1140.

What to Do When the Intervals Are Different

In actuality, the interval of a Poisson problem is used to assure the statistician that the lambda value and the value of x can be compared because they are recorded on the same basis. That is, having the same interval assures us of a "level playing field". Note that in the bank example shown in above, both λ and x were over a 4-minute interval. Suppose, however, the intervals are in the same units (minutes, county, manufactured item), but are not equal (e.g., 2 minutes for lambda but 5 minutes for x)? How do we account for this? Because lambda is a long-run average, we adjust lambda and its interval so that the interval for lambda is the same as the interval for x. If a bank is averaging 3.2 customers in 4 minutes, then it is also averaging 6.4 customers in 8 minutes and 1.6 customers in 2 minutes. **Never change the x interval!** Just because 3 customers arrive in 10 minutes does not mean that 6 customers will arrive in 20 minutes.

As an example, suppose that on Saturday mornings, a specialty clothing store averages 2.4 customer arrivals every 10 minutes. What is the probability that, on a given Saturday morning, 2 customers will arrive at the store in a 6-minute interval? The problem can be summarized as:

$$\lambda = 2.4 \, \text{customers}/10 \, \text{minutes}$$
$$x = 2 \, \text{customers}/6 \, \text{minutes}$$

Since the intervals are not the same, they must be reconciled. Remember, do not change the x interval—only the interval for lambda. Thus, we need to change the λ interval from 10 minutes to 6 minutes to match the x interval. One way is to recognize that 6 minutes (x interval) is 0.6 of 10 minutes. If we take 0.6 of both the number of customers and the interval for lambda, we compute the new lambda as:

$$0.6(2.4 \, \text{customers}) = 1.44 \, \text{customers and } 0.6(10 \, \text{minutes}) = 6 \, \text{minutes}$$
$$\lambda = 1.44 \, \text{customers}/6 \, \text{minutes}$$

We can use this new lambda and the old x interval of $x = 2$ customers/6 minutes to solve the problem as:

$$\frac{\lambda^x \cdot e^{-\lambda}}{x!} = \frac{1.44^2 \cdot e^{-1.44}}{2!} = .2456$$

In this case, it was relatively easy to change the interval for lambda into the x interval. Suppose, on the other hand, $\lambda = 2.8$ customers/7 minutes and $x = 4$ customers/11 minutes. While there are at least a couple of ways to reconcile the two intervals, one sure way is to divide the lambda interval by itself first. As an example, divide this lambda value and the interval by 7, resulting in $\lambda = 0.4$ customers/1 minute. Now multiply this interval by the x interval, which in this case is 11, resulting in a new lambda of $\lambda = 4.4$ customers/11 minutes. This new problem could be worked as:

$$\lambda = 4.4 \, \text{customers}/11 \, \text{minutes}$$
$$x = 4 \, \text{customers}/11 \, \text{minutes}$$

Using the Poisson Tables

For every new and different value of lambda, there is a different Poisson distribution. However, the Poisson distribution for a particular lambda is the same regardless of the nature of the interval associated with that lambda. Because of this, over time statisticians have recorded the probabilities of various Poisson distribution problems and organized these into what we refer to as the Poisson tables. More recently, computers have been used to solve virtually any Poisson distribution problem, adding to the size and potential of such Poisson tables. In Table A.3 of Appendix A, Poisson distribution tables are given for selected values of lambda. These tables can be used to solve many different Poisson problems and are especially useful when a researcher is working a cumulative problem. Table 5.10 presents a portion of Table A.3 that contains the probabilities of $x \leq 9$ if lambda is 1.6.

TABLE 5.10

Poisson Table for $\lambda = 1.6$

x	PROBABILITY
0	.2019
1	.3230
2	.2584
3	.1378
4	.0551
5	.0176
6	.0047
7	.0011
8	.0002
9	.0000

DEMONSTRATION PROBLEM 5.6

Suppose that during the noon hour in the holiday season, a UPS store averages 2.3 customers every minute and that arrivals at such a store are Poisson distributed. During such a season and time, what is the probability that more than four customers will arrive in a given minute?

Solution: This is a Poisson probability problem with $\lambda = 2.3$ and $x > 4$. To work this problem using the Poisson probability formula would involve many steps because the formula can only calculate probabilities for one x value at a time. Thus, to solve this problem using the formula, we would have to solve for each x of 5, 6, 7, 8, 9, 10, 11, 12, etc. and sum the answers. However, using the Poisson table for $\lambda = 2.3$, we need merely look up the answers in the table and sum them. Shown below are the Poisson table values for $\lambda = 2.3$ and the solution to this problem.

X	$\lambda = 2.3$
0	.1003
1	.2306
2	.2652
3	.2033
4	.1169
5	.0538
6	.0206
7	.0068
8	.0019
9	.0005
10	.0001
11	.0000
12	.0000

$X > 4$

.0837

If a store is averaging 2.3 customers per minute, the probability that more than four customers would arrive in any one minute is the sum of these table values, or **.0837**.

Mean and Standard Deviation of a Poisson Distribution

The mean or expected value of a Poisson distribution is λ. It is the long-run average of occurrences for an interval if many random samples are taken. Lambda usually is not a whole number, so most of the time actually observing lambda occurrences in an interval is impossible.

For example, suppose $\lambda = 6.5$/interval for some Poisson-distributed phenomenon. The resulting numbers of x occurrences in 20 different random samples from a Poisson distribution with $\lambda = 6.5$ might be as follows.

6 9 7 4 8 7 6 6 10 6 5 5 8 4 5 8 5 4 9 10

Computing the mean number of occurrences from this group of 20 intervals gives 6.6. In theory, for infinite sampling the long-run average is 6.5. Note from the samples that, when λ is 6.5, several 5s and 6s occur. Rarely would sample occurrences of 1, 2, 3, 11, 12, 13, . . . occur when $\lambda = 6.5$. Understanding the mean of a Poisson distribution gives a feel for the actual occurrences that are likely to happen.

The variance of a Poisson distribution also is λ. The standard deviation is $\sqrt{\lambda}$. Thus, for the Poisson distribution with $\lambda = 6.5$, the variance is 6.5 and the standard deviation is $\sqrt{6.5} = 2.55$.

Thinking Critically About Statistics in Business Today

Air Passengers' Complaints

In recent months, airline passengers have expressed much more dissatisfaction with airline service than ever before. Complaints include flight delays, lost baggage, long runway delays with little or no onboard service, overbooked flights, cramped space due to fuller flights, canceled flights, and grumpy airline employees. A majority of dissatisfied fliers merely grin and bear it. In fact, in the mid-1990s, the average number of complaints per 100,000 passengers boarded was only 0.66. For several years, the average number of complaints increased to 0.74, 0.86, 1.08, and 1.21.

In 2014, according to the Department of Transportation, the industrywide figure is an average of 1.34 complaints per 100,000 passengers. Alaska Airlines had the fewest average number of complaints per 100,000 with 0.42, followed by Southwest Airlines with 0.53. Frontier Airlines had the highest average number of complaints per 100,000 with 3.91 followed by United Airlines with 2.71. Because these average numbers of complaints per 100,000 are relatively small and occur randomly, such complaints may follow a Poisson distribution. In such a case, λ represents

the average number of complaints; and the interval is 100,000 passengers.

For example, using $\lambda = 1.34$ complaints (average for all airlines), if 100,000 boarded passengers were contacted, the probability that exactly three of them logged a complaint to the Department of Transportation could be computed as

$$\frac{(1.34)^3 e^{-1.34}}{3!} = .1050$$

That is, if 100,000 boarded passengers were contacted over and over, 10.50% of the time exactly three would have logged complaints with the Department of Transportation.

THINGS TO PONDER

1. Based on the figures given in this feature, can you reach any conclusions about the rate of passenger complaints in general?

2. Passenger complaints appear to be rare occurrences. Can you suggest some reasons why this is the case?

Graphing Poisson Distributions

The values in Table A.3, Appendix A, can be used to graph a Poisson distribution. The x values are on the x-axis and the probabilities are on the y-axis. **Figure 5.3** is a Minitab graph for the distribution of values for $\lambda = 1.6$.

The graph reveals a Poisson distribution skewed to the right. With a mean of 1.6 and a possible range of x from zero to infinity, the values obviously will "pile up" at 0, 1, and 2. Consider, however, the Minitab graph of the Poisson distribution for $\lambda = 6.5$ in **Figure 5.4**. Note that with $\lambda = 6.5$, the probabilities are greatest for the values of 5, 6, and 7. The graph has less skewness, because the probability of occurrence of values near zero is small, as are the probabilities of large values of x.

Using the Computer to Generate Poisson Distributions

Using the Poisson formula to compute probabilities can be tedious when one is working problems with cumulative probabilities. The Poisson tables in Table A.3, Appendix A, are faster to use than the Poisson formula. However, Poisson tables are limited by the amount of space available, and Table A.3 only includes probability values for Poisson distributions with lambda values to the tenths place in most cases. For researchers who want to use lambda

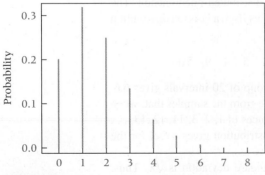

FIGURE 5.3 **Minitab Graph of the Poisson Distribution for $\lambda = 1.6$**

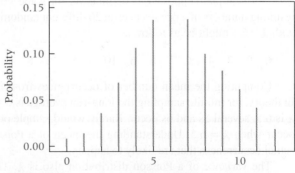

FIGURE 5.4 **Minitab Graph of the Poisson Distribution for $\lambda = 6.5$**

values with more precision or who feel that the computer is more convenient than textbook tables, some statistical computer software packages are an attractive option.

Minitab will produce a Poisson distribution for virtually any value of lambda. For example, one study by the National Center for Health Statistics claims that, on average, an American has 1.9 acute illnesses or injuries per year. If these cases are Poisson distributed, lambda is 1.9 per year. What does the Poisson probability distribution for this lambda look like? Table 5.11 contains the Minitab computer output for this distribution.

Excel can also generate probabilities of different values of *x* for any Poisson distribution. Table 5.12 displays the probabilities produced by Excel for a poisson distribution with a lambda of 3.7.

Approximating Binomial Problems by the Poisson Distribution

Certain types of binomial distribution problems can be approximated by using the Poisson distribution. Binomial problems with large sample sizes and small values of *p*, which then generate rare events, are potential candidates for use of the Poisson distribution. As a rule of thumb, if $n > 20$ and $n \cdot p \leq 7$, the approximation is close enough to use the Poisson distribution for binomial problems.

If these conditions are met and the binomial problem is a candidate for this process, the procedure begins with computation of the mean of the binomial distribution, $\mu = n \cdot p$. Because μ is the expected value of the binomial, it translates to the expected value, λ, of the Poisson distribution. Using μ as the λ value and using the *x* value of the binomial problem allows approximation of the probability from a Poisson table or by the Poisson formula.

Large values of *n* and small values of *p* usually are not included in binomial distribution tables, thereby precluding the use of binomial computational techniques. Using the Poisson distribution as an approximation to such a binomial problem in such cases is an attractive alternative; and indeed, when a computer is not available, it can be the only alternative.

As an example, the following binomial distribution problem can be worked by using the Poisson distribution: $n = 50$ and $p = .03$. What is the probability that $x = 4$? That is, $P(x = 4 | n = 50 \text{ and } p = .03) = ?$

To solve this equation, first determine lambda:

$$\lambda = \mu = n \cdot p = (50)(.03) = 1.5$$

TABLE 5.11	Minitab Output for the Poisson Distribution $\lambda = 1.9$
PROBABILITY DENSITY FUNCTION	
Poisson with mean = 1.9	
x	$P(X = x)$
0	0.149569
1	0.284180
2	0.269971
3	0.170982
4	0.081216
5	0.030862
6	0.009773
7	0.002653
8	0.000630
9	0.000133
10	0.000025

TABLE 5.12

Excel Output for the Poisson Distribution $\lambda = 3.7$

x	PROBABILITY
0	0.0247
1	0.0915
2	0.1692
3	0.2087
4	0.1931
5	0.1429
6	0.0881
7	0.0466
8	0.0215
9	0.0089
10	0.0033
11	0.0011
12	0.0003
13	0.0001
14	0.0000

As $n > 20$ and $n \cdot p \le 7$, this problem is a candidate for the Poisson approximation. For $x = 4$, Table A.3 yields a probability of .0471 for the Poisson approximation. For comparison, working the problem by using the binomial formula yields the following results:

$$_{50}C_4(.03)^4(.97)^{46} = .0459$$

The Poisson approximation is .0012 different from the result obtained by using the binomial formula to work the problem.

A Minitab graph of this binomial distribution ($n = 50$, $p = .03$) follows.

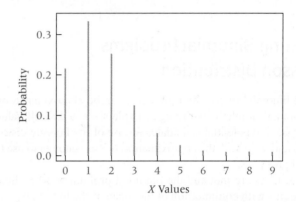

With $\lambda = 1.5$, the Poisson distribution can be generated. A Minitab graph of this Poisson distribution follows.

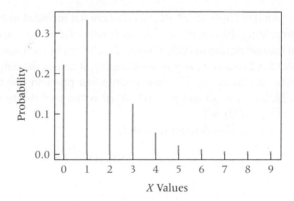

In comparing the two graphs, it is difficult to tell the difference between the binomial distribution and the Poisson distribution because the approximation of the binomial distribution by the Poisson distribution is close.

DEMONSTRATION PROBLEM 5.7

Suppose the probability of a bank making a mistake in processing a deposit is .0003. If 10,000 deposits (n) are audited, what is the probability that more than six mistakes were made in processing deposits?

Solution:

$$\lambda = \mu = n \cdot p = (10,000)(.0003) = 3.0$$

Because $n > 20$ and $n \cdot p \le 7$, the Poisson approximation is close enough to analyze $x > 6$. Table A.3 yields the following probabilities for $\lambda = 3.0$ and $x \ge 7$.

$\lambda = 3.0$	
x	PROBABILITY
7	.0216
8	.0081
9	.0027
10	.0008
11	.0002
12	.0001
	$x > 6 = .0335$

To work this problem by using the binomial formula requires starting with $x = 7$.

$$_{10,000}C_7(.0003)^7(.9997)^{9993}$$

This process would continue for x values of 8, 9, 10, 11, . . . , until the probabilities approach zero. Obviously, this process is impractical, making the Poisson approximation an attractive alternative.

5.4 Problems

5.17. Find the following values by using the Poisson formula.

  a. $P(x = 5 | \lambda = 2.3)$

  b. $P(x = 2 | \lambda = 3.9)$

  c. $P(x \leq 3 | \lambda = 4.1)$

  d. $P(x = 0 | \lambda = 2.7)$

  e. $P(x = 1 | \lambda = 5.4)$

  f. $P(4 < x < 8 | \lambda = 4.4)$

5.18. Find the following values by using the Poisson tables in Appendix A.

  a. $P(x = 6 | \lambda = 3.8)$

  b. $P(x > 7 | \lambda = 2.9)$

  c. $P(3 \leq x \leq 9 | \lambda = 4.2)$

  d. $P(x = 0 | \lambda = 1.9)$

  e. $P(x \leq 6 | \lambda = 2.9)$

  f. $P(5 < x \leq 8 | \lambda = 5.7)$

5.19. Sketch the graphs of the following Poisson distributions. Compute the mean and standard deviation for each distribution. Locate the mean on the graph. Note how the probabilities are graphed around the mean.

  a. $\lambda = 6.3$

  b. $\lambda = 1.3$

  c. $\lambda = 8.9$

  d. $\lambda = 0.6$

5.20. On Monday mornings, the First National Bank only has one teller window open for deposits and withdrawals. Experience has shown that the average number of arriving customers in a four-minute interval on Monday mornings is 2.8, and each teller can serve more than that number efficiently. These random arrivals at this bank on Monday mornings are Poisson distributed.

  a. What is the probability that on a Monday morning exactly six customers will arrive in a four-minute interval?

  b. What is the probability that no one will arrive at the bank to make a deposit or withdrawal during a four-minute interval?

  c. Suppose the teller can serve no more than four customers in any four-minute interval at this window on a Monday morning. What is the probability that, during any given four-minute interval, the teller will be unable to meet the demand? What is the probability that the teller will be able to meet the demand? When demand cannot be met during any given interval, a second window is opened. What percentage of the time will a second window have to be opened?

  d. What is the probability that exactly three people will arrive at the bank during a two-minute period on Monday mornings to make a deposit or a withdrawal? What is the probability that five or more customers will arrive during an eight-minute period?

5.21. A restaurant manager is interested in taking a more statistical approach to predicting customer load. She begins the process by gathering data. One of the restaurant hosts or hostesses is assigned to count customers every five minutes from 7 P.M. until 8 P.M. every Saturday night for three weeks. The data are shown here. After the data are gathered, the manager computes lambda using the data from all three weeks as one data set as a basis for probability analysis. What value of lambda did she find? Assume that these customers randomly arrive and that the arrivals are Poisson distributed. Use the value of lambda computed by the manager and help the manager calculate the probabilities in parts (a) through (e) for any given five-minute interval between 7 P.M. and 8 P.M. on Saturday night.

NUMBER OF ARRIVALS		
WEEK 1	WEEK 2	WEEK 3
3	1	5
6	2	3
4	4	5
6	0	3
2	2	5
3	6	4
1	5	7
5	4	3
1	2	4
0	5	8
3	3	1
3	4	3

a. What is the probability that no customers arrive during any given five-minute interval?

b. What is the probability that six or more customers arrive during any given five-minute interval?

c. What is the probability that during a 10-minute interval fewer than four customers arrive?

d. What is the probability that between three and six (inclusive) customers arrive in any 10-minute interval?

e. What is the probability that exactly eight customers arrive in any 15-minute interval?

5.22. According to the United National Environmental Program and World Health Organization, in Mumbai, India, air pollution standards for particulate matter are exceeded an average of 5.6 days in every three-week period. Assume that the distribution of number of days exceeding the standards per three-week period is Poisson distributed.

a. What is the probability that the standard is not exceeded on any day during a three-week period?

b. What is the probability that the standard is exceeded exactly six days of a three-week period?

c. What is the probability that the standard is exceeded 15 or more days during a three-week period? If this outcome actually occurred, what might you conclude?

5.23. Ship collisions in the Houston Ship Channel are rare. Suppose the number of collisions are Poisson distributed, with a mean of 1.2 collisions every four months.

a. What is the probability of having no collisions occur over a four-month period?

b. What is the probability of having exactly two collisions in a two-month period?

c. What is the probability of having one or fewer collisions in a six-month period? If this outcome occurred, what might you conclude about ship channel conditions during this period? What might you conclude about ship channel safety awareness during this period? What might you conclude about weather conditions during this period? What might you conclude about lambda?

5.24. A pen company averages 1.2 defective pens per carton produced (200 pens). The number of defects per carton is Poisson distributed.

a. What is the probability of selecting a carton and finding no defective pens?

b. What is the probability of finding eight or more defective pens in a carton?

c. Suppose a purchaser of these pens will quit buying from the company if a carton contains more than three defective pens. What is the probability that a carton contains more than three defective pens?

5.25. A medical researcher estimates that .00004 of the population has a rare blood disorder. If the researcher randomly selects 100,000 people from the population,

a. What is the probability that seven or more people will have the rare blood disorder?

b. What is the probability that more than 10 people will have the rare blood disorder?

c. Suppose the researcher gets more than 10 people who have the rare blood disorder in the sample of 100,000 but that the sample was taken from a particular geographic region. What might the researcher conclude from the results?

5.26. A data firm records a large amount of data. Historically, .9% of the pages of data recorded by the firm contain errors. If 200 pages of data are randomly selected,

a. What is the probability that six or more pages contain errors?

b. What is the probability that more than 10 pages contain errors?

c. What is the probability that none of the pages contain errors?

d. What is the probability that fewer than five pages contain errors?

5.5 | Hypergeometric Distribution

Another discrete statistical distribution is the hypergeometric distribution. Statisticians often use the **hypergeometric distribution** to complement the types of analyses that can be made by using the binomial distribution. Recall that the binomial distribution applies, in theory, only to experiments in which the trials are done with replacement (independent events). The hypergeometric distribution applies only to experiments in which the trials are done without replacement.

The hypergeometric distribution, like the binomial distribution, consists of two possible outcomes: success and failure. However, the user must know the size of the population and the proportion of successes and failures in the population to apply the hypergeometric distribution. In other words, because the hypergeometric distribution is used when sampling is done without replacement, information about population makeup must be known in order to redetermine the probability of a success in each successive trial as the probability changes.

The hypergeometric distribution has the following characteristics:

- It is a discrete distribution.
- Each outcome consists of either a success or a failure.
- Sampling is done without replacement.
- The population, N, is finite and known.
- The number of successes in the population, A, is known.

Hypergeometric Formula

$$P(x) = \frac{_{A}C_{x} \cdot {}_{N-A}C_{n-x}}{_{N}C_{n}}$$

where

N = size of the population
n = sample size
A = number of successes in the population
x = number of successes in the sample; sampling is done *without* replacement

A hypergeometric distribution is characterized or described by three parameters: N, A, and n. Because of the multitude of possible combinations of these three parameters, creating tables for the hypergeometric distribution is practically impossible. Hence, the researcher who selects the hypergeometric distribution for analyzing data must use the hypergeometric formula to calculate each probability. Because this task can be tedious and time-consuming, most researchers use the hypergeometric distribution as a fallback position when working binomial problems without replacement. Even though the binomial distribution theoretically applies only when sampling is done with replacement and p stays constant, recall that, if the population is large enough in comparison with the sample size, the impact of sampling without replacement on p is minimal. Thus the binomial distribution can be used in some situations when sampling is done without replacement. Because of the tables available, using the binomial distribution instead of the hypergeometric distribution whenever possible is preferable. As a rule of thumb, if the sample size is less than 5% of the population, use of the binomial distribution rather than the hypergeometric distribution is acceptable when sampling is done without replacement. The hypergeometric distribution yields the exact probability, and the binomial distribution yields a good approximation of the probability in these situations.

In summary, the hypergeometric distribution should be used instead of the binomial distribution when the following conditions are present:

1. Sampling is being done without replacement.
2. $n \geq 5\% N$.

Hypergeometric probabilities are calculated under the assumption of equally likely sampling of the remaining elements of the sample space.

As an application of the hypergeometric distribution, consider the following problem. Twenty-four people, of whom eight are women, apply for a job. If five of the applicants are sampled randomly, what is the probability that exactly three of those sampled are women?

This problem contains a small, finite population of 24, or $N = 24$. A sample of five applicants is taken, or $n = 5$. The sampling is being done without replacement, because the five applicants selected for the sample are five different people. The sample size is 21% of the population, which is greater than 5% of the population $(n/N = 5/24 = .21)$. The hypergeometric distribution is the appropriate distribution to use. The population breakdown is $A = 8$

women (successes) and $N - A = 24 - 8 = 16$ men. The probability of getting $x = 3$ women in the sample of $n = 5$ is

$$\frac{_8C_3 \cdot _{16}C_2}{_{24}C_5} = \frac{(56)(120)}{42,504} = .1581$$

Conceptually, the combination in the denominator of the hypergeometric formula yields all the possible ways of getting n samples from a population, N, including the ones with the desired outcome. In this problem, there are 42,504 ways of selecting five people from 24 people. The numerator of the hypergeometric formula computes all the possible ways of getting x successes from the A successes available and $n - x$ failures from the $N - A$ available failures in the population. There are 56 ways of getting three women from a pool of eight, and there are 120 ways of getting two men from a pool of 16. The combinations of each are multiplied in the numerator because the joint probability of getting x successes and $n - x$ failures is being computed.

DEMONSTRATION PROBLEM 5.8

Suppose 18 major computer companies operate in the United States and 12 are located in California's Silicon Valley. If three computer companies are selected randomly from the entire list, what is the probability that one or more of the selected companies are located in the Silicon Valley?

Solution:

$$N = 18, \ n = 3, \ A = 12, \text{ and } x \geq 1$$

This problem is actually three problems in one: $x = 1$, $x = 2$, and $x = 3$. Sampling is being done without replacement, and the sample size is 16.6% of the population. Hence this problem is a candidate for the hypergeometric distribution. The solution follows.

$$
\begin{array}{ccccc}
x = 1 & & x = 2 & & x = 3 \\[4pt]
\dfrac{_{12}C_1 \cdot _6C_2}{_{18}C_3} & + & \dfrac{_{12}C_2 \cdot _6C_1}{_{18}C_3} & + & \dfrac{_{12}C_3 \cdot _6C_0}{_{18}C_3} = \\[12pt]
.2206 & + & .4853 & + & .2696 \quad = .9755
\end{array}
$$

An alternative solution method using the law of complements would be one minus the probability that none of the companies is located in Silicon Valley, or

$$1 - P(x = 0 \mid N = 18, \ n = 3, \ A = 12)$$

Thus,

$$1 - \frac{_{12}C_0 \cdot _6C_3}{_{18}C_3} = 1 - .0245 = .9755$$

Using the Computer to Solve for Hypergeometric Distribution Probabilities

Using Minitab or Excel, it is possible to solve for hypergeometric distribution probabilities on the computer. Both software packages require the input of N, A, n, and x. In either package, the resulting output is the exact probability for that particular value of x. The Minitab output for the example presented in this section, where $N = 24$ people of whom $A = 8$ are women, $n = 5$

TABLE 5.13 Minitab Output for Hypergeometric Problem

PROBABILITY DENSITY FUNCTION	
Hypergeometric with $N = 24$, $M = 8$ and $n = 5$	
x	$P(X = x)$
3	0.158103

TABLE 5.14 Excel Output for a Hypergeometric Problem

The probability of $x = 3$ when $N = 24$, $n = 5$, and $A = 8$ is: 0.158103

are randomly selected, and $x = 3$ are women, is displayed in Table 5.13. Note that Minitab represents successes in the population as "M." The Excel output for this same problem is presented in Table 5.14.

5.5 Problems

5.27. Compute the following probabilities by using the hypergeometric formula.

a. The probability of $x = 3$ if $N = 11$, $A = 8$, and $n = 4$
b. The probability of $x < 2$ if $N = 15$, $A = 5$, and $n = 6$
c. The probability of $x = 0$ if $N = 9$, $A = 2$, and $n = 3$
d. The probability of $x > 4$ if $N = 20$, $A = 5$, and $n = 7$

5.28. Shown here are the top 19 companies in the world in terms of oil refining capacity. Some of the companies are privately owned and others are state owned. Suppose six companies are randomly selected.

a. What is the probability that exactly one company is privately owned?
b. What is the probability that exactly four companies are privately owned?
c. What is the probability that all six companies are privately owned?
d. What is the probability that none of the companies is privately owned?

COMPANY	OWNERSHIP STATUS
ExxonMobil	Private
Royal Dutch/Shell	Private
Sinopec	Private
British Petroleum	Private
ConocoPhillips	Private
Petroleos de Venezuela	State
Total	Private
Valero Energy	Private
China National	State
Saudi Arabian	State
Petroleo Brasilerio	State
Chevron	Private
Petroleos Mexicanos	State
National Iranian	State

Nippon	Private
Rosneft (Russia)	State
OAO Lukoil	Private
Repsol YPF	Private
Kuwait National	State

5.29. Bloomberg L.P. lists the top 20 U.S. companies by revenue. Walmart stores is number one followed by Exxon Mobil and Chevron. Of the 20 companies on the list, 8 are in some type of electronics-related business. Suppose four firms are randomly selected.

a. What is the probability that none of the firms is in some type of electronics-related business?
b. What is the probability that all four of the firms is in some type of electronics-related business?
c. What is the probability that exactly two of the firms is in some type of electronics-related business?

5.30. W. Edwards Deming in his red bead experiment had a box of 4,000 beads, of which 800 were red and 3,200 were white.* Suppose a researcher were to conduct a modified version of the red bead experiment. In her experiment, she has a bag of 20 beads, of which 4 are red and 16 are white. This experiment requires a participant to reach into the bag and randomly select five beads, one at a time, without replacement.

a. What is the probability that the participant will select exactly four white beads?
b. What is the probability that the participant will select exactly four red beads?
c. What is the probability that the participant will select all red beads?

5.31. Shown here are the top 10 U.S. cities ranked by number of hotel rooms sold in a recent year.

RANK	CITY	NUMBER OF ROOMS SOLD
1	Las Vegas (NV)	40,000,000
2	Orlando (FL)	27,200,000
3	Los Angeles (CA)	25,500,000

*Mary Walton, "Deming's Parable of Red Beads," Across the Board (February 1987): 43–48.

4	Chicago (IL)	24,800,000
5	New York City (NY)	23,900,000
6	Washington (DC)	22,800,000
7	Atlanta (GA)	21,500,000
8	Dallas (TX)	15,900,000
9	Houston (TX)	14,500,000
10	San Diego (CA)	14,200,000

Suppose four of these cities are selected randomly.

a. What is the probability that exactly two cities are in California?

b. What is the probability that none of the cities is east of the Mississippi River?

c. What is the probability that exactly three of the cities are ones with more than 24 million rooms sold?

5.32. A company produces and ships 16 personal computers knowing that four of them have defective wiring. The company that purchased the computers is going to thoroughly test three of the computers. The purchasing company can detect the defective wiring. What is the probability that the purchasing company will find the following?

a. No defective computers

b. Exactly three defective computers

c. Two or more defective computers

d. One or fewer defective computer

5.33. A western city has 18 police officers eligible for promotion. Eleven of the 18 are Hispanic. Suppose only five of the police officers are chosen for promotion and that one is Hispanic. If the officers chosen for promotion had been selected by chance alone, what is the probability that one or fewer of the five promoted officers would have been Hispanic? What might this result indicate?

Decision Dilemma Solved

Life with a Cell Phone

Suppose that 44% of cell phone owners in the United States use only cellular phones. If 20 Americans are randomly selected, what is the probability that more than 12 use only cell phones? Converting the 44% to a proportion, the value of p is .44 and this is a classic binomial distribution problem with $n = 20$ and $x > 12$. Because the binomial distribution probability tables (Appendix A, Table A.2) do not include $p = .44$, the problem will have to be solved using the binomial formula for each of $x = 13, 14, 15, \ldots, 20$.

$$\text{For } x = 13: \quad {}_{20}C_{13}(.44)^{13}(.56)^7 = .0310$$

Solving for $x = 14, 15, 16, 17,$ and 18 in a similar manner results in probabilities of .0122, .0038, .0009, .0002, and .0000 respectively. Since the probabilities "zero out" (four decimal places) at $x = 18$, we need not proceed on to $x = 19$ and 20. Summing the probabilities for $x = 13$ through $x = 18$ results in a total probability of .0481 as the answer to the posed question. To further understand these probabilities, we can calculate the expected value of this distribution as:

$$\mu = n \cdot p = 20(.44) = 8.8$$

In the long run, one would expect to average about 8.8 Americans out of every 20 who consider their cell phone as their primary phone. In light of this, there is a small probability (.0481) that more than 12 Americans would do so.

It was reported that 90% of American adults own a cell phone. On the basis of this, if you were to randomly select 25 American adults, what is the probability that fewer than 20 own a cell phone? This problem is a binomial distribution problem with $n = 25$, $p = .90$, and $x < 20$. Because this is a cumulative problem and because $p = .90$ can be found in the binomial distribution tables, we can use Table A.2 to help us solve this problem:

x	PROBABILITY
19	.024
18	.007
17	.002
16	.000

The total of these probabilities is .033. Probabilities for all other values ($x \leq 15$) are displayed as .000 in the binomial probability table and are not included here. If 90% of American adults own a cell phone, the probability is very small (.033) that out of 25 randomly selected American adults, less than 20 would own a cell phone. The expected number is 25(.90) = 22.5.

Suppose, on average, mobile phone users receive 1.5 calls every two hours. Given that information, what is the probability that a mobile phone user would receive no calls in a two-hour period? Since random phone calls are generally thought to be Poisson distributed, this problem can be solved by using either the Poisson probability formula or the Poisson tables (A.3, Appendix A). In this problem, $\lambda = 1.5$ and $x = 0$; and the probability associated with this is:

$$\frac{\lambda^x e^{-\lambda}}{x!} = \frac{1.5^0 e^{-1.5}}{0!} = .2231$$

What is the probability that a mobile phone user receives five or more calls in a two-hour period? Since this is a cumulative probability question ($x \geq 5$), the best option is to use the Poisson probability tables (A.3, Appendix A) to obtain:

x	PROBABILITY
5	.0141
6	.0035
7	.0008
8	.0001
9	.0000
	.0185

There is a 1.85% chance that a mobile phone user will receive five or more calls in two hours if, on average, such a mobile phone user averages 1.5 calls per two hours.

Summary

Probability experiments produce random outcomes. A variable that contains the outcomes of a random experiment is called a random variable. Random variables such that the set of all possible values is at most a finite or countably infinite number of possible values are called discrete random variables. Random variables that take on values at all points over a given interval are called continuous random variables. Discrete distributions are constructed from discrete random variables. Continuous distributions are constructed from continuous random variables. Three discrete distributions are the binomial distribution, Poisson distribution, and hypergeometric distribution.

The binomial distribution fits experiments when only two mutually exclusive outcomes are possible. In theory, each trial in a binomial experiment must be independent of the other trials. However, if the population size is large enough in relation to the sample size ($n < 5\% \, N$), the binomial distribution can be used where applicable in cases where the trials are not independent. The probability of getting a desired outcome on any one trial is denoted as p, which is denoted as the probability of getting a success. The binomial formula is used to determine the probability of obtaining x outcomes in n trials. Binomial distribution problems can be solved more rapidly with the use of binomial tables than by formula. Table A.2 of Appendix A contains binomial tables for selected values of n and p.

The Poisson distribution usually is used to analyze phenomena that produce rare occurrences over some interval. The only information required to generate a Poisson distribution is the long-run average, which is denoted by lambda (λ). The assumptions are that each occurrence is independent of other occurrences and that the value of lambda remains constant throughout the experiment. Poisson probabilities can be determined by either the Poisson formula or the Poisson tables in Table A.3 of Appendix A. The Poisson distribution can be used to approximate binomial distribution problems when n is large ($n > 20$), p is small, and $n \cdot p \leq 7$.

The hypergeometric distribution is a discrete distribution that is usually used for binomial-type experiments when the population is small and finite and sampling is done without replacement. Because using the hypergeometric distribution is a tedious process, using the binomial distribution whenever possible is generally more advantageous.

Key Terms

binomial distribution
continuous distributions
continuous random variables

discrete distributions
discrete random variables
hypergeometric distribution

lambda (λ)
mean or expected value

Poisson distribution
random variable

Formulas

Mean (expected) value of a discrete distribution

$$\mu = E(x) = \Sigma[x \cdot P(x)]$$

Variance of a discrete distribution

$$\sigma^2 = \Sigma[(x - \mu)^2 \cdot P(x)]$$

Standard deviation of a discrete distribution

$$\sigma = \sqrt{\Sigma[(x - \mu)^2 \cdot P(x)]}$$

Binomial formula

$$_nC_x \cdot p^x \cdot q^{n-x} = \frac{n!}{x!(n-x)!} \cdot p^x \cdot q^{n-x}$$

Mean of a binomial distribution

$$\mu = n \cdot p$$

Standard deviation of a binomial distribution

$$\sigma = \sqrt{n \cdot p \cdot q}$$

Poisson formula

$$P(x) = \frac{\lambda^x e^{-\lambda}}{x!}$$

Hypergeometric formula

$$P(x) = \frac{_AC_x \cdot {}_{N-A}C_{n-x}}{_NC_n}$$

Ethical Considerations

Several points must be emphasized about the use of discrete distributions to analyze data. The independence and/or size assumptions must be met in using the binomial distribution in situations where sampling is done without replacement. Size and λ assumptions must be satisfied in using the Poisson distribution to approximate binomial problems. In either case, failure to meet such assumptions can result in spurious conclusions.

As n increases, the use of binomial distributions to study exact x-value probabilities becomes questionable in decision making. Although the probabilities are mathematically correct, as n becomes larger, the probability of any particular x value becomes lower because there are more values among which to split the probabilities. For example, if $n = 100$ and $p = .50$, the probability of $x = 50$ is .0796. This probability of occurrence appears quite low, even though $x = 50$ is the expected value of this distribution and is also the value most likely to occur. It is more useful to decision makers and, in a sense, probably more ethical to present

cumulative values for larger sizes of n. In this example, it is probably more useful to examine $P(x > 50)$ than $P(x = 50)$.

The reader is warned in the chapter that the value of λ is assumed to be constant in a Poisson distribution experiment. Researchers may produce spurious results because the λ value changes during a study. For example, suppose the value of λ is obtained for the number of customer arrivals at a toy store between 7 P.M. and 9 P.M. in the month of December. Because December is an active month in terms of traffic volume through a toy store, the use of such a λ to analyze arrivals at the same store between noon and 2 P.M. in February would be inappropriate and, in a sense, unethical.

Errors in judgment such as these are probably more a case of misuse than lack of ethics. However, it is important that statisticians and researchers adhere to assumptions and appropriate applications of these techniques. The inability or unwillingness to do so opens the way for unethical decision making.

Supplementary Problems

Calculating the Statistics

5.34. Solve for the probabilities of the following binomial distribution problems by using the binomial formula.

    a. If $n = 11$ and $p = .23$, what is the probability that $x = 4$?

    b. If $n = 6$ and $p = .50$, what is the probability that $x \geq 1$?

    c. If $n = 9$ and $p = .85$, what is the probability that $x > 7$?

    d. If $n = 14$ and $p = .70$, what is the probability that $x \leq 3$?

5.35. Use Table A.2, Appendix A, to find the values of the following binomial distribution problems.

    a. $P(x = 14 | n = 20$ and $p = .60)$

    b. $P(x < 5 | n = 10$ and $p = .30)$

    c. $P(x \geq 12 | n = 15$ and $p = .60)$

    d. $P(x > 20 | n = 25$ and $p = .40)$

5.36. Use the Poisson formula to solve for the probabilities of the following Poisson distribution problems.

    a. If $\lambda = 1.25$, what is the probability that $x = 4$?

    b. If $\lambda = 6.37$, what is the probability that $x \leq 1$?

    c. If $\lambda = 2.4$, what is the probability that $x > 5$?

5.37. Use Table A.3, Appendix A, to find the following Poisson distribution values.

    a. $P(x = 3 | \lambda = 1.8)$

    b. $P(x < 5 | \lambda = 3.3)$

    c. $P(x \geq 3 | \lambda = 2.1)$

    d. $P(2 < x \leq 5 | \lambda = 4.2)$

5.38. Solve the following problems by using the hypergeometric formula.

    a. If $N = 6$, $n = 4$, and $A = 5$, what is the probability that $x = 3$?

    b. If $N = 10$, $n = 3$, and $A = 5$, what is the probability that $x \leq 1$?

    c. If $N = 13$, $n = 5$, and $A = 3$, what is the probability that $x \geq 2$?

Testing Your Understanding

5.39. In a study by Peter D. Hart Research Associates for the Nasdaq Stock Market, it was determined that 20% of all stock investors are retired people. In addition, 40% of all U.S. adults invest in mutual funds. Suppose a random sample of 25 stock investors is taken.

    a. What is the probability that exactly seven are retired people?

    b. What is the probability that 10 or more are retired people?

    c. How many retired people would you expect to find in a random sample of 25 stock investors?

    d. Suppose a random sample of 20 U.S. adults is taken. What is the probability that exactly eight adults invested in mutual funds?

    e. Suppose a random sample of 20 U.S. adults is taken. What is the probability that fewer than six adults invested in mutual funds?

    f. Suppose a random sample of 20 U.S. adults is taken. What is the probability that none of the adults invested in mutual funds?

    g. Suppose a random sample of 20 U.S. adults is taken. What is the probability that 12 or more adults invested in mutual funds?

    h. For parts e–g, what exact number of adults would produce the highest probability? How does this compare to the expected number?

5.40. A service station has a pump that distributes diesel fuel to automobiles. The station owner estimates that only about 3.2 cars use the diesel pump every 2 hours. Assume the arrivals of diesel pump users are Poisson distributed.

    a. What is the probability that three cars will arrive to use the diesel pump during a one-hour period?

    b. Suppose the owner needs to shut down the diesel pump for half an hour to make repairs. However, the owner hates to lose any business. What is the probability that no cars will arrive to use the diesel pump during a half-hour period?

c. Suppose five cars arrive during a one-hour period to use the diesel pump. What is the probability of five or more cars arriving during a one-hour period to use the diesel pump? If this outcome actually occurred, what might you conclude?

5.41. In a particular manufacturing plant, two machines (A and B) produce a particular part. One machine (B) is newer and faster. In one five-minute period, a lot consisting of 32 parts is produced. Twenty-two are produced by machine B and the rest by machine A. Suppose an inspector randomly samples a dozen of the parts from this lot.

a. What is the probability that exactly three parts were produced by machine A?

b. What is the probability that half of the parts were produced by each machine?

c. What is the probability that all of the parts were produced by machine B?

d. What is the probability that seven, eight, or nine parts were produced by machine B?

5.42. Suppose that, for every lot of 100 computer chips a company produces, an average of 1.4 are defective. Another company buys many lots of these chips at a time, from which one lot is selected randomly and tested for defects. If the tested lot contains more than three defects, the buyer will reject all the lots sent in that batch. What is the probability that the buyer will accept the lots? Assume that the defects per lot are Poisson distributed.

5.43. The National Center for Health Statistics reports that 25% of all Americans between the ages of 65 and 74 have a chronic heart condition. Suppose you live in a state where the environment is conducive to good health and low stress and you believe the conditions in your state promote healthy hearts. To investigate this theory, you conduct a random telephone survey of 20 persons 65 to 74 years of age in your state.

a. On the basis of the figure from the National Center for Health Statistics, what is the expected number of persons 65 to 74 years of age in your survey who have a chronic heart condition?

b. Suppose only one person in your survey has a chronic heart condition. What is the probability of getting one or fewer people with a chronic heart condition in a sample of 20 if 25% of the population in this age bracket has this health problem? What do you conclude about your state from the sample data?

5.44. A survey conducted for the Northwestern National Life Insurance Company revealed that 70% of American workers say job stress caused frequent health problems. One in three said they expected to burn out in the job in the near future. Thirty-four percent said they thought seriously about quitting their job last year because of workplace stress. Fifty-three percent said they were required to work more than 40 hours a week very often or somewhat often.

a. Suppose a random sample of 10 American workers is selected. What is the probability that more than seven of them say job stress caused frequent health problems? What is the expected number of workers who say job stress caused frequent health problems?

b. Suppose a random sample of 15 American workers is selected. What is the expected number of these sampled workers who say they will burn out in the near future? What is the probability that none of the workers say they will burn out in the near future?

c. Suppose a sample of seven workers is selected randomly. What is the probability that all seven say they are asked very often or somewhat often to work more than 40 hours a week? If this outcome actually happened, what might you conclude?

5.45. According to Padgett Business Services, 20% of all small-business owners say the most important advice for starting a business is to prepare for long hours and hard work. Twenty-five percent say the most important advice is to have good financing ready. Nineteen percent say having a good plan is the most important advice; 18% say studying the industry is the most important advice; and 18% list other advice. Suppose 12 small business owners are contacted, and assume that the percentages hold for all small-business owners.

a. What is the probability that none of the owners would say preparing for long hours and hard work is the most important advice?

b. What is the probability that six or more owners would say preparing for long hours and hard work is the most important advice?

c. What is the probability that exactly five owners would say having good financing ready is the most important advice?

d. What is the expected number of owners who would say having a good plan is the most important advice?

5.46. According to a recent survey, the probability that a passenger files a complaint with the Department of Transportation about a particular U.S. airline is .000014. Suppose 100,000 passengers who flew with this particular airline are randomly contacted.

a. What is the probability that exactly five passengers filed complaints?

b. What is the probability that none of the passengers filed complaints?

c. What is the probability that more than six passengers filed complaints?

5.47. A hair stylist has been in business one year. Sixty percent of his customers are walk-in business. If he randomly samples eight of the people from last week's list of customers, what is the probability that three or fewer were walk-ins? If this outcome actually occurred, what would be some of the explanations for it?

5.48. A Department of Transportation survey showed that 60% of U.S. residents over 65 years of age oppose use of cell phones in flight even if there were no issues with the phones interfering with aircraft communications systems. If this information is correct and if a researcher randomly selects 25 U.S. residents who are over 65 years of age,

a. What is the probability that exactly 12 oppose the use of cell phones in flight?

b. What is the probability that more than 17 oppose the use of cell phones in flight?

c. What is the probability that less than eight oppose the use of cell phones in flight? If the researcher actually got less than eight, what might she conclude about the Department of Transportation survey?

5.49. A survey conducted by the Consumer Reports National Research Center reported, among other things, that women spend an average of 1.2 hours per week shopping online. Assume that hours per week shopping online are Poisson distributed. If this survey result is true for all women and if a woman is randomly selected,

a. What is the probability that she did not shop at all online over a one-week period?

b. What is the probability that a woman would shop three or more hours online during a one-week period?

c. What is the probability that a woman would shop fewer than five hours in a three-week period?

5.50. According to the Audit Bureau of Circulations, the top 25 city newspapers in the United States ranked according to circulation are:

RANK	NEWSPAPER
1	New York Times (NY)
2	Los Angeles Times (CA)
3	San Jose Mercury News (CA)
4	New York Daily News (NY)
5	New York Post (NY)
6	Washington Post (DC)
7	Chicago Sun Times (IL)
8	Chicago Tribune (IL)
9	Long Island Newsday (NY)
10	Denver Post (CO)
11	Dallas Morning News (TX)
12	Houston Chronicle (TX)
13	Arizona Republic (AZ)
14	Oregonian (OR)
15	Cleveland Plain Dealer (OH)
16	Minneapolis Star Tribune (MN)
17	Newark Star-Ledger (NJ)
18	Orange County Register (CA)
19	San Diego Union-Tribune (CA)
20	Boston Globe (MA)
21	Tampa Bay Times (FL)
22	Detroit Free Press (MI)
23	Atlanta Journal Constitution (GA)
24	Seattle Times (WA)
25	San Francisco Chronicle (CA)

Suppose a researcher wants to sample a portion of these newspapers and compare the sizes of the business sections of the Sunday papers. She randomly samples eight of these newspapers.

a. What is the probability that the sample contains exactly one newspaper located in New York state?

b. What is the probability that half of the sampled newspapers are ranked in the top 10 by circulation?

c. What is the probability that none of the newspapers is located in California?

d. What is the probability that exactly three of the newspapers are located in states that begin with the letter *M*?

5.51. An office in Albuquerque has 24 workers including management. Eight of the workers commute to work from the west side of the Rio Grande River. Suppose six of the office workers are randomly selected.

a. What is the probability that all six workers commute from the west side of the Rio Grande?

b. What is the probability that none of the workers commute from the west side of the Rio Grande?

c. Which probability from parts (a) and (b) was greatest? Why do you think this is?

d. What is the probability that half of the workers do not commute from the west side of the Rio Grande?

5.52. According to the U.S. Census Bureau, 20% of the workers in Atlanta use public transportation. If 25 Atlanta workers are randomly

selected, what is the expected number to use public transportation? Graph the binomial distribution for this sample. What are the mean and the standard deviation for this distribution? What is the probability that more than 12 of the selected workers use public transportation? Explain conceptually and from the graph why you would get this probability. Suppose you randomly sample 25 Atlanta workers and actually get 14 who use public transportation. Is this outcome likely? How might you explain this result?

5.53. One of the earliest applications of the Poisson distribution was in analyzing incoming calls to a telephone switchboard. Analysts generally believe that random phone calls are Poisson distributed. Suppose phone calls to a switchboard arrive at an average rate of 2.4 calls per minute.

a. If an operator wants to take a one-minute break, what is the probability that there will be no calls during a one-minute interval?

b. If an operator can handle at most five calls per minute, what is the probability that the operator will be unable to handle the calls in any one-minute period?

c. What is the probability that exactly three calls will arrive in a two-minute interval?

d. What is the probability that one or fewer calls will arrive in a 15-second interval?

5.54. A survey by Frank N. Magid Associates revealed that 3% of Americans are not connected to the Internet at home. Another researcher randomly selects 70 Americans.

a. What is the expected number of these who would not be connected to the Internet at home?

b. What is the probability that eight or more are not connected to the Internet at home?

c. What is the probability that between three and six (inclusive) are not connected to the Internet at home?

5.55. Suppose that in the bookkeeping operation of a large corporation the probability of a recording error on any one billing is .005. Suppose the probability of a recording error from one billing to the next is constant, and 1,000 billings are randomly sampled by an auditor.

a. What is the probability that fewer than four billings contain a recording error?

b. What is the probability that more than 10 billings contain a billing error?

c. What is the probability that all 1,000 billings contain no recording errors?

5.56. According to the American Medical Association, about 36% of all U.S. physicians under the age of 35 are women. Your company has just hired eight physicians under the age of 35 and none is a woman. If a group of women physicians under the age of 35 want to sue your company for discriminatory hiring practices, would they have a strong case based on these numbers? Use the binomial distribution to determine the probability of the company's hiring result occurring randomly, and comment on the potential justification for a lawsuit.

5.57. The following table lists the 25 largest U.S. higher education institutions according to enrollment figures from U.S. Department of Education. The state of location is given in parenthesis.

RANK	UNIVERSITY	ENROLLMENT
1	University of Phoenix (AZ)	442,033
2	Ivy Tech Community College (IN)	175,313
3	Ashford University (IA)	169,843

4	American Public University System (WV)	110,644
5	Miami Dade College (FL)	100,855
6	Lone Star College System (TX)	98,313
7	Liberty University (VA)	95,639
8	Houston Community College (TX)	93,625
9	Arizona State University (AZ)	81,789
10	Kaplan University (IA)	77,566
11	Northern Virginia Community College (VA)	76,552
12	Walden University (MN)	75,895
13	Tarrant County College District (TX)	75,547
14	Grand Canyon University (AZ)	71,712
15	Austin Community College District (TX)	70,452
16	University of Central Florida (FL)	69,086
17	Ohio State University (OH)	64,930
18	University of Maryland (MD)	64,737
19	University of Minnesota (MN)	63,929
20	Broward College (FL)	62,796
21	Florida International University (FL)	60,592
22	Valencia College (FL)	60,469
23	University of Florida (FL)	56,683
24	East Los Angeles College (CA)	56,395
25	College of Southern Nevada (NV)	56,364

a. If five different universities are selected randomly from the list, what is the probability that three of them have enrollments of 70,000 or more?

b. If eight different universities are selected randomly from the list, what is the probability that two or fewer are universities in Florida?

c. Suppose universities are being selected randomly from this list with replacement. If five universities are sampled, what is the probability that the sample will contain exactly two universities in Texas?

5.58. In one midwestern city, the government has 14 repossessed houses, which are evaluated to be worth about the same. Ten of the houses are on the north side of town and the rest are on the west side. A local contractor submitted a bid to purchase four of the houses. Which houses the contractor will get is subject to a random draw.

a. What is the probability that all four houses selected for the contractor will be on the north side of town?

b. What is the probability that all four houses selected for the contractor will be on the west side of town?

c. What is the probability that half of the houses selected for the contractor will be on the west side and half on the north side of town?

5.59. The Public Citizen's Health Research Group studied the serious disciplinary actions that were taken during a recent year on nonfederal medical doctors in the United States. The national average was 3.05 serious actions per 1000 doctors. The state with the lowest number was Minnesota with only 1.07 serious actions per 1000

doctors. Assume that the numbers of serious actions per 1000 doctors in both the United States and in Minnesota are Poisson distributed.

a. What is the probability of randomly selecting 1000 U.S. doctors and finding no serious actions taken?

b. What is the probability of randomly selecting 2000 U.S. doctors and finding six serious actions taken?

c. What is the probability of randomly selecting 3000 Minnesota doctors and finding fewer than seven serious actions taken?

Interpreting the Output

5.60. Study the Minitab output. Discuss the type of distribution, the mean, standard deviation, and why the probabilities fall as they do.

PROBABILITY DENSITY FUNCTION	
Binomial with $n = 15$ and $n = 0.36$	
x	$P(X = x)$
0	0.001238
1	0.010445
2	0.041128
3	0.100249
4	0.169170
5	0.209347
6	0.196263
7	0.141940
8	0.079841
9	0.034931
10	0.011789
11	0.003014
12	0.000565
13	0.000073
14	0.000006
15	0.000000

5.61. Study the Excel output. Explain the distribution in terms of shape and mean. Are these probabilities what you would expect? Why or why not?

x VALUES	POISSON PROBABILITIES: $\lambda = 2.78$
0	0.0620
1	0.1725
2	0.2397
3	0.2221
4	0.1544
5	0.0858
6	0.0398
7	0.0158
8	0.0055
9	0.0017
10	0.0005
11	0.0001

5.62. Study the graphical output from Excel. Describe the distribution and explain why the graph takes the shape it does.

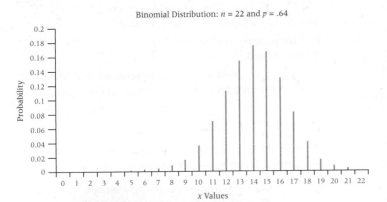

Binomial Distribution: $n = 22$ and $p = .64$

5.63. Study the Minitab graph. Discuss the distribution including type, shape, and probability outcomes.

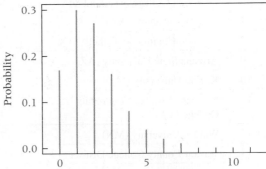

Poisson Distribution: Lambda = 1.784

Analyzing the Databases

See **www.wiley.com/college/black**

1. Use the Consumer Food database. What proportion of the database households are in the Metro area? Use this as the value of p in a binomial distribution. If you were to randomly select 12 of these households, what is the probability that fewer than 3 would be households in the Metro area? If you were to randomly select 25 of these households, what is the probability that exactly 8 would be in the Metro area?

2. Use the Hospital database. What is the breakdown between hospitals that are general medical hospitals and those that are psychiatric hospitals in this database of 200 hospitals? (Hint: In Service, 1 = general medical and 2 = psychiatric.) Using these figures and the hypergeometric distribution, determine the probability of randomly selecting 16 hospitals from the database and getting exactly 9 that are psychiatric hospitals. Now, determine the number of hospitals in this database that are for-profit (Hint: In Control, 3 = for-profit.) From this number, calculate p, the proportion of hospitals that are for-profit. Using this value of p and the binomial distribution, determine the probability of randomly selecting 30 hospitals and getting exactly 10 that are for-profit.

Case

Whole Foods Market Grows Through Mergers and Acquisitions

Over three decades ago, four businesspeople who had experience in retailing natural foods through food stores believed that there was a demand for a supermarket for natural foods. As a result, in 1980 in Austin, Texas, they founded the first Whole Foods Market store in a building that had around 10,000 square feet and a staff of 19. This store was quite large compared to health food stores at the time. By 1984, the company was successful enough to expand to Houston and Dallas. In 1988, they purchased the Whole Food Company in New Orleans and expanded there. The next year, they moved into the West Coast with a store in Palo Alto, California. Even though the company has built a number of its own stores, much of the company growth has come through mergers and acquisitions, many of which came in the 1990s in such places as North Carolina, Massachusetts, Rhode Island, both Northern and Southern California, and Michigan. After the turn of the century, Whole Foods Market established a presence in Manhattan (NY), followed by a move into Canada and later into the United Kingdom.

Presently, Whole Foods Market has 433 stores including 414 stores in 42 U.S. states and the District of Columbia, 10 stores in Canada, and 9 stores in the United Kingdom. There are over 91,000 team members, many of whom are full-time employees. Existing stores now average 43,000 square feet in size, about four times as large as the original "supermarket". Whole Foods Market is the eighth largest food and drug store in the United States with over $14 billion in sales last year and ranks 218 on the list of Fortune 500 companies.

Whole Food Markets is the largest retailer of natural and organic foods and prides itself in doing the research necessary to assure customers that offered products are free of artificial flavors, colors, sweeteners, preservatives, or hydrogenated fats. The company attempts to customize each store by stocking it with products that are most in demand in any given community. Whole Foods Market management cares about their employees, and the company has been named by *Fortune* magazine as one of the "100 Best Companies to Work For" in the United States every year since the list was first compiled 18 years ago. The company attempts to be a good community citizen, and it gives back at least 5% of after-tax profits to the communities in which they operate. In January 2008, Whole Foods Market was the first U.S. supermarket to commit to completely eliminating disposable plastic bags. The Core Values of the company are "Whole Foods, Whole People, and Whole Planet." The Whole Foods Market searches "for the highest quality, least processed, most flavorful and natural foods possible . . ." The company attempts to "create a respectful workplace where people are treated fairly and are highly motivated to succeed." In addition, the company is committed to the world around us and protecting the planet.

Discussion

1. Whole Foods Market has shown steady growth at a time when traditional supermarkets have been flat. This could be attributed to a growing awareness of and demand for more natural foods. According to a study by Mintel in 2006, 30% of consumers have a high level of concern about the safety of the food they eat. Suppose we want to test this figure to determine if consumers have changed since then. Assuming that the 30% figure still holds, what is the probability of randomly sampling 25 consumers and having 12 or more respond that they have a high level of concern about the safety of the food they eat? What would the expected number be? If a researcher actually got 12 or more out of 25 to respond that they have a high level of concern about the safety of the food they eat, what might this mean?

2. Suppose that, on average, in a Whole Foods Market in Dallas, 3.4 customers want to check out every minute. Based on this figure, store management wants to staff checkout lines such that less than 1% of the time demand for checkout cannot be met. In this case, store management would have to staff for what number of customers? Based on the 3.4 customer average per minute, what percentage of the time would the store have 12 or more customers who want to check out in any two-minute period?

3. Suppose a survey is taken of 30 managers of Whole Foods Market stores and it is determined that 17 are at least 40 years old. If another researcher randomly selects 10 of these 30 managers to interview, what is the probability that 3 or fewer are at least 40 years old? Suppose 9 of the 30 surveyed managers are female. What is the probability of randomly selecting 10 managers from the 30 and finding out that 7 of the 10 are female?

Sources: Adapted from: Whole Foods Market website at http://www. wholefoodsmarket.com; William A. Knudson, "The Organic Food Market," a working paper from the Strategic Marketing Institute, Michigan State University, 2007; media.wholefoodsmarket.com/.

Continuous Distributions

LEARNING OBJECTIVES

The primary learning objective of Chapter 6 is to help you understand continuous distributions, thereby enabling you to:

1. Solve for probabilities in a continuous uniform distribution.

2. Solve for probabilities in a normal distribution using z scores and for the mean, the standard deviation, or a value of x in a normal distribution when given information about the area under the normal curve.

3. Solve problems from the discrete binomial distribution using the continuous normal distribution and correcting for continuity.

4. Solve for probabilities in an exponential distribution and contrast the exponential distribution to the discrete Poisson distribution.

Decision Dilemma

CSX Corporation

The CSX Corporation is a leading rail transportation company in the U.S., moving cargo through traditional rail service and shipping goods using intermodal containers and trailers. Based in Jacksonville, Florida, the CSX Transportation network has 21,000 miles of track spread across the eastern half of the United States and the Canadian provinces of Ontario and Quebec.

Founded in 1827 when America's first common carrier railroad, the Baltimore & Ohio, was founded, CSX presently has over 36,000 employees, $31 billion in total assets and an annual revenue of over $12 billion. CSX has access to over 70 water terminals in the United States and Canada and moves a broad range of products across its service area. In its intermodal shipping, CSX uses special containers such that goods and products can be transferred from ship to rail to truck without having to be repacked.

Since 1999, CSX and five other North American freight railroads have voluntarily reported three weekly performance measures—Cars On Line, Train Speed, and Terminal Dwell—to the Railroad Performance Measures website in an effort to improve communications with their customers. In addition, CSX keeps data on such variables as Network Velocity (in mph), % On-Time Arrivals, % On-Time Originations, Average Daily Trains Holding for Power, and Train Crew Delay Hours by Week.

© Ken MacKay/Alamy Stock Photo

MANAGERIAL AND STATISTICAL QUESTIONS

1. Suppose the average rail freight line-haul speed in any given year is 23.7 mph. If rail freight line-haul speeds are uniformly distributed in a year with a minimum of 21 mph and a maximum of 26.4 mph, what percentage of line-hauls would have speeds between 22 and 24 mph? What percentage of line-hauls would have speeds of more than 25 mph?

2. Terminal dwell time, typically measured in hours, is the time a rail car resides in a rail terminal on the same train (excluding cars on run-through trains). Suppose terminal dwell time is normally distributed for rail cars in the United States with a mean of 27.5 hours and a standard deviation of 2.6 hours. Based on these statistics, what is the probability that a randomly selected rail car has a terminal dwell time of more than 32.4 hours? What is the probability that a randomly selected rail car has a terminal dwell time of less than 26 hours?

3. Suppose that 45% of all freight trains arrive on time. If this is true, what is the probability of randomly selecting 120 trains and finding out that more than 65 were on time?

4. Suppose that at a relatively small railroad, on average, 1.7 employees call in sick per day. What is the probability that at least two days go by with no worker calling in sick?

Sources: www.csx.com; U.S. Department of Transportation, Research and Innovative Technology Administration, Bureau of Transportation Statistics; www.railroadpm.org/.

Whereas Chapter 5 focused on the characteristics and applications of discrete distributions, Chapter 6 concentrates on information about continuous distributions. Continuous distributions are constructed from continuous random variables in which values are taken on for every point over a given interval and are usually generated from experiments in which things are "measured" as opposed to "counted." With continuous distributions, probabilities of outcomes occurring between particular points are determined by calculating the area under the curve between those points. In addition, the entire area under the whole curve is equal to 1. **Figure 6.1** highlights these points. The many continuous distributions in statistics include the uniform distribution, the normal distribution, the exponential distribution, the t distribution, the chi-square distribution, and the F distribution. This chapter presents the uniform distribution, the normal distribution, and the exponential distribution.

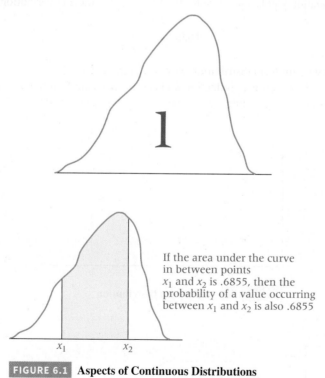

If the area under the curve in between points x_1 and x_2 is .6855, then the probability of a value occurring between x_1 and x_2 is also .6855

FIGURE 6.1 **Aspects of Continuous Distributions**

1. Continuous distributions are created from "measured" variables; *volume, distance, temperature, weight, . . . ,* E.g. 16.429 cubic feet, 7.3852 km, 81.36 degrees, 2.6641 kg

2. Area under a continuous distribution curve is 1

3. Probabilities in a continuous distribution are found by determining the area:

6.1 The Uniform Distribution

Perhaps the simplest of all continuous distributions is the uniform or rectangular distribution. A uniform distribution is a continuous distribution in which the same height is obtained over a range of values.

Shown in Figure 6.2 is a uniform distribution. Note that through the entire distribution from point a to point b, the height of the distribution remains constant and that the distribution takes the shape of a rectangle.

Can you think of phenomena in business that might be uniformly distributed? Consider the demand for breakfast cereal over time. Could it be relatively uniform? What about the demand for some clothing items like dress socks?

Solving for the Height and Length of a Uniform Distribution

Consider again the uniform distribution shown in Figure 6.2. A uniform distribution takes on the shape of a rectangle. The length of the rectangle shown in Figure 6.2 is $(b - a)$, the distance between the two points defining the ends of the rectangle.

Recall that the area under a continuous distribution curve is by definition equal to 1. But the area of a rectangle is length times width. In the graph displayed in Figure 6.2, the width of the rectangle is actually the height of the curve. Thus, the area of a uniform distribution is the length times the height and is equal to one:

$$\text{Area} = (\text{length})(\text{height}) = 1$$

But the length is $(b - a)$. Thus, $\text{Area} = (b - a)(\text{height}) = 1$

Solving this equation yields a formula for the height of a uniform distribution:

$$\text{Height} = \frac{1}{b - a}$$

Figure 6.3 shows a uniform distribution with its length and height.

As an example, suppose a production line is set up to manufacture machine braces in lots of five per minute during a shift. When the lots are weighed, variation among the weights

FIGURE 6.2 A Uniform Distribution

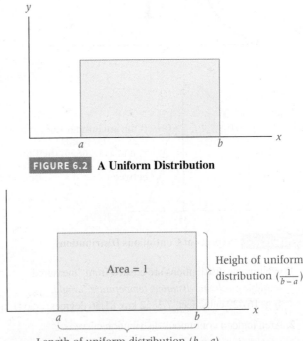

FIGURE 6.3 A Uniform Distribution with Length and Height

is detected, with lot weights ranging from 41 to 47 grams in a uniform distribution. In this example, $a = 41$, $b = 47$, and the length of the uniform distribution is $b - a = 47 - 41 = 6$. The height of the distribution is equal to $\dfrac{1}{b - a} = \dfrac{1}{47 - 41} = \dfrac{1}{6}$. **Figure 6.4** shows this uniform distribution with the length and height.

The Mean and Standard Deviation of a Uniform Distribution

The mean and the standard deviation of a uniform distribution can be calculated using formula 6.1.

Formula 6.1 Mean and Standard Deviation of a Uniform Distribution

$$\mu = \frac{a + b}{2} \qquad \sigma = \frac{b - a}{\sqrt{12}}$$

The mean and the standard deviation can be computed for the machine braces example as

$$\mu = \frac{a + b}{2} = \frac{41 + 47}{2} = 44$$

$$\sigma = \frac{b - a}{\sqrt{12}} = \frac{47 - 41}{3.4641} = 1.732$$

Figure 6.5 shows the uniform distribution for the braces example with the mean and the standard deviation

Determining Probabilities in a Uniform Distribution

Unlike discrete distributions, which have probability functions to yield probability values and in which it is possible to have a probability for a single point, in continuous distributions, probabilities are calculated by determining the area under the curve (or function) over an interval. As an example, note the second curve shown in Figure 6.1. Formula 6.2 is used to determine the probabilities of x for a uniform distribution between a and b.

Formula 6.2 Probabilities in a Uniform Distribution

$$P(x) = \frac{x_2 - x_1}{b - a}$$

where:

$$a \leq x_1 \leq x_2 \leq b$$

In a uniform distribution, since a and b define the outer boundaries of the distribution, the area between a and b is equal to one. For values of x between a and b, Formula 6.2 computes the proportion of the total area that lies between two values of x. Consider the machine

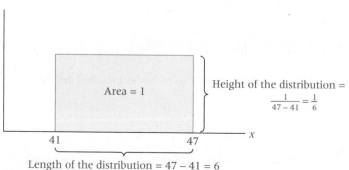

FIGURE 6.4 Uniform Distribution of Braces with Length and Height

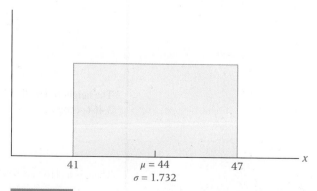

FIGURE 6.5 Mean and Standard Deviation of Braces

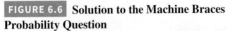

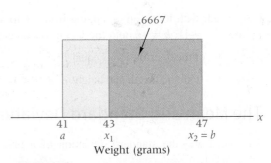

.5000

41 42   45   47
Weight (grams)

FIGURE 6.6 **Solution to the Machine Braces Probability Question**

.6667

41   43   47
a x_1 $x_2 = b$
Weight (grams)

FIGURE 6.7 **Solution to the Second Machine Braces Probability Question**

braces problem with lot weights ranging from 41 to 47 grams ($a = 41$ and $b = 47$) in a uniform distribution. What is the probability that a randomly selected brace weighs between 42 and 45 grams ($x_1 = 42$ and $x_2 = 45$)? Using Formula 6.2, this probability can be computed as:

$$P(x) = \frac{x_2 - x_1}{b - a} = \frac{45 - 42}{47 - 41} = \frac{3}{6} = .5000$$

This solution is displayed in **Figure 6.6**.

Typically, the values of x_1 and x_2, lie between a and b. What is the probability if $x_1 = a$ and $x_2 = b$? The probability of $x \geq b$ or of $x \leq a$ is zero because there is no area above b or below a. If part of the range between x_1 and x_2 lies outside of the area between a and b, that portion will not be considered part of the probability.

As a second example using the machine braces problem, what is the probability that a randomly selected brace weighs more than 43 grams ($x_1 > 43$)? Because the uniform distribution's upper bound is 47 grams ($b = 47$), there is no area beyond $x = 47$. Thus, x_2 is 47 and using Formula 6.2, the probability can be computed as:

$$P(x) = \frac{x_2 - x_1}{b - a} = \frac{47 - 43}{47 - 41} = \frac{4}{6} = .6667$$

This solution is displayed in **Figure 6.7**.

DEMONSTRATION PROBLEM 6.1

Suppose the amount of time it takes to assemble a plastic module ranges from 27 to 39 seconds and that assembly times are uniformly distributed. Describe the distribution. What is the probability that a given assembly will take between 30 and 35 seconds? Fewer than 30 seconds?

Solution:

$$f(x) = \frac{1}{39 - 27} = \frac{1}{12}$$

$$\mu = \frac{a + b}{2} = \frac{39 + 27}{2} = 33$$

$$\sigma = \frac{b - a}{\sqrt{12}} = \frac{39 - 27}{\sqrt{12}} = \frac{12}{\sqrt{12}} = 3.464$$

The height of the distribution is $1/12$. The mean time is 33 seconds with a standard deviation of 3.464 seconds.

$$P(30 \leq x \leq 35) = \frac{35 - 30}{39 - 27} = \frac{5}{12} = .4167$$

There is a .4167 probability that it will take between 30 and 35 seconds to assemble the module.

$$P(x < 30) = \frac{30 - 27}{39 - 27} = \frac{3}{12} = .2500$$

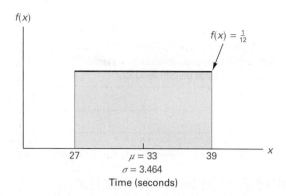

There is a .2500 probability that it will take less than 30 seconds to assemble the module. Because there is no area less than 27 seconds, $P(x < 30)$ is determined by using only the interval $27 \leq x < 30$. In a continuous distribution, there is no area at any one point (only over an interval). Thus the probability $x < 30$ is the same as the probability of $x \leq 30$.

DEMONSTRATION PROBLEM 6.2

According to the National Association of Insurance Commissioners, the average annual cost for automobile insurance in the United States in a recent year was $691. Suppose automobile insurance costs are uniformly distributed in the United States with a range of from $200 to $1,182. What is the standard deviation of this uniform distribution? What is the height of the distribution? What is the probability that a person's annual cost for automobile insurance in the United States is between $410 and $825?

Solution: The mean is given as $691. The value of a is $200 and b is $1,182.

$$\sigma = \frac{b - a}{\sqrt{12}} = \frac{1,182 - 200}{\sqrt{12}} = 283.5$$

The height of the distribution is $\dfrac{1}{1,182 - 200} = \dfrac{1}{982} = .001$

$$x_1 = 410 \text{ and } x_2 = 825$$

$$P(410 \leq x \leq 825) = \frac{825 - 410}{1,182 - 200} = \frac{415}{982} = .4226$$

The probability that a randomly selected person pays between $410 and $825 annually for automobile insurance in the United States is .4226. That is, about 42.26% of all people in the United States pay in that range.

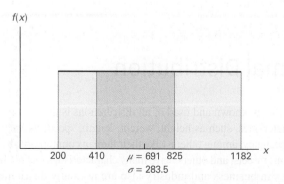

TABLE 6.1 Minitab Output for Uniform Distribution

CUMULATIVE DISTRIBUTION FUNCTION	
Continuous uniform on 200 to 1182	
x	$P(X <= x)$
825	0.636456
410	0.213849

Using the Computer to Solve for Uniform Distribution Probabilities

Using the values of a, b, and x, Minitab has the capability of computing probabilities for the uniform distribution. The resulting computation is a cumulative probability from the left end of the distribution to each x value. As an example, the probability question, $P(410 \leq x \leq 825)$, from Demonstration Problem 6.2 can be worked using Minitab. Minitab computes the probability of $x \leq 825$ and the probability of $x \leq 410$, and these results are shown in Table 6.1. The final answer to the probability question from Demonstration Problem 6.2 is obtained by subtracting these two probabilities:

$$P(410 \leq x \leq 825) = .636456 - .213849 = .422607$$

Excel does not have the capability of directly computing probabilities for the uniform distribution.

6.1 Problems

6.1. Values are uniformly distributed between 200 and 240.

a. What is the value of $f(x)$ for this distribution?

b. Determine the mean and standard deviation of this distribution.

c. Probability of $(x > 230) = ?$

d. Probability of $(205 \leq x \leq 220) = ?$

e. Probability of $(x \leq 225) = ?$

6.2. x is uniformly distributed over a range of values from 8 to 21.

a. What is the value of $f(x)$ for this distribution?

b. Determine the mean and standard deviation of this distribution.

c. Probability of $(10 \leq x < 17) = ?$

d. Probability of $(x < 22) = ?$

e. Probability of $(x \geq 7) = ?$

6.3. The retail price of a medium-sized box of a well-known brand of cornflakes ranges from $2.80 to $3.14. Assume these prices are uniformly distributed. What are the average price and standard deviation

of prices in this distribution? If a price is randomly selected from this list, what is the probability that it will be between $3.00 and $3.10?

6.4. The average fill volume of a regular can of soft drink is 12 ounces. Suppose the fill volume of these cans ranges from 11.97 to 12.03 ounces and is uniformly distributed. What is the height of this distribution? What is the probability that a randomly selected can contains more than 12.01 ounces of fluid? What is the probability that the fill volume is between 11.98 and 12.01 ounces?

6.5. According to the U.S. Department of Labor, the average American household spends $639 on household supplies per year. Suppose annual expenditures on household supplies per household are uniformly distributed between the values of $253 and $1,025. What are the standard deviation and the height of this distribution? What proportion of households spend more than $850 per year on household supplies? What proportion of households spend more than $1,200 per year on household supplies? What proportion of households spend between $350 and $480 on household supplies?

6.2 Normal Distribution

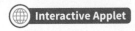

Probably the most widely known and used of all distributions is the **normal distribution**. It fits many human characteristics, such as height, weight, length, speed, IQ, scholastic achievement, and years of life expectancy, among others. Like their human counterparts, living things in nature, such as trees, animals, insects, and others, have many characteristics that are normally distributed.

Many variables in business and industry also are normally distributed. Some examples of variables that could produce normally distributed measurements include the annual cost of household insurance, the cost per square foot of renting warehouse space, and managers' satisfaction with support from ownership on a five-point scale. In addition, most items produced or filled by machines are normally distributed.

Because of its many applications, the normal distribution is an extremely important distribution. Besides the many variables mentioned that are normally distributed, the normal distribution and its associated probabilities are an integral part of statistical process control (see Chapter 18). When large enough sample sizes are taken, many statistics are normally distributed regardless of the shape of the underlying distribution from which they are drawn (as discussed in Chapter 7). Figure 6.8 is the graphic representation of the normal distribution: the normal curve.

FIGURE 6.8 The Normal Curve

Characteristics of the Normal Distribution

Figure 6.9 displays the characteristics of the normal distribution. Several of these will be useful to us in solving for probabilities under the normal curve. In addition, the normal distribution is a family of curves each defined by a particular combination of mean and standard deviation.

The normal distribution exhibits the following characteristics:

- It is a continuous distribution.
- It is a symmetrical distribution about its mean.
- It is asymptotic to the horizontal axis.
- It is unimodal.
- It is a family of curves.
- Area under the curve is 1.

The normal distribution is symmetrical. Each half of the distribution is a mirror image of the other half. Many normal distribution tables contain probability values for only one side of the distribution because probability values for the other side of the distribution are identical because of symmetry.

In theory, the normal distribution is asymptotic to the horizontal axis. That is, it does not touch the x-axis, and it goes forever in each direction. The reality is that most applications of the normal curve are experiments that have finite limits of potential outcomes. For example, even though GMAT scores are analyzed by the normal distribution, the range of scores on the GMAT is from 200 to 800.

The normal curve sometimes is referred to as the *bell-shaped curve*. It is unimodal in that values *mound up* in only one portion of the graph—the center of the curve. The normal distribution actually is a family of curves. Every unique value of the mean and every unique value of the standard deviation result in a different normal curve. In addition, *the total area under any normal distribution is 1*. The area under the curve yields the probabilities, so the total of all probabilities for a normal distribution is 1. Because the distribution is symmetric, the area of the distribution on each side of the mean is 0.5.

History of the Normal Distribution

Discovery of the normal curve of errors is generally credited to mathematician and astronomer Karl Gauss (1777–1855), who recognized that the errors of repeated measurement of objects

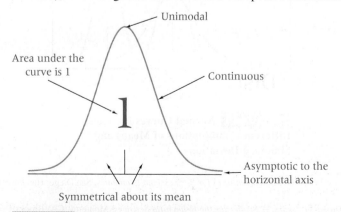

FIGURE 6.9 Characteristics of the Normal Distribution

are often normally distributed.* Thus the normal distribution is sometimes referred to as the *Gaussian distribution* or the *normal curve of error.* A modern-day analogy of Gauss's work might be the distribution of measurements of machine-produced parts, which often yield a normal curve of error around a mean specification.

To a lesser extent, some credit has been given to Pierre-Simon de Laplace (1749–1827) for discovering the normal distribution. However, many people now believe that Abraham de Moivre (1667–1754), a French mathematician, first understood the normal distribution. De Moivre determined that the binomial distribution approached the normal distribution as a limit. De Moivre worked with remarkable accuracy. His published table values for the normal curve are only a few ten-thousandths off the values of currently published tables.[†]

Probability Density Function of the Normal Distribution

The normal distribution is described or characterized by two parameters: the mean, μ, and the standard deviation, σ. The values of μ and σ produce a normal distribution. The density function of the normal distribution is

$$f(x) = \frac{1}{\sigma\sqrt{2\pi}} e^{-1/2[(x-\mu)/\sigma)]^2}$$

where

μ = mean of x
σ = standard deviation of x
π = 3.14159 . . . , and
e = 2.71828. . . .

Using integral calculus to determine areas under the normal curve from this function is difficult and time-consuming; therefore, virtually all researchers use table values to analyze normal distribution problems rather than this formula.

Standardized Normal Distribution

The normal distribution is described or characterized by two parameters, the mean, μ, and the standard deviation, σ. That is, every unique pair of the values of μ and σ defines a different normal distribution. **Figure 6.10** shows the Minitab graphs of normal distributions for the following three pairs of parameters.

1. $\mu = 50$ and $\sigma = 5$
2. $\mu = 80$ and $\sigma = 5$
3. $\mu = 50$ and $\sigma = 10$

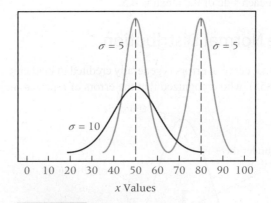

FIGURE 6.10 **Normal Curves for Three Different Combinations of Means and Standard Deviations**

*John A. Ingram and Joseph G. Monks, *Statistics for Business and Economics.* San Diego: Harcourt Brace Jovanovich, 1989.
† Roger E. Kirk, *Statistical Issues: A Reader for the Behavioral Sciences.* Monterey, CA: Brooks/Cole, 1972.

Note that every change in a parameter (μ or σ) determines a different normal distribution. This characteristic of the normal curve (a family of curves) could make analysis by the normal distribution tedious because volumes of normal curve tables—one for each different combination of μ and σ—would be required. Fortunately, a mechanism was developed by which all normal distributions can be converted into a single distribution: the z distribution. This process yields the **standardized normal distribution** (or curve). The conversion formula for any x value of a given normal distribution follows.

---

z Formula

$$z = \frac{x - \mu}{\sigma}, \qquad \sigma \neq 0$$

A z **score** is *the number of standard deviations that a value, x, is above or below the mean.* If the value of x is less than the mean, the z score is negative; if the value of x is more than the mean, the z score is positive; and if the value of x equals the mean, the associated z score is zero. This formula allows conversion of the distance of any x value from its mean into standard deviation units. A standard z score table can be used to find probabilities for any normal curve problem that has been converted to z scores. The z **distribution** is *a normal distribution with a mean of 0 and a standard deviation of 1.* Any value of x at the mean of a normal curve is zero standard deviations from the mean. Any value of x that is one standard deviation above the mean has a z value of 1. The empirical rule, introduced in Chapter 3, is based on the normal distribution in which about 68% of all values are within one standard deviation of the mean regardless of the values of μ and σ. In a z distribution, about 68% of the z values are between $z = -1$ and $z = +1$.

The z distribution probability values are given in Table A.5. Because it is so frequently used, the z distribution is also printed inside the cover of this text. For discussion purposes, a list of z distribution values is presented in Table 6.2.

Table A.5 gives the total area under the z curve between 0 and any point on the positive z-axis. Since the curve is symmetric, the area under the curve between z and 0 is the same whether z is positive or negative (the sign on the z value designates whether the z score is above or below the mean). The table areas or probabilities are always positive.

Solving for Probabilities Using the Normal Curve

Probabilities for intervals of any particular values of a normal distribution can be determined by using the mean, the standard deviation, the z formula, and the z distribution table. As an example, let's consider information collected and reported by the U.S. Environmental Protection Agency (EPA) on the generation and disposal of waste. According to EPA data, on average there is 4.43 pounds of waste generated per person in the U.S. per day. Suppose waste generated per person per day in the U.S. is normally distributed with a standard deviation of 1.32 pounds. If a U.S. person is randomly selected, what is the probability that the person generates more than 6.00 pounds of waste per day?

We can summarize this problem as:

$$P(x > 6.00 \,|\, \mu = 4.43 \text{ and } \sigma = 1.32) = ?$$

Figure 6.11 displays a graphical representation of the problem. Note that the area under the curve for which we are interested in solving is the tail of the distribution.

We begin the process by solving for the z value:

$$z = \frac{x - \mu}{\sigma} = \frac{6.00 - 4.43}{1.32} = 1.19$$

The z of 1.19 indicates that the value of x (6.00) is 1.19 standard deviations above the mean (4.43). Looking this z value up in the z distribution table yields a probability of .3830. Is this the

TABLE 6.2 *z* Distribution

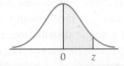

	SECOND DECIMAL PLACE IN *z*									
z	0.00	0.01	0.02	0.03	0.04	0.05	0.06	0.07	0.08	0.09
0.0	.0000	.0040	.0080	.0120	.0160	.0199	.0239	.0279	.0319	.0359
0.1	.0398	.0438	.0478	.0517	.0557	.0596	.0636	.0675	.0714	.0753
0.2	.0793	.0832	.0871	.0910	.0948	.0987	.1026	.1064	.1103	.1141
0.3	.1179	.1217	.1255	.1293	.1331	.1368	.1406	.1443	.1480	.1517
0.4	.1554	.1591	.1628	.1664	.1700	.1736	.1772	.1808	.1844	.1879
0.5	.1915	.1950	.1985	.2019	.2054	.2088	.2123	.2157	.2190	.2224
0.6	.2257	.2291	.2324	.2357	.2389	.2422	.2454	.2486	.2517	.2549
0.7	.2580	.2611	.2642	.2673	.2704	.2734	.2764	.2794	.2823	.2852
0.8	.2881	.2910	.2939	.2967	.2995	.3023	.3051	.3078	.3106	.3133
0.9	.3159	.3186	.3212	.3238	.3264	.3289	.3315	.3340	.3365	.3389
1.0	.3413	.3438	.3461	.3485	.3508	.3531	.3554	.3577	.3599	.3621
1.1	.3643	.3665	.3686	.3708	.3729	.3749	.3770	.3790	.3810	.3830
1.2	.3849	.3869	.3888	.3907	.3925	.3944	.3962	.3980	.3997	.4015
1.3	.4032	.4049	.4066	.4082	.4099	.4115	.4131	.4147	.4162	.4177
1.4	.4192	.4207	.4222	.4236	.4251	.4265	.4279	.4292	.4306	.4319
1.5	.4332	.4345	.4357	.4370	.4382	.4394	.4406	.4418	.4429	.4441
1.6	.4452	.4463	.4474	.4484	.4495	.4505	.4515	.4525	.4535	.4545
1.7	.4554	.4564	.4573	.4582	.4591	.4599	.4608	.4616	.4625	.4633
1.8	.4641	.4649	.4656	.4664	.4671	.4678	.4686	.4693	.4699	.4706
1.9	.4713	.4719	.4726	.4732	.4738	.4744	.4750	.4756	.4761	.4767
2.0	.4772	.4778	.4783	.4788	.4793	.4798	.4803	.4808	.4812	.4817
2.1	.4821	.4826	.4830	.4834	.4838	.4842	.4846	.4850	.4854	.4857
2.2	.4861	.4864	.4868	.4871	.4875	.4878	.4881	.4884	.4887	.4890
2.3	.4893	.4896	.4898	.4901	.4904	.4906	.4909	.4911	.4913	.4916
2.4	.4918	.4920	.4922	.4925	.4927	.4929	.4931	.4932	.4934	.4936
2.5	.4938	.4940	.4941	.4943	.4945	.4946	.4948	.4949	.4951	.4952
2.6	.4953	.4955	.4956	.4957	.4959	.4960	.4961	.4962	.4963	.4964
2.7	.4965	.4966	.4967	.4968	.4969	.4970	.4971	.4972	.4973	.4974
2.8	.4974	.4975	.4976	.4977	.4977	.4978	.4979	.4979	.4980	.4981
2.9	.4981	.4982	.4982	.4983	.4984	.4984	.4985	.4985	.4986	.4986
3.0	.4987	.4987	.4987	.4988	.4988	.4989	.4989	.4989	.4990	.4990
3.1	.4990	.4991	.4991	.4991	.4992	.4992	.4992	.4992	.4993	.4993
3.2	.4993	.4993	.4994	.4994	.4994	.4994	.4994	.4995	.4995	.4995
3.3	.4995	.4995	.4995	.4996	.4996	.4996	.4996	.4996	.4996	.4997
3.4	.4997	.4997	.4997	.4997	.4997	.4997	.4997	.4997	.4997	.4998
3.5	.4998									
4.0	.49997									
4.5	.499997									
5.0	.4999997									
6.0	.499999999									

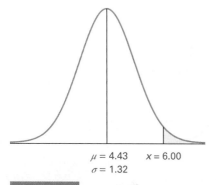

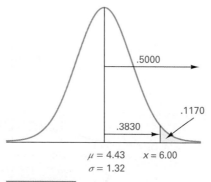

FIGURE 6.11 **Graphical Depiction of the Waste-Generation Problem with** $x > 6.00$

FIGURE 6.12 **Solution of the Waste-Generation Problem with** $x > 6.00$

answer? A cursory glance at the top of the z distribution table shows that the probability given in the table is for the area between a z of 0 and the given z value. Thus there is .3830 area (probability) between the mean of the z distribution ($z = 0$) and the z value of interest (1.19). However, we want to solve for the tail of the distribution or the area above $z = 1.19$. The normal curve has an area of 1 and is symmetrical. Thus, the area under the curve in the upper half is .5000. Subtracting .3830 from .5000 results in .1170 for the area of the upper tail of the distribution. The probability that a randomly selected person in the U.S. generates more than 6.00 pounds of waste per day is .1170 or 11.70%. **Figure 6.12** displays the solution to this problem.

DEMONSTRATION PROBLEM 6.3

Using this same waste-generation example, if a U.S. person is randomly selected, what is the probability that the person generates between 3.60 and 5.00 pounds of waste per day?

We can summarize this problem as:

$$P(3.60 < x < 5.00 \,|\, \mu = 4.43 \text{ and } \sigma = 1.32 = ?$$

Figure 6.13 displays a graphical representation of the problem. Note that the area under the curve for which we are solving crosses over the mean of the distribution. Note that there are two x values in this problem ($x_1 = 3.60$ and $x_2 = 5.00$). The z formula can handle only one x value at a time. Thus, this problem needs to be worked out as two separate problems and the resulting probabilities added together. We begin the process by solving for each z value:

$$z = \frac{x - \mu}{\sigma} = \frac{3.60 - 4.43}{1.32} = -0.63$$

$$z = \frac{x - \mu}{\sigma} = \frac{5.00 - 4.43}{1.32} = 0.43$$

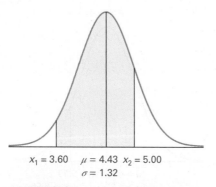

FIGURE 6.13 **Graphical Depiction of the Waste-Generation Problem with** $3.60 < x < 5.00$

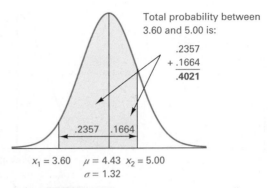

Total probability between
3.60 and 5.00 is:

.2357
+ .1664
———
.4021

.2357 | .1664

$x_1 = 3.60$ $\mu = 4.43$ $x_2 = 5.00$
$\sigma = 1.32$

FIGURE 6.14 **Solution of the Waste-Generation
Problem with 3.60 < x < 5.00**

Next, we look up each z value in the z distribution table. Since the normal distribution is symmetrical, the probability associated with $z = -0.63$ is the same as the probability associated with $z = 0.63$. Looking up $z = 0.63$ in the table yields a probability of .2357. The probability associated with $z = 0.43$ is .1664. Using these two probability values, we can get the probability that $3.60 < x < 5.00$ by summing the two areas:

$$P(3.60 < x < 5.00 \mid \mu = 4.43 \text{ and } \sigma = 1.32) = .2357 + .1664 = .4021$$

The probability that a randomly selected person in the U.S. has between 3.60 and 5.00 pounds of waste generation per day is .4021 or 40.21%. Figure 6.14 displays the solution to this problem.

DEMONSTRATION PROBLEM 6.4

Using this same waste-generation example, if a U.S. person is randomly selected, what is the probability that the person generates between 5.30 and 6.50 pounds of waste per day? We can summarize this problem as:

$$P(5.30 < x < 6.50 \mid \mu = 4.43 \text{ and } \sigma = 1.32) = ?$$

Figure 6.15 displays a graphical representation of the problem. Note that the area under the curve for which we are solving lies completely on one side of the mean of the distribution.

There are two x values in this problem ($x_1 = 5.30$ and $x_2 = 6.50$). The z formula can handle only one x value at a time. Thus, this problem needs to be worked out as two separate problems. However, in this problem, the x values are on the same side of the mean. To solve for this probability, we will need to find the area (probability) between $x_2 = 6.50$ and the mean and the area

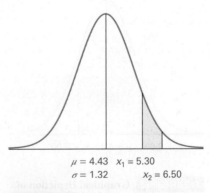

$\mu = 4.43$ $x_1 = 5.30$
$\sigma = 1.32$ $x_2 = 6.50$

FIGURE 6.15 **Graphical Depiction of
the Waste-Generation Problem with
5.30 < x < 6.50**

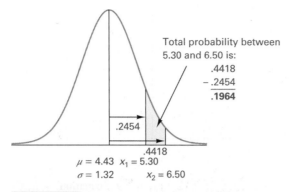

Total probability between
5.30 and 6.50 is:
.4418
− .2454
.1964

.2454

.4418

$\mu = 4.43$ $x_1 = 5.30$
$\sigma = 1.32$ $x_2 = 6.50$

FIGURE 6.16 **Solution of the Waste-Generation Problem with $5.30 < x < 6.50$**

(probability) between $x_1 = 5.30$ and the mean, and then subtract the two areas (probabilities). We begin the process by solving for each z value:

$$z = \frac{x - \mu}{\sigma} = \frac{6.50 - 4.43}{1.32} = 1.57$$

$$z = \frac{x - \mu}{\sigma} = \frac{5.30 - 4.43}{1.32} = 0.66$$

Next, we look up each z value in the z distribution table. The probability associated with $z = 1.57$ is .4418. The probability associated with $z = 0.66$ is .2454. Using these two probability values, we can get the probability that $5.30 < x < 6.50$ by subtracting the two areas (probabilities):

$$P(5.30 < x < 6.50 | \mu = 4.43 \text{ and } \sigma = 1.32) = .4418 - .2454 = .1964.$$

The probability that a randomly selected person in the United States has between 5.30 and 6.50 pounds of waste generation per day is .1964 or 19.64%. **Figure 6.16** displays the solution to this problem.

Using Probabilities to Solve for the Mean, the Standard Deviation, or an x Value in a Normal Distribution

Note that the z formula contains four variables: μ, σ, z, and x. In solving for probabilities, the researcher has knowledge of μ, σ, x and enters those values into the z formula:

$$z = \frac{x - \mu}{\sigma}$$

Looking up the resulting computed value of z in the z distribution table yields a probability value.

There are times, however, when a business researcher has probability information but wants to solve for one of the mean, the standard deviation, or an x value of a normal distribution. That is, we sometimes want to solve for one of the three variables in the right-hand side of the z formula. Typically, in such problems, we are given two of the three variables along with probability information that will help us solve for z.

As an example, Runzheimer International publishes business travel costs for various cities throughout the world. In particular, they publish per diem totals that represent the average costs for the typical business traveler, including three meals a day in business-class restaurants and single-rate lodging in business-class hotels. Suppose 86.65% of the per diem costs in Buenos Aires, Argentina, are less than $449. Assuming that per diem costs are normally distributed and that the standard deviation of per diem costs in Buenos Aires is $36, what is the average per diem cost in Buenos Aires?

What is given in this problem? The standard deviation, σ, is 36. The value of $449 is the particular value of x that we are working with in this problem, $x = 449$. The mean is unknown. Entering these two values into the z formula results in:

$$z = \frac{449 - \mu}{36}$$

We need only secure the value of z, and μ can be solved for. To do this, we must use the probability information given and the z distribution table to find the value of z.

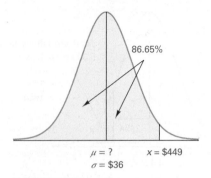

86.65%

$\mu = ?$ $x = \$449$
$\sigma = \$36$

FIGURE 6.17 **Layout of Information for Per Diem Problem**

Study the layout of this problem in **Figure 6.17** in order to determine how to proceed. Think about how probabilities are given in the z distribution table.

How can we use the fact that 86.65% of the per diem rates are less than $449, as shown in Figure 6.17? Recall that the z distribution table associated with this text always gives probability values for areas between a given x value and the mean. In this problem, if we subtract off the 50% of the area less than the mean, it leaves an area of 36.65% between the mean and $x = \$449$. Converting this to a proportion, we can say that .3665 of the area lies between the mean and x. Now, we can look up this value as an area (probability) in the z distribution table and back out the associated value of z as shown in **Figure 6.18**.

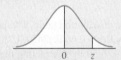

0   z

The entries in this table are the probabilities that a standard normal random variable is between 0 and z (the shaded area)

z	0.00	0.01	0.02	0.03	0.04	0.05	0.06	0.07	0.08	0.09
0.0	.0000		.0080	.0120	.0160	.0199	.0239	.0279	.0319	.0359
0.1	.0398		.0478	.0517	.0557	.0596	.0636	.0675	.0714	.0753
0.2	.0793		.0871	.0910	.0948	.0987	.1026	.1064	.1103	.1141
0.3	.1179		.1255	.1293	.1331	.1368	.1406	.1443	.1480	.1517
0.4	.1554		.1628	.1664	.1700	.1736	.1772	.1808	.1844	.1879
0.5	.1915						.2123	.2157	.2190	.2224
0.6	.2257						.2454	.2486	.2517	.2549
0.7	.2580						.2764	.2794	.2823	.2852
0.8	.2881		.2939	.2967	.2995	.3023	.3051	.3078	.3106	.3133
0.9	.3159		.3212	.3238	.3264	.3289	.3315	.3340	.3365	.3389
1.0	.3413		.3461	.3485	.3508	.3531	.3554	.3577	.3599	.3621
1.1		(.3665)	.3686	.3708	.3729	.3749	.3770	.3790	.3810	.3830
1.2	.3849	.3869	.3888	.3907	.3925	.3944	.3962	.3980	.3997	.4015
1.3	.4032	.4049	.4066	.4082	.4099	.4115	.4131	.4147	.4162	.4177
1.4	.4192	.4207	.4222	.4236	.4251	.4265	.4279	.4292	.4306	.4319
1.5	.4332	.4345	.4357	.4370	.4382	.4394	.4406	.4418	.4429	.4441
1.6	.4452	.4463	.4474	.4484	.4495	.4505	.4515	.4525	.4535	.4545
1.7	.4554	.4564	.4573	.4582	.4591	.4599	.4608	.4616	.4625	.4633
1.8	.4641	.4649	.4656	.4664	.4671	.4678	.4686	.4693	.4699	.4706
1.9	.4713	.4719	.4726	.4732	.4738	.4744	.4750	.4756	.4761	.4767
2.0	.4772	.4778	.4783	.4788	.4793	.4798	.4803	.4808	.4812	.4817
2.1	.4821	.4826	.4830	.4834	.4838	.4842	.4846	.4850	.4854	.4857
2.2	.4861	.4864	.4868	.4871	.4875	.4878	.4881	.4884	.4887	.4890
2.3	.4893	.4896	.4898	.4901	.4904	.4906	.4909	.4911	.4913	.4916
2.4	.4918	.4920	.4922	.4925	.4927	.4929	.4931	.4932	.4934	.4936

The z value associated with an area of .3665 is $z = 1.11$

FIGURE 6.18 **Using the z Distribution Table to Locate the z Value Associated with an Area of .3665.**

The resulting z, as shown in Figure 6.18, is $z = 1.11$. In problems such as this (solving for x, μ, or σ), the sign on the z value can matter. In this particular example, x is in the upper half of the distribution and is therefore positive. The standard deviation, σ, is 36, the value of $x = 449$, and $z = 1.11$. Using these values, μ can now be solved for as follows:

$$1.11 = \frac{449 - \mu}{36}$$

$$\mu = 409.04$$

DEMONSTRATION PROBLEM 6.5

As a second example, a particular ten-inch (diameter) clay pipe weighs, on average, 44 pounds, and pipe weights are normally distributed in the population. If 74.22% of the pipe weights are more than 40 pounds, what is the value of the standard deviation?

The mean, μ, is 44. The value of x is 40. The standard deviation is unknown. Entering these two values into the z formula results in:

$$z = \frac{40 - 44}{\sigma}$$

We need only secure the value of z, and σ can be solved for. To do this, we must use the probability information given and the z distribution table to find the value of z.

Study the layout of this problem in **Figure 6.19** in order to determine how to proceed. Think about how probabilities are given in the z distribution table.

How can we use the fact that 74.22% of the weights are more than 40 as shown in Figure 6.19? Recall that the z distribution table associated with this text always gives probability values for areas between a given x value and the mean. In this problem, if we subtract off the 50% of the area greater than the mean, it leaves an area of 24.22% between the mean and $x = 40$. Converting this to a proportion, we can say that .2422 of the area lies between the mean and x. Now, we can look up this value as an area (probability) in the z distribution table and back out the associated value of z, which is 0.65. In this example, since the value of x is to the left of the mean, we must manually assign a negative sign to the z value, resulting in $z = -0.65$.

The mean, μ, is 44, the value of $x = 40$, and $z = -0.65$. Using these values, σ can now be solved for as follows:

$$-0.65 = \frac{40 - 44}{\sigma}$$

$$\sigma = 6.154$$

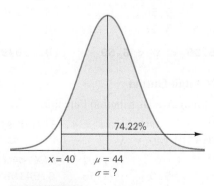

$$x = 40 \qquad \mu = 44$$
$$\sigma = ?$$

74.22%

FIGURE 6.19   **Layout for the Clay Pipe Problem**

Thinking Critically About Statistics in Business Today

Warehousing

Tompkins Associates conducted a national study of warehousing in the United States. The study revealed many interesting facts. Warehousing is a labor-intensive industry that presents considerable opportunity for improvement in productivity. What does the "average" warehouse look like? The construction of new warehouses is restricted by prohibitive expense. Perhaps for that reason, the average age of a warehouse is 19 years. Warehouses vary in size, but the average size is about 50,000 square feet. To visualize such an "average" warehouse, picture one that is square with about 224 feet on each side or a rectangle that is 500 feet by 100 feet. The average clear height of a warehouse in the United States is 22 feet.

Suppose the ages of warehouses, the sizes of warehouses, and the clear heights of warehouses are normally distributed. Using the mean values already given and the standard deviations, techniques presented in this section could be used to determine, for example, the probability that a randomly selected warehouse is less than 15 years old, is larger than 60,000 square feet, or has a clear height between 20 and 25 feet.

THINGS TO PONDER

1. The feature states that "Warehousing is a labor-intensive industry that presents considerable opportunity for improvement in productivity." How might there be opportunities for improvement in productivity of warehousing?

2. What are some reasons why new warehouses might be prohibitively expensive?

3. With current technology, what are some ways that warehousing may be changing?

Using the Computer to Solve for Normal Distribution Probabilities

Both Excel and Minitab can be used to solve for normal distribution probabilities. In each case, the computer package uses μ, σ, and the value of x to compute a cumulative probability from the left. Shown in Table 6.3 are Excel and Minitab output for the probability question addressed in Demonstration Problem 6.4: $P(5.30 < x < 6.50 | \mu = 4.43$ and $\sigma = 1.32)$. Since both computer packages yield probabilities cumulated from the left, this problem is solved manually with the computer output by finding the difference in $P(x < 6.50)$ and $P(x < 5.30)$.

TABLE 6.3	Excel and Minitab Normal Distribution Output for Demonstration Problem 6.4

Excel Output

x Value	Probability
6.50	0.941581
5.30	0.745081
5.30 < x < 6.50	**0.196499**

Minitab Output

Cumulative Distribution Function

Normal with mean = 4.43 and standard deviation = 1.32

x	P(X <= x)
6.5	0.941581
5.3	0.745081

Prob (5.3 < x < 6.5) = 0.196500

6.2 Problems

6.6. Determine the probabilities for the following normal distribution problems.

a. $\mu = 604$, $\sigma = 56.8$, $x \leq 635$

b. $\mu = 48$, $\sigma = 12$, $x < 20$

c. $\mu = 111$, $\sigma = 33.8$, $100 \leq x < 150$

d. $\mu = 264$, $\sigma = 10.9$, $250 < x < 255$

e. $\mu = 37$, $\sigma = 4.35$, $x > 35$

f. $\mu = 156$, $\sigma = 11.4$, $x \geq 170$

6.7. Tompkins Associates reports that the mean clear height for a Class A warehouse in the United States is 22 feet. Suppose clear heights are normally distributed and that the standard deviation is 4 feet. A Class A warehouse in the United States is randomly selected.

a. What is the probability that the clear height is greater than 17 feet?

b. What is the probability that the clear height is less than 13 feet?

c. What is the probability that the clear height is between 25 and 31 feet?

6.8. According to CBS Money Watch, the average monthly household cellular phone bill is $100. Suppose monthly household cell phone bills are normally distributed with a standard deviation of $11.35.

a. What is the probability that a randomly selected monthly cell phone bill is more than $127?

b. What is the probability that a randomly selected monthly cell phone bill is between $87 and $110?

c. What is the probability that a randomly selected monthly cell phone bill is between $107 and $117?

d. What is the probability that a randomly selected monthly cell phone bill is no more than $82?

6.9. According to the Internal Revenue Service, income tax returns one year averaged $1,332 in refunds for taxpayers. One explanation of this figure is that taxpayers would rather have the government keep back too much money during the year than to owe it money at the end of the year. Suppose the average amount of tax at the end of a year is a refund of $1,332, with a standard deviation of $725. Assume that amounts owed or due on tax returns are normally distributed.

a. What proportion of tax returns show a refund greater than $2,000?

b. What proportion of the tax returns show that the taxpayer owes money to the government?

c. What proportion of the tax returns show a refund between $100 and $700?

6.10. Toolworkers are subject to work-related injuries. One disorder, caused by strains to the hands and wrists, is called carpal tunnel syndrome. It strikes as many as 23,000 workers per year. The U.S. Labor Department estimates that the average cost of this disorder to

employers and insurers is approximately $30,000 per injured worker. Suppose these costs are normally distributed, with a standard deviation of $9,000.

a. What proportion of the costs are between $15,000 and $45,000?

b. What proportion of the costs are greater than $50,000?

c. What proportion of the costs are between $5,000 and $20,000?

d. Suppose the standard deviation is unknown, but the mean is still $30,000 and 90.82% of the costs are more than $7,000. What would be the value of the standard deviation?

e. Suppose the mean value is unknown, but the standard deviation is still $9,000. How much would the average cost be if 79.95% of the costs were less than $33,000?

6.11. Suppose you are working with a data set that is normally distributed, with a mean of 200 and a standard deviation of 47. Determine the value of x from the following information.

a. 60% of the values are greater than x.

b. x is below 17% of the values.

c. 22% of the values are less than x.

d. x is greater than 55% of the values.

6.12. Suppose the annual employer 401(k) cost per participant is normally distributed with a standard deviation of $625, but the mean is unknown.

a. If 73.89% of such costs are greater than $1,700, what is the mean annual employer 401(k) cost per participant?

b. Suppose the mean annual employer 401(k) cost per participant is $2,258 and the standard deviation is $625. If such costs are normally distributed, 31.56% of the costs are greater than what value?

6.13. Based on annual driving of 15,000 miles and fuel efficiency of 20 mpg, a car in the United States uses, on average, 750 gallons of gasoline per year. If annual automobile fuel usage is normally distributed, and if 29.12% of cars in the United States use less than 500 gallons of gasoline per year, what is the standard deviation?

6.14. The U.S. national average door-to-doctor wait time for patients to see a doctor is now 21.3 minutes. Suppose such wait times are normally distributed with a standard deviation of 6.7 minutes. Some patients will have to wait much longer than the mean to see the doctor. In fact, based on this information, 3% of patients still have to wait more than how many minutes to see a doctor?

6.15. Suppose commute times in a large city are normally distributed and that 62.5% of commuters in this city take more than 21 minutes to commute one-way. If the standard deviation of such commutes is 6.2 minutes, what is the mean commute?

6.16. According to Student Monitor, a New Jersey research firm, the average cumulated college student loan debt for a graduating senior is $25,760. Assume that the standard deviation of such student loan debt is $5,684. Thirty percent of these graduating seniors owe more than what amount?

6.3 Using the Normal Curve to Approximate Binomial Distribution Problems

For certain types of binomial distribution problems, the normal distribution can be used to approximate the probabilities. As sample sizes become large, binomial distributions approach the normal distribution in shape regardless of the value of p. This phenomenon occurs faster (for smaller values of n) when p is near .50. Figures 6.20 through 6.22 show three binomial distributions. Note in Figure 6.20 that even though the sample size, n, is only 10, the binomial graph bears a strong resemblance to a normal curve.

The graph in Figure 6.21 ($n = 10$ and $p = .20$) is skewed to the right because of the low p value and the small size. For this distribution, the expected value is only 2 and the

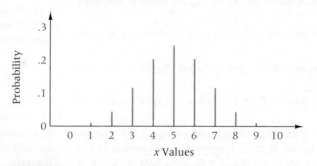

FIGURE 6.20 The Binomial Distribution for $n = 10$ and $p = .50$

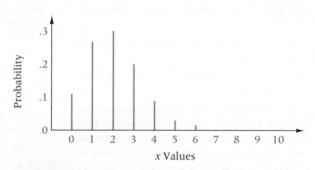

FIGURE 6.21 The Binomial Distribution for $n = 10$ and $p = .20$

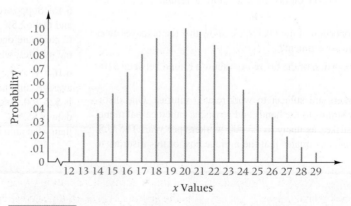

FIGURE 6.22 The Binomial Distribution for $n = 100$ and $p = .20$

probabilities pile up at $x = 0$ and 1. However, when n becomes large enough, as in the binomial distribution ($n = 100$ and $p = .20$) presented in Figure 6.22, the graph is relatively symmetric around the mean ($\mu = n \cdot p = 20$) because enough possible outcome values to the left of $x = 20$ allow the curve to fall back to the x-axis.

For large n values, the binomial distribution is cumbersome to analyze without a computer. Table A.2 goes only to $n = 25$. The normal distribution is a good approximation for binomial distribution problems for large values of n.

To work a binomial problem by the normal curve requires a translation process. The first part of this process is to convert the two parameters of a binomial distribution, n and p, to the two parameters of the normal distribution, μ and σ. This process utilizes formulas from Chapter 5:

$$\mu = n \cdot p \text{ and } \sigma = \sqrt{n \cdot p \cdot q}$$

After completion of this, a test must be made to determine whether the normal distribution is a good enough approximation of the binomial distribution:

$$\text{Does the interval } \mu \pm 3\sigma \text{ lie between 0 and } n?$$

Recall that the empirical rule states that approximately 99.7%, or almost all, of the values of a normal curve are within three standard deviations of the mean. For a normal curve approximation of a binomial distribution problem to be acceptable, all possible x values should be between 0 and n, which are the lower and upper limits, respectively, of a binomial distribution. If $\mu \pm 3\sigma$ is not between 0 and n, do *not* use the normal distribution to work a binomial problem because the approximation is not good enough. Upon demonstration that the normal curve is a good approximation for a binomial problem, the procedure continues. Another rule of thumb for determining when to use the normal curve to approximate a binomial problem is that the approximation is good enough if both $n \cdot p > 5$ and $n \cdot q > 5$.

The process can be illustrated in the solution of the binomial distribution problem.

$$P(x \geq 25 | n = 60 \text{ and } p = .30) = ?$$

Note that this binomial problem contains a relatively large sample size and that none of the binomial tables in Appendix A.2 can be used to solve the problem. This problem is a good candidate for use of the normal distribution.

Translating from a binomial problem to a normal curve problem gives

$$\mu = n \cdot p = (60)(.30) = 18 \text{ and } \sigma = \sqrt{n \cdot p \cdot q} = 3.55$$

The binomial problem becomes a normal curve problem.

$$P(x \geq 25 | \mu = 18 \text{ and } \sigma = 3.55) = ?$$

Next, the test is made to determine whether the normal curve sufficiently fits this binomial distribution to justify the use of the normal curve.

$$\mu \pm 3\sigma = 18 \pm 3(3.55) = 18 \pm 10.65$$

$$7.35 \leq \mu \pm 3\sigma \leq 28.65$$

This interval is between 0 and 60, so the approximation is sufficient to allow use of the normal curve. Figure 6.23 is a Minitab graph of this binomial distribution. Notice how closely it resembles the normal curve. Figure 6.24 is the apparent graph of the normal curve version of this problem.

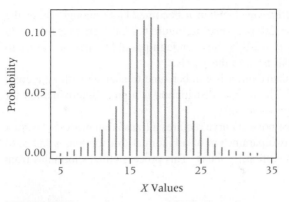

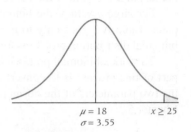

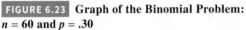

FIGURE 6.23 Graph of the Binomial Problem: $n = 60$ and $p = .30$

FIGURE 6.24 Graph of Apparent Solution of Binomial Problem Worked by the Normal Curve

Correcting for Continuity

The translation of a discrete distribution to a continuous distribution is not completely straightforward. A correction of +.50 or −.50 or ±.50, depending on the problem, is required. This correction ensures that most of the binomial problem's information is correctly transferred to the normal curve analysis. This correction is called the **correction for continuity**, which is *made during conversion of a discrete distribution into a continuous distribution.*

Figure 6.25 is a portion of the graph of the binomial distribution, $n = 60$ and $p = .30$. Note that with a binomial distribution, all the probabilities are concentrated on the whole numbers. Thus, the answers for $x \geq 25$ are found by summing the probabilities for $x = 25, 26, 27, \ldots ,$ 60. There are no values between 24 and 25, 25 and 26, $\ldots$, 59, and 60. Yet, the normal distribution is continuous, and values are present all along the x-axis. A correction must be made for this discrepancy for the approximation to be as accurate as possible.

As an analogy, visualize the process of melting iron rods in a furnace. The iron rods are like the probability values on each whole number of a binomial distribution. Note that the binomial graph in Figure 6.25 looks like a series of iron rods in a line. When the rods are placed in a furnace, they melt down and spread out. Each rod melts and moves to fill the area between it and the adjacent rods. The result is a continuous sheet of solid iron (continuous iron) that looks like the normal curve. The melting of the rods is analogous to spreading the binomial distribution to approximate the normal distribution.

How far does each rod spread toward the others? A good estimate is that each rod goes about halfway toward the adjacent rods. In other words, a rod that was concentrated at $x = 25$ spreads to cover the area from 24.5 to 25.5; $x = 26$ becomes continuous from 25.5 to 26.5; and so on. For the problem $P(x \geq 25 | n = 60$ and $p = .30)$, conversion to a continuous normal curve problem yields $P(x \geq 24.5 | \mu = 18$ and $\sigma = 3.55)$. The correction for continuity was

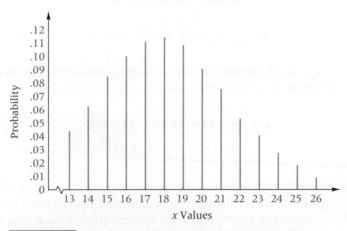

FIGURE 6.25 Graph of a Portion of the Binomial Problem: $n = 60$ and $p = .30$

TABLE 6.4	Rules of Thumb for the Correction for Continuity
VALUES BEING DETERMINED	CORRECTIONS
$x >$	+.50
$x \geq$	−.50
$x <$	−.50
$x \leq$	+.50
$\leq x \leq$	−.50 and +.50
$< x <$	+.50 and −.50
$x =$	−.50 and +.50

−.50 because the problem called for the inclusion of the value of 25 along with all greater values; the binomial value of $x = 25$ translates to the normal curve value of 24.5 to 25.5. Had the binomial problem been to analyze $P(x > 25)$, the correction would have been +.50, resulting in a normal curve problem of $P(x \geq 25.5)$. The latter case would begin at more than 25 because the value of 25 would not be included.

The decision as to how to correct for continuity depends on the equality sign and the direction of the desired outcomes of the binomial distribution. Table 6.4 lists some rules of thumb that can help in the application of the correction for continuity.

For the binomial problem $P(x \geq 25 | n = 60$ and $p = .30)$, the normal curve becomes $P(x \geq 24.5 | \mu = 18$ and $\sigma = 3.55)$, as shown in Figure 6.26, and

$$z = \frac{x - \mu}{\sigma} = \frac{24.5 - 18}{3.55} = 1.83$$

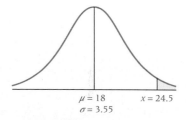

$\mu = 18$ $x = 24.5$
$\sigma = 3.55$

FIGURE 6.26 Graph of the Solution to the Binomial Problem Worked by the Normal Curve

The probability (Table 6.2) of this z value is .4664. The answer to this problem lies in the tail of the distribution, so the final answer is obtained by subtracting.

```
 .5000
−.4664
 .0336
```

Had this problem been worked by using the binomial formula, the solution would have been as shown in Table 6.5. The difference between the normal distribution approximation and the actual binomial values is only .0025 (.0361 − .0336).

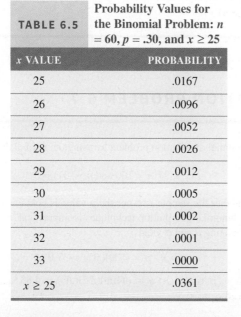

TABLE 6.5	Probability Values for the Binomial Problem: $n = 60$, $p = .30$, and $x \geq 25$
x VALUE	PROBABILITY
25	.0167
26	.0096
27	.0052
28	.0026
29	.0012
30	.0005
31	.0002
32	.0001
33	.0000
$x \geq 25$	.0361

DEMONSTRATION PROBLEM 6.6

Work the following binomial distribution problem by using the normal distribution.

$$P(x = 12 | n = 25 \text{ and } p = .40) = ?$$

Solution: Find μ and σ.

$$\mu = n \cdot p = (25)(.40) = 10.0$$
$$\sigma = \sqrt{n \cdot p \cdot q} = \sqrt{(25)(.40)(.60)} = 2.45$$
$$\text{test} : \mu \pm 3\sigma = 10.0 \pm 3(2.45) = 2.65 \text{ to } 17.35$$

This range is between 0 and 25, so the approximation is close enough. Correct for continuity next. Because the problem is to determine the probability of x being exactly 12, the correction entails both −.50 and +.50. That is, a binomial probability at $x = 12$ translates to a continuous normal curve area that lies between 11.5 and 12.5. The graph of the problem follows:

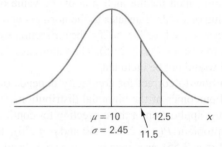

Then,

$$z = \frac{x - \mu}{\sigma} = \frac{12.5 - 10}{2.45} = 1.02$$

and

$$z = \frac{x - \mu}{\sigma} = \frac{11.5 - 10}{2.45} = 0.61$$

$$z = 1.02 \text{ produces a probability of } .3461.$$
$$z = 0.61 \text{ produces a probability of } .2291.$$

The difference in areas yields the following answer:

$$.3461 - .2291 = .1170$$

Had this problem been worked by using the binomial tables, the resulting answer would have been .114. The difference between the normal curve approximation and the value obtained by using binomial tables is only .003.

DEMONSTRATION PROBLEM 6.7

Solve the following binomial distribution problem by using the normal distribution.

$$P(x < 27 | n = 100 \text{ and } p = .37) = ?$$

Solution: Because neither the sample size nor the p value is contained in Table A.2, working this problem by using binomial distribution techniques is impractical. It is a good candidate for the normal curve. Calculating μ and σ yields

$$\mu = n \cdot p = (100)(.37) = 37.0$$
$$\sigma = \sqrt{n \cdot p \cdot q} = \sqrt{(100)(.37)(.63)} = 4.83$$

Testing to determine the closeness of the approximation gives

$$\mu \pm 3\sigma = 37 \pm 3(4.83) = 37 \pm 14.49$$

The range 22.51 to 51.49 is between 0 and 100. This problem satisfies the conditions of the test. Next, correct for continuity: $x < 27$ as a binomial problem translates to $x \le 26.5$ as a normal distribution problem. The graph of the problem follows.

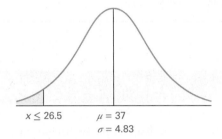

$x \le 26.5$ $\mu = 37$
$\sigma = 4.83$

Then,

$$z = \frac{x - \mu}{\sigma} = \frac{26.5 - 37}{4.83} = -2.17$$

Table 6.2 shows a probability of .4850. Solving for the tail of the distribution gives

$$.5000 - .4850 = .0150$$

which is the answer.

Had this problem been solved by using the binomial formula, the probabilities would have been the following.

x VALUE	PROBABILITY
26	.0059
25	.0035
24	.0019
23	.0010
22	.0005
21	.0002
20	.0001
x < 27	.0131

The answer obtained by using the normal curve approximation (.0150) compares favorably to this exact binomial answer. The difference is only .0019.

Thinking Critically About Statistics in Business Today

Teleworking Facts

There are many interesting statistics about teleworkers. In a recent year, there were 45 million teleworkers in the United States, and more than 18% of employed adult Americans telework from home during business hours at least one day per month. Fifty-seven percent of HR professionals indicate that their organizations offer some form of telecommuting. The typical teleworker works an average of 5.5 days at home per month. The average commuting distance of a teleworker when he/she is not teleworking is 18 miles. Teleworkers save an average of 53 minutes commuting each day, saving them the equivalent of one extra day of work for every nine days of commuting. Thirty-three percent of Canadians would prefer to telework over a 10% wage increase, and 43% would change jobs to an employer allowing telework. Sixty-five percent of home teleworkers are males versus 44% of non-teleworkers. Among 20 United States government agencies, the average per-user cost of setting up telecommuting is $1,920. Telecommuting saves

840 million gallons of fuel annually in the United States, and telecommuting saves the equivalent of 9 to 14 billion kilowatt-hours of electricity per year—the same amount of energy used by roughly 1 million United States households every year.

THINGS TO PONDER

1. What are some of the impacts of telecommuting on the company, the worker, and the product or service? That is, what are some of the pros and cons of telecommuting on the various constituencies?

2. What are some aspects of our culture that have facilitated the advent of telecommuting?

Source: Telecommuting and Remote Work Statistics site, http://www.suitecommute.com/Statistics.htm; and Telework Facts, http://www.telcoa.org/id33_m.htm.

6.3 Problems

6.17. Convert the following binomial distribution problems to normal distribution problems. Use the correction for continuity.

a. $P(x \leq 16 \mid n = 30$ and $p = .70)$

b. $P(10 < x \leq 20) \mid n = 25$ and $p = .50)$

c. $P(x = 22 \mid n = 40$ and $p = .60)$

d. $P(x > 14 \mid n = 16$ and $p = .45)$

6.18. Use the test $\mu \pm 3\sigma$ to determine whether the following binomial distributions can be approximated by using the normal distribution.

a. $n = 8$ and $p = .50$

b. $n = 18$ and $p = .80$

c. $n = 12$ and $p = .30$

d. $n = 30$ and $p = .75$

e. $n = 14$ and $p = .50$

6.19. Where appropriate, work the following binomial distribution problems by using the normal curve. Also, use Table A.2 to find the answers by using the binomial distribution and compare the answers obtained by the two methods.

a. $P(x = 8 \mid n = 25$ and $p = .40) = ?$

b. $P(x \geq 13 \mid n = 20$ and $p = .60) = ?$

c. $P(x = 7 \mid n = 15$ and $p = .50) = ?$

d. $P(x < 3 \mid n = 10$ and $p = .70) = ?$

6.20. The Zimmerman Agency conducted a study for Residence Inn by Marriott of business travelers who take trips of five nights or more. According to this study, 37% of these travelers enjoy sightseeing more than any other activity that they do not get to do as much at home. Suppose 120 randomly selected business travelers who take trips of five nights or more are contacted. What is the probability that fewer than 40 enjoy sightseeing more than any other activity that they do not get to do as much at home?

6.21. One study on managers' satisfaction with management tools reveals that 59% of all managers use self-directed work teams as a management tool. Suppose 70 managers selected randomly in the United States are interviewed. What is the probability that fewer than 35 use self-directed work teams as a management tool?

6.22. According to the Yankee Group, 53% of all cable households rate cable companies as good or excellent in quality transmission. Sixty percent of all cable households rate cable companies as good or excellent in having professional personnel. Suppose 300 cable households are randomly contacted.

a. What is the probability that more than 175 cable households rate cable companies as good or excellent in quality transmission?

b. What is the probability that between 165 and 170 (inclusive) cable households rate cable companies as good or excellent in quality transmission?

c. What is the probability that between 155 and 170 (inclusive) cable households rate cable companies as good or excellent in having professional personnel?

d. What is the probability that fewer than 200 cable households rate cable companies as good or excellent in having professional personnel?

6.23. According to the International Data Corporation, HP is the leading company in the United States in PC sales with about 26% of the market share. Suppose a business researcher randomly selects 130 recent purchasers of PCs in the United States.

a. What is the probability that more than 39 PC purchasers bought an HP computer?

b. What is the probability that between 28 and 38 PC purchasers (inclusive) bought an HP computer?

c. What is the probability that fewer than 23 PC purchasers bought an HP computer?

d. What is the probability that exactly 33 PC purchasers bought an HP computer?

6.24. A study about strategies for competing in the global marketplace states that 52% of the respondents agreed that companies need to make direct investments in foreign countries. It also states that about 70% of those responding agree that it is attractive to have a joint venture to increase global competitiveness. Suppose CEOs of 95 manufacturing companies are randomly contacted about global strategies.

a. What is the probability that between 44 and 52 (inclusive) CEOs agree that companies should make direct investments in foreign countries?

b. What is the probability that more than 56 CEOs agree with that assertion?

c. What is the probability that fewer than 60 CEOs agree that it is attractive to have a joint venture to increase global competitiveness?

d. What is the probability that between 55 and 62 (inclusive) CEOs agree with that assertion?

6.4 | Exponential Distribution

Another useful continuous distribution is the exponential distribution. It is closely related to the Poisson distribution. Whereas the Poisson distribution is discrete and describes random occurrences over some interval, the exponential distribution is *continuous and describes a probability distribution of the times between random occurrences.* The following are the characteristics of the exponential distribution.

- It is a continuous distribution.
- It is a family of distributions.
- It is skewed to the right.
- The x values range from zero to infinity.
- Its apex is always at $x = 0$.
- The curve steadily decreases as x gets larger.

The exponential probability distribution is determined by the following.

Exponential Probability Density Function

$$f(x) = \lambda e^{-\lambda x}$$

where

$x \geq 0$

$\lambda > 0$

and $e = 2.71828\ldots$

An exponential distribution can be characterized by the one parameter, λ. Each unique value of λ determines a different exponential distribution, resulting in a family of exponential distributions. **Figure 6.27** shows graphs of exponential distributions for four values of λ. The points on the graph are determined by using λ and various values of x in the probability density formula. The mean of an exponential distribution is $\mu = 1/\lambda$, and the standard deviation of an exponential distribution is $\sigma = 1/\lambda$.

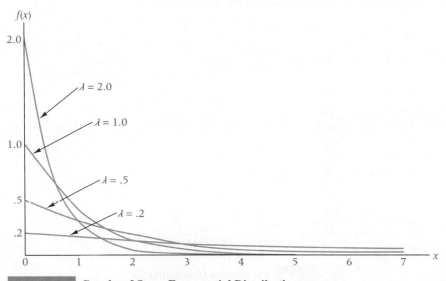

FIGURE 6.27 **Graphs of Some Exponential Distributions**

Probabilities of the Exponential Distribution

Probabilities are computed for the exponential distribution by determining the area under the curve between two points. Applying calculus to the exponential probability density function produces a formula that can be used to calculate the probabilities of an exponential distribution.

Probabilities of the Right Tail of the Exponential Distribution

$$P(x \geq x_0) = e^{-\lambda x_0}$$

where

$$x_0 \geq 0$$

To use this formula requires finding values of e^{-x}. These values can be computed on most calculators or obtained from Table A.4, which contains the values of e^{-x} for selected values of x. x_0 is the fraction of the interval or the number of intervals between arrivals in the probability question and λ is the average arrival rate.

As an example, arrivals at a bank are Poisson distributed with a λ of 1.2 customers every minute. What is the average time between arrivals and what is the probability that at least 2 minutes will elapse between one arrival and the next arrival? Since the interval for lambda is 1 minute and we want to know the probability that at least 2 minutes transpire between arrivals (twice the lambda interval), x_0 is 2.

Interarrival times of random arrivals are exponentially distributed. The mean of this exponential distribution is $\mu = 1/\lambda = 1/1.2 = .833$ minute (50 seconds). On average, .833 minute, or 50 seconds, will elapse between arrivals at the bank. The probability of an interval of 2 minutes or more between arrivals can be calculated by

$$P(x \geq 2 \mid \lambda = 1.2) = e^{-1.2(2)} = .0907.$$

About 9.07% of the time when the rate of random arrivals is 1.2 per minute, 2 minutes or more will elapse between arrivals, as shown in **Figure 6.28**.

This problem underscores the potential of using the exponential distribution in conjunction with the Poisson distribution to solve problems. In operations research and management science, these two distributions are used together to solve queuing problems (theory of waiting lines). The Poisson distribution can be used to analyze the arrivals to the queue, and the exponential distribution can be used to analyze the interarrival time.

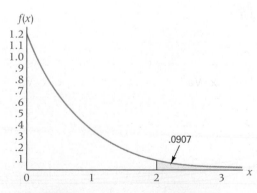

FIGURE 6.28 **Exponential Distribution for** $\lambda = 1.2$ **and Solution for** $x \geq 2$

DEMONSTRATION PROBLEM 6.8

A manufacturing firm has been involved in statistical quality control for several years. As part of the production process, parts are randomly selected and tested. From the records of these tests, it has been established that a defective part occurs in a pattern that is Poisson distributed on the average of 1.38 defects every 20 minutes during production runs. Use this information to determine the probability that less than 15 minutes will elapse between any two defects.

Solution: The value of λ is 1.38 defects per 20-minute interval. The value of μ can be determined by

$$\mu = \frac{1}{\lambda} = \frac{1}{1.38} = .7246$$

On the average, it is .7246 of the interval, or $(.7246)(20 \text{ minutes}) = 14.49$ minutes, between defects. The value of x_0 represents the desired number of intervals between arrivals or occurrences for the probability question. In this problem, the probability question involves 15 minutes and the interval is 20 minutes. Thus x_0 is $15/20$, or .75 of an interval. The question here is to determine the probability of there being less than 15 minutes between defects. The probability formula always yields the right tail of the distribution—in this case, the probability of there being 15 minutes or more between arrivals. By using the value of x_0 and the value of λ, the probability of there being 15 minutes or more between defects can be determined.

$$P(x \geq x_0) = P(x \geq .75) = e^{-\lambda x_0} = e^{(-1.38)(.75)} = e^{-1.035} = .3552$$

The probability of .3552 is the probability that at least 15 minutes will elapse between defects. To determine the probability of there being less than 15 minutes between defects, compute $1 - P(x)$. In this case, $1 - .3552 = .6448$. There is a probability of .6448 that less than 15 minutes will elapse between two defects when there is an average of 1.38 defects per 20-minute interval or an average of 14.49 minutes between defects.

Using the Computer to Determine Exponential Distribution Probabilities

Both Excel and Minitab can be used to solve for exponential distribution probabilities. Excel uses the value of λ and x_0, but Minitab requires μ (equals $1/\lambda$) and x_0. In each case, the computer yields the cumulative probability from the left (the complement of what the probability formula shown in this section yields). Table 6.6 provides Excel and Minitab output for the probability question addressed in Demonstration Problem 6.8.

TABLE 6.6	Excel and Minitab Output for Exponential Distribution

Excel Output

```
x Value  Probability < x Value
0.75       0.6448
```

Minitab Output

Cumulative Distribution Function

```
Exponential with mean = 0.7246

x       P(X <= x)
0.75  0.644793
```

6.4 Problems

6.25. Use the probability density formula to sketch the graphs of the following exponential distributions.

   a. $\lambda = 0.1$

   b. $\lambda = 0.3$

   c. $\lambda = 0.8$

   d. $\lambda = 3.0$

6.26. Determine the mean and standard deviation of the following exponential distributions.

   a. $\lambda = 3.25$

   b. $\lambda = 0.7$

   c. $\lambda = 1.1$

   d. $\lambda = 6.0$

6.27. Determine the following exponential probabilities.

   a. $P(x \geq 5 | \lambda = 1.35)$

   b. $P(x < 3 | \lambda = 0.68)$

   c. $P(x > 4 | \lambda = 1.7)$

   d. $P(x < 6 | \lambda = 0.80)$

6.28. The average length of time between arrivals at a turnpike tollbooth is 23 seconds. Assume that the time between arrivals at the tollbooth is exponentially distributed.

   a. What is the probability that a minute or more will elapse between arrivals?

   b. If a car has just passed through the tollbooth, what is the probability that no car will show up for at least 3 minutes?

6.29. A busy restaurant determined that between 6:30 P.M. and 9:00 P.M. on Friday nights, the arrivals of customers are Poisson distributed with an average arrival rate of 2.44 per minute.

   a. What is the probability that at least 10 minutes will elapse between arrivals?

   b. What is the probability that at least 5 minutes will elapse between arrivals?

   c. What is the probability that at least 1 minute will elapse between arrivals?

   d. What is the expected amount of time between arrivals?

6.30. During the summer at a small private airport in western Nebraska, the unscheduled arrival of airplanes is Poisson distributed with an average arrival rate of 1.12 planes per hour.

   a. What is the average interarrival time between planes?

   b. What is the probability that at least 2 hours will elapse between plane arrivals?

   c. What is the probability of two planes arriving less than 10 minutes apart?

6.31. The exponential distribution can be used to solve Poisson-type problems in which the intervals are not time. The Air Travel Consumer Report published by the U.S. Department of Transportation reported that in a recent year, Virgin America led the nation in fewest occurrences of mishandled baggage, with a mean rate of 0.95 per 1,000 passengers. Assume that mishandled baggage occurrences are Poisson distributed. Using the exponential distribution to analyze this problem, determine the average number of passengers between occurrences. Suppose baggage has just been mishandled.

   a. What is the probability that at least 500 passengers will have their baggage handled properly before the next mishandling occurs?

   b. What is the probability that the number will be fewer than 200 passengers?

6.32. The Foundation Corporation specializes in constructing the concrete foundations for new houses in the South. The company knows that because of soil types, moisture conditions, variable construction, and other factors, eventually most foundations will need major repair. On the basis of its records, the company's president believes that a new house foundation on average will not need major repair for 20 years. If she wants to guarantee the company's work against major repair but wants to have to honor no more than 10% of its guarantees, for how many years should the company guarantee its work? Assume that occurrences of major foundation repairs are Poisson distributed.

6.33. During the dry month of August, one U.S. city has measurable rain on average only two days per month. If the arrival of rainy days is Poisson distributed in this city during the month of August, what is the average number of days that will pass between measurable rain? What is the standard deviation? What is the probability during this month that there will be a period of less than two days between rain?

Decision Dilemma Solved

CSX Corporation

If rail freight line-haul speeds are uniformly distributed with an average speed of 23.7 mph and if the minimum and maximum speeds are 21 mph and 26.4 mph respectively, what percentage of line-hauls would have speeds of between 22 and 24 mph? Using techniques presented in Section 6.1, this uniform distribution can be described by $a = 21$, $b = 26.4$, and $\mu = 23.7$. The probability that a line-haul would have a speed between 22 and 24 mph can be determined by the following calculation assuming that $x_1 = 22$ and $x_2 = 24$:

$$P(x) = \frac{x_2 - x_1}{b - a} = \frac{24 - 22}{26.4 - 21} = \frac{2}{5.4} = .3704$$

Thus, 37.04% of the time, the line-haul speed is between 22 and 24 mph.

What percentage of the time would the line-haul speed be more than 25 mph? The probability of this occurring is:

$$P(x) = \frac{x_2 - x_1}{b - a} = \frac{26.4 - 25}{26.4 - 21} = \frac{1.4}{5.4} = .2593$$

Therefore, 25.93% of the time, the line-haul speed is more than 25 mph.

If terminal dwell time is normally distributed with a mean of 27.5 hours and a standard deviation of 2.6 hours, what is the probability that a randomly selected rail car has a terminal dwell time of more than 32.4 hours? We can solve this problem using techniques presented in Section 6.2 as:

$$z = \frac{x - \mu}{\sigma} = \frac{32.4 - 27.5}{2.6} = 1.88$$

The area associated with this z value is .4699 and the tail of the distribution is $.5000 - .4699 = .0301$. That is, the probability that a randomly selected rail car has a terminal dwell time of more than 32.4 hours is .0301.

What is the probability that a randomly selected rail car has a terminal dwell time of less than 26 hours? This probability can be solved in a similar manner using techniques from Section 6.2:

$$z = \frac{x - \mu}{\sigma} = \frac{26 - 27.5}{2.6} = -0.58$$

The area associated with this z value is .2190 and the tail of the distribution is $.5000 - .2190 = .2810$. That is, the probability that a randomly selected rail car has a terminal dwell time of less than 26 hours is .2810.

Suppose that 45% of all freight trains arrive on time. Based on this, what is the probability of randomly selecting 120 trains and finding out that more than 65 were on time? This is a binomial distribution problem with $n = 120$, $p = .45$, and $x > 65$. Using techniques presented in Section 6.3, the probability that $x > 65$ can be solved by converting the problem into a normal curve problem:

$$\mu = n \cdot p = (120)(.45) = 54$$

and

$$\sigma = \sqrt{n \cdot p \cdot q} = \sqrt{(120)(.45)(.55)} = 5.45$$

Since $54 \pm 3(5.45)$ is between 0 and 120, it is appropriate to use the normal distribution to approximate this binomial problem. Applying the correction for continuity, $x \geq 65.5$. The z value is calculated as:

$$z = \frac{x - \mu}{\sigma} = \frac{65.5 - 54}{5.45} = 2.11$$

The area associated with this z value is .4826 and the tail of the distribution is $.5000 - .4826 = .0174$. That is, 1.74% of the time, more than 65 trains out of 120 trains will arrive on time.

Suppose that at a relatively small railroad, on average, 1.7 employees call in sick per day and that the number of employees calling in sick per day is Poisson distributed. What is the probability that at least two days go by with no worker calling in sick? Using techniques from Section 6.4, this is an exponential distribution problem with a lambda of 1.7 per day. This problem is a right-side probability question with $x_0 = 2$ (since two days is twice the lambda). Using $\lambda = 1.7$ and $x_0 = 2$, the probability can be solved as:

$$P(x_0 \geq 2 \mid \lambda = 1.7) = e^{-2(1.7)} = e^{-3.4} = .0334.$$

If, on average, 1.7 employees call in sick per day, there is only a .0334 probability that two days would go by without anyone calling in sick.

Ethical Considerations

Several points must be considered in working with continuous distributions. Is the population being studied the same population from which the parameters (mean, standard deviation, λ) were determined? If not, the results may not be valid for the analysis being done. Invalid or spurious results can be obtained by using the parameters from one population to analyze another population. For example, a market study in New England may result in the conclusion that the amount of fish eaten per month by adults is normally distributed with the average of 2.3 pounds of fish per month. A market researcher in the Southwest should not assume that these figures apply to her population. People in the Southwest probably have quite different fish-eating habits than people in New England, and the application of New England population parameters to the Southwest probably will result in questionable conclusions.

As was true with the Poisson distribution in Chapter 5, the use of λ in the exponential distribution should be judicious because a λ for one interval in a given time period or situation may not be the same as the λ for the same interval in a different time period or situation. For example, the number of arrivals per five-minute time period at a restaurant on Friday night is not likely to be the same as the number of arrivals in a five-minute time period at that same restaurant from 2 P.M. to 4 P.M. on weekdays. In using established parameters such as μ and λ, a researcher should be certain that the population from which the parameter was determined is, indeed, the same population being studied.

Sometimes a normal distribution is used to analyze data when, in fact, the data are not normal. Such an analysis can contain bias and produce false results. Certain techniques for testing a distribution of data can determine whether they are distributed a certain way. Some of the techniques are presented in Chapter 16. In general, Chapter 6 techniques can be misused if the wrong type of distribution is applied to the data or if the distribution used for analysis is the right one but the parameters (μ, σ, λ) do not fit the data of the population being analyzed.

Summary

This chapter discussed three different continuous distributions: the uniform distribution, the normal distribution, and the exponential distribution. With continuous distributions, the value of the probability density function does not yield the probability but instead gives the height of the curve at any given point. In fact, with continuous distributions, the probability at any discrete point is .0000. Probabilities are determined over an interval. In each case, the probability is the area under the curve for the interval being considered. In each distribution, the probability or total area under the curve is 1.

Probably the simplest of these distributions is the uniform distribution, sometimes referred to as the rectangular distribution. The uniform distribution is determined from a probability density function that contains equal values along some interval between the points a and b. Basically, the height of the curve is the same everywhere between these two points. Probabilities are determined by calculating the portion of the rectangle between the two points a and b that is being considered.

The most widely used of all distributions is the normal distribution. Many phenomena are normally distributed, including characteristics of most machine-produced parts, many measurements of the biological and natural environment, and many human characteristics such as height, weight, IQ, and achievement test scores. The normal curve is continuous, symmetrical, unimodal, and asymptotic to the axis; actually, it is a family of curves.

The parameters necessary to describe a normal distribution are the mean and the standard deviation. For convenience, data that are being analyzed by the normal curve should be standardized by using the mean and the standard deviation to compute z scores. A z score is the distance that an x value is from the mean, μ, in units of standard deviations. With the z score of an x value, the probability of that value occurring by chance from a given normal distribution can be determined by using a table of z scores and their associated probabilities.

The normal distribution can be used to work certain types of binomial distribution problems. Doing so requires converting the n and p values of the binomial distribution to μ and σ of the normal distribution. When worked by using the normal distribution, the binomial distribution solution is only an approximation. If the values of $\mu \pm 3\sigma$ are within a range from 0 to n, the approximation is reasonably accurate. Adjusting for the fact that a discrete distribution problem is being worked by using a continuous distribution requires a correction for continuity. The correction for continuity involves adding or subtracting .50 to the x value being analyzed. This correction usually improves the normal curve approximation.

Another continuous distribution is the exponential distribution. It complements the discrete Poisson distribution. The exponential distribution is used to compute the probabilities of times between random occurrences. The exponential distribution is a family of distributions described by one parameter, λ. The distribution is skewed to the right and always has its highest value at $x = 0$.

Key Terms

correction for continuity	normal distribution	standardized normal distribution	z distribution
exponential distribution	rectangular distribution	uniform distribution	z score

Formulas

Probability density function of a uniform distribution

$$f(x) = \begin{cases} \dfrac{1}{b-a} & \text{for } a \le x < b \\ 0 & \text{for all others values} \end{cases}$$

Mean and standard deviation of a uniform distribution

$$\mu = \frac{a+b}{2}$$

$$\sigma = \frac{b-a}{\sqrt{12}}$$

Probability density function of the normal distribution

$$f(x) = \frac{1}{\sigma\sqrt{2\pi}} e^{-(1/2)[(x-\mu)/\sigma]^2}$$

z formula

$$z = \frac{x - \mu}{\sigma}$$

Conversion of a binomial problem to the normal curve

$$\mu = n \cdot p \text{ and } \sigma = \sqrt{n \cdot p \cdot q}$$

Exponential probability density function

$$f(x) = \lambda e^{-\lambda x}$$

Probabilities of the right tail of the exponential distribution

$$P(x \ge x_0) = e^{-\lambda x_0}$$

Supplementary Problems

Calculating the Statistics

6.34. Data are uniformly distributed between the values of 6 and 14. Determine the value of $f(x)$. What are the mean and standard deviation of this distribution? What is the probability of randomly selecting a value greater than 11? What is the probability of randomly selecting a value between 7 and 12?

6.35. Assume a normal distribution and find the following probabilities.

   a. $P(x < 21 | \mu = 25 \text{ and } \sigma = 4)$

   b. $P(x \geq 77 | \mu = 50 \text{ and } \sigma = 9)$

   c. $P(x > 47 | \mu = 50 \text{ and } \sigma = 6)$

   d. $P(13 < x < 29 | \mu = 23 \text{ and } \sigma = 4)$

   e. $P(x \geq 105 | \mu = 90 \text{ and } \sigma = 2.86)$

6.36. Work the following binomial distribution problems by using the normal distribution. Check your answers by using Table A.2 to solve for the probabilities.

   a. $P(x = 12 | n = 25 \text{ and } p = .60)$

   b. $P(x > 5 | n = 15 \text{ and } p = .50)$

   c. $P(x \leq 3 | n = 10 \text{ and } p = .50)$

   d. $P(x \geq 8 | n = 15 \text{ and } p = .40)$

6.37. Find the probabilities for the following exponential distribution problems.

   a. $P(x \geq 3 | \lambda = 1.3)$

   b. $P(x < 2 | \lambda = 2.0)$

   c. $P(1 \leq x \leq 3 | \lambda = 1.65)$

   d. $P(x > 2 | \lambda = .405)$

Testing Your Understanding

6.38. The U.S. Bureau of Labor Statistics reports that of persons who usually work full-time, the average number of hours worked per week is 43.4. Assume that the number of hours worked per week for those who usually work full-time is normally distributed. Suppose 12% of these workers work more than 48 hours. Based on this percentage, what is the standard deviation of number of hours worked per week for these workers?

6.39. A U.S. Bureau of Labor Statistics survey showed that one in five people 16 years of age or older volunteers some of his or her time. If this figure holds for the entire population and if a random sample of 150 people 16 years of age or older is taken, what is the probability that more than 50 of those sampled do volunteer work?

6.40. An entrepreneur opened a small hardware store in a strip mall. During the first few weeks, business was slow, with the store averaging only one customer every 20 minutes in the morning. Assume that the random arrival of customers is Poisson distributed.

   a. What is the probability that at least one hour would elapse between customers?

   b. What is the probability that 10 to 30 minutes would elapse between customers?

   c. What is the probability that less than five minutes would elapse between customers?

6.41. According to an NRF survey conducted by BIGresearch, the average family spends about $237 on electronics (computers, cell phones, etc.) in back-to-college spending per student. Suppose back-to-college family spending on electronics is normally distributed with a standard deviation of $54. If a family of a returning college student is randomly selected, what is the probability that:

   a. They spend less than $150 on back-to-college electronics?

   b. They spend more than $400 on back-to-college electronics?

   c. They spend between $120 and $185 on back-to-college electronics?

6.42. According to the U.S. Department of Agriculture, Alabama egg farmers produce millions of eggs every year. Suppose egg production per year in Alabama is normally distributed, with a standard deviation of 83 million eggs. If during only 3% of the years Alabama egg farmers produce more than 2,655 million eggs, what is the mean egg production by Alabama farmers?

6.43. The U.S. Bureau of Labor Statistics releases figures on the number of full-time wage and salary workers with flexible schedules. The numbers of full-time wage and salary workers in each age category are almost uniformly distributed by age, with ages ranging from 18 to 65 years. If a worker with a flexible schedule is randomly drawn from the U.S. workforce, what is the probability that he or she will be between 25 and 50 years of age? What is the mean value for this distribution? What is the height of the distribution?

6.44. A business convention holds its registration on Wednesday morning from 9:00 A.M. until 12:00 noon. Past history has shown that registrant arrivals follow a Poisson distribution at an average rate of 1.8 every 15 seconds. Fortunately, several facilities are available to register convention members.

   a. What is the average number of seconds between arrivals to the registration area for this conference based on past results?

   b. What is the probability that 25 seconds or more would pass between registration arrivals?

   c. What is the probability that less than five seconds will elapse between arrivals?

   d. Suppose the registration computers went down for a one-minute period. Would this condition pose a problem? What is the probability that at least one minute will elapse between arrivals?

6.45. The Zumper National Rent Report lists the average monthly apartment rent in various locations in the United States. According to their report, the average cost of renting a one-bedroom apartment in Houston is $1,090. Suppose that the standard deviation of the cost of renting a one-bedroom apartment in Houston is $96 and that such apartment rents in Houston are normally distributed. If a one-bedroom apartment in Houston is randomly selected, what is the probability that the price is:

   a. $1150 or more?

   b. Between $1000 and $1200?

   c. Between $950 and $1050?

   d. Less than $800?

6.46. According to *The Wirthlin Report*, 24% of all workers say that their job is very stressful. If 60 workers are randomly selected:

   a. What is the probability that 17 or more say that their job is very stressful?

b. What is the probability that more than 22 say that their job is very stressful?

c. What is the probability that between 8 and 12 (inclusive) say that their job is very stressful?

6.47. According to Bureau of Labor Statistics data, the average income for a worker in the metropolitan Boston area is $61,162. Suppose average income for a worker in the metropolitan Boston area is normally distributed with a standard deviation of $4,246. A metropolitan Boston area worker is randomly selected.

a. What is the probability that the worker's income is more than $70,000?

b. What is the probability that the worker's income is less than $55,000?

c. What is the probability that the worker's income is more than $50,000?

d. What is the probability that the worker's income is between $57,000 and $65,000?

6.48. Suppose interarrival times at a hospital emergency room during a weekday are exponentially distributed, with an average interarrival time of nine minutes. If the arrivals are Poisson distributed, what would the average number of arrivals per hour be? What is the probability that less than five minutes will elapse between any two arrivals?

6.49. Suppose the average speeds of passenger trains traveling from Newark, New Jersey, to Philadelphia, Pennsylvania, are normally distributed, with a mean average speed of 88 miles per hour and a standard deviation of 6.4 miles per hour.

a. What is the probability that a train will average less than 70 miles per hour?

b. What is the probability that a train will average more than 80 miles per hour?

c. What is the probability that a train will average between 90 and 100 miles per hour?

6.50. The Conference Board published information on why companies expect to increase the number of part-time jobs and reduce full-time positions. Eighty-one percent of the companies said the reason was to get a flexible work-force. Suppose 200 companies that expect to increase the number of part-time jobs and reduce full-time positions are identified and contacted. What is the expected number of these companies that would agree that the reason is to get a flexible workforce? What is the probability that between 150 and 155 (not including the 150 or the 155) would give that reason? What is the probability that more than 158 would give that reason? What is the probability that fewer than 144 would give that reason?

6.51. According to the U.S. Bureau of the Census, about 75% of commuters in the United States drive to work alone. Suppose 150 U.S. commuters are randomly sampled.

a. What is the probability that fewer than 105 commuters drive to work alone?

b. What is the probability that between 110 and 120 (inclusive) commuters drive to work alone?

c. What is the probability that more than 95 commuters drive to work alone?

6.52. According to figures released by the National Agricultural Statistics Service of the U.S. Department of Agriculture, the U.S. production of wheat over the past 20 years has been approximately uniformly distributed. Suppose the mean production over this period was 2.165 billion bushels. If the height of this distribution is .862 billion bushels, what are the values of a and b for this distribution?

6.53. The Federal Reserve System publishes data on family income based on its Survey of Consumer Finances. When the head of the household has a college degree, the mean before-tax family income is $85,200. Suppose that 60% of the before-tax family incomes when the head of the household has a college degree are between $75,600 and $94,800 and that these incomes are normally distributed. What is the standard deviation of before-tax family incomes when the head of the household has a college degree?

6.54. According to the Polk Company, a survey of households using the Internet in buying or leasing cars reported that 81% were seeking information about prices. In addition, 44% were seeking information about products offered. Suppose 75 randomly selected households who are using the Internet in buying or leasing cars are contacted.

a. What is the expected number of households who are seeking price information?

b. What is the expected number of households who are seeking information about products offered?

c. What is the probability that 67 or more households are seeking information about prices?

d. What is the probability that fewer than 23 households are seeking information about products offered?

6.55. Coastal businesses along the Gulf of Mexico from Texas to Florida worry about the threat of hurricanes during the season from June through October. Businesses become especially nervous when hurricanes enter the Gulf of Mexico. Suppose the arrival of hurricanes during this season is Poisson distributed, with an average of three hurricanes entering the Gulf of Mexico during the five-month season. If a hurricane has just entered the Gulf of Mexico:

a. What is the probability that at least one month will pass before the next hurricane enters the Gulf?

b. What is the probability that another hurricane will enter the Gulf of Mexico in two weeks or less?

c. What is the average amount of time between hurricanes entering the Gulf of Mexico?

6.56. With the growing emphasis on technology and the changing business environment, many workers are discovering that training such as reeducation, skill development, and personal growth are of great assistance in the job marketplace. A recent Gallup survey found that 80% of Generation Xers considered the availability of company-sponsored training as a factor to weigh in taking a job. If 50 Generation Xers are randomly sampled, what is the probability that fewer than 35 consider the availability of company-sponsored training as a factor to weigh in taking a job? What is the expected number? What is the probability that between 42 and 47 (inclusive) consider the availability of company-sponsored training as a factor to weigh in taking a job?

6.57. According to the Air Transport Association of America, the average operating cost of an MD-80 jet airliner is $2,087 per hour. Suppose the operating costs of an MD-80 jet airliner are normally distributed with a standard deviation of $175 per hour. At what operating cost would only 20% of the operating costs be less? At what operating cost would 65% of the operating costs be more? What operating cost would be more than 85% of operating costs?

6.58. Supermarkets usually become busy at about 5 P.M. on weekdays, because many workers stop by on the way home to shop. Suppose at that time arrivals at a supermarket's express checkout station are Poisson distributed, with an average of .8 person/minute. If the clerk has just checked out the last person in line, what is the probability that at least one minute will elapse before the next customer arrives? Suppose the clerk wants to go to the manager's office to ask a quick question and needs 2.5 minutes to do so. What is the probability that the clerk will get back before the next customer arrives?

6.59. In a recent year, the average daily circulation of the Wall Street Journal was 2,276,207. Suppose the standard deviation is 70,940. Assume the paper's daily circulation is normally distributed. On what percentage of days would circulation pass 2,400,000? Suppose the paper cannot support the fixed expenses of a full-production setup if the circulation drops below 2,100,000. If the probability of this even occurring is low, the production manager might try to keep the full crew in place and not disrupt operations. How often will this even happen, based on this historical information?

6.60. Incoming phone calls generally are thought to be Poisson distributed. If an operator averages 2.2 phone calls every 30 seconds, what is the expected (average) amount of time between calls? What is the probability that a minute or more would elapse between incoming calls? Two minutes?

Interpreting the Output

6.61. Shown here is a Minitab output. Suppose the data represent the number of sales associates who are working in a department store in any given retail day. Describe the distribution including the mean and standard deviation. Interpret the shape of the distribution and the mean in light of the data being studied. What do the probability statements mean?

CUMULATIVE DISTRIBUTION FUNCTION	
Continuous uniform on 11 to 32	
x	$P(X <= x)$
28	0.80952
34	1.00000
16	0.23810
21	0.47619

6.62. A manufacturing company produces a metal rod. Use the Excel output shown here to describe the weight of the rod. Interpret the probability values in terms of the manufacturing process.

NORMAL DISTRIBUTION	
Mean = 227 mg.	
Standard Deviation = 2.3 mg.	
x Value	Probability < x Value
220	0.0012
225	0.1923
227	0.5000
231	0.9590
238	1.0000

6.63. Suppose the Minitab output shown here represents the analysis of the length of home-use cell phone calls in terms of minutes. Describe the distribution of cell phone call lengths and interpret the meaning of the probability statements.

CUMULATIVE DISTRIBUTION FUNCTION	
Normal with mean = 2.35 and standard deviation = 0.11	
x	$P(X <= x)$
2.60	0.988479
2.45	0.818349
2.30	0.324718
2.00	0.000732

6.64. A restaurant averages 4.51 customers per 10 minutes during the summer in the late afternoon. Shown here are Excel and Minitab output for this restaurant. Discuss the type of distribution used to analyze the data and the meaning of the probabilities.

EXPONENTIAL DISTRIBUTION	
x Value	Probability < x Value
0.1	0.3630
0.2	0.5942
0.5	0.8951
1.0	0.9890
2.4	1.0000

CUMULATIVE DISTRIBUTION FUNCTION	
Exponential with mean = 0.221729	
x	$P(X <= x)$
0.1	0.363010
0.2	0.594243
0.5	0.895127
1.0	0.989002
2.4	0.999980

Analyzing the Databases

See **www.wiley.com/college/black**

1. The Consumer Food database contains a variable, Annual Food Spending, which represents the amount spent per household on food for a year. Calculate the mean and standard deviation for this variable that is approximately normally distributed in this database. Using the mean and standard deviation, calculate the probability that a randomly selected household spends more than $10,000 annually on food. What is the probability that a randomly selected household spends less than $5,000 annually on food? What is the probability that a randomly selected household spends between $8,000 and $11,000 annually on food?

2. Select the Agribusiness time-series database. Create a histogram graph for onions and for broccoli. Each of these variables is approximately normally distributed. Compute the mean and the standard deviation for each distribution. The data in this database represent the monthly weight (in thousands of pounds) of each vegetable. In terms of monthly weight, describe each vegetable (onions and broccoli). If a month were randomly selected from the onion distribution, what is the probability that the weight would be more than 50,000? What is the probability that the weight would be between 25,000 and 35,000?

If a month were randomly selected from the broccoli distribution, what is the probability that the weight would be more than 100,000? What is the probability that the weight would be between 135,000 and 170,000?

3. From the Hospital database, it can be determined that some hospitals admit around 50 patients per day. Suppose we select a hospital that admits 50 patients per day. Assuming that admittance only occurs within a 12-hour time period each day and that admittance is Poisson distributed, what is the value of lambda per hour for this hospital? What is the interarrival time for admittance based on this figure? Suppose a person was just admitted to the hospital. What the probability that it would be more than 30 minutes before the next person was admitted? What is the probability that there would be less than 10 minutes before the next person was admitted?

Case

USAA

USAA, the United Services Automobile Association, is a diversified financial services group of companies based in San Antonio, Texas. Currently, ranked 57th in net worth ($25 billion) and 141st in revenue in Fortune 500 companies, USAA offers banking, investing, and insurance to people and families that serve, or served, in the United States military. At the end of last year, there were 10.7 million members, 42.6 million products, and 26,300 employees. It is the 5th largest homeowners' insurer and the 6th largest auto insurer.

USAA was founded in 1922 by 25 army officers who came together in San Antonio and decided to insure each other's automobiles. In the 1930s, even with the great depression, the number of employees doubled from 46 to 99. By 1940, there were 30,000 members including 60% of all eligible U.S. military officers. During the 1940s, in spite of a decrease in driving due to wartime restrictions on gasoline, spare parts, and tires, USAA grew rapidly and reported a profit of over $3 million. At the end of the 1950s, profits were over $14 million. In 1961, USAA's bylaws were changed such that membership no longer had to be relinquished when an officer leaves the service. In 1963, the USAA Life Insurance Company was formed; and by the end of 1969, there were 700,000 members producing a profit of almost $24 million.

In 1977, USAA reached $1 billion in assets; and in 1983 they opened the USAA Federal Savings Bank. *Fortune* magazine named USAA one of "America's Most Admired Companies" in 1992 and Money magazine named USAA Federal Savings Bank the best bank in America. By the turn of the century, USAA owned and operated a total of $58.9 billion assets. By 2003, 96% of all active-duty officers and 44% of enlisted personnel were USAA members. USAA introduced a car-buying service in 2008; and in 2009, the company expanded its eligibility to all who are serving or have honorably served our nation in the U.S. military and their families. In 2011, Fortune magazine included USAA on its list of "100 Best Companies to Work For" for the third straight year.

According to their mission statement, "USAA's mission is to facilitate the financial security of its members, associates and their families by providing a full range of highly competitive financial products and services. In so doing, we seek to be the provider of choice for the military community."

Discussion

1. According to the National Association of Insurance Commissioners (NAIC), the average premium for homeowner's insurance in the United States in a recent year was $1,034. Suppose these premium rates are uniformly distributed across the country from $535 to $1533. What percentage rates are between $800 and $1200? What percentage are more than $1350?

2. A study by Quadrant Information Services commissioned by Insure.com calculated auto insurance rates for each of the 50 states; and as a result, the average annual rate for the United States was $1317. Suppose annual rates of auto insurance in the United States are normally distributed with a standard deviation of $324. Based on these data, what is the probability that a randomly selected auto insurance rate in the United States would be greater than $1750? What percentage of auto insurance rates would be less than $1200? What percentage of auto insurance rates would be between $1100 and $1500?

3. Homeowners do not make insurance claims very often. In fact, the Oregon Insurance Division says that, on average, a homeowner makes one claim every nine years. Suppose such homeowner claims are Poisson distributed. What is the probability that it would be 15 years or more between claims for a homeowner? What percentage of the time would it be less than 5 years between claims? According to data released by the Insurance Information Institute, the claim frequency for automobile collisions is 5.59 per 100 car years (a car year is equal to 365 days of insured coverage for one vehicle). What is the average "inter arrival time" for auto collisions in car years? What do you think this average means? Assume that auto collisions are Poisson distributed.

Sources: Adapted from the USAA website, www.usaa.com; homeowner's insurance figures from the Insurance Information Institute website, www. iii.org/ Facts+Statistics and from www.naic.org/; auto insurance rates from a study commissioned by www.insure.com/. Oregon Insurance Division information from finance.zacks.com

CHAPTER 7

Sampling and Sampling Distributions

LEARNING OBJECTIVES

The two main objectives for Chapter 7 are to give you an appreciation for the proper application of sampling techniques and an understanding of the sampling distributions of two statistics, thereby enabling you to:

1. Contrast sampling to census and differentiate among different methods of sampling, which include simple, stratified, systematic, and cluster random sampling; and convenience, judgment, quota, and snowball nonrandom sampling, by assessing the advantages associated with each.

2. Describe the distribution of a sample's mean using the central limit theorem, correcting for a finite population if necessary.

3. Describe the distribution of a sample's proportion using the z formula for sample proportions.

Decision Dilemma

Toro

Bloomberg/Getty Images, Inc.

On July 10, 2014, The Toro Company celebrated 100 years of providing business solutions for the outdoor environment including turf, snow, and ground-engaging equipment along with irrigation and outdoor lighting solutions. Founded in 1914 in St. Paul, Minnesota, the company began by building engines for The Bull Tractor Company. When The Bull Tractor Company folded in 1916, Toro adapted by building engines for other companies in both the farm and truck industries. In 1919, Toro developed its first Toro-branded piece of equipment, the Toro TO-RO Utility Tractor, which was a two-row power cultivator thereby enabling farmers to perform multiple tasks while ploughing. In the next decade, Toro developed equipment for manicuring golf fairways including a motorized fairway mower and a fairway sprinkler system. In 1928, the company introduced the Silver Flash push reel mower which has been dubbed as "America's finest hand lawn mower"; and in 1930, Toro introduced its first gas-powered greens mower.

In 1940, Toro revolutionized commercial mowing by introducing the 76-inch Professional known as "the power mower with wings". This product was the top seller for Toro until 1975.

In 1951, Toro created and marketed its first snowblower, the Snow Boy, which is said to have "taken the place of 50 men" in clearing snow from streets. In the 1950's, Toro created an expansive R & D unit to test new product concepts and conduct agronomic research. In 1956, Toro became the first company in the lawn and garden industry to advertise on television; and in 1959, they introduced the Wind Tunnel housing on rotary mowers making possible the first bagging lawnmower. In 1962, Toro acquired an irrigation equipment manufacturer providing entry into the underground irrigation business; and in 1966, Toro began its long partnership with the Super Bowl by preparing the field for Super Bowl I. Toro introduced a revolutionary mulching mower that virtually eliminates the need to bag grass clippings in 1990. In 2003, the company entered the market with the Toro Ultra Blower and sold one million units in one year. In 2008, they introduced a series of spray nozzles that turned out to be one of the most significant breakthroughs in irrigation nozzle technology in 60 years thereby helping to reduce water usage by up to 30 percent.

Today, The Toro Company has its world headquarters in Bloomington, Minnesota, and manufacturing plants in California, Nebraska, Texas, Wisconsin, and Mexico. Now a global company, Toro has manufacturing and sales in Australia, Belgium, China, Italy, Japan, and the United Kingdom.

According to The Toro Company website, its purpose is "To help our customers enrich the beauty, productivity, and sustainability of the land" and its vision is "To be the most trusted leader in solutions for the outdoor environment. Every day. Everywhere." The company has 5,900 employees worldwide with revenues of $2.2 billion. Revenues by geography are 71% United States and 29% international, by market are 68% professional and 31% residential, and by product are 81% equipment and 19% irrigation.

MANAGERIAL AND STATISTICAL QUESTIONS

1. Suppose researchers decide to survey U.S. households to ascertain information about consumer spending on landscape services. Is it possible to take a census of all households or should just a sample be taken? If a sample is taken, what type of sampling technique would gain the most valid information? How can researchers be certain that the sample of households is representative of all households?

2. According to gardenresearch.com, the average household in the United States spends $449 per year on their lawns and gardens. If a random sample of 35 U.S. households is taken, what is the probability that the sample mean amount spent on lawns and gardens per year is more than $500 assuming that the standard deviation is about $120?

3. According to the National Association of Landscape Professionals, thirty-five percent of U.S. adults who have a lawn/landscape purchased lawn/landscaping services in the past year. Assuming this figure is true for this year, if a business researcher randomly samples 350 U.S. adults who have a lawn/landscape, what is the probability that less than thirty-two percent purchased lawn/landscaping services?

Sources: Company information adapted from The Toro Company website, www.thetorocompany.com/. Household spending data from www.gardenresearch.com/index.php?q=show&id=2542. Information about lawn/landscape services from https://www.loveyourlandscape.com/.../National-Survey-on-Consumer-Spe. . .

This chapter explores the process of sampling and the sampling distributions of some statistics. How do we obtain the data used in statistical analysis? Why do researchers often take a sample rather than conduct a census? What are the differences between random and nonrandom sampling? This chapter addresses these and other questions about sampling.

In addition to sampling theory, the distributions of two statistics: the sample mean and the sample proportion are presented. Knowledge of the uses of the sample mean and sample proportion is important in the study of statistics and is basic to much of statistical analysis.

7.1 | Sampling

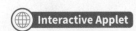

Sampling is widely used in business as a means of gathering useful information about a population. Data are gathered from samples and conclusions are drawn about the population as a part of the inferential statistics process. In the Decision Dilemma, it is mentioned that the Toro Company created a research and development unit in the 1950s to test new product concepts and conduct agronomic research. In studying the effectiveness of its equipment in irrigating, mowing, mulching, snow removing and other tasks in the lawn and garden industry, this R & D unit could sample customer preferences for brand preference, machine features, and equipment usages. Their agronomic researchers might sample plots of land in studying soil management issues, crop production, grass growth rates, fertilizer effectiveness, and other land-use concerns. Often, a sample provides a reasonable means for gathering such useful decision-making information that might be otherwise unattainable and unaffordable.

Reasons for Sampling

Taking a sample instead of conducting a census offers several advantages.

1. The sample can save money.

2. The sample can save time.

3. For given resources, the sample can broaden the scope of the study.

4. Because the research process is sometimes destructive, the sample can save product.

5. If accessing the population is impossible, the sample is the only option.

For a given number of questions from a survey or a given set of measurements obtained in a study, taking a sample versus a census can result in a savings of both money and time. For example, suppose an eight-minute telephone interview is conducted as part of a survey. Conducting such interviews with a sample of 100 customers is substantially less expensive and time-consuming than taking a census of 100,000 customers. If obtaining the outcomes of a study is a matter of urgency, sampling can produce results more quickly. With the volatility of the marketplace and the constant barrage of new competition and new ideas, sampling has a strong advantage over a census in terms of research turnaround time.

If resources allocated to a research project are fixed, more detailed information can be gathered by taking a sample than by conducting a census. With resources concentrated on fewer individuals or items, a study can be broadened in scope to allow more specialized questions and deeper investigation. As an example, one organization budgeted $80,000 to survey the opinions of its customers and opted to take a census instead of a sample by sending a mail survey to the entire population. The researchers mass-mailed thousands of copies of a brief 20-question survey in which each question could be answered with a Yes or No response. One of the questions was, "Are you satisfied with the service that you received at the XYZ store?" For the same amount of money, the company could have taken a random sample from the population, held interactive one-on-one sessions with highly trained interviewers, and gathered detailed information about customer opinions and attitudes towards products, service, layout, availability, etc.

Some research processes are destructive to the product or item being studied. For example, if light bulbs are being tested to determine how long they burn or batteries are being discharged to determine how long they last, the light bulbs and/or the batteries being analyzed for longevity are ruined in the testing process. By using a sample in destructive testing, only a portion of the population is ruined.

Sometimes a population is virtually impossible to access for research. For example, some people refuse to answer sensitive questions, some telephone numbers are unlisted, and some executives are virtually impossible to access. In such cases, sampling is the only option.

Reasons for Taking a Census

Sometimes it is preferable to conduct a census of the entire population rather than taking a sample. There are at least three reasons why a business researcher may opt to take a census rather than a sample, provided there is adequate time and money available to conduct such a census: (1) to eliminate the possibility that by chance a randomly selected sample may not be representative of the population, (2) for the safety of the consumer, and (3) to benchmark data for future studies.

Even when proper sampling techniques are implemented in a study, there is the possibility a sample could be selected by chance that does not represent the population. For example, if the population of interest is all truck owners in the state of Colorado, a random sample of truck owners could yield mostly ranchers when, in fact, many of the truck owners in Colorado are urban dwellers. If the researcher or study sponsor cannot tolerate such a possibility, then taking a census may be the only option.

Sometimes a census is taken to protect the safety of the consumer. For example, there are some products, such as airplanes or heart defibrillators, in which the performance of such is so critical to the consumer that 100% of the products are tested, and sampling is not a reasonable option. In addition, companies often want to establish performance baselines in areas like cost, time, and quality by taking a census at least one time. On the basis of such a baseline, future managers can compare their results with past baselines to determine how well their processes are performing.

Thinking Critically About Statistics in Business Today

Sampling Canadian Manufacturers

Statistics Canada, Canada's national statistical agency, administers a monthly survey of manufacturing for Canada. This Monthly Survey of Manufacturing (MSM) includes information on such variables as sales of goods manufactured, inventories, and orders. The MSM data are used as indicators of the economic condition of manufacturing industries in Canada along with inputs for Canada's gross domestic product, economic studies, and econometric models. The sampling frame for the MSM is the Business Register of Statistics Canada. The target population consists of all statistical establishments on the business register that are classified as being in the manufacturing sector. The frame is further reduced by eliminating the smallest units of the survey population. As a result, there are 27,000 establishments in the sampling frame, of which approximately 10,500 units are sampled. Before the sample is taken, the sampling frame is stratified by both industry and province. Further stratification is then made within each combination of industry and province by company size so that similar-sized companies are grouped together. Selected establishments are required to respond to the survey, and data are collected directly from survey respondents and extracted from administrative files. Sampled companies are contacted either by mail or telephone, whichever they prefer.

THINGS TO PONDER

1. According to the information presented, the MSM sample is stratified by province, industry, and size. Do you think that these strata make sense? If so, why? Can you think of other strata that might be used in this survey?

2. Sampled companies are contacted either by mail or telephone. Do you think that survey responses might differ by whether they were obtained by mail or by telephone? Explain why or why not.

Source: Statistics Canada Web site at: http://www.statcan.gc.ca/cgibin/imdb/p2SV.pl?Function=getSurvey&SurvId=32686&SurvVer=2&Instal d=32690&InstaVer=98&DispYear=2008&SDDS=2101&lang=en&db=imdb&adm=8&dis=2.

Frame

Every research study has a target population that consists of the individuals, institutions, or entities that are the object of investigation. When a sample is drawn from a population, it is actually selected from a list, map, directory, or some other source that represents the population. This list, map, or directory is called the frame. Thus, a **frame** is a list, map, directory, or some other source used in the sampling process to represent the population. Because the sample is drawn from the frame, the frame is sometimes referred to as the working population. Examples of frames can include phone directories, trade association lists, company human resource records, or even lists sold by list brokers. Ideally, a one-to-one correspondence exists between the frame units and the target population units. That is, the frame and the target population are congruent. In reality, the frame and the target population are often different, as shown in **Figure 7.1**. In such cases, a frame can be *overregistered* in that it contains units that are not in the target population; and it can be *underregistered* because it does not contain some of the units in the target population.

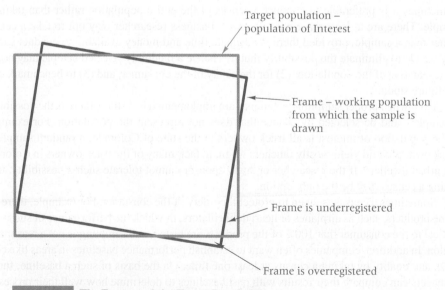

Target population – population of Interest

Frame – working population from which the sample is drawn

Frame is underregistered

Frame is overregistered

FIGURE 7.1 The Frame and the Target Population

Suppose the target population is all families living in Detroit. A feasible frame might be the residential pages of the Detroit telephone books. How might the frame differ from the target population? A growing number of families have no "land-line" phone. Other families have unlisted numbers. Still other families might have moved and/or changed numbers since the directory was printed. Some families even have multiple listings under different names.

Random Versus Nonrandom Sampling

The two main types of sampling are random and nonrandom. In **random sampling** *every unit of the population has the same probability of being selected into the sample.* Random sampling implies that chance enters into the process of selection. For example, most Americans would like to believe that winners of nationwide magazine sweepstakes or numbers selected as state lottery winners are selected by some random draw of numbers, hence, random sampling.

In **nonrandom sampling** *not every unit of the population has the same probability of being selected into the sample.* Members of nonrandom samples are not selected by chance. For example, they might be selected because they are at the right place at the right time or because they know the people conducting the research.

Sometimes random sampling is called *probability sampling* and nonrandom sampling is called *nonprobability sampling.* Because every unit of the population is not equally likely to be selected, assigning a probability of occurrence in nonrandom sampling is impossible. The statistical methods presented and discussed in this text are based on the assumption that the data come from random samples. *Nonrandom sampling methods are not appropriate techniques for gathering data to be analyzed by most of the statistical methods presented in this text.* However, several nonrandom sampling techniques are described in this section, primarily to alert you to their characteristics and limitations.

Random Sampling Techniques

The four basic random sampling techniques are simple random sampling, stratified random sampling, systematic random sampling, and cluster (or area) random sampling. Each technique offers advantages and disadvantages. Some techniques are simpler to use, some are less costly, and others show greater potential for reducing sampling error.

Simple Random Sampling The most elementary random sampling technique is **simple random sampling**. Simple random sampling can be viewed as the basis for other random sampling techniques. With simple random sampling, each unit of the frame is numbered from 1 to N (where N is the size of the population). Next, a table of random numbers or a random number generator is used to select n items into the sample. A random number generator is usually a computer program that allows computer-calculated output to yield random numbers. Table 7.1 contains a brief table of random numbers. Table A.1 in Appendix A contains a full table of random numbers. These numbers are random in all

TABLE 7.1 **A Brief Table of Random Numbers**

91567	42595	27958	30134	04024	86385	29880	99730
46503	18584	18845	49618	02304	51038	20655	58727
34914	63974	88720	82765	34476	17032	87589	40836
57491	16703	23167	49323	45021	33132	12544	41035
30405	83946	23792	14422	15059	45799	22716	19792
09983	74353	68668	30429	70735	25499	16631	35006
85900	07119	97336	71048	08178	77233	13916	47564

directions. The spaces in the table are there only for ease of reading the values. For each number, any of the 10 digits (0–9) is equally likely, so getting the same digit twice or more in a row is possible.

As an example, from the population frame of companies listed in Table 7.2, we will use simple random sampling to select a sample of six companies. First, we number every member of the population. We select as many digits for each unit sampled as there are in the largest number in the population. For example, if a population has 2,000 members, we select four-digit numbers. Because the population in Table 7.2 contains 30 members, only two digits need be selected for each number. The population is numbered from 01 to 30, as shown in Table 7.3.

The object is to sample six companies, so six different two-digit numbers must be selected from the table of random numbers. Because this population contains only 30 companies, all numbers greater than 30 (31–99) must be ignored. If, for example, the number 67 is selected, we discard the number and continue the process until a value between 01 and 30 is obtained. If the same number occurs more than once, we proceed to another number. For ease of understanding, we start with the first pair of digits in Table 7.1 and proceed across the first row until $n = 6$ different values between 01 and 30 are selected. If additional numbers are needed, we proceed across the second row, and so on. Often a researcher will start at some randomly selected location in the table and proceed in a predetermined direction to select numbers.

In the first row of digits in Table 7.1, the first number is 91. This number is out of range so it is cast out. The next two digits are 56. Next is 74, followed by 25, which is the first usable number. From Table 7.3, we see that 25 is the number associated with Occidental Petroleum, so Occidental Petroleum is the first company selected into the sample. The next number is 95, unusable, followed by 27, which is usable. Twenty-seven is the number for Procter & Gamble, so this company is selected. Continuing the process, we pass over the numbers 95 and 83. The

TABLE 7.2	A Population Frame of 30 Companies	
Alaska Airlines	DuPont	Lubrizol
Alcoa	ExxonMobil	Mattel
Ashland	General Dynamics	Merck
Bank of America	General Electric	Microsoft
Boeing	General Mills	Occidental Petroleum
Chevron	Halliburton	JCPenney
Citigroup	IBM	Procter & Gamble
Clorox	Kellogg's	Ryder
Delta Air Lines	Kroger	Sears
Disney	Lowe's	Time Warner

TABLE 7.3	Numbered Population of 30 Companies	
01 Alaska Airlines	11 DuPont	21 Lubrizol
02 Alcoa	12 ExxonMobil	22 Mattel
03 Ashland	13 General Dynamics	23 Merck
04 Bank of America	14 General Electric	24 Microsoft
05 Boeing	15 General Mills	25 Occidental Petroleum
06 Chevron	16 Halliburton	26 JCPenney
07 Citigroup	17 IBM	27 Procter & Gamble
08 Clorox	18 Kellogg	28 Ryder
09 Delta Air Lines	19 Kroger	29 Sears
10 Disney	20 Lowe's	30 Time Warner

next usable number is 01, which is the value for Alaska Airlines. Thirty-four is next, followed by 04 and 02, both of which are usable. These numbers are associated with Bank of America and Alcoa, respectively. Continuing along the first row, the next usable number is 29, which is associated with Sears. Because this selection is the sixth, the sample is complete. The following companies constitute the final sample.

Alaska Airlines
Alcoa
Bank of America
Occidental Petroleum
Procter & Gamble
Sears

Simple random sampling is easier to perform on small than on large populations. The process of numbering all the members of the population and selecting items is cumbersome for large populations.

Stratified Random Sampling

A second type of random sampling is stratified random sampling, in which the population is divided into nonoverlapping subpopulations called strata. The researcher then extracts a random sample from each of the subpopulations (strata). The main reason for using stratified random sampling is that it has the potential for reducing sampling error. Sampling error occurs when, by chance, the sample does not represent the population. With stratified random sampling, the potential to match the sample closely to the population is greater than it is with simple random sampling because portions of the total sample are taken from different population subgroups. However, stratified random sampling is generally more costly than simple random sampling because each unit of the population must be assigned to a stratum before the random selection process begins.

Strata selection is usually based on available information. Such information may have been gleaned from previous censuses or surveys. Stratification benefits increase as the strata differ more. Internally, a stratum should be relatively homogeneous; externally, strata should contrast with each other. Stratification is often done by using demographic variables, such as sex, socioeconomic class, geographic region, religion, and ethnicity. For example, if a U.S. presidential election poll is to be conducted by a market research firm, what important variables should be stratified? The sex of the respondent might make a difference because a gender gap in voter preference has been noted in past elections; that is, men and women tended to vote differently in national elections. Geographic region also provides an important variable in national elections because voters are influenced by local cultural values that differ from region to region.

In FM radio markets, age of listener is an important determinant of the type of programming used by a station. **Figure 7.2** contains a stratification by age with three strata, based on

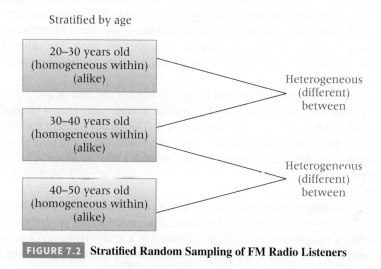

FIGURE 7.2 **Stratified Random Sampling of FM Radio Listeners**

the assumption that age makes a difference in programming preference. This stratification implies that listeners 20 to 30 years of age tend to prefer the same type of programming, which is different from that preferred by listeners 30 to 40 and 40 to 50 years of age. Within each age subgroup (stratum), *homogeneity* or alikeness is present; between each pair of subgroups a difference, or *heterogeneity,* is present.

Stratified random sampling can be either proportionate or disproportionate. **Proportionate stratified random sampling** occurs *when the percentage of the sample taken from each stratum is proportionate to the percentage that each stratum is within the whole population.* For example, suppose voters are being surveyed in Boston and the sample is being stratified by religion as Catholic, Protestant, Jewish, and others. If Boston's population is 90% Catholic and if a sample of 1,000 voters is taken, the sample would require inclusion of 900 Catholics to achieve proportionate stratification. Any other number of Catholics would be disproportionate stratification. The sample proportion of other religions would also have to follow population percentages. Or consider the city of El Paso, Texas, where the population is approximately 80% Hispanic. If a researcher is conducting a citywide poll in El Paso and if stratification is by ethnicity, a proportionate stratified random sample should contain 80% Hispanics. Hence, an ethnically proportionate stratified sample of 160 residents from El Paso's 660,000 residents should contain approximately 128 Hispanics. *Whenever the proportions of the strata in the sample are different from the proportions of the strata in the population,* **disproportionate stratified random sampling** occurs.

Systematic Sampling

Systematic sampling is a third random sampling technique. Unlike stratified random sampling, systematic sampling is not done in an attempt to reduce sampling error. Rather, systematic sampling is used because of its convenience and relative ease of administration. With **systematic sampling**, *every kth item is selected to produce a sample of size n from a population of size N.* The value of *k*, sometimes called the sampling cycle, can be determined by the following formula. If *k* is not an integer value, the whole-number value should be used.

Determining the Value of *k* (7.1)

$$k = \frac{N}{n}$$

where

n = sample size
N = population size
k = size of interval for selection

As an example of systematic sampling, a business researcher wanted to sample Texas manufacturers as part of a management study. She had enough financial support to sample 1,000 companies. Her frame was the most recent edition of the Texas Manufacturers Register® which listed 26,000 manufacturing companies in alphabetic order. The value of *k* was 26 (26,000/1,000) and the researcher selected every 26th company in the Texas Manufacturers Register® for her sample.

Did the researcher begin with the first company listed or the 26th or one somewhere between? In selecting every *k*th value, a simple random number table should be used to select a value between 1 and *k* inclusive as a starting point. The second element for the sample is the starting point plus *k*. In the example, *k* = 26, so the researcher would have gone to a table of random numbers to determine a starting point between 1 and 26. Suppose he selected the number 5. He would have started with the 5th company, then selected the 31st (5 + 26), and then the 57th, and so on.

Besides convenience, systematic sampling has other advantages. Because systematic sampling is evenly distributed across the frame, a knowledgeable person can easily determine whether a sampling plan has been followed in a study. However, a problem with systematic sampling can occur if the data are subject to any periodicity, and the sampling interval is in syncopation with it. In such a case, the sampling would be nonrandom. For example, if a list of 150 college students is actually a merged list of five classes with 30 students in each class and if each of the lists of the five classes has been ordered with the names of top students first and bottom students last, then systematic sampling of every 30th student could cause selection of all top students, all bottom students, or all mediocre students; that is, the original list is subject to a cyclical or periodic organization. Systematic sampling methodology is based on the assumption that the source of population elements is random.

Cluster (or Area) Sampling

Cluster (or area) sampling is a fourth type of random sampling. Cluster (or area) sampling involves dividing the population into nonoverlapping areas, or clusters. However, in contrast to stratified random sampling where strata are homogeneous within, cluster sampling identifies clusters that tend to be internally heterogeneous. In theory, each cluster contains a wide variety of elements, and the cluster is a miniature, or microcosm, of the population. Examples of clusters are towns, companies, homes, colleges, areas of a city, and geographic regions. Often clusters are naturally occurring groups of the population and are already identified, such as states or Standard Metropolitan Statistical Areas. Although area sampling usually refers to clusters that are areas of the population, such as geographic regions and cities, the terms *cluster sampling* and *area sampling* are used interchangeably in this text.

After randomly selecting clusters from the population, the business researcher either selects all elements of the chosen clusters or randomly selects individual elements into the sample from the clusters. One example of business research that makes use of clustering is test marketing of new products. Often in test marketing, the United States is divided into clusters of test market cities, and individual consumers within the test market cities are surveyed. Figure 7.3 shows some of the top U.S. cities that are used as clusters to test products. The Thinking Critically About Statistics in Business Today feature on test market cities elaborates more on the concept of test market cities and how they are selected.

Sometimes the clusters are too large, and a second set of clusters is taken from each original cluster. This technique is called two-stage sampling. For example, a researcher could divide the United States into clusters of cities. She could then divide the cities into clusters of

FIGURE 7.3 **Some Top-Rated Test Market Cities in the United States**

Thinking Critically About Statistics in Business Today

Test Market Cities

Companies that intend to introduce a new product across a country will often use test market cities to help determine how well the product will sell in the country and to gain insight into how to better market the product to consumers. Test market cities serve as a sample of the entire country, thereby reducing the cost of testing the product throughout the entire country and minimizing the time to do so. In the sense that test market cities are randomly selected areas from the country, such sampling could be viewed as a form of area or cluster sampling. However, there are other reasons (besides random selection) that test market cities are chosen, including demographics, familiarity, convenience, and psychographics. Sometimes a test market city is chosen because the company has used that city in a previous test and the product went on to be successful. Still, others are chosen because market researchers are comfortable there.

In cluster or area sampling, each area or cluster is ideally a miniature or microcosm of the population. This being the case for a test market city, a business researcher can gain the benefits of test marketing a product in an environment that closely resembles the population and, at the same time, realize cost and time savings benefits associated with sampling. Josh Herman, Product Manager of Acxiom Corp, reports that companies in the United States have begun utilizing life-stage-based consumer segmentation to identify test market cities that most effectively represent the market

makeup of consumers in the United States. One of these systems suggests that the 110 million U.S. households consist of 70 different life-stage segments, including "getting married," "having children," "raising kids," "launching the kids out of the house," "retiring," etc. Since such life-stage changes greatly impact our consumer behavior, it is important that market researchers who are interested in test marketing products to the entire country select test market cities that most closely parallel the overall U.S. profile in life-stage segments.

Figure 7.3 displays some of the top-rated test market cities in the United States.

THINGS TO PONDER

1. Think about your home city. What characteristics of it would lend themselves to making your city an effective test market for the entire country? What characteristics would hinder the use of your city as a test market?

2. Select a product or service and suppose that it is going to be test marketed in a test market city. What characteristics (demographics) would a test market city have to have in order to conduct a successful market test?

Source: Adapted from "Marketing News: Albany, N.Y. Reflects True Test Market," located at the Acxiom Corp's Web site: http://www.acxiom.com/default.aspx?ID=2428&DisplayID=18.

---

blocks and randomly select individual houses from the block clusters. The first stage is selecting the test cities and the second stage is selecting the blocks.

Cluster or area sampling offers several advantages. Two of the foremost advantages are convenience and cost. Clusters are usually convenient to obtain, and the cost of sampling from the entire population is reduced because the scope of the study is reduced to the clusters. The cost per element is usually lower in cluster or area sampling than in stratified sampling because of lower element listing or locating costs. The time and cost of contacting elements of the population can be reduced, especially if travel is involved, because clustering reduces the distance to the sampled elements. In addition, administration of the sample survey can be simplified. Sometimes cluster or area sampling is the only feasible approach because the sampling frames of the individual elements of the population are unavailable, and therefore other random sampling techniques cannot be used.

Cluster or area sampling also has several disadvantages. If the elements of a cluster are similar, cluster sampling may be statistically less efficient than simple random sampling. In an extreme case—when the elements of a cluster are the same—sampling from the cluster may be no better than sampling a single unit from the cluster. Moreover, the costs and problems of statistical analysis are greater with cluster or area sampling than with simple random sampling.

Nonrandom Sampling

Sampling techniques used to select elements from the population by any mechanism that does not involve a random selection process are called **nonrandom sampling techniques**. Because chance is not used to select items from the samples, these techniques are non-probability techniques and are not desirable for use in gathering data to be analyzed by the methods of inferential statistics presented in this text. Sampling error cannot be determined objectively for these sampling techniques. Four nonrandom sampling techniques are presented here: convenenience sampling, judgment sampling, quota sampling, and snow-ball sampling.

Convenience Sampling

In convenience sampling, *elements for the sample are selected for the convenience of the researcher.* The researcher typically chooses elements that are readily available, nearby, or willing to participate. The sample tends to be less variable than the population because in many environments the extreme elements of the population are not readily available. The researcher will select more elements from the middle of the population. For example, a convenience sample of homes for door-to-door interviews might include houses where people are at home, houses with no dogs, houses near the street, first-floor apartments, and houses with friendly people. In contrast, a random sample would require the researcher to gather data only from houses and apartments that have been selected randomly, no matter how inconvenient or unfriendly the location. If a research firm is located in a mall, a convenience sample might be selected by interviewing only shoppers who pass the shop and look friendly.

Judgment Sampling

Judgment sampling occurs when *elements selected for the sample are chosen by the judgment of the researcher.* Researchers often believe they can obtain a representative sample by using sound judgment, which will result in saving time and money. Sometimes ethical, professional researchers might believe they can select a more representative sample than the random process will provide. They might be right! However, some studies show that random sampling methods outperform judgment sampling in estimating the population mean even when the researcher who is administering the judgment sampling is trying to put together a representative sample. When sampling is done by judgment, calculating the probability that an element is going to be selected into the sample is not possible. The sampling error cannot be determined objectively because probabilities are based on *nonrandom* selection.

Other problems are associated with judgment sampling. The researcher tends to make errors of judgment in one direction. These systematic errors lead to what are called *biases*. The researcher also is unlikely to include extreme elements. Judgment sampling provides no objective method for determining whether one person's judgment is better than another's.

Quota Sampling

A third nonrandom sampling technique is quota sampling, which appears to be similar to stratified random sampling. Certain population subclasses, such as age group, gender, or geographic region, are used as strata. However, instead of randomly sampling from each stratum, the researcher uses a nonrandom sampling method to gather data from a stratum until the desired quota of samples is filled. Quotas are described by quota controls, which set the sizes of the samples to be obtained from the subgroups. Generally, a quota is based on the proportions of the subclasses in the population. In this case, the quota concept is similar to that of proportional stratified sampling.

Quotas are often filled by using available, recent, or applicable elements. Table 7.4 shows how quota sampling might be used to fill quotas of consumers by age.

TABLE 7.4	Using Quota Sampling to Fill Quotas of Consumers by Age	
AGE CATEGORY	**QUOTA**	**HOW SAMPLE IS OBTAINED**
14–18 years old	70	Go to the nearest high school and survey willing students as they leave school until you have surveyed 70 students
25–39 years old	30	Go to junior soccer matches and survey parents in the stands until you have 30 surveys
Over 65 years old	40	Go to the activity center of a retirement community and survey whomever will talk to you

Note from studying Table 7.4 that the researcher is using strata similar to stratified random sampling. However, the quotas are filled in each case by using convenience sampling, and the result, while appearing to be scientific, is actually nonrandom sampling.

Quota sampling can be useful if no frame is available for the population. For example, suppose a researcher wants to stratify the population into owners of different types of cars but fails to find any lists of Toyota van owners. Through quota sampling, the researcher would proceed by interviewing all car owners and casting out non–Toyota van owners until the quota of Toyota van owners is filled.

Quota sampling is less expensive than most random sampling techniques because it essentially is a technique of convenience. However, cost may not be meaningful because the quality of nonrandom and random sampling techniques cannot be compared. Another advantage of quota sampling is the speed of data gathering. The researcher does not have to call back or send out a second questionnaire if he does not receive a response; he just moves on to the next element. Also, preparatory work for quota sampling is minimal.

The main problem with quota sampling is that, when all is said and done, it still is only a *nonrandom* sampling technique. Some researchers believe that if the quota is filled by *randomly* selecting elements and discarding those not from a stratum, quota sampling is essentially a version of stratified random sampling. However, most quota sampling is carried out by the researcher going where the quota can be filled quickly. The object is to gain the benefits of stratification without the high field costs of stratification. Ultimately, it remains a nonprobability sampling method.

Snowball Sampling

Snowball Sampling   Another nonrandom sampling technique is snowball sampling, in which *survey subjects are selected based on referral from other survey respondents*. The researcher identifies a person who fits the profile of subjects wanted for the study. The researcher then asks this person for the names and locations of others who would also fit the profile of subjects wanted for the study. Through these referrals, survey subjects can be identified cheaply and efficiently, which is particularly useful when survey subjects are difficult to locate. It is the main advantage of snowball sampling; its main disadvantage is that it is nonrandom.

Sampling Error

Sampling error occurs *when the sample is not representative of the population*. When random sampling techniques are used to select elements for the sample, sampling error occurs by chance. Many times the statistic computed on the sample is not an accurate estimate of the population parameter because the sample was not representative of the population. This result is caused by sampling error. With random samples, sampling error can be computed and analyzed.

Nonsampling Errors

All errors other than sampling errors are nonsampling errors. The many possible nonsampling errors include missing data, recording errors, input processing errors, and analysis errors. Other nonsampling errors result from the measurement instrument, such as errors of unclear definitions, defective questionnaires, and poorly conceived concepts. Improper definition of the frame is a nonsampling error. In many cases, finding a frame that perfectly fits the population is impossible. Insofar as it does not fit, a nonsampling error has been committed.

Response errors are also nonsampling errors. They occur when people do not know, will not say, or overstate. Virtually no statistical method is available to measure or control for nonsampling errors. The statistical techniques presented in this text are based on the assumption that none of these nonsampling errors were committed. The researcher must eliminate these errors through carefully planning and executing the research study.

7.1 Problems

7.1. Develop a frame for the population of each of the following research projects.

  a. Measuring the job satisfaction of all union employees in a company

  b. Conducting a telephone survey in Utica, New York, to determine the level of interest in opening a new hunting and fishing specialty store in the mall

  c. Interviewing passengers of a major airline about its food service

  d. Studying the quality control programs of boat manufacturers

  e. Attempting to measure the corporate culture of cable television companies

7.2. Make a list of 20 people you know. Include men and women, various ages, various educational levels, and so on. Number the list and then use the random number list in Table 7.1 to select six people randomly from your list. How representative of the population is the sample? Find the proportion of men in your population and in your sample. How do the proportions compare? Find the proportion of 20-year-olds in your sample and the proportion in the population. How do they compare?

7.3. Use the random numbers in Table A.1 of Appendix A to select 10 of the companies from the 30 companies listed in Table 7.2. Compare the types of companies in your sample with the types in the population. How representative of the population is your sample?

7.4. For each of the following research projects, list three variables for stratification of the sample.

  a. A nationwide study of motels and hotels is being conducted. An attempt will be made to determine the extent of the availability of online links for customers. A sample of motels and hotels will be taken.

  b. A consumer panel is to be formed by sampling people in Michigan. Members of the panel will be interviewed periodically in an effort to understand current consumer attitudes and behaviors.

  c. A large soft drink company wants to study the characteristics of its U.S. bottlers, but the company does not want to conduct a census.

  d. The business research bureau of a large university is conducting a project in which the bureau will sample paper-manufacturing companies.

7.5. In each of the following cases, the variable represents one way that a sample can be stratified in a study. For each variable, list some strata into which the variable can be divided.

  a. Age of respondent (person)

  b. Size of company (sales volume)

  c. Size of retail outlet (square feet)

  d. Geographic location

  e. Occupation of respondent (person)

  f. Type of business (company)

7.6. A city's telephone book lists 100,000 people. If the telephone book is the frame for a study, how large would the sample size be if systematic sampling were done on every 200th person?

7.7. If every 11th item is systematically sampled to produce a sample size of 75 items, approximately how large is the population?

7.8. If a company employs 3500 people and if a random sample of 175 of these employees has been taken by systematic sampling, what is the value of k? The researcher would start the sample selection between what two values? Where could the researcher obtain a frame for this study?

7.9. For each of the following research projects, list at least one area or cluster that could be used in obtaining the sample.

  a. A study of road conditions in the state of Missouri

  b. A study of U.S. offshore oil wells

  c. A study of the environmental effects of petrochemical plants west of the Mississippi River

7.10. Give an example of how judgment sampling could be used in a study to determine how district attorneys feel about attorneys advertising on television.

7.11. Give an example of how convenience sampling could be used in a study of *Fortune* 500 executives to measure corporate attitude toward paternity leave for employees.

7.12. Give an example of how quota sampling could be used to conduct sampling by a company test marketing a new personal computer.

7.2   Sampling Distribution of $\bar{x}$

In this section, we explore aspects of the sample mean, $\bar{x}$. The sample mean is one of the more common statistics used in the inferential process. To compute and assign the probability of occurrence of a particular value of a sample mean, the researcher must know the distribution of the sample means. One way to examine the distribution possibilities is to take a population with a particular distribution, randomly select samples of a given size, compute the sample means, and attempt to determine how the means are distributed.

    Suppose a small finite population consists of only $N = 8$ numbers:

$$54 \quad 55 \quad 59 \quad 63 \quad 64 \quad 68 \quad 69 \quad 70$$

Using an Excel-produced histogram, we can see the shape of the distribution of this population of data.

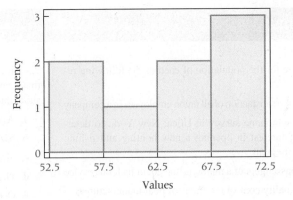

Suppose we take all possible samples of size $n = 2$ from this population with replacement. The result is the following pairs of data.

(54, 54)	(55, 54)	(59, 54)	(63, 54)
(54, 55)	(55, 55)	(59, 55)	(63, 55)
(54, 59)	(55, 59)	(59, 59)	(63, 59)
(54, 63)	(55, 63)	(59, 63)	(63, 63)
(54, 64)	(55, 64)	(59, 64)	(63, 64)
(54, 68)	(55, 68)	(59, 68)	(63, 68)
(54, 69)	(55, 69)	(59, 69)	(63, 69)
(54, 70)	(55, 70)	(59, 70)	(63, 70)
(64, 54)	(68, 54)	(69, 54)	(70, 54)
(64, 55)	(68, 55)	(69, 55)	(70, 55)
(64, 59)	(68, 59)	(69, 59)	(70, 59)
(64, 63)	(68, 63)	(69, 63)	(70, 63)
(64, 64)	(68, 64)	(69, 64)	(70, 64)
(64, 68)	(68, 68)	(69, 68)	(70, 68)
(64, 69)	(68, 69)	(69, 69)	(70, 69)
(64, 70)	(68, 70)	(69, 70)	(70, 70)

The means of each of these samples follow.

54	54.5	56.5	58.5	59	61	61.5	62
54.5	55	57	59	59.5	61.5	62	62.5
56.5	57	59	61	61.5	63.5	64	64.5
58.5	59	61	63	63.5	65.5	66	66.5
59	59.5	61.5	63.5	64	66	66.5	67
61	61.5	63.5	65.5	66	68	68.5	69
61.5	62	64	66	66.5	68.5	69	69.5
62	62.5	64.5	66.5	67	69	69.5	70

Again using an Excel-produced histogram, we can see the shape of the distribution of these sample means.

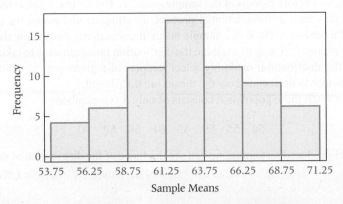

Notice that the shape of the histogram for sample means is quite unlike the shape of the histogram for the population. The sample means appear to "pile up" toward the middle of the distribution and "tail off" toward the extremes.

As another example, consider Figure 7.4, which contains an Excel-produced histogram of a Poisson population with a mean (λ) of 1.3 produced from 5,000 data points. Describe the shape of the population. Is it approximately symmetrical or is it skewed to the right or to the left?

Note that this graph is skewed to the right with a mode of 1 with the numbers 0 and 2 also occurring in large numbers.

Now consider Figure 7.5, which displays the Excel-produced histogram of sample means computed on 1,000 random samples of size 30 taken from a Poisson population with $\lambda = 1.3$. Is the graph also skewed to the right like the Poisson population from which the samples are drawn? Or is something else happening here?

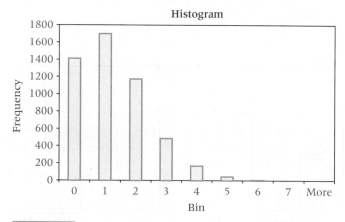

FIGURE 7.4 **An Excel-Produced Histogram of 5,000 Random Numbers Generated from a Poisson Population with $\lambda = 1.3$**

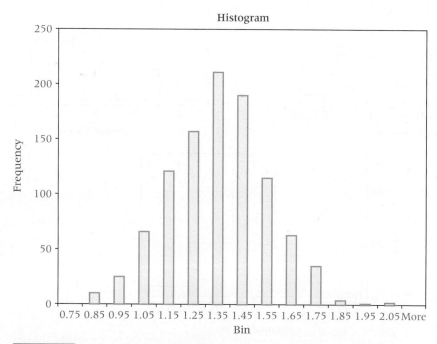

FIGURE 7.5 **An Excel-Produced Histogram of the Sample Means from 1,000 Samples Taken from a Poisson Population with $\lambda = 1.3$**

Observe that even though these 1,000 samples (size $n = 30$) were taken from a skewed Poisson distribution with a λ of 1.3, the distribution of sample means is nearly symmetrical and is approaching the shape of the normal distribution.

Suppose a population is uniformly distributed. If samples are selected randomly from a population with a uniform distribution, how are the sample means distributed? Figure 7.6 displays the Minitab histogram distributions of sample means from five different sample sizes. Each of these histograms represents the distribution of sample means from 90 samples generated randomly from a uniform distribution in which $a = 10$ and $b = 30$. Observe the shape of the distributions. Notice that even for small sample sizes, the distributions of sample means for samples taken from the uniformly distributed population begin to "pile up" in the middle. As sample sizes become much larger, the sample mean distributions begin to approach a normal distribution and the variation among the means decreases.

So far, we examined three populations with different distributions. However, the sample means for samples taken from these populations appear to be approximately normally distributed, especially as the sample sizes become larger. What would happen to the distribution of sample means if we studied populations with differently shaped distributions? The answer to that question is given in the **central limit theorem**.

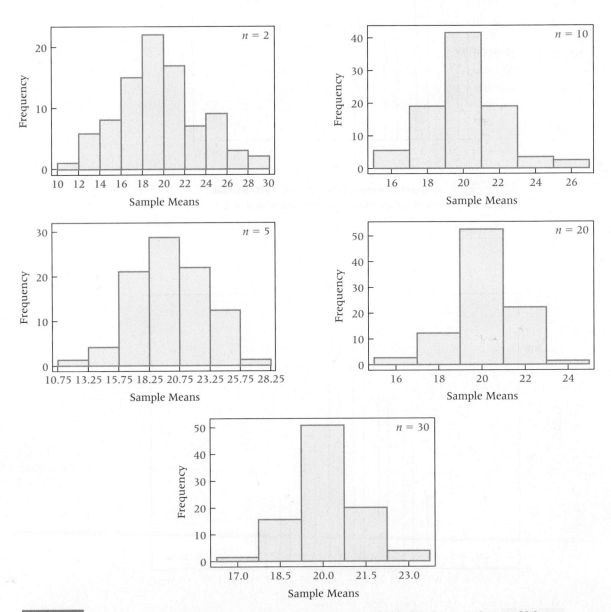

FIGURE 7.6   **Minitab Outputs for Sample Means from 90 Samples Ranging in Size from $n = 2$ to $n = 30$ from a Uniformly Distributed Population with $a = 10$ and $b = 30$**

Central Limit Theorem

If random samples of size n are repeatedly drawn from a population that has a mean of μ and a standard deviation of σ, the sample means, $\bar{x}$, are approximately normally distributed for sufficiently large sample sizes ($n \geq 30$) regardless of the shape of the population distribution. If the population is normally distributed, the sample means are normally distributed for any size sample.

From mathematical expectation,* it can be shown that the mean of the sample means is the population mean

$$\mu_{\bar{x}} = \mu$$

and the standard deviation of the sample means (called the standard error of the mean) is the standard deviation of the population divided by the square root of the sample size.

$$\sigma_{\bar{x}} = \frac{\sigma}{\sqrt{n}}$$

The central limit theorem creates the potential for applying the normal distribution to many problems when sample size is sufficiently large. Sample means that have been computed for random samples drawn from normally distributed populations are normally distributed. However, the real advantage of the central limit theorem comes when sample data drawn from populations not normally distributed or from populations of unknown shape also can be analyzed by using the normal distribution because the sample means are normally distributed for sufficiently large sample sizes.* Column 1 of **Figure 7.7** shows four different population

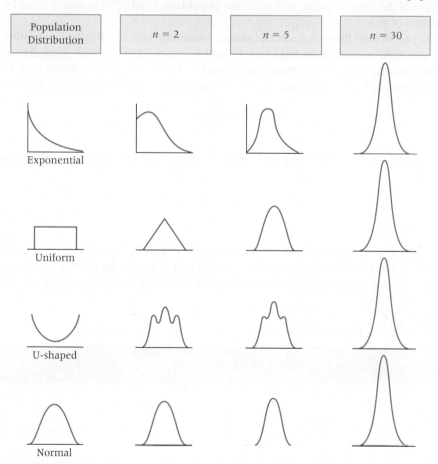

FIGURE 7.7   **Shapes of the Distributions of Sample Means for Three Sample Sizes Drawn from Four Different Population Distributions**

*The derivations are beyond the scope of this text and are not shown.
*The actual form of the central limit theorem is a limit function of calculus. As the sample size increases to infinity, the distribution of sample means literally becomes normal in shape.

distributions. Each succeeding column displays the shape of the distribution of the sample means for a particular sample size. Note in the bottom row for the normally distributed population that the sample means are normally distributed even for $n = 2$. Note also that with the other population distributions, the distribution of the sample means begins to approximate the normal curve as n becomes larger. For all four distributions, the distribution of sample means is approximately normal for $n = 30$.

How large must a sample be for the central limit theorem to apply? The sample size necessary varies according to the shape of the population. However, in this text (as in many others), a sample of *size 30 or larger* will suffice. Recall that if the population is normally distributed, the sample means are normally distributed for sample sizes as small as $n = 1$.

The shapes displayed in Figure 7.7 coincide with the results obtained empirically from the random sampling shown in Figures 7.5 and 7.6. As shown in Figure 7.7, and as indicated in Figure 7.6, as sample size increases, the distribution narrows, or becomes more leptokurtic. This trend makes sense because the standard deviation of the mean is $\sigma/\sqrt{n}$. This value will become smaller as the size of n increases.

In Table 7.5, the means and standard deviations of the means are displayed for random samples of various sizes ($n = 2$ through $n = 30$) drawn from the uniform distribution of $a = 10$ and $b = 30$ shown in Figure 7.6. The population mean is 20, and the standard deviation of the population is 5.774. Note that the mean of the sample means for each sample size is approximately 20 and that the standard deviation of the sample means for each set of 90 samples is approximately equal to $\sigma/\sqrt{n}$. A small discrepancy occurs between the standard deviation of the sample means and $\sigma/\sqrt{n}$, because not all possible samples of a given size were taken from the population (only 90). In theory, if all possible samples for a given sample size are taken exactly once, the mean of the sample means will equal the population mean and the standard deviation of the sample means will equal the population standard deviation divided by the square root of n.

The central limit theorem states that sample means are normally distributed regardless of the shape of the population for large samples and for any sample size with normally distributed populations. Thus, sample means can be analyzed by using z scores. Recall from Chapters 3 and 6 the formula to determine z scores for individual values from a normal distribution:

$$z = \frac{x - \mu}{\sigma}$$

If sample means are normally distributed, the z score formula applied to sample means would be

$$z = \frac{\bar{x} - \mu_{\bar{x}}}{\sigma_{\bar{x}}}$$

This result follows the general pattern of z scores: the difference between the statistic and its mean divided by the statistic's standard deviation. In this formula, the mean of the statistic of interest is $\mu_{\bar{x}}$, and *the standard deviation of the statistic of interest is* $\sigma_{\bar{x}}$, sometimes referred

TABLE 7.5 $\mu_{\bar{x}}$ and $\sigma_{\bar{x}}$ of 90 Random Samples for Five Different Sizes[*]

SAMPLE SIZE	MEAN OF SAMPLE MEANS	STANDARD DEVIATION OF SAMPLE MEANS	μ	$\dfrac{\sigma}{\sqrt{n}}$
$n = 2$	19.92	3.87	20	4.08
$n = 5$	20.17	2.65	20	2.58
$n = 10$	20.04	1.96	20	1.83
$n = 20$	20.20	1.37	20	1.29
$n = 30$	20.25	0.99	20	1.05

[*]Randomly generated by using Minitab from a uniform distribution with $a = 10$, $b = 30$.

to as **the standard error of the mean**. To determine $\mu_{\bar{x}}$, the researcher would randomly draw out all possible samples of the given size from the population, compute the sample means, and average them. This task is virtually impossible to accomplish in any realistic period of time. Fortunately, $\mu_{\bar{x}}$ equals the population mean, μ, which is easier to access. Likewise, to determine directly the value of $\sigma_{\bar{x}}$, the researcher would take all possible samples of a given size from a population, compute the sample means, and determine the standard deviation of sample means. This task also is practically impossible. Fortunately, $\sigma_{\bar{x}}$ can be computed by using the population standard deviation divided by the square root of the sample size.

As sample size increases, the standard deviation of the sample means becomes smaller and smaller because the population standard deviation is being divided by larger and larger values of the square root of n. The ultimate benefit of the central limit theorem is a practical, useful version of the z formula for sample means.

> **z Formula for Sample Means (7.2)**
>
> $$z = \frac{\bar{x} - \mu}{\frac{\sigma}{\sqrt{n}}}$$

When the population is normally distributed and the sample size is 1, this formula for sample means becomes the z formula for individual values that we used in Chapter 6. The reason is that the mean of one value is that value, and when $n = 1$ the value of $\sigma/\sqrt{n} = \sigma$.

As an example of the application of this z formula for sample means (Formula 7.2), suppose the population mean expenditure per customer at a tire store is \$125 and the population standard deviation is \$30. If a random sample of 40 customers is taken, what is the probability that the sample mean expenditure is more than \$133? Because the sample size is greater than 30, the central limit theorem can be used and the sample means are normally distributed allowing us to use Formula 7.2. With $\mu = \$125$, $\sigma = \$30$, and a sample mean, $\bar{x}$, of \$133, z can be computed with Formula 7.2 as:

$$z = \frac{\bar{x} - \mu}{\frac{\sigma}{\sqrt{n}}} = \frac{\$133 - \$125}{\frac{\$30}{\sqrt{40}}} = 1.69$$

From the z distribution (Table A.5), $z = 1.69$ produces a probability of .4545. This is the probability of getting a sample mean between \$125 and \$133. Solving for the tail of the distribution yields

$$.5000 - .4545 = .0455$$

which is the probability of $\bar{x} > \$133$. That is, 4.55% of the time, a random sample of 40 customers from this population would yield a sample mean expenditure of \$133 or more when the population mean is \$125. **Figure 7.8** shows the problem and its solution.

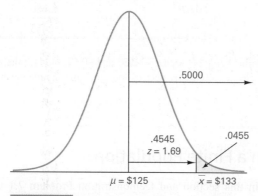

FIGURE 7.8 **Graphical Solution to the Tire Store Problem**

DEMONSTRATION PROBLEM 7.1

Suppose that during any hour in a large department store, the average number of shoppers is 448, with a standard deviation of 21 shoppers. What is the probability that a random sample of 49 different shopping hours will yield a sample mean between 441 and 446 shoppers?

Solution: For this problem, $\mu = 448$, $\sigma = 21$, and $n = 49$. The problem is to determine $P(441 \leq \bar{x} \leq 446)$. The following diagram depicts the problem.

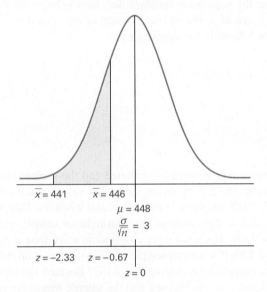

Solve this problem by calculating the z scores and using Table A.5 to determine the probabilities.

$$z = \frac{441 - 448}{\frac{21}{\sqrt{49}}} = \frac{-7}{3} = -2.33$$

and

$$z = \frac{446 - 448}{\frac{21}{\sqrt{49}}} = \frac{-2}{3} = -0.67$$

Z VALUE	PROBABILITY
−2.33	.4901
−0.67	−.2486
	.2415

The probability of a value being between $z = -2.33$ and -0.67 is .2415; that is, there is a 24.15% chance of randomly selecting 49 hourly periods for which the sample mean is between 441 and 446 shoppers.

Sampling from a Finite Population

The example shown in this section and Demonstration Problem 7.1 was based on the assumption that the population was infinitely or extremely large. In cases of a finite population, *a statistical adjustment can be made to the z formula for sample means*. The adjustment is called the **finite correction factor**: $\sqrt{\dfrac{N-n}{N-1}}$. It operates on the standard deviation of sample mean, $\sigma_{\bar{x}}$. Following is the z formula for sample means when samples are drawn from finite populations.

---

z Formula for Sample Means of a Finite Population (7.3)

$$z = \frac{\bar{x} - \mu}{\dfrac{\sigma}{\sqrt{n}} \sqrt{\dfrac{N-n}{N-1}}}$$

If a random sample of size 35 were taken from a finite population of only 500, the sample mean would be less likely to deviate from the population mean than would be the case if a sample of size 35 were taken from an infinite population. For a sample of size 35 taken from a finite population of size 500, the finite correction factor is

$$\sqrt{\frac{500-35}{500-1}} = \sqrt{\frac{465}{499}} = .965$$

Thus the standard deviation of the mean—sometimes referred to as the standard error of the mean—is adjusted downward by using .965. As the size of the finite population becomes larger in relation to sample size, the finite correction factor approaches 1. In theory, whenever researchers are working with a finite population, they can use the finite correction factor. A rough rule of thumb for many researchers is that, if the sample size is less than 5% of the finite population size or $n/N < 0.05$, the finite correction factor does not significantly modify the solution. Table 7.6 contains some illustrative finite correction factors.

TABLE 7.6   Finite Correction Factor for Some Sample Sizes

POPULATION SIZE	SAMPLE SIZE	VALUE OF CORRECTION FACTOR
2000	30(<5% N)	.993
2000	500	.866
500	30	.971
500	200	.775
200	30	.924
200	75	.793

DEMONSTRATION PROBLEM 7.2

A production company's 350 hourly employees average 37.6 years of age, with a standard deviation of 8.3 years. If a random sample of 45 hourly employees is taken, what is the probability that the sample will have an average age of less than 40 years?

Solution: The population mean is 37.6, with a population standard deviation of 8.3; that is, $\mu = 37.6$ and $\sigma = 8.3$. The sample size is 45, but it is being drawn from a finite population of 350; that is, $n = 45$ and $N = 350$. The sample mean under consideration is 40, or $\bar{x} = 40$. The following diagram depicts the problem on a normal curve.

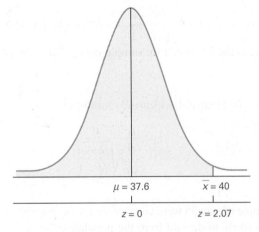

$\mu = 37.6$ $\bar{x} = 40$

$z = 0$ $z = 2.07$

Using the z formula with the finite correction factor gives

$$z = \frac{40 - 37.6}{\dfrac{8.3}{\sqrt{45}}\sqrt{\dfrac{350 - 45}{350 - 1}}} = \frac{2.4}{1.157} = 2.07$$

This z value yields a probability (Table A.5) of .4808. Therefore, the probability of getting a sample average age of less than 40 years is $.4808 + .5000 = .9808$. Had the finite correction factor not been used, the z value would have been 1.94, and the final answer would have been .9738.

7.2 Problems

7.13. A population has a mean of 50 and a standard deviation of 10. If a random sample of 64 is taken, what is the probability that the sample mean is each of the following?

  a. Greater than 52

  b. Less than 51

  c. Less than 47

  d. Between 48.5 and 52.4

  e. Between 50.6 and 51.3

7.14. A population is normally distributed, with a mean of 23.45 and a standard deviation of 3.8. What is the probability of each of the following?

  a. Taking a sample of size 10 and obtaining a sample mean of 22 or more

  b. Taking a sample of size 4 and getting a sample mean of more than 26

7.15. Suppose a random sample of size 36 is drawn from a population with a mean of 278. If 86% of the time the sample mean is less than 280, what is the population standard deviation?

7.16. A random sample of size 81 is drawn from a population with a standard deviation of 12. If only 18% of the time a sample mean greater than 300 is obtained, what is the mean of the population?

7.17. Find the probability in each case.

  a. $N = 1000$, $n = 60$, $\mu = 75$, and $\sigma = 6$; $P(\bar{x} < 76.5) = ?$

  b. $N = 90$, $n = 36$, $\mu = 108$, and $\sigma = 3.46$; $P(107 < \bar{x} < 107.7) = ?$

  c. $N = 250$, $n = 100$, $\mu = 35.6$, and $\sigma = 4.89$; $P(\bar{x} \geq 36) = ?$

  d. $N = 5000$, $n = 60$, $\mu = 125$, and $\sigma = 13.4$; $P(\bar{x} \leq 123) = ?$

7.18. The Statistical Abstract of the United States published by the U.S. Census Bureau reports that the average annual consumption of fresh fruit per person is 99.9 pounds. The standard deviation of fresh fruit consumption is about 30 pounds. Suppose a researcher took a random sample of 38 people and had them keep a record of the fresh fruit they ate for one year.

  a. What is the probability that the sample average would be less than 90 pounds?

  b. What is the probability that the sample average would be between 98 and 105 pounds?

  c. What is the probability that the sample average would be less than 112 pounds?

  d. What is the probability that the sample average would be between 93 and 96 pounds?

7.19. Suppose a subdivision on the southwest side of Denver, Colorado, contains 1,500 houses. The subdivision was built in 1983. A sample of 100 houses is selected randomly and evaluated by an appraiser. If the mean appraised value of a house in this subdivision for all houses is $227,000, with a standard deviation of $8,500, what is the probability that the sample average is greater than $229,000?

7.20. Suppose the average checkout tab at a large supermarket is $65.12, with a standard deviation of $21.45. Twenty-three percent of the time when a random sample of 45 customer tabs is examined, the sample average should exceed what value?

7.21. According to Nielsen Media Research, the average number of hours of TV viewing by adults (18 and over) per week in the United States is 36.07 hours. Suppose the standard deviation is 8.4 hours and a random sample of 42 adults is taken.

  a. What is the probability that the sample average is more than 38 hours?

  b. What is the probability that the sample average is less than 33.5 hours?

  c. What is the probability that the sample average is less than 26 hours? If the sample average actually is less than 26 hours, what would it mean in terms of the Nielsen Media Research figures?

  d. Suppose the population standard deviation is unknown. If 71% of all sample means are greater than 35 hours and the population mean is still 36.07 hours, what is the value of the population standard deviation?

7.3 Sampling Distribution of $\hat{p}$

Sometimes a business researcher will choose to use a sample proportion, denoted as $\hat{p}$, in the analysis of data rather than a sample mean, $\bar{x}$. If research produces *measurable* data such as weight, distance, time, and income, the sample mean is often the statistic of choice. However, if research results in *countable* items, such as how many people in a sample choose Dr. Pepper as their soft drink or how many people in a sample have a flexible work schedule, the sample proportion is often the statistic of choice. Whereas the mean is computed by averaging a set of values, the **sample proportion** is *computed by dividing the frequency with which a given characteristic occurs in a sample by the number of items in the sample.*

Sample Proportion (7.4)

$$\hat{p} = \frac{x}{n}$$

where

  x = number of items in a sample that have the characteristic
  n = number of items in the sample

For example, in a sample of 100 factory workers, 30 workers might belong to a union. The value of $\hat{p}$ for this characteristic, union membership, is 30/100 = .30. In a sample of 500 businesses in suburban malls, if 10 are shoe stores, then the sample proportion of shoe stores is 10/500 = .02. The sample proportion is a widely used statistic and is usually computed on questions involving Yes or No answers. For example, do you have at least a high school education? Are you predominantly right-handed? Are you female? Do you belong to the student accounting association?

How does a researcher use the sample proportion in analysis? The central limit theorem applies to sample proportions in that the normal distribution approximates the shape of the distribution of sample proportions if $n \cdot p > 5$ and $n \cdot q > 5$ (p is the population proportion and $q = 1 - p$). The mean of sample proportions for all samples of size n randomly drawn from a population is p (the population proportion) and the standard deviation of sample proportions is $\sqrt{\frac{p \cdot q}{n}}$, sometimes referred to as the **standard error of the proportion**.

Using this information, a z formula (7.5) for sample proportions can be developed.

z Formula for Sample Proportions for $n \cdot p > 5$ and $n \cdot q > 5$ (7.5)

$$z = \frac{\hat{p} - p}{\sqrt{\frac{p \cdot q}{n}}}$$

where

  $\hat{p}$ = sample proportion
  n = sample size
  p = population proportion
  $q = 1 - p$

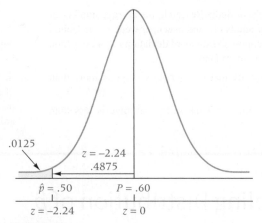

FIGURE 7.9 **Graphical Solution to the Electrical Contractor Example**

Suppose 60% of the electrical contractors in a region use a particular brand of wire. What is the probability of taking a random sample of size 120 from these electrical contractors and finding that .50 or less use that brand of wire? For this problem,

$$p = .60 \quad \hat{p} = .50 \quad n = 120$$

The z formula yields

$$z = \frac{.50 - .60}{\sqrt{\dfrac{(.60)(.40)}{120}}} = \frac{-.10}{.0447} = -2.24$$

From Table A.5, the probability corresponding to $z = -2.24$ is .4875. For $z < -2.24$ (the tail of the distribution), the answer is $.5000 - .4875 = .0125$. **Figure 7.9** shows the problem and solution graphically.

This answer indicates that a researcher would have difficulty (probability of .0125) finding that 50% or less of a sample of 120 contractors use a given brand of wire if indeed the population market share for that wire is .60. If this sample result actually occurs, either it is a rare chance result, the .60 proportion does not hold for this population, or the sampling method may not have been random.

DEMONSTRATION PROBLEM 7.3

If 10% of a population of parts is defective, what is the probability of randomly selecting 80 parts and finding that 12 or more parts are defective?

Solution: Here, $p = .10$, $\hat{p} = 12/80 = .15$, and $n = 80$. Entering these values in the z formula yields

$$z = \frac{.15 - .10}{\sqrt{\dfrac{(.10)(.90)}{80}}} = \frac{.05}{.0335} = 1.49$$

Table A.5 gives a probability of .4319 for a z value of 1.49, which is the area between the sample proportion, .15, and the population proportion, .10. The answer to the question is

$$P(\hat{p} \geq .15) = .5000 - .4319 = .0681.$$

Thus, about 6.81% of the time, 12 or more defective parts would appear in a random sample of 80 parts when the population proportion is .10. If this result actually occurred, the 10% proportion for population defects would be open to question. The diagram shows the problem graphically.

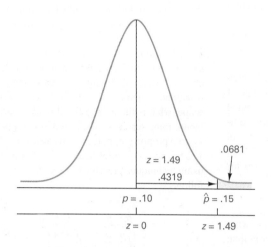

7.3 Problems

7.22. A given population proportion is .25. For the given value of n, what is the probability of getting each of the following sample proportions?

    a. $n = 110$ and $\hat{p} \leq .21$

    b. $n = 33$ and $\hat{p} > .24$

    c. $n = 59$ and $.24 \leq \hat{p} < .27$

    d. $n = 80$ and $\hat{p} < .30$

    e. $n = 800$ and $\hat{p} < .30$

7.23. A population proportion is .58. Suppose a random sample of 660 items is sampled randomly from this population.

    a. What is the probability that the sample proportion is greater than .60?

    b. What is the probability that the sample proportion is between .55 and .65?

    c. What is the probability that the sample proportion is greater than .57?

    d. What is the probability that the sample proportion is between .53 and .56?

    e. What is the probability that the sample proportion is less than .48?

7.24. Suppose a population proportion is .40, and 80% of the time when you draw a random sample from this population you get a sample proportion of .35 or more. How large a sample were you taking?

7.25. If a population proportion is .28 and if the sample size is 140, 30% of the time the sample proportion will be less than what value if you are taking random samples?

7.26. According to a study by Decision Analyst, 21% of the people who have credit cards are very close to the total limit on the card(s). Suppose a random sample of 600 credit card users is taken. What is the probability that more than 150 credit card users are very close to the total limit on their card(s)?

7.27. According to a survey by Accountemps, 48% of executives believe that employees are most productive on Tuesdays. Suppose 200 executives are randomly surveyed.

    a. What is the probability that fewer than 90 of the executives believe employees are most productive on Tuesdays?

    b. What is the probability that more than 100 of the executives believe employees are most productive on Tuesdays?

    c. What is the probability that more than 80 of the executives believe employees are most productive on Tuesdays?

7.28. A Travel Weekly International Air Transport Association survey asked business travelers about the purpose for their most recent business trip. Nineteen percent responded that it was for an internal company visit. Suppose 950 business travelers are randomly selected.

    a. What is the probability that more than 25% of the business travelers say that the reason for their most recent business trip was an internal company visit?

    b. What is the probability that between 15% and 20% of the business travelers say that the reason for their most recent business trip was an internal company visit?

    c. What is the probability that between 133 and 171 of the business travelers say that the reason for their most recent business trip was an internal company visit?

Decision Dilemma Solved

Toro

Because of limited resources, limited time, and a large population of potential consumers (many U.S. households), landscape services research will almost assuredly be accomplished through the use of random sampling. To ensure the inclusion of certain groups in an effort to reduce sampling error, a proportionate stratified random sampling technique might be selected. Such a sampling plan could include as strata such things as geographic location, type of housing (house, apartment, etc.), business vs. residential, annual rainfall, size of yard, average annual temperature, and many others. By using stratified random sampling, the researcher can, in theory, reduce sampling error by sampling from a variety of strata known to have an impact on the impact of and expenditures for landscaping services.

According to gardenresearch.com, the average household in the United States spends $449 per year on their lawns and gardens. Suppose a random sample of 35 U.S. households is taken, what is the probability that these households would average more than $500 spent on lawns and gardens if the population standard deviation is about $120? Using techniques presented in section 7.2, we can solve for a z score as follows:

$$z = \frac{\bar{x} - \mu}{\sigma/\sqrt{n}} = \frac{500 - 449}{120/\sqrt{35}} = \frac{51}{20.28} = 2.51$$

From Table A.5, we obtain a probability of .4940 for $z = 2.51$. In solving for the probability of $\bar{x} > \$500$, we are solving for the tail of the distribution: $.5000 - .4940 = .0060$. If the average household in the U.S. is spending $449 per year on their lawns and gardens and we randomly select 35 U.S. households, we would only get a sample mean of $500 or more 0.6% of the time.

According to the National Association of Landscape Professionals, 35% of U.S. adults who have a lawn or landscape purchased lawn/landscaping services in the past year. If a business researcher randomly sampled 350 adults who have a lawn or landscape, what is the probability that less than 32% purchased lawn/landscaping services? The population proportion, p, is .35 and the sample proportion, $\hat{p}$, is .32. Because $n = 350$, $n \cdot p = (350)(.35) = 122.5$, and $n \cdot q = (350)(.65) = 227.5$, this problem can be solved using techniques presented in section 7.3 and with formula 7.5 as follows:

$$z = \frac{\hat{p} - p}{\sqrt{\dfrac{p \cdot q}{n}}} = \frac{.32 - .35}{\sqrt{\dfrac{(.35)(.65)}{350}}} = \frac{-.03}{.0255} = -1.18$$

From Table A.5, we obtain a probability of .3810 for $z = -1.18$. In solving for the probability of $\hat{p} < .32$, we are solving for the tail of the distribution: $.5000 - .3810 = .1190$. Given that 35% of the adult population who has a lawn or landscape purchases lawn/landscaping services and if a business researcher randomly samples 350 such adults, there is only a .1190 or 11.90% chance that the sample percentage would be 32% or less.

Ethical Considerations

The art and science of sampling has potential for breeding unethical behavior. Considerable research is reported under the guise of random sampling when, in fact, nonrandom sampling is used. Remember, if nonrandom sampling is used, probability statements about sampling error are not appropriate. Some researchers purport to be using stratified random sampling when they are actually using quota sampling. Others claim to be using systematic random sampling when they are actually using convenience or judgment sampling.

In the process of inferential statistics, researchers use sample results to make conclusions about a population. These conclusions are disseminated to the interested public. The public often assumes that sample results truly reflect the state of the population.

If the sample does not reflect the population because questionable sampling practices were used, it could be argued that unethical research behavior occurred. Valid, representative sampling is not an easy task. Researchers and statisticians should exercise extreme caution in taking samples to be sure the results obtained reflect the conditions in the population as nearly as possible.

The central limit theorem is based on large samples unless the population is normally distributed. In analyzing small-sample data, it is an unethical practice to assume a sample mean is from a normal distribution unless the population can be shown with some confidence to be normally distributed. Using the normal distribution to analyze sample proportions is also unethical if sample sizes are smaller than those recommended by the experts.

Summary

For much business research, successfully conducting a census is virtually impossible and the sample is a feasible alternative. Other reasons for sampling include cost reduction, potential for broadening the scope of the study, and loss reduction when the testing process destroys the product.

To take a sample, a population must be identified. Often the researcher cannot obtain an exact roster or list of the population and so must find some way to identify the population as closely as possible. The final list or directory used to represent the population and from which the sample is drawn is called the frame.

The two main types of sampling are random and nonrandom. Random sampling occurs when each unit of the population has the same probability of being selected for the sample. Nonrandom sampling is any sampling that is not random. The four main types of random sampling discussed are simple random sampling, stratified sampling, systematic sampling, and cluster or area, sampling.

In simple random sampling, every unit of the population is numbered. A table of random numbers or a random number generator is used to select n units from the population for the sample.

Stratified random sampling uses the researcher's prior knowledge of the population to stratify the population into subgroups. Each subgroup is internally homogeneous but different from the others. Stratified random sampling is an attempt to reduce sampling error and ensure that at least some of each of the subgroups appears in the sample. After the strata are identified, units can be sampled randomly from each stratum. If the proportions of units selected from each subgroup for the sample are the same as the proportions of the subgroups in the population, the process is called proportionate stratified sampling. If not, it is called disproportionate stratified sampling.

With systematic sampling, every kth item of the population is sampled until n units have been selected. Systematic sampling is used because of its convenience and ease of administration.

Cluster or area sampling involves subdividing the population into nonoverlapping clusters or areas. Each cluster or area is a microcosm of the population and is usually heterogeneous within. A sample of clusters is randomly selected from the population. Individual units are then selected randomly from the clusters or areas to get the final sample. Cluster or area sampling is usually done to reduce costs.

If a set of second clusters or areas is selected from the first set, the method is called two-stage sampling.

Four types of nonrandom sampling were discussed: convenience, judgment, quota, and snowball. In convenience sampling, the researcher selects units from the population to be in the sample for convenience. In judgment sampling, units are selected according to the judgment of the researcher. Quota sampling is similar to stratified sampling, with the researcher identifying subclasses or strata. However, the researcher selects units from each stratum by some nonrandom technique until a specified quota from each stratum is filled. With snowball sampling, the researcher obtains additional sample members by asking current sample members for referral information.

Sampling error occurs when the sample does not represent the population. With random sampling, sampling error occurs by chance. Nonsampling errors are all other research and analysis errors that occur in a study. They can include recording errors, input errors, missing data, and incorrect definition of the frame.

According to the central limit theorem, if a population is normally distributed, the sample means for samples taken from that population also are normally distributed regardless of sample size. The central limit theorem also says that if the sample sizes are large ($n \geq 30$), the sample mean is approximately normally distributed regardless of the distribution shape of the population. This theorem is extremely useful because it enables researchers to analyze sample data by using the normal distribution for virtually any type of study in which means are an appropriate statistic, as long as the sample size is large enough. The central limit theorem states that sample proportions are normally distributed for large sample sizes.

Key Terms

central limit theorem
cluster (or area) sampling
convenience sampling
disproportionate stratified
    random sampling
finite correction factor
frame

judgment sampling
nonrandom sampling
nonrandom sampling techniques
nonsampling errors
overregistration
proportionate stratified random
    sampling

quota sampling
random sampling
sample proportion
sampling error
simple random sampling
snowball sampling
standard error of the mean

standard error of the
    proportion
stratified random sampling
systematic sampling
two-stage sampling
underregistration

Formulas

Determining the value of k

$$k = \frac{N}{n}$$

z formula for sample means

$$z = \frac{\bar{x} - \mu}{\frac{\sigma}{\sqrt{n}}}$$

z formula for sample means when there is a finite population

$$z = \frac{\bar{x} - \mu}{\frac{\sigma}{\sqrt{n}} \sqrt{\frac{N - n}{N - 1}}}$$

Sample proportion

$$\hat{p} = \frac{x}{n}$$

z formula for sample proportions

$$z = \frac{\hat{p} - p}{\sqrt{\frac{p \cdot q}{n}}}$$

Supplementary Problems

Calculating the Statistics

7.29. The mean of a population is 76 and the standard deviation is 14. The shape of the population is unknown. Determine the probability of each of the following occurring from this population.

  a. A random sample of size 35 yielding a sample mean of 79 or more

  b. A random sample of size 140 yielding a sample mean of between 74 and 77

  c. A random sample of size 219 yielding a sample mean of less than 76.5

7.30. Forty-six percent of a population possesses a particular characteristic. Random samples are taken from this population. Determine the probability of each of the following occurrences.

  a. The sample size is 60 and the sample proportion is between .41 and .53.

  b. The sample size is 458 and the sample proportion is less than .40.

  c. The sample size is 1350 and the sample proportion is greater than .49.

Testing Your Understanding

7.31. Suppose the age distribution in a city is as follows.

Under 18	22%
18–25	18%
26–50	36%
51–65	10%
Over 65	14%

  A researcher is conducting proportionate stratified random sampling with a sample size of 250. Approximately how many people should he sample from each stratum?

7.32. Candidate Jones believes she will receive .55 of the total votes cast in her county. However, in an attempt to validate this figure, her pollster contacts a random sample of 600 registered voters in the county. The poll results show that 298 of the voters say they are committed to voting for her. If she actually has .55 of the total vote, what is the probability of getting a sample proportion this small or smaller? Do you think she actually has 55% of the vote? Why or why not?

7.33. Determine a possible frame for conducting random sampling in each of the following studies.

  a. The average amount of overtime per week for production workers in a plastics company in Pennsylvania

  b. The average number of employees in all Ralphs supermarkets in Southern California

  c. A survey of commercial lobster catchers in Maine

7.34. A particular automobile costs an average of $21,755 in the Pacific Northwest. The standard deviation of prices is $650. Suppose a random sample of 30 dealerships in Washington and Oregon is taken, and their managers are asked what they charge for this automobile. What is the probability of getting a sample average cost of less than $21,500? Assume that only 120 dealerships in the entire Pacific Northwest sell this automobile.

7.35. A company has 1,250 employees, and you want to take a simple random sample of $n = 60$ employees. Explain how you would go about selecting this sample by using the table of random numbers. Are there numbers that you cannot use? Explain.

7.36. Suppose the average client charge per hour for out-of-court work by lawyers in the state of Iowa is $125. Suppose further that a random telephone sample of 32 lawyers in Iowa is taken and that the sample average charge per hour for out-of-court work is $110. If the population variance is $525, what is the probability of getting a sample mean of $110 or larger? What is the probability of getting a sample mean larger than $135 per hour? What is the probability of getting a sample mean of between $120 and $130 per hour?

7.37. A survey of 2645 consumers by DDB Needham Worldwide of Chicago for public relations agency Porter/Novelli showed that how a company handles a crisis when at fault is one of the top influences in consumer buying decisions, with 73% claiming it is an influence. Quality of product was the number one influence, with 96% of consumers stating that quality influences their buying decisions. How a company handles complaints was number two, with 85% of consumers reporting it as an influence in their buying decisions. Suppose a random sample of 1100 consumers is taken and each is asked which of these three factors influence their buying decisions.

  a. What is the probability that more than 810 consumers claim that how a company handles a crisis when at fault is an influence in their buying decisions?

  b. What is the probability that fewer than 1030 consumers claim that quality of product is an influence in their buying decisions?

  c. What is the probability that between 82% and 84% of consumers claim that how a company handles complaints is an influence in their buying decisions?

7.38. Suppose you are sending out questionnaires to a randomly selected sample of 100 managers. The frame for this study is the membership list of the American Managers Association. The questionnaire contains demographic questions about the company and its top manager. In addition, it asks questions about the manager's leadership style. Research assistants are to score and enter the responses into the computer as soon as they are received. You are to conduct a statistical analysis of the data. Name and describe four nonsampling errors that could occur in this study.

7.39. A researcher is conducting a study of a *Fortune* 500 company that has factories, distribution centers, and retail outlets across the country. How can she use cluster or area sampling to take a random sample of employees of this firm?

7.40. A directory of personal computer retail outlets in the United States contains 12,080 alphabetized entries. Explain how systematic sampling could be used to select a sample of 300 outlets.

7.41. In an effort to cut costs and improve profits, many U.S. companies have been turning to outsourcing. In fact, according to *Purchasing* magazine, 54% of companies surveyed outsourced some part of their manufacturing process in the past two to three years. Suppose 565 of these companies are contacted.

  a. What is the probability that 339 or more companies outsourced some part of their manufacturing process in the past two to three years?

  b. What is the probability that 288 or more companies outsourced some part of their manufacturing process in the past two to three years?

c. What is the probability that 50% or less of these companies outsourced some part of their manufacturing process in the past two to three years?

7.42. The average cost of a one-bedroom apartment in a town is $650 per month. What is the probability of randomly selecting a sample of 50 one-bedroom apartments in this town and getting a sample mean of less than $630 if the population standard deviation is $100?

7.43. The Aluminum Association reports that the average American uses 56.8 pounds of aluminum in a year. A random sample of 51 households is monitored for one year to determine aluminum usage. If the population standard deviation of annual usage is 12.3 pounds, what is the probability that the sample mean will be each of the following?

a. More than 60 pounds

b. More than 58 pounds

c. Between 56 and 57 pounds

d. Less than 55 pounds

e. Less than 50 pounds

7.44. Use Table A.1 to select 20 three-digit random numbers. Did any of the numbers occur more than once? How is it possible for a number to occur more than once? Make a stem-and-leaf plot of the numbers with the stem being the left digit. Do the numbers seem to be equally distributed, or are they bunched together?

7.45. Direct marketing companies are turning to the Internet for new opportunities. A recent study by Gruppo, Levey, & Co. showed that 73% of all direct marketers conduct transactions on the Internet. Suppose a random sample of 300 direct marketing companies is taken.

a. What is the probability that between 210 and 234 (inclusive) direct marketing companies are turning to the Internet for new opportunities?

b. What is the probability that 78% or more of direct marketing companies are turning to the Internet for new opportunities?

c. Suppose a random sample of 800 direct marketing companies is taken. Now what is the probability that 78% or more are turning to the Internet for new opportunities? How does this answer differ from the answer in part (b)? Why do the answers differ?

7.46. According to the U.S. Bureau of Labor Statistics, 20% of all people 16 years of age or older do volunteer work. In this age group, women volunteer slightly more than men, with 22% of women volunteering and 19% of men volunteering. What is the probability of randomly sampling 140 women 16 years of age or older and getting 35 or more who do volunteer work? What is the probability of getting 21 or fewer from this group? Suppose a sample of 300 men and women 16 years of age or older is selected randomly from the U.S. population. What is the probability that the sample proportion of those who do volunteer work is between 18% and 25%?

7.47. Suppose you work for a large firm that has 20,000 employees. The CEO calls you in and asks you to determine employee attitudes toward the company. She is willing to commit $100,000 to this project. What are the advantages of taking a sample versus conducting a census? What are the trade-offs?

7.48. In a particular area of the Northeast, an estimated 75% of the homes use heating oil as the principal heating fuel during the winter. A random telephone survey of 150 homes is taken in an attempt to determine whether this figure is correct. Suppose 120 of the 150 homes surveyed use heating oil as the principal heating fuel. What is the probability of getting a sample proportion this large or larger if the population estimate is true?

7.49. The U.S. Bureau of Labor Statistics released hourly wage figures for various countries for workers in the manufacturing sector. The hourly wage was $30.67 for Switzerland, $20.20 for Japan, and $23.82 for the U.S. Assume that in all three countries, the standard deviation of hourly labor rates is $3.00.

a. Suppose 40 manufacturing workers are selected randomly from across Switzerland and asked what their hourly wage is. What is the probability that the sample average will be between $30.00 and $31.00?

b. Suppose 35 manufacturing workers are selected randomly from across Japan. What is the probability that the sample average will exceed $21.00?

c. Suppose 50 manufacturing workers are selected randomly from across the United States What is the probability that the sample average will be less than $22.75?

7.50. Give a variable that could be used to stratify the population for each of the following studies. List at least four subcategories for each variable.

a. A political party wants to conduct a poll prior to an election for the office of U.S. senator in Minnesota.

b. A soft drink company wants to take a sample of soft drink purchases in an effort to estimate market share.

c. A retail outlet wants to interview customers over a one-week period.

d. An eyeglasses manufacturer and retailer wants to determine the demand for prescription eyeglasses in its marketing region.

7.51. According to Runzheimer International, a typical business traveler spends an average of $281 per day in Chicago. This cost includes hotel, meals, car rental, and incidentals. A survey of 65 randomly selected business travelers who have been to Chicago on business recently is taken. For the population mean of $281 per day, what is the probability of getting a sample average of more than $273 per day if the population standard deviation is $47?

Analyzing the Databases

See **www.wiley.com/college/black**

1. Let the Manufacturing database be the frame for a population of manufacturers to be studied. This database has 140 different SIC codes. Explain how you would take a systematic sample of size 10 from this frame. Examining the variables in the database, name two variables that could be used to stratify the population. Explain how these variables could be used in stratification and why each variable might produce important strata.

2. Consider the Consumer Food database. Compute the mean and standard deviation for annual food spending for this population. Now take a random sample of 32 of the households in this database and compute the sample mean. Using techniques presented in this chapter, determine the probability of getting a mean this large or larger from the population. Work this problem both with and without the finite correction factor and compare the results by discussing the differences in answers.

3. Use the Hospital database and determine the proportion of hospitals that are under the control of nongovernment not-for-profit organizations (category 2). Assume that this proportion represents the entire population of all hospitals. If you randomly selected 500 hospitals from across the United States, what is the probability that 45% or more are under the control of nongovernment not-for-profit organizations? If you randomly selected 100 hospitals, what is the probability that less than 40% are under the control of nongovernment not-for-profit organizations?

Case

3M

The 3M company is a global innovation company with over 100,000 patents, $31 billion in sales, and 90,000 employees. 3M has 27 business units organized under five business groups: consumer, electronics & energy, health care, industrial, and safety & graphics. It has 46 technology platforms including adhesives, abrasives, electronics & software, light management, microreplication, nanotechnology, nonwoven materials, and surface modification. Related to this, 3M has 8,500 researchers worldwide and its products are sold in nearly 200 countries. Included in 3M's more widely-known products are Scotch® Tape, Post-it® Notes, and Ace™ bandages.

3M was born as a small-scale mining company in 1902 when the five founders invested in harvesting a mineral known as corundum from a mine in Minnesota on the shores of Lake Superior. The mine ultimately did not produce much corundum but the company used a spirit of innovation, collaboration, and technology to discover other materials and products that could be of use to consumers and companies. In 1910, the company, then known as Minnesota Mining and Manufacturing (3M), moved its headquarters to St. Paul where it is today. In the early 1920s, 3M created the world's first waterproof sandpaper which helped open up opportunities for the company in the automotive industry. In 1925, a young lab assistant invented masking tape thereby helping to diversify the company's offering. Over the next few decades, many of the "Scotch™" products were developed and marketed including Scotch® Tape, Scotchlite™, and Scotchgard™. In the 1960's, 3M introduced dry-silver microfilm, photographic products, carbonless papers, overhead projection systems, and numerous health care and dental products. In 1980, 3M introduced Post-it® Notes creating a new category in the marketplace. By the year 2000, there were new products such as Post-it® Super Sticky Notes, Scotch® Transparent Duct Tape, optical films for LCD televisions and a family of new Scotch-Brite™ Cleaning Products. In 2009, 3M introduced a new line of stethoscopes in health care and introduced new produces in the grinding industry. In later years, 3M developed 3M® Solar Mirror Film 1100 for concentrated solar power.

Today, one-third of 3M's sales come from products invented within the past five years during which time over $8 billion has been invested in R&D and related expenditures. According to company information sources, the global 3M team is committed to creating the technology and products that advance every company, enhance every home and improve every life. 3M has been listed on the Dow Jones Sustainability Index for 15 consecutive years.

Discussion

1. 3M has developed a composite measure, a 3M™ Value Index Score, which provides a standard metric to assess accountable value in health care. This index score is a composite measure based on six critical primary care domains derived from 16 measures of key processes and outcomes that effect value in health care. According to 3M, this Value Index Score can increase the understanding of provider and system performance thereby accelerating and prioritizing the areas where improvement is needed. This measure can be used by both providers and payers to help improve patient outcomes and to control costs. Suppose you were asked to develop a sampling plan for a study to determine the value of the index, usage rates of the index, and general attitudes toward the index, what sampling plan would you use? What is the target population (or are there multiple target populations)? What might you use for the frame(s)? Which of the four types of random sampling discussed in the chapter would you use and why? If you were to use stratified random sampling, what would be your strata?

2. In 2009, the Global Strategy Group conducted an online survey commissioned by Scotch® Tape of adults nationwide in the United States about their personal gift-wrapping behaviors and trends. One finding was that the average number of presents wrapped by adults in a typical December holiday season is 15.3. In addition, the study found that women wrap more presents than men with women averaging 20.3 and men averaging 9.9. Suppose that these figures obtained from a sample are actually true for the entire population and that the standard deviation for all adults, for women, and for men is 2.5. If a random sample of 35 U.S. adults is taken, what is the probability that the sample mean number of presents wrapped in a typical December holiday season is more than 16? If a random sample of 60 U.S. men is taken, what is the probability that the sample mean number of presents wrapped by a man in a typical December holiday season is less than 10? If a random sample of 43 U.S. women is taken, what is the probability that the sample mean number of presents wrapped by a woman in a typical December holiday season is between 20.0 and 20.8?

3. In 2015, 3M commissioned a survey conducted by Wakefield Research regarding color quality in electronic devices (phones, tablets, notebook PC's and LCD TVs). Among the results of the survey are that 62% of device owners wish there was better color quality on their display devices. Twenty-nine percent want more realistic colors, eighteen percent want bolder colors, and fourteen percent want richer dark colors. Assume these figures are true for the general population of device owners. If a random sample of 450 device owners is taken, what is the probability that more than 65% wish there was better color quality on their display devices? If a random sample of 270 device owners is taken, what is the probability that 25% or fewer want more realistic colors? If a random sample of 950 device owners is taken, what is the probability that between 152 and 200 want bolder colors?

Sources: Adapted from information at: www.3m.com/and www.3m.com/3M/en_US/company-us/all-3m-products

CHAPTER 8

Statistical Inference: Estimation for Single Populations

LEARNING OBJECTIVES

The overall learning objective of Chapter 8 is to help you understand estimating parameters of single populations, thereby enabling you to:

1. Estimate the population mean with a known population standard deviation using the *z* statistic, correcting for a finite population if necessary.

2. Estimate the population mean with an unknown population standard deviation using the *t* statistic and properties of the *t* distribution.

3. Estimate a population proportion using the *z* statistic.

4. Use the chi-square distribution to estimate the population variance given the sample variance.

5. Determine the sample size needed in order to estimate the population mean and population proportion.

Decision Dilemma

Batteries and Bulbs: How Long Do They Last?

What is the average life of a battery? As you can imagine, the answer depends on the type of battery, what it is used for, and how it is used. Car batteries are different from iPhone batteries, which are different from flashlight batteries. Nevertheless, a few statistics are available on the life of batteries. For example, according to Apple, an iPhone 6 has up to 240 hours of life if kept in standby, without making any calls or running any applications. In a *PCWorld* study, several smartphones were tested to determine battery life. In the tests, a video file was played at maximum brightness looped over and over with the audio set played very loud. As a result, the average battery life without recharge for the brand with the top battery life was 7.37 hours, with other brands varying from 4.23 hours to 6.55 hours. According to another study, the average battery life of a tablet computer is 8.78 hours. Overall, a laptop computer battery should last through around 1,000 charges. Another source says that the typical AA battery used in such things as flashlights, digital cameras, etc. will last two

© DBURKE/Alamy

hours in straight constant use. According to a source at the Sears Automotive Group, heat is a factor in the average life expectancy of a car battery. The average life of a battery in the northern United States is five years, but the average life of a battery in the South may only be around two years. According to BatteryStuff. com, only 30% of car batteries make it to age four before dying.

Furthermore, 78% of customers wait for a car battery to fail or an incident to occur before replacing a battery.

The life of a light bulb varies with the type of bulb. For example, the typical incandescent bulb lasts between 1,000 and 2,000 hours. One source says that the average life of an incandescent 60-watt bulb is 1.4 years based on a 3-hours-per-day usage (1533 hours). The estimated yearly energy cost of such a bulb is $7.23. Another source says that the average lifespan of a compact fluorescent light is about 10,000 hours, halogen bulbs have a lifespan ranging from 4,000 to 8,000 hours, and light-emitting diodes (LEDs) have a lifespan ranging from 30,000 to 50,000 hours. In terms of switching over from traditional light bulbs to CFLs (compact fluorescent lamp), 72% of Socket Survey respondents said that they use CFLs in their home. However, many of these respondents use a variety of types of bulbs including incandescent light bulbs.

MANAGERIAL AND STATISTICAL QUESTIONS

1. According to a study mentioned here, the average battery life of a tablet computer is 8.78 hours. Undoubtedly, this figure was obtained by testing a sample of tablet computers. Suppose the 8.78 hour average was obtained by sampling 60 tablet computers. If a second sample of 60 tablet computers was selected, do you think that the average battery life would also be 8.78 hours? How could this figure be used to estimate the average battery life of all tablet computers?

2. One source says that the average life of an incandescent 60-watt bulb is 1.4 years based on a 3-hours-per-day usage (1533 hours). Do you think that the 1533 hours figure was obtained from a sample or from the population of all incandescent 60-watt bulbs? Why or why not? Suppose the 1533 hours average was computed from a sample of 41 light bulbs; how

can it be used to estimate the average number of hours of burn for all 60 watt bulbs?

3. According to BatteryStuff.com, only 30% of car batteries make it to age four before dying. If this figure was obtained by studying 280 car batteries over a four-year period, how could these results be used to estimate the percent of all car batteries that make it to age four before dying? According to a Socket Survey, 72% of respondents said that they use CFLs in their home. Suppose there were 900 respondents in this survey; how could the results be used to estimate the percentage for all homes?

Sources: Figures obtained from: information on average battery life of a tablet computer obtained at the Web site for FindTheBest, 2013 located at http://tablets.findthebest.com/app-question/301/What-is-the-average-battery-life-of-a-tablet-computer; information on laptop computer batteries obtained at the Computer Hope Web site, 2012, at http://www.computerhope.com/issues/ch001236.htm; "What is the average life of AA battery?", Answers Corporation, 2012 at http://wiki.answers.com/Q/What_is_the_average_life_of_AA_battery; "How Long Did You Say That Bulb Would Last?" by Eric A. Taub, NY Times BITS, February 11, 2009, at http://bits.blogs.nytimes.com/2009/02/11/how-long-did-you-say-that-bulb-will-last/; "Learn Your Lumens, New Light Bulb Labeling in 2011:, Mark Schrieber, September 28, 2010 at http://blog.cleantechies.com/2010/09/28/learn-your-lumens-new-light-bulb-labeling-in-2011/; "Summer Heat Can Destroy Automotive Batteries", PR Newswire, July 20, 2012, at http://www.marketwatch.com/story/summer-heat-can-destroy-automotive-batteries-2012-07-20; "Reasons for a Car Battery Dying," by Chris Joseph, eHow, at http://www.ehow.com/list_5982917_reasons-car-battery-dying.html; "More Americans Aware of Traditional Light Bulb Phaseout", by Leslie Guevarra, GreenBiz.com, December 16, 2010, at http://www.greenbiz.com/news/2010/12/16/more-americans-aware-traditional-light-bulb-phaseout. www.apple.com/iphone/compare/

Displayed in **Figure 8.1** is a tree diagram displaying the confidence interval techniques presented in Chapter 8. This tree diagram contains all statistical techniques for constructing confidence intervals from one-sample data presented in this text. Note that at the bottom of each tree branch in Figure 8.1, the title of the statistical technique along with its respective section number is given for ease of identification and use. In Chapter 8, techniques are presented that allow a business researcher to estimate a population mean, proportion, or variance by taking a sample from the population, analyzing data from the sample, and projecting the resulting statistics back onto the population, thereby reaching conclusions about the population. Because it is often extremely difficult to obtain and analyze population data for a variety of reasons mentioned in Chapter 7, the importance of the ability to estimate population parameters from sample statistics cannot be underestimated. **Figure 8.2** depicts this process. If a business researcher is estimating a population mean and the population standard deviation is known, then he will use the z confidence interval for μ contained in Section 8.1. If the population standard deviation is unknown and therefore the researcher is using the sample standard deviation, then the appropriate technique is the t confidence interval for μ contained in Section 8.2. If a business researcher is estimating a population proportion, then he will use the z confidence interval for p presented in Section 8.3. If the researcher desires to estimate a population variance with a single sample, then he will use the χ^2 confidence interval for σ^2 presented in Section 8.4. Section 8.5 contains techniques for determining how large a sample to take in order to ensure a given level of confidence within a targeted level of error.

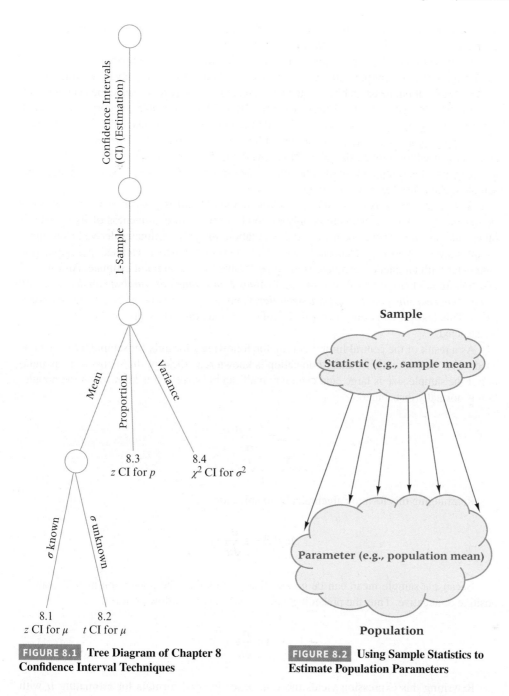

FIGURE 8.1 **Tree Diagram of Chapter 8 Confidence Interval Techniques**

FIGURE 8.2 **Using Sample Statistics to Estimate Population Parameters**

8.1 Estimating the Population Mean Using the *z* Statistic (σ Known)

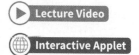

On many occasions estimating the population mean is useful in business research. For example, the manager of human resources in a company might want to estimate the average number of days of work an employee misses per year because of illness. If the firm has thousands of employees, direct calculation of a population mean such as this may be practically impossible. Instead, a random sample of employees can be taken, and the sample mean number of sick days can be used to estimate the population mean. Suppose another company developed a new process for prolonging the shelf life of a loaf of bread. The company wants to be able to date each loaf for freshness, but company officials do not know exactly how long the bread will stay fresh. By taking a random sample and determining the sample mean shelf life, they can estimate the average shelf life for the population of bread.

As the cellular telephone industry has grown and matured, it is apparent that the use of texting has increased dramatically. Suppose a large cellular phone company in wanting to meet the needs of cell phone users hires a business research company to estimate the average number of texts used per month by Americans in the 18-to-24-years-of-age category. The research company studies the phone records of 85 randomly sampled Americans in the 18-to-24-years-of-age category and computes a sample monthly mean of 1300 texts. This mean, which is a statistic, is used to estimate the population mean, which is a parameter. If the cellular phone company uses the sample mean of 1300 texts as an estimate for the population mean, the same sample mean is used as a *point estimate*.

A **point estimate** is *a statistic taken from a sample that is used to estimate a population parameter*. A point estimate is only as good as the representativeness of its sample. If other random samples are taken from the population, the point estimates derived from those samples are likely to vary. Because of variation in sample statistics, estimating a population parameter with an interval estimate is often preferable to using a point estimate. An **interval estimate** (confidence interval) is *a range of values within which the analyst can declare, with some confidence, the population parameter lies*. Confidence intervals can be two-sided or one-sided. This text presents only two-sided confidence intervals. How are confidence intervals constructed?

As a result of the central limit theorem, the following z formula for sample means can be used when the population standard deviation is known regardless of the shape of the population if the sample size is large, and even for small sample sizes if it is known that the population is normally distributed.

$$z = \frac{\bar{x} - \mu}{\frac{\sigma}{\sqrt{n}}}$$

Rearranging this formula algebraically to solve for μ gives

$$\mu = \bar{x} - z\frac{\sigma}{\sqrt{n}}$$

Because a sample mean can be greater than or less than the population mean, z can be positive or negative. Thus the preceding expression takes the following form:

$$\bar{x} \pm z\frac{\sigma}{\sqrt{n}}$$

Rewriting this expression yields the confidence interval formula for estimating μ with large sample sizes if the population standard deviation is known.

100(1 − α)% Confidence Interval to Estimate μ: σ known

$$\bar{x} \pm z_{\alpha/2}\frac{\sigma}{\sqrt{n}}$$

or

(8.1)

$$\bar{x} - z_{\alpha/2}\frac{\sigma}{\sqrt{n}} \leq \mu \leq \bar{x} + z_{\alpha/2}\frac{\sigma}{\sqrt{n}}$$

where

α = the area under the normal curve outside the confidence interval area
$\alpha/2$ = the area in one end (tail) of the distribution outside the confidence interval

Alpha (α) is the area under the normal curve in the tails of the distribution outside the area defined by the confidence interval. We will focus more on α in Chapter 9. Here we use α to locate the z value in constructing the confidence interval as shown in **Figure 8.3**. Because the standard normal table is based on areas between a z of 0 and $z_{\alpha/2}$, the table z value is found by locating the area of $.5000 - \alpha/2$, which is the part of the normal curve between the middle of the curve and one of the tails. Another way to locate this z value is to change the confidence level from percentage to proportion, divide it in half, and go to the table with this value. The results are the same.

The confidence interval formula (8.1) yields a range (interval) within which we feel with some confidence that the population mean is located. It is not certain that the population mean is in the interval unless we have a 100% confidence interval that is infinitely wide. If we want to construct a 95% confidence interval, the level of confidence is 95%, or .95. If 100 such intervals are constructed by taking random samples from the population, it is likely that 95 of the intervals would include the population mean and 5 would not.

As an example, in the cellular telephone company's effort to estimate the population monthly mean number of texts in the 18-to-24-year-old age category, from a sample of 85 bills it is determined that the sample mean is 1300 texts. Using this sample mean, a confidence interval can be calculated within which the researcher is relatively confident that the actual population mean is located. To make this calculation using Formula 8.1, the value of the population standard deviation and the value of z (in addition to the sample mean, 1300, and the sample size, 85) must be known. Suppose past history and similar studies indicate that the population standard deviation is about 160.

The value of z is driven by the level of confidence. An interval with 100% confidence is so wide that it is meaningless. Some of the more common levels of confidence used by business researchers are 90%, 95%, 98%, and 99%. Why would a business researcher not just select the highest confidence and always use that level? The reason is that trade-offs between sample size, interval width, and level of confidence must be considered. For example, as the level of confidence is increased, the interval gets wider, provided the sample size and standard deviation remain constant.

For the cellular telephone problem, suppose the business researcher decided on a 95% confidence interval for the results. **Figure 8.4** shows a normal distribution of sample means

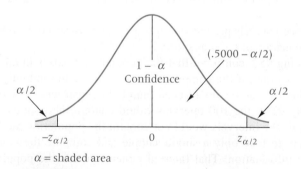

FIGURE 8.3 z Scores for Confidence Intervals in Relation to α

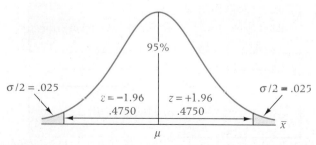

FIGURE 8.4   **Distribution of Sample Means for 95% Confidence**

about the population mean. When using a 95% level of confidence, the researcher selects an interval centered on μ within which 95% of all sample mean values will fall and then uses the width of that interval to create an interval around the *sample mean* within which he has some confidence the population mean will fall.

For 95% confidence, $\alpha = .05$ and $\alpha/2 = .025$. The value of $z_{\alpha/2}$ or $z_{.025}$ is found by looking in the standard normal table under $.5000 - .0250 = .4750$. This area in the table is associated with a z value of 1.96. Another way can be used to locate the table z value. Because the distribution is symmetric and the intervals are equal on each side of the population mean, ½(95%), or .4750, of the area is on each side of the mean. Table A.5 yields a z value of 1.96 for this portion of the normal curve. Thus the z value for a 95% confidence interval is always 1.96. In other words, of all the possible $\bar{x}$ values along the horizontal axis of the diagram, 95% of them should be within a z score of 1.96 from the population mean.

The business researcher can now complete the cellular telephone problem. To determine a 95% confidence interval for $\bar{x} = 1300$, $\sigma = 160$, $n = 85$, and $z = 1.96$, the researcher estimates the average number of texts by including the value of z in Formula 8.1.

$$1300 - 1.96\frac{160}{\sqrt{85}} \leq \mu \leq 1300 + 1.96\frac{160}{\sqrt{85}}$$

$$1300 - 34.01 \leq \mu \leq 1300 + 34.01$$

$$1265.99 \leq \mu \leq 1334.01$$

From this interval, the research company can conclude with 95% confidence that the population mean number of texts per month for an American in the 18-to-24-years-of-age category is between 1265.99 texts and 1334.01 texts. Note that actually the confidence interval is constructed from two values, the point estimate (1300), and another value (34.01) that is added and subtracted from the point estimate. This value, 34.01, or $\pm(1.96)\frac{160}{\sqrt{85}}$, is the **margin of error of the interval** and is the distance between the statistic computed to estimate a parameter and the parameter. The margin of error takes into account the desired level of confidence, sample size, and standard deviation. When the margin of error is added to the point estimate, the result is the **upper bound of the confidence interval**. When the margin of error is subtracted from the point estimate, the result is the **lower bound of the confidence interval**.

Most confidence intervals presented in this text are constructed from the point estimate plus and minus the margin of error, as shown in **Figure 8.5**.

What does being 95% confident that the population mean is in an interval actually indicate? It indicates that, if the company researcher were to randomly select 100 samples of 85 bills and use the results of each sample to construct a 95% confidence interval, approximately 95 of the 100 intervals would contain the population mean. It also indicates that 5% of the intervals would not contain the population mean. The company researcher is likely to take only a single sample and compute the confidence interval from that sample information. That interval either contains the population mean or it

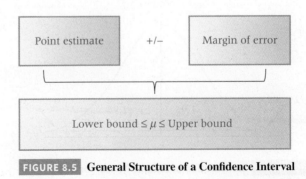

FIGURE 8.5 **General Structure of a Confidence Interval**

does not. **Figure 8.6** depicts the meaning of a 95% confidence interval for the mean. Note that if 20 random samples are taken from the population, 19 of the 20 are likely to contain the population mean if a 95% confidence interval is used $(19/20 = 95\%)$. If a 90% confidence interval is constructed, only 18 of the 20 intervals are likely to contain the population mean.

DEMONSTRATION PROBLEM 8.1

A survey was taken of U.S. companies that do business with firms in India. One of the questions on the survey was: Approximately how many years has your company been trading with firms in India? A random sample of 44 responses to this question yielded a mean of 10.455 years. Suppose the population standard deviation for this question is 7.7 years. Using this information, construct a 90% confidence interval for the mean number of years that a company has been trading in India for the population of U.S. companies trading with firms in India.

Solution: Here, $n = 44$, $\bar{x} = 10.455$, and $\sigma = 7.7$. To determine the value of $Z_{\alpha/2}$, divide the 90% confidence in half, or take $.5000 - \alpha/2 = .5000 - .0500$ where $\alpha = 10\%$. *Note:* The *z*-distribution of $\bar{x}$ around μ contains .4500 of the area on each side of μ, or ½(90%). Table A.5 yields a *z* value of 1.645 for the area of .4500 (interpolating between .4495 and .4505). The confidence interval is

$$\bar{x} - z\frac{\sigma}{\sqrt{n}} \leq \mu \leq \bar{x} + z\frac{\sigma}{\sqrt{n}}$$

$$10.455 - 1.645\frac{7.7}{\sqrt{44}} \leq \mu \leq 10.455 + 1.645\frac{7.7}{\sqrt{44}}$$

$$10.455 - 1.910 \leq \mu \leq 10.455 + 1.910$$

$$8.545 \leq \mu \leq 12.365$$

The analyst is 90% confident that if a census of all U.S. companies trading with firms in India were taken at the time of this survey, the actual population mean number of years a company would have been trading with firms in India would be between 8.545 and 12.365. The point estimate is 10.455 years and the margin of error is 1.910 years.

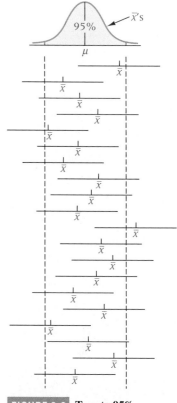

FIGURE 8.6   **Twenty 95% Confidence Intervals of μ**

For convenience, **Table 8.1** contains some of the more common levels of confidence and their associated *z* values.

Finite Correction Factor

Recall from Chapter 7 that if the sample is taken from a finite population, a finite correction factor may be used to increase the accuracy of the solution. In the case of interval estimation, the finite correction factor is used to reduce the width of the interval. As stated in Chapter 7, if the sample size is less than 5% of the population, the finite correction factor does not significantly alter the solution. If Formula 8.1 is modified to include the finite correction factor, the result is Formula 8.2.

Confidence Interval to Estimate μ Using the Finite Correction Factor

$$\bar{x} - z_{\alpha/2}\frac{\sigma}{\sqrt{n}}\sqrt{\frac{N-n}{N-1}} \leq \mu \leq \bar{x} + z_{\alpha/2}\frac{\sigma}{\sqrt{n}}\sqrt{\frac{N-n}{N-1}} \qquad (8.2)$$

Demonstration Problem 8.2 shows how the finite correction factor can be used.

TABLE 8.1

Values of *z* for Common Levels of Confidence

CONFIDENCE LEVEL	*z* VALUE
90%	1.645
95%	1.96
98%	2.33
99%	2.575

DEMONSTRATION PROBLEM 8.2

A study is conducted in a company that employs 800 engineers. A random sample of 50 of these engineers reveals that the average sample age is 34.30 years. Historically, the population standard deviation of the age of the company's engineers is approximately 8 years. Construct a 98% confidence interval to estimate the average age of all the engineers in this company.

Solution: This problem has a finite population. The sample size, 50, is greater than 5% of the population, so the finite correction factor may be helpful. In this case $N = 800$, $n = 50$, $\bar{x} = 34.30$, and $\sigma = 8$. The z value for a 98% confidence interval is 2.33 (.98 divided into two equal parts yields .4900; the z value is obtained from Table A.5 by using .4900). Substituting into Formula 8.2 and solving for the confidence interval gives

$$34.30 - 2.33 \frac{8}{\sqrt{50}} \sqrt{\frac{750}{799}} \leq \mu \leq 34.30 + 2.33 \frac{8}{\sqrt{50}} \sqrt{\frac{750}{799}}$$

$$34.30 - 2.55 \leq \mu \leq 34.30 + 2.55$$

$$31.75 \leq \mu \leq 36.85$$

Without the finite correction factor, the result would have been

$$34.30 - 2.64 \leq \mu \leq 34.30 + 2.64$$

$$31.66 \leq \mu \leq 36.94$$

The finite correction factor takes into account the fact that the population is only 800 instead of being infinitely large. The sample, $n = 50$, is a greater proportion of the 800 than it would be of a larger population, and thus the width of the confidence interval is reduced when using the finite correction factor.

Estimating the Population Mean Using the *z* Statistic When the Sample Size Is Small

In the formulas and problems presented so far in the section, sample size was large $(n \geq 30)$. However, quite often in the business world, sample sizes are small. While the central limit theorem applies only when sample size is large, the distribution of sample means is approximately normal even for small sizes *if the population is normally distributed*. This is visually displayed in the bottom row of Figure 7.6 in Chapter 7. Thus, if it is known that the population from which the sample is being drawn is normally distributed and if σ is known, the z formulas presented in this section can still be used to estimate a population mean even if the sample size is small $(n < 30)$.

As an example, suppose a U.S. car rental firm wants to estimate the average number of miles traveled per day by each of its cars rented in California. A random sample of 20 cars rented in California reveals that the sample mean travel distance per day is 85.5 miles, with a population standard deviation of 19.3 miles. Assume that number of miles traveled per day is normally distributed in the population. Compute a 99% confidence interval to estimate μ.

Here, $n = 20$, $\bar{x} = 85.5$, and $\sigma = 19.3$. For a 99% level of confidence, a z value of 2.575 is obtained. The confidence interval is

$$\bar{x} - z_{\alpha/2} \frac{\sigma}{\sqrt{n}} \leq \mu \leq \bar{x} + z_{\alpha/2} \frac{\sigma}{\sqrt{n}}$$

$$85.5 - 2.575 \frac{19.3}{\sqrt{20}} \leq \mu \leq 85.5 + 2.575 \frac{19.3}{\sqrt{20}}$$

$$85.5 - 11.1 \leq \mu \leq 85.5 + 11.1$$

$$74.4 \leq \mu \leq 96.6$$

Excel Output

The sample mean is:	1300
The error of the interval is:	34.014
The confidence interval is:	1300 ± 34.014
The confidence interval is:	$1265.986 \leq \mu \leq 1334.014$

Minitab Output

One-Sample Z

```
The assumed standard deviation = 160
N    Mean      SE Mean   95% CI
85   1300.00   17.35     (1265.99, 1334.01)
```

FIGURE 8.7 **Excel and Minitab Output for the Cellular Telephone Example**

The point estimate indicates that the average number of miles traveled per day by a rental car in California is 85.5 with a margin of error of 11.1 miles. With 99% confidence, we estimate that the population mean is somewhere between 74.4 and 96.6 miles per day.

Using the Computer to Construct z Confidence Intervals for the Mean

It is possible to construct a z confidence interval for the mean with either Excel or Minitab. Excel yields the ± error portion of the confidence interval that must be placed with the sample mean to construct the complete confidence interval. Minitab constructs the complete confidence interval. Figure 8.7 shows both the Excel output and the Minitab output for the cellular telephone example.

8.1 Problems

8.1. Use the following information to construct the confidence intervals specified to estimate μ.

a. 95% confidence for $\bar{x} = 25$, $\sigma = 3.5$, and $n = 60$

b. 98% confidence for $\bar{x} = 119.6$, $\sigma = 23.89$, and $n = 75$

c. 90% confidence for $\bar{x} = 3.419$, $\sigma = 0.974$, and $n = 32$

d. 80% confidence for $\bar{x} = 56.7$, $\sigma = 12.1$, $N = 500$, and $n = 47$

8.2. For a random sample of 36 items and a sample mean of 211, compute a 95% confidence interval for μ if the population standard deviation is 23.

8.3. A random sample of 81 items is taken, producing a sample mean of 47. The population standard deviation is 5.89. Construct a 90% confidence interval to estimate the population mean.

8.4. A random sample of size 70 is taken from a population that has a variance of 49. The sample mean is 90.4. What is the point estimate of μ? Construct a 94% confidence interval for μ.

8.5. A random sample of size 39 is taken from a population of 200 members. The sample mean is 66 and the population standard deviation is 11. Construct a 96% confidence interval to estimate the population mean. What is the point estimate of the population mean?

8.6. A candy company fills a 20-ounce package of Halloween candy with individually wrapped pieces of candy. The number of pieces of candy per package varies because the package is sold by weight. The company wants to estimate the number of pieces per package. Inspectors randomly sample 120 packages of this candy and count the number of pieces in each package. They find that the sample mean number of pieces is 18.72. Assuming a population standard deviation of .8735, what is the point estimate of the number of pieces per package? Construct a 99% confidence interval to estimate the mean number of pieces per package for the population.

8.7. A small lawnmower company produced 1,500 lawnmowers in 2005. In an effort to determine how maintenance-free these units were, the company decided to conduct a multiyear study of the 2005 lawnmowers. A sample of 200 owners of these lawnmowers was drawn randomly from company records and contacted. The owners were given an 800 number and asked to call the company when the first major repair was required for the lawnmowers. Owners who no longer used the lawnmower to cut their grass were disqualified. After many years, 187 of the owners had reported. The other 13 disqualified themselves. The average number of years until the first major repair was 5.3 for the 187 owners reporting. It is believed that the population standard deviation was 1.28 years. If the company wants to advertise an average number of years of repair-free lawn mowing for this lawnmower, what is the point estimate? Construct a 95% confidence interval for the average number of years until the first major repair.

8.8. The average total dollar purchase at a convenience store is less than that at a supermarket. Despite smaller-ticket purchases, convenience stores can still be profitable because of the size of operation, volume of business, and the markup. A researcher is interested in estimating the average purchase amount for convenience stores in suburban Long Island. To do so, she randomly sampled 24 purchases from several convenience stores in suburban Long Island and tabulated the amounts to the nearest dollar. Use the following data to construct a 90% confidence interval for the population average amount of purchases. Assume that the population standard deviation is 3.23 and the population is normally distributed.

$2	$11	$8	$7	$9	$3
5	4	2	1	10	8
14	7	6	3	7	2
4	1	3	6	8	4

8.9. A community health association is interested in estimating the average number of maternity days women stay in the local hospital. A random sample is taken of 36 women who had babies in the hospital during the past year. The following numbers of maternity days each woman was in the hospital are rounded to the nearest day.

3	3	4	3	2	5	3	1	4	3
4	2	3	5	3	2	4	3	2	4
1	6	3	4	3	3	5	2	3	2
3	5	4	3	5	4				

Use these data and a population standard deviation of 1.17 to construct a 98% confidence interval to estimate the average maternity stay in the hospital for all women who have babies in this hospital.

8.10. A meat-processing company in the Midwest produces and markets a package of eight small sausage sandwiches. The product is nationally distributed, and the company is interested in knowing the average retail price charged for this item in stores across the country. The company cannot justify a national census to generate this information. Based on the company information system's list of all retailers who carry the product, a researcher for the company contacts 36 of these retailers and ascertains the selling prices for the product. Use the following price data and a population standard deviation of 0.113 to determine a point estimate for the national retail price of the product. Construct a 90% confidence interval to estimate this price.

$2.23	$2.11	$2.12	$2.20	$2.17	$2.10
2.16	2.31	1.98	2.17	2.14	1.82
2.12	2.07	2.17	2.30	2.29	2.19
2.01	2.24	2.18	2.18	2.32	2.02
1.99	1.87	2.09	2.22	2.15	2.19
2.23	2.10	2.08	2.05	2.16	2.26

8.11. According to the U.S. Census Bureau, the average travel time to work in Philadelphia is 27.4 minutes. Suppose a business researcher wants to estimate the average travel time to work in Cleveland using a 95% level of confidence. A random sample of 45 Cleveland commuters is taken and the travel time to work is obtained from each. The data follow. Assuming a population standard deviation of 5.124, compute a 95% confidence interval on the data. What is the point estimate and what is the error of the interval? Explain what these results means in terms of Philadelphia commuters.

27	25	19	21	24	27	29	34	18	29	16	28
20	32	27	28	22	20	14	15	29	28	29	33
16	29	28	28	27	23	27	20	27	25	21	18
26	14	23	27	27	21	25	28	30			

8.12. Suppose a random sample of turkey prices is taken from across the nation in an effort to estimate the average turkey price per pound in the United States. Shown here is the Minitab output for such a sample. Examine the output. What is the point estimate? What is the value of the assumed population standard deviation? How large is the sample? What level of confidence is being used? What table value is associated with this level of confidence? What is the confidence interval? Often the portion of the confidence interval that is added and subtracted from the mean is referred to as the margin of error of the estimate. How much is the margin of error of the estimate in this problem?

```
One-Sample Z

The assumed standard deviation = 0.14

N    Mean       SE Mean    95% CI
41   0.960000   0.021864   (0.917147, 1.002853)
```

8.2 Estimating the Population Mean Using the t Statistic (σ Unknown)

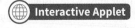

In Section 8.1, we learned how to estimate a population mean by using the sample mean when the population standard deviation is known. In most instances, if a business researcher desires to estimate a population mean, the population standard deviation will be unknown and thus techniques presented in Section 8.1 will not be applicable. When the population standard deviation is unknown, the sample standard deviation must be used in the estimation process. In this section, a statistical technique is presented to estimate a population mean using the sample mean when the population standard deviation is unknown.

Suppose a business researcher is interested in estimating the average flying time of a 757 jet from New York to Los Angeles. Since the business researcher does not know the population mean or average time, it is likely that she also does not know the population standard deviation. By taking a random sample of flights, the researcher can compute a sample mean and a sample standard deviation from which the estimate can be constructed. Another business researcher wants to estimate the mean number of work hours lost annually per worker due to illness, using a random sample, but the researcher has no idea what is the population standard deviation. He will have the sample mean and sample standard deviation available to perform this analysis.

The *z* formulas presented in Section 8.1 are inappropriate for use when the population standard deviation is unknown (and is replaced by the sample standard deviation). Instead, another mechanism to handle such cases was developed by a British statistician, William S. Gosset.

Gosset was born in 1876 in Canterbury, England. He studied chemistry and mathematics and in 1899 went to work for the Guinness Brewery in Dublin, Ireland. Gosset was involved in quality control at the brewery, studying variables such as raw materials and temperature. Because of the circumstances of his experiments, Gosset conducted many studies where the population standard deviation was unavailable. He discovered that using the standard *z* test with a sample standard deviation produced inexact and incorrect distributions. This finding led to his development of the distribution of the sample standard deviation and the *t* test.

Gosset was a student and close personal friend of Karl Pearson. When Gosset's first work on the *t* test was published, he used the pen name "Student." As a result, the *t* test is sometimes referred to as the Student's *t* test. Gosset's contribution was significant because it led to more exact statistical tests, which some scholars say marked the beginning of the modern era in mathematical statistics.*

The *t* Distribution

Gosset developed the *t* **distribution**, which is used instead of the *z* distribution for performing inferential statistics on the population mean when the population standard deviation is unknown and the population is normally distributed. The formula for the *t* statistic is

$$t = \frac{\bar{x} - \mu}{\frac{s}{\sqrt{n}}}$$

This formula is essentially the same as the *z* formula, but the distribution table values are different. The *t* distribution values are contained in Table A.6 and, for convenience, inside the front of the text.

The *t* distribution actually is a series of distributions because every sample size has a different distribution, thereby creating the potential for many *t* tables. To make these *t* values more manageable, only select key values are presented in this text; each line in the table contains values from a different *t* distribution. An assumption underlying the use of the *t* statistic is that the population is normally distributed. If the population distribution is not normal or is unknown, nonparametric techniques (presented in Chapter 17) should be used.

Robustness

Most statistical techniques have one or more underlying assumptions. If a statistical technique is relatively insensitive to minor violations in one or more of its underlying assumptions, the technique is said to be **robust** to that assumption. The *t* statistic for estimating a population mean is relatively robust to the assumption that the population is normally distributed.

---

*Adapted from Arthur L. Dudycha and Linda W. Dudycha,"Behavioral Statistics: An Historical Perspective," in *Statistical Issues: A Reader for the Behavioral Sciences,* Roger Kirk, ed. (Monterey, CA: Brooks/Cole, 1972).

Some statistical techniques are not robust, and a statistician should exercise extreme caution to be certain that the assumptions underlying a technique are being met before using it or interpreting statistical output resulting from its use. A business analyst should always beware of statistical assumptions and the robustness of techniques being used in an analysis.

Characteristics of the *t* Distribution

Figure 8.8 displays two *t* distributions superimposed on the standard normal distribution. Like the standard normal curve, *t* distributions are symmetric, unimodal, and a family of curves. The *t* distributions are flatter in the middle and have more area in their tails than the standard normal distribution.

An examination of *t* distribution values reveals that the *t* distribution approaches the standard normal curve as *n* becomes large. The *t* distribution is the appropriate distribution to use any time the population variance or standard deviation is unknown, regardless of sample size, so long as it is known that the population of interest is normally distributed.

Reading the *t* Distribution Table

To find a value in the *t* distribution table requires knowing the degrees of freedom; each different value of degrees of freedom is associated with a different *t* distribution. The *t* distribution table used here is a compilation of many *t* distributions, with each line of the table having different degrees of freedom and containing *t* values for different *t* distributions. The degrees of freedom for the *t* statistic presented in this section are computed by $n - 1$. The term degrees of freedom refers to *the number of independent observations for a source of variation minus the number of independent parameters estimated in computing the variation.** In this case, one independent parameter, the population mean, μ, is being estimated by $\bar{x}$ in computing *s*. Thus, the degrees of freedom formula is *n* independent observations minus one independent parameter being estimated $(n - 1)$. Because the degrees of freedom are computed differently for various *t* formulas, a degrees of freedom formula is given along with each *t* formula in the text.

In Table A.6, the degrees of freedom are located in the left column. The *t* distribution table in this text does not use the area between the statistic and the mean as does the *z* distribution (standard normal distribution). Instead, the *t* table uses the area in the tail of the distribution. The emphasis in the *t* table is on α, and each tail of the distribution contains $\alpha/2$ of the area under the curve when confidence intervals are constructed. For confidence intervals, the table *t* value is found in the column under the value of $\alpha/2$ and in the row of the degrees of freedom (df) value.

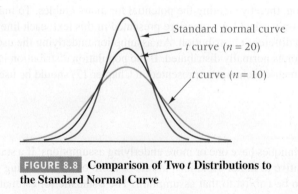

FIGURE 8.8 **Comparison of Two *t* Distributions to the Standard Normal Curve**

---

*Roger E. Kirk. *Experimental Design: Procedures for the Behavioral Sciences.* Belmont, California: Brooks/ Cole, 1968.

For example, if a 90% confidence interval is being computed, the total area in the two tails is 10%. Thus, α is .10 and $\alpha/2$ is .05, as indicated in **Figure 8.9**. The *t* distribution table shown in **Table 8.2** contains only six values of $\alpha/2$ (.10, .05, .025, .01, .005, .001). The *t* value is located at the intersection of the df value and the selected $\alpha/2$ value. So if the degrees of freedom for a given *t* statistic are 24 and the desired $\alpha/2$ value is .05, the *t* value is 1.711.

Confidence Intervals to Estimate the Population Mean Using the *t* Statistic

The *t* formula

$$t = \frac{\bar{x} - \mu}{\frac{s}{\sqrt{n}}}$$

can be manipulated algebraically to produce a formula for estimating the population mean when σ is unknown and the population is normally distributed. The results are the formulas given next.

Confidence Interval to Estimate μ: Population Standard Deviation Unknown and the Population Normally Distributed

$$\bar{x} \pm t_{\alpha/2, n-1} \frac{s}{\sqrt{n}}$$

$$\bar{x} - t_{\alpha/2, n-1} \frac{s}{\sqrt{n}} \leq \mu \leq \bar{x} + t_{\alpha/2, n-1} \frac{s}{\sqrt{n}} \qquad (8.3)$$

$$df = n - 1$$

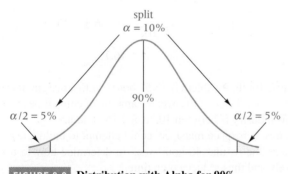

FIGURE 8.9 **Distribution with Alpha for 90% Confidence**

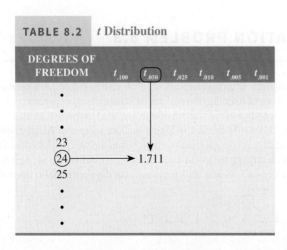

TABLE 8.2 *t* Distribution

DEGREES OF FREEDOM	$t_{.100}$	$t_{.050}$	$t_{.025}$	$t_{.010}$	$t_{.005}$	$t_{.001}$
.						
.						
.						
23						
24	1.711					
25						
.						
.						
.						

Formula 8.3 can be used in a manner similar to methods presented in Section 8.1 for constructing a confidence interval to estimate μ. For example, in the aerospace industry some companies allow their employees to accumulate extra working hours beyond their 40-hour week. These extra hours sometimes are referred to as *green* time, or *comp* time. Many managers work longer than the eight-hour workday preparing proposals, overseeing crucial tasks, and taking care of paperwork. Recognition of such overtime is important. Most managers are usually not paid extra for this work, but a record is kept of this time and occasionally the manager is allowed to use some of this comp time as extra leave or vacation time. Suppose a researcher wants to estimate the average amount of comp time accumulated per week for managers in the aerospace industry. He randomly samples 18 managers and measures the amount of extra time they work during a specific week and obtains the results shown (in hours).

6	21	17	20	7	0	8	16	29
3	8	12	11	9	21	25	15	16

He constructs a 90% confidence interval to estimate the average amount of extra time per week worked by a manager in the aerospace industry. He assumes that comp time is normally distributed in the population. The sample size is 18, so df = 17. A 90% level of confidence results in $\alpha/2 = .05$ area in each tail. The table t value is

$$t_{.05,17} = 1.740$$

The subscripts in the t value denote to other researchers the area in the right tail of the t distribution (for confidence intervals $\alpha/2$) and the number of degrees of freedom. The sample mean is 13.56 hours, and the sample standard deviation is 7.80 hours. The confidence interval is computed from this information as

$$\bar{x} \pm t_{\alpha/2,\ n-1} \frac{s}{\sqrt{n}}$$

$$13.56 \pm 1.740 \frac{7.80}{\sqrt{18}} = 13.56 \pm 3.20$$

$$10.36 \le \mu \le 16.76$$

The point estimate for this problem is 13.56 hours, with a margin of error of ±3.20 hours. The researcher is 90% confident that the average amount of comp time accumulated by a manager per week in this industry is between 10.36 and 16.76 hours.

From these figures, aerospace managers could attempt to build a reward system for such extra work or evaluate the regular 40-hour week to determine how to use the normal work hours more effectively and thus reduce comp time.

DEMONSTRATION PROBLEM 8.3

The owner of a large equipment rental company wants to make a rather quick estimate of the average number of days a piece of ditchdigging equipment is rented out per person per time. The company has records of all rentals, but the amount of time required to conduct an audit of *all* accounts would be prohibitive. The owner decides to take a random sample of rental invoices. Fourteen different rentals of ditchdiggers are selected randomly from the files, yielding the following data. She uses these data to construct a 99% confidence interval to estimate the average number of days that a ditchdigger is rented and assumes that the number of days per rental is normally distributed in the population.

3 1 3 2 5 1 2 1 4 2 1 3 1 1

Solution: As $n = 14$, the df $= 13$. The 99% level of confidence results in $\alpha/2 = .005$ area in each tail of the distribution. The table *t* value is

$$t_{.005, 13} = 3.012$$

The sample mean is 2.14 and the sample standard deviation is 1.29. The confidence interval is

$$\bar{x} \pm t \frac{s}{\sqrt{n}}$$

$$2.14 \pm 3.012 \frac{1.29}{\sqrt{14}} = 2.14 \pm 1.04$$

$$1.10 \le \mu \le 3.18$$

The point estimate of the average length of time per rental is 2.14 days, with a margin of error of ±1.04. With a 99% level of confidence, the company's owner can estimate that the average length of time per rental is between 1.10 and 3.18 days. Combining this figure with variables such as frequency of rentals per year can help the owner estimate potential profit or loss per year for such a piece of equipment.

Using the Computer to Construct *t* Confidence Intervals for the Mean

Both Excel and Minitab can be used to construct confidence intervals for μ using the *t* distribution. Figure 8.10 displays Excel output and Minitab output for the aerospace comp time problem. The Excel output includes the mean, the standard error, the sample standard deviation, and the error of the confidence interval, referred to by Excel as the "confidence level." The standard error of the mean is computed by dividing the standard deviation (7.8006) by the square root of *n* (4.243). When using the Excel output, the confidence interval must be computed from the sample mean and the confidence level (error of the interval).

The Minitab output yields the confidence interval endpoints (10.36, 16.75). The "SE Mean" is the standard error of the mean. The error of the confidence interval is computed by multiplying the standard error of the mean by the table value of *t*. Adding and subtracting this error from the mean yields the confidence interval endpoints produced by Minitab.

Excel Output

	Comp Time
Mean	13.560
Standard Error	1.839
Standard Deviation	7.801
Confidence Level (90.0%)	3.200

Minitab Output

One-Sample T: Comp Time

Variable	N	Mean	StDev	SE Mean	90% CI
Comp Time	18	13.56	7.80	1.84	(10.36, 16.76)

FIGURE 8.10 **Excel and Minitab Output for the Comp Time Example**

Thinking Critically About Statistics in Business Today

Canadian Grocery Shopping Statistics

A study of 1,000 adult Canadians was conducted by the Environics Research Group in a recent year on behalf of Master Card World-wide to ascertain information about Canadian shopping habits. Canadian shopping activities were divided into two core categories: (1) the "quick" trip for traditional staples, convenience items, or snack foods, and (2) the "stock-up" trip that generally occurs once per week and is approximately two and a half times longer than a quick trip. As a result, many interesting statistics were reported. Canadians take a mean of 37 stock-up trips per year, spending an average of 44 minutes in the store, and they take a mean of 76 quick trips per year, spending an average of 18 minutes in the store. Forty-six percent of households with kids usually take them on quick trips, as do 51% on stock-up trips. On average, Canadians spend four times more money on a stock-up trip than on a quick trip. Some other interesting statistics from this survey include: 23% often buy items that are not on their list but catch

their eye, 28% often go to a store to buy an item that is on sale, 24% often switch to another checkout lane to get out faster, and 45% often bring their own bag. Since these statistics are based on a sample of 1,000 shoppers, it is virtually certain that the statistics given here are point estimates.

THINGS TO PONDER

1. Suppose a Canadian chain of large supermarkets wants to specifically appeal to customers making quick trips. What are some steps that the supermarkets could take to appeal more to customers making quick trips?

2. Since 23% of buyers in this survey buy items that are not on their lists, what are some things that a store can do to encourage even more buyers to purchase items not on their lists?

Source: 2008 MASTERINDEX Report: *Checking Out the Canadian Grocery Shopping Experience*, located at: http://www.mastercard.com/ca/wce/PDF/TRANSACTOR_REPORT_E.pdf.

8.2 Problems

8.13. Suppose the following data are selected randomly from a population of normally distributed values.

40	51	43	48	44	57	54
39	42	48	45	39	43	

Construct a 95% confidence interval to estimate the population mean.

8.14. Assuming x is normally distributed, use the following information to compute a 90% confidence interval to estimate μ.

313	320	319	340	325	310
321	329	317	311	307	318

8.15. If a random sample of 41 items produces $\bar{x} = 128.4$ and $s = 20.6$, what is the 98% confidence interval for μ? Assume x is normally distributed for the population. What is the point estimate?

8.16. A random sample of 15 items is taken, producing a sample mean of 2.364 with a sample variance of .81. Assume x is normally distributed and construct a 90% confidence interval for the population mean.

8.17. Use the following data to construct a 99% confidence interval for μ.

16.4	17.1	17.0	15.6	16.2
14.8	16.0	15.6	17.3	17.4
15.6	15.7	17.2	16.6	16.0
15.3	15.4	16.0	15.8	17.2
14.6	15.5	14.9	16.7	16.3

Assume x is normally distributed. What is the point estimate for μ?

8.18. According to Runzheimer International, the average cost of a domestic trip for business travelers in the financial industry is $1,250.

Suppose another travel industry research company takes a random sample of 51 business travelers in the financial industry and determines that the sample average cost of a domestic trip is $1,192, with a sample standard deviation of $279. Construct a 98% confidence interval for the population mean from these sample data. Assume that the data are normally distributed in the population. Now go back and examine the $1,250 figure published by Runzheimer International. Does it fall into the confidence interval computed from the sample data? What does this tell you?

8.19. A valve manufacturer produces a butterfly valve composed of two semicircular plates on a common spindle that is used to permit flow in one direction only. The semicircular plates are supplied by a vendor with specifications that the plates be 2.37 millimeters thick and have a tensile strength of five pounds per millimeter. A random sample of 20 such plates is taken. Electronic calipers are used to measure the thickness of each plate; the measurements are given here. Assuming that the thicknesses of such plates are normally distributed, use the data to construct a 95% level of confidence for the population mean thickness of these plates. What is the point estimate? How much is the error of the interval?

2.4066	2.4579	2.6724	2.1228	2.3238
2.1328	2.0665	2.2738	2.2055	2.5267
2.5937	2.1994	2.5392	2.4359	2.2146
2.1933	2.4575	2.7956	2.3353	2.2699

8.20. Some fast-food chains offer a lower-priced combination meal in an effort to attract budget-conscious customers. One chain test-marketed a burger, fries, and a drink combination for $1.71. The weekly sales volume for these meals was impressive. Suppose the chain wants to estimate the average amount its customers spent on a meal at their restaurant while this combination offer was in effect. An analyst gathers data from 28 randomly selected customers. The following data represent the sample meal totals.

$3.21 5.40 3.50 4.39 5.60 8.65 5.02 4.20 1.25 7.64
3.28 5.57 3.26 3.80 5.46 9.87 4.67 5.86 3.73 4.08
5.47 4.49 5.19 5.82 7.62 4.83 8.42 9.10

Use these data to construct a 90% confidence interval to estimate the population mean value. Assume the amounts spent are normally distributed.

8.21. The marketing director of a large department store wants to estimate the average number of customers who enter the store every five minutes. She randomly selects five-minute intervals and counts the number of arrivals at the store. She obtains the figures 58, 32, 41, 47, 56, 80, 45, 29, 32, and 78. The analyst assumes the number of arrivals is normally distributed. Using these data, the analyst computes a 95% confidence interval to estimate the mean value for all five-minute intervals. What interval values does she get?

8.22. Suppose a company from the United States does considerable business in the city of Johannesburg, South Africa, and wishes to establish a per diem rate for employee travel to that city. The company researcher is assigned this task, and in an effort to determine this figure, she obtains a random sample of 14 business travelers staying in Johannesburg. The result is the data presented below. Use these data to construct a 98% confidence interval to estimate the average per diem expense for business people traveling to Johannesburg. What is the point estimate? Assume per diem rates for any locale are approximately normally distributed.

418.42   229.06   396.48   326.21   435.57   363.38   426.57
607.69   372.80   583.10   253.67   332.25   350.81   362.37

8.23. How much experience do supply-chain transportation managers have in their field? Suppose in an effort to estimate this, 41 supply-chain transportation managers are surveyed and asked how many

years of managerial experience they have in transportation. Survey results (in years) are shown below. Use these data to construct a 99% confidence interval to estimate the mean number of years of experience in transportation. Assume that years of experience in transportation is normally distributed in the population.

5	8	10	21	20
25	14	6	19	3
1	9	11	2	3
13	2	4	9	4
5	4	21	7	6
3	28	17	32	2
25	8	13	17	27
7	3	15	4	16
6				

8.24. Cycle time in manufacturing can be viewed as the total time it takes to complete a product from the beginning of the production process. The concept of cycle time varies according to the industry and product or service being offered. Suppose a boat manufacturing company wants to estimate the mean cycle time it takes to produce a 16-foot skiff. A random sample of such skiffs is taken, and the cycle times (in hours) are recorded for each skiff in the sample. The data are analyzed using Minitab and the results are shown below in hours. What is the point estimate for cycle time? How large was the sample size? What is the level of confidence, and what is the confidence interval? What is the margin of error of the confidence interval?

One-Sample T

N	Mean	StDev	SE Mean	98% CI
26	25.41	5.34	1.05	(22.81, 28.01)

Estimating the Population Proportion

Business decision makers and researchers often need to be able to estimate a population proportion. For example, what proportion of the market does our company control (market share)? What proportion of our products is defective? What proportion of customers will call customer service with complaints? What proportion of our customers is in the 20-to-30 age group? What proportion of our workers speaks Spanish as a first language?

Methods similar to those in Section 8.1 can be used to estimate the population proportion. The central limit theorem for sample proportions led to the following formula in Chapter 7.

$$z = \frac{\hat{p} - p}{\sqrt{\frac{p \cdot q}{n}}}$$

where $q = 1 - p$. Recall that this formula can be applied only when $n \cdot p$ and $n \cdot q$ are greater than 5.

Algebraically manipulating this formula to estimate p involves solving for p. However, p is in both the numerator and the denominator, which complicates the resulting formula. For this reason—for confidence interval purposes only and for large sample sizes—$\hat{p}$ is substituted for p in the denominator, yielding

$$z = \frac{\hat{p} - p}{\sqrt{\frac{\hat{p} \cdot \hat{q}}{n}}}$$

Thinking Critically About Statistics in Business Today

Coffee Consumption in the United States

What is the state of coffee consumption in the United States today? According to a recent Gallup poll of 1,009 adults living in all 50 states and the District of Columbia, sixty-four percent of adults in the United States drink one or more cups of coffee per day, and regular coffee drinkers consume an average of around three cups per day. While around 50% of those in the 18- to 34-year-old bracket are coffee drinkers, the figure is much higher (74%) for adults over 55. While there are fewer coffee drinkers in the lower-income brackets, those who do drink coffee tend to drink more (3.8 cups per day) than coffee drinkers in higher-income brackets (2.4 cups per day).

Is there a difference between men and women in U.S. coffee consumption? According to the poll, 62% of men drink one or more cups of coffee per day as compared to 66% of women. The average number of cups per day among coffee drinkers is 2.6 for men and 2.9 for women. Geographically, 70% of people in the East drink one or more cups per day versus 65% in the Midwest,

63% in the South, and 62% in the West. The survey source reported that these data were based on a 95% confidence interval with a ±4 percentage error.

THINGS TO PONDER

1. What might be some reasons why a lower percentage of young adults drink coffee than do older adults? Of those young adults who do drink coffee, consumption is higher than for other groups. Why might this be?

2. Note that the figures reported here are from a Gallup poll of around 1,000 respondents based on a 95% confidence interval with a ±4 percentage error. This report includes both means and percentages. In what ways do the statistics in this report tie-in to the information presented in this chapter?

Source: Adapted from Lydia Saad, "Americans' Coffee Consumption is Steady, Few Want to Cut Back", WELL-BEING, July 29, 2015, www.gallup.com/.../americans-coffee-consumption-steady-few-cut-back.as

where $\hat{q} = 1 - \hat{p}$. Solving for p results in the confidence interval in formula (8.4).*

Confidence Interval to Estimate p

$$\hat{p} - z_{\alpha/2}\sqrt{\frac{\hat{p} \cdot \hat{q}}{n}} \leq p \leq \hat{p} + z_{\alpha/2}\sqrt{\frac{\hat{p} \cdot \hat{q}}{n}} \qquad (8.4)$$

where

$\hat{p}$ = sample proportion
$\hat{q} = 1 - \hat{p}$
p = population proportion
n = sample size

In this formula, $\hat{p}$ is the point estimate and $\pm z_{\alpha/2}\sqrt{\frac{\hat{p} \cdot \hat{q}}{n}}$ is the margin of error of the estimation. **Figure 8.11** underscores this structure.

As an example, a study of 87 randomly selected companies with a telemarketing operation revealed that 39% of the sampled companies used telemarketing to assist them in order processing. Using this information, how could a researcher estimate the population proportion of telemarketing companies that use their telemarketing operation to assist them in order processing?

The sample proportion, $\hat{p} = .39$, is the *point estimate* of the population proportion, p. For $n = 87$ and $\hat{p} = .39$, a 95% confidence interval can be computed to determine the interval

---

*Because we are not using the true standard deviation of $\hat{p}$, the correct divisor of the standard error of $\hat{p}$ is $n - 1$. However, for large sample sizes, the effect is negligible. Although technically the minimal sample size for the techniques presented in this section is $n \cdot p$ and $n \cdot q$ greater than 5, in actual practice sample sizes of several hundred are more commonly used. As an example, for $\hat{p}$ and $\hat{q}$ of .50 and $n = 300$, the standard error of $\hat{p}$ is .02887 using n and .02892 using $n - 1$, a difference of only .00005.

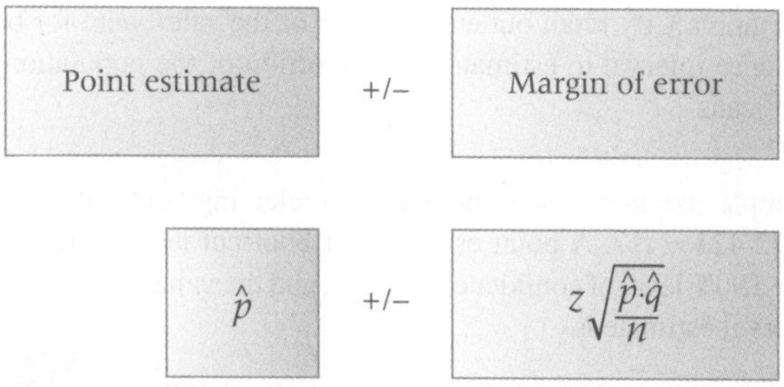

FIGURE 8.11 **Structure of a Confidence Interval for Estimating a Population Proportion**

estimation of p. The z value for 95% confidence is 1.96. The value of $\hat{q} = 1 - \hat{p} = 1 - .39 = .61$. The confidence interval estimate is

$$.39 - 1.96\sqrt{\frac{(.39)(.61)}{87}} \le p \le .39 + 1.96\sqrt{\frac{(.39)(.61)}{87}}$$

$$.39 - .10 \le p \le .39 + .10$$

$$.29 \le p \le .49$$

This interval suggests that the population proportion of telemarketing firms that use their operation to assist order processing is somewhere between .29 and .49, based on the point estimate of .39 with a margin of error of ±.10. This result has a 95% level of confidence.

DEMONSTRATION PROBLEM 8.4

Coopers & Lybrand surveyed 210 chief executives of fast-growing small companies. Only 51% of these executives had a management succession plan in place. A spokesperson for Cooper & Lybrand said that many companies do not worry about management succession unless it is an immediate problem. However, the unexpected exit of a corporate leader can disrupt and unfocus a company for long enough to cause it to lose its momentum.

Use the data given to compute a 92% confidence interval to estimate the proportion of *all* fast-growing small companies that have a management succession plan.

Solution: The point estimate is the sample proportion given to be .51. It is estimated that .51, or 51% of all fast-growing small companies have a management succession plan. Realizing that the point estimate might change with another sample selection, we calculate a confidence interval.

The value of n is 210; $\hat{p}$ is .51, and $\hat{q} = 1 - \hat{p} = .49$. Because the level of confidence is 92%, the value of $z_{.04} = 1.75$. The confidence interval is computed as

$$.51 - 1.75\sqrt{\frac{(.51)(.49)}{210}} \le p \le .51 + 1.75\sqrt{\frac{(.51)(.49)}{210}}$$

$$.51 - .06 \le p \le .51 + .06$$

$$.45 \le p \le .57$$

It is estimated with 92% confidence that the proportion of the population of fast-growing small companies that have a management succession plan is between .45 and .57.

DEMONSTRATION PROBLEM 8.5

A clothing company produces men's jeans. The jeans are made and sold with either a regular cut or a boot cut. In an effort to estimate the proportion of their men's jeans market in Oklahoma City that prefers boot-cut jeans, the analyst takes a random sample of 423 jeans sales from the company's two Oklahoma City retail outlets. Only 72 of the sales were for boot-cut jeans. Construct a 90% confidence interval to estimate the proportion of the population in Oklahoma City who prefer boot-cut jeans.

Solution: The sample size is 423, and the number preferring boot-cut jeans is 72. The sample proportion is $\hat{p} = 72/423 = .17$. A point estimate for boot-cut jeans in the population is .17, or 17%. The z value for a 90% level of confidence is 1.645, and the value of $\hat{q} = 1 - \hat{p} = 1 - .17 = .83$. The confidence interval estimate is

$$.17 - 1.645\sqrt{\frac{(.17)(.83)}{423}} \le p \le .17 + 1.645\sqrt{\frac{(.17)(.83)}{423}}$$

$$.17 - .03 \le p \le .17 + .03$$

$$.14 \le p \le .20$$

The analyst estimates that the population proportion of boot-cut jeans purchases is between .14 and .20. The level of confidence in this result is 90%.

Using the Computer to Construct Confidence Intervals of the Population Proportion

Minitab has the capability of producing confidence intervals for proportions, and Excel does not. Figure 8.12 contains Minitab output for Demonstration Problem 8.5. The Minitab output contains the sample size (labeled as N), the number in the sample containing the characteristic of interest (X), the sample proportion, the level of confidence, and the endpoints of the confidence interval. Note that the endpoints of the confidence interval are essentially the same as those computed in Demonstration Problem 8.5.

Minitab Output

Test and CI for One Proportion

Sample	X	N	Sample p	90% CI
1	72	423	0.170213	(0.140156, 0.200269)

FIGURE 8.12 **Minitab Output for Demonstration Problem 8.5**

8.3 Problems

8.25. Use the information about each of the following samples to compute the confidence interval to estimate p.

a. $n = 44$ and $\hat{p} = .51$; compute a 90% confidence interval.

b. $n = 300$ and $\hat{p} = .82$; compute a 95% confidence interval.

c. $n = 1,150$ and $\hat{p} = .48$; compute a 90% confidence interval.

d. $n = 95$ and $\hat{p} = .32$; compute an 88% confidence interval.

8.26. Use the following sample information to calculate the confidence interval to estimate the population proportion. Let x be the number of items in the sample having the characteristic of interest.

a. $n = 116$ and $x = 57$, with 99% confidence

b. $n = 800$ and $x = 479$, with 97% confidence

c. $n = 240$ and $x = 106$, with 85% confidence

d. $n = 60$ and $x = 21$, with 90% confidence

8.27. Suppose a random sample of 85 items has been taken from a population and 40 of the items contain the characteristic of interest. Use this information to calculate a 90% confidence interval to estimate the proportion of the population that has the characteristic of interest. Calculate a 95% confidence interval. Calculate a 99% confidence interval. As the level of confidence changes and the other sample information stays constant, what happens to the confidence interval?

8.28. According to the annual survey by Ovum publication *Music & Copyright 2014*, Universal Music Group is the music leader in combined physical and digital recorded music trade revenue. Suppose a researcher wants to determine what market share the company holds in the city of St. Louis by randomly selecting 1003 people who purchased CD last month. In addition, suppose 25.5% of the purchases made by these people were for products manufactured and distributed by the Universal Music Group.

a. Based on these data, construct a 99% confidence interval to estimate the proportion of the CD sales market in St. Louis that is held by the Universal Music Group.

b. Suppose that the survey had been taken with 10,000 people. Recompute the confidence interval and compare your results with the first confidence interval. How did they differ? What might you conclude from this about sample size and confidence intervals?

8.29. According to the Stern Marketing Group, 9 out of 10 professional women say that financial planning is more important today than it was five years ago. Where do these women go for help in financial planning? Forty-seven percent use a financial advisor (broker, tax consultant, financial planner). Twenty-eight percent use written sources such as magazines, books, and newspapers. Suppose these figures were obtained by taking a sample of 560 professional women who said that financial planning is more important today than it was five years ago.

a. Construct a 95% confidence interval for the proportion of professional women who use a financial advisor. Use the percentage given in this problem as the point estimate.

b. Construct a 90% confidence interval for the proportion of professional women who use written sources. Use the percentage given in this problem as the point estimate.

8.30. What proportion of pizza restaurants that are primarily for walk-in business have a salad bar? Suppose that, in an effort to determine this figure, a random sample of 1,250 of these restaurants across the United States based on the Yellow Pages is called. If 997 of the restaurants sampled have a salad bar, what is the 98% confidence interval for the population proportion?

8.31. The highway department wants to estimate the proportion of vehicles on Interstate 25 between the hours of midnight and 5:00 A.M. that are 18-wheel tractor trailers. The estimate will be used to determine highway repair and construction considerations and in highway patrol planning. Suppose researchers for the highway department counted vehicles at different locations on the interstate for several nights during this time period. Of the 3,481 vehicles counted, 927 were 18-wheelers.

a. Determine the point estimate for the proportion of vehicles traveling Interstate 25 during this time period that are 18-wheelers.

b. Construct a 99% confidence interval for the proportion of vehicles on Interstate 25 during this time period that are 18-wheelers.

8.32. What proportion of commercial airline pilots are more than 40 years of age? Suppose a researcher has access to a list of all pilots who are members of the Commercial Airline Pilots Association. If this list is used as a frame for the study, she can randomly select a sample of pilots, contact them, and ascertain their ages. From 89 of these pilots so selected, she learns that 48 are more than 40 years of age. Construct an 85% confidence interval to estimate the population proportion of commercial airline pilots who are more than 40 years of age.

8.33. According to Runzheimer International, in a survey of relocation administrators 63% of all workers who rejected relocation offers did so for family considerations. Suppose this figure was obtained by using a random sample of the files of 672 workers who had rejected relocation offers. Use this information to construct a 95% confidence interval to estimate the population proportion of workers who reject relocation offers for family considerations.

8.34. Suppose a survey of 275 executives is taken in an effort to determine what qualities are most important for an effective CEO to possess. The survey participants are offered several qualities as options, one of which is "communication." One hundred twenty-one of the surveyed respondents select "communicator" as the most important quality for an effective CEO. Use these data to construct a 98% confidence interval to estimate the population proportion of executives who believe that "communicator" is the most important quality of an effective CEO.

| 8.4 | # Estimating the Population Variance |

At times in statistical analysis, the researcher is more interested in the population variance than in the population mean or population proportion. For example, in the total quality movement, suppliers who want to earn world-class supplier status or even those who want to maintain customer contracts are often asked to show continual reduction of variation on supplied parts. Tests are conducted with samples in efforts to determine lot variation and to determine whether variability goals are being met.

Estimating the variance is important in many other instances in business. For example, variations among airplane altimeter readings need to be minimal. It is not enough just to know that, on the average, a particular brand of altimeter produces the correct altitude. It is also important that the variation between instruments be small. Thus measuring the variation of altimeters is critical. Parts being used in engines must fit tightly on a consistent basis. A wide variability among parts can result in a part that is too large to fit into its slots or so small that it results in too much tolerance, which causes vibrations. How can variance be estimated?

You may recall from Chapter 3 that sample variance is computed by using the formula

$$s^2 = \frac{\Sigma(x - \bar{x})^2}{n - 1}$$

Because sample variances are typically used as estimators or estimations of the population variance, as they are here, a mathematical adjustment is made in the denominator by using $n - 1$ to make the sample variance an unbiased estimator of the population variance.

Suppose a researcher wants to estimate the population variance from the sample variance in a manner that is similar to the estimation of the population mean from a sample mean. The relationship of the sample variance to the population variance is captured by the **chi-square distribution** (χ^2). The ratio of the sample variance (s^2), multiplied by $n-1$, to the population variance (σ^2) is approximately chi-square distributed, as shown in Formula 8.5, if the population from which the values are drawn is normally distributed.

Caution: *Use of the chi-square statistic to estimate the population variance is extremely sensitive to violations of the assumption that the population is normally distributed. For that reason, some researchers do not include this technique among their statistical repertoire. Although the technique is still rather widely presented as a mechanism for constructing confidence intervals to estimate a population variance, you should proceed with extreme caution and apply the technique only in cases where the population is known to be normally distributed. We can say that this technique lacks robustness.*

Like the t distribution, the chi-square distribution varies by sample size and contains a degrees-of-freedom value. The number of degrees of freedom for the chi-square formula (8.5) is $n-1$.

χ^2 **Formula for Single Variance**

$$\chi^2 = \frac{(n-1)s^2}{\sigma^2}$$

(8.5)

$$df = n - 1$$

The chi-square distribution is not symmetrical, and its shape will vary according to the degrees of freedom. **Figure 8.13** shows the shape of chi-square distributions for three different degrees of freedom.

Formula 8.5 can be rearranged algebraically to produce a formula that can be used to construct confidence intervals for population variances. This new formula is shown as Formula 8.6.

Confidence Interval to Estimate the Population Variance

$$\frac{(n-1)s^2}{\chi^2_{\alpha/2}} \le \sigma^2 \le \frac{(n-1)s^2}{\chi^2_{1-\alpha/2}}$$

(8.6)

$$df = n - 1$$

The value of alpha (α) is equal to $1 -$ (level of confidence expressed as a proportion). Thus, if we are constructing a 90% confidence interval, alpha is 10% of the area and is expressed in proportion form: $\alpha = .10$.

How can this formula be used to estimate the population variance from a sample variance? Suppose eight purportedly 7-centimeter aluminum cylinders in a sample are measured in diameter, resulting in the following values:

6.91 cm	6.93 cm	7.01 cm	7.02 cm
7.05 cm	7.00 cm	6.98 cm	7.01 cm

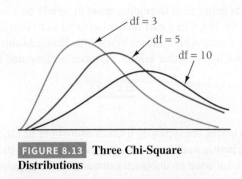

FIGURE 8.13 **Three Chi-Square Distributions**

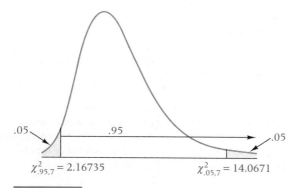

FIGURE 8.14   **Two Table Values of Chi-Square**

In estimating a population variance from these values, the sample variance must be computed. This value is $s^2 = .0022125$. If a point estimate is all that is required, the point estimate is the sample variance, .0022125. However, realizing that the point estimate will probably change from sample to sample, we want to construct an interval estimate. To do this, we must know the degrees of freedom and the table values of the chi-squares. Because $n = 8$, the degrees of freedom are df $= n - 1 = 7$. What are the chi-square values necessary to complete the information needed in Formula 8.6? Assume the population of cylinder diameters is normally distributed.

Suppose we are constructing a 90% confidence interval. The value of α is $1 - .90 = .10$ which is the portion of the area under the chi-square curve that is outside the confidence interval. This outside area is needed because the chi-square table values given in Table A.8 are listed according the area in the right tail of the distribution. In a 90% confidence interval, $\alpha/2$ or .05 of the area is in the right tail of the distribution and .05 is in the left tail of the distribution. The chi-square value for the .05 area on the right tail of the distribution can be obtained directly from the table by using the degrees of freedom, which in this case are 7. Thus the right-side chi-square, $\chi^2_{.05,7}$, is 14.0671. Because Table A.8 lists chi-square values for areas in the right tail, the chi-square value for the left tail must be obtained by determining how much area lies to the right of the left tail. If .05 is to the left of the confidence interval, then $1 - .05 = .95$ of the area is to the right of the left tail. This calculation is consistent with the $1 - \alpha/2$ expression used in formula (8.6). Thus the chi-square for the left tail is $\chi^2_{.95,7} = 2.16735$. Figure 8.14 shows the two table values of χ^2 on a chi-square distribution.

Incorporating these values into the formula, we can construct the 90% confidence interval to estimate the population variance of the 7-centimeter aluminum cylinders.

$$\frac{(n - 1)s^2}{\chi^2_{\alpha/2}} \le \sigma^2 \le \frac{(n - 1)s^2}{\chi^2_{1-\alpha/2}}$$

$$\frac{(7)(.0022125)}{14.0671} \le \sigma^2 \le \frac{(7)(.0022125)}{2.16735}$$

$$.001101 \le \sigma^2 \le .007146$$

The confidence interval says that with 90% confidence, the population variance is somewhere between .001101 and .007146.

DEMONSTRATION PROBLEM 8.6

The U.S. Bureau of Labor Statistics publishes data on the hourly compensation costs for production workers in manufacturing for various countries. The latest figures published for Greece show that the average hourly wage for a production worker in manufacturing is $21.78. Suppose the business council of Greece wants to know how consistent this figure is. It randomly selects

25 production workers in manufacturing from across the country and determines that the standard deviation of hourly wages for such workers is \$1.12. Use this information to develop a 95% confidence interval to estimate the population variance for the hourly wages of production workers in manufacturing in Greece. Assume that the hourly wages for production workers across the country in manufacturing are normally distributed.

Solution: By squaring the standard deviation, $s = 1.12$, we can obtain the sample variance, $s^2 = 1.2544$. This figure provides the point estimate of the population variance. Because the sample size, n, is 25, the degrees of freedom, $n - 1$, are 24. A 95% confidence means that alpha is $1 - .95 = .05$. This value is split to determine the area in each tail of the chi-square distribution: $\alpha/2 = .025$. The values of the chi-squares obtained from Table A.8 are

$$\chi^2_{.025,24} = 39.3641 \text{ and } \chi^2_{.975,24} = 12.40115$$

From this information, the confidence interval can be determined.

$$\frac{(n-1)s^2}{\chi^2_{\alpha/2}} \leq \sigma^2 \leq \frac{(n-1)s^2}{\chi^2_{1-\alpha/2}}$$

$$\frac{(24)(1.2544)}{39.3641} \leq \sigma^2 \leq \frac{(24)(1.2544)}{12.40115}$$

$$0.7648 \leq \sigma^2 \leq 2.4276$$

The business council can estimate with 95% confidence that the population variance of the hourly wages of production workers in manufacturing in Greece is between 0.7648 and 2.4276.

8.4 Problems

8.35. For each of the following sample results, construct the requested confidence interval. Assume the data come from normally distributed populations.

    a. $n = 12$, $\bar{x} = 28.4$, $s^2 = 44.9$; 99% confidence for σ^2

    b. $n = 7$, $\bar{x} = 4.37$, $s = 1.24$; 95% confidence for σ^2

    c. $n = 20$, $\bar{x} = 105$, $s = 32$; 90% confidence for σ^2

    d. $n = 17$, $s^2 = 18.56$; 80% confidence for σ^2

8.36. Use the following sample data to estimate the population variance. Produce a point estimate and a 98% confidence interval. Assume the data come from a normally distributed population.

27	40	32	41	45	29	33	39
30	28	36	32	42	40	38	46

8.37. The Interstate Conference of Employment Security Agencies says the average workweek in the United States is down to only 35 hours, largely because of a rise in part-time workers. Suppose this figure was obtained from a random sample of 20 workers and that the standard deviation of the sample was 4.3 hours. Assume hours worked per week are normally distributed in the population. Use this sample information to develop a 98% confidence interval for the population variance of the number of hours worked per week for a worker. What is the point estimate?

8.38. A manufacturing plant produces steel rods. During one production run of 20,000 such rods, the specifications called for rods that were 46 centimeters in length and 3.8 centimeters in width. Fifteen of these rods comprising a random sample were measured for length; the resulting measurements are shown here. Use these data to estimate the population variance of length for the rods. Assume rod length is normally distributed in the population. Construct a 99% confidence interval. Discuss the ramifications of the results.

44 cm	47 cm	43 cm	46 cm	46 cm
45 cm	43 cm	44 cm	47 cm	46 cm
48 cm	48 cm	43 cm	44 cm	45 cm

8.39. Suppose a random sample of 14 people 30–39 years of age produced the household incomes shown here. Use these data to determine a point estimate for the population variance of household incomes for people 30–39 years of age and construct a 95% confidence interval. Assume household income is normally distributed.

$37,500	44,800
33,500	36,900
42,300	32,400
28,000	41,200
46,600	38,500
40,200	32,000
35,500	36,800

Estimating Sample Size

In most business research that uses sample statistics to infer about the population, being able to *estimate the size of sample necessary to accomplish the purposes of the study* is important. The need for this sample-size estimation is the same for the large corporation investing tens of thousands of dollars in a massive study of consumer preference and for students undertaking a small case study and wanting to send questionnaires to local business people. In either case, such things as level of confidence, sampling error, and width of estimation interval are closely tied to sample size. If the large corporation is undertaking a market study, should it sample 40 people or 4,000 people? The question is an important one. In most cases, because of cost considerations, business researchers do not want to sample any more units or individuals than necessary.

Sample Size When Estimating μ

In research studies when μ is being estimated, the size of sample can be determined by using the z formula for sample means and solving for n. Consider,

$$z = \frac{\bar{x} - \mu}{\frac{\sigma}{\sqrt{n}}}$$

The difference between $\bar{x}$ and μ is the margin of error of estimation resulting from the sampling process. Let $E = (\bar{x} - \mu) =$ the margin of error of estimation. Substituting E into the preceding formula yields

$$z = \frac{E}{\frac{\sigma}{\sqrt{n}}}$$

Solving for n yields a formula that can be used to determine sample size.

Sample Size When Estimating μ

$$n = \frac{z_{\alpha/2}^2 \sigma^2}{E^2} = \left(\frac{z_{\alpha/2}\sigma}{E}\right)^2 \tag{8.7}$$

Sometimes in estimating sample size the population variance is known or can be determined from past studies. Other times, the population variance is unknown and must be estimated to determine the sample size. In such cases, it is acceptable to use the following estimate to represent σ.

$$\sigma \approx \frac{1}{4}(range)$$

Using formula (8.7), the business researcher can estimate the sample size needed to achieve the goals of the study before gathering data. For example, suppose a researcher wants to estimate the average monthly expenditure on bread by a family in Chicago. She wants to be 90% confident of her results. How much error is she willing to tolerate in the results? Suppose she wants the estimate to be within $1.00 of the actual figure (error) and the standard deviation of average monthly bread purchases is $4.00. What is the sample size estimation for this problem? The value of z for a 90% level of confidence is 1.645. Using formula (8.7) with $E = \$1.00$, $\sigma = \$4.00$, and $z = 1.645$ gives

$$n = \frac{z_{\alpha/2}^2 \sigma^2}{E^2} = \frac{(1.645)^2 (4)^2}{1^2} = 43.30$$

That is, at least $n = 43.3$ must be sampled randomly to attain a 90% level of confidence and produce an error within $1.00 for a standard deviation of $4.00. Sampling 43.3 units is impossible, so this result should be rounded up to $n = 44$ units.

In this approach to estimating sample size, we view the error of the estimation as the amount of difference between the statistic (in this case, $\bar{x}$) and the parameter (in this case, μ). The error could be in either direction; that is, the statistic could be over or under the parameter. Thus, the error, E, is actually $\pm E$ as we view it. So when a problem states that the researcher wants to be within $1.00 of the actual monthly family expenditure for bread, it means that the researcher is willing to allow a tolerance within $\pm\$1.00$ of the actual figure. Another name for this error is the **bounds** of the interval.

DEMONSTRATION PROBLEM 8.7

Suppose you want to estimate the average age of all Boeing 737-300 airplanes now in active domestic U.S. service. You want to be 95% confident, and you want your estimate to be within one year of the actual figure. The 737-300 was first placed in service about 24 years ago, but you believe that no active 737-300s in the U.S. domestic fleet are more than 20 years old. How large of a sample should you take?

Solution: Here, $E = 1$ year, the z value for 95% is 1.96, and σ is unknown, so it must be estimated by using $\sigma \approx (1/4) \cdot (\text{range})$. As the range of ages is 0 to 20 years, $\sigma = (1/4)(20) = 5$. Use formula (8.7).

$$n = \frac{z^2\sigma^2}{E^2} = \frac{(1.96)^2 (5)^2}{1^2} = 96.04$$

Because you cannot sample 96.04 airplanes, the required sample size is 97. If you randomly sample 97 airplanes, you have an opportunity to estimate the average age of active 737-300s within one year and be 95% confident of the results.

Note: *Sample-size estimates for the population mean where σ is unknown using the t distribution are not shown here. Because a sample size must be known to determine the table value of t, which in turn is used to estimate the sample size, this procedure usually involves an iterative process.*

Determining Sample Size when Estimating p

Determining the sample size required to estimate the population proportion, p, also is possible. The process begins with the z formula for sample proportions.

$$z = \frac{\hat{p} - p}{\sqrt{\dfrac{p \cdot q}{n}}}$$

where $q = 1 - p$.

As various samples are taken from the population, $\hat{p}$ will rarely equal the population proportion, p, resulting in an error of estimation. The difference between $\hat{p}$ and p is the margin of error of estimation, so $E = \hat{p} - p$.

$$z = \frac{E}{\sqrt{\dfrac{p \cdot q}{n}}}$$

Solving for n yields the formula for determining sample size.

Sample Size When Estimating P

$$n = \frac{z^2 pq}{E^2}$$

(8.8)

where

p = population proportion
$q = 1 - p$
E = error of estimation
n = sample size

How can the value of n be determined prior to a study if the formula requires the value of p and the study is being done to estimate p? Although the actual value of p is not known prior to the study, similar studies might have generated a good approximation for p. If no previous value is available for use in estimating p, some possible p values, as shown in Table 8.3, might be considered.

Note that, as $p \cdot q$ is in the numerator of the sample size formula, $p = .5$ will result in the largest sample sizes. Often *if p is unknown, researchers use .5 as an estimate of p* in Formula 8.8. This selection results in the largest sample size that could be determined from Formula 8.8 for a given z value and a given error value.

TABLE 8.3

$p \cdot q$ for Various Selected Values of p

p	$p \cdot q$
.9	.09
.8	.16
.7	.21
.6	.24
.5	.25
.4	.24
.3	.21
.2	.16
.1	.09

DEMONSTRATION PROBLEM 8.8

Hewitt Associates conducted a national survey to determine the extent to which employers are promoting health and fitness among their employees. One of the questions asked was, Does your company offer on-site exercise classes? Suppose it was estimated before the study that no more than 40% of the companies would answer yes. How large a sample would Hewitt Associates have to take in estimating the population proportion to ensure a 98% confidence in the results and to be within .03 of the true population proportion?

Solution: The value of E for this problem is .03. Because it is estimated that no more than 40% of the companies would say yes, $p = .40$ can be used. A 98% confidence interval results in a z value of 2.33. Inserting these values into formula (8.8) yields

$$n = \frac{(2.33)^2(.40)(.60)}{(.03)^2} = 1447.7$$

Hewitt Associates would have to sample 1,448 companies to be 98% confident in the results and maintain an error of .03.

DEMONSTRATION PROBLEM 8.9

Suppose a researcher wants to estimate what proportion of refinery workers in the U.S. are contract workers. The researcher wants to be 99% confident of her results and be within .05 of the actual proportion. In addition, suppose that there have been no previous or similar studies to this, and therefore the researcher has no idea what is the actual population proportion. How large a sample size should be taken?

Solution: The value of E for this problem is .05. The value of z for a 99% confidence interval is 2.575. Because no estimate of the population proportion is available, the researcher will use $p = .50$ and $q = .50$. Placing these values into Formula 8.8:

$$n = \frac{z^2 pq}{E^2} = \frac{(2.575^2)(.50)(.50)}{(.05)^2} = 663.1$$

The researcher would have to sample at least 664 workers to attain a 99% level of confidence and produce an error no bigger than .05 if the population proportion is approximately .50.

8.5 Problems

8.40. Determine the sample size necessary to estimate μ for the following information.

a. $\sigma = 36$ and $E = 5$ at 95% confidence

b. $\sigma = 4.13$ and $E = 1$ at 99% confidence

c. Values range from 80 to 500, error is to be within 10, and the confidence level is 90%

d. Values range from 50 to 108, error is to be within 3, and the confidence level is 88%

8.41. Determine the sample size necessary to estimate p for the following information.

a. $E = .02$, p is approximately .40, and confidence level is 96%

b. E is to be within .04, p is unknown, and confidence level is 95%

c. E is to be within 5%, p is approximately 55%, and confidence level is 90%

d. E is to be no more than .01, p is unknown, and confidence level is 99%

8.42. A bank officer wants to determine the amount of the average total monthly deposits per customer at the bank. He believes an estimate of this average amount using a confidence interval is sufficient. How large a sample should he take to be within $200 of the actual average with 99% confidence? He assumes the standard deviation of total monthly deposits for all customers is about $1,000.

8.43. Suppose you have been following a particular airline stock for many years. You are interested in determining the average daily price of this stock in a 10-year period and you have access to the stock reports for these years. However, you do not want to average all the daily prices over 10 years because there are several thousand data points, so you decide to take a random sample of the daily prices and estimate the average. You want to be 90% confident of

your results, you want the estimate to be within $2.00 of the true average, and you believe the standard deviation of the price of this stock is about $12.50 over this period of time. How large a sample should you take?

8.44. A group of investors wants to develop a chain of fast-food restaurants. In determining potential costs for each facility, they must consider, among other expenses, the average monthly electric bill. They decide to sample some fast-food restaurants currently operating to estimate the monthly cost of electricity. They want to be 90% confident of their results and want the error of the interval estimate to be no more than $100. They estimate that such bills range from $600 to $2,500. How large a sample should they take?

8.45. Suppose a production facility purchases a particular component part in large lots from a supplier. The production manager wants to estimate the proportion of defective parts received from this supplier. She believes the proportion defective is no more than .20 and wants to be within .02 of the true proportion of defective parts with a 90% level of confidence. How large a sample should she take?

8.46. What proportion of secretaries of *Fortune* 500 companies has a personal computer at his or her workstation? You want to answer this question by conducting a random survey. How large a sample should you take if you want to be 95% confident of the results and you want the error of the confidence interval to be no more than .05? Assume no one has any idea of what the proportion actually is.

8.47. What proportion of shoppers at a large appliance store actually makes a large-ticket purchase? To estimate this proportion within 10% and be 95% confident of the results, how large a sample should you take? Assume you have no idea what proportion of all shoppers actually make a large-ticket purchase.

Decision Dilemma Solved

Batteries and Bulbs: How Long Do They Last?

According to a study mentioned in the Decision Dilemma, the average battery life of a tablet computer is 8.78 hours. Assuming that this figure is not actually the population mean battery life but rather is a sample mean obtained from a sample of 60 tablet computers, we could use the sample mean, $\bar{x} = 8.78$, as a point estimate for the population mean. However, we realize that the 8.78 figure is merely a function of the particular 60 tablet computers that were selected for the study. A different sample of 60 tablet computers would likely produce a different sample mean. In order to account for this, we can compute a margin of error for this analysis and combining it with the point estimate produce a confidence interval. Suppose the population standard deviation is 1.46 hours and that we want to be 98% confident of our results. To determine the value of z, divide the 98% confidence in half, $.98/2 = .4900$. Table A.5 yields a z value of 2.33 for the area of .4900. Summarizing what we now know,

$n = 60$, $\bar{x} = 8.78$, $\sigma = 1.46$, and $z = 2.33$. Entering these values into Formula 8.1 yields

$$\bar{x} - z\frac{\sigma}{\sqrt{n}} \leq \mu \leq \bar{x} + z\frac{\sigma}{\sqrt{n}}$$

$$8.78 - 2.33\frac{1.46}{\sqrt{60}} \leq \mu \leq 8.78 + 2.33\frac{1.46}{\sqrt{60}}$$

$$8.78 - 0.44 \leq \mu \leq 8.78 + 0.44$$

$$8.34 \leq \mu \leq 9.22$$

We are 98% confident that the population mean battery life of a tablet computer is between 8.34 and 9.22 hours. The margin of error in this estimation is 0.44 hours.

One source in the Decision Dilemma says that the average life of an incandescent 60-watt bulb is 1.4 years based on a 3-hours-per-day usage (1533 hours). It is highly unlikely that this figure is a population mean because in order to determine the population mean life of all incandescent 60-watt bulbs, company researchers would have to test all such bulbs, in which case they would be destroying all product (burning all bulbs until they quit giving light). Suppose, instead, the 1533-hour average was computed from a sample of 41 light bulbs, in which case the 1553-hour average life is a point estimate, not the actual population mean. Suppose also that the sample standard deviation for the 41 bulbs is 78 hours. Using these statistics, a 90% confidence interval for the average burn life for all such 60-watt incandescent bulbs can be computed.

Summarizing the sample information, $n = 41$, df $= 40$, $\bar{x} = 1553$, and $s = 78$. The table t value is $t_{.05,40} = 1.684$. From this information, we can construct the 90% confidence interval as:

$$\bar{x} - t\frac{s}{\sqrt{n}} \leq \mu \leq \bar{x} + t\frac{s}{\sqrt{n}}$$

$$1553 - 1.684\frac{78}{\sqrt{41}} \leq \mu \leq 1553 + 1.684\frac{78}{\sqrt{41}}$$

$$1553 - 20.5 \leq \mu \leq 1553 + 20.5$$

The point estimate number of hours of bulb life is 1553 hours—the figure given in the chapter opener—with a margin of error is 20.5 hours. Combining these, we can construct the 90% confidence interval for the mean number of hours of burn of a 60-watt incandescent bulb as:

$$1532.5 \leq \mu \leq 1573.5$$

From this, researchers are 90% confident that the population mean life of a 60-watt incandescent bulb is between 1532.5 hours and 1573.5 hours.

As presented in the Decision Dilemma, according to Socket Survey, 72 percent of respondents said that they use CFLs in their home. Suppose there were 900 homes in this survey, how could the results be used to estimate the percentage for all homes?

Converting the 72 percent to a proportion of .72, we can construct a confidence interval to estimate the population proportion of homes that use CFLs. The sample proportion, $\hat{p} = .72$, came from a sample of $n = 900$. Suppose we want the level of confidence to be 99%. To determine the value of z, divide the 99% confidence in half, $.99/2 = .4950$. Table A.5 yields a z value of 2.575 for the area of .4950 (interpolating between .4949 and .4951). In addition, we solve for $\hat{q}$ as $1 - \hat{p} = 1 - .72 = .28$. Entering these values into Formula 8.4, gives us

$$\hat{p} - z\sqrt{\frac{\hat{p} \cdot \hat{q}}{n}} \leq p \leq \hat{p} + z\sqrt{\frac{\hat{p} \cdot \hat{q}}{n}}$$

$$.72 - 2.575\sqrt{\frac{(.72)(.28)}{900}} \leq p \leq .72 + 2.575\sqrt{\frac{(.72)(.28)}{900}}$$

$$.72 - .04 \leq p \leq .72 + .04$$

$$.68 \leq p \leq .76$$

From this, a researcher is 99% confident that if a study of all homes was undertaken, the actual population proportion of homes using CFLs would be between .68 and .76. Note that the final confidence interval is constructed from the point estimate, .72, and the margin of error, .04.

Ethical Considerations

Using sample statistics to estimate population parameters poses a couple of ethical concerns. Many survey reports and advertisers use point estimates as the values of the population parameter. Often, no error value is stated, as would have been the case if a confidence interval had been computed. These point estimates are subject to change if another sample is taken. It is probably unethical to state as a conclusion that a point estimate is the population parameter without some sort of disclaimer or explanation about what a point estimate is.

The misapplication of t formulas when data are not normally distributed in the population is also of concern. Although some studies have shown that the t formula analyses are robust, a researcher should be careful not to violate the assumptions underlying the use of the t formulas. An even greater potential for misuse lies in using the chi-square for the estimation of a population variance because this technique is highly sensitive to violations of the assumption that the data are normally distributed.

Summary

Techniques for estimating population parameters from sample statistics are important tools for business research. These tools include techniques for estimating population means, techniques for estimating the population proportion and the population variance, and methodology for determining how large a sample to take.

At times in business research a product is new or untested or information about the population is unknown. In such cases, gathering data from a sample and making estimates about the population is useful and can be done with a point estimate or an interval estimate. A point estimate is the use of a statistic from the sample as an estimate for a parameter of the population. Because point estimates vary with each sample, it is usually best to construct an interval estimate. An interval estimate is a range of values computed from the sample within which the researcher believes with some confidence that the population parameter lies. Certain levels of confidence seem to be used more than others: 90%, 95%, 98%, and 99%.

If the population standard deviation is known, the z statistic is used to estimate the population mean. If the population standard deviation is unknown, the t distribution should be used instead of the z distribution. It is assumed when using the t distribution that the population from which the samples are drawn is normally distributed. However, the technique for estimating a population mean by using the *t* test is robust, which means it is relatively insensitive to minor violations to the assumption. The population variance can be estimated by using sample variance and the chi-square distribution. The chi-square technique for estimating the population variance is not robust; it is sensitive to violations of the assumption that the population is normally distributed. Therefore, extreme caution must be exercised in using this technique.

The formulas in Chapter 7 resulting from the central limit theorem can be manipulated to produce formulas for estimating sample size for large samples. Determining the sample size necessary to estimate a population mean, if the population standard deviation is unavailable, can be based on one-fourth the range as an approximation of the population standard deviation. Determining sample size when estimating a population proportion requires the value of the population proportion. If the population proportion is unknown, the population proportion from a similar study can be used. If none is available, using a value of .50 will result in the largest sample size estimation for the problem if other variables are held constant. Sample size determination is used mostly to provide a ballpark figure to give researchers some guidance. Larger sample sizes usually result in greater costs.

Key Terms

Bounds	Lower bound of the confidence	Point estimate	*t* distribution
Chi-square distribution	interval	Robust	*t* value
Degrees of freedom (df)	Margin of error of the	Sample size	Upper bound of the
Interval Estimate	interval	estimation	confidence interval

Formulas

$100(1 - \alpha)\%$ confidence interval to estimate μ: population standard deviation known

$$\bar{x} - z_{\alpha/2} \frac{\sigma}{\sqrt{n}} \leq \mu \leq \bar{x} + z_{\alpha/2} \frac{\sigma}{\sqrt{n}}$$

Confidence interval to estimate μ using the finite correction factor

$$\bar{x} - z_{\alpha/2} \frac{\sigma}{\sqrt{n}} \sqrt{\frac{N - n}{N - 1}} \leq \mu \leq \bar{x} + z_{\alpha/2} \frac{\sigma}{\sqrt{n}} \sqrt{\frac{N - n}{N - 1}}$$

Confidence interval to estimate μ: population standard deviation unknown

$$\bar{x} - t_{\alpha/2, n-1} \frac{s}{\sqrt{n}} \leq \mu \leq \bar{x} + t_{\alpha/2, n-1} \frac{s}{\sqrt{n}}$$

$$df = n - 1$$

Confidence interval to estimate *p*

$$\hat{p} - z_{\alpha/2} \sqrt{\frac{\hat{p} \cdot \hat{q}}{n}} \leq p \leq \hat{p} + z_{\alpha/2} \sqrt{\frac{\hat{p} \cdot \hat{q}}{n}}$$

χ^2 formula for single variance

$$\chi^2 = \frac{(n - 1)s^2}{\sigma^2}$$

$$df = n - 1$$

Confidence interval to estimate the population variance

$$\frac{(n - 1)s^2}{\chi^2_{\alpha/2}} \leq \sigma^2 \leq \frac{(n - 1)s^2}{\chi^2_{1-\alpha/2}}$$

$$df = n - 1$$

Sample size when estimating μ

$$n = \frac{z^2_{\alpha/2}\sigma^2}{E^2} = \left(\frac{z_{\alpha/2}\sigma}{E}\right)^2$$

Sample size when estimating *p*

$$n = \frac{z^2 pq}{E^2}$$

Supplementary Problems

Calculating the Statistics

8.48. Use the following data to construct 80%, 94%, and 98% confidence intervals to estimate μ. Assume that σ is 7.75. State the point estimate.

44	37	49	30	56	48	53	42	51
38	39	45	47	52	59	50	46	34
39	46	27	35	52	51	46	45	58
51	37	45	52	51	54	39	48	

8.49. Construct 90%, 95%, and 99% confidence intervals to estimate μ from the following data. State the point estimate. Assume the data come from a normally distributed population.

12.3	11.6	11.9	12.8	12.5	11.4	12.0
11.7	11.8	12.3				

8.50. Use the following information to compute the confidence interval for the population proportion.

a. $n = 715$ and $x = 329$, with 95% confidence

b. $n = 284$ and $\hat{p} = .71$, with 90% confidence

c. $n = 1250$ and $\hat{p} = .48$, with 95% confidence

d. $n = 457$ and $x = 270$, with 98% confidence

8.51. Use the following data to construct 90% and 95% confidence intervals to estimate the population variance. Assume the data come from a normally distributed population.

212	229	217	216	223	219	208
214	232	219				

8.52. Determine the sample size necessary under the following conditions.

a. To estimate μ with $\sigma = 44$, $E = 3$, and 95% confidence

b. To estimate μ with a range of values from 20 to 88 with $E = 2$ and 90% confidence

c. To estimate p with p unknown, $E = .04$, and 98% confidence

d. To estimate p with $E = .03$, 95% confidence, and p thought to be approximately .70

Testing Your Understanding

8.53. In planning both market opportunity and production levels, being able to estimate the size of a market can be important. Suppose a diaper manufacturer wants to know how many diapers a one-month-old baby uses during a 24-hour period. To determine this usage, the manufacturer's analyst randomly selects 17 parents of one-month-olds and asks them to keep track of diaper usage for 24 hours. The results are shown. Construct a 99% confidence interval to estimate the average daily diaper usage of a one-month-old baby. Assume diaper usage is normally distributed.

12	8	11	9	13	14	10
10	9	13	11	8	11	15
10	7	12				

8.54. Suppose you want to estimate the proportion of cars that are sport utility vehicles (SUVs) being driven in Kansas City, Missouri, at rush hour by standing on the corner of I-70 and I-470 and counting SUVs. You believe the figure is no higher than .40. If you want the error of the confidence interval to be no greater than .03, how many cars should you randomly sample? Use a 90% level of confidence.

8.55. Use the data in Problem 8.53 to construct a 99% confidence interval to estimate the population variance for the number of diapers used during a 24-hour period for one-month-olds. How could information about the population variance be used by a manufacturer or marketer in planning?

8.56. What is the average length of a company's policy book? Suppose policy books are sampled from 45 medium-sized companies. The average number of pages in the sample books is 213, and the population standard deviation of 48. Use this information to construct a 98% confidence interval to estimate the mean number of pages for the population of medium-sized company policy books.

8.57. A random sample of small-business managers was given a leadership style questionnaire. The results were scaled so that each manager received a score for initiative. Suppose the following data are a random sample of these scores.

37	42	40	39	38	31	40
37	35	45	30	33	35	44
36	37	39	33	39	40	41
33	35	36	41	33	37	38
40	42	44	35	36	33	38
32	30	37	42			

Assuming σ is 3.891, use these data to construct a 90% confidence interval to estimate the average score on initiative for all small-business managers.

8.58. A national beauty spa chain wants to estimate the number of times per year a woman has her nails done at one of their spas if she uses one at least once a year. The chain's researcher estimates that, of those women who use a beauty spa at least once a year to get their nails done, the standard deviation of number of times of usage is approximately 6. The national chain wants the estimate to be within one time of the actual mean value. How large a sample should the researcher take to obtain a 98% confidence level?

8.59. Is the environment a major issue with Americans? To answer that question, a researcher conducts a survey of 1255 randomly selected Americans. Suppose 714 of the sampled people replied that the environment is a major issue with them. Construct a 95% confidence interval to estimate the proportion of Americans who feel that the environment is a major issue with them. What is the point estimate of this proportion?

8.60. According to a survey by Topaz Enterprises, a travel auditing company, the average error by travel agents is $128. Suppose this figure was obtained from a random sample of 41 travel agents and the sample standard deviation is $21. What is the point estimate of the national average error for all travel agents? Compute a 98% confidence interval for the national average error based on these sample results. Assume the travel agent errors are normally distributed in the population. How wide is the interval? Interpret the interval.

8.61. A national survey on telemarketing was undertaken. One of the questions asked was: How long has your organization had a telemarketing operation? Suppose the following data represent some of the answers received to this question. Suppose further that only 300 telemarketing firms comprised the population when this survey was taken. Use the following data to compute a 98% confidence interval to estimate the average number of years an organization has had a telemarketing operation. The population standard deviation is 3.06.

5	5	6	3	6	7	5
5	6	8	4	9	6	4
10	5	10	11	5	14	7
5	9	6	7	3	4	3
7	5	9	3	6	8	16
12	11	5	4	3	6	5
8	3	5	9	7	13	4
6	5	8	3	5	8	7
11	5	14	4			

8.62. An entrepreneur wants to open an appliance repair shop. She would like to know about what the average home repair bill is, including the charge for the service call for appliance repair in the area. She wants the estimate to be within $20 of the actual figure. She believes the range of such bills is between $30 and $600. How large a sample should the entrepreneur take if she wants to be 95% confident of the results?

8.63. A national survey of insurance offices was taken, resulting in a random sample of 245 companies. Of these 245 companies, 189 responded that they were going to purchase new software for their offices in the next year. Construct a 90% confidence interval to estimate the population proportion of insurance offices that intend to purchase new software during the next year.

8.64. A national survey of companies included a question that asked whether the company had at least one bilingual telephone operator. The sample results of 90 companies follow (Y denotes that the company does have at least one bilingual operator; N denotes that it does not).

N	N	N	N	Y	N	Y	N	N
Y	N	N	N	Y	Y	N	N	N
N	N	Y	N	Y	N	Y	N	Y
Y	Y	N	Y	N	N	N	Y	N
N	Y	N	N	N	N	N	N	N
Y	N	Y	Y	N	N	Y	N	Y
N	N	Y	Y	N	N	N	N	N
Y	N	N	N	N	Y	N	N	N
Y	Y	Y	N	N	Y	N	N	N
N	N	N	Y	Y	N	N	Y	N

Use this information to estimate with 95% confidence the proportion of the population that does have at least one bilingual operator.

8.65. A movie theater has had a poor accounting system. The manager has no idea how many large containers of popcorn are sold per movie showing. She knows that the amounts vary by day of the week and hour of the day. However, she wants to estimate the overall average per movie showing. To do so, she randomly selects 12 movie performances and counts the number of large containers of popcorn sold between 30 minutes before the movie showing and 15 minutes after the movie showing. The sample average was 43.7 containers, with a sample variance of 228. Construct a 95% confidence interval to estimate the mean number of large containers of popcorn sold during a movie showing. Assume the number of large containers of popcorn sold per movie is normally distributed in the population. Use this information to construct a 98% confidence interval to estimate the population variance.

8.66. According to a survey by Runzheimer International, the average cost of a fast-food meal (quarter-pound cheese-burger, large fries, medium soft drink, excluding taxes) in Seattle is $4.82. Suppose this figure was based on a sample of 27 different establishments and the sample standard deviation was $0.37. Construct a 95% confidence interval for the population mean cost for all fast-food meals in Seattle. Assume the costs of a fast-food meal in Seattle are normally distributed. Using the interval as a guide, is it likely that the population mean is really $4.50? Why or why not?

8.67. A survey of 77 commercial airline flights of under 2 hours resulted in a sample average late time for a flight of 2.48 minutes. The population standard deviation was 12 minutes. Construct a 95% confidence interval for the average time that a commercial flight of under 2 hours is late. What is the point estimate? What does the interval tell about whether the average flight is late?

8.68. A regional survey of 560 companies asked the vice president of operations how satisfied he or she was with the software support received from the computer staff of the company. Suppose 33% of the 560 vice presidents said they were satisfied. Construct a 99% confidence interval for the proportion of the population of vice presidents who would have said they were satisfied with the software support if a census had been taken.

8.69. A research firm has been asked to determine the proportion of all restaurants in the state of Ohio that serve alcoholic beverages. The firm wants to be 98% confident of its results but has no idea of what the actual proportion is. The firm would like to report an error of no more than .05. How large a sample should it take?

8.70. A national magazine marketing firm attempts to win subscribers with a mail campaign that involves a contest using magazine stickers. Often when people subscribe to magazines in this manner they sign up for multiple magazine subscriptions. Suppose the marketing firm wants to estimate the average number of subscriptions per customer of those who purchase at least one subscription. To do

so, the marketing firm's researcher randomly selects 27 entries with subscription requests. Of these, the average number of subscriptions is 2.10, with a sample standard deviation of .86. The researcher uses this information to compute a 98% confidence interval to estimate μ and assumes that x is normally distributed. What does the researcher find?

8.71. A national survey showed that Hillshire Farm Deli Select cold cuts were priced, on the average, at $5.20 per pound. Suppose a national survey of 23 retail outlets was taken and the price per pound of Hillshire Farm Deli Select cold cuts was ascertained. If the following data represent these prices, what is a 90% confidence interval for the population variance of these prices? Assume prices are normally distributed in the population.

5.18	5.22	5.25	5.19	5.30
5.17	5.15	5.28	5.20	5.14
5.05	5.19	5.26	5.23	5.19
5.22	5.08	5.21	5.24	5.33
5.22	5.19	5.19		

8.72. The price of a head of iceberg lettuce varies greatly with the season and the geographic location of a store. During February a researcher contacts a random sample of 39 grocery stores across the United States and asks the produce manager of each to state the current price charged for a head of iceberg lettuce. Using the researcher's results that follow, construct a 99% confidence interval to estimate the mean price of a head of iceberg lettuce in February in the United States. Assume that σ is 0.205.

1.59	1.25	1.65	1.40	0.89
1.19	1.50	1.49	1.30	1.39
1.29	1.60	0.99	1.29	1.19
1.20	1.50	1.49	1.29	1.35
1.10	0.89	1.10	1.39	1.39
1.50	1.50	1.55	1.20	1.15
0.99	1.00	1.30	1.25	1.10
1.00	1.55	1.29	1.39	

8.73. A study of 1,000 adult Canadians was undertaken in an effort to obtain information about Canadian shopping habits. One of the results of this survey was that 23% often buy items that are not on their shopping list but catch their eye. Use this study result to estimate with an 80% level of confidence the population proportion of Canadian shoppers who buy items that are not on their shopping list but catch their eye.

Interpreting the Output

8.74. A soft drink company produces a cola in a 12-ounce can. Even though their machines are set to fill the cans with 12 ounces, variation due to calibration, operator error, and other things sometimes precludes the cans having the correct fill. To monitor the can fills, a quality team randomly selects some filled 12-ounce cola cans and measures their fills in the lab. A confidence interval for the population mean is constructed from the data. Shown here is the Minitab output from this effort. Discuss the output.

```
One-Sample Z

The assumed standard deviation = 0.0536

N     Mean      SE Mean    99% CI
58    11.9788   0.0070     (11.9607, 11.99691)
```

8.75. A company has developed a new light bulb that seems to burn longer than most residential bulbs. To determine how long these bulbs burn, the company randomly selects a sample of these bulbs and burns them in the laboratory. The Excel output shown here is a portion of the analysis from this effort. Discuss the output.

Bulb Burn	
Mean	2198.217
Standard deviation	152.9907
Count	84
Confidence level (90.0%)	27.76691

8.76. Suppose a researcher wants to estimate the average age of a person who is a first-time home buyer. A random sample of first-time home buyers is taken and their ages are ascertained. The Minitab output shown here is an analysis of that data. Study the output and explain its implication.

```
One-Sample T

N    Mean   StDev  SE Mean    99% CI
21   27.63  6.54   1.43       (23.57, 31.69)
```

8.77. What proportion of all American workers drive their cars to work? Suppose a poll of American workers is taken in an effort to answer that question, and the Minitab output shown here is an analysis of the data from the poll. Explain the meaning of the output in light of the question.

```
Test and CI for One Proportion

Sample  X    N    Sample p  95% CI
1       506  781  0.647887  (0.613240, 0.681413)
```

Analyzing the Databases

see **www.wiley.com/college/black**

1. Using the Manufacturing database as a sample, construct a 95% confidence interval for the population mean number of production workers. What is the point estimate? How much is the error of the estimate? Comment on the results.

2. Using the Hospital database, construct a 90% confidence interval to estimate the average census for hospitals. Change the level of confidence to 99%. What happened to the interval? Did the point estimate change?

3. The Financial database contains financial data on 100 companies. Use this database as a sample and estimate the earnings per share for all corporations from these data. Select several levels of confidence and compare the results.

4. Using the frequency feature of the computer software, determine the sample proportion of the Hospital database under the variable "service" that are "general medical" (category 1). From this statistic, construct a 95% confidence interval to estimate the population proportion of hospitals that are "general medical." What is the point estimate? How much error is there in the interval?

Case

The Container Store

In the late 1970s, Kip Tindell (chairman and CEO), Garrett Boone (Chairman Emeritus), and John Mullen (architect) drew up plans for a first of a kind retail store specializing in storage solutions for both the home and the office. The vision that they created was realized when on July 1, 1978, the Container Store opened its doors in a small 1600-square-foot retail space in Dallas. The store was stocked with products that were devoted to simplifying people's lives, such as commercial parts bins, wire drawers, mailboxes, milk crates, wire leaf burners, and many others. Some critics questioned whether a store selling "empty boxes" could survive. However, the concept took off, and in the past 37 years, the company has expanded coast to coast in the United States with stores in 49 locations. Now headquartered in Coppell, Texas, the Container Store has 6000 employees and annual revenues of over $780 million.

Besides their innovative product mix, some of the keys to the success of the Container Store are the enthusiasm with which their employees work, the care that employees give to the customer, and employee knowledge of their products. For 16 straight years, the Container Store has made *Fortune* magazine's list of "100 Best Companies to Work For." Generally rated in the top 40 of this list each year, the company was number 1 for the first two years that they applied for consideration. Their current president and C.O.O., Melissa Reiff, credits the company's devotion to recruiting and retaining a highly qualified workforce as one of the keys to its success. Company sources say that the Container Store offers more than 240 hours of formal training for full-time employees the first year of employment with the company and that this compares to about 8 hours of such training with other companies in the industry. According to company sources, the Container Store believes that their employees are their number one stakeholder and "The Container Store is an absolutely exhilarating and inspiring place to shop and an equally exciting place to work."

In addition to innovative products and motivated employees, the Container Store has embraced a commitment to the environment. Chairman Emeritus Garrett Boone says that they firmly believe that there is no conflict between economic prosperity and environmental stewardship. The Container Company is embracing sustainability as a key to their economic future. As part of this effort, they sell eco-friendly products, use highly efficient HVAC units in their stores and warehouses, sponsor an employee purchase program for compact fluorescent lights, are switching from neon to LED lighting in all exterior signage, and offer an employee battery and light bulb recycling program.

Discussion

1. Among other things, the Container Store has grown and flourished because of strong customer relationships, which include listening to customer needs, containing products that meet customer needs, having salespeople who understand both customer needs and the products, and creating a store environment that is customer friendly both in layout and in culture. Suppose company management wants to formally measure customer satisfaction at least once a year and develops a brief survey that includes the following four questions. Suppose that the survey was administered to 115 customers with the following results. Use techniques presented in this chapter to analyze the data to estimate the population responses to these questions.

QUESTION	YES	NO
1. Compared to most other stores that you shop in, is the Container Store more customer friendly?	73	42
2. Most of the time, this store has the number and type of home or office storage solution that I need.	81	34
3. The salespeople at this store appear the be particularly knowledgeable of their products.	88	27
4. Store hours are particularly convenient for me.	66	49

2. The Container Store is well known as a great company to work for. In addition, company management states that their employee is their number one stakeholder. Suppose in spite of their history as an employee-friendly company, management wants to measure employee satisfaction this year to determine if they are maintaining this culture. A researcher is hired by the company who randomly selects 21 employees and asks them to complete a satisfaction survey under the supervision of an independent testing organization. As part of this survey, employees are asked to respond to questions by providing a score of from 0 to 50 along a continuous scale, where 0 denotes no satisfaction and 50 denotes the utmost satisfaction. Assume that the data are normally distributed in the population. The questions and the results of the survey are shown below. Analyze the results by using techniques from this chapter. Discuss your findings.

QUESTION	MEAN	STANDARD DEVIATION
1. Are you treated fairly by the company as an employee?	42.4	5.2
2. Has the company given you the training that you need to do the job adequately?	44.9	3.1
3. Does management seriously consider your input in making decisions about the store?	38.7	7.5
4. Is your physical work environment acceptable?	35.6	9.2
5. Is the compensation for your work adequate and fair?	34.5	12.4
6. Overall, do you feel that company management really cares about you as a person?	41.8	6.3

Sources: fortune.com/best-companies/the-container-store-27/; investor.containerstore.com/financial-reports/annual/default.aspx; http://www.containerstore.com/

CHAPTER 9

Statistical Inference: Hypothesis Testing for Single Populations

LEARNING OBJECTIVES

The main objective of Chapter 9 is to help you to learn how to test hypotheses on single populations, thereby enabling you to:

1. Develop both one- and two-tailed statistical hypotheses that can be tested in a business setting by examining the rejection and nonrejection regions in light of Type I and Type II errors.

2. Reach a statistical conclusion in hypothesis testing problems about a population mean with a known population standard deviation using the z statistic.

3. Reach a statistical conclusion in hypothesis testing problems about a population mean with an unknown population standard deviation using the t statistic.

4. Reach a statistical conclusion in hypothesis testing problems about a population proportion using the z statistic.

5. Reach a statistical conclusion in hypothesis testing problems about a population variance using the chi-square statistic.

6. Solve for possible Type II errors when failing to reject the null hypothesis.

Decision Dilemma

Valero: Refining and Retailing

Annie Wells/Getty Images, Inc.

The Valero Energy Corporation, a Fortune 500 company based in San Antonio, is a major success story both in refining and in retailing. Valero, named after the mission—San Antonio de Valero—more commonly known as the Alamo, is a relatively young company, having been created in 1980 as a result of a court settlement approved in 1978 by the Texas Railroad Commission, the natural gas regulatory agency in Texas. In refining, Valero has grown from a humble beginning with a single refinery purchased in the mid-1980s to the world's largest independent refiner, with 15 refineries stretching from California to Canada to the United Kingdom. Valero has a combined throughput capacity of 2.9 million barrels per day. Its refinery products are used in dozens of diversified industries, ranging from health care and plastics to transportation, beauty products, and manufacturing. In addition, Valero has 11 ethanol plants with a combined capacity of 1.3 billion U.S. gallons per year and a 30-turbine 50 megawatt wind farm in Sunray, Texas. Presently, Valero has a work force of over 10,000 employees.

In addition to its rapid growth in refining, Valero has developed an impressive assembly of almost 7,400 retail gas stations (see photo) in the United States, Canada, and the Caribbean. Besides gasoline, Valero's retail stores typically sell a large variety of convenience store goods. Valero's entry into retailing did not begin until the year 2000 when it acquired a 270-store retail distribution chain and 80 company-operated sites in the San Francisco area. On December 31, 2001, Valero acquired Ultramar Diamond Shamrock, adding over 4,700 retail sites in the United States, Canada, and the Caribbean to its portfolio. While Valero branding is taking over most of these sites in the United States, Ultramar will still be used in Canada as the brand name. In 2007, Valero introduced its updated "Corner Store" retail concept by opening its first 5,500-square-foot prototype in western San Antonio. The Corner Store concept includes a variety of family products, fresh (hot) Cibolo Mountain Premium Blend coffee, fresh doughnuts and pastries baked daily, and hot sandwiches and hot dogs, among other items.

MANAGERIAL AND STATISTICAL QUESTIONS

1. The refining aspect of Valero's company brings to mind the fact that there are many possible research hypotheses that could be generated in the oil-refining business. For example, suppose it was determined that oil refineries have been running below capacity for the last two months. What are at least four research hypotheses that might explain this?

2. According to industry sources, the average barrel of crude oil contains 42 U.S. gallons. However, the weight of such barrels varies based on the quality and type of oil. A barrel of light, sweet crude oil weighs about 294 U.S. lbs. whereas heavy oil might weigh as much as 350 U.S. lbs. Suppose a petroleum company is using a mix of quality of crude oil, and they just received a shipment of thousands of barrels of oil. It knows from the past that the average weight of a barrel for all oil is 320 lbs. with a standard deviation of 7 lbs., and it wants to test to determine if the average weight of the present shipment is the same or different from 320 lbs. How does it go about conducting such a test?

3. According to *Convenience Store News,* the average in-store transaction for a convenience store was $7.47 in 2010. Suppose you believe that the average is now higher than that figure. While the population average ($7.47) was known, there was no information about the population standard deviation. However, it is generally thought that in-store transactions for convenience stores are approximately normally distributed in the population. How do you test to determine if the average is now higher?

4. According to the National Association of Convenience Stores, 62% of all convenience stores in the United States are owned and operated by someone who has only one store. Suppose you live in a city that seemingly has fewer entrepreneurs and more corporate influence and you believe that in your city, significantly fewer than 62% of all convenience stores are owned and operated by someone who has only one store. You set out to "prove" your theory by taking a random sample of 328 convenience stores; it turns out that 187 of them are owned and operated by someone who has only one store. Is this enough evidence to declare that in your city, a significantly lower percentage of convenience stores are owned and operated by someone who has only one store?

Sources: http://www.valero.com/OurBusiness/Pages/CompanyHistory.aspx

A foremost statistical mechanism for decision making is the hypothesis test. The concept of hypothesis testing lies at the heart of inferential statistics, and the use of statistics to "prove" or "disprove" claims hinges on it. With **hypothesis testing**, business researchers are able *to structure problems in such a way that they can use statistical evidence to test various theories about business phenomena.* Business applications of statistical hypothesis testing run the gamut from determining whether a production line process is out of control to providing conclusive evidence that a new management leadership approach is significantly more effective than an old one.

While Chapter 8 presents techniques that can be used for estimating a mean, a proportion, or a variance for a population with a single sample, Chapter 9 contains techniques used for testing hypotheses about a population mean, a population proportion, and a population variance using a single sample. **Figure 9.1** is a tree diagram displaying the hypothesis testing techniques presented in Chapter 9. Note that at the bottom of each tree branch in Figure 9.1, the title of the statistical technique along with its respective section number is given for ease of identification and use. If a business researcher is testing a population mean and the population standard deviation is known, then she will use the z test for μ contained in Section 9.2. If the population standard deviation is unknown and therefore the researcher is using the sample standard deviation, then the appropriate technique is the t test for μ contained in Section 9.3. If a business researcher is testing a population proportion, then she will use the z test for p presented in Section 9.4. If the researcher desires to test a population variance from a single sample, then she will use the χ^2 test for σ^2 presented in Section 9.5. Section 9.6 contains techniques for solving for Type II errors.

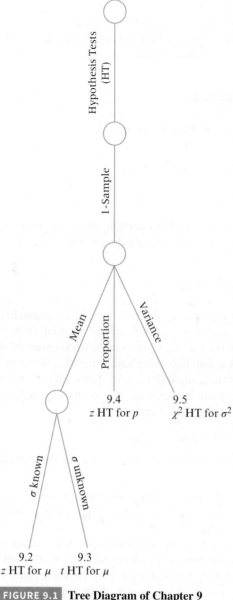

FIGURE 9.1   **Tree Diagram of Chapter 9 Hypothesis Testing Techniques**

9.1 | Introduction to Hypothesis Testing

In the field of business, decision makers are continually attempting to find answers to questions such as the following:

- What container shape is most economical and reliable for shipping a product?
- Which management approach best motivates employees in the retail industry?
- How can the company's retirement investment financial portfolio be diversified for optimum performance?
- What is the best way to link client databases for fast retrieval of useful information?
- Which indicator best predicts the general state of the economy in the next six months?
- What is the most effective means of advertising in a business-to-business setting?

Business researchers are often called upon to provide insights and information to decision makers to assist them in answering such questions. In searching for answers to questions and in attempting to find explanations for business phenomena, business researchers often develop "hypotheses" that can be studied and explored. **Hypotheses** are *tentative explanations of a principle operating in nature.** In this text, we will explore various types of hypotheses, how to test them, and how to interpret the results of such tests so that useful information can be brought to bear on the business decision-making process.

Types of Hypotheses

Three types of hypotheses will be explored here:

1. *Research* hypotheses
2. *Statistical* hypotheses
3. *Substantive* hypotheses

Although much of the focus will be on testing statistical hypotheses, it is also important for business decision makers to have an understanding of both research and substantive hypotheses.

Research Hypotheses

Of the three types of hypotheses discussed in this section, a research hypothesis is most similar to the general definition of hypotheses given earlier. A **research hypothesis** is *a statement of what the researcher believes will be the outcome of an experiment or a study.* Before studies are undertaken, business researchers often have some idea or theory based on experience or previous work as to how the study will turn out. These ideas, theories, or notions established before an experiment or study is conducted are research hypotheses. Some examples of research hypotheses in business might include:

- Older workers are more loyal to a company.
- Bigger companies spend a higher percentage of their annual budget on advertising than do smaller companies.
- Using a Six Sigma quality approach to manufacturing results in greater productivity.
- Scrap metal price is a good leading indicator of the Industrial Production Index.

Virtually, all inquisitive thinking business people have similar research hypotheses concerning relationships, approaches, and techniques in business. Such hypotheses can lead decision makers to new and better ways to accomplish business goals. However, to formally test research hypotheses, it is generally best to state them as statistical hypotheses.

Statistical Hypotheses

In order to scientifically test research hypotheses, a more formal hypothesis structure needs to be set up using **statistical hypotheses**. A statistical hypothesis is a formal hypothesis structure set up with a null and an alternative hypothesis to scientifically test research hypotheses. Suppose business researchers want to "prove" the research hypothesis that older workers are more loyal to a company. The researchers either develop or obtain a "loyalty" survey instrument. If this instrument is administered to a sample of both older and younger workers, how much higher do older workers have to score (assuming higher scores indicate more loyal) than younger workers to prove the research hypothesis? What is the "proof threshold"? Instead of attempting to prove or disprove research hypotheses directly in this manner, business researchers convert their research hypotheses to statistical hypotheses and then test the statistical hypotheses using standard procedures. What are these procedures, and how is this done?

All statistical hypotheses consist of two parts, a null hypothesis and an alternative hypothesis. These two parts are constructed to contain all possible outcomes of the experiment

---

*Paraphrasing of definition published in *Merriam Webster's Collegiate Dictionary*, 10th ed. Springfield, MA: Merriam Webster, Inc., 1983.

or study. Generally, the **null hypothesis** *states that the "null" condition exists; that is, there is nothing new happening, the old theory is still true, the old standard is correct, and the system is in control.* The **alternative hypothesis**, on the other hand, *states that the new theory is true, there are new standards, the system is out of control, and/or something is happening.*

As an example, suppose flour packaged by a manufacturer is sold by weight, and a particular size of package is supposed to average 80 oz. Suppose the manufacturer wants to test to determine whether their packaging process is out of control as determined by the weight of the flour packages. The null hypothesis for this experiment is that the average weight of the flour packages is 80 oz. (no problem). The alternative hypothesis is that the average is not 80 oz. (process is out of control).

It is common symbolism to represent the null hypothesis as H_0 and the alternative hypothesis as H_a. The null and alternative hypotheses for the flour example can be restated using these symbols and μ for the population mean as:

$$H_0: \mu = 80 \text{ oz.}$$

$$H_a: \mu \neq 80 \text{ oz.}$$

Note that the alternative hypothesis is the "complement" of the null hypothesis and contains everything that is not in the null hypothesis. Thus, between the null and alternative hypotheses all possibilities are being considered.

Statistical hypotheses are written so that they will produce either a one-tailed or a two-tailed test. The hypotheses shown here for the flour packaging manufacturing study are two-tailed because there is no stipulation that researchers believe that the packages are overfilled or that they are underfilled. That is, there is no "directional" hypothesis. By conducting a two-tailed test such as this, researchers allow for the possibility that either $\mu > 80$ oz. or $\mu < 80$ oz. could occur.

A **two-tailed test** is a statistical test wherein the researcher is interested in testing both sides of the distribution. Two-tailed tests always use = and ≠ in the statistical hypotheses and are directionless in that the alternative hypothesis allows either the greater than (>) or the less than (<) possibility.

 ▶ **Applied Skills Video**

As an example of a one-tailed test, suppose a company has held an 18% share of the market. However, because of an increased marketing effort, company officials believe the company's market share is now greater than 18%, and the officials would like to prove it. The null hypothesis is that the market share is still 18%. Converting the 18% to a proportion and using p to represent the population proportion results in the following null hypothesis:

$$H_0: p = .18$$

The alternative hypothesis is that the population proportion is now greater than .18:

$$H_a: p > .18$$

Note that the "new idea" or "new theory" that company officials want to "prove" is stated in the alternative hypothesis. The null hypothesis states that the old market share of 18% is still true.

A **one-tailed test** is a statistical test wherein the researcher is interested in testing only one side of the distribution. One-tailed tests are always directional, and the alternative hypothesis uses either the greater than (>) or the less than (<) sign. Notice that even though the market share problem is a one-tailed test, the null hypothesis has an = sign, as does the null hypothesis for the two-tailed test (flour problem). The difference in the one-tailed test and the two-tailed test lies in the alternative hypothesis. While the alternative hypothesis in a two-tailed test is always ≠, the alternative hypothesis in a one-tailed test has a directional sign (< or >). Note that in a one-tailed test, even though the null hypothesis is written with an equal sign (=), it is assumed that the direction not being tested in the alternative hypothesis is included in the null hypothesis. For example, in the market share problem, even though business researchers are interested in showing that the market share has increased, there is the possibility that it actually decreased. This possibility is included in the null hypothesis even though the null

Thinking Critically About Statistics in Business Today

Consumer Attitudes Toward Food in the United States

The average American eats 1996.3 pounds of food per year, including over 600 pounds of non-cheese dairy products, 110 pounds of red meat, over 273 pounds of fruit, over 415 pounds of vegetables, 29 pounds of french fries, 23 pounds of pizza, 24 pounds of ice cream, and 53 gallons of soda. On average, a person in the United States consumes 2770 calories of food daily.

About 70% of Americans say that they are concerned about their weight, and around 77% are trying to lose or maintain their weight. About 65% of Americans rate weight loss as their number one way to improve their health. Sixteen percent plan to use an improved diet to maintain their weight. Only 19% of those trying to lose weight actually keep track of their caloric intake. Around half of all Americans are trying to consume more protein, partly because 68% of Americans believe that protein builds muscle. A great percentage of Americans (88%) do their food shopping at supermarkets and grocery stores.

THINGS TO PONDER

1. Think about the abundance of food in the United States, the high percentage of Americans who seem to be concerned about weight, and the various types of food that are being consumed in large quantities. Brainstorm a half dozen or so business opportunities that this might present to American entrepreneurs in terms of products, programs, or services.

2. A high percentage of Americans want to maintain or lose weight. What are some ways that employers/managers can help workers in this regard?

Sources: International Food Information Council (IFIC) Foundation, "2010 Food & Health Survey," Executive Summary & Key Trends, http://www.foodinsight.org/Content/3651/FINAL%202010%20Food%20 and%20Health%20Exec%20Summary%20Final.pdf; "Food Consumption in America," January 30, 2011, http://www.visualeconomics.com/food-consumption-in-america_2010-07-12/.

hypothesis is written with = and not as ≤. Table 9.1 points out the differences between a one-tailed and a two-tailed test.

Generally speaking, new hypotheses are stated in the alternative hypothesis. Because many business researchers undertake an experiment only to determine whether their new hypothesis is correct, they are hoping that the alternative hypothesis will be "proven" true. An exception to this might be in manufacturing where a business researcher is testing to determine if a process is out of control. Of course, the manufacturer hopes that the system is not out of control.

A one-tailed test should be used only when the researcher feels certain that the outcome of an experiment is going to occur in one direction or the researcher is only interested in one direction of the experiment, as in the case of the market share problem. In business research, the conservative approach is to conduct a two-tailed test because sometimes study results can be obtained that are opposite to what researchers thought would

TABLE 9.1   Differences Between One-Tailed and Two-Tailed Tests

ONE-TAILED TESTS	TWO-TAILED TESTS
• Null hypothesis has an = sign	• Null hypothesis has an = sign
• Directional	• Nondirectional
• Cues in problem are *directional* words such as: higher, lower, older, younger, more, less, longer, shorter, etc.	• Cues in problem are *nondirectional* words such as: same, different, equal, not equal, control, out-of-control
• Alternative hypothesis has either > or < sign	• Alternative hypothesis can have only ≠ sign
• The direction (> or <) not included in the alternative hypotheses is assumed to be included in the null hypothesis—although not shown	• Null and alternative hypotheses include all possible cases
• Hypothesis possibilities:	• Hypotheses are always written as:

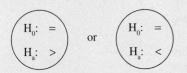

occur. For example, in the market share problem, it might turn out that the company had actually lost market share, and even though company officials were not interested in "proving" such a case, they may need to know that it is true. It is recommended that, if in doubt, business researchers should use a two-tailed test.

Substantive Hypotheses

In testing a statistical hypothesis, a business researcher reaches a conclusion based on the data obtained in the study. If the null hypothesis is rejected and therefore the alternative hypothesis is accepted, it is common to say that a statistically significant result has been obtained. For example, in the market share problem, if the null hypothesis is rejected, the result is that the market share is "significantly greater" than 18%. The word *significant* to statisticians and business researchers merely means that the result of the experiment is unlikely due to chance and a decision has been made to reject the null hypothesis. However, in everyday business life, the word *significant* is more likely to connote "important" or "a large amount." One problem that can arise in testing statistical hypotheses is that particular characteristics of the data can result in a statistically significant outcome that is not a significant business outcome.

As an example, consider the market share study. Suppose a large sample of potential customers is taken, and a sample market share of 18.2% is obtained. Suppose further that a statistical analysis of these data results in statistical significance. We would conclude statistically that the market share is significantly higher than 18%. This finding actually means that it is unlikely that the difference between the sample proportion and the population proportion is due just to chance. However, to the business decision maker, a market share of 18.2% might not be significantly higher than 18%. Because of the way the word *significant* is used to denote rejection of the null hypothesis rather than an important business difference, business decision makers need to exercise caution in interpreting the outcomes of statistical tests.

In addition to understanding a statistically significant result, business decision makers need to determine what, to them, is a *substantive* result. A **substantive result** is *when the outcome of a statistical study produces results that are important to the decision maker*. The importance to the researcher will vary from study to study. As an example, in a recent year, one healthcare administrator was excited because patient satisfaction had significantly increased (statistically) from one year to the next. However, an examination of the data revealed that on a five-point scale, their satisfaction ratings had gone up from 3.61 to only 3.63. Is going from a 3.61 rating to a 3.63 rating in one year really a substantive increase? On the other hand, increasing the average purchase at a large, high-volume store from $55.45 to $55.50 might be substantive as well as significant if volume is large enough to drive profits higher. Both business researchers and decision makers should be aware that statistically significant results are not always substantive results.

Eight-Step Process for Testing Hypotheses

Research hypotheses are tested using a variation of the scientific method. In each hypothesis test, a business researcher goes through the same eight-step process. **Figure 9.2** displays these steps.

At step 1, establishing a null and an alternative hypothesis, it is important that the business researcher clearly identify what is being tested and whether the hypotheses are one-tailed or two-tailed. In the hypothesis testing process, it is *always assumed that the null hypothesis is true at the beginning of the study*. In other words, it is assumed that the process is in control (no problems in the process), the market share has not increased, older workers are not more loyal to a company than younger workers, and so on. This process is analogous to the U.S. trial system in which the accused is presumed innocent at the beginning of the trial.

Step 2 is to select the most appropriate statistical test to use for the analysis. In selecting such a test, the business researcher needs to consider the type, number, and level of data being used in the study along with the statistic used in the analysis (mean, proportion, etc.). In addition, business researchers should consider the assumptions underlying certain statistical tests and determine whether they can be met in the study before using such tests.

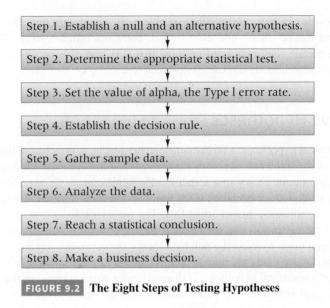

Step 1. Establish a null and an alternative hypothesis.

Step 2. Determine the appropriate statistical test.

Step 3. Set the value of alpha, the Type I error rate.

Step 4. Establish the decision rule.

Step 5. Gather sample data.

Step 6. Analyze the data.

Step 7. Reach a statistical conclusion.

Step 8. Make a business decision.

FIGURE 9.2   **The Eight Steps of Testing Hypotheses**

At step 3, the value of alpha is set. Alpha is the probability of committing a Type I error and will be discussed later. Common values of alpha include .05, .01, .10, and .001.

Step 4 is to establish the decision rule, which should be done before the study is undertaken. Using alpha and the test statistic, **critical values** can be determined. These critical values are used at the decision step (step 7) to determine whether the null hypothesis is rejected or not. If the p-value method (discussed later) is utilized, the value of alpha is used as a critical probability value. The process begins by assuming that the null hypothesis is true. Data are gathered and statistics computed. If the evidence is away from the null hypothesis, the business researcher begins to doubt that the null hypothesis is really true. If the evidence is far enough away from the null hypothesis that the critical value is surpassed, the business researcher will reject the null hypothesis and declare that a statistically significant result has been attained.

The first four steps in testing hypotheses should *always* be completed before the study is undertaken. It is not sound research to gather data first and then try to determine what to do with them.

Step 5 is to gather sample data. This step might include the construction and implementation of a survey, conducting focus groups, randomly sampling items from an assembly line, or even sampling from secondary data sources (e.g., financial databases). In gathering data, the business researcher is cautioned to recall the proper techniques of random sampling (see Chapter 7, Section 7.1). Care should be taken in establishing a frame, determining the sampling technique, and constructing the measurement device. A strong effort should be made to avoid all nonsampling errors.

After the data are sampled, the test statistic can be calculated (step 6).

Step 7 is reaching a statistical conclusion. Using step 4 (decision rule) and the value of the test statistic (step 6), the business researcher can draw a statistical conclusion. In all hypothesis tests, the business researcher needs to conclude whether the null hypothesis is rejected or is not rejected.

Step 8 is determining the business implications of the statistical decision. That is, after a statistical decision is made, the business researcher or decision maker decides what business implications the study results contain. If the statistical decision is to fail to reject the null hypothesis, then typically the business decision maker is left with the status quo. However, if the statistical decision is to reject the null hypothesis, it is at this step that the business decision maker must decide if the results are substantive. In either case, there may be business decisions to be made. For example, if the hypothesis-testing procedure results in a conclusion that train passengers are significantly older today than they were in the past, the manager may decide to cater to these older customers or to draw up a strategy to make ridership more appealing to younger people.

Rejection and Nonrejection Regions

Using the critical values established at step 4 of the hypothesis testing process, the possible statistical outcomes of a study can be divided into two groups:

1. Those that cause the rejection of the null hypothesis
2. Those that do not cause the rejection of the null hypothesis

Conceptually and graphically, statistical outcomes that result in the rejection of the null hypothesis lie in what is termed the **rejection region**. Statistical outcomes that fail to result in the rejection of the null hypothesis lie in what is termed the **nonrejection region**.

As an example, consider the flour-packaging manufacturing example. The null hypothesis is that the average fill for the population of packages is 80 oz. Suppose a sample of 100 such packages is randomly selected, and a sample mean of 80.1 oz. is obtained. Because this mean is not 80 oz., should the business researcher decide to reject the null hypothesis? In the hypothesis testing process we are using sample statistics (in this case, the sample mean of 80.1 oz.) to make decisions about population parameters (in this case, the population mean of 80 oz.). It makes sense that in taking random samples from a population with a mean of 80 oz. not all sample means will equal 80 oz. In fact, the central limit theorem (see Chapter 7) states that for large sample sizes, sample means are normally distributed around the population mean. Thus, even when the population mean is 80 oz., a sample mean might still be 80.1, 78.6, or even 84.2. However, suppose a sample mean of 90 oz. is obtained from 100 packages. This sample mean may be so far from what is reasonable to expect for a population with a mean of 80 oz. that the decision is made to reject the null hypothesis. This prompts the question: When is the sample mean so far away from the population mean that the null hypothesis is rejected? The critical values established at step 4 of the hypothesis testing process are used to divide the means that lead to the rejection of the null hypothesis from those that do not. **Figure 9.3** displays a normal distribution of sample means around a population mean of 80 oz. Note the critical values in each end (tail) of the distribution. In each direction beyond the critical values lie the rejection regions. Any sample mean that falls in that region will lead the business researcher to reject the null hypothesis. Sample means that fall between the two critical values are close enough to the population mean that the business researcher will decide not to reject the null hypothesis. These means are in the nonrejection region.

Type I and Type II Errors

Because the hypothesis testing process uses sample statistics calculated from random data to reach conclusions about population parameters, it is possible to make an incorrect decision about the null hypothesis. In particular, two types of errors can be made in testing hypotheses: Type I error and Type II error.

A **Type I error** is committed by *rejecting a true null hypothesis.* With a Type I error, the null hypothesis is true, but the business researcher decides that it is not. As an example, suppose the flour-packaging process actually is "in control" and is averaging 80 oz. of flour per package.

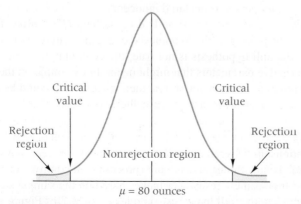

FIGURE 9.3   **Rejection and Nonrejection Regions**

Suppose also that a business researcher randomly selects 100 packages, weighs the contents of each, and computes a sample mean. It is possible, by chance, to randomly select 100 of the more extreme packages (mostly heavy weighted or mostly light weighted) resulting in a mean that falls in the rejection region. The decision is to reject the null hypothesis even though the population mean is actually 80 oz. In this case, the business researcher has committed a Type I error.

The notion of a Type I error can be used outside the realm of statistical hypothesis testing in the business world. For example, if a manager fires an employee because some evidence indicates that she is stealing from the company and if she really is not stealing from the company, then the manager has committed a Type I error. As another example, suppose a worker on the assembly line of a large manufacturer hears an unusual sound and decides to shut the line down (reject the null hypothesis). If the sound turns out not to be related to the assembly line and no problems are occurring with the assembly line, then the worker has committed a Type I error. In U.S. industries in the 1950s, 1960s, and 1970s, when U.S. products were in great demand, workers were strongly discouraged from making such Type I errors because the production downtime was so expensive. An analogous courtroom example of a Type I error is when an innocent person is sent to jail.

In Figure 9.3, the rejection regions represent the possibility of committing a Type I error. Means that fall beyond the critical values will be considered so extreme that the business researcher chooses to reject the null hypothesis. However, if the null hypothesis is true, any mean that falls in a rejection region will result in a decision that produces a Type I error. The *probability of committing a Type I error* is called **alpha** (α) or **level of significance**. Alpha equals the area under the curve that is in the rejection region beyond the critical value(s). The value of alpha is always set before the experiment or study is undertaken. As mentioned previously, common values of alpha are .05, .01, .10, and .001.

A **Type II error** is committed when a business researcher *fails to reject a false null hypothesis*. In this case, the null hypothesis is false, but a decision is made to not reject it. Suppose in the case of the flour problem that the packaging process is actually producing a population mean of 81 oz. even though the null hypothesis is 80 oz. A sample of 100 packages yields a sample mean of 80.2 oz., which falls in the nonrejection region. The business decision maker decides not to reject the null hypothesis. A Type II error has been committed. The packaging procedure is out of control and the hypothesis testing process does not identify it.

Suppose in the business world an employee is stealing from the company. A manager sees some evidence that the stealing is occurring but lacks enough evidence to conclude that the employee is stealing from the company. The manager decides not to fire the employee based on theft. The manager has committed a Type II error. Consider the manufacturing line with the noise. Suppose the worker decides not enough noise is heard to shut the line down, but in actuality, one of the cords on the line is unraveling, creating a dangerous situation. The worker is committing a Type II error. Beginning in the 1980s, U.S. manufacturers started protecting more against Type II errors. They found that in many cases, it was more costly to produce bad product (e.g., scrap/rework costs and loss of market share due to poor quality) than it was to make it right the first time. They encouraged workers to shut down the line if the quality of work was seemingly not what it should be (risking a Type I error) rather than allowing poor quality product to be shipped. In a court of law, a Type II error is committed when a guilty person is declared innocent.

The probability of committing a Type II error is **beta** (β). Unlike alpha, beta is not usually stated at the beginning of the hypothesis testing procedure. Actually, because beta occurs only when the null hypothesis is not true, the computation of beta varies with the many possible alternative parameters that might occur. For example, in the flour-packaging problem, if the population mean is not 80 oz., then what is it? It could be 81, 78, or 82 oz. A value of beta is associated with each of these alternative means.

Comparing Type I and Type II Errors
How are alpha and beta related? **Figure 9.4** shows the relationship between alpha, beta, and another concept, power. In Figure 9.4, the "state of nature" is how things actually are (process is in control, etc.) and the "action" is the decision that the business researcher makes based on the sample statistic. Alpha can only be committed when the null hypothesis is rejected (row 2 of Figure 9.4) and beta can only be committed when the null hypothesis is not rejected (row 1 of Figure 9.4). Thus, because the business researcher is the one who takes the "action" shown in Figure 9.4, the

		State of nature: Null true	State of nature: Null false
Action	Fail to reject null	Correct decision	Type II error (β)
	Reject null	Type I error (α)	Correct decision (power)

FIGURE 9.4 Alpha, Beta, and Power

business researcher cannot commit both a Type I and a Type II error on the same hypothesis test (researcher's action is either in row 1 or row 2 but not both).

Generally speaking, alpha and beta are inversely related. That is, if alpha is reduced, beta is increased, and vice versa. In terms of the manufacturing assembly line, if management makes it harder for workers to shut down the assembly line (protect against Type I errors), then there is a greater chance that bad product will be made or that a serious problem with the line will arise (an increase in Type II errors). Legally, if the courts make it harder to send innocent people to jail, then they have made it easier to let guilty people go free. One way to reduce both errors simultaneously is to increase the sample size. If a larger sample is taken, it is more likely that it is representative of the population, which translates into a better chance that a business researcher will make a correct choice (and less chance of either a Type I or a Type II error). **Power**, which is equal to $1 - \beta$, is *the probability of a statistical test rejecting the null hypothesis when the null hypothesis is false*. More is said about the concept of power in Section 9.6.

9.1 Problems

9.1. Read each of the following statements. Assuming that statistical hypotheses are set up to test them, classify each as a one-tailed or a two-tailed test.

a. Maritz Marketing Research reports that 42% of all adults seek advice from others in selecting a lawyer. A business researcher wants to test this claim.

b. A study reported by Roper Starch Worldwide states that, on average, an influential person makes 5.8 recommendations about office equipment per year. You believe that this figure is too high and you want to test your belief.

c. The results of a survey conducted by *Purchasing* revealed that the mean age of a purchasing manager is 46.2. This seems too young to you and you want to conduct a test to determine if the average age of a purchasing manager is older than 46.2.

d. According to the U.S. Department of Labor Statistics Consumer Expenditure Survey, the average family spends $3,465 annually on meals at home. A business researcher would like to conduct a survey of families in her state to determine if this figure is true for her state, but she does not really have any idea whether or not the average might be higher or lower in her state.

9.2. In each of the following scenarios, tell if the researcher has committed a Type I error, a Type II error, or made a correct decision.

a. A researcher is testing to determine if .31 of all families own more than one car. His null hypothesis is that the population proportion is .31. He randomly samples 600 families and obtains a sample proportion of .33 that own more than one car. Based on this sample data, his decision is to fail to reject the null hypothesis. The actual population proportion is .31.

b. Suppose it is generally known that the average price per square foot for a home in a particular U.S. suburb is $73. A researcher believes that due to the economy, the average may now be less than that. To test her belief, she takes a random sample of 45 homes in this community, resulting in a sample mean of $70 per square foot. The researcher's decision based on this sample information is to fail to reject the null hypothesis. The actual average price per square foot is now $68.

c. Suppose a utility researcher knows from past experience that the average water bill for a 2000-square-foot home in a large Midwest city is $25 per month. The utility researcher wants to test to determine if this figure is still true today. Her null hypothesis is that the population mean is $25. To test this, she randomly samples 63 homes, resulting in a sample mean of $29. From this, she decides to reject the null hypothesis. The actual average is $27.

d. According to *PR Newswire*, 71% of all expectant mothers wish they had to go to only one source to get their baby information. Suppose in your region of the country, you think that this figure is too high so you conduct a test of 358 expectant mothers. In your study, only 66% of the expectant mothers wish they had to go to only one source to get their baby information. Based on this, your decision is to reject the null hypothesis. It turns out that in actuality, 71% of all expectant mothers in your region of the country wish they had to go to only one source to get their information.

9.2 Testing Hypotheses About a Population Mean Using the z Statistic (σ Known)

One of the most basic hypothesis tests is a test about a population mean. A business researcher might be interested in testing to determine whether an established or accepted mean value for an industry is still true or in testing a hypothesized mean value for a new theory or product. As an example, a computer products company sets up a telephone service to assist customers by providing technical support. The average wait time during weekday hours is 37 minutes. However, a recent hiring effort added technical consultants to the system; management believes that the average wait time decreased, and they want to prove it. Other business scenarios resulting in hypothesis tests of a single mean might include the following:

- A financial investment firm wants to test to determine whether the average hourly change in the Dow Jones Average over a 10-year period is +0.25.
- A manufacturing company wants to test to determine whether the average thickness of a plastic bottle is 2.4 millimeters.
- A retail store wants to test to determine whether the average age of its customers is less than 40 years.

Formula 9.1 can be used to test hypotheses about a single population mean when σ is known if the sample size is large ($n \geq 30$) for any population and for small samples ($n < 30$) if x is known to be normally distributed in the population.

z Test for a Single Mean

$$z = \frac{\bar{x} - \mu}{\frac{\sigma}{\sqrt{n}}}$$

(9.1)

An Example Using the Eight-Step Approach   A survey of CPAs across the United States found that the average net income for sole-proprietor CPAs is $98,500. Because this survey is over a decade old, an accounting researcher wants to test this figure by taking a random sample of 112 sole-proprietor accountants in the United States to determine whether the net income figure has changed or not. The researcher is using the eight-step approach to hypothesis testing to accomplish this. It is assumed that the population standard deviation of net incomes for sole-proprietor CPAs is $14,530.

Step 1   At step 1, the hypotheses must be established. Because the researcher is testing to determine whether the figure has changed, the alternative hypothesis is that the mean net income is not $98,500. The null hypothesis is that the mean still equals $98,500. The statistical hypotheses are:

$$H_0: \mu = \$98,500$$

$$H_a: \mu \neq \$98,500$$

Step 2   At step 2, the appropriate statistical test and sampling distribution is determined. Because the population standard deviation is known ($14,530), the sample size is greater than 30, and the researcher is using the sample mean as the statistic, the z test in Formula 9.1 is the appropriate test statistic:

$$z = \frac{\bar{x} - \mu}{\frac{\sigma}{\sqrt{n}}}$$

Source: Adapted from Daniel J. Flaherty, Raymond A. Zimmerman, and Mary Ann Murray, "Benchmarking Against the Best," *Journal of Accountancy* (July 1995), pp. 85–88.

Step 3 At step 3, the Type I error rate, or alpha, which is .05, is specified for this problem.

Step 4 At step 4, the decision rule is stated for the problem. Because the test is two-tailed and alpha is .05, there is $\alpha/2$ or .025 of the area in each of the tails of the distribution. Thus, the rejection region is in the two ends of the distribution with 2.5% of the area in each tail. There is a .4750 area between the mean and each of the critical values that separate the tails of the distribution (the rejection region) from the nonrejection region. By using this .4750 area and Table A.5, the critical *z* value can be obtained:

$$z_{\alpha/2} = \pm 1.96$$

Figure 9.5 displays the problem with the rejection regions and the critical values of *z*. The decision rule is that if the data gathered produce a *z* value greater than 1.96 or less than −1.96, the test statistic is in one of the rejection regions and the decision is to reject the null hypothesis. If the observed *z* value calculated from the data is between −1.96 and +1.96, the decision is to not reject the null hypothesis because the observed *z* value is in the nonrejection region.

Step 5 Gather the data. Suppose the 112 CPAs who respond to the survey produce a sample mean of $102,220.

Step 6 The value of the test statistic is calculated by using $\bar{x} = \$102,220$, $n = 112$, $\sigma = \$14,530$, and a hypothesized $\mu = \$98,500$:

$$z = \frac{102,220 - 98,500}{\dfrac{14,530}{\sqrt{112}}} = 2.71$$

Step 7 Reach a statistical conclusion. Because this test statistic, $z = 2.71$, is greater than the critical value of *z* (+1.96) in the upper tail of the distribution, the statistical conclusion reached at step 7 is to reject the null hypothesis. The "calculated" test statistic, in this case $z = 2.71$, is often referred to as the *observed value*. Thus, the observed value of *z* for this problem is 2.71 and the critical value of *z* for this problem is 1.96. The **observed value** is a statistic computed from data gathered in an experiment that is used in the determination of whether to reject or not reject the null hypothesis.

Step 8 At step 8, a managerial decision is made. The manager asks the researcher, "What does this result mean?" Statistically, the researcher has enough evidence to reject the figure of $98,500 as the true population average net income for sole-proprietor CPAs. Although the researcher conducted a two-tailed test, the evidence gathered indicates that the population average may have increased, and the sample mean of $102,220 is $3,720 higher than the national mean being tested. While the researcher can conclude that the population average is more than before, because the $102,220 is only a sample mean, it offers no guarantee that the population average for all sole-proprietor CPAs is

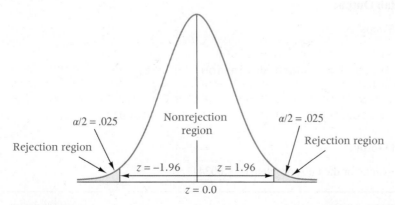

FIGURE 9.5 **CPA Net Income Example Showing the Locations of the Decision Rule**

$3,720 more. Other samples might produce different sample means. Managerially, this statistical finding may mean that CPAs will be more expensive to hire either as full-time employees or as consultants. It may mean that consulting services have gone up in price. For new accountants, it may mean the potential for greater earning power.

Using the *p*-Value to Test Hypotheses

Another way to reach a statistical conclusion in hypothesis testing problems is by using the *p*-value method. The *p*-value method is a method of testing hypotheses in which there is no preset level of α nor critical values of the test statistic. Decisions about rejecting or failing to reject the null hypothesis are made using a *p*-value, which is the probability of getting a test statistic at least as extreme as the observed test statistic computed under the assumption that the null hypothesis is true. The *p*-value is sometimes referred to as the observed significance level.

The *p*-value method has grown in importance with the increasing use of statistical computer packages to test hypotheses. The beauty of this method is that most computer statistical packages yield a *p*-value for virtually every analysis. *The p-value defines the smallest value of alpha for which the null hypothesis can be rejected.* For example, if the *p*-value of a test is .038, the null hypothesis cannot be rejected at $\alpha = .01$ because .038 is the smallest value of alpha for which the null hypothesis can be rejected and is larger than .01. However, the null hypothesis can be rejected for $\alpha = .05$ because the *p*-value = .038 is smaller than $\alpha = .05$.

How does one manually solve for a *p*-value? Suppose a researcher is conducting a one-tailed test with a rejection region in the upper tail, and the researcher obtains an observed test statistic of $z = 2.04$ from the sample data. Using the standard normal table, Table A.5, we find that the probability of randomly obtaining a *z* value this great or greater by chance is .0207 (.5000 − .4793). Thus, the *p*-value for this problem is .0207. Using this information, the researcher would reject the null hypothesis for $\alpha = .05$ or .10 or any value larger than .0207. The researcher would *not* reject the null hypothesis for any alpha value less than .0207 (in particular, $\alpha = .01$, .001, etc.). When conducting two-tailed tests, recall that we split alpha to determine the critical value of the test statistic. For a two-tailed test, the *p*-value can be compared to $\alpha/2$ to reach a statistical conclusion. If the *p*-value is less than $\alpha/2$, the decision is to reject the null hypothesis.

Note: The business researcher should be cautioned that some statistical computer packages are programmed to double the observed probability and report that value as the *p*-value when the user signifies that a two-tailed test is being requested. The researcher then compares this *p*-value to alpha values (rather than $\alpha/2$) to decide whether to reject the null hypothesis.

As an example of using *p*-values with a two-tailed test, consider the CPA net income problem. The observed test statistic for this problem is $z = 2.71$. Using Table A.5, we can calculate the probability of obtaining a test statistic at least this extreme if the null hypothesis is true as .5000 − .4966 = .0034. The *p*-value for this problem is .0034. In the Minitab output shown in Figure 9.6, the *p*-value is .0068 (but rounded to .0070). Minitab doubles

---

Minitab Output

One-Sample Z

Test of μ = 98500 vs ≠ 98500
The assumed standard deviation = 14530

N	Mean	SE Mean	95% CI	Z	P
112	102220	1373	(99529, 104911)	2.71	0.007

Excel Output

The *p*-value for the CPA problem is .0034

FIGURE 9.6 Minitab and Excel Output for CPA Problem Displaying *p*-Values

the *p*-value on a two-tailed test so that the researcher can compare the *p*-value to α to reach a statistical conclusion. On the other hand, when Excel yields a *p*-value in its output, it always gives the one-tailed value, which in this case is .0034 (see output in Figure 9.6). To reach a statistical conclusion from an Excel-produced *p*-value when doing a two-tailed test, the researcher must compare the *p*-value to $\alpha/2$. If alpha is .05, then $\alpha/2 = .025$. If alpha is .01, then $\alpha/2$ is .0050. Since the *p*-value of .0034 is less than both of these, we select the smallest value of alpha for which $\alpha/2$ is greater than the *p*-value. We can say that the null hypothesis is rejected using $\alpha = .01$.

Table 9.2 summarizes the decisions that can be made using various *p*-values for a one-tailed test. To use this for a two-tailed test, compare the *p*-value to $\alpha/2$. Because $\alpha = .10$ is usually the largest value of alpha used by most researchers, if a *p*-value is not less than .10 for a one-tailed test, then the decision is made to fail to reject the null hypothesis. In other words, the null hypothesis is not rejected for *p*-values of .579 or .106 or .283, etc. If a *p*-value is less than .10 but not less than .05, then the null hypothesis can be rejected for $\alpha = .10$. If it is less than .05 but not less than .01, then the null hypothesis can be rejected for $\alpha = .05$, and so on.

Testing the Mean with a Finite Population

If the hypothesis test for the population mean is being conducted with a known finite population, the population information can be incorporated into the hypothesis-testing formula. Doing so can increase the potential for rejecting the null hypothesis. However, remember from Chapter 7 that if the sample size is less than 5% of the population, the finite correction factor does not significantly alter the solution. Formula 9.1 can be amended to include the population information where *N* equals the size of the population.

Formula to Test Hypotheses About μ with a Finite Population

$$z = \frac{\bar{x} - \mu}{\dfrac{\sigma}{\sqrt{n}}\sqrt{\dfrac{N - n}{N - 1}}} \tag{9.2}$$

In the CPA net income example, suppose only 600 sole-proprietor CPAs practice in the United States. A sample of 112 CPAs taken from a population of only 600 CPAs is 18.67% of the population and therefore is much more likely to be representative of the population than a sample of 112 CPAs taken from a population of 20,000 CPAs (.56% of the population). The finite correction factor takes this difference into consideration and allows for an increase in the observed value of *z*. The observed *z* value would change to

$$z = \frac{\bar{x} - \mu}{\dfrac{\sigma}{\sqrt{n}}\sqrt{\dfrac{N - n}{N - 1}}} = \frac{102,220 - 98,500}{\dfrac{14,530}{\sqrt{112}}\sqrt{\dfrac{600 - 112}{600 - 1}}} = \frac{3,720}{1,239.2} = 3.00$$

TABLE 9.2 Rejecting Null Hypothesis Using *p*-Values for One-Tailed Tests

RANGE OF *p*-VALUES	REJECTION RANGE
p-value > .10	Cannot reject the null hypothesis for commonly accepted values of alpha
.05 < *p*-value ≤ .10	Reject the null hypothesis for $\alpha = .10$
.01 < *p*-value ≤ .05	Reject the null hypothesis for $\alpha = .05$
.001 < *p*-value ≤ .01	Reject the null hypothesis for $\alpha = .01$
.0001 < *p*-value ≤ .001	Reject the null hypothesis for $\alpha = .001$

Use of the finite correction factor increased the observed z value from 2.71 to 3.00. The decision to reject the null hypothesis does not change with this new information. However, on occasion, the finite correction factor can make the difference between rejecting and failing to reject the null hypothesis.

Using the Critical Value Method to Test Hypotheses

Another method of testing hypotheses is the critical value method. In the CPA income example, the null hypothesis was rejected because the computed value of z was in the rejection zone. What mean income would it take to cause the observed z value to be in the rejection zone? The **critical value method** *determines the critical mean value required for z to be in the rejection region and uses it to test the hypotheses.*

This method also uses Formula 9.1. However, instead of an observed z, a critical $\bar{x}$ value, $\bar{x}_c$, is determined. The critical table value of z_c is inserted into the formula, along with μ and σ. Thus,

$$z_c = \frac{\bar{x}_c - \mu}{\dfrac{\sigma}{\sqrt{n}}}$$

Substituting values from the CPA income example gives

$$\pm 1.96 = \frac{\bar{x}_c - 98,500}{\dfrac{14,530}{\sqrt{112}}}$$

or

$$\bar{x}_c = 98,500 \pm 1.96\frac{14,530}{\sqrt{112}} = 98,500 \pm 2691$$

$$\text{lower } \bar{x}_c = 95,809 \text{ and upper } \bar{x}_c = 101,191.$$

Figure 9.7 depicts graphically the rejection and nonrejection regions in terms of means instead of z scores.

With the critical value method, most of the computational work is done ahead of time. In this problem, before the sample means are computed, the analyst knows that a sample mean value of greater than \$101,191 or less than \$95,809 must be attained to reject the hypothesized population mean. Because the sample mean for this problem was \$102,220, which is greater than \$101,191, the analyst rejects the null hypothesis. This method is particularly attractive in industrial settings where standards can be set ahead of time and then quality control technicians can gather data and compare actual measurements of products to specifications.

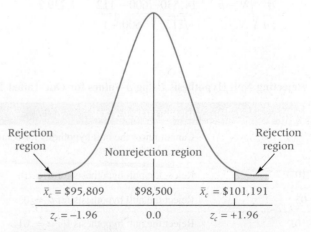

FIGURE 9.7   **Rejection and Nonrejection Regions for Critical Value Method**

DEMONSTRATION PROBLEM 9.1

According to Consumer Reports National Research Center, the average out-of-pocket expenditure in the United States for a dental tooth filling procedure if a person is insured is $141. Suppose a consumer researcher believes that such a procedure is more expensive now, and she wants to conduct a hypothesis to confirm her belief. She sets up a study in which a random sample of 32 recent tooth fillings is taken from across the United States. The resulting out-of-pocket expenditures for such fillings are given below. Previous studies reveal that the population standard deviation for such data is $30. The value of alpha for her study is set at .05. Use these data and the eight-step approach for testing her hypotheses on these data.

147	152	119	142	163	151	123	118
145	166	149	130	158	175	142	160
175	125	147	210	132	156	139	122
163	175	120	135	207	141	170	110

Solution

Step 1. Establish the hypotheses. Because the researcher wants to prove that this procedure is more expensive, she is conducting a one-tailed test in the upper tail. Her alternative hypothesis is that the mean expense is more than $141. The null hypothesis is that the mean still equals $141. The statistical hypotheses are:

$$H_0: \mu = \$141$$
$$H_a: \mu > \$141$$

Step 2. Determine the appropriate statistical test and sampling distribution. Because the population standard deviation is known ($30), the sample size is greater than 30, and the researcher is using the mean as the statistic, the z test in Formula 9.1 is the appropriate test statistic.

$$z = \frac{\bar{x} - \mu}{\dfrac{\sigma}{\sqrt{n}}}$$

Step 3. Specify the Type I error rate. Alpha is .05 for this problem.

Step 4. Establish the decision rule. Because this test is one-tailed, alpha = .05 is in the upper tail of the distribution. Thus, the rejection region is in the upper tail of the distribution and contains 5% of the area of the distribution. There is .4500 of the area between the mean and the critical value that separates the tail of the distribution (the rejection region) from the nonrejection region. By using this .4500 and Table A.5, the critical z value can be obtained.

$$z_{.05} = +1.645$$

Shown in Figure 9.8 is a graph of the problem with the rejection region and the critical value of z. The decision rule is that if the data gathered produce an observed z value greater than 1.645, the

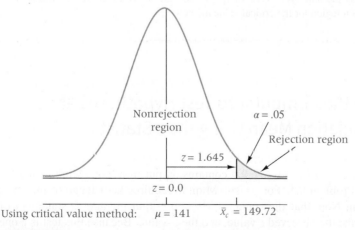

FIGURE 9.8 **Graph of the Dental Problem Rejection and Nonrejection Regions**

test statistic is in the rejection region and the decision is to reject the null hypothesis. If the observed z value is less than $+1.645$, the decision is to fail to reject the null hypothesis because the observed z value is in the nonrejection region.

Step 5. Gather the data. The 32 observed expense values are given. The sample mean of these data is $148.97.

Step 6. The value of the test statistic is calculated by using $\bar{x} = 148.97$, $n = 32$, and $\sigma = \$30$, and a hypothesized $\mu = \$141$:

$$z = \frac{148.97 - 141}{\frac{30}{\sqrt{32}}} = 1.50$$

Step 7. Statistical conclusion. Because this test statistic, $z = 1.50$, is less than the critical value of $z(+1.645)$ in the upper tail of the distribution, the statistical conclusion is to fail to reject the null hypothesis. The same conclusion can be reached using the p-value method. The observed test statistic is $z = 1.50$. From Table A.5, the probability of getting a z value at least this extreme when the null hypothesis is true is $.5000 - .4332 = .0668$. Since the p-value is greater than $\alpha = .05$, the decision is to fail to reject the null hypothesis. Remember, the p-value, in this case $.0668$, is the smallest value of alpha for which the null hypothesis can be rejected. If alpha had been $.10$, then the decision based on this p-value would have been to reject the null hypothesis. Note that we reach the same conclusion whether we use the critical value or the p-value.

Step 8. Managerial implications. The consumer researcher does not have the statistical evidence to declare that the average out-of-pocket expense of getting a tooth filling is higher than $141. One might use the results of this study to argue that dentists are holding the line on expenses and/or that there is little or no inflation in the area of dental work.

Using the critical value method: For what sample mean (or more extreme) value would the null hypothesis be rejected? This critical sample mean can be determined by using the critical z value associated with alpha, $z_{.05} = 1.645$.

$$z_c = \frac{\bar{x}_c - \mu}{\frac{\sigma}{\sqrt{n}}}$$

$$1.645 = \frac{\bar{x}_c - 141}{\frac{30}{\sqrt{32}}}$$

$$\bar{x}_c = 149.72$$

The decision rule is that a sample mean more than 149.72 would be necessary to reject the null hypothesis. Because the mean obtained from the sample data is 148.97, the researchers fail to reject the null hypothesis. Figure 9.8 includes a scale with the critical sample mean and the rejection region for the critical value method.

Using the Computer to Test Hypotheses About a Population Mean Using the z Statistic

Both Minitab and Excel can be used to test hypotheses about a single population mean using the z statistic. **Figure 9.9** contains output from both Minitab and Excel for Demonstration Problem 9.1. For z tests, Minitab requires knowledge of the population standard deviation. Note that the standard Minitab output includes a statement of the one-tailed hypothesis, the observed z value, and the p-value. Because this test is a one-tailed test, the p-value was not doubled. The Excel output contains only the right-tailed p-value of the z statistic.

Minitab Output

One-Sample Z: Cost

Test of μ = 141 vs > 141
The assumed standard deviation = 30

Variable	N	Mean	StDev	SE Mean	95% Lower Bound	Z	P
Cost	32	148.97	23.99	5.30	(140.25)	1.50	0.066

Excel Output

The *p*-value for the dental cost problem is   .0665

FIGURE 9.9   **Minitab and Excel Output for Demonstration Problem 9.1**

9.2 Problems

9.3. a. Use the data given to test the following hypotheses.

$$H_0: \mu = 25 \qquad H_a: \mu \neq 25$$

$$\bar{x} = 28.1, \, n = 57, \qquad \sigma = 8.46, \, \alpha = .01$$

b. Use the *p*-value to reach a statistical conclusion.

c. Using the critical value method, what are the critical sample mean values?

9.4. Use the data given to test the following hypotheses. Assume the data are normally distributed in the population.

$$H_0: \mu = 7.48 \qquad H_a: \mu < 7.48$$

$$\bar{x} = 6.91, \, n = 24, \qquad \sigma = 1.21, \, \alpha = .01$$

9.5. a. Use the data given to test the following hypotheses.

$$H_0: \mu = 1200 \qquad H_a: \mu > 1200$$

$$\bar{x} = 1215, \, n = 113, \qquad \sigma = 100, \, \alpha = .10$$

b. Use the *p*-value to obtain the results.

c. Solve for the critical value required to reject the mean.

9.6. The Environmental Protection Agency releases figures on urban air soot in selected cities in the United States. For the city of St. Louis, the EPA claims that the average number of micrograms of suspended particles per cubic meter of air is 82. Suppose St. Louis officials have been working with businesses, commuters, and industries to reduce this figure. These city officials hire an environmental company to take random measures of air soot over a period of several weeks. The resulting data follow. Assume that the population standard deviation is 9.184. Use these data to determine whether the urban air soot in St. Louis is significantly lower than it was when the EPA conducted its measurements. Let $\alpha = .01$. If the null hypothesis is rejected, discuss the substantive hypothesis.

81.6	66.6	70.9	82.5	58.3	71.6	72.4
96.6	78.6	76.1	80.0	73.2	85.5	73.2
68.6	74.0	68.7	83.0	86.9	94.9	75.6
77.3	86.6	71.7	88.5	87.0	72.5	83.0
85.8	74.9	61.7	92.2			

9.7. According to the U.S. Bureau of Labor Statistics, the average weekly earnings of a production worker in manufacturing in the United States as of October 2014 was $827.27. Suppose a labor researcher wants to test to determine whether this figure is still accurate today. The researcher randomly selects 54 production workers from across the United States and obtains a representative earnings statement for one week from each worker. The resulting sample average is $843.56. Assuming a population standard deviation of $63.90 and a 5% level of significance, determine whether the mean weekly earnings of a production worker have changed.

9.8. According to a study several years ago by the Personal Communications Industry Association, the average cell phone user earns $62,600 per year. Suppose a researcher believes that the average annual earnings of a cell phone user are lower now, and he sets up a study in an attempt to prove his theory. He randomly samples 18 cell phone users and finds out that the average annual salary for this sample is $58,974, with a population standard deviation of $7,810. Use $\alpha = .01$ to test the researcher's theory. Assume wages of cell phone users are normally distributed in the population.

9.9. A manufacturing company produces valves in various sizes and shapes. One particular valve plate is supposed to have a tensile strength of 5 pounds per millimeter (lbs/mm). The company tests a random sample of 42 such valve plates from a lot of 650 valve plates. The sample mean is a tensile strength of 5.0611 lbs/mm, and the population standard deviation is 0.2803 lbs/mm. Use $\alpha = .10$ and test to determine whether the lot of valve plates has an average tensile strength of 5 lbs/mm.

9.10. According to a report released by CIBC entitled "Women Entrepreneurs: Leading the Charge," the average age for Canadian businesswomen in 2008 was 41. In the report, there was some indication that researchers believed that this mean age will increase. Suppose now, a few years later, business researchers in Canada want to test to determine if, indeed, the mean age of Canadian businesswomen has increased. The researchers randomly sample 97 Canadian businesswomen and ascertain that the sample mean age is 43.4. From past experience, it is known that the population standard deviation is 8.95. Test to determine if the mean age of Canadian businesswomen has increased using a 1% level of significance. What is the *p*-value for this test? What is the decision? If the null hypothesis is rejected, is the result substantive?

9.11. According to HowtoAdvice.com, the average price charged to a customer to have a 12′ by 18′ wall-to-wall carpet shampoo cleaned is about $50. Suppose that a start-up carpet-cleaning company believes that in the region in which it operates, the average price for this service is higher. To test this hypothesis, the carpet-cleaning company randomly contacts 23 customers who have recently had a 12′ by 18′ wall-to-wall carpet shampoo cleaned and asks the customers how much they were charged for the job. Suppose the resulting data are given below and that the population standard deviation price is $3.49. Use a 10% level of significance to test the hypothesis. Assume that such prices are normally distributed in the population. What is the observed value? What is the *p*-value? What is the decision? If the null hypothesis is rejected, is the result substantive?

$52	52	56	50	50	51	49	49	54	51	51	48
56	52	52	53	56	52	52	56	57	48	53	

9.12. The American Water Works Association estimates that the average person in the United States uses 123 gallons of water per day.

Suppose some researchers believe that more water is being used now and want to test to determine whether this is so. They randomly select a sample of Americans and carefully keep track of the water used by each sample member for a day, then analyze the results by using a statistical computer software package. The output is given here. Assume $\alpha = .05$. How many people were sampled? What were the sample mean? Was this a one- or two-tailed test? What was the result of the study? What decision could be stated about the null hypothesis from these results?

```
One-Sample Z: C1

Test of μ = 123 vs > 123
The assumed standard deviation = 27.68

                              95% Lower
N     Mean    SE Mean    Bound      Z      P
40   132.360   4.38     (123.78)   2.14   0.016
```

9.3 Testing Hypotheses About a Population Mean Using the *t* Statistic (σ Unknown)

Very often when a business researcher is gathering data to test hypotheses about a single population mean, the value of the population standard deviation is unknown and the researcher must use the sample standard deviation as an estimate of it. In such cases, the *z* test cannot be used.

Chapter 8 presented the *t* distribution, which can be used to analyze hypotheses about a single population mean when σ is unknown if the population is normally distributed for the measurement being studied. In this section, we will examine the *t* test for a single population mean. In general, this *t* test is applicable whenever the researcher is drawing a single random sample to test the value of a population mean (μ), the population standard deviation is unknown, and the population is normally distributed for the measurement of interest. Recall from Chapter 8 that the assumption that the data be normally distributed in the population is rather robust.

The formula for testing such hypotheses follows.

***t* Test for μ**

$$t = \frac{\bar{x} - \mu}{\frac{s}{\sqrt{n}}}$$

(9.3)

$$\text{df} = n - 1$$

Table 9.3 highlights the differences between the *z* test and the *t* test for single means.

The U.S. Farmers' Production Company builds large harvesters. For a harvester to be properly balanced when operating, a 25-pound plate is installed on its side. The machine that produces these plates is set to yield plates that average 25 pounds. The distribution of plates produced from the machine is normal. However, the shop supervisor is worried that the machine is out of adjustment and is producing plates that do not average 25 pounds. To test this concern, he randomly selects 20 of the plates produced the day before and weighs them.

TABLE 9.3 *z* Test vs. *t* Test for a Single Mean

	z TEST	*t* TEST
BASIC FORMULA:	$z = \dfrac{\bar{x} - \mu}{\dfrac{\sigma}{\sqrt{n}}}$	$t = \dfrac{\bar{x} - \mu}{\dfrac{s}{\sqrt{n}}}$
DEGREES OF FREEDOM (df):	Does not use degrees of freedom (df)	$df = n - 1$
POPULATION STANDARD DEVIATION (σ):	Must know the population standard deviation, σ	Do not know σ. Uses sample standard deviation, *s*
SAMPLE SIZE:	$n \geq 30$ always okay $n < 30$ okay only if population is normally distributed	Any size sample
ASSUMPTIONS:	No assumptions unless $n < 30$. If $n < 30$, population must be normally distributed	Population must be normally distributed in all cases

Table 9.4 shows the weights obtained, along with the computed sample mean and sample standard deviation.

We will use the eight-step process to test the shop supervisor's hypothesis.

Step 1 Establish the hypotheses. The test is being conducted to determine whether the machine is out of control, and the shop supervisor has not specified whether he believes the machine is producing plates that are too heavy or too light. Thus, a two-tailed test is appropriate. The statistical hypotheses for this problem are:

$$H_0: \mu = 25 \text{ pounds}$$
$$H_a: \mu \neq 25 \text{ pounds}$$

Step 2 Determine the appropriate statistical test and sampling distribution. Because the researcher is using the mean as the statistic, the population standard deviation is unknown, and the population is normally distributed, the *t* test in Formula 9.3 is the appropriate test statistic.

$$t = \frac{\bar{x} - \mu}{\dfrac{s}{\sqrt{n}}}$$

Step 3 Specify the Type I error rate. Alpha is .05 for this problem.

Step 4 At step 4, the decision rule is stated for the problem. Because $n = 20$, the degrees of freedom are 19 ($20 - 1$). The *t* distribution table is a one-tailed table but the test for this problem is two-tailed, so alpha must be split, which yields $\alpha/2 = .025$, the value in each tail. (Note: To obtain the table *t* value when conducting a two-tailed test, always split alpha and use $\alpha/2$.) Using $\alpha/2 = .025$ and $df = 19$, from Appendix A.6, we can obtain the critical *t* value: $t_{.025,19} = \pm2.093$.

TABLE 9.4 Weights in Pounds of a Sample of 20 Plates

22.6	22.2	23.2	27.4	24.5
27.0	26.6	28.1	26.9	24.9
26.2	25.3	23.1	24.2	26.1
25.8	30.4	28.6	23.5	23.6

$\bar{x} = 25.51, \ s = 2.19, \ n = 20$

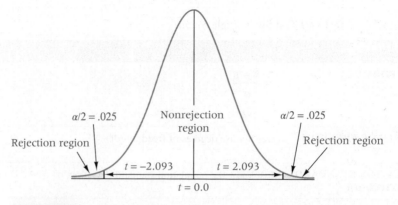

FIGURE 9.10 Rejection Regions, Nonrejection Region, and Critical Values for the Plate Problem

Figure 9.10 displays the problem with the rejection regions and the critical values of t. The decision rule is that if the data gathered produce a t value greater than $+2.093$ or less than -2.093, the test statistic is in one of the rejection regions and the decision is to reject the null hypothesis. If the observed t value calculated from the data is between -2.093 and $+2.093$, the decision is to not reject the null hypothesis because the observed t value is in the nonrejection region.

Step 5   Gather the data. The data are displayed in Table 9.4.

Step 6   The value of the test statistic is calculated by using $\bar{x} = 25.51$, $n = 20$, $s = 2.19$, and a hypothesized $\mu = 25$:

$$t = \frac{25.51 - 25}{\dfrac{2.19}{\sqrt{20}}} = 1.04$$

Step 7   Reach a statistical conclusion. Because this test statistic, $t = 1.04$, is less than the critical value of $t = 2.093$ in the upper tail of the distribution, the statistical conclusion reached is to fail to reject the null hypothesis. There is not enough evidence found in this sample to reject the null hypothesis that the population mean is 25 pounds. Table A.6, the table of critical values for the t distribution, is not complete enough to yield exact p-values for t statistics. However, Excel yields a one-tailed p-value of .1557 for an observed t of 1.04. Since this p-value is greater than $\alpha/2 = .025$, the decision using the p-value method is to fail to reject the null hypothesis. **Figure 9.11** depicts the t

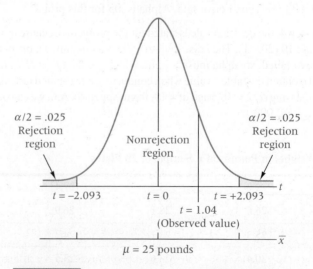

FIGURE 9.11 Graph of Observed and Critical t Values for the Machine Plate Example

Minitab Output

One-Sample T: Weight

Test of $\mu = 25$ vs $\neq 25$

Variable	N	Mean	StDev	SE Mean	95% CI	T	P
Weight	20	25.510	2.193	0.490	(24.484, 26.536)	1.04	0.311

Excel Output

t-Test: Two-Sample Assuming Unequal Variances

	Weight
Mean	25.51
Variance	4.8104
Observations	20
df	19
t Stat	1.04
P(T<=t) one-tail	0.1557
t Critical one-tail	1.73
P(T<=t) two-tail	0.3114
t Critical two-tail	2.09

FIGURE 9.12 **Minitab and Excel Output for the Machine Plate Example**

distribution for this example along with the critical values, the observed *t* value, and the rejection region.

Step 8 Managerial implications. Since the decision is to fail to reject the null hypothesis, there is not enough evidence for the shop supervisor to say that the machines are producing plates that do not average 25 lbs. In a sense, the results of the study are that the process is in control. However, the shop supervisor may still wish to monitor the process and retest the plates at a later time.

Figure 9.12 shows Minitab and Excel output for this example. Note that the Minitab output includes the observed *t* value (1.04) and the *p*-value (.311). Since this test is a two-tailed test, Minitab has doubled the one-tailed *p*-value for $t = 1.04$. Thus, the *p*-value of .311 can be compared directly to $\alpha = .05$ to reach the conclusion to fail to reject the null hypothesis.

The Excel output contains the observed *t* value (1.04) plus the *p*-value and the critical table *t* value for both a one-tailed and a two-tailed test. For the two-tailed test in the machine plate problem, Excel gives a table value of 2.09. Since the observed *t* value of 1.04 is less than this table value (2.09), the decision is to fail to reject the null hypothesis. This conclusion is confirmed by examining the Excel produced *p*-value of .1557 (for one-tail) which is greater than $\alpha/2 = .025$.

DEMONSTRATION PROBLEM 9.2

Figures released by the U.S. Department of Agriculture show that the average size of farms has increased since 1940. In 1940, the mean size of a farm was 174 acres; by 1997, the average size was 471 acres. Between those years, the number of farms decreased but the amount of tillable land remained relatively constant, so now farms are bigger. This trend might be explained, in part, by the inability of small farms to compete with the prices and costs of large-scale operations and to produce a level of income necessary to support the farmers' desired standard of living. Suppose an agribusiness researcher believes the average size of farms has now increased from the 1997 mean figure of 471 acres. To test this notion, she randomly sampled 23 farms across the United States and ascertained the size of each farm from county records. The data she gathered follow. Use a 5% level of significance to test her hypothesis. Assume that number of acres per farm is normally distributed in the population.

445	489	474	505	553	477	454	463	466
557	502	449	438	500	466	477	557	433
545	511	590	561	560				

Solution

Step 1. Establish the hypotheses. The researcher's hypothesis is that the average size of a U.S. farm is more than 471 acres. Because this theory is unproven, it is the alternate hypothesis. The null hypothesis is that the mean is still 471 acres.

$$H_0: \mu = 471 \text{ acres}$$

$$H_a: \mu > 471 \text{ acres}$$

Step 2. Determine the appropriate statistical test and sampling distribution. Because the researcher is using the mean as the statistic, the population standard deviation is unknown, and the population is normally distributed, the t test in Formula 9.3 is the appropriate test statistic.

$$t = \frac{\bar{x} - \mu}{\frac{s}{\sqrt{n}}}$$

Step 3. Specify the Type I error rate. Alpha is .05 for this problem.

Step 4. The decision rule. Because $n = 23$, the degrees of freedom are 22. This test is one-tailed, and the critical table t value is

$$t_{.05,22} = 1.717$$

Figure 9.13 displays the problem with the rejection region and the critical value of t. The decision rule is that if the data gathered produce a t value greater than 1.717, the test statistic is in the rejection region and the decision is to reject the null hypothesis. If the observed t value is less than 1.717, the decision is to fail to reject the null hypothesis.

Step 5. Gather the data. The data are given in the problem above.

Step 6. The value of the test statistic is calculated by using $\bar{x} = 498.78$, $n = 23$, $s = 46.94$, and a hypothesized $\mu = 471$:

$$t = \frac{498.78 - 471}{\frac{46.94}{\sqrt{23}}} = 2.84$$

Step 7. Reach a statistical conclusion. Because this test statistic, $t = 2.84$, is greater than the critical value of $t = 1.717$ in the upper tail of the distribution, the statistical conclusion reached is to reject the null hypothesis. The agribusiness researcher concludes that the average size of a farm is now greater than 471 acres.

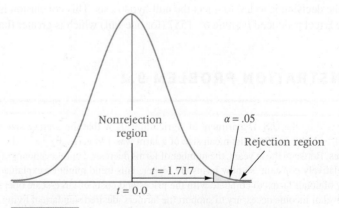

Nonrejection region

$\alpha = .05$

Rejection region

$t = 1.717$

$t = 0.0$

FIGURE 9.13 Location of Rejection Region, Nonrejection Region, and Critical Value for the Farm Problem

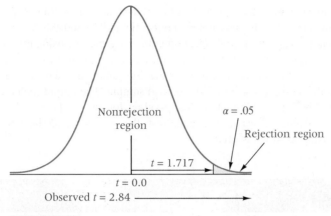

FIGURE 9.14 **Graphical Depiction of the Results of the Farm Problem**

Figure 9.14 shows where the observed *t* value falls relative to the critical value in the rejection region.

Step 8.   Managerial implications. Agribusiness researchers can speculate about what it means to have larger farms. The increase in average farm size from 471 acres to almost 500 acres may be substantive. It could mean that small farms are not financially viable. It might mean that corporations are buying out small farms and that large company farms are on the increase. Such a trend might spark legislative movements to protect the small farm. Larger farm sizes might also affect commodity trading.

Using the Computer to Test Hypotheses About a Population Mean Using the *t* Test

Minitab has the capability of computing a one-sample *t* test for means. **Figure 9.15** contains Minitab output for Demonstration Problem 9.2. The output contains the hypotheses being

Minitab Output

One-Sample T: Acres

Test of μ = 471 vs > 471

Variable	N	Mean	StDev	SE Mean	95% Lower Bound	T	P
Acres	23	498.78	46.94	9.79	481.97	2.84	0.005

Excel Output

t-Test: Two-Sample Assuming Unequal Variances

	Acres
Mean	498.783
Variance	2203.632
Observations	23
df	22
t Stat	2.84
P(T<=t)one-tail	0.0048
t Critical one-tail	1.72
P(T<=t)two-tail	0.0096
t Critical two-tail	2.07

FIGURE 9.15 **Minitab and Excel Output for Demonstration Problem 9.2**

tested, the sample statistics, the observed t value (2.84), and the p-value (.005). Because the p-value is less than $\alpha = .05$, the decision is to reject the null hypothesis.

Excel does not have a one-sample t test function. However, by using the two-sample t test for means with unequal variances, the results for a one-sample test can be obtained. This is accomplished by inputting the sample data for the first sample and the value of the parameter being tested (in this case, $\mu = 471$) for the second sample. The output includes the observed t value (2.84) and both the table t values and p-values for one- and two-tailed tests. Because Demonstration Problem 9.2 was a one-tailed test, the p-value of .0048, which is the same value obtained using Minitab, is used.

9.3 Problems

9.13. A random sample of size 20 is taken, resulting in a sample mean of 16.45 and a sample standard deviation of 3.59. Assume x is normally distributed and use this information and $\alpha = .05$ to test the following hypotheses.

$$H_0: \mu = 16 \qquad H_a: \mu \neq 16$$

9.14. A random sample of 51 items is taken, with $\bar{x} = 58.42$ and $s^2 = 25.68$. Use these data to test the following hypotheses, assuming you want to take only a 1% risk of committing a Type I error and that x is normally distributed.

$$H_0: \mu = 60 \qquad H_a: \mu < 60$$

9.15. The following data were gathered from a random sample of 11 items.

1200	1175	1080	1275	1201	1387
1090	1280	1400	1287	1225	

Use these data and a 5% level of significance to test the following hypotheses, assuming that the data come from a normally distributed population.

$$H_0: \mu = 1160 \qquad H_a: \mu > 1160$$

9.16. The following data (in pounds), which were selected randomly from a normally distributed population of values, represent measurements of a machine part that is supposed to weigh, on average, 8.3 pounds.

8.1	8.4	8.3	8.2	8.5	8.6	8.4	8.3	8.4	8.2
8.8	8.2	8.2	8.3	8.1	8.3	8.4	8.5	8.5	8.7

Use these data and $\alpha = .01$ to test the hypothesis that the parts average 8.3 pounds.

9.17. A hole-punch machine is set to punch a hole 1.84 centimeters in diameter in a strip of sheet metal in a manufacturing process. The strip of metal is then creased and sent on to the next phase of production, where a metal rod is slipped through the hole. It is important that the hole be punched to the specified diameter of 1.84 cm. To test punching accuracy, technicians have randomly sampled 12 punched holes and measured the diameters. The data (in centimeters) follow. Use an alpha of .10 to determine whether the holes are being punched an average of 1.84 centimeters. Assume the punched holes are normally distributed in the population.

1.81	1.89	1.86	1.83
1.85	1.82	1.87	1.85
1.84	1.86	1.88	1.85

9.18. Suppose a study reports that the average price for a gallon of self-serve regular unleaded gasoline is $3.76. You believe that the figure is higher in your area of the country. You decide to test this claim for your part of the United States by randomly calling gasoline stations. Your random survey of 25 stations produces the following prices.

$3.87	$3.89	$3.76	$3.80	$3.97
3.80	3.83	3.79	3.80	3.84
3.76	3.67	3.87	3.69	3.95
3.75	3.83	3.74	3.65	3.95
3.81	3.74	3.74	3.67	3.70

Assume gasoline prices for a region are normally distributed. Do the data you obtained provide enough evidence to reject the null hypothesis? Use a 1% level of significance.

9.19. Suppose that in past years the average price per square foot for warehouses in the United States has been $32.28. A national real estate investor wants to determine whether that figure has changed now. The investor hires a researcher who randomly samples 49 warehouses that are for sale across the United States and finds that the mean price per square foot is $31.67, with a sample standard deviation of $1.29. Assume that prices of warehouse footage are normally distributed in population. If the researcher uses a 5% level of significance, what statistical conclusion can be reached? What are the hypotheses?

9.20. Major cities around the world compete with each other to attract new businesses. Some of the criteria that businesses use to judge cities as potential locations for their headquarters might include the labor pool; the environment, including work, governmental, and living; the tax structure; the availability of skilled/educated labor; housing; education; medical care; and others. Suppose in a study done several years ago, the city of Atlanta received a mean rating of 3.51 (on a scale of 1 to 5 and assuming an interval level of data) on housing, but that since that time, considerable residential building has occurred in the Atlanta area such that city leaders feel the mean might now be higher. They hire a team of researchers to conduct a survey of businesses around the world to determine how businesses now rate the city on housing (and other variables). Sixty-one businesses take part in the new survey, with a result that Atlanta receives a mean response of 3.72 on housing with a sample standard deviation of 0.65. Assuming that such responses are normally distributed, use a 1% level of significance and these data to test to determine if the mean housing rating for the city of Atlanta by businesses has significantly increased.

9.21. Based on population figures and other general information on the U.S. population, suppose it has been estimated that, on average, a family of four in the United States spends about $1,135 annually on dental procedures. Suppose further that a regional dental association wants to test to determine if this figure is accurate for its area of the country. To test this, 22 families of four are randomly selected from the population in that area of the country and a log is kept of the family's dental expenditures for one year. The resulting data are given below. Assuming that dental expenditures are normally distributed in the population, use the data and an alpha of .05 to test the dental association's hypothesis.

1008	812	1117	1323	1308	1415
831	1021	1287	851	930	730
699	872	913	944	954	987
1695	995	1003	994		

9.22. According to data released by the World Bank, the mean PM10 (particulate matter) concentration for the city of Kabul, Afghanistan, in 1999 was 46. Suppose that because of efforts to improve air quality in Kabul, increases in modernization, and efforts to establish environmental-friendly businesses, city leaders believe rates of particulate matter in Kabul have decreased. To test this notion, they randomly sample 12 readings over a one-year period with the resulting readings shown below. Do these data present enough evidence to determine that PM10 readings are significantly less now in Kabul? Assume that particulate readings are normally distributed and that $\alpha = .01$.

| 31 | 44 | 35 | 53 | 57 | 47 |
| 32 | 40 | 31 | 38 | 53 | 45 |

9.23. According to a National Public Transportation survey, the average commuting time for people who commute to a city with a population of 1 to 3 million is 19.0 minutes. Suppose a researcher lives in a city with a population of 2.4 million and wants to test this claim in her city. Assume that commuter times are normally distributed in the population. She takes a random sample of commuters and gathers data. The data are analyzed using both Minitab and Excel, and the output is shown here. What are the results of the study? What are the hypotheses?

Minitab Output

One-Sample T

```
Test of μ = 19 vs ≠ 19
N   Mean   StDev SE Mean  95% CI              T    P
26  19.534 4.100 0.804    (17.878, 21.190)  0.66 0.513
```

Excel Output

Mean	19.534
Variance	16.813
Observations	26
df	25
t Stat	0.66
P (T<=t)one-tail	0.256
t Critical one-tail	1.71
P (T<=t)two-tail	0.513
t Critical two-tail	2.06

9.4 Testing Hypotheses About a Proportion

Data analysis used in business decision making often contains proportions to describe such aspects as market share, consumer makeup, quality defects, on-time delivery rate, profitable stocks, and others. Business surveys often produce information expressed in proportion form, such as .45 of all businesses offer flexible hours to employees or .88 of all businesses have Web sites. Business researchers conduct hypothesis tests about such proportions to determine whether they have changed in some way. As an example, suppose a company held a 26%, or .26, share of the market for several years. Due to a massive marketing effort and improved product quality, company officials believe that the market share increased, and they want to prove it. Other examples of hypothesis testing about a single population proportion might include:

- A market researcher wants to test to determine whether the proportion of new car purchasers who are female has increased.
- A financial researcher wants to test to determine whether the proportion of companies that were profitable last year in the average investment officer's portfolio is .60.
- A quality manager for a large manufacturing firm wants to test to determine whether the proportion of defective items in a batch is less than .04.

Formula 9.4 for inferential analysis of a proportion was introduced in Section 7.3 of Chapter 7. Based on the central limit theorem, this formula makes possible the testing of hypotheses about the population proportion in a manner similar to that of the formula used to test sample means. Recall that $\hat{p}$ denotes a sample proportion and p denotes the population proportion. To validly use this test, the sample size must be large enough such that $n \cdot p \geq 5$ and $n \cdot q \geq 5$.

z Test of a Population Proportion

$$z = \frac{\hat{p} - p}{\sqrt{\dfrac{p \cdot q}{n}}}$$ (9.4)

where

$\hat{p}$ = sample proportion
p = population proportion
$q = 1 - p$

A manufacturer believes exactly 8% of its products contain at least one minor flaw. Suppose a company researcher wants to test this belief. The researcher will randomly select a sample of 200 product items for the test and will use the eight-step approach to test this hypothesis.

Step 1 Establish the hypotheses. The null and alternative hypotheses are:

$$H_0: p = .08$$

$$H_a: p \neq .08$$

Step 2 Determine the appropriate statistical test and sampling distribution. Because we are testing a single population proportion and the sample size is 200, the z test in Formula 9.4 is the appropriate test statistic.

$$z = \frac{\hat{p} - p}{\sqrt{\dfrac{p \cdot q}{n}}}$$

Step 3 Specify the Type I error rate. Alpha is .10 for this problem.

Step 4 Establish the decision rule. Because the test is two-tailed and alpha is .10, there is $\alpha/2$ or .05 area in each of the tails of the distribution. Thus, the rejection region is in the two ends of the distribution with 5% of the area in each tail. There is a .4500 area between the middle of the distribution and each of the critical values that separate the tails of the distribution (the rejection region) from the nonrejection region. Using a .4500 area and Table A.5, the critical z value can be obtained:

$$z_{\alpha/2} = \pm 1.645$$

Figure 9.16 displays the problem with the rejection regions and the critical values of z. The decision rule is that if the data gathered produce a z value greater than +1.645 or less than −1.645, the test statistic is in one of the rejection regions and the decision is to reject the null hypothesis. If the observed z value calculated from the data is between −1.645 and +1.645, the decision is to not reject the null hypothesis because the observed z value is in the nonrejection region.

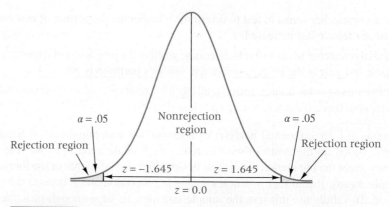

FIGURE 9.16 **Graph of the Manufacturing Flaw Problem Rejection and Nonrejection Regions and Critical Values**

Step 5   Gather the data. The company researcher has randomly selected a sample of 200 product items, inspected each one for flaws, and determined that 24 items have at least one minor flaw.

Step 6   Calculate the value of the test statistic. The sample proportion is determined by:

$$\hat{p} = \frac{x}{n} = \frac{24}{200} = .12$$

The value of the test statistic is calculated by using $\hat{p} = .12$, $n = 200$, $p = .08$, and $q = 1 - p = 1 - .08 = .92$:

$$z = \frac{\hat{p} - p}{\sqrt{\dfrac{p \cdot q}{n}}} = \frac{.12 - .08}{\sqrt{\dfrac{(.08)(.92)}{200}}} = 2.09$$

Step 7   Statistical conclusion. Because this test statistic, $z = 2.09$, is greater than the critical value of z (+1.645) in the upper tail of the distribution, the statistical conclusion is to reject the null hypothesis. The same conclusion can be reached using the p-value method. The observed test statistic is $z = 2.09$. From Table A.5, the probability of getting a z value at least this extreme when the null hypothesis is true is $.5000 - .4817 = .0183$. Since the p-value is less than $\alpha/2 = .05$, the decision is to reject the null hypothesis. Note that we reach the same conclusion whether we use the critical value or the p-value.

Step 8   Managerial implications. The company researcher has the statistical evidence to declare that the proportion of product items with at least one minor flaw is higher than .08. The quality control people, management, and process engineers need to take a hard look at the processes involved in producing these items to determine why more than 8% of the product items have at least one flaw. There is indication from the sample results that the percent may be as high as 12% or even higher.

The Minitab output shown in **Figure 9.17** displays a p-value of .037 (two-tailed p-value) for this problem.

Suppose the researcher wanted to use the critical value method. He would enter the table values of $z_{.05} = \pm 1.645$ in the z formula for single sample proportions, along with the hypothesized population proportion and n, and solve for the critical value denoted as $\hat{p}_c$. The result is

$$z_{\alpha/2} = \frac{\hat{p}_c - p}{\sqrt{\dfrac{p \cdot q}{n}}}$$

$$\pm 1.645 = \frac{\hat{p}_c - .08}{\sqrt{\dfrac{(.08)(.92)}{200}}}$$

$$\hat{p}_c = .08 \pm 1.645 \sqrt{\frac{(.08)(.92)}{200}} = .08 \pm .032$$

$$= .048 \text{ and } .112$$

Using the critical value method, if the sample proportion is less than .048 or greater than .112, the decision will be to reject the null hypothesis. Since the sample proportion, $\hat{p}$, is .12, which

```
Test and CI for One Proportion

Test of p = 0.08 vs p ≠ 0.08

Sample   X    N    Sample p   90% CI                 Z-Value   P-Value
1        24   200  0.120000   (0.082204, 0.157796)   2.09      0.037

using the normal approximation.
```

FIGURE 9.17   **Minitab Output for the Flawed-Product Example**

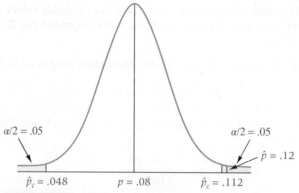

FIGURE 9.18 **Distribution Using Critical Value Method for the Flawed-Product Example**

is greater than .112, the decision here is to reject the null hypothesis. The proportion of products with at least one flaw is not .08. Figure 9.18 shows these critical values, the observed value and the rejection regions.

Thinking Critically About Statistics in Business Today

Testing Hypotheses About Commuting

How do Americans commute to work? A National Public Transportation survey taken a few years ago indicated that almost 80% of U.S. commuters drive alone to work, more than 11% use carpool, and approximately 5% use public transportation. Using hypothesis testing methodology presented in this chapter, researchers can test whether these proportions still hold true today as well as how these figures vary by region. For example, in New York City it is almost certain that the proportion of commuters using public transportation is much higher than 5%. In rural parts of the country where public transportation is unavailable, the proportion of commuters using public transportation would be zero.

What is the average travel time of a commute to work in the United States? According to the National Public Transportation Survey, travel time varies according to the type of transportation used. For example, the average travel time of a commute using a private vehicle is 20 minutes as compared to 42 minutes using

public transportation. In part, this difference can be accounted for by the travel speed in miles per hour: private vehicles average 35 miles per hour over a commute compared to 19 miles per hour averaged by public transportation vehicles. It is possible to test any of these means using hypothesis testing techniques presented in this chapter to either validate the figures or to determine whether the figures are no longer true.

THINGS TO PONDER

1. According to the statistics presented here, 80% of U.S. commuters drive alone to work. Why is this so? What are some reasons why Americans drive to work alone? Is it a good thing that Americans drive to work alone? What are some reasons why Americans might not want to drive to work alone?

2. The mean commute time for a private vehicle in the United States is about 20 minutes. Can you think of some reasons why Americans might want to reduce this figure? What are some ways that this figure might be reduced?

DEMONSTRATION PROBLEM 9.3

A survey of the morning beverage market shows that the primary breakfast beverage for 17% of Americans is milk. A milk producer in Wisconsin, where milk is plentiful, believes the figure is higher for Wisconsin. To test this idea, she contacts a random sample of 550 Wisconsin residents and asks which primary beverage they consumed for breakfast that day. Suppose 116 replied that milk was the primary beverage. Using a level of significance of .01 and the eight-step approach, test the idea that the milk figure is higher for Wisconsin.

Solution

Step 1. Establish the hypotheses. The milk producer's theory is that the proportion of Wisconsin residents who drink milk for breakfast is higher than the national proportion, which is the alternative hypothesis. The null hypothesis is that the proportion in Wisconsin does not differ from the national average. The null and alternative hypotheses are:

$$H_0: p = .17$$

$$H_a: p > .17$$

Step 2.   Determine the appropriate statistical test and sampling distribution. Because we are testing a single population proportion and the sample size is 550, the z test in Formula 9.4 is the appropriate test statistic.

$$z = \frac{\hat{p} - p}{\sqrt{\dfrac{p \cdot q}{n}}}$$

Step 3.   At step 3, the Type I error rate, or alpha, which is .01 is specified for this problem.

Step 4.   Establish the decision rule. Because the test is one-tailed and alpha is .01, there is .01 of the area in the upper tail of the distribution. Thus, the rejection region is in the upper end of the distribution with 1% of the area in the tail. There is .4900 area between the center of distribution and the critical value. By using this .4900 and Table A.5, the critical z value can be obtained:

$$z_{.01} = +2.33$$

Figure 9.19 displays the problem with the rejection region and the critical value of z. The decision rule is that if the data gathered produce a z value greater than +2.33, the test statistic is in the rejection region and the decision is to reject the null hypothesis. If the observed z value calculated from the data is less than +2.33, the decision is to not reject the null hypothesis because the observed z value is in the nonrejection region.

Step 5.   Gather the data. The researcher has randomly selected a sample of 550 Wisconsin residents and determined that 116 replied that milk was their primary breakfast beverage.

Step 6.   Calculate the value of the test statistic. The sample proportion is determined by:

$$\hat{p} = \frac{x}{n} = \frac{116}{550} = .211$$

The value of the test statistic is calculated by using $\hat{p} = .211$, $n = 550$, $p = .17$, and $q = 1 - p = 1 - .17 = .83$:

$$z = \frac{\hat{p} - p}{\sqrt{\dfrac{p \cdot q}{n}}} = \frac{.211 - .17}{\sqrt{\dfrac{(.17)(.83)}{550}}} = 2.56$$

Step 7.   Statistical conclusion. Because this test statistic, $z = 2.56$, is greater than the critical value of $z = 2.33$ in the upper tail of the distribution, the statistical conclusion is to reject the null hypothesis. The same conclusion can be reached using the p-value method. The observed test statistic is $z = 2.56$. From Table A.5, the probability of getting a z value at least this extreme when the null hypothesis is true is $.5000 - .4948 = .0052$. Since the p-value is less than $\alpha = .01$, the decision is to reject the null hypothesis.

Step 8.   Managerial implications. If the proportion of residents who drink milk for breakfast is higher in Wisconsin than in other parts of the United States, milk producers might have a market opportunity in Wisconsin that is not available in other parts of the country. The fact that more milk is sold in Wisconsin might mean that if Wisconsin milk producers appeal to markets outside Wisconsin in the same way they do inside the state, they might increase their market share of the breakfast beverage market in other states.

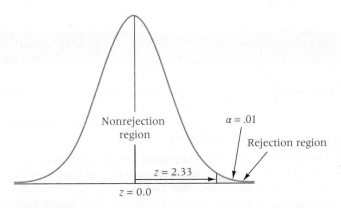

FIGURE 9.19   **Graph of the Wisconsin Milk Problem Rejection and Nonrejection Regions**

Is a sample proportion of almost .21 a substantive increase of .17? Certainly in a market of any size at all, an increase of almost 4% of the market share could be worth millions of dollars; in such a case, the significant increase might also be substantive.

A critical proportion can be solved for by

$$z_{.01} = \frac{\hat{p}_c - p}{\sqrt{\dfrac{p \cdot q}{n}}}$$

$$2.33 = \frac{\hat{p}_c - .17}{\sqrt{\dfrac{(.17)(.83)}{550}}}$$

$$\hat{p}_c = .17 + 2.33\sqrt{\frac{(.17)(.83)}{550}} = .17 + .037 = .207$$

With the critical value method, a sample proportion greater than .207 must be obtained to reject the null hypothesis. The sample proportion for this problem is .211, so the null hypothesis is also rejected with the critical value method.

Using the Computer to Test Hypotheses About a Population Proportion

Minitab has the capability of testing hypotheses about a population proportion. **Figure 9.20** shows the Minitab output for Demonstration Problem 9.3. Notice that the output includes a restatement of the hypotheses, the sample proportion, and the p-value. From this information, a decision regarding the null hypothesis can be made by comparing the p-value (.005) to α (.01). Because the p-value is less than α, the decision is to reject the null hypothesis.

Test and CI for One Proportion

Test of p = 0.17 vs p > 0.17

Sample	X	N	Sample p	99% Lower Bound	Z-Value	P-Value
1	116	550	0.210909	0.170442	2.55	0.005

Using the normal approximation.

FIGURE 9.20 **Minitab Output for Demonstration Problem 9.3**

9.4 Problems

9.24. Suppose you are testing H_0: $p = .45$ versus H_a: $p > .45$. A random sample of 310 people produces a value of $\hat{p} = .465$. Use $\alpha = .05$ to test this hypothesis.

9.25. Suppose you are testing H_0: $p = .63$ versus H_a: $p < .63$. For a random sample of 100 people, $x = 55$, where x denotes the number in the sample that have the characteristic of interest. Use a .01 level of significance to test this hypothesis.

9.26. Suppose you are testing H_0: $p = .29$ versus H_a: $p \neq .29$. A random sample of 740 items shows that 207 have this characteristic. With a .05 probability of committing a Type I error, test the hypothesis. For

the p-value method, what is the probability of the observed z value for this problem? If you had used the critical value method, what would the two critical values be? How do the sample results compare with the critical values?

9.27. The Independent Insurance Agents of America conducted a survey of insurance consumers and discovered that 48% of them always reread their insurance policies, 29% sometimes do, 16% rarely do, and 7% never do. Suppose a large insurance company invests considerable time and money in rewriting policies so that they will be more attractive and easy to read and understand. After using the new policies for a year, company managers want to determine whether rewriting the policies significantly changed the proportion of policy-holders who always reread their insurance policy. They contact 380 of the company's insurance consumers who purchased a policy in the past year and ask them whether they always reread their insurance policies. One hundred and sixty-four respond that they do. Use a 1% level of significance to test the hypothesis.

9.28. A study by Hewitt Associates showed that 79% of companies offer employees flexible scheduling. Suppose a researcher believes that in accounting firms this figure is lower. The researcher randomly selects 415 accounting firms and through interviews determines that 303 of these firms have flexible scheduling. With a 1% level of significance, does the test show enough evidence to conclude that a significantly lower proportion of accounting firms offer employees flexible scheduling?

9.29. A survey was undertaken by Bruskin/Goldring Research for Quicken to determine how people plan to meet their financial goals in the next year. Respondents were allowed to select more than one way to meet their goals. Thirty-one percent said that they were using a financial planner to help them meet their goals. Twenty-four percent were using family/friends to help them meet their financial goals, followed by broker/accountant (19%), computer software (17%), and books (9%). Suppose another researcher takes a similar survey of 600 people to test these results. If 200 people respond that they are going to use a financial planner to help them meet their goals, is this proportion enough evidence to reject the 31% figure generated in the Bruskin/Goldring survey using $\alpha = .10$? If 158 respond that they are going to use family/friends to help them meet their financial goals, is this result enough evidence to declare that the proportion is significantly higher than Bruskin/Goldring's figure of .24 if $\alpha = .05$?

9.30. Eighteen percent of U.S.-based multinational companies provide an allowance for personal long-distance calls for executives living overseas, according to the Institute for International Human Resources and the National Foreign Trade Council. Suppose a researcher thinks that U.S.-based multinational companies are having a more difficult time recruiting executives to live overseas and that an increasing number of these companies are providing an allowance for personal long-distance calls to these executives to ease the burden of living away from home. To test this hypothesis, a new study is conducted by contacting 376 multinational companies. Twenty-two percent of these surveyed companies are providing an allowance for personal long-distance calls to executives living overseas. Does the test show enough evidence to declare that a significantly higher proportion of multinational companies provide a long-distance call allowance? Let $\alpha = .01$.

9.31. A large manufacturing company investigated the service it received from suppliers and discovered that, in the past, 32% of all materials shipments were received late. However, the company recently installed a just-in-time system in which suppliers are linked more closely to the manufacturing process. A random sample of 118 deliveries since the just-in-time system was installed reveals that 22 deliveries were late. Use this sample information to test whether the proportion of late deliveries was reduced significantly. Let $\alpha = .05$.

9.32. Where do CFOs get their money news? According to Robert Half International, 47% get their money news from newspapers, 15% get it from communication/colleagues, 12% get it from television, 11% from the Internet, 9% from magazines, 5% from radio, and 1% don't know. Suppose a researcher wants to test these results. She randomly samples 67 CFOs and finds that 40 of them get their money news from newspapers. Does the test show enough evidence to reject the findings of Robert Half International? Use $\alpha = .05$.

9.5 Testing Hypotheses About a Variance

At times a researcher needs to test hypotheses about a population variance. For example, in the area of statistical quality control, manufacturers try to produce equipment and parts that are consistent in measurement. Suppose a company produces industrial wire that is specified to be a particular thickness. Because of the production process, the thickness of the wire will vary slightly from one end to the other and from lot to lot and batch to batch. Even if the average thickness of the wire as measured from lot to lot is on specification, the variance of the measurements might be too great to be acceptable. In other words, on the average the wire is the correct thickness, but some portions of the wire might be too thin and others unacceptably thick. By conducting hypothesis tests for the variance of the thickness measurements, the quality control people can monitor for variations in the process that are too great.

The procedure for testing hypotheses about a population variance is similar to the techniques presented in Chapter 8 for estimating a population variance from the sample variance. Formula 9.5 used to conduct these tests assumes a normally distributed population.

Formula for Testing Hypotheses About a Population Variance

$$\chi^2 = \frac{(n-1)s^2}{\sigma^2}$$

$$df = n - 1$$

(9.5)

Note: *As was mentioned in Chapter 8, the chi-square test of a population variance is extremely sensitive to violations of the assumption that the population is normally distributed.*

As an example, a manufacturing firm has been working diligently to implement a just-in-time inventory system for its production line. The final product requires the installation of a pneumatic tube at a particular station on the assembly line. With the just-in-time inventory system, the company's goal is to minimize the number of pneumatic tubes that are piled up at the station waiting to be installed. Ideally, the tubes would arrive just as the operator needs them. However, because of the supplier and the variables involved in getting the tubes to the line, most of the time there will be some buildup of tube inventory. The company expects that, on the average, about 20 pneumatic tubes will be at the station. However, the production superintendent does not want the variance of this inventory to be greater than 4. On a given day, the number of pneumatic tubes piled up at the workstation is determined eight different times and the following number of tubes are recorded.

23   17   20   29   21   14   19   24

Using these sample data, we can test to determine whether the variance is greater than 4. The hypothesis test is one tailed. Assume the number of tubes is normally distributed. The null hypothesis is that the variance is acceptable—the variance is equal to (or less than) 4. The alternative hypothesis is that the variance is greater than 4.

$$H_0: \sigma^2 = 4$$

$$H_a: \sigma^2 > 4$$

Suppose alpha is .05. Because the sample size is 8, the degrees of freedom for the critical table chi-square value are $8 - 1 = 7$. Using Table A.8, we find the critical chi-square value:

$$\chi^2_{.05,7} = 14.0671$$

Because the alternative hypothesis is greater than 4, the rejection region is in the upper tail of the chi-square distribution. The sample variance is calculated from the sample data to be

$$s^2 = 20.9821$$

The observed chi-square value is calculated as

$$\chi^2 = \frac{(8-1)(20.9821)}{4} = 36.72$$

Because this observed chi-square value, $\chi^2 = 36.72$, is greater than the critical chi-square table value, $\chi^2_{.05,7} = 14.0671$, the decision is to reject the null hypothesis. On the basis of this sample of eight data measurements, the population variance of inventory at this workstation is greater than 4. Company production personnel and managers might want to investigate further to determine whether they can find a cause for this unacceptable variance. **Figure 9.21** shows a chi-square distribution with the critical value, the rejection region, the nonrejection region, the value of α, and the observed chi-square value.

Using Excel, the p-value of the observed chi-square, 36.72, is determined to be .0000053. Because this value is less than $\alpha = .05$ the conclusion is to reject the null hypothesis using the p-value. In fact, using this p-value, the null hypothesis could be rejected for

$$\alpha = .00001$$

This null hypothesis can also be tested by the critical value method. Instead of solving for an observed value of chi-square, the critical chi-square value for alpha is inserted into Formula 9.5 along with the hypothesized value of σ^2 and the degrees of freedom $(n - 1)$.

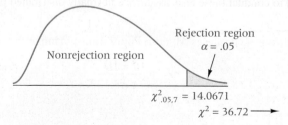

FIGURE 9.21 **Hypothesis Test Distribution for Pneumatic Tube Example**

Solving for s^2 yields a critical sample variance value, s_c^2.

$$\chi_c^2 = \frac{(n-1)s_c^2}{\sigma^2}$$

$$s_c^2 = \frac{\chi_c^2 \cdot \sigma^2}{(n-1)} = \frac{(14.0671)(4)}{7} = 8.038$$

The critical value of the sample variance is $s_c^2 = 8.038$. Because the observed sample variance actually was 20.9821, which is larger than the critical variance, the null hypothesis is rejected.

DEMONSTRATION PROBLEM 9.4

A small business has 37 employees. Because of the uncertain demand for its product, the company usually pays overtime on any given week. The company assumed that about 50 total hours of overtime per week is required and that the variance on this figure is about 25. Company officials want to know whether the variance of overtime hours has changed. Given here is a sample of 16 weeks of overtime data (in hours per week). Assume hours of overtime are normally distributed. Use these data to test the null hypothesis that the variance of overtime data is 25. Let $\alpha = .10$.

57	56	52	44
46	53	44	44
48	51	55	48
63	53	51	50

Solution

Step 1. This test is a two-tailed test. The null and alternative hypotheses are

$$H_0: \sigma^2 = 25$$
$$H_a: \sigma^2 \neq 25$$

Step 2. The test statistic is

$$\chi^2 = \frac{(n-1)s^2}{\sigma^2}$$

Step 3. Because this test is two tailed, $\alpha = .10$ must be split: $\alpha/2 = .05$

Step 4. The degrees of freedom are $16 - 1 = 15$. The two critical chi-square values are

$$\chi_{(1-.05),15}^2 = \chi_{.95,15}^2 = 7.26093$$
$$\chi_{.05,15}^2 = 24.9958$$

The decision rule is to reject the null hypothesis if the observed value of the test statistic is less than 7.26093 or greater than 24.9958.

Step 5. The data are as listed previously.

Step 6. The sample variance is

$$s^2 = 28.0625$$

The observed chi-square value is calculated as

$$\chi^2 = \frac{(n-1)s^2}{\sigma^2} = \frac{(15)(28.0625)}{25} - 16.84$$

Step 7. This observed chi-square value is in the nonrejection region because $\chi_{.95,15}^2 = 7.26094 < \chi_{observed}^2 = 16.84 < \chi_{.05,15}^2 = 24.9958$. The company fails to reject the null hypothesis. There is not enough evidence to declare that the population variance is different from 25.

Step 8. Managerial implications. This result indicates to the company managers that the variance of weekly overtime hours is about what they expected.

9.5 Problems

9.33. Test each of the following hypotheses by using the given information. Assume the populations are normally distributed.

a. $H_0: \sigma^2 = 20$
   $H_a: \sigma^2 > 20$
   $\alpha = .05$, $n = 15$, $s^2 = 32$

b. $H_0: \sigma^2 = 8.5$
   $H_a: \sigma^2 \neq 8.5$
   $\alpha = .10$, $n = 22$, $s^2 = 17$

c. $H_a: \sigma^2 = 45$
   $H_a: \sigma^2 < 45$
   $\alpha = .01$, $n = 8$, $s = 4.12$

d. $H_a: \sigma^2 = 5$
   $H_a: \sigma^2 \neq 5$
   $\alpha = .05$, $n = 11$, $s^2 = 1.2$

9.34. Previous experience shows the variance of a given process to be 14. Researchers are testing to determine whether this value has changed. They gather the following dozen measurements of the process. Use these data and $\alpha = .05$ to test the null hypothesis about the variance. Assume the measurements are normally distributed.

52	44	51	58	48	49
38	49	50	42	55	51

9.35. A manufacturing company produces bearings. One line of bearings is specified to be 1.64 centimeters (cm) in diameter. A major customer requires that the variance of the bearings be no more than .001 cm². The producer is required to test the bearings before they are shipped, and so the diameters of 16 bearings are measured with a precise instrument, resulting in the following values. Assume bearing diameters are normally distributed. Use the data and $\alpha = .01$ to test to determine whether the population of these bearings is to be rejected because of too high a variance.

1.69	1.62	1.63	1.70
1.66	1.63	1.65	1.71
1.64	1.69	1.57	1.64
1.59	1.66	1.63	1.65

9.36. A savings and loan averages about $100,000 in deposits per week. However, because of the way pay periods fall, seasonality, and erratic fluctuations in the local economy, deposits are subject to a wide variability. In the past, the variance for weekly deposits has been about $199,996,164. In terms that make more sense to managers, the standard deviation of weekly deposits has been $14,142. Shown here are data from a random sample of 13 weekly deposits for a recent period. Assume weekly deposits are normally distributed. Use these data and $\alpha = .10$ to test to determine whether the variance for weekly deposits has changed.

$93,000	$135,000	$112,000
68,000	46,000	104,000
128,000	143,000	131,000
104,000	96,000	71,000
87,000		

9.37. A company produces industrial wiring. One batch of wiring is specified to be 2.16 centimeters (cm) thick. A company inspects the wiring in seven locations and determines that, on the average, the wiring is about 2.16 cm thick. However, the measurements vary. It is unacceptable for the variance of the wiring to be more than .04 cm². The standard deviation of the seven measurements on this batch of wiring is .34 cm. Use $\alpha = .01$ to determine whether the variance on the sample wiring is too great to meet specifications. Assume wiring thickness is normally distributed.

9.6 | Solving for Type II Errors

If a researcher reaches the statistical conclusion to fail to reject the null hypothesis, he makes either a correct decision or a Type II error. If the null hypothesis is true, the researcher makes a correct decision. If the null hypothesis is false, then the result is a Type II error.

In business, failure to reject the null hypothesis may mean staying with the status quo, not implementing a new process, or not making adjustments. If a new process, product, theory, or adjustment is not significantly better than what is currently accepted practice, the decision maker makes a correct decision. However, if the new process, product, theory, or adjustment would significantly improve sales, the business climate, costs, or morale, the decision maker makes an error in judgment (Type II). In business, Type II errors can translate to lost opportunities, poor product quality (as a result of failure to discern a problem in the process), or failure to react to the marketplace. Sometimes the ability to react to changes, new developments, or new opportunities is what keeps a business moving and growing. Thus Type II error plays an important role in business statistical decision making.

Determining the probability of committing a Type II error is more complex than finding the probability of committing a Type I error. The probability of committing a Type I error either is given in a problem or is stated by the researcher before proceeding with the study. A Type II error, β, varies with possible values of the alternative parameter. For example, suppose a researcher is conducting a statistical test on the following hypotheses regarding 12-oz. cans of soft drink beverage:

$$H_0: \mu = 12 \text{ oz.}$$

$$H_a: \mu < 12 \text{ oz.}$$

A Type II error can be committed only when the researcher fails to reject the null hypothesis and the null hypothesis is false. In these hypotheses, if the null hypothesis, $\mu = 12$ ounces, is false, what is the true value for the population mean? Is the mean really 11.99 or 11.90 or 11.5 or 10 ounces? For each of these possible values of the population mean, the researcher can compute the probability of committing a Type II error. Often, when the null hypothesis is false, the value of the alternative mean is unknown, so the researcher will compute the probability of committing Type II errors for several possible values. How can the probability of committing a Type II error be computed for a specific alternative value of the mean?

Suppose that, in testing the preceding hypotheses, a sample of 60 cans of beverage yields a sample mean of 11.985 ounces. Assume that the population standard deviation is 0.10 ounces. From $\alpha = .05$ and a one-tailed test, the table $z_{.05}$ value is -1.645. The observed z value from sample data is

$$z = \frac{11.985 - 12.00}{\frac{.10}{\sqrt{60}}} = -1.16$$

From this observed value of z, the researcher determines not to reject the null hypothesis. By not rejecting the null hypothesis, the researcher either makes a correct decision or commits a Type II error. What is the probability of committing a Type II error in this problem if the population mean actually is 11.99?

The first step in determining the probability of a Type II error is to calculate a critical value for the sample mean, $\bar{x}_c$. In testing the null hypothesis by the critical value method, this value is used as the cutoff for the nonrejection region. For any sample mean obtained that is less than $\bar{x}_c$ (or greater for an upper-tail rejection region), the null hypothesis is rejected. Any sample mean greater than $\bar{x}_c$ (or less for an upper-tail rejection region) causes the researcher to fail to reject the null hypothesis. Solving for the critical value of the mean gives

$$z_c = \frac{\bar{x}_c - \mu}{\frac{\sigma}{\sqrt{n}}}$$

$$-1.645 = \frac{\bar{x}_c - 12}{\frac{.10}{\sqrt{60}}}$$

$$\bar{x}_c = 11.979$$

Figure 9.22(a) shows the distribution of values when the null hypothesis is true. It contains a critical value of the mean, $\bar{x}_c = 11.979$ oz., below which the null hypothesis will be rejected. Figure 9.22(b) shows the distribution when the alternative mean, $\mu_1 = 11.99$ oz., is true. How often will the business researcher fail to reject the top distribution as true when, in reality, the bottom distribution is true? If the null hypothesis is false, the researcher will fail to reject the null hypotheses whenever $\bar{x}$ is in the nonrejection region, $\bar{x} \geq 11.979$ oz. If μ actually equals 11.99 oz., what is the probability of failing to reject $\mu - 12$ oz. when 11.979 oz. is the critical value? The business researcher calculates this probability by extending the critical value ($\bar{x}_c = 11.979$ oz.) from distribution (a) to distribution (b) and solving for the area to the right of $\bar{x}_c = 11.979$.

$$z_1 = \frac{\bar{x}_c - \mu_1}{\frac{\sigma}{\sqrt{n}}} = \frac{11.979 - 11.99}{\frac{.10}{\sqrt{60}}} = -0.85$$

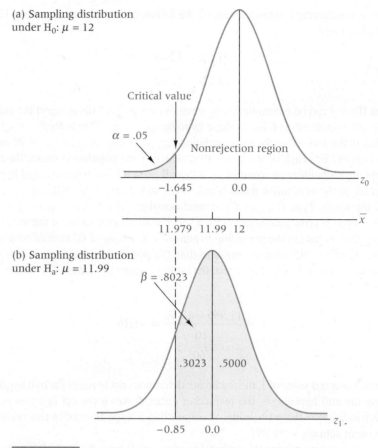

(a) Sampling distribution under H_0: $\mu = 12$

Critical value

$\alpha = .05$

Nonrejection region

-1.645 0.0 z_0

11.979 11.99 12 $\bar{x}$

(b) Sampling distribution under H_a: $\mu = 11.99$

$\beta = .8023$

.3023   .5000

-0.85 0.0 z_1

FIGURE 9.22 **Type II Error for Soft Drink Example with Alternative Mean = 11.99 oz.**

This value of z yields an area of .3023. The probability of committing a Type II error is all the area to the right of $\bar{x}_c = 11.979$ in distribution (b), or $.3023 + .5000 = .8023$. Hence there is an 80.23% chance of committing a Type II error if the alternative mean is 11.99 oz.

DEMONSTRATION PROBLEM 9.5

Recompute the probability of committing a Type II error for the soft drink example if the alternative mean is 11.96 oz.

Solution

Everything in distribution (a) of Figure 9.22 stays the same. The null hypothesized mean is still 12 oz., the critical value is still 11.979 oz., and $n = 60$. However, distribution (b) of Figure 9.22 changes with $\mu_1 = 11.96$ oz., as the following diagram shows.

The z formula used to solve for the area of distribution (b), $\mu_1 = 11.96$, to the right of 11.979 is

$$z_1 = \frac{\bar{x}_c - \mu_1}{\frac{\sigma}{\sqrt{n}}} = \frac{11.979 - 11.96}{\frac{.10}{\sqrt{60}}} = 1.47$$

From Table A.5, only .0708 of the area is to the right of the critical value. Thus the probability of committing a Type II error is only .0708, as illustrated in the following diagram.

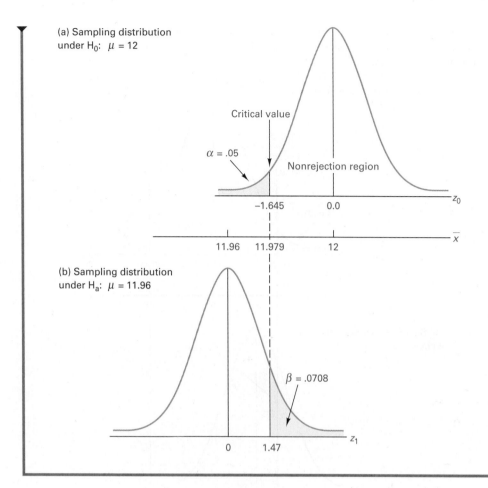

(a) Sampling distribution
under H_0: $\mu = 12$

Critical value

$\alpha = .05$

Nonrejection region

−1.645   0.0 z_0

11.96   11.979   12 $\bar{x}$

(b) Sampling distribution
under H_a: $\mu = 11.96$

$\beta = .0708$

0   1.47 z_1

DEMONSTRATION PROBLEM 9.6

Suppose you are conducting a two-tailed hypothesis test of proportions. The null hypothesis is that the population proportion is .40. The alternative hypothesis is that the population proportion is not .40. A random sample of 250 produces a sample proportion of .44. With alpha of .05, the table z value for $\alpha/2$ is ± 1.96. The observed z from the sample information is

$$z_c = \frac{\hat{p} - p}{\sqrt{\dfrac{p \cdot q}{n}}} = \frac{.44 - .40}{.031} = 1.29$$

Thus the null hypothesis is not rejected. Either a correct decision is made or a Type II error is committed. Suppose the alternative population proportion really is .36. What is the probability of committing a Type II error?

Solution

Solve for the critical value of the proportion.

$$z_c = \frac{\hat{p}_c - p}{\sqrt{\dfrac{p \cdot q}{n}}}$$

$$\pm 1.96 = \frac{\hat{p}_c - .40}{\sqrt{\dfrac{(.40)(.60)}{250}}}$$

$$\hat{p}_c = .40 \pm .06$$

The critical values are .34 on the lower end and .46 on the upper end. The alternative population proportion is .36. The following diagram illustrates these results and the remainder of the solution to this problem.

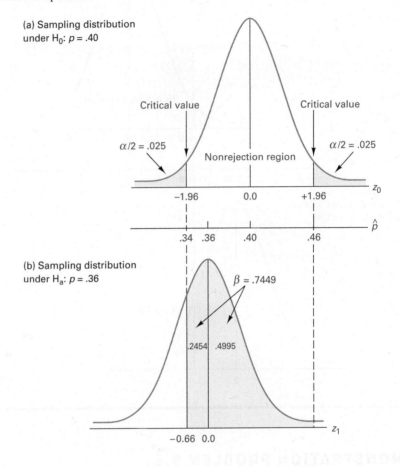

(a) Sampling distribution under H_0: $p = .40$

(b) Sampling distribution under H_a: $p = .36$

Solving for the area between $\hat{p}_c = .34$ and $p_1 = .36$ yields

$$z_1 = \frac{.34 - .36}{\sqrt{\dfrac{(.36)(.64)}{250}}} = -0.66$$

The area associated with $z_1 = -0.66$ is .2454.

The area between .36 and .46 of the sampling distribution under H_a: $p = .36$ (graph (b)) can be solved for by using the following z value:

$$z = \frac{.46 - .36}{\sqrt{\dfrac{(.36)(.64)}{250}}} = 3.29$$

The area from Table A.5 associated with $z = 3.29$ is .4995. Combining this value with the .2454 obtained from the left side of the distribution in graph (b) yields the total probability of committing a Type II error:

$$.2454 + .4995 = .7449$$

With two-tailed tests, both tails of the distribution contain rejection regions. The area between the two tails is the nonrejection region and the region where Type II errors can occur. If the alternative hypothesis is true, the area of the sampling distribution under H_a between the locations where the critical values from H_0 are located is β. In theory, both tails of the sampling distribution under H_a would be non-β area. However, in this problem, the right critical value is so far away from the alternative proportion ($p_1 = .36$) that the area between the right critical value and the alternative proportion is near .5000 (.4995) and virtually no area falls in the upper right tail of the distribution (.0005).

Some Observations About Type II Errors

Type II errors are committed only when the researcher fails to reject the null hypothesis but the alternative hypothesis is true. If the alternative mean or proportion is close to the hypothesized value, the probability of committing a Type II error is high. If the alternative value is relatively far away from the hypothesized value, as in the problem with $\mu = 12$ ounces and $\mu_a = 11.96$ ounces, the probability of committing a Type II error is small. The implication is that when a value is being tested as a null hypothesis against a true alternative value that is relatively far away, the sample statistic obtained is likely to show clearly which hypothesis is true. For example, suppose a researcher is testing to determine whether a company really is filling 2-liter bottles of cola with an average of 2 liters. If the company decides to underfill the bottles by filling them with only 1 liter, a sample of 50 bottles is likely to average a quantity near the 1-liter fill rather than near the 2-liter fill. Committing a Type II error is highly unlikely. Even a customer probably could see by looking at the bottles on the shelf that they are underfilled. However, if the company fills 2-liter bottles with 1.99 liters, the bottles are close in fill volume to those filled with 2.00 liters. In this case, the probability of committing a Type II error is much greater. A customer probably could not catch the underfill just by looking.

In general, if the alternative value is relatively far from the hypothesized value, the probability of committing a Type II error is smaller than it is when the alternative value is close to the hypothesized value. The probability of committing a Type II error decreases as alternative values of the hypothesized parameter move farther away from the hypothesized value. This situation is shown graphically in operating characteristic curves and power curves.

Operating Characteristic and Power Curves

Because the probability of committing a Type II error changes for each different value of the alternative parameter, it is best in managerial decision making to examine a series of possible alternative values. For example, Table 9.5 shows the probabilities of committing a Type II error (β) for several different possible alternative means for the soft drink example discussed in Demonstration Problem 9.5, in which the null hypothesis was H_0: $\mu = 12$ oz. and $\alpha = .05$.

As previously mentioned, power is the probability of rejecting the null hypothesis when it is false and represents the correct decision of selecting the alternative hypothesis when it is true. Power is equal to $1 - \beta$. Note that Table 9.5 also contains the power values for the alternative means and that the β and power probabilities sum to 1 in each case.

TABLE 9.5 β Values and Power Values for the Soft Drink Example

ALTERNATIVE MEAN	PROBABILITY OF COMMITTING A TYPE II ERROR, β	POWER
$\mu_a = 11.999$	.94	.06
$\mu_a = 11.995$	.89	.11
$\mu_a = 11.99$	.80	.20
$\mu_a = 11.98$	.53	.47
$\mu_a = 11.97$	.24	.76
$\mu_a = 11.96$	.07	.93
$\mu_a = 11.95$	.01	.99

These values can be displayed graphically as shown in **Figures 9.23** and **9.24**. Figure 9.23 is a Minitab-generated **operating characteristic (OC) curve** *constructed by plotting the β values against the various values of the alternative hypothesis.* Notice that when the alternative means are near the value of the null hypothesis, $\mu = 12$, the probability of committing a Type II error is high because it is difficult to discriminate between a distribution with a mean of 12 and a distribution with a mean of 11.999. However, as the values of the alternative means move away from the hypothesized value, $\mu = 12$, the values of β drop. This visual representation underscores the notion that it is easier to discriminate between a distribution with $\mu = 12$ and a distribution with $\mu = 11.95$ than between distributions with $\mu = 12$ and $\mu = 11.999$.

Figure 9.24 is an Excel **power curve** constructed by *plotting the power values* $(1 - \beta)$ *against the various values of the alternative hypotheses.* Note that the power increases as the alternative mean moves away from the value of μ in the null hypotheses. This relationship makes sense. As the alternative mean moves farther and farther away from the null hypothesized mean, a correct decision to reject the null hypothesis becomes more likely.

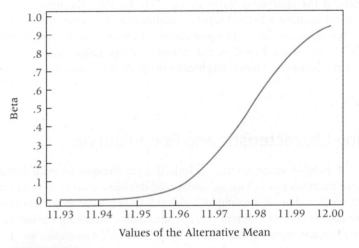

FIGURE 9.23 **Minitab Operating-Characteristic Curve for the Soft Drink Example**

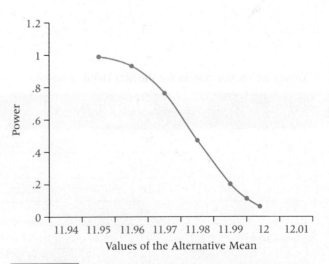

FIGURE 9.24 **Excel Power Curve for the Soft Drink Example**

Effect of Increasing Sample Size on the Rejection Limits

The size of the sample affects the location of the rejection limits. Consider the soft drink example in which we were testing the following hypotheses:

$$H_0: \mu = 12 \text{ oz.}$$

$$H_a: \mu < 12 \text{ oz.}$$

Sample size was 60 ($n = 60$) and the standard deviation was .10 ($\sigma = .10$). With $\alpha = .05$, the critical value of the test statistic was $z_{.05} = -1.645$. From this information, a critical raw score value was computed:

$$z_c = \frac{\bar{x}_c - \mu}{\dfrac{\sigma}{\sqrt{n}}}$$

$$-1.645 = \frac{\bar{x}_c - 12}{\dfrac{.10}{\sqrt{60}}}$$

$$\bar{x}_c = 11.979$$

Any sample mean obtained in the hypothesis-testing process that is less than 11.979 will result in a decision to reject the null hypothesis.

Suppose the sample size is increased to 100. The critical raw score value is

$$-1.645 = \frac{\bar{x}_c - 12}{\dfrac{.10}{\sqrt{100}}}$$

$$\bar{x}_c = 11.984$$

Notice that the critical mean value is nearer to the hypothesized value ($\mu = 12$) for the larger sample size than it was for a sample size of 60. Because n is in the denominator of the standard error of the mean ($\sigma/\sqrt{n}$), an increase in n results in a decrease in the standard error of the mean, which when multiplied by the critical value of the test statistic ($z_{\alpha/2}$) results in a critical mean value that is closer to the hypothesized value. For $n = 500$, the critical raw score value for this problem is 11.993.

Increased sample size not only affects the distance of the critical mean value from the hypothesized value of the distribution, but also can result in reducing β for a given value of α. Examine Figure 9.22. Note that the critical mean value is 11.979 with alpha equal to .05 for $n = 60$. The value of β for an alternative mean of 11.99 is .8023. Suppose the sample size is 100. The critical mean value (already solved) is 11.984. The value of β is now .7257. The computation is

$$z = \frac{11.984 - 11.99}{\dfrac{.10}{\sqrt{100}}} = -0.60$$

The area under the standard normal curve for $z = -0.60$ is .2257. Adding .2257 + .5000 (from the right half of the H_a sampling distribution) results in a β of .7257. Figure 9.25 shows the sampling distributions with α and β for this problem. In addition, by increasing sample size a business researcher could reduce alpha without necessarily increasing beta. It is possible to reduce the probabilities of committing Type I and Type II errors simultaneously by increasing sample size.

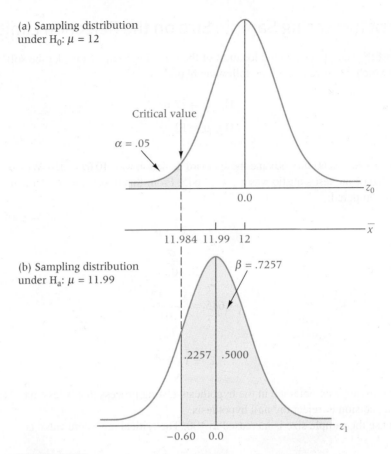

(a) Sampling distribution under H_0: $\mu = 12$

(b) Sampling distribution under H_a: $\mu = 11.99$

FIGURE 9.25 Type II Error for Soft Drink Example with n Increased to 100

9.6 Problems

9.38. Suppose a null hypothesis is that the population mean is greater than or equal to 100. Suppose further that a random sample of 48 items is taken and the population standard deviation is 14. For each of the following α values, compute the probability of committing a Type II error if the population mean actually is 99.

   a. $\alpha = .10$

   b. $\alpha = .05$

   c. $\alpha = .01$

   d. Based on the answers to parts (a), (b), and (c), what happens to the value of β as α gets smaller?

9.39. For Problem 9.38, use $\alpha = .05$ and solve for the probability of committing a Type II error for the following possible true alternative means.

   a. $\mu_a = 98.5$

   b. $\mu_a = 98$

   c. $\mu_a = 97$

   d. $\mu_a = 96$

   e. What happens to the probability of committing a Type II error as the alternative value of the mean gets farther from the null hypothesized value of 100?

9.40. Suppose a hypothesis states that the mean is exactly 50. If a random sample of 35 items is taken to test this hypothesis, what is the value of β if the population standard deviation is 7 and the alternative mean is 53? Use $\alpha = .01$

9.41. An alternative hypothesis is that $p < .65$ To test this hypothesis, a random sample of size 360 is taken. What is the probability of committing a Type II error if $\alpha = .05$ and the alternative proportion is as follows?

   a. $p_a = .60$

   b. $p_a = .55$

   c. $p_a = .50$

9.42. The New York Stock Exchange recently reported that the average age of a female shareholder is 44 years. A broker in Chicago wants to know whether this figure is accurate for the female shareholders in Chicago. The broker secures a master list of shareholders in Chicago and takes a random sample of 58 women. Suppose the average age for shareholders in the sample is 45.1 years, with a population standard deviation of 8.7 years. Test to determine whether the broker's sample data differ significantly enough from the 44-years figure released by the New York Stock Exchange to declare that Chicago female shareholders are different in age from female shareholders in general. Use $\alpha = .05$. If no significant difference is noted, what is the broker's probability of committing a Type II error if the average age of a female Chicago shareholder is actually 45 years? 46 years? 47 years? 48 years? Construct an OC curve for these data. Construct a power curve for these data.

9.43. A Harris poll was taken to determine which of 13 major industries are doing a good job of serving their customers. Among the industries rated most highly by Americans for serving their customers were computer hardware and software companies, car manufacturers, and airlines. The industries rated lowest on serving their customers were tobacco companies, managed care providers, and health insurance companies. Seventy-one percent of those polled responded that airlines are doing a good job serving their customers. Suppose due to rising ticket prices, a researcher feels that this figure is now too high.

He takes a poll of 463 Americans, and 324 say that the airlines are doing a good job of serving their customers. Does the survey show enough evidence to declare that the proportion of Americans saying that the airlines are doing a good job of serving their customers is significantly lower than stated in the Harris poll? Let alpha equal .10. If the researcher fails to reject the null hypothesis and if the figure is actually 69% now, what is the probability of committing a Type II error? What is the probability of committing a Type II error if the figure is really 66%? 60%?

Decision Dilemma Solved

Valero: Refining and Retailing

In the Decision Dilemma, it was noted that there are many possible research hypotheses that could be generated in the oil refining business. As an example, there are several research hypotheses that might explain why refineries have been running below capacity for the last two months; (1) There is less demand for gasoline; (2) There is a shortage of oil supply; (3) The supply of crude oil has been below standards; (4) There has been infrastructure damage to the refinery; (5) There is a shortage of qualified workers; and (6) Management is attempting to manipulate the market.

A barrel of light, sweet crude oil weighs about 294 U.S. lbs. whereas heavy oil might weigh as much as 350 U.S. lbs. Suppose a petroleum company is using a mix of quality of crude oil, and they just received a shipment of thousands of barrels of oil. They know from the past that the average weight of a barrel for all oil is 320 lbs. with a standard deviation of 7 lbs. They decide to test the shipment by randomly sampling 45 barrels of crude oil and the resulting sample mean of weight is 317 lbs. Since they are testing a mean, the population standard deviation is known ($\sigma = 7$), and n is 45, they can use the z test for sample means to analyze the data. Because they did not know before they took the sample whether the sample mean would be less than or greater than 320 lbs., they conducted a two-tailed test with $\alpha = .05$. Thus, the critical z values are ±1.96.

The observed z is:

$$z = \frac{317 - 320}{\frac{7}{\sqrt{45}}} = -2.87$$

Because this test statistic, $z = -2.87$, is less than the critical value of $z = -1.96$ in the lower tail of the distribution, the statistical conclusion reached is to reject the null hypothesis. The p-value for $z = -2.87$ is calculated using Table A.5 as .5000 − .4979 = .0021. This p-value (.0021) is less than $\alpha/2$ (.025), so the decision based on the p-value method is to reject the null hypothesis. The mean weight of a barrel of oil in the sample is significantly lower than 320 lbs., although it is arguable whether or not the result is substantive.

In the Decision Dilemma according to *Convenience Store News*, the average in-store transaction for a convenience store was $7.47 in 2010. Suppose a consumer researcher believes that the average is now higher than that figure and want to test it. However, while the population average ($7.47) was known, there was no information about the population standard deviation. Suppose further it is agreed that in-store transactions for convenience stores

are approximately normally distributed in the population. To test this hypothesis, the consumer researcher randomly samples seventeen in-store transactions from convenience stores across the United States, with the resulting data:

$ 9.49	$ 7.12	$ 8.31	$ 7.04	$ 7.96	$10.69
$ 7.03	$ 9.78	$ 6.66	$ 7.07	$ 9.45	$ 8.84
$ 6.36	$10.38	$ 9.42	$ 6.80	$ 8.26	

She uses a 1% level of significance to test the hypotheses. Because the researcher is using the mean as the statistic, the population standard deviation is unknown, and the population is normally distributed, the t test in Formula 9.3 is the appropriate test statistic. Since $n = 17$, the degrees of freedom are 16. This test is one-tailed (only testing for higher transactions), and the critical table t value is $t_{.01,16} = 2.583$. The sample mean of the data is $\bar{x} = \$8.27$ and the sample standard deviation is $s = \$1.40$. From this, the observed t value can be computed as:

$$t = \frac{\$8.27 - \$7.47}{\frac{\$1.40}{\sqrt{17}}} = 2.36$$

Because this test statistic, $t = 2.36$, is less than the critical value of $t = 2.583$ in the upper tail of the distribution, the statistical conclusion reached is to fail to reject the null hypothesis. The consumer researcher concludes that there is not enough evidence to say that the average in-store transaction is now greater than $7.47.

According to the National Association of Convenience Stores, 62% of all convenience stores in the United States are owned and operated by someone who has only one store. Suppose you live in a city that seemingly has fewer entrepreneurs and more corporate influence and you believe that in your city, significantly fewer than 62% of all convenience stores are owned and operated by someone who has only one store. You set out to "prove" your theory by taking a random sample of 328 convenience stores; it turns out that 187 of them are owned and operated by someone who has only one store. Because we are testing a single population proportion and the sample size is 328, the z test in Formula 9.4 is the appropriate test statistic. You are conducting a one-tailed test (fewer) with the alternative hypothesis as $p < .62$. Using $\alpha = .10$, the critical z value is -1.28.

The sample proportion is determined by:

$$\hat{p} = \frac{x}{n} = \frac{187}{328} = .57$$

The value of the test statistic is calculated by using $\hat{p} = .57$, $n = 328$, $p = .62$, and $q = 1 - p = 1 - .62 = .38$:

$$z = \frac{\hat{p} - p}{\sqrt{\frac{p \cdot q}{n}}} = \frac{.57 - .62}{\sqrt{\frac{(.62)(.38)}{328}}} = -1.87$$

Because this test statistic, $z = -1.87$, is less than the critical value of $z = -1.28$ in the lower tail of the distribution, the statistical conclusion is to reject the null hypothesis. This study shows that significantly fewer convenience stores are operated by single-store owners in this city.

Ethical Considerations

The process of hypothesis testing encompasses several areas that could potentially lead to unethical activity, beginning with the null and alternative hypotheses. In the hypothesis-testing approach, the preliminary assumption is that the null hypothesis is true. If a researcher has a new theory or idea that he or she is attempting to prove, it is somewhat unethical to express that theory or idea as the null hypothesis. In doing so, the researcher is assuming that what he or she is trying to prove is true and the burden of proof is on the data to reject this idea or theory. The researcher must take great care not to assume that what he or she is attempting to prove is true.

Hypothesis testing through random sampling opens up many possible unethical situations that can occur in sampling, such as identifying a frame that is favorable to the outcome the researcher is seeking or using nonrandom sampling techniques to test hypotheses. In addition, the researcher should be careful to use the proper test statistic for tests of a population mean, particularly when σ is unknown. If t tests are used, or in testing a population variance, the researcher should be careful to apply the techniques only when it can be shown with some confidence that the population is normally distributed. The chi-square test of a population variance has been shown to be extremely sensitive to the assumption that the population is normally distributed. Unethical usage of this technique occurs when the statistician does not carefully check the population distribution shape for compliance with this assumption. Failure to do so can easily result in the reporting of spurious conclusions.

It can be unethical from a business decision-making point of view to knowingly use the notion of statistical significance to claim business significance when the results are not substantive. Therefore, it is unethical to intentionally attempt to mislead the business user by inappropriately using the word *significance*.

Summary

Three types of hypotheses were presented in this chapter: research hypotheses, statistical hypotheses, and substantive hypotheses. Research hypotheses are statements of what the researcher believes will be the outcome of an experiment or study. In order to test hypotheses, business researchers formulate their research hypotheses into statistical hypotheses. All statistical hypotheses consist of two parts, a null hypothesis and an alternative hypothesis. The null and alternative hypotheses are structured so that either one or the other is true but not both. In testing hypotheses, the researcher assumes that the null hypothesis is true. By examining the sampled data, the researcher either rejects or does not reject the null hypothesis. If the sample data are significantly in opposition to the null hypothesis, the researcher rejects the null hypothesis and accepts the alternative hypothesis by default.

Hypothesis tests can be one-tailed or two-tailed. Two-tailed tests always utilize = and ≠ in the null and alternative hypotheses. These tests are nondirectional in that significant deviations from the hypothesized value that can occur in either the upper or the lower rejection regions. The one-tailed test is directional, and the alternative hypothesis contains < or > signs. In these tests, only one end or tail of the distribution contains a rejection region. In a one-tailed test, the researcher is interested only in deviations from the hypothesized value that are either greater than or less than the value but not both.

Not all statistically significant outcomes of studies are important business outcomes. A substantive result is when the outcome of a statistical study produces results that are important to the decision maker.

When a business researcher reaches a decision about the null hypothesis, the researcher makes either a correct decision or an error. If the null hypothesis is true, the researcher can make a Type I error by rejecting the null hypothesis. The probability of making a Type I error is alpha (α). Alpha is usually set by the researcher when establishing the hypotheses. Another expression sometimes used for the value of α is level of significance.

If the null hypothesis is false and the researcher fails to reject it, a Type II error is committed. Beta (β) is the probability of committing a Type II error. Type II errors must be computed from the hypothesized value of the parameter, α, and a specific alternative value of the parameter being examined. There are as many possible Type II errors in a problem as there are possible alternative statistical values.

If a null hypothesis is true and the researcher fails to reject it, no error is committed, and the researcher makes a correct decision. Similarly, if a null hypothesis is false and it is rejected, no error is committed. Power $(1 - \beta)$ is the probability of a statistical test rejecting the null hypothesis when the null hypothesis is false.

An operating characteristic (OC) curve is a graphical depiction of values of β that can occur as various values of the alternative hypothesis are explored. This graph can be studied to determine what happens to β as one moves away from the value of the null hypothesis. A power curve is used in conjunction with an operating characteristic curve. The power curve is a graphical depiction of the values of power as various values of the alternative hypothesis are examined. The researcher can view the increase in power as values of the alternative hypothesis diverge from the value of the null hypothesis.

Included in this chapter were hypothesis tests for a single mean when σ is known and when σ is unknown, a test of a single population proportion, and a test for a population variance. Three different analytic decision making approaches were presented: (1) standard method, (2) the p-value; and (3) the critical value method.

Key Terms

alpha (α)	level of significance	operating characteristic	statistical hypothesis
alternative hypothesis	nonrejection region	(OC) curve	substantive result
beta (β)	null hypothesis	p-value method	two-tailed test
critical value	observed significance	power	Type I error
critical value method	level	power curve	Type II error
hypothesis	observed value	rejection region	
hypothesis testing	one-tailed test	research hypothesis	

Formulas

z test for a single mean (9.1)

$$z = \frac{\bar{x} - \mu}{\frac{\sigma}{\sqrt{n}}}$$

Formula to test hypotheses about μ with a finite population (9.2)

$$z = \frac{\bar{x} - \mu}{\frac{\sigma}{\sqrt{n}} \sqrt{\frac{N - n}{N - 1}}}$$

t test for a single mean (9.3)

$$t = \frac{\bar{x} - \mu}{\frac{s}{\sqrt{n}}}$$

$$df = n - 1$$

z test of a population proportion (9.4)

$$z = \frac{\hat{p} - p}{\sqrt{\frac{p \cdot q}{n}}}$$

Formula for testing hypotheses about a population variance (9.5)

$$\chi^2 = \frac{(n - 1)s^2}{\sigma^2}$$

$$df = n - 1$$

Supplementary Problems

Calculating the Statistics

9.44. Use the information given and the eight-step approach to test the hypotheses. Let $\alpha = .01$.

$$H_0: \mu = 36 \quad H_a: \mu \neq 36 \quad n = 36 \quad \bar{x} = 38.4 \quad \sigma = 5.93$$

9.45. Use the information given and the eight-step approach to test the hypotheses. Let $\alpha = .05$. Assume that the population is normally distributed.

$$H_0: \mu = 7.82 \quad H_a: \mu < 7.82 \quad n = 17 \quad \bar{x} = 7.01 \quad s = 1.69$$

9.46. For each of the following problems, use the eight-step approach to test the hypotheses.

a. $H_0: p = .28 \quad H_a: p > .28 \quad n = 783 \quad x = 230 \quad \alpha = .10$.

b. $H_0: p = .61 \quad H_a: p \neq .61 \quad n = 401 \quad \hat{p} = .56 \quad \alpha = .05$.

9.47. Test the following hypotheses by using the information given and the eight-step approach. Let alpha be .01. Assume the population is normally distributed.

$$H_0: \sigma^2 = 15.4 \quad H_a: \sigma^2 > 15.4 \quad n = 18 \quad s^2 = 29.6$$

9.48. Solve for the value of beta in each of the following problems.

a. $H_0: \mu = 130 \quad H_a: \mu > 130 \quad n = 75 \quad \sigma = 12 \quad \alpha = .01$.
  The alternative mean is actually 135.

b. $H_0: p - .44 \quad H_a: p < .44 \quad n = 1095 \quad \alpha = .05$.
  The alternative proportion is actually .42.

Testing Your Understanding

9.49. According to a Gallup survey two years ago, 32% of American households use a computer or online financial program to manage their money. Suppose researchers believe that this figure has increased recently, and they test their theory by randomly sampling 80 American households. Of the 80 households, 38% respond that they do use a computer or online financial program to manage their money. Is this result enough evidence to conclude that a significantly higher proportion of American households use a computer or online financial program to manage their money? Let $\alpha = .10$.

9.50. According to Zero Population Growth, the average urban U.S. resident consumes 3.3 pounds of food per day. Is this figure accurate for rural U.S. residents? Suppose 64 rural U.S. residents are identified by a random procedure and their average consumption per day is 3.60 pounds of food. Assume a population variance of 1.31 pounds of food per day. Use a 5% level of significance to determine whether the Zero Population Growth figure for urban U.S. residents also is true for rural U.S. residents on the basis of the sample data.

9.51. Brokers generally agree that bonds are a better investment during times of low interest rates than during times of high interest rates. A survey of executives during a time of low interest rates showed that 57% of them had some retirement funds invested in bonds. Assume this percentage is constant for bond market investment by executives with retirement funds. Suppose interest rates have risen lately and the proportion of executives with retirement investment money in the bond market may have dropped. To test this idea, a researcher randomly samples 210 executives who have retirement funds. Of these, 93 now have retirement funds invested in bonds. For $\alpha = .10$, does the test show enough evidence to declare that the proportion of executives with retirement fund investments in the bond market is significantly lower than .57?

9.52. Highway engineers in Ohio are painting white stripes on a highway. The stripes are supposed to be approximately 10 feet long. However, because of the machine, the operator, and the motion of the vehicle carrying the equipment, considerable variation occurs among the stripe lengths. Engineers claim that the variance of stripes is not more than 16 inches. Use the sample lengths given here from 12 measured stripes to test the variance claim. Assume stripe length is normally distributed. Let $\alpha = .05$.

STRIPE LENGTHS IN FEET

10.3	9.4	9.8	10.1
9.2	10.4	10.7	9.9
9.3	9.8	10.5	10.4

9.53. A computer manufacturer estimates that its line of minicomputers has, on average, 8.4 days of downtime per year. To test this claim, a researcher contacts seven companies that own one of these computers and is allowed to access company computer records. It is determined that, for the sample, the average number of downtime days is 5.6, with a sample standard deviation of 1.3 days. Assuming that number of downtime days is normally distributed, test to determine whether these minicomputers actually average 8.4 days of downtime in the entire population. Let $\alpha = .01$.

9.54. Life insurance experts have been claiming that the average worker in the city of Cincinnati has no more than $25,000 of personal life insurance. An insurance researcher believes that this is not true and sets out to prove that the average worker in Cincinnati has more than $25,000 of personal life insurance. To test this claim, she randomly samples 100 workers in Cincinnati and interviews them about their personal life insurance coverage. She discovers that the average amount of personal life insurance coverage for this sample group is $26,650. The population standard deviation is $12,000.

a. Determine whether the test shows enough evidence to reject the null hypothesis posed by the salesperson. Assume the probability of committing a Type I error is .05.

b. If the actual average for this population is $30,000, what is the probability of committing a Type II error?

9.55. A financial analyst watched a particular stock for several months. The price of this stock remained fairly stable during this time. In fact, the financial analyst claims that the variance of the price of this stock did not exceed $4 for the entire period. Recently, the market heated up, and the price of this stock appears more volatile. To determine whether it is more volatile, a sample of closing prices of this stock for eight days is taken randomly. The sample mean price is $36.25, with a sample standard deviation of $7.80. Using a level of significance of .10, test to determine whether the financial analyst's previous variance figure is now too low. Assume stock prices are normally distributed.

9.56. A study of MBA graduates by Universum for the American Graduate Survey 1999 revealed that MBA graduates had several expectations of prospective employers beyond their base pay. In particular, according to the study 46% expect a performance-related bonus, 46% expect stock options, 42% expect a signing bonus, 28% expect profit sharing, 27% expect extra vacation/personal days, 25% expect tuition reimbursement, 24% expect health benefits, and 19% expect guaranteed annual bonuses. Suppose a study was conducted last year to see whether these expectations have changed. If 125 MBA graduates were randomly selected last year, and if 66 expected stock options, does this result provide enough evidence to declare that a significantly higher proportion of MBAs expect stock options? Let $\alpha = .05$. If the proportion really is .50, what is the probability of committing a Type II error?

9.57. Suppose the number of beds filled per day in a mediumsized hospital is normally distributed. A hospital administrator tells the board of directors that, on the average, at least 185 beds are filled on any given day. One of the board members believes that the average is less than 185 and she sets out to test to determine if she is correct. She secures a random sample of 16 days of data (shown below). Use $\alpha = .05$ and the sample data to test the board member's theory. Assume the number of filled beds per day is normally distributed in the population.

NUMBER OF BEDS OCCUPIED PER DAY

173	149	166	180
189	170	152	194
177	169	188	160
199	175	172	187

9.58. According to Gartner Inc., the second largest share of the worldwide PC market is held by Hewlett-Packard with 17.3%. Suppose that a market researcher believes that Hewlett-Packard holds a higher share of the market in the western region of the United States. To verify this theory, he randomly selects 428 people who purchased a personal computer in the last month in the western region of the United States. Eighty of these purchases were Hewlett-Packard computers. Using a 1% level of significance, test the market researcher's theory. If the market share is really .24 in the southwestern region of the United States, what is the probability of making a Type II error?

9.59. A national publication reported that a college student living away from home spends, on average, no more than $15 per month on laundry. You believe this figure is too low and want to disprove the publication's claim. To conduct the test, you randomly select 17 college students and ask them to keep track of the amount of money they spend during a given month for laundry. The sample produces an average expenditure on laundry of $19.34. Assume a population standard deviation of $4.52. Use these sample data to conduct the hypothesis test. Assume you are willing to take a 10% risk of making a Type I error and that spending on laundry per month is normally distributed in the population.

9.60. A local company installs natural-gas grills. As part of the installation, a ditch is dug to lay a small natural-gas line from the grill to the main line. On the average, the depth of these lines seems to run about 1 foot. The company claims that the depth does not vary by more than 16 square inches (the variance). To test this claim, a researcher randomly took 22 depth measurements at different locations. The sample average depth was 13.4 inches with a standard deviation of 6 inches. Is this enough evidence to reject the company's claim about the variance? Assume line depths are normally distributed. Let $\alpha = .05$.

9.61. A study of pollutants showed that certain industrial emissions should not exceed 2.5 parts per million. You believe a particular company may be exceeding this average. To test this supposition, you randomly take a sample of nine air tests. The sample average is 3.4 parts per million, with a sample standard deviation of 0.6. Does this result provide enough evidence for you to conclude that the company is exceeding the safe limit? Use $\alpha = .01$. Assume emissions are normally distributed.

9.62. The average cost per square foot for office rental space in the central business district of Philadelphia is $23.58, according to Cushman & Wakefield. A large real estate company wants to confirm this figure. The firm conducts a telephone survey of 95 offices in the central business district of Philadelphia and asks the office managers how much they pay in rent per square foot. Suppose the sample average is $22.83 per square foot. The population standard deviation is $5.11.

    a. Conduct a hypothesis test using $\alpha = .05$ to determine whether the cost per square foot reported by Cushman & Wakefield should be rejected.

    b. If the decision in part (a) is to fail to reject and if the actual average cost per square foot is $22.30, what is the probability of committing a Type II error?

9.63. The American Water Works Association reports that, on average, men use between 10 and 15 gallons of water daily to shave when they leave the water running. Suppose the following data are the numbers of gallons of water used in a day to shave by 12 randomly selected men and the data come from a normal distribution of data. Use these data and a 5% level of significance to test to determine whether the population variance for such water usage is 2.5 gallons squared.

10	8	13	17	13	15
12	13	15	16	9	7

9.64. Downtime in manufacturing is costly and can result in late deliveries, backlogs, failure to meet orders, and even loss of market share. Suppose a manufacturing plant has been averaging 23 minutes of downtime per day for the past several years, but during the past year, there has been a significant effort by both management and production workers to reduce downtime. In an effort to determine if downtime has been significantly reduced, company productivity researchers have randomly sampled 31 days over the past several months from company records and have recorded the daily downtimes shown below in minutes. Use these data and an alpha of .01 to test to determine if downtime has been significantly reduced. Assume that daily downtimes are normally distributed in the population.

19	22	17	19	32	24	16	18	27	17
24	19	23	27	28	19	17	18	26	22
19	15	18	25	23	19	26	21	16	21
24

Interpreting the Output

9.65. According to the U.S. Census Bureau, the average American generates 4.4 pounds of garbage per day. Suppose we believe that because of recycling and a greater emphasis on the environment, the figure is now lower. To test this notion, we take a random sample of Americans and have them keep a log of their garbage for a day. We record and analyze the results by using a statistical computer package. The output follows. Describe the sample. What statistical decisions can be made on the basis of this analysis? Let alpha be .05. Assume that pounds of garbage per day are normally distributed in the population. Discuss any substantive results.

```
One-Sample Z

Test of μ = 4.4 vs < 4.4
The assumed standard deviation = 0.866

                          95%
                          Upper
  N    Mean   SE Mean    Bound      Z       P
  22   3.969   0.185     4.273    -2.33   0.010
```

9.66. One survey conducted by RHI Management Resources determined that the Lexus is the favorite luxury car for 25% of CFOs. Suppose a financial management association conducts its own survey of CFOs in an effort to determine whether this figure is correct. They use an alpha of .05. Following is the Minitab output with the results of the survey. Discuss the findings, including the hypotheses, one- or two-tailed tests, sample statistics, and the conclusion. Explain from the data why you reached the conclusion you did. Are these results substantive?

```
Test and CI for One Proportion

Test of p = 0.25 vs p ≠ 0.25

                                                  Exact
Sample  X    N    Sample p   95% CI              P-Value
1       79   384  0.205729   (0.166399, 0.2496663)  0.045
```

9.67. In a recent year, published statistics by the National Cattlemen's Beef Association claimed that the average retail beef price for USDA All Fresh beef was $2.51. Suppose a survey of retailers is conducted this year to determine whether the price of USDA All Fresh beef has increased. The Excel output of the results of the survey are shown here. Analyze the output and explain what it means in this study. An alpha of .05 was used in this analysis. Assume that beef prices are normally distributed in the population. Comment on any substantive results.

Mean	2.55
Variance	0.0218
Observations	26
df	25
t Stat	1.51
$P (T <= t)$ one-tail	0.072
t Critical one-tail	1.71
$P (T <= t)$ two-tail	0.144
t Critical two-tail	2.06

9.68. The American Express Retail Index states that the average U.S. household will spend $2747 on home improvement projects this year. Suppose a large national home improvement company wants to test that figure in the West, theorizing that the average might be lower in the West. The research firm hired to conduct the study arrives at the results shown here. Analyze the data and explain the results. Comment on any substantive findings.

```
One-Sample Z

Test of μ = 2747 vs < 2747
The assumed standard deviation = 1557

                            95%
                            Upper
  N   Mean   SE Mean      Bound     Z       P
  67  2349    190          2662   -2.09   0.018
```

Analyzing the Databases

See www.wiley.com/college/black

1. Suppose the average number of employees per industry group in the manufacturing database is believed to be less than 150 (1000s). Test this belief as the alternative hypothesis by using the 140 SIC Code industries given in the database as the sample. Let $\alpha = .10$. Assume that the number of employees per industry group are normally distributed in the population. What did you decide and why?

2. Examine the hospital database. Suppose you want to "prove" that the average hospital in the United States averages more than 700 births per year. Use the hospital database as your sample and test this hypothesis. Let alpha be .01. On average, do hospitals in the United States employ fewer than 900 personnel? Use the hospital database as your sample and an alpha of .10 to test this figure as the alternative hypothesis. Assume that the number of births and number of employees in the hospitals are normally distributed in the population.

3. Consider the financial database. Are the average earnings per share for companies in the stock market less than $2.50? Use the sample of companies represented by this database to test that hypothesis. Let $\alpha = .05$. Test to determine whether the average return on equity for all companies is equal to 21. Use this database as the sample and $\alpha = .10$. Assume that the earnings per share and return on equity are normally distributed in the population.

4. Suppose a researcher wants to test to determine if the average annual food spending for a household in the Midwest region of the U.S. is more than $8,000. Use the Midwest region data from the Consumer Food database and a 1% level of significance to test this hypothesis. Assume that annual food spending is normally distributed in the population.

Case

Frito-Lay Targets the Hispanic Market

Frito Company was founded in 1932 in San Antonio, Texas, by Elmer Doolin. H. W. Lay & Company was founded in Atlanta, Georgia, by Herman W. Lay in 1938. In 1961, the two companies merged to form Frito-Lay, Inc., with headquarters in Texas. Frito-Lay produced, distributed, and marketed snack foods with particular emphasis on various types of chips. In 1965, the company merged with Pepsi-Cola to form PepsiCo, Inc. Three decades later, Pepsi-Cola combined its domestic and international snack food operations into one business unit called Frito-Lay Company. Today, Frito-Lay brands account for 59% of the U.S. snack chip industry, and there are more than 50,000 Frito-Lay employees in the United States and Canada.

In the late 1990s, despite its overall popularity, Frito-Lay faced a general lack of appeal to Hispanics, a fast-growing U.S. market. In an effort to better penetrate that market, Frito-Lay hired various market researchers to determine why Hispanics were not purchasing their products as often as company officials had hoped and what could be done about the problem. In the studies, market researchers discovered that Hispanics thought Frito-Lay products were too bland, Frito-Lay advertisements were not being widely viewed by Hispanics, and Hispanics tended to purchase snacks in small bags at local grocery stores rather than in the large family-style bags sold at large supermarkets.

Focus groups composed of male teens and male young adults—a group that tends to consume a lot of chips—were formed. The researchers determined that even though many of the teens spoke English at school, they spoke Spanish at home with their family. From this discovery, it was concluded that Spanish advertisements would be needed to reach Hispanics. In addition, the use of Spanish rock music, a growing movement in the Hispanic youth culture, could be effective in some ads.

Researchers also found that using a "Happy Face" logo, which is an icon of Frito-Lay's sister company in Mexico, was effective. Because it reminded the 63% of all Hispanics in the United States who are Mexican American of snack foods from home, the logo increased product familiarity.

As a result of this research, Frito-Lay launched its first Hispanic products in San Antonio, in 1997. Within a few years, sales of the Doritos brand improved 32% in Hispanic areas. In May 2002, Frito-Lay teamed up with its Mexican affiliate, Sabritas, to launch a new line of products to further appeal to Hispanic customers. Included in these offerings are Sabritas Adobadas tomato and chile potato chips, Sabritones Churrumais fried corn strips with chile and lime seasonings, Crujitos queso and chile flavor puffed corn twists, Fritos Sabrositas lime and chile chips, El Isleno Plantains, and others.

More recently, Frito-Lay has been relying on input and guidance from the Adelante employee network, which is a multicultural Latina/

Hispanic professional organization associated with PepsiCo. At Frito-Lay, the organization's mission is to help develop a diverse, inclusive culture accelerating growth opportunities for associates while providing a competitive advantage in an increasingly diverse marketplace. As part of this effort, Adelante has been used to help develop new flavors and advertising programs for Hispanics. Based on information gleaned from Adelante members, new Frito-Lay snack products are being test marketed in several states, and guacamole-flavored Doritos became one of the most successful new-product launches in the company's history.

Discussion

In the research process for Frito-Lay Company, many different numerical questions were raised regarding Frito-Lay products, advertising techniques, and purchase patterns among Hispanics. In each of these areas, statistics—in particular, hypothesis testing—plays a central role. Using the case information and the concepts of statistical hypothesis testing, discuss the following:

1. Many proportions were generated in the focus groups and market research that were conducted for this project, including the proportion of the market that is Hispanic, the proportion of Hispanic grocery shoppers that are women, the proportion of chip purchasers that are teens, and so on. Use techniques presented in this chapter to analyze each of the following and discuss how the results might affect marketing decision makers regarding the Hispanic market.

   a. Suppose that in the past, 94% of all Hispanic grocery shoppers were women. Perhaps due to changing cultural values, we believe that more Hispanic men are now grocery shopping. We randomly sample 689 Hispanic grocery shoppers from around the United States and 606 are women. Does this result provide enough evidence to conclude that a lower proportion of Hispanic grocery shoppers now are women?

   b. What proportion of Hispanics listen primarily to advertisements in Spanish? Suppose one source says that in the past the proportion has been about .83. We want to test to determine whether this figure is true. A random sample of 438 Hispanics is selected, and the Minitab results of testing this hypothesis are shown here. Discuss and explain this output and the implications of this study using $\alpha = .05$.

```
Test and CI for One Proportion

Test of p = 0.83 vs p ≠ 0.83

                                                   Exact
Sample  X    N    Sample p  95% CI                 P-Value
1       347  438  0.792237  (0.751184, 0.829290)   0.042
```

2. The statistical mean can be used to measure various aspects of the Hispanic culture and the Hispanic market, including size of purchase, frequency of purchase, age of consumer, size of store, and so on. Use techniques presented in this chapter to analyze each of the following and discuss how the results might affect marketing decisions.

   a. What is the average age of a purchaser of Doritos Salsa Verde? Suppose initial tests indicate that the mean age is 31. Is this figure really correct? To test whether it is, a researcher randomly contacts 24 purchasers of Doritos Salsa Verde with results shown in the following Excel output. Discuss the output in terms of a hypothesis test to determine whether the mean age is actually 31. Let α be .01. Assume that ages of purchasers are normally distributed in the population.

Mean	28.81
Variance	50.2651
Observations	24
df	23
t Stat	−1.52
$P (T <= t)$ one-tail	0.0716
t Critical one-tail	2.50
$P (T < \neq t)$ two-tail	0.1431
t Critical two-tail	2.81

   b. What is the average expenditure of a Hispanic customer on chips per year? Suppose it is hypothesized that the figure is $45 per year. A researcher who knows the Hispanic market believes that this figure is too high and wants to prove her case. She randomly selects 18 Hispanics, has them keep a log of grocery purchases for one year, and obtains the following figures. Analyze the data using techniques from this chapter and an alpha of .05. Assume that expenditures per customer are normally distributed in the population.

$55	37	59	57	27	28
16	46	34	62	9	34
4	25	38	58	3	50

Source: Adapted from "From Bland to Brand," *American Demographics*, (March 1999) p. 57; Ronald J. Alsop, ed., *The Wall Street Journal Almanac 1999*. New York: Ballantine Books, 1998, p. 202; and the 2011 Frito-Lay Web site at http://www.fritolay.com/index.html. The Adelante Group (San Antonio, Texas) January 30, 2011, http://adelante-sa.com/history.htm; "Diversity Finds Its Place: More Organizations Are Dedicating Senior-Level Executives to Drive Diversity Initiatives for Bottom-Line Effect," *HR Magazine*, August 2006, http://findarticles.com/p/articles/mi_m3495/is_8_51/ai_n26968947/; Snack Chat, "Reaching Out to Hispanic Consumers," March 11, 2009, http://www.snacks.com/good_fun_fritolay/2009/03/reaching-out-to-mexican-consumers.html; www.fritolay.com/

CHAPTER 10

Statistical Inferences About Two Populations

LEARNING OBJECTIVES

The general focus of Chapter 10 is on testing hypotheses and constructing confidence intervals about parameters from two populations, thereby enabling you to:

1. Test hypotheses and develop confidence intervals about the difference in two means with known population variances using the z statistic.

2. Test hypotheses and develop confidence intervals about the difference in two means of independent samples with unknown population variances using the t test.

3. Test hypotheses and develop confidence intervals about the difference in two dependent populations.

4. Test hypotheses and develop confidence intervals about the difference in two population proportions.

5. Test hypotheses about the difference in two population variances using the F distribution.

Decision Dilemma

L. L. Bean

L. L. Bean, with headquarters in Freeport, Maine, began as a one-man operation in 1912 by selling hunting boots from a circular entitled "The Maine Hunting Shoe" and has evolved into the leading U.S. catalog company and the largest supplier of outdoor gear in the world, with annual sales of $1.44 billion. The company's founder, Leon Leonwood (L. L.) Bean, was a Maine outdoorsman and hunter and an entrepreneur. As a result of one cold, wet hunting trip from which he returned with damp feet, he developed a new style of hunting boot with leather uppers and a rubber base. This new hunting boot, the Maine Hunting Shoe[R], "changed outdoor footwear forever." He offered the new boots to other hunters and outdoorsmen by sending a letter to sportsmen from outside Maine who had purchased a Maine hunting license. He promised a money-back guarantee on sales that has become a mainstay of the company to this day. After some adjustments and restarts, sales of the boots took off and the company began.

Bean established his factory directly above the post office so that orders could be conveniently filled and shipped. Because he knew that hunters from out of state interested in seeing his operation might be passing through Freeport in the middle of the night on their way to hunting stands, he opened for business 24 hours a day—a policy that is still a distinctive feature of its flagship store today. In 1920, Bean opened a showroom adjacent to his factory, and by 1922, company sales had reached $135,000 annually. As the company grew, other outdoor products were added. The company built its success, in part, through

Matthew Wiley/Masterfile

high-quality products offered at reasonable prices and through excellent customer service.

For the next 30 years, L. L. Bean increased sales through product innovation and word-of-mouth and print advertising. The company expanded its catalog offerings, publishing several per year so as to offer products for different seasons. It built the company's reputation from its Maine outdoor image, the appeal of its catalogs, and free shipping. In 1954, L. L. Bean introduced its first women's department. In the 1960s, with the grandson of the founder, Leon A. Gorman, the company expanded both its target demographic group and its advertising budget along with implementing more competitive pricing. By 1975, annual sales had reached $30 million; by the end of the decade, L. L. Bean had built a distribution center with over 300,000 square feet.

L. L. Bean achieved remarkable growth in the 1980s, due in part to several trends. The Bean label became affiliated with prep culture and clothing, the national health and fitness boom sparked greater interest in the active lifestyle promoted by outdoor activities, and there was a surge in mail-order shopping, especially by women. In the early 1990s, the company opened its first Japanese store followed by 10 others by the end of the decade. Today, L. L. Bean employs over 5,000 people year-round and over 10,000 during the holiday season. In 2010, L. L. Bean produced 50 different catalogs distributed to all 50 U.S. states and over 160 countries. According to company sources, over 11 million customer contacts are received per year with over 130,000 orders placed online in a single day.

L. L. Bean has become quite fast in its mobile retail performance. Recent statistics show that its e-commerce site home page loaded on average in 7.28 seconds, placing the company in the top 10 of the Keynote Mobile Commerce Performance Index in a recent week. The average order size at L. L. Bean is $76.55, and the number of coupon clicks in a recent month was 6,454.

MANAGERIAL AND STATISTICAL QUESTIONS

1. Recent statistics have shown that L. L. Bean's e-commerce site home page loaded, on average, in 7.28 seconds. Suppose the company did not have that figure broken down by daytime (between 8 A.M. and 5 P.M.) and nighttime (after 5 P.M. and before 8 A.M.) but held the theory that due to a slower volume at night, the home page might load faster at night. To test this theory, a random sample of 37 uploads is taken during the daytime with a resultant mean time of 7.46 seconds. A second random sample of 45 uploads is taken at night with a resulting mean time of 7.11 seconds. Previous studies indicate that the population standard deviation both during the daytime and at night is 0.83 seconds. From this information, how would a statistician go about testing the proposed theory?

2. Is the average order size for women greater than the average order size for men? Suppose researchers at L. L. Bean want to test this question by taking a random sample of 44 orders from women and a random sample of 48 orders from men. Suppose that the sample mean for women is $80 with a sample standard deviation of $18. Suppose furthermore that the sample mean for men is $72 with a sample standard deviation of $16. How could we set up and carry out a hypothesis test to answer the question about order size using these data?

3. According to a survey conducted by comScore for UPS, about 41% of shoppers said that "receiving my product when expected" led them to recommend an online retailer. Suppose another researcher wanted to compare this result for L. L. Bean purchasers and a competitor. Suppose a random sample of 310 L. L. Bean purchasers is obtained and asked this question, with the result that 136 agreed with this statement. Suppose a random sample of 195 competitor purchasers is obtained and asked this question, with the result that 72 agreed with this statement. If we wanted to use these data to determine if there is a significant difference between L. L. Bean purchasers and the competitor's purchasers on this issue, how would we go about doing it?

Sources: About L. L. Bean: company history: http://www.llbean.com/customerService/aboutLLBean/company_history.html; about L. L. Bean: companyinformation:http://www.llbean.com/customerService/aboutLLBean/company_information.html; UPS site at: https://thenewlogistics.ups.com/retail/comscore-survey/; "L. L. Bean shows other mobile retailers how to speed things up," Mobile Commerce, May 3, 2012, at http://www.internetretailer.com/2012/05/03/ll-bean-shows-other-mobile-retailers-how-speed-things; "L. L. Bean Coupons," Coupon Cabin, September 28, 2012 at http://www.couponcabin.com/coupons/ll-bean/; L. L. Bean at Encyclopedia.com at http://www.encyclopedia.com/topic/L.L._Bean.aspx

To this point, all discussion of confidence intervals and hypothesis tests has centered on single population parameters. That is, a single sample is randomly drawn from a population, and using data from that sample, a population mean, proportion, or variance is estimated or tested. Chapter 8 presents statistical techniques for constructing confidence intervals to estimate a population mean, a population proportion, or a population variance. Chapter 9 presents statistical techniques for testing hypotheses about a population mean, a population proportion, or a population variance. Often, it is of equal interest to make inferences about two populations. A retail analyst might want to compare per person annual expenditures on shoes in the year 2016 with those in the year 2011 to determine whether a change has occurred over time. A market researcher might want to estimate or test to determine the proportion of market share of one company in two different regions.

In this chapter, we will consider several different techniques for analyzing data that come from two samples. One technique is used with proportions, one is used with variances, and the others are used with means. The techniques for analyzing means are separated into those using the *z* statistic and those using the *t* statistic. In four of the five techniques presented in this chapter, the two samples are assumed to be **independent samples**. The samples are independent because *the items or people sampled in each group are in no way related to those in the other group.* Any similarity between items or people in the two samples is coincidental and due to chance. One of the techniques presented in the chapter is for analyzing data from dependent, or related, samples in which items or persons in one sample are matched in some way with items or persons in the other sample. For four of the five techniques, we will examine both hypothesis tests and confidence intervals.

Chapter 10 contains techniques for constructing confidence intervals and testing hypotheses about the differences in two population means and two population proportions and, in addition, testing hypotheses about two population variances. **Figure 10.1** displays a tree diagram of Chapter 10 confidence interval techniques. **Figure 10.2** displays a tree diagram of Chapter 10 hypothesis testing techniques. Note that at the bottom of each tree branch in Figures 10.1 and 10.2, the title of the statistical technique along with its respective section number is given for ease of identification and use. If a business researcher is constructing confidence intervals or testing hypotheses about the difference in two population means and the population standard deviations or variances are known, then he will use the z test for $\mu_1 - \mu_2$ contained in

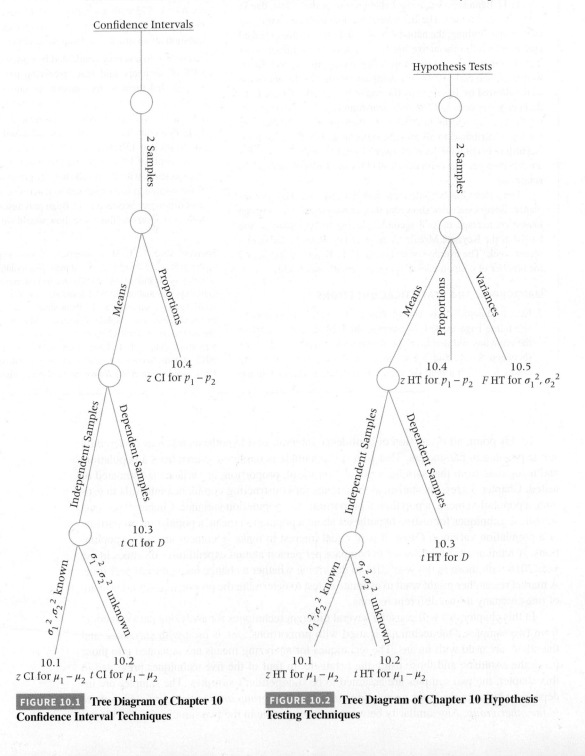

FIGURE 10.1 **Tree Diagram of Chapter 10 Confidence Interval Techniques**

FIGURE 10.2 **Tree Diagram of Chapter 10 Hypothesis Testing Techniques**

Section 10.1. If the population standard deviations or variances are unknown, then the appropriate technique is the *t* test for $\mu_1 - \mu_2$ contained in Section 10.2. If a business researcher is constructing confidence intervals or testing hypotheses about the difference in two related populations, then he will use the *t* test presented in Section 10.3. If a business researcher is constructing a confidence interval or testing a hypothesis about the difference in two population proportions, then he will use the *z* test for $p_1 - p_2$ presented in Section 10.4. If the researcher desires to test a hypothesis about two population variances, then he will use the *F* test presented in Section 10.5.

10.1 Hypothesis Testing and Confidence Intervals About the Difference in Two Means Using the *z* Statistic (Population Variances Known)

In some research designs, the sampling plan calls for selecting two independent samples, calculating the sample means and using the difference in the two sample means to estimate or test the difference in the two population means. The object might be to determine whether the two samples come from the same population or, if they come from different populations, to determine the amount of difference in the populations. This type of analysis can be used to determine, for example, whether the effectiveness of two brands of toothpaste differs or whether two brands of tires wear differently. Business research might be conducted to study the difference in the productivity of men and women on an assembly line under certain conditions. An engineer might want to determine differences in the strength of aluminum produced under two different temperatures. Does the average cost of a two-bedroom, one-story house differ between Boston and Seattle? If so, how much is the difference? These and many other interesting questions can be researched by comparing the difference in two sample means.

▶ Lecture Video

How does a researcher analyze the difference in two samples by using sample means? The central limit theorem states that the difference in two sample means, $\bar{x}_1 - \bar{x}_2$, is normally distributed for large sample sizes (both n_1 and $n_2 \geq 30$) regardless of the shape of the populations. It can also be shown that

$$\mu_{\bar{x}_1 - \bar{x}_2} = \mu_1 - \mu_2$$

$$\sigma_{\bar{x}_1 - \bar{x}_2} = \sqrt{\frac{\sigma_1^2}{n_1} + \frac{\sigma_2^2}{n_2}}$$

These expressions lead to a *z* formula for the difference in two sample means.

z Formula for the Difference in Two Sample Means (Independent Samples and Population Variances Known)

$$z = \frac{(\bar{x}_1 - \bar{x}_2) - (\mu_1 - \mu_2)}{\sqrt{\dfrac{\sigma_1^2}{n_1} + \dfrac{\sigma_2^2}{n_2}}} \tag{10.1}$$

where

μ_1 = the mean of population 1
μ_2 = the mean of population 2
n_1 = size of sample 1
n_2 = size of sample 2
σ_1^2 = the variance of population 1
σ_2^2 = the variance of population 2

This formula is the basis for statistical inferences about the difference in two means using two random independent samples.

Note: *If the populations are normally distributed on the measurement being studied and if the population variances are known, Formula 10.1 can be used for small sample sizes.*

Hypothesis Testing

In many instances, a business researcher wants to test the differences in the mean values of two populations. As an example, a consumer organization might want to test two brands of light bulbs to determine whether one burns longer than the other. A company wanting to relocate might want to determine whether a significant difference separates the average price of a home in Newark, New Jersey, from house prices in Cleveland, Ohio. Formula 10.1 can be used to test the difference between two population means.

As a specific example, suppose we want to conduct a hypothesis test to determine whether the average annual wage for an advertising manager is different from the average annual wage of an auditing manager. Because we are testing to determine whether the means are different, it might seem logical that the null and alternative hypotheses would be

$$H_0: \mu_1 = \mu_2$$
$$H_a: \mu_1 \neq \mu_2$$

where advertising managers are population 1 and auditing managers are population 2. However, statisticians generally construct these hypotheses as

$$H_0: \mu_1 - \mu_2 = \delta$$
$$H_a: \mu_1 - \mu_2 \neq \delta$$

This format not only allows the business analyst to test if the population means are equal but also affords her the opportunity to hypothesize about a particular difference in the means (δ). Generally speaking, most business analysts are only interested in testing whether the difference in the means is different. Thus, δ is set equal to zero, resulting in the following hypotheses, which we will use for this problem and most others.

$$H_0: \mu_1 - \mu_2 = 0$$
$$H_a: \mu_1 - \mu_2 \neq 0$$

Note, however, that a business researcher could be interested in testing to determine if there is, for example, a difference of means equal to, say, 10, in which case, $\delta = 10$.

A random sample of 32 advertising managers from across the United States is taken. The advertising managers are contacted by telephone and asked what is their annual salary. A similar random sample is taken of 34 auditing managers. The resulting salary data are listed in Table 10.1, along with the sample means, the population standard deviations, and the population variances.

In this problem, the business analyst is testing whether there is a difference in the average wage of an advertising manager and an auditing manager; therefore the test is two-tailed. If the business analyst had hypothesized that one was paid more than the other, the test would have been one tailed.

Suppose $\alpha = .05$. Because this test is a two-tailed test, each of the two rejection regions has an area of .025, leaving .475 of the area in the distribution between each critical value and the mean of the distribution. The associated critical table value for this area is $z_{.025} = \pm 1.96$. Figure 10.3 shows the critical table z value along with the rejection regions.

Formula 10.1 and the data in Table 10.1 yield a z value to complete the hypothesis test

$$z = \frac{(70.700 - 62.187) - (0)}{\sqrt{\dfrac{264.160}{32} + \dfrac{166.410}{34}}} = 2.35$$

The observed value of 2.35 is greater than the critical value obtained from the z table, 1.96. The business researcher rejects the null hypothesis and can say that there is a significant

TABLE 10.1	Wages for Advertising Managers and Auditing Managers ($1,000)		
ADVERTISING MANAGERS		**AUDITING MANAGERS**	
74.256	64.276	69.962	67.160
96.234	74.194	55.052	37.386
89.807	65.360	57.828	59.505
93.261	73.904	63.362	72.790
103.030	54.270	37.194	71.351
74.195	59.045	99.198	58.653
75.932	68.508	61.254	63.508
80.742	71.115	73.065	43.649
39.672	67.574	48.036	63.369
45.652	59.621	60.053	59.676
93.083	62.483	66.359	54.449
63.384	69.319	61.261	46.394
57.791	35.394	77.136	71.804
65.145	86.741	66.035	72.401
96.767	57.351	54.335	56.470
77.242		42.494	67.814
67.056		83.849	71.492

$$n_1 = 32 \qquad\qquad n_2 = 34$$

$$\bar{x}_1 = 70.700 \qquad\qquad \bar{x}_2 = 62.187$$

$$\sigma_1 = 16.253 \qquad\qquad \sigma_2 = 12.900$$

$$\sigma_1^2 = 264.160 \qquad\qquad \sigma_2^2 = 166.410$$

difference between the average annual wage of an advertising manager and the average annual wage of an auditing manager. The business researcher then examines the sample means (70.700 for advertising managers and 62.187 for auditing managers) and uses common sense to conclude that advertising managers earn more, on the average, than do auditing managers. Figure 10.4 shows the relationship between the observed z and $z_{\alpha/2}$.

This conclusion could have been reached by using the p-value. Looking up the probability of $z \geq 2.35$ in the z distribution table in Appendix A.5 yields an area of $.5000 - .4906 = .0094$. This p-value ($.0094$) is less than $\alpha/2 = .025$. The decision is to reject the null hypothesis.

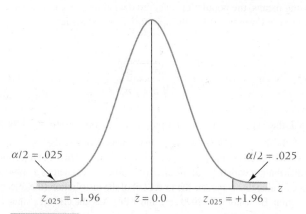

$\alpha/2 = .025$ $\alpha/2 = .025$

$z_{.025} = -1.96$ $z = 0.0$ $z_{.025} = +1.96$

FIGURE 10.3 **Critical Values and Rejection Regions for the Wage Example**

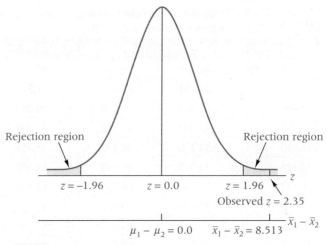

Rejection region   Rejection region

$z = -1.96$ $z = 0.0$ $z = 1.96$

Observed $z = 2.35$

$\mu_1 - \mu_2 = 0.0$ $\bar{x}_1 - \bar{x}_2 = 8.513$ $\bar{x}_1 - \bar{x}_2$

FIGURE 10.4 **Location of Observed z Value for the Wage Example**

DEMONSTRATION PROBLEM 10.1

A women's activist group wants to "prove" that women do not pay as much per year as men into private pension funds. They hire a business researcher to test their theory. The business researcher takes a random sample of 87 professional working women, and from information provided by them, she determines that the sample average annual amount paid into a private pension fund per person is $3,352. Assume that the standard deviation for this population is $1,100. She also takes a random sample of 76 professional working men, and from information provided by them, she determines that the sample average annual amount paid into a private pension fund per person is $5,727. Assume that the standard deviation for this population is $1,700. Using this data, $\alpha = .001$, and the eight-step approach to hypothesis testing, the business researcher will test the hypothesis that women do pay less per year into private pension funds than do men.

Solution:

Step 1. At step 1, the hypotheses must be established. We let women be population 1 and men be population 2. Because the women's activist group wants to prove that women pay less than men into private pension funds annually, the alternative hypothesis should be $\mu_1 - \mu_2 < 0$ and the null hypothesis is $\mu_1 - \mu_2 = 0$. Note that the case where women pay more than men is included in the null hypothesis. Summarizing the hypotheses:

$$H_0: \mu_1 - \mu_2 = 0$$
$$H_a: \mu_1 - \mu_2 < 0$$

Step 2. At step 2, the appropriate statistical test and sampling distribution is determined. Because we are testing means, the population standard deviations are known, and both sample sizes are over 30, the z test in Formula 10.1 is the appropriate test statistic:

$$z = \frac{(\bar{x}_1 - \bar{x}_2) - (\mu_1 - \mu_2)}{\sqrt{\dfrac{\sigma_1^2}{n_1} + \dfrac{\sigma_2^2}{n_2}}}$$

Step 3. At step 3, the Type I error rate, or alpha, which is .001, is specified for this problem.

Step 4. At step 4, the decision rule is stated for the problem. Because the test is one tailed and alpha is .001, there is .001 of the area in the lower tail of the distribution. Thus, the rejection region is in the lower end of the distribution with 0.1% of the area in the lower tail. There is a .4990 area between the mean and the critical value that separates the lower tail of the distribution (the rejection region) from the nonrejection region. By using this .4990 area and Table A.5, the critical z value can be obtained:

$$z_\alpha = -3.08$$

The decision rule is that if the data gathered produce a z value less than -3.08, the test statistic is in the rejection region and the decision is to reject the null hypothesis. If the observed z value calculated from the data is greater than -3.08, the decision is not to reject the null hypothesis because the observed z value is in the non-rejection region.

Step 5.   Gather the data. Data for the problem are summarized as:

WOMEN	MEN
$n_1 = 87$	$n_2 = 76$
$\bar{x}_1 = \$3,352$	$\bar{x}_2 = \$5,727$
$\sigma_1 = \$1,100$	$\sigma_2 = \$1,700$

Step 6.   Using these values and a null hypothesis of zero, the value of the test statistic can be calculated as:

$$z = \frac{(3,352 - 5,727) - (0)}{\sqrt{\dfrac{1,100^2}{87} + \dfrac{1,700^2}{76}}} = -10.42$$

Step 7.   Reach a statistical conclusion. Because this test statistic, $z = -10.42$, is less than the critical value of z (-3.08) in the lower tail of the distribution, the statistical conclusion reached at step 7 is to reject the null hypothesis.

Step 8.   At step 8, a managerial decision is made. The evidence is substantial that annually women, on average, pay less than men into private pension funds.

The following diagram displays these results.

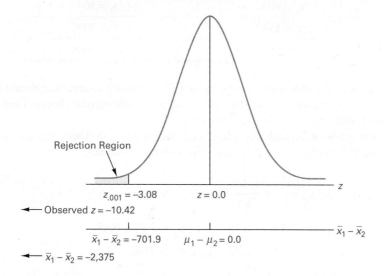

The probability of obtaining an observed z value of -10.42 by chance is virtually zero, because the value is beyond the limits of the z table. By the p-value, the null hypothesis is rejected because the probability is .0000, or less than $\alpha = .001$.

If this problem were worked by the critical value method, what critical value of the difference in the two means would have to be surpassed to reject the null hypothesis for a table z value of -3.08? The answer is:

$$(\bar{x}_1 - \bar{x}_2)_c = (\mu_1 - \mu_2) + z\sqrt{\frac{\sigma_1^2}{n_1} + \frac{\sigma_2^2}{n_2}}$$
$$= 0 - 3.08(227.9) = -701.9$$

The difference in sample means would need to be at least 701.9 to reject the null hypothesis. The actual sample difference in this problem was $-2,375$ $(3,352 - 5,727)$, which is considerably larger than the critical value of difference. Thus, with the critical value method also, the null hypothesis is rejected.

Confidence Intervals

Sometimes being able to estimate the difference in the means of two populations is valuable. By how much do two populations differ in size or weight or age? By how much do two products differ in effectiveness? Do two different manufacturing or training methods produce different mean results? The answers to these questions are often difficult to obtain through census techniques. The alternative is to take a random sample from each of the two populations and study the difference in the sample means.

Algebraically, Formula 10.1 can be manipulated to produce a formula for constructing confidence intervals for the difference in two population means.

Confidence Interval to Estimate $\mu_1 - \mu_2$

$$(\bar{x}_1 - \bar{x}_2) - z\sqrt{\frac{\sigma_1^2}{n_1} + \frac{\sigma_2^2}{n_2}} \leq \mu_1 - \mu_2 \leq (\bar{x}_1 - \bar{x}_2) + z\sqrt{\frac{\sigma_1^2}{n_1} + \frac{\sigma_2^2}{n_2}} \tag{10.2}$$

Suppose a study is conducted to estimate the difference between middle-income shoppers and low-income shoppers in terms of the average amount saved on grocery bills per week by using coupons. Random samples of 60 middle-income shoppers and 80 low-income shoppers are taken, and their purchases are monitored for one week. The average amounts saved with coupons, as well as sample sizes and population standard deviations, are in the table below.

MIDDLE-INCOME SHOPPERS	LOW-INCOME SHOPPERS
$n_1 = 60$	$n_1 = 80$
$\bar{x}_1 = \$5.84$	$\bar{x}_2 = \$2.67$
$\sigma_1 = \$1.41$	$\sigma_2 = \$0.54$

This information can be used to construct a 98% confidence interval to estimate the difference between the mean amount saved with coupons by middle-income shoppers and the mean amount saved with coupons by low-income shoppers.

The z_c value associated with a 98% level of confidence is 2.33. This value, the data shown, and Formula 10.2 can be used to determine the confidence interval.

$$(5.84 - 2.67) - 2.33\sqrt{\frac{1.41^2}{60} + \frac{0.54^2}{80}} \leq \mu_1 - \mu_2 \leq (5.84 - 2.67) + 2.33\sqrt{\frac{1.41^2}{60} + \frac{0.54^2}{80}}$$

$$3.17 - 0.45 \leq \mu_1 - \mu_2 \leq 3.17 + 0.45$$

$$2.72 \leq \mu_1 - \mu_2 \leq 3.62$$

There is a 98% level of confidence that the actual difference in the population mean coupon savings per week between middle-income and low-income shoppers is between $2.72 and $3.62. That is, the difference could be as little as $2.72 or as great as $3.62. The point estimate for the difference in mean savings is $3.17. Note that a zero difference in the population means of these two groups is unlikely, because zero is not in the 98% range.

DEMONSTRATION PROBLEM 10.2

A consumer test group wants to determine the difference in gasoline mileage of cars using regular unleaded gas and cars using premium unleaded gas. Researchers for the group divided a fleet of 100 cars of the same make in half and tested each car on one tank of gas. Fifty of the cars were filled with regular unleaded gas and 50 were filled with premium unleaded gas. The sample average for the regular gasoline group was 21.45 miles per gallon (mpg), and the sample average for the premium gasoline group was 24.60 mpg. Assume that the population standard deviation of the regular unleaded gas population is 3.46 mpg, and that the population standard deviation of the premium unleaded gas population is 2.99 mpg. Construct a 95% confidence interval to estimate the difference in the mean gas mileage between the cars using regular gasoline and the cars using premium gasoline.

Solution: The *z* value for a 95% confidence interval is 1.96. The other sample information follows.

REGULAR	PREMIUM
$n_r = 50$	$n_p = 50$
$\bar{x}_r = 21.45$	$\bar{x}_p = 24.60$
$\sigma_r = 3.46$	$\sigma_p = 2.99$

Based on this information, the confidence interval is

$$(21.45 - 24.60) - 1.96\sqrt{\frac{3.46^2}{50} + \frac{2.99^2}{50}} \le \mu_1 - \mu_2 \le (21.45 - 24.60) + 1.96\sqrt{\frac{3.46^2}{50} + \frac{2.99^2}{50}}$$

$$-3.15 - 1.27 \le \mu_1 - \mu_2 \le -3.15 + 1.27$$

$$-4.42 \le \mu_1 - \mu_2 \le -1.88$$

We are 95% confident that the actual difference in mean gasoline mileage between the two types of gasoline is between −1.88 mpg and −4.42 mpg. The point estimate is −3.15 mpg.

Designating one group as group 1 and another group as group 2 is an arbitrary decision. If the two groups in Demonstration Problem 10.2 were reversed, the confidence interval would be the same, but the signs would be reversed and the inequalities would be switched. Thus the researcher must interpret the confidence interval in light of the sample information. For the confidence interval in Demonstration Problem 10.2, the population difference in mean mileage between regular and premium could be as much as −4.42 mpg. This result means that the premium gasoline could average 4.42 mpg more than regular gasoline. The other side of the interval shows that, on the basis of the sample information, the difference in favor of premium gasoline could be as little as 1.88 mpg.

If the confidence interval were being used to test the hypothesis that there is a difference in the average number of miles per gallon between regular and premium gasoline, the interval would tell us to reject the null hypothesis because the interval does *not* contain zero. When both ends of a confidence interval have the same sign, zero is not in the interval. In Demonstration Problem 10.2, the interval signs are both negative. We are 95% confident that the true difference in population means is negative. Hence, we are 95% confident that there is nonzero difference in means. For such a test, $\alpha = 1 - .95 = .05$. If the signs of the confidence interval for the difference of the sample means are different, the interval includes zero, and finding no significant difference in population means is possible.

Using the Computer to Test Hypotheses About the Difference in Two Population Means Using the *z* Test

Excel has the capability of testing hypotheses about two population means using a *z* test, but Minitab does not. **Figure 10.5** shows Excel output for the advertising manager and auditing manager wage problem. For *z* tests, Excel requires knowledge of the population variances. The standard output includes the sample means and population variances, the sample sizes, the hypothesized mean difference (which here, as in most cases, is zero), the observed *z* value, and the *p*-values and critical table *z*-values for both a one-tailed and a two-tailed test. Note that the *p*-value for this two-tailed test is .0189, which is less than $\alpha = .05$ and thus indicates that the decision should be to reject the null hypothesis.

z-Test: Two Sample for Means

	Ad Mgr	Aud Mgr
Mean	70.700	62.187
Known Variance	264.160	166.411
Observations	32	34
Hypothesized Mean Difference	0	
z	2.35	
P(Z<=z) one-tail	0.0094	
z Critical one-tail	1.64	
P(Z<=z) two-tail	0.0189	
z Critical two-tail	1.96	

FIGURE 10.5 **Excel Output for the Advertising Manager and Auditing Manager Wage Problem**

10.1 Problems

10.1. a. Test the following hypotheses of the difference in population means by using the following data $(\alpha = .10)$ and the eight-step process.

$$H_0: \mu_1 - \mu_2 = 0 \qquad H_a: \mu_1 - \mu_2 < 0$$

SAMPLE 1	SAMPLE 2
$n_1 = 31$	$n_2 = 32$
$\bar{x}_1 = 51.3$	$\bar{x}_2 = 53.2$
$\sigma_1^2 = 52$	$\sigma_2^2 = 60$

b. Use the critical value method to find the critical difference in the mean values required to reject the null hypothesis.

c. What is the p-value for this problem?

10.2. Use the following sample information to construct a 90% confidence interval for the difference in the two population means.

SAMPLE 1	SAMPLE 2
$n_1 = 32$	$n_2 = 31$
$\bar{x}_1 = 70.4$	$\bar{x}_2 = 68.7$
$\sigma_1 = 5.76$	$\sigma_2 = 6.1$

10.3. Examine the following data. Assume the variances for the two populations are 22.74 and 26.65, respectively.

a. Use the data to test the following hypotheses $(\alpha = .02)$.

$$H_0: \mu_1 - \mu_2 = 0 \qquad H_a: \mu_1 - \mu_2 \neq 0$$

SAMPLE 1						SAMPLE 2					
90	88	80	88	83	94	78	85	82	81	75	76
88	87	91	81	83	88	90	80	76	83	88	77
81	84	84	87	87	93	77	75	79	86	90	75
88	90	91	88	84	83	82	83	88	80	80	74
89	95	97	95	93	97	80	90	74	89	84	79

b. Construct a 98% confidence interval to estimate the difference in population means using these data. How does your result validate the decision you reached in part (a)?

10.4. The Trade Show Bureau conducted a survey to determine why people go to trade shows. The respondents were asked to rate a series of reasons on a scale from 1 to 5, with 1 representing little importance and 5 representing great importance. One of the reasons suggested was general curiosity. The following responses for 50 people from the computers/electronics industry and 50 people from the food/beverage industry were recorded for general curiosity. Use these data and $\alpha = .01$ to determine whether there is a significant difference between people in these two industries on this question. Assume the variance for the computer/electronics population is 1.0188 and the variance for the food/beverage population is 0.9180 and the data are interval in level.

COMPUTERS/ELECTRONICS					FOOD/BEVERAGE				
1	2	1	3	2	3	3	2	4	3
0	3	3	2	1	4	5	2	4	3
3	3	1	2	2	3	2	3	2	3
3	2	2	2	2	4	3	3	3	3
1	2	3	2	1	2	4	2	3	3
1	1	3	3	2	2	4	4	4	4
2	1	4	1	4	3	5	3	3	2
2	3	0	1	0	2	0	2	2	5
3	3	2	2	3	4	3	3	2	3
2	1	0	2	3	4	3	3	3	2

10.5. Suppose you own a plumbing repair business and employ 15 plumbers. You are interested in estimating the difference in the average number of calls completed per day between two of the plumbers. A random sample of 40 days of plumber A's work results in a sample average of 5.3 calls, with a population variance of 1.99. A random sample of 37 days of plumber B's work results in a sample mean of 6.5 calls, with a population variance of 2.36. Use this information and a 95% level of confidence to estimate the difference in population mean daily efforts between plumber A and plumber B. Interpret the results. Is it possible that, for these populations of days, the average number of calls completed between plumber A and plumber B do not differ?

10.6. The Bureau of Labor Statistics shows that the average insurance cost to a company per hour worked for an employee by major industry group, is $2.94 for construction workers and $3.76 for manufacturing workers. Suppose these figures were obtained from 14 construction workers and 15 manufacturing workers and that their respective population standard deviations are $1.38 and $1.51. Assume that such insurance costs are normally distributed in the population.

 a. Calculate a 98% confidence interval to estimate the difference in the mean hourly company expenditures for insurance for these two groups. What is the value of the point estimate?

 b. Test to determine whether there is a significant difference in the hourly rates employers pay for insurance between construction workers and manufacturing workers. Use a 2% level of significance.

10.7. A company's auditor believes the per diem cost in Nashville, Tennessee, rose significantly between 2005 and 2016. To test this belief, the auditor samples 51 business trips from the company's records for 2005 the sample average was $190 per day, with a population standard deviation of $18.50. The auditor selects a second random sample of 47 business trips from the company's records for 2016 the sample average was $198 per day, with a population standard deviation of $15.60. If he uses a risk of committing a Type I error of .01, does the auditor find that the per diem average expense in Nashville has gone up significantly?

10.8. Suppose a market analyst wants to determine the difference in the average price of a gallon of whole milk in Seattle and Atlanta. To do so, he takes a telephone survey of 21 randomly selected consumers in Seattle who have purchased a gallon of milk and asks how much they paid for it. The analyst undertakes a similar survey in Atlanta with 18 respondents. Assume the population variance for Seattle is 0.03, the population variance for Atlanta is 0.015, and that the price of milk is normally distributed. Using the resulting sample information that follows,

 a. Compute a 99% confidence interval to estimate the difference in the mean price of a gallon of milk between the two cities.

 b. Using a 1% level of significance, test to determine if there is a significant difference in the price of a gallon of milk between the two cities.

SEATTLE			ATLANTA		
$2.55	$2.36	$2.43	$2.25	$2.40	$2.39
2.67	2.54	2.43	2.30	2.33	2.40
2.50	2.54	2.38	2.49	2.29	2.23
2.61	2.80	2.49	2.41	2.48	2.29
2.43	2.61	2.57	2.39	2.59	2.53
2.36	2.56	2.71	2.26	2.38	2.45
2.50	2.64	2.27			

10.9. Employee suggestions can provide useful and insightful ideas for management. Some companies solicit and receive employee suggestions more than others, and company culture influences the use of employee suggestions. Suppose a study is conducted to determine whether there is a significant difference in mean number of suggestions per year per employee between the Canon Corporation and the Pioneer Electronic Corporation. The study shows that the average number of suggestions per year per employee is 1.3 at Canon and 1.0 at Pioneer. Suppose these figures were obtained from random samples of 36 and 45 employees, respectively. If the population standard deviations of suggestions per employee are 0.7 and 0.4 for Canon and Pioneer, respectively, is there a significant difference in the population means? Use $\alpha = .05$.

10.10. Two processes in a manufacturing line are performed manually: operation A and operation B. A random sample of 50 different assemblies using operation A shows that the sample average time per assembly is 8.05 minutes, with a population standard deviation of 1.36 minutes. A random sample of 38 different assemblies using operation B shows that the sample average time per assembly is 7.26 minutes, with a population standard deviation of 1.06 minutes. For $\alpha = .10$, is there enough evidence in these samples to declare that operation A takes significantly longer to perform than operation B?

10.2 Hypothesis Testing and Confidence Intervals About the Difference in Two Means: Independent Samples and Population Variances Unknown

The techniques presented in Section 10.1 are for use whenever the population variances are known. On many occasions, statisticians test hypotheses or construct confidence intervals about the difference in two population means and the population variances are not known. If the population variances are not known, the *z* methodology is not appropriate. This section presents methodology for handling the situation when the population variances are unknown.

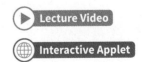

Hypothesis Testing

The hypothesis test presented in this section is a test that compares the means of two samples to determine whether there is a difference in the two population means from which the samples come. This technique is used whenever the population variances are unknown (and hence the sample variances must be used) and the samples are independent (not related in any way). *An assumption underlying this technique is that the measurement or characteristic being studied is normally distributed for both populations.* In Section 10.1, the difference in large sample means was analyzed by Formula 10.1:

$$z = \frac{(\bar{x}_1 - \bar{x}_2) - (\mu_1 - \mu_2)}{\sqrt{\dfrac{\sigma_1^2}{n_1} + \dfrac{\sigma_2^2}{n_2}}}$$

If $\sigma_1^2 = \sigma_2^2$, Formula 10.1 algebraically reduces to

$$z = \frac{(\bar{x}_1 - \bar{x}_2) - (\mu_1 - \mu_2)}{\sigma \sqrt{\dfrac{1}{n_1} + \dfrac{1}{n_2}}}$$

If σ is unknown, it can be estimated by *pooling* the two sample variances and computing a pooled sample standard deviation.

$$\sigma \approx s_p = \sqrt{\frac{s_1^2(n_1 - 1) + s_2^2(n_2 - 1)}{n_1 + n_2 - 2}}$$

s_p^2 is the weighted average of the two sample variances, s_1^2 and s_2^2. Substituting this expression for σ and changing z to t produces a formula to test the difference in means.

---

t Formula to Test the Difference in Means Assuming σ_1^2, σ_2^2, are Equal

$$t = \frac{(\bar{x}_1 - \bar{x}_2) - (\mu_1 - \mu_2)}{\sqrt{\dfrac{s_1^2(n_1 - 1) + s_2^2(n_2 - 1)}{n_1 + n_2 - 2}} \sqrt{\dfrac{1}{n_1} + \dfrac{1}{n_2}}} \qquad (10.3)$$

$$\text{df} = n_1 + n_2 - 2$$

Formula 10.3 is constructed by assuming that the two population variances, σ_1^2 and σ_2^2, are equal. Thus, when using Formula 10.3 to test hypotheses about the difference in two means for independent samples when the population variances are unknown, we must assume that the two samples come from populations in which the variances are essentially equal.

At the Hernandez Manufacturing Company, an application of this test arises. New employees are expected to attend a three-day seminar to learn about the company. At the end of the seminar, they are tested to measure their knowledge about the company. The traditional training method has been lecture and a question-and-answer session. Management decided to experiment with a different training procedure that processes new employees in two days by using DVDs and having no question-and-answer session. If this procedure works, it could save the company thousands of dollars over a period of several years. However, there is some concern about the effectiveness of the two-day method, and company managers would like to know whether there is any difference in the effectiveness of the two training methods.

To test the difference in the two methods, the managers randomly select one group of 15 newly hired employees to take the three-day seminar (method A) and a second group of 12 new employees for the two-day DVD method (method B). Table 10.2 shows the test scores of the two groups. Using $\alpha = .05$, the managers want to determine whether there is a significant difference in the mean scores of the two groups. They assume that the scores for this test are normally distributed and that the population variances are approximately equal.

TABLE 10.2   **Test Scores for New Employees After Training**

TRAINING METHOD A					TRAINING METHOD B			
56	50	52	44	52	59	54	55	65
47	47	53	45	48	52	57	64	53
42	51	42	43	44	53	56	53	57

Step 1   At step 1, the hypotheses must be established. Because they are testing to determine if the average scores for method A are different from the average scores for method B, the null and alternate hypotheses are:

$$H_0: \mu_1 - \mu_2 = 0$$
$$H_a: \mu_1 - \mu_2 \neq 0$$

Step 2   At step 2, the appropriate statistical test and sampling distribution are determined. The population variances (and standard deviations) are not known. Because it was assumed that the scores for this test are normally distributed and that the population variances are approximately equal, the researchers can use Formula 10.3.

Step 3   At step 3, the Type I error rate, or alpha, which is .05, is specified for this problem.

Step 4   At step 4, the decision rule is stated for the problem. Because the test is two-tailed and alpha is .05, there is $\alpha/2$ or .025 of the area in each of the tails of the distribution. In addition, since we are using a *t* test in this analysis, we must compute the degrees of freedom by df $= n_1 + n_2 - 2$. From the data in Table 10.2, n_1 is 15 and n_2 is 12; thus, the degrees of freedom are $15 + 12 - 2 = 25$. Using Table A.6, the critical *t* value can be obtained.

$$t_{.025,25} = \pm 2.060$$

The null hypothesis will be rejected if the observed *t* value is less than −2.060 or greater than +2.060.

Step 5   Gather the data. Data for the problem are summarized as:

METHOD A	METHOD B
$n_1 = 15$	$n_2 = 12$
$\bar{x}_1 = 47.73$	$\bar{x}_2 = 56.50$
$s_1^2 = 19.495$	$s_2^2 = 18.273$

Note: If the equal variances assumption cannot be met, the following formula should be used.

t Formula to Test the Difference in Means

$$t = \frac{(\bar{x}_1 - \bar{x}_2) - (\mu_1 - \mu_2)}{\sqrt{\dfrac{s_1^2}{n_1} + \dfrac{s_2^2}{n_2}}} \qquad df = \frac{\left[\dfrac{s_1^2}{n_1} + \dfrac{s_2^2}{n_2}\right]^2}{\dfrac{\left(\dfrac{s_1^2}{n_1}\right)^2}{n_1 - 1} + \dfrac{\left(\dfrac{s_2^2}{n_2}\right)^2}{n_2 - 1}}$$

Because this formula requires a more complex degrees-of-freedom component, it may be unattractive to some users. Many statistical computer software packages offer the user a choice of the "pooled" formula or the "unpooled" formula. The "pooled" formula in the computer packages is Formula 10.3, in which equal population variances are assumed. Excel refers to Formula 10.3 as a *t*-Test: Two-Sample Assuming Equal Variances. The formula shown just above is the "unpooled" formula used when population variances cannot be assumed to be equal. Excel refers to this as a *t*-Test: Two-Sample Assuming Unequal Variances. Again, in each of these formulas, the populations from which the two samples are drawn are assumed to be normally distributed for the phenomenon being measured.

Step 6 Using these values (step 5) and a hypothesized difference of zero, the value of the test statistic can be calculated as:

$$t = \frac{(47.73 - 56.50) - (0)}{\sqrt{\dfrac{(19.495)(15-1) + (18.273)(12-1)}{15 + 12 - 2}} \sqrt{\dfrac{1}{15} + \dfrac{1}{12}}} = -5.20$$

Step 7 Reach a statistical conclusion. Because this test statistic, $t = -5.20$, is less than the critical value of t (−2.060) in the lower tail of the distribution, the statistical conclusion reached at step 7 is to reject the null hypothesis. There is a significant difference in the mean scores of the two tests.

Step 8 At step 8, a managerial decision is made. **Figure 10.6** shows the critical areas and the observed t value. Note that the computed t value is −5.20, which is enough to cause the managers of the Hernandez Manufacturing Company to reject the null hypothesis. Their conclusion is that there is a significant difference in the effectiveness of the training methods. Upon examining the sample means, they realize that method B (the two-day DVD method) actually produced an average score that was more than eight points higher than that for the group trained with method A. Given that training method B scores are significantly higher and that the seminar is a day shorter than method A (thereby saving both time and money), it makes business sense to adopt method B as the standard training method.

In a test of this sort, which group is group 1 and which is group 2 is an arbitrary decision. If the two samples had been designated in reverse, the observed t value would have been $t = +5.20$ (same magnitude but different sign), and the decision would have been the same.

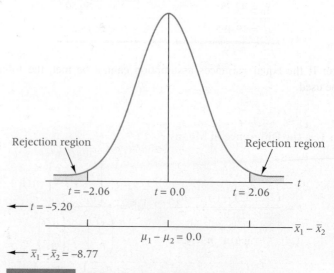

FIGURE 10.6 *t* Values for the Training Methods Example

Using the Computer to Test Hypotheses and Construct Confidence Intervals About the Difference in Two Population Means Using the *t* Test

Both Excel and Minitab have the capability of analyzing *t* tests for the difference in two means. The two computer packages yield similar output. **Figure 10.7** contains Excel and Minitab output for the Hernandez Manufacturing Company training methods example. Notice that both outputs contain the same sample means, the degrees of freedom (df = 25), the observed *t* value −5.20 and the *p*-value (.000022 on Excel as two-tailed *p* and .000 on Minitab). This *p*-value can be compared directly with $\alpha = .05$ for decision-making purposes (reject the null hypothesis).

Each package offers other information. Excel displays the sample variances whereas Minitab displays sample standard deviations. Excel displays the pooled variance whereas Minitab displays the pooled standard deviation. Excel prints out *p*-values for both a one-tailed test and a two-tailed test, and the user must select the appropriate value for his or her test. Excel also prints out the critical *t* values for both one- and two-tailed tests. Notice that the critical *t* value for a two-tailed test (2.06) is the same as the critical *t* value obtained by using the *t* table (±2.060). Minitab yields the standard errors of the mean for each sample. Minitab uses the same command for hypothesis testing and confidence interval estimation for the two-sample case. For this reason, Minitab output for this type of problem always contains both the hypothesis-testing and confidence interval results.

Excel Output

t-Test: Two-Sample Assuming Equal Variances

	Method A	Method B
Mean	47.73	56.50
Variance	19.495	18.273
Observations	15	12
Pooled Variance	18.957	
Hypothesized Mean Difference	0	
df	25	
t Stat	−5.20	
P(T<=t) one-tail	0.000011	
t Critical one-tail	1.71	
P(T<=t) two-tail	0.000022	
t Critical two-tail	2.06	

Minitab Output

Two-Sample T-Test and CI: Method A, Method B

Two-sample T for Method A vs Method B

	N	Mean	StDev	SE Mean
Method A	15	47.73	4.42	1.1
Method B	12	56.50	4.27	1.2

Difference = μ (Method A) − μ (Method B)

Estimate for difference: −8.77

95% CI for difference: (−12.24, −5.29)

T-Test of difference = 0 (vs ≠): T-Value = −5.20 P-Value = 0.000 DF = 25

Both use Pooled StDev = 4.3540

FIGURE 10.7   **Excel and Minitab Output for the Training Methods Example**

DEMONSTRATION PROBLEM 10.3

Is there a difference in the way Chinese cultural values affect the purchasing strategies of industrial buyers in Taiwan and mainland China? A study by researchers at the National Chiao-Tung University in Taiwan attempted to determine whether there is a significant difference in the purchasing strategies of industrial buyers between Taiwan and mainland China based on the cultural dimension labeled "integration." Integration is being in harmony with one's self, family, and associates. For the study, 46 Taiwanese buyers and 26 mainland Chinese buyers were contacted and interviewed. Buyers were asked to respond to 35 items using a 9-point scale with possible answers ranging from no importance (1) to extreme importance (9). The resulting statistics for the two groups are shown in step 5. Using $\alpha = .01$, test to determine whether there is a significant difference between buyers in Taiwan and buyers in mainland China on integration. Assume that integration scores are normally distributed in the population and are interval in level of measurement.

Solution:

Step 1. At step 1, the hypotheses must be established. Because they are testing to determine if there is a difference between Taiwan and mainland China (no direction), the null and alternate hypotheses are:

$$H_0: \mu_1 - \mu_2 = 0$$
$$H_a: \mu_1 - \mu_2 \neq 0$$

Step 2. At step 2, the appropriate statistical test and sampling distribution are determined. The population variances (and standard deviations) are not known. Because it was assumed that the scores for this test are normally distributed and that the population variances are approximately equal, the researchers can use Formula 10.3.

Step 3. At step 3, the Type I error rate, or alpha, which is .01, is specified for this problem.

Step 4. At step 4, the decision rule is stated for the problem. Because the test is two tailed and alpha is .01, there is $\alpha/2$ or .005 of the area in each of the tails of the distribution. In addition, since we are using a t test in this analysis, we must compute the degrees of freedom by df $= n_1 + n_2 - 2$. In this problem, n_1 is 46 and n_2 is 26; thus, the degrees of freedom are $46 + 26 - 2 = 70$. Using Table A.6, the critical t values can be obtained.

$$t_{.005,70} = \pm 2.648$$

The null hypothesis will be rejected if the observed t value is less than -2.648 or greater than $+2.648$.

Step 5. Gather the data. The sample data for this problem are:

TAIWAN	MAINLAND CHINA
$n_1 = 46$	$n_2 = 26$
$\bar{x}_1 = 5.42$	$\bar{x}_2 = 5.04$
$s_1^2 = (.58)^2 = .3364$	$s_2^2 = (.49)^2 = .2401$

Step 6. Analyzing the data. Using these values and a hypothesized difference of zero, the value of the test statistic can be calculated as:

$$t = \frac{(5.42 - 5.04) - (0)}{\sqrt{\dfrac{0.3364(46 - 1) + 0.2401(26 - 1)}{46 + 26 - 2}}\sqrt{\dfrac{1}{46} + \dfrac{1}{26}}} = 2.82$$

Step 7. Reach a statistical conclusion. Because this test statistic, $t = 2.82$, is greater than the critical value of t (2.648) in the upper tail of the distribution, the statistical conclusion reached at step 7 is to reject the null hypothesis. There is a significant difference in the mean scores of Taiwan and mainland China.

Step 8. At step 8, a managerial decision is made. The Taiwan industrial buyers scored significantly higher than the mainland China industrial buyers on integration. Managers should keep in mind in dealing with Taiwanese buyers that they may be more likely to place value on personal virtue and social hierarchy than do the mainland Chinese buyers.

The following graph shows the critical *t* values, the rejection regions, the observed *t* value, and the difference in the raw means.

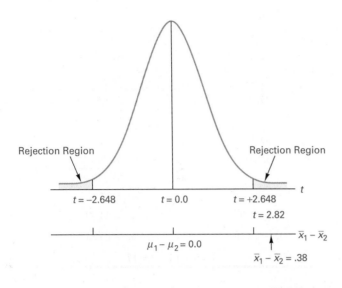

Confidence Intervals

Confidence interval formulas can be derived to estimate the difference in the population means for independent samples when the population variances are unknown. The focus in this section is only on confidence intervals when approximately equal population variances and normally distributed populations can be assumed.

Confidence Interval to Estimate $\mu_1 - \mu_2$ Assuming the Population Variances are Unknown and Equal

$$(\bar{x}_1 - \bar{x}_2) - t\sqrt{\frac{s_1^2(n_1 - 1) + s_2^2(n_2 - 1)}{n_1 + n_2 - 2}}\sqrt{\frac{1}{n_1} + \frac{1}{n_2}} \le \mu_1 - \mu_2 \le \qquad (10.4)$$

$$(\bar{x}_1 - \bar{x}_2) + t\sqrt{\frac{s_1^2(n_1 - 1) + s_2^2(n_2 - 1)}{n_1 + n_2 - 2}}\sqrt{\frac{1}{n_1} + \frac{1}{n_2}}$$

$$df = n_1 + n_2 - 2$$

One group of researchers set out to determine whether there is a difference between "average Americans" and those who are "phone survey respondents."* Their study was based on a well-known personality survey that attempted to assess the personality profile of both average Americans and phone survey respondents. Suppose they sampled nine phone survey respondents and 10 average Americans in this survey and obtained the results on one personality factor, conscientiousness, that are displayed in Table 10.3. Assume that conscientiousness scores are normally distributed in the population.

---

*Source: Data adapted from David Whitlark and Michael Geurts, "Phone Surveys: How Well Do Respondents Represent Average Americans?" *Marketing Research* (Fall 1998), pp. 13–17. Note that the results on this portion of the actual study are about the same as those shown here except that in the actual study the sample sizes were in the 500–600 range.

TABLE 10.3	Conscientiousness Data on Phone Survey Respondents and Average Americans
PHONE SURVEY RESPONDENTS	**AVERAGE AMERICANS**
35.38	35.03
37.06	33.90
37.74	34.56
36.97	36.24
37.84	34.59
37.50	34.95
40.75	33.30
35.31	34.73
35.30	34.79
	37.83
$n_1 = 9$	$n_2 = 10$
$\bar{x}_1 = 37.09$	$\bar{x}_2 = 34.99$
$s_1 = 1.727$	$s_2 = 1.253$
df = 9 + 10 − 2 = 17	

The table t value for a 99% level of confidence and 17 degrees of freedom is $t_{.005,17} = 2.898$. The confidence interval is

$$(37.09 - 34.99) \pm 2.898 \sqrt{\frac{(1.727)^2(8) + (1.253)^2(9)}{9 + 10 - 2}} \sqrt{\frac{1}{9} + \frac{1}{10}}$$

$$2.10 \pm 1.99$$

$$0.11 \le \mu_1 - \mu_2 \le 4.09$$

The researchers are 99% confident that the true difference in population mean personality scores for conscientiousness between phone survey respondents and average Americans is between .11 and 4.09. Zero is not in this interval, so they can conclude that there is a significant difference in the average scores of the two groups. Higher scores indicate more conscientiousness. Therefore, it is possible to conclude from Table 10.3 and this confidence interval that phone survey respondents are significantly more conscientious than average Americans. These results indicate that researchers should be careful in using phone survey results to reach conclusions about average Americans.

Figure 10.8 contains Minitab output for this problem. Note that the Minitab output includes both the confidence interval (.112 to 4.093) and the observed t value (3.06) for

```
Two-Sample T-Test and CI: Phone Survey Respondent, Average American

Two-Sample T for Phone Survey Respondent vs Average American

                          N   Mean   StDev  SE Mean
Phone Survey Respondent   9   37.09  1.73   0.58
Average American          10  34.99  1.25   0.40

Difference = μ (Phone Survey Respondent) − μ (Average American)

Estimate for difference: 2.102

99% CI for difference: (0.112, 4.093)

T-Test of difference = 0 (vs ≠): T-Value = 3.06

P-Value = 0.007 DF = 17

Both use Pooled StDev = 1.4949
```

FIGURE 10.8 Minitab Output for the Phone Survey Respondent and Average American Example

hypothesis testing. Because the *p*-value is .007, which is less than .01, the Minitab hypothesis-testing information validates the conclusion reached that there is a significant difference in the scores of the two groups.

DEMONSTRATION PROBLEM 10.4

A coffee manufacturer is interested in estimating the difference in the average daily coffee consumption of regular-coffee drinkers and decaffeinated-coffee drinkers. Its researcher randomly selects 13 regular-coffee drinkers and asks how many cups of coffee per day they drink. He randomly locates 15 decaffeinated-coffee drinkers and asks how many cups of coffee per day they drink. The average for the regular-coffee drinkers is 4.35 cups, with a standard deviation of 1.20 cups. The average for the decaffeinated-coffee drinkers is 6.84 cups, with a standard deviation of 1.42 cups. The researcher assumes, for each population, that the daily consumption is normally distributed, and he constructs a 95% confidence interval to estimate the difference in the averages of the two populations.

Solution: The table *t* value for this problem is $t_{.025,26} = 2.056$. The confidence interval estimate is

$$(4.35 - 6.84) \pm 2.056 \sqrt{\frac{(1.20)^2(12) + (1.42)^2(14)}{13 + 15 - 2}} \sqrt{\frac{1}{13} + \frac{1}{15}}$$

$$-2.49 \pm 1.03$$

$$-3.52 \le \mu_1 - \mu_2 \le -1.46$$

The researcher is 95% confident that the difference in population average daily consumption of cups of coffee between regular- and decaffeinated-coffee drinkers is between 1.46 cups and 3.52 cups. The point estimate for the difference in population means is 2.49 cups, with an error of 1.03 cups.

Thinking Critically About Statistics in Business Today

Beverage Consumption: America vs. Europe

How does America compare to Europe in the consumption of beverages? In many categories, including coffee, milk, juice, bottled water, and liquor, consumption is similar. However, according to statistics from the Wine Institute, Americans drink nearly five times as much soda as do Europeans and almost twice as much beer. On the other hand, Europeans drink more than twice as much tea (hot or iced), more than three times as much wine, and over four times as much tap water as do Americans. Statistics show that the average American consumes forty-eight 12 oz. containers of carbonated soda per month compared to only ten for Europeans. On the other hand, Europeans consume an average of sixteen 4 oz. containers of wine per month compared to an average of only five for Americans. According to the study, Americans have a slight edge over Europeans in the consumption of milk, with Americans drinking an average of seventeen 12 oz. containers of milk per month compared

to fifteen for Europeans. This study contained comparisons between Americans and Europeans on 11 different beverages.

THINGS TO PONDER

1. Suppose the figures given in this feature are actually only sample data. Would any of the techniques presented in this chapter be appropriate for conducting hypothesis tests to determine if there is a significant difference between Americans and Europeans on the consumption of various beverages? If so, what additional information would be needed?

2. Can you think of some reasons why Americans consume more carbonated soda pop and beer than Europeans, but less wine, hot or iced tea, or tap water? Do you think that these outcomes may change in time? Why or why not?

Source: "Wine and Other Beverage Consumption in America," http://www.beekmanwine.com/prevtopat.htm, 2011.

10.2 Problems

10.11. Use the data given and the eight-step process to test the following hypotheses.

$$H_0: \mu_1 - \mu_2 = 0 \qquad H_a: \mu_1 - \mu_2 < 0$$

SAMPLE 1	SAMPLE 2
$n_1 = 8$	$n_2 = 11$
$\bar{x}_1 = 24.56$	$\bar{x}_2 = 26.42$
$s_1^2 = 12.4$	$s_2^2 = 15.8$

Use a 1% level of significance, and assume that x is normally distributed.

10.12. a. Use the following data and $\alpha = .10$ to test the stated hypotheses. Assume x is normally distributed in the populations and the variances of the populations are approximately equal.

$$H_0: \mu_1 - \mu_2 = 0 \qquad H_a: \mu_1 - \mu_2 \neq 0$$

SAMPLE 1	SAMPLE 2
$n_1 = 20$	$n_2 = 20$
$\bar{x}_1 = 118$	$\bar{x}_2 = 113$
$s_1 = 23.9$	$s_2 = 21.6$

b. Use these data to construct a 90% confidence interval to estimate $\mu_1 - \mu_2$.

10.13. Suppose that for years the mean of population 1 has been accepted as the same as the mean of population 2, but that now population 1 is believed to have a greater mean than population 2. Letting $\alpha = .05$ and assuming the populations have equal variances and x is approximately normally distributed, use the following data to test this belief.

SAMPLE 1		SAMPLE 2	
43.6	45.7	40.1	36.4
44.0	49.1	42.2	42.3
45.2	45.6	43.1	38.8
40.8	46.5	37.5	43.3
48.3	45.0	41.0	40.2

10.14. a. Suppose you want to determine whether the average values for populations 1 and 2 are different, and you randomly gather the following data.

SAMPLE 1						SAMPLE 2					
2	10	7	8	2	5	10	12	8	7	9	11
9	1	8	0	2	8	9	8	9	10	11	10
11	2	4	5	3	9	11	10	7	8	10	10

Test your conjecture, using a probability of committing a Type I error of .01. Assume the population variances are the same and x is normally distributed in the populations.

b. Use these data to construct a 98% confidence interval for the difference in the two population means.

10.15. Suppose a realtor is interested in comparing the asking prices of midrange homes in Peoria, Illinois, and Evansville, Indiana. The realtor conducts a small telephone survey in the two cities, asking the prices of midrange home. A random sample of 21 listings in Peoria resulted in a sample average price of $88,400, with a standard deviation of $4500. A random sample of 26 listings in Evansville resulted in a sample average price of $96,800, with a standard deviation of $4400. The realtor assumes prices of midrange homes are normally distributed and the variance in prices in the two cities is about the same.

a. What would he obtain for a 90% confidence interval for the difference in mean prices of midrange homes between Peoria and Evansville?

b. Test whether there is any difference in the mean prices of midrange homes of the two cities for $\alpha = .10$.

10.16. According to the National Association of Colleges and Employers, the average hourly wage of an undergraduate college student working as a co-op is $17.27 and the average hourly wage of college student working as an intern is $16.57. Assume that such wages are normally distributed in the population and that the population variances are equal. Suppose these figures were actually obtained from the data below:

a. Use these data and $\alpha = .10$ to test to determine if there is a significant difference in the mean hourly wage of a college co-op student and the mean hourly wage of a college intern.

b. Using these same data, construct a 90% confidence interval to estimate the difference in the population mean hourly wages of college co-ops and interns.

CO-OPS	INTERNS
16.97	16.23
16.38	15.58
17.51	17.34
18.55	16.04
18.47	14.93
19.00	17.15
15.68	17.38
17.04	17.02
18.37	15.12
16.18	17.61
16.88	16.88
16.27	17.55

10.17. Based on an indication that mean daily car rental rates may be higher for Boston than for Dallas, a survey of eight car rental companies in Boston is taken and the sample mean car rental rate is $47, with a sample standard deviation of $3. Further, suppose a survey of nine car rental companies in Dallas results in a sample mean of $44 and a sample standard deviation of $3. Use $\alpha = .05$ to test to determine whether the average daily car rental rates in Boston are significantly higher than those in Dallas. Assume car rental rates are normally distributed and the population variances are equal.

10.18. What is the difference in average daily hotel room rates between Minneapolis and New Orleans? Suppose we want to estimate this difference by taking hotel rate samples from each city and using a 98% confidence level. The data for such a study follow. Use these data to produce a point estimate for the mean difference in the hotel rates for the two cities. Assume the population variances are approximately equal and hotel rates in any given city are normally distributed.

MINNEAPOLIS	NEW ORLEANS
$n_M = 20$	$n_{NO} = 22$
$\bar{x}_M = \$128$	$\bar{x}_{NO} = \$144$
$s_M = \$24$	$s_{NO} = \$29$

10.19. A study was made to compare the costs of supporting a family of four Americans for a year in different foreign cities. The lifestyle of living in the United States on an annual income of $75,000 was the standard against which living in foreign cities was compared. A comparable living standard in Toronto and Mexico City was attained for about $64,000. Suppose an executive wants to determine whether there is any difference in the average annual cost of supporting her family of four in the manner to which they are accustomed between Toronto and Mexico City. She uses the following data, randomly gathered from 11 families in each city, and an alpha of .01 to test this difference. She assumes the annual cost is normally distributed and the population variances are equal. What does the executive find?

TORONTO	MEXICO CITY
$69,000	$65,000
64,500	64,000
67,500	66,000
64,500	64,900
66,700	62,000
68,000	60,500
65,000	62,500

69,000	63,000
71,000	64,500
68,500	63,500
67,500	62,400

Use the data from the previous table to construct a 95% confidence interval to estimate the difference in average annual costs between the two cities.

10.20. Some studies have shown that in the United States, men spend more than women buying gifts and cards on Valentine's Day. Suppose a researcher wants to test this hypothesis by randomly sampling 9 men and 10 women with comparable demographic characteristics from various large cities across the United States to be in a study. Each study participant is asked to keep a log beginning one month before Valentine's Day and record all purchases made for Valentine's Day during that one-month period. The resulting data are shown below. Use these data and a 1% level of significance to test to determine if, on average, men actually do spend significantly more than women on Valentine's Day. Assume that such spending is normally distributed in the population and that the population variances are equal.

MEN	WOMEN
$107.48	$125.98
143.61	45.53
90.19	56.35
125.53	80.62
70.79	46.37
83.00	44.34
129.63	75.21
154.22	68.48
93.80	85.84
	126.11

10.3 Statistical Inferences For Two Related Populations

In the preceding section, hypotheses were tested and confidence intervals constructed about the difference in two population means when the samples are independent. In this section, a method is presented to analyze **dependent samples** or related samples. Some researchers refer to this test as the **matched-pairs** test. Others call it the *t test for related measures* or the **correlated t test**.

What are some types of situations in which the two samples being studied are related or dependent? Let's begin with the before-and-after study. Sometimes as an experimental control mechanism, the same person or object is measured both before and after a treatment. Certainly, the after measurement is *not* independent of the before measurement because the measurements are taken on the same person or object in both cases. Table 10.4 gives data from a hypothetical study in which people were asked to rate a company before and after one week of viewing a 15-minute DVD of the company twice a day. The before scores are one sample and the after scores are a second sample, but each pair of scores is related because the two measurements apply to the same person. The before scores and the after scores are not likely to

TABLE 10.4	Rating of a Company (on a Scale from 0 to 50)	
INDIVIDUAL	**BEFORE**	**AFTER**
1	32	39
2	11	15
3	21	35
4	17	13
5	30	41
6	38	39
7	14	22

vary from each other as much as scores gathered from independent samples because individuals bring their biases about businesses and the company to the study. These individual biases affect both the before scores and the after scores in the same way because each pair of scores is measured on the same person.

Other examples of related measures samples include studies in which twins, siblings, or spouses are matched and placed in two different groups. For example, a fashion merchandiser might be interested in comparing men's and women's perceptions of women's clothing. If the men and women selected for the study are spouses or siblings, a built-in relatedness to the measurements of the two groups in the study is likely. Their scores are more apt to be alike or related than those of randomly chosen independent groups of men and women because of similar backgrounds or tastes.

Hypothesis Testing

To ensure the use of the proper hypothesis-testing techniques, the researcher must determine whether the two samples being studied are dependent or independent. The approach to analyzing two *related* samples is different from the techniques used to analyze independent samples. Use of the techniques in Section 10.2 to analyze related group data can result in a loss of power and an increase in Type II errors.

The matched-pairs test for related samples requires that the two samples be the same size and that the individual related scores be matched. Formula 10.5 is used to test hypotheses about dependent populations.

t **Formula to Test the Difference in Two Dependent Populations**

$$t = \frac{\bar{d} - D}{\frac{s_d}{\sqrt{n}}}$$

$$df = n - 1$$

(10.5)

where

n = number of pairs
d = sample difference in pairs
D = mean population difference
s_d = standard deviation of sample difference
$\bar{d}$ = mean sample difference

This *t* test for dependent measures uses the sample difference, *d*, between individual matched sample values as the basic measurement of analysis instead of individual sample values. Analysis of the *d* values effectively converts the problem from a two-sample problem to a single sample of differences, which is an adaptation of the single-sample means formula. This test utilizes the sample mean of differences, and the standard deviation of differences, s_d, which can be computed by using Formulas 10.6 and 10.7.

Formulas for $\bar{d}$ and s_d

$$\bar{d} = \frac{\Sigma d}{n}$$

$$s_d = \sqrt{\frac{\Sigma(d - \bar{d})^2}{n - 1}} = \sqrt{\frac{\Sigma d^2 - \frac{(\Sigma d)^2}{n}}{n - 1}} \qquad (10.6 \text{ and } 10.7)$$

An assumption for this test is that the differences of the two populations are normally distributed.

Analyzing data by this method involves calculating a t value with Formula 10.5 and comparing it with a critical t value obtained from the table. The critical t value is obtained from the t distribution table in the usual way, with the exception that, in the degrees of freedom $(n - 1)$, n is the number of matched pairs of scores.

Suppose a stock market investor is interested in determining whether there is a significant difference in the P/E (price to earnings) ratio for companies from one year to the next. In an effort to study this question, the investor randomly samples nine companies from the *Handbook of Common Stocks* and records the P/E ratios for each of these companies at the end of year 1 and at the end of year 2. The data are shown in Table 10.5.

These data are related data because each P/E value for year 1 has a corresponding year 2 measurement on the same company. Because no prior information indicates whether P/E ratios have gone up or down, the hypothesis tested is two tailed. Assume $\alpha = .01$. Assume that differences in P/E ratios are normally distributed in the population.

Step 1 At step 1, the hypotheses must be established. The null and alternate hypotheses are:

$$\text{H}_0: D = 0$$
$$\text{H}_a: D \neq 0$$

Step 2 At step 2, the appropriate statistical test and sampling distribution are determined. Because the data are related and are normally distributed in the population, Formula 10.5 is the appropriate statistical test:

$$t = \frac{\bar{d} - D}{\frac{s_d}{\sqrt{n}}}$$

Step 3 At step 3, the Type I error rate, or alpha, which is .01, is specified for this problem.

Step 4 At step 4, the decision rule is stated for the problem. Because the test is two tailed and alpha is .01, there is $\alpha/2$ or .005 of the area in each of the tails of the distribution. In addition, since we are using a t test in this analysis, we must compute the degrees

TABLE 10.5 **P/E Ratios for Nine Randomly Selected Companies**

COMPANY	YEAR 1 P/E RATIO	YEAR 2 P/E RATIO
1	8.9	12.7
2	38.1	45.4
3	43.0	10.0
4	34.0	27.2
5	34.5	22.8
6	15.2	24.1
7	20.3	32.3
8	19.9	40.1
9	61.9	106.5

of freedom, df $= n - 1$. In this problem, there are nine pairs of numbers, so n is 9 and the degrees of freedom are $9 - 1 = 8$. Using Table A.6, the critical t values can be obtained.

$$t_{.005, 8} = \pm 3.355$$

The null hypothesis will be rejected if the observed t value is less than -3.355 or greater than $+3.355$.

Step 5 Gather the data. The sample data for this problem are given in Table 10.5.

Step 6 Analyzing the data. Table 10.6 shows the calculations to obtain the observed value of the test statistic, which is $t = -0.70$.

Step 7 Reach a statistical conclusion. Because this test statistic, $t = -0.70$, is greater than the critical value of t (-3.355) in the lower tail of the distribution and less than the critical value of t $(+3.355)$ in the upper tail of the distribution, it falls in the nonrejection region and the statistical conclusion is to fail to reject the null hypothesis.

Step 8 At step 8, a managerial decision is made. There is not enough evidence from the data to declare that there is a significant difference in the average P/E ratios between year 1 and year 2. The graph in Figure 10.9 depicts the rejection regions, the critical values of t, and the observed value of t for this example.

TABLE 10.6 Analysis of P/E Ratio Data

COMPANY	YEAR 1 P/E	YEAR 2 P/E	d
1	8.9	12.7	−3.8
2	38.1	45.4	−7.3
3	43.0	10.0	33.0
4	34.0	27.2	6.8
5	34.5	22.8	11.7
6	15.2	24.1	−8.9
7	20.3	32.3	−12.0
8	19.9	40.1	−20.2
9	61.9	106.5	−44.6

$\bar{d} = -5.033, \quad s_d = 21.599, \quad n = 9$

$$\text{Observed } t = \frac{-5.033 - 0}{\dfrac{21.599}{\sqrt{9}}} = -0.70$$

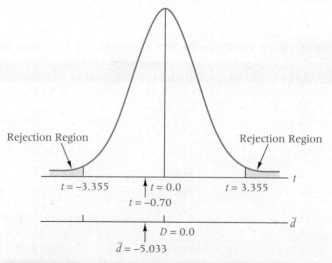

FIGURE 10.9 Graphical Depiction of P/E Ratio Analysis

Minitab Output

Paired T-Test and CI: Year 1, Year 2

```
Paired T for Year 1 - Year 2
             N      Mean     StDev    SE Mean
Year 1       9      30.64    16.37    5.46
Year 2       9      35.68    28.94    9.65
Difference   9      -5.03    21.60    7.20
```

```
99% CI for mean difference: (-29.19, 19.12)
T-Test of mean difference = 0 (vs ≠ 0):
T-Value = -0.70 P-Value = 0.504
```

Excel Output

t-Test: Paired Two Sample for Means

	Year 1	Year 2
Mean	30.64	35.68
Variance	268.135	837.544
Observations	9	9
Pearson Correlation	0.674	
Hypothesized Mean Difference	0	
df	8	
t Stat	-0.70	
P(T<=t) one-tail	0.252	
t Critical one-tail	2.90	
P(T<=t) two-tail	0.504	
t Critical two-tail	3.36	

FIGURE 10.10 **Minitab and Excel Output for the P/E Ratio Example**

Using the Computer to Make Statistical Inferences about Two Related Populations

Both Minitab and Excel can be used to make statistical inferences about two related populations. Figure 10.10 shows Minitab and Excel output for the P/E Ratio problem. The Minitab output contains summary data for each sample and the difference of the two samples along with a confidence interval of the difference, a restating of the tested hypotheses, the observed t value, and the p-value. Because the p-value (0.504) is greater than the value of alpha (.01), the decision is to fail to reject the null hypothesis.

The Excel output contains the hypothesized mean difference, the observed t value (-0.70), and the critical t values and their associated p-values for both a one-tailed and a two-tailed test. The p-value for a two-tailed test is the same as that produced by Minitab, indicating that the decision is to fail to reject the null hypothesis.

DEMONSTRATION PROBLEM 10.5

Let us revisit the hypothetical study discussed earlier in the section in which consumers are asked to rate a company both before and after viewing a video on the company twice a day for a week. The data from Table 10.4 are displayed again here. Use an alpha of .05 to test to determine whether there is a significant increase in the ratings of the company after the one-week video treatment. Assume that differences in ratings are normally distributed in the population.

INDIVIDUAL	BEFORE	AFTER
1	32	39
2	11	15
3	21	35
4	17	13
5	30	41
6	38	39
7	14	22

Solution: Because the same individuals are being used in a before-and-after study, it is a related measures study. The desired effect is to increase ratings, which means the hypothesis test is one tailed.

Step 1.   At step 1, the hypotheses must be established. Because the researchers are testing to determine if there is a significant increase in ratings from before to after, a one-tailed test is being conducted. In computing the difference, the after scores will be subtracted from the before scores, resulting in an anticipated negative difference. The null and alternate hypotheses are:

$$H_0: D = 0$$

$$H_a: D < 0$$

Step 2.   At step 2, the appropriate statistical test and sampling distribution are determined. Because the data are related (before and after) and are normally distributed in the population, Formula 10.5 is the appropriate statistical test:

$$t = \frac{\bar{d} - D}{\dfrac{s_d}{\sqrt{n}}}$$

Step 3.   At step 3, the Type I error rate, or alpha, which is .05, is specified for this problem.

Step 4.   At step 4, the decision rule is stated for the problem. The degrees of freedom are $n - 1 = 7 - 1 = 6$. For $\alpha = .05$, the table t value is $t_{.05,6} = -1.943$. The decision rule is to reject the null hypothesis if the observed value is less than -1.943.

Step 5.   Gather the data. The sample data and some calculations follow.

INDIVIDUAL	BEFORE	AFTER	d
1	32	39	−7
2	11	15	−4
3	21	35	−14
4	17	13	+4
5	30	41	−11
6	38	39	−1
7	14	22	−8
$\bar{d} = -5.857$		$s_d = 6.0945$	

Step 6.   Analyzing the data. The observed t value is:

$$t = \frac{-5.857 - 0}{\dfrac{6.0945}{\sqrt{7}}} = -2.54$$

Computer analysis of this problem reveals that the p-value is .022.

Step 7. Reach a statistical conclusion. Because the observed value of −2.54 is less than the critical, table value of −1.943 and the *p*-value (.022) is less than alpha (.05), the decision is to reject the null hypothesis.

Step 8. At step 8, a managerial decision is made. There is enough evidence to conclude that, on average, the ratings have increased significantly. This result might be used by managers to support a decision to continue using the videos or expand the use of such videos in an effort to increase public support for their company.

The following graph depicts the observed value, the rejection region, and the critical *t* value for the problem.

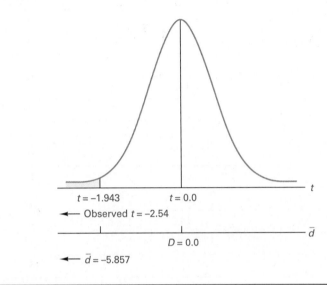

Confidence Intervals

Sometimes a researcher is interested in estimating the mean difference in two populations for related samples. A confidence interval for *D*, the mean population difference of two related samples, can be constructed by algebraically rearranging Formula 10.5, which was used to test hypotheses about *D*. Again the assumption is that the differences are normally distributed in the population.

Confidence Interval Formula to Estimate the Difference in Related Populations, *D*

$$\bar{d} - t\frac{s_d}{\sqrt{n}} \le D \le \bar{d} + t\frac{s_d}{\sqrt{n}}$$

$$\text{df} = n - 1$$

(10.8)

The following housing industry example demonstrates the application of Formula 10.8. The sale of new houses apparently fluctuates seasonally. Superimposed on the seasonality are economic and business cycles that also influence the sale of new houses. In certain parts of the country, new-house sales increase in the spring and early summer and drop off in the fall. Suppose a national real estate association wants to estimate the average difference in the number of new-house sales per company in Indianapolis between 2015 and 2016. To do so, the association randomly selects 18 real estate firms in the Indianapolis area and obtains their new-house sales figures for May 2015 and May 2016. The numbers of sales per company are shown in Table 10.7. Using these data, the association's analyst estimates the average difference in the number of sales per real estate company in Indianapolis for May 2015 and May 2016 and constructs a 99% confidence interval. The analyst assumes that differences in sales are normally distributed in the population.

The number of pairs, *n*, is 18, and the degrees of freedom are 17. For a 99% level of confidence and these degrees of freedom, the table *t* value is $t_{.005,17} = 2.898$. The values for $\bar{d}$, and s_d are shown in Table 10.8.

TABLE 10.7   Number of New House Sales in Indianapolis

REALTOR	MAY 2015	MAY 2016
1	8	11
2	19	30
3	5	6
4	9	13
5	3	5
6	0	4
7	13	15
8	11	17
9	9	12
10	5	12
11	8	6
12	2	5
13	11	10
14	14	22
15	7	8
16	12	15
17	6	12
18	10	10

TABLE 10.8   Differences in Number of New House Sales, 2015–2016

REALTOR	MAY 2015	MAY 2016	d
1	8	11	−3
2	19	30	−11
3	5	6	−1
4	9	13	−4
5	3	5	−2
6	0	4	−4
7	13	15	−2
8	11	17	−6
9	9	12	−3
10	5	12	−7
11	8	6	+2
12	2	5	−3
13	11	10	+1
14	14	22	−8
15	7	8	−1
16	12	15	−3
17	6	12	−6
18	10	10	0

$\bar{d} = -3.389$ and $s_d = 3.274$

```
Paired T-Test and CI: 2015, 2016

Paired T for 2015 - 2016
                N       Mean      StDev     SE Mean
2015            18      8.44      4.64      1.09
2016            18      11.83     6.54      1.54
Difference      18      -3.389    3.274     0.772

99% CI for mean difference: (-5.626, -1.152)
T-Test of mean difference = 0 (vs ≠ 0):
T-Value = -4.39 P-Value = 0.000
```

FIGURE 10.11 **Minitab Output for the New House Sales Example**

The point estimate of the difference is $\bar{d} = -3.389$. The 99% confidence interval is

$$\bar{d} - t\frac{s_d}{\sqrt{n}} \leq D \leq \bar{d} + t\frac{s_d}{\sqrt{n}}$$

$$-3.389 - 2.898\frac{3.274}{\sqrt{18}} \leq D \leq -3.389 + 2.898\frac{3.274}{\sqrt{18}}$$

$$-3.389 - 2.236 \leq D \leq -3.389 + 2.236$$

$$-5.625 \leq D \leq -1.153$$

The analyst estimates with a 99% level of confidence that the average difference in new-house sales for a real estate company in Indianapolis between 2015 and 2016 in May is somewhere between −5.625 and −1.153 houses. Because 2016 sales were subtracted from 2015 sales, the minus signs indicate more sales in 2016 than in 2015. Note that both ends of the confidence interval contain negatives. This result means that the analyst can be 99% confident that zero difference is not the average difference. If the analyst were using this confidence interval to test the hypothesis that there is no significant mean difference in average new-house sales per company in Indianapolis between May 2015 and May 2016, the null hypothesis would be rejected for $\alpha = .01$. The point estimate for this example is −3.389 houses, with an error of 2.236 houses. Figure 10.11 is the Minitab computer output for the confidence interval.

10.3 Problems

10.21. Use the data given and a 1% level of significance to test the following hypotheses. Assume the differences are normally distributed in the population.

$$H_0: D = 0 \qquad H_a: D > 0$$

PAIR	SAMPLE 1	SAMPLE 2
1	38	22
2	27	28
3	30	21
4	41	38
5	36	38
6	38	26
7	33	19
8	35	31
9	44	35

10.22. Use the data given to test the following hypotheses ($\alpha = .05$). Assume the differences are normally distributed in the population.

$$H_0: D = 0 \qquad H_a: D \neq 0$$

INDIVIDUAL	BEFORE	AFTER
1	107	102
2	99	98
3	110	100
4	113	108
5	96	89
6	98	101
7	100	99
8	102	102
9	107	105
10	109	110
11	104	102
12	99	96
13	101	100

10.23. Construct a 98% confidence interval to estimate D from the following sample information. Assume the differences are normally distributed in the population.

$$\bar{d} = 40.56, \qquad s_d = 26.58, \qquad n = 22$$

10.24. Construct a 90% confidence interval to estimate D from the following sample information. Assume the differences are normally distributed in the population.

CLIENT	BEFORE	AFTER
1	32	40
2	28	25
3	35	36
4	32	32
5	26	29
6	25	31
7	37	39
8	16	30
9	35	31

10.25. Because of uncertainty in real estate markets, many home-owners are considering remodeling and constructing additions rather than selling. Probably the most expensive room in the house to re-model is the kitchen, with an average cost of about $23,400. In terms of resale value, is remodeling the kitchen worth the cost? The following cost and resale figures are published by *Remodeling* magazine for 11 cities. Use these data to construct a 99% confidence interval for the difference between cost and added resale value of kitchen remodeling. Assume the differences are normally distributed in the population.

CITY	COST	RESALE
Atlanta	$20,427	$25,163
Boston	27,255	24,625
Des Moines	22,115	12,600
Kansas City, MO	23,256	24,588
Louisville	21,887	19,267
Portland, OR	24,255	20,150
Raleigh-Durham	19,852	22,500
Reno	23,624	16,667
Ridgewood, NJ	25,885	26,875
San Francisco	28,999	35,333
Tulsa	20,836	16,292

10.26. The vice president of marketing brought to the attention of sales managers that most of the company's manufacturer representatives contacted clients and maintained client relationships in a disorganized, haphazard way. The sales managers brought the reps in for a three-day seminar and training session on how to use an organizer to schedule visits and recall pertinent information about each client more effectively. Sales reps were taught how to schedule visits most efficiently to maximize their efforts. Sales managers were given data on the number of site visits by sales reps on a randomly selected day both before and after the seminar. Use the following data to test whether significantly more site visits were made after the seminar ($\alpha = .05$). Assume the differences in the number of site visits are normally distributed.

REP	BEFORE	AFTER
1	2	4
2	4	5
3	1	3
4	3	3
5	4	3
6	2	5
7	2	6
8	3	4
9	1	5

10.27. Eleven employees were put under the care of the company nurse because of high cholesterol readings. The nurse lectured them on the dangers of this condition and put them on a new diet. Shown are the cholesterol readings of the 11 employees both before the new diet and one month after use of the diet began. Construct a 98% confidence interval to estimate the population mean difference of cholesterol readings for people who are involved in this program. Assume differences in cholesterol readings are normally distributed in the population.

EMPLOYEE	BEFORE	AFTER
1	255	197
2	230	225
3	290	215
4	242	215
5	300	240
6	250	235
7	215	190
8	230	240
9	225	200
10	219	203
11	236	223

10.28. Lawrence and Glover published the results of a study in the *Journal of Managerial Issues* in which they examined the effects of accounting firm mergers on auditing delay. Auditing delay is the time between a company's fiscal year-end and the date of the auditor's report. The hypothesis is that with the efficiencies gained through mergers the length of the audit delay would decrease. Suppose that to test their hypothesis, they examined the audit delays on 27 clients of Big Six firms from both before and after the Big Six firm merger (a span of five years). Suppose further that the mean difference in audit delay for these clients from before merger to after merger was a decrease in 3.71 days and the standard deviation of difference was five days. Use these data and $\alpha = .01$ to test whether the audit delays after the merger were significantly lower than before the merger. Assume that the differences in auditing delay are normally distributed in the population.

10.29. A nationally known supermarket decided to promote its own brand of soft drinks on TV for two weeks. Before the ad campaign, the company randomly selected 21 of its stores across the United States to be part of a study to measure the campaign's effectiveness.

During a specified half-hour period on a certain Monday morning, all the stores in the sample counted the number of cans of its own brand of soft drink sold. After the campaign, a similar count was made. The average difference was an increase of 75 cans, with a standard deviation of difference of 30 cans. Using this information, construct a 90% confidence interval to estimate the population average difference in soft drink sales for this company's brand before and after the ad campaign. Assume the differences in soft drink sales for the company's brand are normally distributed in the population.

10.30. Is there a significant difference in the gasoline mileage of a car for regular unleaded and premium unleaded? To test this question, a researcher randomly selected 15 drivers for a study. They were to drive their cars for one month on regular unleaded and for one month on premium unleaded gasoline. The participants drove their own cars for this experiment. The average sample difference was 2.85 miles per gallon in favor of the premium unleaded, and the sample standard deviation of difference was 1.9 miles per gallon. For $\alpha = .01$, does the test show enough evidence for the researcher to conclude that there is a significant difference in mileage between regular unleaded and premium unleaded gasoline? Assume the differences in gasoline mileage figures are normally distributed in the population.

10.4 Statistical Inferences About Two Population Proportions, $p_1 - p_2$

Sometimes a researcher wishes to make inferences about the difference in two population proportions. This type of analysis has many applications in business, such as comparing the market share of a product for two different markets, studying the difference in the proportion of female customers in two different geographic regions, or comparing the proportion of defective products from one period to another. In making inferences about the difference in two population proportions, the statistic normally used is the difference in the sample proportions: $\hat{p}_1 - \hat{p}_2$. This statistic is computed by taking random samples and determining $\hat{p}$ for each sample for a given characteristic, then calculating the difference in these sample proportions.

The central limit theorem states that for large samples (each of $n_1 \cdot \hat{p}_1$, $n_1 \cdot \hat{q}_1$, $n_2 \cdot \hat{p}_2$, and $n_2 \cdot \hat{q}_2 > 5$, where $\hat{q} = 1 - \hat{p}$), the difference in sample proportions is normally distributed with a mean difference of

$$\mu_{\hat{p}_1 - \hat{p}_2} = p_1 - p_2$$

and a standard deviation of the difference of sample proportions of

$$\sigma_{\hat{p}_1 - \hat{p}_2} = \sqrt{\frac{p_1 \cdot q_1}{n_1} + \frac{p_2 \cdot q_2}{n_2}}$$

From this information, a z formula for the difference in sample proportions can be developed.

> **z Formula for the Difference in Two Population Proportions**
>
> $$z = \frac{(\hat{p}_1 - \hat{p}_2) - (p_1 - p_2)}{\sqrt{\frac{p_1 \cdot q_1}{n_1} + \frac{p_2 \cdot q_2}{n_2}}} \tag{10.9}$$
>
> where
>
> $\hat{p}_1 =$ proportion from sample 1
> $\hat{p}_2 =$ proportion from sample 2
> $n_1 =$ size of sample 1
> $n_2 =$ size of sample 2
> $p_1 =$ proportion from population 1
> $p_2 =$ proportion from population 2
> $q_1 = 1 - p_1$
> $q_2 = 1 - p_2$

Hypothesis Testing

Formula 10.9 is the formula that can be used to determine the probability of getting a particular difference in two sample proportions when given the values of the population proportions. In testing hypotheses about the difference in two population proportions, particular values of the population proportions are not usually known or assumed. Rather, the hypotheses are about the difference in the two population proportions $(p_1 - p_2)$. Note that Formula 10.9 requires knowledge of the values of p_1 and p_2. Hence, a modified version of Formula 10.9 is used when testing hypotheses about $p_1 - p_2$. This formula utilizes a pooled value obtained from the sample proportions to replace the population proportions in the denominator of Formula 10.9.

The denominator of Formula 10.9 is the standard deviation of the difference in two sample proportions and uses the population proportions in its calculations. However, the population proportions are unknown, so an estimate of the standard deviation of the difference in two sample proportions is made by using sample proportions as point estimates of the population proportions. The sample proportions are combined by using a weighted average to produce $\bar{p}$, which, in conjunction with $\bar{q}$ and the sample sizes, produces a point estimate of the standard deviation of the difference in sample proportions. The result is Formula 10.10, which we shall use to test hypotheses about the difference in two population proportions.

z Formula to Test the Difference in Population Proportions

$$z = \frac{(\hat{p}_1 - \hat{p}_2) - (p_1 - p_2)}{\sqrt{(\bar{p} \cdot \bar{q})\left(\dfrac{1}{n_1} + \dfrac{1}{n_2}\right)}}$$ (10.10)

where $\bar{p} = \dfrac{x_1 + x_2}{n_1 + n_2} = \dfrac{n_1 \hat{p}_1 + n_2 \hat{p}_2}{n_1 + n_2}$ and $\bar{q} = 1 - \bar{p}$

Testing the difference in two population proportions is useful whenever the researcher is interested in comparing the proportion of one population that has a certain characteristic with the proportion of a second population that has the same characteristic. For example, a researcher might be interested in determining whether the proportion of people driving new cars (less than one year old) in Houston is different from the proportion in Denver. A study could be conducted with a random sample of Houston drivers and a random sample of Denver drivers to test this idea. The results could be used to compare the new-car potential of the two markets and the propensity of drivers in these areas to buy new cars.

As another example, do consumers and CEOs have different perceptions of ethics in business? A group of researchers attempted to determine whether there was a difference in the proportion of consumers and the proportion of CEOs who believe that fear of getting caught or losing one's job is a strong influence of ethical behavior. In their study, they found that 57% of consumers said that fear of getting caught or losing one's job was a strong influence on ethical behavior, but only 50% of CEOs felt the same way.

Suppose these data were determined from a sample of 755 consumers and 616 CEOs. Does this result provide enough evidence to declare that a significantly higher proportion of consumers than of CEOs believe fear of getting caught or losing one's job is a strong influence on ethical behavior?

> **Step 1** At step 1, the hypotheses must be established. We will let consumers be population 1 and CEOs be population 2. Because we are interested in proving that a higher proportion of consumers believe fear of getting caught or losing one's job is a strong influence on ethical behavior than the proportion of CEOs, the alternative hypothesis should be $p_1 - p_2 > 0$ and the null hypothesis is $p_1 - p_2 = 0$. Summarizing the hypotheses:
>
> $$H_0: p_1 - p_2 = 0$$
>
> $$H_a: p_1 - p_2 > 0$$

Step 2   At step 2, the appropriate statistical test and sampling distribution are determined. Because we are testing the difference in two population proportions, the z test in Formula 10.10 is the appropriate test statistic.

$$z = \frac{(\hat{p}_1 - \hat{p}_2) - (p_1 - p_2)}{\sqrt{(\bar{p} \cdot \bar{q})\left(\dfrac{1}{n_1} + \dfrac{1}{n_2}\right)}}$$

Step 3   At step 3, the Type I error rate, or alpha, is .10.

Step 4   At step 4, the decision rule is stated for the problem. Because this test is a one-tailed test, the critical table z value is $z_c = 1.28$. If an observed value of z of more than 1.28 is obtained, the null hypothesis will be rejected. **Figure 10.12** shows the rejection region and the critical value for this problem.

Step 5   Gather the data. The sample information follows.

CONSUMERS	CEOs
$n_1 = 755$	$n_2 = 616$
$\hat{p}_1 = .57$	$\hat{p}_2 = .50$

Step 6   The value of the test statistic can be calculated as:

$$\bar{p} = \frac{n_1\hat{p}_1 + n_2\hat{p}_2}{n_1 + n_2} = \frac{(755)(.57) + (616)(.50)}{755 + 616} = .539$$

If the statistics had been given as raw data instead of sample proportions, we would have used the following formula.

$$\bar{p} = \frac{x_1 + x_2}{n_1 + n_2}$$

The observed z value is

$$z = \frac{(.57 - .50) - (0)}{\sqrt{(.539)(.461)\left(\dfrac{1}{755} + \dfrac{1}{616}\right)}} = 2.59$$

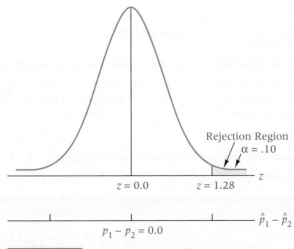

Rejection Region
$\alpha = .10$

$z = 0.0$ $z = 1.28$ z

$p_1 - p_2 = 0.0$ $\hat{p}_1 - \hat{p}_2$

FIGURE 10.12   **Rejection Region for the Ethics Example**

Step 7 Reach a statistical conclusion. Because this test statistic, $z = 2.59$, is greater than the critical value of z (1.28) in the upper tail of the distribution, the statistical conclusion reached at step 7 is to reject the null hypothesis. The same conclusion can be reached using the p-value method. For an observed test statistic $z = 2.59$, the p-value is .0048. Since this p-value is less than $\alpha = .10$, the decision is to reject the null hypothesis.

Step 8 At step 8, a managerial decision is made. A significantly higher proportion of consumers than of CEOs believe fear of getting caught or losing one's job is a strong influence on ethical behavior. CEOs might want to take another look at ways to influence ethical behavior. If employees are more like consumers than CEOs, CEOs might be able to use fear of getting caught or losing one's job as a means of ensuring ethical behavior on the job. Retailers might use fear of being caught and prosecuted to retard shoplifting in the retail trade. On the other hand, one could argue that on this question, the sample difference of 7% is not substantive. Indeed, around 50% of both groups believe that fear of getting caught or losing one's job is a strong influence on ethical behavior.

DEMONSTRATION PROBLEM 10.6

A study of female entrepreneurs was conducted to determine their definition of success. The women were offered optional choices such as happiness/self-fulfillment, sales/profit, and achievement/challenge. The women were divided into groups according to the gross sales of their businesses. A significantly higher proportion of female entrepreneurs in the $100,000 to $500,000 category than in the less than $100,000 category seemed to rate sales/profit as a definition of success.

Suppose you decide to test this result by taking a survey of your own and identify female entrepreneurs by gross sales. You interview 100 female entrepreneurs with gross sales of less than $100,000, and 24 of them define sales/profit as success. You then interview 95 female entrepreneurs with gross sales of $100,000 to $500,000, and 39 cite sales/profit as a definition of success. Use this information to test to determine whether there is a significant difference in the proportions of the two groups that define success as sales/profit. Use $\alpha = .01$.

Solution:

Step 1. At step 1, the hypotheses must be established. Since we are testing to determine whether there is a difference between the two groups of entrepreneurs, a two-tailed test is required. The hypotheses follow.

$$H_0: p_1 - p_2 = 0$$
$$H_a: p_1 - p_2 \neq 0$$

Step 2. At step 2, the appropriate statistical test and sampling distribution are determined. Because we are testing the difference in two population proportions, the z test in Formula 10.10 is the appropriate test statistic.

Step 3. At step 3, the Type I error rate, or alpha, which is .01, is specified for this problem.

Step 4. At step 4, the decision rule is stated for the problem. This problem requires a two-tailed test. With $\alpha = .01$, the critical z value can be obtained from Table A.5 for $\alpha/2 = .005$, $z_{.005} = \pm2.575$. The decision rule is that if the data produce a z value greater than 2.575 or less than -2.575, the test statistic is in the rejection region and the decision is to reject the null hypothesis. If the observed z value is less than 2.575 but greater than -2.575, the decision is to not reject the null hypothesis because the observed z value is in the nonrejection region.

Step 5. Gather the data. Data for the problem are summarized as:

LESS THAN $100,000 IN SALES	$100,000 – $500,000 IN SALES
$n_1 = 100$	$n_2 = 95$
$x_1 = 24$	$x_2 = 39$

From this, we calculate $\hat{p}_1$ and $\hat{p}_2$:

$$\hat{p}_1 = \frac{x_1}{n_1} = \frac{24}{100} = .24$$

$$\hat{p}_2 = \frac{x_2}{n_2} = \frac{39}{95} = .41$$

Step 6.   Using these values and a null hypothesis of zero, the value of the test statistic can be calculated as follows. First, we solve for $\bar{p}$:

$$\bar{p} = \frac{x_1 + x_2}{n_1 + n_2} = \frac{24 + 39}{100 + 95} = .323$$

$$\bar{q} = 1 - \bar{p} - 1 - .323 = .677$$

Then solve for the z:

$$z = \frac{(.24 - .41) - (0)}{\sqrt{(.323)(.677)\left(\dfrac{1}{100} + \dfrac{1}{95}\right)}} = -2.54$$

Step 7.   Reach a statistical conclusion. Because this test statistic, $z = -2.54$, is more than the critical value of z (−2.575) in the lower tail of the distribution and less than the critical value of z (2.575) in the upper tail, the statistical conclusion reached at step 7 is to fail to reject the null hypothesis. The same conclusion can be reached using the p-value method. The observed test statistic is $z = -2.54$. From Table A.5, the probability of getting a z value at least this extreme when the null hypothesis is true is $.5000 - .4945 = .0055$. Since this p-value is more than $\alpha/2 = .005$, the decision is to fail to reject the null hypothesis.

The following diagram shows the critical values, the rejection regions, and the observed value for this problem.

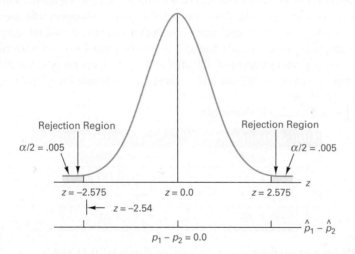

Step 8.   At step 8, a managerial decision is made. We cannot statistically conclude that a greater proportion of female entrepreneurs in the higher gross sales category define success as sales/profit. One of the payoffs of such a determination is to find out what motivates the people with whom we do business. If sales/profits motivate people, offers or promises of greater sales and profits can be a means of attracting their services, their interest, or their business. If sales/profits do not motivate people, such offers would not generate the kind of response wanted and we would need to look for other ways to motivate them.

Confidence Intervals

Sometimes in business research the investigator wants to estimate the difference in two population proportions. For example, what is the difference, if any, in the population proportions of workers in the Midwest who favor union membership and workers in the South who favor union membership? In studying two different suppliers of the same part, a large manufacturing company might want to estimate the difference between suppliers in the proportion of parts that meet specifications. These and other situations requiring the estimation of the difference in two population proportions can be solved by using confidence intervals.

The formula for constructing confidence intervals to estimate the difference in two population proportions is a modified version of Formula 10.9. Formula 10.9 for two proportions requires knowledge of each of the population proportions. Because we are attempting to estimate the difference in these two proportions, we obviously do not know their value. To overcome this lack of knowledge in constructing a confidence interval formula, we substitute the sample proportions in place of the population proportions and use these sample proportions in the estimate, as follows.

$$z = \frac{(\hat{p}_1 - \hat{p}_2) - (p_1 - p_2)}{\sqrt{\dfrac{\hat{p}_1 \cdot \hat{q}_1}{n_1} + \dfrac{\hat{p}_2 \cdot \hat{q}_2}{n_2}}}$$

Solving this equation for $p_1 - p_2$ produces the formula for constructing confidence intervals for $p_1 - p_2$.

Confidence Interval to Estimate $p_1 - p_2$

$$(\hat{p}_1 - \hat{p}_2) - z\sqrt{\frac{\hat{p}_1 \cdot \hat{q}_1}{n_1} + \frac{\hat{p}_2 \cdot \hat{q}_2}{n_2}} \leq p_1 - p_2 \leq (\hat{p}_1 - \hat{p}_2) + z\sqrt{\frac{\hat{p}_1 \cdot \hat{q}_1}{n_1} + \frac{\hat{p}_2 \cdot \hat{q}_2}{n_2}} \qquad (10.11)$$

To see how this formula is used, suppose that in an attempt to target its clientele, managers of a supermarket chain want to determine the difference between the proportion of morning shoppers who are men and the proportion of after–5 P.M. shoppers who are men. Over a period of two weeks, the chain's researchers conduct a systematic random sample survey of 400 morning shoppers, which reveals that 352 are women and 48 are men. During this same period, a systematic random sample of 480 after–5 P.M. shoppers reveals that 293 are women and 187 are men. Construct a 98% confidence interval to estimate the difference in the population proportions of men.

The sample information is shown here.

MORNING SHOPPERS	AFTER–5 P.M. SHOPPERS
$n_1 = 400$	$n_2 = 480$
$x_1 = 48$ men	$x_2 = 187$ men
$\hat{p}_1 = .12$	$\hat{p}_2 = .39$
$\hat{q}_1 = .88$	$\hat{q}_2 = .61$

For a 98% level of confidence, $z = 2.33$. Using Formula 10.11 yields

$$(.12 - .39) - 2.33\sqrt{\frac{(.12)(.88)}{400} + \frac{(.39)(.61)}{480}} \leq p_1 - p_2$$

$$\leq (.12 - .39) + 2.33\sqrt{\frac{(.12)(.88)}{400} + \frac{(.39)(.61)}{480}}$$

$$-.27 - .064 \geq p_1 - p_2 \geq -.27 + .064$$

$$-.334 \geq p_1 - p_2 \geq -.206$$

There is a 98% level of confidence that the difference in population proportions is between −.334 and −.206. Because the after–5 P.M. shopper proportion was subtracted from the morning shoppers, the negative signs in the interval indicate a higher proportion of men in the

```
Test and CI For Two Proportions

Sample   X     N     Sample p
1        48    400   0.120000
2        187   480   0.389583

Difference = p(1) - p(2)

Estimate for difference: -0.269583

98% CI for difference: (-0.333692, -0.205474)

Test for difference = 0 (vs ≠ 0):

Z = -9.78 P-Value = 0.000

Fisher's exact test: P-Value = 0.000
```

FIGURE 10.13 **Minitab Output for the Shopping Example**

after–5 P.M. shoppers than in the morning shoppers. Thus the confidence level is 98% that the difference in proportions is at least .206 and may be as much as .334.

Using the Computer to Analyze the Difference in Two Proportions

Minitab has the capability of testing hypotheses or constructing confidence intervals about the difference in two proportions. Figure 10.13 shows Minitab output for the shopping example. Notice that the output contains a summary of sample information along with the difference in sample proportions, the confidence interval, the computer z value for a hypothesis test, and the p-value. The confidence interval shown here is the same as the one we just computed except for rounding differences.

10.4 Problems

10.31. Using the given sample information, test the following hypotheses.

a. $H_0: p_1 - p_2 = 0$ $H_a: p_1 - p_2 \neq 0$

SAMPLE 1	SAMPLE 2
$n_1 = 368$	$n_2 = 405$
$x_1 = 175$	$x_2 = 182$ Let $\alpha = .05$.

Note that x is the number in the sample having the characteristic of interest.

b. $H_0: p_1 - p_2 = 0$ $H_a: p_1 - p_2 > 0$

SAMPLE 1	SAMPLE 2
$n_1 = 649$	$n_2 = 558$
$\hat{p}_1 = .38$	$\hat{p}_2 = .25$ Let $\alpha = .10$.

10.32. In each of the following cases, calculate a confidence interval to estimate $p_1 - p_2$.

a. $n_1 = 85$, $n_2 = 90$, $\hat{p}_1 = .75$, $\hat{p}_2 = .67$; level of confidence = 90%

b. $n_1 = 1100$, $n_2 = 1300$, $\hat{p}_1 = .19$, $\hat{p}_2 = .17$; level of confidence = 95%

c. $n_1 = 430$, $n_2 = 399$, $x_1 = 275$, $x_2 = 275$; level of confidence = 85%

d. $n_1 = 1500$, $n_2 = 1500$, $x_1 = 1050$, $x_2 = 1100$; level of confidence = 80%

10.33. According to a study conducted by a major computer company, 59% of men and 70% of women say that weight is an extremely/very important factor in purchasing a laptop computer. Suppose this survey was conducted using 374 men and 481 women. Do these data show enough evidence to declare that a significantly higher proportion of women than men believe that weight is an extremely/very important factor in purchasing a laptop computer? Use a 5% level of significance.

10.34. Does age make a difference in the amount of savings a worker feels is needed to be secure at retirement? A study by CommSciences for Transamerica Asset Management found that .24 of workers in the 25–33 age category feel that $250,000 to $500,000 is enough to be secure at retirement. However, .35 of the workers in the 34–52 age category feel that this amount is enough. Suppose 210 workers in the 25–33 age category and 176 workers in the 34–52 age category were involved in this study. Use these data to construct a 90% confidence interval to estimate the difference in population proportions on this question.

10.35. Companies that recently developed new products were asked to rate which activities are most difficult to accomplish with new products. Options included such activities as assessing market potential, market testing, finalizing the design, developing a business plan, and the like. A researcher wants to conduct a similar study to compare the results between two industries: the computer hardware industry and the banking industry. He takes a random sample of 56 computer firms and 89 banks. The researcher asks whether market testing is the most difficult activity to accomplish in developing a new product. Some 48% of the sampled computer companies and 56% of the sampled banks respond that it is the most difficult activity. Use a level of significance of .20 to test whether there is a significant difference in the responses to the question from these two industries.

10.36. A large production facility uses two machines to produce a key part for its main product. Inspectors have expressed concern about the quality of the finished product. Quality control investigation has revealed that the key part made by the two machines is defective at times. The inspectors randomly sampled 35 units of the key part from each machine. Of those produced by machine A, five were defective. Seven of the 35 sampled parts from machine B were defective. The production manager is interested in estimating the difference in

proportions of the populations of parts that are defective between machine A and machine B. From the sample information, compute a 98% confidence interval for this difference.

10.37. According to a CCH Unscheduled Absence survey, 9% of small businesses use telecommuting of workers in an effort to reduce unscheduled absenteeism. This proportion compares to 6% for all businesses. Is there really a significant difference between small businesses and all businesses on this issue? Use these data and an alpha of .10 to test this question. Assume that there were 780 small businesses and 915 other businesses in this survey.

10.38. Many Americans spend time worrying about paying their bills. A survey by Fleishman-Hilliard Research for MassMutual discovered that 60% of Americans with kids say that paying bills is a major concern. This proportion compares to 52% of Americans without kids. Suppose 850 Americans with kids and 910 without kids were contacted for this study. Use these data to construct a 95% confidence interval to estimate the difference in population proportions between Americans with kids and Americans without kids on this issue.

10.5 | Testing Hypotheses About Two Population Variances

Sometimes we are interested in studying the variance of a population rather than a mean or proportion. Section 9.5 discussed how to test hypotheses about a single population variance, but on some occasions business researchers are interested in testing hypotheses about the difference in two population variances. In this section, we examine how to conduct such tests. When would a business researcher be interested in the variances from two populations?

In quality control, analysts often examine both a measure of central tendency (mean or proportion) and a measure of variability. Suppose a manufacturing plant made two batches of an item, produced items on two different machines, or produced items on two different shifts. It might be of interest to management to compare the variances from two batches or two machines to determine whether there is more variability in one than another.

Variance is sometimes used as a measure of the risk of a stock in the stock market. The greater the variance, the greater the risk. By using techniques discussed here, a financial researcher could determine whether the variances (or risk) of two stocks are the same.

In testing hypotheses about two population variances, the sample variances are used. It makes sense that if two samples come from the same population (or populations with equal variances), the ratio of the sample variances, s_1^2/s_2^2, should be about 1. However, because of sampling error, sample variances even from the same population (or from two populations with equal variances) will vary. This *ratio of two sample variances* formulates what is called an *F value*.

$$F = \frac{s_1^2}{s_2^2}$$

These ratios, if computed repeatedly for pairs of sample variances taken from a population, are distributed as an *F distribution*. The F distribution will vary by the sizes of the samples, which are converted to degrees of freedom.

With the F distribution, there are degrees of freedom associated with the numerator (of the ratio) and the denominator. An assumption underlying the F distribution is that the populations from which the samples are drawn are normally distributed for x. *The F test of two population variances is extremely sensitive to violations of the assumption that the populations are normally distributed.* The statistician should carefully investigate the shape of the distributions of the populations from which the samples are drawn to be certain the populations are normally distributed. The formula used to test hypotheses comparing two population variances follows.

F Test for Two Population Variances

$$F = \frac{s_1^2}{s_2^2}$$

$$\text{df}_{\text{numerator}} = v_1 = n_1 - 1$$

$$\text{df}_{\text{denominator}} = v_2 = n_2 - 1$$

(10.12)

Table A.7 contains F distribution table values for $\alpha = .10$, $.05$, $.025$, $.01$, and $.005$. Figure 10.14 shows an F distribution for $v_1 = 6$ and $v_2 = 30$. Notice that the distribution is nonsymmetric, which can be a problem when we are conducting a two-tailed test and want to determine the critical value for the lower tail. Table A.7 contains only F values for the upper tail. However, the F distribution is not symmetric nor does it have a mean of zero as do the z and t distributions; therefore, we cannot merely place a minus sign on the upper-tail critical value and obtain the lower-tail critical value (in addition, the F ratio is always positive—it is the ratio of two variances). This dilemma can be solved by using Formula 10.13, which essentially states that the critical F value for the lower tail $(1 - \alpha)$ can be solved for by taking the inverse of the F value for the upper tail (α). The degrees of freedom numerator for the upper-tail critical value is the degrees of freedom denominator for the lower-tail critical value, and the degrees of freedom denominator for the upper-tail critical value is the degrees of freedom numerator for the lower-tail critical value.

Formula for Determining the Critical Value for the Lower-Tail F

$$F_{1-\alpha, v_2, v_1} = \frac{1}{F_{\alpha, v_1, v_2}}$$

(10.13)

A hypothesis test can be conducted using two sample variances and Formula 10.12. The following example illustrates this process.

Suppose a machine produces metal sheets that are specified to be 22 millimeters thick. Because of the machine, the operator, the raw material, the manufacturing environment, and other factors, there is variability in the thickness. Two machines produce these sheets. Operators are concerned about the consistency of the two machines. To test consistency, they randomly sample 10 sheets produced by machine 1 and 12 sheets produced by machine 2. The thickness measurements of sheets from each machine are given in the table in Step 5. Assume sheet thickness is normally distributed in the population. How can we test to determine whether the variance from each sample comes from the same population variance (population variances are equal) or from different population variances (population variances are not equal)?

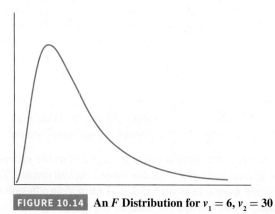

FIGURE 10.14   An F Distribution for $v_1 = 6$, $v_2 = 30$

Step 1 Determine the null and alternative hypotheses. In this case, we are conducting a two-tailed test (variances are the same or not), and the following hypotheses are used.

$$H_0: \sigma_1^2 = \sigma_2^2$$
$$H_a: \sigma_1^2 \neq \sigma_2^2$$

Step 2 The appropriate statistical test is

$$F = \frac{s_1^2}{s_2^2}$$

Step 3 Let $\alpha = .05$.

Step 4 Because we are conducting a two-tailed test, $\alpha/2 = .025$. Because $n_1 = 10$ and $n_2 = 12$, the degrees of freedom numerator for the upper-tail critical value is $v_1 = n_1 - 1 = 10 - 1 = 9$ and the degrees of freedom denominator for the upper-tail critical value is $v_2 = n_2 - 1 = 12 - 1 = 11$. The critical F value for the upper tail obtained from Table A.7 is

$$F_{.025,9,11} = 3.59$$

Table 10.9 is a copy of the F distribution for a one-tailed $\alpha = .025$ (which yields equivalent values for two-tailed $\alpha = .05$ where the upper tail contains .025 of the area). Locate $F_{.025,9,11} = 3.59$ in the table. The lower-tail critical value can be calculated from the upper-tail value by using Formula 10.13.

$$F_{.975,11,9} = \frac{1}{F_{.025,9,11}} = \frac{1}{3.59} = .28$$

The decision rule is to reject the null hypothesis if the observed F value is greater than 3.59 or less than .28.

Step 5 Next we compute the sample variances. The data are shown here.

MACHINE 1		MACHINE 2	
22.3	21.9	22.0	21.7
21.8	22.4	22.1	21.9
22.3	22.5	21.8	22.0
21.6	22.2	21.9	22.1
21.8	21.6	22.2	21.9
		22.0	22.1
$s_1^2 = .11378$		$s_2^2 = .02023$	
$n_1 = 10$		$n_2 = 12$	

Step 6

$$F = \frac{s_1^2}{s_2^2} = \frac{.11378}{.02023} = 5.62$$

The ratio of sample variances is 5.62.

Step 7 The observed F value is 5.62, which is greater than the upper-tail critical value of 3.59. As Figure 10.15 shows, this F value is in the rejection region. Thus, the decision is to reject the null hypotheses. The population variances are not equal.

Step 8 An examination of the sample variances reveals that the variance from machine 1 measurements is greater than that from machine 2 measurements. The operators and process managers might want to examine machine 1 further; an adjustment may be needed or some other reason may be causing the seemingly greater variations on that machine.

TABLE 10.9   **A Portion of the F Distribution Table**

PERCENTAGE POINTS OF THE F DISTRIBUTION

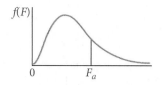

$\alpha = .025$

v_2 \ v_1	NUMERATOR DEGREES OF FREEDOM								
	1	2	3	4	5	6	7	8	9
1	647.8	799.5	864.2	899.6	921.8	937.1	948.2	956.7	963.3
2	38.51	39.00	39.17	39.25	39.30	39.33	39.36	39.37	39.39
3	17.44	16.04	15.44	15.10	14.88	14.73	14.62	14.54	14.47
4	12.22	10.65	9.98	9.60	9.36	9.20	9.07	8.98	8.90
5	10.01	8.43	7.76	7.39	7.15	6.98	6.85	6.76	6.68
6	8.81	7.26	6.60	6.23	5.99	5.82	5.70	5.60	5.52
7	8.07	6.54	5.89	5.52	5.29	5.12	4.99	4.90	4.82
8	7.57	6.06	5.42	5.05	4.82	4.65	4.53	4.43	4.36
9	7.21	5.71	5.08	4.72	4.48	4.32	4.20	4.10	4.03
10	6.94	5.46	4.83	4.47	4.24	4.07	3.95	3.85	3.78
11	6.72	5.26	4.63	4.28	4.04	3.88	3.76	3.66	3.59
12	6.55	5.10	4.47	4.12	3.89	3.73	3.61	3.51	3.44
13	6.41	4.97	4.35	4.00	3.77	3.60	3.48	3.39	3.31
14	6.30	4.86	4.24	3.89	3.66	3.50	3.38	3.29	3.21
15	6.20	4.77	4.15	3.80	3.58	3.41	3.29	3.20	3.12
16	6.12	4.69	4.08	3.73	3.50	3.34	3.22	3.12	3.05
17	6.04	4.62	4.01	3.66	3.44	3.28	3.16	3.06	2.98
18	5.98	4.56	3.95	3.61	3.38	3.22	3.10	3.01	2.93
19	5.92	4.51	3.90	3.56	3.33	3.17	3.05	2.96	2.88
20	5.87	4.46	3.86	3.51	3.29	3.13	3.01	2.91	2.84
21	5.83	4.42	3.82	3.48	3.25	3.09	2.97	2.87	2.80
22	5.79	4.38	3.78	3.44	3.22	3.05	2.93	2.84	2.76
23	5.75	4.35	3.75	3.41	3.18	3.02	2.90	2.81	2.73
24	5.72	4.32	3.72	3.38	3.15	2.99	2.87	2.78	2.70
25	5.69	4.29	3.69	3.35	3.13	2.97	2.85	2.75	2.68
26	5.66	4.27	3.67	3.33	3.10	2.94	2.82	2.73	2.65
27	5.63	4.24	3.65	3.31	3.08	2.92	2.80	2.71	2.63
28	5.61	4.22	3.63	3.29	3.06	2.90	2.78	2.69	2.61
29	5.59	4.20	3.61	3.27	3.04	2.88	2.76	2.67	2.59
30	5.57	4.18	3.59	3.25	3.03	2.87	2.75	2.65	2.57
40	5.42	4.05	3.46	3.13	2.90	2.74	2.62	2.53	2.45
60	5.29	3.93	3.34	3.01	2.79	2.63	2.51	2.41	2.33
120	5.15	3.80	3.23	2.89	2.67	2.52	2.39	2.30	2.22
∞	5.02	3.69	3.12	2.79	2.57	2.41	2.29	2.19	2.11

Denominator Degrees of Freedom

$F_{.025,9,11}$

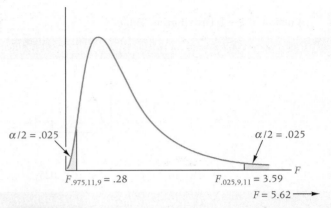

$\alpha/2 = .025$ $\alpha/2 = .025$

$F_{.975,11,9} = .28$ $F_{.025,9,11} = 3.59$

$F = 5.62 \longrightarrow$

FIGURE 10.15 **Minitab Graph of F Values and Rejection Region for the Sheet Metal Example**

Using the Computer to Test Hypotheses About Two Population Variances

Both Excel and Minitab have the capability of directly testing hypotheses about two population variances. Figure 10.16 shows Minitab and Excel output for the sheet metal example. The Minitab output contains the observed F value and its associated p-value along with the sample standard

---

Minitab Output

Test and CI for Two Variances: Machine 1, Machine 2

Statistics

Variable	N	StDev	Variance	95% CI for Variances
Machine 1	10	0.337	0.114	(0.054, 0.379)
Machine 2	12	0.142	0.020	(0.010, 0.058)

Ratio of standard deviations = 2.372
Ratio of variances = 5.625

95% Confidence Intervals

Method	CI for StDev Ratio	CI for Variance Ratio
F	(1.252, 4.691)	(1.568, 22.005)

Tests

Method	DF1	DF2	Test Statistic	P-Value
F	9	11	5.62	0.009

Excel Output

F- Test Two-Sample for Variances

	Machine 1	*Machine 2*
Mean	22.04	21.98
Variance	0.11378	0.02023
Observations	10	12
df	9	11
F	5.62	
P(F<=f) one-tail	0.0047	
F Critical one-tail	2.90	

FIGURE 10.16 **Minitab and Excel Output for the Sheet Metal Example**

deviations and variances. The Excel output contains the two sample means, the two sample variances, the observed F value, the p-value for a one-tailed test, and the critical F value for a one-tailed test. Because the sheet metal example is a two-tailed test, compare the p-value of .0047 to $\alpha/2 = .025$. Because this value (.0047) is less than $\alpha/2 = .025$, the decision is to reject the null hypothesis.

DEMONSTRATION PROBLEM 10.7

According to Runzheimer International, a family of four in Manhattan with $60,000 annual income spends more than $22,000 a year on basic goods and services. In contrast, a family of four in San Antonio with the same annual income spends only $15,460 on the same items. Suppose we want to test to determine whether the variance of money spent per year on the basics by families across the United States is greater than the variance of money spent on the basics by families in Manhattan—that is, whether the amounts spent by families of four in Manhattan are more homogeneous than the amounts spent by such families nationally. Suppose a random sample of eight Manhattan families produces the figures in the table, which are given along with those reported from a random sample of seven families across the United States. Complete a hypothesis-testing procedure to determine whether the variance of values taken from across the United States can be shown to be greater than the variance of values obtained from families in Manhattan. Let $\alpha = .01$. Assume the amount spent on the basics is normally distributed in the population.

Amount Spent on Basics by Family of Four with $60,000 Annual Income

AMOUNT SPENT ON BASICS BY FAMILY OF FOUR WITH $60,000 ANNUAL INCOME	
ACROSS UNITED STATES	MANHATTAN
$18,500	$23,000
19,250	21,900
16,400	22,500
20,750	21,200
17,600	21,000
21,800	22,800
14,750	23,100
	21,300

Solution:

Step 1. This is a one-tailed test with the following hypotheses.

$$H_0: \sigma_1^2 = \sigma_2^2$$
$$H_a: \sigma_1^2 > \sigma_2^2$$

Note that what we are trying to prove—that the variance for the U.S. population is greater than the variance for families in Manhattan—is in the alternative hypothesis.

Step 2. The appropriate statistical test is

$$F = \frac{s_1^2}{s_2^2}$$

Step 3. The Type I error rate is .01.

Step 4. This test is a one-tailed test, so we will use the F distribution table in Appendix A.7 with $\alpha = .01$. The degrees of freedom for $n_1 = 7$ and $n_2 = 8$ are $v_1 = 6$ and $v_2 = 7$. The critical F value for the upper tail of the distribution is

$$F_{.01,6,7} = 7.19.$$

The decision rule is to reject the null hypothesis if the observed value of F is greater than 7.19.

Step 5. The following sample variances are computed from the data.

$$s_1^2 = 5,961,428.6$$

$$n_1 = 7$$

$$s_2^2 = 737,142.9$$

$$n_2 = 8$$

Step 6.   The observed F value can be determined by

$$F = \frac{s_1^2}{s_2^2} = \frac{5,961,428.6}{737,142.9} = 8.09$$

Step 7.   Because the observed value of $F = 8.09$ is greater than the table critical F value of 7.19, the decision is to reject the null hypothesis.

Step 8.   The variance for families in the United States is greater than the variance of families in Manhattan. Families in Manhattan are more homogeneous in amount spent on basics than families across the United States. Marketing managers need to understand this homogeneity as they attempt to find niches in the Manhattan population. Manhattan may not contain as many subgroups as can be found across the United States. The task of locating market niches may be easier in Manhattan than in the rest of the country because fewer possibilities are likely. The following Minitab graph shows the rejection region as well as the critical and observed values of F.

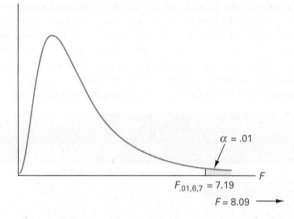

Note: *Some authors recommend the use of this F test to determine whether the data being analyzed by a t test for two population means are meeting the assumption of equal population variances. However, some statistical researchers suggest that for equal sample sizes, the t test is insensitive to the equal variance assumption, and therefore the F test is not needed in that situation. For unequal sample sizes, the F test of variances is "not generally capable of detecting assumption violations that lead to poor performance" with the t test.* This text does not present the application of the F test to determine whether variance assumptions for the t test have been met.*

10.5 Problems

10.39. Test the following hypotheses by using the given sample information and $\alpha = .01$. Assume the populations are normally distributed.

$$H_0: \sigma_1^2 = \sigma_2^2 \qquad H_a: \sigma_1^2 < \sigma_2^2$$

$$n_1 = 10, \qquad n_2 = 11, \qquad s_1^2 = 562, \qquad s_2^2 = 1013$$

10.40. Test the following hypotheses by using the given sample information and $\alpha = .05$. Assume the populations are normally distributed.

$$H_0: \sigma_1^2 = \sigma_2^2 \qquad H_a: \sigma_1^2 \neq \sigma_2^2$$

$$n_1 = 5, \qquad n_2 = 19, \qquad s_1 = 4.68, \qquad s_2 = 2.78$$

10.41. Suppose the data shown here are the results of a survey to investigate gasoline prices. Ten service stations were selected randomly in each of two cities and the figures represent the prices of a gallon of unleaded regular gasoline on a given day. Use the F test to determine whether there is a significant difference in the variances of the prices of unleaded regular gasoline between these two cities. Let $\alpha = .01$. Assume gasoline prices are normally distributed.

CITY 1			CITY 2		
3.43	3.32	3.38	3.33	3.30	3.44
3.40	3.39	3.38	3.42	3.46	3.37
3.39	3.38	3.28	3.39	3.39	3.38
3.34			3.36		

*Carol A. Markowski and Edward P. Markowski, "Conditions for the Effectiveness of a Preliminary Test of Variance," *The American Statistician,* vol. 44 (November 1990), pp. 322–326.

10.42. How long are resale houses on the market? One survey by the Houston Association of Realtors reported that in Houston, resale houses are on the market an average of 112 days. Of course, the length of time varies by market. Suppose random samples of 13 houses in Houston and 11 houses in Chicago that are for resale are traced. The data shown here represent the number of days each house was on the market before being sold. Use the given data and a 1% level of significance to determine whether the population variances for the number of days until resale are different in Houston than in Chicago. Assume the numbers of days resale houses are on the market are normally distributed.

HOUSTON		CHICAGO	
132	126	118	56
138	94	85	69
131	161	113	67
127	133	81	54
99	119	94	137
126	88	93	
134			

10.43. One recent study showed that the average annual amount spent by an East Coast household on frankfurters was $23.84 compared with an average of $19.83 for West Coast households. Suppose a random sample of 11 East Coast households showed that the standard deviation of these purchases (frankfurters) was $7.52, whereas a random sample of 15 West Coast households resulted in a standard deviation of $6.08. Do these samples provide enough evidence to conclude that the variance of annual frankfurter purchases for East Coast households is greater than the variance of annual frankfurter purchases for West Coast households? Let alpha be .05. Assume amounts spent per year on frankfurters are normally distributed. Suppose the data did show that the variance among East Coast households is greater than that among West Coast households. What might this variance mean to decision makers in the frankfurter industry?

10.44. According to the General Accounting Office of the U.S. government, the average age of a male federal worker is 43.6 years and that of a male worker in the nonfederal sector is 37.3 years. Is there any difference in the variation of ages of men in the federal sector and men in the nonfederal sector? Suppose a random sample of 15 male federal workers is taken and the variance of their ages is 91.5. Suppose also a random sample of 15 male nonfederal workers is taken and the variance of their ages is 67.3. Use these data and $\alpha = .01$ to answer the question. Assume ages are normally distributed.

Decision Dilemma Solved

L. L. Bean

Various techniques in Chapter 10 can be used to analyze the L. L. Bean managerial and statistical questions and their associated data. Question 1 asks if, due to a smaller online volume at night, the home page might load faster at night. To test this hypothesis, a random sample of 37 uploads is taken during the daytime with a resultant mean time of 7.46 seconds. A second random sample of 45 uploads is taken at nighttime with a resultant mean time of 7.11 seconds. Previous studies indicate that the population standard deviation in both the daytime and the nighttime is 0.83 seconds. Because the business statistician is testing the difference in sample means taken from independent populations and the population standard deviations are known, the z test featured in Section 10.1 is the appropriate test. A one-tailed test is set up because the business researcher is testing to determine if the upload time at night is faster. Using an alpha of .01, a critical z of 2.33 is obtained. From the data given in question 1 of the decision dilemma, an observed z of 1.90 is computed. Because this test statistic, $z = 1.90$, is less than the critical value of z (2.33) in the upper tail of the distribution, the statistical conclusion is to fail to reject the null hypothesis. There is not enough evidence to conclude that, on average, daytime uploads are slower than nighttime uploads.

In the second managerial and statistical question of the Decision Dilemma, it is asked if the average order size for women is greater than is the average order size for men. Suppose researchers at L. L. Bean want to test this question by taking a random sample of 44 orders from women and a random sample of 48 orders from men. Suppose that the sample mean for women is $80 with a sample standard deviation of $18. Suppose furthermore that the sample mean for men is $72 with a sample standard deviation of $16. Using this information and statistical techniques learned in Chapter 10, how could the researchers set up and carry out a hypothesis

test to answer this question about order size? Because the business statistician is testing the difference in sample means taken from independent populations and the population standard deviations are not known, the t test featured in Section 10.2 is the appropriate test provided that it can be demonstrated that order sizes are normally distributed in the population. A one-tailed test is set up because the researchers are testing to determine if the average order size for women is greater than the average order size for men. Using an alpha of .05 and degrees of freedom of 90, a critical t of 1.662 is obtained. From the data given in question 2 of the decision dilemma, an observed t of 2.26 is computed. Because this test statistic, $t = 2.26$, is greater than the critical value of t (1.662) in the upper tail of the distribution, the statistical conclusion to reject the null hypothesis. There is enough evidence to conclude that the average order size for women is greater than the average order size for men.

In managerial and statistical question three of the Decision Dilemma, it is reported that about 41% of shoppers said that "receiving my product when expected" led them to recommend an online retailer. Suppose a business researcher wants to compare the proportion of L. L. Bean purchasers who agree with this statement to the proportion of a competitor's purchasers who agree with this statement. Suppose that a random sample of 310 L. L. Bean purchasers is obtained and each purchaser is asked this question, with the result that 136 agreed with this statement. Suppose a random sample of 195 competitor purchasers is obtained and each purchaser is asked this question, with the result that 72 agreed with this statement. If we want to use these data to test to determine if there is a significant difference between L. L. Bean purchasers and the competitor's purchasers on this issue, how would we go about doing it? Because the business researcher is testing the difference in sample proportions instead of means, the z test featured in Section 10.4 is the appropriate test. Since there is no idea as to which company might have a higher proportion of purchasers who agree with the statement, a two-tailed test is set up. Using an alpha of .05 and an $\alpha/2$ of .025 in each tail, critical z values of ±1.96 are obtained. From the data given in question 3 of the decision dilemma, an observed z of 1.56 is computed. Because this test statistic, $z = 1.56$, is less than

the critical value of z (1.96) in the upper tail of the distribution, the statistical conclusion is to fail to reject the null hypothesis. There is not enough evidence to conclude that the proportion of L. L. Bean purchasers who agree with the statement is different from the proportion of the competitor's purchasers who agree with the statement.

Ethical Considerations

The statistical techniques presented in this chapter share some of the pitfalls of confidence interval methodology and hypothesis-testing techniques mentioned in preceding chapters. Included among these pitfalls are assumption violations. Remember, if small sample sizes are used in analyzing means, the z tests are valid only when the population is normally distributed and the population variances are known. If the population variances are unknown, a t test can be used if the population is normally distributed and if the population variances can be assumed to be equal.

The z tests and confidence intervals for two population proportions also have a minimum sample-size requirement that should be met. In addition, it is assumed that both populations are normally distributed when the F test is used for two population variances.

Use of the t test for two independent populations is not unethical when the populations are related, but it is likely to result in a loss of power. As with any hypothesis-testing procedure, in determining the null and alternative hypotheses, make certain you are not assuming true what you are trying to prove.

Summary

Business research often requires the analysis of two populations. Three types of parameters can be compared: means, proportions, and variances. Except for the F test for population variances, all techniques presented contain both confidence intervals and hypothesis tests. In each case, the two populations are studied through the use of sample data randomly drawn from each population.

The population means are analyzed by comparing two sample means. When sample sizes are large ($n \geq 30$) and population variances are known, a z test is used. When sample sizes are small, the population variances are known, and the populations are normally distributed, the z test is used to analyze the population means. If the

population variances are unknown and the populations are normally distributed, the t test of means for independent samples is used. For populations that are related on some measure, such as twins or before-and-after, a t test for dependent measures (matched pairs) is used. The difference in two population proportions can be tested or estimated using a z test.

The population variances are analyzed by an F test when the assumption that the populations are normally distributed is met. The F value is a ratio of the two variances. The F distribution is a distribution of possible ratios of two sample variances taken from one population or from two populations containing the same variance.

Key Terms

dependent samples	F value	matched-pairs test	related measures
F distribution	independent samples		

Formulas

z test for the difference in two independent sample means

$$z = \frac{(\bar{x}_1 - \bar{x}_2) - (\mu_1 - \mu_2)}{\sqrt{\dfrac{\sigma_1^2}{n_1} + \dfrac{\sigma_2^2}{n_2}}}$$

Confidence interval for estimating the difference in two independent population means using z

$$(\bar{x}_1 - \bar{x}_2) - z\sqrt{\frac{\sigma_1^2}{n_1} + \frac{\sigma_2^2}{n_2}} \leq \mu_1 - \mu_2 \leq (\bar{x}_1 - \bar{x}_2)$$
$$+ z\sqrt{\frac{\sigma_1^2}{n_1} + \frac{\sigma_2^2}{n_2}}$$

t test for two independent sample means, and population variances unknown but assumed to be equal (assume also that the two populations are normally distributed)

$$t = \frac{(\bar{x}_1 - \bar{x}_2) - (\mu_1 - \mu_2)}{\sqrt{\dfrac{s_1^2(n_1 - 1) + s_2^2(n_2 - 1)}{n_1 + n_2 - 2}} \sqrt{\dfrac{1}{n_1} + \dfrac{1}{n_2}}}$$

$$df = n_1 + n_2 - 2$$

Confidence interval for estimating the difference in two independent means, and population variances unknown but assumed to be equal (assume also that two populations are normally distributed)

$$(\bar{x}_1 - \bar{x}_2) \pm t\sqrt{\frac{s_1^2(n_1 - 1) + s_2^2(n_2 - 1)}{n_1 + n_2 - 2}} \sqrt{\frac{1}{n_1} + \frac{1}{n_2}}$$

$$df = n_1 + n_2 - 2$$

t test for the difference in two related samples (the differences are normally distributed in the population)

$$t = \frac{\bar{d} - D}{\dfrac{s_d}{\sqrt{n}}}$$

$$df = n - 1$$

Formulas for $\bar{d}$ and s_d

$$\bar{d} = \frac{\Sigma d}{n}$$

$$s_d = \sqrt{\frac{\Sigma(d - \bar{d})^2}{n - 1}} = \sqrt{\frac{\Sigma d^2 - \dfrac{(\Sigma d)^2}{n}}{n - 1}}$$

Confidence interval formula for estimating the difference in related samples (the differences are normally distributed in the population)

$$\bar{d} - t\frac{s_d}{\sqrt{n}} \le D \le \bar{d} + t\frac{s_d}{\sqrt{n}}$$

$$df = n - 1$$

z formula for testing the difference in population proportions

$$z = \frac{(\hat{p}_1 - \hat{p}_2) - (p_1 - p_2)}{\sqrt{(\bar{p} \cdot \bar{q})\left(\dfrac{1}{n_1} + \dfrac{1}{n_2}\right)}}$$

where $\bar{p} = \dfrac{x_1 + x_2}{n_1 + n_2} = \dfrac{n_1\hat{p}_1 + n_2\hat{p}_2}{n_1 + n_2}$ and $\bar{q} = 1 - \bar{p}$

Confidence interval to estimate $p_1 - p_2$

$$(\hat{p}_1 - \hat{p}_2) - z\sqrt{\frac{\hat{p}_1 \cdot \hat{q}_1}{n_1} + \frac{\hat{p}_2 \cdot \hat{q}_2}{n_2}} \le p_1 - p_2$$

$$\le (\hat{p}_1 - \hat{p}_2) + z\sqrt{\frac{\hat{p}_1 \cdot \hat{q}_1}{n_1} + \frac{\hat{p}_2 \cdot \hat{q}_2}{n_2}}$$

F test for two population variances (assume the two populations are normally distributed)

$$F = \frac{s_1^2}{s_2^2}$$

$$df_{numerator} = v_1 = n_1 - 1$$

$$df_{denominator} = v_2 = n_2 - 1$$

Formula for determining the critical value for the lower-tail F

$$F_{1-\alpha, v_2, v_1} = \frac{1}{F_{\alpha, v_1, v_2}}$$

Supplementary Problems

Calculating the Statistics

10.45. Test the following hypotheses with the data given. Let $\alpha = .10$.

$$H_0: \mu_1 - \mu_2 = 0 \qquad H_a: \mu_1 - \mu_2 \ne 0$$

SAMPLE 1	SAMPLE 2
$\bar{x}_1 = 138.4$	$\bar{x}_2 = 142.5$
$\sigma_1 = 6.71$	$\sigma_2 = 8.92$
$n_1 = 48$	$n_2 = 39$

10.46. Use the following data to construct a 98% confidence interval to estimate the difference between μ_1 and μ_2.

SAMPLE 1	SAMPLE 2
$\bar{x}_1 = 34.9$	$\bar{x}_2 = 27.6$
$\sigma_1^2 = 2.97$	$\sigma_2^2 = 3.50$
$n_1 = 34$	$n_2 = 31$

10.47. The following data come from independent samples drawn from normally distributed populations. Use these data to test the following hypotheses. Let the Type I error rate be .05.

$$H_0: \mu_1 - \mu_2 = 0$$
$$H_a: \mu_1 - \mu_2 > 0$$

SAMPLE 1	SAMPLE 2
$\bar{x}_1 = 2.06$	$\bar{x}_2 = 1.93$
$s_1^2 = .176$	$s_2^2 = .143$
$n_1 = 12$	$n_2 = 15$

10.48. Construct a 95% confidence interval to estimate $\mu_1 - \mu_2$ by using the following data. Assume the populations are normally distributed.

SAMPLE 1	SAMPLE 2
$\bar{x}_1 = 74.6$	$\bar{x}_2 = 70.9$
$s_1^2 = 10.5$	$s_2^2 = 11.4$
$n_1 = 18$	$n_2 = 19$

10.49. The following data have been gathered from two related samples. The differences are assumed to be normally distributed in the population. Use these data and alpha of .01 to test the following hypotheses.

$$H_0: D = 0$$
$$H_a: D < 0$$
$$n = 21, \quad \bar{d} = -1.16, \quad s_d = 1.01$$

10.50. Use the following data to construct a 99% confidence interval to estimate D. Assume the differences are normally distributed in the population.

RESPONDENT	BEFORE	AFTER
1	47	63
2	33	35
3	38	36
4	50	56
5	39	44
6	27	29
7	35	32
8	46	54
9	41	47

10.51. Test the following hypotheses by using the given data and alpha equal to .05.

$$H_0: p_1 - p_2 = 0$$
$$H_a: p_1 - p_2 \neq 0$$

SAMPLE 1	SAMPLE 2
$n_1 = 783$	$n_2 = 896$
$x_1 = 345$	$x_2 = 421$

10.52. Use the following data to construct a 99% confidence interval to estimate $p_1 - p_2$.

SAMPLE 1	SAMPLE 2
$n_1 = 409$	$n_2 = 378$
$\hat{p}_1 = .71$	$\hat{p}_2 = .67$

10.53. Test the following hypotheses by using the given data. Let alpha = .05.

$$H_0: \sigma_1^2 = \sigma_2^2$$
$$H_a: \sigma_1^2 \neq \sigma_2^2$$
$$n_1 = 8, \quad n_2 = 10, \quad s_1^2 = 46, \quad s_2^2 = 37$$

Testing Your Understanding

10.54. Suppose a large insurance company wants to estimate the difference between the average amount of term life insurance purchased per family and the average amount of whole life insurance purchased per family. To obtain an estimate, one of the company's actuaries randomly selects 27 families who have term life insurance only and 29 families who have whole life policies only. Each sample is taken from families in which the leading provider is younger than 45 years of age. Use the data obtained to construct a 95% confidence interval to estimate the difference in means for these two groups. Assume the amount of insurance is normally distributed.

TERM	WHOLE LIFE
$n_T = 27$	$n_W = 29$
$\bar{x}_T = \$75,000$	$\bar{x}_W = \$45,000$
$s_T = \$22,000$	$s_W = \$15,500$

10.55. A study is conducted to estimate the average difference in bus ridership for a large city during the morning and afternoon rush hours. The transit authority's researcher randomly selects nine buses because of the variety of routes they represent. On a given day the number of riders on each bus is counted at 7:45 A.M. and at 4:45 P.M., with the following results.

BUS	MORNING	AFTERNOON
1	43	41
2	51	49
3	37	44
4	24	32
5	47	46
6	44	42
7	50	47
8	55	51
9	46	49

Use the data to compute a 90% confidence interval to estimate the population average difference. Assume ridership is normally distributed.

10.56. There are several methods used by people to organize their lives in terms of keeping track of appointments, meetings, and deadlines. Some of these include using a desk calendar, using informal notes of scrap paper, keeping them "in your head," using a day planner, and keeping a formal "to do" list. Suppose a business researcher wants to test the hypothesis that a greater proportion of marketing managers keep track of such obligations "in their head" than do accountants. To test this, a business researcher samples 400 marketing managers and 450 accountants. Of those sampled, 220 marketing managers keep track "in their head" while 216 of the accountants do so. Using a 1% level of significance, what does the business researcher find?

10.57. A study was conducted to compare the salaries of accounting clerks and data entry operators. One of the hypotheses to be tested is that the variability of salaries among accounting clerks is the same as the variability of salaries of data entry operators. To test this hypothesis, a random sample of 16 accounting clerks was taken, resulting in a sample mean salary of $26,400 and a sample standard deviation of $1,200. A random sample of 14 data entry operators was taken as well, resulting in a sample mean of $25,800 and a sample standard deviation of $1,050. Use these data and $\alpha = .05$ to test to determine whether the population variance of salaries is the same for accounting clerks as it is for data entry operators. Assume that salaries of data entry operators and accounting clerks are normally distributed in the population.

10.58. A study was conducted to develop a scale to measure stress in the workplace. Respondents were asked to rate 26 distinct work events. Each event was to be compared with the stress of the first week on the job, which was awarded an arbitrary score of 500. Sixty professional men and 41 professional women participated in the study. One of the stress events was "lack of support from the boss." The men's sample average rating of this event was 631 and the women's sample average rating was 848. Suppose the population standard deviations for men and for women both were about 100. Construct a 95% confidence interval to estimate the difference in the population mean scores on this event for men and women.

10.59. A national grocery store chain wants to test the difference in the average weight of turkeys sold in Detroit and the average weight of turkeys sold in Charlotte. According to the chain's researcher, a random sample of 20 turkeys sold at the chain's stores in Detroit yielded a sample mean of 17.53 pounds, with a sample standard deviation of 3.2 pounds. Her random sample of 24 turkeys sold at the chain's stores in Charlotte yielded a sample mean of 14.89 pounds, with a sample standard deviation of 2.7 pounds. Use a 1% level of significance to determine whether there is a difference in the mean weight of turkeys sold in these two cities. Assume the population variances are approximately the same and that the weights of turkeys sold in the stores are normally distributed.

10.60. A tree nursery has been experimenting with fertilizer to increase the growth of seedlings. A sample of 35 two-year-old pine trees is grown for three more years with a cake of fertilizer buried in the soil near the trees' roots. A second sample of 35 two-year-old pine trees is grown for three more years under identical conditions (soil, temperature, water) as the first group, but not fertilized. Tree growth is measured over the three-year period with the following results.

TREES WITH FERTILIZER	TREES WITHOUT FERTILIZER
$n_1 = 35$	$n_2 = 35$
$\bar{x}_1 = 38.4$ inches	$\bar{x}_2 = 23.1$ inches
$\sigma_1 = 9.8$ inches	$\sigma_2 = 7.4$ inches

Do the data support the theory that the population of trees with the fertilizer grew significantly larger during the period in which they were fertilized than the nonfertilized trees? Use $\alpha = .01$.

10.61. One of the most important aspects of a store's image is the perceived quality of its merchandise. Other factors include merchandise pricing, assortment of products, convenience of location, and service. Suppose image perceptions of shoppers of specialty stores and shoppers of discount stores are being compared. A random sample of shoppers is taken at each type of store, and the shoppers are asked whether the quality of merchandise is a determining factor in their perception of the store's image. Some 75% of the 350 shoppers at the specialty stores say yes, but only 52% of the 500 shoppers at the discount store say yes. Use these data to test to determine if there is a significant difference between the proportion of shoppers at specialty stores and the proportion of shoppers at discount stores who say that quality of merchandise is a determining factor in their perception of a store's image. Let alpha equal .10.

10.62. Is there more variation in the output of one shift in a manufacturing plant than in another shift? In an effort to study this question, plant managers gathered productivity reports from the 8 A.M. to 4 P.M. shift for eight days. The reports indicated that the following numbers of units were produced on each day for this shift.

5528	4779	5112	5380
4918	4763	5055	5106

Productivity information was also gathered from seven days for the 4 P.M. to midnight shift, resulting in the following data.

4325	4016	4872	4559
3982	4754	4116	

Use these data and $\alpha = .01$ to test to determine whether the variances of productivity for the two shifts are the same. Assume productivity is normally distributed in the population.

10.63. What is the average difference between the price of name-brand soup and the price of store-brand soup? To obtain an estimate, an analyst randomly samples eight stores. Each store sells its own brand and a national name brand. The prices of a can of name-brand tomato soup and a can of the store-brand tomato soup follow.

STORE	NAME BRAND	STORE BRAND
1	54¢	49¢
2	55	50
3	59	52
4	53	51
5	54	50
6	61	56
7	51	47
8	53	49

Construct a 90% confidence interval to estimate the average difference. Assume that the differences in prices of tomato soup are normally distributed in the population.

10.64. As the prices of heating oil and natural gas increase, consumers become more careful about heating their homes. Researchers want to know how warm homeowners keep their houses in January and how the results from Wisconsin and Tennessee compare. The researchers randomly call 23 Wisconsin households between 7 P.M. and 9 P.M. on January 15 and ask the respondent how warm the house is according to the thermostat. The researchers then call 19 households in Tennessee the same night and ask the same question. The results follow.

WISCONSIN				TENNESSEE			
71	71	65	68	73	75	74	71
70	61	67	69	74	73	74	70
75	68	71	73	72	71	69	72
74	68	67	69	74	73	70	72
69	72	67	72	69	70	67	
70	73	72					

For $\alpha = .01$, is the average temperature of a house in Tennessee significantly higher than that of a house in Wisconsin on the evening of January 15? Assume the population variances are equal and the house temperatures are normally distributed in each population.

10.65. In manufacturing, does worker productivity drop on Friday? In an effort to determine whether it does, a company's personnel analyst randomly selects from a manufacturing plant five workers who make the same part. He measures their output on Wednesday and again on Friday and obtains the following results.

WORKER	WEDNESDAY OUTPUT	FRIDAY OUTPUT
1	71	53
2	56	47
3	75	52
4	68	55
5	74	58

The analyst uses $\alpha = .05$ and assumes the difference in productivity is normally distributed. Do the samples provide enough evidence to show that productivity drops on Friday?

10.66. A manufacturer uses two machines to drill holes in pieces of sheet metal used in engine construction. The workers who attach the sheet metal to the engine become inspectors in that they reject sheets so poorly drilled that they cannot be attached. The production manager is interested in knowing whether one machine produces more defective drillings than the other machine. As an experiment, employees mark the sheets so that the manager can determine which machine was used to drill the holes. A random sample of 191 sheets of metal drilled by machine 1 is taken, and 38 of the sheets are defective. A random sample of 202 sheets of metal drilled by machine 2 is taken, and 21 of the sheets are defective. Use $\alpha = .05$ to determine whether there is a significant difference in the proportion of sheets drilled with defective holes between machine 1 and machine 2.

10.67. Is there a difference in the proportion of construction workers who are under 35 years of age and the proportion of telephone repair people who are under 35 years of age? Suppose a study is conducted in Calgary, Alberta, using random samples of 338 construction workers and 281 telephone repair people. The sample of construction workers includes 297 people under 35 years of age and the sample of telephone repair people includes 192 people under that age. Use these data to construct a 90% confidence interval to estimate the difference in proportions of people under 35 years of age among construction workers and telephone repair people.

10.68. Executives often spend so many hours in meetings that they have relatively little time to manage their individual areas of operation. What is the difference in mean time spent in meetings by executives of the aerospace industry and executives of the automobile industry? Suppose random samples of 33 aerospace executives and 35 automobile executives are monitored for a week to determine how much time they spend in meetings. The results follow.

AEROSPACE	AUTOMOBILE
$n_1 = 33$	$n_2 = 35$
$\bar{x}_1 = 12.4\,\text{hours}$	$\bar{x}_2 = 4.6\,\text{hours}$
$\sigma_1 = 2.9\,\text{hours}$	$\sigma_2 = 1.8\,\text{hours}$

Use the data to estimate the difference in the mean time per week executives in these two industries spend in meetings. Use a 99% level of confidence.

10.69. Various types of retail outlets sell toys during the holiday season. Among them are specialty toy stores, large discount toy stores, and other retailers that carry toys as only one part of their stock of goods. Is there any difference in the dollar amount of a customer purchase between a large discount toy store and a specialty toy store if they carry relatively comparable types of toys? Suppose in December a random sample of 60 sales slips is selected from a large discount toy outlet and a random sample of 40 sales slips is selected from a specialty toy store. The data gathered from these samples follow.

LARGE DISCOUNT TOY STORE	SPECIALTY TOY STORE
$\bar{x}_D = \$47.20$	$\bar{x}_S = \$27.40$
$\sigma_D = \$12.45$	$\sigma_S = \$9.82$

Use $\alpha = .01$ and the data to determine whether there is a significant difference in the average size of purchases at these stores.

10.70. One of the thrusts of quality control management is to examine the process by which a product is produced. This approach also applies to paperwork. In industries where large long-term projects are undertaken, days and even weeks may elapse as a change order makes its way through a maze of approvals before receiving final approval. This process can result in long delays and stretch schedules to the breaking point. Suppose a quality control consulting group claims that it can significantly reduce the number of days required for such paperwork to receive approval. In an attempt to "prove" its case, the group selects five jobs for which it revises the paperwork system. The following data show the number of days required for a change order to be approved before the group intervened and the number of days required for a change order to be approved after the group instituted a new paperwork system.

BEFORE	AFTER
12	8
7	3
10	8
16	9
8	5

Use $\alpha = .01$ to determine whether there was a significant drop in the number of days required to process paperwork to approve change orders. Assume that the differences in days are normally distributed.

10.71. For the two large newspapers in your city, you are interested in knowing whether there is a significant difference in the average number of pages in each dedicated solely to advertising. You randomly select 10 editions of newspaper A and 6 editions of newspaper B (excluding weekend editions). The data follow. Use $\alpha = .01$ to test whether there is a significant difference in averages. Assume the number of pages of advertising per edition is normally distributed and the population variances are approximately equal.

A		B	
17	17	8	14
21	15	11	10
11	19	9	6
19	22		
26	16		

Interpreting the Output

10.72. A study by Colliers International presented the highest and the lowest global rental rates per year per square foot of office space. Among the cities with the lowest rates were Perth, Australia; Edmonton, Alberta, Canada; and Calgary, Alberta, Canada, with rates of $8.81, $9.55, and $9.69, respectively. At the high end were Hong Kong; Mumbai, India; and Tokyo, Japan, with rates over $100. Suppose a researcher conducted her own survey of businesses renting office space to determine whether one city is significantly more expensive than another. The data are tallied and analyzed by using Minitab. The results follow. Discuss the output. Assume that rental rates are normally distributed in the population. What cities were studied? How large were the samples? What were the sample statistics? What was the value of alpha? What were the hypotheses, and what was the conclusion?

```
Two-Sample T-Test and CI

Sample        N     Mean    StDev    SE Mean
Hong Kong    19    130.4    12.9     3.0
Mumbai       23    128.4    13.9     2.9

Difference = μ (Hong Kong) − μ (Mumbai)
Estimate for difference: 2.00
98% CI for difference: (−8.11, 12.11)
T-Test of difference = 0 (vs ≠):
T-Value = 0.48 P-Value = 0.634 DF = 40
Both use Pooled StDev = 13.4592
```

10.73. Why do employees "blow the whistle" on other employees for unethical or illegal behavior? One study conducted by the AICPA reported the likelihood that employees would blow the whistle on another employee for such things as unsafe working conditions, unsafe products, and poorly managed operations. On a scale from 1 to 7, with 1 denoting highly improbable and 7 denoting highly probable, unnecessary purchases received a 5.72 in the study. Suppose this study was administered at a company and then all employees were subjected to a one-month series of seminars on reasons to blow the whistle on fellow employees. One month later the study was administered again to the same employees at the company in an effort to determine whether the treatment had any effect. The following Excel output shows the results of the study. What were the sample sizes? What might the hypotheses have been? If $\alpha = .05$, what conclusions could be made? Which of the statistical tests presented in this chapter is likely to have been used? Assume that differences in scores are normally distributed.

t-Test: Paired Two Sample for Means

	Variable 1	Variable 2
Mean	3.991	5.072
Variance	1.898	0.785
Observations	14	14
Pearson Correlation	−0.04585	
Hypothesized Mean Difference	0	
df	13	
t Stat	−2.47	
P(T<=t) one-tail	0.0102	
t Critical one-tail	1.77	
P(T<=t) two-tail	0.00204	
t Critical two-tail	2.16	

10.74. A large manufacturing company produces computer printers that are distributed and sold all over the United States. Due to lack of industry information, the company has a difficult time ascertaining its market share in different parts of the country. They hire a market research firm to estimate their market share in a northern city and a southern city. They would also like to know whether there is a difference in their market shares in these two cities; if so, they want to estimate how much. The market research firm randomly selects printer customers from different locales across both cities and determines what brand of computer printer they purchased. The following Minitab output shows the results from this study. Discuss the results including sample sizes, estimation of the difference in proportions, and any significant differences determined. What were the hypotheses tested?

```
Test and CI for Two Proportions

Sample           X      N      Sample P
Northern City   147    473    0.310782
Southern City   104    385    0.270130

Difference = p (Northern City) − p
(Southern City)
Estimate for difference: 0.0406524
99% CI for difference: (−0.0393623,
0.120667)
Test for difference = 0 (vs ≠ 0):
Z = 1.31 P-Value = 0.191
```

10.75. A manufacturing company produces plastic pipes that are specified to be 10 inches long and 1/8 inch thick with an opening of 3/4 inch. These pipes are molded on two different machines. To maintain consistency, the company periodically randomly selects pipes for testing. In one specific test, pipes were randomly sampled from each machine and the lengths were measured. A statistical test was computed using Excel in an effort to determine whether the variance for machine 1 was significantly greater than the variance for machine 2. The results are shown here. Discuss the outcome of this test along with some of the other information given in the output.

F-Test Two-Sample for Variances

	Variable 1	Variable 2
Mean	10.03	9.97
Variance	0.02920	0.01965
Observations	26	28
df	25	27
F	1.49	
P(F<=f) one-tail	0.15766	
F Critical one-tail	1.92	

Analyzing the Databases

See **www.wiley.com/college/black**

1. Test to determine whether there is a significant difference between mean Value Added by the Manufacturer and the mean Cost of Materials in manufacturing. Use the Manufacturing database as the sample data and let alpha be .01.

2. Use the Manufacturing database to test to determine whether there is a significantly greater variance among the values of End-of-Year Inventories than among Cost of Materials. Let α = .05.

3. Is there a difference between the average Number of Admissions at a general medical hospital and a psychiatric hospital? Use the Hospital database to test this hypothesis with α = .10. The variable Service in the Hospital database differentiates general medical hospitals

(coded 1) and psychiatric hospitals (coded 2). Now test to determine whether there is a difference between these two types of hospitals on the variables Beds and Total Expenses.

4. Use the Financial database to test whether there is a significant difference in the proportion of companies whose earnings per share are more than $2.00 and the proportion of companies whose dividends per share are between $1.00 and $2.00. Let α = .05.

5. Using the appropriate technique selected from this chapter and the Consumer Food database, test to determine if there is a significant difference between households in a metro area and households outside metro areas in annual food spending. Let α = .01.

Case

Five Guys

In 1986 for a little less than $70,000, the first Five Guys hamburger restaurant was opened in Arlington, Virginia. Though originally named after Jerry Murrell, founder and chief executive, and his four sons, after a fifth son was born in 1987, the restaurant name reflects Murrell's five sons. Their philosophy was to serve fresh, hand-cooked burgers with "all the toppings you could stuff between fresh-baked buns" along with fresh-cut fries cooked in peanut oil. The business was take-out only with no delivery and no drive-through service.

Building on a company philosophy that the customer is their best salesperson, their small restaurant quickly enjoyed a cult-like following in the Washington, D.C. area where they were voted the number 1 burger in the metro area. As word-of-mouth spread, they opened four more restaurants with sit-down seating.

Even though the company has grown and expanded, they still use only fresh ground beef in their hamburgers; and there are no freezers in Five Guys locations – just coolers – because nothing is ever frozen. Because they use high quality foods and processes, Five Guys charges a little more for their product and are considered to be in the "better burger" category where they rank number one. With 17 possible toppings to choose from, there are over 250,000 possible ways to order a burger at Five Guys.

The Five Guys are widely known for their hand-cut fries which contain no cholesterol and served in ample portions. Jerry Murrell said that because fries are much harder to cook than burgers, they read French cookbooks and figured out how to make the perfect French

fry. Most of their potatoes come from Idaho – about 8 percent of the Idaho potato crop – and, they like northern potatoes because they grow during the day when it is warm and stop at night when it cools down. They do not serve dehydrated fries but rather soak their fries in water and prefry them forming a seal so that when they get fried a second time, they do not absorb any oil and are not greasy. Chad Murrell leads "fry calibration" classes to drill into workers the proper mix of starch, water and temperature needed to make the perfect fry.

In 2002, when the family had five restaurants in northern Virginia and after much discussion and consideration, the family decided to sell franchises but only if the franchisees agreed to abide by Five Guys' high quality standards. Within three days of this decision, the franchising rights to Virginia were sold out. In the next few years, hundreds of Five Guys' franchises were established across the United States. The hardest part for the Murrell family was assuring that each franchise stuck to the company formula and menu.

In the past 30 years, the company has grown to 1,163 U.S. units (around 20% company-owned and 80% franchises) with a U.S. system wide sales of $1.21 billion. In addition, there are Five Guys restaurants in six Canadian provinces, the United Kingdom, and potentially in the Middle East. The family is still heavily involved in the business with Jerry as CEO, Jim helping manage the entire operation, Matt opening new restaurants, Chad overseeing management training, Ben overseeing IT, Tyler overseeing the bakeries that provide Five Guys buns, and Janie running the books. Each has equal share in the company. Around 50 percent of Five Guys' current staffers have been promoted due to robust reviewing procedures and all staffers receive paid sick leave.

Discussion

1. Suppose a fast-food researcher is interested in determining if there is a difference between Denver and Chicago in the average price of a comparable hamburger. There is some indication, based on information published by Grub Hub, that the average price of a hamburger in Denver may be more than it is in Chicago. Suppose further that the prices of hamburgers in any given city are approximately normally distributed with a population standard deviation of $0.64. A random sample of 15 different fast-food hamburger restaurants is taken in Denver and the average price of a hamburger for these restaurants is $9.11. In addition, a random sample of 18 different fast-food hamburger restaurants is taken in Chicago and the average price of a hamburger for these restaurants is $8.62. Use techniques presented in this chapter to answer the researcher's question. Explain your results.

2. According to Beef Producer.com, there has been a gradual, relatively consistent drop in the consumption of beef in the United States over the past few years. Suppose researchers randomly sampled 18 American adults six years ago and measured the amount of beef that they consumed in one year. Suppose also that five years later, these same researchers identified 18 closely matching American adults and measured the amount of beef that they consumed last year. The data were entered into a Minitab spreadsheet and the following output was obtained. Study the output and write a paragraph on your findings.

```
Paired T-Test and CI: Early Year, Late Year
Paired T for Early Year – Late Year

             N     Mean    StDev    SE Mean
Early Year   18    59.58   11.58    2.73
Late Year    18    58.60   11.58    2.73
Difference   18    0.986   1.619    0.381

95% CI for mean difference: (0.181, 1.791)
T-Test of mean difference = 0 (vs ≠ 0):
T-Value = 2.59  P-Value = 0.019
```

3. Are the percentages of men and women who cut their hamburgers in half about the same? Suppose a random sample of men is taken and a random sample of women is taken, and respondents in each group are asked if they cut their hamburgers in half. The results are analyzed using Minitab and the output is presented here. Explain these results. What conclusions can be reached?

```
Test and CI for Two Proportions

Sample      X       N       Sample p
Men         128     203     0.630542
Women       153     214     0.714953

Difference = p (1) – p (2)
Estimate for difference: –0.0844114
95% CI for difference: (–0.174226,
0.00540317)
Test for difference = 0 (vs ≠ 0):  Z = –1.84
P-Value = 0.065

Fisher's exact test: P-Value = 0.076
```

Sources: www.fiveguys.com/; "How I Did It: Jerry Murrell, Five Guys, Burgers and Fries" at www.inc.dom/.../jerry-murrell-five-guys-burgers-and-fries.html-Inc.; Nation's Restaurant News at nrn.com/top-100/five-guys-burgers-and-fries; "Burger Consumption Stays Strong" at BurgerBusiness.com; "Average Price of Hamburgers By City" at www.foxnews.com/leisure/ . . . /average-price-burger-around-country-varies/.www.foodbeast.com/news/american-consumption-in-pounds-and-money/

CHAPTER 11

Analysis of Variance and Design of Experiments

LEARNING OBJECTIVES

The focus of this chapter is the design of experiments and the analysis of variance, thereby enabling you to:

1. Describe an experimental design and its elements, including independent variables—both treatment and classification—and dependent variables.

2. Test a completely randomized design using a one-way analysis of variance.

3. Use multiple comparison techniques, including Tukey's honestly significant difference test and the Tukey-Kramer procedure, to test the difference in two treatment means

when there is overall significant difference between treatments.

4. Test a randomized block design that includes a blocking variable to control for confounding variables.

5. Test a factorial design using a two-way analysis of variance, noting the advantages and applications of such a design and accounting for possible interaction between two treatment variables.

Decision Dilemma

Job and Career Satisfaction of Foreign Self-Initiated Expatriates

Because of worker shortages in some industries, in a global business environment, firms around the world sometimes must compete with each other for workers. This is especially true in industries and job designations where specialty skills are required. In order to fill such needs, companies sometimes turn to self-initiated expatriates. Self-initiated expatriates (SEs) are defined to be workers who are hired as individuals on a contractual basis to work in a foreign country as "guest workers"—in contrast to individuals who are given overseas transfers by a parent organization, "corporation-assigned expatriates" (AEs). Some examples of SEs could be computer experts from India, China, and Japan being hired by Silicon Valley companies; American engineers working with Russian companies to extract oil and gas; or financial experts from England who are hired by Singapore companies to help manage the stock market. Studies have been conducted to compare SEs to AEs, particularly in the area of career orientation over time. However, since here we focus only on SEs, how satisfied are SEs with their jobs and their careers?

Peter Charlesworth/Getty Images, Inc.

In an attempt to answer that question, suppose a study was conducted by randomly sampling SEs in five industries: information technology (IT), finance, education, healthcare, and consulting. Each is asked to rate his or her present job satisfaction on a 7-point Likert scale, with 7 being very satisfied and 1 being very unsatisfied. Suppose the data shown below are a portion of the study.

IT	FINANCE	EDUCATION	HEALTHCARE	CONSULTING
5	3	2	3	6
6	4	3	2	7
5	4	3	4	5
7	5	2	3	6
	4	2	5	
		3		

Suppose, in addition, self-initiated expatriates are asked to re-port their overall satisfaction with their career on the same 7-point scale. The ratings are broken down by the respondent's experience in the host country and age and the resultant data are shown below.

		TIME IN HOST COUNTRY			
		< 1 YEAR	1–2 YEARS	3–4 YEARS	≥5 YEARS
Age	30–39	3	4	3	6
		2	5	4	4
		3	3	5	5
		4	3	4	4
	40–49	3	4	4	6
		2	3	5	5
		4	4	5	6
	Over 50	3	4	4	5
		4	5	5	6

MANAGERIAL AND STATISTICAL QUESTIONS

1. Is there a difference in the job satisfaction ratings of SEs by industry? If we were to use the t test for the difference of two independent population means presented in Chapter 10 to analyze these data, we would need to do 10 different t tests since there are five different industries. Is there a better, more parsimonious way to analyze this data? Can the analysis be done simultaneously using one technique?

2. The second table in the Decision Dilemma displays career sat-isfaction data broken down two different ways, age and time in country. How does a researcher analyze such data when there are two different types of groups or classifications? What if one variable, like age, acts on another variable, like time in the country, such that there is an interaction? That is, time in the country might matter more in one category than in another. Can this effect be measured and if so, how?

Source: Concepts adapted from Chay Hoon Lee, "A Study of Underem-ployment Among Self-Initiated Expatriates," *Journal of World Business* vol. 40, no. 2 (May 2005), pp. 172–187; Biemann, T., & Andresen, M. (2010). "Self-initiated Foreign Work Experience Versus Expatriate Assignment: A Distinct Group of International Careerists?" *Journal of Managerial Psychology*, vol. 25, pp. 430–448.

Sometimes business research entails more complicated hypothesis-testing scenarios than those presented to this point in the text. Instead of comparing the wear of tire tread for two brands of tires to determine whether there is a significant difference between the brands, as we could have done using Chapter 10 techniques, a tire researcher may choose to compare three, four, or even more brands of tires at the same time. In addition, the researcher may want to include different levels of quality of tires in the experiment, such as low-quality, medium-quality, and high-quality tires. Tests may be conducted under varying conditions of temperature, precipitation, or road surface. Such experiments involve selecting and analyzing more than two samples of data.

Techniques for testing hypotheses using a *single* sample are presented in Chapter 9; tech-niques for testing hypotheses about the differences in two populations using *two* samples are pre-sented in Chapter 10. The far right branch of the tree diagram taxonomy shown in Figure 11.1 contains techniques presented in Chapter 11 for testing hypotheses about *three or more* samples.

11.1 Introduction to Design of Experiments

An **experimental design** is *a plan and a structure to test hypotheses in which the researcher either controls or manipulates one or more variables*. It contains independent and dependent variables. In an experimental design, an **independent variable** may be either a treatment vari-able or a classification variable. A **treatment variable** is *a variable the experimenter controls or modifies in the experiment*. A **classification variable** is *some characteristic of the experi-mental subject that was present prior to the experiment and is not a result of the experimenter's manipulations or control*. Independent variables are sometimes also referred to as **factors**. Wal-Mart executives might sanction an in-house study to compare daily sales volumes for a

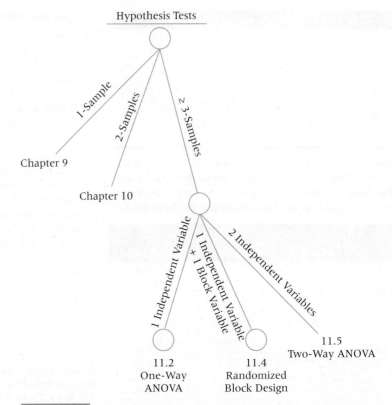

FIGURE 11.1 **Tree Diagram Taxonomy of Hypothesis Testing Techniques**

given size store in four different demographic settings: (1) inner-city stores (large city), (2) suburban stores (large city), (3) stores in a medium-sized city, and (4) stores in a small town. Managers might also decide to compare sales on the five different weekdays (Monday through Friday). In this study, the independent variables are store demographics and day of the week.

A finance researcher might conduct a study to determine whether there is a significant difference in application fees for home loans in five geographic regions of the United States and might include three different types of lending organizations. In this study, the independent variables are geographic region and types of lending organizations. Or suppose a manufacturing organization produces a valve that is specified to have an opening of 6.37 centimeters. Quality controllers within the company might decide to test to determine how the openings for produced valves vary among four different machines on three different shifts. This experiment includes the independent variables of type of machine and work shift.

Whether an independent variable can be manipulated by the researcher depends on the concept being studied. Independent variables such as work shift, gender of employee, geographic region, type of machine, and quality of tire are classification variables with conditions that existed prior to the study. The business researcher cannot change the characteristic of the variable, so he or she studies the phenomenon being explored under several conditions of the various aspects of the variable. As an example, the valve experiment is conducted under the conditions of all three work shifts.

However, some independent variables can be manipulated by the researcher. For example, in the well-known Hawthorne studies of the Western Electric Company in the 1920s in Illinois, the amount of light in production areas was varied to determine the effect of light on productivity. In theory, this independent variable could be manipulated by the researcher to allow any level of lighting. Other examples of independent variables that can be manipulated include the size of bonuses offered workers, temperature in the plant, amount of on-the-job training, number of hours of overtime, degree of encouragement by management, and many others. These are examples of treatment variables.

Each independent variable has two or more levels, or classifications. **Levels**, or **classifications**, of independent variables are *the subcategories of the independent variable used by the researcher in the experimental design.* For example, the different demographic settings listed for the Wal-Mart study are four levels, or classifications, of the independent variable store

TABLE 11.1	Valve Opening Measurements (in cm) for 24 Valves Produced on an Assembly Line			
6.26	6.19	6.33	6.26	6.50
6.19	6.44	6.22	6.54	6.23
6.29	6.40	6.23	6.29	6.58
6.27	6.38	6.58	6.31	6.34
6.21	6.19	6.36	6.56	

$\bar{x} = 6.34$. Total Sum of Squares Deviation = SST = $\Sigma(x_i - \bar{x})^2$ = .3915

demographics: (1) inner-city store, (2) suburban store, (3) store in a medium-sized city, and (4) store in small town. In the valve experiment, four levels or classifications of machines within the independent variable machine type are used: machine 1, machine 2, machine 3, and machine 4.

The other type of variable in an experimental design is a **dependent variable**. A dependent variable is *the response to the different levels of the independent variables*. It is the measurement taken under the conditions of the experimental design that reflect the effects of the independent variable(s). In the Wal-Mart study, the dependent variable is the dollar amount of daily total sales. For the study on loan application fees, the fee charged for a loan application is probably the dependent variable. In the valve experiment, the dependent variable is the size of the opening of the valve.

Experimental designs in this chapter are analyzed statistically by a group of techniques referred to as **analysis of variance**, or **ANOVA**. The analysis of variance concept begins with the notion that dependent variable responses (measurements, data) are not all the same in a given study. That is, dependent variable measures such as employee output, sales, length of stay, customer satisfaction, and product viscosity will often vary from item to item or observation to observation. Note the measurements for the openings of 24 valves randomly selected from an assembly line that are given in Table 11.1. The mean opening is 6.34 centimeters (cm). Only one of the 24 valve openings is actually the mean. Why do the valve openings vary? The total sum of squares of deviation of these valve openings around the mean is .3915 cm². Why is this value not zero? Using various types of experimental designs, we can explore some possible reasons for this variance with analysis of variance techniques. As we explore each of the experimental designs and their associated analysis, note that the statistical technique is attempting to "break down" the total variance among the objects being studied into possible causes. In the case of the valve openings, this variance of measurements might be due to such variables as machine, operator, shift, supplier, and production conditions, among others.

Many different types of experimental designs are available to researchers. In this chapter, we will present and discuss three specific types of experimental designs: completely randomized design, randomized block design, and factorial experiments.

11.1 Problems

11.1. Some New York Stock Exchange analysts believe that 24-hour trading on the stock exchange is the wave of the future. As an initial test of this idea, the New York Stock Exchange opened two after-hour "crossing sections" in the early 1990s and studied the results of these extra-hour sessions for one year.

   a. State an independent variable that could have been used for this study.

   b. List at least two levels, or classifications, for this variable.

   c. Give a dependent variable for this study.

11.2. Southwest Airlines is able to keep fares low, in part because of relatively low maintenance costs on its airplanes. One of the main

reasons for the low maintenance costs is that Southwest flies only one type of aircraft, the Boeing 737. However, Southwest flies three different versions of the 737. Suppose Southwest decides to conduct a study to determine whether there is a significant difference in the average annual maintenance costs for the three types of 737s used.

   a. State an independent variable for such a study.

   b. What are some of the levels or classifications that might be studied under this variable?

   c. Give a dependent variable for this study.

11.3. A large multinational banking company wants to determine whether there is a significant difference in the average dollar amounts purchased by users of different types of credit cards. Among the credit cards being studied are MasterCard, Visa, Discover, and American Express.

a. If an experimental design were set up for such a study, what are some possible independent variables?

b. List at least three levels, or classifications, for each independent variable.

c. What are some possible dependent variables for this experiment?

11.4. Is there a difference in the family demographics of people who stay at motels? Suppose a study is conducted in which three categories of motels are used: economy motels, modestly priced chain motels, and exclusive motels. One of the dependent variables studied might be the number of children in the family of the person staying in the motel. Name three other dependent variables that might be used in this study.

11.2 The Completely Randomized Design (One-Way Anova)

One of the simplest experimental designs is the completely randomized design. In the **completely randomized design**, *subjects are assigned randomly to treatments.* The completely randomized design contains only one independent variable, with two or more treatment levels, or classifications. If only two treatment levels, or classifications, of the independent variable are present, the design is the same one used to test the difference in means of two independent populations presented in Chapter 10, which used the *t* test to analyze the data.

In this section, we will focus on completely randomized designs with three or more classification levels. Analysis of variance, or ANOVA, will be used to analyze the data that result from the treatments.

A completely randomized design could be structured for a tire-quality study in which tire quality is the independent variable and the treatment levels are low, medium, and high quality. The dependent variable might be the number of miles driven before the tread fails state inspection. A study of daily sales volumes for Wal-Mart stores could be undertaken by using a completely randomized design with demographic setting as the independent variable. The treatment levels, or classifications, would be inner-city stores, suburban stores, stores in medium-sized cities, and stores in small towns. The dependent variable would be sales dollars.

As an example of a completely randomized design, suppose a researcher decides to analyze the effects of the machine operator on the valve opening measurements of valves produced in a manufacturing plant, like those shown in Table 11.1. The independent variable in this design is machine operator. Suppose further that four different operators run the machines. These four machine operators are the levels of treatment, or classification, of the independent variable. The dependent variable is the opening measurement of the valve. Figure 11.2 shows the structure of this completely randomized design. Is there a significant difference in the mean valve openings of 24 valves produced by the four operators? Table 11.2 contains the valve opening measurements for valves produced under each operator.

TABLE 11.2 **Valve Openings by Operator**

1	2	3	4
6.33	6.26	6.44	6.29
6.26	6.36	6.38	6.23
6.31	6.23	6.58	6.19
6.29	6.27	6.54	6.21
6.40	6.19	6.56	
	6.50	6.34	
	6.19	6.58	
	6.22		

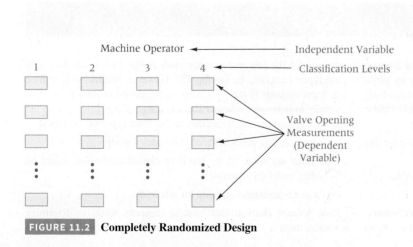

FIGURE 11.2 **Completely Randomized Design**

One-Way Analysis of Variance

In the machine operator example, is it possible to analyze the four samples by using a t test for the difference in two sample means? These four samples would require ${}_4C_2 = 6$ individual t tests to accomplish the analysis of two groups at a time. Recall that if $\alpha = .05$ for a particular test, there is a 5% chance of rejecting a null hypothesis that is true (i.e., committing a Type I error). If enough tests are done, eventually one or more null hypotheses will be falsely rejected by chance. Hence, $\alpha = .05$ is valid only for one t test. In this problem, with six t tests, the error rate compounds, so when the analyst is finished with the problem there is a much greater than .05 chance of committing a Type I error. Fortunately, a technique has been developed that analyzes all the sample means at one time and thus precludes the buildup of error rate: analysis of variance (ANOVA). A completely randomized design is analyzed by a **one-way analysis of variance**.

In general, if k samples are being analyzed, the following hypotheses are being tested in a one-way ANOVA.

$$H_0: \mu_1 = \mu_2 = \mu_3 = \ldots = \mu_k$$

$$H_a: \text{At least one of the means is different from the others.}$$

The null hypothesis states that the population means for all treatment levels are equal. Because of the way the alternative hypothesis is stated, if even one of the population means is different from the others, the null hypothesis is rejected.

Testing these hypotheses by using one-way ANOVA is accomplished by partitioning the total variance of the data into the following two variances:

1. The variance resulting from the treatment (columns)

2. The error variance, or that portion of the total variance unexplained by the treatment

As part of this process, the total sum of squares of deviation of values around the mean can be divided into two additive and independent parts.

$$\text{SST} \quad = \quad \text{SSC} \quad + \quad \text{SSE}$$

$$\sum_{j=1}^{C}\sum_{i=1}^{n_j}(x_{ij} - \overline{x})^2 = \sum_{j=1}^{C}n_j(\overline{x}_j - \overline{x})^2 + \sum_{j=1}^{C}\sum_{i=1}^{n_j}(x_{ij} - \overline{x}_j)^2$$

where

SST = total sum of squares
SSC = sum of squares column (treatment)
SSE = sum of squares error
i = particular member of a treatment level
j = a treatment level
C = number of treatment levels
n_j = number of observations in a given treatment level
$\overline{x}$ = grand mean
$\overline{x}_j$ = mean of a treatment group or level
x_{ij} = individual value

This relationship is shown in **Figure 11.3**. Observe that the total sum of squares of variation is partitioned into the sum of squares of treatment (columns) and the sum of squares of error.

The formulas used to accomplish one-way analysis of variance are developed from this relationship. The double summation sign indicates that the values are summed within a treatment level and across treatment levels. Basically, ANOVA compares the relative sizes of the *treatment* variation and the *error* variation (within-group variation). The error variation is unaccounted-for variation and can be viewed at this point as variation due to individual differences within treatment groups. If a significant difference in treatments is present, the treatment variation should be large relative to the error variation.

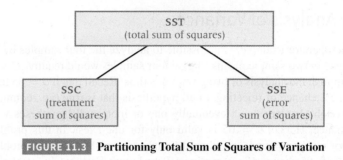

FIGURE 11.3   **Partitioning Total Sum of Squares of Variation**

Figure 11.4 displays the data from the machine operator example in terms of treatment level. Note the variation of values (x) *within* each treatment level. Now examine the variation between levels 1 through 4 (the difference in the machine operators). In particular, note that values for treatment level 3 seem to be located differently from those of levels 2 and 4. This difference is also underscored by the mean values for each treatment level:

$$\bar{x}_1 = 6.318 \quad \bar{x}_2 = 6.2775 \quad \bar{x}_3 = 6.488571 \quad \bar{x}_4 = 6.23$$

Analysis of variance is used to determine statistically whether the variance between the treatment level means is greater than the variances within levels (error variance). Several important assumptions underlie analysis of variance:

1. Observations are drawn from normally distributed populations.
2. Observations represent random samples from the populations.
3. Variances of the populations are equal.

These assumptions are similar to those for using the *t* test for independent samples in Chapter 10 where it is assumed that the populations are normally distributed and that the population variances are equal. These techniques should be used only with random samples.

An ANOVA is computed with the three sums of squares: total, treatment (columns), and error. Shown here are the formulas to compute a one-way analysis of variance. The term SS represents sum of squares, and the term MS represents mean square. SSC is the sum of squares columns, which yields the sum of squares between treatments. It measures the variation between columns or between treatments since the independent variable treatment levels are presented as columns. SSE is the sum of squares of error, which yields the variation within treatments (or columns). Some say that it is a measure of the individual differences unaccounted for by the treatments. SST is the total sum of squares and is a measure of all variation in the dependent variable. As shown previously, SST contains both SSC and SSE and can be partitioned into SSC and SSE. MSC and MSE are the mean squares of column and error, respectively. Mean square is an average and is computed by dividing the sum of squares by the degrees of freedom. Finally, the *F* value is determined by dividing the treatment variance (MSC) by the error variance (MSE). As discussed in Chapter 10, the *F* is a ratio of two variances. In the ANOVA situation, the *F* value is *a ratio of the treatment variance to the error variance.*

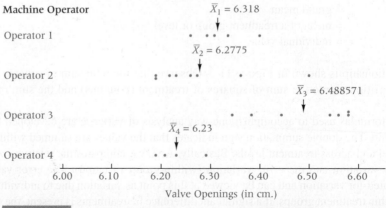

FIGURE 11.4   **Location of Mean Value Openings by Operator**

Formulas for Computing a One-Way ANOVA

$$SSC = \sum_{j=1}^{C} n_j (\bar{x}_j - \bar{x})^2$$

$$SSE = \sum_{j=1}^{C} \sum_{i=1}^{n_j} (x_{ij} - \bar{x}_j)^2$$

$$SST = \sum_{j=1}^{C} \sum_{i=1}^{n_j} (x_{ij} - \bar{x})^2$$

$$df_C = C - 1$$

$$df_E = N - C$$

$$df_T = N - 1$$

$$MSC = \frac{SSC}{C-1}$$

$$MSE = \frac{SSE}{N-C}$$

$$F = \frac{MSC}{MSE}$$

where

i = a particular member of a treatment level
j = a treatment level
C = number of treatment levels
n_j = number of observations in a given treatment level
$\bar{x}$ = grand mean
$\bar{x}_j$ = column mean
x_{ij} = individual value

Performing these calculations for the machine operator example yields the following.

MACHINE OPERATOR			
1	2	3	4
6.33	6.26	6.44	6.29
6.26	6.36	6.38	6.23
6.31	6.23	6.58	6.19
6.29	6.27	6.54	6.21
6.40	6.19	6.56	
	6.50	6.34	
	6.19	6.58	
	6.22		

n_j: $n_1 = 5$ $n_2 = 8$ $n_3 = 7$ $n_4 = 4$ $N = 24$
$\bar{x}_j$: $\bar{x}_1 = 6.318$ $\bar{x}_2 = 6.2775$ $\bar{x}_3 = 6.488571$ $\bar{x}_4 = 6.23$ $\bar{x} = 6.339583$

$$SSC = \sum_{j=1}^{C} n_j (\bar{x}_j - \bar{x})^2 = [5(6.318 - 6.339583)^2 + 8(6.2775 - 6.339583)^2$$
$$+ 7(6.488571 - 6.339583)^2 + 4(6.23 - 6.339583)^2]$$
$$= 0.00233 + 0.03083 + 0.15538 + 0.04803$$
$$= 0.23658$$

$$\text{SSE} = \sum_{j=1}^{C}\sum_{i=1}^{n_j}(x_{ij} - \overline{x}_j)^2 = [(6.33 - 6.318)^2 + (6.26 - 6.318)^2 + (6.31 - 6.318)^2$$
$$+ (6.29 - 6.318)^2 + (6.40 - 6.318)^2 + (6.26 - 6.2775)^2$$
$$+ (6.36 - 6.2775)^2 + \ldots + (6.19 - 6.23)^2 + (6.21 - 6.23)^2$$
$$= 0.15492$$

$$\text{SST} = \sum_{j=1}^{C}\sum_{i=1}^{n_j}(x_{ij} - \overline{\overline{x}}_j)^2 = [(6.33 - 6.339583)^2 + (6.26 - 6.339583)^2$$
$$+ (6.31 - 6.339583)^2 + \ldots + (6.19 - 6.339583)^2$$
$$+ (6.21 - 6.339583)^2$$
$$= 0.39150$$

$$\text{df}_C = C - 1 = 4 - 1 = 3$$
$$\text{df}_E = N - C = 24 - 4 = 20$$
$$\text{df}_T = N - 1 = 24 - 1 = 23$$

$$\text{MSC} = \frac{\text{SSC}}{\text{df}_C} = \frac{0.23658}{3} = 0.078860$$

$$\text{MSE} = \frac{\text{SSE}}{\text{df}_E} = \frac{0.15492}{20} = 0.007746$$

$$F = \frac{0.078860}{0.007746} = 10.18$$

From these computations, an analysis of variance chart can be constructed, as shown in Table 11.3. The observed F value is 10.18. It is compared to a critical value from the F table to determine whether there is a significant difference in treatment or classification.

Reading the F Distribution Table

The **F distribution** table is in Table A.7. Associated with every F value in the table are two unique df values: degrees of freedom in the numerator (df_C) and degrees of freedom in the denominator (df_E). To look up a value in the F distribution table, the researcher must know both degrees of freedom. Because each F distribution is determined by a unique pair of degrees of freedom, many F distributions are possible. Space constraints limit Table A.7 to F values for only $\alpha = .005, .01, .025, .05,$ and $.10$. However, statistical computer software packages for computing ANOVAs usually give a probability for the F value, which allows a hypothesis-testing decision for any alpha based on the p-value method.

In the one-way ANOVA, the df_C values are the treatment (column) degrees of freedom, $C - 1$. The df_E values are the error degrees of freedom, $N - C$. For the machine operator example, $\alpha = .05$, $\text{df}_C = 3$ and $\text{df}_E = 20$, $F_{.05,3,20}$ from Table 11.4 is 3.10. Table 11.4 contains a partial view of the F distribution table for $\alpha = .05$ with the critical F value for the machine operator example highlighted. This value is the critical value of the F test. Analysis of variance tests are always one-tailed tests with the rejection region in the upper tail. The decision rule is to reject the null hypothesis if the observed F value is greater than the

TABLE 11.3　Analysis of Variance for the Machine Operator Example

SOURCE OF VARIANCE	df	SS	MS	F
Between	3	0.23658	0.078860	10.18
Error	20	0.15492	0.007746	
Total	23	0.39150		

TABLE 11.4 A partial F Table for $\alpha = .05$

v_1 / v_2	1	2	3	4	5	6	7	8	9
			NUMERATOR DEGREES OF FREEDOM						
1	161.45	199.50	215.71	224.58	230.16	233.99	236.77	238.88	240.54
2	18.51	19.00	19.16	19.25	19.30	19.33	19.35	19.37	19.38
3	10.13	9.55	9.28	9.12	9.01	8.94	8.89	8.85	8.81
4	7.71	6.94	6.59	6.39	6.26	6.16	6.09	6.04	6.00
5	6.61	5.79	5.41	5.19	5.05	4.95	4.88	4.82	4.77
6	5.99	5.14	4.76	4.53	4.39	4.28	4.21	4.15	4.10
7	5.59	4.74	4.35	4.12	3.97	3.87	3.79	3.73	3.68
8	5.32	4.46	4.07	3.84	3.69	3.58	3.50	3.44	3.39
9	5.12	4.26	3.86	3.63	3.48	3.37	3.29	3.23	3.18
10	4.96	4.10	3.71	3.48	3.33	3.22	3.14	3.07	3.02
11	4.84	3.98	3.59	3.36	3.20	3.09	3.01	2.95	2.90
12	4.75	3.89	3.49	3.26	3.11	3.00	2.91	2.85	2.80
13	4.47	3.81	3.41	3.18	3.03	2.92	2.83	2.77	2.71
14	4.60	3.74	3.34	3.11	2.96	2.85	2.76	2.70	2.65
15	4.54	3.68	3.29	3.06	2.90	2.79	2.71	2.64	2.59
16	4.49	3.63	3.24	3.01	2.85	2.74	2.66	2.59	2.54
17	4.45	3.59	3.20	2.96	2.81	2.70	2.61	2.55	2.49
18	4.41	3.55	3.16	2.93	2.77	2.66	2.58	2.51	2.46
19	4.38	3.52	3.13	2.90	2.74	2.63	2.54	2.48	2.42
20	4.35	3.49	3.10	2.87	2.71	2.60	2.51	2.45	2.39
21	4.32	3.47	3.07	2.84	2.68	2.57	2.49	2.42	2.37
22	4.30	3.44	3.05	2.82	2.66	2.55	2.46	2.40	2.34

Denominator Degrees of Freedom

$\alpha = .05$

Critical F value: $F_{.05, 3, 20} = 3.10$

critical F value ($F_{.05,3,20} = 3.10$). For the machine operator problem, the observed F value of 10.18 is larger than the table F value of 3.10. The null hypothesis is rejected. Not all means are equal, so there is a significant difference in the mean valve openings by machine operator. **Figure 11.5** is a Minitab graph of an F distribution showing the critical F value for this example and the rejection region. Note that the F distribution begins at zero and contains no negative values because the F value is the ratio of two variances, and variances are always positive.

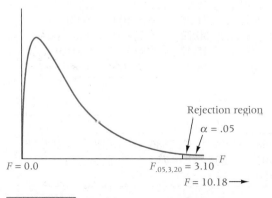

Rejection region
$\alpha = .05$

$F = 0.0$

$F_{.05, 3, 20} = 3.10$

$F = 10.18 \longrightarrow$

FIGURE 11.5 Minitab Graph of F Values for the Machine Operator Example

Using the Computer for One-Way ANOVA

Many researchers use the computer to analyze data with a one-way ANOVA. Figure 11.6 shows the Minitab and Excel output of the ANOVA computed for the machine operator example. The output includes the analysis of variance table presented in Table 11.3. Both Minitab and Excel ANOVA tables display the observed F value, mean squares, sum of squares,

Minitab Output

One-way ANOVA: Operator 1, Operator 2, Operator 3, Operator 4

Analysis of Variance

Source	DF	Seq SS	Contribution	Adj SS	Adj MS	F-Value	P-Value
Factor	3	0.2366	60.43%	0.2366	0.078860	10.18	0.000
Error	20	0.1549	39.57%	0.1549	0.007746		
Total	23	0.3915	100.00%				

Means

Factor	N	Mean	StDev	95% CI
Operator 1	5	6.3180	0.0526	(6.2359, 6.4001)
Operator 2	8	6.2775	0.1053	(6.2126, 6.3424)
Operator 3	7	6.4886	0.1006	(6.4192, 6.5580)
Operator 4	4	6.2300	0.0432	(6.1382, 6.3218)

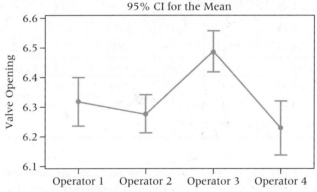

Interval Plot of Operator 1, Operator 2, ...
95% CI for the Mean

The pooled standard deviation is to calculate the intervals.

Excel Output

Anova: Single Factor

SUMMARY

Groups	Count	Sum	Average	Variance
Operator 1	5	31.59	6.31800	0.00277
Operator 2	8	50.22	6.27750	0.01108
Operator 3	7	45.42	6.48857	0.01011
Operator 4	4	24.92	6.23000	0.00187

ANOVA

Source of Variation	SS	df	MS	F	P-value	F crit
Between Groups	0.23658	3	0.07886	10.18	0.000279	3.10
Within Groups	0.15492	20	0.00775			
Total	0.39150	23				

FIGURE 11.6 **Minitab and Excel Analysis of the Machine Operator Problem**

degrees of freedom, and a value of p. The value of p is the probability of an F value of 10.18 occurring by chance in an ANOVA with this structure (same degrees of freedom) even if there is no difference between means of the treatment levels. Using the p-value method of testing hypotheses presented in Chapter 9, we can easily see that because this p-value is only .000279, the null hypothesis would be rejected using $\alpha = .05$. Most computer output yields the value of p, so there is no need to look up a table value of F against which to compare the observed F value. The Excel output also includes the critical table F value for this problem, $F_{.05,3,20} = 3.10$.

The second part of the Minitab output in Figure 11.6 contains the size of samples and sample means for each of the treatment levels along with a 95% confidence interval for the mean of each operator. Displayed graphically are the 95% confidence levels for the population means of each treatment level group. These levels are computed by using a pooled standard deviation from all the treatment level groups. The researcher can visually observe the confidence intervals and make a subjective determination about the relative difference in the population means. More rigorous statistical techniques for testing the differences in pairs of groups are given in Section 11.3.

Comparison of F and t Values

Analysis of variance can be used to test hypotheses about the difference in two sample means from independent populations (Section 10.2). This t test of independent samples is actually a special case of one-way ANOVA when there are only two treatment levels ($df_C = 1$). In this case, $F = t^2$.

The t test is computationally simpler than ANOVA for two groups. However, some statistical computer software packages do not contain a t test. In these cases, the researcher can perform a one-way ANOVA and then either take the square root of the F value to obtain the value of t or use the generated probability with the p-value method to reach conclusions.

DEMONSTRATION PROBLEM 11.1

A company has three manufacturing plants, and company officials want to determine whether there is a difference in the average age of workers at the three locations. The following data are the ages of five randomly selected workers at each plant. Perform a one-way ANOVA to determine whether there is a significant difference in the mean ages of the workers at the three plants. Use $\alpha = .01$ and note that the sample sizes are equal.

Solution:

Step 1. The hypotheses follow.

$$H_0: \mu_1 = \mu_2 = \mu_3$$

H_a: At least one of the means is different from the others.

Step 2. The appropriate test statistic is the F test calculated from ANOVA.

Step 3. The value of α is .01.

Step 4. The degrees of freedom for this problem are $3 - 1 = 2$ for the numerator and $15 - 3 = 12$ for the denominator. The critical F value is $F_{.01,2,12} = 6.93$.

Because ANOVAs are always one tailed with the rejection region in the upper tail, the decision rule is to reject the null hypothesis if the observed value of F is greater than 6.93.

Step 5.

PLANT (EMPLOYEE AGES)		
1	2	3
29	32	25
27	33	24
30	31	24
27	34	25
28	30	26

Step 6.

$$n_j: \quad n_1 = 5 \qquad n_2 = 5 \qquad n_3 = 5 \qquad N = 15$$
$$\bar{x}_j: \quad \bar{x}_1 = 28.2 \quad \bar{x}_2 = 32.0 \quad \bar{x}_3 = 24.8 \quad \bar{x}_4 = 28.33$$

$$SSC = 5(28.2 - 28.33)^2 + 5(32.0 - 28.33)^2 + 5(24.8 - 28.33)^2 = 129.73$$

$$SSE = (29 - 28.2)^2 + (27 - 28.2)^2 + \cdots + (25 - 24.8)^2 + (26 - 24.8)^2 = 19.60$$

$$SST = (29 - 28.33)^2 + (27 - 28.33)^2 + \cdots + (25 - 28.33)^2$$
$$+ (26 - 28.33)^2 = 149.33$$

$$df_C = 3 - 1 = 2$$
$$df_E = 15 - 3 = 12$$
$$df_T = 15 - 1 = 14$$

SOURCE OF VARIANCE	SS	df	MS	F
Between	129.73	2	64.865	39.72
Error	19.60	12	1.633	
Total	149.33	14		

Step 7. The decision is to reject the null hypothesis because the observed F value of 39.72 is greater than the critical table F value of 6.93.

Step 8. There is a significant difference in the mean ages of workers at the three plants. This difference can have hiring implications. Company leaders should understand that because motivation, discipline, and experience may differ with age, the differences in ages may call for different managerial approaches in each plant.

The chart shown below displays the dispersion of the ages of workers from the three samples, along with the mean age for each plant sample. Note the difference in group means. The significant F value says that the differences between the mean ages are relatively greater than the differences of ages within each group.

Following are the Minitab and Excel output for this problem.

Minitab Output

One-way ANOVA: Plant 1, Plant 2, Plant 3

Analysis of Variance

Source	DF	Adj SS	Adj MS	F-Value	P-Value
Factor	2	129.73	64.867	39.71	0.000
Error	12	19.60	1.633		
Total	14	149.33			

Means

Factor	N	Mean	StDev	95% CI
Plant 1	5	28.200	1.304	(26.955, 29.445)
Plant 2	5	32.000	1.581	(30.755, 33.245)
Plant 3	5	24.800	0.837	(23.555, 26.045)

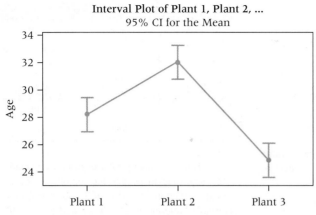

Interval Plot of Plant 1, Plant 2, ...
95% CI for the Mean

The pooled standard deviation used to calculate the intervals.

Excel Output

Anova: Single Factor

SUMMARY

Groups	Count	Sum	Average	Variance
Plant 1	5	141	28.2	1.7
Plant 2	5	160	32	2.5
Plant 3	5	124	24.8	0.7

ANOVA

Source of Variation	SS	df	MS	F	P-value	F crit
Between Groups	129.73333	2	64.8667	39.71	0.0000051	6.93
Within Groups	19.6	12	1.6333			
Total	149.33333	14				

11.2 Problems

11.5. Compute a one-way ANOVA on the following data.

1	2	3
2	5	3
1	3	4
3	6	5
3	4	5
2	5	3
1		5

Determine the observed F value. Compare the observed F value with the critical table F value and decide whether to reject the null hypothesis. Use $\alpha = .05$.

11.6. Compute a one-way ANOVA on the following data.

1	2	3	4	5
14	10	11	16	14
13	9	12	17	12
10	12	13	14	13
	9	12	16	13
	10		17	12
				14

Determine the observed F value. Compare the observed F value with the critical table F value and decide whether to reject the null hypothesis. Use $\alpha = .01$.

11.7. Develop a one-way ANOVA on the following data.

1	2	3	4
113	120	132	122
121	127	130	118
117	125	129	125
110	129	135	125

Determine the observed F value. Compare it to the critical F value and decide whether to reject the null hypothesis. Use a 1% level of significance.

11.8. Compute a one-way ANOVA on the following data.

1	2
27	22
31	27
31	25
29	23
30	26
27	27
28	23

Determine the observed F value. Compare it to the critical table F value and decide whether to reject the null hypothesis. Perform a t test for independent measures on the data. Compare the t and F values. Are the results different? Use $\alpha = .05$.

11.9. Suppose you are using a completely randomized design to study some phenomenon. There are five treatment levels and a total of 55 people in the study. Each treatment level has the same sample size. Complete the following ANOVA.

SOURCE OF VARIANCE	SS	df	MS	F
Treatment	583.39			
Error	972.18			
Total	1555.57			

11.10. Suppose you are using a completely randomized design to study some phenomenon. There are three treatment levels and a total of 17 people in the study. Complete the following ANOVA table. Use = .05 to find the table F value and use the data to test the null hypothesis.

SOURCE OF VARIANCE	SS	df	MS	F
Treatment	29.64			
Error	68.42			
Total				

11.11. A milk company has four machines that fill gallon jugs with milk. The quality control manager is interested in determining whether the average fill for these machines is the same. The following data represent random samples of fill measures (in quarts) for 19 jugs of milk filled by the different machines. Use $\alpha = .01$ to test the hypotheses. Discuss the business implications of your findings.

MACHINE 1	MACHINE 2	MACHINE 3	MACHINE 4
4.05	3.99	3.97	4.00
4.01	4.02	3.98	4.02
4.02	4.01	3.97	3.99
4.04	3.99	3.95	4.01
	4.00	4.00	
	4.00		

11.12. That the starting salaries of new accounting graduates would differ according to geographic regions of the United States seems logical. A random selection of accounting firms is taken from three geographic regions, and each is asked to state the starting salary for a new accounting graduate who is going to work in auditing. The data obtained follow. Use a one-way ANOVA to analyze these data. Note that the data can be restated to make the computations more reasonable (example: $42,500 = 4.25$). Use a 1% level of significance. Discuss the business implications of your findings.

SOUTH	NORTHEAST	WEST
$48,600	$59,100	$53,600
49,600	57,600	51,600
48,100	57,100	53,100
49,100	56,100	54,600
49,600	57,600	54,100

11.13. A management consulting company presents a three-day seminar on project management to various clients. The seminar is basically the same each time it is given. However, sometimes it is presented to high-level managers, sometimes to midlevel managers, and sometimes to low-level managers. The seminar facilitators believe evaluations of the seminar may vary with the audience. Suppose the following data are some randomly selected evaluation scores from different levels of managers who attended the seminar. The ratings are on a scale from 1 to 10, with 10 being the highest. Use a one-way ANOVA to determine whether there is a significant difference in the evaluations according to manager level. Assume $\alpha = .05$. Discuss the business implications of your findings.

HIGH LEVEL	MIDLEVEL	LOW LEVEL
7	8	5
7	9	6
8	8	5
7	10	7
9	9	4
	10	8
	8	

11.14. Family transportation costs are usually higher than most people believe because those costs include car payments, insurance, fuel costs, repairs, parking, and public transportation. Twenty randomly selected families in four major cities are asked to use their records to estimate a monthly figure for transportation cost. Use the data obtained and ANOVA to test whether there is a significant difference in monthly transportation costs for families living in these cities. Assume that $\alpha = .05$. Discuss the business implications of your findings.

ATLANTA	NEW YORK	LOS ANGELES	CHICAGO
$850	$450	$1050	$740
680	725	900	650
750	500	1150	875
800	375	980	750
875	700	800	800

11.15. Shown here is the Minitab output for a one-way ANOVA. Analyze the results. Include the number of treatment levels, the sample sizes, the F value, the overall statistical significance of the test, and the values of the means.

```
Analysis of Variance

Source   DF   Adj SS   Adj MS   F-Value   P-Value
Factor    3   1071     357.1    2.84      0.045
Error    61   7669     125.7
Total    64   8740

Means

Factor   N    Mean     StDev    95% CI
C1       18   230.11    7.06    (224.83, 235.40)
C2       15   238.17    8.38    (232.38, 243.96)
C3       21   235.18   12.69    (230.29, 240.07)
C4       11   241.83   16.17    (235.07, 248.59)

Pooled StDev = 11.2124
```

11.16. Business is very good for a chemical company. In fact, it is so good that workers are averaging more than 40 hours per week at each of the chemical company's five plants. However, management is not certain whether there is a difference between the five plants in the average number of hours worked per week per worker. Random samples of data are taken at each of the five plants. The data are analyzed using Excel. The results follow. Explain the design of the study and determine whether there is an overall significant difference between the means at $\alpha = .05$. Why or why not? What are the values of the means? What are the business implications of this study to the chemical company?

Anova: Single Factor

SUMMARY

Groups	Count	Sum	Average	Variance
Plant 1	11	636.5577	57.87	63.5949
Plant 2	12	601.7648	50.15	62.4813
Plant 3	8	491.7352	61.47	47.4772
Plant 4	5	246.0172	49.20	65.6072
Plant 5	7	398.6368	56.95	140.3540

ANOVA

Source of Variation	SS	df	MS	F	P-value	F crit
Between Groups	900.086	4	225.022	3.10	0.0266	2.62
Within Groups	2760136	38	72.635			
Total	3660.223	42				

11.3   Multiple Comparison Tests

Analysis of variance techniques are particularly useful in testing hypotheses about the differences of means in multiple groups because ANOVA utilizes only one single overall test. The advantage of this approach is that the probability of committing a Type I error, α, is controlled. As noted in Section 11.2, if four groups are tested two at a time, it takes six t tests ($_4C_2$) to analyze hypotheses between all possible pairs. In general, if k groups are tested two at a time, $_kC_2 = k(k-1)/2$ paired comparisons are possible.

Suppose alpha for an experiment is .05. If two different pairs of comparisons are made in the experiment using alpha of .05 in each, there is a .95 probability of not making a Type I error in each comparison. This approach results in a .9025 probability of not making a Type I error in either comparison (.95 × .95), and a .0975 probability of committing a Type I error in at least one comparison (1 − .9025). Thus, the probability of committing a Type I error for this experiment is not .05 but .0975. In an experiment where the means of four groups are being tested two at a time, six different tests are conducted. If each is analyzed using $\alpha = .05$, the probability that no Type I error will be committed in any of the six tests is .95 × .95 × .95 × .95 × .95 × .95 = .735 and the probability of committing at least one Type I error in the six tests is 1 − .735 = .265. If an ANOVA is computed on all groups simultaneously using $\alpha = .05$, the value of alpha is maintained in the experiment.

Sometimes the researcher is satisfied with conducting an overall test of differences in groups such as the one ANOVA provides. However, when it is determined that there is an overall difference in population means, it is often desirable to go back to the groups and determine from the data which pairs of means are significantly different. Such pairwise analyses can lead to a buildup of the Type I experimental error rate, as mentioned. Fortunately, several techniques, referred to as **multiple comparisons**, have been developed to handle this problem.

Multiple comparisons are to be used only when an overall significant difference between groups has been obtained by using the F value of the analysis of variance. Some of these techniques protect more for Type I errors and others protect more for Type II errors. Some multiple comparison techniques require equal sample sizes. There seems to be some difference of opinion in the literature about which techniques are most appropriate. Here we will consider only a posteriori or post hoc pairwise comparisons.

A posteriori or post hoc pairwise comparisons are made *after the experiment when the researcher decides to test for any significant differences in the samples based on a significant overall F value.* In contrast, a priori comparisons are made when the researcher *determines before the experiment which comparisons are to be made.* The error rates for these two types of comparisons are different, as are the recommended techniques. In this text, we only consider pairwise (two-at-a-time) multiple comparisons. Other types of comparisons are possible but belong in a more advanced presentation. The two multiple comparison tests discussed here are Tukey's HSD test for designs with equal sample sizes and the Tukey-Kramer procedure for situations in which sample sizes are unequal. Minitab yields computer output for each of these tests.

Tukey's Honestly Significant Difference (HSD) Test: The Case of Equal Sample Sizes

Tukey's honestly significant difference (HSD) test, sometimes known as Tukey's T method, is a popular test for pairwise a posteriori multiple comparisons. This test, developed by John W. Tukey and presented in 1953, is somewhat limited by the fact that it requires equal sample sizes.

Tukey's HSD test takes into consideration the number of treatment levels, the value of mean square error, and the sample size. Using these values and a table value, q, the HSD determines the critical difference necessary between the means of any two treatment levels for the means to be significantly different. Once the HSD is computed, the researcher can examine the absolute value of any or all differences between pairs of means from treatment levels to determine whether there is a significant difference. The formula to compute a Tukey's HSD test follows.

Tukey's HSD Test

$$HSD = q_{\alpha,C,N-C}\sqrt{\frac{MSE}{n}}$$

where

$$MSE = \text{mean square error}$$
$$n = \text{sample size}$$
$$q_{\alpha,C,N-C} = \text{critical value of the studentized range distribution from Table A.10}$$

In Demonstration Problem 11.1, an ANOVA test was used to determine that there was an overall significant difference in the mean ages of workers at the three different plants, as evidenced by the F value of 39.72. The sample data for this problem follow.

	PLANT		
	1	2	3
	29	32	25
	27	33	24
	30	31	24
	27	34	25
	28	30	26
Group Means	28.2	32.0	24.8
n_j	5	5	5

Because the sample sizes are equal in this problem, Tukey's HSD test can be used to compute multiple comparison tests between groups 1 and 2, 2 and 3, and 1 and 3. To compute the HSD, the values of MSE, n, and q must be determined. From the solution presented in Demonstration Problem 11.1, the value of MSE is 1.633. The sample size, n_j, is 5. The value of q is obtained from Table A.10 by using

$$\text{Number of Populations} = \text{Number of Treatment Means} = C$$

along with $\text{df}_E = N - C$.

In this problem, the values used to look up q are

$$C = 3$$

$$\text{df}_E = N - C = 12$$

Table A.10 has a q table for $\alpha = .05$ and one for $\alpha = .01$. In this problem, $\alpha = .01$. Shown in Table 11.5 is a portion of Table A.10 for $\alpha = .01$.

For this problem, $q_{.01,3,12} = 5.04$. HSD is computed as

$$\text{HSD} = q\sqrt{\frac{\text{MSE}}{n}} = 5.04\sqrt{\frac{1.633}{5}} = 2.88$$

Using this value of HSD, the business researcher can examine the differences between the means from any two groups of plants. Any of the pairs of means that differ by more than 2.88 are significantly different at $\alpha = .01$. Here are the differences for all three possible pairwise comparisons.

$$|\bar{x}_1 - \bar{x}_2| = |28.2 - 32.0| = 3.8$$

$$|\bar{x}_1 - \bar{x}_3| = |28.2 - 24.8| = 3.4$$

$$|\bar{x}_2 - \bar{x}_3| = |32.0 - 24.8| = 7.2$$

All three comparisons are greater than the value of HSD, which is 2.88. Thus, the mean ages between any and all pairs of plants are significantly different.

Using the Computer to Do Multiple Comparisons

Table 11.6 shows the Minitab output from computing a Tukey's HSD test. The computer output contains the sample means, grouping information, the difference of means, the confidence intervals for the differences of means, a t value for the difference of means, and the adjusted p-value for the difference of means. The grouping information assigns a letter (A, B, and C) to the mean of each factor (plant). If the means do not share a letter, then they are significantly different. Note that none of the means share a letter; and thus, they are all significantly different from each other. The t-values and their associated p-values

TABLE 11.5 Some q Values for $\alpha = .01$

DEGREES OF FREEDOM	NUMBER OF POPULATIONS				
	2	3	4	5	...
1	90	135	164	186	
2	14	19	22.3	24.7	
3	8.26	10.6	12.2	13.3	
4	6.51	8.12	9.17	9.96	
.					
.					
.					
11	4.39	5.14	5.62	5.97	
12	4.32	5.04	5.50	5.84	

Critical q value: $q_{.01,3,12} = 5.04$

TABLE 11.6	Minitab Output for Tukey's HSD

Tukey Pairwise Comparisons

Grouping Information Using the Tukey Method and 99% Confidence

Factor	N	Mean	Grouping
Plant 2	5	32.000	A
Plant 1	5	28.200	B
Plant 3	5	24.800	C

Means that do not share a letter are significantly different.

Tukey Simultaneous Tests for Differences of Means

Difference of Levels	Difference of Means	SE of Difference	99% CI	T-Value	Adjusted P-Value
Plant 2 - Plant 1	3.800	0.808	(0.914, 6.686)	4.70	0.001
Plant 3 - Plant 1	-3.400	0.808	(-6.286, -0.514)	-4.21	0.003
Plant 3 - Plant 2	-7.200	0.808	(-10.086, -4.314)	-8.91	0.000

indicated that all three tests for differences of means are significant at $\alpha = .01$. In addition, in examining the confidence intervals for the differences of means, if the confidence interval includes zero, there is no significant difference in the pair of means. (If the interval contains zero, there is a possibility of no difference in the means.) Note in Table 11.6 that all three pairs of confidence intervals contain the same sign throughout the interval. For example, the confidence interval for estimating the difference in means from 1 and 2 is $0.914 \leq \mu_1 - \mu_2 \leq 6.686$. This interval does not contain zero, so we are confident that there is more than a zero difference in the two means. The same holds true for levels 1 and 3 and levels 2 and 3.

DEMONSTRATION PROBLEM 11.2

A metal-manufacturing firm wants to test the tensile strength of a given metal under varying conditions of temperature. Suppose that in the design phase, the metal is processed under five different temperature conditions and that random samples of size five are taken under each temperature condition. The data follow.

TENSILE STRENGTH OF METAL PRODUCED UNDER FIVE DIFFERENT TEMPERATURE SETTINGS				
1	2	3	4	5
2.46	2.38	2.51	2.49	2.56
2.41	2.34	2.48	2.47	2.57
2.43	2.31	2.46	2.48	2.53
2.47	2.40	2.49	2.46	2.55
2.46	2.32	2.50	2.44	2.55

A one-way ANOVA is performed on these data by using Minitab, with the resulting analysis shown here.

```
Analysis of Variance

Source    DF    Adj SS      Adj MS       F-Value     P-Value
Factor     4    0.10802     0.027006     43.70       0.000
Error     20    0.01236     0.000618
Total     24    0.12038

Model Summary

S             R-sq      R-sq(adj)    R-sq(pred)
0.0248596     89.73%    87.68%       83.96%
```

Note from the ANOVA table that the F value of 43.70 is statistically significant at $\alpha = .01$. There is an overall difference in the population means of metal produced under the five temperature settings. Use the data to compute a Tukey's HSD to determine which of the five groups are significantly different from the others.

Solution: From the ANOVA table, the value of MSE is .000618. The sample size, n_j, is 5. The number of treatment means, C, is 5, and the df_E are 20. With these values and $\alpha = .01$, the value of q can be obtained from Table A.10.

$$q_{.01,5,20} = 5.29$$

HSD can be computed as

$$HSD = q\sqrt{\frac{MSE}{n}} = 5.29\sqrt{\frac{.000618}{5}} = .0588$$

The treatment group means for this problem follow.

$$Group\,1 = 2.446$$
$$Group\,2 = 2.350$$
$$Group\,3 = 2.488$$
$$Group\,4 = 2.468$$
$$Group\,5 = 2.552$$

Computing all pairwise differences between these means (in absolute values) produces the following data.

	GROUP				
	1	2	3	4	5
1	—	.096	.042	.022	.106
2	.096	—	.138	.118	.202
3	.042	.138	—	.020	.064
4	.022	.118	.020	—	.084
5	.106	.202	.064	.084	—

Comparing these differences to the value of HSD = .0588, we can determine that the differences between groups 1 and 2 (.096), 1 and 5 (.106), 2 and 3 (.138), 2 and 4 (.118), 2 and 5 (.202), 3 and 5 (.064), and 4 and 5 (.084) are significant at $\alpha = .01$.

Not only is there an overall significant difference in the treatment levels as shown by the ANOVA results, but there is a significant difference in the tensile strength of metal between seven pairs of levels. By studying the magnitudes of the individual treatment levels' means, the steel-manufacturing firm can determine which temperatures result in the greatest tensile strength. The Minitab output for this Tukey's HSD is shown below. Note that the grouping information shows that means 1 and 2, 1 and 5, 2 and 3, 2 and 4, 2 and 5, 3 and 5, and 4 and 5 are significantly different because they do not share a letter. The same statistical conclusions can be reached by examining the p-values associated with the t tests.

Tukey Pairwise Comparisons

Grouping Information Using the Tukey Method and 99% Confidence

Factor	N	Mean	Grouping		
5	5	2.55200	A		
3	5	2.48800		B	
4	5	2.46800		B	
1	5	2.4460		B	
2	5	2.3500			C

Means that do not share a letter are significantly different.

Tukey Simultaneous Tests for Differences of Means

Difference of Levels	Difference of Means	SE of Difference	99% CI	T-Value	Adjusted P-Value
2 - 1	-0.0960	0.0157	(-0.1548, -0.0372)	-6.11	0.000
3 - 1	0.0420	0.0157	(-0.0168, 0.1008)	2.67	0.095
4 - 1	0.0220	0.0157	(-0.0368, 0.0808)	1.40	0.635
5 - 1	0.1060	0.0157	(0.0472, 0.1648)	6.74	0.000
3 - 2	0.1380	0.0157	(0.0792, 0.1968)	8.78	0.000
4 - 2	0.1180	0.0157	(0.0592, 0.1768)	7.51	0.000
5 - 2	0.2020	0.0157	(0.1432, 0.2608)	12.85	0.000
4 - 3	-0.0200	0.0157	(-0.0788, 0.0388)	-1.27	0.711
5 - 3	0.0640	0.0157	(0.0052, 0.1228)	4.07	0.005
5 - 4	0.0840	0.0157	(0.0252, 0.1428)	5.34	0.000

Tukey-Kramer Procedure: The Case of Unequal Sample Sizes

Tukey's HSD was modified by C. Y. Kramer in the mid-1950s to handle situations in which the sample sizes are unequal. The modified version of HSD is sometimes referred to as the **Tukey-Kramer procedure**. The formula for computing the significant differences with this procedure is similar to that for the equal sample sizes, with the exception that the mean square error is divided in half and weighted by the sum of the inverses of the sample sizes under the root sign.

Tukey-Kramer Formula

$$q_{\alpha,C,N-C}\sqrt{\frac{\text{MSE}}{2}\left(\frac{1}{n_r}+\frac{1}{n_s}\right)}$$

where

MSE = mean square error
n_r = sample size for rth sample
n_s = sample size for sth sample
$q_{\alpha,C,N-C}$ = critical value of the studentized range distribution from Table A.10

As an example of the application of the Tukey-Kramer procedure, consider the machine operator example in Section 11.2. A one-way ANOVA was used to test for any difference in the mean valve openings produced by four different machine operators. An overall F of 10.18 was computed, which was significant at $\alpha = .05$. Because the ANOVA hypothesis test is significant and the null hypothesis is rejected, this problem is a candidate for multiple comparisons. Because the sample sizes are not equal, Tukey's HSD cannot be used to determine which pairs are significantly different. However, the Tukey-Kramer procedure can be applied. Shown in Table 11.7 are the means and sample sizes for the valve openings for valves produced by the four different operators.

The mean square error for this problem, MSE, is shown in Table 11.3 as .007746. The four operators in the problem represent the four levels of the independent variable, machine operator. Thus, $C = 4$, $N = 24$, and $N - C = 20$. The value of alpha in the problem is .05. With this information, the value of q is obtained from Table A.10 as

$$q_{.05,4,20} = 3.96$$

The distance necessary for the difference in the means of two samples to be statistically significant must be computed by using the Tukey-Kramer procedure for each pair because the sample sizes differ. In this problem with $C = 4$, there are $C(C - 1)/2$ or six possible pairwise comparisons. The computations follow.

For operators 1 and 2,

$$3.96\sqrt{\frac{.007746}{2}\left(\frac{1}{5} + \frac{1}{8}\right)} = .1405$$

The difference between the means of operator 1 and operator 2 is

$$6.3180 - 6.2775 = .0405.$$

Because this result is less than the critical difference of .1405, there is no significant difference between the average valve openings of valves produced by machine operators 1 and 2.

Table 11.8 reports the critical differences for each of the six pairwise comparisons as computed by using the Tukey-Kramer procedure, along with the absolute value of the actual distances between the means. Any actual distance between means that is greater than the critical distance is significant. As shown in the table, the means of three pairs of samples, operators 1 and 3, operators 2 and 3, and operators 3 and 4 are significantly different.

TABLE 11.7	Means and Sample Sizes for the Valves Produced by Four Operators	
OPERATOR	SAMPLE SIZE	MEAN
1	5	6.3180
2	8	6.2775
3	7	6.4886
4	4	6.2300

TABLE 11.8	Results of Pairwise Comparisons for the Machine Operators Example Using the Tukey-Kramer Procedure	
PAIR	CRITICAL DIFFERENCE	ACTUAL DIFFERENCE
1 and 2	.1405	.0405
1 and 3	.1443	.1706*
1 and 4	.1653	.0880
2 and 3	.1275	.2111*
2 and 4	.1509	.0475
3 and 4	.1545	.2586*

*Significant at $\alpha = .05$.

TABLE 11.9   Minitab Multiple Comparisons in the Machine Operator Example Using the Tukey-Kramer Procedure

Tukey Pairwise Comparisons

Grouping Information Using the Tukey Method and 95% Confidence

Factor	N	Mean	Grouping
Operator 3	7	6.4886	A
Operator 1	5	6.3180	B
Operator 2	8	6.2775	B
Operator 4	4	6.2300	B

Means that do not share a letter are significantly different.

Tukey Simultaneous Tests for Differences of Means

Difference of Levels	Difference of Means	SE of Difference	95% CI	T-Value	Adjusted P-Value
Operator 2 - Operator 1	-0.0405	0.0502	(-0.1810, 0.1000)	-0.81	0.850
Operator 3 - Operator 1	0.1706	0.0515	(0.0263, 0.3149)	3.31	0.017
Operator 4 - Operator 1	-0.0880	0.0590	(-0.2533, 0.0773)	-1.49	0.461
Operator 3 - Operator 2	0.2111	0.0455	(0.0835, 0.3386)	4.63	0.001
Operator 4 - Operator 2	-0.0475	0.0539	(-0.1984, 0.1034)	-0.88	0.814
Operator 4 - Operator 3	-0.2586	0.0552	(-0.4130,-0.1041)	-4.69	0.001

Table 11.9 shows the Minitab output for this problem. The grouping information indicates that pairs 1 and 3, 2 and 3, and 3 and 4 do not share a letter and thus, contain significant differences. This is underscored by the *t* tests in which these three comparisons produce *p*-values of .017, .001, and .001 respectively – all significant at $\alpha = .05$.

11.3 Problems

11.17. Suppose an ANOVA has been performed on a completely randomized design containing six treatment levels. The mean for group 3 is 15.85, and the sample size for group 3 is eight. The mean for group 6 is 17.21, and the sample size for group 6 is seven. MSE is .3352. The total number of observations is 46. Compute the significant difference for the means of these two groups by using the Tukey-Kramer procedure. Let $\alpha = .05$.

11.18. A completely randomized design has been analyzed by using a one-way ANOVA. There are four treatment groups in the design, and each sample size is six. MSE is equal to 2.389. Using $\alpha = .05$, compute Tukey's HSD for this ANOVA.

11.19. Using the results of problem 11.5, compute a critical value by using the Tukey-Kramer procedure for groups 1 and 2. Use $\alpha = .05$. Determine whether there is a significant difference between these two groups.

11.20. Use the Tukey-Kramer procedure to determine whether there is a significant difference between the means of groups 2 and 5 in problem 11.6. Let $\alpha = .01$.

11.21. Using the results from problem 11.7, compute a Tukey's HSD to determine whether there are any significant differences between group means. Let $\alpha = .01$.

11.22. Using problem 11.8, compute Tukey's HSD and determine whether there is a significant difference in means by using this methodology. Let $\alpha = .05$.

11.23. Use the Tukey-Kramer procedure to do multiple comparisons for problem 11.11. Let $\alpha = .01$. State which pairs of machines, if any, produce significantly different mean fills.

11.24. Use Tukey's HSD test to compute multiple comparisons for the data in problem 11.12. Let $\alpha = .01$. State which regions, if any, are significantly different from other regions in mean starting salary figures.

11.25. Using $\alpha = .05$, compute critical values using the Tukey-Kramer procedure for the pairwise groups in problem 11.13. Determine which pairs of groups are significantly different, if any.

11.26. Do multiple comparisons on the data in problem 11.14 using Tukey's HSD test and $\alpha = .05$. State which pairs of cities, if any, have significantly different mean costs.

11.27. Problem 11.16 analyzed the number of weekly hours worked per person at five different plants. An *F* value of 3.10 was obtained with a probability of .0266. Because the probability is less than .05, the null hypothesis is rejected at $\alpha = .05$. There is an overall difference in the mean weekly hours worked by plant. Which pairs of plants have significant differences in the means, if any? To answer this question, a Minitab computer analysis was done. The data follow. Study the output in light of problem 11.16 and discuss the results.

Tukey Pairwise Comparisons

```
Grouping Information Using the Tukey Method and 95% Confidence

Factor    N    Mean    Grouping
Plant 3   8    61.47   A
Plant 1   11   57.87   A B
Plant 5   7    56.95   A B
Plant 2   12   50.15     B
Plant 4   5    49.20   A B

Means that do not share a letter are significantly different.
```

Tukey Simultaneous Tests for Differences of Means

Difference of Levels	Difference of Means	SE of Difference	95% CI	T-Value	Adjusted P-Value
Plant 2 - Plant 1	-7.72	3.56	(-17.91, 2.47)	-2.17	0.213
Plant 3 - Plant 1	3.60	3.96	(-7.74, 14.94)	0.91	0.892
Plant 4 - Plant 1	-8.67	4.60	(-21.83, 4.50)	-1.89	0.343
Plant 5 - Plant 1	-0.92	4.12	(-12.72, 10.88)	-0.22	0.999
Plant 3 - Plant 2	11.32	3.89	(0.18, 22.46)	2.91	0.045
Plant 4 - Plant 2	-0.94	4.54	(-13.94, 12.05)	-0.21	1.000
Plant 5 - Plant 2	6.80	4.05	(-4.81, 18.41)	1.68	0.459
Plant 4 - Plant 3	-12.26	4.86	(-26.18, 1.65)	-2.52	0.106
Plant 5 - Plant 3	-4.52	4.41	(-17.15, 8.11)	-1.02	0.842
Plant 5 - Plant 4	7.74	4.99	(-6.55, 22.04)	1.55	0.536

Thinking Critically About Statistics in Business Today

Does National Ideology Affect a Firm's Definition of Success?

One researcher, G. C. Lodge, proposed that companies pursue different performance goals based on the ideology of their home country. L. Thurow went further by suggesting that such national ideologies drive U.S. firms to be short-term profit maximizers, Japanese firms to be growth maximizers, and European firms to be a mix of the two.

Three other researchers, J. Katz, S. Werner, and L. Brouthers, decided to test these suggestions by studying 114 international banks from the United States, the European Union (EU), and Japan listed in the Global 1000. Specifically, there were 34 banks from the United States, 45 banks from the European Union, and 35 banks from Japan in the study. Financial and market data were gathered and averaged on each bank over a five-year period to limit the effect of single-year variations.

The banks were compared on general measures of success such as profitability, capitalization, growth, size, risk, and earnings distribution by specifically examining 11 measures. Eleven one-way analyses of variance designs were computed, one for each dependent variable. These included return on equity, return on assets, yield, capitalization, assets, market value, growth, Tobin's Q, price-to-earnings ratio, payout ratio, and risk. The independent variable in each ANOVA was country, with three levels: U.S., EU, and Japan.

In all 11 ANOVAs, there was a significant difference between banks in the three countries ($\alpha = .01$) supporting the theme of different financial success goals for different national cultures. Because of the overall significant difference attained in the ANOVAs, each analysis of variance was followed by a multiple comparison test to determine which, if any, of the pairs were significantly different. These comparisons revealed that U.S. and EU banks maintained significantly higher levels than Japanese banks on return on equity, return on assets, and yield. This result underscores the notion that U.S. and EU banks have more of a short-term profit orientation than do Japanese banks. There was a significant difference in banks from each of the three countries on amount of capitalization. U.S. banks had the highest level of capitalization followed by EU banks and then Japanese banks. This result may reflect the cultural attitude about how much capital is needed to ensure a sound economy, with U.S. banks maintaining higher levels of capital.

The study found that Japanese banks had significantly higher levels on growth, Tobin's Q, and price-to-earnings ratio than did the other two national entities. This result confirms the hypothesis that Japanese firms are more interested in growth. In addition, Japanese banks had a significantly higher asset size and market value of equity than did U.S. banks. The researchers had hypothesized that EU banks would have a greater portfolio risk than that of U.S. or Japanese banks. They found that EU banks did have significantly higher risk and paid out significantly higher dividends than did either Japanese or U.S. banks.

THINGS TO PONDER

1. If you represent an American company wanting to do business in Japan, what are some points from this study that might guide you in your endeavor?

2. What did you learn about EU banks in this study that may set them apart from U.S. banks?

Source: Adapted from Jeffrey P. Katz, Steve Werner, and Lance Brouthers, "Does Winning Mean the Same Thing Around the World? National Ideology and the Performance of Global Competitors," *Journal of Business Research*, vol. 44, no. 2 (February 1999), pp. 117–126.

11.4 The Randomized Block Design

A second research design is the **randomized block design**. The randomized block design is similar to the completely randomized design in that it focuses on one independent variable (treatment variable) of interest. However, the randomized block design also includes a second variable, referred to as a blocking variable, that can be used to control for confounding or concomitant variables.

Confounding variables, or **concomitant variables**, are *variables that are not being controlled by the researcher in the experiment but can have an effect on the outcome of the treatment being studied.* For example, Demonstration Problem 11.2 showed how a completely randomized design could be used to analyze the effects of temperature on the tensile strengths of metal. However, other variables not being controlled by the researcher in this experiment may affect the tensile strength of metal, such as humidity, raw materials, machine, and shift. One way to control for these variables is to include them in the experimental design. The randomized block design has the capability of adding one of these variables into the analysis as a blocking variable. A **blocking variable** is *a variable that the researcher wants to control but is not the treatment variable of interest.*

One of the first people to use the randomized block design was Sir Ronald A. Fisher. He applied the design to the field of agriculture, where he was interested in studying the growth patterns of varieties of seeds for a given type of plant. The seed variety was his independent variable. However, he realized that as he experimented on different plots of ground, the "block" of ground might make some difference in the experiment. Fisher designated several different plots of ground as blocks, which he controlled as a second variable. Each of the seed varieties was planted on each of the blocks. The main thrust of his study was to compare the seed varieties (independent variable). He merely wanted to control for the difference in plots of ground (blocking variable).

In Demonstration Problem 11.2, examples of blocking variables might be machine number (if several machines are used to make the metal), worker, shift, or day of the week. The researcher probably already knows that different workers or different machines will produce at least slightly different metal tensile strengths because of individual differences. However, designating the variable (machine or worker) as the blocking variable and computing a randomized block design affords the potential for a more powerful analysis. In other experiments, some other possible variables that might be used as blocking variables include sex of subject, age of subject, intelligence of subject, economic level of subject, brand, supplier, or vehicle.

A special case of the randomized block design is the repeated measures design. The **repeated measures design** is a randomized block design in which each block level is an individual item or person, and that person or item is measured across all treatments. Thus, where a block level in a randomized block design is night shift and items produced under different treatment levels on the night shift are measured, in a repeated measures design, a block level might be an individual machine or person; items produced by that person or machine are then randomly chosen across all treatments. Thus, a repeated measure of the person or machine is made across all treatments. This repeated measures design is an extension of the *t* test for dependent samples presented in Section 10.3.

The sum of squares in a completely randomized design is

$$SST = SSC + SSE$$

In a randomized block design, the sum of squares is

$$SST = SSC + SSR + SSE$$

where

SST = sum of squares total

SSC = sum of squares columns (treatment)

SSR = sum of squares rows (blocking)

SSE = sum of squares error

SST and SSC are the same for a given analysis whether a completely randomized design or a randomized block design is used. For this reason, the SSR (blocking effects) comes out of the SSE; that is, some of the error variation in the completely randomized design is accounted for in the blocking effects of the randomized block design, as shown in **Figure 11.7**. By reducing the error term, it is possible that the value of F for treatment will increase (the denominator of the F value is decreased). However, if there is not sufficient difference between levels of the blocking variable, the use of a randomized block design can lead to a less powerful result than would a completely randomized design computed on the same problem. Thus, the researcher should seek out blocking variables that he or she believes are significant contributors to variation among measurements of the dependent variable. **Figure 11.8** shows the layout of a randomized block design.

In each of the intersections of independent variable and blocking variable in Figure 11.8, one measurement is taken. In the randomized block design, one measurement is given for each treatment level under each blocking level.

The null and alternate hypotheses for the treatment effects in the randomized block design are

$$H_0\!: \mu_{._1} = \mu_{._2} = \mu_{._3} = \ldots = \mu_{._c}$$

H_a: At least one of the treatment means is different from the others.

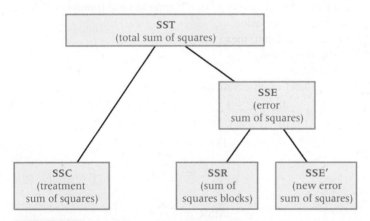

FIGURE 11.7   **Partitioning the Total Sum of Squares in a Randomized Block Design**

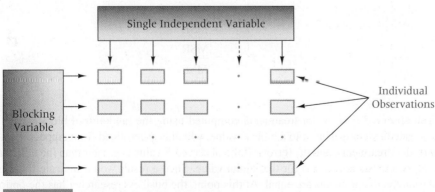

FIGURE 11.8   **A Randomized Block Design**

For the blocking effects, they are

$$H_0: \mu_1. = \mu_2. = \mu_3. = \ldots = \mu_R.$$

$$H_a: \text{At least one of the blocking means is different from the others.}$$

Essentially, we are testing the null hypothesis that the population means of the treatment groups are equal. If the null hypothesis is rejected, at least one of the population means does not equal the others.

The formulas for computing a randomized block design follow.

Formulas for Computing a Randomized Block Design

$$SSC = n\sum_{j=1}^{C}(\bar{x}_j - \bar{x})^2$$

$$SSR = C\sum_{i=1}^{n}(\bar{x}_i - \bar{x})^2$$

$$SSE = \sum_{j=1}^{C}\sum_{i=1}^{n}(x_{ij} - \bar{x}_j - \bar{x}_i + \bar{x})^2$$

$$SST = \sum_{j=1}^{C}\sum_{i=1}^{n}(x_{ij} - \bar{x})^2$$

where

i = block group (row)
j = treatment level (column)
C = number of treatment levels (columns)
n = number of observations in each treatment level (number of blocks or rows)
x_{ij} = individual observation
$\bar{x}_j$ = treatment (column) mean
$\bar{x}_i$ = block (row) mean
$\bar{x}$ = grand mean
N = total number of observations

$$df_C = C - 1$$
$$df_R = n - 1$$
$$df_E = (C-1)(n-1) = N - n - C + 1$$

$$MSC = \frac{SSC}{C-1}$$

$$MSR = \frac{SSR}{n-1}$$

$$MSE = \frac{SSE}{N - n - C + 1}$$

$$F_{treatments} = \frac{MSC}{MSE}$$

$$F_{blocks} = \frac{MSR}{MSE}$$

The observed F value for treatments computed using the randomized block design formula is tested by comparing it to a table F value, which is ascertained from Appendix A.7 by using α, df_C (treatment), and df_E (error). If the observed F value is greater than the table value, the null hypothesis is rejected for that alpha value. Such a result would indicate that not all population treatment means are equal. At this point, the business researcher has the option of computing multiple comparisons if the null hypothesis has been rejected.

Some researchers also compute an F value for blocks even though the main emphasis in the experiment is on the treatments. The observed F value for blocks is compared to a critical table F value determined from Appendix A.7 by using α, df_R (blocks), and df_E (error). If the F value for blocks is greater than the critical F value, the null hypothesis that all block population means are equal is rejected. This result tells the business researcher that including the blocking in the design was probably worthwhile and that a significant amount of variance was drawn off from the error term, thus increasing the power of the treatment test. In this text, we have omitted F_{blocks} from the normal presentation and problem solving. We leave the use of this F value to the discretion of the reader.

As an example of the application of the randomized block design, consider a tire company that developed a new tire. The company conducted tread-wear tests on the tire to determine whether there is a significant difference in tread wear if the average speed with which the automobile is driven varies. The company set up an experiment in which the independent variable was speed of automobile. There were three treatment levels: slow speed (car is driven 20 miles per hour), medium speed (car is driven 40 miles per hour), and high speed (car is driven 60 miles per hour). Company researchers realized that several possible variables could confound the study. One of these variables was supplier. The company uses five suppliers to provide a major component of the rubber from which the tires are made. To control for this variable experimentally, the researchers used supplier as a blocking variable. Fifteen tires were randomly selected for the study, three from each supplier. Each of the three was assigned to be tested under a different speed condition. The data are given here, along with treatment and block totals. These figures represent tire wear in units of 10,000 miles.

SUPPLIER	SLOW	SPEED MEDIUM	FAST	BLOCK MEANS $\bar{x}_i$
1	3.7	4.5	3.1	3.77
2	3.4	3.9	2.8	3.37
3	3.5	4.1	3.0	3.53
4	3.2	3.5	2.6	3.10
5	3.9	4.8	3.4	4.03
Treatment Means $\bar{x}_j$	3.54	4.16	2.98	$\bar{x} = 3.56$

To analyze this randomized block design using $\alpha = .01$, the computations are as follows.

$$C = 3$$
$$n = 5$$
$$N = 15$$

$$SSC = n\sum_{j=1}^{C}(\bar{x}_j - \bar{x})^2$$
$$= 5[(3.54 - 3.56)^2 + (4.16 - 3.56)^2 + (2.98 - 3.56)^2]$$
$$= 3.484$$

$$SSR = C\sum_{i=1}^{n}(\bar{x}_i - \bar{x})^2$$
$$= 3[(3.77 - 3.56)^2 + (3.37 - 3.56)^2 + (3.53 - 3.56)^2 + (3.10 - 3.56)^2 + (4.03 - 3.56)^2]$$
$$= 1.549$$

$$SSE = \sum_{j=1}^{C}\sum_{i=1}^{n}(x_{ij} - \bar{x}_j - \bar{x}_i + \bar{x})^2$$
$$= (3.7 - 3.54 - 3.77 + 3.56)^2 + (3.4 - 3.54 - 3.37 + 3.56)^2$$
$$+ \cdots + (2.6 - 2.98 - 3.10 + 3.56)^2 + (3.4 - 2.98 - 4.03 + 3.56)^2$$
$$= .14267$$

$$SST = \sum_{j=1}^{C} \sum_{i=1}^{n} (\bar{x}_{ij} - \bar{x})^2$$

$$= (3.7 - 3.56)^2 + (3.4 - 3.56)^2 + \cdots + (2.6 - 3.56)^2 + (3.4 - 3.56)^2$$

$$= 5.176$$

$$MSC = \frac{SSC}{C - 1} = \frac{3.484}{2} = 1.742$$

$$MSR = \frac{SSR}{n - 1} = \frac{1.549}{4} = .38725$$

$$MSE = \frac{SSE}{N - n - C + 1} = \frac{.14267}{8} = .017833$$

$$F = \frac{MSC}{MSE} = \frac{1.742}{.017833} = 97.68$$

SOURCE OF VARIATION	SS	df	MS	F
Treatment	3.484	2	1.742	97.68
Block	1.549	4	.38725	
Error	.14267	8	.017833	
Total	5.176	14		

For alpha of .01, the critical F value is

$$F_{.01,2,8} = 8.65$$

Because the observed value of F for treatment (97.68) is greater than this critical F value, the null hypothesis is rejected. At least one of the population means of the treatment levels is not the same as the others; that is, there is a significant difference in tread wear for cars driven at different speeds. If this problem had been set up as a completely randomized design, the SSR would have been a part of the SSE. The degrees of freedom for the blocking effects would have been combined with degrees of freedom of error. Thus, the value of SSE would have been $1.549 + .14267 = 1.692$, and df_E would have been $4 + 8 = 12$. These would then have been used to recompute $MSE = 1.692/12 = .141$. The value of F for treatments would have been

$$F = \frac{MSC}{MSE} = \frac{1.742}{0.141} = 12.35$$

Thus, the F value for treatment with the blocking was 97.68 and *without* the blocking was 12.35. By using the random block design, a much larger observed F value was obtained.

Using the Computer to Analyze Randomized Block Designs

Both Minitab and Excel have the capability of analyzing a randomized block design. The computer output from each of these software packages for the tire tread wear example is displayed in Table 11.10.

The Minitab output includes F values and their associated p-values for both the treatment and the blocking effects. As with most standard ANOVA tables, the sum of squares, mean squares, and degrees of freedom for each source of variation are included.

TABLE 11.10 Minitab and Excel Output for the Tread Wear Example

Minitab Output

Analysis of Variance for Mileage

```
Source      DF     SS          MS         F        P
Speed       2      3.48400     1.74200    97.68    0.000
Supplier    4      1.54933     0.38733    21.72    0.000
Error       8      0.14267     0.01783
Total       14     5.17600
```

S = 0.133542   R-Sq = 97.24%   R-Sq(adj) = 95.18%

Excel Output

Anova: Two-factor Without Replication

SUMMARY	Count	Sum	Average	Variance
Supplier 1	3	11.3	3.767	0.4933
Supplier 2	3	10.1	3.367	0.3033
Supplier 3	3	10.6	3.533	0.3033
Supplier 4	3	9.3	3.100	0.2100
Supplier 5	3	12.1	4.033	0.5033
Slow	5	17.7	3.54	0.073
Medium	5	20.8	4.16	0.258
Fast	5	14.9	2.98	0.092

ANOVA

Source of Variation	SS	df	MS	F	P-value	F crit
Rows	1.549333	4	0.387333	21.72	0.0002357	7.01
Columns	3.484000	2	1.742000	97.68	0.0000024	8.65
Error	0.142667	8	0.017833			
Total	5.176000	14				

Excel treats a randomized block design as a two-way ANOVA (Section 11.5) that has only one observation per cell. The Excel output includes sums, averages, and variances for each row and column. The Excel ANOVA table displays the observed F values for the treatment (columns) and the blocks (rows). An important inclusion in the Excel output is the p-value for each F, along with the critical (table) F values.

DEMONSTRATION PROBLEM 11.3

Suppose a national travel association studied the cost of premium unleaded gasoline in the United States during the summer of 2016. From experience, association directors believed there was a significant difference in the average cost of a gallon of premium gasoline among urban areas in different parts of the country. To test this belief, they placed random calls to gasoline stations in five different cities. In addition, the researchers realized that the brand of gasoline might make a difference. They were mostly interested in the differences between cities, so they made city their treatment variable. To control for the fact that pricing varies with brand, the researchers included brand as a blocking variable and selected six different brands to participate. The researchers randomly telephoned one gasoline station for each brand in each city, resulting in 30 measurements (five cities and six brands). Each station operator was asked to report the current cost of a gallon of premium unleaded gasoline at that station. The data are shown here. Test these data by using a randomized block design analysis to determine whether there is a significant difference in the average cost of premium unleaded gasoline by city. Let $\alpha = .01$.

			GEOGRAPHIC REGION			
BRAND	MIAMI	PHILADELPHIA	MINNEAPOLIS	SAN ANTONIO	OAKLAND	$\bar{x}_i$
A	3.47	3.40	3.38	3.32	3.50	3.414
B	3.43	3.41	3.42	3.35	3.44	3.410
C	3.44	3.41	3.43	3.36	3.45	3.418
D	3.46	3.45	3.40	3.30	3.45	3.412
E	3.46	3.40	3.39	3.39	3.48	3.424
F	3.44	3.43	3.42	3.39	3.49	3.434
$\bar{x}_j$	3.450	3.4167	3.4067	3.3517	3.4683	$\bar{x} = 3.4187$

Solution:

Step 1. The hypotheses follow.

For treatments,

$$H_0: \mu_{\cdot 1} = \mu_{\cdot 2} = \mu_{\cdot 3} = \mu_{\cdot 4} = \mu_{\cdot 5}$$

H_a: At least one of the treatment means is different from the others.

For blocks,

$$H_0: \mu_{1 \cdot} = \mu_{2 \cdot} = \mu_{3 \cdot} = \mu_{4 \cdot} = \mu_{5 \cdot} = \mu_{6 \cdot}.$$

H_a: At least one of the blocking means is different from the others.

Step 2. The appropriate statistical test is the F test in the ANOVA for randomized block designs.

Step 3. Let $\alpha = .01$.

Step 4. There are four degrees of freedom for the treatment ($C - 1 = 5 - 1 = 4$), five degrees of freedom for the blocks ($n - 1 = 6 - 1 = 5$), and 20 degrees of freedom for error [$(C - 1)(n - 1) = (4)(5) = 20$]. Using these, $\alpha = .01$, and Table A.7, we find the critical F values.

$$F_{.01,4,20} = 4.43 \text{ for treatments}$$

$$F_{.01,5,20} = 4.10 \text{ for blocks}$$

The decision rule is to reject the null hypothesis for treatments if the observed F value for treatments is greater than 4.43 and to reject the null hypothesis for blocking effects if the observed F value for blocks is greater than 4.10.

Step 5. The sample data including row and column means and the grand mean are given in the preceding table.

Step 6.

$$SSC = n \sum_{j=1}^{C} (\bar{x}_j - \bar{x})^2$$

$$= 6[(3.450 - 3.4187)^2 + (3.4167 - 3.4187)^2 + (3.4067 - 3.4187)^2$$
$$+ (3.3517 - 3.4187)^2 + (3.4683 - 3.4187)^2]$$

$$= .04846$$

$$SSR = C \sum_{j=1}^{n} (\bar{x}_i - \bar{x})^2$$

$$= 5[(3.414 - 3.4187)^2 + (3.410 - 3.4187)^2 + (3.418 - 3.4187)^2$$
$$+ (3.412 - 3.4187)^2 + (3.424 - 3.4187)^2 + (3.434 - 3.4187)^2]$$

$$= .00203$$

$$SSE = \sum_{i=1}^{n} \sum_{j=1}^{C} (x_{ij} - \bar{x}_j - \bar{x}_i + \bar{x})^2$$

$$= (3.47 - 3.450 - 3.414 + 3.4187)^2 + (3.43 - 3.450 - 3.410 + 3.4187)^2 + \ldots$$
$$+ (3.48 - 3.4683 - 3.424 + 3.4187)^2 + (3.49 - 3.4683 - 3.434 + 3.4187)^2$$

$$= .01281$$

$$SST = \sum_{i=1}^{n} \sum_{j=1}^{C} (x_{ij} - \bar{x})^2$$

$$= (3.47 - 3.4187)^2 + (3.43 - 3.4187)^2 + \ldots + (3.48 - 3.4187)^2 + (3.49 - 3.4187)^2$$

$$= .06330$$

$$MSC = \frac{SSC}{C-1} = \frac{.04846}{4} = .01212$$

$$MSR = \frac{SSR}{n-1} = \frac{.00203}{5} = .00041$$

$$MSE = \frac{SSE}{(C-1)(n-1)} = \frac{.01281}{20} = .00064$$

$$F = \frac{MSC}{MSE} = \frac{.01212}{.00064} = 18.94$$

SOURCE OF VARIANCE	SS	df	MS	F
Treatment	.04846	4	.01212	18.94
Block	.00203	5	.00041	
Error	.01281	20	.00064	
Total	.06330	29		

Step 7. Because $F_{treat} = 18.94 > F_{.01,4,20} = 4.43$, the null hypothesis is rejected for the treatment effects. There is a significant difference in the average price of a gallon of premium unleaded gasoline in various cities.

A glance at the MSR reveals that there appears to be relatively little blocking variance. The result of determining an F value for the blocking effects is

$$F = \frac{MSR}{MSE} = \frac{.00041}{.00064} = 0.64$$

The value of F for blocks is not significant at $\alpha = .01$ ($F_{.01,5,20} = 4.10$). This result indicates that the blocking portion of the experimental design did not contribute significantly to the analysis. If the blocking effects (SSR) are added back into SSE and the df_R are included with df_E, the MSE becomes .00059 instead of .00064. Using the value .00059 in the denominator for the treatment F increases the observed treatment F value to 20.54. Thus, including nonsignificant blocking effects in the original analysis caused a loss of power.

Shown here are the Minitab and Excel ANOVA table outputs for this problem.

Minitab Output

Analysis of Variance for Gas Prices

```
Source   DF    SS           MS           F        P
City     4     0.0485133    0.0121283    18.94    0.000
Brand    5     0.0020267    0.0004053     0.63    0.677
Error    20    0.0128067    0.0006403
Total    29    0.0633467
```

Excel Output

Anova: Two-Factor Without Replication

ANOVA

Source of Variation	SS	df	MS	F	P-value	F crit
Rows	0.002027	5	0.000405	0.63	0.6768877	4.10
Columns	0.048513	4	0.012128	18.94	0.0000014	4.43
Error	0.012807	20	0.000640			
Total	0.063347	29				

> **Step 8.** The fact that there is a significant difference in the price of gasoline in different parts of the country can be useful information to decision makers. For example, companies in the ground transportation business are greatly affected by increases in the cost of fuel. Knowledge of price differences in fuel can help these companies plan strategies and routes. Fuel price differences can sometimes be indications of cost-of-living differences or distribution problems, which can affect a company's relocation decision or cost-of-living increases given to employees who transfer to the higher-priced locations. Knowing that the price of gasoline varies around the country can generate interest among market researchers who might want to study why the differences are there and what drives them. This information can sometimes result in a better understanding of the marketplace.

11.4 Problems

11.28. Use ANOVA to analyze the data from the randomized block design given here. Let $\alpha = .05$. State the null and alternative hypotheses and determine whether the null hypothesis is rejected.

		TREATMENT LEVEL			
		1	*2*	*3*	*4*
	1	23	26	24	24
	2	31	35	32	33
Block	3	27	29	26	27
	4	21	28	27	22
	5	18	25	27	20

11.29. The following data were gathered from a randomized block design. Use $\alpha = .01$ to test for a significant difference in the treatment levels. Establish the hypotheses and reach a conclusion about the null hypothesis.

		TREATMENT LEVEL		
		1	*2*	*3*
	1	1.28	1.29	1.29
Block	2	1.40	1.36	1.35
	3	1.15	1.13	1.19
	4	1.22	1.18	1.24

11.30. A randomized block design has a treatment variable with six levels and a blocking variable with 10 blocks. Using this information and $\alpha = .05$, complete the following table and reach a conclusion about the null hypothesis.

SOURCE OF VARIANCE	SS	df	MS	F
Treatment	2,477.53			
Blocks	3,180.48			
Error	11,661.38			
Total				

11.31. A randomized block design has a treatment variable with four levels and a blocking variable with seven blocks. Using this information and $\alpha = .01$, complete the following table and reach a conclusion about the null hypothesis.

SOURCE OF VARIANCE	SS	df	MS	F
Treatment	199.48			
Blocks	265.24			
Error	306.59			
Total				

11.32. Safety in motels and hotels is a growing concern among travelers. Suppose a survey was conducted by the National Motel and Hotel Association to determine U.S. travelers' perception of safety in various motel chains. The association chose four different national chains from the economy lodging sector and randomly selected 10 people who had stayed overnight in a motel in each of the four chains in the past two years. Each selected traveler was asked to rate each motel chain on a scale from 0 to 100 to indicate how safe he or she felt at that motel. A score of 0 indicates completely unsafe and a score of 100 indicates perfectly safe. The scores follow. Test this randomized block design to determine whether there is a significant difference in the safety ratings of the four motels. Use $\alpha = .05$.

TRAVELER	MOTEL 1	MOTEL 2	MOTEL 3	MOTEL 4
1	40	30	55	45
2	65	50	80	70
3	60	55	60	60
4	20	40	55	50
5	50	35	65	60
6	30	30	50	50
7	55	30	60	55
8	70	70	70	70
9	65	60	80	75
10	45	25	45	50

11.33. In recent years, the debate over the U.S. economy has been constant. The electorate seems somewhat divided as to whether the economy is in a recovery or not. Suppose a survey was undertaken to ascertain whether the perception of economic recovery differs according to political affiliation. People were selected for the survey from the Democratic Party, the Republican Party, and those classifying themselves as independents. A 25-point scale was developed in which respondents gave a score of 25 if they felt the economy was definitely in complete recovery, a 0 if the economy was definitely not in a recovery, and some value in between for more uncertain responses. To control for differences in socioeconomic class, a blocking variable was maintained using five different socioeconomic categories. The data are given here in the form of a randomized block design. Use $\alpha = .01$ to determine whether there is a significant difference in mean responses according to political affiliation.

SOCIOECONOMIC CLASS	POLITICAL AFFILIATION		
	DEMOCRAT	REPUBLICAN	INDEPENDENT
Upper	11	5	8
Upper middle	15	9	8
Middle	19	14	15
Lower middle	16	12	10
Lower	9	8	7

11.34. As part of a manufacturing process, a plastic container is supposed to be filled with 46 ounces of saltwater solution. The plant has three machines that fill the containers. Managers are concerned that the machines might not be filling the containers with the same amount of saltwater solution, so they set up a randomized block design to test this concern. A pool of five machine operators operates each of the three machines at different times. Company technicians randomly select five containers filled by each machine (one container for each of the five operators). The measurements are gathered and analyzed. The Minitab output from this analysis follows. What was the structure of the design? How many blocks were there? How many treatment classifications? Is there a statistical difference in the

treatment means? Are the blocking effects significant? Discuss the implications of the output.

```
Two-way ANOVA: Measurement versus Machine, Operator
Source    DF    SS      MS      F      P
Machine    2    78.30   39.15   6.72   .019
Operator   4     5.09    1.27   0.22   .807
Error      8    46.66    5.83
Total     14   130.06
```

11.35. The comptroller of a company is interested in determining whether the average length of long-distance calls by managers varies according to type of telephone. A randomized block design experiment is set up in which a long-distance call by each of five managers is sampled for four different types of telephones: cellular, computer, regular, and cordless. The treatment is type of telephone and the blocks are the managers. The results of analysis by Excel are shown here. Discuss the results and any implications they might have for the company.

Anova: Two-Factor Without Replication

ANOVA

Source of Variation	SS	df	MS	F	P-value	F crit
Managers	11.3346	4	2.8336	12.74	0.00028	3.26
Phone Type	10.6043	3	3.5348	15.89	0.00018	3.49
Error	2.6696	12	0.2225			
Total	24.6085	19				

 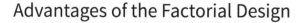

A Factorial Design (Two-Way Anova)

Some experiments are designed so that *two or more treatments* (independent variables) *are explored simultaneously.* Such experimental designs are referred to as **factorial designs.** In factorial designs, *every level of each treatment is studied under the conditions of every level of all other treatments.* Factorial designs can be arranged such that three, four, or *n* treatments or independent variables are studied simultaneously in the same experiment. As an example, consider the valve opening data in Table 11.1. The mean valve opening for the 24 measurements is 6.34 centimeters. However, every valve but one in the sample measures something other than the mean. Why? Company management realizes that valves at this firm are made on different machines, by different operators, on different shifts, on different days, with raw materials from different suppliers. Business researchers who are interested in finding the sources of variation might decide to set up a factorial design that incorporates all five of these independent variables in one study. In this text, we explore the factorial designs with two treatments only.

Advantages of the Factorial Design

If two independent variables are analyzed by using a completely randomized design, the effects of each variable are explored separately (one per design). Thus, it takes two completely randomized designs to analyze the effects of the two independent variables. By using a factorial design, the business researcher can analyze both variables at the same time in one design, saving the time and effort of doing two different analyses and minimizing the experiment-wise error rate.

Some business researchers use the factorial design as a way to control confounding or concomitant variables in a study. By building variables into the design, the researcher attempts to control for the effects of multiple variables *in* the experiment. With the completely randomized design, the variables are studied in isolation. With the factorial design, there is potential for increased power over the completely randomized design because the additional effects of the second variable are removed from the error sum of squares.

The researcher can explore the possibility of interaction between the two treatment variables in a two-factor factorial design if multiple measurements are taken under every combination of levels of the two treatments. Interaction will be discussed later.

Factorial designs with two treatments are similar to randomized block designs. However, whereas randomized block designs focus on one treatment variable and control for a blocking effect, a two-treatment factorial design focuses on the effects of both variables. Because the randomized block design contains only one measure for each (treatment-block) combination, interaction cannot be analyzed in randomized block designs.

Factorial Designs with Two Treatments

The structure of a two-treatment factorial design is featured in **Figure 11.9**. Note that there are two independent variables (two treatments) and that there is an intersection of each level of each treatment. These intersections are referred to as *cells*. One treatment is arbitrarily designated as *row* treatment (forming the rows of the design) and the other treatment is designated as *column* treatment (forming the columns of the design). Although it is possible to analyze factorial designs with unequal numbers of items in the cells, the analysis of unequal cell designs is beyond the scope of this text. All factorial designs discussed here have cells of equal size.

Treatments (independent variables) of factorial designs must have at least two levels each. The simplest factorial design is a 2×2 factorial design, where each treatment has two levels. If such a factorial design were diagrammed in the manner of Figure 11.9, it would include two rows and two columns, forming four cells.

In this section, we study only factorial designs with $n > 1$ measurements for each combination of treatment levels (cells). This approach allows us to attempt to measure the interaction of the treatment variables. As with the completely randomized design and the randomized block design, a factorial design contains only one dependent variable.

Applications

Many applications of the factorial design are possible in business research. For example, the natural gas industry can design an experiment to study usage rates and how they are affected by temperature and precipitation. Theorizing that the outside temperature and type of precipitation make a difference in natural gas usage, industry researchers can gather usage measurements for a given community over a variety of temperature and precipitation conditions. At the same time, they can make an effort to determine whether certain types of precipitation, combined with certain temperature levels, affect usage rates differently from other combinations of temperature and precipitation (interaction effects).

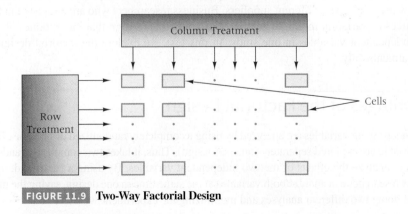

FIGURE 11.9 **Two-Way Factorial Design**

Stock market analysts can select a company from an industry such as the construction industry and observe the behavior of its stock under different conditions. A factorial design can be set up by using volume of the stock market and prime interest rate as two independent variables. For volume of the market, business researchers can select some days when the volume is up from the day before, some days when the volume is down from the day before, and some other days when the volume is essentially the same as on the preceding day. These groups of days would constitute three levels of the independent variable, market volume. Business researchers can do the same thing with prime rate. Levels can be selected such that the prime rate is (1) up, (2) down, and (3) essentially the same. For the dependent variable, the researchers would measure how much the company's stock rises or falls on those randomly selected days (stock change). Using the factorial design, the business researcher can determine whether stock changes are different under various levels of market volume, whether stock changes are different under various levels of the prime interest rate, and whether stock changes react differently under various combinations of volume and prime rate (interaction effects).

Statistically Testing the Factorial Design

Analysis of variance is used to analyze data gathered from factorial designs. For factorial designs with two factors (independent variables), a **two-way analysis of variance (two-way ANOVA)** is used to test hypotheses statistically. The following hypotheses are tested by a two-way ANOVA.

Row effects:	H_0: Row means all are equal.
	H_a: At least one row mean is different from the others.
Column effects:	H_0: Column means are all equal.
	H_a: At least one column mean is different from the others.
Interaction effects:	H_0: The interaction effects are zero.
	H_a: An interaction effect is present.

Formulas for computing a two-way ANOVA are given in the following box. These formulas are computed in a manner similar to computations for the completely randomized design and the randomized block design. F values are determined for three effects:

1. Row effects

2. Column effects

3. Interaction effects

The row effects and the column effects are sometimes referred to as the main effects. Although F values are determined for these main effects, an F value is also computed for interaction effects. Using these observed F values, the researcher can make a decision about the null hypotheses for each effect.

Each of these observed F values is compared to a table F value. The table F value is determined by α, df_{num}, and df_{denom}. The degrees of freedom for the numerator (df_{num}) are determined by the effect being studied. If the observed F value is for columns, the degrees of freedom for the numerator are $C - 1$. If the observed F value is for rows, the degrees of freedom for the numerator are $R - 1$. If the observed F value is for interaction, the degrees of freedom for the numerator are $(R - 1)(C - 1)$. The number of degrees of freedom for the denominator of the table value for each of the three effects is the same, the error degrees of freedom, $RC(n - 1)$. The table F values (critical F) for a two-way ANOVA follow.

Table F Values for a Two-Way Anova

Row effects:	$F_{\alpha, R-1, RC(n-1)}$
Column effects:	$F_{\alpha, C-1, RC(n-1)}$
Interaction effects:	$F_{\alpha, (R-1)(C-1), RC(n-1)}$

Formulas for Computing a Two-Way ANOVA

$$SSR = nC\sum_{i=1}^{R}(\bar{x}_i - \bar{x})^2$$

$$SSC = nR\sum_{j=1}^{C}(\bar{x}_j - \bar{x})^2$$

$$SSI = n\sum_{i=1}^{R}\sum_{j=1}^{C}(\bar{x}_{ij} - \bar{x}_i - \bar{x}_j + \bar{x})^2$$

$$SSE = \sum_{i=1}^{R}\sum_{j=1}^{C}\sum_{k=1}^{n}(x_{ijk} - \bar{x}_{ij})^2$$

$$SST = \sum_{i=1}^{R}\sum_{j=1}^{C}\sum_{k=1}^{n}(x_{ijk} - \bar{x})^2$$

$$df_R = R - 1$$

$$df_C = C - 1$$

$$df_I = (R - 1)(C - 1)$$

$$df_E = RC(n - 1)$$

$$df_T = N - 1$$

$$MSR = \frac{SSR}{R - 1}$$

$$MSC = \frac{SSC}{C - 1}$$

$$MSI = \frac{SSI}{(R - 1)(C - 1)}$$

$$MSE = \frac{SSE}{RC(n - 1)}$$

$$F_R = \frac{MSR}{MSE}$$

$$F_C = \frac{MSC}{MSE}$$

$$F_I = \frac{MSI}{MSE}$$

where

n = number of observations per cell
C = number of column treatments
R = number of row treatments
i = row treatment level
j = column treatment level
k = cell member
x_{ijk} = individual observation
$\bar{x}_{ij}$ = cell mean
$\bar{x}_i$ = row mean
$\bar{x}_j$ = column mean
$\bar{x}$ = grand mean

Interaction

As noted before, along with testing the effects of the two treatments in a factorial design, it is possible to test for the interaction effects of the two treatments whenever multiple measures are taken in each cell of the design. **Interaction** occurs *when the effects of one treatment vary according to the levels of treatment of the other effect*. For example, in a study examining the impact of temperature and humidity on a manufacturing process, it is possible that temperature and humidity will interact in such a way that the effect of temperature on the process varies with the humidity. Low temperatures might not be a significant manufacturing factor when humidity is low but might be a factor when humidity is high. Similarly, high temperatures might be a factor with low humidity but not with high humidity.

As another example, suppose a business researcher is studying the amount of red meat consumed by families per month and is examining economic class and religion as two independent variables. Class and religion might interact in such a way that with certain religions, economic class does not matter in the consumption of red meat, but with other religions, class does make a difference.

In terms of the factorial design, interaction occurs when the pattern of cell means in one row (going across columns) varies from the pattern of cell means in other rows. This variation indicates that the differences in column effects depend on which row is being examined. Hence, an interaction of the rows and columns occurs. The same thing can happen when the pattern of cell means within a column is different from the pattern of cell means in other columns.

Interaction can be depicted graphically by plotting the cell means within each row (and can also be done by plotting the cell means within each column). The means within each row (or column) are then connected by a line. If the broken lines for the rows (or columns) are parallel, no interaction is indicated.

Figure 11.10 is a graph of the means for each cell in each row in a 2×3 (2 rows, 3 columns) factorial design with interaction. Note that the lines connecting the means in each row cross each other. In Figure 11.11 the lines converge, indicating the likely presence of some interaction. Figure 11.12 depicts a 2×3 factorial design with no interaction.

When the interaction effects are significant, the main effects (row and column) are confounded and should not be analyzed in the usual manner. In this case, it is not possible to state unequivocally that the row effects or the column effects are significantly different because the difference in means of one main effect varies according to the level of the other main effect (interaction is present). Some specific procedures are recommended for examining main effects when significant interaction is present. However, these techniques are beyond the scope of material presented here. Hence, in this text, whenever interaction effects are present (F_{inter} is significant), the researcher should *not* attempt to interpret the main effects (F_{row} and F_{col}).

As an example of a factorial design, consider the fact that at the end of a financially successful fiscal year, CEOs often must decide whether to award a dividend to stockholders or to make a company investment. One factor in this decision would seem to be whether attractive investment opportunities are available.* To determine whether this factor is important, business

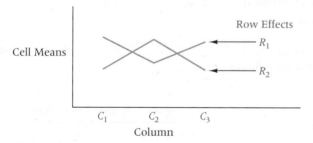

FIGURE 11.10 A 2×3 **Factorial Design with Interaction**

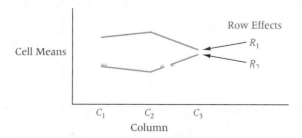

FIGURE 11.11 A 2×3 **Factorial Design with Some Interaction**

*Adapted from H. Kent Baker, "Why Companies Pay No Dividends," *Akron Business and Economic Review*, vol. 20 (Summer 1989), pp. 48–61.

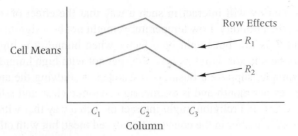

FIGURE 11.12 **A 2 × 3 Factorial Design with No Interaction**

researchers randomly select 24 CEOs and ask them to rate how important "availability of profitable investment opportunities" is in deciding whether to pay dividends or invest. The CEOs are requested to respond to this item on a scale from 0 to 4, where 0 = no importance, 1 = slight importance, 2 = moderate importance, 3 = great importance, and 4 = maximum importance. The 0–4 response is the dependent variable in the experimental design.

The business researchers are concerned that where the company's stock is traded (New York Stock Exchange, American Stock Exchange, and over-the-counter) might make a difference in the CEOs' response to the question. In addition, the business researchers believe that how stockholders are informed of dividends (annual reports versus presentations) might affect the outcome of the experiment. Thus, a two-way ANOVA is set up with "where the company's stock is traded" and "how stockholders are informed of dividends" as the two independent variables. The variable "how stockholders are informed of dividends" has two treatment levels, or classifications.

1. Annual/quarterly reports

2. Presentations to analysts

The variable "where company stock is traded" has three treatment levels, or classifications.

1. New York Stock Exchange

2. American Stock Exchange

3. Over-the-counter

This factorial design is a 2 × 3 design (2 rows, 3 columns) with four measurements (ratings) per cell, as shown in the following table.

		Where Company Stock Is Traded			
		New York Stock Exchange	*American Stock Exchange*	*Over the Counter*	$\overline{X}_i =$
How Stockholders Are Informed of Dividends	*Annual Quarterly Reports*	2 1 2 1 $\overline{X}_{11} = 1.5$	2 3 3 2 $\overline{X}_{12} = 2.5$	4 3 4 3 $\overline{X}_{13} = 3.5$	2.5
	Presentations to Analysts	2 3 1 2 $\overline{X}_{21} = 2.0$	3 3 2 4 $\overline{X}_{22} = 3.0$	4 4 3 4 $\overline{X}_{23} = 3.75$	2.9167
	$\overline{X}_j =$	1.75	2.75	3.625	

$$\overline{X} = 2.7083$$

These data are analyzed by using a two-way analysis of variance and $\alpha = .05$.

$$SSR = nC\sum_{i=1}^{R}(\bar{x}_i - \bar{x})^2$$
$$= 4(3)[(2.5 - 2.7083)^2 + (2.9167 - 2.7083)^2] = 1.0418$$

$$SSC = nR\sum_{j=1}^{C}(\bar{x}_i - \bar{x})^2$$
$$= 4(2)[(1.75 - 2.7083)^2 + (2.75 - 2.7083)^2 + (3.625 - 2.7083)^2] = 14.0833$$

$$SSI = n\sum_{i=1}^{R}\sum_{j=1}^{C}(\bar{x}_{ij} - \bar{x}_i - \bar{x}_j + \bar{x})^2$$
$$= 4[(1.5 - 2.5 - 1.75 + 2.7083)^2 + (2.5 - 2.5 - 2.75 + 2.7083)^2$$
$$+ (3.5 - 2.5 - 3.625 + 2.7083)^2 + (2.0 - 2.9167 - 1.75 + 2.7083)^2$$
$$+ (3.0 - 2.9167 - 2.75 + 2.7083)^2 + (3.75 - 2.9167 - 3.625 + 2.7083)^2] = .0833$$

$$SSE = \sum_{i=1}^{R}\sum_{j=1}^{C}\sum_{k=1}^{n}(x_{ijk} - \bar{x}_{ij})^2$$
$$= (2 - 1.5)^2 + (1 - 1.5)^2 + \cdots + (3 - 3.75)^2 + (4 - 3.75)^2 = 7.7500$$

$$SST = \sum_{i=1}^{R}\sum_{j=1}^{C}\sum_{k=1}^{n}(x_{ijk} - \bar{x})^2$$
$$= (2 - 2.7083)^2 + (1 - 2.7083)^2 + \cdots + (3 - 2.7083)^2 + (4 - 2.7083)^2 = 22.9583$$

$$MSR = \frac{SSR}{R-1} = \frac{1.0418}{1} = 1.0418$$

$$MSC = \frac{SSC}{C-1} = \frac{14.0833}{2} = 7.0417$$

$$MSI = \frac{SSI}{(R-1)(C-1)} = \frac{.0833}{2} = .0417$$

$$MSE = \frac{SSE}{RC(n-1)} = \frac{7.7500}{18} = .4306$$

$$F_R = \frac{MSR}{MSE} = \frac{1.0418}{.4306} = 2.42$$

$$F_C = \frac{MSC}{MSE} = \frac{7.0417}{.4306} = 16.35$$

$$F_I = \frac{MSI}{MSE} = \frac{.0417}{.4306} = 0.10$$

SOURCE OF VARIATION	SS	df	MS	F
Row	1.0418	1	1.0418	2.42
Column	14.0833	2	7.0417	16.35*
Interaction	.0833	2	.0417	0.10
Error	7.7500	18	.4306	
Total	22.9583	23		

*Denotes significance at $\alpha = .05$.

The critical F value for the interaction effects at $\alpha = .05$ is
$$F_{.05,2,18} = 3.55.$$

The observed F value for interaction effects is 0.10. Because this value is less than the critical table value (3.55), no significant interaction effects are evident. Because no significant interaction effects are present, it is possible to examine the main effects.

The critical F value of the row effects at $\alpha = .05$ is $F_{.05,1,18} = 4.41$. The observed F value of 2.42 is less than the table value. Hence, no significant row effects are present.

The critical F value of the column effects at $\alpha = .05$ is $F_{.05,2,18} = 3.55$. This value is coincidently the same as the critical table value for interaction because in this problem the degrees of freedom are the same for interaction and column effects. The observed F value for columns (16.35) is greater than this critical value. Hence, a significant difference in column effects is evident at $\alpha = .05$.

A significant difference is noted in the CEOs' mean ratings of the item "availability of profitable investment opportunities" according to where the company's stock is traded. A cursory examination of the means for the three levels of the column effects (where stock is traded) reveals that the lowest mean was from CEOs whose company traded stock on the New York Stock Exchange. The highest mean rating was from CEOs whose company traded stock over-the-counter. Using multiple comparison techniques, the business researchers can statistically test for differences in the means of these three groups.

Because the sample sizes within each column are equal, Tukey's HSD test can be used to compute multiple comparisons. The value of MSE is .431 for this problem. In testing the column means with Tukey's HSD test, the value of n is the number of items in a column, which is eight. The number of treatments is $C = 3$ for columns and $N - C = 24 - 3 = 21$.

With these two values and $\alpha = .05$, a value for q can be determined from Table A.10:

$$q_{.05,3,21} = 3.58$$

From these values, the honestly significant difference can be computed:

$$\text{HSD} = q\sqrt{\frac{\text{MSE}}{n}} = 3.58\sqrt{\frac{.431}{8}} = .831$$

The mean ratings for the three columns are

$$\bar{x}_1 = 1.75, \quad \bar{x}_2 = 2.75, \quad \bar{x}_3 = 3.625$$

The absolute value of differences between means are as follows:

$$|\bar{x}_1 - \bar{x}_2| = |1.75 - 2.75| = 1.00$$
$$|\bar{x}_1 - \bar{x}_3| = |1.75 - 3.625| = 1.875$$
$$|\bar{x}_2 - \bar{x}_3| = |2.75 - 3.625| = .875$$

All three differences are greater than .831 and are therefore significantly different at $\alpha = .05$ by the HSD test. Where a company's stock is traded makes a difference in the way a CEO responds to the question.

Using a Computer to Do a Two-Way ANOVA

A two-way ANOVA can be computed by using either Minitab or Excel. **Figure 11.13** displays the Minitab and Excel output for the CEO example. The Minitab output contains an ANOVA table with each of the three F values and their associated p-values.

The Excel output for two-way ANOVA with replications on the CEO dividend example is included in Figure 11.13. The Excel output contains cell, column, and row means along with observed F values for rows (sample), columns, and interaction. The Excel output also contains p-values and critical F values for each of these F's. Note that the output here is virtually identical to the findings obtained by the manual calculations.

Minitab Output

Analysis of Variance

```
Source          DF    SS        MS       F       P
Where Traded     2    14.0833   7.0417   16.35   0.000
How Reported     1     1.0417   1.0417    2.42   0.137
Interaction      2     0.0833   0.0417    0.10   0.908
Error           18     7.7500   0.4306
Total           23    22.9583

S = 0.656167   R-Sq = 66.24%   R-Sq(adj) = 56.87%
```

Excel Output

Anova: Two-factor With Replication

SUMMARY	NYSE	ASE	OTC	Total
A.Q. Reports				
Count	4	4	4	12
sum	6	10	14	30
Average	1.5	2.5	3.5	2.5
Variance	0.3333	0.3333	0.3333	1
Pres. to Analysis				
Count	4	4	4	12
sum	8	12	15	35
Average	2	3	3.75	2.9167
Variance	0.6667	0.6667	0.25	0.9924
Total				
Count	8	8	8	
sum	14	22	29	
Average	1.75	2.75	3.625	
Variance	0.5	0.5	0.2679	

ANOVA

Source of Variation	SS	df	MS	F	P-value	F crit
Sample	1.0417	1	1.0417	2.42	0.13725	4.41
Columns	14.0833	2	7.0417	16.35	0.00009	3.55
Interaction	0.0833	2	0.0417	0.10	0.90823	3.55
Within	7.7500	18	0.4306			
Total	22.9583	23				

FIGURE 11.13 **Minitab and Excel Output for the CEO Dividend Problem**

DEMONSTRATION PROBLEM 11.4

Some theorists believe that training warehouse workers can reduce absenteeism.* Suppose an experimental design is structured to test this belief. Warehouses in which training sessions have been held for workers are selected for the study. The four types of warehouses are (1) general merchandise, (2) commodity, (3) bulk storage, and (4) cold storage. The training sessions are differentiated by length. Researchers identify three levels of training sessions according to the length

*Adapted from Paul R. Murphy and Richard F. Poist, "Managing the Human Side of Public Warehousing: An Overview of Modern Practices," *Transportation Journal*, vol. 31 (Spring 1992), pp. 54–63.

of sessions: (1) 1–20 days, (2) 21–50 days, and (3) more than 50 days. Three warehouse workers are selected randomly for each particular combination of type of warehouse and session length. The workers are monitored for the next year to determine how many days they are absent. The resulting data are in the following 4×3 design (4 rows, 3 columns) structure. Using this information, calculate a two-way ANOVA to determine whether there are any significant differences in effects. Use $\alpha = .05$.

Solution:

Step 1. The following hypotheses are being tested.

For row effects:

$$H_0: \mu_1. = \mu_2. = \mu_3. = \mu_4.$$

$$H_a: \text{At least one of the row means is different from the others.}$$

For column effects:

$$H_0: \mu._1 = \mu._2 = \mu._3$$

$$H_a: \text{At least one of the column means is different from the others.}$$

For interaction effects:

$$H_0: \text{The interaction effects are zero.}$$

$$H_a: \text{There is an interaction effect.}$$

Step 2. The two-way ANOVA with the F test is the appropriate statistical test.

Step 3. $\alpha = .05$.

Step 4.

$$df_{rows} = 4 - 1 = 3$$
$$df_{columns} = 3 - 1 = 2$$
$$df_{interaction} = (3)(2) = 6$$
$$df_{error} = (4)(3)(2) = 24$$

For row effects, $F_{.05,3,24} = 3.01$; for column effects, $F_{.05,2,24} = 3.40$; and for interaction effects, $F_{.05,6,24} = 2.51$. For each of these effects, if any observed F value is greater than its associated critical F value, the respective null hypothesis will be rejected.

Step 5.

			Length of Training Session (Days)		
		1–20	21–50	More than 50	$\overline{X}_r$
	General Merchandise	3 4.5 4	2 2.5 2	2.5 1 1.5	2.5556
	Commodity	5 4.5 4	1 3 2.5	0 1.5 2	2.6111
Types of Warehouses	Bulk Storage	2.5 3 3.5	1 3 1.5	3.5 3.5 4	2.8333
	Cold Storage	2 2 3	5 4.5 2.5	4 4.5 5	3.6111
	$\overline{X}_c$	3.4167	2.5417	2.75	

$$\overline{X} = 2.9028$$

Step 6. The Minitab and Excel (ANOVA table only) output for this problem follows

Minitab Output

```
Two-way ANOVA: Absences versus Type of Ware, Length
   Source          DF   SS        MS         F       P
   Type of ware     3   6.4097    2.13657    3.46    0.032
   Length           2   5.0139    2.50694    4.06    0.030
   Interaction      6  33.1528    5.52546    8.94    0.000
   Error           24  14.8333    0.61806
   Total           35  59.4097
```

Excel Output

ANOVA

Source of Variation	SS	df	MS	F	P-value	F crit
Types of Warehouses	6.40972	3	2.13657	3.46	0.03221	3.01
Length of Training Session	5.01389	2	2.50694	4.06	0.03037	3.40
Interaction	33.15278	6	5.52546	8.94	0.00004	2.51
Within	14.83333	24	0.61806			
Total	59.40972	35				

Step 7.   Looking at the source of variation table, we must first examine the interaction effects. The observed F value for interaction is 8.94 for both Excel and Minitab. The observed F value for interaction is greater than the critical F value. The interaction effects are statistically significant at $\alpha = .05$. The p-value for interaction shown in Excel is .00004. The interaction effects are significant at $\alpha = .0001$. The business researcher should not bother to examine the main effects because the significant interaction confounds the main effects.

Step 8.   The significant interaction effects indicate that certain warehouse types in combination with certain lengths of training session result in different absenteeism rates than do other combinations of levels for these two variables. Using the cell means shown here, we can depict the interactions graphically.

		Length of Training Session (Days)		
		1–20	21–50	More than 50
Type of Warehouse	General Merchandise	3.8	2.2	1.7
	Commodity	4.5	2.2	1.2
	Bulk Storage	3.0	1.8	3.7
	Cold Storage	2.3	4.0	4.5

Minitab produces the following graph of the interaction.

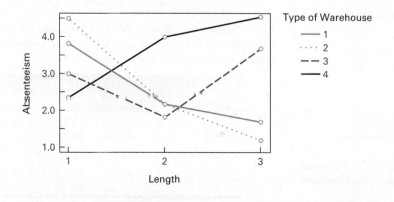

Note the intersecting and crossing lines, which indicate interaction. Under the short-length training sessions, 1, cold-storage workers had the lowest rate of absenteeism and workers at commodity warehouses had the highest. However, for medium-length sessions, 2, cold-storage workers had the highest rate of absenteeism and bulk-storage had the lowest. For the longest training sessions, 3, commodity warehouse workers had the lowest rate of absenteeism, even though these workers had the highest rate of absenteeism for short-length sessions. Thus, the rate of absenteeism for workers at a particular type of warehouse depended on length of session. There was an interaction between type of warehouse and length of session. This graph could be constructed with the row levels along the bottom axis instead of column levels.

11.5 Problems

11.36. Describe the following factorial design. How many independent and dependent variables are there? How many levels are there for each treatment? If the data were known, could interaction be determined from this design? Compute all degrees of freedom. Each data value is represented by an x.

	VARIABLE 1			
Variable 2	x_{111}	x_{121}	x_{131}	x_{141}
	x_{112}	x_{122}	x_{132}	x_{142}
	x_{113}	x_{123}	x_{133}	x_{143}
	x_{211}	x_{221}	x_{231}	x_{241}
	x_{212}	x_{222}	x_{232}	x_{242}
	x_{213}	x_{223}	x_{233}	x_{243}

11.37. Describe the following factorial design. How many independent and dependent variables are there? How many levels are there for each treatment? If the data were known, could interaction be determined from this design? Compute all degrees of freedom. Each data value is represented by an x.

	VARIABLE 1		
Variable 2	x_{111}	x_{121}	x_{131}
	x_{112}	x_{122}	x_{132}
	x_{211}	x_{221}	x_{231}
	x_{212}	x_{222}	x_{232}
	x_{311}	x_{321}	x_{331}
	x_{312}	x_{322}	x_{332}
	x_{411}	x_{421}	x_{431}
	x_{412}	x_{422}	x_{432}

11.38. Complete the following two-way ANOVA table. Determine the critical table F values and reach conclusions about the hypotheses for effects. Let $\alpha = .05$.

SOURCE OF VARIANCE	SS	df	MS	F
Row	126.98	3		
Column	37.49	4		
Interaction	380.82			
Error	733.65	60		
Total				

11.39. Complete the following two-way ANOVA table. Determine the critical table F values and reach conclusions about the hypotheses for effects. Let $\alpha = .05$.

SOURCE OF VARIANCE	SS	df	MS	F
Row	1.047	1		
Column	3.844	3		
Interaction	0.773			
Error				
Total	12.632	23		

11.40. The data gathered from a two-way factorial design follow. Use the two-way ANOVA to analyze these data. Let $\alpha = .01$.

		TREATMENT 1		
		A	*B*	*C*
Treatment 2	A	23	21	20
		25	21	22
	B	27	24	26
		28	27	27

11.41. Suppose the following data have been gathered from a study with a two-way factorial design. Use $\alpha = .05$ and a two-way ANOVA to analyze the data. State your conclusions.

		TREATMENT 2			
		A	*B*	*C*	D
Treatment 1	*X*	1.2 1.3	2.2 2.1	1.7 1.8	2.4 2.3
		1.3 1.5	2.0 2.3	1.7 1.6	2.5 2.4
	Y	1.9 1.6	2.7 2.5	1.9 2.2	2.8 2.6
		1.7 2.0	2.8 2.8	1.9 2.0	2.4 2.8

11.42. Children are generally believed to have considerable influence over their parents in the purchase of certain items, particularly food and beverage items. To study this notion further, a study is conducted in which parents are asked to report how many food and beverage items purchased by the family per week are purchased mainly because of the influence of their children. Because the age of the child may have an effect on the study, parents are asked to focus on one particular child in the family for the week, and to report the age of the child. Four age categories are selected for the children: 4–5 years, 6–7 years, 8–9 years, and 10–12 years. Also, because the number of children in the family might make a difference, three different sizes of families are chosen for the study: families with one child, families with two children, and families with three or more children. Suppose the following data represent the reported number of child-influenced buying incidents per week. Use the data to compute a two-way ANOVA. Let $\alpha = .05$.

| | | NUMBER OF CHILDREN IN FAMILY | | |
		1	2	3 OR MORE
	4–5	2	1	1
		4	2	1
Age of Child (years)	6–7	5	3	2
		4	1	1
	8–9	8	4	2
		6	5	3
	10–12	7	3	4
		8	5	3

11.43. A shoe retailer conducted a study to determine whether there is a difference in the number of pairs of shoes sold per day by stores according to the number of competitors within a 1-mile radius and the location of the store. The company researchers selected three types of stores for consideration in the study: stand-alone suburban stores, mall stores, and downtown stores. These stores vary in the numbers of competing stores within a 1-mile radius, which have been reduced to four categories: 0 competitors, 1 competitor, 2 competitors, and 3 or more competitors. Suppose the following data represent the number of pairs of shoes sold per day for each of these types of stores with the given number of competitors. Use $\alpha = .05$ and a two-way ANOVA to analyze the data.

| | | NUMBER OF COMPETITORS | | | |
		0	1	2	3 OR MORE
	Stand-Alone	41	38	59	47
		30	31	48	40
		45	39	51	39
Store Location	Mall	25	29	44	43
		31	35	48	42
		22	30	50	53
	Downtown	18	22	29	24
		29	17	28	27
		33	25	26	32

11.44. Study the following analysis of variance table produced by using Minitab. Describe the design (number of treatments, sample sizes, etc.). Are there any significant effects? Discuss the output.

```
Analysis of Variance for DV

Source      DF    SS       MS       F       P
RowEffect    2    92.31    46.16    13.23   0.000
ColEffect    4   998.80   249.70    71.57   0.000
Row*Column   8   442.13    55.27    15.84   0.000
Error       30   104.67     3.49
Total       44  1637.91

S = 1.86786  R-Sq = 93.61%  R-Sq(adj) = 90.63%
```

11.45. Consider the valve opening data displayed in Table 11.1. Suppose the data represent valves produced on four different machines on three different shifts and that the quality controllers want to know whether there is any difference in the mean measurements of valve openings by shift or by machine. The data are given here, organized by machine and shift. In addition, Excel has been used to analyze the data with a two-way ANOVA. What are the hypotheses for this problem? Study the output in terms of significant differences. Discuss the results obtained. What conclusions might the quality controllers reach from this analysis?

| | | VALVE OPENINGS (cm) | | |
		SHIFT 1	SHIFT 2	SHIFT 3
	1	6.56	6.38	6.29
		6.40	6.19	6.23
	2	6.54	6.26	6.19
Machine		6.34	6.23	6.33
	3	6.58	6.22	6.26
		6.44	6.27	6.31
	4	6.36	6.29	6.21
		6.50	6.19	6.58

ANOVA: Two-Factor with Replication

ANOVA

Source of Variation	SS	df	MS	F	P-value	F crit
Sample	0.00538	3	0.00179	0.14	0.9368	3.49
Columns	0.19731	2	0.09865	7.47	0.0078	3.89
Interaction	0.03036	6	0.00506	0.38	0.8760	3.00
Within	0.15845	12	0.01320			
Total	0.39150	23				

11.46. Finish the computations in the Minitab ANOVA table shown below and determine the critical table F values. Interpret the analysis. Discuss this problem, including the structure of the design, the sample sizes, and decisions about the hypotheses.

```
Analysis of Variance for depvar

Source        DF    SS       MS
Row            2    0.296    0.148
Column         2    1.852    0.926
Interaction    4    4.370    1.093
Error         18   14.000    0.778
Total         26   20.519
```

Decision Dilemma Solved

Is there a difference in the job satisfaction ratings of self-initiated expatriates by industry? The data presented in the Decision Dilemma to study this question represent responses on a seven-point Likert scale by 24 self-initiated expatriates from five different industries. The Likert scale score is the dependent variable. There is only one independent variable, industry, with five classification levels: IT, finance, education, healthcare, and consulting. If a series of t tests for the difference of two means from independent populations were used to analyze these data, there would be $_5C_2$ or 10 different t tests on this one problem. Using $\alpha = .05$ for each test, the probability of at least one of the 10 tests being significant by chance when the null hypothesis is true is $1 - (.95)^{10} = .4013$. That is, performing 10 t tests on this problem could result in an overall probability of committing a Type I error equal to .4013, not .05. In order to control the overall error, a one-way ANOVA is used on this completely randomized design to analyze these data by producing a single value of F and holding the probability of committing a Type I error at .05. Both Excel and Minitab have the capability of analyzing these data, and Minitab output for this problem is shown below.

```
Analysis of Variance
Source  DF  Adj SS  Adj MS   F-Value  P-Value
Factor   4  43.18   10.7938  15.25    0.000
Error   19  13.45    0.7079
Total   23  56.63

Model Summary
S         R-sq    R-sq(adj)  R-sq(pred)
0.841365  76.25%  71.25%     61.40%
```

With an F value of 15.25 and a p-value of 0.000, the results of the one-way ANOVA show that there is an overall significant difference in job satisfaction between the five industries. Examining the Minitab confidence intervals shown graphically suggests that there might be a significant difference between some pairs of industries. Because there was an overall significant difference in the industries, it is appropriate to use Tukey's HSD test to determine which of the pairs of industries are significantly different. Tukey's test controls for the overall error so that the problem mentioned previously arising from computing ten t tests is avoided. The Minitab output for Tukey's test is:

```
Tukey Pairwise Comparisons
Grouping Information Using the Tukey
Method and 95% Confidence

Factor        N    Mean     Grouping
Consulting    4    6.000    A
It            4    5.750    A
Finance       5    4.000         B
Healthcare    5    3.400         B
Education     6    2.500         B

Means that do not share a letter are
significantly different.
```

The grouping information reveals that there are significant differences between consulting and finance, consulting and healthcare, consulting and education, IT and finance, IT and healthcare, and IT and education because the members in each pair did not share a letter.

In analyzing career satisfaction, self-initiated expatriates were sampled from three age categories and four categories of time in the host country. This experimental design is a two-way factorial design with age and time in the host country as independent variables and individual scores on the seven-point Likert scale being the dependent variable. There are three classification levels under the independent variable Age: 30–39, 40–49, and over 50, and there are four classifications under the independent variable Time in Host Country: <1 year, 1 to 2 years, 3 to 4 years, and 5 or more years. Because there is more than one score per cell, interaction can be analyzed. A two-way ANOVA with replication is run in Excel to analyze the data and the result is shown below.

An examination of this output reveals no significant interaction effects (p-value of 0.929183). Since there are no significant interaction effects, it is appropriate to examine the main effects. Because of a p-value of 0.00008, there is a significant difference in Time in Host Country using an alpha of 0.0001. Multiple comparison analysis could be done to determine which, if any, pairs of Time in Host Country are significantly different. The p-value for Age is 0.07392, indicating that there is a significant difference between Age classifications at alpha 0.10 but not at alpha of 0.05.

Excel Output:

ANOVA

Source of Variation	SS	df	MS	F	P-value	F crit
Age	3.5556	2	1.7778	2.91	0.07392	3.40
Time in Host Country	20.9722	3	6.9907	11.44	0.00008	3.01
Interaction	1.1111	6	0.1852	0.30	0.92918	2.51
Within	14.6667	24	0.6111			
Total	40.3056	35				

Ethical Considerations

In theory, any phenomenon that affects the dependent variable in an experiment should be either entered into the experimental design or controlled in the experiment. Researchers will sometimes report statistical findings from an experiment and fail to mention the possible concomitant variables that were neither controlled by the experimental setting nor controlled by the experimental design. The findings from such studies are highly questionable and often lead to spurious conclusions. Scientifically, the researcher needs to conduct the experiment in an environment such that as many concomitant variables are controlled as possible. To the extent that they are not controlled, the researcher has an ethical responsibility to report that fact in the findings.

Other ethical considerations enter into conducting research with experimental designs. Selection of treatment levels should be done with fairness or even randomness in cases where the treatment has several possibilities for levels. A researcher can build in skewed views of the treatment effects by erroneously selecting treatment levels to be studied. Some researchers believe that reporting significant main effects from a factorial design when there are confounding interaction effects is unethical or at least misleading.

Another ethical consideration is the leveling of sample sizes. Some designs, such as the two-way factorial design or completely randomized design with Tukey's HSD, require equal sample sizes. Sometimes unequal sample sizes arise either through the selection process or through attrition. A number of techniques for approaching this problem are not presented in this book. It remains highly unethical to make up data values or to eliminate values arbitrarily to produce equal sample sizes.

Summary

Sound business research requires that the researcher plan a design for the experiment before a study is undertaken. The design of the experiment should encompass the treatment variables to be studied, manipulated, and controlled. These variables are often referred to as the independent variables. It is possible to study several independent variables and several levels, or classifications, of each of those variables in one design. In addition, the researcher selects one measurement to be taken from sample items under the conditions of the experiment. This measurement is referred to as the dependent variable because if the treatment effect is significant, the measurement of the dependent variable will "depend" on the independent variable(s) selected. This chapter explored three types of experimental designs: completely randomized design, randomized block design, and the factorial experimental designs.

The completely randomized design is the simplest of the experimental designs presented in this chapter. It has only one independent, or treatment, variable. With the completely randomized design, subjects are assigned randomly to treatments. If the treatment variable has only two levels, the design becomes identical to the one used to test the difference in means of independent populations presented in Chapter 10. The data from a completely randomized design are analyzed by a one-way analysis of variance (ANOVA). A one-way ANOVA produces an F value that can be compared to table F values in Appendix A.7 to determine whether the ANOVA F value is statistically significant. If it is, the null hypothesis that all population means are equal is rejected and at least one of the means is different from the others. Analysis of variance does not tell the researcher which means, if any, are significantly different from others. Although the researcher can visually examine means to determine which ones are greater and lesser, statistical techniques called multiple comparisons must be used to determine statistically whether pairs of means are significantly different.

Two types of multiple comparison techniques are presented and used in this chapter: Tukey's HSD test and the Tukey-Kramer procedure. Tukey's HSD test requires that equal sample sizes be used. It utilizes the mean square of error from the ANOVA, the sample size, and a q value that is obtained from Table A.10 to solve for the least difference between a pair of means that would be significant (HSD). The absolute value of the difference in sample means is compared to the HSD value to determine statistical significance. The Tukey-Kramer procedure is used in the case of unequal sample sizes.

A second experimental design is the randomized block design. This design contains a treatment variable (independent variable) and a blocking variable. The independent variable is the main variable of interest in this design. The blocking variable is a variable the researcher is interested in controlling rather than studying. A special case of randomized block design is the repeated measures design, in which the blocking variable represents subjects or items for which repeated measures are taken across the full range of treatment levels.

In randomized block designs, the variation of the blocking variable is removed from the error variance. This approach can potentially make the test of treatment effects more powerful. If the blocking variable contains no significant differences, the blocking can make the treatment effects test less powerful. Usually an F is computed only for the treatment effects in a randomized block design. Sometimes an F value is computed for blocking effects to determine whether the blocking was useful in the experiment.

A third experimental design is the factorial design. A factorial design enables the researcher to test the effects of two or more independent variables simultaneously. In complete factorial designs, every treatment level of each independent variable is studied under the conditions of every other treatment level for all independent variables. This chapter focused only on factorial designs with two independent variables. Each independent variable can have two or more treatment levels. These two-way factorial designs are analyzed by two-way analysis of variance (ANOVA). This analysis produces an F value for each of the two treatment effects and for interaction. Interaction is present when the results of one treatment vary significantly according to the levels of the other treatment. At least two measurements per cell must be present in order to compute interaction. If the F value for interaction is statistically significant, the main effects of the experiment are confounded and should not be examined in the usual manner.

Key Terms

a posteriori	concomitant variables	factors	randomized block design
a priori	confounding variables	independent variable	repeated measures design
analysis of variance (ANOVA)	dependent variable	interaction	treatment variable
blocking variable	experimental design	levels	Tukey-Kramer procedure
classification variable	F distribution	multiple comparisons	Tukey's HSD test
classifications	F value	one-way analysis of variance	two-way analysis
completely randomized design	factorial design	post hoc	of variance

Formulas

Formulas for computing a one-way ANOVA

$$SSC = \sum_{j=1}^{C} n_j (\bar{x}_j - \bar{x})^2$$

$$SSE = \sum_{j=1}^{C} \sum_{i=1}^{n_j} (x_{ij} - \bar{x}_j)^2$$

$$SST = \sum_{j=1}^{C} \sum_{i=1}^{n_j} (x_{ij} - \bar{x})^2$$

$$df_C = C - 1$$

$$df_E = N - C$$

$$df_T = N - 1$$

$$MSC = \frac{SSC}{C - 1}$$

$$MSE = \frac{SSE}{N - C}$$

$$F = \frac{MSC}{MSE}$$

Tukey's HSD test

$$HSD = q_{\alpha,C,N-C} \sqrt{\frac{MSE}{n}}$$

Tukey-Kramer formula

$$q_{\alpha,C,N-C} \sqrt{\frac{MSE}{2} \left(\frac{1}{n_r} + \frac{1}{n_s} \right)}$$

Formulas for computing a randomized block design

$$SSC = n \sum_{j=1}^{C} (\bar{x}_j - \bar{x})^2$$

$$SSR = C \sum_{i=1}^{n} (\bar{x}_i - \bar{x})^2$$

$$SSE = \sum_{j=1}^{C} \sum_{i=1}^{n} (x_{ij} - \bar{x}_j - \bar{x}_i + \bar{x})^2$$

$$SST = \sum_{j=1}^{C} \sum_{i=1}^{n} (x_{ij} - \bar{x})^2$$

$$df_C = C - 1$$

$$df_R = n - 1$$

$$df_E = (C - 1)(n - 1) = N - n - C + 1$$

$$MSC = \frac{SSC}{C - 1}$$

$$MSR = \frac{SSR}{n - 1}$$

$$MSE = \frac{SSE}{N - n - C + 1}$$

$$F_{treatments} = \frac{MSC}{MSE}$$

$$F_{blocks} = \frac{MSR}{MSE}$$

Formulas for computing a two-way ANOVA

$$SSR = nC \sum_{i=1}^{R} (\bar{x}_i - \bar{x})^2$$

$$SSC = nR \sum_{j=1}^{C} (\bar{x}_j - \bar{x})^2$$

$$SSI = n \sum_{i=1}^{R} \sum_{j=1}^{C} (\bar{x}_{ij} - \bar{x}_i - \bar{x}_j + \bar{x})^2$$

$$SSE = \sum_{i=1}^{R} \sum_{j=1}^{C} \sum_{k=1}^{n} (x_{ijk} - \bar{x}_{ij})^2$$

$$SST = \sum_{i=1}^{R} \sum_{j=1}^{C} \sum_{k=1}^{n} (x_{ijk} - \bar{x})^2$$

$$df_R = R - 1$$

$$df_C = C - 1$$

$$df_I = (R - 1)(C - 1)$$

$$df_E = RC(n - 1)$$

$$df_T = N - 1$$

$$MSR = \frac{SSR}{R - 1}$$

$$MSC = \frac{SSC}{C - 1}$$

$$MSI = \frac{SSI}{(R - 1)(C - 1)}$$

$$MSE = \frac{SSE}{RC(n - 1)}$$

$$F_R = \frac{MSR}{MSE}$$

$$F_C = \frac{MSC}{MSE}$$

$$F_I = \frac{MSI}{MSE}$$

Supplementary Problems

Calculating the Statistics

11.47. Compute a one-way ANOVA on the following data. Use $\alpha = .05$. If there is a significant difference in treatment levels, use Tukey's HSD to compute multiple comparisons. Let $\alpha = .05$ for the multiple comparisons.

TREATMENT			
1	*2*	*3*	*4*
10	9	12	10
12	7	13	10
15	9	14	13
11	6	14	12

11.48. Complete the following ANOVA table.

SOURCE OF VARIANCE	SS	df	MS	F
Treatment				
Error	249.61	19		
Total	317.80	25		

11.49. You are asked to analyze a completely randomized design that has six treatment levels and a total of 42 measurements. Complete the following table, which contains some information from the study.

SOURCE OF VARIANCE	SS	df	MS	F
Treatment	210			
Error	655			
Total				

11.50. Compute a one-way ANOVA on the following data. Let $\alpha = .01$. Use the Tukey-Kramer procedure to conduct multiple comparisons for the means.

TREATMENT		
1	*2*	*3*
7	11	8
12	17	6
9	16	10

11	13	9
8	10	11
9	15	7
11	14	10
10	18	
7		
8		

11.51. Examine the structure of the following experimental design. Determine which of the three designs presented in the chapter would be most likely to characterize this structure. Discuss the variables and the levels of variables. Determine the degrees of freedom.

	METHODOLOGY		
PERSON	METHOD 1	METHOD 2	METHOD 3
1	x_{11}	x_{12}	x_{13}
2	x_{21}	x_{22}	x_{23}
3	x_{31}	x_{32}	x_{33}
4	x_{41}	x_{42}	x_{43}
5	x_{51}	x_{52}	x_{53}
6	x_{61}	x_{62}	x_{63}

11.52. Complete the following ANOVA table and determine whether there is any significant diffrence in treatment effects. Let $\alpha = .05$.

SOURCE OF VARIANCE	SS	df	MS	F
Treatment	20,994	3		
Blocking		9		
Error	33,891			
Total	71,338			

11.53. Analyze the following data, gathered from a randomized block design using $\alpha = .05$. If there is a significant difference in the treatment effects, use Tukey's HSD test to do multiple comparisons.

	TREATMENT			
	A	*B*	*C*	*D*
	1	17	10	9	21
	2	13	9	8	16
Blocking	3	20	17	18	22
Variable	4	11	6	5	10
	5	16	13	14	22
	6	23	19	20	28

11.54. A two-way ANOVA has been computed on a factorial design. Treatment 1 has five levels and treatment 2 has two levels. Each cell contains four measures. Complete the following ANOVA table. Use $\alpha = .05$ to test to determine significance of the effects. Comment on your findings.

SOURCE OF VARIANCE	SS	df	MS	F
Treatment 1	29.13			
Treatment 2	12.67			
Interaction	73.49			
Error	110.38			
Total				

11.55. Compute a two-way ANOVA on the following data ($\alpha = .01$).

		TREATMENT 1		
		A	*B*	*C*
		5	2	2
	A	3	4	3
		6	4	5
		11	9	13
	B	8	10	12
Treatment 2		12	8	10
		6	7	4
	C	4	6	6
		5	7	8
		9	8	8
	D	11	12	9
		9	9	11

Testing Your Understanding

11.56. A company conducted a consumer research project to ascertain customer service ratings from its customers. The customers were asked to rate the company on a scale from 1 to 7 on various quality characteristics. One question was the promptness of company response to a repair problem. The following data represent customer responses to this question. The customers were divided by geographic region and by age. Use analysis of variance to analyze the responses. Let $\alpha = .05$. Compute multiple comparisons where they are appropriate. Graph the cell means and observe any interaction.

GEOGRAPHIC REGION			
SOUTHEAST	*WEST*	*MIDWEST*	*NORTHEAST*
3	2	3	2
21–35	2	4	3	3

	3	3	2	2
	5	4	5	6
Age 36–50	5	4	6	4
	4	6	5	5
	3	2	3	3
Over 50	1	2	2	2
	2	3	3	1

11.57. A major automobile manufacturer wants to know whether there is any difference in the average mileage of four different brands of tires (A, B, C, and D), because the manufacturer is trying to select the best supplier in terms of tire durability. The manufacturer selects comparable levels of tires from each company and tests some on comparable cars. The mileage results follow.

A	B	C	D
31,000	24,000	30,500	24,500
25,000	25,500	28,000	27,000
28,500	27,000	32,500	26,000
29,000	26,500	28,000	21,000
32,000	25,000	31,000	25,500
27,500	28,000		26,000
	27,500		

Use $\alpha = .05$ to test whether there is a significant difference in the mean mileage of these four brands. Assume tire mileage is normally distributed.

11.58. Agricultural researchers are studying three different ways of planting peanuts to determine whether significantly different levels of production yield will result. The researchers have access to a large peanut farm on which to conduct their tests. They identify six blocks of land. In each block of land, peanuts are planted in each of the three different ways. At the end of the growing season, the peanuts are harvested and the average number of pounds per acre is determined for peanuts planted under each method in each block. Using the following data and $\alpha = .01$, test to determine whether there is a significant difference in yields among the planting methods.

BLOCK	METHOD 1	METHOD 2	METHOD 3
1	1310	1080	850
2	1275	1100	1020
3	1280	1050	780
4	1225	1020	870
5	1190	990	805
6	1300	1030	910

11.59. The Construction Labor Research Council lists a number of construction labor jobs that seem to pay approximately the same wages per hour. Some of these are bricklaying, iron working, and crane operation. Suppose a labor researcher takes a random sample of workers from each of these types of construction jobs and from across the country and asks what are their hourly wages? If this survey yields the following data, is there a significant difference in mean hourly wages for these three jobs? If there is a significant difference, use the Tukey-Kramer procedure to determine which pairs, if any, are also significantly different. Let $\alpha = .05$.

JOB TYPE		
BRICKLAYING	*IRON WORKING*	*CRANE OPERATION*
19.25	26.45	16.20
17.80	21.10	23.30
20.50	16.40	22.90
24.33	22.86	19.50
19.81	25.55	27.00
22.29	18.50	22.95
21.20		25.52
		21.20

11.60. Why are mergers attractive to CEOs? One of the reasons might be a potential increase in market share that can come with the pooling of company markets. Suppose a random survey of CEOs is taken, and they are asked to respond on a scale from 1 to 5 (5 representing strongly agree) whether increase in market share is a good reason for considering a merger of their company with another. Suppose also that the data are as given here and that CEOs have been categorized by size of company and years they have been with their company. Use a two-way ANOVA to determine whether there are any significant differences in the responses to this question. Let $\alpha = .05$.

		COMPANY SIZE ($ MILLION PER YEAR IN SALES)			
		0–5	*6–20*	*21–100*	*>100*
		2	2	3	3
		3	1	4	4
	0–2	2	2	4	4
		2	3	5	3
Years		2	2	3	3
with the		1	3	2	3
Company	3–5	2	2	4	3
		3	3	4	4
		2	2	3	2
		1	3	2	3
	Over 5	1	1	3	2
		2	2	3	3

11.61. Are some office jobs viewed as having more status than others? Suppose a study is conducted in which eight unemployed people are interviewed. The people are asked to rate each of five positions on a scale from 1 to 10 to indicate the status of the position, with 10 denoting most status and 1 denoting least status. The resulting data are given below. Use $\alpha = .05$ to analyze the repeated measures randomized block design data.

	JOB				
	MAIL CLERK	*DATA ENTRY*	*RECEP- TIONIST*	*SECRE- TARY*	*ADMIN. ASST.*
1	4	5	3	7	6
2	2	4	4	5	4

	3	3	3	2	6	7
Respondent	4	4	4	4	5	4
	5	3	5	1	3	5
	6	3	4	2	7	7
	7	2	2	2	4	4
	8	3	4	3	6	6

Interpreting the Output

11.62. Analyze the following Minitab output. Describe the design of the experiment. Using $\alpha = .05$ determine whether there are any significant effects; if so, explain why. Discuss any other ramifications of the output.

```
Analysis of Variance

Source   DF   Adj SS   Adj MS   F-Value   P-Value
Factor    3    876.6    292.2     3.01     0.045
Error    32   3107.5     97.1
Total    35   3984.1
```

11.63. Following is Excel output for an ANOVA problem. Describe the experimental design. The given value of alpha was .05. Discuss the output in terms of significant findings.

```
Anova: Two-Factor Without Replication

ANOVA
```

Source of Variation	SS	df	MS	F	P-value	F crit
Rows	48.278	5	9.656	3.16	0.057	3.33
Columns	10.111	2	5.056	1.65	0.230	4.10
Error	30.556	10	3.056			
Total	88.944	17				

11.64. Study the following Minitab output and graph. Discuss the meaning of the output.

```
Analysis of Variance for Dependent Variable

Source         DF    SS     MS     F      P
Row Effects     4   4.70   1.17   0.98   0.461
Col Effects     1   3.20   3.20   2.67   0.134
Interaction     4  22.30   5.57   4.65   0.022
Error          10  12.00   1.20
Total          19  42.20
```

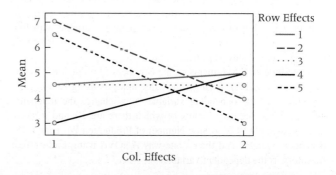

11.65. Interpret the following Excel output. Discuss the structure of the experimental design and any significant effects. Alpha is .05.

Anova: Two-Factor Without Replication

ANOVA

Source of Variation	SS	df	MS	F	P-value	F crit
Sample	2913.889	3	971.296	4.30	0.0146	3.01
Columns	240.389	2	120.194	0.53	0.5940	3.40
Interaction	1342.944	6	223.824	0.99	0.4533	2.51
Within	5419.333	24	225.806			
Total	9916.556	35				

11.66. Study the following Minitab output. Determine whether there are any significant effects and discuss the results. What kind of design was used and what was the size of it?

Analysis of Variance

Source	DF	SS	MS
Blocking	4	41.44	10.36
Treatment	4	143.93	35.98
Error	16	117.82	7.36
Total	24	303.19	

11.67. Discuss the following Minitab output.

Analysis of Variance

Source	DF	Adj SS	Adj MS	F-Value	P-Value
Factor	3	138.0	46.0	3.51	0.034
Error	20	262.2	13.1		
Total	23	400.3			

Means

Factor	N	Mean	StDev	95% CI
1	6	53.778	5.470	(6.2359, 6.4001)
2	6	54.665	1.840	(6.2126, 6.3424)
3	6	59.911	3.845	(6.4192, 6.5580)
4	6	57.293	2.088	(6.1382, 6.3218)

Pooled StDev = 3.621

Tukey Pairwise Comparisons

Grouping Information Using the Tukey Method and 95% Confidence

Factor	N	Mean	Grouping	
3	6	59.911	A	
4	6	57.293	A	B
2	6	54.665	A	B
1	6	53.778		B

Means that do not share a letter are significantly different.

Analyzing the Databases

See **www.wiley.com/college/black**

1. Do various financial indicators differ significantly according to type of company? Use a one-way ANOVA and the financial database to answer this question. Let Type of Company be the independent variable with seven levels (Apparel, Chemical, Electric Power, Grocery, Healthcare Products, Insurance, and Petroleum). Compute three one-way ANOVAs, one for each of the following dependent variables: Earnings Per Share, Dividends Per Share, and Average P/E Ratio. On each ANOVA, if there is a significant overall difference between Type of Company, compute multiple comparisons to determine which pairs of types of companies, if any, are significantly different.

2. In the Manufacturing database, the Value of Industrial Shipments has been recoded into four classifications (1–4) according to magnitude of value. Let this value be the independent variable with four levels of classifications. Compute a one-way ANOVA to determine whether there is any significant difference in classification of the Value of Industrial Shipments on the Number of Production Workers (dependent variable). Perform the same analysis using End-of-Year Inventories as the dependent variable. Now change the independent variable to Industry Group, of which there are 20, and perform first a one-way ANOVA using Number of Production Workers as the dependent variable and then a one-way ANOVA using End-of-Year Inventory as the dependent variable.

3. The hospital database contains data on hospitals from seven different geographic regions. Let this variable be the independent variable. Determine whether there is a significant difference in Admissions for these geographic regions using a one-way ANOVA. Perform the same analysis using Births as the dependent variable. Control is a variable with four levels of classification denoting the type of control the hospital is under (such as federal government or for-profit). Use this variable as the independent variable and test to determine whether there is a significant difference in the Admissions of a hospital by Control. Perform the same test using Births as the dependent variable.

4. The Consumer Food database contains data on Annual Food Spending, Annual Household Income, and Non-Mortgage Household Debt broken down by Region and Location. Using Region as an independent variable with four classification levels (four regions of the U.S.), perform three different one-way ANOVA's—one for each of the three dependent variables (Annual Food Spending, Annual Household Income, Non-Mortgage Household Debt). Did you find any significant differences by region? If so, conduct multiple comparisons to determine which regions, if any, are significantly different.

Case

The Clarkson Company: A Division of Tyco International

In 1950, J. R. Clarkson founded a family-owned industrial valve design and manufacturing company in Sparks, Nevada. For almost a half century, the company, known as the Clarkson Company, worked on advancing metal and mineral processing. The Clarkson Company became known for its knife-gate and control valves, introduced in the 1970s, that are able to halt and isolate sections of slurry flow. By the late 1990s, the company had become a key supplier of knife-gate valves, helping to control the flow in many of the piping systems around the world in different industries, including mining, energy, and wastewater treatment.

The knife-gate valve uses a steel gate like a blade that lowers into a slurry flow to create a bubble-tight seal. While conventional metal gates fill with hardened slurry and fail easily thereby requiring high maintenance, Clarkson's design introduced an easily replaceable snap-in elastomer sleeve that is durable, versatile, and handles both high pressure and temperature variation. Pipeline operators value Clarkson's elastomer sleeve because traditional seals have cost between $75 and $500 to replace, and considerable revenue is lost when a slurry system is stopped for maintenance repairs. Clarkson's product lasts longer and is easier to replace.

In the late 1990s, the Clarkson Company was acquired by Tyco Valves & Controls, a division of Tyco International, Ltd. In 2012, Pentair acquired the valve and flow control operations of Tyco International in a deal worth around $5 billion. This acquisition fit quite well with Pentair's main business of providing products and systems that control the filtration, treatment and storage of water and other fluids. The Clarkson wafer style slurry knife gate valve is still an important product for Pentair in this effort.

Discussion

1. The successful Clarkson knife-gate valve contains a wafer that is thin and light. Yet, the wafer is so strong it can operate with up to 150 pounds-per-square-inch (psi) of pressure on it, making it much stronger than those of competing brands. Suppose Tyco engineers have developed a new wafer that is even stronger. They want to set up an experimental design to test the strength of the wafer but they want to conduct the tests under three different temperature conditions, 70°, 110°, and 150°. In addition, suppose Tyco uses two different suppliers (company A and company B) of the synthetic materials that are used to manufacture the wafers. Some wafers are made primarily of raw materials supplied by company A, and some are made primarily of raw materials from company B. Thus, the engineers have set up a 2×3 factorial design with temperature and supplier as the independent variables and pressure (measured in psi) as the dependent variable. Data are gathered and are shown here. Analyze the data and discuss the business implications of the findings. If you were conducting the study, what would you report to the engineers?

	TEMPERATURE		
	70°	*110°*	*150°*
Supplier A	163	157	146
	159	162	137
	161	155	140
	158	159	150
Supplier B	154	157	142
	164	160	155

2. Pipeline operators estimate that it costs between $75 and $500 in U.S. currency to replace each seal, thus making the Clarkson longer-lasting valves more attractive. Tyco does business with pipeline companies around the world. Suppose in an attempt to develop marketing materials, Tyco marketers are interested in determining whether there is a significant difference in the cost of replacing pipeline seals in different countries. Four countries—Canada, Colombia, China, and the United States—are chosen for the study. Pipeline operators from equivalent operations are selected from companies in each country. The operators keep a cost log of seal replacements. A random sample of the data follows. Use these data to help Tyco determine whether there is a difference in the cost of seal replacements in the various countries. Explain your answer and tell how Tyco might use the information in their marketing materials.

CANADA	COLOMBIA	CHINA	UNITED STATES
$215	$355	$170	$230
205	280	190	190
245	300	235	225
270	330	195	220
290	360	205	215
260	340	180	245
225	300	190	230

3. In the late 1980s, the Clarkson Company installed a manufacturing resource planning system. Using this and other quality improvement approaches, the company was able to reduce lead-time from six to eight weeks to less than two weeks. Suppose that Tyco now uses a similar system and wants to test to determine whether lead-times differ significantly according to the type of valve it is manufacturing. As a control of the experiment, they are including in the study, as a blocking variable, the day of the week the valve was ordered. One lead-time was selected per valve per day of the week. The data are given here in weeks. Analyze the data and discuss your findings.

	TYPE OF VALVE					
	SAFETY	*BUTTERFLY*	*CLACK*	*SLIDE*	*POPPET*	*NEEDLE*
Monday	1.6	2.2	1.3	1.8	2.5	0.8
Tuesday	1.8	2.0	1.4	1.5	2.4	1.0
Wednesday	1.0	1.8	1.0	1.6	2.0	0.8
Thursday	1.8	2.2	1.4	1.6	1.8	0.6
Friday	2.0	2.4	1.5	1.8	2.2	1.2

Source: Adapted from "J. R. Clarkson Co., From Afterthought to Forethought," Real-World Lessons for America's Small Businesses: Insights from the Blue Chip Enterprise Initiative. Published by *Nation's Business* magazine on behalf of Connecticut Mutual Life Insurance Company and the U.S. Chamber of Commerce in association with the Blue Chip Enterprise Initiative, 1992; "The Clarkson Company Saves Time and Money Improving Piping Valves," ALGOR, pp. 1–4, available at http://www.algor.com; "Controlling the Flow," *Mechanical Engineering*, December 1998, pp. 1–5, available at http://www.memagazine. org. Tyco Valves & Controls Web site at www.tycovalves.com, and http://www. tycoflowcontrol.com/valves/products/slurry_valves/knife_gate_valves/2011, http://valves.pentair.com/valves//resources/VCIOM-06600-EN.pdf.

CHAPTER 12

Simple Regression Analysis and Correlation

LEARNING OBJECTIVES

The overall objective of this chapter is to give you an understanding of bivariate linear regression analysis and correlation, thereby enabling you to:

1. Calculate the Pearson product-moment correlation coefficient to determine if there is a correlation between two variables.

2. Explain what regression analysis is and the concepts of independent and dependent variable.

3. Calculate the slope and y-intercept of the least squares equation of a regression line and from those, determine the equation of the regression line.

4. Calculate the residuals of a regression line and from those determine the fit of the model, locate outliers, and test the assumptions of the regression model.

5. Calculate the standard error of the estimate using the sum of squares of error, and use the standard error of the estimate to determine the fit of the model.

6. Calculate the coefficient of determination to measure the fit for regression models, and relate it to the coefficient of correlation.

7. Use the t and F tests to test hypotheses for both the slope of the regression model and the overall regression model.

8. Calculate confidence intervals to estimate the conditional mean of the dependent variable and prediction intervals to estimate a single value of the dependent variable.

9. Determine the equation of the trend line to forecast outcomes for time periods in the future, using alternate coding for time periods if necessary.

10. Use a computer to develop a regression analysis, and interpret the output that is associated with it.

Decision Dilemma

Predicting International Hourly Wages by the Price of a Big Mac

The McDonald's Corporation is the leading global foodservice retailer with more than 36,000 local restaurants serving nearly 69 million people in more than 100 countries each day. This global presence, in addition to its consistency in food offerings and restaurant operations, makes McDonald's a unique and attractive setting for economists to make salary and price comparisons around the world. Because the Big Mac hamburger is a standardized hamburger produced and sold in virtually every McDonald's around the world, the *Economist*, a weekly newspaper

©Antonella Carri/Age Fotostock America, Inc.

focusing on international politics and business news and opinion, was compiling as early as 1986 information about Big Mac prices as an indicator of exchange rates. Building on this idea, researchers Ashenfelter and Jurajda proposed comparing wage rates across countries using the price of a Big Mac hamburger. Shown below are Big Mac prices and net hourly wage figures (in U.S. dollars) for 20 countries.

COUNTRY	BIG MAC PRICE (U.S. $)	NET HOURLY WAGE (U.S. $)
Argentina	4.84	15.91
Australia	4.94	46.29
Brazil	6.16	11.65
Canada	5.00	36.56
Czech Republic	4.07	13.13
Denmark	5.48	51.67
Hungary	4.04	9.17
Israel	4.67	21.42
Japan	4.08	36.71
Mexico	2.74	6.48
New Zealand	4.41	23.38
Philippines	2.78	2.01
Poland	3.09	8.83
Singapore	3.65	22.60
South Korea	3.50	18.91
Sweden	7.64	49.12
Switzerland	8.06	60.40
Taiwan	2.60	9.34
United Kingdom	3.89	30.77
United States	4.07	35.53

MANAGERIAL AND STATISTICAL QUESTIONS

1. Is there a relationship between the price of a Big Mac and the net hourly wages of workers around the world? If so, how strong is the relationship?

2. Is it possible to develop a model to predict or determine the net hourly wage of a worker around the world by the price of a Big Mac hamburger in that country? If so, how good is the model?

3. If a model can be constructed to determine the net hourly wage of a worker around the world by the price of a Big Mac hamburger, what would be the predicted net hourly wage of a worker in a country if the price of a Big Mac hamburger was $3.00?

Sources: McDonald's Web site, at http://www.aboutmcdonalds.com/; Michael R. Pakko and Patricia S. Pollard, "Burgernomics: A Big Mac Guide to Purchasing Power Parity," research publication by the St. Louis Federal Reserve Bank, at https://research.stlouisfed.org/publications/review/03/11/pakko.pdf; Orley Ashenfelter and Stepan Jurajda, "Cross Country Comparisons of Wage Rates: The Big Mac Index," unpublished manuscript, Princeton University and CERGEEI/Charles University, October 2001; http:www.bls.gov/news.release/ichcc.t01.htm; http://www.economist.com/blogs/dailychart/2001/07/big-mac-index

In business, the key to decision making often lies in the understanding of the relationships between two or more variables. For example, a company in the distribution business may determine that there is a relationship between the price of crude oil and the company's transportation costs. Financial experts, in studying the behavior of the bond market, might find it useful to know if the interest rates on bonds are related to the prime interest rate set by the Federal Reserve. A marketing executive might want to know how strong the relationship is between advertising dollars and sales dollars for a product or a company.

In this chapter, we will study the concept of correlation and how it can be used to estimate the relationship between two variables. We will also explore simple regression analysis through which mathematical models can be developed to predict one variable by another. We will examine tools for testing the strength and predictability of regression models, and we will learn how to use regression analysis to develop a forecasting trend line.

12.1 Correlation

Correlation is *a measure of the degree of relatedness of variables.* It can help a business researcher determine, for example, whether the stocks of two airlines rise and fall in any related manner. For a sample of pairs of data, correlation analysis can yield a numerical value that represents the degree of relatedness of the two stock prices over time. In the transportation industry, is a correlation evident between the price of transportation and the weight of the object being shipped? If so, how strong are the correlations? In economics, how strong is the correlation between the producer price index and the unemployment rate? In retail sales, are

 Interactive Applet

sales related to population density, number of competitors, size of the store, amount of advertising, or other variables?

Several measures of correlation are available, the selection of which depends mostly on the level of data being analyzed. Ideally, researchers would like to solve for ρ, the population coefficient of correlation. However, because researchers virtually always deal with sample data, this section introduces a widely used sample **coefficient of correlation**, r. This measure is applicable only if both variables being analyzed have at least an interval level of data. Chapter 17 presents a correlation measure that can be used when the data are ordinal.

The statistic r is the **Pearson product-moment correlation coefficient**, named after Karl Pearson (1857–1936), an English statistician who developed several coefficients of correlation along with other significant statistical concepts. The term r is a *measure of the linear correlation of two variables*. It is a number that ranges from −1 to 0 to +1, representing the strength of the relationship between the variables. An r value of +1 denotes a perfect positive relationship between two sets of numbers. An r value of −1 denotes a perfect negative correlation, which indicates an inverse relationship between two variables: as one variable gets larger, the other gets smaller. An r value of 0 means no linear relationship is present between the two variables.

Pearson Product-Moment Correlation Coefficient

$$r = \frac{\Sigma(x - \bar{x})(y - \bar{y})}{\sqrt{\Sigma(x - \bar{x})^2 \, \Sigma(y - \bar{y})^2}} = \frac{\Sigma xy - \dfrac{(\Sigma x \Sigma y)}{n}}{\sqrt{\left[\Sigma x^2 - \dfrac{(\Sigma x)^2}{n}\right]\left[\Sigma y^2 - \dfrac{(\Sigma y)^2}{n}\right]}} \tag{12.1}$$

Figure 12.1 depicts five different degrees of correlation: (a) represents strong negative correlation, (b) represents moderate negative correlation, (c) represents moderate positive correlation, (d) represents strong positive correlation, and (e) contains no correlation.

What is the measure of correlation between the interest rate of federal funds and the commodities futures index? With data such as those shown in **Table 12.1**, which represent the

TABLE 12.1   Data for the Economics Example

DAY	INTEREST RATE	FUTURES INDEX
1	7.43	221
2	7.48	222
3	8.00	226
4	7.75	225
5	7.60	224
6	7.63	223
7	7.68	223
8	7.67	226
9	7.59	226
10	8.07	235
11	8.03	233
12	8.00	241

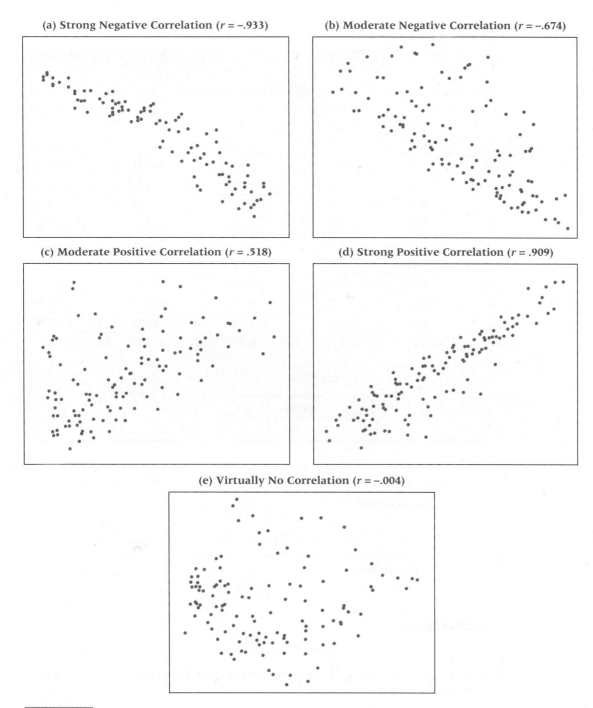

(a) Strong Negative Correlation ($r = -.933$)

(b) Moderate Negative Correlation ($r = -.674$)

(c) Moderate Positive Correlation ($r = .518$)

(d) Strong Positive Correlation ($r = .909$)

(e) Virtually No Correlation ($r = -.004$)

FIGURE 12.1 **Five Correlations**

values for interest rates of federal funds and commodities futures indexes for a sample of 12 days, a correlation coefficient, r, can be computed.

Examination of the formula for computing a Pearson product-moment correlation coefficient (12.1) reveals that the following values must be obtained to compute r: Σx, Σx^2, Σy, Σy^2, Σxy, and n. In correlation analysis, it does not matter which variable is designated x and which is designated y. For this example, the correlation coefficient is computed as shown in Table 12.2. The r value obtained ($r = .815$) represents a relatively strong positive relationship between interest rates and commodities futures index over this 12-day period.

Figure 12.2 shows both Excel and Minitab output for this problem.

TABLE 12.2 Computation of r for the Economics Example

DAY	INTEREST RATE x	FUTURES INDEX y	x^2	y^2	xy
1	7.43	221	55.205	48,841	1,642.03
2	7.48	222	55.950	49,284	1,660.56
3	8.00	226	64.000	51,076	1,808.00
4	7.75	225	60.063	50,625	1,743.75
5	7.60	224	57.760	50,176	1,702.40
6	7.63	223	58.217	49,729	1,701.49
7	7.68	223	58.982	49,729	1,712.64
8	7.67	226	58.829	51,076	1,733.42
9	7.59	226	57.608	51,076	1,715.34
10	8.07	235	65.125	55,225	1,896.45
11	8.03	233	64.481	54,289	1,870.99
12	8.00	241	64.000	58,081	1,928.00
	$\Sigma x = 92.93$	$\Sigma y = 2{,}725$	$\Sigma x^2 = 720.220$	$\Sigma y^2 = 619{,}207$	$\Sigma xy = 21{,}115.07$

$$r = \dfrac{(21{,}115.07) - \dfrac{(92.93)(2725)}{12}}{\sqrt{\left[(720.22) - \dfrac{(92.93)^2}{12}\right]\left[(619{,}207) - \dfrac{(2725)^2}{12}\right]}} = .815$$

Excel Output

	Interest Rate	Futures Index
Interest Rate	1	
Futures Index	0.815	1

Minitab Output

Correlations: Interest Rate, Futures Index

Pearson correlation of Interest Rate and Futures Index = 0.815
p-Value = 0.001

FIGURE 12.2 Excel and Minitab Output for the Economics Example

12.1 Problems

12.1. Determine the value of the coefficient of correlation, r, for the following data.

X	4	6	7	11	14	17	21
Y	18	12	13	8	7	7	4

12.2. Determine the value of r for the following data.

X	158	296	87	110	436
Y	349	510	301	322	550

12.3. In an effort to determine whether any correlation exists between the price of stocks of airlines, an analyst sampled six days of activity of the stock market spread out over 4 months. Using the following prices of Delta stock and Southwest stock, compute the coefficient of correlation. Stock prices have been rounded off to the nearest tenth for ease of computation.

DELTA	SOUTHWEST
45.96	38.76
50.14	45.41
47.93	45.74
51.78	49.58
52.17	44.34
46.96	42.68

Oklahoma	258	31
Texas	894	141

Use the data to compute a correlation coefficient, r, to determine the correlation between claims and surplus.

12.5. The National Safety Council released the following data on the incidence rates for fatal or lost-worktime injuries per 100 employees for several industries in three recent years.

12.4. The following data are the claims (in $ millions) for BlueCross BlueShield benefits for nine states, along with the surplus (in $ millions) that the company had in assets in those states.

STATE	CLAIMS	SURPLUS
Alabama	$1,425	$277
Colorado	273	100
Florida	915	120
Illinois	1,687	259
Maine	234	40
Montana	142	25
North Dakota	259	57

INDUSTRY	YEAR 1	YEAR 2	YEAR 3
Textile	.46	.48	.69
Chemical	.52	.62	.63
Communication	.90	.72	.81
Machinery	1.50	1.74	2.10
Services	2.89	2.03	2.46
Nonferrous metals	1.80	1.92	2.00
Food	3.29	3.18	3.17
Government	5.73	4.43	4.00

Compute r for each pair of years and determine which years are most highly correlated.

12.2 Introduction to Simple Regression Analysis

Regression analysis is *the process of constructing a mathematical model or function that can be used to predict or determine one variable by another variable or other variables.* The most elementary regression model is called **simple regression** or **bivariate regression** involving two variables in which one variable is predicted by another variable. In simple regression, *the variable to be predicted* is called the **dependent variable** and is designated as y. The *predictor* is called the **independent variable**, or *explanatory variable*, and is designated as x. In simple regression analysis, only a straight-line relationship between two variables is examined. Nonlinear relationships and regression models with more than one independent variable can be explored by using multiple regression models, which are presented in Chapters 13 and 14.

Can the cost of flying a commercial airliner be predicted using regression analysis? If so, what variables are related to such cost? A few of the many variables that can potentially contribute are type of plane, distance, number of passengers, amount of luggage/freight, weather conditions, direction of destination, and perhaps even pilot skill. Suppose a study is conducted using only Boeing 737s traveling 500 miles on comparable routes during the same season of the year. Can the number of passengers predict the cost of flying such routes? It seems logical that more passengers result in more weight and more baggage, which could, in turn, result in increased fuel consumption and other costs. Suppose the data displayed in Table 12.3 are the costs and associated number of passengers for twelve 500-mile commercial airline flights using Boeing 737s during the same season of the year. We will use these data to develop a regression model to predict cost by number of passengers.

Usually, the first step in simple regression analysis is to construct a **scatter plot** (or scatter diagram), discussed in Chapter 2. Graphing the data in this way yields preliminary information about the shape and spread of the data. **Figure 12.3** is an Excel scatter plot of the data in Table 12.3. **Figure 12.4** is a close-up view of the scatter plot produced by Minitab. Try to

TABLE 12.3

Airline Cost Data

NUMBER OF PASSENGERS	COST ($1,000)
61	4.280
63	4.080
67	4.420
69	4.170
70	4.480
74	4.300
76	4.820
81	4.700
86	5.110
91	5.130
95	5.640
97	5.560

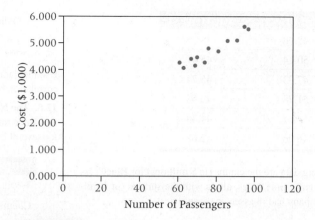

FIGURE 12.3 **Excel Scatter Plot of Airline Cost Data**

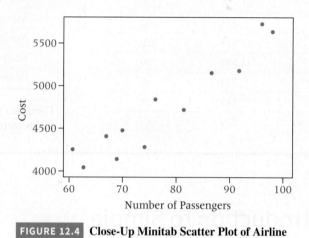

FIGURE 12.4 **Close-Up Minitab Scatter Plot of Airline Cost Data**

imagine a line passing through the points. Is a linear fit possible? Would a curve fit the data better? The scatter plot gives some idea of how well a regression line fits the data. Later in the chapter, we present statistical techniques that can be used to determine more precisely how well a regression line fits the data.

12.3 | Determining the Equation of the Regression Line

The first step in determining the equation of the regression line that passes through the sample data is to establish the equation's form. Several different types of equations of lines are discussed in algebra, finite math, or analytic geometry courses. Recall that among these equations of a line are the two-point form, the point-slope form, and the slope-intercept form. In regression analysis, researchers use the slope-intercept equation of a line. In math courses, the slope-intercept form of the equation of a line often takes the form

$$y = mx + b$$

where

m = slope of the line
b = y intercept of the line

In statistics, the slope-intercept form of the equation of the regression line through the population points is

$$\hat{y} = \beta_0 + \beta_1 x$$

where

$\hat{y}$ = the predicted value of y
β_0 = the population y intercept
β_1 = the population slope

For any specific dependent variable value, y_i,

$$y_i = \beta_0 + \beta_1 x_i + \epsilon_i$$

where

x_i = the value of the independent variable for the ith value
y_i = the value of the dependent variable for the ith value
β_0 = the population y intercept
β_1 = the population slope
ϵ_i = the error of prediction for the ith value

Unless the points being fitted by the regression equation are in perfect alignment, the regression line will miss at least some of the points. In the preceding equation, ϵ_i represents the error of the regression line in fitting these points. If a point is on the regression line, $\epsilon_i = 0$.

These mathematical models can be either deterministic models or probabilistic models. **Deterministic models** are *mathematical models that produce an "exact" output for a given input.* For example, suppose the equation of a regression line is

$$y = 1.68 + 2.40x$$

For a value of $x = 5$, the exact predicted value of y is

$$y = 1.68 + 2.40(5) = 13.68$$

We recognize, however, that most of the time the values of y will not equal exactly the values yielded by the equation. Random error will occur in the prediction of the y values for values of x because it is likely that the variable x does not explain all the variability of the variable y. For example, suppose we are trying to predict the volume of sales (y) for a company through regression analysis by using the annual dollar amount of advertising (x) as the predictor. Although sales are often related to advertising, other factors related to sales are not accounted for by amount of advertising. Hence, a regression model to predict sales volume by amount of advertising probably involves some error. For this reason, in regression, we present the general model as a probabilistic model. A **probabilistic model** is *one that includes an error term that allows the y values to vary for any given value of x.*

A deterministic regression model is

$$y = \beta_0 + \beta_1 x$$

The probabilistic regression model is

$$y = \beta_0 + \beta_1 x + \epsilon$$

$\beta_0 + \beta_1 x$ is the deterministic portion of the probabilistic model, $\beta_0 + \beta_1 x + \epsilon$. In a deterministic model, all points are assumed to be on the line and in all cases ϵ is zero.

Virtually all regression analyses of business data involve sample data, not population data. As a result, β_0 and β_1 are unattainable and must be estimated by using the sample statistics, b_0 and b_1. Hence the equation of the regression line contains the sample y intercept, b_0, and the sample slope, b_1.

Equation of the Simple Regression Line

$$\hat{y} = b_0 + b_1 x$$

where

b_0 = the sample y intercept
b_1 = the sample slope

To determine the equation of the regression line for a sample of data, the researcher must determine the values for b_0 and b_1. This process is sometimes referred to as least squares analysis. **Least squares analysis** is *a process whereby a regression model is developed by producing the minimum sum of the squared error values.* On the basis of this premise and calculus, a particular set of equations has been developed to produce components of the regression model.*

Examine the regression line fit through the points in **Figure 12.5**. Observe that the line does not actually pass through any of the points. The vertical distance from each point to the line is the error of the prediction. In theory, an infinite number of lines could be constructed to pass through these points in some manner. The least squares regression line is the regression line that results in the smallest sum of errors squared.

Formula 12.2 is an equation for computing the value of the sample slope. Several versions of the equation are given to afford latitude in doing the computations.

Slope of the Regression Line

$$b_1 = \frac{\Sigma(x - \overline{x})(y - \overline{y})}{\Sigma(x - \overline{x})^2} = \frac{\Sigma xy - n\overline{x}\,\overline{y}}{\Sigma x^2 - n\overline{x}^2} = \frac{\Sigma xy - \dfrac{(\Sigma x)(\Sigma y)}{n}}{\Sigma x^2 - \dfrac{(\Sigma x)^2}{n}}$$

(12.2)

The expression in the numerator of the slope Formula 12.2 appears frequently in this chapter and is denoted as SS_{xy}.

$$SS_{xy} = \Sigma(x - \overline{x})(y - \overline{y}) = \Sigma xy - \frac{(\Sigma x)(\Sigma y)}{n}$$

The expression in the denominator of the slope Formula 12.2 also appears frequently in this chapter and is denoted as SS_{xx}.

$$SS_{xx} = \Sigma(x - \overline{x})^2 = \Sigma x^2 - \frac{(\Sigma x)^2}{n}$$

With these abbreviations, the equation for the slope can be expressed as in Formula 12.3.

Alternative Formula for Slope

$$b_1 = \frac{SS_{xy}}{SS_{xx}}$$

(12.3)

Formula 12.4 is used to compute the sample y intercept. The slope must be computed before the y intercept.

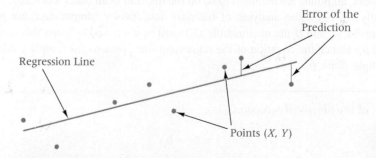

FIGURE 12.5 **Minitab Plot of a Regression Line**

*Derivation of these formulas is beyond our scope here but is presented in WileyPLUS.

y Intercept of the Regression Line

$$b_0 = \bar{y} - b_1\bar{x} = \frac{\Sigma y}{n} - b_1\frac{(\Sigma x)}{n} \qquad (12.4)$$

Formulas 12.2, 12.3, and 12.4 show that the following data are needed from sample information to compute the slope and intercept: Σx, Σy, Σx^2, and, Σxy, unless sample means are used. Table 12.4 contains the results of solving for the slope and intercept and determining the equation of the regression line for the data in Table 12.3.

The least squares equation of the regression line for this problem is

$$\hat{y} = 1.57 + .0407x$$

The slope of this regression line is .0407. Because the x values were recoded for the ease of computation and are actually in \$1,000 denominations, the slope is actually \$40.70. One interpretation of the slope in this problem is that for every unit increase in x (every person added to the flight of the airplane), there is a \$40.70 increase in the cost of the flight. The y-intercept is the point where the line crosses the y-axis (where x is zero). Sometimes in regression analysis, the y-intercept is meaningless in terms of the variables studied. However, in this problem, one interpretation of the y-intercept, which is 1.570 or \$1,570, is that even if there were no passengers on the commercial flight, it would still cost \$1,570. In other words, there are costs associated with a flight that carries no passengers.

TABLE 12.4	Solving for the Slope and the *y* Intercept of the Regression Line for the Airline Cost Example		
NUMBER OF PASSENGERS	**COST (\$1,000)**		
x	*y*	*x²*	*xy*
61	4.280	3,721	261.080
63	4.080	3,969	257.040
67	4.420	4,489	296.140
69	4.170	4,761	287.730
70	4.480	4,900	313.600
74	4.300	5,476	318.200
76	4.820	5,776	366.320
81	4.700	6,561	380.700
86	5.110	7,396	439.460
91	5.130	8,281	466.830
95	5.640	9,025	535.800
97	5.560	9,409	539.320
$\Sigma x = 930$	$\Sigma y = 56.690$	$\Sigma x^2 = 73{,}764$	$\Sigma xy = 4462.220$

$$SS_{xy} = \Sigma xy - \frac{(\Sigma x)(\Sigma y)}{n} = 4462.22 - \frac{(930)(56.69)}{12} = 68.745$$

$$SS_{xx} = \Sigma x^2 - \frac{(\Sigma x)^2}{n} = 73{,}764 - \frac{(930)^2}{12} = 1689$$

$$b_1 = \frac{SS_{xy}}{SS_{xx}} = \frac{68.745}{1689} = .0407$$

$$b_0 = \frac{\Sigma y}{n} - b_1\frac{\Sigma x}{n} = \frac{56.69}{12} - (.0407)\frac{930}{12} = 1.57$$

$$\hat{y} = 1.57 + .0407x$$

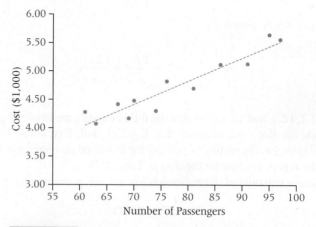

FIGURE 12.6 **Excel Graph of Regression Line for the Airline Cost Example**

Superimposing the line representing the least squares equation for this problem on the scatter plot indicates how well the regression line fits the data points, as shown in the Excel graph in Figure 12.6. The next several sections explore mathematical ways of testing how well the regression line fits the points.

DEMONSTRATION PROBLEM 12.1

A specialist in hospital administration stated that the number of FTEs (full-time employees) in a hospital can be estimated by counting the number of beds in the hospital (a common measure of hospital size). A healthcare business researcher decided to develop a regression model in an attempt to predict the number of FTEs of a hospital by the number of beds. She surveyed 12 hospitals and obtained the following data. The data are presented in sequence, according to the number of beds.

NUMBER OF BEDS	FTEs	NUMBER OF BEDS	FTEs
23	69	50	138
29	95	54	178
29	102	64	156
35	118	66	184
42	126	76	176
46	125	78	225

Solution: The following Minitab graph is a scatter plot of these data. Note the linear appearance of the data.

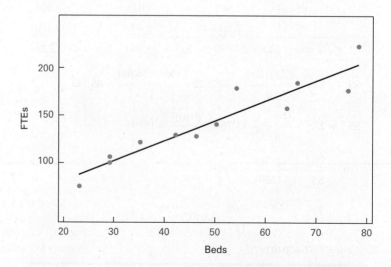

Next, the researcher determined the values of Σx, Σy, Σx^2, and Σxy.

HOSPITAL	NUMBER OF BEDS x	FTEs y	x^2	xy
1	23	69	529	1,587
2	29	95	841	2,755
3	29	102	841	2,958
4	35	118	1,225	4,130
5	42	126	1,764	5,292
6	46	125	2,116	5,750
7	50	138	2,500	6,900
8	54	178	2,916	9,612
9	64	156	4,096	9,984
10	66	184	4,356	12,144
11	76	176	5,776	13,376
12	78	225	6,084	17,550
	$\Sigma x = 592$	$\Sigma y = 1{,}692$	$\Sigma x^2 = 33{,}044$	$\Sigma xy = 92{,}038$

Using these values, the researcher solved for the sample slope (b_1) and the sample y-intercept (b_0).

$$SS_{xy} = \Sigma xy - \frac{(\Sigma x)(\Sigma y)}{n} = 92{,}038 - \frac{(592)(1692)}{12} = 8566$$

$$SS_{xx} = \Sigma x^2 - \frac{(\Sigma x)^2}{n} = 33{,}044 - \frac{(592)^2}{12} = 3838.667$$

$$b_1 = \frac{SS_{xy}}{SS_{xx}} = \frac{8566}{3838.667} = 2.232$$

$$b_0 = \frac{\Sigma y}{n} - b_1 \frac{\Sigma x}{12} = \frac{1692}{12} - (2.232)\frac{592}{12} = 30.888$$

The least squares equation of the regression line is

$$\hat{y} = 30.888 + 2.232x$$

The slope of the line, $b_1 = 2.232$, means that for every unit increase of x (every additional bed), y (number of FTEs) is predicted to increase by 2.232. Even though the y-intercept helps the researcher sketch the graph of the line by being one of the points on the line (0, 30.888), it has limited usefulness in terms of this solution because $x = 0$ denotes a hospital with no beds. On the other hand, it could be interpreted that a hospital has to have at least 31 FTEs to open its doors even with no patients—a sort of "fixed cost" of personnel.

12.3 Problems

12.6. Sketch a scatter plot from the following data, and determine the equation of the regression line.

x	12	21	28	8	20
y	17	15	22	19	24

12.7. Sketch a scatter plot from the following data, and determine the equation of the regression line.

x	140	119	103	91	65	29	24
y	25	29	46	70	88	112	128

12.8. A corporation owns several companies. The strategic planner for the corporation believes dollars spent on advertising can to some extent be a predictor of total sales dollars. As an aid in long-term planning, she gathers the following sales and advertising information from several of the companies for 2016 ($ millions).

ADVERTISING	SALES
12.5	148
3.7	55
21.6	338
60.0	994
37.6	541
6.1	89
16.8	126
41.2	379

Develop the equation of the simple regression line to predict sales from advertising expenditures using these data.

12.9. Investment analysts generally believe the interest rate on bonds is inversely related to the prime interest rate for loans; that is, bonds perform well when lending rates are down and perform poorly when interest rates are up. Can the bond rate be predicted by the prime interest rate? Use the following data to construct a least squares regression line to predict bond rates by the prime interest rate.

BOND RATE	PRIME INTEREST RATE
5%	16%
12	6
9	8
15	4
7	7

12.10. Is it possible to predict the annual number of business bankruptcies by the number of firm births (business starts) in the United States? The following data, published by the U.S. Small Business Administration, Office of Advocacy, are pairs of the number of business bankruptcies (1000s) and the number of firm births (10,000s) for a six-year period. Use these data to develop the equation of the regression model to predict the number of business bankruptcies by the number of firm births. Discuss the meaning of the slope.

BUSINESS BANKRUPTCIES (1000)	FIRM BIRTHS (10,000)
34.3	58.1
35.0	55.4
38.5	57.0
40.1	58.5
35.5	57.4
37.9	58.0

12.11. It appears that over the past 50 years, the number of farms in the United States declined while the average size of farms increased. The following data provided by the U.S. Department of Agriculture show five-year interval data for U.S. farms. Use these data to develop the equation of a regression line to predict the average size of a farm by the number of farms. Discuss the slope and y-intercept of the model.

YEAR	NUMBER OF FARMS (MILLIONS)	AVERAGE SIZE (ACRES)
1960	3.96	297
1965	3.36	340
1970	2.95	374
1975	2.52	420
1980	2.44	426
1985	2.29	441
1990	2.15	460
1995	2.07	469
2000	2.17	434
2005	2.10	444
2010	2.19	419
2015	2.08	438

12.12. Can the annual new orders for manufacturing in the United States be predicted by the raw steel production in the United States? Shown below are the annual new orders for 10 years according to the U.S. Census Bureau and the raw steel production for the same 10 years as published by the American Iron & Steel Institute. Use these data to develop a regression model to predict annual new orders by raw steel production. Construct a scatter plot and draw the regression line through the points.

RAW STEEL PRODUCTION (100,000s OF NET TONS)	NEW ORDERS ($ TRILLIONS)
99.9	2.74
97.9	2.87
98.9	2.93
87.9	2.87
92.9	2.98
97.9	3.09
100.6	3.36
104.9	3.61
105.3	3.75
108.6	3.95

12.4 Residual Analysis

How does a business researcher test a regression line to determine whether the line is a good fit of the data other than by observing the fitted line plot (regression line fit through a scatter plot of the data)? One particularly popular approach is to use the *historical data* (x and y values used to construct the regression model) to test the model. With this approach, the values of the independent variable (x values) are inserted into the regression model and a predicted value ($\hat{y}$) is obtained for each x value. These predicted values ($\hat{y}$) are then compared to the actual y values to determine how much error the equation of the regression line produced. *Each difference between the actual y values and the predicted y values is the error of the regression line at a given point, $y - \hat{y}$, and is referred to as the* **residual**. It is the sum of squares of these residuals that is minimized to find the least squares line.

Table 12.5 shows $\hat{y}$ values and the residuals for each pair of data for the airline cost regression model developed in Section 12.3. The predicted values are calculated by inserting an x value into the equation of the regression line and solving for $\hat{y}$. For example, when $x = 61$, $\hat{y} = 1.57 + .0407(61) = 4.053$, as displayed in column 3 of the table. Each of these predicted y values is subtracted from the actual y value to determine the error, or residual. For example, the first y value listed in the table is 4.280 and the first predicted value is 4.053, resulting in a residual of $4.280 - 4.053 = .227$. The residuals for this problem are given in column 4 of the table.

Note that the sum of the residuals is approximately zero. Except for rounding error, the sum of the residuals is *always zero*. A residual is geometrically the vertical distance from the regression line to a data point. The equations used to solve for the slope and intercept place the line geometrically in the middle of all points. Therefore, vertical distances from the line to the points will cancel each other and sum to zero. Figure 12.7 is a Minitab-produced scatter plot of the data and the residuals for the airline cost example.

An examination of the residuals may give the researcher an idea of how well the regression line fits the historical data points. The largest residual for the airline cost example is $-.282$, and the smallest is .040. Because the objective of the regression analysis was to predict the cost of flight in \$1,000s, the regression line produces an error of \$282 when there are 74 passengers and an error of only \$40 when there are 86 passengers. This result presents the *best* and *worst* cases for the residuals. The researcher must examine other residuals to determine how well the regression model fits other data points.

Sometimes residuals are used to locate outliers. **Outliers** are *data points that lie apart from the rest of the points*. Outliers can produce residuals with large magnitudes and are usually easy to identify on scatter plots. Outliers can be the result of misrecorded or miscoded data, or they may simply be data points that do not conform to the general trend. The equation of the regression line is influenced by every data point used in its calculation in a manner similar to the arithmetic mean. Therefore, outliers sometimes can unduly influence the regression line by "pulling" the line toward the outliers. The origin of outliers must be investigated to determine whether they should be retained or whether the regression equation should be recomputed without them.

TABLE 12.5	Predicted Values and Residuals for the Airline Cost Example		
NUMBER OF PASSENGERS x	COST (\$1,000) y	PREDICTED VALUE $\hat{y}$	RESIDUAL $y - \hat{y}$
61	4.280	4.053	.227
63	4.080	4.134	$-.054$
67	4.420	4.297	.123
69	4.170	4.378	$-.208$
70	4.480	4.419	.061
74	4.300	4.582	$-.282$
76	4.820	4.663	.157
81	4.700	4.867	$-.167$
86	5.110	5.070	.040
91	5.130	5.274	$-.144$
95	5.640	5.436	.204
97	5.560	5.518	.042
			$\Sigma(y - \hat{y}) = -.001$

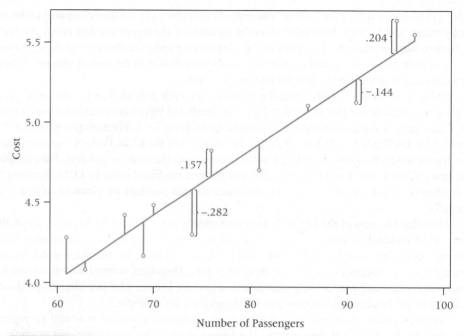

FIGURE 12.7 **Close-Up Minitab Scatter Plot with Residuals for the Airline Cost Example**

Residuals are usually plotted against the *x*-axis, which reveals a view of the residuals as *x* increases. **Figure 12.8** shows the residuals plotted by Excel against the *x*-axis for the airline cost example.

Using Residuals to Test the Assumptions of the Regression Model

One of the major uses of residual analysis is to test some of the assumptions underlying regression. The following are the assumptions of simple regression analysis.

1. The model is linear.
2. The error terms have constant variances.
3. The error terms are independent.
4. The error terms are normally distributed.

A particular method for studying the behavior of residuals is the residual plot. The **residual plot** is *a type of graph in which the residuals for a particular regression model are plotted along with their associated value of x as an ordered pair* $(x, y - \hat{y})$. Information about how

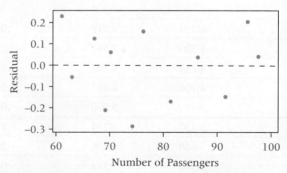

FIGURE 12.8 **Excel Graph of Residuals for the Airline Cost Example**

well the regression assumptions are met by the particular regression model can be gleaned by examining the plots. Residual plots are more meaningful with larger sample sizes. For small sample sizes, residual plot analyses can be problematic and subject to over-interpretation. Hence, because the airline cost example is constructed from only 12 pairs of data, one should be cautious in reaching conclusions from Figure 12.8. The residual plots in Figures 12.9, 12.10, and 12.11, however, represent large numbers of data points and therefore are more likely to depict overall trends accurately.

If a residual plot such as the one in **Figure 12.9** appears, the assumption that the model is linear does not hold. Note that the residuals are negative for low and high values of x and are positive for middle values of x. The graph of these residuals is parabolic, not linear. The residual plot does not have to be shaped in this manner for a nonlinear relationship to exist. Any significant deviation from an approximately linear residual plot may mean that a nonlinear relationship exists between the two variables.

The assumption of *constant error variance* sometimes is called **homoscedasticity**. If *the error variances are not constant* (called **heteroscedasticity**), the residual plots might look like one of the two plots in **Figure 12.10**. Note in Figure 12.10(a) that the error variance is greater for small values of x and smaller for large values of x. The situation is reversed in Figure 12.10(b).

If the error terms are not independent, the residual plots could look like one of the graphs in **Figure 12.11**. According to these graphs, instead of each error term being independent of the one next to it, the value of the residual is a function of the residual value next to it. For example, a large positive residual is next to a large positive residual and a small negative residual is next to a small negative residual.

The graph of the residuals from a regression analysis that meets the assumptions—a *healthy residual graph*—might look like the graph in **Figure 12.12**. The plot is relatively linear; the variances of the errors are about equal for each value of x, and the error terms do not appear to be related to adjacent terms.

Using the Computer for Residual Analysis

Some computer programs contain mechanisms for analyzing residuals for violations of the regression assumptions. Minitab has the capability of providing graphical analysis of residuals. **Figure 12.13** displays Minitab's residual graphic analyses for a regression model developed to predict the production of carrots in the United States per month by the total production of sweet corn. The data were gathered over a time period of 168 consecutive months (see Wiley-PLUS for the agricultural database).

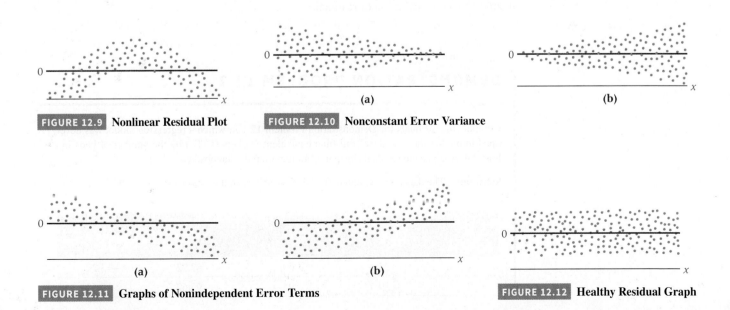

FIGURE 12.9 **Nonlinear Residual Plot**

(a)

(b)

FIGURE 12.10 **Nonconstant Error Variance**

(a)

(b)

FIGURE 12.11 **Graphs of Nonindependent Error Terms**

FIGURE 12.12 **Healthy Residual Graph**

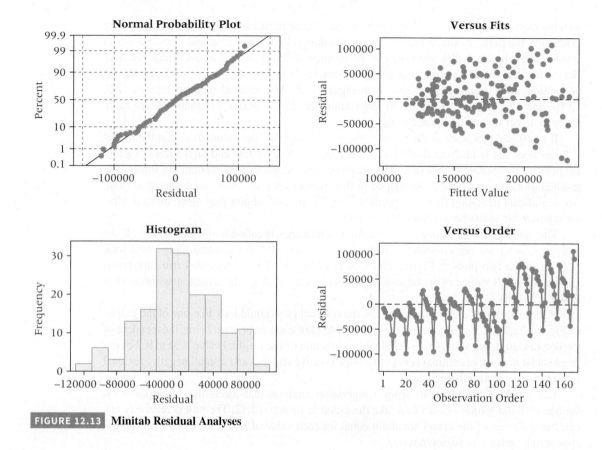

FIGURE 12.13 Minitab Residual Analyses

These Minitab residual model diagnostics consist of four different plots. The graph on the upper right is a plot of the residuals versus the fits. Note that this residual plot "flares-out" as *x* gets larger. This pattern is an indication of heteroscedasticity, which is a violation of the assumption of constant variance for error terms. The graph in the upper left is a normal probability plot of the residuals. A straight line indicates that the residuals are normally distributed. Observe that this normal plot is relatively close to being a straight line, indicating that the residuals are nearly normal in shape. This normal distribution is confirmed by the graph on the lower left, which is a histogram of the residuals. The histogram groups residuals in classes so the researcher can observe where groups of the residuals lie without having to rely on the residual plot and to validate the notion that the residuals are approximately normally distributed. In this problem, the pattern is indicative of at least a mound-shaped distribution of residuals.

DEMONSTRATION PROBLEM 12.2

Compute the residuals for Demonstration Problem 12.1 in which a regression model was developed to predict the number of full-time equivalent workers (FTEs) by the number of beds in a hospital. Analyze the residuals by using Minitab graphic diagnostics.

Solution: The data and computed residuals are shown in the following table.

HOSPITAL	NUMBER OF BEDS x	FTES y	PREDICTED VALUE $\hat{y}$	RESIDUALS $y - \hat{y}$
1	23	69	82.22	−13.22
2	29	95	95.62	−.62

3	29	102	95.62	6.38
4	35	118	109.01	8.99
5	42	126	124.63	1.37
6	46	125	133.56	−8.56
7	50	138	142.49	−4.49
8	54	178	151.42	26.58
9	64	156	173.74	−17.74
10	66	184	178.20	5.80
11	76	176	200.52	−24.52
12	78	225	204.98	<u>20.02</u>

$$\Sigma(y - \hat{y}) = -.01$$

Note that the regression model fits these particular data well for hospitals 2 and 5, as indicated by residuals of −.62 and 1.37 FTEs, respectively. For hospitals 1, 8, 9, 11, and 12, the residuals are relatively large, indicating that the regression model does not fit the data for these hospitals well. The Residuals Versus the Fitted Values graph indicates that the residuals seem to increase as x increases, indicating a potential problem with heteroscedasticity. The normal plot of residuals indicates that the residuals are nearly normally distributed. The histogram of residuals shows that the residuals pile up in the middle, but are somewhat skewed toward the larger positive values.

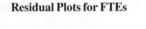

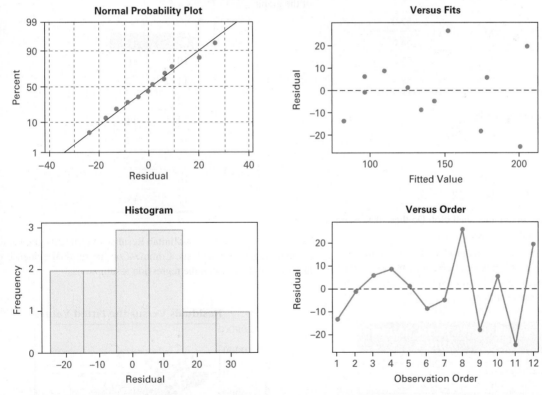

12.4 Problems

12.13. Determine the equation of the regression line for the following data, and compute the residuals.

x	15	8	19	12	5
y	47	36	56	44	21

12.14. Solve for the predicted values of y and the residuals for the data in Problem 12.6. The data are provided here again:

x	12	21	28	8	20
y	17	15	22	19	24

12.15. Solve for the predicted values of y and the residuals for the data in Problem 12.7. The data are provided here again:

x	140	119	103	91	65	29	24
y	25	29	46	70	88	112	128

12.16. Solve for the predicted values of y and the residuals for the data in Problem 12.8. The data are provided here again:

Advertising	12.5	3.7	21.6	60.0	37.6	6.1	16.8	41.2
Sales		148	55	338	994	541	89	126	379

12.17. Solve for the predicted values of y and the residuals for the data in Problem 12.9. The data are provided here again:

Bond Rate	5%	12%	9%	15%	7%
Prime Interest Rate	16%	6%	8%	4%	7%

12.18. In problem 12.10, you were asked to develop the equation of a regression model to predict the number of business bankruptcies by the number of firm births. Using this regression model and the data given in problem 12.10 (and provided here again), solve for the predicted values of y and the residuals. Comment on the size of the residuals.

BUSINESS BANKRUPTCIES (1,000)	FIRM BIRTHS (10,000)
34.3	58.1
35.0	55.4
38.5	57.0
40.1	58.5
35.5	57.4
37.9	58.0

12.19. The equation of a regression line is

$$\hat{y} = 50.506 - 1.646x$$

and the data are as follows.

x	5	7	11	12	19	25
y	47	38	32	24	22	10

Solve for the residuals and graph a residual plot. Do these data seem to violate any of the assumptions of regression?

12.20. Wisconsin is an important milk-producing state. Some people might argue that because of transportation costs, the cost of milk increases with the distance of markets from Wisconsin. Suppose the milk prices in eight cities are as follows.

COST OF MILK (PER GALLON)	DISTANCE FROM MADISON (MILES)
$2.64	1,245
2.31	425
2.45	1,346
2.52	973
2.19	255
2.55	865
2.40	1,080
2.37	296

Use the prices along with the distance of each city from Madison, Wisconsin, to develop a regression line to predict the price of a gallon of milk by the number of miles the city is from Madison. Use the data and the regression equation to compute residuals for this model. Sketch a graph of the residuals in the order of the x values. Comment on the shape of the residual graph.

12.21. Graph the following residuals, and indicate which of the assumptions underlying regression appear to be in jeopardy on the basis of the graph.

x	$y - \hat{y}$
213	−11
216	−5
227	−2
229	−1
237	+6
247	+10
263	+12

12.22. Graph the following residuals, and indicate which of the assumptions underlying regression appear to be in jeopardy on the basis of the graph.

x	$y - \hat{y}$
10	+6
11	+3
12	−1
13	−11
14	−3
15	+2
16	+5
17	+8

12.23. Study the following Minitab Residuals Versus Fits graphic for a simple regression analysis. Comment on the residual evidence of lack of compliance with the regression assumptions.

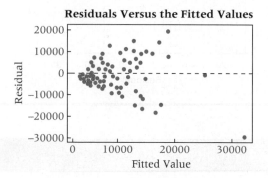

Residuals Versus the Fitted Values

12.5 Standard Error of the Estimate

Residuals represent errors of estimation for individual points. With large samples of data, residual computations become laborious. Even with computers, a researcher sometimes has difficulty working through pages of residuals in an effort to understand the error of the regression model. An alternative way of examining the error of the model is the standard error of the estimate, which provides a single measurement of the regression error.

Because the sum of the residuals is zero, attempting to determine the total amount of error by summing the residuals is fruitless. This zero-sum characteristic of residuals can be avoided by squaring the residuals and then summing them.

Table 12.6 contains the airline cost data from Table 12.3, along with the residuals and the residuals squared. The *total of the residuals squared* column is called the **sum of squares of error (SSE)**.

Sum of Squares of Error

$$SSE = \Sigma(y - \hat{y})^2$$

In theory, infinitely many lines can be fit to a sample of points. However, Formulas 12.2 and 12.4 produce a line of best fit for which the SSE is the smallest for any line that can be fit to the sample data. This result is guaranteed, because Formulas 12.2 and 12.4 are derived from calculus to minimize SSE. For this reason, the regression process used in this chapter is called *least squares* regression.

A computational version of the equation for computing SSE is less meaningful in terms of interpretation than $\Sigma(y - \hat{y})^2$ but it is usually easier to compute. The computational formula for SSE follows.

Computational Formula for SSE

$$SSE = \Sigma y^2 - b_0 \Sigma y - b_1 \Sigma xy$$

TABLE 12.6 Determining SSE for the Airline Cost Example

NUMBER OF PASSENGERS x	COST ($1,000) y	RESIDUAL $y - \hat{y}$	$(y - \hat{y})^2$
61	4.280	.227	.05153
63	4.080	−.054	.00292
67	4.420	.123	.01513
69	4.170	−.208	.04326
70	4.480	.061	.00372
74	4.300	−.282	.07952
76	4.820	.157	.02465
81	4.700	−.167	.02789
86	5.110	.040	.00160
91	5.130	−.144	.02074
95	5.640	.204	.04162
97	5.560	.042	.00176
		$\Sigma(y - \hat{y}) = -.001$	$\Sigma(y - \hat{y})^2 = .31434$

Sum of squares of error = SSE = .31434

For the airline cost example,

$$\Sigma y^2 = \Sigma[(4.280)^2 + (4.080)^2 + (4.420)^2 + (4.170)^2 + (4.480)^2 + (4.300)^2 + (4.820)^2$$
$$+ (4.700)^2 + (5.110)^2 + (5.130)^2 + (5.640)^2 + (5.560)^2] = 270.9251$$

$$b_0 = 1.5697928$$

$$b_1 = .0407016*$$

$$\Sigma y = 56.69$$

$$\Sigma xy = 4462.22$$

$$SSE = \Sigma y^2 - b_0\,\Sigma y - b_1\,\Sigma xy$$
$$= 270.9251 - (1.5697928)(56.69) - (.0407016)(4462.22) = .31405$$

The slight discrepancy between this value and the value computed in Table 12.6 is due to rounding error.

The sum of squares error is in part a function of the number of pairs of data being used to compute the sum, which lessens the value of SSE as a measurement of error. A more useful measurement of error is the standard error of the estimate. The **standard error of the estimate**, denoted s_e, is *a standard deviation of the error of the regression model*. The standard error of the estimate follows.

Standard Error of the Estimate

$$s_e = \sqrt{\frac{SSE}{n-2}}$$

The standard error of the estimate for the airline cost example is

$$s_e = \sqrt{\frac{SSE}{n-2}} = \sqrt{\frac{.31434}{10}} = .1773$$

How is the standard error of the estimate used? As previously mentioned, the standard error of the estimate is a standard deviation of error. Recall from Chapter 3 that if data are approximately normally distributed, the empirical rule states that about 68% of all values are within $\mu \pm 1\sigma$ and that about 95% of all values are within $\mu \pm 2\sigma$. One of the assumptions for regression states that for a given x the error terms are normally distributed. Because the error terms are normally distributed, s_e is the standard deviation of error, and the average error is zero, approximately 68% of the error values (residuals) should be within $0 \pm 1s_e$ and 95% of the error values (residuals) should be within $0 \pm 2s_e$. By having knowledge of the variables being studied and by examining the value of s_e, the researcher can often make a judgment about the fit of the regression model to the data by using s_e. How can the s_e value for the airline cost example be interpreted?

The regression model here is used to predict airline cost by number of passengers. Note that the range of the airline cost data in Table 12.3 is from 4.08 to 5.64 ($4,080 to $5,640). The regression model for the data yields an s_e of .1773. An interpretation of s_e is that the standard deviation of error for the airline cost example is $177.30. If the error terms were normally distributed about the given values of x, approximately 68% of the error terms would be within ±$177.30 and 95% would be within ±2($177.30) = ±$354.60. Examination of the residuals reveals that 8 out of 12 (67%) of the residuals are within ±$1s_e$ and 100% of the residuals are within $2s_e$. The standard error of the estimate provides a single measure of error, which, if the researcher has enough background in the area being analyzed, can be used to understand the magnitude of errors in the model. In addition, some researchers use the standard error of the estimate to identify outliers. They do so by looking for data that are outside ±$2s_e$ or ±$3s_e$.

---

*Note: In previous sections, the values of the slope and intercept were rounded off for ease of computation and interpretation. They are shown here with more precision in an effort to reduce rounding error.

DEMONSTRATION PROBLEM 12.3

Compute the sum of squares of error and the standard error of the estimate for Demonstration Problem 12.1, in which a regression model was developed to predict the number of FTEs at a hospital by the number of beds.

Solution:

HOSPITAL	NUMBER OF BEDS x	FTES y	RESIDUALS $y - \hat{y}$	$(y - \hat{y})^2$
1	23	69	−13.22	174.77
2	29	95	−.62	0.38
3	29	102	6.38	40.70
4	35	118	8.99	80.82
5	42	126	1.37	1.88
6	46	125	−8.56	73.27
7	50	138	−4.49	20.16
8	54	178	26.58	706.50
9	64	156	−17.74	314.71
10	66	184	5.80	33.64
11	76	176	−24.52	601.23
12	78	225	20.02	400.80
	$\Sigma x = 592$	$\Sigma y = 1692$	$\Sigma(y - \hat{y}) = -.01$	$\Sigma(y - \hat{y})^2 = 2448.86$

SSE = 2448.86

$$S_e = \sqrt{\frac{SSE}{n-2}} = \sqrt{\frac{2448.86}{10}} = 15.65$$

The standard error of the estimate is 15.65 FTEs. An examination of the residuals for this problem reveals that 8 of 12 (67%) are within $\pm 1s_e$ and 100% are within $\pm 2s_e$. Is this size of error acceptable? Hospital administrators probably can best answer that question.

12.5 Problems

12.24. Determine the sum of squares of error (SSE) and the standard error of the estimate (s_e) for Problem 12.6. Determine how many of the residuals computed in Problem 12.14 (for Problem 12.6) are within one standard error of the estimate. If the error terms are normally distributed, approximately how many of these residuals should be within $\pm 1s_e$?

12.25. Determine the SSE and the s_e for Problem 12.7. Use the residuals computed in Problem 12.15 (for Problem 12.7) and determine how many of them are within $\pm 1s_e$ and $\pm 2s_e$. How do these numbers compare with what the empirical rule says should occur if the error terms are normally distributed?

12.26. Determine the SSE and the s_e for Problem 12.8. Think about the variables being analyzed by regression in this problem and comment on the value of s_e.

12.27. Determine the SSE and s_e for Problem 12.9. Examine the variables being analyzed by regression in this problem and comment on the value of s_e.

12.28. In Problem 12.10, you were asked to develop the equation of a regression model to predict the number of business bankruptcies by the number of firm births. For this regression model, solve for the standard error of the estimate and comment on it.

12.29. Use the data from Problem 12.19 and determine the s_e.

12.30. Determine the SSE and the s_e for Problem 12.20. Comment on the size of s_e for this regression model, which is used to predict the cost of milk.

12.31. Determine the equation of the regression line to predict annual sales of a company from the yearly stock market volume of shares sold in a recent year. Compute the standard error of the estimate for this model. Does volume of shares sold appear to be a good predictor of a company's sales? Why or why not?

ANNUAL SALES ($ BILLIONS)	ANNUAL VOLUME (MILLIONS OF SHARES)
10.5	728.6
48.1	497.9
64.8	439.1
20.1	377.9
11.4	375.5
123.8	363.8
89.0	276.3

12.6 | Coefficient of Determination

A widely used measure of fit for regression models is the **coefficient of determination**, or r^2. The coefficient of determination is *the proportion of variability of the dependent variable (y) accounted for or explained by the independent variable (x)*.

The coefficient of determination ranges from 0 to 1. An r^2 of zero means that the predictor accounts for none of the variability of the dependent variable and that there is no regression prediction of y by x. An r^2 of 1 means perfect prediction of y by x and that 100% of the variability of y is accounted for by x. Of course, most r^2 values are between the extremes. The researcher must interpret whether a particular r^2 is high or low, depending on the use of the model and the context within which the model was developed.

In exploratory research where the variables are less understood, low values of r^2 are likely to be more acceptable than they are in areas of research where the parameters are more developed and understood. One NASA researcher who uses vehicular weight to predict mission cost searches for the regression models to have an r^2 of .90 or higher. However, a business researcher who is trying to develop a model to predict the motivation level of employees might be pleased to get an r^2 near .50 in the initial research.

The dependent variable, y, being predicted in a regression model has a variation that is measured by the sum of squares of y (SS$_{yy}$):

$$SS_{yy} = \Sigma(y - \bar{y})^2 = \Sigma y^2 - \frac{(\Sigma y)^2}{n}$$

and is the sum of the squared deviations of the y values from the mean value of y. This variation can be broken into two additive variations: the *explained variation*, measured by the sum of squares of regression (SSR), and the *unexplained variation*, measured by the sum of squares of error (SSE). This relationship can be expressed in equation form as

$$SS_{yy} = SSR + SSE$$

If each term in the equation is divided by SS$_{yy}$, the resulting equation is

$$1 = \frac{SSR}{SS_{yy}} + \frac{SSE}{SS_{yy}}$$

The term r^2 is the proportion of the y variability that is explained by the regression model and represented here as

$$r^2 = \frac{SSR}{SS_{yy}}$$

Substituting this equation into the preceding relationship gives

$$1 = r^2 + \frac{SSE}{SS_{yy}}$$

Solving for r^2 yields Formula 12.5.

Coefficient of Determination

$$r^2 = 1 - \frac{SSE}{SS_{yy}} = 1 - \frac{SSE}{\Sigma y^2 - \frac{(\Sigma y)^2}{n}} \qquad (12.5)$$

Note: $0 \le r^2 \le 1$

The value of r^2 for the airline cost example is solved as follows:

$$SSE = .31434$$

$$SS_{yy} = \Sigma y^2 - \frac{(\Sigma y)^2}{n} = 270.9251 - \frac{(56.69)^2}{12} = 3.11209$$

$$r^2 = 1 - \frac{SSE}{SS_{yy}} = 1 - \frac{.31434}{3.11209} = .899$$

That is, 89.9% of the variability of the cost of flying a Boeing 737 airplane on a commercial flight is explained by variations in the number of passengers. This result also means that 10.1% of the variance in airline flight cost, y, is unaccounted for by x or unexplained by the regression model.

The coefficient of determination can be solved for directly by using

$$r^2 = \frac{SSR}{SS_{yy}}$$

It can be shown through algebra that

$$SSR = b_1^2 SS_{xx}$$

From this equation, a computational formula for r^2 can be developed.

Computational Formula for r^2

$$r^2 = \frac{b_1^2 SS_{xx}}{SS_{yy}}$$

For the airline cost example, $b_1 = .0407016$, $SS_{xx} = 1689$, and $SS_{yy} = 3.11209$. Using the computational formula for r^2 yields

$$r^2 = \frac{(.0407016)^2(1689)}{3.11209} = .899$$

DEMONSTRATION PROBLEM 12.4

Compute the coefficient of determination (r^2) for Demonstration Problem 12.1, in which a regression model was developed to predict the number of FTEs of a hospital by the number of beds.

Solution:

$$SSE = 2448.86$$

$$SS_{yy} = 260,136 - \frac{(1692)^2}{12} = 21,564$$

$$r^2 = 1 - \frac{SSE}{SS_{yy}} = 1 - \frac{2448.86}{21,564} = .886$$

This regression model accounts for 88.6% of the variance in FTEs, leaving only 11.4% unexplained variance.

Using $SS_{xx} = 3838.667$ and $b_1 = 2.232$ from Demonstration Problem 12.1, we can solve for r^2 with the computational formula:

$$r^2 = \frac{b_1^2 SS_{xx}}{SS_{yy}} = \frac{(2.232)^2(3838.667)}{21,564} = .886$$

Relationship Between r and r^2

Is r, the coefficient of correlation (introduced in Section 12.1), related to r^2, the coefficient of determination in linear regression? The answer is yes: r^2 equals $(r)^2$. The coefficient of determination is the square of the coefficient of correlation. In Demonstration Problem 12.1, a regression model was developed to predict FTEs by number of hospital beds. The r^2 value for the model was .886. Taking the square root of this value yields $r = .941$, which is the correlation between the sample number of beds and FTEs. A word of caution here: Because r^2 is always positive, solving for r by taking $\sqrt{r^2}$ gives the correct magnitude of r but may give the wrong sign. The researcher must examine the sign of the slope of the regression line to determine whether a positive or negative relationship exists between the variables and then assign the appropriate sign to the correlation value.

12.6 Problems

12.32. Compute r^2 for Problem 12.24 (Problem 12.6). Discuss the value of r^2 obtained.

12.33. Compute r^2 for Problem 12.25 (Problem 12.7). Discuss the value of r^2 obtained.

12.34. Compute r^2 for Problem 12.26 (Problem 12.8). Discuss the value of r^2 obtained.

12.35. Compute r^2 for Problem 12.27 (Problem 12.9). Discuss the value of r^2 obtained.

12.36. In Problem 12.10, you were asked to develop the equation of a regression model to predict the number of business bankruptcies by the number of firm births. For this regression model, solve for the coefficient of determination and comment on it.

12.37. The Conference Board produces a Consumer Confidence Index (CCI) that reflects people's feelings about general business conditions, employment opportunities, and their own income prospects. Some researchers may feel that consumer confidence is a function of the median household income. Shown here are the CCIs for nine years and the median household incomes for the same nine years published by the U.S. Census Bureau. Determine the equation of the regression line to predict the CCI from the median household income. Compute the standard error of the estimate for this model. Compute the value of r^2. Does median household income appear to be a good predictor of the CCI? Why or why not?

CCI	MEDIAN HOUSEHOLD INCOME ($1,000)
116.8	37.415
91.5	36.770
68.5	35.501
61.6	35.047
65.9	34.700
90.6	34.942
100.0	35.887
104.6	36.306
125.4	37.005

12.7 | Hypothesis Tests for the Slope of the Regression Model and Testing the Overall Model

Testing the Slope

A hypothesis test can be conducted on the sample slope of the regression model to determine whether the population slope is significantly different from zero. This test is another way to determine how well a regression model fits the data. Suppose a researcher decides that it is not worth the effort to develop a linear regression model to predict y from x. An alternative approach might be to average the y values and use $\bar{y}$ as the predictor of y for all values of x. For the airline cost example, instead of using number of passengers as the predictor, the researcher would use the average value of airline cost, $\bar{y}$, as the predictor. In this case the average value of y is

$$\bar{y} = \frac{56.69}{12} = 4.7242, \text{ or } \$4,724.20$$

Using this result as a model to predict y, if the number of passengers is 61, 70, or 95—or any other number—the predicted value of y is still 4.7242. Essentially, this approach fits the line of $\bar{y} = 4.7242$ through the data, which is a horizontal line with a slope of zero. Would a regression analysis offer anything more than the $\bar{y}$ model? Using this nonregression model (the $\bar{y}$ model) as a worst case, the researcher can analyze the regression line to determine whether it adds a more significant amount of predictability of y than does the $\bar{y}$ model. Because the slope of the $\bar{y}$ line is zero, one way to determine whether the regression line adds significant predictability is to test the population slope of the regression line to find out whether the slope is different from zero. As the slope of the regression line diverges from zero, the regression model is adding predictability that the $\bar{y}$ line is not generating. For this reason, testing the slope of the regression line to determine whether the slope is different from zero is important. If the slope is not different from zero, the regression line is doing nothing more than the $\bar{y}$ line in predicting y.

How does the researcher go about testing the slope of the regression line? Why not just examine the observed sample slope? For example, the slope of the regression line for the airline cost data is .0407. This value is obviously not zero. The problem is that this slope is obtained from a sample of 12 data points; and if another sample was taken, it is likely that a different slope would be obtained. For this reason, the population slope is statistically tested using the sample slope. The question is: If all the pairs of data points for the population were available, would the slope of that regression line be different from zero? Here the sample slope, b_1, is used as evidence to test whether the population slope is different from zero. The hypotheses for this test follow.

$$H_0: \beta_1 = 0$$
$$H_a: \beta_1 \neq 0$$

Note that this test is two-tailed. The null hypothesis can be rejected if the slope is either negative or positive. A negative slope indicates an inverse relationship between x and y. That is, larger values of x are related to smaller values of y, and vice versa. Both negative and positive slopes can be different from zero. To determine whether there is a significant *positive* relationship between two variables, the hypotheses would be one tailed, or

$$H_0: \beta_1 = 0$$
$$H_a: \beta_1 > 0$$

To test for a significant *negative* relationship between two variables, the hypotheses also would be one tailed, or

$$H_0: \beta_1 = 0$$
$$H_a: \beta_1 < 0$$

In each case, testing the null hypothesis involves a t test of the slope.

t Test of Slope

$$t = \frac{b_1 - \beta_1}{s_b}$$

where

$$s_b = \frac{s_e}{\sqrt{SS_{xx}}}$$

$$s_e = \sqrt{\frac{SSE}{n - 2}}$$

$$SS_{xx} = \Sigma x^2 - \frac{(\Sigma x)^2}{n}$$

$\beta_1 =$ the hypothesized slope
$df = n - 2$

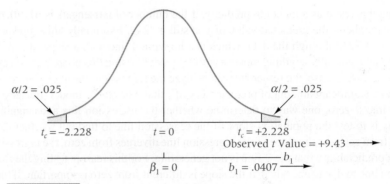

t **Test of Slope from Airline Cost Example**

The test of the slope of the regression line for the airline cost regression model for $\alpha = .05$ follows. The regression line derived for the data is

$$\hat{y} = 1.57 + .0407x$$

The sample slope is $.0407 = b_1$. The value of s_e is .1773, $\Sigma x = 930$, $\Sigma x^2 = 73{,}764$, and $n = 12$. The hypotheses are

$$H_0: \beta_1 = 0$$

$$H_a: \beta_1 \neq 0$$

The df $= n - 2 = 12 - 2 = 10$. As this test is two tailed, $\alpha/2 = .025$. The table *t* value is $t_{.025,10} = \pm 2.228$. The observed *t* value for this sample slope is

$$t = \frac{.0407 - 0}{.1773 \Big/ \sqrt{73{,}764 - \dfrac{(930)^2}{12}}} = 9.43$$

As shown in Figure 12.14, the *t* value calculated from the sample slope falls in the rejection region and the *p*-value is .0000027. The null hypothesis that the population slope is zero is rejected. This linear regression model is adding significantly more predictive information to the $\bar{y}$ model (no regression).

It is desirable to reject the null hypothesis in testing the slope of the regression model. In rejecting the null hypothesis of a zero population slope, we are stating that the regression model is adding something to the explanation of the variation of the dependent variable that the average value of *y* model does not. Failure to reject the null hypothesis in this test causes the researcher to conclude that the regression model has no predictability of the dependent variable, and the model, therefore, has little or no use.

Thinking Critically About Statistics in Business Today

Are Facial Characteristics Correlated with CEO Traits?

Researchers John R. Graham, Campbell R. Harvey, and Manju Puri, all of the Fuqua School of Business at Duke, conducted a study using almost 2,000 participants in an effort to determine if facial characteristics are related to various CEO traits. In one experiment of the study, the researchers showed pictures of 138 CEOs to 230 study participants who were asked to rate each CEO picture in terms of four attributes: competence, attractiveness, trustworthiness, and likeability. The results of the study

showed that all four traits are positively correlated. That is, if a CEO (based on the picture) was rated as high on competence, he was also rated high on each of attractiveness, trustworthiness, and likeability. The largest correlation was between trustworthiness and likeability, and the smallest correlation was between trustworthiness and attractiveness. These ratings on each of the four traits were also analyzed to determine if there was a correlation with total sales of the CEO's firm and with CEO income. The results showed that there was a small positive correlation between CEO ratings on competence and company sales. There was also a small positive correlation between CEO ratings on competence and their income. In another experiment, 138 CEOs were rated on being "baby-faced." Analysis of the study data showed that there was a positive correlation between CEOs' baby-faced rating and likability. That is, the more CEOs appeared to be baby-faced, the higher they were rated in likeability. However, there was a negative correlation between CEOs' baby-faced rating and competence.

THINGS TO PONDER

1. Similar studies have been conducted in the area of political science to determine the electability of people running for office. What do you think is the real impact of studies like this in business?

2. The authors of the study suggest that baby-faced people tend to have large, round eyes, high eyebrows and a small chin, thereby giving the perception of a baby-faced appearance. In this study, baby-faced CEOs were rated more highly on one attribute and low on another attribute. Based on these results, what advice would you give to a "baby-faced" business manager who aspires to be a CEO?

Source: John R. Graham, Campbell R. Harvey, and Manju Puri. "A Corporate Beauty Contest," working paper (15906) in the NBER Working Paper Series, National Bureau of Economic Research, at http://www.nber.org/papers/w15906, April 2010.

DEMONSTRATION PROBLEM 12.5

Test the slope of the regression model developed in Demonstration Problem 12.1 to predict the number of FTEs in a hospital from the number of beds to determine whether there is a significant positive slope. Use $\alpha = .01$.

Solution: The hypotheses for this problem are

$$H_0: \beta_1 = 0$$

$$H_a: \beta_1 > 0$$

The level of significance is .01. With 12 pairs of data, df = 10. The critical table t value is $t_{.01,10} = 2.764$. The regression line equation for this problem is

$$\hat{y} = 30.888 + 2.232x$$

The sample slope, b_1, is 2.232, and $s_e = 15.65$, $\Sigma x = 592$, $\Sigma x^2 = 33,044$, and $n = 12$. The observed t value for the sample slope is

$$t = \frac{2.232 - 0}{15.65 \Big/ \sqrt{33,044 - \frac{(592)^2}{12}}} = 8.84$$

The observed t value (8.84) is in the rejection region because it is greater than the critical table t value of 2.764 and the p-value is .0000024. The null hypothesis is rejected. The population slope for this regression line is significantly different from zero in the positive direction. This regression model is adding significant predictability over the $\overline{y}$ model.

Testing the Overall Model

It is common in regression analysis to compute an F test to determine the overall significance of the model. Most computer software packages include the F test and its associated ANOVA table as standard regression output. In multiple regression (Chapters 13 and 14), this test determines whether at least one of the regression coefficients (from multiple predictors) is different from zero. Simple regression provides only one predictor and only one regression coefficient to test. Because the regression coefficient is the slope of the regression line, the F test for overall significance is testing the same thing as the t test in simple regression. The hypotheses being tested in simple regression by the F test for overall significance are

$$H_0: \beta_1 = 0$$
$$H_a: \beta_1 \neq 0$$

In the case of simple regression analysis, $F = t^2$. Thus, for the airline cost example, the F value is

$$F = t^2 = (9.43)^2 = 88.92$$

The F value is computed directly by

$$F = \frac{SS_{reg}/df_{reg}}{SS_{err}/df_{err}} = \frac{MS_{reg}}{MS_{err}}$$

where
$$df_{reg} = k$$
$$df_{err} = n - k - 1$$
$$k = \text{the number of independent variables}$$

The values of the sum of squares (SS), degrees of freedom (df), and mean squares (MS) are obtained from the analysis of variance table, which is produced with other regression statistics as standard output from statistical software packages. Shown here is the analysis of variance table produced by Minitab for the airline cost example.

Analysis of Variance					
Source	DF	SS	MS	F	p
Regression	1	2.7980	2.7980	89.09	0.000
Residual Error	10	0.3141	0.0314		
Total	11	3.1121			

The F value for the airline cost example is calculated from the analysis of variance table information as

$$F = \frac{2.7980/1}{.3141/10} = \frac{2.7980}{.03141} = 89.08$$

The difference between this value (89.08) and the value obtained by squaring the t statistic (88.92) is due to rounding error. The probability of obtaining an F value this large or larger by chance if there is no regression prediction in this model is .000, according to the ANOVA output (the p-value). This output value means it is highly unlikely that the population slope is zero and also unlikely that there is no prediction due to regression from this model, given the sample statistics obtained. Hence, it is highly likely that this regression model adds significant predictability of the dependent variable.

Note from the ANOVA table that the degrees of freedom due to regression are equal to 1. Simple regression models have only one independent variable; therefore, $k = 1$. The degrees of freedom error in simple regression analysis is always $n - k - 1 = n - 1 - 1 = n - 2$. With the degrees of freedom due to regression (1) as the numerator degrees of freedom and the degrees of freedom due to error $(n - 2)$ as the denominator degrees of freedom, Table A.7 can be used to obtain the critical F value $(F_{\alpha,1,n-2})$ to help make the hypothesis testing decision about the overall regression model if the p-value of F is not given in the computer output. This critical F value is always found in the right tail of the distribution. In simple regression, the relationship between the critical t value to test the slope and the critical F value of overall significance is

$$t^2_{\alpha/2,n-2} = F_{\alpha,1,n-2}$$

For the airline cost example with a two-tailed test and $\alpha = .05$, the critical value of $t_{.025,10}$ is ± 2.228 and the critical value of $F_{.05,1,10}$ is 4.96.

$$t^2_{.025,10} = (\pm 2.228)^2 = 4.96 = F_{.05,1,10}$$

12.7 Problems

12.38. Test the slope of the regression line determined in Problem 12.6. Use $\alpha = .05$.

12.39. Test the slope of the regression line determined in Problem 12.7. Use $\alpha = .01$.

12.40. Test the slope of the regression line determined in Problem 12.8. Use $\alpha = .10$.

12.41. Test the slope of the regression line determined in Problem 12.9. Use a 5% level of significance.

12.42. Test the slope of the regression line developed in Problem 12.10. Use a 5% level of significance.

12.43. Study the following analysis of variance table which was generated from a simple regression analysis. Discuss the F test of the overall model. Determine the value of t and test the slope of the regression line.

Analysis of Variance

Source	DF	SS	MS	F	p
Regression	1	116.65	116.65	8.26	0.021
Error	8	112.95	14.12		
Total	9	229.60			

12.8 Estimation

One of the main uses of regression analysis is as a prediction tool. If the regression function is a good model, the researcher can use the regression equation to determine values of the dependent variable from various values of the independent variable. For example, financial brokers would like to have a model with which they could predict the selling price of a stock on a certain day by a variable such as unemployment rate or producer price index. Marketing managers would like to have a site location model with which they could predict the sales volume of a new location by variables such as population density or number of competitors. The airline cost example presents a regression model that has the potential to predict the cost of flying an airplane by the number of passengers.

In simple regression analysis, a point estimate prediction of y can be made by substituting the associated value of x into the regression equation and solving for y. From the airline cost example, if the number of passengers is $x = 73$, the predicted cost of the airline flight can be computed by substituting the x value into the regression equation determined in Section 12.3:

$$\hat{y} = 1.57 + .0407x = 1.57 + .0407(73) = 4.5411$$

The point estimate of the predicted cost is 4.5411 or \$4,541.10.

Confidence Intervals to Estimate the Conditional Mean of y: $\mu_{y|x}$

Although a point estimate is often of interest to the researcher, the regression line is determined by a sample set of points; and if a different sample is taken, a different line will result, yielding a different point estimate. Hence computing a *confidence interval* for the estimation is often useful. Because for any value of x (independent variable) there can be many values of y (dependent variable), one type of **confidence interval** is *an estimate of the average value of* *y for a given x.* This average value of *y* is denoted $E(y_x)$—the expected value of *y*—and can be computed using Formula 12.6.

> **Confidence Interval to Estimate $E(y_x)$ for a Given Value of *x***
>
> $$\hat{y} \pm t_{\alpha/2, n-2} s_e \sqrt{\frac{1}{n} + \frac{(x_0 - \bar{x})^2}{SS_{xx}}}$$ (12.6)
>
> where
>
> x_0 = a particular value of *x*
>
> $$SS_{xx} = \Sigma x^2 - \frac{(\Sigma x)^2}{n}$$

The application of this formula can be illustrated with construction of a 95% confidence interval to estimate the average value of *y* (airline cost) for the airline cost example when *x* (number of passengers) is 73. For a 95% confidence interval, $\alpha = .05$ and $\alpha/2 = .025$. The df $= n - 2 = 12 - 2 = 10$. The table *t* value is $t_{.025,10} = 2.228$. Other needed values for this problem, which were solved for previously, are

$$s_e = .1773 \quad \Sigma x = 930 \quad \bar{x} = 77.5 \quad \Sigma x^2 = 73,764$$

For $x_0 = 73$, the value of $\hat{y}$ is 4.5411. The computed confidence interval for the average value of *y*, $E(y_{73})$, is

$$4.5411 \pm (2.228)(.1773) \sqrt{\frac{1}{12} + \frac{(73 - 77.5)^2}{73,764 - \frac{(930)^2}{12}}} = 4.5411 \pm .1220$$

$$4.4191 \le E(y_{73}) \le 4.6631$$

That is, with 95% confidence the average value of *y* for $x = 73$ is between 4.4191 and 4.6631.

Table 12.7 shows confidence intervals computed for the airline cost example for several values of *x* to estimate the average value of *y*. Note that as *x* values get farther from the mean *x* value (77.5), the confidence intervals get wider; as the *x* values get closer to the mean, the confidence intervals narrow. The reason is that the numerator of the second term under the radical sign approaches zero as the value of *x* nears the mean and increases as *x* departs from the mean.

Prediction Intervals to Estimate a Single Value of *y*

A second type of interval in regression estimation is a **prediction interval** to *estimate a single value of y for a given value of x.*

TABLE 12.7	Confidence Intervals to Estimate the Average Value of *y* for Some *x* Values in the Airline Cost Example	
x	CONFIDENCE INTERVAL	
62	$4.0934 \pm .1876$	3.9058 to 4.2810
68	$4.3376 \pm .1461$	4.1915 to 4.4837
73	$4.5411 \pm .1220$	4.4191 to 4.6631
85	$5.0295 \pm .1349$	4.8946 to 5.1644
90	$5.2330 \pm .1656$	5.0674 to 5.3986

Prediction Interval to Estimate y for a Given Value of x

$$\hat{y} \pm t_{\alpha/2,n-2} s_e \sqrt{1 + \frac{1}{n} + \frac{(x_0 - \bar{x})^2}{SS_{xx}}} \qquad (12.7)$$

where

x_0 = a particular value of x

$$SS_{xx} = \Sigma x^2 - \frac{(\Sigma x)^2}{n}$$

Formula 12.7 is virtually the same as Formula 12.6, except for the additional value of 1 under the radical. This additional value widens the prediction interval to estimate a single value of y from the confidence interval to estimate the average value of y. This result seems logical because the average value of y is toward the middle of a group of y values. Thus, the confidence interval to estimate the average need not be as wide as the prediction interval produced by Formula 12.7, which takes into account all the y values for a given x.

A 95% prediction interval can be computed to estimate the single value of y for $x = 73$ from the airline cost example by using Formula 12.7. The same values used to construct the confidence interval to estimate the average value of y are used here.

$$t_{.025,10} = 2.228, \ s_e = .1773, \ \Sigma x = 930, \ \bar{x} = 77.5, \ \Sigma x^2 = 73,764$$

For $x_0 = 73$, the value of $\hat{y} = 4.5411$. The computed prediction interval for the single value of y is

$$4.5411 \pm (2.228)(.1773) \sqrt{1 + \frac{1}{12} + \frac{(73 - 77.5)^2}{73,764 - \frac{(930)^2}{12}}} = 4.5411 \pm .4134$$

$$4.1277 \le y \le 4.9545$$

Prediction intervals can be obtained by using the computer. Shown in **Figure 12.15** is the Minitab computer output for the airline cost example. The output displays the predicted value for $x = 73$ ($\hat{y} = 4.5411$), a 95% confidence interval for the average value of y for $x = 73$, and a 95% prediction interval for a single value of y for $x = 73$. Note that the resulting values are virtually the same as those calculated in this section.

Figure 12.16 displays Minitab confidence intervals for various values of x for the average y value and the prediction intervals for a single y value for the airline example. Note that the intervals flare out toward the ends, as the values of x depart from the average x value. Note also that the intervals for a single y value are always wider than the intervals for the average y value for any given value of x.

An examination of the prediction interval formula to estimate y for a given value of x explains why the intervals flare out.

$$\hat{y} \pm t_{\alpha/2,n-2} s_e \sqrt{1 + \frac{1}{n} + \frac{(x_0 - \bar{x})^2}{SS_{xx}}}$$

As we enter different values of x_0 from the regression analysis into the equation, the only thing that changes in the equation is $(x_0 - \bar{x})^2$. This expression increases as individual values

```
Fit        StDev Fit   95.0% CI            95.0 PI
4.5410     0.0547      (4.4191, 4.6629)    (4.1278, 4.9543)
```

FIGURE 12.15 Minitab Output for Prediction Intervals

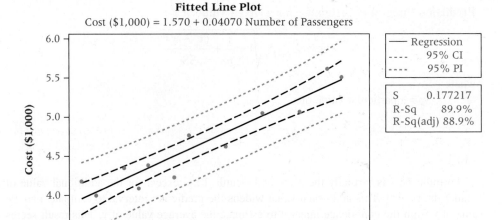

FIGURE 12.16 Minitab Intervals for Estimation

of x_0 get farther from the mean, resulting in an increase in the width of the interval. The interval is narrower for values of x_0 nearer $\bar{x}$ and wider for values of x_0 further from $\bar{x}$.

Caution: *A regression line is determined from a sample of points. The line, the r^2, the s_e, and the confidence intervals change for different sets of sample points. That is, the linear relationship developed for a set of points does not necessarily hold for values of x outside the domain of those used to establish the model. In the airline cost example, the domain of x values (number of passengers) varied from 61 to 97. The regression model developed from these points may not be valid for flights of say 40, 50, or 100 because the regression model was not constructed with x values of those magnitudes. However, decision makers sometimes extrapolate regression results to values of x beyond the domain of those used to develop the formulas (often in time-series sales forecasting). Understanding the limitations of this type of use of regression analysis is essential.*

DEMONSTRATION PROBLEM 12.6

Construct a 95% confidence interval to estimate the average value of y (FTEs) for Demonstration Problem 12.1 when $x = 40$ beds. Then construct a 95% prediction interval to estimate the single value of y for $x = 40$ beds.

Solution: For a 95% confidence interval, $\alpha = .05$, $n = 12$, and df = 10. The table t value is $t_{.025,10} = 2.228$; $s_e = 15.65$, $\Sigma x = 592$, $\bar{x} = 49.33$, and $\Sigma x^2 = 33,044$. For $x_0 = 40$, $\hat{y} = 120.17$. The computed confidence interval for the average value of y is

$$120.17 \pm (2.228)(15.65)\sqrt{\frac{1}{12} + \frac{(40 - 49.33)^2}{33,044 - \frac{(592)^2}{12}}} = 120.17 \pm 11.35$$

$$108.82 \leq E(y_{40}) \leq 131.52$$

With 95% confidence, the statement can be made that the average number of FTEs for a hospital with 40 beds is between 108.82 and 131.52.

The computed prediction interval for the single value of y is

$$120.17 \pm (2.228)(15.65) \sqrt{1 + \frac{1}{12} + \frac{(40 - 49.33)^2}{33,044 - \frac{(592)^2}{12}}} = 120.17 \pm 36.67$$

$$83.5 \le y \le 156.84$$

With 95% confidence, the statement can be made that a single number of FTEs for a hospital with 40 beds is between 83.5 and 156.84. Obviously, this interval is much wider than the 95% confidence interval for the average value of y for $x = 40$.

The following Minitab graph depicts the 95% interval bands for both the average y value and the single y values for all 12 x values in this problem. Note once again the flaring out of the bands near the extreme values of x.

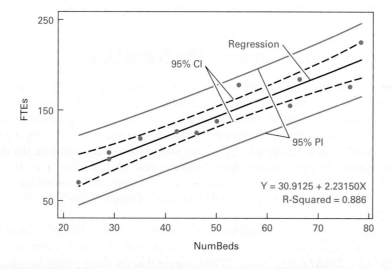

12.8 Problems

12.44. Construct a 95% confidence interval for the average value of y for Problem 12.6. Use $x = 25$.

12.45. Construct a 90% prediction interval for a single value of y for Problem 12.7 using $x = 100$. Construct a 90% prediction interval for a single value of y for Problem 12.7 using $x = 130$. Compare the results. Which prediction interval is greater? Why?

12.46. Construct a 98% confidence interval for the average value of y for Problem 12.8 using $x = 20$. Construct a 98% prediction interval for a single value of y for Problem 12.8 using $x = 20$. Which is wider? Why?

12.47. Construct a 99% confidence interval for the average bond rate in Problem 12.9 for a prime interest rate of 10%. Discuss the meaning of this confidence interval.

12.9   Using Regression to Develop a Forecasting Trend Line

Business researchers often use historical data with measures taken over time in an effort to forecast what might happen in the future. A particular type of data that often lends itself well to this analysis is **time-series data**, defined as *data gathered on a particular characteristic over a period of time at regular intervals*. Some examples of time-series data are 10 years of weekly Dow Jones Industrial Averages, twelve months of daily oil production, or monthly consumption of coffee over a two-year period. To be useful to forecasters, time-series measurements need to be made in regular time intervals and arranged according to time of

TABLE 12.8

Ten-Year Sales Data for Huntsville Chemicals

YEAR	SALES ($ MILLIONS)
2007	7.84
2008	12.26
2009	13.11
2010	15.78
2011	21.29
2012	25.68
2013	23.80
2014	26.43
2015	29.16
2016	33.06

occurrence. As an example, consider the time-series sales data over a 10-year time period for the Huntsville Chemical Company shown in Table 12.8. Note that the measurements (sales) are taken over time and that the sales figures are given on a yearly basis. Time-series data can also be reported daily, weekly, monthly, quarterly, semi-annually, or for other defined time periods.

It is generally believed that time-series data contain any one or combination of four elements: trend, cyclicality, seasonality, and irregularity. While each of these four elements will be discussed in greater detail in Chapter 15, Time-Series Forecasting and Index Numbers, here we examine **trend** and define it as *the long-term general direction of data*. Observing the scatter plot of the Huntsville Chemical Company's sales data shown in Figure 12.17, it is apparent that there is positive trend in the data. That is, there appears to be a long-term upward general direction of sales over time. How can trend be expressed in mathematical terms? In the field of forecasting, it is common to attempt to fit a trend line through time-series data by determining the equation of the trend line and then using the equation of the trend line to predict future data points. How does one go about developing such a line?

Determining the Equation of the Trend Line

Developing the equation of a linear trend line in forecasting is actually a special case of simple regression where the y or dependent variable is the variable of interest that a business analyst wants to forecast and for which a set of measurements has been taken over a period of time. For example, with the Huntsville Chemicals Company data, if company forecasters want to predict sales for the year 2019 using these data, sales would be the dependent variable in the simple regression analysis. In linear trend analysis, the time period is used as the x, the independent or predictor variable, in the analysis to determine the equation of the trend line. In the case of the Huntsville Chemicals Company, the x variable represents the years 2007–2016.

Using sales as the y variable and time (year) as the x variable, the equation of the trend line can be calculated in the usual way as shown in Table 12.9 and is determined to be: $\hat{y} = -5,347.65 + 2.6687x$. The slope, 2.6687, means that for every yearly increase in time, sales increases by an average of $2.6687 (million). The intercept would represent company sales in the year 0, which, of course, in this problem has no meaning since the Huntsville Chemical Company was not in existence in the year 0. Figure 12.18 is a Minitab display of the Huntsville sales data with the fitted trend line. Note that the output contains the equation of the trend line along with the values of s (standard error of the estimate) and R-Sq (r^2). As is typical with data that have a relatively strong trend, the r^2 value (.963) is quite high.

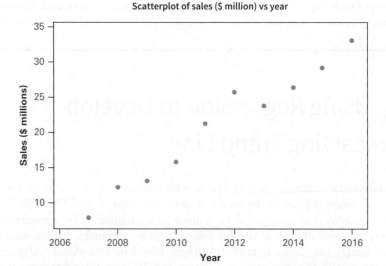

Scatterplot of sales ($ million) vs year

FIGURE 12.17 **Minitab Scatter Plot of Huntsville Chemicals Data**

YEAR	SALES		
x	y	x^2	xy
2007	7.84	4,028,049	15,734.88
2008	12.26	4,032,064	24,618.08
2009	13.11	4,036,081	26,337.99
2010	15.78	4,040,100	31,717.80
2011	21.29	4,044,121	42,814.19
2012	25.68	4,048,144	51,668.16
2013	23.80	4,052,169	47,909.40
2014	26.43	4,052,169	53,230.02
2015	29.16	4,060,225	58,757.40
2016	33.06	4,064,256	66,648.96

TABLE 12.9 Determining the Equation of the Trend Line for the Huntsville Chemical Company Sales Data

$\Sigma x = 20{,}115 \qquad \Sigma y = 208.41 \qquad \Sigma x^2 = 40{,}461{,}405 \qquad \Sigma xy = 419{,}436.9$

$$b_1 = \frac{\Sigma xy - \dfrac{(\Sigma x)(\Sigma y)}{n}}{\Sigma x^2 - \dfrac{(\Sigma x)^2}{n}} = \frac{419{,}436.9 - \dfrac{(20{,}115)(208.41)}{10}}{40{,}461{,}405 - \dfrac{(20{,}115)^2}{10}} = \frac{220.185}{82.5} = 2.6689$$

$$b_0 = \frac{\Sigma y}{n} - b_1 \frac{\Sigma x}{n} = \frac{208.41}{10} - (2.6689)\frac{20{,}115}{10} = -5{,}347.65$$

Equation of the Trend Line: $\quad \hat{y} = -5{,}347.65 + 2.6689\,x$

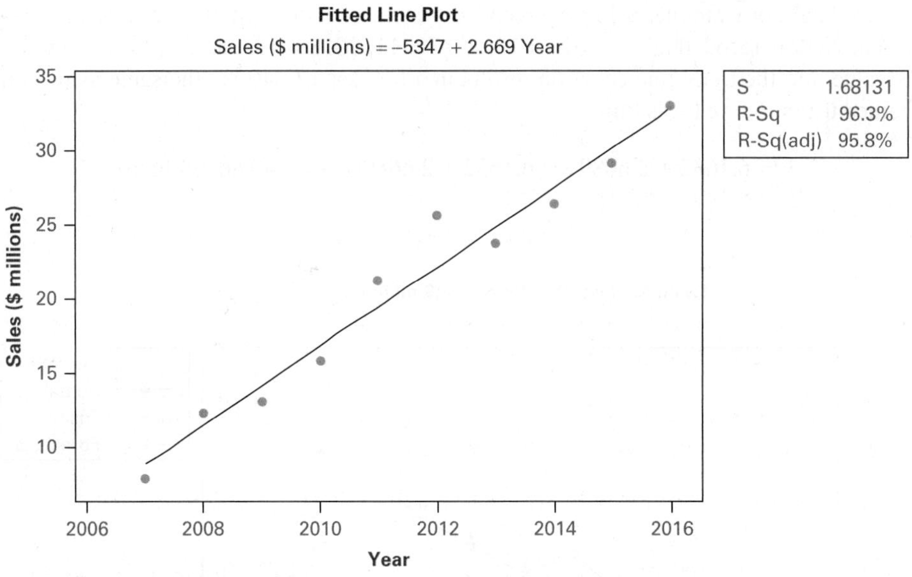

FIGURE 12.18 Minitab Graph of Huntsville Sales Data with a Fitted Trend Line

Forecasting Using the Equation of the Trend Line

The main use of the equation of a trend line by business analysts is for forecasting outcomes for time periods in the future. Recall the caution from Section 12.8 that using a regression model to predict y values for x values outside the domain of those used to develop the model may not be valid. Despite this caution and understanding the potential drawbacks, business forecasters nevertheless extrapolate trend lines beyond the most current time periods of the data and attempt to predict outcomes for time periods in the future. To forecast for future time periods using a trend line, insert the time period of interest into the equation of the trend line and solve for $\hat{y}$. For example, suppose forecasters for the Huntsville Chemicals Company want to predict sales for the year 2019 using the equation of the trend line developed from their historical time series data. Replacing x in the equation of the sales trend line with 2019, results in a forecast of $40.86 (million):

$$\hat{y}(2019) = -5{,}347.65 + 2.6689(2019) = 40.86$$

Figure 12.19 shows Minitab output for the Huntsville Chemicals Company data with the trend line through the data and graphical forecasts for the next three periods (2017, 2018, and 2019). Observe from the graph that the forecast for 2019 is about $41 (million).

Alternate Coding for Time Periods

If you manually calculate the equation of a trend line when the time periods are years, you notice that the calculations can get quite large and cumbersome (observe Table 12.9). However, if the years are consecutive, they can be recoded using many different possible schemes and still produce a meaningful trend line equation (albeit a different y intercept value). For example, instead of using the years 2007–2016, suppose we use the years 1 to 10. That is, 2007 = 1 (first year), 2008 = 2, 2009 = 3, and so on, to 2016 = 10. This recoding scheme produces the trend line equation of: $\hat{y} = 6.1632 + 2.6689x$ as shown in Table 12.10. Notice that the slope of the trend line is the same whether the years 2007 through 2016 are used or the recoded years of 1 through 10, but the y intercept (6.1632) is different. This needs to be taken into consideration when using the equation of the trend line for forecasting. Since the new trend equation was derived from recoded data, forecasts will also need to be made using recoded data. For example, using the recoded system of 1 through 10 to represent "years," the year 2019 is recoded as 13 (2016 = 10, 2017 = 11, 2018 = 12, and 2019 = 13). Inserting this value into the trend line equation results in a forecast of $40.86, the same as the value obtained using raw years as time.

$$\hat{y} = 6.1632 + 2.6689x = 6.1632 + 2.6689(13) = \$40.86 \text{ (million)}.$$

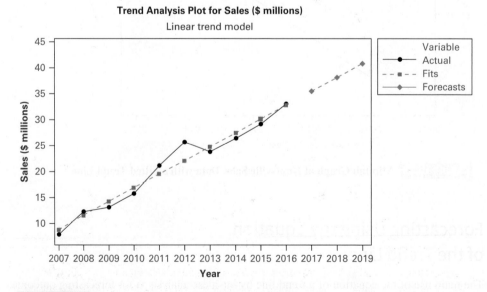

Trend Analysis Plot for Sales ($ millions)
Linear trend model

FIGURE 12.19   **Minitab Output for Trend Line and Forecasts**

TABLE 12.10   **Using Recoded Data to Calculate the Trend Line Equation**

YEAR x	SALES y	x^2	xy
1	7.84	1	7.84
2	12.26	4	24.52
3	13.11	9	39.33
4	15.78	16	63.12
5	21.29	25	106.45
6	25.68	36	154.08
7	23.80	49	166.60
8	26.43	64	211.44
9	29.16	81	262.44
10	33.06	100	330.60
$\Sigma x = 55$	$\Sigma y = 208.41$	$\Sigma x^2 = 385$	$\Sigma xy = 1,366.42$

$$b_1 = \frac{\Sigma xy - \frac{(\Sigma x)(\Sigma y)}{n}}{\Sigma x^2 - \frac{(\Sigma x)^2}{n}} = \frac{(1,366.42) - \frac{(55)(208.41)}{10}}{385 - \frac{(55)^2}{10}} = \frac{220.165}{82.5} = 2.6689$$

$$b_0 = \frac{\Sigma y}{n} - b_1 \frac{\Sigma x}{n} = \frac{208.41}{10} - (2.6689)\frac{55}{10} = 6.1632$$

Equation of the Trend Line: $\hat{y} = 6.1632 + 2.6689x$

Similar time recoding schemes can be used in calculating trend line equations when the time variable is something other than years. For example, in the case of monthly time series data, the time periods can be recoded as:

$$\text{January} = 1, \text{ February} = 2, \text{ March} = 3, \ldots, \text{ December} = 12.$$

In the case of quarterly data over a two-year period, the time periods can be recoded with a scheme such as:

TIME PERIOD		RECODED TIME PERIOD
Year 1:	Quarter 1	1
	Quarter 2	2
	Quarter 3	3
	Quarter 4	4
Year 2:	Quarter 1	5
	Quarter 2	6
	Quarter 3	7
	Quarter 4	8

DEMONSTRATION PROBLEM 12.7

Shown below are monthly food and beverage sales in the United States during a recent year over an eight-month period ($ million). Develop the equation of a trend line through these data and use the equation to forecast sales for October.

MONTH	SALES ($ MILLION)
January	32,569
February	32,274
March	32,583
April	32,304
May	32,149
June	32,077
July	31,989
August	31,977

Solution: Shown here is a Minitab-produced scatter diagram of these time series data:

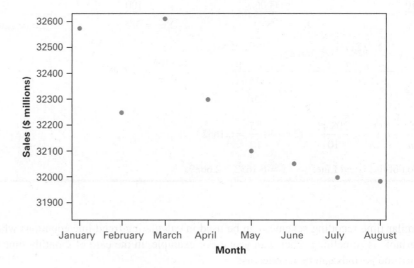

The months of January through August can be coded using the numbers of 1 through 8, respectively. Using these numbers as the time period values (x) and sales as the dependent variable (y), the following output was obtained from Minitab:

Regression Analysis: Sales ($ million) versus Month

The regression equation is

Sales ($ million) = 32628 − 86.21 Month

S = 119.708   R-Sq = 78.4%   R-Sq(adj) = 74.8%

The equation of the trend line is: $\hat{y} = 32,628 − 86.21x$. A slope of −86.21 indicates that there is a downward trend in food and beverage sales over this period of time at a rate of $86.21 (million) per month. The y intercept of 32,628 represents what the trend line would estimate the sales to have been in period 0 or December of the previous year. The sales figure for October can be forecast by inserting $x = 10$ into this model and obtaining:

$$\hat{y}(10) = 32,628 − 86.21(10) = 31,765.9$$

12.9 Problems

12.48. Determine the equation of the trend line for the data shown below on U.S. exports of fertilizers to Indonesia over a five-year period provided by the U.S. Census Bureau. Using the trend line equation, forecast the value for the year 2017.

YEAR	FERTILIZER ($ MILLIONS)
2010	51.5
2011	52.2
2012	72.0
2013	61.1
2014	65.0

12.49. Shown below are rental and leasing revenue figures for office machinery and equipment in the United States over a seven-year period according to the U.S. Census Bureau. Use these data to construct a trend line and forecast the rental and leasing revenue for the year 2017 using these data.

YEAR	RENTAL AND LEASING ($ MILLIONS)
2007	2138
2008	2051
2009	1744
2010	1684
2011	1727
2012	1711
2013	1704

12.50. After a somewhat uncertain start, e-commerce sales in the United States have been growing for the past several years. Shown below are quarterly adjusted e-commerce sales figures ($ billions) released by the Census Bureau for the United States over a three-year period. Use these data to determine the equation of a trend line for e-commerce sales during this time and use the trend "model" to forecast e-commerce sales for the third quarter of the year 2015.

YEAR	QUARTER	SALES ($ BILLIONS)
2012	1	54.6
	2	55.7
	3	57.8
	4	60.4
2013	1	61.9
	2	64.0
	3	65.9
	4	68.0
2014	1	70.1
	2	73.5
	3	76.2

12.10   Interpreting the Output

Although manual computations can be done, most regression problems are analyzed by using a computer. In this section, computer output from both Minitab and Excel will be presented and discussed.

At the top of the Minitab regression output, shown in **Figure 12.20**, is the Analysis of Variance table. Note that the value of $F = 89.09$ along with its associated p-value is used to test the overall model of the regression line. The next row of output, Model Summary, contains various statistics summarizing the model including the standard error of the estimate, $S = 0.177217$; the coefficient of determination, r^2, R-sq = 89.91%; and the adjusted value of r^2, R-sq(adj) = 88.90% (adjusted r^2 will be discussed in Chapter 13). Next is a table that describes the model in more detail. "Coef" stands for coefficient of the regression terms. The coefficient of Number of Passengers, the x variable, is 0.04070. This value is equal to the slope of the regression line and is reflected in the regression equation. The coefficient shown next to the constant term (1.570) is the value of the constant, which is the y intercept and also a part of the regression equation. The "T" values are a t test for the slope and a t test for the intercept or constant. (We generally do not interpret the t test for the constant.) The t value for the slope, $t = 9.44$ with an associated probability of .000, is the same as the value obtained manually in section 12.7. Because the probability of the t value is given, the p-value method can be used to interpret the t value. At the bottom of the output is the regression equation.

Although the Excel regression output, shown in **Figure 12.21** for Demonstration Problem 12.1, is somewhat different from the Minitab output, the same essential regression features are present. The regression equation is found under Coefficients at the bottom of ANOVA. The slope or coefficient of x is 2.2315 and the y-intercept is 30.9125. The standard

Regression Analysis: Cost ($1,000) versus Number of Passengers

```
Analysis of Variance

Source                DF   Adj SS   Adj MS   F-Value  P-Value
Regression             1   2.7980   2.79803    89.09    0.000
Number of Passengers   1   2.7980   2.79803    89.09    0.000
Error                 10   0.3141   0.03141
Total                 11   3.1121

Model Summary

        S        R-sq     R-sq(adj)      R-sq(pred)
 0.177217     89.91%       88.90%          85.52%

Coefficients

Term                    Coef   SE Coef  T-Value  P-Value   VIF
Constant               1.570     0.338     4.64    0.001
Number of Passengers 0.04070   0.00431     9.44    0.000  1.00

Regression Equation
Cost ($1,000) = 1.570 + 0.04070 Number of Passengers
```

FIGURE 12.20 **Minitab Regression Analysis of the Airline Cost Example**

SUMMARY OUTPUT

Regression Statistics	
Multiple R	0.942
R Square	0.886
Adjusted R Square	0.875
Standard Error	15.6491
Observations	12

ANOVA

	df	*SS*	*MS*	*F*	*Significance F*
Regression	1	19115.06322	19115.06	78.05	0.000005
Residual	10	2448.94	244.89		
Total	11	21564			

	Coefficients	*Standard Error*	*t Stat*	*P-value*
Intercept	30.9125	13.2542	2.33	0.041888
Number of Beds	2.2315	0.2526	8.83	0.000005

RESIDUAL OUTPUT

Observation	*Predicted FTEs*	*Residuals*
1	82.237	−13.237
2	95.626	−0.626
3	95.626	6.374
4	109.015	8.985
5	124.636	1.364
6	133.562	−8.562
7	142.488	−4.488
8	151.414	26.586
9	173.729	−17.729
10	178.192	5.808
11	200.507	−24.507
12	204.970	20.030

FIGURE 12.21 **Excel Regression Output for Demonstration Problem 12.1**

error of the estimate for the hospital problem is given as the fourth statistic under Regression Statistics at the top of the output, Standard Error = 15.6491. The r^2 value is given as 0.886 on the second line. The t test for the slope is found under t Stat near the bottom of the ANOVA section on the "Number of Beds" (x variable) row, $t = 8.83$. Adjacent to the t Stat is the p-value, which is the probability of the t statistic occurring by chance if the null hypothesis is true. For this slope, the probability shown is 0.000005. The ANOVA table is in the middle of the output with the F value having the same probability as the t statistic, 0.000005, and equaling t^2. The predicted values and the residuals are shown in the Residual Output section.

Decision Dilemma Solved

Predicting International Hourly Wages by the Price of a Big Mac

In the Decision Dilemma, questions were raised about the relationship between the price of a Big Mac hamburger and net hourly wages around the world and if a model could be developed to predict net hourly wages by the price of a Big Mac. Data were given for a sample of 20 countries. In exploring the possibility that there is a relationship between these two variables, a Pearson product-moment correlation coefficient, r, was computed to be .733. This r value indicates that there is a relatively high correlation between the two variables and that developing a regression model to predict one variable by the other has potential. Designating net hourly wages as the y or dependent variable and the price of a Big Mac as the x or predictor variable, the following regression output was obtained for these data using Excel.

REGRESSION STATISTICS	
Multiple R	0.733
R Square	0.538
Adjusted R Square	0.512
Standard Error	11.8803
Observations	20

ANOVA

	df	SS	MS	F	SIGNIFICANCE F
Regression	1	2957.87	2957.87	20.96	0.00023
Residual	18	2540.53	141.14		
Total	19	5498.40			

	COEFFICIENTS	STANDARD ERROR	t STAT	P-VALUE
Intercept	−12.444	8.703	−1.43	0.16987
Big Mac Price (U.S. $)	8.458	1.848	4.58	0.00023

Taken from this output, the regression model is:

Net Hourly Wage = −12.444 + 8.458 (Price of Big Mac)

While the y-intercept has virtually no practical meaning in this analysis, the slope indicates that for every dollar increase in the

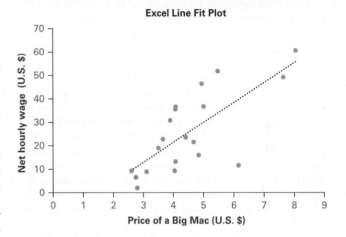

Excel Line Fit Plot

Net hourly wage (U.S. $) vs. Price of a Big Mac (U.S. $)

price of a Big Mac, there is an incremental increase of $8.458 in net hourly wages for a country. It is worth underscoring here that just because there is a relationship between two variables, it does not mean there is a cause-and-effect relationship. That is, McDonald's cannot raise net hour wages in a country just by increasing the cost of a Big Mac!

Using this regression model, the net hourly wage for a country with a $3.00 Big Mac can be predicted by substituting $x = 3$ into the model:

Net Hourly Wage = −12.444 + 8.458(3) = $12.93

That is, the model predicts that the net hourly wage for a country is $12.93 when the price of a Big Mac is $3.00.

How good a fit is the regression model to the data? Observe from the Excel output that the F value for testing the overall significance of the model (20.96) is highly significant with a p-value of .00023, and that the t statistic for testing to determine if the slope is significantly different from zero is 4.58 with a p-value of .00023. In simple regression, the t statistic is the square root of the F value and these statistics relate essentially the same information—that there are significant regression effects in the model. The r^2 value is 53.8%, indicating that the model has moderate predictability. The standard error of the model, $s = 11.88$, indicates that if the error terms are approximately normally distributed, about 68% of the predicted net hourly wages would fall within ±$11.88.

Shown here is an Excel-produced line fit plot. Note from the plot that there generally appears be a linear relationship between the variables but that many of the data points fall considerably away from the fitted regression line, indicating that the price of a Big Mac only partially accounts for net hourly wages.

Ethical Considerations

Regression analysis offers several opportunities for unethical behavior. One way is to present a regression model in isolation from information about the fit of the model. That is, the regression model is represented as a valid tool for prediction without any regard for how well it actually fits the data. While it is true that least squares analysis can produce a line of best fit through virtually any set of points, it does not necessarily follow that the regression model is a good predictor of the dependent variable. For example, sometimes business consultants sell regression models to companies as forecasting tools or market predictors without disclosing to the client that the r^2 value is very low, the slope of the regression line is not significant, the residuals are large, and the standard error of the estimate is large. This is unethical behavior.

Another unethical use of simple regression analysis is stating or implying a cause-and-effect relationship between two variables just because they are highly correlated and produce a high r^2 in regression. The Decision Dilemma presents a good example of this with the regression analysis of the price of a Big Mac hamburger and the net hourly wages in a country. While the coefficient of determination is 53.8% and there appears to be a modest fit of the regression line to the data, that does not mean that increasing the price of a Big Mac in a given country will increase the country's net hourly wages. Often, two correlated variables are related to a third variable that drives the two of them but is not included in the regression analysis. In the Decision Dilemma example, both Big Mac prices and net hourly wages may be related to exchange rates or a country's economic condition.

A third way that business analysts can act unethically in using regression analysis is to knowingly violate the assumptions underlying regression. Regression analysis requires equal error variance, independent error terms, and error terms that are normally distributed. Through the use of residual plots and other statistical techniques, a business researcher can test these assumptions. To present a regression model as fact when the assumptions underlying it are being grossly violated is unethical behavior.

It is important to remember that since regression models are developed from sample data, when an x value is entered into a simple regression model, the resulting prediction is only a point estimate. While business people often use regression models as predicting tools, it should be kept in mind that the prediction value is an estimate, not a guaranteed outcome. By utilizing or at least pointing out confidence intervals and prediction intervals, such as those presented in Section 12.8, the business researcher places the predicted point estimate within the context of inferential estimation and is thereby acting more ethically.

And lastly, another ethical problem that arises in regression analysis is using the regression model to predict values of the independent variable that are outside the domain of values used to develop the model. The airline cost model used in this chapter was built with between 61 and 97 passengers. A linear relationship appeared to be evident between flight costs and number of passengers over this domain. This model is not guaranteed to fit values outside the domain of 61 to 97 passengers, however. In fact, either a nonlinear relationship or no relationship may be present between flight costs and number of passengers if values from outside this domain are included in the model-building process. It is a mistake and probably unethical behavior to make claims for a regression model outside the purview of the domain of values for which the model was developed.

Summary

Correlation measures the degree of relatedness of variables. The most well-known measure of correlation is the Pearson product-moment coefficient of correlation, r. This value ranges from −1 to 0 to +1. An r value of +1 is perfect positive correlation and an r value of −1 is perfect negative correlation. Positive correlation means that as one variable increases in value, the other variable tends to increase. Negative correlation means that as one variable increases in value, the other variable tends to decrease. For r values near zero, little or no correlation is present.

Regression is a procedure that produces a mathematical model (function) that can be used to predict one variable by other variables. Simple regression is bivariate (two variables) and linear (only a line fit is attempted). Simple regression analysis produces a model that attempts to predict a y variable, referred to as the dependent variable, by an x variable, referred to as the independent variable. The general form of the equation of the simple regression line is the slope-intercept equation of a line. The equation of the simple regression model consists of a slope of the line as a coefficient of x and a y-intercept value as a constant.

After the equation of the line has been developed, several statistics are available that can be used to determine how well the line fits the data. Using the historical data values of x, predicted values of y (denoted as $\hat{y}$) can be calculated by inserting values of x into the regression equation. The predicted values can then be compared to the actual values of y to determine how well the regression equation fits the known data. The difference between a specific y value and its associated predicted y value is called the residual or error of prediction. Examination of the residuals can offer insight into the magnitude of the errors produced by a model. In addition, residual analysis can be used to help determine whether the assumptions underlying the regression analysis have been met. Specifically, graphs of the residuals can reveal (1) lack of linearity, (2) lack of homogeneity of error variance, and (3) independence of error terms. Geometrically, the residuals are the vertical distances from the y values to the regression line. Because the equation that yields the regression line is derived in such a way that the line is in the geometric middle of the points, the sum of the residuals is zero.

A single value of error measurement called the standard error of the estimate, s_e, can be computed. The standard error of the estimate is the standard deviation of error of a model. The value of s_e can be used as a single guide to the magnitude of the error produced by the regression model as opposed to examining all the residuals.

Another widely used statistic for testing the strength of a regression model is r^2, or the coefficient of determination. The coefficient of determination is the proportion of total variance of the y variable accounted for or predicted by x. The coefficient of determination ranges from 0 to 1. The higher the r^2 is, the stronger is the predictability of the model.

Testing to determine whether the slope of the regression line is different from zero is another way to judge the fit of the regression model to the data. If the population slope of the regression line is not different from zero, the regression model is not adding significant predictability to the dependent variable. A t statistic is used to test the significance of the slope. The overall significance of the regression model can be tested using an F statistic. In simple regression, because only one predictor is present, this test accomplishes the same thing as the t test of the slope and $F = t^2$.

One of the most prevalent uses of a regression model is to predict the values of y for given values of x. Recognizing that the predicted value is often not the same as the actual value, a confidence interval has been developed to yield a range within which the mean y value for a given x should fall. A prediction interval for a single y value for a given x value also is specified. This second interval is wider because it allows for the wide diversity of individual values, whereas the confidence interval for the mean y value reflects only the range of average y values for a given x.

Time-series data are data that are gathered over a period of time at regular intervals. Developing the equation of a forecasting trend line for time-series data is a special case of simple regression analysis where the time factor is the predictor variable. The time variable can be in units of years, months, weeks, quarters, and others.

Key Terms

coefficient of determination (r^2)	homoscedasticity	probabilistic model	simple regression
confidence interval	independent variable	regression analysis	standard error of the
dependent variable	least squares analysis	residual	estimate (s_e)
deterministic model	outliers	residual plot	sum of squares of error
heteroscedasticity	prediction interval	scatter plot	(SSE)

Formulas

Pearson's product-moment correlation coefficient

$$r = \frac{\Sigma(x - \bar{x})(y - \bar{y})}{\sqrt{\Sigma(x - \bar{x})^2 \, \Sigma(y - \bar{y})^2}}$$

$$= \frac{\Sigma xy - \dfrac{(\Sigma x \Sigma y)}{n}}{\sqrt{\left[\Sigma x^2 - \dfrac{(\Sigma x)^2}{n}\right]\left[\Sigma y^2 - \dfrac{(\Sigma y)^2}{n}\right]}}$$

Equation of the simple regression line

$$\hat{y} = \beta_0 + \beta_1 x$$

Sum of squares

$$SS_{xx} = \Sigma x^2 - \frac{(\Sigma x)^2}{n}$$

$$SS_{yy} = \Sigma y^2 - \frac{(\Sigma y)^2}{n}$$

$$SS_{xy} = \Sigma xy - \frac{\Sigma x \Sigma y}{n}$$

Slope of the regression line

$$b_1 = \frac{\Sigma(x - \bar{x})(y - \bar{y})}{\Sigma(x - \bar{x})^2} = \frac{\Sigma xy - n\bar{x}\,\bar{y}}{\Sigma x^2 - n\bar{x}^2}$$

$$= \frac{\Sigma xy - \dfrac{(\Sigma x)(\Sigma y)}{n}}{\Sigma x^2 - \dfrac{(\Sigma x)^2}{n}}$$

y-intercept of the regression line

$$b_0 = \bar{y} - b_1\bar{x} = \frac{\Sigma y}{n} - b_1\frac{(\Sigma x)}{n}$$

Sum of squares of error

$$SSE = \Sigma(y - \hat{y})^2 = \Sigma y^2 - b_0\Sigma y - b_1\Sigma xy$$

Standard error of the estimate

$$s_e = \sqrt{\frac{SSE}{n - 2}}$$

Coefficient of determination

$$r^2 = 1 - \frac{SSE}{SS_{yy}} = 1 - \frac{SSE}{\Sigma y^2 - \dfrac{(\Sigma y)^2}{n}}$$

Computational formula for r^2

$$r^2 = \frac{b_1^2 SS_{xx}}{SS_{yy}}$$

t test of slope

$$t = \frac{b_1 - \beta_1}{s_b}$$

$$s_b = \frac{s_e}{\sqrt{SS_{xx}}}$$

Confidence interval to estimate $E(y_x)$ for a given value of x

$$\hat{y} \pm t_{\alpha/2, n-2} s_e \sqrt{\frac{1}{n} + \frac{(x_0 - \bar{x})^2}{SS_{xx}}}$$

Prediction interval to estimate y for a given value of x

$$\hat{y} \pm t_{\alpha/2, n-2} s_e \sqrt{1 + \frac{1}{n} + \frac{(x_0 - \bar{x})^2}{SS_{xx}}}$$

Supplementary Problems

Calculating the Statistics

12.51. Determine the Pearson product-moment correlation coefficient for the following data.

x	1	10	9	6	5	3	2
y	8	4	4	5	7	7	9

12.52. Use the following data for parts (a) through (f).

x	5	7	3	16	12	9
y	8	9	11	27	15	13

a. Determine the equation of the least squares regression line to predict y by x.

b. Using the x values, solve for the predicted values of y and the residuals.

c. Solve for s_e.

d. Solve for r^2.

e. Test the slope of the regression line. Use $\alpha = .01$

f. Comment on the results determined in parts (b) through (e), and make a statement about the fit of the line.

12.53. Use the following data for parts (a) through (g).

x	53	47	41	50	58	62	45	60
y	5	5	7	4	10	12	3	11

a. Determine the equation of the simple regression line to predict y from x.

b. Using the x values, solve for the predicted values of y and the residuals.

c. Solve for SSE.

d. Calculate the standard error of the estimate.

e. Determine the coefficient of determination.

f. Test the slope of the regression line. Assume $\alpha = .05$. What do you conclude about the slope?

g. Comment on parts (d) and (e).

12.54. If you were to develop a regression line to predict y by x, what value would the coefficient of determination have?

x	213	196	184	202	221	247
y	76	65	62	68	71	75

12.55. Determine the equation of the least squares regression line to predict y from the following data.

x	47	94	68	73	80	49	52	61
y	14	40	34	31	36	19	20	21

a. Construct a 95% confidence interval to estimate the mean y value for $x = 60$.

b. Construct a 95% prediction interval to estimate an individual y value for $x = 70$.

c. Interpret the results obtained in parts (a) and (b).

12.56. Determine the equation of the trend line through the following cost data. Use the equation of the line to forecast cost for year 7.

YEAR	COST ($ MILLIONS)
1	56
2	54
3	49
4	46
5	45

Testing Your Understanding

12.57. A manager of a car dealership believes there is a relationship between the number of salespeople on duty and the number of cars sold. Suppose the following sample is used to develop a simple regression model to predict the number of cars sold by the number of salespeople. Solve for r^2 and explain what r^2 means in this problem.

WEEK	NUMBER OF CARS SOLD	NUMBER OF SALESPEOPLE
1	79	6
2	64	6
3	49	4
4	23	2
5	52	3

12.58. The American Research Group, Inc. conducted a telephone survey of a random sample of 1,100 U.S. adults in a recent year and determined that the average amount of planned spending on gifts for the holiday season was $854 and that 40% of the purchases would be made from catalogs. Shown below are the average amounts of planned spending on gifts for the holiday season for 11 years along with the associated percentages to be made from catalogs. Develop a regression model to predict the amount of planned spending in a given year by the associated percentage to be made from catalogs for that year. Comment of the strength of the model and the output.

YEAR	AVERAGE SPENDING ($)	PERCENTAGE PURCHASES TO BE MADE FROM CATALOGS
1	1,037	44
2	976	42
3	1,004	47
4	942	47
5	907	50
6	859	51
7	431	43
8	417	36
9	658	26
10	646	42
11	854	40

12.59. It seems logical that restaurant chains with more units (restaurants) would have greater sales. This assumption is mitigated, however, by several possibilities: some units may be more profitable than others, some units may be larger, some units may serve more meals, some units may serve more expensive meals, and so on. The data shown here were published by OSR 50. Perform a simple regression analysis to predict a food chain's sales by its number of units. How strong is the relationship?

CHAIN	SALES ($ BILLION)	NUMBER OF UNITS (1000)
McDonalds	35.45	14.4
Starbucks	12.69	12.1
Subway	11.90	27.2
Burger King	8.64	7.1
Wendy's	8.51	5.8
Taco Bell	8.20	5.9
Dunkin' Donuts	7.18	8.1
Chick-Fil-A	5.78	1.9
Pizza Hut	5.50	7.9
Panera Bread	4.50	1.9
KFC	4.20	4.4
Domino's Pizza	4.10	5.1
SONIC Drive-Ins	4.09	3.5
Chipotle Mexican Grill	4.05	1.8
Carl's Jr./Hardee's	3.57	2.9

12.60. Shown here are the labor force figures (in millions) published by the World Bank for the country of Bangladesh over a 10-year period. Develop the equation of a trend line through these data and use the equation to predict the labor force of Bangladesh for the year 2017.

YEAR	LABOR FORCE (MILLION)
2005	66.49
2006	67.83
2007	69.11
2008	70.37
2009	71.66
2010	73.01
2011	74.55
2012	76.04
2013	77.61
2014	78.62

12.61. How strong is the correlation between the inflation rate and 30-year treasury yields? The following data published by Fuji Securities are given as pairs of inflation rates and treasury yields for selected years over a 35-year period.

INFLATION RATE	30-YEAR TREASURY YIELD
1.57%	3.05%
2.23	3.93
2.17	4.68
4.53	6.57
7.25	8.27
9.25	12.01
5.00	10.27
4.62	8.45

Compute the Pearson product-moment correlation coefficient to determine the strength of the correlation between these two variables. Comment on the strength and direction of the correlation.

12.62. Shown below are data on the total sales generated by the seafood industry and the corresponding jobs supported by the seafood industry in the top 15 states by seafood sales. The data are published by the National Marine Fisheries Service of the National Oceanic and Atmospheric Administration of the U.S. Department of Commerce. Develop a simple regression model to predict the number of jobs supported by the seafood industry for a state from the total sales generated by the seafood industry of a state. Construct a confidence interval for the average y value for sales of $3,000 (million). Use the t statistic to test to determine whether the slope is significantly different from zero using $\alpha = .05$.

STATE	TOTAL SALES GENERATED BY THE SEAFOOD INDUSTRY (IN $ MILLION)	JOBS SUPPORTED BY THE SEAFOOD INDUSTRY (1,000)
California	20,054	122.1
Florida	14,250	72.3
Washington	8,026	67.0
Massachusetts	7,754	98.4
New Jersey	6,564	43.6
New York	5,103	41.8
Alaska	4,685	63.3
Texas	2,278	27.7
Virginia	1,867	22.1
Louisiana	1,802	32.8
Maryland	1,743	15.3
Maine	1,734	31.1
Georgia	1,490	11.1
Oregon	1,351	18.6
Rhode Island	1,025	9.2

12.63. People in the aerospace industry believe the cost of a space project is a function of the weight of the major object being sent into space. Use the following data to develop a regression model to predict the cost of a space project by the weight of the space object. Determine r^2 and s_e.

WEIGHT (TONS)	COST ($ MILLIONS)
1.897	$ 53.6
3.019	184.9
0.453	6.4
0.988	23.5
1.058	33.4
2.100	110.4
2.387	104.6

12.64. The following data represent a breakdown of state banks and all savings organizations in the United States every 5 years over a 60-year span, according to the Federal Reserve System.

TIME PERIOD	STATE BANKS	ALL SAVINGS
1	1342	2330
2	1864	2667
3	1912	3054
4	1847	3764
5	1641	4423
6	1405	4837
7	1147	4694
8	1046	4407
9	997	4328
10	1070	3626
11	1009	2815
12	1042	2030
13	992	1779

Develop a regression model to predict the total number of state banks by the number of all savings organizations. Comment on the strength of the model. Develop a time-series trend line for All Savings using the time periods given. Forecast All Savings for period 15 using this equation.

12.65. Is the amount of money spent by companies on advertising a function of the total revenue of the company? Shown are revenue and advertising cost data for ten companies published by *Advertising Age*.

COMPANY	ADVERTISING ($ MILLIONS)	REVENUES ($ BILLIONS)
Procter & Gamble	4.6	80.5
AT&T	3.3	132.0
General Motors Co.	3.1	155.0
Comcast Corp.	3.0	64.7
Verizon Communications	2.5	127.1
Ford Motor Co.	2.5	144.0
American Express Co.	2.4	34.3
Fiat Chrysler Automobiles	2.2	116.9
L'Oréal	2.2	30.0
Walt Disney Co.	2.1	48.8

Use the data to develop a regression line to predict the amount of advertising by revenues. Compute s_e and r^2. Assuming $\alpha = .05$, test the slope of the regression line. Comment on the strength of the regression model.

12.66. Can the consumption of water in a city be predicted by air temperature? The following data represent a sample of a day's water consumption and the high temperature for that day.

WATER USE (MILLIONS OF GALLONS)	TEMPERATURE (DEGREES FAHRENHEIT)
219	103°
56	39
107	77
129	78
68	50
184	96
150	90
112	75

Develop a least squares regression line to predict the amount of water used in a day in a city by the high temperature for that day. What would be the predicted water usage for a temperature of 100°? Evaluate the regression model by calculating s_e, by calculating r^2, and by testing the slope. Let $\alpha = .01$.

Interpreting the Output

12.67. Study the following Minitab output from a regression analysis to predict y from x.

    a. What is the equation of the regression model?

    b. What is the meaning of the coefficient of x?

    c. What is the result of the test of the slope of the regression model? Let $\alpha = .10$. Why is the t ratio negative?

    d. Comment on r^2 and the standard error of the estimate.

    e. Comment on the relationship of the F value to the t ratio for x.

    f. The correlation coefficient for these two variables is $-.7918$. Is this result surprising to you? Why or why not?

```
Regression Analysis: Y versus X

The regression equation is
Y = 67.2 - 0.0565 X

Predictor   Coef       SE Coef    T       P
Constant    67.231     5.046      13.32   0.000
X           -0.05650   0.01027    -5.50   0.000
S = 10.32   R-Sq = 62.7%   R-Sq(adj) = 60.6%

Analysis of Variance

Source           DF  SS      MS      F      P
Regression        1  3222.9  3222.9  30.25  0.000
Residual Error   18  1918.0  106.6
Total            19  5141.0
```

12.68. Study the following Excel regression output for an analysis attempting to predict the number of union members in the United States by the size of the labor force for selected years over a 30-year period from data published by the U.S. Bureau of Labor Statistics. Analyze the computer output. Discuss the strength of the model in terms of proportion of variation accounted for, slope, and overall predictability. Using the equation of the regression line, attempt to predict the number of union members when the labor force is 110,000. Note that the model was developed with data already recorded in 1,000 units. Use the data in the model as is.

SUMMARY OUTPUT

Regression Statistics	
Multiple R	0.798
R Square	0.636
Adjusted R Square	0.612
Standard Error	258.632
Observations	17

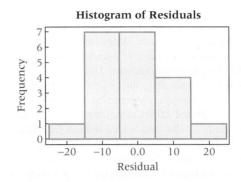

ANOVA					
	df	SS	MS	F	Significance F
Regression	1	1756035.529	1756036	26.25	0.00012
Residual	15	1003354.471	66890.3		
Total	16	2759390			

	Coefficients	Standard Error	t Stat	P-value
Intercept	20704.3805	879.6067	23.54	0.00000
Total Employment	−0.0390	0.0076	−5.12	0.00012

12.69. Study the following Minitab residual diagnostic graphs. Comment on any possible violations of regression assumptions.

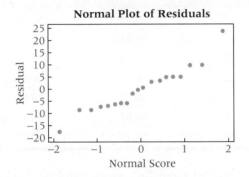

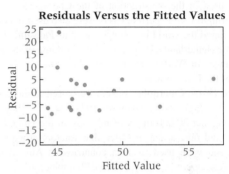

Analyzing the Databases

See **www.wiley.com/college/black** and **WileyPLUS**

1. Develop a regression model from the Consumer Food database to predict Annual Food Spending by Annual Household Income. Discuss the model and its strength on the basis of statistics presented in this chapter. Now develop a regression model to predict Non-Mortgage Household Debt by Annual Household Income. Discuss this model and its strengths. Compare the two models. Does it make sense that Annual Food Spending and Non-Mortgage Household Debt could each be predicted by Annual Household Income? Why or why not?

2. Using the Hospital database, develop a regression model to predict the number of Personnel by the number of Births. Now develop a regression model to predict number of Personnel by number of Beds. Examine the regression output. Which model is stronger in predicting number of Personnel? Explain why, using techniques presented in this chapter. Use the second regression model to predict the number of Personnel in a hospital that has 110 beds. Construct a 95% confidence interval around this prediction for the average value of y.

3. Analyze all the variables except Type in the Financial database by using a correlation matrix. The seven variables in this database are capable of producing 21 pairs of correlations. Which are most highly correlated? Select the variable that is most highly correlated with P/E ratio and use it as a predictor to develop a regression model to predict P/E ratio. How did the model do?

4. Construct a correlation matrix for the six U.S. and international stock indicators. Describe what you find. That is, what indicators seem to be most strongly related to other indicators? Now focus on the three international stock indicators. Which pair of these stock indicators is most correlated? Develop a regression model to predict the DJIA by the Nikkei 225. How strong is the model? Develop a regression model to predict the DJIA by the Hang Seng. How strong is the model? Develop a regression model to predict the DJIA by the Mexico IPC. How strong is the model? Compare the three models.

Case

Caterpillar, Inc.

Caterpillar, Inc., headquartered in Peoria, Illinois, is an American corporation with a worldwide dealer network which sells machinery, engines, financial products and insurance. Caterpillar is the world's leading manufacturer of construction and mining equipments, diesel and natural gas engines, industrial gas turbines and diesel-electric locomotives. Although providing financial services through its

Financial Products segment, Caterpillar primarily operates through its three product segments of Construction Industries Resource Industries, and Energy & Transportation. Founded in 1925, the company presently has sales and revenues of $55.2 billion, total assets of $78.5 billion, and 114,000 employees. Caterpillar machinery are commonly recognized by its trademark "Caterpillar Yellow" and it's "CAT" logo. Some of its manufactured construction products include: mini excavators, small-wheel loaders, backhoe loaders, multi-terrain loaders, and compact-wheel loaders. Other products include: machinery in mining and quarrying applications, reciprocating engines and turbines in power systems, the remanufacturing of CAT engines and components, and a wide range of financial alternatives to customers and dealers for Caterpillar machinery and engines.

Caterpillar tractors have undertaken and completed many difficult tasks since the company's beginning. In the late 1920s, the Soviet Grain Trust purchased 2,050 Caterpillar machines for use on its large farm cooperatives. This sale helped to keep Caterpillar's factories busy during the Great Depression. In the 1930s, Caterpillar track-type tractors helped construct the Hoover Dam, worked on the Mississippi Levee construction project, helped construct the Golden Gate Bridge, and were used in the construction of the Chesapeake & Delaware Canal. During this time period, CATs were also used in construction projects around the world in countries such as Palestine, Iraq, India, Canada, the Netherlands, Belgium and the building of the Pan American Highway. In World War II, Caterpillar built 51,000 track-type tractors for the U.S. military.

In the 1940s, Caterpillar tractors were used in the construction of the Alaskan highway; and between 1944 and 1956, they were used to help construct 70,000 miles of highway in the United States. In the 1950s and 60s, usage of Caterpillar tractors around the world exploded and were used in such countries as Australia, Austria, Ceylon, France, Germany, Italy, Nigeria, Philippines, Rhodesia, Russia, Sweden, Switzerland, Uganda, and Venezuela, in a wide variety of projects. In addition, Caterpillar products were used to help construct the St. Lawrence Seaway between Canada and the United States. In the 1970s and 80s, Caterpillar equipment were used in numerous dam, power, and pipeline projects. Since then, Caterpillars have been used in the construction of several projects such as Japan's Kansai International Airport as a marine airport approximately three miles offshore in Osaka Bay, the Chunnel between France and England, the "Big Dig" in Boston, Panama Canal expansion, and several Olympic Games sites.

Discussion

1. The United States Department of Agriculture (USDA), in conjunction with the Forest Service, publishes information to assist companies in estimating the cost of building a temporary road for such activities as a timber sale. Such roads are generally built for one or two seasons of use for limited traffic and are designed with the goal of reestablishing vegetative cover on the roadway and adjacent disturbed area within ten years after the termination of the contract, permit, or lease. The timber sale contract requires out sloping, removal of culverts and ditches, and building water bars or cross ditches after the road is no longer needed. As part of this estimation process, the company needs to estimate haul costs. The USDA publishes variable costs in dollars per cubic-yard-mile of hauling dirt according to the speed with which the vehicle can drive. Speeds are mainly determined by the road width, the sight distance, the grade, the curves and the turnouts. Thus, on a steep, narrow, winding road, the speed is slow; and

on a flat, straight, wide road, the speed is faster. Shown below are data on speed, cost per cubic yard for a 12 cubic yard end-dump vehicle, and cost per cubic yard for a 20 cubic yard bottom-dump vehicle. Use these data and simple regression analysis to develop models for predicting the haul cost by speed for each of these two vehicles. Discuss the strength of the models. Based on the models, predict the haul cost for 35 mph and for 45 mph for each of these vehicles.

SPEED (MPH)	HAUL COST 12-CUBIC-YARD END-DUMP VEHICLE $ PER CUBIC YD.	HAUL COST 20-CUBIC-YARD BOTTOM-DUMP VEHICLE $ PER CUBIC YD.
10	$2.46	$1.98
15	$1.64	$1.31
20	$1.24	$0.98
25	$0.98	$0.77
30	$0.82	$0.65
40	$0.62	$0.47
50	$0.48	$0.40

2. Shown here are Caterpillar's annual global sales and revenue streams for the years 2004 through 2014. By observing the data graphically and analyzing the data statistically using techniques and concepts from this chapter, share your insights and conclusions about Caterpillar's annual global sales and revenue streams over this period of time.

YEAR	SALES AND REVENUE STREAMS ($ BILLIONS)
2004	30.31
2005	36.34
2006	41.52
2007	44.96
2008	51.32
2009	32.40
2010	42.59
2011	60.14
2012	65.88
2013	55.66
2014	55.18

Source: Adapted from www.cat.com/

CHAPTER 13

Multiple Regression Analysis

LEARNING OBJECTIVES

This chapter presents the potential of multiple regression analysis as a tool in business decision making and its applications, thereby enabling you to:

1. Explain how, by extending the simple regression model to a multiple regression model with two or more independent variables, it is possible to determine the multiple regression equation for any number of unknowns.

2. Examine significance tests of both the overall regression model and the regression coefficients.

3. Calculate the residual, standard error of the estimate, coefficient of multiple determination, and adjusted coefficient of multiple determination of a regression model.

4. Use a computer to find and interpret multiple regression outputs.

Decision Dilemma

Are You Going to Hate Your New Job?

Getting a new job can be an exciting and energizing event in your life.

But what if you discover after a short time on the job that you hate your job? Is there any way to determine ahead of time whether you will love or hate your job? Sue Shellenbarger of *The Wall Street Journal* discusses some of the things to look for when interviewing for a position that may provide clues as to whether you will be happy on that job.

Among other things, work cultures vary from hip, freewheeling start-ups to old-school organizational-driven domains. Some organizations place pressure on workers to feel tense and to work long hours while others place more emphasis on creativity and the bottom line. Shellenbarger suggests that job interviewees pay close attention to how they are treated in an interview. Are they just another cog in the wheel or are they valued as an individual? Is a work-life balance apparent within the company? Ask what a typical workday is like at that firm. Inquire about the values that undergird the management by asking questions such as, "What is your proudest accomplishment?" Ask about flexible schedules and how job training is managed. For example, do workers have to go to job training on their own time?

A "Work Trends" survey undertaken by the John J. Heldrich Center for Workforce Development at Rutgers University and the Center for Survey Research and Analysis at the University of

Jacob Wackerhausen/iStockphoto

Connecticut posed several questions to employees in a survey to ascertain their job satisfaction. Some of the themes included in these questions were relationship with your supervisor, overall quality of the work environment, total hours worked each week, and opportunities for advancement at the job.

Suppose another researcher gathered survey data from 19 employees on these questions and also asked the employees to rate their job satisfaction on a scale from 0 to 100 (with 100 being perfectly satisfied). Suppose the following data represent the results of this survey. Assume that relationship with supervisor is rated on a scale from 0 to 50 (0 represents poor relationship and 50 represents an excellent relationship), overall quality of the work environment is rated on a scale from 0 to 100 (0 represents poor work environment and 100 represents an excellent work environment), and opportunities for advancement is rated on a scale from 0 to 50 (0 represents no opportunities and 50 represents excellent opportunities).

JOB SATIS-FACTION	RELATION-SHIP WITH SUPER-VISOR	OVERALL QUALITY OF WORK ENVIRON-MENT	TOTAL HOURS WORKED PER WEEK	OPPOR-TUNITIES FOR ADVANCE-MENT
55	27	65	50	42
20	•12	13	60	28
85	40	79	45	7
65	35	53	65	48
45	29	43	40	32
70	42	62	50	41
35	22	18	75	18
60	34	75	40	32
95	50	84	45	48
65	33	68	60	11
85	40	72	55	33
10	5	10	50	21
75	37	64	45	42
80	42	82	40	46
50	31	46	60	48
90	47	95	55	30
75	36	82	70	39
45	20	42	40	22
65	32	73	55	12

MANAGERIAL AND STATISTICAL QUESTIONS

1. Several variables are presented that may be related to job satisfaction. Which variables are stronger predictors of job satisfaction? Might other variables not mentioned here be related to job satisfaction?

2. Is it possible to develop a mathematical model to predict job satisfaction using the data given? If so, how strong is the model? With four independent variables, will we need to develop four different simple regression models and compare their results?

Source: Adapted from Sue Shellenbarger, "How to Find Out if You're Going to Hate a New Job Before You Agree to Take It," *The Wall Street Journal*, June 13, 2002, p. D1; www.heldrich.rutgers.edu/research/topics/work-trends-surveys.

Simple regression analysis (discussed in Chapter 12) is bivariate linear regression in which one **dependent variable**, *y*, is predicted by one **independent variable**, *x*. Examples of simple regression applications include models to predict retail sales by population density, Dow Jones averages by prime interest rates, crude oil production by energy consumption, and CEO compensation by quarterly sales. However, in many cases, other independent variables, taken in conjunction with these variables, can make the regression model a better fit in predicting the dependent variable. For example, sales could be predicted by the size of store and number of competitors in addition to population density. A model to predict the Dow Jones average of 30 industrials could include, in addition to the prime interest rate, such predictors as yesterday's volume, the bond interest rate, and the producer price index. A model to predict CEO compensation could be developed by using variables such as company earnings per share, age of CEO, and size of company, in addition to quarterly sales. A model could perhaps be developed to predict the cost of outsourcing by such variables as unit price, export taxes, cost of money, damage in transit, and other factors. Each of these examples contains only one dependent variable, *y*, as with simple regression analysis. However, multiple independent variables, *x* (predictors), are involved. *Regression analysis with two or more independent variables or with at least one nonlinear predictor* is called **multiple regression** analysis.

13.1 | The Multiple Regression Model

Multiple regression analysis is similar in principle to simple regression analysis. However, it is more complex conceptually and computationally. Recall from Chapter 12 that the equation of the probabilistic simple regression model is

$$y = \beta_0 + \beta_1 x + \epsilon$$

where

y = the value of the dependent variable
β_0 = the population y intercept
β_1 = the population slope
$\in$ = the error of prediction

Extending this notion to multiple regression gives the general equation for the probabilistic multiple regression model.

$$y = \beta_0 + \beta_1 x_1 + \beta_2 x_2 + \beta_3 x_3 + \cdots + \beta_k x_k + \in$$

where

y = the value of the dependent variable
β_0 = the regression constant
β_1 = the partial regression coefficient for independent variable 1
β_2 = the partial regression coefficient for independent variable 2
β_3 = the partial regression coefficient for independent variable 3
β_k = the partial regression coefficient for independent variable k
k = the number of independent variables

In multiple regression analysis, the dependent variable, y, is sometimes referred to as the **response variable**. The **partial regression coefficient** of an independent variable, β_i, *represents the increase that will occur in the value of y from a one-unit increase in that independent variable if all other variables are held constant.* The "full" (versus partial) regression coefficient of an independent variable is a coefficient obtained from the bivariate model (simple regression) in which the independent variable is the sole predictor of y. The partial regression coefficients occur because more than one predictor is included in a model. The partial regression coefficients are analogous to β_1, the slope of the simple regression model in Chapter 12.

In actuality, the partial regression coefficients and the regression constant of a multiple regression model are population values and are unknown. In virtually all research, these values are estimated by using sample information. Shown here is the form of the equation for estimating y with sample information.

$$\hat{y} = b_0 + b_1 x_1 + b_2 x_2 + b_3 x_3 + \cdots + b_k x_k$$

where

$\hat{y}$ = the predicted value of y
b_0 = the estimate of the regression constant
b_1 = the estimate of regression coefficient 1
b_2 = the estimate of regression coefficient 2
b_3 = the estimate of regression coefficient 3
b_k = the estimate of regression coefficient k
k = the number of independent variables

Multiple Regression Model with Two Independent Variables (First-Order)

The simplest multiple regression model is one constructed with two independent variables, where the highest power of either variable is 1 (first-order regression model). This regression model is

$$y = \beta_0 + \beta_1 x_1 + \beta_2 x_2 + \in$$

The constant and coefficients are estimated from sample information, resulting in the following model.

$$\hat{y} = b_0 + b_1 x_1 + b_2 x_2$$

Figure 13.1 is a three-dimensional graph of a series of points (x_1, x_2, y) representing values from three variables used in a multiple regression model to predict the sales price of a house by the number of square feet in the house and the age of the house. Simple regression models yield a line that is fit through data points in the xy plane. In multiple regression analysis, the resulting model produces a **response surface**. In the multiple regression model shown here with two independent first-order variables, the response surface is a **response plane**. The response plane for such a model is fit in a three-dimensional space (x_1, x_2, y).

If such a response plane is fit into the points shown in Figure 13.1, the result is the graph in Figure 13.2. Notice that most of the points are not on the plane. As in simple regression, an error in the fit of the model in multiple regression is usually present. The distances shown in the graph from the points to the response plane are the errors of fit, or residuals $(y - \hat{y})$. Multiple regression models with three or more independent variables involve more than three dimensions and are difficult to depict geometrically.

Observe in Figure 13.2 that the regression model attempts to fit a plane into the three-dimensional plot of points. Notice that the plane intercepts the y axis. Figure 13.2 depicts some values of y for various values of x_1 and x_2. The error of the response plane $(\in)$ in predicting or determining the y values is the distance from the points to the plane.

Determining the Multiple Regression Equation

The simple regression equations for determining the sample slope and intercept given in Chapter 12 are the result of using methods of calculus to minimize the sum of squares of error for the regression model. The procedure for developing these equations involves solving two simultaneous equations with two unknowns, b_0 and b_1. Finding the sample slope and intercept from these formulas requires the values of Σx, Σy, Σxy, and Σx^2.

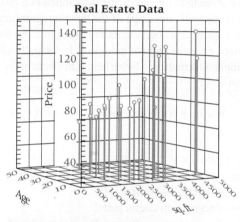

FIGURE 13.1 **Points in a Sample Space**

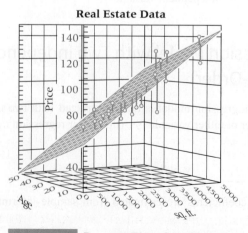

FIGURE 13.2 **Response Plane for a First- Order Two-Predictor Multiple Regression Model**

The procedure for determining formulas to solve for multiple regression coefficients is similar. The formulas are established to meet an objective of *minimizing the sum of squares of error for the model*. Hence, the regression analysis shown here is referred to as **least squares analysis**. Methods of calculus are applied, resulting in $k + 1$ equations with $k + 1$ unknowns (b_0 and k values of b_i) for multiple regression analyses with k independent variables. Thus, a regression model with six independent variables will generate seven simultaneous equations with seven unknowns (b_0, b_1, b_2, b_3, b_4, b_5, b_6).

For multiple regression models with two independent variables, the result is three simultaneous equations with three unknowns (b_0, b_1, and b_2).

$$b_0 n + b_1 \Sigma x_1 + b_2 \Sigma x_2 = \Sigma y$$

$$b_0 \Sigma x_1 + b_1 \Sigma x_1^2 + b_2 \Sigma x_1 x_2 = \Sigma x_1 y$$

$$b_0 \Sigma x_2 + b_1 \Sigma x_1 x_2 + b_2 \Sigma x_2^2 = \Sigma x_2 y$$

The process of solving these equations by hand is tedious and time-consuming. Solving for the regression coefficients and regression constant in a multiple regression model with two independent variables requires Σx_1, Σx_2, Σy, Σx_1^2, Σx_2^2, $\Sigma x_1 x_2$, $\Sigma x_1 y$, and $\Sigma x_2 y$. In actuality, virtually all business researchers use computer statistical software packages to solve for the regression coefficients, the regression constant, and other pertinent information. In this chapter, we will discuss computer output and assume little or no hand calculation. The emphasis will be on the interpretation of the computer output.

A Multiple Regression Model

A real estate study was conducted in a small Louisiana city to determine what variables, if any, are related to the market price of a home. Several variables were explored, including the number of bedrooms, the number of bathrooms, the age of the house, the number of square feet of living space, the total number of square feet of space, and the number of garages. Suppose the researcher wants to develop a regression model to predict the market price of a home by two variables, "total number of square feet in the house" and "the age of the house." Listed in Table 13.1 are the data for these three variables.

A number of statistical software packages can perform multiple regression analysis, including Excel and Minitab. The output for the Minitab multiple regression analysis on the real estate data is given in Figure 13.3. (Excel output is shown in Demonstration Problem 13.1.)

This Minitab output for regression analysis ends with "Regression Equation." From Figure 13.3, the regression equation for the real estate data in Table 13.1 is

$$\hat{y} = 57.4 + .0177 x_1 - .666 x_2$$

The regression constant, 57.4, is the y-intercept. The y-intercept is the value of $\hat{y}$ if both x_1 (number of square feet) and x_2 (age) are zero. In this example, a practical understanding of the y-intercept is meaningless. It makes little sense to say that a house containing no square feet ($x_1 = 0$) and no years of age ($x_2 = 0$) would cost \$57,400. Note in Figure 13.2 that the response plane crosses the y-axis (price) at 57.4.

The coefficient of x_1 (total number of square feet in the house) is .0177, which means that a one-unit increase in square footage would result in a predicted increase of $.0177 \cdot (\$1,000) = \$17.70$ in the price of the home if age were held constant. All other variables being held constant, the addition of 1 square foot of space in the house results in a predicted increase of \$17.70 in the price of the home.

The coefficient of x_2 (age) is $-.666$. The negative sign on the coefficient denotes an inverse relationship between the age of a house and the price of the house: the older the house, the lower the price. In this case, if the total number of square feet in the house is kept constant, a one-unit increase in the age of the house (1 year) will result in $-.666 \cdot (\$1,000) = -\$666$, a predicted \$666 drop in the price.

TABLE 13.1 Real Estate Data

MARKET PRICE ($1,000)	TOTAL NUMBER OF SQUARE FEET	AGE OF HOUSE (YEARS)
y	x_1	x_2
63.0	1605	35
65.1	2489	45
69.9	1553	20
76.8	2404	32
73.9	1884	25
77.9	1558	14
74.9	1748	8
78.0	3105	10
79.0	1682	28
83.4	2470	30
79.5	1820	2
83.9	2143	6
79.7	2121	14
84.5	2485	9
96.0	2300	19
109.5	2714	4
102.5	2463	5
121.0	3076	7
104.9	3048	3
128.0	3267	6
129.0	3069	10
117.9	4765	11
140.0	4540	8

```
Regression Analysis: Price versus Square Feet, Age

Analysis of Variance

Source          DF    Adj SS    Adj MS    F-Value    P-Value
Regression       2      8190    4094.9      28.63      0.000
  Square Feet    1      4538    4538.5      31.73      0.000
  Age            1      1222    1221.9       8.54      0.008
Error           20      2861     143.1
Total           22     11051

Model Summary

S          R-sq      R-sq(adj)
11.9604    74.11%     71.52%

Coefficients

Term          Coef      SE Coef    T-Value    P-Value
Constant      57.4        10.0       5.73      0.000
Square Feet   0.0177      0.0032     5.63      0.000
Age          -0.666       0.228     -2.92      0.008

Regression Equation

Price = 57.4 + 0.0177 Square Feet - 0.666 Age
```

FIGURE 13.3 Minitab Output of Regression for the Real Estate Example

In examining the regression coefficients, it is important to remember that the independent variables are often measured in different units. It is usually not wise to compare the regression coefficients of predictors in a multiple regression model and decide that the variable with the largest regression coefficient is the best predictor. In this example, the two variables are in different units, square feet and years. Just because x_2 has the larger coefficient (.666) does not necessarily make x_2 the strongest predictor of y.

This regression model can be used to predict the price of a house in this small Louisiana city. If the house has 2500 square feet total and is 12 years old, $x_1 = 2500$ and $x_2 = 12$. Substituting these values into the regression model yields

$$\hat{y} = 57.4 + .0177x_1 - .666x_2$$
$$= 57.4 + .0177(2500) - .666(12) = 93.658$$

The predicted price of the house is $93,658. Figure 13.2 is a graph of these data with the response plane and the residual distances.

DEMONSTRATION PROBLEM 13.1

Since 1980, the prime interest rate in the United States has varied from less than 5% to over 15%. What factor in the U.S. economy seems to be related to the prime interest rate? Two possible predictors of the prime interest rate are the annual unemployment rate and the savings rate in the United States. Shown below are data for the annual prime interest rate for the even-numbered years over a 28-year period in the United States along with the annual unemployment rate and the annual average personal saving (as a percentage of disposable personal income). Use these data to develop a multiple regression model to predict the annual prime interest rate by the unemployment rate and the average personal saving. Determine the predicted prime interest rate if the unemployment rate is 6.5 and the average personal saving is 5.0.

YEAR	PRIME INTEREST RATE	UNEMPLOYMENT RATE	PERSONAL SAVING
1986	8.33	7.0	8.2
1988	9.32	5.5	7.3
1990	10.01	5.6	7.0
1992	6.25	7.5	7.7
1994	7.15	6.1	4.8
1996	8.27	5.4	4.0
1998	8.35	4.5	4.3
2000	9.23	4.0	2.3
2002	4.67	5.8	2.4
2004	4.34	5.5	2.1
2006	7.96	4.6	0.7
2008	5.09	5.8	1.8
2010	3.25	9.6	5.8
2012	3.25	8.1	7.6
2014	3.25	6.2	4.8

Solution: The following output shows the results of analyzing the data by using the regression portion of Excel.

▼ SUMMARY OUTPUT

Regression Statistics

Multiple R	0.820
R Square	0.672
Adjusted R Square	0.617
Standard Error	1.496
Observations	15

ANOVA

	df	SS	MS	F	Significance F
Regression	2	54.9835	27.4917	12.29	0.0012
Residual	12	26.8537	2.2378		
Total	14	81.8372			

	Coefficients	Standard Error	t Stat	P-value
Intercept	13.5786	1.728	7.86	0.0000
Unemployment Rates	−1.6622	0.337	−4.93	0.0003
Personal Savings	0.6586	0.199	3.31	0.0062

The regression equation is

$$\hat{y} = 13.5786 - 1.6622x_1 + 0.6586x_2$$

where:

$\hat{y}$ = prime interest rate

x_1 = unemployment rate

x_2 = personal saving

The model indicates that for every one-unit (1%) increase in the unemployment rate, the predicted prime interest rate decreases by 1.6622%, if personal saving is held constant. The model also indicates that for every one-unit (1%) increase in personal saving, the predicted prime interest rate increases by 0.6586%, if unemployment is held constant.

If the unemployment rate is 6.5 and the personal saving rate is 5.0, the predicted prime interest rate is 7.35%:

$$\hat{y} = 13.5786 - 1.6622(6.5) + 0.6586(5.0) = 6.07$$

13.1 Problems

13.1. Use a computer to develop the equation of the regression model for the following data. Comment on the regression coefficients. Determine the predicted value of y for $x_1 = 200$ and $x_2 = 7$.

y	x_1	x_2
12	174	3
18	281	9
31	189	4
28	202	8
52	149	9
47	188	12
38	215	5
22	150	11
36	167	8
17	135	5

13.2. Use a computer to develop the equation of the regression model for the following data. Comment on the regression coefficients. Determine the predicted value of y for $x_1 = 33$, $x_2 = 29$, and $x_3 = 13$.

y	x_1	x_2	x_3
114	21	6	5
94	43	25	8
87	56	42	25
98	19	27	9
101	29	20	12

85	34	45	21
94	40	33	14
107	32	14	11
119	16	4	7
93	18	31	16
108	27	12	10
117	31	3	8

13.3. Using the following data, determine the equation of the regression model. How many independent variables are there? Comment on the meaning of these regression coefficients.

PREDICTOR	COEFFICIENT
Constant	121.62
x_1	−.174
x_2	6.02
x_3	.00026
x_4	.0041

13.4. Use the following data to determine the equation of the multiple regression model. Comment on the regression coefficients.

PREDICTOR	COEFFICIENT
Constant	31,409.5
x_1	.08425
x_2	289.62
x_3	−.0947

13.5. Is there a particular product that is an indicator of per capita personal consumption for countries around the world? Shown here are data on per capita personal consumption, paper consumption, fish consumption, and gasoline consumption for 11 countries. Use the data to develop a multiple regression model to predict per capita personal consumption by paper consumption, fish consumption, and gasoline consumption. Discuss the meaning of the partial regression weights.

COUNTRY	PER CAPITA PERSONAL CONSUMPTION ($ U.S.)	PAPER CONSUMPTION (KG PER PERSON)	FISH CONSUMPTION (LBS PER PERSON)	GASOLINE CONSUMPTION (LITERS PER PERSON)
Bangladesh	836	1	23	2
Greece	3,145	85	53	394
Italy	21,785	204	48	368
Japan	37,931	250	141	447
Kenya	276	4	12	16
Norway	1,913	156	113	477
Philippines	2,195	19	65	43
Portugal	3,154	116	133	257
United Kingdom	19,539	207	44	460
United States	109,521	308	47	1,624
Venezuela	622	27	40	528

13.6. Jensen, Solberg, and Zorn investigated the relationship of insider ownership, debt, and dividend policies in companies. One of their findings was that firms with high insider ownership choose lower levels of both debt and dividends. Shown here is a sample of data of these three variables for 11 different industries. Use the data to develop the equation of the regression model to predict insider ownership by debt ratio and dividend payout. Comment on the regression coefficients.

INDUSTRY	INSIDER OWNERSHIP	DEBT RATIO	DIVIDEND PAYOUT
Mining	8.2	14.2	10.4
Food and beverage	18.4	20.8	14.3
Furniture	11.8	18.6	12.1
Publishing	28.0	18.5	11.8
Petroleum refining	7.4	28.2	10.6
Glass and cement	15.4	24.7	12.6
Motor vehicle	15.7	15.6	12.6
Department store	18.4	21.7	7.2
Restaurant	13.4	23.0	11.3
Amusement	18.1	46.7	4.1
Hospital	10.0	35.8	9.0

13.2 | Significance Tests of the Regression Model and Its Coefficients

Multiple regression models can be developed to fit almost any data set if the level of measurement is adequate and enough data points are available. Once a model has been constructed, it is important to test the model to determine whether it fits the data well and whether the assumptions underlying regression analysis are met. Assessing the adequacy of the regression model can be done in several ways, including testing the overall significance of the model, studying the significance tests of the regression coefficients, computing the residuals, examining the standard error of the estimate, and observing the coefficient of determination. In this section, we examine significance tests of the regression model and of its coefficients.

Testing the Overall Model

With simple regression, a t test of the slope of the regression line is used to determine whether the population slope of the regression line is different from zero—that is, whether the independent variable contributes significantly in linearly predicting the dependent variable.

The hypotheses for this test, presented in Chapter 12 are

$$H_0: \beta_1 = 0$$
$$H_a: \beta_1 \neq 0$$

For multiple regression, an analogous test makes use of the F statistic. The overall significance of the multiple regression model is tested with the following hypotheses.

$$H_0: \beta_1 = \beta_2 = \beta_3 = \cdots = \beta_k = 0$$
$$H_a: \text{At least one of the regression coefficients is} \neq 0.$$

If we fail to reject the null hypothesis, we are stating that the regression model has no significant predictability for the dependent variable. A rejection of the null hypothesis indicates that at least one of the independent variables is adding significant predictability for y.

This F test of overall significance is often given as a part of the standard multiple regression output from statistical software packages. The output appears as an analysis of variance (ANOVA) table. Shown here is the ANOVA table for the real estate example taken from the Minitab output in Figure 13.3.

Analysis of Variance

Source	DF	SS	MS	F	p
Regression	2	8189.7	4094.9	28.63	0.000
Residual Error	20	2861.0	143.1		
Total	22	11050.7			

The F value is 28.63; because $p = .000$, the F value is significant at $\alpha = .001$. The null hypothesis is rejected, and there is at least one significant predictor of house price in this analysis.

The F value is calculated by the following equation:

$$F = \frac{MS_{reg}}{MS_{err}} = \frac{SS_{reg}/df_{reg}}{SS_{err}/df_{err}} = \frac{SSR/k}{SSE/(N-k-1)}$$

where

$$MS = \text{mean square}$$
$$SS = \text{sum of squares}$$
$$df = \text{degrees of freedom}$$
$$k = \text{number of independent variables}$$
$$N = \text{number of observations}$$

Note that in the ANOVA table for the real estate example, $df_{reg} = 2$. The degrees of freedom formula for regression is the number of regression coefficients plus the regression constant minus 1. The net result is the number of regression coefficients, which equals the number of independent variables, k. The real estate example uses two independent variables, so $k = 2$. Degrees of freedom error in multiple regression equals the total number of observations minus the number of regression coefficients minus the regression constant, or $N - k - 1$. For the real estate example, $N = 23$; thus, $df_{err} = 23 - 2 - 1 = 20$.

As shown in Chapter 11, $MS = SS/df$. The F ratio is formed by dividing MS_{reg} by MS_{err}. In using the F distribution table to determine a critical value against which to test the observed F value, the degrees of freedom numerator is df_{reg} and the degrees of freedom denominator is df_{err}. The table F value is obtained in the usual manner, as presented in Chapter 11. With $\alpha = .01$ for the real estate example, the table value is

$$F_{.01,2,20} = 5.85$$

Comparing the observed F of 28.63 to this table value shows that the decision is to reject the null hypothesis. This same conclusion was reached using the p-value method from the computer output.

If a regression model has only one linear independent variable, it is a simple regression model. In that case, the F test for the overall model is the same as the t test for significance of the population slope. The F value displayed in the regression ANOVA table is related to the t test for the slope in the simple regression case as follows:

$$F = t^2$$

In simple regression, the F value and the t value give redundant information about the overall test of the model.

Most researchers who use multiple regression analysis will observe the value of F and its p-value rather early in the process. If F is not significant, then no population regression coefficient is significantly different from zero, and the regression model has no predictability for the dependent variable.

Significance Tests of the Regression Coefficients

In multiple regression, individual significance tests can be computed for each regression coefficient using a t test. Each of these t tests is analogous to the t test for the slope used in Chapter 12 for simple regression analysis. The hypotheses for testing the regression coefficient of each independent variable take the following form:

$$H_0: \beta_1 = 0$$
$$H_a: \beta_1 \neq 0$$

$$H_0: \beta_2 = 0$$
$$H_a: \beta_2 \neq 0$$
$$\vdots$$
$$H_0: \beta_k = 0$$
$$H_a: \beta_k \neq 0$$

Most multiple regression computer packages yield observed t values to test the individual regression coefficients as standard output. Shown here are the t values and their associated probabilities for the real estate example as displayed with the multiple regression output in Figure 13.3.

VARIABLE	T	P
Square feet	5.63	.000
Age	−2.92	.008

At $\alpha = .05$, the null hypothesis is rejected for both variables because the probabilities (p) associated with their t values are less than .05. If the t ratios for any predictor variables are not significant (fail to reject the null hypothesis), the researcher might decide to drop that variable(s) from the analysis as a nonsignificant predictor(s). Other factors can enter into this decision. In Chapter 14, we will explore techniques for model building in which some variable sorting is required.

The degrees of freedom for each of these individual tests of regression coefficients are $n - k - 1$. In this particular example because there are $k = 2$ predictor variables, the degrees of freedom are $23 - 2 - 1 = 20$. With $\alpha = .05$ and a two-tailed test, the critical table t value is

$$t_{.025, 20} = \pm 2.086$$

Notice from the t ratios shown here that if this critical table t value had been used as the hypothesis test criterion instead of the p-value method, the results would have been the same. Testing the regression coefficients not only gives the researcher some insight into the fit of the regression model, but it also helps in the evaluation of how worthwhile individual independent variables are in predicting y.

13.2 Problems

13.7. Examine the Minitab output shown here for a multiple regression analysis. How many predictors were there in this model? Comment on the overall significance of the regression model. Discuss the t ratios of the variables and their significance.

The regression equation is

$Y = 4.096 - 5.111X_1 + 2.662X_2 + 1.557X_3 + 1.141X_4 + 1.650X_5$
$\quad - 1.248X_6 + 0.436X_7 + 0.962X_8 + 1.289X_9$

Predictor	Coef	Stdev	T	p
Constant	4.096	1.2884	3.24	.006
X_1	-5.111	1.8700	2.73	.011
X_2	2.662	2.0796	1.28	.212
X_3	1.557	1.2811	1.22	.235
X_4	1.141	1.4712	0.78	.445
X_5	1.650	1.4994	1.10	.281
X_6	-1.248	1.2735	0.98	.336
X_7	0.436	0.3617	1.21	.239
X_8	0.962	1.1896	0.81	.426
X_9	1.289	1.9182	0.67	.508

$S = 3.503$ $R\text{-sq} = 40.8\%$ $R\text{-sq(adj.)} = 20.3\%$

Analysis of Variance

Source	DF	SS	MS	F	p
Regression	9	219.746	24.416	1.99	.0825
Error	26	319.004	12.269		
Total	35	538.750			

13.8. Displayed here is the Minitab output for a multiple regression analysis. Study the ANOVA table and the t ratios and use these to discuss the strengths of the regression model and the predictors. Does this model appear to fit the data well? From the information here, what recommendations would you make about the predictor variables in the model?

The regression equation is

$Y = 34.7 + 0.0763X_1 + 0.00026X_2 - 1.12X_3$

Predictor	Coef	Stdev	T	p
Constant	34.672	5.256	6.60	.000
X_1	0.07629	0.02234	3.41	.005
X_2	0.000259	0.001031	0.25	.805
X_3	-1.1212	0.9955	-1.13	.230

$S = 9.722$ $R\text{-sq} = 51.5\%$ $R\text{-sq(adj)} = 40.4\%$

Analysis of Variance

Source	DF	SS	MS	F	p
Regression	3	1306.99	435.66	4.61	.021
Error	13	1228.78	94.52		
Total	16	2535.77			

13.9. Using the data in Problem 13.5, develop a multiple regression model to predict per capita personal consumption by the consumption of paper, fish, and gasoline. Discuss the output and pay particular attention to the F test and the t tests.

13.10. Using the data from Problem 13.6, develop a multiple regression model to predict insider ownership from debt ratio and dividend payout. Comment on the strength of the model and the predictors by examining the ANOVA table and the t tests.

13.11. Develop a multiple regression model to predict y from x_1, x_2, and x_3 using the following data. Discuss the values of F and t.

y	x_1	x_2	x_3
5.3	44	11	401
3.6	24	40	219
5.1	46	13	394
4.9	38	18	362
7.0	61	3	453
6.4	58	5	468
5.2	47	14	386
4.6	36	24	357
2.9	19	52	206
4.0	31	29	301
3.8	24	37	243
3.8	27	36	228
4.8	36	21	342
5.4	50	11	421
5.8	55	9	445

13.12. Use the following data to develop a regression model to predict y from x_1 and x_2. Comment on the output. Develop a regression model to predict y from x_1 only. Compare the results of this model with those of the model using both predictors. What might you conclude by examining the output from both regression models?

y	x_1	x_2
28	12.6	134
43	11.4	126
45	11.5	143
49	11.1	152
57	10.4	143
68	9.6	147
74	9.8	128
81	8.4	119
82	8.8	130
86	8.9	135
101	8.1	141
112	7.6	123
114	7.8	121
119	7.4	129
124	6.4	135

13.13. Study the following Excel multiple regression output. How many predictors are in this model? How many observations? What is the equation of the regression line? Discuss the strength of the model in terms F. Which predictors, if any, are significant? Why or why not? Comment on the overall effectiveness of the model.

SUMMARY OUTPUT

Regression Statistics

Multiple R	0.842
R Square	0.710
Adjusted R Square	0.630
Standard Error	109.430
Observations	15

ANOVA

	df	SS	MS	F	Significance F
Regression	3	321946.82	107315.6	8.96	0.0027
Residual	11	131723.20	11974.8		
Total	14	453670.00			

	Coefficients	Standard Error	t Stat	P-value
Intercept	657.053	167.46	3.92	0.0024
x Variable 1	5.7103	1.792	3.19	0.0087
x Variable 2	−0.4169	0.322	−1.29	0.2222
x Variable 3	−3.4715	1.443	−2.41	0.0349

13.3 Residuals, Standard Error of the Estimate, and R^2

Three more statistical tools for examining the strength of a regression model are the residuals, the standard error of the estimate, and the coefficient of multiple determination.

Residuals

The **residual**, or error, of the regression model is *the difference between the y value and the predicted value, $\hat{y}$.*

$$\text{Residual} = y - \hat{y}$$

The residuals for a multiple regression model are solved for in the same manner as they are with simple regression. First, a predicted value, $\hat{y}$, is determined by entering the value for each independent variable for a given set of observations into the multiple regression equation and solving for $\hat{y}$. Next, the value of $y - \hat{y}$ is computed for each set of observations. Shown here are the calculations for the residuals of the first set of observations from Table 13.1. The predicted value of y for $x_1 = 1605$ and $x_2 = 35$ is

$$\hat{y} = 57.4 + .0177\left(1605\right) - .666\left(35\right) = 62.499$$

Actual value of $y = 63.0$
Residual $= y - \hat{y} = 63.0 - 62.499 = 0.501$

All residuals for the real estate data and the regression model displayed in Table 13.1 and Figure 13.3 are displayed in Table 13.2.

An examination of the residuals in Table 13.2 can reveal some information about the fit of the real estate regression model. The business researcher can observe the residuals and decide whether the errors are small enough to support the accuracy of the model. The house

TABLE 13.2   **Residuals for the Real Estate Regression Model**

y	$\hat{y}$	$y - \hat{y}$
63.0	62.499	.501
65.1	71.485	−6.385
69.9	71.568	−1.668
76.8	78.639	−1.839
73.9	74.097	−.197
77.9	75.653	2.247
74.9	83.012	−8.112
78.0	105.699	−27.699
79.0	68.523	10.477
83.4	81.139	2.261
79.5	88.282	−8.782
83.9	91.335	−7.435
79.7	85.618	−5.918
84.5	95.391	−10.891
96.0	85.456	10.544
109.5	102.774	6.726
102.5	97.665	4.835
121.0	107.183	13.817
104.9	109.352	−4.452
128.0	111.230	16.770
129.0	105.061	23.939
117.9	134.415	−16.515
140.0	132.430	7.570

price figures are in units of $1,000. Two of the 23 residuals are more than 20.00, or more than $20,000 off in their prediction. On the other hand, two residuals are less than 1, or $1,000 off in their prediction.

Residuals are also helpful in locating outliers. **Outliers** are *data points that are apart, or far, from the mainstream of the other data.* They are sometimes data points that were mistakenly recorded or measured. Because every data point influences the regression model, outliers can exert an overly important influence on the model based on their distance from other points. In examining the residuals in Table 13.2 for outliers, the eighth residual listed is −27.699. This error indicates that the regression model was not nearly as successful in predicting house price on this particular house as it was with others (an error of more than $27,000). For whatever reason, this data point stands somewhat apart from other data points and may be considered an outlier.

Residuals are also useful in testing the assumptions underlying regression analysis. **Figure 13.4** displays Minitab diagnostic techniques for the real estate example. In the top right is a graph of the residuals. Notice that residual variance seems to increase in the right half of the plot, indicating potential heteroscedasticity. As discussed in Chapter 12, one of the assumptions underlying regression analysis is that the error terms have homoscedasticity or homogeneous variance. That assumption might be violated in this example. The normal plot of residuals is nearly a straight line, indicating that the assumption of normally distributed error terms probably has not been violated.

SSE and Standard Error of the Estimate

One of the properties of a regression model is that the residuals sum to zero. As pointed out in Chapter 12, this property precludes the possibility of computing an "average" residual as a single measure of error. In an effort to compute a single statistic that can represent the error in a regression analysis, the zero-sum property can be overcome by *squaring the residuals and then summing the squares.* Such an operation produces the **sum of squares of error (SSE)**.

The formula for computing the sum of squares error (SSE) for multiple regression is the same as it is for simple regression.

$$SSE = \Sigma(y - \hat{y})^2$$

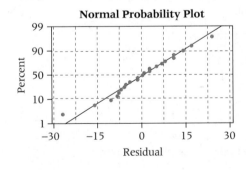

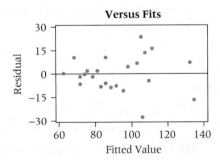

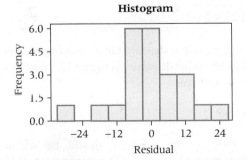

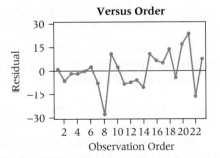

FIGURE 13.4   **Minitab Residual Diagnosis for the Real Estate Example**

For the real estate example, SSE can be computed by squaring and summing the residuals displayed in Table 13.2.

$$
\begin{aligned}
\text{SSE} = [&(.501)^2 + (-6.385)^2 + (-1.668)^2 + (-1.839)^2 \\
&+ (-.197)^2 + (2.247)^2 + (-8.112)^2 + (-27.699)^2 \\
&+ (10.477)^2 + (2.261)^2 + (-8.782)^2 + (-7.435)^2 \\
&+ (-5.918)^2 + (-10.891)^2 + (10.544)^2 + (6.726)^2 \\
&+ (4.835)^2 + (13.817)^2 + (-4.452)^2 + (16.770)^2 \\
&+ (23.939)^2 + (-16.515)^2 + (7.570)^2] \\
= &\ 2861.0
\end{aligned}
$$

SSE can also be obtained directly from the multiple regression computer output by selecting the value of SS (sum of squares) listed beside error. Shown here is the ANOVA portion of the output displayed in Figure 13.3, which is the result of a multiple regression analysis model developed to predict house prices. Note that the SS for error shown in the ANOVA table equals the value of $\Sigma(y - \hat{y})^2$ just computed (2861.0).

Analysis of Variance				SSE		
Source	DF	SS		MS	F	P
Regression	2	818.7		4094.9	28.63	.000
Error	20	2861.0		143.1		
Total	22	11050.7				

SSE has limited usage as a measure of error. However, it is a tool used to solve for other, more useful measures. One of those is the **standard error of the estimate**, s_e, which is essentially *the standard deviation of residuals (error) for the regression model*. As explained in Chapter 12, an assumption underlying regression analysis is that the error terms are approximately normally distributed with a mean of zero. With this information and by the empirical rule, approximately 68% of the residuals should be within $\pm 1 s_e$ and 95% should be within $\pm 2 s_e$. This property makes the standard error of the estimate a useful tool in estimating how accurately a regression model is fitting the data.

The standard error of the estimate is computed by dividing SSE by the degrees of freedom of error for the model and taking the square root.

$$
s_e = \sqrt{\frac{\text{SSE}}{n - k - 1}}
$$

where

n = number of observations
k = number of independent variables

The value of s_e can be computed for the real estate example as follows:

$$
s_e = \sqrt{\frac{\text{SSE}}{n - k - 1}} = \sqrt{\frac{2861}{23 - 2 - 1}} = 11.96
$$

The standard error of the estimate, s_e, is usually given as standard output from regression analysis by computer software packages. The Minitab output displayed in Figure 13.3 contains the standard error of the estimate for the real estate example.

$$
S = 11.96
$$

By the empirical rule, approximately 68% of the residuals should be within $\pm 1 s_e = \pm 1(11.96) = \pm 11.96$. Because house prices are in units of $1,000, approximately 68% of the predictions are within $\pm 1.96(\$1,000)$, or $\pm\$11,960$. Examining the output displayed in

Table 13.2, 18/23, or about 78%, of the residuals are within this span. According to the empirical rule, approximately 95% of the residuals should be within $\pm 2s_e$, or $\pm 2(11.96) = \pm 23.92$. Further examination of the residual values in Table 13.2 shows that 21 of 23, or 91%, fall within this range. The business researcher can study the standard error of the estimate and these empirical rule–related ranges and decide whether the error of the regression model is sufficiently small to justify further use of the model.

Coefficient of Multiple Determination (R^2)

The **coefficient of multiple determination (R^2)** is analogous to the coefficient of determination (r^2) discussed in Chapter 12. R^2 represents *the proportion of variation of the dependent variable, y, accounted for by the independent variables in the regression model.* As with r^2, the range of possible values for R^2 is from 0 to 1. An R^2 of 0 indicates no relationship between the predictor variables in the model and y. An R^2 of 1 indicates that 100% of the variability of y has been accounted for by the predictors. Of course, it is desirable for R^2 to be high, indicating the strong predictability of a regression model. The coefficient of multiple determination can be calculated by the following formula:

$$R^2 = \frac{SSR}{SS_{yy}} = 1 - \frac{SSE}{SS_{yy}}$$

R^2 can be calculated in the real estate example by using the sum of squares regression (SSR), the sum of squares error (SSE), and sum of squares total (SS_{yy}) from the ANOVA portion of Figure 13.3.

Analysis of Variance			$\overset{SSE}{}\overset{SS_{yy}}{}$			
Source	DF	SS	$\overset{SSR}{}$ MS	F	P	
Regression	2	(8189.7)	4094.9	28.63	.000	
Error	20	(2861.0)	143.1			
Total	22	(11050.7)				

$$R^2 = \frac{SSR}{SS_{yy}} = \frac{8189.7}{11050.7} = .741$$

or

$$R^2 = 1 - \frac{SSE}{SS_{yy}} = 1 - \frac{2861.0}{11050.7} = .741$$

In addition, virtually all statistical software packages print out R^2 as standard output with multiple regression analysis. A reexamination of Figure 13.3 reveals that R^2 is given as

$$R\text{-sq} = 74.1\%$$

This result indicates that a relatively high proportion of the variation of the dependent variable, house price, is accounted for by the independent variables in this regression model.

Adjusted R^2

As additional independent variables are added to a regression model, the value of R^2 cannot decrease, and in most cases it will increase. In the formulas for determining R^2,

$$R^2 = \frac{SSR}{SS_{yy}} = 1 - \frac{SSE}{SS_{yy}}$$

the value of SS_{yy} for a given set of observations will remain the same as independent variables are added to the regression analysis because SS_{yy} is the sum of squares for the dependent variable. Because additional independent variables are likely to increase SSR at least by some amount, the value of R^2 will probably increase for any additional independent variables.

However, sometimes additional independent variables add no *significant* information to the regression model, yet R^2 increases. R^2 therefore may yield an inflated figure. Statisticians have developed an **adjusted R^2** *to take into consideration both the additional information each new independent variable brings to the regression model and the changed degrees of freedom of regression.* Many standard statistical computer packages now compute and report adjusted R^2 as part of the output. The formula for computing adjusted R^2 is

$$\text{Adjusted } R^2 = 1 - \frac{\text{SSE}/\left(n - k - 1\right)}{\text{SS}_{yy}/\left(n - 1\right)}$$

The value of adjusted R^2 for the real estate example can be solved by using information from the ANOVA portion of the computer output in Figure 13.3.

```
                           n - 1        SS_yy
              n - k - 1 /           SSE /

Analysis of Variance /

Source      DF  //   SS     /  MS      F      p
Regression  2  //  8189.7 //4094.9   28.63  .000
Error      (20)//  (2861.0)/  143.1
Total      (22)  (11050.7)/
─────────────────────────────────────────────
SSE = 2861    SS_YY = 11050.7   n - k - 1 = 20   n - 1 = 22
```

Thinking Critically About Statistics in Business Today

Assessing Property Values Using Multiple Regression

According to county assessor sources, Colorado state statute requires that all county assessors in the state value residential real property solely by a market approach. Furthermore, in the statute, it is stated that such a market approach will be based on a representative body of sales sufficient to set a pattern. No specifics on market analysis methods are given in the statutes, but there are several commonly used methods, including multiple regression. In the multiple regression approach, an attempt is made to develop a model to predict recent sales (dependent variable) by such property characteristics (independent variables) as location, lot size, building square feet, construction quality, property type (single family, condominium, townhouse), garage size, basement type, and other features. One county Web site states that "regression does not require strict similarity between property sales because it estimates the value contribution (coefficient) for each attribute. . . ." In producing a sound multiple regression model to predict property values, several models are developed, refined, and compared using the typical indicators of a good fit, such as R^2, standard error of the estimate, F test for the overall model, and p-values associated with the t tests of significance for predictors. The final multiple regression model is then used in the estimation of property values by the appraiser, who enters into the regression model (equation) the specific measure of each independent (predictor) variable for a given property, resulting in a predicted appraised property value for tax purposes. The models are updated for currency and based on data that are never more than two years old.

THINGS TO PONDER

1. How does the multiple regression method improve the validity of property value assessments over typical standard methods? Do you think it is more fair and equitable? If so, why?

2. Can you think of other similar possible applications of multiple regression in business?

Source: Douglas County, Colorado, Assessor's Office, at http:/www.douglas.co.us/assessor/Multiple_Regression.html, March 20, 2011, and Gunnison County Assessor's Office, at http://www.gunnisoncounty.org/assessor_assessment_process.html, March 20, 2011.

$$\text{Adj.}\,R^2 = 1 - \left[\frac{2861/20}{11050.7/22}\right] = 1 - .285 = .715$$

The standard Minitab regression output in Figure 13.3 contains the value of the adjusted R^2 already computed. For the real estate example, this value is shown as

$$R\text{-sq(adj.)} = 71.5\%$$

A comparison of R^2 (.741) with the adjusted R^2 (.715) for this example shows that the adjusted R^2 reduces the overall proportion of variation of the dependent variable accounted for by the independent variables by a factor of .026, or 2.6%. The gap between the R^2 and adjusted R^2 tends to increase as nonsignificant independent variables are added to the regression model. As n increases, the difference between R^2 and adjusted R^2 becomes less.

13.3 Problems

13.14. Study the Minitab output shown in Problem 13.7. Comment on the overall strength of the regression model in light of S, R^2, and adjusted R^2.

13.15. Study the Minitab output shown in Problem 13.8. Comment on the overall strength of the regression model in light of S, R^2, and adjusted R^2.

13.16. Using the regression output obtained by working Problem 13.5, comment on the overall strength of the regression model using S, R^2, and adjusted R^2.

13.17. Using the regression output obtained by working Problem 13.6, comment on the overall strength of the regression model using S, R^2, and adjusted R^2.

13.18. Using the regression output obtained by working Problem 13.11, comment on the overall strength of the regression model using S, R^2, and adjusted R^2.

13.19. Using the regression output obtained by working Problem 13.12, comment on the overall strength of the regression model using S, R^2, and adjusted R^2.

13.20. Study the Excel output shown in Problem 13.13. Comment on the overall strength of the regression model in light of S, R^2, and adjusted R^2.

13.21. Study the Minitab residual diagnostic output that follows. Discuss any potential problems with meeting the regression assumptions for this regression analysis based on the residual graphics.

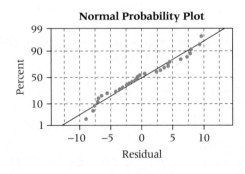

Normal Probability Plot

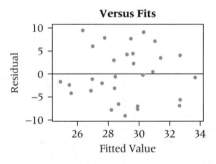

Versus Fits

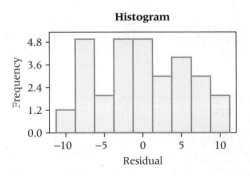

Histogram

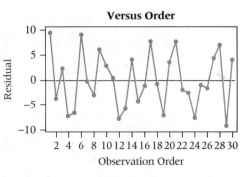

Versus Order

$$\boxed{13.4}$$ Interpreting Multiple Regression Computer Output

A Reexamination of the Multiple Regression Output

Figure 13.5 shows again the Minitab multiple regression output for the real estate example. Many of the concepts discussed thus far in the chapter are highlighted. Note the following items:

1. The equation of the regression model
2. The ANOVA table with the F value for the overall test of the model
3. The t ratios, which test the significance of the regression coefficients
4. The value of SSE
5. The value of s_e
6. The value of R^2
7. The value of adjusted R^2

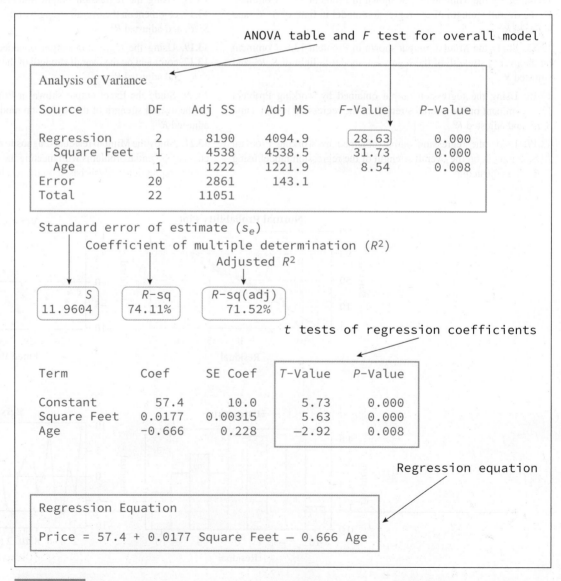

ANOVA table and F test for overall model

Analysis of Variance

Source	DF	Adj SS	Adj MS	F-Value	P-Value
Regression	2	8190	4094.9	28.63	0.000
Square Feet	1	4538	4538.5	31.73	0.000
Age	1	1222	1221.9	8.54	0.008
Error	20	2861	143.1		
Total	22	11051			

Standard error of estimate (s_e)
Coefficient of multiple determination (R^2)
Adjusted R^2

S	R-sq	R-sq(adj)
11.9604	74.11%	71.52%

t tests of regression coefficients

Term	Coef	SE Coef	T-Value	P-Value
Constant	57.4	10.0	5.73	0.000
Square Feet	0.0177	0.00315	5.63	0.000
Age	-0.666	0.228	-2.92	0.008

Regression equation

Regression Equation

Price = 57.4 + 0.0177 Square Feet − 0.666 Age

FIGURE 13.5   **Annotated Version of the Minitab Output of Regression for the Real Estate Example**

DEMONSTRATION PROBLEM 13.2

Discuss the Excel multiple regression output for Demonstration Problem 13.1. Comment on the F test for the overall significance of the model, the t tests of the regression coefficients, and the values of s_e, R^2, and adjusted R^2.

Solution: This multiple regression analysis was done to predict the prime interest rate using the predictors of unemployment and personal saving. The equation of the regression model was presented in the solution of Demonstration Problem 13.1. Shown here is the complete multiple regression output from the Excel analysis of the data.

The value of F for this problem is 12.29, with a p-value of .0012, which is significant at $\alpha = .01$. On the basis of this information, the null hypothesis is rejected for the overall test of significance. At least one of the predictor variables is **statistically significant**, and there is significant predictability of the prime interest rate by this model.

An examination of the t ratios reveals that unemployment rate is a significant predictor at $\alpha = .001$ ($t = -4.93$ with a p-value of .0003) and that personal savings is a significant predictor at $\alpha = .01$ ($t = 3.31$ with a p-value of .0062). The positive signs on the regression coefficient and the t value for personal savings indicate that as personal savings increase, the prime interest rate tends to get higher. On the other hand, the negative signs on the regression coefficient and the t value for unemployment rates indicate that as the unemployment rate increases, the prime interest rate tends to decrease.

The standard error of the estimate is $s_e = 1.496$, indicating that approximately 68% of the residuals are within ± 1.496. An examination of the Excel-produced residuals shows that actually 11 out of 15, or 73.3%, fall in this interval. Approximately 95% of the residuals should be within $\pm 2(1.496) = \pm 2.992$, and an examination of the Excel-produced residuals shows that 14 out of 15, or 93.3%, of the residuals are within this interval.

R^2 for this regression analysis is .672, or 67.2%. The adjusted R^2 is .617, indicating that there is some inflation in the R^2 value. Overall, there is modest predictability in this model.

SUMMARY OUTPUT

Regression Statistics

Multiple R	0.820
R Square	0.672
Adjusted R Square	0.617
Standard Error	1.496
Observations	15

ANOVA

	df	SS	MS	F	Significance F
Regression	2	54.9835	27.4917	12.29	0.0012
Residual	12	26.8537	2.2378		
Total	14	81.8372			

	Coefficients	Standard Error	t Stat	P-value
Intercept	13.5786	1.728	7.86	0.0000
Unemployment Rates	−1.6622	0.337	−4.93	0.0003
Personal Savings	0.6586	0.199	3.31	0.0062

RESIDUAL OUTPUT

Observation	Predicted Prime Interest Rate	Residuals
1	7.3441	0.9859
2	9.2446	0.0754
3	8.8808	1.1292
4	6.1837	0.0663

5	6.6008	0.5492
6	7.2374	1.0326
7	8.9309	−0.5809
8	8.4448	0.7852
9	5.5187	−0.8487
10	5.8198	−1.4798
11	6.3937	1.5663
12	5.1236	−0.0336
13	1.4418	1.8082
14	5.1206	−1.8706
15	6.4346	−3.1846

13.4 Problems

13.22. Study the Minitab regression output that follows. How many predictors are there? What is the equation of the regression model? Using the key statistics discussed in this chapter, discuss the strength of the model and the predictors.

Regression Analysis: Y versus X_1, X_2, X_3, X_4

```
Analysis of Variance
Source       DF  Adj SS   Adj MS  F-Value  P-Value
Regression    4  18088.5  4522.13  55.52    0.000
Error        55   4479.7    81.45
Total        59  22568.2

  S       R-sq   R-sq(adj)
 9.025    80.2%   78.7%

Coefficients
Term       Coef     SE Coef  T-Value  P-Value
Constant  -55.93    24.22    -2.31    0.025
X₁         0.01049  0.02100   0.50    0.619
X₂        -0.10720  0.03503  -3.06    0.003
X₃         0.57922  0.07633   7.59    0.000
X₄        -0.8695   0.1498   -5.81    0.000

Regression Equation
   Y = -55.9 + 0.0105 X₁ - 0.107 X₂
       + 0579 X₃ - 0.870 X₄
```

13.23. Study the Excel regression output that follows. How many predictors are there? What is the equation of the regression model? Using the key statistics discussed in this chapter, discuss the strength of the model and its predictors.

SUMMARY OUTPUT

Regression Statistics	
Multiple R	0.814
R Square	0.663
Adjusted R Square	0.636
Standard Error	51.761
Observations	28

ANOVA

	df	*SS*	*MS*	*F*	*Significance F*
Regression	2	131567.02	65783.51	24.55	0.0000013
Residual	25	66979.65	2679.19		
Total	27	198546.68			

	Coefficients	*Standard Error*	*t Stat*	*P-value*
Intercept	203.3937	67.518	3.01	0.0059
X_1	1.1151	0.528	2.11	0.0448
X_2	−2.2115	0.567	−3.90	0.0006

Decision Dilemma Solved

Are You Going to Hate Your New Job?

In the Decision Dilemma, several variables are considered in attempting to determine whether a person will like his or her new job. Four predictor (independent) variables are given with the data set: relationship with supervisor, overall quality of work environment, total hours worked per week, and opportunities for advancement. Other possible variables might include openness of work culture, amount of pressure, how the interviewee is treated during the interview, availability of flexible scheduling, size of office, amount of time allotted for lunch, availability of management, interesting work, and many others.

Using the data that are given, a multiple regression model can be developed to predict job satisfaction from the four independent variables. Such an analysis allows the business researcher to study the entire data set in one model rather than constructing four different simple regression models, one for each independent variable. In the multiple regression model, job satisfaction is the dependent variable. There are 19 observations. The Excel regression output for this problem follows.

The test for overall significance of the model produced an F of 87.79 with a p-value of .000000001 (significant at $\alpha = .00000001$). The R^2 of .962 and adjusted R^2 of .951 indicate very strong predictability in the model. The standard error of the estimate, 5.141, can be viewed in light of the job satisfaction values that ranged from 10 to 95 and the residuals, which are not shown here. Fourteen of the 19 residuals (73.7%) are within the standard error of the estimate. Examining the t statistics and their associated p-values reveals that two independent variables, relationship with supervisor ($t = 5.33$, p-value $= .0001$) and overall quality of work environment ($t = 2.73$, p-value $= .0162$) are significant predictors at $\alpha = .05$. Judging by their large p-values, it appears that total hours worked per week and opportunities for advancement are not good predictors of job satisfaction.

SUMMARY OUTPUT

Regression Statistics

Multiple R	0.981
R Square	0.962
Adjusted R Square	0.951
Standard Error	5.141
Observations	19

ANOVA

	df	SS	MS	F	Significance F
Regression	4	9282.569	2320.642	87.79	0.000000001
Residual	14	370.062	26.433		
Total	18	9652.632			

	Coefficients	Standard Error	t Stat	P-value
Intercept	−1.469	8.116	−0.18	0.8590
Relationship with Supervisor	1.391	0.261	5.33	0.0001
Overall Quality of Work Environment	0.317	0.116	2.73	0.0162
Total Hours Worked per Week	0.043	0.121	0.36	0.7263
Opportunities for Advancement	−0.094	0.102	−0.92	0.3711

Ethical Considerations

Multiple regression analysis can be used either intentionally or unintentionally in questionable or unethical ways. When degrees of freedom are small, an inflated value of R^2 can be obtained, leading to overenthusiastic expectations about the predictability of a regression model. To prevent this type of reliance, a researcher should take into account the nature of the data, the variables, and the value of the adjusted R^2.

Another misleading aspect of multiple regression can be the tendency of researchers to assume cause-and-effect relationships between the dependent variable and predictors. Just because independent variables produce a significant R^2 does not necessarily mean those variables are causing the deviation of the y values. Indeed, some other force not in the model may be driving both the independent variables and the dependent variable over the range of values being studied.

Some people use the estimates of the regression coefficients to compare the worth of the predictor variables; the larger the coefficient, the greater is its worth. At least two problems can be found in this approach. The first is that most variables are measured in different units. Thus, regression coefficient weights are partly a function of the unit of measurement of the variable. Second, if multicollinearity (discussed in Chapter 14) is present, the interpretation of the regression coefficients is questionable. In addition, the presence of multicollinearity raises several issues about the interpretation of other regression output. Researchers who ignore this problem are at risk of presenting spurious results.

Another danger in using regression analysis is in the extrapolation of the model to values beyond the range of values used to derive the model. A regression model that fits data within a given range does not necessarily fit data outside that range. One of the uses of regression analysis is in the area of forecasting. Users need to be aware that what has occurred in the past is not guaranteed to continue to occur in the future. Unscrupulous and sometimes even well-intentioned business decision makers can use regression models to project conclusions about the future that have little or no basis. The receiver of such messages should be cautioned that regression models may lack validity outside the range of values in which the models were developed.

Summary

Multiple regression analysis is a statistical tool in which a mathematical model is developed in an attempt to predict a dependent variable by two or more independent variables or in which at least one predictor is nonlinear. Because doing multiple regression analysis by hand is extremely tedious and time-consuming, it is almost always done on a computer.

The standard output from a multiple regression analysis is similar to that of simple regression analysis. A regression equation is produced with a constant that is analogous to the y-intercept in simple regression and with estimates of the regression coefficients that are analogous to the estimate of the slope in simple regression. An F test for the overall model is computed to determine whether at least one of the regression coefficients is significantly different from zero. This F value is usually displayed in an ANOVA table, which is part of the regression output. The ANOVA table also contains the sum of squares of error and sum of squares of regression, which are used to compute other statistics in the model.

Most multiple regression computer output contains t values, which are used to determine the significance of the regression coefficients. Using these t values, statisticians can make decisions about including or excluding variables from the model.

Residuals, standard error of the estimate, and R^2 are also standard computer regression output with multiple regression. The coefficient of determination for simple regression models is denoted r^2, whereas for multiple regression it is R^2. The interpretation of residuals, standard error of the estimate, and R^2 in multiple regression is similar to that in simple regression. Because R^2 can be inflated with nonsignificant variables in the mix, an adjusted R^2 is often computed. Unlike R^2, adjusted R^2 takes into account the degrees of freedom and the number of observations.

Key Terms

adjusted R^2	independent variable	partial regression coefficient R^2	response variable
coefficient of multiple	least squares analysis	residual	standard error of the
determination (R^2)	multiple regression	response plane	estimate (s_e)
dependent variable	outliers	response surface	sum of squares of error (SSE)

Formulas

The F value

$$F = \frac{MS_{reg}}{MS_{err}} = \frac{SS_{reg}/df_{reg}}{SS_{err}/df_{err}} = \frac{SSR/k}{SSE/(N - k - 1)}$$

Sum of squares of error

$$SSE = \Sigma(y - \hat{y})^2$$

Standard error of the estimate

$$s_e = \sqrt{\frac{SSE}{n - k - 1}}$$

Coefficient of multiple determination

$$R^2 = \frac{SSR}{SS_{yy}} = 1 - \frac{SSE}{SS_{yy}}$$

Adjusted R^2

$$\text{Adjusted } R^2 = 1 - \frac{SSE/(n - k - 1)}{SS_{yy}/(n - 1)}$$

Supplementary Problems

Calculating the Statistics

13.24. Use the following data to develop a multiple regression model to predict y from x_1 and x_2. Discuss the output, including comments about the overall strength of the model, the significance of the regression coefficients, and other indicators of model fit.

y	x_1	x_2
198	29	1.64
214	71	2.81
211	54	2.22
219	73	2.70
184	67	1.57
167	32	1.63
201	47	1.99
204	43	2.14
190	60	2.04
222	32	2.93
197	34	2.15

13.25. Given here are the data for a dependent variable, y, and independent variables. Use these data to develop a regression model to predict y. Discuss the output.

y	x_1	x_2	x_3
14	51	16.4	56
17	48	17.1	64
29	29	18.2	53
32	36	17.9	41
54	40	16.5	60
86	27	17.1	55
117	14	17.8	71
120	17	18.2	48
194	16	16.9	60
203	9	18.0	77
217	14	18.9	90
235	11	18.5	67

Testing Your Understanding

13.26. The U.S. Bureau of Mines produces data on the price of minerals. Shown here are the average prices per year for several minerals over a decade. Use these data and multiple regression to produce a model to predict the average price of gold from the other variables. Comment on the results of the process.

GOLD ($ PER OZ.)	COPPER (CENTS PER LB.)	SILVER ($ PER OZ.)	ALUMINUM (CENTS PER LB.)
161.1	64.2	4.4	39.8
308.0	93.3	11.1	61.0
613.0	101.3	20.6	71.6
460.0	84.2	10.5	76.0
376.0	72.8	8.0	76.0
424.0	76.5	11.4	77.8
361.0	66.8	8.1	81.0
318.0	67.0	6.1	81.0
368.0	66.1	5.5	81.0
448.0	82.5	7.0	72.3
438.0	120.5	6.5	110.1
382.6	130.9	5.5	87.8

13.27. The Shipbuilders Council of America in Washington, D.C., publishes data about private shipyards. Among the variables reported by this organization are the employment figures (per 1000), the number of naval vessels under construction, and the number of repairs or conversions done to commercial ships (in $ millions). Shown here are the data for these three variables over a seven-year period. Use the data to develop a regression model to predict private shipyard employment from number of naval vessels under construction and repairs or conversions of commercial ships. Comment on the regression model and its strengths and its weaknesses.

	COMMERCIAL SHIP	
EMPLOYMENT	NAVAL VESSELS	REPAIRS OR CONVERSIONS
133.4	108	431
177.3	99	1335
143.0	105	1419
142.0	111	1631
130.3	100	852
120.6	85	847
120.4	79	806

13.28. The U.S. Bureau of Labor Statistics produces consumer price indexes for several different categories. Shown here are the percentage changes in consumer price indexes over a period of 20 years for food, shelter, apparel, and fuel oil. Also displayed are the percentage changes in consumer price indexes for all commodities. Use these data and multiple regression to develop a model that attempts to predict all commodities by the other four variables. Comment on the result of this analysis.

ALL COMMODITIES	FOOD	SHELTER	APPAREL	FUEL OIL
.9	1.0	2.0	1.6	3.7
.6	1.3	.8	.9	2.7
.9	.7	1.6	.4	2.6
.9	1.6	1.2	1.3	2.6
1.2	1.3	1.5	.9	2.1
1.1	2.2	1.9	1.1	2.4
2.6	5.0	3.0	2.5	4.4
1.9	.9	3.6	4.1	7.2
3.5	3.5	4.5	5.3	6.0
4.7	5.1	8.3	5.8	6.7
4.5	5.7	8.9	4.2	6.6
3.6	3.1	4.2	3.2	6.2
3.0	4.2	4.6	2.0	3.3
7.4	14.5	4.7	3.7	4.0
11.9	14.3	9.6	7.4	9.3
8.8	8.5	9.9	4.5	12.0
4.3	3.0	5.5	3.7	9.5
5.8	6.3	6.6	4.5	9.6
7.2	9.9	10.2	3.6	8.4
11.3	11.0	13.9	4.3	9.2

13.29. The U.S. Department of Agriculture publishes data annually on various selected farm products. Shown here are the unit production figures (in millions of bushels) for three farm products for 10 years during a 20-year period. Use these data and multiple regression analysis to predict corn production by the production of soybeans and wheat. Comment on the results.

CORN	SOYBEANS	WHEAT
4152	1127	1352
6639	1798	2381
4175	1636	2420
7672	1861	2595
8876	2099	2424
8226	1940	2091
7131	1938	2108
4929	1549	1812
7525	1924	2037
7933	1922	2739

13.30. The American Chamber of Commerce Researchers Association compiles cost-of-living indexes for selected metropolitan areas. Shown here are cost-of-living indexes for 25 different cities on five different items for a recent year. Use the data to develop a regression model to predict the grocery cost-of-living index by the indexes of housing, utilities, transportation, and healthcare. Discuss the results, highlighting both the significant and nonsignificant predictors.

CITY	GROCERY ITEMS	HOUSING	UTILITIES	TRANSPORTATION	HEALTHCARE
Albany	108.3	106.8	127.4	89.1	107.5
Albuquerque	96.3	105.2	98.8	100.9	102.1
Augusta, GA	96.2	88.8	115.6	102.3	94.0
Austin	98.0	83.9	87.7	97.4	94.9
Baltimore	106.0	114.1	108.1	112.8	111.5
Buffalo	103.1	117.3	127.6	107.8	100.8
Colorado Springs	94.5	88.5	74.6	93.3	102.4
Dallas	105.4	98.9	108.9	110.0	106.8
Denver	91.5	108.3	97.2	105.9	114.3
Des Moines	94.3	95.1	111.4	105.7	96.2
El Paso	102.9	94.6	90.9	104.2	91.4
Indianapolis	96.0	99.7	92.1	102.7	97.4
Jacksonville	96.1	90.4	96.0	106.0	96.1
Kansas City	89.8	92.4	96.3	95.6	93.6
Knoxville	93.2	88.0	91.7	91.6	82.3
Los Angeles	103.3	211.3	75.6	102.1	128.5
Louisville	94.6	91.0	79.4	102.4	88.4
Memphis	99.1	86.2	91.1	101.1	85.5
Miami	100.3	123.0	125.6	104.3	137.8
Minneapolis	92.8	112.3	105.2	106.0	107.5
Mobile	99.9	81.1	104.9	102.8	92.2
Nashville	95.8	107.7	91.6	98.1	90.9
New Orleans	104.0	83.4	122.2	98.2	87.0
Oklahoma City	98.2	79.4	103.4	97.3	97.1
Phoenix	95.7	98.7	96.3	104.6	115.2

Interpreting the Output

13.31. Shown here are the data for y and three predictors, x_1, x_2, and x_3. A multiple regression analysis has been done on these data; the Minitab results are given. Comment on the outcome of the analysis in light of the data.

y	x_1	x_2	x_3
94	21	1	204
97	25	0	198
93	22	1	184
95	27	0	200
90	29	1	182
91	20	1	159
91	18	1	147
94	25	0	196
98	26	0	228
99	24	0	242
90	28	1	162
92	23	1	180
96	25	0	219

Regression Analysis: Y versus X_1, X_2, X_3

```
Analysis of Variance

Source       DF   Adj SS   Adj MS   F-Value  P-Value
Regression    3  103.185  34.3950    47.57    0.000
X₁            1    6.857   6.8570     9.48    0.013
X₂            1    9.975   9.9752    13.80    0.005
X₃            1   19.685  19.6849    27.23    0.001
Error         9    6.507   0.7230
Total        12  109.692

S         R-sq    R-sq(adj)  R-sq(pred)
0.850311  94.07%    92.09%     88.90%

Coefficients

Term       Coef     SE Coef  T-Value  P-Value
Constant   87.89     3.45     25.51    0.000
X₁        -0.2561   0.0832    -3.08    0.013
X₂        -2.714    0.731     -3.71    0.005
X₃         0.0706   0.0135     5.22    0.001

Regression Equation

  Y = 87.89 − 0.2561 X₁ − 2.714 X₂ + 0.0706 X₃
```

13.32. Minitab residual diagnostic output from the multiple regression analysis for the data given in Problem 13.30 follows. Discuss any potential problems with meeting the regression assumptions for this regression analysis based on the residual graphics.

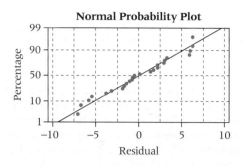

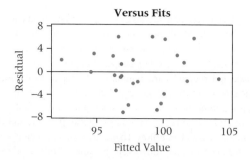

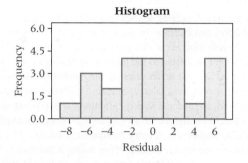

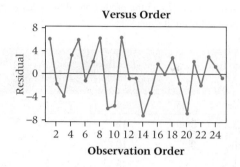

Analyzing the Databases

See **www.wiley.com/college/black**

1. Use the Manufacturing database to develop a multiple regression model to predict Cost of Materials by Number of Employees, New Capital Expenditures, Value Added by Manufacture, and End-of-Year Inventories. Discuss the results of the analysis.

2. Develop a regression model using the Financial database. Use Total Revenues, Total Assets, Return on Equity, Earnings Per Share, Average Yield, and Dividends Per Share to predict the average P/E ratio for a company. How strong is the model? Which variables seem to be the best predictors?

3. Using the International Stock Market database, develop a multiple regression model to predict the Nikkei by the DJIA, the Nasdaq, the S&P 500, the Hang Seng, the FTSE 100, and the IPC. Discuss the outcome, including the model, the strength of the model, and the strength of the predictors.

4. Develop a multiple regression model to predict Annual Food Spending by Annual Household Income and Non-Mortgage Household Debt using the Consumer Food database. How strong is the model? Which of the two predictors seems to be stronger? Why?

Case

Starbucks Introduces Debit Card

Starbucks is a resounding restaurant success story. Beginning with its first coffee house in 1971, Starbucks has grown to more than 22,500 stores. Opening up its first international outlet in the mid-1990s, Starbucks now operates in more than 67 countries outside of North America. Besides selling beverages, pastries, confections, and coffee-related accessories and equipment at its retail outlets, Starbucks also purchases and roasts high quality coffee beans in several locations. The company's objective is to become the most recognized and respected brand in the world. Starbucks maintains a strong environmental orientation and is committed to taking a leadership position environmentally. In addition, the company has won awards for corporate social responsibility through its community-building programs, its strong

commitment to its origins (coffee producers, family, community), and the Starbucks Foundation, which is dedicated to creating hope, discovery, and opportunity in the communities where Starbucks resides.

In November 2001, Starbucks launched its prepaid (debit) Starbucks Card. The card, which holds between $5 and $500, can be used at virtually any Starbucks location. The card was so popular when it first was released that many stores ran out. By mid-2002, Starbucks had activated more than 5 million of these cards. The Starbucks Card has surpassed the $25 billion mark for total activations and reloads since its introduction. As customers "reload" the cards, it appears they are placing more money on them than the initial value of the card.

Starbucks has gone on to promote their Starbucks Card as a flexible marketing tool that can be used by individuals as a gift of thanks and appreciation for friendship or service and can be used by companies to reward loyal customers and as an incentive to employees.

Discussion

1. Starbucks enjoyed considerable success with its debit cards, which they sell for $5 to $500. Suppose Starbucks management wants to study the reasons why some people purchase debit cards with higher prepaid amounts than do other people. Suppose a study of 25 randomly selected prepaid card purchasers is taken. Respondents are asked the amount of the prepaid card, the customer's age, the number of days per month the customer makes a purchase at Starbucks, the number of cups of coffee the customer drinks per day, and the customer's income. The data follow. Using these data, develop a multiple regression model to study how well the amount of the prepaid card can be predicted by the other variables and which variables seem to be more promising in doing the prediction. What sales implications might be evident from this analysis?

AMOUNT OF PREPAID CARD ($)	AGE	DAYS PER MONTH AT STARBUCKS	CUPS OF COFFEE PER DAY	INCOME ($1,000)
5	25	4	1	20
25	30	12	5	35
10	27	10	4	30
5	42	8	5	30
15	29	11	8	25
50	25	12	5	60
10	50	8	3	30
15	45	6	5	35
5	32	16	7	25
5	23	10	1	20
20	40	18	5	40
35	35	12	3	40
40	28	10	3	50
15	33	12	2	30
200	40	15	5	80
15	37	3	1	30
40	51	10	8	35
5	20	8	4	25
30	26	15	5	35
100	38	19	10	45
30	27	12	3	35
25	29	14	6	35
25	34	10	4	45
50	30	6	3	55
15	22	8	5	30

2. Suppose marketing wants to be able to profile frequent visitors to a Starbucks store. Using the same data set already provided, develop a multiple regression model to predict Days per month at Starbucks by Age, Income, and Number of cups of coffee per day. How strong is the model? Which particular independent variables seem to have more promise in predicting how many days per month a customer visits Starbucks? What marketing implications might be evident from this analysis?

3. Over the past decade or so, Starbucks has grown quite rapidly. As they add stores and increase the number of drinks, their sales revenues increase. In reflecting about this growth, think about some other variables that might be related to the increase in Starbucks sales revenues. Some data for the past seven years on the number of Starbucks stores (worldwide), approximate sales revenue (in $ millions), number of different drinks sold, and average weekly earnings of U.S. production workers are given here. Most figures are approximate. Develop a multiple regression model to predict sales revenue by number of drinks sold, number of stores, and average weekly earnings. How strong is the model? What are the key predictors, if any? How might this analysis help Starbucks management in attempting to determine what drives sales revenues?

SALES YEAR	REVENUE	NUMBER OF STORES	NUMBER OF DRINKS	AVERAGE WEEKLY EARNINGS
1	400	676	15	386
2	700	1015	15	394
3	1000	1412	18	407
4	1350	1886	22	425
5	1650	2135	27	442
6	2200	3300	27	457
7	2600	4709	30	474

Source: Adapted from Shirley Leung, "Starbucks May Indeed Be a Robust Staple," *The Wall Street Journal,* July 26, 2002, p. B4; James Peters, "Starbucks' Growth Still Hot; Gift Card Jolts Chain's Sales," *Nation's Restaurant News,* February 11, 2002, pp. 1–2. https://www.starbucks.com/ card, Starbucks' Web site (2016) at http://www.starbucks.com/about-us; https://news.starbucks.com/

CHAPTER 14

Building Multiple Regression Models

LEARNING OBJECTIVES

This chapter presents several advanced topics in multiple regression analysis, enabling you to:

1. Generalize linear regression models as polynomial regression models using model transformation and Tukey's ladder of transformation, accounting for possible interaction among the independent variables.

2. Examine the role of indicator, or dummy, variables as predictors or independent variables in multiple regression analysis.

3. Use all possible regressions, stepwise regression, forward selection, and backward elimination search procedures to develop regression models that account for the greatest variation in the dependent variable and are parsimonious.

4. Recognize when multicollinearity is present, understanding general techniques for preventing and controlling it.

5. Explain when to use logistic regression, and interpret its results.

Predicting CEO Salaries

Chief executive officers for large companies receive widely varying salaries for their work. What are some of the variables that seem to contribute to the size of a CEO salary? Some possible company factors might include assets, sales, number of employees, type of industry, ownership structure, performance of the firm, and company location. Are any of these variables a determining factor in establishing a CEO salary? Do CEOs' personal characteristics such as age, experience, reputation, or degrees matter in determining salary?

According to PayScale.com, skills that affect a CEO's salary can include team building, business strategy, strategic planning, and leadership. Generally, Chief Executive Officers who have more years of relevant experience have higher salaries although even those with less experience can enjoy high salaries. Forty-five percent of CEOs have twenty or more years of experience. PayScale.com also reports that CEO pay varies with location. For example, the pay rates for CEOs in New York City average 44% more than the national average in contrast to Austin where CEO salaries are 11% below the national average.

Shown here are data created for illustration purposes from twenty companies on four variables: 1) CEO Salary ($ millions),

Yuri_Arcurs/Getty Images, Inc.

2) Annual Company Revenue ($ billions), 3) Number of Company Employees (1,000s), and 4) if the company is in Manufacturing or Not.

CEO SALARY ($ MILLIONS)	COMPANY ANNUAL REVENUE ($ BILLIONS)	NUMBER OF EMPLOYEES (1,000S)	MANUFACTURING COMPANY 1 = YES
6.327	49.5	47.200	1
2.208	30.6	29.250	0
3.847	39.5	44.000	0
4.467	32.6	37.925	1
2.569	21.7	13.440	0
5.809	37.5	81.500	1
3.512	16.7	43.000	0
8.624	51.2	104.000	1
4.716	56.8	74.500	1
3.863	29.1	52.000	0
2.970	35.4	36.700	0
1.091	27.2	44.700	0
6.513	67.2	126.500	1
9.376	82.3	62.000	1
4.530	41.1	43.000	1
5.724	35.7	82.000	1
7.015	48.9	61.800	1
3.667	27.1	29.480	0
1.983	24.0	30.040	0
4.716	55.6	60.142	1

MANAGERIAL AND STATISTICAL QUESTIONS

1. Can a model be developed from these data and variables to predict CEO salaries?
2. If a model is developed, how can the model be evaluated to determine how strong it is?
3. Is it possible to sort out variables that appear to be related to CEO salary and determine which variables are more significant predictors?
4. Are some of the variables related to CEO salary but in a nonlinear manner?
5. Are some of the variables highly interrelated and redundant in their potential for determining CEO compensation?

Sources: CEO information adapted from PayScale.com at: www.payscale.com/data-packages/ceo-income/full-list; http://www.payscale.com/research/US/Job=Chief_Executive_Officer_(CEO)/Salary

Note: Data was created by the author for illustrative purposes and does not necessarily reflect actual market conditions.

14.1 Nonlinear Models: Mathematical Transformation

The regression models presented thus far are based on the general linear regression model, which has the form

General Linear Regression Model

$$y = \beta_0 + \beta_1 x_1 + \beta_2 x_2 + \cdots + \beta_k x_k + \epsilon, \qquad (14.1)$$

where

β_0 = the regression constant

$\beta_1, \beta_2 ..., \beta_k$ are the partial regression coefficients for the k independent variables

$x_1, \ldots, x_k$ are the independent variables

k = the number of independent variables

In this general linear model, the parameters β_i are linear. This does not mean, however, that the dependent variable, y, is necessarily linearly related to the predictor variables. Scatter plots sometimes reveal a curvilinear relationship between x and y. Multiple regression response surfaces are not restricted to linear surfaces and may be curvilinear.

To this point in the text, the variables, x_i, have represented different predictors. For example, in the real estate example presented in Chapter 13, the variables—x_1, x_2—represented two predictors: number of square feet in the house and the age of the house, respectively. Certainly, regression models can be developed for more than two predictors. For example, a marketing site location model could be developed in which sales, as the response variable, is predicted by population density, number of competitors, size of the store, and number of salespeople. Such a model could take the form

$$y = \beta_0 + \beta_1 x_1 + \beta_2 x_2 + \beta_3 x_3 + \beta_4 x_4 + \epsilon$$

This regression model has four x_i variables, each of which represents a different predictor.

The general linear model also applies to situations in which some x_i represent recoded data from a predictor variable already represented in the model by another independent variable. In some models, x_i represents variables that have undergone a mathematical transformation to allow the model to follow the form of the general linear model.

In this section, we explore some of these other models, including polynomial regression models, regression models with interaction, and models with transformed variables.

Polynomial Regression

Regression models in which the highest power of any predictor variable is 1 and in which there are no interaction terms—cross products $(x_i \cdot x_j)$—are referred to as *first-order models*. Simple regression models like those presented in Chapter 12 are *first-order models with one independent variable*. The general model for simple regression is

$$y = \beta_0 + \beta_1 x_1 + \epsilon$$

If a second independent variable is added, the model is referred to as a first-order model with two independent variables and appears as

$$y = \beta_0 + \beta_1 x_1 + \beta_2 x_2 + \epsilon$$

Polynomial regression models are regression models that are second- or higher-order models. They contain squared, cubed, or higher powers of the predictor variable(s) and contain response surfaces that are curvilinear. Yet, they are still special cases of the general linear model given in Formula 14.1.

Consider a regression model with one independent variable where the model includes a second predictor, which is the independent variable squared. Such a model is referred to as a second-order model with one independent variable because the highest power among the predictors is 2, but there is still only one independent variable. The model takes the following form:

$$y = \beta_0 + \beta_1 x_1 + \beta_2 x_1^2 + \epsilon$$

This model can be used to explore the possible fit of a quadratic model in predicting a dependent variable. A **quadratic model** is *a multiple regression model in which the predictors are a variable and the square of the variable*. How can this be a special case of the general linear model? Let x_2 of the general linear model be equal to x_1^2: then $y = \beta_0 + \beta_1 x_1 + \beta_2 x_1^2 + \epsilon$, becomes $y = \beta_0 + \beta_1 x_1 + \beta_2 x_2 + \epsilon$. Through what process does a researcher go to develop the regression constant and coefficients for a curvilinear model such as this one?

Multiple regression analysis assumes a linear fit of the regression coefficients and regression constant, but not necessarily a linear relationship of the independent variable values (x). Hence, a researcher can often accomplish curvilinear regression by recoding the data before the multiple regression analysis is attempted.

As an example, consider the data given in Table 14.1. This table contains sales volumes (in $ millions) for 13 manufacturing companies along with the number of manufacturer's representatives associated with each firm. A simple regression analysis to predict sales by the number of manufacturer's representatives results in the Excel output in Figure 14.1.

This regression output shows a regression model with an r^2 of 87.0%, a standard error of the estimate equal to 51.10, a significant overall F test for the model, and a significant t ratio for the predictor' number of manufacturer's representatives.

TABLE 14.1   Sales Data for 13 Manufacturing Companies

MANUFACTURER	SALES ($ MILLIONS)	NUMBER OF MANUFACTURING REPRESENTATIVES
1	2.1	2
2	3.6	1
3	6.2	2
4	10.4	3
5	22.8	4
6	35.6	4
7	57.1	5
8	83.5	5
9	109.4	6
10	128.6	7
11	196.8	8
12	280.0	10
13	462.3	11

SUMMARY OUTPUT

Regression Statistics

Multiple R	0.933
R Square	0.870
Adjusted R Square	0.858
Standard Error	51.098
Observations	13

ANOVA

	df	SS	MS	F	Significance F
Regression	1	192395.416	192395.416	73.69	0.0000033
Residual	11	28721.452	2611.041		
Total	12	221116.868			

	Coefficients	Standard Error	t Stat	P-value
Intercept	−107.029	28.737	−3.72	0.0033561
Reps	41.026	4.779	8.58	0.0000033

FIGURE 14.1   Excel Simple Regression Output for Manufacturing Example

Figure 14.2(a) is a scatter plot for the data in Table 14.1. Notice that the plot of number of representatives and sales is not a straight line and is an indication that the relationship between the two variables may be curvilinear. To explore the possibility that a quadratic relationship may exist between sales and number of representatives, the business researcher creates a second predictor variable, (number of manufacturer's representatives)^2, to use in the regression analysis to predict sales along with number of manufacturer's representatives, as shown in Table 14.2. Thus, a variable can be created to explore second-order parabolic relationships by squaring the data from the independent variable of the linear model and entering it into the analysis. Figure 14.2(b) is a scatter plot of sales with (number of manufacturer's reps)^2. Note that this graph, with the squared term, more closely approaches a straight line than does the graph in Figure 14.2(a). By recoding the predictor variable, the researcher creates a potentially better regression fit.

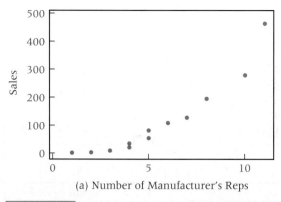 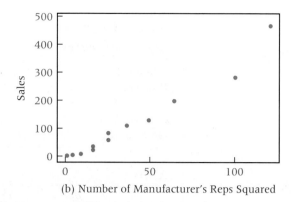

(a) Number of Manufacturer's Reps   (b) Number of Manufacturer's Reps Squared

FIGURE 14.2 **Minitab Scatter Plots of Manufacturing Data**

TABLE 14.2 **Display of Manufacturing Data with Newly Created Variable**

MANUFACTURER	SALES ($ MILLIONS) y	NUMBER OF MGFR. REPS x_1	NUMBER OF (MGFR. REPS)^2 $x_2 = (x_1)^2$
1	2.1	2	4
2	3.6	1	1
3	6.2	2	4
4	10.4	3	9
5	22.8	4	16
6	35.6	4	16
7	57.1	5	25
8	83.5	5	25
9	109.4	6	36
10	128.6	7	49
11	196.8	8	64
12	280.0	10	100
13	462.3	11	121

With these data (Table 14.2), a multiple regression model can be developed. **Figure 14.3** shows the Excel output for the regression analysis to predict sales by number of manufacturer's representatives and (number of manufacturer's representatives)^2.

Examine the output in Figure 14.3 and compare it with the output in Figure 14.1 for the simple regression model. The R^2 for this model is 97.3%, which is an increase from the r^2 of 87.0% for the single linear predictor model. The standard error of the estimate for this model is 24.59, which is considerably lower than the 51.10 value obtained from the simple regression model. Remember, the sales figures were $ millions. The quadratic model reduced the standard error of the estimate by 26.51($1,000,000), or $26,510,000. It appears that the quadratic model is a better model for predicting sales.

An examination of the t statistic for the squared term and its associated probability in Figure 14.3 shows that it is statistically significant at $\alpha = .001$ ($t = 6.12$ with a probability of .0001). If this t statistic were not significant, the researcher would most likely drop the squared term and revert to the first-order model (simple regression model).

In theory, third- and higher-order models can be explored. Generally, business researchers tend to utilize first- and second-order regression models more than higher-order models. Remember that most regression analysis is used in business to aid decision making. Higher-power models (third, fourth, etc.) become difficult to interpret and difficult to explain to decision makers. In addition, the business researcher is usually looking for trends and general directions. The higher the order in regression modeling, the more the model tends to follow irregular fluctuations rather than meaningful directions.

SUMMARY OUTPUT

Regression Statistics

Multiple R	0.986
R Square	0.973
Adjusted R Square	0.967
Standard Error	24.593
Observations	13

ANOVA

	df	SS	MS	F	Significance F
Regression	2	215068.600	107534.300	177.79	0.000000015
Residual	10	6048.268	604.827		
Total	12	221116.868			

	Coefficients	Standard Error	t Stat	P-value
Intercept	18.067	24.673	0.73	0.48082
Reps	−15.723	9.550	−1.65	0.13070
Reps Squared	4.750	0.776	6.12	0.00011

FIGURE 14.3 **Excel Output for Quadratic Model of Manufacturing Example**

Tukey's Ladder of Transformations

As just shown with the manufacturing example, recoding data can be a useful tool in improving the regression model fit. Many other ways of recoding data can be explored in this process. John W. Tukey* presented a "ladder of expressions" that can be explored to straighten out a plot of x and y, thereby offering potential improvement in the predictability of the regression model. **Tukey's ladder of transformations** gives the following expressions for both x and y.

Ladder for x

$\leftarrow$ Up Ladder $\qquad \downarrow$ Neutral $\qquad$ Down Ladder $\rightarrow$

$$..., x^4, x^3, x^2, x, \sqrt{x}, x, \log x, -\frac{1}{\sqrt{x}}, -\frac{1}{x}, -\frac{1}{x^2}, -\frac{1}{x^3}, -\frac{1}{x^4}, ...$$

Ladder for y

$\leftarrow$ Up Ladder $\qquad \downarrow$ Neutral $\qquad$ Down Ladder $\rightarrow$

$$..., y^4, y^3, y^2, y, \sqrt{y}, y, \log y, -\frac{1}{\sqrt{y}}, -\frac{1}{y}, -\frac{1}{y^2}, -\frac{1}{y^3}, -\frac{1}{y^4}, ...$$

These ladders suggest to the user potential ways to recode the data. Tukey published a **four-quadrant approach** to determining which expressions on the ladder are more appropriate for a given situation. This approach is based on the shape of the scatter plot of x and y. **Figure 14.4** shows the four quadrants and the associated recoding expressions. For example, if the scatter plot of x and y indicates a shape like that shown in the upper left quadrant, recoding should move "down the ladder" for the x variable toward

$$\log x, -\frac{1}{\sqrt{x}}, -\frac{1}{x}, -\frac{1}{x^2}, -\frac{1}{x^3}, -\frac{1}{x^4}, ...$$

*John W. Tukey, *Exploratory Data Analysis*. Reading, MA: Addison-Wesley, 1977.

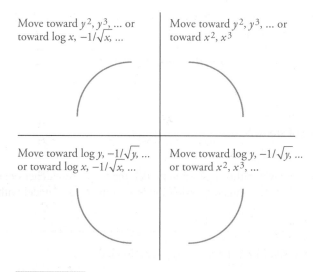

FIGURE 14.4 Tukey's Four-Quadrant Approach

or "up the ladder" for the y variable toward

$$y^2, y^3, y^4, \ldots$$

Or, if the scatter plot of x and y indicates a shape like that of the lower right quadrant, the recoding should move "up the ladder" for the x variable toward

$$x^2, x^3, x^4, \ldots$$

or "down the ladder" for the y variable toward

$$\log y, \; -\frac{1}{\sqrt{y}}, \; -\frac{1}{y}, \; -\frac{1}{y^2}, \; -\frac{1}{y^3}, \; -\frac{1}{y^4}, \ldots$$

In the manufacturing example, the graph in Figure 14.2(a) is shaped like the curve in the lower right quadrant of Tukey's four-quadrant approach. His approach suggests that the business researcher move "up the ladder" on x, as was done by using the squared term. The researcher could have explored other options such as continuing on up the ladder of x or going down the ladder of y. Tukey's ladder is a continuum and leaves open other recoding possibilities between the expressions. For example, between x^2 and x^3 are many possible powers of x that can be explored, such as $x^{2.1}$, $x^{2.5}$, or $x^{2.86}$.

Regression Models with Interaction

Sometimes when two different independent variables are used in a regression analysis, an *interaction* occurs between the two variables. This interaction was discussed in Chapter 11 in two-way analysis of variance, where one variable will act differently over a given range of values for the second variable than it does over another range of values for the second variable. For example, in a manufacturing plant, temperature and humidity might interact in such a way as to affect the hardness of the raw material. The air humidity may affect the raw material differently at different temperatures.

In regression analysis, interaction can be examined as a separate independent variable. An interaction predictor variable can be designed by multiplying the data values of one variable by the values of another variable, thereby creating a new variable. One model that includes an interaction variable is

$$y = \beta_0 + \beta_1 x_1 + \beta_2 x_2 + \beta_3 x_1 x_2 + \epsilon$$

The $x_1 x_2$ term is the interaction term. Even though this model has 1 as the highest power of any one variable, it is considered to be a second-order equation because of the $x_1 x_2$ term.

Suppose the data in Table 14.3 represent the closing stock prices for three corporations over a period of 15 months. An investment firm wants to use the prices for stocks 2 and 3

TABLE 14.3

Prices of Three Stocks over a 15-Month Period

STOCK 1	STOCK 2	STOCK 3
41	36	35
39	36	35
38	38	32
45	51	41
41	52	39
43	55	55
47	57	52
49	58	54
41	62	65
35	70	77
36	72	75
39	74	74
33	83	81
28	101	92
31	107	91

to develop a regression model to predict the price of stock 1. The form of the general linear regression equation for this model is

$$y = \beta_0 + \beta_1 x_1 + \beta_2 x_2 + \epsilon$$

where

y = price of stock 1

x_1 = price of stock 2

x_2 = price of stock 3

Using Minitab to develop this regression model, the firm's researcher obtains the first output displayed in **Figure 14.5.** This regression model is a first-order model with two predictors,

Regression Analysis: Stock 1 versus Stock 2, Stock 3

Analysis of Variance

Source	DF	Adj SS	Adj MS	F-Value	P-Value
Regression	2	224.29	112.15	5.37	0.022
Error	12	250.64	20.89		
Total	14	474.93			

S	R-sq	R-sq(adj)
4.57020	47.23%	38.43%

Coefficients

Term	Coef	SE Coef	T-Value	P-Value
Constant	50.86	3.79	13.41	0.000
Stock 2	−0.119	0.193	−0.62	0.549
Stock 3	−0.071	0.199	−0.36	0.728

Regression Equation

Stock 1 = 50.86 − 0.119 Stock 2 − 0.071 Stock 3

Regression Analysis: Stock 1 versus Stock 2, Stock 3, Interaction

Analysis of Variance

Source	DF	Adj SS	Adj MS	F-Value	P-Value
Regression	3	381.847	127.282	15.04	0.000
Error	11	93.087	8.462		
Total	14	474.933			

S	R-sq	R-sq(adj)
2.90902	80.40%	75.05%

Coefficients

Term	Coef	SE Coef	T-Value	P-Value
Constant	12.05	9.31	1.29	0.222
Stock 2	0.879	0.262	3.36	0.006
Stock 3	0.220	0.144	1.54	0.153
Interaction	−0.00998	0.00231	−4.31	0.001

Regression Equation

Stock 1 = 12.05 + 0.879 Stock 2 + 0.220 Stock 3 − 0.00998 Interaction

FIGURE 14.5 Two Minitab Regression Outputs—Without and with Interaction

x_1 and x_2. This model produced a modest R^2 of .472. Both of the t ratios are small and statistically nonsignificant ($t = -.62$ with a p-value of .549 and $t = -.36$ with a p-value of .728). Although the overall model is statistically significant, $F = 5.37$ with probability of .022, neither predictor is significant.

Sometimes the effects of two variables are not additive because of the interacting effects between the two variables. In such a case, the researcher can use multiple regression analysis to explore the interaction effects by including an interaction term in the equation:

$$y = \beta_0 + \beta_1 x_1 + \beta_2 x_2 + \beta_3 x_1 x_2 + \epsilon$$

The equation fits the form of the general linear model

$$y = \beta_0 + \beta_1 x_1 + \beta_2 x_2 + \beta_3 x_3 + \epsilon$$

where $x_3 = x_1 x_2$. Each individual observation of x_3 is obtained through a recoding process by multiplying the associated observations of x_1 and x_2.

Applying this procedure to the stock example, the researcher uses the interaction term and Minitab to obtain the second regression output shown in Figure 14.5. This output contains x_1, x_2, and the interaction term, $x_1 x_2$. Observe the R^2, which equals .804 for this model. The introduction of the interaction term caused the R^2 to increase from 47.2% to 80.4%. In addition, the standard error of the estimate decreased from 4.570 in the first model to 2.909 in the second model. The t ratios for both the x_1 term (stock 2) and the interaction term are statistically significant in the second model ($t = 3.36$ with a p-value of .006 for x_1 and $t = -4.31$ with a probability of .001 for $x_1 x_2$). The inclusion of the interaction term helped the regression model account for a substantially greater amount of the dependent variable and is a significant contributor to the model.

Figure 14.6(a) is the response surface for the first regression model presented in Figure 14.5 (the model without interaction). As you observe the response plane with stock 3 as the point of reference, you see the plane moving upward with increasing values of stock 1 as the plane moves away from you toward smaller values of stock 2. Now examine **Figure 14.6(b)**, the response surface for the second regression model presented in Figure 14.5 (the model with interaction). Note how the response plane is twisted, with its slope changing as it moves along stock 2. This pattern is caused by the interaction effects of stock 2 prices and stock 3 prices. A cross-section of the plane taken from left to right at any given stock 2 price produces a line that attempts to predict the price of stock 3 from the price of stock 1. As you move back through different prices of stock 2, the slope of that line changes, indicating that the relationship between stock 1 and stock 3 varies according to stock 2.

A researcher also could develop a model using two independent variables with their squares and interaction. Such a model would be a second-order model with two independent variables. The model would look like this:

$$y = \beta_0 + \beta_1 x_1 + \beta_2 x_2 + \beta_3 x_1^2 + \beta_4 x_2^2 + \beta_5 x_1 x_2 + \epsilon$$

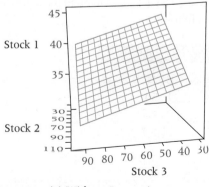

(a) Without Interaction

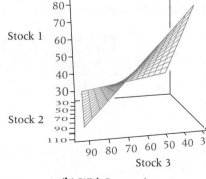

(b) With Interaction

FIGURE 14.6 **Response Surfaces for the Stock Example—Without and with Interaction**

Model Transformation

To this point in examining polynomial and interaction models, the focus has been on recoding values of x variables. Some multiple regression situations require that the dependent variable, y, be recoded. To examine different relationships between x and y, Tukey's four-quadrant analysis and ladder of transformations can be used to explore ways to recode x or y in attempting to construct regression models with more predictability. Included on the ladder are such y transformations as log y and $1/y$.

Suppose the following data represent the annual sales and annual advertising expenditures for seven companies. Can a regression model be developed from these figures that can be used to predict annual sales by annual advertising expenditures?

COMPANY	SALES ($ MILLION/YEAR)	ADVERTISING ($ MILLION/YEAR)
1	2,580	1.2
2	11,942	2.6
3	9,845	2.2
4	27,800	3.2
5	18,926	2.9
6	4,800	1.5
7	14,550	2.7

One mathematical model that is a good candidate for fitting these data is an exponential model of the form

$$y = \beta_0 \beta_1^x \in$$

This model can be transformed (by taking the log of each side) so that it is in the form of the general linear equation:

$$\log y = \log \beta_0 + x \log \beta_1$$

This transformed model requires a recoding of the y data through the use of logarithms. Notice that x is not recoded but that the regression constant and coefficient are in logarithmic scale. If we let $y' = \log y$, $\beta_0' = \log \beta_0$, and $\beta_1' = \log \beta_1$, the exponential model is in the form of the general linear model:

$$y' = \beta_0' + \beta_1' x$$

The process begins by taking the log of the y values. The data used to build the regression model and the Excel regression output for these data follow.

LOG SALES (y)	ADVERTISING (x)
3.4116	1.2
4.0771	2.6
3.9932	2.2
4.4440	3.2
4.2771	2.9
3.6812	1.5
4.1629	2.7

SUMMARY OUTPUT

Regression Statistics

Multiple R	0.990
R Square	0.980
Adjusted R Square	0.977
Standard Error	0.0543
Observations	7

ANOVA

	df	SS	MS	F	Significance F
Regression	1	0.7392	0.7392	250.36	0.000018
Residual	5	0.0148	0.0030		
Total	6	0.7540			

	Coefficients	Standard Error	t Stat	P-value
Intercept	2.9003	0.0729	39.80	0.00000019
Advertising	0.4751	0.0300	15.82	0.00001834

A simple regression model (without the log recoding of the y variable) yields an R^2 of 87%, whereas the exponential model R^2 is 98%. The t statistic for advertising is 15.82 with a p-value of 0.00001834 in the exponential model and 5.77 with a p-value of 0.00219 in the simple regression model. Thus the exponential model gives a better fit than does the simple regression model. An examination of (x^2, y) and (x^3, y) models reveals R^2 of .930 and .969, respectively, which are quite high but still not as good as the R^2 yielded by the exponential model (the output for these models is not shown here).

The resulting equation of the exponential regression model is

$$y = 2.9003 + .4751x$$

In using this regression equation to determine predicted values of y for x, remember that the resulting predicted y value is in logarithmic form and the antilog of the predicted y must be taken to get the predicted y value in raw units. For example, to get the predicted y value (sales) for an advertising figure of 2.0 ($ million), substitute $x = 2.0$ into the regression equation.

$$y = 2.9003 + .4751x = 2.9003 + .4751(2.0) = 3.8505$$

The log of sales is 3.8505. Taking the antilog of 3.8505 results in the predicted sales in raw units.

$$antilog(3.8505) = 7087.61 (\$ \text{million})$$

Thus, the exponential regression model predicts that $2.0 million of advertising will result in $7,087.61 million of sales.

Other ways can be used to transform mathematical models so that they can be treated like the general linear model. One example is an inverse model such as

$$y = \frac{1}{\beta_0 + \beta_1 x_1 + \beta_2 x_2 + \in}$$

Such a model can be manipulated algebraically into the form

$$\frac{1}{y} = \beta_0 + \beta_1 x_1 + \beta_2 x_2 + \in$$

Substituting $y' = 1/y$ into this equation results in an equation that is in the form of the general linear model.

$$y' = \beta_0 + \beta_1 x_1 + \beta_2 x_2 + \in$$

To use this "inverse" model, recode the data values for y by using $1/y$. The regression analysis is done on the $1/y$, x_1, and x_2 data. To get predicted values of y from this model, enter the raw values of x_1 and x_2. The resulting predicted value of y from the regression equation will be the inverse of the actual predicted y value.

DEMONSTRATION PROBLEM 14.1

In the aerospace and defense industry, some cost estimators predict the cost of new space projects by using mathematical models that take the form

$$y = \beta_0 x^{\beta_1} \in$$

These cost estimators often use the weight of the object being sent into space as the predictor (x) and the cost of the object as the dependent variable (y). Quite often β_1 turns out to be a value between 0 and 1, resulting in the predicted value of y equaling some root of x.

Use the sample cost data given here to develop a cost regression model in the form just shown to determine the equation for the predicted value of y. Use this regression equation to predict the value of y for $x = 3,000$.

y (COST IN BILLIONS)	x (WEIGHT IN TONS)
1.2	450
9.0	20,200
4.5	9,060
3.2	3,500
13.0	75,600
0.6	175
1.8	800
2.7	2,100

Solution: The equation

$$y = \beta_0 x^{\beta_1} \in$$

is not in the form of the general linear model, but it can be transformed by using logarithms:

$$\log y = \log \beta_0 + \beta_1 \log x + \in$$

which takes on the general linear form

$$y' = \beta_0' + \beta_1 x'$$

where

$$y' = \log y$$
$$\beta_0' = \log \beta_0$$
$$x' = \log x$$

This equation requires that both x and y be recoded by taking the logarithm of each.

LOG y	LOG x
.0792	2.6532
.9542	4.3054
.6532	3.9571
.5051	3.5441
1.1139	4.8785
−.2218	2.2430
.2553	2.9031
.4314	3.3222

Using these data, the computer produces the following regression constant and coefficient:

$$b_0' = -1.25292 \quad b_1 = .49606$$

From these values, the equation of the predicted y value is determined to be

$$\log \hat{y} = -1.25292 + .49606 \ \log \ x$$

If $x = 3,000$, $\log x = 3.47712$, and

$$\log \hat{y} = -1.25292 + .49606(3.47712) = .47194$$

then

$$\hat{y} = \text{antilog}(\log \hat{y}) = \text{antilog}(.47194) = 2.9644$$

The predicted value of y is \$2.9644 billion for $x = 3000$ tons of weight.

Taking the antilog of $b_0' = -1.25292$ yields .055857. From this and $b_1 = .49606$, the model can be written in the original form:

$$y = (.055857)x^{.49606}$$

Substituting $x = 3000$ into this formula also yields \$2.9644 billion for the predicted value of y.

14.1 Problems

14.1. Use the following data to develop a quadratic model to predict y from x. Develop a simple regression model from the data and compare the results of the two models. Does the quadratic model seem to provide any better predictability? Why or why not?

x	y	x	y
14	200	15	247
9	74	8	82
6	29	5	21
21	456	10	94
17	320		

14.2. Develop a multiple regression model of the form

$$y = b_0 b_1^x \varepsilon$$

using the following data to predict y from x. From a scatter plot and Tukey's ladder of transformation, explore ways to recode the data and develop an alternative regression model. Compare the results.

y	x	y	x
2485	3.87	740	2.83
1790	3.22	4010	3.62
874	2.91	3629	3.52
2190	3.42	8010	3.92
3610	3.55	7047	3.86
2847	3.61	5680	3.75
1350	3.13	1740	3.19

14.3. The Publishers Information Bureau in New York City released magazine advertising expenditure data compiled by leading national advertisers. The data were organized by product type over several years. Shown here are data on total magazine advertising expenditures and household equipment and supplies advertising expenditures. Using these data, develop a regression model to predict total magazine advertising expenditures by household equipment and supplies advertising expenditures and by (household equipment and supplies advertising expenditures)². Compare this model to a regression model to predict total magazine advertising expenditures by only household equipment and supplies advertising expenditures. Construct a scatter plot of the data. Does the shape of the plot suggest some alternative models in light of Tukey's four-quadrant approach? If so, develop at least one other model and compare the model to the other two previously developed.

TOTAL MAGAZINE ADVERTISING EXPENDITURES ($ MILLIONS)	HOUSEHOLD EQUIPMENT AND SUPPLIES EXPENDITURES ($ MILLIONS)
1193	34
2846	65
4668	98
5120	93
5943	102
6644	103

14.4. Dun & Bradstreet reports, among other things, information about new business incorporations and number of business failures over several years. Shown here are data on business failures and current liabilities of the failing companies over several years. Use these data and the following model to predict current liabilities of the failing companies by the number of business failures. Discuss the strength of the model.

$$y = b_0 b_1^x \epsilon$$

Now develop a different regression model by recoding x. Use Tukey's four-quadrant approach as a resource. Compare your models.

RATE OF BUSINESS FAILURES (10,000)	CURRENT LIABILITIES OF FAILING COMPANIES ($ MILLIONS)
44	1,888
43	4,380
42	4,635
61	6,955
88	15,611
110	16,073
107	29,269
115	36,937
120	44,724
102	34,724
98	39,126
65	44,261

14.5. Use the following data to develop a curvilinear model to predict y. Include both x_1 and x_2 in the model in addition to x_1^2 and x_2^2, and the interaction term $x_1 x_2$. Comment on the overall strength of the model and the significance of each predictor. Develop a regression model with the same independent variables as the first model but without the interaction variable. Compare this model to the model with interaction.

y	x_1	x_2
47.8	6	7.1
29.1	1	4.2
81.8	11	10.0
54.3	5	8.0
29.7	3	5.7
64.0	9	8.8
37.4	3	7.1
44.5	4	5.4
42.1	4	6.5
31.6	2	4.9
78.4	11	9.1
71.9	9	8.5
17.4	2	4.2
28.8	1	5.8
34.7	2	5.9
57.6	6	7.8
84.2	12	10.2
63.2	8	9.4
39.0	3	5.7
47.3	5	7.0

14.6. What follows is Excel output from a regression model to predict y using x_1, x_2, x_1^2, x_2^2, and the interaction term, $x_1 x_2$. Comment on the overall strength of the model and the significance of each predictor. The data follow the Excel output. Develop a regression model with the same independent variables as the first model but without the interaction variable. Compare this model to the model with interaction.

SUMMARY OUTPUT

Regression Statistics

Multiple R	0.954
R Square	0.910
Adjusted R Square	0.878
Standard Error	7.544
Observations	20

ANOVA

	df	SS	MS	F	Significance F
Regression	5	8089.275	1617.855	28.43	0.00000073
Residual	14	796.725	56.909		
Total	19	8886.000			

	Coefficients	Standard Error	t Stat	P-value
Intercept	464.4433	503.0955	0.92	0.3716
X1	−10.5101	6.0074	−1.75	0.1021
X2	−1.2212	1.9791	−0.62	0.5471
X1Sq	0.0357	0.0195	1.84	0.0876
X2Sq	−0.0002	0.0021	−0.08	0.9394
X1*X2	0.0243	0.0107	2.28	0.0390

y	x_1	x_2	y	x_1	x_2
34	120	190	45	96	245
56	105	240	34	79	288
78	108	238	23	66	312
90	110	250	89	88	315
23	78	255	76	80	320
34	98	230	56	73	335
45	89	266	43	69	335
67	92	270	23	75	250
78	95	272	45	63	372
65	85	288	56	74	360

14.2 Indicator (Dummy) Variables

Some variables are referred to as **qualitative variables** (as opposed to *quantitative* variables) because qualitative variables do not yield quantifiable outcomes. Instead, *qualitative variables yield nominal- or ordinal-level information*, which is used more to categorize items. These variables have a role in multiple regression and are referred to as **indicator** or **dummy variables**. In this section, we will examine the role of indicator, or dummy, variables as predictors or independent variables in multiple regression analysis.

Indicator variables arise in many ways in business research. Questionnaire or personal interview demographic questions are prime candidates because they tend to generate qualitative measures on such items as sex, geographic region, occupation, marital status, level of education, economic class, political affiliation, religion, management/nonmanagement status, buying/leasing a home, method of transportation, or type of broker. In one business study, business researchers were attempting to develop a multiple regression model to predict the distances shoppers drive to malls in the greater Cleveland area. One independent variable was whether the mall was located on the shore of Lake Erie. In a second study, a site location model for pizza restaurants included indicator variables for (1) whether the restaurant served beer and (2) whether the restaurant had a salad bar.

These indicator variables are qualitative in that no interval or ratio level measurement is assigned to a response. For example, if a mall is located on the shore of Lake Erie, awarding it a score of 20 or 30 or 75 because of its location makes no sense. In terms of sex, what value would you assign to a man or a woman in a regression study? Yet these types of indicator, or dummy, variables are often useful in multiple regression studies and can be included if they are coded in the proper format.

Most researchers code indicator variables by using 0 or 1. For example, in the shopping mall study, malls located on the shore of Lake Erie could be assigned a 1, and all other malls would then be assigned a 0. The assignment of 0 or 1 is arbitrary, with the number merely holding a place for the category. For this reason, the coding is referred to as "dummy" coding; the number represents a category by holding a place and is not a measurement.

Many indicator, or dummy, variables are dichotomous, such as male/female, salad bar/ no salad bar, employed/not employed, and rent/own. For these variables, a value of 1 is arbitrarily assigned to one category and a value of 0 is assigned to the other category. Some qualitative variables contain several categories, such as the variable "type of job," which might have the categories of assembler, painter, and inspector. In this case, using a coding of 1, 2, and 3, respectively, is tempting. However, that type of coding creates problems for multiple regression analysis. For one thing, the category "inspector" might receive a value that is three times that of "assembler." In addition, the values of 1, 2, and 3 indicate a hierarchy of job types: assembler < painter < inspector. The proper way to code such indicator variables is with the 0, 1 coding. Two separate independent variables should be used to code the three categories of type of job. The first variable is assembler, where a 1 is recorded if the person's job is assembler and a 0 is recorded if not. The second variable is painter, where a 1 is recorded if the person's job is painter and a 0 is recorded if not. A variable should not be assigned to inspector, because all workers in the study for whom a 1 was not recorded either for the assembler variable or the painter variable must be inspectors. Thus, coding the inspector variable would result in redundant information and is not necessary. This reasoning holds for all indicator variables with more than two categories. If an indicator variable has c categories, then $c - 1$ dummy variables must be created and inserted into the regression analysis in order to include the indicator variable in the multiple regression.[†]

An example of an indicator variable with more than two categories is the result of the following question taken from a typical questionnaire.

Your office is located in which region of the country?

_____ Northeast _____ Midwest _____ South _____ West

[†] If c indicator variables are included in the analysis, no unique estimator of the regression coefficients can be found. [J. Neter, M. H. Kuter, W. Wasserman, and C. Nachtsheim, *Applied Linear Regression Models,* 3rd ed. Chicago: Richard D. Irwin, 1996.]

Suppose a researcher is using a multiple regression analysis to predict the cost of doing business and believes geographic location of the office is a potential predictor. How does the researcher insert this qualitative variable into the analysis? Because $c = 4$ for this question, three dummy variables are inserted into the analysis. Table 14.4 shows one possible way this process works with 13 respondents. Note that rows 2, 7, and 11 contain all zeros, which indicate that those respondents have offices in the West. Thus, a fourth dummy variable for the West region is not necessary and, indeed, should not be included because the information contained in such a fourth variable is contained in the other three variables.

A word of caution is in order. Because of degrees of freedom and interpretation considerations, it is important that a multiple regression analysis have enough observations to handle adequately the number of independent variables entered. Some researchers recommend as a rule of thumb at least three observations per independent variable. If a qualitative variable has multiple categories, resulting in several dummy independent variables, and if several qualitative variables are being included in an analysis, the number of predictors can rather quickly exceed the recommended number of variables per number of observations. Nevertheless, dummy variables can be useful and are a way in which nominal or ordinal information can be recoded and incorporated into a multiple regression model.

As an example, consider the issue of sex discrimination in the salary earnings of workers in some industries. In examining this issue, suppose a random sample of 15 workers is drawn from a pool of employed laborers in a particular industry and the workers' average monthly salaries are determined, along with their age and sex. The data are shown in Table 14.5. As sex can be only male or female, this variable is a dummy variable requiring 0, 1 coding. Suppose we arbitrarily let 1 denote male and 0 denote female. Figure 14.7 is the multiple regression model developed from the data of Table 14.5 by using Minitab to predict the dependent variable, monthly salary, by two independent variables, age and sex.

The computer output in Figure 14.7 contains the regression equation for this model.

$$\text{Salary} = 1.732 + 0.111\,\text{Age} + 0.459\,\text{Sex}$$

An examination of the t ratios reveals that the dummy variable "sex" has a regression coefficient that is significant at $\alpha = .001$ ($t = 8.58$, $p = .000$). The overall model is significant at $\alpha = .001$ ($F = 48.54$, $p = .000$). The standard error of the estimate, $s_e = .09679$, indicates that approximately 68% of the errors of prediction are within $\pm\$96.79\,(.09679 \cdot \$1,000)$. The R^2 is relatively high at 89.0%, and the adjusted R^2 is 87.2%.

TABLE 14.4 Coding for the Indicator Variable of Geographic Location for Regression Analysis

NORTHEAST x_1	MIDWEST x_2	SOUTH x_3
1	0	0
0	0	0
1	0	0
0	0	1
0	1	0
0	1	0
0	0	0
0	0	1
1	0	0
1	0	0
0	0	0
0	1	0
0	0	1

TABLE 14.5 Data for the Monthly Salary Example

MONTHLY SALARY ($1,000)	AGE (10 YEARS)	SEX (1 = MALE, 0 = FEMALE)
2.548	3.2	1
2.629	3.8	1
2.011	2.7	0
2.229	3.4	0
2.746	3.6	1
2.528	4.1	1
2.018	3.8	0
2.190	3.4	0
2.551	3.3	1
1.985	3.2	0
2.610	3.5	1
2.432	2.9	1
2.215	3.3	0
1.990	2.8	0
2.585	3.5	1

Regression Analysis: Salary versus Age, Sex

Analysis of Variance

Source	DF	Adj SS	Adj MS	F-Value	P-Value
Regression	2	0.90949	0.454744	48.54	0.000
Error	12	0.11242	0.009369		
Total	14	1.02191			

S	R-sq	R-sq(adj)
0.0967916	89.0%	87.2%

Coefficients

Term	Coef	SE Coef	T-Value	P-Value
Constant	1.732	0.236	7.35	0.000
Age	0.1112	0.0721	1.54	0.149
Sex	0.4587	0.0535	8.58	0.000

Regression Equation

Salary = 1.732 + 0.111 Age + 0.459 Sex

FIGURE 14.7 **Minitab Regression Output for the Monthly Salary Example**

The *t* value for sex indicates that it is a significant predictor of monthly salary in this model. This significance is apparent when one looks at the effects of this dummy variable another way. **Figure 14.8** shows the graph of the regression equation when sex = 1 (male) and the graph of the regression equation when sex = 0 (female). When sex = 1 (male), the regression equation becomes

$$1.732 + .111(\text{Age}) + .459(1) = 2.191 + .111(\text{Age})$$

When sex = 0 (female), the regression equation becomes

$$1.732 + .111(\text{Age}) + .459(0) = 1.732 + .111(\text{Age}).$$

The full regression model (with both predictors) has a response surface that is a plane in a three-dimensional space. However, if a value of 1 is entered for sex into the full regression model, as just shown, the regression model is reduced to a line passing through the plane formed by monthly salary and age. If a value of 0 is entered for sex, as shown, the full regression model also reduces to a line passing through the plane formed by monthly salary and age. Figure 14.8 displays these two lines. Notice that the only difference in the two lines

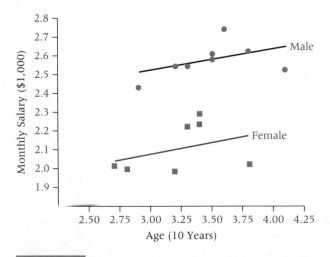

FIGURE 14.8 **Minitab Graph of Regression Lines for Males and Females**

is the y-intercept. Observe the monthly salary with male sex, as depicted by ●, versus the monthly salary with female sex, depicted by ■. The difference in the y-intercepts of these two lines is .459, which is the value of the regression coefficient for sex. This intercept figure signifies that, on average, men earn $459 per month more than women for this population.

Thinking Critically About Statistics in Business Today

Predicting Export Intensity of Chinese Manufacturing Firms Using Multiple Regression Analysis

According to business researchers Hongxin Zhao and Shaoming Zou, little research has been done on the impact of external or uncontrollable variables on the export performance of a company. These two researchers conducted a study of Chinese manufacturing firms and used multiple regression to determine whether both domestic market concentration and firm location are good predictors of a firm's export intensity. The study included 999 Chinese manufacturing firms that exported. The dependent variable was "export intensity," which was defined to be the proportion of production output that is exported and was computed by dividing the firm's export value by its production output value. The higher the proportion was, the higher the export intensity. Zhao and Zou used covariate techniques (beyond the scope of this text) to control for the fact that companies in the study varied by size, capital intensity, innovativeness, and industry. The independent variables were industry concentration and location. Industry concentration was computed as a ratio, with higher values indicating more

concentration in the industry. The location variable was a composite index taking into account total freight volume, available modes of transportation, number of telephones, and size of geographic area.

The multiple regression model produced an R^2 of approximately 52%. Industry concentration was a statistically significant predictor at $\alpha = .01$, and the sign on the regression coefficient indicated that a negative relationship may exist between industry concentration and export intensity. It means export intensity is lower in highly concentrated industries and higher in lower concentrated industries. The researchers believe that in a more highly concentrated industry, the handful of firms dominating the industry will stifle the export competitiveness of firms. In the absence of dominating firms in a more fragmented setting, more competition and an increasing tendency to export are noted. The location variable was also a significant predictor at $\alpha = .01$. Firms located in coastal areas had higher export intensities than did those located in inland areas.

Source: Hongxin Zhao and Shaoming Zou, "The Impact of Industry Concentration and Firm Location on Export Propensity and Intensity: An Empirical Analysis of Chinese Manufacturing Firms," *Journal of International Marketing*, vol. 10, no. 1 (2002), pp. 52–71.

14.2 Problems

14.7. Analyze the following data by using a multiple regression computer software package to predict y using x_1 and x_2. Notice that x_2 is a dummy variable. Discuss the output from the regression analysis; in particular, comment on the predictability of the dummy variable.

y	x_1	x_2
16.8	27	1
13.2	16	0
14.7	13	0
15.4	11	1
11.1	17	0
16.2	19	1
14.9	24	1
13.3	21	0
17.8	16	1
17.1	23	1
14.3	18	0
13.9	16	0

14.8. Given here are the data from a dependent variable and two independent variables. The second independent variable is an indicator variable with several categories. Hence, this variable is represented by x_2, x_3, and x_4. How many categories are there for this independent variable? Use a computer to perform a multiple regression analysis

on this data to predict y from the x values. Discuss the output and pay particular attention to the dummy variables.

y	x_1	x_2	x_3	x_4
11	1.9	1	0	0
3	1.6	0	1	0
2	2.3	0	1	0
5	2.0	0	0	1
9	1.8	0	0	0
14	1.9	1	0	0
10	2.4	1	0	0
8	2.6	0	0	0
4	2.0	0	1	0
9	1.4	0	0	0
11	1.7	1	0	0
4	2.5	0	0	1
6	1.0	1	0	0
10	1.4	0	0	0
3	1.9	0	1	0
4	2.3	0	1	0
9	2.2	0	0	0
6	1.7	0	0	1

14.9. The Minitab output displayed here is the result of a multiple regression analysis with three independent variables. Variable x_1 is a dummy variable. Discuss the computer output and the role x_1 plays in this regression model.

```
Analysis of Variance

Source       DF  Adj SS  Adj MS  F-Value  P-Value
Regression    3  2491.98  830.66   16.76    0.000
Error        13   644.49   49.58
Total        16  3136.47

    S       R-sq     R-sq(adj)
  7.041     79.5%      74.7%

Coefficients

Term      Coef    SE Coef  T-Value  P-Value
Constant  121.31   11.56    10.50    0.000
X₁         13.355    4.714    2.83    0.014
X₂         -0.6322  0.2270   -2.79    0.015
X₃          1.421    3.342    0.43    0.678

Regression Equation

Y = 121 + 13.4 X₁ - 0.632 X₂ + 1.42 X₃
```

14.10. Given here is Excel output for a multiple regression model that was developed to predict y from two independent variables, x_1 and x_2. Variable x_2 is a dummy variable. Discuss the strength of the multiple regression model on the basis of the output. Focus on the contribution of the dummy variable. Plot x_1 and y with x_2 as 0, and then plot x_1 and y with x_2 as 1. Compare the two lines and discuss the differences.

SUMMARY OUTPUT

Regression Statistics

Multiple R	0.623
R Square	0.388
Adjusted R Square	0.341
Standard Error	11.744
Observations	29

ANOVA

	df	SS	MS	F	Significance F
Regression	2	2270.11	1135.05	8.23	0.0017
Residual	26	3585.75	137.91		
Total	28	5855.86			

	Coefficients	Standard Error	t Stat	P-value
Intercept	41.225	6.380	6.46	0.00000076
X₁	1.081	1.353	0.80	0.4316
X₂	−18.404	4.5470	−4.05	0.0004

14.11. Falvey, Fried, and Richards developed a multiple regression model to predict the average price of a meal at New Orleans restaurants. The variables explored included such indicator variables as the following: Accepts reservations, Has its own parking lot, Has a separate bar or lounge, Has a maitre d', Has a dress code, Is candlelit, Has live entertainment, Serves alcoholic beverages, Is a steakhouse, Is in the French Quarter. Suppose a relatively simpler model is developed to predict the average price of a meal at a restaurant in New Orleans from the number of hours the restaurant is open per week, the probability of being seated upon arrival, and whether the restaurant is located in the French Quarter. Use the following data and a computer to develop such a model. Comment on the output.

PRICE	HOURS	PROBABILITY OF BEING SEATED	FRENCH QUARTER
$ 8.52	65	.62	0
21.45	45	.43	1
16.18	52	.58	1
6.21	66	.74	0
12.19	53	.19	1
25.62	55	.49	1
13.90	60	.80	0
18.66	72	.75	1
5.25	70	.37	0
7.98	55	.64	0
12.57	48	.51	1
14.85	60	.32	1
8.80	52	.62	0
6.27	64	.83	0

14.12. A researcher gathered 155 observations on four variables: job satisfaction, occupation, industry, and marital status. She wants to develop a multiple regression model to predict job satisfaction by the other three variables. All three predictor variables are qualitative variables with the following categories.

1. Occupation: accounting, management, marketing, finance
2. Industry: manufacturing, healthcare, transportation
3. Marital status: married, single

How many variables will be in the regression model? Delineate the number of predictors needed in each category and discuss the total number of predictors.

14.3 Model-Building: Search Procedures

To this point in the chapter, we have explored various types of multiple regression models. We evaluated the strengths of regression models and learned how to understand more about the output from multiple regression computer packages. In this section we examine procedures for developing several multiple regression model options to aid in the decision-making process.

Suppose a researcher wants to develop a multiple regression model to predict the world production of crude oil. The researcher realizes that much of the world crude oil market is driven by variables related to usage and production in the United States. The researcher decides to use as predictors the following five independent variables.

1. U.S. energy consumption
2. Gross U.S. nuclear electricity generation
3. U.S. coal production
4. Total U.S. dry gas (natural gas) production
5. Fuel rate of U.S.-owned automobiles

The researcher measured data for each of these variables for the year preceding each data point of world crude oil production, figuring that the world production is driven by the previous year's activities in the United States. It would seem that as the energy consumption of the United States increases, so would world production of crude oil. In addition, it makes sense that as nuclear electricity generation, coal production, dry gas production, and fuel rates increase, world crude oil production would decrease if energy consumption stays approximately constant.

Table 14.6 shows data for the five independent variables along with the dependent variable, world crude oil production. Using the data presented in Table 14.6, the researcher attempted to develop a multiple regression model using five different independent variables. The result

TABLE 14.6 Data for Multiple Regression Model to Predict Crude Oil Production

WORLD CRUDE OIL PRODUCTION (MILLION BARRELS PER DAY)	U.S. ENERGY CONSUMPTION (QUADRILLION BTUs GENERATION PER YEAR)	U.S. NUCLEAR ELECTRICITY (BILLION KILOWATT-HOURS)	U.S. COAL GROSS PRODUCTION (MILLION SHORT-TONS)	U.S. TOTAL DRY GAS PRODUCTION (TRILLION CUBIC FEET)	U.S. FUEL RATE FOR AUTOMOBILES (MILES PER GALLON)
55.7	74.3	83.5	598.6	21.7	13.4
55.7	72.5	114.0	610.0	20.7	13.6
52.8	70.5	172.5	654.6	19.2	14.0
57.3	74.4	191.1	684.9	19.1	13.8
59.7	76.3	250.9	697.2	19.2	14.1
60.2	78.1	276.4	670.2	19.1	14.3
62.7	78.9	255.2	781.1	19.7	14.6
59.6	76.0	251.1	829.7	19.4	16.0
56.1	74.0	272.7	823.8	19.2	16.5
53.5	70.8	282.8	838.1	17.8	16.9
53.3	70.5	293.7	782.1	16.1	17.1
54.5	74.1	327.6	895.9	17.5	17.4
54.0	74.0	383.7	883.6	16.5	17.5
56.2	74.3	414.0	890.3	16.1	17.4
56.7	76.9	455.3	918.8	16.6	18.0
58.7	80.2	527.0	950.3	17.1	18.8
59.9	81.4	529.4	980.7	17.3	19.0
60.6	81.3	576.9	1029.1	17.8	20.3
60.2	81.1	612.6	996.0	17.7	21.2
60.2	82.2	618.8	997.5	17.8	21.0
60.2	83.9	610.3	945.4	18.1	20.6
61.0	85.6	640.4	1033.5	18.8	20.8
62.3	87.2	673.4	1033.0	18.6	21.1
64.1	90.0	674.7	1063.9	18.8	21.2
66.3	90.6	628.6	1089.9	18.9	21.5
67.0	89.7	666.8	1109.8	18.9	21.6

```
Regression Analysis: CrOilPrd versus USEnCons, USNucGen, USCoalPr,
USDryGas, FuelRate

Analysis of Variance

Source          DF    Adj SS    Adj MS    F-Value    P-Value
Regression       5   343.916   68.7833     46.62      0.000
Error           20    29.510    1.4755
Total           25   373.427

S          R-sq      R-sq(adj)
1.21470    92.10%      90.12%

Coefficients

Term          Coef     SE Coef    T-Value    P-Value
Constant      2.71        8.91       0.30      0.764
USEnCons     0.836       0.180       4.64      0.000
USNucGen  -0.00654     0.00985      -0.66      0.514
USCoalPr   0.00983     0.00729       1.35      0.193
USDryGas    -0.143       0.448      -0.32      0.753
FuelRate    -0.734       0.549      -1.34      0.196

Regression Equation

CrOilPrd = 2.71 + 0.836 USEnCons - 0.00654 USNucGen + 0.00983
USCoalPr - 0.143 USDryGas - 0.734 FuelRate
```

FIGURE 14.9 **Minitab Output of Regression for Crude Oil Production Example**

of this process was the Minitab output in Figure 14.9. Examining the output, the researcher can reach some conclusions about that particular model and its variables.

The output contains an R^2 value of 92.1%, a standard error of the estimate of 1.215, and an overall significant F value of 46.62. Notice from Figure 14.9 that the t ratios indicate that the regression coefficients of four of the predictor variables, nuclear, coal, dry gas, and fuel rate, are not significant at $\alpha = .05$. If the researcher were to drop these four variables out of the regression analysis and rerun the model with the other predictor only, what would happen to the model? What if the researcher ran a regression model with only three predictors? How would these models compare to the full model with all five predictors? Are all the predictors necessary?

Developing regression models for business decision making involves at least two considerations. The first is to develop a regression model that accounts for the most variation of the dependent variable—that is, develop models that maximize the explained proportion of the deviation of the y values. At the same time, the regression model should be as parsimonious (simple and economical) as possible. The more complicated a quantitative model becomes, the harder it is for managers to understand and implement the model. In addition, as more variables are included in a model, it becomes more expensive to gather historical data or update present data for the model. These two considerations (dependent variable explanation and parsimony of the model) are quite often in opposition to each other. Hence the business researcher, as the model builder, often needs to explore many model options.

In the world crude oil production regression model, if three variables explain the deviation of world crude oil production nearly as well as five variables, the simpler model is more attractive. How might researchers conduct regression analysis so that they can examine several models and then choose the most attractive one? The answer is to use search procedures.

Search Procedures

Search procedures are processes *whereby more than one multiple regression model is developed for a given database, and the models are compared and sorted by different criteria,* depending on the given procedure. Virtually all search procedures are done on a computer.

Several search procedures are discussed in this section, including all possible regressions, stepwise regression, forward selection, and backward elimination.

All Possible Regressions

The **all possible regressions** search procedure *computes all possible linear multiple regression models from the data using all combinations of the variables.* If a data set contains k independent variables, all possible regressions will determine $2^k - 1$ different models.

For the crude oil production example, the procedure of all possible regressions would produce $2^5 - 1 = 31$ different models from the $k = 5$ independent variables. With $k = 5$ predictors, the procedure produces all single-predictor models, all models with two predictors, all models with three predictors, all models with four predictors, and all models with five predictors, as shown in Table 14.7.

The all possible regressions procedure enables the business researcher to examine every model. In theory, this method eliminates the chance that the business researcher will never consider some models, as can be the case with other search procedures. On the other hand, the search through all possible models can be tedious, time-consuming, inefficient, and perhaps overwhelming.

Stepwise Regression

Perhaps the most widely known and used of the search procedures is stepwise regression. **Stepwise regression** is *a step-by-step process that begins by developing a regression model with a single predictor variable and adds and deletes predictors one step at a time,* examining the fit of the model at each step until no more significant predictors remain outside the model.

Step 1 In step 1 of a stepwise regression procedure, the k independent variables are examined one at a time by developing a simple regression model for each independent variable to predict the dependent variable. The model containing the largest absolute value of t for an independent variable is selected, and the independent variable associated with the model is selected as the "best" single predictor of y at the first step. Some computer software packages use an F value instead of a t value to make this determination. Most of these computer programs allow the researcher to predetermine critical values for t or F, but also contain a default value as an option. If the first independent variable selected at step 1 is denoted x_1, the model appears in the form

$$\hat{y} = b_0 + b_1 x_1$$

If, after examining all possible single-predictor models, it is concluded that none of the independent variables produces a t value that is significant at α, then the search procedure stops at step 1 and recommends no model.

TABLE 14.7 Predictors for All Possible Regressions with Five Independent Variables

SINGLE PREDICTOR	TWO PREDICTORS	THREE PREDICTORS	FOUR PREDICTORS	FIVE PREDICTORS
x_1	x_1, x_2	x_1, x_2, x_3	x_1, x_2, x_3, x_4	x_1, x_2, x_3, x_4, x_5
x_2	x_1, x_3	x_1, x_2, x_4	x_1, x_2, x_3, x_5	
x_3	x_1, x_4	x_1, x_2, x_5	x_1, x_2, x_4, x_5	
x_4	x_1, x_5	x_1, x_3, x_4	x_1, x_3, x_4, x_5	
x_5	x_2, x_3	x_1, x_3, x_5	x_2, x_3, x_4, x_5	
	x_2, x_4	x_1, x_4, x_5		
	x_2, x_5	x_2, x_3, x_4		
	x_3, x_4	x_2, x_3, x_5		
	x_3, x_5	x_2, x_4, x_5		
	x_4, x_5	x_3, x_4, x_5		

Step 2   In step 2, the stepwise procedure examines all possible two-predictor regression models with x_1 as one of the independent variables in the model and determines which of the other $k - 1$ independent variables in conjunction with x_1 produces the highest absolute t value in the model. If this other variable selected from the remaining independent variables is denoted x_2 and is included in the model selected at step 2 along with x_1, the model appears in the form

$$\hat{y} = b_0 + b_1 x_1 + b_2 x_2$$

At this point, stepwise regression pauses and examines the t value of the regression coefficient for x_1. Occasionally, the regression coefficient for x_1 will become statistically nonsignificant when x_2 is entered into the model. In that case, stepwise regression will drop x_1 out of the model and go back and examine which of the other $k - 2$ independent variables, if any, will produce the largest significant absolute t value when that variable is included in the model along with x_2. If no other variables show significant t values, the procedure halts. It is worth noting that the regression coefficients are likely to change from step to step to account for the new predictor being added in the process. Thus, if x_1 stays in the model at step 2, the value of b_1 at step 1 will probably be different from the value of b_1 at step 2.

Step 3   Step 3 begins with independent variables, x_1 and x_2 (the variables that were finally selected at step 2), in the model. At this step, a search is made to determine which of the $k - 2$ remaining independent variables in conjunction with x_1 and x_2 produces the largest significant absolute t value in the regression model. Let us denote the one that is selected as x_3. If no significant t values are acknowledged at this step, the process stops here and the model determined in step 2 is the final model. At step 3, the model appears in the form

$$\hat{y} = b_0 + b_1 x_1 + b_2 x_2 + b_3 x_3$$

In a manner similar to step 2, stepwise regression now goes back and examines the t values of the regression coefficients of x_1 and x_2 in this step 3 model. If either or both of the t values are now nonsignificant, the variables are dropped out of the model and the process calls for a search through the remaining $k - 3$ independent variables to determine which, if any, in conjunction with x_3 produce the largest significant t values in this model. The stepwise regression process continues step by step until no significant independent variables remain that are not in the model.

In the crude oil production example, recall that Table 14.6 contained data that can be used to develop a regression model to predict world crude oil production from as many as five different independent variables. Figure 14.9 displayed the results of a multiple regression analysis to produce a model using all five predictors. Suppose the researcher were to use a stepwise regression search procedure on these data to find a regression model. Recall that the following independent variables were being considered.

1. U.S. energy consumption
2. U.S. nuclear generation
3. U.S. coal production
4. U.S. dry gas production
5. U.S. fuel rate

Step 1   Each of the independent variables is examined one at a time to determine the strength of each predictor in a simple regression model. The results are reported in Table 14.8.

Note that the independent variable "energy consumption" was selected as the predictor variable, x_1, in step 1. An examination of Table 14.8 reveals that energy consumption produced the largest absolute t value (11.77) of the single predictors. By itself, energy consumption accounted for 85.2% of the variation of the y values (world crude oil production). The regression equation taken from the computer output for this model is

$$y = 13.075 + .580 x_1$$

TABLE 14.8	Step 1: Results of Simple Regression Using Each Independent Variable to Predict Oil Production		
DEPENDENT VARIABLE	**INDEPENDENT VARIABLE**	***t* RATIO**	R^2
Oil production	Energy consumption	11.77	85.2%
Oil production	Nuclear	4.43	45.0
Oil production	Coal	3.91	38.9
Oil production	Dry gas	1.08	4.6
Oil production	Fuel rate	3.54	34.2

→ Variable selected to serve as x_1

where

y = world crude oil production

x_1 = U.S. energy consumption

Step 2 In step 2, x_1 was retained initially in the model and a search was conducted among the four remaining independent variables to determine which of those variables in conjunction with x_1 produced the largest significant *t* value. Table 14.9 reports the results of this search.

The information in Table 14.9 shows that the model selected in step 2 includes the independent variables "energy consumption" and "fuel rate." Fuel rate has the largest absolute *t* value (−3.75), and it is significant at α = .05. Other variables produced varying sizes of *t* values. The model produced at step 2 has an R^2 of 90.8%. These two variables taken together account for almost 91% of the variation of world crude oil production in this sample.

From other computer information, it is ascertained that the *t* value for the x_1 variable in this model is 11.91, which is even higher than in step 1. Therefore, x_1 will not be dropped from the model by the stepwise regression procedure. The step 2 regression model from the computer output is

$$y = 7.14 + 0.772x_1 - 0.517x_2$$

where

y = world crude oil production

x_1 = U.S. energy consumption

x_2 = U.S. fuel rate

Note that the regression coefficient for x_1 changed from .580 at step 1 in the model to .772 at step 2.

The R^2 for the model in step 1 was 85.2%. Notice that none of the R^2 values produced from step 2 models is less than 85.2%. The reason is that x_1 is still in the model, so the R^2 at this step must be at least as high as it was in step 1, when only x_1 was in the model. In addition, by examining the R^2 values in Table 14.9, you can get a feel for how much the prospective new

TABLE 14.9	Step 2: Regression Results with Two Predictors			
DEPENDENT VARIABLE y	**INDEPENDENT VARIABLE** x_1	**INDEPENDENT VARIABLE** x_2	***t* RATIO OF x_2**	R^2
Oil production	Energy consumption	Nuclear	−3.60	90.6%
Oil production	Energy consumption	Coal	−2.44	88.3
Oil production	Energy consumption	Dry gas	2.23	87.9
Oil production	Energy consumption	Fuel rate	−3.75	90.8

→ Variable selected at step 2

predictor adds to the model by seeing how much R^2 increases from 85.2%. For example, with x_2 (fuel rate) added to the model, the R^2 goes up to 90.8%. However, adding the variable "dry gas" to x_1 increases R^2 very little (it goes up to 87.9%).

Step 3 In step 3, the search procedure continues to look for an additional predictor variable from the three independent variables remaining out of the solution. Variables x_1 and x_2 are retained in the model. Table 14.10 reports the result of this search.

In this step, regression models are explored that contain x_1 (energy consumption) and x_2 (fuel rate) in addition to one of the three remaining variables. None of the three models produces t ratios that are significant at $\alpha = .05$. No new variables are added to the model produced in step 2. The stepwise regression process ends.

Figure 14.10 shows the Minitab stepwise regression output for the world crude oil production example. The results printed in the table are virtually identical to the step-by-step results discussed in this section but are in a different format.

Each column in Figure 14.10 contains information about the regression model at each step with each step highlighted here by a box. Thus, column 1 contains data on the regression model for step 1. In each column at each step you can see the variables in the model. As an example, at step 2, energy consumption and fuel rate are in the model. The numbers in the Coef column are the regression coefficients. The coefficients and the constant in column 2, for example, yield the regression model equation values for step 2.

$$\hat{y} = 7.140 + 0.772x_1 - 0.52x_2$$

TABLE 14.10 **Step 3: Regression Results with Three Predictors**

DEPENDENT VARIABLE y	INDEPENDENT VARIABLE x_1	INDEPENDENT VARIABLE x_2	INDEPENDENT VARIABLE x_3	t RATIO OF x_3	R^2
Oil production	Energy consumption	Fuel rate	Nuclear	−0.43	90.9%
Oil production	Energy consumption	Fuel rate	Coal	1.71	91.9
Oil production	Energy consumption	Fuel rate	Dry gas	−0.46	90.9

No t ratio is significant at $\alpha = .05$.
No new variables are added to the model.

```
Regression Analysis: CrOilPrd versus USEnCons, USNucGen, USCoalPr,
USDryGas, FuelRate

Stepwise Selection of Terms

Candidate terms: USEnCons, USNucGen, USCoalPr, USDryGas,
FuelRate

                -----Step 1----          -----Step 2----
                Coef        P            Coef        P
Constant        13.07                     7.14
USEnCons        0.5801      0.000        0.7720      0.000
FuelRate                                -0.517       0.001

S                           1.51548                 1.22012
R-sq                        85.24%                  90.03%
R-sq(adj)                   84.62%                  90.03%

α to enter = 0.05, α to remove = 0.05
```

FIGURE 14.10 **Minitab Stepwise Regression Output for the Crude Oil Production Example**

The values of R^2 (R-Sq) and the standard error of the estimate (S) for each step are displayed along with the adjusted value of R^2. Note that the t-ratios are not included in the output, but the p-values associated with each predictor variable at each step are included.

Forward Selection

Another search procedure is forward selection. **Forward selection** is essentially the same as stepwise regression, but once a variable is entered into the process, it is never dropped out. Forward selection begins by finding the independent variable that will produce the largest absolute value of t (and largest R^2) in predicting y. The selected variable is denoted here as x_1 and is part of the model:

$$\hat{y} = b_0 + b_1 x_1$$

Forward selection proceeds to step 2. While retaining x_1, it examines the other $k - 1$ independent variables and determines which variable in the model with x_1 produces the highest absolute value of t that is significant. Thus far, forward selection is the same as stepwise regression. If this second variable is designated x_2, the model is:

$$\hat{y} = b_0 + b_1 x_1 + b_2 x_2$$

At this point, forward selection does not reexamine the t value of x_1. Both x_1 and x_2 remain in the model as other variables are examined and included. When independent variables are correlated in forward selection, the overlapping of information can limit the potential predictability of two or more variables in combination. Stepwise regression takes this into account, in part, when it goes back to reexamine the t values of predictors already in the model to determine whether they are still significant predictors of y given the variables that have now entered the process. In other words, stepwise regression acknowledges that the strongest single predictor of y that is selected at step 1 may not be a significant predictor of y when taken in conjunction with other variables.

Using a forward selection procedure to develop multiple regression models for the world crude oil production example would result in the same outcome as that provided by stepwise regression because neither x_1 nor x_2 were removed from the model in that particular stepwise regression. The difference in the two procedures is more apparent in examples where variables selected at earlier steps in the process are removed during later steps in stepwise regression.

Backward Elimination

The **backward elimination** search procedure is *a step-by-step process that begins with the "full" model (all k predictors)*. Using the t values, a search is made to determine whether any nonsignificant independent variables are in the model. If no nonsignificant predictors are found, the backward process ends with the full model. If nonsignificant predictors are found, the predictor with the smallest absolute value of t is eliminated and a new model is developed with $k - 1$ independent variables.

This model is then examined to determine whether it contains any independent variables with nonsignificant t values. If it does, the predictor with the smallest absolute t value is eliminated from the process and a new model is developed for the next step.

This procedure of identifying the smallest nonsignificant t value and eliminating that variable continues until all variables left in the model have significant t values. Sometimes this process yields results similar to those obtained from forward selection and other times it does not. A word of caution is in order. Backward elimination always begins with all possible predictors in the model. Sometimes the sample data do not provide enough observations to justify the use of all possible predictors at the same time in the model. In this case, backward elimination is not a suitable option with which to build regression models.

The following steps show how the backward elimination process can be used to develop multiple regression models to predict world crude oil production using the data and five predictors displayed in Table 14.6.

TABLE 14.11	Step 1: Backward Elimination, Full Model		
PREDICTOR	COEFFICIENT	t RATIO	p
Energy consumption	.8357	4.64	.000
Nuclear	−.00654	−0.66	.514
Coal	.00983	1.35	.193
Dry gas	−.1432	−0.32	.753
Fuel rate	−.7341	−1.34	.196

Variable to be dropped from the model

TABLE 14.12	Step 2: Backward Elimination, Four Predictors		
PREDICTOR	COEFFICIENT	t RATIO	p
Energy consumption	.7843	9.85	.000
Nuclear	−.004261	−0.64	.528
Coal	.010933	1.74	.096
Fuel rate	−.8253	−1.80	.086

Variable to be dropped from the model

Step 1 A full model is developed with all predictors. The results are shown in Table 14.11. The R^2 for this model is 92.1%. A study of Table 14.11 reveals that the predictor "dry gas" has the smallest absolute value of a nonsignificant t ($t = -.32$, $p = .753$). In step 2, this variable will be dropped from the model.

Step 2 A second regression model is developed with $k - 1 = 4$ predictors. Dry gas has been eliminated from consideration. The results of this multiple regression analysis are presented in Table 14.12. The computer results in Table 14.12 indicate that the variable "nuclear" has the smallest absolute value of a nonsignificant t of the variables remaining in the model ($t = -.64$, $p = .528$). In step 3, this variable will be dropped from the model.

Step 3 A third regression model is developed with $k - 2 = 3$ predictors. Both nuclear and dry gas variables have been removed from the model. The results of this multiple regression analysis are reported in Table 14.13. The computer results in Table 14.13 indicate that the variable "coal" has the smallest absolute value of a nonsignificant t of the variables remaining in the model ($t = 1.71$, $p = .102$). In step 4, this variable will be dropped from the model.

Step 4 A fourth regression model is developed with $k - 3 = 2$ predictors. Nuclear, dry gas, and coal variables have been removed from the model. The results of this multiple regression analysis are reported in Table 14.14. Observe that all p-values are less than $\alpha = .05$, indicating that all t values are significant, so no additional independent variables need to be removed. The backward elimination process ends with two predictors in the model. The final model obtained from this backward elimination process is the same model as that obtained by using stepwise regression.

TABLE 14.13	Step 3: Backward Elimination, Three Predictors		
PREDICTOR	COEFFICIENT	t RATIO	p
Energy consumption	.75394	11.94	.000
Coal	.010479	1.71	.102
Fuel rate	−1.0283	−3.14	.005

Variable to be dropped from the model

TABLE 14.14	Step 4: Backward Elimination, Two Predictors		
PREDICTOR	COEFFICIENT	t RATIO	p
Energy consumption	.77201	11.91	.000
Fuel rate	−.5173	−3.75	.001

All variables are significant at = .05.
No variables will be dropped from this model.
The process stops.

14.3 Problems

14.13. Use a stepwise regression procedure and the following data to develop a multiple regression model to predict y. Discuss the variables that enter at each step, commenting on their t values and on the value of R^2.

y	x_1	x_2	x_3	y	x_1	x_2	x_3
21	5	108	57	22	13	105	51
17	11	135	34	20	10	111	43

14	14	113	21	16	20	140	20
13	9	160	25	13	19	150	14
19	16	122	43	18	14	126	29
15	18	142	40	12	21	175	22
24	7	93	52	23	6	98	38
17	9	128	38	18	15	129	40

14.14. Given here are data for a dependent variable and four potential predictors. Use these data and a stepwise regression procedure to develop a multiple regression model to predict y. Examine the values of t and R^2 at each step and comment on those values. How many steps did the procedure use? Why do you think the process stopped?

y	x_1	x_2	x_3	x_4
101	2	77	1.2	42
127	4	72	1.7	26
98	9	69	2.4	47
79	5	53	2.6	65
118	3	88	2.9	37
114	1	53	2.7	28
110	3	82	2.8	29
94	2	61	2.6	22
96	8	60	2.4	48
73	6	64	2.1	42
108	2	76	1.8	34
124	5	74	2.2	11
82	6	50	1.5	61
89	9	57	1.6	53
76	1	72	2.0	72
109	3	74	2.8	36
123	2	99	2.6	17
125	6	81	2.5	48

14.15. The computer output given here is the result of a stepwise multiple regression analysis to predict a dependent variable by using six predictor variables. The number of observations was 108. Study the output and discuss the results. How many predictors ended up in the model? Which predictors, if any, did not enter the model?

14.16. Study the output given here from a stepwise multiple regression analysis to predict y from four variables. Comment on the output at each step.

```
Stepwise Selection of Terms

Candidate terms: X₁, X₂, X₃, X₄
           -----Step 1-----      -----Step 2----
           Coef       P          Coef       P
Constant   27.88                 22.30
X₃         0.89       0.028
X₂                               12.38      0.011
X₄                               0.0047     0.049
S                     16.52                 9.47
R-sq                  42.39%               68.20%
```

14.17. The National Underwriter Company in Cincinnati, Ohio, publishes property and casualty insurance data. Given here is a portion of the data published. These data include information from the U.S. insurance industry about (1) net income after taxes, (2) dividends to policyholders, (3) net underwriting gain/loss, and (4) premiums earned. Use the data and stepwise regression to predict premiums earned from the other three variables.

PREMIUMS EARNED	NET INCOME	DIVIDENDS	UNDERWRITING GAIN/LOSS
30.2	1.6	.6	.1
47.2	.6	.7	−3.6
92.8	8.4	1.8	−1.5
95.4	7.6	2.0	−4.9
100.4	6.3	2.2	−8.1
104.9	6.3	2.4	−10.8
113.2	2.2	2.3	−18.2
130.3	3.0	2.4	−21.4
161.9	13.5	2.3	−12.8
182.5	14.9	2.9	−5.9
193.3	11.7	2.9	−7.6

```
Stepwise Selection of Terms

Candidate terms: X₁, X₂, X₃, X₄, X₅, X₆
           -----Step 1-----    -----Step 2-----   -----Step 3-----   -----Step 4-----
           Coef      P         Coef      P         Coef      P        Coef      P
Constant   8.71                6.82                6.57               5.96
X₃         -2.85     0.005     -4.92     0.000     -4.97     0.000    -5.00     0.000
X₁                             4.42      0.000     3.72      0.000    3.22      0.002
X₂                                                 2.41      0.018    2.19      0.031
X₆                                                                    1.99      0.049
S                    3.81                3.51                3.43               3.36
R-sq                 85.24%             90.83%
R-sq(adj)            29.20%             49.45%              54.72%             59.29%

α to enter = 0.05, α to remove = 0.05
```

14.18. The U.S. Energy Information Administration releases figures in their publication, *Monthly Energy Review*, about the cost of various fuels and electricity. Shown here are the figures for four different items over a 12-year period. Use the data and stepwise regression to predict the cost of residential electricity from the cost of residential natural gas, residual fuel oil, and leaded regular gasoline. Examine the data and discuss the output.

RESIDENTIAL ELECTRICITY (kWh)	RESIDENTIAL NATURAL GAS (1000 ft³)	RESIDUAL FUEL OIL (gal)	LEADED REGULAR GASOLINE (gal)
2.54	1.29	.21	.39
3.51	1.71	.31	.57
4.64	2.98	.44	.86
5.36	3.68	.61	1.19
6.20	4.29	.76	1.31
6.86	5.17	.68	1.22
7.18	6.06	.65	1.16
7.54	6.12	.69	1.13
7.79	6.12	.61	1.12
7.41	5.83	.34	.86
7.41	5.54	.42	.90
7.49	4.49	.33	.90

14.4 Multicollinearity

One problem that can arise in multiple regression analysis is multicollinearity. **Multicollinearity** is *when two or more of the independent variables of a multiple regression model are highly correlated*. Technically, if two of the independent variables are correlated, we have collinearity; when three or more independent variables are correlated, we have multicollinearity. However, the two terms are frequently used interchangeably.

The reality of business research is that much of the time some correlation between predictors (independent variables) will be present. The problem of multicollinearity arises when the intercorrelation between predictor variables is high. This relationship causes several other problems, particularly in the interpretation of the analysis.

1. It is difficult, if not impossible, to interpret the estimates of the regression coefficients.
2. Inordinately small t values for the regression coefficients may result.
3. The standard deviations of regression coefficients are overestimated.
4. The algebraic sign of estimated regression coefficients may be the opposite of what would be expected for a particular predictor variable.

The problem of multicollinearity can arise in regression analysis in a variety of business research situations. For example, suppose a model is being developed to predict salaries in a given industry. Independent variables such as years of education, age, years in management, experience on the job, and years of tenure with the firm might be considered as predictors. It is obvious that several of these variables are correlated (virtually all of these variables have something to do with number of years, or time) and yield redundant information. Suppose a financial regression model is being developed to predict bond market rates by such independent variables as Dow Jones average, prime interest rates, GNP, producer price index, and consumer price index. Several of these predictors are likely to be intercorrelated.

In the world crude oil production example used in section 14.3, several of the independent variables are intercorrelated, leading to the potential of multicollinearity problems. Table 14.15

TABLE 14.15 **Correlations Among Oil Production Predictor Variables**

	ENERGY CONSUMPTION	NUCLEAR	COAL	DRY GAS	FUEL RATE
Energy consumption	1	.856	.791	.057	.791
Nuclear	.856	1	.952	−.404	.972
Coal	.791	.952	1	−.448	.968
Dry gas	.057	−.404	−.448	1	−.423
Fuel rate	.791	.972	.968	−.423	1

gives the correlations of the predictor variables for this example. Note that r values are quite high ($r > .90$) for fuel rate and nuclear (.972), fuel rate and coal (.968), and coal and nuclear (.952).

Table 14.15 shows that fuel rate and coal production are highly correlated. Using fuel rate as a single predictor of crude oil production produces the following simple regression model.

$$\hat{y} = 44.869 + .7838 \text{ (fuel rate)}$$

Notice that the estimate of the regression coefficient, .7838, is positive, indicating that as fuel rate increases, oil production increases. Using coal as a single predictor of crude oil production yields the following simple regression model.

$$\hat{y} = 45.072 + .0157 \text{ (coal)}$$

The multiple regression model developed using both fuel rate and coal to predict crude oil production is

$$\hat{y} = 45.806 + .0227(\text{coal}) - .3934 \text{ (fuel rate)}$$

Observe that this regression model indicates a *negative* relationship between fuel rate and oil production (−.3934), which is in opposition to the *positive* relationship shown in the regression equation for fuel rate as a single predictor. Because of the multicollinearity between coal and fuel rate, these two independent variables interact in the regression analysis in such a way as to produce regression coefficient estimates that are difficult to interpret. Extreme caution should be exercised before interpreting these regression coefficient estimates.

The problem of multicollinearity can also affect the t values that are used to evaluate the regression coefficients. Because the problems of multicollinearity among predictors can result in an overestimation of the standard deviation of the regression coefficients, the t values tend to be underrepresentative when multicollinearity is present. In some regression models containing multicollinearity in which all t values are nonsignificant, the overall F value for the model is highly significant. In Section 14.1, an example was given of how including interaction when it is significant strengthens a regression model. The computer output for the regression models both with and without the interaction term was shown in Figure 14.5. The model without interaction produced a statistically significant F value but neither predictor variable was significant. Further investigation of this model reveals that the correlation between the two predictors, x_1 and x_2, is .945. This extremely high correlation indicates a strong collinearity between the two predictor variables.

This collinearity may explain the fact that the overall model is significant but neither predictor is significant. It also underscores one of the problems with multicollinearity: underrepresented t values. The t values test the strength of the predictor given the other variables in the model. If a predictor is highly correlated with other independent variables, it may appear not to add much to the explanation of y and produce a low t value. However, had the predictor not been in the presence of these other correlated variables, the predictor might have explained a high proportion of variation of y.

Many of the problems created by multicollinearity are interpretation problems. The business researcher should be alert to and aware of multicollinearity potential with the predictors in the model and view the model outcome in light of such potential.

The problem of multicollinearity is not a simple one to overcome. However, several methods offer an approach to the problem. One way is to examine a correlation matrix like the one in Table 14.15 to search for possible intercorrelations among potential predictor variables. If several variables are highly correlated, the researcher can select the variable that is most correlated to the dependent variable and use that variable to represent the others in the analysis. One problem with this idea is that correlations can be more complex than simple correlation among variables. In other words, simple correlation values do not always reveal multiple correlation between variables. In some instances, variables may not appear to be correlated as pairs, but one variable is a linear combination of several other variables. This situation is also an example of multicollinearity, and a cursory observation of the correlation matrix will probably not reveal the problem.

Stepwise regression is another way to prevent the problem of multicollinearity. The search process enters the variables one at a time and compares the new variable to those in solution. If a new variable is entered and the t values on old variables become nonsignificant, the old variables are dropped out of solution. In this manner, it is more difficult for the problem of multicollinearity to affect the regression analysis. Of course, because of multicollinearity, some important predictors may not enter in to the analysis.

Other techniques are available to attempt to control for the problem of multicollinearity. One is called a **variance inflation factor**, in which a regression analysis is conducted to predict an independent variable by the other independent variables. In this case, the independent variable being predicted becomes the dependent variable. As this process is done for each of the independent variables, it is possible to determine whether any of the independent variables are a function of the other independent variables, yielding evidence of multicollinearity. By using the results from such a model, a variance inflation factor (VIF) can be computed to determine whether the standard errors of the estimates are inflated:

$$VIF = \frac{1}{1 - R_i^2}$$

where R_i^2 is the coefficient of determination for any of the models, used to predict an independent variable by the other $k - 1$ independent variables. Some researchers follow a guideline that any variance inflation factor greater than 10 or R_i^2 value more than .90 for the largest variance inflation factors indicates a severe multicollinearity problem.*

14.4 Problems

14.19. Develop a correlation matrix for the independent variables in Problem 14.13. Study the matrix and make a judgment as to whether substantial multicollinearity is present among the predictors. Why or why not?

14.20. Construct a correlation matrix for the four independent variables for Problem 14.14 and search for possible multicollinearity. What did you find, and why?

14.21. In Problem 14.17, you were asked to use stepwise regression to predict premiums earned by net income, dividends, and underwriting gain or loss. Study the stepwise results, including the regression coefficients, to determine whether there may be a problem with multicollinearity. Construct a correlation matrix of the three variables to aid you in this task.

14.22. Study the three predictor variables in Problem 14.18 and attempt to determine whether substantial multicollinearity is present among the predictor variables. If there is a problem of multicollinearity, how might it affect the outcome of the multiple regression analysis?

14.5 Logistic Regression

There are times when business statisticians need to develop models to predict dependent variables that are dichotomous (have only two outcomes). For example, a major bank sends out credit cards to selected pre-qualified people. To use the credit card, the person must call a national telephone number and activate it. Why do some people activate the card and others do not? Can a model be developed to predict whether a person will activate the card? A financial institution is trying to get people to invest in a new annuity product. What variables seem to be related to whether a person invests? Can a model be developed to predict whether someone will invest? There are many other instances in business where it can be interesting and informative to develop a regression-type model to predict a dichotomous outcome.

In such models, a 0, 1 coding is used for the dependent variable in a manner similar to the coding used for dummy (qualitative) independent variables in regression analysis. However, unlike the use of dummy variables as predictors in regression, developing regression models to predict a dichotomous dependent variable is problematic. Such models violate assumptions underlying multiple regression because 1.) the error terms do not follow a normal distribution, 2.) the error terms are not independent, and 3.) there is heteroscedasticity of error variances.

---

*William Mendenhall and Terry Sincich, *A Second Course in Business Statistics: Regression Analysis*. San Francisco: Dellen Publishing Company, 1989; John Neter, William Wasserman, and Michael H. Kutner, *Applied Linear Regression Models*, 2nd ed. Homewood, IL: Richard D. Irwin, 1989.

In addition, even with transformations accounting for nonlinear effects, there is no guarantee with multiple regression that the predicted values would always be between 0 and 1. For these reasons, a different methodology, **logistic regression**, is commonly used to develop models to predict dichotomous dependent variables.

The methods used in logistic regression have some properties similar to those used in multiple regression; however, there are differences. Logistic regression does not assume a linear relationship between the dependent and independent variables. The independent variables do not have to be interval/ratio in data level, the data need not be normally distributed, and within-group variances need not be equal. In addition, because of the methodology used, sample size requirements for logistic regression are larger than for multiple regression. Generally, there should be at least 50 observations for each predictor variable in logistic regression.

An Example

Suppose an auto club mails a flier to its members offering to send more information on a supplemental health insurance plan if the club member returns a brief form in an enclosed envelope. Why do some club members return the form and others do not? Can a model be developed to predict whether a club member will return the form? One theory is that older people are more likely to return the form inquiring about additional health insurance because they are more concerned about their health and they may have more disposable income to afford such coverage. Suppose a random sample of 92 club members is taken and club members are asked their age and if they have returned the form. The resulting data are shown in Table 14.16. For clarity of understanding, the data are organized by whether or not the club member returned the form.

TABLE 14.16   Data on Auto Club Members

REQUESTED ADDITIONAL INFORMATION?		REQUESTED ADDITIONAL INFORMATION?	
(1 = YES, 0 = NO)	AGE OF CLUB MEMBER	(1 = YES, 0 = NO)	AGE OF CLUB MEMBER
1	52	1	53
1	57	1	46
1	53	1	45
1	57	1	53
1	48	1	47
1	50	1	50
1	54	1	47
1	47	1	55
1	45	1	65
1	66	1	56
1	61	1	50
1	60	1	51
1	53	1	64
1	66	1	54
1	56	0	52
1	58	0	42
1	45	0	45
1	62	0	33
1	51	0	42
1	52	0	51
1	57	0	43
1	48	0	40

0	50	0	43
0	29	0	47
0	41	0	37
0	39	0	30
0	33	0	39
0	39	0	50
0	45	0	36
0	37	0	28
0	45	0	34
0	34	0	51
0	45	0	43
0	30	0	34
0	41	0	45
0	39	0	31
0	48	0	29
0	41	0	24
0	47	0	36
0	28	0	43
0	45	0	39
0	37	0	42
0	48	0	39
0	38	0	32
0	39	0	29
0	41	0	34

Figure 14.11 displays a scatter plot of the data.

The Logistic Regression Model

Note that in the graph of the data in Figure 14.11 there are only two y values, 0 and 1. Imagine trying to fit a line through the data. Among other problems, the line would not begin nor end at 0 and 1. Over time, statisticians have experimented with various curves that might fit this type of data and have determined that the following function models these types of data well:

$$f(x) = p = \frac{e^u}{1 + e^u}$$

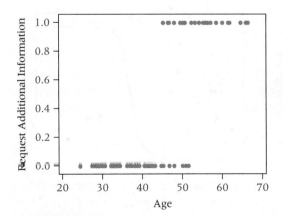

FIGURE 14.11   **Scatter Plot of Auto Club Member Data**

This particular function, which results in an "s-shaped" curve, is called the logistic model. It approaches 0 at the lower end and 1 at the upper end. Figure 14.12 contains the same scatter plot of the auto club data with such a curve fit to the data.

In a manner analogous to simple regression where there is only one predictor variable and the model is first order, we begin with the simplest model, $\mu = \beta_0 + \beta_1 x_1$. Substituting this expression for μ in the equation results in

$$f(x) = p = \frac{e^{\beta_0 + \beta_1 x_1}}{1 + e^{\beta_0 + \beta_1 x_1}}$$

where p is the probability that a club member fits into group 1 (returns the form). In general for multiple predictors, the logistic model is:

$$f(x) = p = \frac{e^{\beta_0 + \beta_1 x_1 + \cdots + \beta_k x_k}}{1 + e^{\beta_0 + \beta_1 x_1 + \cdots + \beta_k x_k}}$$

For ease of computation in logistic regression, this expression is transformed into an odds ratio. Recall that the odds of an event occurring are computed by dividing the probability of the event occurring by the probability that the event will not occur. For example, if there is a .60 probability that it will rain, then there is a $1 - .60 = .40$ probability that it will not rain. The odds that it will rain are: Prob. (rain)/Prob. (not rain) or $.60/.40 = 1.50$. In transforming the logistic model, the function is converted to an odds ratio:

$$S = \text{Odds radio} = \frac{p}{1 - p}$$

$$S = \text{Odds radio} = \frac{\dfrac{e^{\beta_0 + \beta_1 x_1 + \cdots + \beta_k x_k}}{1 + e^{\beta_0 + \beta_1 x_1 + \cdots + \beta_k x_k}}}{1 - \dfrac{e^{\beta_0 + \beta_1 x_1 + \cdots + \beta_k x_k}}{1 + e^{\beta_0 + \beta_1 x_1 + \cdots + \beta_k x_k}}}$$

Rearranging and reducing this by algebra results in:

$$S = \text{Odds ratio} = e^{\beta_0 + \beta_1 x_1 + \cdots + \beta_k x_k}$$

The transformation is completed by taking the natural log of each side of the equation, resulting in:

$$\ln(S) = \ln(e^{\beta_0 + \beta_1 x_1 + \cdots + \beta_k x_k}) = \beta_0 + \beta_1 x_1 + \cdots + \beta_k x_k$$

This log of the odds ratio is called the logit, and the transformed model is now linear in the β's. In logistic regression, for reasons mentioned before, least squares regression methodology is not used to develop the model but rather a maximum likelihood method, which maximizes the probability of getting the observed results, is employed. Maximum likelihood

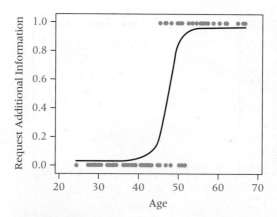

FIGURE 14.12 **Scatter Plot of Auto Club Data with Logistic Model**

estimation is an iterative process using the computer and is not described here. Minitab uses a maximum likelihood procedure to produce logistic regression results. We will now focus on interpreting the results of such an analysis.

Interpreting the Output

Figure 14.13 contains Minitab output from its binary logistic regression analysis of the auto club data. The model was developed in an attempt to predict whether an auto club member would send in a form asking for additional health insurance information by the age of the member.

Notice that in the Minitab summary of information, 36 of the 92 auto club members sent in the form (a little over 39%) and 56 of the members did not (almost 61%).

Determining Logistic Regression Model   Found in the column Coef are the coefficients of the resulting logistic model: −20.7540 for Constant and 0.433680 for Age.

Thus, the log of the odds ratio or logit equation is:

$$\ln(S) = -20.7540 + 0.433680 \text{ Age}$$

Binary Logistic Regression: Request Additional Information versus Age

Response Information

Variable	Value	Count
Request Additional Information	1	36 (Event)
	0	56
	Total	92

Deviance Table

Source	DF	Seq Dev	Contribution	Adj Dev	Adj Mean	Chi-Square	P-Value
Regression	1	73.74	59.87%	73.74	73.7394	73.74	0.000
Error	90	49.42	40.13%	49.42	0.5491		
Total	91	123.16	100.00%				

Model Summary

Deviance R-Sq	Deviance R-Sq(adj)
59.87%	59.06%

Coefficients

Term	Coef	SE Coef	95% CI	Z-Value	P-Value
Constant	-20.75	4.62	(-29.80, -11.70)	-4.49	0.000
Age	0.4337	0.0969	(0.2437, 0.6237)	4.47	0.000

Odds Ratios for Continuous Predictors

	Odds Ratio	95% CI
Age	1.5429	(1.2759, 1.8658)

Regression Equation

P(1) = exp(Y')/(1 + exp(Y'))

Y' = -20.75 + 0.4337 Age

FIGURE 14.13 Minitab Binary Logistic Regression Output for the Auto Club Example

As an example, suppose we want to determine the probability that a 50-year-old auto club member will return the form. Inserting Age = 50 into the logit equation, $\ln(S) = -20.7540 + 0.433680$ Age, results in a ln odds of $-20.7540 + 0.433680(50) = 0.93$.

Taking the antilog of this value results in the odds, S:

$$S = e^{0.93} = 2.535$$

The odds that a 50-year-old returns the form are 2.535 to 1. From this, we can compute the probability that a 50-year-old returns the form as:

$$\hat{p} = \frac{S}{S+1} = \frac{2.535}{2.535+1} = .7171$$

How can the probability that an auto club member will return the form be computed directly? The logistic model to predict the probability of returning the form is determined by:

$$\hat{p} = \frac{e^{-20.7540+0.433680\,\text{Age}}}{1+e^{-20.7540+0.433680\,\text{Age}}}$$

For the 50-year-old, the predicted probability is:

$$\hat{p} = \frac{e^{-20.7540+0.433680(50)}}{1+e^{-20.7540+0.433680(50)}} = \frac{e^{.93}}{1+e^{.93}} = \frac{2.53451}{3.53451} = .7171$$

The predicted probability that the 50-year-old returns the form is .7171. Using a probability of .50 as a cutoff between predicting a 0 or a 1, the 50-year-old would be classified as a 1 (a member who will return the form). The predicted probability that he/she will not return the form is $1 - .7171 = .2829$. Computing the odds from these probability values:

$$\text{Odds} = \frac{.7171}{.2829} = 2.535.$$

This answer agrees with the odds calculated above using the odds ratio. In summary, with the logistic regression equation, one can calculate the probability, determine the $\log_e$ of the odds, and compute the odds of being in the 1 group.

Testing the Overall Model

In regression analysis, an F test is computed to determine if there is overall significance in the model. In multiple regression, this test determines whether or not at least one of the regression coefficients is different from zero. Logistic regression has an analogous test, the Chi-square statistic. Displayed in the Minitab output given in Figure 14.13 for the auto club example problem, is a Chi-square value of 73.74 with an associated p-value of 0.000. This result indicates that the logistic regression model has overall significance and there is at least one significant predictor variable.

Logistic regression can be run for models with more than one predictor. In these models, the Chi-square statistic yields the same information as the single-predictor model. However, for multiple-predictor models, the degrees of freedom are equal to p, which equals the number of predictors in the model. Thus, if there are four predictors in the model, the degrees of freedom are 4. In the case of multiple predictors, a significant Chi-square statistic indicates that at least one of the predictor variables is significant.

Testing Individual Predictor Variables

Determining the significance of individual predictor variables in logistic regression can be done by studying z values and their associated p-values. Minitab output contains the z value and its associated *p*-value for each predictor variable. Note in Figure 14.13 that the *z* value for Age is 4.47 with a *p*-value of .000. This indicates that age is a significant predictor in the model. With the single-predictor model, this information is similar to that gleaned from the test of the overall model. However, in models with multiple predictors, such *z* statistics and their associated *p*-values can help determine which variables are significant and are contributing to the model and which are not.

14.5 Problems

14.23. The Hospital database associated with this text and found in WileyPLUS contains a dichotomous variable, Service, that represents two types of hospitals, general medical and psychiatric. In the database, general medical hospitals are coded as 1 and psychiatric hospitals as 2. However, to run a logistic regression model to predict service, the data were recoded so that general medical hospitals are 0 and psychiatric hospitals are 1. Shown below is Minitab output from a logistic regression attempt to predict service by payroll expenditures. Study the output. What is the model? Comment on the strength of the predictor. Thinking about hospitals, does the model make sense to you? Use the model to estimate the probability that a hospital is a psychiatric hospital if the payroll expenditures are $80,000. (Note that payroll expenditures are actually in units of $1,000)

```
Variable            Value    Count
Service               1         32 (Event)
                      0        168
                    Total      200

Coefficients

Term         Coef        SE Coef     Z-Value  P-Value
Constant    -0.932546    0.289749    -3.22    0.001
Payroll Exp. -0.0000323  0.0000123    2.64    0.008

Regression Equation

P(1) = exp(Y')/(1 + exp(Y'))

Y' = -0.932546 - 0.0000323 Payroll Exp.
```

14.24. Another database associated with this text and found in WileyPLUS is the Consumer Food database. There is a dichotomous variable in this database, and that is whether a family lives in a metro area or outside. In the database, metro is coded as 1 and outside metro as 2. However, to run a logistic regression model to predict service, the data were recoded so that families in metro areas are 0 and families outside of metro areas are 1. Shown below is Minitab output from a logistic regression attempt to predict if a family is from outside a metro area by annual food spending by household. Study the output. What is the model? How good is the overall fit of the model? Comment on the strength of the predictor. Thinking about households and metro areas, does the model make sense to you? Use the model to estimate the probability that a household is from outside a metro area if their annual food spending by household is $12,000.

```
Variable            Value    Count
Service               1         80 (Event)
                      0        120
                    Total      200
```

```
Coefficients

Term           Coef        SE Coef     Z-Value  P-Value
Constant      0.705987    0.451245     1.56     0.118
Annual Food
Spending     -0.0001257   0.0000489   -2.57     0.010

Regression Equation

P(1) = exp(Y')/(1 + exp(Y'))

Y' = 0.705987 - 0.0000489 Annual Food Spending
```

14.25 The Manufacturing database associated with this text and found in WileyPLUS has a variable, Value of Industrial Shipments, that is coded 0 if the value is small and 1 if the value is large. Using Minitab, a logistic regression analysis was done in an attempt to predict the value of industrial shipments by the number of production workers. The Minitab output is given below. Study the output. What is the model? How good is the overall fit of the model? Comment on the strength of the predictor. Use the model to estimate the probability that a selected company has a large value of industrial shipments if their number of production workers is 30. (Note that number of production workers is in units of 1,000)

```
Coefficients

Term           Coef       SE Coef    Z-Value  P-Value
Constant      -3.07942    0.535638   -5.75    0.000
No. Prod. Wkrs. 0.0544532 0.0096833   5.62    0.000

Regression Equation

P(1) = exp(Y')/(1 + exp(Y'))

Y' = -3.07942 + 0.0544532 No. Prod. Wkrs.
```

14.26. Suppose logistic regression is used to develop a second model from the Manufacturing database discussed in problem 14.25 to predict the value of industrial shipments by two variables, Number of Production Workers and New Capital Expenditures. The Minitab output for this analysis is given below. Since number of production workers was used as the single predictor in Problem 14.25, how does this output compare to that given in Problem 14.25?

```
Coefficients

Term           Coef        SE Coef    Z-Value  P-Value
Constant      -5.40701     1.08209    -5.00    0.000
No. Prod. Wkrs. 0.0295051  0.0095208   3.10    0.002
New Cap. Exp.  0.0074783   0.0010749   3.99    0.000

Regression Equation

P(1) = exp(Y')/(1 + exp(Y'))

Y' = -5.40701 + 0.0295051 No. Prod. Wkrs. + 0.0074783
New Cap. Exp.
```

Use the model to estimate the probability that a selected company has a large value of industrial shipments if their number of production workers is 80 and new capital expenditures are 1,000. New capital expenditures are in million-dollar units.

Sources for Section 14.5

1. Alfred, DeMaris, "A Tutorial in Logistic Regression," *Journal of Marriage and Family,* vol. 57, no. 4, November 1995, 956–968.

2. Joseph F. Hair Jr., William C. Black, Barry J. Babin, and Rolph E. Anderson, *Multivariate Data Analysis,* 7th ed., Saddle River, NJ: Pearson, 2010.

3. David W. Hosmer and Stanley Lemeshow, *Applied Logistic Regression,* 2nd ed., New York: John Wiley & Sons, 2000.

4. David G. Kleinbaum and Mitchel Klein, *Logistic Regression: A Self-Learning Text,* 2nd ed., New York: Springer Science Productions, 2002.

5. Fred C. Pampel, *Logistic Regression: A Primer.* Thousand Oaks, CA: Sage, 2000.

Decision Dilemma Solved

Predicting CEO Salaries

Models to predict CEO salaries can be developed using multiple regression and such possible predictor variables as age, years of experience, worth of company and others. Search procedures such as stepwise regression can be used to sort out the more significant predictors of CEO salaries. In the Decision Dilemma, data was given for three possible predictors: Annual Revenue, Number of Employees, and if the company is in manufacturing or not, along with corresponding data on CEO salaries.

Using these data and Minitab, a stepwise regression procedure was conducted on the Decision Dilemma data in an attempt to predict CEO salary by the three independent variables of Revenue, Employees, and Manufacturing (or not). An alpha of .10 was used as a cut-off for entry into the model. The result of the initial analysis is:

Candidate terms: Employees, Revenue, Mgfr				
	----Step 1----		----Step 2---	
	Coef	P	Coef	P
Constant	0.462		1.109	
Revenue	0.1041	0.000	0.0626	0.018
Mgfr			1.878	0.026
S		1.36412		1.20883
R-sq		62.35%		72.08%
R-sq(adj)		60.26%		68.79%
R-sq(pred)		54.94%		60.19%
Mallows' Cp		6.80		2.91
α to enter = 0.1, α to remove = 0.1				

Company Revenue enters the model at step 1 producing an R^2 of 62.35%. At step 2, the qualitative variable, Manufacturing or Not, enters the model joining Company Revenue; and the R^2 increases to 72.08%. No other variables enter into the stepwise process, and the regression equation is:

$$\text{CEO Salary} = 1.109 + 0.0626 \text{ Revenue} + 1.878 \text{ Manufacturing}$$

In considering the possibility that there might be multicollinearity in these data, a modest correlation between Company Revenue and Number of Employees ($r = .63$) was observed. Because of this correlation, an interaction term was created for Company Revenue and Number of Employees. A second stepwise regression was then conducted using Minitab and including a new predictor variable, Interaction of Revenue and Employees, along with the three original predictors. The result of this new analysis is:

Candidate terms: Employees, Revenue, Mgfr, Inter R&E				
	-----Step 1-----		----Step 2---	
	Coef	P	Coef	P
Constant	3.005		2.480	
Inter R&E	0.000555	0.000	0.000369	0.001
Mgfr			1.974	0.003
S		1.30069		1.02161
R-sq		65.77%		80.06%
R-sq(adj)		63.87%		77.71%
R-sq(pred)		53.36%		74.52%
Mallows' Cp		11.00		1.73
α to enter = 0.1, α to remove = 0.1				

Note that the interaction variable, Interaction of Revenue and Employees, enters the stepwise procedure at Step 1 producing an R^2 of 65.77% which is higher than the R^2 for the first model (62.35%). At step 2, the interaction variable is retained in the model and the Manufacturing variable enters the model. The resulting R^2 for the new model at step 2 is 80.06% which is considerably higher than the R^2 for the first analysis (72.08%). No other variables enter into this stepwise process, and the final regression equation is:

$$\text{CEO Salary} = 2.480 + 0.000369 \text{ Interaction of Revenue and Employees} + 1.974 \text{ Manufacturing}$$

Ethical Considerations

Some business researchers misuse the results of search procedures by using the order in which variables come into a model (on stepwise and forward selection) to rank the variables in importance. They state that the variable entered at step 1 is the most important predictor of y, the variable entering at step 2 is second most important, and so on. In actuality, variables entering the analysis after step 1 are being analyzed by how much of the unaccounted-for variation (residual variation) they are explaining, not how much they are related to y by themselves. A variable that comes into the model at the fourth step is the variable that most greatly accounts for the variation of the y values left over after the first three variables have explained the rest. However, the fourth variable taken by itself might explain more variation of y than the second or third variable when seen as single predictors.

Some people use the estimates of the regression coefficients to compare the worth of the predictor variables: the larger the coefficient is, the greater its worth. At least two problems plague this approach. The first is that most variables are measured in different units. Thus, regression coefficient weights are partly a function of the unit of measurement of the variable. Second, if multicollinearity is present, the interpretation of the regression coefficients is questionable. In addition, the presence of multicollinearity raises several issues about the interpretation of other regression output. Researchers who ignore this problem are at risk of presenting spurious results. Because of assumption violations, it is greatly frowned upon by statisticians to use least squares multiple regression to develop regression models to predict dichotomous variables. To do so could be considered a form of unethical behavior, especially by knowledgeable business researchers.

Summary

Multiple regression analysis can handle nonlinear independent variables. One way to accommodate this issue is to recode the data and enter the variables into the analysis in the normal way. Other nonlinear regression models, such as exponential models, require that the entire model be transformed. Often the transformation involves the use of logarithms. In some cases, the resulting value of the regression model is in logarithmic form and the antilogarithm of the answer must be taken to determine the predicted value of y.

Indicator, or dummy, variables are qualitative variables used to represent categorical data in the multiple regression model. These variables are coded as 0, 1 and are often used to represent nominal or ordinal classification data that the researcher wants to include in the regression analysis. If a qualitative variable contains more than two categories, it generates multiple dummy variables. In general, if a qualitative variable contains c categories, $c - 1$ dummy variables should be created.

Search procedures are used to help sort through the independent variables as predictors in the examination of various possible models. Several search procedures are available, including all possible regressions, stepwise regression, forward selection, and backward elimination. The all possible regressions procedure computes every possible regression model for a set of data. The drawbacks of this procedure include the time and energy required to compute all possible regressions and the difficulty of deciding which models are most appropriate. The stepwise regression procedure involves selecting and adding one independent variable at a time to the regression process after beginning with a one-predictor model. Variables are added to the model at each step if they contain the most significant t value associated with the remaining variables. If no additional t value is statistically significant at any given step, the procedure stops. With stepwise regression, at each step the process examines the variables already in the model to determine whether their t values are still significant. If

not, they are dropped from the model, and the process searches for other independent variables with large, significant t values to replace the variable(s) dropped. The forward selection procedure is the same as stepwise regression but does not drop variables from the model once they have been included. The backward elimination procedure begins with a "full" model, a model that contains all the independent variables. The sample size must be large enough to justify a full model, which can be a limiting factor. Backward elimination drops out the least important predictors one at a time until only significant predictors are left in the regression model. The variable with the smallest absolute t value of the statistically nonsignificant t values is the independent variable that is dropped out of the model at each step.

One of the problems in using multiple regression is multicollinearity, or correlations among the predictor variables. This problem can cause overinflated estimates of the standard deviations of regression coefficients, misinterpretation of regression coefficients, undersized t values, and misleading signs on the regression coefficients. It can be lessened by using an intercorrelation matrix of independent variables to help recognize bivariate correlation, by using stepwise regression to sort the variables one at a time, or by using statistics such as a variance inflation factor. For a variety of reasons, including assumption violations, statisticians do not recommend using least squares regression analysis to develop models to predict dichotomous dependent variables. A commonly used methodology for developing such models is logistic regression, which has some properties similar to multiple regression. However, logistic regression does not assume a linear relationship between the dependent and independent variables, and several of the assumptions underlying least squares regression need not be met. Sample size requirements for logistic regression are larger than for multiple regression, and it is recommended that there be at least 50 observations for each predictor variable in logistic regression.

Key Terms

all possible regressions	indicator variable	qualitative variable	Tukey's ladder of
backward elimination	logistic regression	search procedures	transformations
dummy variable	multicollinearity	stepwise regression	variance inflation factor
forward selection	quadratic model	Tukey's four-quadrant approach	

Formulas

Variance inflation factor

$$VIF = \frac{1}{1 - R_i^2}$$

General logistic model:

$$p = \frac{e^u}{1 + e^u}$$

Logistic model for multiple predictors:

$$p = \frac{e^{\beta_0 + \beta_1 x_1 + \cdots + \beta_k x_k}}{1 + e^{\beta_0 + \beta_1 x_1 + \cdots + \beta_k x_k}}$$

Odds ratio:

$$Odds\ ratio = \frac{p}{1 - p}$$

Logit:

$$\ln(S) = \ln(e^{\beta_0 + \beta_1 x_1 + \cdots + \beta_k x_k}) = \beta_0 + \beta_1 x_1 + \cdots + \beta_k x_k$$

Supplementary Problems

Calculating the Statistics

14.27. Given here are the data for a dependent variable, y, and independent variables. Use these data to develop a regression model to predict y. Discuss the output. Which variable is an indicator variable? Was it a significant predictor of y?

x_1	x_2	x_3	y
0	51	16.4	14
0	48	17.1	17
1	29	18.2	29
0	36	17.9	32
0	40	16.5	54
1	27	17.1	86
1	14	17.8	117
0	17	18.2	120
1	16	16.9	194
1	9	18.0	203
1	14	18.9	217
0	11	18.5	235

14.28. Use the following data and a stepwise regression analysis to predict y. In addition to the two independent variables given here, include three other predictors in your analysis: the square of each x as a predictor and an interaction predictor. Discuss the results of the process.

x_1	x_2	y	x_1	x_2	y
10	3	2002	5	12	1750
5	14	1747	6	8	1832
8	4	1980	5	18	1795
7	4	1902	7	4	1917
6	7	1842	8	5	1943

7	6	1883	6	9	1830
4	21	1697	5	12	1786
11	4	2021			

14.29. Use the x_1 values and the log of the x_1 values given here to predict the y values by using a stepwise regression procedure. Discuss the output. Were either or both of the predictors significant?

y	x_1	y	x_1
20.4	850	13.2	204
11.6	146	17.5	487
17.8	521	12.4	192
15.3	304	10.6	98
22.4	1029	19.8	703
21.9	910	17.4	394
16.4	242	19.4	647

Testing Your Understanding

14.30. The U.S. Commodities Futures Trading Commission reports on the volume of trading in the U.S. commodity futures exchanges. Shown here are the figures for grain, oilseeds, and livestock products over a period of several years. Use these data to develop a multiple regression model to predict grain futures volume of trading from oilseeds volume and livestock products volume. All figures are given in units of millions. Graph each of these predictors separately with the response variable and use Tukey's four-quadrant approach to explore possible recoding schemes for nonlinear relationships. Include any of these in the regression model. Comment on the results.

GRAIN	OILSEEDS	LIVESTOCK
2.2	3.7	3.4
18.3	15.7	11.8
19.8	20.3	9.8

14.9	15.8	11.0
17.8	19.8	11.1
15.9	23.5	8.4
10.7	14.9	7.9
10.3	13.8	8.6
10.9	14.2	8.8
15.9	22.5	9.6
15.9	21.1	8.2

14.31. The U.S. Bureau of Mines produces data on the price of minerals. Shown here are the average prices per year for several minerals over a decade. Use these data and a stepwise regression procedure to produce a model to predict the average price of gold from the other variables. Comment on the results of the process.

GOLD ($ PER OZ.)	COPPER (CENTS PER LB.)	SILVER ($ PER OZ.)	ALUMINUM (CENTS PER LB.)
161.1	64.2	4.4	39.8
308.0	93.3	11.1	61.0
613.0	101.3	20.6	71.6
460.0	84.2	10.5	76.0
376.0	72.8	8.0	76.0
424.0	76.5	11.4	77.8
361.0	66.8	8.1	81.0
318.0	67.0	6.1	81.0
368.0	66.1	5.5	81.0
448.0	82.5	7.0	72.3
438.0	120.5	6.5	110.1
382.6	130.9	5.5	87.8

14.32. The Shipbuilders Council of America in Washington, D.C., publishes data about private shipyards. Among the variables reported by this organization are the employment figures (per 1000), the number of naval vessels under construction, and the number of repairs or conversions done to commercial ships (in $ millions). Shown here are the data for these three variables over a seven-year period. Use the data to develop a regression model to predict private shipyard employment from number of naval vessels under construction and repairs or conversions of commercial ships. Graph each of these predictors separately with the response variable and use Tukey's four-quadrant approach to explore possible recoding schemes for nonlinear relationships. Include any of these in the regression model. Comment on the regression model and its strengths and its weaknesses.

EMPLOYMENT	NAVAL VESSELS	COMMERCIAL SHIP REPAIRS OR CONVERSIONS
133.4	108	431
177.3	99	1335
143.0	105	1419
142.0	111	1631
130.3	100	852
120.6	85	847
120.4	79	806

14.33. The U.S. Bureau of Labor Statistics produces consumer price indexes for several different categories. Shown here are the percentage changes in consumer price indexes over a period of 20 years for food, shelter, apparel, and fuel oil. Also displayed are the percentage changes in consumer price indexes for all commodities. Use these data and a stepwise regression procedure to develop a model that attempts to predict all commodities by the other four variables. Construct scatter plots of each of these variables with all commodities. Examine the graphs in light of Tukey's four-quadrant approach. Develop any other appropriate predictor variables by recoding data and include them in the analysis. Comment on the result of this analysis.

ALL COMMODITIES	FOOD	SHELTER	APPAREL	FUEL OIL
.9	1.0	2.0	1.6	3.7
.6	1.3	.8	.9	2.7
.9	.7	1.6	.4	2.6
.9	1.6	1.2	1.3	2.6
1.2	1.3	1.5	.9	2.1
1.1	2.2	1.9	1.1	2.4
2.6	5.0	3.0	2.5	4.4
1.9	.9	3.6	4.1	7.2
3.5	3.5	4.5	5.3	6.0
4.7	5.1	8.3	5.8	6.7
4.5	5.7	8.9	4.2	6.6
3.6	3.1	4.2	3.2	6.2
3.0	4.2	4.6	2.0	3.3
7.4	14.5	4.7	3.7	4.0
11.9	14.3	9.6	7.4	9.3
8.8	8.5	9.9	4.5	12.0
4.3	3.0	5.5	3.7	9.5
5.8	6.3	6.6	4.5	9.6
7.2	9.9	10.2	3.6	8.4
11.3	11.0	13.9	4.3	9.2

14.34. The U.S. Department of Agriculture publishes data annually on various selected farm products. Shown here are the unit production figures for three farm products for 10 years during a 20-year period. Use these data and a stepwise regression analysis to predict corn production by the production of soybeans and wheat. Comment on the results.

CORN (MILLION BUSHELS)	SOYBEANS (MILLION BUSHELS)	WHEAT (MILLION BUSHELS)
4152	1127	1352
6639	1798	2381
4175	1636	2420
7672	1861	2595
8876	2099	2424
8226	1940	2091
7131	1938	2108
4929	1549	1812
7525	1924	2037
7933	1922	2739

14.35. The American Chamber of Commerce Researchers Association compiles cost-of-living indexes for selected metropolitan areas. Shown here are cost-of-living indexes for 25 different cities on five different items for a recent year. Use the data to develop a regression model to predict the grocery cost-of-living index by the indexes of housing, utilities, transportation, and healthcare. Discuss the results, highlighting both the significant and nonsignificant predictors.

CITY	GROCERY ITEMS	HOUSING	UTILITIES	TRANSPOR-TATION	HEALTH-CARE
Albany	108.3	106.8	127.4	89.1	107.5
Albuquerque	96.3	105.2	98.8	100.9	102.1
Augusta, GA	96.2	88.8	115.6	102.3	94.0
Austin	98.0	83.9	87.7	97.4	94.9
Baltimore	106.0	114.1	108.1	112.8	111.5
Buffalo	103.1	117.3	127.6	107.8	100.8
Colorado Springs	94.5	88.5	74.6	93.3	102.4
Dallas	105.4	98.9	108.9	110.0	106.8
Denver	91.5	108.3	97.2	105.9	114.3
Des Moines	94.3	95.1	111.4	105.7	96.2
El Paso	102.9	94.6	90.9	104.2	91.4
Indianapolis	96.0	99.7	92.1	102.7	97.4
Jacksonville	96.1	90.4	96.0	106.0	96.1
Kansas City	89.8	92.4	96.3	95.6	93.6
Knoxville	93.2	88.0	91.7	91.6	82.3
Los Angeles	103.3	211.3	75.6	102.1	128.5
Louisville	94.6	91.0	79.4	102.4	88.4
Memphis	99.1	86.2	91.1	101.1	85.5
Miami	100.3	123.0	125.6	104.3	137.8
Minneapolis	92.8	112.3	105.2	106.0	107.5
Mobile	99.9	81.1	104.9	102.8	92.2
Nashville	95.8	107.7	91.6	98.1	90.9
New Orleans	104.0	83.4	122.2	98.2	87.0
Oklahoma City	98.2	79.4	103.4	97.3	97.1
Phoenix	95.7	98.7	96.3	104.6	115.2

Interpreting the Output

14.36. A stepwise regression procedure was used to analyze a set of 20 observations taken on four predictor variables to predict a dependent variable. The results of this procedure are given next. Discuss the results.

```
Candidate terms: X₁, X₂, X₃, X₄

                ----Step 1----      ----Step 2----
                Coef      P         Coef      P
Constant        152.2               124.5
X₁              -50.6     0.000     -43.4     0.000
X₂                                  1.36      0.051

S                         15.5                13.9
R-sq                      75.39%              80.59%

α to enter = 0.1, α to remove = 0.1
```

14.37. Shown here are the data for y and three predictors, x_1, x_2, and x_3. A stepwise regression procedure has been done on these data; the results are also given. Comment on the outcome of the stepwise analysis in light of the data.

y	x_1	x_2	x_3
94	21	1	204
97	25	0	198
93	22	1	184
95	27	0	200
90	29	1	182
91	20	1	159
91	18	1	147
94	25	0	196
98	26	0	228
99	24	0	242
90	28	1	162
92	23	1	180
96	25	0	219

```
Candidate terms: X₁, X₂, X₃

            ----Step 1---  ----Step 2----  ----Step 3----
            Coef     P      Coef     P      Coef     P
Constant    74.81           82.18           87.89
X₃          0.0989   0.000  0.0670   0.004  0.0706   0.001
X₂                         -2.261    0.043  -2.714   0.005
X₁                                          -0.2561  0.013

S           1.36777         1.15604         0.850311
R-sq        81.24%          87.82%          94.07%
```

14.38. Shown below is output from two Excel regression analyses on the same problem. The first output was done on a "full" model. In the second output, the variable with the smallest absolute t value has been removed, and the regression has been rerun as a second step of a backward elimination process. Examine the two outputs. Explain what happened, what the results mean, and what might happen in a third step.

FULL MODEL

Regression Statistics

Multiple R	0.567
R Square	0.321
Adjusted R Square	0.208
Standard Error	159.681
Observations	29

ANOVA

	df	SS	MS	F	Significance F
Regression	4	289856.08	72464.02	2.84	0.046
Residual	24	611955.23	25498.13		
Total	28	901811.31			

	Coefficients	Standard Error	t Stat	P-value
Intercept	336.79	124.0800	2.71	0.012
X_1	1.65	1.7800	0.93	0.363
X_2	−5.63	13.4700	−0.42	0.680
X_3	0.26	1.6800	0.16	0.878
X_4	185.50	66.2200	2.80	0.010

SECOND MODEL

Regression Statistics

Multiple R	0.566
R Square	0.321
Adjusted R Square	0.239
Standard Error	156.534
Observations	29

ANOVA

	df	SS	MS	F	Significance F
Regression	3	289238.10	96412.70	3.93	0.020
Residual	25	612573.20	24502.90		
Total	28	901811.30			

	Coefficients	Standard Error	t Stat	P-value
Intercept	342.92	115.34	2.97	0.006
X_1	1.83	1.31	1.40	0.174
X_2	−5.75	13.18	−0.44	0.667
X_4	181.22	59.05	3.07	0.005

14.39. Shown below is Minitab output from a logistic regression analysis to develop a model to predict whether a shopper in a mall store will purchase something by the number of miles the shopper drives to get to the mall store. The original data were coded as 1 if the shopper purchases something and 0 if they do not. Study the output and determine the model. Discuss the strength or lack of strength of the model and the predictor. Use the output to compute the predicted probability that a person would purchase something if he/she drives 5 miles to get to the store. Now calculate the probabilities for 4 miles, 3 miles, 2 miles, and 1 mile. What happens to the probability over these values?

```
Variable        Value       Count
Service           1            65 (Event)
                  0            55
                Total         120

Coefficients

Term           Coef      SE Coef   Z-Value  P-Value
Constant      -3.94828   0.736737  -5.36    0.000
Miles to Store 1.36988   0.255838   5.35    0.000

Regression Equation

P(1) = exp(Y')/(1 + exp(Y'))

Y' = -3.94828 + 1.36988 Miles to Store
```

Analyzing the Databases

see www.wiley.com/college/black and **WileyPlus**

1. Use the Manufacturing database to develop a multiple regression model to predict Cost of Materials by Number of Employees, New Capital Expenditures, Value Added by Manufacture, Value of Industry Shipments, and End-of- Year Inventories. Create indicator variables for values of industry shipments that have been coded from 1 to 4. Use a stepwise regression procedure. Does multicollinearity appear to be a problem in this analysis? Discuss the results of the analysis.

2. Construct a correlation matrix for the Hospital database variables. Are some of the variables highly correlated? Which ones and why? Perform a stepwise multiple regression analysis to predict Personnel by Control, Service, Beds, Admissions, Census, Outpatients, and Births. The variables Control and Service will need to be coded as indicator variables. Control has four subcategories, and Service has two.

3. Develop a regression model using the Financial database. Use Total Revenues, Total Assets, Return on Equity, Earnings per Share, Average Yield, and Dividends per Share to predict the average P/E ratio for a company. How strong is the model? Use stepwise regression to help sort out the variables. Several of these variables may be measuring similar things. Construct a correlation matrix to explore the possibility of multicollinearity among the predictors.

4. Using the International Stock Market database, conduct a stepwise multiple regression procedure to predict the DJIA by the Nasdaq, the S&P 500, the Nikkei, the Hang Seng, the FTSE 100, and the IPC. Discuss the outcome of the analysis including the model, the strength of the model, and the predictors.

Case

Virginia Semiconductor

Virginia Semiconductor, Inc. is a leading manufacturer of prime silicon substrates and is the top on-line source for silicon wafers and substrates in the World. The company, situated in Fredericksburg,

Virginia, was founded in 1978 by Dr. Thomas G. Digges and his brother, Robert.

Virginia Semiconductor was growing and prospering in the early 1980s by selling a high volume of low-profit-margin wafers in the microelectronic industry. However, in 1985, without notice, the company lost two major customers that represented 65% of its business. Left with only 35% of its sales base, the company desperately needed customers.

Dr. Digges, CEO of Virginia Semiconductor, decided to seek markets where his company's market share would be small but profit margin would be high because of the value of its engineering research and its expertise. This decision turned out to be a wise direction for the small, versatile company. Virginia Semiconductor developed a silicon wafer that was two inches in diameter, 75 microns thick, and polished off on both sides. Such wafers were needed by several customers but had never been produced before. They produced a number of these wafers and sold them for more than 10 times the price of conventional wafers.

Soon the company was making wafers from 2 to 4 microns thick (extremely thin), wafers with textured surfaces for infrared applications, and wafers with micro-machined holes or shapes and selling them in specialized markets. The company was able to deliver these products faster than competitors were able to deliver standard wafers.

Having made inroads at replacing lost sales, Virginia Semiconductor still had to streamline operations and control inventory and expenses. No layoffs occurred, but the average work week dropped to 32 hours and the president took an 80% pay reduction for a time. Expenses were cut as far as seemed possible. The company had virtually no long-term debt and fortunately was able to make it through this period without incurring any additional significant debt. The absence of large monthly debt payments enabled the company to respond quickly to new production needs.

Virginia Semiconductor improved production quality by cross-training employees. In addition, the company participated in the state of Virginia's economic development efforts to find markets in Europe, Japan, Korea, and Israel. Exports, which were only 1% of the company's business in 1985, grew to over 40%.

The company continues to find new customers because of product development. Virginia Semiconductor has a worldwide distribution network in 29 countries on four continents. Today, SOI (silicon on insulator) substrates are its fastest growing product. Virginia Semiconductor has received numerous business awards and holds over 15 U.S. Patents and Trademarks.

Discussion

1. It is often useful to decision makers at a company to determine what factors enter into the size of a customer's purchase. Suppose decision makers at Virginia Semiconductor want to determine from past data what variables might be predictors of size of purchase and are able to gather some data on various customer companies. Assume the following data represent information gathered for 16 companies on five variables: the total amount of purchases made during a one-year period (size of purchase), the size of the purchasing company (in total sales volume), the percentage of all purchases made by the customer company that were imports, the distance of the customer company from Virginia Semiconductor, and whether the customer company had a single central purchasing agent. Use these data to generate a multiple regression model to predict size of purchase by the other variables. Summarize your findings in terms of the strength of the model, significant predictor variables, and any new variables generated by recoding.

SIZE OF PURCHASE ($1,000)	COMPANY SIZE ($ MILLION SALES)	PERCENT OF CUSTOMER IMPORTS	DISTANCE FROM VIRGINIA SEMICONDUCTOR	CENTRAL PURCHASER?
27.9	25.6	41	18	1
89.6	109.8	16	75	0
12.8	39.4	29	14	0
34.9	16.7	31	117	0
408.6	278.4	14	209	1
173.5	98.4	8	114	1
105.2	101.6	20	75	0
510.6	139.3	17	50	1
382.7	207.4	53	35	1
84.6	26.8	27	15	1
101.4	13.9	31	19	0
27.6	6.8	22	7	0
234.8	84.7	5	89	1
464.3	180.3	27	306	1
309.8	132.6	18	73	1
294.6	118.9	16	11	1

2. Suppose that the next set of data is Virginia Semiconductor's sales figures for the past 11 years, along with the average number of hours worked per week by a full-time employee and the number of different customers the company has for its unique wafers. How do the average workweek length and number of customers relate to total sales figures? Use scatter plots to examine possible relationships between sales and hours per week and sales and number of customers. Use Tukey's four-quadrant approach for possible ways to recode the data. Use stepwise regression analysis to explore the relationships. Let the response variable be "sales" and the predictors be "average number of hours worked per week," "number of customers," and any new variables created by recoding. Explore quadratic relationships, interaction, and other relationships that seem appropriate by using stepwise regression. Summarize your findings in terms of model strength and significant predictors.

AVERAGE SALES ($ MILLION)	HOURS WORKED PER WEEK	NUMBER OF CUSTOMERS
15.6	44	54
15.7	43	52
15.4	41	55
14.3	41	55
11.8	40	39
9.7	40	28
9.6	40	37
10.2	38	58
11.3	38	67
14.3	32	186
14.8	37	226

3. As Virginia Semiconductor continues to grow and prosper, the potential for slipping back into inefficient ways is always present. Suppose that after a few years the company's sales begin to level off, but it continues hiring employees. Such figures over a 10-year period of time may look like the data given here. Graph these data, using sales as the response variable and number of employees as the predictor. Study the graph in light of Tukey's four-quadrant approach. Using the information learned, develop a regression model to predict sales by the number of employees. On the basis of what you find, what would you recommend to management about the trend if it were to continue? What do you see in these data that would concern management?

SALES ($ MILLION)	NUMBER OF EMPLOYEES
20.2	120
24.3	122
28.6	127
33.7	135
35.2	142
35.9	156
36.3	155
36.2	167
36.5	183
36.6	210

Source: Adapted from the Virginia Semiconductor Inc. website, https://www.virginiasemi.com/ and from "Virginia Semiconductor: A New Beginning." *Real World Lessons for America's Small Businesses: Insights from the Blue Chip Enterprise Initiative 1994.* Published by *Nation's Business* magazine on behalf of Connecticut Mutual Life Insurance Company and the U.S. Chamber of Commerce in association with the Blue Chip Enterprise Initiative, 1994.

CHAPTER 15

Time-Series Forecasting and Index Numbers

LEARNING OBJECTIVES

This chapter discusses the general use of forecasting in business, several tools that are available for making business forecasts, the nature of time-series data, and the role of index numbers in business, thereby enabling you to:

1. Differentiate among various measurements of forecasting error, including mean absolute deviation and mean square error, in order to assess which forecasting method to use.

2. Describe smoothing techniques for forecasting models, including naïve, simple average, moving average, weighted moving average, and exponential smoothing.

3. Determine trend in time-series data by using linear regression trend analysis, quadratic model trend analysis, and Holt's two-parameter exponential smoothing method.

4. Account for seasonal effects of time-series data by using decomposition and Winters' three-parameter exponential smoothing method.

5. Test for autocorrelation using the Durbin-Watson test, overcoming autocorrelation by adding independent variables and transforming variables, and taking advantage of autocorrelation with autoregression.

6. Differentiate among simple index numbers, unweighted aggregate price index numbers, weighted aggregate price index numbers, Laspeyres price index numbers, and Paasche price index numbers by defining and calculating each.

Decision Dilemma

Forecasting Air Pollution

For the past two decades, there has been a heightened awareness of and increased concern over pollution in various forms in the United States. One of the main areas of environmental concern is air pollution, and the U.S. Environmental Protection Agency (EPA) regularly monitors the quality of air around the country. Some of the air pollutants monitored include carbon monoxide emissions, nitrogen oxide emissions, volatile organic compounds, sulfur dioxide emissions, particulate matter, fugitive dust, and lead emissions. Shown below are emission data for two of these air pollution variables, carbon monoxide and nitrogen oxides, over a 24-year period reported by the EPA in millions short-tons.

All Canada Photos/Alamy

YEAR	CARBON MONOXIDE	NITROGEN OXIDES
1991	147.13	25.18
1992	140.90	25.26
1993	135.90	25.36
1994	133.56	25.35
1995	126.78	24.96
1996	128.86	24.79
1997	117.91	24.71
1998	115.38	24.35
1999	114.54	22.85
2000	114.47	22.60
2001	106.26	21.55
2002	102.03	23.96
2003	99.60	22.65
2004	97.15	21.33
2005	88.55	20.36
2006	85.84	19.23
2007	83.13	18.10
2008	79.66	16.91
2009	72.75	15.77
2010	73.77	14.85
2011	73.76	14.52
2012	71.76	13.66
2013	69.76	13.07
2014	67.76	12.41

MANAGERIAL AND STATISTICAL QUESTIONS

1. Is it possible to forecast the emissions of carbon monoxide or nitrogen oxides for the year 2017, 2021, or even 2029 using these data?

2. What techniques best forecast the emissions of carbon monoxide or nitrogen oxides for future years from these data?

Source: National Emissions Inventory (NEI) Air Pollutant Emissions Trends Data. Retrieved October 28, 2015, from http://www3.epa.gov/ttnchie1/trends.

Every day, **forecasting**—*the art or science of predicting the future*—is used in the decision-making process to help business people reach conclusions about buying, selling, producing, hiring, and many other actions. As an example, consider the following items:

- Market watchers predict a resurgence of stock values next year.
- Future brightens for wind power.
- Economist says other sectors to feel oil's decline.
- The baby care market will grow in the next decade.
- CEO says difficult times won't be ending soon for U.S. airline industry.
- Life insurance outlook fades.
- Increased competition from overseas businesses will result in significant layoffs in the U.S. computer chip industry.

How are these and other conclusions reached? What forecasting techniques are used? Are the forecasts accurate? In this chapter we discuss several forecasting techniques, how to measure the error of a forecast, and some of the problems that can occur in forecasting. In addition, this chapter will focus only on data that occur over time, time-series data.

Time-series data are *data gathered on a given characteristic over a period of time at regular intervals.* Time-series forecasting techniques attempt to account for changes over time by examining patterns, cycles, or trends, or using information about previous time periods to predict the outcome for a future time period. Time-series methods include naïve methods, averaging, smoothing, regression trend analysis, and the decomposition of the possible time-series factors, all of which are discussed in subsequent sections.

15.1 Introduction to Forecasting

Virtually all areas of business, including production, sales, employment, transportation, distribution, and inventory, produce and maintain time-series data. Table 15.1 provides an example of time-series data released by the Office of Market Finance, U.S. Department of the Treasury. The table contains the bond yield rates of three-month Treasury Bills for a 17-year period.

TABLE 15.1

Bond Yields of Three-Month Treasury Bills

YEAR	AVERAGE YIELD
1	14.03%
2	10.69
3	8.63
4	9.58
5	7.48
6	5.98
7	5.82
8	6.69
9	8.12
10	7.51
11	5.42
12	3.45
13	3.02
14	4.29
15	5.51
16	5.02
17	5.07

Why does the average yield differ from year to year? Is it possible to use these time series data to predict average yields for year 18 or ensuing years? **Figure 15.1** is a graph of these data over time. Often graphical depiction of time-series data can give a clue about any trends, cycles, or relationships that might be present. Does the graph in Figure 15.1 show that bond yields are decreasing? Will next year's yield rate be lower or is a cycle occurring in these data that will result in an increase? To answer such questions, it is sometimes helpful to determine which of the four components of time-series data exist in the data being studied.

Time-Series Components

It is generally believed that time-series data are composed of four elements: trend, cycles, seasonal effects, and irregular fluctuations. Not all time-series data have all these elements. Consider **Figure 15.2**, which shows the effects of these time-series elements on data over a period of 13 years.

The long-term general direction of data is referred to as **trend**. Notice that even though the data depicted in Figure 15.2 move through upward and downward periods, the general direction or trend is increasing (denoted in Figure 15.2 by the line). **Cycles** are *patterns of highs and lows through which data move over time periods usually of more than a year*. Notice that the data in Figure 15.2 seemingly move through two periods or cycles of highs and lows over a 13-year period. Time-series data that do not extend over a long period of time may not have enough "history" to show **cyclical effects**. **Seasonal effects**, on the other hand, are *shorter cycles, which usually occur in time periods of less than one year*. Often seasonal effects are measured by the month, but they may occur by quarter, or may be measured in as small a time frame as a week or even a day. Note the seasonal effects shown in Figure 15.2 as up and down cycles, many of which occur during a 1-year period. **Irregular fluctuations** are *rapid changes or "bleeps" in the data, which occur in even shorter time frames than seasonal effects*. Irregular fluctuations can happen as often as day to day. They are subject to momentary change and are often unexplained. Note the irregular fluctuations in the data of Figure 15.2.

Observe again the bond yield data depicted in Figure 15.1. The general trend seems to move downward and contain two cycles. Each of the cycles traverses approximately 5 to 8 years. It is possible, although not displayed here, that seasonal periods of highs and lows within each year result in seasonal bond yields. In addition, irregular daily fluctuations of bond yield rates may occur but are unexplainable.

Time-series data that contain no trend, cyclical, or seasonal effects are said to be **stationary**. Techniques used to forecast stationary data analyze only the irregular fluctuation effects.

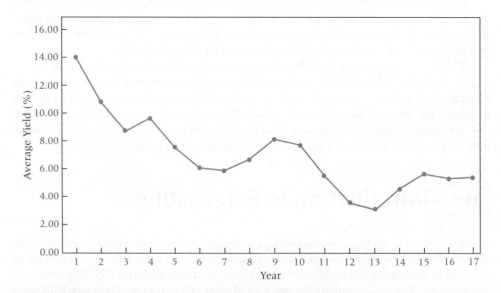

FIGURE 15.1 **Excel Graph of Bond Yield Time-Series Data (new)**

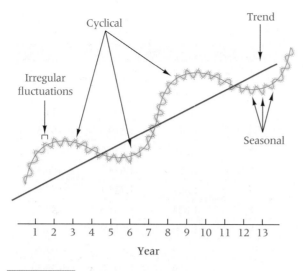

FIGURE 15.2 Time-Series Effects

The Measurement of Forecasting Error

In this chapter, several forecasting techniques will be introduced that typically produce different forecasts. How does a decision maker know which forecasting technique is doing the best job in predicting the future? One way is to compare forecast values with actual values and determine the amount of **forecasting error** a technique produces. An examination of individual errors gives some insight into the accuracy of the forecasts. However, this process can be tedious, especially for large data sets, and often a single measurement of overall forecasting error is needed for the entire set of data under consideration. Any of several methods can be used to compute error in forecasting. The choice depends on the forecaster's objective, the forecaster's familiarity with the technique, and the method of error measurement used by the computer forecasting software. Several techniques can be used to measure overall error, including mean error (ME), mean absolute deviation (MAD), mean square error (MSE), mean percentage error (MPE), and mean absolute percentage error (MAPE). Here we will consider the mean absolute deviation (MAD) and the mean square error (MSE).

Error

The **error of an individual forecast** is *the difference between the actual value and the forecast of that value.*

Error of an Individual Forecast

$$e_t = x_t - F_t$$

where

e_t = the error of the forecast
x_t = the actual value
F_t = the forecast value

Mean Absolute Deviation (MAD)

One measure of overall error in forecasting is the mean absolute deviation, MAD. The **mean absolute deviation (MAD)** is *the mean, or average, of the absolute values of the errors.* Table 15.2 presents the nonfarm partnership tax returns (1000) in the United States over an 11-year period along with the forecast for each year and the error of the forecast. An examination of these data reveals that some of the forecast errors are positive and some are negative. In summing these errors in an attempt to compute an overall measure of error, the

TABLE 15.2	Nonfarm Partnership Tax Returns		
YEAR	ACTUAL	FORECAST	ERROR
1	1,402	—	—
2	1,458	1,402	56.0
3	1,553	1,441.2	111.8
4	1,613	1,519.5	93.5
5	1,676	1,585.0	91.0
6	1,755	1,648.7	106.3
7	1,807	1,723.1	83.9
8	1,824	1,781.8	42.2
9	1,826	1,811.3	14.7
10	1,780	1,821.6	−41.6
11	1,759	1,792.5	−33.5

negative and positive values offset each other, resulting in an underestimation of the total error. The mean absolute deviation overcomes this problem by taking the absolute value of the error measurement, thereby analyzing the magnitude of the forecast errors without regard to direction.

Mean Absolute Deviation

$$MAD = \frac{\Sigma |e_i|}{\text{Number of Forecasts}}$$

The mean absolute error can be computed for the forecast errors in Table 15.2 as follows.

$$MAD = \frac{|56.0| + |111.8| + |93.5| + |91.0| + |106.3| + |83.9| + |42.2| + |14.7| + |-41.6| + |-33.5|}{10} = 67.45$$

Mean Square Error (MSE)

The **mean square error (MSE)** is another way to circumvent the problem of the canceling effects of positive and negative forecast errors. The MSE is *computed by squaring each error (thus creating a positive number) and averaging the squared errors.* The following formula states it more formally.

Mean Square Error

$$MSE = \frac{\Sigma e_i^2}{\text{Number of Forecasts}}$$

The mean square error can be computed for the errors shown in Table 15.2 as follows.

$$MSE = \frac{(56.0)^2 + (111.8)^2 + (93.5)^2 + (91.0)^2 + (106.3)^2 + (83.9)^2 + (42.2)^2 + (14.7)^2 + (-41.6)^2 + (-33.5)^2}{10} = 5,584.7$$

Selection of a particular mechanism for computing error is up to the forecaster. It is important to understand that different error techniques will yield different information. The business researcher should be informed enough about the various error measurement techniques to make an educated evaluation of the forecasting results.

15.1. Use the forecast errors given here to compute MAD and MSE. Discuss the information yielded by each type of error measurement.

PERIOD	e
1	2.3
2	1.6
3	−1.4
4	1.1
5	.3
6	−.9
7	−1.9
8	−2.1
9	.7

15.2. Determine the error for each of the following forecasts. Compute MAD and MSE.

PERIOD	VALUE	FORECAST	ERROR
1	202	—	—
2	191	202	
3	173	192	
4	169	181	
5	171	174	
6	175	172	
7	182	174	
8	196	179	
9	204	189	
10	219	198	
11	227	211	

15.3. Using the following data, determine the values of MAD and MSE. Which of these measurements of error seems to yield the best information about the forecasts? Why?

PERIOD	VALUE	FORECAST
1	19.4	16.6
2	23.6	19.1
3	24.0	22.0
4	26.8	24.8
5	29.2	25.9
6	35.5	28.6

15.4. Figures for acres of tomatoes harvested in the United States from an 11-year period follow. The data are published by the U.S. Department of Agriculture. With these data, forecasts have been made by using techniques presented later in this chapter. Compute MAD and MSE on these forecasts. Comment on the errors.

YEAR	NUMBER OF ACRES	FORECAST
1	140,000	—
2	141,730	140,000
3	134,590	141,038
4	131,710	137,169
5	131,910	133,894
6	134,250	132,704
7	135,220	133,632
8	131,020	134,585
9	120,640	132,446
10	115,190	125,362
11	114,510	119,259

15.2 Smoothing Techniques

Several techniques are available to forecast time-series data that are stationary or that include no significant trend, cyclical, or seasonal effects. These techniques are often referred to as **smoothing techniques** because they *produce forecasts based on "smoothing out" the irregular fluctuation effects in the time-series data.* Three general categories of smoothing techniques are presented here: (1) naïve forecasting models, (2) averaging models, and (3) exponential smoothing.

Naïve Forecasting Models

Naïve forecasting models are *simple models in which it is assumed that the more recent time periods of data represent the best predictions or forecasts for future outcomes.* Naïve models do not take into account data trend, cyclical effects, or seasonality. For this reason, naïve models seem to work better with data that are reported on a daily or weekly basis or in situations that show no trend or seasonality. The simplest of the naïve forecasting methods is the model in which the forecast for a given time period is the value for the previous time period.

$$F_t = x_{t-1}$$

where

F_t = the forecast value for time period t

x_{t-1} = the value for time period $t - 1$

As an example, if 532 pairs of shoes were sold by a retailer last week, this naïve forecasting model would predict that the retailer will sell 532 pairs of shoes this week. With this naïve model, the actual sales for this week will be the forecast for next week.

Observe the agricultural data in Table 15.3 representing the total reported domestic rail, truck, and air shipments of bell peppers in the United States for a given year reported by the U.S. Department of Agriculture. Figure 15.3 presents an Excel graph of these shipments over the 12-month period. From these data, we can make a naïve forecast of the total number of reported shipments of bell peppers for January of the next year by using the figure for December, which is 412.

Another version of the naïve forecast might be to use the number of shipments for January of the previous year as the forecast for January of next year, because the business researcher may believe a relationship exists between bell pepper shipments and the month of the year. In this case, the naïve forecast for next January from Table 15.3 is 336 (January of the previous year). The forecaster is free to be creative with the naïve forecast model method and search for other relationships or rationales within the limits of the time-series data that would seemingly produce a valid forecast.

Averaging Models

Many naïve model forecasts are based on the value of one time period. Often such forecasts become a function of irregular fluctuations of the data; as a result, the forecasts are "over-steered." Using averaging models, a forecaster enters information from several time periods into the forecast and "smoothes" the data. Averaging models are computed by *averaging data from several time periods and using the average as the forecast for the next time period.*

TABLE 15.3	Total Reported Domestic Shipments of Bell Peppers
MONTH	**SHIPMENTS (millions of pounds)**
January	336
February	308
March	582
April	771
May	935
June	808
July	663
August	380
September	333
October	412
November	458
December	412

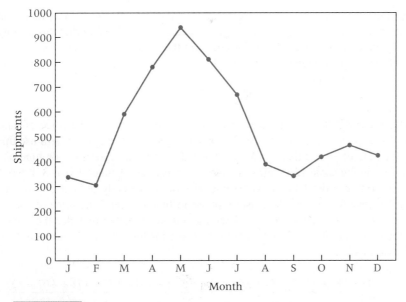

FIGURE 15.3 **Excel Graph of Shipments of Bell Peppers over a 12-Month Period**

Simple Averages

The most elementary of the averaging models is the **simple average model**. With this model, *the forecast for time period t is the average of the values for a given number of previous time periods,* as shown in the following equation:

$$F_t = \frac{X_{t-1} + X_{t-2} + X_{t-3} + \cdots + X_{t-n}}{n}$$

The data in Table 15.4 provide the prices of natural gas in the United States for 3 years. Figure 15.4 displays a Minitab graph of these data.

A simple 12-month average could be used to forecast the price of natural gas for June of year 3 from the data in Table 15.4 by averaging the values for June of year 2 through May of year 3 (the preceding 12 months).

$$F_{June, year 3} = \frac{2.50 + 2.96 + 2.81 + 2.92 + 3.50 + 3.69 + 3.44 + 3.35 + 3.31 + 3.77 + 4.16 + 4.07}{12} = 3.37$$

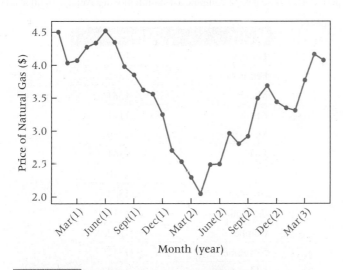

FIGURE 15.4 **Minitab Graph of Natural Gas Futures Data**

TABLE 15.4	
Prices of Natural Gas Futures ($)	
TIME FRAME	PRICE OF NATURAL GAS ($)
January (year 1)	4.50
February	4.04
March	4.07
April	4.27
May	4.34
June	4.52
July	4.35
August	3.98
September	3.85
October	3.62
November	3.56
December	3.25
January (year 2)	2.71
February	2.53
March	2.30
April	2.05
May	2.49
June	2.50
July	2.96
August	2.81
September	2.92
October	3.50
November	3.69
December	3.44
January (year 3)	3.35
February	3.31
March	3.77
April	4.16
May	4.07

With this **simple average**, the forecast for the year 3 June price of natural gas is $3.37. Note that none of the previous 12-month figures equal this value and that this average is not necessarily more closely related to values early in the period than to those late in the period. The use of the simple average over 12 months tends to smooth the variations, or fluctuations, that occur during this time.

Moving Averages

Suppose we were to attempt to forecast the price of natural gas for July of year 3 by using averages as the forecasting method. Would we still use the simple average for June of year 2 through May of year 3 as we did to forecast for June of year 3? Instead of using the same 12 months' average used to forecast June of year 3, it would seem to make sense to use the 12 months prior to July of year 3 (July of year 2 through June of year 3) to average for the new forecast. Suppose in June of year 3 the price of natural gas is $3.37. We could forecast July of year 3 with a new average that includes the same months used to forecast June of year 3, but without the value for June of year 2 and with the value of June of year 3 added.

$$F_{July, year 3} = \frac{2.96 + 2.81 + 2.92 + 3.50 + 3.69 + 3.44 + 3.35 + 3.31 + 3.77 + 4.16 + 4.07 + 3.37}{12} = 3.45$$

Computing an average of the values from July of year 2 through June of year 3 produces a **moving average**, which can be used to forecast the price of natural gas for July of year 3. In computing this moving average, the earliest of the previous 12 values, June of year 2, is dropped and the most recent value, June of year 3, is included.

A **moving average** is *an average that is updated or recomputed for every new time period being considered*. The most recent information is utilized in each new moving average. This advantage is offset by the disadvantages that (1) it is difficult to choose the optimal length of time for which to compute the moving average, and (2) moving averages do not usually adjust for such time-series effects as trend, cycles, or seasonality. To determine the more optimal lengths for which to compute the moving averages, we would need to forecast with several different average lengths and compare the errors produced by them.

DEMONSTRATION PROBLEM 15.1

Shown here are shipments (in millions of dollars) for electric lighting and wiring equipment over a 12-month period. Use these data to compute a 4-month moving average for all available months.

MONTH	SHIPMENTS
January	1056
February	1345
March	1381
April	1191
May	1259
June	1361
July	1110
August	1334
September	1416
October	1282
November	1341
December	1382

Solution: The first moving average is

$$\text{4-Month Moving Average} = \frac{1056 + 1345 + 1381 + 1191}{4} = 1243.25$$

This first 4-month moving average can be used to forecast the shipments in May. Because 1259 shipments were actually made in May, the error of the forecast is

$$\text{Error}_{\text{May}} = 1259 - 1243.25 = 15.75$$

Shown next, along with the monthly shipments, are the 4-month moving averages and the errors of forecast when using the 4-month moving averages to predict the next month's shipments. The first moving average is displayed beside the month of May because it is computed by using January, February, March, and April and because it is being used to forecast the shipments for May. The rest of the 4-month moving averages and errors of forecast are as shown.

4-MONTH MOVING FORECAST			
MONTH	SHIPMENTS	AVERAGE	ERROR
January	1056	—	—
February	1345	—	—
March	1381	—	—
April	1191	—	—
May	1259	1243.25	15.75
June	1361	1294.00	67.00
July	1110	1298.00	−188.00
August	1334	1230.25	103.75
September	1416	1266.00	150.00
October	1282	1305.25	−23.25
November	1341	1285.50	55.50
December	1382	1343.25	38.75

The following Minitab graph shows the actual shipment values and the forecast shipment values based on the 4-month moving averages. Notice that the moving averages are "smoothed" in comparison with the individual data values. They appear to be less volatile and seem to be attempting to follow the general trend of the data.

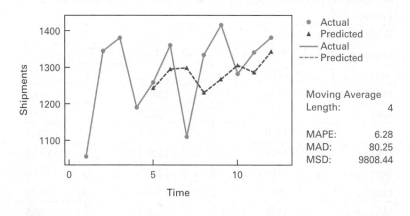

Weighted Moving Averages A forecaster may want to place more weight on certain periods of time than on others. For example, a forecaster might believe that the previous month's value is three times as important in forecasting as other months. *A moving average in which some time periods are weighted differently than others* is called a **weighted moving average**.

As an example, suppose a 3-month weighted average is computed by weighting last month's value by 3, the value for the previous month by 2, and the value for the month before that by 1. This weighted average is computed as

$$\bar{x}_{weighted} = \frac{3(M_{t-1}) + 2(M_{t-2}) + 1(M_{t-3})}{6}$$

where

M_{t-1} = last month's value
M_{t-2} = value for the previous month
M_{t-3} = value for the month before the previous month

Notice that the divisor is 6. With a weighted average, the divisor always equals the total number of weights. In this example, the value of M_{t-1} counts three times as much as the value for M_{t-3}.

DEMONSTRATION PROBLEM 15.2

Compute a 4-month weighted moving average for the electric lighting and wiring data from Demonstration Problem 15.1, using weights of 4 for last month's value, 2 for the previous month's value, and 1 for each of the values from the 2 months prior to that.

Solution: The first weighted average is

$$\frac{4(1191) + 2(1381) + 1(1345) + 1(1056)}{8} = 1240.875$$

This moving average is recomputed for each ensuing month. Displayed next are the monthly values, the weighted moving averages, and the forecast error for the data.

MONTH	SHIPMENTS	4-MONTH WEIGHTED MOVING AVERAGE FORECAST	ERROR
January	1056	—	—
February	1345	—	—
March	1381	—	—
April	1191	—	—
May	1259	1240.9	18.1
June	1361	1268.0	93.0
July	1110	1316.8	−206.8
August	1334	1201.5	132.5
September	1416	1272.0	144.0
October	1282	1350.4	−68.4
November	1341	1300.5	40.5
December	1382	1334.8	47.2

Note that in this problem the errors obtained by using the 4-month weighted moving average were greater than most of the errors obtained by using an unweighted 4-month moving average, as shown here.

FORECAST ERROR, UNWEIGHTED 4-MONTH MOVING AVERAGE	FORECAST ERROR, WEIGHTED 4-MONTH MOVING AVERAGE
—	—
—	—
—	—
—	—
15.8	18.1
67.0	93.0
−188.0	−206.8
103.8	132.5
150.0	144.0
−23.3	−68.4
55.5	40.5
38.8	47.2

Larger errors with weighted moving averages are not always the case. The forecaster can experiment with different weights in using the weighted moving average as a technique. Many possible weighting schemes can be used.

Exponential Smoothing

Another forecasting technique, **exponential smoothing**, is *used to weight data from previous time periods with exponentially decreasing importance in the forecast.* Exponential smoothing is accomplished by multiplying the actual value for the present time period, X_t, by a value between 0 and 1 (the exponential smoothing constant) referred to as α (not the same α used for a Type I error) and adding that result to the product of the present time period's forecast, F_t, and $(1 - \alpha)$. The following is a more formalized version.

Exponential Smoothing

$$F_{t+1} = \alpha \cdot X_t + (1 - \alpha) \cdot F_t$$

where

F_{t+1} = the forecast for the next time period $(t + 1)$
F_t = the forecast for the present time period (t)
X_t = the actual value for the present time period
α = a value between 0 and 1 referred to as the exponential smoothing constant.

The value of α is determined by the forecaster. The essence of this procedure is that the new forecast is a combination of the present forecast and the present actual value. If α is chosen to be less than .5, less weight is placed on the actual value than on the forecast of that value. If α is chosen to be greater than .5, more weight is being put on the actual value than on the forecast value.

As an example, suppose the prime interest rate for a time period is 5% and the forecast of the prime interest rate for this time period was 6%. If the forecast of the prime interest rate for the next period is determined by exponential smoothing with $\alpha = .3$, the forecast is

$$F_{t+1} = (.3)(5\%) + (1.0 - .3)(6\%) = 5.7\%$$

Notice that the forecast value of 5.7% for the next period is weighted more toward the previous forecast of 6% than toward the actual value of 5% because α is .3. Suppose we use $\alpha = .7$ as the exponential smoothing constant. Then,

$$F_{t+1} = (.7)(5\%) + (1.0 - .7)(6\%) = 5.3\%$$

This value is closer to the actual value of 5% than the previous forecast of 6% because the exponential smoothing constant, α, is greater than .5.

To see why this procedure is called exponential smoothing, examine the formula for exponential smoothing again.

$$F_{t+1} = \alpha \cdot X_t + (1 - \alpha) \cdot F_t$$

If exponential smoothing has been used over a period of time, the forecast for F_t will have been obtained by

$$F_t = \alpha \cdot X_{t-1} + (1 - \alpha) \cdot F_{t-1}$$

Substituting this forecast value, F_t, into the preceding equation for F_{t+1} produces

$$F_{t+1} = \alpha \cdot X_t + (1 - \alpha)[\alpha \cdot X_{t-1} + (1 - \alpha) \cdot F_{t-1}]$$
$$= \alpha \cdot X_t + \alpha(1 - \alpha) \cdot X_{t-1} + (1 - \alpha)^2 F_{t-1}$$

but

$$F_{t-1} = \alpha \cdot X_{t-2} + (1 - \alpha)F_{t-2}$$

Substituting this value of F_{t-1} into the preceding equation for F_{t+1} produces

$$F_{t+1} = \alpha \cdot X_t + \alpha(1 - \alpha) \cdot X_{t-1} + (1 - \alpha)^2 F_{t-1}$$
$$= \alpha \cdot X_t + \alpha(1 - \alpha) \cdot X_{t-1} + (1 - \alpha)^2[\alpha \cdot X_{t-2} + (1 - \alpha)F_{t-2}]$$
$$= \alpha \cdot X_t + \alpha(1 - \alpha) \cdot X_{t-1} + \alpha(1 - \alpha)^2 \cdot X_{t-2} + (1 - \alpha)^3 F_{t-2}$$

Continuing this process shows that the weights on previous-period values and forecasts include $(1 - \alpha)^n$ (exponential values). The following chart shows the values of α, $(1 - \alpha)$, $(1 - \alpha)^2$, and $(1 - \alpha)^3$ for three different values of α. Included is the value of $\alpha(1 - \alpha)^3$, which is the weight of the actual value for three time periods back. Notice the rapidly decreasing emphasis on values for earlier time periods. The impact of exponential smoothing on time-series data is to place much more emphasis on recent time periods. The choice of α determines the amount of emphasis.

α	$1 - \alpha$	$(1 - \alpha)^2$	$(1 - \alpha)^3$	$\alpha(1 - \alpha)^3$
.2	.8	.64	.512	.1024
.5	.5	.25	.125	.0625
.8	.2	.04	.008	.0064

Some forecasters use the computer to analyze time-series data for various values of α. By setting up criteria with which to judge the forecasting errors, forecasters can select the value of α that best fits the data.

The exponential smoothing formula

$$F_{t+1} = \alpha \cdot X_t + (1 - \alpha) \cdot F_t$$

can be rearranged algebraically as

$$F_{t+1} = F_t + \alpha(X_t - F_t)$$

This form of the equation shows that the new forecast, F_{t+1}, equals the old forecast, F_t, plus an adjustment based on α times the error of the old forecast $(X_t - F_t)$. The smaller α is, the less impact the error has on the new forecast and the more the new forecast is like the old. It demonstrates the dampening effect of α on the forecasts.

DEMONSTRATION PROBLEM 15.3

The U.S. Census Bureau reports on the total units of new privately owned housing started over a 16-year recent period in the United States are given here. Use exponential smoothing to forecast the values for each ensuing time period. Work the problem using $\alpha = .2, .5,$ and $.8$.

YEAR	TOTAL UNITS (1000)
1	1193
2	1014
3	1200
4	1288
5	1457
6	1354
7	1477
8	1474
9	1617
10	1641
11	1569
12	1603
13	1705
14	1848
15	1956
16	2068

Solution: An Excel graph of these data is shown here.

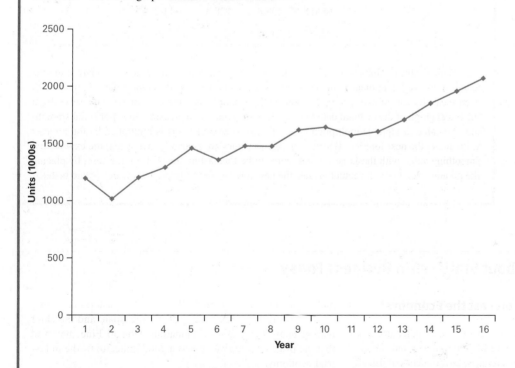

The following table provides the forecasts with each of the three values of alpha. Note that because no forecast is given for the first time period, we cannot compute a forecast based on exponential smoothing for the second period. Instead, we use the actual value for the first period as the forecast for the second period to get started. As examples, the forecasts for the third, fourth, and fifth periods are computed for $\alpha = .2$ as follows.

$$F_3 = .2(1014) + .8(1193) = 1157.2$$

$$F_4 = .2(1200) + .8(1157.2) = 1165.8$$

$$F_5 = .2(1288) + .8(1165.8) = 1190.2$$

YEAR	TOTAL UNITS (1000)	$\alpha = .2$ F	$\alpha = .2$ e	$\alpha = .5$ F	$\alpha = .5$ e	$\alpha = .8$ F	$\alpha = .8$ e
1	1193	—	—	—	—	—	—
2	1014	1193.0	−179.0	1193.0	−179.0	1193.0	−179.0
3	1200	1157.2	42.8	1103.5	96.5	1049.8	150.2
4	1288	1165.8	122.2	1151.8	136.2	1170.0	118.0
5	1457	1190.2	266.8	1219.9	237.1	1264.4	192.6
6	1354	1243.6	110.4	1338.4	15.6	1418.5	−64.5
7	1477	1265.7	211.3	1346.2	130.8	1366.9	110.1
8	1474	1307.9	166.1	1411.6	62.4	1455.0	19.0
9	1617	1341.1	275.9	1442.8	174.2	1470.2	146.8
10	1641	1396.3	244.7	1529.9	111.1	1587.6	53.4
11	1569	1445.2	123.8	1585.5	−16.5	1630.3	−61.3
12	1603	1470.0	133.0	1577.2	25.8	1581.3	21.7
13	1705	1496.6	208.4	1590.1	114.9	1598.7	106.3
14	1848	1538.3	309.7	1647.6	200.4	1683.7	164.3
15	1956	1600.2	355.8	1747.8	208.2	1815.1	140.9
16	2068	1671.4	396.6	1851.9	216.1	1927.8	140.2

	$\alpha = .2$	$\alpha = .5$	$\alpha = .8$
MAD:	209.8	128.3	111.2
MSE:	53,110.5	21,626.7	15,246.4

Which value of alpha works best on the data? At the bottom of the preceding analysis are the values of two different measurements of error for each of the three different values of alpha. With each measurement of error, $\alpha = .8$ produces the smallest measurement of error. Observe from the Excel graph of the original data that the data are generally increasing. In exponential smoothing, the value of alpha is multiplied by the actual value and $1 - \alpha$ is multiplied by the forecast value to get the next forecast. Because the actual values are generally increasing, the exponential smoothing value with the largest alpha seems to be forecasting the best. In this case, by placing the greatest weight on the actual values, the new forecast seems to predict the new value better.

Thinking Critically About Statistics in Business Today

Can Scrap Metal Prices Forecast the Economy?

Economists are constantly on the lookout for valid indicators of a country's economy. Forecasters have sifted through oil indicators, the price of gold, the Dow Jones averages, government-published indexes, and practically anything else that might seem related in some way to the economy.

One rather promising indicator of economic activity in the United States back in the 1990s was the price of scrap metal. At the time, several well-known forecasters, including the Federal Reserve chairman, Alan Greenspan, and the chief market analyst for Chase Manhattan, Donald Fine, believed that the price of scrap metal was a good indicator of the industrial economy.

Scrap metal is leftover copper, steel, aluminum, and other metals. The theory was that as U.S. manufacturing increases, the demand for scrap metals increases, as does their price, because as the industrial economy heats up, inventories of readily available metals are reduced, thereby increasing the demand for scrap metal. In the past, in some cases, the price of scrap metal correctly predicted no economic recovery when some government measures indicated that a recovery was underway.

Now, 20 years later, it is a new world economy and the United States is impacted by growth and demand for metals in other countries. Demand for steel and other metals in China, India, Turkey, the Middle East, and other emerging areas of the world has helped drive up the price of scrap metal in the United States even when the U.S. economy has been somewhat stagnant. That is, perhaps the price of scrap metal in the United States is now more of a forecaster of the world economy than the U.S. economy.

As a side note, as the U.S. economy has gone through a down cycle, supplies of scrap metal from individual sellers have increased. In tough economic times, instead of trashing old bicycles, appliances, and other items containing metals, people have been selling them to scrap-metal recyclers to earn extra household income.

THINGS TO PONDER

1. According to the Institute of Scrap Recycling Industries (ISRI), the U.S.-based scrap recycling industry meets 40% of the global raw materials needs. If this is so, the scrap recycling industry is heavily involved in world industrial growth. Do you think that this source will continually replenish itself or eventually dry up? Why or why not? What are some factors?

2. If U.S.-based scrap metal is reduced in the coming years, how might this impact world construction? Are there replacement sources? Where might such sources come from?

Source: Anita Raghavan and David Wessel, "In Scraping Together Economic Data, Forecasters Turn to Scrap-Metal Prices," *Wall Street Journal* (April 27, 1992), C1; "Scrap-Metal Recycling Grows as Economy Shrinks", WRAL.com at http://www.wral.com/news/local/story/3187137/July 2008; Industry Facts, Web site for ISRI, at http://www.isri.org/iMIS15_PROD/ISRI/About_ISRI/Industry_Facts/ISRI/Navigation/AboutISRI/Industry_Facts.aspx?hkey=9e68d6a2-7b25-4a0e-ac22-06a259f893cc, March 28, 2011.

15.2 Problems

15.5. Use the following time-series data to answer the given questions.

TIME PERIOD	VALUE	TIME PERIOD	VALUE
1	27	6	66
2	31	7	71
3	58	8	86
4	63	9	101
5	59	10	97

a. Develop forecasts for periods 5 through 10 using 4-month moving averages.

b. Develop forecasts for periods 5 through 10 using 4-month weighted moving averages. Weight the most recent month by a factor of 4, the previous month by 2, and the other months by 1.

c. Compute the errors of the forecasts in parts (a) and (b) and observe the differences in the errors forecast by the two different techniques.

15.6. Following are time-series data for eight different periods. Use exponential smoothing to forecast the values for periods 3 through 8. Use the value for the first period as the forecast for the second period. Compute forecasts using two different values of alpha, $\alpha = .1$ and $\alpha = .8$. Compute the errors for each forecast and compare the errors produced by using the two different exponential smoothing constants.

TIME PERIOD	VALUE	TIME PERIOD	VALUE
1	211	5	242
2	228	6	227
3	236	7	217
4	241	8	203

15.7. Following are time-series data for nine time periods. Use exponential smoothing with constants of .3 and .7 to forecast time periods 3 through 9. Let the value for time period 1 be the forecast for time period 2. Compute additional forecasts for time periods 4 through 9 using a 3-month moving average. Compute the errors for the forecasts and discuss the size of errors under each method.

TIME PERIOD	VALUE	TIME PERIOD	VALUE
1	9.4	6	11.0
2	8.2	7	10.3
3	7.9	8	9.5
4	9.0	9	9.1
5	9.8		

15.8. The U.S. Census Bureau publishes data on factory orders for all manufacturing, durable goods, and nondurable goods industries. Shown here are factory orders in the United States over a 13-year period ($ billion).

a. Use these data to develop forecasts for the years 6 through 13 using a 5-year moving average.

b. Use these data to develop forecasts for the years 6 through 13 using a 5-year weighted moving average. Weight the most recent year by 6, the previous year by 4, the year before that by 2, and the other years by 1.

c. Compute the errors of the forecasts in parts (a) and (b) and observe the differences in the errors of the forecasts.

YEAR	FACTORY ORDERS ($ billion)
1	2,512.7
2	2,739.2
3	2,874.9
4	2,934.1
5	2,865.7

6	2,978.5
7	3,092.4
8	3,356.8
9	3,607.6
10	3,749.3
11	3,952.0
12	3,949.0
13	4,137.0

YEAR	NUMBER OF ISSUES
1	332
2	694
3	518
4	222
5	209
6	172
7	366
8	512
9	667
10	571
11	575
12	865
13	609

15.9. The following data show the number of issues from initial public offerings (IPOs) for a 13-year period released by the Securities Data Company. Use these data to develop forecasts for the years 3 through 13 using exponential smoothing techniques with alpha values of .2 and .9. Let the forecast for year 2 be the value for year 1. Compare the results by examining the errors of the forecasts.

15.3 | Trend Analysis

There are several ways to determine trend in time-series data, and one of the more prominent is by using regression analysis. In Section 12.9, we explored the use of simple regression analysis in determining the equation of a trend line. In time-series regression trend analysis, the response variable, Y, is the variable being forecast, and the independent variable, X, represents time.

Many possible trend fits can be explored with time-series data. In this section we examine only the linear model and the quadratic model because they are the easiest to understand and simplest to compute. Because seasonal effects can confound trend analysis, it is assumed here that no seasonal effects occur in the data or they were removed prior to determining the trend.

Linear Regression Trend Analysis

The data in Table 15.5 represent 35 years of data on the average length of the workweek in Canada for manufacturing workers. A regression line can be fit to these data by using the time periods as the independent variable and length of workweek as the dependent variable. Because the time periods are consecutive, they can be entered as X along with the time-series data (Y) into a regression analysis. The linear model explored in this example is

$$Y_i = \beta_0 + \beta_1 X_{ti} + \epsilon_i$$

where

Y_i = data value for period i
X_{ti} = ith time period

Figure 15.5 shows the Excel regression output for this example. By using the coefficients of the X variable and intercept, the equation of the trend line can be determined to be

$$\hat{Y} = 37.4161 - .0614X_t$$

The slope indicates that for every unit increase in time period, X_t, a predicted decrease of .0614 occurs in the length of the average workweek in manufacturing. Because the workweek is measured in hours, the length of the average workweek decreases by an average of (.0614)(60 minutes) = 3.7 minutes each year in Canada in manufacturing. The Y intercept, 37.4161, indicates that in the year prior to the first period of these data the average workweek was 37.4161 hours.

TABLE 15.5 Average Hours per Week in Manufacturing by Canadian Workers

TIME PERIOD	HOURS	TIME PERIOD	HOURS
1	37.2	19	36.0
2	37.0	20	35.7
3	37.4	21	35.6
4	37.5	22	35.2
5	37.7	23	34.8
6	37.7	24	35.3
7	37.4	25	35.6
8	37.2	26	35.6
9	37.3	27	35.6
10	37.2	28	35.9
11	36.9	29	36.0
12	36.7	30	35.7
13	36.7	31	35.7
14	36.5	32	35.5
15	36.3	33	35.6
16	35.9	34	36.3
17	35.8	35	36.5
18	35.9		

Source: Data prepared by the U.S. Bureau of Labor Statistics, Office of Productivity and Technology.

SUMMARY OUTPUT

Regression Statistics

Multiple R	0.782
R Square	0.611
Adjusted R Square	0.600
Standard Error	0.509
Observations	35

ANOVA

	df	SS	MS	F	Significance F
Regression	1	13.447	13.447	51.91	0.00000003
Residual	33	8.549	0.259		
Total	34	21.995			

	Coefficients	Standard Error	t Stat	P-value
Intercept	37.4161	0.1758	212.81	0.000000000
Year	−0.0614	0.0085	−7.20	0.00000003

FIGURE 15.5 Excel Regression Output for Hours Worked Using Linear Trend

The probability of the t ratio (.00000003) indicates that significant linear trend is present in the data. In addition, $R^2 = .611$ indicates considerable predictability in the model. Inserting the various period values (1, 2, 3, . . . , 35) into the preceding regression equation produces the predicted values of Y that are the trend. For example, for period 23 the predicted value is

$$\hat{Y} = 37.4161 - .0614(23) = 36.0 \text{ hours}$$

The model was developed with 35 periods (years). From this model, the average workweek in Canada in manufacturing for period 41 (the 41st year) can be forecast:

$$\hat{Y} = 37.4161 - .0614(41) = 34.9 \text{ hours}$$

Figure 15.6 presents an Excel scatter plot of the average workweek lengths over the 35 periods (years). In this Excel plot, the trend line has been fitted through the points. Observe the general downward trend of the data, but also note the somewhat cyclical nature of the points. Because of this pattern, a forecaster might want to determine whether a quadratic model is a better fit for trend.

Regression Trend Analysis Using Quadratic Models

In addition to linear regression, forecasters can explore using quadratic regression models to predict data by using the time-series periods. The quadratic regression model is

$$Y_i = \beta_0 + \beta_1 X_{ti} + \beta_2 X_{ti}^2 + \epsilon_i$$

where

Y_i = the time-series data value for period i
X_{ti} = the ith period
X_{ti}^2 = the square of the ith period

This model can be implemented in time-series trend analysis by using the time periods squared as an additional predictor. Thus, in the hours worked example, besides using $X_t = 1, 2, 3, 4, \ldots, 35$ as a predictor, we would also use $X_t^2 = 1,4,9,16, \ldots, 1225$ as a predictor.

Table 15.6 provides the data needed to compute a quadratic regression trend model on the manufacturing workweek data. Note that the table includes the original data, the time periods, and the time periods squared.

The Excel computer output for this quadratic trend regression analysis is shown in Figure 15.7. We see that the quadratic regression model produces an R^2 of .761 with both

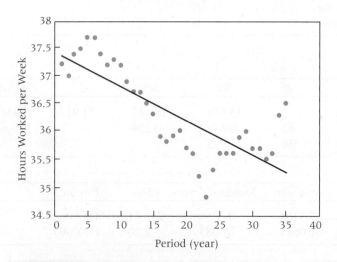

FIGURE 15.6 **Excel Graph of Canadian Manufacturing Data with Trend Line**

TABLE 15.6   Data for Quadratic Fit of Manufacturing Workweek Example

TIME PERIOD	(TIME PERIOD)²	HOURS	TIME PERIOD	(TIME PERIOD)²	HOURS
1	1	37.2	19	361	36.0
2	4	37.0	20	400	35.7
3	9	37.4	21	441	35.6
4	16	37.5	22	484	35.2
5	25	37.7	23	529	34.8
6	36	37.7	24	576	35.3
7	49	37.4	25	625	35.6
8	64	37.2	26	676	35.6
9	81	37.3	27	729	35.6
10	100	37.2	28	784	35.9
11	121	36.9	29	841	36.0
12	144	36.7	30	900	35.7
13	169	36.7	31	961	35.7
14	196	36.5	32	1024	35.5
15	225	36.3	33	1089	35.6
16	256	35.9	34	1156	36.3
17	289	35.8	35	1225	36.5
18	324	35.9			

Source: Data prepared by the U.S. Bureau of Labor Statistics, Office of Productivity and Technology.

SUMMARY OUTPUT

Regression Statistics

Multiple R	0.873
R Square	0.761
Adjusted R Square	0.747
Standard Error	0.405
Observations	35

ANOVA

	df	SS	MS	F	Significance F
Regression	2	16.748	8.374	51.07	0.0000000001
Residual	32	5.247	0.164		
Total	34	21.995			

	Coefficients	Standard Error	t Stat	P-value
Intercept	38.1644	0.2177	175.34	0.000000
Year	−0.1827	0.0279	−6.55	0.000000
Year Sq.	0.0034	0.0008	4.49	0.000088

FIGURE 15.7   Excel Regression Output for Canadian Manufacturing Example with Quadratic Trend

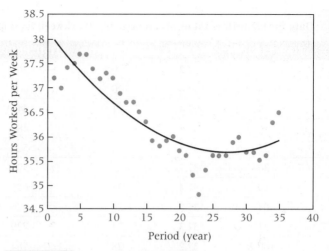

FIGURE 15.8 Excel Graph of Canadian Manufacturing Data with a Second-Degree Polynomial Fit

X_t and X_t^2 in the model. The linear model produced an R^2 of .611 with X_t alone. The quadratic regression seems to add some predictability to the trend model. **Figure 15.8** displays an Excel scatter plot of the work week data with a second-degree polynomial fit through the data.

DEMONSTRATION PROBLEM 15.4

Following are data on the employed U.S. civilian labor force (100,000) for 1993 through 2014 obtained from the U.S. Bureau of Labor Statistics. Use regression analysis to fit a trend line through the data. Explore a quadratic regression trend also. Does either model do well? Compare the two models.

YEAR	LABOR FORCE (100,000)
1993	120.26
1994	123.06
1995	124.90
1996	126.71
1997	129.56
1998	131.46
1999	133.49
2000	136.89
2001	136.93
2002	136.49
2003	137.74
2004	139.25
2005	141.73
2006	144.43
2007	146.05
2008	145.36
2009	139.90
2010	139.10
2011	139.90
2012	142.50
2013	143.93
2014	146.31

Solution: Recode the time periods as 1 through 22 and let that be X. Run the regression analysis with the labor force members as Y, the dependent variable, and the time period as the independent variable. Now square all the X values, resulting in 1, 4, 9, . . . , 400, 441, 484, and let those formulate a second predictor (X^2). Run the regression analysis to predict the number in the labor force with both the time period variable (X) and the (time period)^2 variable. The Minitab output for each of these regression analyses follows.

Regression Analysis: Labor Force (100,000) versus Year

Analysis of Variance

Source	DF	Adj SS	Adj MS	F-Value	P-Value
Regression	1	1001.2	1001.22	82.58	0.000
Error	20	242.5	12.12		
Total	21	1243.7			

Model Summary

S	R-sq	R-sq(adj)
3.48196	80.50%	79.53%

Coefficients

Term	Coef	SE Coef	T-Value	P-Value
Constant	124.41	1.54	80.95	0.000
Year	1.063	0.117	9.09	0.000

Regression Equation

Labor Force (100,000) = 124.41 + 1.063 Year

Regression Analysis: Labor Force (100,000) versus Year, Year Sq

Analysis of Variance

Source	DF	Adj SS	Adj MS	F-Value	P-Value
Regression	2	1151.25	575.625	118.30	0.000
Error	19	92.45	4.866		
Total	21	1243.70			

Model Summary

S	R-sq	R-sq(adj)
2.20589	92.57%	91.78%

Coefficients

Term	Coef	SE Coef	T-Value	P-Value
Constant	117.71	1.55	75.96	0.000
Year	2.737	0.310	8.82	0.000
Year Sq	-0.0728	0.0131	-5.55	0.000

Regression Equation

Labor Force (100,000) = 117.71 + 2.737 Year - 0.0728 Year Sq

A comparison of the models shows that the linear model accounts for 80.50% of the variability of the labor force figures. The quadratic model increases the R^2 to 92.57%. Shown next are Minitab scatter plots of the data. First is the linear model, and then the quadratic model is presented. Note the considerable reduction in forecasting error when using the quadratic model.

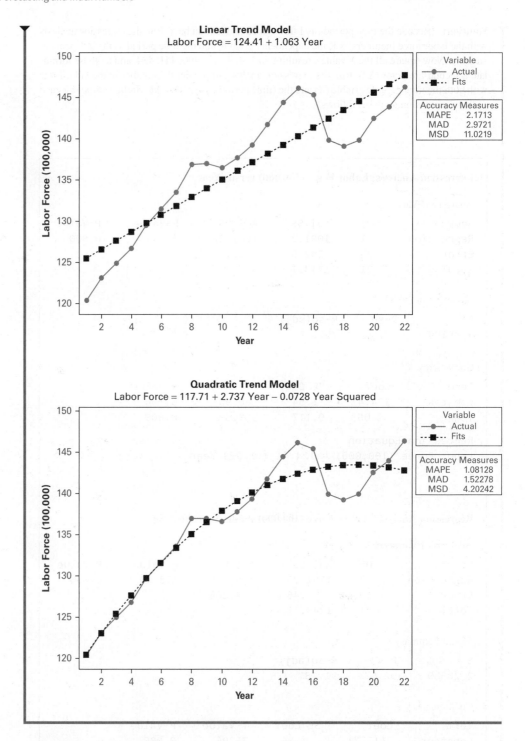

Holt's Two-Parameter Exponential Smoothing Method

The exponential smoothing technique presented in Section 15.2 (single exponential smoothing) is appropriate to use in forecasting stationary time-series data but is ineffective in forecasting time-series data with a trend because the forecasts will lag behind the trend. However, another exponential smoothing technique, Holt's two-parameter exponential smoothing method, can be used for trend analysis. Holt's technique uses weights (β) to smooth the trend in a manner similar to the smoothing used in single exponential smoothing (α). Using these two weights and several equations, Holt's method is able to develop forecasts that include both a smoothing value and a trend value. A more detailed explanation of Holt's two-parameter exponential smoothing method, along with examples and practice problems, can be accessed at WileyPLUS and at the Wiley Web site for this text.

15.3 Problems

15.10. The "Economic Report to the President of the United States" included data on the amounts of manufacturers' new and unfilled orders in millions of dollars. Shown here are the figures for new orders over a 21-year period. Use a computer to develop a regression model to fit the trend effects for these data. Use a linear model and then try a quadratic model. How well does either model fit the data?

YEAR	TOTAL NUMBER OF NEW ORDERS	YEAR	TOTAL NUMBER OF NEW ORDERS
1	55,022	12	168,025
2	55,921	13	162,140
3	64,182	14	175,451
4	76,003	15	192,879
5	87,327	16	195,706
6	85,139	17	195,204
7	99,513	18	209,389
8	115,109	19	227,025
9	131,629	20	240,758
10	147,604	21	243,643
11	156,359		

15.11. The following data on the number of union members in the United States for the years 1986 through 2014 are provided by the U.S. Bureau of Labor Statistics. Using regression techniques discussed in this section, analyze the data for trend. Develop a scatter plot of the data and fit the trend line through the data. Discuss the strength of the model.

YEAR	UNION MEMBERS (1000s)	YEAR	UNION MEMBERS (1000s)
1986	16,975	1990	16,740
1987	16,913	1991	16,568
1988	17,002	1992	16,390
1989	16,960	1993	16,598
1994	16,748	2005	15,685
1995	16,360	2006	15,359
1996	16,269	2007	15,670
1997	16,110	2008	16,098
1998	16,211	2009	15,327
1999	16,447	2010	14,715
2000	16,334	2011	14,764
2001	16,305	2012	14,366
2002	15,145	2013	14,528
2003	15,776	2014	14,576
2004	15,472		

15.12. Shown below are dollar figures for commercial and industrial loans at all commercial banks in the United States as recorded for the month of April during a recent 9-year period and published by the Federal Reserve Bank of St. Louis. Plot the data, fit a trend line, and discuss the strength of the regression model. In addition, explore a quadratic trend and compare the results of the two models.

YEAR	LOANS ($ billions)
1	741.0
2	807.4
3	871.3
4	951.6
5	1,033.6
6	1,089.8
7	1,002.6
8	940.8
9	888.5

15.4 Seasonal Effects

Earlier in the chapter, we discussed the notion that time-series data consist of four elements: trend, cyclical effects, seasonality, and irregularity. In this section, we examine techniques for identifying seasonal effects. **Seasonal effects** are *patterns of data behavior that occur in periods of time of less than one year.* How can we separate out the seasonal effects?

TABLE 15.7

Shipments of Household Appliances

YEAR	QUARTER	SHIPMENTS
1	1	4009
	2	4321
	3	4224
	4	3944
2	1	4123
	2	4522
	3	4657
	4	4030
3	1	4493
	2	4806
	3	4551
	4	4485
4	1	4595
	2	4799
	3	4417
	4	4258
5	1	4245
	2	4900
	3	4585
	4	4533

Decomposition

One of the main techniques for isolating the effects of seasonality is **decomposition**. The decomposition methodology presented here uses the multiplicative model as its basis. The multiplicative model is:

$$T \cdot C \cdot S \cdot I$$

where

T = trend
C = cycles
S = seasonal effects
I = irregular fluctuations

To illustrate the decomposition process, we will use the 5-year quarterly time-series data on U.S. shipments of household appliances given in Table 15.7. Figure 15.9 provides a graph of these data.

According to the multiplicative time-series model, $T \cdot C \cdot S \cdot I$, the data can contain the elements of trend, cycles, seasonal effects, and irregular fluctuations. The process of isolating the seasonal effects begins by determining $T \cdot C$ for each value and dividing the time-series data ($T \cdot C \cdot S \cdot I$) by $T \cdot C$. The result is

$$\frac{T \cdot C \cdot S \cdot I}{T \cdot C} = S \cdot I$$

The resulting expression contains seasonal effects along with irregular fluctuations. After reducing the time-series data to the effects of *SI* (seasonal effects and irregular fluctuations), a method for eliminating the irregular fluctuations can be applied, leaving only the seasonal effects.

Suppose we start with time-series data that cover several years and are measured in quarterly increments. If we average the data over four quarters, we will have "dampened" the seasonal effects of the data because the rise and fall of values during the quarterly periods will have been averaged out over the year.

We begin by computing a 4-quarter moving average for quarter 1 through quarter 4 of year 1, using the data from Table 15.7.

$$\text{4-quarter average} = \frac{4{,}009 + 4{,}321 + 4{,}224 + 3{,}944}{4} = 4{,}124.5$$

The 4-quarter moving average for quarter 1 through quarter 4 of year 1 is 4,124.5 ($ million) worth of shipments. Because the 4-quarter average is in the middle of the four quarters, it would be placed in the decomposition table between quarter 2 and quarter 3.

Quarter 1
Quarter 2
——— 4,124.5
Quarter 3
Quarter 4

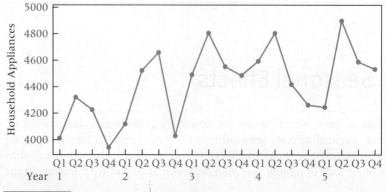

FIGURE 15.9 **Minitab Time-Series Graph of Household Appliance Data**

To remove seasonal effects, we need to determine a value that is "centered" with each quarter. To find this value, instead of using a 4-quarter moving average, we use 4-quarter moving totals and then sum two consecutive moving totals. This 8-quarter total value is divided by 8 to produce a "centered" 4-quarter moving average that lines up across from a quarter. Using this method is analogous to computing two consecutive 4-quarter moving averages and averaging them, thus producing a value that falls on line with a quarter, in between the two averages. The results of using this procedure on the data from Table 15.7 are shown in Table 15.8 in column 5.

A 4-quarter moving total can be computed on these data starting with quarter 1 of year 1 through quarter 4 of year 1 as follows:

$$\text{First Moving Total} = 4{,}009 + 4{,}321 + 4{,}224 + 3{,}944 = 16{,}498$$

In Table 15.8, 16,498 is between quarter 2 and quarter 3 of year 1. The 4-month moving total for quarter 2 of year 1 through quarter 1 of year 2 is

$$\text{Second Moving Total} = 4{,}321 + 4{,}224 + 3{,}944 + 4{,}123 = 16{,}612$$

In Table 15.8, this value is between quarter 3 and quarter 4 of year 1. The 8-quarter (2-year) moving total is computed for quarter 3 of year 1 as

$$\text{8-Quarter Moving Total} = 16{,}498 + 16{,}612 = 33{,}110$$

Notice that in Table 15.8 this value is centered with quarter 3 of year 1 because it is between the two adjacent 4-quarter moving totals. Dividing this total by 8 produces the 4-quarter moving average for quarter 3 of year 1 shown in column 5 of Table 15.8.

$$\frac{33{,}110}{8} = 4{,}139$$

TABLE 15.8 Development of 4-Quarter Moving Averages for the Household Appliance Data

QUARTER	ACTUAL VALUES $(T \cdot C \cdot S \cdot I)$	4-QUARTER MOVING TOTAL	4-QUARTER 2-YEAR MOVING TOTAL	RATIOS OF ACTUAL CENTERED MOVING AVERAGE $(T \cdot C)$	VALUES TO MOVING AVERAGES $(S \cdot I) \cdot (100)$
1 (year 1)	4,009				
2	4,321				
		16,498			
3	4,224		33,110	4,139	102.05
		16,612			
4	3,944		33,425	4,178	94.40
		16,813			
1 (year 2)	4,123		34,059	4,257	96.85
		17,246			
2	4,522		34,578	4,322	104.63
		17,332			
3	4,657		35,034	4,379	106.35
		17,702			
4	4,030		35,688	4,461	90.34
		17,986			
1 (year 3)	4,493		35,866	4,483	100.22
		17,880			
2	4,806		36,215	4,527	106.16
		18,335			
3	4,551		36,772	4,597	99.00
		18,437			
4	4,485		36,867	4,608	97.33
		18,430			
1 (year 4)	4,595		36,726	4,591	100.09
		18,296			
2	4,799		36,365	4,546	105.57
		18,069			
3	4,417		35,788	4,474	98.73
		17,719			
4	4,258		35,539	4,442	95.86
		17,820			
1 (year 5)	4,245		35,808	4,476	94.84
		17,988			
2	4,900		36,251	4,531	108.14
		18,263			
3	4,585				
4	4,533				

Column 3 contains the uncentered 4-quarter moving totals, column 4 contains the 2-year centered moving totals, and column 5 contains the 4-quarter centered moving averages.

The 4-quarter centered moving averages shown in column 5 of Table 15.8 represent $T \cdot C$. Seasonal effects have been removed from the original data (actual values) by summing across the 4-quarter periods. Seasonal effects are removed when the data are summed across the time periods that include the seasonal periods and the irregular effects are smoothed, leaving only trend and cycle.

Column 2 of Table 15.8 contains the original data (actual values), which include all effects ($T \cdot C \cdot S \cdot I$). Column 5 contains only the trend and cyclical effects, $T \cdot C$. If column 2 is divided by column 5, the result is $S \cdot I$, which is displayed in column 6 of Table 15.8.

The values in column 6, sometimes called ratios of actuals to moving average, have been multiplied by 100 to index the values. These values are thus seasonal indexes. An **index number** is *a ratio of a measure taken during one time frame to that same measure taken during another time frame, usually denoted as the base period.* Often the ratio is multiplied by 100 and expressed as a percentage. Index numbers will be discussed more fully in Section 15.6. Column 6 contains the effects of seasonality and irregular fluctuations. Now we must remove the irregular effects.

Table 15.9 contains the values from column 6 of Table 15.8 organized by quarter and year. Each quarter in these data has four seasonal indexes. Throwing out the high and low index for each quarter eliminates the extreme values. The remaining two indexes are averaged as follows for quarter 1.

$$\text{Quarter 1:} \quad 96.85 \quad 100.22 \quad 100.09 \quad 94.84$$
$$\text{Eliminate:} \quad 94.84 \quad \text{and} \quad 100.22$$

Average the Remaining Indexes:

$$\bar{X}_{Q1index} = \frac{96.85 + 100.09}{2} = 98.47$$

Table 15.10 gives the final seasonal indexes for all the quarters of these data.

After the final adjusted seasonal indexes are determined, the original data can be **deseasonalized**. The deseasonalization of actual values is relatively common with data published by the government and other agencies. Data can be deseasonalized by dividing the actual values, which consist of $T \cdot C \cdot S \cdot I$, by the final adjusted seasonal effects.

$$\text{Deseasonalized Data} = \frac{T \cdot C \cdot S \cdot I}{S} = T \cdot C \cdot I$$

Because the seasonal effects are in terms of index numbers, the seasonal indexes must be divided by 100 before deseasonalization. Shown here are the computations for deseasonalizing the household appliance data from Table 15.7 for quarter 1 of year 1.

$$\text{Year 1 Quarter 1 Actual} = 4,009$$

$$\text{Year 1 Quarter 1 Seasonal Index} = 98.47$$

$$\text{Year 1 Quarter 1 Deseasonalized Value} = \frac{4,009}{.9847} = 4,071.3$$

TABLE 15.9   **Seasonal Indexes for the Household Appliance Data**

QUARTER	YEAR 1	YEAR 2	YEAR 3	YEAR 4	YEAR 5
1	—	96.85	100.22	100.09	94.84
2	—	104.63	106.16	105.57	108.14
3	102.05	106.35	99.00	98.73	—
4	94.40	90.34	97.33	95.86	—

TABLE 15.10

Final Seasonal Indexes for the Household Appliance Data

QUARTER	INDEX
1	98.47
2	105.87
3	100.53
4	95.13

TABLE 15.11   Deseasonalized Household Appliance Data

YEAR	QUARTER	SHIPMENTS ACTUAL VALUES ($T \cdot C \cdot S \cdot I$)	SEASONAL INDEXES S	DESEASONALIZED DATA $T \cdot C \cdot I$
1	1	4,009	98.47	4,071
	2	4,321	105.87	4,081
	3	4,224	100.53	4,202
	4	3,944	95.13	4,146
2	1	4,123	98.47	4,187
	2	4,522	105.87	4,271
	3	4,657	100.53	4,632
	4	4,030	95.13	4,236
3	1	4,493	98.47	4,563
	2	4,806	105.87	4,540
	3	4,551	100.53	4,527
	4	4,485	95.13	4,715
4	1	4,595	98.47	4,666
	2	4,799	105.87	4,533
	3	4,417	100.53	4,394
	4	4,258	95.13	4,476
5	1	4,245	98.47	4,311
	2	4,900	105.87	4,628
	3	4,585	100.53	4,561
	4	4,533	95.13	4,765

Table 15.11 gives the deseasonalized data for this example for all years. Figure 15.10 is a graph of the deseasonalized data.

Finding Seasonal Effects with the Computer

Through Minitab, decomposition can be performed on the computer with relative ease. Figure 15.11 displays Minitab output for seasonal decomposition of the household appliance example. Note that the seasonal indexes are virtually identical to those shown in Table 15.10 computed by hand.

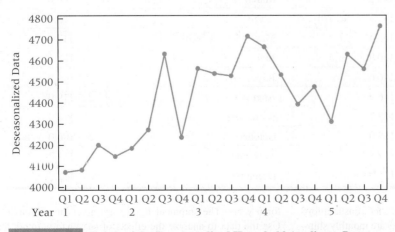

FIGURE 15.10   **Graph of the Deseasonalized Household Appliance Data**

Time Series Decomposition for Household Appliances

Multiplicative Model

```
Data        Household Appliances
Length      20
N Missing    0

Seasonal    Indices
  Period    Index
       1    0.98469
       2    1.05871
       3    1.00536
       4    0.95124
```

FIGURE 15.11 Minitab Output for Seasonal Decomposition of the Household Appliance Data

Winters' Three-Parameter Exponential Smoothing Method

Holt's two-parameter exponential smoothing method can be extended to include seasonal analysis. This technique, referred to as Winters' method, not only smoothes observations and trend but also smoothes the seasonal effects. In addition to the single exponential smoothing weight of α and the trend weight of β, Winters' method introduces γ, a weight for seasonality. Using these three weights and several equations, Winters' method is able to develop forecasts that include a smoothing value for observations, a trend value, and a seasonal value. A more detailed explanation of Winters' three-parameter exponential smoothing method along with examples and practice problems is presented in WileyPLUS and at the Wiley Web site for this text.

15.4 Problems

15.13. The U.S. Department of Agriculture publishes statistics on the production of various types of food commodities by month. Shown here are the production figures on broccoli for January of a recent year through December of the next year. Use these data to compute 12-month centered moving averages $(T \cdot C)$. Using these computed values, determine the seasonal effects $(S \cdot I)$.

MONTH	BROCCOLI (million pounds)	MONTH	BROCCOLI (million pounds)
January (1st year)	132.5	January (2nd year)	104.9
February	164.8	February	99.3
March	141.2	March	102.0
April	133.8	April	122.4
May	138.4	May	112.1
June	150.9	June	108.4
July	146.6	July	119.0
August	146.9	August	119.0
September	138.7	September	114.9
October	128.0	October	106.0
November	112.4	November	111.7
December	121.0	December	112.3

15.14. The U.S. Department of Commerce publishes census information on manufacturing. Included in these figures are monthly shipment data for the paperboard container and box industry shown below for 6 years. The shipment figures are given in millions of dollars. Use the data to analyze the effects of seasonality, trend, and cycle. Develop the trend model with a linear model only.

MONTH	SHIPMENTS	MONTH	SHIPMENTS
January (year 1)	1,891	January (year 4)	2,336
February	1,986	February	2,474
March	1,987	March	2,546
April	1,987	April	2,566
May	2,000	May	2,473
June	2,082	June	2,572
July	1,878	July	2,336
August	2,074	August	2,518
September	2,086	September	2,454
October	2,045	October	2,559
November	1,945	November	2,384
December	1,861	December	2,305
MONTH	**SHIPMENTS**	**MONTH**	**SHIPMENTS**
January (year 2)	1,936	January (year 5)	2,389
February	2,104	February	2,463
March	2,126	March	2,522
April	2,131	April	2,417
May	2,163	May	2,468
June	2,346	June	2,492
July	2,109	July	2,304
August	2,211	August	2,511
September	2,268	September	2,494
October	2,285	October	2,530
November	2,107	November	2,381
December	2,077	December	2,211
MONTH	**SHIPMENTS**	**MONTH**	**SHIPMENTS**
January (year 3)	2,183	January (year 6)	2,377
February	2,230	February	2,381
March	2,222	March	2,268
April	2,319	April	2,407
May	2,369	May	2,367
June	2,529	June	2,446
July	2,267	July	2,341
August	2,457	August	2,491
September	2,524	September	2,452
October	2,502	October	2,561
November	2,314	November	2,377
December	2,277	December	2,277

15.5 | Autocorrelation and Autoregression

Data values gathered over time are often correlated with values from past time periods. This characteristic can cause problems in the use of regression in forecasting and at the same time can open some opportunities. One of the problems that can occur in regressing data over time is autocorrelation.

Autocorrelation

Autocorrelation, or **serial correlation**, occurs in data *when the error terms of a regression forecasting model are correlated.* The likelihood of this occurring with business data increases over time, particularly with economic variables. Autocorrelation can be a problem in using regression analysis as the forecasting method because one of the assumptions underlying regression analysis is that the error terms are independent or random (not correlated). In most business analysis situations, the correlation of error terms is likely to occur as positive autocorrelation (positive errors are associated with positive errors of comparable magnitude and negative errors are associated with negative errors of comparable magnitude).

When autocorrelation occurs in a regression analysis, several possible problems might arise. First, the estimates of the regression coefficients no longer have the minimum variance property and may be inefficient. Second, the variance of the error terms may be greatly underestimated by the mean square error value. Third, the true standard deviation of the estimated regression coefficient may be seriously underestimated. Fourth, the confidence intervals and tests using the t and F distributions are no longer strictly applicable.

First-order autocorrelation results from correlation between the error terms of adjacent time periods (as opposed to two or more previous periods). If first-order autocorrelation is present, the error for one time period, e_t, is a function of the error of the previous time period, e_{t-1}, as follows:

$$e_t = \rho e_{t-1} + v_t$$

The first-order autocorrelation coefficient, ρ, measures the correlation between the error terms. It is a value that lies between −1 and 0 and +1, as does the coefficient of correlation discussed in Chapter 12. v_t is a normally distributed independent error term. If positive autocorrelation is present, the value of ρ is between 0 and +1. If the value of ρ is 0, $e_t = v_t$, which means there is no autocorrelation and e_t is just a random, independent error term.

One way to *test to determine whether autocorrelation is present in a time-series regression analysis* is by using the **Durbin-Watson test** for autocorrelation. Shown next is the formula for computing a Durbin-Watson test for autocorrelation.

Durbin-Watson Test

$$D = \frac{\sum_{t=2}^{n}(e_t - e_{t-1})^2}{\sum_{t=1}^{n}e_t^2}$$

where

n = the number of observations

Note from the formula that the Durbin-Watson test involves finding the difference between successive values of error $(e_t - e_{t-1})$. If errors are positively correlated, this difference will be smaller than with random or independent errors. Squaring this term eliminates the cancellation effects of positive and negative terms.

The null hypothesis for this test is that there is *no* autocorrelation. For a two-tailed test, the alternative hypothesis is that there *is* autocorrelation.

$$H_0: \rho = 0$$
$$H_a: \rho \neq 0$$

As mentioned before, most business forecasting autocorrelation is positive autocorrelation. In most cases, a one-tailed test is used.

$$H_0: \rho = 0$$
$$H_a: \rho > 0$$

In the Durbin-Watson test, D is the observed value of the Durbin-Watson statistic using the residuals from the regression analysis. A critical value for D can be obtained from the values of α, n, and k by using Table A.9 in the appendix, where α is the level of significance, n is the number of data items, and k is the number of predictors. Two Durbin-Watson tables are given in the appendix. One table contains values for $\alpha = .01$ and the other for $\alpha = .05$. The Durbin-Watson tables in Appendix A include values for d_U and d_L. These values range from 0 to 4. If the observed value of D is above d_U, we fail to reject the null hypothesis and there is no significant autocorrelation. If the observed value of D is below d_L, the null hypothesis is rejected and there is autocorrelation. Sometimes the observed statistic, D, is between the values of d_U and d_L. In this case, the Durbin-Watson test is inconclusive.

As an example, consider Table 15.12, which contains crude oil production and natural gas withdrawal data for the United States over a 25-year period published by the Energy Information Administration in its Annual Energy Review. A regression line can be fit through these data to determine whether the amount of natural gas withdrawals can be predicted by the amount of crude oil production. The resulting errors of prediction can be tested by the Durbin-Watson statistic for the presence of significant positive autocorrelation by using $\alpha = .05$. The hypotheses are

$$H_0: \rho = 0$$
$$H_a: \rho > 0$$

TABLE 15.12	U.S. Crude Oil Production and Natural Gas Withdrawals over a 25-Year Period	
YEAR	CRUDE OIL PRODUCTION (1000s)	NATURAL GAS WITHDRAWALS FROM NATURAL GAS WELLS (1000s)
1	8.597	17.573
2	8.572	17.337
3	8.649	15.809
4	8.688	14.153
5	8.879	15.513
6	8.971	14.535
7	8.680	14.154
8	8.349	14.807
9	8.140	15.467
10	7.613	15.709
11	7.355	16.054
12	7.417	16.018
13	7.171	16.165
14	6.847	16.691
15	6.662	17.351
16	6.560	17.282
17	6.465	17.737
18	6.452	17.844
19	6.252	17.729
20	5.881	17.590
21	5.822	17.726
22	5.801	18.129
23	5.746	17.795
24	5.681	17.819
25	5.430	17.739

The following regression equation was obtained by means of a Minitab computer analysis.

$$\text{Natural Gas Withdrawals} = 22.7372 - 0.8507 \text{ Crude Oil Production}$$

Using the values for crude oil production (X) from Table 15.12 and the regression equation shown here, predicted values of Y (natural gas withdrawals) can be computed. From the predicted values and the actual values, the errors of prediction for each time interval, e_t, can be calculated. Table 15.13 shows the values of $\hat{Y}$, e_t, e_t^2, $(e_t - e_{t-1})$, and $(e_t - e_{t-1})^2$ for this example. Note that the first predicted value of Y is

$$\hat{Y}_1 = 22.7372 - 0.8507(8.597) = 15.4237$$

The error for year 1 is

$$\text{Actual}_1 - \text{Predicted}_1 = 17.573 - 15.4237 = 2.1493$$

The value of $e_t - e_{t-1}$ for year 1 and year 2 is computed by subtracting the error for year 1 from the error of year 2.

$$e_{\text{year 2}} - e_{\text{year 1}} = 1.8920 - 2.1493 = -0.2573$$

TABLE 15.13	Predicted Values and Error Terms for the Crude Oil Production and Natural Gas Withdrawal Data				
YEAR	$\hat{Y}$	e_t	e_t^2	$e_t - e_{t-1}$	$(e_t - e_{t-1})^2$
1	15.4237	2.1493	4.6195	—	—
2	15.4450	1.8920	3.5797	−0.2573	0.0662
3	15.3795	0.4295	0.1845	−1.4625	2.1389
4	15.3463	−1.1933	1.4240	−1.6228	2.6335
5	15.1838	0.3292	0.1084	1.5225	2.3180
6	15.1056	−0.5706	0.3256	−0.8998	0.8096
7	15.3531	−1.1991	1.4378	−0.6285	0.3950
8	15.6347	−0.8277	0.6851	0.3714	0.1379
9	15.8125	−0.3455	0.1194	0.4822	0.2325
10	16.2608	−0.5518	0.3045	−0.2063	0.0426
11	16.4803	−0.4263	0.1817	0.1255	0.0158
12	16.4276	−0.4096	0.1678	0.0167	0.0003
13	16.6368	−0.4718	0.2226	−0.0622	0.0039
14	16.9125	−0.2215	0.0491	0.2503	0.0627
15	17.0698	0.2812	0.0791	0.5027	0.2527
16	17.1566	0.1254	0.0157	−0.1558	0.0243
17	17.2374	0.4996	0.2496	0.3742	0.1400
18	17.2485	0.5955	0.3546	0.0959	0.0092
19	17.4186	0.3104	0.0963	−0.2851	0.0813
20	17.7342	−0.1442	0.0208	−0.4546	0.2067
21	17.7844	−0.0584	0.0034	0.0858	0.0074
22	17.8023	0.3267	0.1067	0.3851	0.1483
23	17.8491	−0.0541	0.0029	−0.3808	0.1450
24	17.9044	−0.0854	0.0073	−0.0313	0.0010
25	18.1179	−0.3789	0.1436	−0.2935	0.0861
			$\Sigma e_t^2 = 14.4897$		$\Sigma(e_t - e_{t-1})^2 = 9.9589$

The Durbin-Watson statistic can now be computed:

$$D = \frac{\sum_{t=2}^{n}(e_t - e_{t-1})^2}{\sum_{t=1}^{n}e_t^2} = \frac{9.9589}{14.4897} = 0.6873$$

Because we used a simple linear regression, the value of k is 1. The sample size, n, is 25, and $\alpha = .05$. The critical values in Table A.9 are

$$d_L = 1.29 \text{ and } d_U = 1.45$$

Because the computed D statistic, 0.6873, is less than the value of $d_L = 1.29$, the null hypothesis is rejected. A positive autocorrelation is present in this example.

Ways to Overcome the Autocorrelation Problem

Several approaches to data analysis can be used when autocorrelation is present. One uses additional independent variables and another transforms the independent variable.

Addition of Independent Variables   Often the reason autocorrelation occurs in regression analyses is that one or more important predictor variables have been left out of the analysis. For example, suppose a researcher develops a regression forecasting model that attempts to predict sales of new homes by sales of used homes over some period of time. Such a model might contain significant autocorrelation. The exclusion of the variable "prime mortgage interest rate" might be a factor driving the autocorrelation between the other two variables. Adding this variable to the regression model might significantly reduce the autocorrelation.

Transforming Variables   When the inclusion of additional variables is not helpful in reducing autocorrelation to an acceptable level, transforming the data in the variables may help to solve the problem. One such method is the **first-differences approach**. With the first-differences approach, *each value of X is subtracted from each succeeding time period value of X*; these "differences" become the new and transformed X variable. The same process is used to transform the Y variable. The regression analysis is then computed on the transformed X and transformed Y variables to compute a new model that is hopefully free of significant autocorrelation effects.

Another way is to generate new variables by using the percentage changes from period to period and regressing these new variables. A third way is to use autoregression models.

Autoregression

A forecasting technique that takes advantage of the relationship of values (Y_t) to previous-period values $(Y_{t-1}, Y_{t-2}, Y_{t-3}, \ldots)$ is called autoregression. **Autoregression** is *a multiple regression technique in which the independent variables are time-lagged versions of the dependent variable*, which means we try to predict a value of Y from values of Y from previous time periods. The independent variable can be lagged for one, two, three, or more time periods. An autoregressive model containing independent variables for three time periods looks like this:

$$\hat{Y} = b_0 + b_1 Y_{t-1} + b_2 Y_{t-2} + b_3 Y_{t-3}$$

As an example, we shall attempt to predict the volume of natural gas withdrawal, displayed in Table 15.12, by using data lagged for both one and two time periods. The data used in this analysis are displayed in Table 15.14. Using Excel, a multiple regression model is developed to predict the values of Y_t by the values of Y_{t-1} and Y_{t-2}. The results appear in Figure 15.12.

TABLE 15.14 Time-Lagged Natural Gas Data

YEAR	NATURAL GAS WITHDRAWAL Y_t	ONE PERIOD LAGGED $Y_{t-1}(X_1)$	TWO PERIOD LAGGED $Y_{t-2}(X_2)$
1	17.573	—	—
2	17.337	17.573	—
3	15.809	17.337	17.573
4	14.153	15.809	17.337
5	15.513	14.153	15.809
6	14.535	15.513	14.153
7	14.154	14.535	15.513
8	14.807	14.154	14.535
9	15.467	14.807	14.154
10	15.709	15.467	14.807
11	16.054	15.709	15.467
12	16.018	16.054	15.709
13	16.165	16.018	16.054
14	16.691	16.165	16.018
15	17.351	16.691	16.165
16	17.282	17.351	16.691
17	17.737	17.282	17.351
18	17.844	17.737	17.282
19	17.729	17.844	17.737
20	17.590	17.729	17.844
21	17.726	17.590	17.729
22	18.129	17.726	17.590
23	17.795	18.129	17.726
24	17.819	17.795	18.129
25	17.739	17.819	17.795

SUMMARY OUTPUT

Regression Statistics

Multiple R	0.864
R Square	0.746
Adjusted R Square	0.721
Standard Error	0.693
Observations	23

ANOVA

	df	SS	MS	F	Significance F
Regression	2	28.3203	14.1602	29.44	0.0000011
Residual	20	9.6187	0.4809		
Total	22	37.9390			

	Coefficients	Standard Error	t Stat	P-value
Intercept	2.4081	1.9608	1.23	0.2337
Lagged 1	0.9678	0.2221	4.36	0.0003
Lagged 2	−0.1128	0.2239	−0.50	0.6201

FIGURE 15.12 Excel Autoregression Results for Natural Gas Withdrawal Data

Note that the regression analysis does not use data from years 1 and 2 of Table 15.14 because there are no values for the two lagged variables for one or both of those years.

The autoregression model is

$$Y_t = 2.4081 + 0.9678Y_{t-1} - 0.1128Y_{t-2}$$

The relatively high value of R^2 (74.6%) and relatively small value of s_e (0.693) indicate that this regression model has fairly strong predictability. Interestingly, the one-period lagged variable is quite significant ($t = 4.36$ with a p-value of 0.0003), but the two-period lagged variable is not significant ($t = -0.50$ with a p-value of 0.6201), indicating the presence of first-order autocorrelation.

Autoregression can be a useful tool in locating seasonal or cyclical effects in time series data. For example, if the data are given in monthly increments, autoregression using variables lagged by as much as 12 months can search for the predictability of previous monthly time periods. If data are given in quarterly time periods, autoregression of up to four periods removed can be a useful tool in locating the predictability of data from previous quarters. When the time periods are in years, lagging the data by yearly periods and using autoregression can help in locating cyclical predictability.

15.5 Problems

15.15. The U.S. Department of Labor publishes consumer price indexes (CPIs) on many commodities. Following are the percentage changes in the CPIs for food and for shelter for the years 1997 through 2014. Use these data to develop a linear regression model to forecast the percentage change in food CPIs by the percentage change in shelter CPIs. Compute a Durbin-Watson statistic to determine whether significant autocorrelation is present in the model. Let $\alpha = .05$.

YEAR	FOOD	SHELTER	YEAR	FOOD	SHELTER
1997	2.6	3.1	2006	2.1	4.2
1998	2.2	3.3	2007	4.9	3.1
1999	2.1	2.9	2008	5.9	1.9
2000	2.3	3.3	2009	−0.5	0.3
2001	3.2	3.7	2010	1.5	0.4
2002	1.8	3.7	2011	4.7	1.9
2003	2.2	2.4	2012	1.8	2.2
2004	2.7	2.7	2013	1.1	2.5
2005	2.3	2.6	2014	3.4	2.9

15.16. Use the data from Problem 15.15 to create a regression forecasting model using the first-differences data transformation. How do the results from this model differ from those obtained in Problem 15.15?

15.17. The Federal Deposit Insurance Corporation (FDIC) releases data on bank failures. Following are data on the number of U.S. bank failures in a given year and the total amount of bank deposits (in $ millions) involved in such failures for a given year. Use these data to develop a simple regression forecasting model that attempts to predict the failed bank assets involved in bank closings by the number of bank failures. Compute a Durbin-Watson statistic for this regression model and determine whether significant autocorrelation is present. Let $\alpha = .05$.

YEAR	FAILURES	FAILED BANK ASSETS
1	11	8,189
2	7	104
3	34	1,862
4	45	4,137
5	79	36,394
6	118	3,034
7	144	7,609
8	201	7,538
9	221	56,620
10	206	28,507
11	159	10,739
12	108	43,552
13	100	16,915
14	42	2,588
15	11	825
16	6	753
17	5	186
18	1	27

15.18. Use the data in Problem 15.17 to compute a regression model after recoding the data by the first-differences approach. Compute a Durbin-Watson statistic to determine whether significant autocorrelation is present in this first-differences model. Compare this model with the model determined in Problem 15.17, and compare the significance of the Durbin-Watson statistics for the two problems. Let $\alpha = .05$.

15.19. *Current Construction Reports* from the U.S. Census Bureau contain data on new privately owned housing units. Data on new privately owned housing units (1000s) built in the West over a 31-year period follow. Use these time-series data to develop an autoregression model with a one-period lag. Now try an autoregression model with a two-period lag. Discuss the results and compare the two models.

YEAR	HOUSING STARTS (1000)	YEAR	HOUSING STARTS (1000)
1	318.9	17	347.4
2	251.3	18	363.5
3	224.1	19	401.2
4	390.4	20	404.3
5	457.3	21	401.5
6	483.9	22	413.0
7	509.7	23	430.9
8	406.0	24	486.5
9	415.6	25	541.9
10	402.1	26	558.6
11	324.9	27	455.2
12	247.9	28	343.9
13	268.6	29	196.7
14	288.2	30	116.7
15	342.4	31	128.3
16	328.5		

15.20. The U.S. Department of Agriculture publishes data on the production, utilization, and value of fruits in the United States. Shown here are the amounts of noncitrus fruit processed into juice (in kilotons) for a 25-year period. Use these data to develop an autoregression forecasting model with a two-period lag. Discuss the results of this analysis.

YEAR	PROCESSED JUICE	YEAR	PROCESSED JUICE
1	598	14	1135
2	768	15	1893
3	863	16	1372
4	818	17	1547
5	841	18	1450
6	1140	19	1557
7	1285	20	1742
8	1418	21	1736
9	1235	22	1886
10	1255	23	1857
11	1445	24	1582
12	1336	25	1675
13	1226		

15.6 | Index Numbers

One particular type of descriptive measure that is useful in allowing comparisons of data over time is the index number. An index number is, in part, a ratio of a measure taken during one time frame to that same measure taken during another time frame, usually denoted as the base period. Often the ratio is multiplied by 100 and is expressed as a percentage. When expressed as a percentage, index numbers serve as an alternative to comparing raw numbers. Index number users become accustomed to interpreting measures for a given time period in light of a base period on a scale in which the base period has an index of 100(%). Index numbers are used to compare phenomena from one time period to another and are especially helpful in highlighting interperiod differences.

Index numbers are widely used around the world to relate information about stock markets, inflation, sales, exports and imports, agriculture, and many other things. Some examples of specific indexes are the employment cost index, price index for construction, index of manufacturing capacity, producer price index, consumer price index, Dow Jones industrial average, index of output, and Nikkei 225 average. This section, although recognizing the importance of stock indexes and others, will focus on price indexes.

The motivation for using an index number is to reduce data to an easier-to-use, more convenient form. As an example, examine the raw data on number of business bankruptcies in the United States from 1990 through 2014 shown in Table 15.15. An analyst can describe these data by observing that, in general, the number of business bankruptcies has been decreasing since 1990. How do the number of business bankruptcies in 2000 compare to 1990? How do the number of business bankruptcies in 2013 compare to 1993 or 1995? To answer these questions without index numbers, a business researcher would probably resort to subtracting the number of business bankruptcies for the years of interest and comparing the corresponding increases or decreases. This process can be tedious and frustrating for decision makers who must maximize their effort in minimal time. Using simple index numbers, the business researcher can transform these data into values that are more usable and make it easier to compare other years to one particular key year.

Simple Index Numbers

How are index numbers computed? The equation for computing a simple index number follows.

Simple Index Number

$$I_i = \frac{X_i}{X_0}(100)$$

where

X_0 = the quantity, price, or cost in the base year
X_i = the quantity, price, or cost in the year of interest
I_i = the index number for the year of interest

Suppose bankruptcy researchers examining the data from Table 15.15 decide to compute index numbers using 1990 as the base year. The index number for the year 2000 is

$$I_{2000} = \frac{X_{2000}}{X_{1990}}(100) = \frac{35,472}{64,853}(100) = 54.7$$

Table 15.16 displays all the index numbers for the data in Table 15.15, with 1990 as the base year, along with the raw data. A cursory glance at these index numbers reveals a decrease in the number of bankruptcies for most of the years since 1990 (because the index has been going down). In particular, the greatest drop in number seems to have occurred between 2005 and 2006—a drop of 30 in the index. Because most people are easily able to understand the concept of 100%, it is likely that decision makers can make quick judgments on the number of business bankruptcies in the United States from one year relative to another by examining the index numbers over this period.

Unweighted Aggregate Price Index Numbers

The use of simple index numbers makes possible the conversion of prices, costs, quantities, and so on for different time periods into a number scale with the base year equaling 100%. One of the drawbacks of simple index numbers, however, is that each time period is represented by only one item or commodity. When multiple items are involved, multiple sets of index numbers are possible. Suppose a decision maker is interested in combining or pooling the prices of several items, creating a "market basket" in order to compare the prices for several years. Fortunately, a technique does exist for combining several items and determining index numbers for the total (aggregate). Because this technique is used mostly in determining price indexes, the focus in this section is on developing aggregate price indexes. The formula for constructing the unweighted aggregate price index number follows.

Unweighted Aggregate Price Index Number

$$I_i = \frac{\Sigma P_i}{\Sigma P_0}(100)$$

where

P_i = the price of an item in the year of interest (i)
P_0 = the price of an item in the base year (0)
I_i = the index number for the year of interest (i)

Suppose a state's department of labor wants to compare the cost of family food buying over the years. Department officials decide that instead of using a single food item to do this comparison, they will use a food basket that consists of five items: eggs, milk, bananas, potatoes,

TABLE 15.15

Business Bankruptcy Filings in the United States

YEAR	BUSINESS BANKRUPTCY FILINGS
1990	64,853
1991	71,549
1992	70,643
1993	62,304
1994	52,374
1995	51,959
1996	53,549
1997	54,027
1998	44,367
1999	37,884
2000	35,472
2001	40,099
2002	38,540
2003	35,037
2004	34,317
2005	39,201
2006	19,695
2007	28,322
2008	43,546
2009	60,837
2010	56,282
2011	47,806
2012	40,075
2013	33,212
2014	26,983

TABLE 15.16	Index Numbers for Business Bankruptcy Filings in the United States	
YEAR	BUSINESS BANKRUPTCY FILINGS	INDEX NUMBERS
1990	64,853	100.0
1991	71,549	110.3
1992	70,643	108.9
1993	62,304	96.1
1994	52,374	80.8
1995	51,959	80.1
1996	53,549	82.6
1997	54,027	83.3
1998	44,367	68.4
1999	37,884	58.4
2000	35,472	54.7
2001	40,099	61.8
2002	38,540	59.4
2003	35,037	54.0
2004	34,317	52.9
2005	39,201	60.4
2006	19,695	30.4
2007	28,322	43.7
2008	43,546	67.1
2009	60,837	93.8
2010	56,282	86.8
2011	47,806	73.7
2012	40,075	61.8
2013	33,212	51.2
2014	26,983	41.6

and sugar. They gathered price information on these five items for the years 1995, 2005, and 2016. The items and the prices are listed in Table 15.17.

From the data in Table 15.17 and the formula, the unweighted aggregate price indexes for the years 1995, 2005, and 2016 can be computed by using 1995 as the base year. The first step is to add together, or aggregate, the prices for all the food basket items in a given year. These totals are shown in the last row of Table 15.17. The index numbers are constructed by using these totals (not individual item prices): $\Sigma P_{1995} = 2.91$, $\Sigma P_{2005} = 3.44$, and $\Sigma P_{2016} = 5.08$. From these figures, the unweighted aggregate price index for 2005 is computed as follows.

$$\text{For 2005: } I_{2005} = \frac{\Sigma P_{2005}}{\Sigma P_{1995}}(100) = \frac{3.44}{2.91}(100) = 118.2$$

Weighted Aggregate Price Index Numbers

A major drawback to unweighted aggregate price indexes is that they are *unweighted*—that is, equal weight is put on each item by assuming the market basket contains only one of each item. This assumption may or may not be true. For example, a household may consume 5 pounds of bananas per year but drink 50 gallons of milk. In addition, unweighted aggregate

TABLE 15.17   Prices for a Basket of Food Items

ITEM	1995	YEAR 2005	2016
Eggs (dozen)	.78	.86	1.55
Milk (1/2 gallon)	1.14	1.39	2.25
Bananas (per lb.)	.36	.46	.49
Potatoes (per lb.)	.28	.31	.36
Sugar (per lb.)	.35	.42	.43
Total of Items	2.91	3.44	5.08

index numbers are dependent on the units selected for various items. For example, if milk is measured in quarts instead of gallons, the price of milk used in determining the index numbers is considerably lower. A class of index numbers that can be used to avoid these problems is weighted aggregate price index numbers.

Weighted aggregate price index numbers are *computed by multiplying quantity weights and item prices in determining the market basket worth for a given year.* Sometimes when price and quantity are multiplied to construct index numbers, the index numbers are referred to as *value indexes*. Thus, weighted aggregate price index numbers are also value indexes.

Including quantities eliminates the problems caused by how many of each item are consumed per time period and the units of items. If 50 gallons of milk but only 5 pounds of bananas are consumed, weighted aggregate price index numbers will reflect those weights. If the business researcher switches from gallons of milk to quarts, the prices will change downward but the quantity will increase fourfold (4 quarts in a gallon).

In general, weighted aggregate price indexes are constructed by multiplying the price of each item by its quantity and then summing these products for the market basket over a given time period (often a year). The ratio of this sum for one time period of interest (year) to a base time period of interest (base year) is multiplied by 100. The following formula reflects a weighted aggregate price index computed by using quantity weights from each time period (year).

$$I_i = \frac{\Sigma P_i Q_i}{\Sigma P_0 Q_0}(100)$$

One of the problems with this formula is the implication that new and possibly different quantities apply for each time period. However, business researchers expend much time and money ascertaining the quantities used in a market basket. Redetermining quantity weights for each year is therefore often prohibitive for most organizations (even the government). Two particular types of weighted aggregate price indexes offer a solution to the problem of which quantity weights to use. The first and most widely used is the Laspeyres price index. The second and less widely used is the Paasche price index.

Laspeyres Price Index

The **Laspeyres price index** is *a weighted aggregate price index computed by using the quantities of the base period (year) for all other years.* The advantages of this technique are that the price indexes for all years can be compared, and new quantities do not have to be determined for each year. The formula for constructing the Laspeyres price index follows.

Laspeyres Price Index

$$I_L = \frac{\Sigma P_i Q_0}{\Sigma P_0 Q_0}(100)$$

Notice that the formula requires the base period quantities (Q_0) in both the numerator and the denominator.

In Table 15.17, a food basket is presented in which aggregate price indexes are computed. This food basket consisted of eggs, milk, bananas, potatoes, and sugar. The prices of these items were combined (aggregated) for a given year and the price indexes were computed from these aggregate figures. The unweighted aggregate price indexes computed on these data gave all items equal importance. Suppose that the business researchers realize that applying equal weight to these five items is probably not a representative way to construct this food basket and consequently ascertain quantity weights on each food item for one year's consumption. Table 15.18 lists these five items, their prices, and their quantity usage weights for the base year (1995). From these data, the business researchers can compute Laspeyres price indexes.

The Laspeyres price index for 2016 with 1995 as the base year is:

$$
\begin{aligned}
\Sigma P_i Q_0 &= \Sigma P_{2016} Q_{1995} \\
&= \Sigma[(1.55)(45) + (2.25)(60) + (.49)(12) + (.36)(55) + (.43)(36)] \\
&= 69.75 + 135.00 + 5.88 + 19.80 + 15.48 = 245.91 \\
\Sigma P_0 Q_0 &= \Sigma P_{1995} Q_{1995} \\
&= \Sigma[(.78)(45) + (1.14)(60) + (.36)(12) + (.28)(55) + (.35)(36)] \\
&= 35.10 + 68.40 + 4.32 + 15.40 + 12.60 = 135.82
\end{aligned}
$$

$$
I_{2016} = \frac{\Sigma P_{2016} Q_{1995}}{\Sigma P_{1995} Q_{1995}}(100) = \frac{245.91}{135.85}(100) = 181.0
$$

Paasche Price Index

The **Paasche price index** is *a weighted aggregate price index computed by using the quantities for the year of interest in computations for a given year.* The advantage of this technique is that it incorporates current quantity figures in the calculations. One disadvantage is that ascertaining quantity figures for each time period is expensive. The formula for computing Paasche price indexes follows.

Paasche Price Index

$$
I_P = \frac{\Sigma P_i Q_i}{\Sigma P_0 Q_i}(100)
$$

Suppose the yearly quantities for the basket of food items listed in Table 15.18 are determined. The result is the quantities and prices shown in Table 15.19 for the years 1995 and 2016 that can be used to compute Paasche price index numbers.

TABLE 15.18   **Food Basket Items with Quantity Weights**

ITEM	QUANTITY	PRICE 1995	PRICE 2016
Eggs (dozen)	45	.78	1.55
Milk (1/2 gal.)	60	1.14	2.25
Bananas (per lb.)	12	.36	.49
Potatoes (per lb.)	55	.28	.36
Sugar (per lb.)	36	.35	.43

TABLE 15.19	Food Basket Items with Yearly Quantity Weights for 1995 and 2016			
ITEM	P_{1995}	Q_{1995}	P_{2016}	Q_{2016}
Eggs (dozen)	.78	45	1.55	42
Milk (1/2 gal.)	1.14	60	2.25	57
Bananas (per lb.)	.36	12	.49	13
Potatoes (per lb.)	.28	55	.36	52
Sugar (per lb.)	.35	36	.43	36

The Paasche price index numbers can be determined for 2016 by using a base year of 1995 as follows.

For 2016:

$$\Sigma P_{2016} Q_{2016} = \Sigma[(1.55)(42) + (2.25)(57) + (.49)(13) + (.36)(52) + (.43)(36)]$$
$$= 65.10 + 128.25 + 6.37 + 18.72 + 15.48 = 233.92$$

$$\Sigma P_{1995} Q_{2016} = [(.78)(42) + (1.14)(57) + (.36)(13) + (.28)(52) + (.35)(36)]$$
$$= 32.76 + 64.98 + 4.68 + 14.56 + 12.60$$
$$= 129.58$$

$$I_{2016} = \frac{\Sigma P_{2016} Q_{2016}}{\Sigma P_{1995} Q_{2016}}(100) = \frac{233.92}{129.58}(100) = 180.5$$

DEMONSTRATION PROBLEM 15.5

The Arapaho Valley Pediatrics Clinic has been in business for 18 years. The office manager noticed that prices of clinic materials and office supplies fluctuate over time. To get a handle on the price trends for running the clinic, the office manager examined prices of six items the clinic uses as part of its operation. Shown here are the items, their prices, and the quantities for the years 2015 and 2016. Use these data to develop unweighted aggregate price indexes for 2016 with a base year of 2015. Compute the Laspeyres price index for the year 2016 using 2015 as the base year. Compute the Paasche index number for 2016 using 2015 as the base year.

	2015		2016	
ITEM	PRICE	QUANTITY	PRICE	QUANTITY
Syringes (dozen)	6.70	150	6.95	135
Cotton swabs (box)	1.35	60	1.45	65
Patient record forms (pad)	5.10	8	6.25	12
Children's Tylenol (bottle)	4.50	25	4.95	30
Computer paper (box)	11.95	6	13.20	8
Thermometers	7.90	4	9.00	2
Totals	37.50		41.80	

Solution: Unweighted Aggregate Index for 2016:

$$I_{2016} = \frac{\Sigma P_{2016}}{\Sigma P_{2015}}(100) = \frac{41.80}{37.50}(100) = 111.5$$

Laspeyres Index for 2016:

$$\Sigma P_{2016} Q_{2015} = [(6.95)(150) + (1.45)(60) + (6.25)(8) + (4.95)(25) + (13.20)(6) + (9.00)(4)]$$
$$= 1,042.50 + 87.00 + 50.00 + 123.75 + 79.20 + 36.00$$
$$= 1,418.45$$

$$\Sigma P_{2015} Q_{2015} = [(6.70)(150) + (1.35)(60) + (5.10)(8) + (4.50)(25) + (11.95)(6) + (7.90)(4)]$$
$$= 1,005.00 + 81.00 + 40.80 + 112.50 + 71.70 + 31.60$$
$$= 1,342.6$$

$$I_{2016} = \frac{\Sigma P_{2016} Q_{2015}}{\Sigma P_{2015} Q_{2015}}(100) = \frac{1,418.45}{1,342.6}(100) = 105.6$$

Passache Index for 2016:

$$\Sigma P_{2016} Q_{2016} = [(6.95)(135) + (1.45)(65) + (6.25)(12) + (4.95)(30) + (13.20)(8) + (9.00)(2)]$$
$$= 938.25 + 94.25 + 75.00 + 148.50 + 105.60 + 18.00$$
$$= 1,379.60$$

$$\Sigma P_{2015} Q_{2016} = [(6.70)(135) + (1.35)(65) + (5.10)(12) + (4.50)(30) + (11.95)(8) + (7.90)(2)]$$
$$= 904.50 + 87.75 + 61.20 + 135.00 + 95.60 + 15.80$$
$$= 1,299.85$$

$$I_{2016} = \frac{\Sigma P_{2016} Q_{2016}}{\Sigma P_{2015} Q_{2016}}(100) = \frac{1,379.60}{1,299.85}(100) = 106.1$$

15.6 Problems

15.21. Suppose the following data represent the price of 20 reams of office paper over a 65-year time frame. Find the simple index numbers for the data.

a. Let 1950 be the base year.

b. Let 1980 be the base year.

YEAR	PRICE	YEAR	PRICE
1950	$22.45	1985	$73.44
1955	31.40	1990	80.05
1960	32.33	1995	84.61
1965	36.50	2000	87.28
1970	44.90	2005	89.56
1975	61.24	2010	93.22
1980	69.75	2015	129.80

15.22. The U.S. Patent and Trademark Office reports fiscal year figures for patents issued in the United States. Following are the numbers of patents issued for the years 1980 through 2014. Using these data and a base year of 1990, determine the simple index numbers for each year.

YEAR	NUMBER OF PATENTS (1000s)	YEAR	NUMBER OF PATENTS (1000s)
1980	66.2	1986	76.9
1981	71.1	1987	89.4
1982	63.3	1988	84.3
1983	62.0	1989	102.5
1984	72.7	1990	99.1
1985	77.2	1991	106.7

1992	107.4	2004	181.3
1993	109.7	2005	157.7
1994	113.6	2006	196.4
1995	113.8	2007	182.9
1996	121.7	2008	185.2
1997	124.1	2009	191.9
1998	163.1	2010	244.3
1999	169.1	2011	247.7
2000	176.0	2012	276.8
2001	184.0	2013	303.0
2002	184.4	2014	326.0
2003	187.0		

15.23. Using the data that follow, compute the aggregate index numbers for the four types of meat. Let 1995 be the base year for this market basket of goods.

	YEAR		
ITEMS	1995	2002	2016
Ground beef (per lb.)	1.53	1.40	2.17
Sausage (per lb.)	2.21	2.15	2.51
Bacon (per lb.)	1.92	2.68	2.60
Round steak (per lb.)	3.38	3.10	4.00

15.24. Suppose the following data are prices of market goods involved in household transportation for the years 2009 through 2016. Using 2011 as a base year, compute aggregate transportation price indexes for this data.

ITEMS	YEAR							
	2009	2010	2011	2012	2013	2014	2015	2016
Gasoline (per gal.)	1.23	1.08	1.56	1.85	2.59	2.89	3.12	3.53
Oil (per qt.)	1.77	1.61	1.71	1.90	2.05	2.64	4.17	4.71
Transmission fluid (per qt.)	1.96	1.94	1.90	2.25	3.10	3.68	3.95	5.10
Radiator coolant (per gal.)	8.21	8.19	8.05	8.12	9.10	10.70	12.40	14.35

15.25. Calculate Laspeyres price indexes for 2014–2016 from the following data. Use 2005 as the base year.

QUANTITY		PRICE			
ITEM	2005	2005	2014	2015	2016
1	21	$0.50	$0.67	$0.68	$0.71
2	6	1.23	1.85	1.90	1.91
3	17	0.84	0.75	0.75	0.80
4	43	0.15	0.21	0.25	0.25

15.26. Calculate Paasche price indexes for 2015 and 2016 using the following data and 2005 as the base year.

	2005	2015		2016	
ITEM	PRICE	PRICE	QUANTITY	PRICE	QUANTITY
1	$22.50	$27.80	13	$28.11	12
2	10.90	13.10	5	13.25	8
3	1.85	2.25	41	2.35	44

Decision Dilemma Solved

Forecasting Air Pollution

In searching for the most effective forecasting technique to use to forecast either the carbon monoxide emission or the nitrogen oxide, it is useful to determine whether a trend is evident in either set of time-series data. Minitab's trend analysis output is presented here for nitrogen oxides.

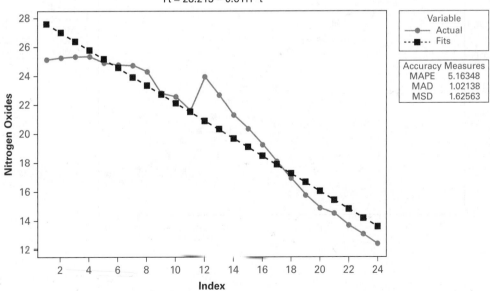

In observing the fit of this trend line and the time-series plot, it is evident that there appears to be more of a quadratic trend than a linear trend. Therefore, a Minitab-produced quadratic trend model was run and the results are presented below. Note that the error measures are all smaller for the quadratic model and that the curve fits the data much better than does the linear model.

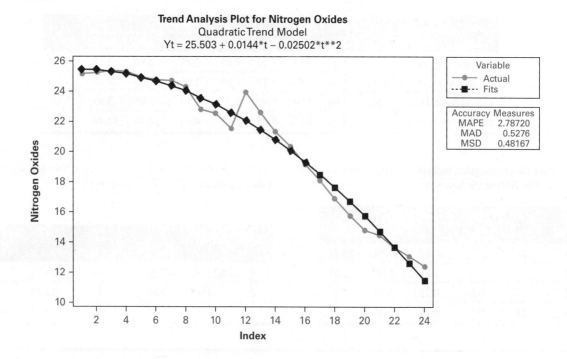

Various smoothing techniques can be used to forecast time-series data. After exploring several moving average models to predict carbon monoxide emissions, it was determined that a 3-year moving average fits the data relatively well. The results of a Minitab moving average graphical analysis of carbon monoxide using a 3-year moving average is shown below. Note that the forecasts shadow the actual values quite well and intersect them in two locations.

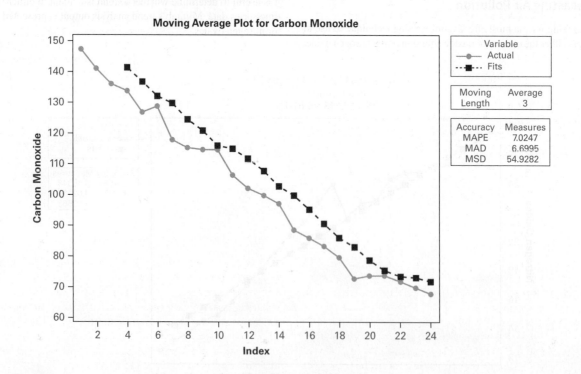

The effectiveness of exponential smoothing as a forecasting tool for nitrogen oxide emissions was tested using Minitab for several values of α. Through this analysis, it was determined that the best forecasts were obtained for values of α near 1, indicating that the actual value for the previous time period was a much stronger contributor to the forecast than the previous time period's forecast. Shown below is a Minitab-produced graphical analysis of an exponential smoothing forecast of the nitrogen oxide data using an alpha of .95. You are encouraged to explore other methods for forecasting nitrogen oxide and carbon monoxide emissions.

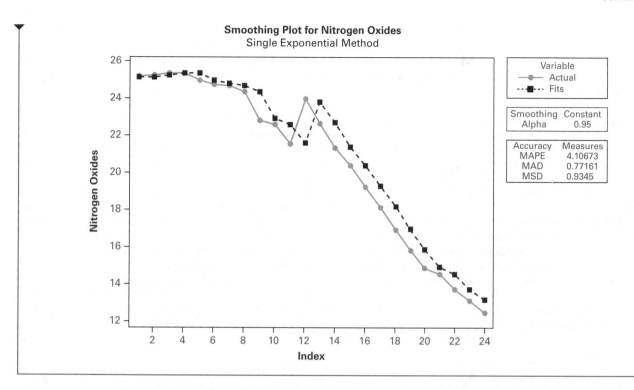

Ethical Considerations

The true test of a forecast is the accuracy of the prediction. Until the actual value is obtained for a given time period, the accuracy of the forecast is unknown. Many forecasters make predictions in society, including card readers, religious leaders, and self-proclaimed prophets. The proof of the forecast is in the outcome. The same holds true in the business world. Forecasts are made about everything from market share to interest rates to number of international air travelers. Some businesses fail because of faulty forecasts.

Forecasting is perhaps as much an art as a science. To keep forecasting ethical, the consumer of the forecast should be given the caveats and limitations of the forecast. The forecaster should be honestly cautious in selling the predictions to a client. In addition, the forecaster should be constantly on the lookout for changes in the business setting being modeled and quickly translate and incorporate those changes into the forecasting model.

Unethical behavior can occur in forecasting when particular data are selected to develop a model that has been predetermined to produce certain results. As mentioned previously, statistics can be used to "prove" almost anything. The ethical forecaster lets the data drive the model and is constantly seeking honest input from new variables to revise the forecast. He or she strives to communicate the limitations of both the forecasts and the models to clients.

Summary

Time-series data are data that have been gathered at regular intervals over a period of time. It is generally believed that time-series data are composed of four elements—trend, cycles, seasonal effects, and irregular fluctuations. Trend is the long-term general direction of the time-series data. Cycles are the business and economic patterns that occur over periods of more than 1 year. Seasonal effects are patterns or cycles of data behavior that occur over time periods of less than 1 year. Irregular fluctuations are unaccounted-for "blips" or variations that occur over short periods of time.

One way to establish the validity of a forecast is to examine the forecasting error. The error of a forecast is the difference between the actual value and the forecast value. Computing a value to measure forecasting error can be done in several different ways. This chapter presents mean absolute deviation and mean square error for this task.

Regression analysis with either linear or quadratic models can be used to explore trend. Regression trend analysis is a special case of regression analysis in which the dependent variable is the data to be forecast and the independent variable is the time periods numbered consecutively from 1 to k, where k is the number of time periods. For the quadratic model, a second independent variable is constructed by squaring the values of the first independent variable, and both independent variables are included in the analysis.

One group of time-series forecasting methods contains smoothing techniques. Among these techniques are naïve models, averaging techniques, and simple exponential smoothing. These techniques do much better if the time series data are stationary or show no significant trend or seasonal effects. Naïve forecasting models are models in which it is assumed that the more recent time periods of data represent the best predictions or forecasts for future outcomes.

Simple averages use the average value for some given length of previous time periods to forecast the value for the next period. Moving averages are time period averages that are revised for each time period by including the most recent value(s) in the computation of the average and deleting the value or values that are farthest away from the present time period. A special case of the moving average is the weighted moving average, in which different weights are placed on the values from different time periods.

Simple (single) exponential smoothing is a technique in which data from previous time periods are weighted exponentially to forecast the value for the present time period. The forecaster has the option of selecting how much to weight more recent values versus those of previous time periods.

Decomposition is a method for isolating the four possible effects in time-series data: trend, cycles, seasonal effects, and irregular fluctuations.

Autocorrelation or serial correlation occurs when the error terms from forecasts are correlated over time. In regression analysis, this effect is particularly disturbing because one of the assumptions is that the error terms are independent. One way to test for autocorrelation is to use the Durbin-Watson test. There are a number of methods that attempt to overcome the effects of autocorrelation on the data.

Autoregression is a forecasting technique in which time-series data are predicted by independent variables that are lagged versions of the original dependent variable data. A variable that is lagged one period is derived from values of the previous time period. Other variables can be lagged two or more periods.

Index numbers can be used to translate raw data into numbers that are more readily comparable. Simple index numbers are constructed by creating the ratio of the raw data value for a given time period to the raw data value for the base period and multiplying the ratio by 100. The index number for the base time period is designated to be 100.

Unweighted aggregate price index numbers are constructed by summing the prices of several items for a time period and comparing that sum to the sum of the prices of the same items during a base time period and multiplying the ratio by 100. Weighted aggregate price indexes are index numbers utilizing the prices of several items, and the items are weighted by their quantity usage.

The Laspeyres price index uses the quantity weights from the base year in all calculations. The Paasche price index uses the quantity weights for the current time period for both the current time period and the base time period in calculations.

Key Terms

autocorrelation	exponential smoothing	mean square error (MSE)	smoothing techniques
autoregression	first-differences approach	moving average	stationary
averaging models	forecasting	naïve forecasting models	time-series data
cycles	forecasting error	Paasche price index	trend
cyclical effects	index number	seasonal effects	unweighted aggregate price
decomposition	irregular fluctuations	serial correlation	index number
deseasonalized data	Laspeyres price index	simple average	weighted aggregate price index
Durbin-Watson test	mean absolute	simple average model	numbers
error of an individual forecast	deviation (MAD)	simple index number	weighted moving average

Formulas

Individual forecast error

$$e_t = X_t - F_t$$

Mean absolute deviation

$$\text{MAD} = \frac{\Sigma |e_i|}{\text{Number of Forecasts}}$$

Mean square error

$$\text{MSE} = \frac{\Sigma e_i^2}{\text{Number of Forecasts}}$$

Exponential smoothing

$$F_{t+1} = \alpha \cdot X_t + (1 - \alpha) \cdot F_t$$

Durbin-Watson test

$$D = \frac{\displaystyle\sum_{t=2}^{n} (e_t - e_{t-1})^2}{\displaystyle\sum_{t=1}^{n} e_t^2}$$

Supplementary Problems

Calculating the Statistics

15.27. Following are the average yields of long-term new corporate bonds over a several-month period published by the Office of Market Finance of the U.S. Department of the Treasury.

MONTH	YIELD	MONTH	YIELD
1	10.08	13	7.91
2	10.05	14	7.73
3	9.24	15	7.39
4	9.23	16	7.48
5	9.69	17	7.52
6	9.55	18	7.48
7	9.37	19	7.35
8	8.55	20	7.04
9	8.36	21	6.88
10	8.59	22	6.88
11	7.99	23	7.17
12	8.12	24	7.22

a. Explore trends in these data by using regression trend analysis. How strong are the models? Is the quadratic model significantly stronger than the linear trend model?

b. Use a 4-month moving average to forecast values for each of the ensuing months.

c. Use simple exponential smoothing to forecast values for each of the ensuing months. Let $\alpha = .3$ and then let $\alpha = .7$. Which weight produces better forecasts?

d. Compute MAD for the forecasts obtained in parts (b) and (c) and compare the results.

e. Determine seasonal effects using decomposition on these data. Let the seasonal effects have four periods. After determining the seasonal indexes, deseasonalize the data.

15.28. Compute index numbers for the following data using 1997 as the base year.

YEAR	QUANTITY	YEAR	QUANTITY
1997	2073	2007	2483
1998	2290	2008	2467
1999	2349	2009	2397
2000	2313	2010	2351
2001	2456	2011	2308
2002	2508	2012	2245
2003	2463	2013	2192
2004	2499	2014	2076
2005	2520	2015	2162
2006	2529		

15.29. Compute unweighted aggregate price index numbers for each of the given years using 2012 as the base year.

ITEM	2012	2013	2014	2015	2016
1	3.21	3.37	3.80	3.73	3.65
2	.51	.55	.68	.62	.59
3	.83	.90	.91	1.02	1.06
4	1.30	1.32	1.33	1.32	1.30
5	1.67	1.72	1.90	1.99	1.98
6	.62	.67	.70	.72	.71

15.30. Using the following data and 2013 as the base year, compute the Laspeyres price index for 2016 and the Paasche price index for 2015.

	2013		2014	
ITEM	PRICE	QUANTITY	PRICE	QUANTITY
1	$2.75	12	$2.98	9
2	0.85	47	0.89	52
3	1.33	20	1.32	28

	2015		2016	
ITEM	PRICE	QUANTITY	PRICE	QUANTITY
1	$3.10	9	$3.21	11
2	0.95	61	0.98	66
3	1.36	25	1.40	32

Testing Your Understanding

15.31. The following data contain the quantity (million pounds) of U.S. domestic fish caught annually over a 25-year period as published by the National Oceanic and Atmospheric Administration.

a. Use a 3-year moving average to forecast the quantity of fish for the years 4 through 25 for these data. Compute the error of each forecast and then determine the mean absolute deviation of error for the forecast.

b. Use exponential smoothing and $\alpha = .2$ to forecast the data from 4 through 25. Let the forecast for 2 equal the actual value for 1. Compute the error of each forecast and then determine the mean absolute deviation of error for the forecast.

c. Compare the results obtained in parts (a) and (b) using MAD. Which technique seems to perform better? Why?

YEAR	QUANTITY	YEAR	QUANTITY
1	6,137	4	8,750
2	7,019	5	9,816
3	7,391	6	9,644

7	9,951	17	9,250
8	9,971	18	9,315
9	10,089	19	9,424
10	9,693	20	9,379
11	9,380	21	9,180
12	9,615	22	9,026
13	8,992	23	7,953
14	9,089	24	7,875
15	8,876	25	7,994
16	9,290		

15.32. The U.S. Department of Commerce publishes a series of census documents referred to as *Current Industrial Reports.* Included in these documents are the manufacturers' shipments, inventories, and orders over a 5-year period. Displayed here is a portion of these data representing the shipments of chemicals and allied products from January of year 1 through December of year 5. Use time-series decomposition methods to develop the seasonal indexes for these data.

TIME PERIOD	CHEMICALS AND ALLIED PRODUCTS ($ billion)	TIME PERIOD	CHEMICALS AND ALLIED PRODUCTS ($ billion)
January (year 1)	23.701	January (year 2)	23.347
February	24.189	February	24.122
March	24.200	March	25.282
April	24.971	April	25.426
May	24.560	May	25.185
June	24.992	June	26.486
July	22.566	July	24.088
August	24.037	August	24.672
September	25.047	September	26.072
October	24.115	October	24.328
November	23.034	November	23.826
December	22.590	December	24.373
January (year 3)	24.207	January (year 4)	25.316
February	25.772	February	26.435
March	27.591	March	29.346
April	26.958	April	28.983
May	25.920	May	28.424
June	28.460	June	30.149
July	24.821	July	26.746
August	25.560	August	28.966
September	27.218	September	30.783
October	25.650	October	28.594
November	25.589	November	28.762
December	25.370	December	29.018

TIME PERIOD	CHEMICALS AND ALLIED PRODUCTS ($ billion)
January (year 5)	28.931
February	30.456
March	32.372
April	30.905
May	30.743
June	32.794
July	29.342
August	30.765
September	31.637
October	30.206
November	30.842
December	31.090

15.33. Use the seasonal indexes computed to deseasonalize the data in Problem 15.32.

15.34. Determine the trend for the data in Problem 15.32 using the deseasonalized data from Problem 15.33. Explore both a linear and a quadratic model in an attempt to develop the better trend model.

15.35. Shown here are retail price figures and quantity estimates for five different food commodities over 3 years. Use these data and a base year of 2014 to compute unweighted aggregate price indexes for this market basket of food. Using a base year of 2014, calculate Laspeyres price indexes and Paasche price indexes for 2015 and 2016.

	2014		2015		2016	
ITEM	PRICE	QUANTITY	PRICE	QUANTITY	PRICE	QUANTITY
Margarine (lb.)	1.26	21	1.32	23	1.39	22
Shortening (lb.)	0.94	5	0.97	3	1.12	4
Milk (1/2 gal.)	1.43	70	1.56	68	1.62	65
Cola (2 liters)	1.05	12	1.02	13	1.25	11
Potato chips (12 oz.)	2.81	27	2.86	29	2.99	28

15.36. Given below are data on the number of business establishments (millions) and the self-employment rate (%) released by the Small Business Administration, Office of Advocacy, for a 21-year period of U.S. business activity. Develop a regression model to predict the self-employment rate by the number of business establishments. Use this model to predict the self-employment rate for a year in which there are 7.0 (million) business establishments. Discuss the strength of the regression model. Use these data and the regression model to compute a Durbin-Watson test to determine whether significant autocorrelation is present. Let alpha be .05.

NUMBER OF ESTABLISHMENTS (millions)	SELF-EMPLOYMENT RATE (%)
4.54317	8.1
4.58651	8.0

4.63396	8.1
5.30679	8.2
5.51772	8.2
5.70149	8.0
5.80697	7.9
5.93706	8.0
6.01637	8.2
6.10692	8.1
6.17556	8.0
6.20086	8.1
6.31930	7.8
6.40123	8.0
6.50907	8.1
6.61272	7.9
6.73848	7.8
6.89487	7.7
6.94182	7.5
7.00844	7.2
7.07005	6.9

15.37. Shown here are the consumer price indexes (CPIs) for housing for the years 1991 through 2014 from the Bureau of Labor Statistics Data Web site. Use the data to answer the following questions.

a. Compute the 4-year moving average to forecast the CPIs from 1995 through 2014.

b. Compute the 4-year weighted moving average to forecast the CPIs from 1995 through 2014. Weight the most recent year by 4, the next most recent year by 3, the next year by 2, and the last year of the four by 1.

c. Determine the errors for parts (a) and (b). Compute MSE for parts (a) and (b). Compare the MSE values and comment on the effectiveness of the moving average versus the weighted moving average for these data.

YEAR	HOUSING CPI	YEAR	HOUSING CPI
1991	133.6	2003	184.8
1992	137.5	2004	189.5
1993	141.2	2005	195.7
1994	144.8	2006	203.2
1995	148.5	2007	209.6
1996	152.8	2008	216.3
1997	156.8	2009	217.1
1998	160.4	2010	216.3
1999	163.9	2011	219.1
2000	169.6	2012	222.7
2001	176.4	2013	227.4
2002	180.3	2014	233.2

15.38. In the *Survey of Current Business,* the U.S. Department of Commerce publishes data on farm commodity prices. Given are the cotton prices from November of year 1 through February of year 4. The prices are indexes with a base of 100 from the period of 1910

through 1914. Use these data to develop autoregression models for a 1-month lag and a 4-month lag. Compare the results of these two models. Which model seems to yield better predictions? Why?

TIME PERIOD	COTTON PRICES
November (year 1)	552
December	519
January (year 2)	505
February	512
March	541
April	549
May	552
June	526
July	531
August	545
September	549
October	570
November	576
December	568
January (year 3)	571
February	573
March	582
April	587
May	592
June	570
July	560
August	565
September	547
October	529
November	514
December	469
January (year 4)	436
February	419

15.39. The U.S. Department of Commerce publishes data on industrial machinery and equipment. Shown here are the shipments (in $ billions) of industrial machinery and equipment from the first quarter of year 1 through the fourth quarter of year 6. Use these data to determine the seasonal indexes for the data through time-series decomposition methods. Use the four-quarter centered moving average in the computations.

TIME PERIOD	INDUSTRIAL MACHINERY AND EQUIPMENT SHIPMENTS
1st quarter (year 1)	54.019
2nd quarter	56.495
3rd quarter	50.169
4th quarter	52.891

1st quarter (year 2)	51.915
2nd quarter	55.101
3rd quarter	53.419
4th quarter	57.236
1st quarter (year 3)	57.063
2nd quarter	62.488
3rd quarter	60.373
4th quarter	63.334
1st quarter (year 4)	62.723
2nd quarter	68.380
3rd quarter	63.256
4th quarter	66.446
1st quarter (year 5)	65.445
2nd quarter	68.011
3rd quarter	63.245
4th quarter	66.872
1st quarter (year 6)	59.714
2nd quarter	63.590
3rd quarter	58.088
4th quarter	61.443

15.40. Use the seasonal indexes computed to deseasonalize the data in Problem 15.39.

15.41. Use both a linear and quadratic model to explore trends in the deseasonalized data from Problem 15.40. Which model seems to produce a better fit of the data?

15.42. The Board of Governors of the Federal Reserve System publishes data on mortgage debt outstanding by type of property and holder. The following data give the amounts of residential nonfarm debt (in $ billions) held by savings institutions in the United States over a 10-year period. Use these data to develop an autoregression model with a one-period lag. Discuss the strength of the model.

YEAR	DEBT
1	529
2	554
3	559
4	602
5	672
6	669
7	600
8	538
9	490
10	470

15.43. Shown here are data from the Investment Company Institute on Total Net Assets and Total Number of Shareholder Accounts of money market funds over a period of 27 years. Use these data to develop a regression model to forecast Total Net Assets by the Total Number of Shareholder Accounts. Total Net Assets is given in billions of dollars and Total Number of Shareholder Accounts is given in millions. Conduct a Durbin-Watson test on the data and the regression model to determine whether significant autocorrelation is present. Let $\alpha = .01$.

YEAR	TOTAL NET ASSETS ($ billions)	TOTAL NUMBER OF SHAREHOLDER ACCOUNTS (millions)
1986	292.2	16.3
1987	316.1	17.7
1988	338.0	18.6
1989	428.1	21.3
1990	498.3	23.0
1991	542.4	23.6
1992	546.2	23.6
1993	565.3	23.6
1994	611.0	25.4
1995	753.0	30.1
1996	901.8	32.2
1997	1,058.9	35.6
1998	1,351.7	38.8
1999	1,613.1	43.6
2000	1,845.2	48.1
2001	2,285.3	47.2
2002	2,265.1	45.4
2003	2,040.0	41.2
2004	1,901.3	37.6
2005	2,026.8	36.8
2006	2,338.5	37.1
2007	3,085.8	39.1
2008	3,832.2	38.1
2009	3,315.9	33.5
2010	2,803.9	30.3
2011	2,691.4	28.7
2012	2,693.5	27.9
2013	2,718.3	26.1

15.44. The purchasing-power value figures for the minimum wage in dollars for the years 1 through 18 are shown here. Use these data and exponential smoothing to develop forecasts for the years 2 through 18. Try $\alpha = .1$, .5, and .8, and compare the results using MAD. Discuss your findings. Select the value of alpha that worked best and use your exponential smoothing results to predict purchasing power for year 19.

YEAR	PURCHASING POWER	YEAR	PURCHASING POWER
1	$6.04	10	$4.34
2	5.92	11	4.67
3	5.57	12	5.01
4	5.40	13	4.86
5	5.17	14	4.72
6	5.00	15	4.60
7	4.91	16	4.48
8	4.73	17	4.86
9	4.55	18	5.15

Interpreting the Output

15.45. Shown below is the Excel output for a regression analysis to predict the number of business bankruptcy filings over a 16-year period by the number of consumer bankruptcy filings. How strong is the model? Note the residuals. Compute a Durbin-Watson statistic from the data and discuss the presence of autocorrelation in this model.

SUMMARY OUTPUT

Regression Statistics

Multiple R	0.529
R Square	0.280
Adjusted R Square	0.228
Standard Error	8179.84
Observations	16

ANOVA

	df	SS	MS	F	Significance F
Regression	1	364069877.4	364069877.4	5.44	0.0351
Residual	14	936737379.6	66909812.8		
Total	15	1300807257			

	Coefficients	Standard Error	t Stat	P-value
Intercept	75532.43621	4980.08791	15.17	0.0000
Year	−0.01574	0.00675	−2.33	0.0351

RESIDUAL OUTPUT

Observation	Predicted Bus. Bankruptcies	Residuals
1	70638.58	−1338.6
2	71024.28	−8588.3
3	71054.61	−7050.6
4	70161.99	1115.0
5	68462.72	12772.3
6	67733.25	14712.8
7	66882.45	−3029.4
8	65834.05	−2599.1
9	64230.61	622.4
10	61801.70	9747.3
11	61354.16	9288.8
12	62738.76	−434.8
13	63249.36	−10875.4
14	61767.01	−9808.0
15	57826.69	−4277.7
16	54283.80	−256.8

Analyzing the Databases

See **www.wiley.com/college/black** and **WileyPLUS**

1. Use the Agricultural time-series database and the variable Green Beans to forecast the number of green beans for period 169 by using following techniques.

   a. Five-period moving average

   b. Simple exponential smoothing with $\alpha = .6$

   c. Time-series linear trend model

   d. Decomposition

2. Use decomposition on Carrots in the Agricultural database to determine the seasonal indexes. These data actually represent 14 years of 12-month data. Do the seasonal indexes indicate the presence of some seasonal effects? Run an autoregression model to predict Carrots by a 1-month lag and another by a 12-month lag. Compare the two models. Because vegetables are somewhat seasonal, is the 12-month lag model significant?

3. Use the Energy database to forecast year 27 U.S. coal production by using simple exponential smoothing of previous U.S. coal production data. Let $\alpha = .2$ and $\alpha = .8$. Compare the forecast with the actual figure. Which of the two models produces the forecast with the least error?

4. Use the International Labor database to develop a regression model to predict the unemployment rate for Germany by the unemployment rate of Italy. Test for autocorrelation and discuss its presence or absence in this regression analysis.

Case

Debourgh Manufacturing Company

The DeBourgh Manufacturing Company was founded in 1909 as a metal-fabricating company in Minnesota by the four Berg brothers. In the 1980s, the company ran into hard times, as did the rest of the metal-fabricating industry. Among the problems that DeBourgh faced were declining sales, deteriorating labor relations, and increasing costs. Labor unions had resisted cost-cutting measures. Losses were piling up in the heavy job-shop fabrication division, which was the largest of the company's three divisions. A division that made pedestrian steel bridges closed in 1990. The remaining company division, producer of All-American lockers, had to move to a lower-cost environment.

In 1990, with the company's survival at stake, the firm made a risky decision and moved everything from its high-cost location in Minnesota to a lower-cost area in La Junta, Colorado. Eighty semi-trailer trucks were used to move equipment and inventory 1000 miles at a cost of $1.2 million. The company was relocated to a building in La Junta that had stood vacant for three years. Only 10 of the Minnesota workers transferred with the company, which quickly hired and trained 80 more workers in La Junta. By moving to La Junta, the company was able to go nonunion.

DeBourgh also faced a financial crisis. A bank that had been loaning the company money for 35 years would no longer do so. In addition, a costly severance package was worked out with Minnesota workers to keep production going during the move. An internal stock-purchase "earnout" was arranged between company president Steven C. Berg and his three aunts, who were the other principal owners.

The roof of the building that was to be the new home of DeBourgh Manufacturing in La Junta was badly in need of repair. During the first few weeks of production, heavy rains fell on the area and production was all but halted. However, DeBourgh was able to overcome these obstacles. One year later, locker sales achieved record-high sales levels each month. The company is now more profitable than ever, with sales topping $10 million. Much credit has been given to the positive spirit of teamwork fostered among its over 100 employees. Emphasis shifted to employee involvement in decision making, quality, teamwork, employee participation in compensation action, and shared profits. In addition, DeBourgh became a more socially responsible company by doing more for the town in which it is located and by using paints that are more environmentally friendly.

Discussion

1. After its move in 1990 to La Junta, Colorado, and its new initiatives, the DeBourgh Manufacturing Company began an upward climb of record sales. Suppose the figures shown here are the DeBourgh monthly sales figures from January 2008 through December 2016 (in $1000s). Are any trends evident in the data? Does DeBourgh have a seasonal component to its sales? Shown after the sales figures is Minitab output from a decomposition analysis of the sales figures using 12-month seasonality. Next an Excel graph displays the data with a trend line. Examine the data, the output, and any additional analysis you feel is helpful, and write a short report on DeBourgh sales. Include a discussion of the general direction of sales and any seasonal tendencies that might be occurring.

MONTH	2008	2009	2010	2011	2012	2013	2014	2015	2016
January	139.7	165.1	177.8	228.6	266.7	431.8	381.0	431.8	495.3
February	114.3	177.8	203.2	254.0	317.5	457.2	406.4	444.5	533.4
March	101.6	177.8	228.6	266.7	368.3	457.2	431.8	495.3	635.0
April	152.4	203.2	279.4	342.9	431.8	482.6	457.2	533.4	673.1
May	215.9	241.3	317.5	355.6	457.2	533.4	495.3	558.8	749.3
June	228.6	279.4	330.2	406.4	571.5	622.3	584.2	647.7	812.8
July	215.9	292.1	368.3	444.5	546.1	660.4	609.6	673.1	800.1
August	190.5	317.5	355.6	431.8	482.6	520.7	558.8	660.4	736.6
September	177.8	203.2	241.3	330.2	431.8	508.0	508.0	609.6	685.8
October	139.7	177.8	215.9	330.2	406.4	482.6	495.3	584.2	635.0
November	139.7	165.1	215.9	304.8	393.7	457.2	444.5	520.7	622.3
December	152.4	177.8	203.2	292.1	406.4	431.8	419.1	482.6	622.3

Time-Series Decomposition for Sales

```
Multiplicative Model
Data:          Sales
Length:        108
NMissing:      0
```

Fitted Trend Equation

$$Y_t = 121.481 + 5.12862 \cdot t$$

Seasonal Indices

Period	Index
1	0.79487
2	0.85125
3	0.92600
4	1.02227
5	1.11591
6	1.24281
7	1.31791
8	1.16422
9	0.99201
10	0.91524
11	0.85071
12	0.80679

```
Accuracy Measures
MAPE:      8.04
MAD:      29.51
MSD:    1407.55
```

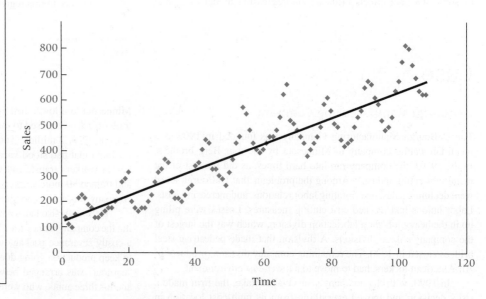

2. Suppose DeBourgh accountants computed a per-unit labor cost of lockers for each year since 2003, as reported here. Use techniques in this chapter to analyze the data. Forecast the per-unit labor costs through the year 2016. Use smoothing techniques, moving averages, trend analysis, and any others that seem appropriate. Calculate the error of the forecasts and determine which forecasting method seems to do the best job of minimizing error. Study the data and explain the behavior of the per-unit labor cost since 2003. Think about the company history and objectives since 2003.

YEAR	PER-UNIT LABOR COST	YEAR	PER-UNIT LABOR COST
2003	$80.15	2010	$59.84
2004	85.29	2011	57.29
2005	85.75	2012	58.74
2006	64.23	2013	55.01
2007	63.70	2014	56.20
2008	62.54	2015	55.93
2009	60.19	2016	55.60

Source: Adapted from "DeBourgh Manufacturing Company: A Move That Saved a Company," *Real-World Lessons for America's Small Businesses: Insights from the Blue Chip Enterprise Initiative*. Published by *Nation's Business* magazine on behalf of Connecticut Mutual Life Insurance Company and the U.S. Chamber of Commerce in association with the Blue Chip Enterprise Initiative, 1992; the Web site containing Colorado Springs top business stories, available at http://www.csbj.com/1998/981113/top_stor.htm, and DeBourgh, available at http://www.debourgh.com, 2016.

CHAPTER 16

Analysis of Categorical Data

LEARNING OBJECTIVES

The overall objective of this chapter is to give you an understanding of two statistical techniques used to analyze categorical data, thereby enabling you to:

1. Use the chi-square goodness-of-fit test to analyze probabilities of multinomial distribution trials along a single dimension.

2. Use the chi-square test of independence to perform contingency analysis.

Decision Dilemma

Selecting Suppliers in the Electronics Industry

What criteria are used in the electronics industry to select a supplier? In years past, price has been the dominant criterion of suppliers in many industries, and the supplier with the low bid often got the job. In more recent years, companies have been forced by global competition and a marked increase in quality to examine other aspects of potential suppliers.

Pearson and Ellram investigated the techniques used by firms in the electronics industry to select suppliers, and they wanted to determine if there is a difference between small and large firms in supplier selection. They sent out a survey instrument with questions about criteria used to select and evaluate suppliers, the participation of various functional areas in the selection process, and the formality of methods used in the selection. Of the 210 survey responses received, 87 were from small companies and 123 from large companies. The average sales were $33 million for the small companies and $583 million for the large companies.

Survey questions were stated in such a way as to generate frequencies. The respondents were given a series of supplier selection and evaluation criteria such as quality, cost, current technology, design capabilities, speed to market, manufacturing process, location, and so on. They were asked to check off the criteria used in supplier selection and evaluation and to rank the criteria that they checked. As part of the analysis, the researchers recorded how many of each of the small and large company respondents ranked a criterion first, how many ranked it second, and how many ranked it third. The results are shown in the following table of raw numbers for the criteria of quality, cost, and current technology.

Chris Knapton/Photo Researchers

QUALITY	COMPANY SIZE	
	Small	Large
1	48	70
2	17	27
3	7	6

COST	COMPANY SIZE	
	Small	Large
1	8	14
2	29	36
3	26	37

CURRENT TECHNOLOGY	COMPANY SIZE	
	Small	Large
1	5	13
2	8	11
3	5	12

Source: Adapted from John N. Pearson and Lisa M. Ellram. "Supplier Selection and Evaluation in Small Versus Large Electronics Firms," *Journal of Small Business Management,* vol. 33, no. 4 (October 1995), pp. 53–65.

MANAGERIAL AND STATISTICAL QUESTIONS

1. Is there a difference between small and large companies in the ranking of criteria for the evaluation and selection of suppliers in the electronics industry?

2. The authors of the study used frequencies to measure the relative rankings of criteria. What is the appropriate statistical technique to analyze these data?

In this chapter, we explore techniques for analyzing categorical data. Categorical data are *nonnumerical data that are frequency counts of categories from one or more variables.* For example, it is determined that of the 790 people attending a convention, 240 are engineers, 160 are managers, 310 are sales reps, and 80 are information technologists. The variable is "position in company" with four categories: engineers, managers, sales reps, and information technologists. The data are not ratings or sales figures but rather frequency counts of how many of each position attended the conference. Research questions producing this type of data are often analyzed using chi-square techniques. The chi-square distribution was introduced in Chapters 8 and 9. The techniques presented here for analyzing categorical data, the *chi-square goodness-of-fit test* and the *chi-square test of independence,* are an outgrowth of the binomial distribution and the inferential techniques for analyzing population proportions.

16.1 Chi-Square Goodness-of-Fit Test

In Chapter 5, we studied the binomial distribution, in which only two possible outcomes could occur on a single trial in an experiment. An extension of the binomial distribution is a multinomial distribution in which more than two possible outcomes can occur in a single trial. The chi-square goodness-of-fit test is *used to analyze probabilities of multinomial distribution trials along a single dimension.* For example, if the variable being studied is economic class with three possible outcomes of lower income class, middle income class, and upper income class, the single dimension is economic class and the three possible outcomes are the three classes. On each trial, one and only one of the outcomes can occur. In other words, a family unit must be classified either as lower income class, middle income class, or upper income class and cannot be in more than one class.

The chi-square goodness-of-fit test compares the *expected,* or theoretical, frequencies of categories from a population distribution to the *observed,* or actual, frequencies from a distribution to determine whether there is a difference between what was expected and what was observed. For example, airline industry officials might theorize that the ages of airline ticket purchasers are distributed in a particular way. To validate or reject this expected distribution, an actual sample of ticket purchaser ages can be gathered randomly, and the observed results can be compared to the expected results with the chi-square goodness-of-fit test. This test also can be used to determine whether the observed arrivals at teller windows at a bank are Poisson distributed, as might be expected. In the paper industry, manufacturers can use the chi-square goodness-of-fit test to determine whether the demand for paper follows a uniform distribution throughout the year.

Formula 16.1 is used to compute a chi-square goodness-of-fit test.

Chi-Square Goodness-of-Fit Test

$$\chi^2 = \sum \frac{(f_o - f_e)^2}{f_e} \tag{16.1}$$

$$df = k - 1 - c$$

where

f_o = frequency of observed values
f_e = frequency of expected values
k = number of categories
c = number of parameters being estimated from the sample data

This formula compares the frequency of observed values to the frequency of the expected values across the distribution. The test loses one degree of freedom because the total number of expected frequencies must equal the number of observed frequencies; that is, the observed total taken from the sample is used as the total for the expected frequencies. In addition, in some instances a population parameter, such as λ, μ, or σ, is estimated from the sample data to determine the frequency distribution of expected values. Each time this estimation occurs, an additional degree of freedom is lost. As a rule, if a uniform distribution is being used as the expected distribution or if an expected distribution of values is given, $k - 1$ degrees of freedom are used in the test. In testing to determine whether an observed distribution is Poisson, the degrees of freedom are $k - 2$ because an additional degree of freedom is lost in estimating λ. In testing to determine whether an observed distribution is normal, the degrees of freedom are $k - 3$ because two additional degrees of freedom are lost in estimating both μ and σ from the observed sample data.

Karl Pearson introduced the chi-square test in 1900. The chi-square distribution is *the sum of the squares of k independent random variables* and therefore can never be less than zero; it extends indefinitely in the positive direction. Actually the chi-square distributions constitute a family, with each distribution defined by the degrees of freedom (df) associated with it. For small df values the chi-square distribution is skewed considerably to the right (positive values). As the df increase, the chi-square distribution begins to approach the normal curve. Table values for the chi-square distribution are given in Appendix A. Because of space limitations, chi-square values are listed only for certain probabilities.

How can the chi-square goodness-of-fit test be applied to business situations? One survey of U.S. consumers conducted by *the Wall Street Journal* and NBC News asked the question: "In general, how would you rate the level of service that American businesses provide?" The distribution of responses to this question was as follows:

Excellent	8%
Pretty good	47%
Only fair	34%
Poor	11%

Suppose a store manager wants to find out whether the results of this consumer survey apply to customers of supermarkets in her city. To do so, she interviews 207 randomly selected consumers as they leave supermarkets in various parts of the city. She asks the customers how they would rate the level of service at the supermarket from which they had just exited. The response categories are excellent, pretty good, only fair, and poor. The observed responses from this study are given in Table 16.1. Now the manager can use a chi-square goodness-of-fit test and the eight-step approach to determine whether the observed frequencies of responses from this survey are the same as the frequencies that would be expected on the basis of the national survey.

Step 1 The hypotheses for this example follows.

H_0: The observed distribution is the same as the expected distribution.

H_a: The observed distribution is not the same as the expected distribution.

Step 2 The statistical test being used is

$$\chi^2 = \sum \frac{(f_o - f_e)^2}{f_e}$$

Step 3 Let $\alpha = .05$.

Step 4 Chi-square goodness-of-fit tests are one tailed because a chi-square of zero indicates perfect agreement between distributions. Any deviation from zero difference occurs in the positive direction only because chi-square is determined by a sum of squared values and can never be negative. With four categories in this example (excellent, pretty good, only fair, and poor), $k = 4$. The degrees of freedom are $k - 1$ because the expected distribution is given: $k - 1 = 4 - 1 = 3$. For $\alpha = .05$ and df = 3, the critical chi-square value is

$$\chi^2_{.05,3} = 7.8147$$

TABLE 16.1

Results of a Local Survey of Consumer Satisfaction

RESPONSE	FREQUENCY (f_o)
Excellent	21
Pretty good	109
Only fair	62
Poor	15

TABLE 16.2	Construction of Expected Values for Service Satisfaction Study		
RESPONSE	**EXPECTED PROPORTION**	**EXPECTED FREQUENCY (f_e)** **(PROPORTION × SAMPLE TOTAL)**	
Excellent	.08	(.08)(207) = 16.56	
Pretty good	.47	(.47)(207) = 97.29	
Only fair	.34	(.34)(207) = 70.38	
Poor	.11	(.11)(207) = 22.77	
		207.00	

TABLE 16.3	Calculation of Chi-Square for Service Satisfaction Example		
RESPONSE	f_o	f_e	$\dfrac{(f_o - f_e)^2}{f_e}$
Excellent	21	16.56	1.19
Pretty good	109	97.29	1.41
Only fair	62	70.38	1.00
Poor	15	22.77	2.65
	207	207.00	6.25

After the data are analyzed, an observed chi-square greater than 7.8147 must be computed in order to reject the null hypothesis.

Step 5   The observed values gathered in the sample data from Table 16.1 sum to 207. Thus $n = 207$. The expected proportions are given, but the expected frequencies must be calculated by multiplying the expected proportions by the sample total of the observed frequencies, as shown in Table 16.2.

Step 6   The chi-square goodness-of-fit can then be calculated, as shown in Table 16.3.

Step 7   Because the observed value of chi-square of 6.25 is not greater than the critical table value of 7.8147, the store manager will not reject the null hypothesis.

Step 8   Thus, the data gathered in the sample of 207 supermarket shoppers indicate that the distribution of responses of supermarket shoppers in the manager's city is not significantly different from the distribution of responses to the national survey.

   The store manager may conclude that her customers do not appear to have attitudes different from those people who took the survey. Figure 16.1 depicts the chi-square distribution produced by using Minitab for this example, along with the observed and critical values.

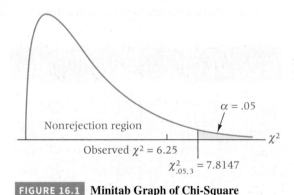

FIGURE 16.1   **Minitab Graph of Chi-Square Distribution for Service Satisfaction Example**

DEMONSTRATION PROBLEM 16.1

Dairies would like to know whether the sales of milk are distributed uniformly over a year so they can plan for milk production and storage. A uniform distribution means that the frequencies are the same in all categories. In this situation, the producers are attempting to determine whether the amounts of milk sold are the same for each month of the year. They ascertain the number of gallons of milk sold by sampling one large supermarket during a year, obtaining the following monthly data. Use $\alpha = .01$ to test whether the data fit a uniform distribution.

MONTH	GALLONS	MONTH	GALLONS
January	1610	August	1350
February	1585	September	1495
March	1649	October	1564
April	1590	November	1602
May	1540	December	1655
June	1397	Total	18,447
July	1410		

Solution:

Step 1. The hypotheses follow.

H_0: The monthly figures for milk sales are uniformly distributed.

H_a: The monthly figures for milk sales are not uniformly distributed.

Step 2. The statistical test used is

$$\chi^2 = \sum \frac{(f_o - f_e)^2}{f_e}$$

Step 3. Alpha is .01.

Step 4. There are 12 categories and a uniform distribution is the expected distribution, so the degrees of freedom are $k - 1 = 12 - 1 = 11$. For $\alpha = .01$, the critical value is $\chi^2_{.01,11} = 24.725$. An observed chi-square value of more than 24.725 must be obtained to reject the null hypothesis.

Step 5. The data are given in the preceding table.

Step 6. The first step in calculating the test statistic is to determine the expected frequencies. The total for the expected frequencies must equal the total for the observed frequencies (18,447). If the frequencies are uniformly distributed, the same number of gallons of milk is expected to be sold each month. The expected monthly figure is

$$\frac{18,447}{12} = 1537.25 \text{ gallons}$$

The following table shows the observed frequencies, the expected frequencies, and the chi-square calculations for this problem.

MONTH	f_o	f_e	$\frac{(f_o - f_e)^2}{f_e}$
January	1610	1537.25	3.44
February	1585	1537.25	1.48
March	1649	1537.25	8.12
April	1590	1537.25	1.81
May	1540	1537.25	0.00
June	1397	1537.25	12.80
July	1410	1537.25	10.53
August	1350	1537.25	22.81
September	1495	1537.25	1.16
October	1564	1537.25	0.47
November	1602	1537.25	2.73
December	1655	1537.25	9.02
Total	18,447	18,447.00	$\chi^2 = 74.37$

Step 7. The observed χ^2 value of 74.37 is greater than the critical table value of $\chi^2_{.01,11} = 24.725$, so the decision is to reject the null hypothesis. This problem provides enough evidence to indicate that the distribution of milk sales is not uniform.

Step 8.   Because retail milk demand is not uniformly distributed, sales and production managers need to generate a production plan to cope with uneven demand. In times of heavy demand, more milk will need to be processed or drawn from reserves; in times of less demand, provision for milk storage or for a reduction in the purchase of milk from dairy farmers will be necessary.

   The following Minitab graph depicts the chi-square distribution, critical chi-square value, and observed chi-square value.

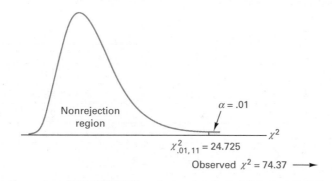

Nonrejection region

$\alpha = .01$

χ^2

$\chi^2_{.01,11} = 24.725$

Observed $\chi^2 = 74.37$ ⟶

DEMONSTRATION PROBLEM 16.2

Chapter 5 indicated that, quite often in the business world, random arrivals are Poisson distributed. This distribution is characterized by an average arrival rate, λ, per some interval. Suppose a teller supervisor believes the distribution of random arrivals at a local bank is Poisson and sets out to test this hypothesis by gathering information. The following data represent a distribution of frequency of arrivals during 1-minute intervals at the bank. Use $\alpha = .05$ and the eight-step approach to test these data in an effort to determine whether they are Poisson distributed.

NUMBER OF ARRIVALS	OBSERVED FREQUENCIES
0	7
1	18
2	25
3	17
4	12
≥5	5

Solution:

Step 1.   The hypotheses follow.

   H_0: The frequency distribution is Poisson.

   H_a: The frequency distribution is not Poisson.

Step 2.   The appropriate statistical test for this problem is

$$\chi^2 = \sum \frac{(f_o - f_e)^2}{f_e}$$

Step 3.   Alpha is .05.

Step 4.   The degrees of freedom are $k - 2 = 6 - 1 - 1 = 4$ because the expected distribution is Poisson. An extra degree of freedom is lost, because the value of lambda must be calculated by using the observed sample data. For $\alpha = .05$, the critical table value is $\chi^2_{.05,4} = 9.4877$. The decision rule is to reject the null hypothesis if the observed chi-square is greater than $\chi^2_{.05,4} = 9.4877$.

Step 5.   To determine the expected frequencies, the supervisor must obtain the probability of each category of arrivals and then multiply each by the total of the observed frequencies. These probabilities are obtained by determining lambda and then using the Poisson table. As it is the mean of a Poisson distribution, lambda can be determined from the observed data by computing the mean of the data. In this case, the supervisor computes a weighted average by summing the product of number of arrivals and frequency of those arrivals and dividing that sum by the total number of observed frequencies.

NUMBER OF ARRIVALS	OBSERVED FREQUENCIES	ARRIVAL × OBSERVED
0	7	0
1	18	18
2	25	50
3	17	51
4	12	48
≥5	5	25
	84	192

$$\lambda = \frac{192}{84} = 2.3$$

With this value of lambda and the Poisson distribution table in Appendix A, the supervisor can determine the probabilities of the number of arrivals in each category. The expected probabilities are determined from Table A.3 by looking up the values of $x = 0$, 1, 2, 3, and 4 in the column under $\lambda = 2.3$, shown in the following table as expected probabilities. The probability for $x \geq 5$ is determined by summing the probabilities for the values of $x = 5$, 6, 7, 8, and so on. Using these probabilities and the total of 84 from the observed data, the supervisor computes the expected frequencies by multiplying each expected probability by the total (84).

ARRIVALS	EXPECTED PROBABILITIES	EXPECTED FREQUENCIES
0	.1003	8.42
1	.2306	19.37
2	.2652	22.28
3	.2033	17.08
4	.1169	9.82
≥5	.0837	7.03
		84.00

Step 6. The supervisor uses these expected frequencies and the observed frequencies to compute the observed value of chi-square.

ARRIVALS	OBSERVED FREQUENCIES	EXPECTED FREQUENCIES	$\frac{(f_o - f_e)^2}{f_e}$
0	7	8.42	.24
1	18	19.37	.10
2	25	22.28	.33
3	17	17.08	.00
4	12	9.82	.48
≥5	5	7.03	.59
	84	84.00	$\chi^2 = 1.74$

Step 7. The observed value of 1.74 is not greater than the critical chi-square value of 9.4877, so the supervisor's decision is to not reject the null hypothesis. In other words, he fails to reject the hypothesis that the distribution of bank arrivals is Poisson.

Step 8. The supervisor can use the Poisson distribution as the basis for other types of analysis, such as queuing modeling.

The following Minitab graph depicts the chi-square distribution, critical value, and computed value.

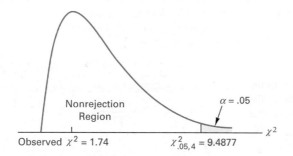

Nonrejection Region

$\alpha = .05$

Observed $\chi^2 = 1.74$

$\chi^2_{.05,4} = 9.4877$

χ^2

Caution: *When the expected value of a category is small, a large chi-square value can be obtained erroneously, leading to a Type I error. To control for this potential error, the chi-square goodness-of-fit test should not be used when any of the expected frequencies is less than 5. If the observed data produce expected values of less than 5, combining adjacent categories (when meaningful) to create larger frequencies may be possible.*

16.1 Problems

16.1. Use a chi-square goodness-of-fit test to determine whether the observed frequencies are distributed the same as the expected frequencies ($\alpha = .05$).

CATEGORY	f_o	f_e
1	53	68
2	37	42
3	32	33
4	28	22
5	18	10
6	15	8

16.2. Use the following data and $\alpha = .01$ to determine whether the observed frequencies represent a uniform distribution.

CATEGORY	f_o
1	19
2	17
3	14
4	18
5	19
6	21
7	18
8	18

16.3. Are the following data Poisson distributed? Use $\alpha = .05$ and the chi-square goodness-of-fit test to answer this question. What is your estimated lambda?

NUMBER OF ARRIVALS	f_o
0	28
1	17
2	11
3	5

16.4. Use the chi-square goodness-of-fit to test to determine if the following observed data are normally distributed. Let $\alpha = .05$. What are your estimated mean and standard deviation?

CATEGORY	OBSERVED
10–under 20	6
20–under 30	14
30–under 40	29
40–under 50	38
50–under 60	25
60–under 70	10
70–under 80	7

16.5. In one survey, successful female entrepreneurs were asked to state their personal definition of success in terms of several categories from which they could select. Thirty-nine percent responded that happiness was their definition of success, 12% said that sales/profit was their definition, 18% responded that helping others was their definition, and 31% responded that achievements/challenge was their definition. Suppose you wanted to determine whether male entrepreneurs felt the same way and took a random sample of men, resulting in the following data. Use the chi-square goodness-of-fit test to determine whether the observed frequency distribution of data for men is the same as the distribution for women. Let $\alpha = .05$.

DEFINITION	f_o
Happiness	42
Sales/profit	95
Helping others	27
Achievements/challenge	63

16.6. The following percentages come from a national survey of the ages of prerecorded-music shoppers. A local survey produced the observed values. Does the evidence in the observed data indicate that we should reject the national survey distribution for local prerecorded-music shoppers? Use $\alpha = .01$.

AGE	PERCENT FROM NATIONAL SURVEY	f_o
10–14	9	22
15–19	23	50
20–24	22	43
25–29	14	29
30–34	10	19
≥35	22	49

16.7. The general manager of a major league baseball team believes the ages of purchasers of game tickets are normally distributed. The following data represent the distribution of ages for a sample of observed purchasers of major league baseball game tickets. Use the chi-square goodness-of-fit test to determine whether this distribution is significantly different from the normal distribution. Assume that $\alpha = .05$.

AGE OF PURCHASER	FREQUENCY
10–under 20	16
20–under 30	44
30–under 40	61
40–under 50	56
50–under 60	35
60–under 70	19

16.8. The Springfield Emergency Medical Service keeps records of emergency telephone calls. A study of 150 five-minute time intervals resulted in the distribution of number of calls that follows. For example, during 18 of the 5-minute intervals, no calls occurred. Use the chi-square goodness-of-fit test and $\alpha = .01$ to determine whether this distribution is Poisson.

NUMBER OF CALLS (PER 5-MINUTE INTERVAL)	FREQUENCY
0	18
1	28
2	47
3	21
4	16
5	11
6 or more	9

16.9. According to a report by the U.S. Environmental Protection Agency (EPA), containers and packaging generated about 30.3% of all municipal solid waste (MSW) in the country in a recent year. This was the largest category of such waste. The next highest group was nondurable goods, which accounted for 21.3% of waste. This was followed by durable goods at 19.6%, yard trimmings/other at 14.9%, and food scraps at 13.9%. Suppose last year, one large midwestern U.S. city processed 300 (1,000 tons) of municipal solid waste (MSW) broken down by categories as follows:

CATEGORY	MSW (1,000 tons)
Containers and Packaging	86
Nondurable Goods	74
Durable Goods	70
Yard Trimmings/Other	41
Food Scraps	29

Use the chi-square goodness-of-fit test to determine if there is a significant difference between the distribution of municipal solid waste in this midwestern city and the distribution released by the EPA. Let $\alpha = .10$.

16.2 Contingency Analysis: Chi-Square Test of Independence

Interactive Applet

The chi-square goodness-of-fit test is used to analyze the distribution of frequencies for categories of *one* variable, such as age or number of bank arrivals, to determine whether the distribution of these frequencies is the same as some hypothesized or expected distribution. However, the goodness-of-fit test cannot be used to analyze *two* variables simultaneously. A different chi-square test, the **chi-square test of independence**, can be *used to analyze the frequencies of two variables with multiple categories to determine whether the two variables are independent.* Many times this type of analysis is desirable. For example, a market researcher might want to determine whether the type of soft drink preferred by a consumer is independent of the consumer's age. An organizational behaviorist might want to know whether absenteeism is independent of job classification. Financial investors might want to determine whether type of preferred stock investment is independent of the region where the investor resides.

The chi-square test of independence can be used to analyze any level of data measurement, but it is particularly useful in analyzing nominal data. Suppose a business researcher is interested in determining whether geographic region is independent of type of financial investment. On a questionnaire, the following two questions might be used to measure geographic region and type of financial investment.

In which region of the country do you reside?

A. Northeast   B. Midwest   C. South   D. West

Which type of financial investment are you most likely to make today?

E. Stocks   F. Bonds   G. Treasury Bills

The business researcher would *tally the frequencies of responses* to these two questions into a two-way table called a **contingency table** (see cross tabulation in Chapter 2). Because the chi-square test of independence uses a contingency table, this test is sometimes referred to as **contingency analysis**.

Depicted in **Table 16.4** is a contingency table for these two variables. Variable 1, geographic region, uses four categories: A, B, C, and D. Variable 2, type of financial investment, uses three categories: E, F, and G. The observed frequency for each cell is denoted as o_{ij}, where i is the row and j is the column. Thus, o_{13} is the observed frequency for the cell in the first row and third column. The expected frequencies are denoted in a similar manner.

If the two variables are independent, they are not related. In a sense, the chi-square test of independence is a test of whether the variables are related. The null hypothesis for a chi-square test of independence is that the two variables are independent (not related). If the null hypothesis is rejected, the conclusion is that the two variables are not independent and are related.

Assume at the beginning that variable 1 and variable 2 are independent. The probability of the intersection of two of their respective categories, *A* and *F*, can be found by using the multiplicative law for independent events presented in Chapter 4:

$$P(A \cap F) = P(A) \cdot P(F)$$

If *A* and *F* are independent, then

$$P(A) = \frac{n_A}{N}, P(F) = \frac{n_F}{N}, \text{ and } P(A \cap F) = \frac{n_A}{N} \cdot \frac{n_F}{N}$$

If $P(A \cap F)$ is multiplied by the total number of frequencies, *N*, the expected frequency for the cell of *A* and *F* can be determined.

$$e_{AF} = \frac{n_A}{N} \cdot \frac{n_F}{N}(N) = \frac{n_A \cdot n_F}{N}$$

In general, if the two variables are independent, the expected frequency values of each cell can be determined by

$$e_{ij} = \frac{n_i \cdot n_j}{N}$$

TABLE 16.4	Contingency Table for the Investment Example

		E	F	G	
	A			o_{13}	n_A
Geographic	B				n_B
Region	C				n_C
	D				n_D
		n_E	n_F	n_G	N

where

i = the row
j = the column
n_i = the total of row i
n_j = the total of column j
N = the total of all frequencies

Using these expected frequency values and the observed frequency values, we can compute a chi-square test of independence to determine whether the variables are independent. Formula 16.2 is the formula for accomplishing this test.

Chi-Square Test of Independence

$$\chi^2 = \sum\sum \frac{(f_o - f_e)^2}{f_e}$$

$$df = (r-1)(c-1)$$

(16.2)

where:

r = number of rows
c = number of columns
f_o = frequency of observed values
f_e = frequency of expected values

The null hypothesis for a chi-square test of independence is that the two variables are independent. The alternative hypothesis is that the variables are not independent. This test is one-tailed. The degrees of freedom are $(r-1)(c-1)$. Note that Formula 16.2 is similar to Formula 16.1, with the exception that the values are summed across both rows and columns and the degrees of freedom are different.

As an example, suppose a business researcher wants to determine whether type of gasoline preferred is independent of a person's income. She takes a random survey of gasoline purchasers, asking them one question about gasoline preference and a second question about income. The respondent is to check whether he or she prefers (1) regular gasoline, (2) premium gasoline, or (3) extra premium gasoline. The respondent also is to check his or her income brackets as being (1) less than \$30,000, (2) \$30,000 to \$49,999, (3) \$50,000 to \$99,999, or (4) more than \$100,000. The business researcher tallies the responses and obtains the results in Table 16.5. Using $\alpha = .01$, she can use the chi-square test of independence and the eight-step approach to determine whether type of gasoline preferred is independent of income level.

Step 1 The hypotheses follow.

H_0: Type of gasoline is independent of income.

H_a: Type of gasoline is not independent of income.

TABLE 16.5 Contingency Table for the Gasoline Consumer Example

		Type of Gasoline			
		Regular	Premium	Extra Premium	
	Less than \$30,000	85	16	6	107
Income	\$30,000 to \$49,999	102	27	13	142
	\$50,000 to \$99,999	36	22	15	73
	More than \$100,000	15	23	25	63
		238	88	59	385

Step 2 The appropriate statistical test is

$$\chi^2 = \sum\sum \frac{(f_o - f_e)^2}{f_e}$$

Step 3 Alpha is .01.

Step 4 Here, there are four rows ($r = 4$) and three columns ($c = 3$). The degrees of freedom are $(4-1)(3-1) = 6$. The critical value of chi-square for $\alpha = .01$ is $\chi^2_{.01,6} = 16.8119$. The decision rule is to reject the null hypothesis if the observed chi-square is greater than 16.8119.

Step 5 The observed data appear in Table 16.5.

Step 6 To determine the observed value of chi-square, the researcher must compute the expected frequencies. The expected values for this example are calculated as follows, with the first term in the subscript (and numerator) representing the row and the second term in the subscript (and numerator) representing the column.

$$e_{11} = \frac{(n_{1.})(n_{.1})}{N} = \frac{(107)(238)}{385} = 66.15 \qquad e_{21} = \frac{(n_{2.})(n_{.1})}{N} = \frac{(142)(238)}{385} = 87.78$$

$$e_{12} = \frac{(n_{1.})(n_{.2})}{N} = \frac{(107)(88)}{385} = 24.46 \qquad e_{22} = \frac{(n_{2.})(n_{.2})}{N} = \frac{(142)(88)}{385} = 32.46$$

$$e_{13} = \frac{(n_{1.})(n_{.3})}{N} = \frac{(107)(59)}{385} = 16.40 \qquad e_{23} = \frac{(n_{2.})(n_{.3})}{N} = \frac{(142)(59)}{385} = 21.76$$

$$e_{31} = \frac{(n_{3.})(n_{.1})}{N} = \frac{(73)(238)}{385} = 45.13 \qquad e_{41} = \frac{(n_{4.})(n_{.1})}{N} = \frac{(63)(238)}{385} = 38.95$$

$$e_{32} = \frac{(n_{3.})(n_{.2})}{N} = \frac{(73)(88)}{385} = 16.69 \qquad e_{42} = \frac{(n_{4.})(n_{.2})}{N} = \frac{(63)(88)}{385} = 14.40$$

$$e_{33} = \frac{(n_{3.})(n_{.3})}{N} = \frac{(73)(59)}{385} = 11.19 \qquad e_{43} = \frac{(n_{4.})(n_{.3})}{N} = \frac{(63)(59)}{385} = 9.65$$

The researcher then lists the expected frequencies in the cells of the contingency tables along with observed frequencies. In this text, expected frequencies are enclosed in parentheses. Table 16.6 provides the contingency table for this example.

TABLE 16.6 Contingency Table of Observed and Expected Frequencies for Gasoline Consumer Example

		Type of Gasoline			
		Regular	Premium	Extra Premium	
Income	Less than $30,000	(66.15) 85	(24.46) 16	(16.40) 6	107
	$30,000 to $49,999	(87.78) 102	(32.46) 27	(21.76) 13	142
	$50,000 to $99,999	(45.13) 36	(16.69) 22	(11.19) 15	73
	More than $100,000	(38.95) 15	(14.40) 23	(9.65) 25	63
		238	88	59	385

Next, the researcher computes the chi-square value by summing $(f_o - f_e)^2/f_e$ for all cells.

$$\chi^2 = \frac{(85 - 66.15)^2}{66.15} + \frac{(16 - 24.46)^2}{24.46} + \frac{(6 - 16.40)^2}{16.40} + \frac{(102 - 87.78)^2}{87.78} + \frac{(27 - 32.46)^2}{32.46}$$

$$+ \frac{(13 - 21.76)^2}{21.76} + \frac{(36 - 45.13)^2}{45.13} + \frac{(22 - 16.69)^2}{16.69} + \frac{(15 - 11.19)^2}{11.19}$$

$$+ \frac{(15 - 38.95)^2}{38.95} + \frac{(23 - 14.40)^2}{14.40} + \frac{(25 - 9.65)^2}{9.65} = 5.37 + 2.93 + 6.60 + 2.30$$

$$+ 0.92 + 3.53 + 1.85 + 1.69 + 1.30 + 14.73 + 5.14 + 24.42 = 70.78$$

Step 7 The observed value of chi-square, 70.78, is greater than the critical value of chi-square, 16.8119, obtained from Table A.8. The business researcher's decision is to reject the null hypothesis; that is, type of gasoline preferred is not independent of income.

Step 8 Having established that conclusion, the business researcher can then examine the outcome to determine which people, by income brackets, tend to purchase which type of gasoline and use this information in market decisions.

Figure 16.2 is the Minitab output for calculating the chi-square value. Figure 16.3 is the Minitab chi-square graph with the critical value, the rejection region, and the observed χ^2.

```
Chi-Square Test: Regular, Premium, Extra Premium

                                            Extra
                     Regular    Premium     Premium     All
<$30K                     85         16           6     107
                       66.15      24.46       16.40

$30K to $49.999K         102         27          13     142
                       87.78      32.46       21.76

$50K to $99.999K          36         22          15      73
                       45.13      16.69       11.19

>$100K                    15         23          25      63
                       38.95      14.40        9.65

All                      238         88          59     385

Cell Contents:        Count
                      Expected count

Pearson Chi-Square = 70.727, DF = 6, P-Value = 0.000
```

FIGURE 16.2 **Minitab Output for Gasoline Consumer Example**

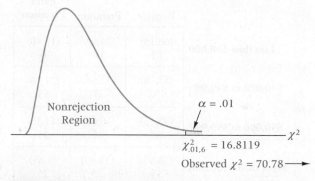

$$\chi^2_{.01,6} = 16.8119$$

Observed $\chi^2 = 70.78 \longrightarrow$

FIGURE 16.3 **Minitab Graph of Chi-Square Distribution for Gasoline Consumer Example**

DEMONSTRATION PROBLEM 16.3

Is the type of beverage ordered with lunch at a restaurant independent of the age of the consumer? A random poll of 309 lunch customers is taken, resulting in the following contingency table of observed values. Use $\alpha = .05$ and the eight-step approach to determine whether the two variables are independent.

Preferred Beverage

		Coffee/Tea	Soft Drink	Other (Milk, etc.)	
	21–34	26	95	18	139
Age	35–55	41	40	20	101
	>55	24	13	32	69
		91	148	70	309

Solution:

Step 1. The hypotheses follow.

H_0: Type of beverage preferred is independent of age.

H_a: Type of beverage preferred is not independent of age.

Step 2. The appropriate statistical test is

$$\chi^2 = \sum\sum \frac{(f_o - f_e)^2}{f_e}$$

Step 3. Alpha is .05.

Step 4. The degrees of freedom are $(3-1)(3-1) = 4$, and the critical value is $\chi^2_{.05,4} = 9.4877$. The decision rule is to reject the null hypothesis if the observed value of chi-square is greater than 9.4877.

Step 5. The sample data were shown previously.

Step 6. The expected frequencies are the product of the row and column totals divided by the grand total. The contingency table, with expected frequencies, follows.

Preferred Beverage

		Coffee/Tea	Soft Drink	Other (Milk, etc.)	
	21–34	(40.94) 26	(66.58) 95	(31.49) 18	139
Age	35–55	(29.74) 41	(48.38) 40	(22.88) 20	101
	>55	(20.32) 24	(33.05) 13	(15.63) 32	69
		91	148	70	309

For these values, the observed χ^2 is

$$\chi^2 = \frac{(26-40.94)^2}{40.94} + \frac{(95-66.58)^2}{66.58} + \frac{(18-31.49)^2}{31.49} + \frac{(41-29.74)^2}{29.74}$$

$$+ \frac{(40-48.38)^2}{48.38} + \frac{(20-22.88)^2}{22.88} + \frac{(24-20.32)^2}{20.32} + \frac{(13-33.05)^2}{33.05}$$

$$+ \frac{(32-15.63)^2}{15.63} = 5.45 + 12.13 + 5.78 + 4.26 + 1.45 + 0.36 + 0.67$$

$$+ 12.16 + 17.15 = 59.41$$

Step 7. The observed value of chi-square, 59.41, is greater than the critical value, 9.4877, so the null hypothesis is rejected.

Step 8. The two variables—preferred beverage and age—are not independent. The type of beverage that a customer orders with lunch is related to or dependent on age. Examination of the categories reveals that younger people tend to prefer soft drinks and older people prefer other types of beverages. Managers of eating establishments and marketers of beverage products can utilize such information in targeting their market and in providing appropriate products.

Caution: *As with the chi-square goodness-of-fit test, small expected frequencies can lead to inordinately large chi-square values with the chi-square test of independence. Hence, contingency tables should not be used with expected cell values of less than 5. One way to avoid small expected values is to collapse (combine) columns or rows whenever possible and whenever doing so makes sense.*

Thinking Critically About Statistics in Business Today

City Images of Cruise Destinations in the Taiwan Strait

A study was conducted by researchers Chiang-Chuan Lu and Ruey-Feng Chen in an effort to determine, in part, if there was a difference in the perceived city images of the Taiwan Strait ports of Hong Kong, Shanghai, and Taipei among cruise passengers. Researchers gathered data by administering questionnaires to cruise passengers over a four-year period. The participating passengers were about half men and half women, and over 50% had college degrees. Slightly over one-half of the respondents were from one of the port cities under study, and 72%, were from Malaysia, Singapore, China, or Taiwan.

One of the hypotheses being studied was if there is a difference in the images of the three cities—Hong Kong, Shanghai, and Taipei—between passengers who resided in those three cities and passengers from other places. A chi-square test of independence

was used to test this hypothesis. Shown here is a 2×2 contingency table with the raw number results:

The null hypothesis for this test is that perceived difference in the three port cities is independent of place of residence. An observed chi-square value of 17.97 is calculated from these data. Using $\alpha = .05$, df = 1, and a critical chi-square of 3.8415, the decision is to reject the null hypothesis. Perceived differences in the three port cities is not independent of place of residence. In fact, over 90% of residents of the three cities perceive that there are differences, but a little less than 60% of residents of other places perceive such differences.

THINGS TO PONDER

1. Why do you think such a high percentage of residents of the three port cities perceive a difference between the three cities, but a much smaller percentage of passengers from outside the three cities do so?

2. How might this problem be worked using techniques given in section 10.4 of the text? Compare the results using those techniques and the chi-square test of independence.

	Perceived Difference in Three Port Cities	No Perceived Difference in Three Port Cities
Resident of One of Three Port Cities	58	5
Not Resident of One of Three Port Cities	37	25

Source: Chiang-Chuan Lu and Ruey-Feng Chen, "Differences in Tourism Image Among Cruise Passengers across the Taiwan Straits," *Global Journal of Business Research,* vol. 5 (2011) 95–108.

16.2 Problems

16.10. Use the following contingency table to test whether variable 1 is independent of variable 2. Let $\alpha = .01$.

Variable 2

Variable 1	203	326
	68	110

16.11. Use the following contingency table to determine whether variable 1 is independent of variable 2. Let $\alpha = .01$.

Variable 2

Variable 1	24	13	47	58
	93	59	187	244

16.12. Use the following contingency table and the chi-square test of independence to determine whether social class is independent of number of children in a family. Let $\alpha = .05$.

		Social Class		
		Lower	Middle	Upper
Number of Children	0	7	18	6
	1	9	38	23
	2 or 3	34	97	58
	More than 3	47	31	30

16.13. A group of 30-year-olds is interviewed to determine whether the type of music most listened to by people in their age category is independent of the geographic location of their residence. Use the chi-square test of independence, $\alpha = .01$, and the following contingency table to determine whether music preference is independent of geographic location.

		Type of Music Preferred			
		Rock	R & B	Country	Classical
	Northeast	140	32	5	18
Geographic Region	South	134	41	52	8
	West	154	27	8	13

16.14. Is the transportation mode used to ship goods independent of type of industry? Suppose the following contingency table represents frequency counts of types of transportation used by the publishing and the computer hardware industries. Analyze the data by using the chi-square test of independence to determine whether type of industry is independent of transportation mode. Let $\alpha = .05$.

		Transportation Mode		
		Air	Train	Truck
	Publishing	32	12	41
Industry	Computer Hardware	5	6	24

16.15. According to data released by the U.S. Department of Housing and Urban Development about new homes built in the United States, there is an almost 50–50 split between one-story and two-story homes. In addition, more than half of all new homes have three bedrooms. Suppose a study is done to determine whether the number of bedrooms in a new home is independent of the number of stories. Use $\alpha = .10$ and the following contingency table to conduct a chi-square test of independence to determine whether, in fact, the number of bedrooms is independent of the number of stories.

		Number of Bedrooms		
		≤2	3	≥4
Number of Stories	1	116	101	57
	2	90	325	160

16.16. A study was conducted to determine the impact of a major Mexican peso devaluation on U.S. border retailers. As a part of the study, data were gathered on the magnitude of business that U.S. border retailers were doing with Mexican citizens. Forty-one shoppers of border city department stores were interviewed; 24 were Mexican citizens, and the rest were U.S. citizens. Thirty-five discount store shoppers were interviewed, as were 30 hardware store and 60 shoe store customers. In these three groups, 20, 11, and 32 were Mexican citizens, and the remaining shoppers were U.S. citizens. Use a chi-square contingency analysis to determine whether the shoppers' citizenship (Mexican versus American) is independent of type of border city retailer (department, discount, hardware, shoe) for these data. Let $\alpha = .05$.

Decision Dilemma Solved

Selecting Suppliers

Pearson and Ellram examined the comparative rankings of selection and evaluation criteria for suppliers of small and large electronics firms. These researchers chose to analyze the relative rankings by using frequency count for various categories of rankings. The three tables of data displayed in the Decision Dilemma contain frequencies for small and large company respondents on three of these criteria: quality, cost, and current technology. Because each of these tables contains categorical data with two variables, company size and rank category, a contingency analysis (chi-square test of independence) is an appropriate statistical technique for analyzing the data. The null hypothesis is that company size is independent of category of rank for each criterion. The alternative hypothesis is that category of rank for each criterion is not independent of company size (company size makes a difference in how the criterion is ranked). Minitab chi-square analysis produced the following output. For quality:

Chi-Sq = 0.991, DF = 2, *P*-Value = 0.609

The *p*-value of .609 indicates that we fail to reject the null hypothesis. On quality as a criterion, rankings of small company

respondents are independent of rankings of large company respondents. There appears to be no difference between small and large company respondents on the importance of quality as a selection and evaluation criterion. Observe in looking at the table that more than half of the respondents for both small and large companies ranked quality as the number 1 criterion.

For cost:

Chi-Sq = 0.483, DF = 2, *P*-Value = 0.785

The *p*-value of .785 indicates failure to reject the null hypothesis. Company size is independent of the ranking of cost as a supplier selection and evaluation tool. In perusing the raw data, it is evident that about one-third of the respondents in both large and small companies ranked cost either as the second or third most important criterion.

For current technology:

Chi-Sq = 1.026, DF = 2, *P*-Value = 0.599

The *p*-value of .599 indicates failure to reject the null hypothesis. Company size is independent of the ranking of this criterion as a supplier selection and evaluation tool.

Ethical Considerations

The usage of chi-square goodness-of-fit tests and chi-square tests of independence becomes an issue when the expected frequencies are too small. Considerable debate surrounds the discussion of how small is too small. In this chapter, we used an expected frequency of less than 5 as too small. As an example, suppose an expected frequency is 2. If the observed value is 6, then the calculation of

$(f_o - f_e)^2/f_e$ results in $(6 - 2)^2/2 = 8$ just for this pair of observed and expected frequencies. Such a contribution to the overall computed chi-square can inordinately affect the total chi-square value and skew the analysis. Researchers should exercise caution in using small expected frequencies with chi-square tests lest they arrive at an incorrect statistical outcome.

Summary

The chapter presented two techniques for analyzing categorical data. Categorical data are nonnumerical data that are frequency counts of categories from one or more variables. Categorical data producing this type of data are often analyzed using chi-square techniques. The two techniques presented for analyzing categorical data are the chi-square goodness-of-fit test and the chi-square test of independence.

The chi-square goodness-of-fit test is used to compare a theoretical or expected distribution of measurements for several categories of a variable with the actual or observed distribution of measurements. It can be used to determine whether a distribution of values fits a given distribution, such as the Poisson or normal distribution.

The chi-square test of independence is used to analyze frequencies for categories of two variables to determine whether the two variables are independent. The data used in analysis by a chi-square test of independence are arranged in a two-dimensional table called a contingency table. For this reason, the test is sometimes referred to as contingency analysis. A chi-square test of independence is computed in a manner similar to that used with the chi-square goodness-of-fit test. Expected values are computed for each cell of the contingency table and then compared to observed values with the chi-square statistic. Both the chi-square test of independence and the chi-square goodness-of-fit test require that expected values be greater than or equal to 5.

Key Terms

categorical data	chi-square goodness-of-fit test	contingency analysis	contingency table
chi-square distribution	chi-square test of independence		

Formulas

χ^2 goodness-of-fit test

$$\chi^2 = \sum \frac{(f_o - f_e)^2}{f_e}$$

$$df = k - 1 - c$$

χ^2 test of independence

$$\chi^2 = \sum\sum \frac{(f_o - f_e)^2}{f_e}$$

$$df = (r - 1)(c - 1)$$

Supplementary Problems

Calculating the Statistics

16.17. Use a chi-square goodness-of-fit test to determine whether the following observed frequencies are distributed the same as the expected frequencies. Let $\alpha = .01$.

CATEGORY	f_o	f_e
1	214	206
2	235	232
3	279	268

4	281	284
5	264	268
6	254	232
7	211	206

16.18. Use the chi-square contingency analysis to test to determine whether variable 1 is independent of variable 2. Use 5% level of significance.

	VARIABLE 2		
	12	23	21
Variable 1	8	17	20
	7	11	18

Testing Your Understanding

16.19. Is a manufacturer's geographic location independent of type of customer? Use the following data for companies with primarily industrial customers and companies with primarily retail customers to test this question. Let $\alpha = .10$.

		Geographic Location		
		Northeast	West	South
Customer Type	Industrial Customer	230	115	68
	Retail Customer	185	143	89

16.20. A national youth organization sells six different kinds of cookies during its annual cookie campaign. A local leader is curious about whether national sales of the six kinds of cookies are uniformly distributed. He randomly selects the amounts of each kind of cookies sold by five youths and combines them into the observed data that follow. Use $\alpha = .05$ to determine whether the data indicate that sales for these six kinds of cookies are uniformly distributed.

KIND OF COOKIE	OBSERVED FREQUENCY
Chocolate chip	189
Peanut butter	168
Cheese cracker	155
Lemon flavored	161
Chocolate mint	216
Vanilla filled	165

16.21. A researcher interviewed 2067 people and asked whether they were the primary decision makers in the household when buying a new car last year. Two hundred seven were men and had bought a new car last year. Sixty-five were women and had bought a new car last year. Eight hundred eleven of the responses were from men who did not buy a car last year. Nine hundred eighty-four were from women who did not buy a car last year. Use these data to determine whether gender is independent of being a major decision maker in purchasing a car last year. Let $\alpha = .05$.

16.22. Are random arrivals at a shoe store at the local mall Poisson distributed? Suppose a mall employee researches this question by gathering data for arrivals during one-minute intervals on a weekday between 6:30 P.M. and 8:00 P.M. The data obtained follow. Use $\alpha = .05$ to determine whether the observed data seem to be from a Poisson distribution.

ARRIVALS PER MINUTE	OBSERVED FREQUENCY
0	26
1	40
2	57
3	32
4	17
5	12
6	8

16.23. According to Beverage Digest, the distribution of market share for the top seven carbonated soft drinks in the United States is: Coke 17.6%, Pepsi-Cola 8.8%, Diet Coke 8.5%, Mt. Dew 6.9%, Dr. Pepper 6.8%, Sprite 6.0%, and Diet Pepsi 4.3%. Others accounted for 41.1% of the market. Suppose a market analyst wants to determine whether this distribution fits her geographic region. She randomly surveys 2,077 people and asks them to name their favorite carbonated soft drink. The responses are: Coke 397, Pepsi-Cola 310, Diet Coke 207, Mt. Dew 160, Dr. Pepper 143, Diet Pepsi 130, Sprite 126, and Others 604. She then tests to determine whether the local distribution of carbonated soft drink preferences is the same or different from the national figures using $\alpha = .05$. What does she find?

16.24. Are the types of professional jobs held in the computing industry independent of the number of years a person has worked in the industry? Suppose 246 workers are interviewed. Use the results obtained to determine whether type of professional job held in the computer industry is independent of years worked in the industry. Let $\alpha = .01$.

	Professional Position			
	Manager	Programmer	Operator	Systems Analyst
Years 0–3	6	37	11	13
Years 4–8	28	16	23	24
Years More than 8	47	10	12	19

16.25. Is the number of children that a college student currently has independent of the type of college or university being attended? Suppose students were randomly selected from three types of colleges and universities and the data shown represent the results of a survey of those students. Use a chi-square test of independence of answer the question. Let $\alpha = .05$.

		Type of College or University		
		Community College	Large University	Small College
Number of Children	0	25	178	31
	1	49	141	12
	2	31	54	8
	3 or more	22	14	6

Interpreting the Output

16.26. A survey by Ipsos-Reid reported in *American Demographics* showed that if a person was given a $1,000 windfall, 36% would spend the money on home improvement, 24% on leisure travel/vacation, 15% on clothing, 15% on home entertainment or electronic products, and 10% on local entertainment including restaurants and movies. Suppose a researcher believes that these results would not be the same if posed to adults between 21 and 30 years of age. The researcher conducts a new survey interviewing 200 adults between 21 and 30 years of age asking these same questions. A chi-square goodness-of-fit test is conducted to compare the results of the new survey to the one taken by Ipsos-Reid. The Excel results follow. The observed and expected values are for the categories as already listed and appear in the same order. Discuss the findings. How did the distribution of results from the new survey compare to the old? Discuss the business implications of this outcome.

21–30 YEARS OF AGE	GENERAL POPULATION
Observed	Expected
36	72
64	48
42	30
38	30
20	20

The *p*-value for the chi-square goodness-of-fit test is: **0.0000043**. The observed chi-square for the goodness-of-fit test is: **30.27**.

16.27. Do men and women prefer the same colors of cars? That is, is sex independent of color preference for cars? Suppose a study is undertaken to address this question. A random sample of men and women are asked which of five colors (silver, white, black, green, blue) they prefer in a car. The results as analyzed using Minitab are shown here. Discuss the test used, the hypotheses, the findings, and the business implications.

```
Chi-Square Test: Men, Women

              Men        Women        All
Silver         90           52        142
            85.20        56.80

White          75           58        133
            79.80        53.20

Black          63           30         93
            55.80        37.20

Green          39           33         72
            43.20        28.80

Blue           33           27         60
            36.00        24.00

All           300          200        500

Cell Contents:     Count
                   Expected count

Pearson Chi-Square = 5.366, DF=4, P-Value=0.252
```

Analyzing the Database

see **www.wiley.com/college/black**

1. The Financial database contains seven different types of companies. These seven are denoted by the variable Type. Use a chi-square goodness-of-fit test to determine whether the seven types of companies are uniformly distributed in this database.

2. In the Manufacturing database, is the Value of Industrial Shipments (a four-category variable) uniformly distributed across the database?

3. Use a chi-square test of independence to determine whether Control is independent of Service in the Hospital database. Comment on the results of this test.

4. In the Consumer database, is Location independent of Region? Use a chi-square test of independence to answer the question.

Case

Foot Locker in the Shoe Mix

Foot Locker, Inc., is the world's number one retailer of athletic footwear and apparel. Headquartered in New York City, the company has over 44,000 employees and 3423 retail stores in 23 countries across North America, Europe, Australia, and New Zealand operating under such brand names as Foot Locker, Lady Foot Locker, Kids Foot Locker, Footaction, Runners Point, and Sidestep. Foot Locker estimates that it controls about 18% of the U.S. $15 billion athletic footwear market. The company intends to increase its share of the worldwide market by adding additional stores and by growing its Internet and catalog business.

In recent years, Foot Locker officials have been rethinking the company's retail mix. Determining the shoe mix that will maximize profits is an important decision for Foot Locker. By the year 2002, in an effort to stock more lower-priced footwear, the company had reduced its inventory of sneakers priced at $120 or more by 50%.

Discussion

Suppose the data presented below represented the number of unit sales (million $) for athletic footwear in the years 2000 and 2016. Use techniques presented in this chapter to analyze these data and discuss the business implications for Foot Locker.

PRICE CATEGORY	2000	2016
Less than $30	115	126
$30–less than $40	38	40
$40–less than $50	37	35
$50–less than $60	30	27
$60–less than $70	22	20
$70–less than $85	21	20
$85–less than $100	11	11
$100 or more	17	18

Suppose Foot Locker strongly encourages its employees to make formal suggestions to improve the store, the product, and the working environment. Suppose a quality auditor keeps records of the suggestions, the persons who submitted them, and the geographic region from which they come. A possible breakdown of the number of suggestions over a 3-year period by employee sex and geographic location follows. Is there any relationship between the sex of the employee and the geographic location in terms of number of suggestions? If they are related, what does this relationship mean to the company? What business implications might there be for such an analysis?

		SEX	
		Male	Female
	U.S. West	29	43
	U.S. South	48	20
Location	U.S. East	52	61
	U.S. North	28	25
	Europe	78	32
	Australia	47	29

Source: Adapted from Christopher Lawton and Maureen Tkacik. "Foot Locker Changes Mix of Sneakers," *The Wall Street Journal* (July 22, 2002), p. B3; Foot Locker, Inc., available at: http://www.footlocker-inc.com; "Venator Group, Inc. Announces Name Change to Foot Locker, Inc.," *PR NEWSWIRE*, (November 1, 2001), p. 1. http://www.footlocker-inc.com/(2016).

CHAPTER 17

Nonparametric Statistics

LEARNING OBJECTIVES

This chapter presents several nonparametric statistics that can be used to analyze data, thereby enabling you to:

1. Use both the small-sample and large-sample runs tests to determine whether the order of observations in a sample is random.

2. Use both the small-sample and large-sample cases of the Mann-Whitney U test to determine if there is a difference in two independent populations.

3. Use both the small-sample and large-sample cases of the Wilcoxon matched-pairs signed rank test to compare the difference in two related samples.

4. Use the Kruskal-Wallis test to determine whether 3 or more samples come from the same or different populations.

5. Use the Friedman test to determine whether different treatment levels come from the same population when a blocking variable is available.

6. Use Spearman's rank correlation to analyze the degree of association of two variables.

Decision Dilemma

How Is the Doughnut Business?

By investing $5,000, William Rosenberg founded the Industrial Luncheon Services company in 1946 to deliver meals and coffee break snacks to customers in suburban Boston, Massachusetts. Building on his success in this venture, Rosenberg opened his first coffee and doughnut shop called "Open Kettle" in 1948. In 1950, Rosenberg changed the name of his shop, located in Quincy, Massachusetts, to Dunkin' Donuts, and thus the first Dunkin' Donuts shop was established. The first Dunkin' Donuts franchise was awarded in 1955; and by 1963, there were 100 Dunkin' Donuts shops. In 1970, the first overseas Dunkin' Donuts shop was opened in Japan; and by 1979, there were 1000 Dunkin' Donuts shops.

Today, there are over 11,000 Dunkin' Donuts franchises in 36 states in the United States and 32 countries around the world. Dunkin' Donuts is the world's largest coffee and baked goods chain, serving more than 3 million customers per day. Dunkin' Donuts sells 52 varieties of doughnuts and more

BryceBridges.com/Alamy

than a dozen coffee beverages as well as an array of bagels, break-fast sandwiches, and other baked goods. Dunkin' Donuts is co-owned along with Baskin-Robbins by Dunkin' Brands Inc., based in Canton, Massachusetts.

Suppose researchers at Dunkin' Donuts are studying several manufacturing and marketing questions in an effort to improve the consistency of their products and understand their market. Manu-facturing engineers are concerned that the various machines produce a consistent doughnut size. In an effort to test this issue, four machines are selected for a study. Each machine is set to produce a doughnut that is supposed to be about 7.62 cm (3 inches) in diam-eter. A random sample of doughnuts is taken from each machine and the diameters of the doughnuts are measured. The result is the data shown as follows:

MACHINE 1	MACHINE 2	MACHINE 3	MACHINE 4
7.58	7.41	7.56	7.72
7.52	7.44	7.55	7.65
7.50	7.42	7.50	7.67
7.52	7.38	7.58	7.70
7.48	7.45	7.53	7.69
	7.40		7.71
			7.73

Suppose Dunkin' Donuts implements a national advertis-ing campaign in the United States. Marketing researchers want to determine whether the campaign has increased the number of doughnuts sold at various outlets around the country. Ten stores are randomly selected and the number of doughnuts sold between 8 and 9 A.M. on a Tuesday is measured both before and after the campaign is implemented. The data follow:

OUTLET	BEFORE	AFTER
1	301	374
2	198	187
3	278	332
4	205	212
5	249	243
6	410	478
7	360	386

8	124	141
9	253	251
10	190	264

Do bigger stores have greater sales? To test this question, suppose sales data were gathered from seven Dunkin' Donuts stores along with store size. These figures are used to rank the seven stores on each variable. The ranked data follow:

STORE	SALES RANK	SIZE RANK
1	6	7
2	2	2
3	3	6
4	7	5
5	5	4
6	1	1
7	4	3

MANAGERIAL AND STATISTICAL QUESTIONS

1. The manufacturing researchers who are testing to determine whether there is a difference in the size of doughnuts by machine want to run a one-way ANOVA, but they have seri-ous doubts that the ANOVA assumptions can be met by these data. Is it still possible to analyze the data using statistics?

2. The market researchers are uncertain that normal distribu-tion assumptions underlying the matched-pairs t test can be met with the number of doughnuts sold data. How can the before-and-after data still be used to test the effectiveness of the advertisements?

3. If the sales and store size data are given as ranks, how do we compute a correlation to answer the research question about the relationship of sales and store size? The Pearson product-moment correlation coefficient requires at least interval-level data, and these data are given as ordinal level.

Source: Adapted from information presented on the Dunkin' Donuts' Web site at: http://www.dunkindonuts.com/aboutus./company/. Please note that the data set forth in the problem are fictional, were not supplied by Dunkin' Donuts, and do not necessarily represent Dunkin' Donuts' experience.

Except for the chi-square analyses presented in Chapter 16, all statistical techniques presented in the text thus far are parametric techniques. **Parametric statistics** are *statistical techniques based on assumptions about the population from which the sample data are selected.* For ex-ample, if a t statistic is being used to conduct a hypothesis test about a population mean, the assumption is that the data being analyzed are randomly selected from a *normally* distributed population. The name *parametric statistics* refers to the fact that an assumption (here, nor-mally distributed data) is being made about the data used to test or estimate the parameter (in this case, the population mean). In addition, the use of parametric statistics requires quantita-tive measurements that yield interval- or ratio-level data.

For data that do not meet the assumptions made about the population, or when the level of data being measured is qualitative, statistical techniques called nonparametric, or distri-bution-free, techniques are used. **Nonparametric statistics** *are based on fewer assumptions* *about the population and the parameters than are parametric statistics.* Sometimes they are referred to as *distribution-free* statistics because many of them can be used regardless of the shape of the population distribution. A variety of nonparametric statistics are available for use with nominal or ordinal data. Some require at least ordinal-level data, but others can be specifically targeted for use with nominal-level data.

Nonparametric techniques have the following advantages.

1. Sometimes there is no parametric alternative to the use of nonparametric statistics.
2. Certain nonparametric tests can be used to analyze nominal data.
3. Certain nonparametric tests can be used to analyze ordinal data.
4. The computations on nonparametric statistics are usually less complicated than those for parametric statistics, particularly for small samples.
5. Probability statements obtained from most nonparametric tests are exact probabilities.

Using nonparametric statistics also has some disadvantages.

1. Nonparametric tests can be wasteful of data if parametric tests are available for use with the data.
2. Nonparametric tests are usually not as widely available and well known as parametric tests.
3. For large samples, the calculations for many nonparametric statistics can be tedious.

Entire courses and texts are dedicated to the study of nonparametric statistics. This text presents only some of the more important techniques: runs test, Mann-Whitney *U* test, Wilcoxon matched-pairs signed ranks test, Kruskal-Wallis test, Friedman test, Spearman's rank correlation coefficient, chi-square test of goodness-of-fit, and chi-square test of independence. The chi-square goodness-of-fit test and the chi-square test of independence were presented in Chapter 16. The others are presented in this chapter.

Figure 17.1 contains a tree diagram that displays all of the nonparametric techniques presented in this chapter, with the exception of Spearman's Rank Correlation, which is used to analyze the degree of association of two variables. As you peruse the tree diagram, you

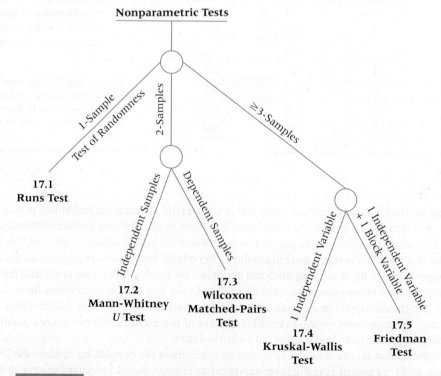

FIGURE 17.1 **Tree Diagram Taxonomy of Nonparametric Inferential Techniques**

will see that there is a test of randomness, the runs test, two tests of the differences of two populations, the Mann-Whitney U test and the Wilcoxon matched-pairs signed rank test, and two tests of the differences of three or more populations—the Kruskal-Wallis test and the Friedman test.

17.1 # Runs Test

The one-sample **runs test** is *a nonparametric test of randomness*. The runs test is *used to determine whether the order or sequence of observations in a sample is random*. The runs test examines the number of "runs" of each of two possible characteristics that sample items may have. A *run* is a succession of observations that have a particular one of the characteristics. For example, if a sample of people contains both men and women, one run could be a continuous succession of women. In tossing coins, the outcome of three heads in a row would constitute a run, as would a succession of seven tails.

Suppose a researcher takes a random sample of 15 people who arrive at a Wal-Mart to shop. Eight of the people are women and seven are men. If these people arrive randomly at the store, it makes sense that the sequence of arrivals would have some mix of men and women, but not probably a perfect mix. That is, it seems unlikely (although possible) that the sequence of a random sample of such shoppers would be first eight women and then seven men. In such a case, there are two runs. Suppose, however, the sequence of shoppers is woman, man, woman, man, woman, and so on all the way through the sample. This would result in 15 "runs." Each of these cases is possible, but neither is highly likely in a random scenario. In fact, if there are just two runs, it seems possible that a group of women came shopping together followed by a group of men who did likewise. In that case, the observations would not be random. Similarly, a pattern of woman-man all the way through may make the business researcher suspicious that what has been observed is not really individual random arrivals, but actually random arrivals of couples.

In a random sample, the number of runs is likely to be somewhere between these extremes. What number of runs is reasonable? The one-sample runs test takes into consideration the size of the sample, n, the number observations in the sample having each characteristic, n_1, n_2 (man, woman, etc.), and the number of runs in the sample, R, to reach conclusions about hypotheses of randomness. The following hypotheses are tested by the one-sample runs test.

H_0: The observations in the sample are randomly generated.

H_a: The observations in the sample are not randomly generated.

The one-sample runs test is conducted differently for small samples than it is for large samples. Each test is presented here. First, we consider the small-sample case.

Small-Sample Runs Test

If each of n_1 and n_2 is less than or equal to 20, the small-sample runs test is appropriate. In the example of shoppers with $n_1 = 7$ men and $n_2 = 8$ women, the small-sample runs test could be used to test for randomness. The test is carried out by comparing the observed number of runs, R, to critical values of runs for the given values of n_1 and n_2. The critical values of R are given in Tables A.11 and A.12 in the Appendix for $\alpha = .05$. Table A.11 contains critical values of R for the lower tail of the distribution in which so few runs occur that the probability of that many runs or fewer runs occurring is less than $.025(\alpha/2)$. Table A.12 contains critical values of R for the upper tail of the distribution in which so many runs occur that the probability of that many runs or more occurring is less than $.025(\alpha/2)$. Any observed value of R that is less than or equal to the critical value of the lower tail (Table A.11) results in the rejection of the null hypothesis and the conclusion that the sample data are not random. Any observed value of R that is equal to or greater than the critical value in the upper tail (Table A.12) also results in the rejection of the null hypothesis and the conclusion that the sample data are not random.

As an example, suppose 26 cola drinkers are sampled randomly to determine whether they prefer regular cola or diet cola. The random sample contains 18 regular cola drinkers and eight diet cola drinkers. Let C denote regular cola drinkers and D denote diet cola drinkers. Suppose the sequence of sampled cola drinkers is DCCCCCDCCDCCCCDCDCCCD-DDCCC. Is this sequence of cola drinkers evidence that the sample is not random? Applying the eight-step approach of hypothesis testing to this problem results in:

Step 1   The hypotheses tested follow.

H_0: The observations in the sample were generated randomly.

H_a: The observations in the sample were not generated randomly.

Step 2   Let n_1 denote the number of regular cola drinkers and n_2 denote the number of diet cola drinkers. Because $n_1 = 18$ and $n_2 = 8$, the small-sample runs test is the appropriate test.

Step 3   Alpha is .05.

Step 4   With $n_1 = 18$ and $n_2 = 8$, Table A.11 yields a critical value of 7 and Table A.12 yields a critical value of 17. If there are seven or fewer runs or 17 or more runs, the decision rule is to reject the null hypothesis.

Step 5   The sample data are given as

$$DCCCCCDCCDCCCCDCDCCCDDDCCC$$

Step 6   Tally the number of runs in this sample.

1	2	3	4	5	6	7	8	9	10	11	12
D	CCCCC	D	CC	D	CCCC	D	C	D	CCC	DDD	CCC

The number of runs, R, is 12.

Step 7   Because the value of R falls between the critical values of 7 and 17, the decision is to not reject the null hypothesis. Not enough evidence is provided to declare that the data are not random.

Step 8   The cola researcher can proceed with the study under the assumption that the sample represents randomly selected cola drinkers.

Minitab has the capability of analyzing data by using the runs test. **Figure 17.2** is the Minitab output for the cola example runs test. Notice that the output includes the number of runs, 12, and the significance level of the test. For this analysis, diet cola was coded as a 1 and regular cola coded as a 2. The Minitab runs test is a two-tailed test, and the reported significance of the test is equivalent to a *p*-value. Because the significance is .9710, the decision is to not reject the null hypothesis.

```
Runs Test: Cola

Runs test for Cola
Runs above and below K = 1.69231

The observed number of runs = 12
The expected number of runs = 12.0769
18 observations above K, 8 below
* N is small, so the following approximation may be invalid.
P-value = 0.971
```

FIGURE 17.2   **Minitab Output for the Cola Example**

Large-Sample Runs Test

Tables A.11 and A.12 do not contain critical values for n_1 and n_2 greater than 20. Fortunately, the sampling distribution of R is approximately normal with a mean and standard deviation of

$$\mu_R = \frac{2n_1 n_2}{n_1 + n_2} + 1 \quad \text{and} \quad \sigma_R = \sqrt{\frac{2n_1 n_2 (2n_1 n_2 - n_1 - n_2)}{(n_1 + n_2)^2 (n_1 + n_2 - 1)}}$$

The test statistic is a z statistic computed as

$$z = \frac{R - \mu_R}{\sigma_R} = \frac{R - \left(\dfrac{2n_1 n_2}{n_1 + n_2} + 1\right)}{\sqrt{\dfrac{2n_1 n_2 (2n_1 n_2 - n_1 - n_2)}{(n_1 + n_2)^2 (n_1 + n_2 - 1)}}}$$

The following hypotheses are being tested.

> H_0: The observations in the sample were generated randomly.
>
> H_a: The observations in the sample were not generated randomly.

The critical z values are obtained in the usual way by using alpha and Table A.5.

Consider the following manufacturing example. A machine produces parts that are occasionally flawed. When the machine is working in adjustment, flaws still occur but seem to happen randomly. A quality-control person randomly selects 50 of the parts produced by the machine today and examines them one at a time in the order that they were made. The result is 40 parts with no flaws and 10 parts with flaws. The sequence of no flaws (denoted by N) and flaws (denoted by F) is shown below. Using an alpha of .05, the quality controller tests to determine whether the machine is producing randomly (the flaws are occurring randomly).

> NNN F NNNNNNN F NN FF NNNNNN F NNNN F NNNNNN
> FFFF NNNNNNNNNNNN

Step 1   The hypotheses follow.

> H_0: The observations in the sample were generated randomly.
>
> H_a: The observations in the sample were not generated randomly.

Step 2   The appropriate statistical test is the large-sample runs test. The test statistic is

$$z = \frac{R - \mu_R}{\sigma_R} = \frac{R - \left(\dfrac{2n_1 n_2}{n_1 + n_2} + 1\right)}{\sqrt{\dfrac{2n_1 n_2 (2n_1 n_2 - n_1 - n_2)}{(n_1 + n_2)^2 (n_1 + n_2 - 1)}}}$$

Step 3   The value of alpha is .05.

Step 4   This test is two tailed. Too few or too many runs could indicate that the machine is not producing flaws randomly. With $\alpha = .05$ and $\alpha/2 = .025$, the critical values are $z_{.025} = \pm 1.96$. The decision rule is to reject the null hypothesis if the observed value of the test statistic is greater than 1.96 or less than -1.96.

Step 5   The preceding sequence provides the sample data. The value of n_1 is 40 and the value of n_2 is 10. The number of runs (R) is 13.

Runs Test: Flaws

```
Runs Test for Flaws
Runs above and below K = 0.2

The observed number of runs = 13
The expected number of runs = 17
10 Observations above K, 40 below
* N is small, so the following approximation may be invalid.
P-value = 0.071
```

FIGURE 17.3 **Minitab Output for the Flawed Parts Example**

Step 6

$$\mu_R = \frac{2(40)(10)}{40+10} + 1 = 17$$

$$\sigma_R = \sqrt{\frac{2(40)(10)[2(40)(10)-40-10]}{(40+10)^2(40+10-1)}} = 2.213$$

$$z = \frac{13-17}{2.213} = -1.81$$

Step 7 Because the observed value of the test statistic, $z = -1.81$, is greater than the lower-tail critical value, $z = -1.96$, the decision is to not reject the null hypothesis.

Step 8 There is no evidence that the machine is not producing flaws randomly. If the null hypothesis had been rejected, there might be concern that the machine is producing flaws systematically and thereby is in need of inspection or repair.

Figure 17.3 is the Minitab output for this example. The value of K is the average of the observations. The data were entered into Minitab with a nonflaw coded as a 0 and a flaw as a 1. The value $K = .20$ is merely the average of these coded values. In Minitab, a run is a sequence of observations above or below this mean, which effectively yields the same thing as the number of 0s in a row (nonflaws) or number of 1s in a row (flaws). The nonflaws and flaws could have been coded as any two different numbers and the same results would have been achieved. The output shows the number of runs as 13 (the same number obtained manually) and a test significance (p-value) equal to .071. The test statistic is not significant at $\alpha = .05$ because the p-value is greater than .05.

17.1 Problems

17.1. Test the following sequence of observations by using the runs test and $\alpha = .05$ to determine whether the process produced random results.

$$X\,X\,X\,Y\,X\,X\,Y\,Y\,Y\,X\,Y\,X\,Y\,X\,X\,Y\,Y\,Y\,X$$

17.2. Test the following sequence of observations by using the runs test and $\alpha = .05$ to determine whether the process produced random results.

$$M\,M\,N\,N\,N\,N\,M\,M\,M\,M\,M\,N\,N\,M\,M\,M\,M\,N\,M\,M$$
$$N\,N\,N\,N\,N\,N\,N\,N\,N\,N\,M\,M\,M\,M\,M\,M\,M\,M\,M$$

17.3. A process produced good parts and defective parts. A sample of 60 parts was taken and inspected. Eight defective parts were found. The sequence of good and defective parts was analyzed by using

Minitab. The output is given here. With a two-tailed test and $\alpha = .05$, what conclusions can be reached about the randomness of the sample?

Runs Test: Defects

```
Runs test for Defects
Runs above and below K = 0.1333

The observed number of runs = 11
The expected number of runs = 14.8667
8 Observations above K, 52 below
P-value = 0.0264
```

17.4. A Watson Wyatt Worldwide survey showed that 58% of all Hispanic Americans are satisfied with their salary. Suppose a researcher randomly samples 27 Hispanic American workers and asks whether they are satisfied with their salary with the result that 15 say yes. The sequence of Yes and No responses is recorded and tested for randomness by means of Minitab. The output follows. Using an alpha of .05 and a two-tailed test, what could you conclude about the randomness of the sample?

```
Runs Test: Yes/No

Runs test for Yes/No
Runs above and below K = 0.5556

The observed number of runs = 18
The expected number of runs = 14.3333
15 Observations above K, 12 below
P-value = 0.1452
```

17.5. A Virginia Slims Opinion Poll by Roper Starch found that more than 70% of the women interviewed believe they have had more opportunity to succeed than their parents. Suppose a researcher in your state conducts a similar poll and asks the same question with the result that of 64 women interviewed, 40 believe they have had more opportunity to succeed than their parents. The sequence of responses to this question is given below with Y denoting Yes and N denoting No. Use the runs test and $\alpha = .05$ to test this sequence and determine whether the responses are random.

Y Y N Y Y N N Y Y Y N N Y N N Y Y Y Y Y N Y Y Y Y
N N Y Y N N N Y Y Y N N Y Y Y Y Y N Y N Y N Y Y Y N N N
Y N N Y Y Y Y Y N N Y Y Y Y

17.6. A survey conducted by the Ethics Resource Center discovered that 35% of all workers say that coworkers have committed some kind of office theft. Suppose a survey is conducted in your large company to ask the same question of 13 randomly selected employees. The results are that five of the sample say coworkers have committed some kind of office theft and eight say they are not aware of such infractions. The sequence of responses follows. (Y denotes a Yes answer and N denotes a No answer.) Use $\alpha = .05$ to test to determine whether this sequence represents a random sample.

N N N N Y Y Y N N N N Y Y

Mann-Whitney *U* Test

The **Mann-Whitney *U* test** is a *nonparametric counterpart of the t test used to compare the means of two independent populations.* This test was developed by Henry B. Mann and D. R. Whitney in 1947. Recall that the *t* test for independent samples presented in Chapter 10 can be used when data are at least interval in measurement and the populations are normally distributed. However, if the assumption of a normally distributed population is invalid or if the data are only ordinal in measurement, the *t* test should not be used. In such cases, the Mann-Whitney *U* test is an acceptable option for analyzing the data. The following assumptions underlie the use of the Mann-Whitney *U* test.

1. The samples are independent.
2. The level of data is at least ordinal.

The two-tailed hypotheses being tested with the Mann-Whitney *U* test are as follows:

H_0: The two populations are identical.

H_a: The two populations are not identical.

Computation of the *U* test begins by arbitrarily designating two samples as group 1 and group 2. The data from the two groups are combined into one group, with each data value retaining a group identifier of its original group. The pooled values are then ranked from 1 to *n*, with the smallest value being assigned a rank of 1. The sum of the ranks of values from group 1 is computed and designated as W_1 and the sum of the ranks of values from group 2 is designated as W_2.

The Mann-Whitney *U* test is implemented differently for small samples than for large samples. If both n_1, $n_2 \leq 10$, the samples are considered small. If either n_1 or n_2 is greater than 10, the samples are considered large.

Small-Sample Case

With small samples, the next step is to calculate a U statistic for W_1 and for W_2 as

$$U_1 = n_1 n_2 + \frac{n_1(n_1+1)}{2} - W_1 \quad \text{and} \quad U_2 = n_1 n_2 + \frac{n_2(n_2+1)}{2} - W_2$$

The test statistic is the smallest of these two U values. Both values do not need to be calculated; instead, one value of U can be calculated and the other can be found by using the transformation

$$U' = n_1 \cdot n_2 - U$$

Table A.13 contains p-values for U. To determine the p-value for a U from the table, let n_1 denote the size of the smaller sample and n_2 the size of the larger sample. Using the particular table in Table A.13 for n_1, n_2, locate the value of U in the left column. At the intersection of the U and n_1 is the p-value for a one-tailed test. For a two-tailed test, double the p-value shown in the table.

DEMONSTRATION PROBLEM 17.1

Is there a difference between health service workers and educational service workers in hourly compensation? Suppose a random sample of seven health service workers is taken along with a random sample of eight educational service workers from different parts of the country. Each of their employers is interviewed and figures are obtained on the amount paid per hour for employee compensation for these workers. The data here indicate total compensation per hour. Use a Mann-Whitney U test and the eight-step approach to determine whether these two populations are different in employee compensation.

HEALTH SERVICE WORKER	EDUCATIONAL SERVICE WORKER
$20.10	$26.19
19.80	23.88
22.36	25.50
18.75	21.64
21.90	24.85
22.96	25.30
20.75	24.12
	23.45

Solution:

Step 1. The hypotheses are as follows.

  H_0: The health service population is identical to the educational service population on employee compensation.

  H_a: The health service population is not identical to the educational service population on employee compensation.

Step 2. Because we cannot be certain the populations are normally distributed, we chose a nonparametric alternative to the t test for independent populations: the small-sample Mann-Whitney U test.

Step 3. Let alpha be .05.

Step 4. If the final p-value from Table A.13 (after doubling for a two-tailed test here) is less than .05, the decision is to reject the null hypothesis.

Step 5. The sample data were already provided.

Step 6. We combine scores from the two groups and rank them from smallest to largest while retaining group identifier information.

TOTAL EMPLOYEE COMPENSATION	RANK	GROUP
$18.75	1	H
19.80	2	H
20.10	3	H
20.75	4	H
21.64	5	E
21.90	6	H
22.36	7	H
22.96	8	H
23.45	9	E
23.88	10	E
24.12	11	E
24.85	12	E
25.30	13	E
25.50	14	E
26.19	15	E

$$W_1 = 1 + 2 + 3 + 4 + 6 + 7 + 8 = 31$$

$$W_2 = 5 + 9 + 10 + 11 + 12 + 13 + 14 + 15 = 89$$

$$U_1 = (7)(8) + \frac{(7)(8)}{2} - 31 = 53$$

$$U_2 = (7)(8) + \frac{(8)(9)}{2} - 89 = 3$$

Because U_2 is the smaller value of U, we use $U = 3$ as the test statistic for Table A.13. Because it is the smallest size, let $n_1 = 7$; $n_2 = 8$.

Step 7. Table A.13 yields a *p*-value of .0011. Because this test is two tailed, we double the table *p*-value, producing a final *p*-value of .0022. Because the *p*-value is less than $\alpha = .05$, the null hypothesis is rejected. The statistical conclusion is that the populations are not identical.

Step 8. An examination of the total compensation figures from the samples indicates that employers pay educational service workers more per hour than they pay health service workers.

As shown in **Figure 17.4**, Minitab has the capability of computing a Mann-Whitney *U* test. The output includes a *p*-value of .0046 for the two-tailed test for Demonstration Problem 17.1. The decision based on the computer output is to reject the null hypothesis, which is consistent with what we computed. The difference in *p*-values is due to rounding error in the table.

```
Mann-Whitney Test and CI: HS Worker, EdS Worker

             N    Median
HS Worker    7    20.750
EdS Worker   8    24.485

Point estimate for η1 - η2 is -3.385
95.7 Percent CI for η1 - η2 is (-5.370,-1.551)
W = 31.0
Test of η1 = η2 vs η1 ≠ η2 is significant at 0.0046
```

FIGURE 17.4 **Minitab Output for Demonstration Problem 17.1**

TABLE 17.1

Income of PBS & Non-PBS Viewers

PBS	NON-PBS
$24,500	$41,000
39,400	32,500
36,800	33,000
43,000	21,000
57,960	40,500
32,000	32,400
61,000	16,000
34,000	21,500
43,500	39,500
55,000	27,600
39,000	43,500
62,500	51,900
61,400	27,800
53,000	
$n_1 = 14$	$n_2 = 13$

Large-Sample Case

For large sample sizes, the value of U is approximately normally distributed. Using an average expected U value for groups of this size and a standard deviation of U's allows computation of a z score for the U value. The probability of yielding a z score of this magnitude, given no difference between the groups, is computed. A decision is then made whether to reject the null hypothesis. A z score can be calculated from U by the following formulas.

Large-Sample Formulas Mann-Whitney U Test

$$\mu_U = \frac{n_1 \cdot n_2}{2}, \quad \sigma_U = \sqrt{\frac{n_1 \cdot n_2 (n_1 + n_2 + 1)}{12}}, \quad z = \frac{U - \mu_U}{\sigma_U} \quad (17.1)$$

For example, the Mann-Whitney U test can be used to determine whether there is a difference in the average income of families who view PBS television and families who do not view PBS television. Suppose a sample of 14 families that have identified themselves as PBS television viewers and a sample of 13 families that have identified themselves as non-PBS television viewers are selected randomly.

Step 1 The hypotheses for this example are as follows.

H_0: The incomes of PBS and non-PBS viewers are identical.

H_a: The incomes of PBS and non-PBS viewers are not identical.

Step 2 Use the Mann-Whitney U test for large samples.

Step 3 Let $\alpha = .05$.

Step 4 Because this test is two-tailed with $\alpha = .05$, the critical values are $z_{.025} = \pm 1.96$. If the test statistic is greater than 1.96 or less than -1.96, the decision is to reject the null hypothesis.

Step 5 The average annual reported income for each family in the two samples is given in Table 17.1.

Step 6 The first step toward computing a Mann-Whitney U test is to combine these two columns of data into one group and rank the data from lowest to highest, while maintaining the identification of each original group. Table 17.2 shows the results of this step.

Note that in the case of a tie, the ranks associated with the tie are averaged across the values that tie. For example, two incomes of $43,500 appear in the sample. These incomes

TABLE 17.2	Ranks of Incomes from Combined Groups of PBS and Non-PBS Viewers				
INCOME	RANK	GROUP	INCOME	RANK	GROUP
$16,000	1	Non-PBS	39,500	15	Non-PBS
21,000	2	Non-PBS	40,500	16	Non-PBS
21,500	3	Non-PBS	41,000	17	Non-PBS
24,500	4	PBS	43,000	18	PBS
27,600	5	Non-PBS	43,500	19.5	PBS
27,800	6	Non-PBS	43,500	19.5	Non-PBS
32,000	7	PBS	51,900	21	Non-PBS
32,400	8	Non-PBS	53,000	22	PBS
32,500	9	Non-PBS	55,000	23	PBS
33,000	10	Non-PBS	57,960	24	PBS
34,000	11	PBS	61,000	25	PBS
36,800	12	PBS	61,400	26	PBS
39,000	13	PBS	62,500	27	PBS
39,400	14	PBS			

represent ranks 19 and 20. Each value therefore is awarded a ranking of 19.5, or the average of 19 and 20.

If PBS viewers are designated as group 1, W_1 can be computed by summing the ranks of all the incomes of PBS viewers in the sample.

$$W_1 = 4 + 7 + 11 + 12 + 13 + 14 + 18 + 19.5 + 22 + 23 + 24 + 25 + 26 + 27 = 245.5$$

Then W_1 is used to compute the U value. Because $n_1 = 14$ and $n_2 = 13$, then

$$U = n_1 n_2 + \frac{n_1(n_1 + 1)}{2} - W_1 = (14)(13) + \frac{(14)(15)}{2} - 245.5 = 41.5$$

Because $n_1, n_2 > 10$, U is approximately normally distributed, with a mean of

$$\mu_U = \frac{n_1 \cdot n_2}{2} = \frac{(14)(13)}{2} = 91$$

and a standard deviation of

$$\sigma_U = \sqrt{\frac{n_1 \cdot n_2 (n_1 + n_2 + 1)}{12}} = \sqrt{\frac{(14)(13)(28)}{12}} = 20.6$$

A z value now can be computed to determine the probability of the sample U value coming from the distribution with $\mu_U = 91$ and $\sigma_U = 20.6$ if there is no difference in the populations.

$$z = \frac{U - \mu_U}{\sigma_U} = \frac{41.5 - 91}{20.6} = \frac{-49.5}{20.6} = -2.40$$

Step 7 The observed value of z is -2.40, which is less than $Z_{\alpha/2} = -1.96$ so the results are in the rejection region. That is, there is a difference between the income of a PBS viewer and that of a non-PBS viewer. Examination of the sample data confirms that in general, the income of a PBS viewer is higher than that of a non-PBS viewer.

Step 8 The fact that PBS viewers have higher average income can affect the type of programming on PBS in terms of both trying to please present viewers and offering programs that might attract viewers of other income levels. In addition, fund-raising drives can be made to appeal to the viewers with higher incomes.

Assignment of PBS viewers to group 1 was arbitrary. If non-PBS viewers had been designated as group 1, the results would have been the same but the observed z value would have been positive.

Figure 17.5 is the Minitab output for this example. Note that Minitab does not produce a z value but rather yields the value of W and the probability of the test results occurring by chance (.0174). Because the p-value (.0174) is less than $\alpha = .05$, the decision based on the computer output is to reject the null hypothesis. The two-tailed p-value of the observed test statistic ($z = -2.40$) is .0164. The difference is likely to be due to rounding error.

```
Mann-Whitney Test and CI: PBS, Non-PBS

                  N     Median
PBS              14     43250
Non-PBS          13     32500

Point estimate for η1 - η2 is 12500
95.1 Percent CI for η1 - η2 is (3000,22000)
W = 245.5
Test of η1 = η2 vs η1 ≠ η2 is significant at 0.0174
The test is significant at 0.0174 (adjusted for ties)
```

FIGURE 17.5 **Minitab Output for the PBS Viewer Example**

DEMONSTRATION PROBLEM 17.2

Do construction workers who purchase lunch from street vendors spend less per meal than construction workers who go to restaurants for lunch? To test this question, a researcher selects two random samples of construction workers, one group that purchases lunch from street vendors and one group that purchases lunch from restaurants. Workers are asked to record how much they spend on lunch that day. The data follow. Use the data, a Mann-Whitney U test, and the eight-step approach to analyze the data to determine whether street-vendor lunches are significantly cheaper than restaurant lunches. Let $\alpha = .01$.

VENDOR	RESTAURANT	VENDOR	RESTAURANT
$2.75	$4.10	4.01	2.70
3.29	4.75	3.68	3.65
4.53	3.95	3.15	5.11
3.61	3.50	2.97	4.80
3.10	4.25	4.05	6.25
4.29	4.98	3.60	3.89
2.25	5.75		4.80
2.97	4.10		5.50
		$n_1 = 14$	$n_2 = 16$

Solution:

Step 1. The hypotheses follow.

H_0: The populations of construction-worker spending for lunch at vendors and restaurants are the same.

H_a: The population of construction-worker spending at vendors is shifted to the left of the population of construction-worker spending at restaurants.

Step 2. The large-sample Mann-Whitney U test is appropriate. The test statistic is the z.

Step 3. Alpha is .01.

Step 4. If the p-value of the sample statistic is less than .01, the decision is to reject the null hypothesis.

Step 5. The sample data are given.

Step 6. Determine the value of W_1 by combining the groups, while retaining group identification and ranking all the values from 1 to 30 (14 + 16), with 1 representing the smallest value.

VALUE	RANK	GROUP	VALUE	RANK	GROUP
$2.25	1	V	$4.01	16	V
2.70	2	R	4.05	17	V
2.75	3	V	4.10	18.5	R
2.97	4.5	V	4.10	18.5	R
2.97	4.5	V	4.25	20	R
3.10	6	V	4.29	21	V
3.15	7	V	4.53	22	V
3.29	8	V	4.75	23	R
3.50	9	R	4.80	24.5	R
3.60	10	V	4.80	24.5	R
3.61	11	V	4.98	26	R
3.65	12	R	5.11	27	R
3.68	13	V	5.50	28	R
3.89	14	R	5.75	29	R
3.95	15	R	6.25	30	R

Summing the ranks for the vendor sample gives

$$W_1 = 1 + 3 + 4.5 + 4.5 + 6 + 7 + 8 + 10 + 11 + 13 + 16 + 17 + 21 + 22 = 144$$

Solving for U, μ_U, and σ_U yields

$$U = (14)(16) + \frac{(14)(15)}{2} - 144 = 185 \qquad \mu_U = \frac{(14)(16)}{2} = 112$$

$$\sigma_U = \sqrt{\frac{(14)(16)(31)}{12}} = 24.1$$

Solving for the observed z value gives

$$z = \frac{185 - 112}{24.1} = 3.03$$

Step 7.   The *p*-value associated with $z = 3.03$ is .0012. The null hypothesis is rejected.

Step 8.   The business researcher concludes that construction-worker spending at vendors is less than the spending at restaurants for lunches.

17.2 Problems

17.7. Use the Mann-Whitney *U* test and the following data to determine whether there is a significant difference between the values of group 1 and group 2. Let $\alpha = .05$.

GROUP 1	GROUP 2
15	23
17	14
26	24
11	13
18	22
21	23
13	18
29	21

17.8. The data shown represent two random samples gathered from two populations. Is there sufficient evidence in the data to determine whether the values of population 1 are significantly larger than the values of population 2? Use the Mann-Whitney *U* test and $\alpha = .01$.

SAMPLE 1	SAMPLE 2
224	203
256	218
231	229
222	230
248	211
283	230
241	209
217	223
240	219
255	236
216	227
	208
	214

17.9. Results of a survey by the National Center for Health Statistics indicated that people between 65 and 74 years of age contact a physician an average of 9.8 times per year. People 75 and older contact doctors an average of 12.9 times per year. Suppose you want to validate these results by taking your own samples. The following data represent the number of annual contacts people make with a physician. The samples are independent. Use a Mann-Whitney *U* test to determine whether the number of contacts with physicians by people 75 and older is greater than the number by people 65 to 74 years old. Let $\alpha = .01$.

65 TO 74	75 AND OLDER
12	16
13	15
8	10
11	17
9	13
6	12
11	14
	9
	13

17.10. Suppose 12 urban households and 12 rural households are selected randomly and each family is asked to report the amount spent on food at home annually. The results follow. Use a Mann-Whitney U test to determine whether there is a significant difference between urban and rural households in the amounts spent for food at home. Use $\alpha = .05$.

URBAN	RURAL
$12,238	$11,890
15,399	16,240
15,718	17,255
14,732	12,035
12,760	14,442
12,615	14,993
11,310	16,066
14,384	17,980
15,254	15,573
15,950	16,182
16,530	17,371
16,530	17,371

17.11. Does the male stock market investor earn significantly more than the female stock market investor? One study by the New York Stock Exchange showed that the male investor has an income of $46,400 and that the female investor has an income of $39,400. Suppose an analyst wanted to "prove" that the male investor earns more than the female investor. The following data represent random samples of male and female investors from across the United States. The analyst uses the Mann-Whitney U test to determine whether the male investor earns significantly more than the female investor for $\alpha = .01$. What does the analyst find?

MALE	FEMALE
$50,100	$41,200
47,800	36,600
45,000	44,500
51,500	47,800

55,000	42,500
53,850	47,500
51,500	40,500
63,900	28,900
57,800	48,000
61,100	42,300
51,000	40,000
	31,400

17.12. According to trulia.com, the average listing price for a home in Albuquerque in a recent week was $221,441 compared to $218,555 for Tulsa that same week. Suppose a survey of 13 randomly selected single-family homes is taken in Albuquerque and a survey of 13 randomly selected single-family homes is taken in Tulsa with the resulting prices shown here. Use a Mann-Whitney U test to determine whether there is a significant difference in the price of a single family home in these two cities. Let $\alpha = .05$.

ALBUQUERQUE	TULSA
$217,200	$226,900
221,000	217,100
218,100	218,200
220,000	220,300
218,900	223,000
219,800	222,100
223,500	225,000
223,100	224,500
239,600	219,400
224,800	220,900
224,400	217,500
215,400	219,300
224,700	227,000

17.3 Wilcoxon Matched-Pairs Signed Rank Test

The Mann-Whitney U test presented in Section 17.2 is a nonparametric alternative to the t test for two *independent* samples. If the two samples are *related*, the U test is not applicable. A test that does handle related data is the Wilcoxon matched-pairs signed rank test, which serves as *a nonparametric alternative to the t test for two related samples*. Developed by Frank Wilcoxon in 1945, the Wilcoxon test, like the t test for two related samples, is used to analyze several different types of studies when the data of one group are related to the data in the other group, including before-and-after studies, studies in which measures are taken on the same person or object under two different conditions, and studies of twins or other relatives.

The Wilcoxon test utilizes the differences of the scores of the two matched groups in a manner similar to that of the t test for two related samples. After the difference scores have been computed, the Wilcoxon test ranks all differences regardless of whether the difference is positive or negative. The values are ranked from smallest to largest, with a rank of 1 assigned to the smallest difference. If a difference is negative, the rank is given a negative sign. The sum of the positive ranks is tallied along with the sum of the negative ranks. Zero differences representing ties between scores from the two groups are ignored, and the value of n is reduced accordingly. When ties occur between ranks, the ranks are averaged over the values. The smallest sum of ranks (either + or −) is used in the analysis and is represented by T. The Wilcoxon matched-pairs signed rank test procedure for determining statistical significance differs with sample size. When the number of matched pairs, n, is greater than 15, the value of T is approximately normally distributed and a z score is computed to test the null hypothesis. When sample size is small, $n \leq 15$, a different procedure is followed.

Two assumptions underlie the use of this technique.

1. The paired data are selected randomly.
2. The underlying distributions are symmetrical.

The following hypotheses are being tested.

For two-tailed tests:

$$H_0: M_d = 0 \quad H_a: M_d \neq 0$$

For one-tailed tests:

$$H_0: M_d = 0 \quad H_a: M_d > 0$$

or

$$H_0: M_d = 0 \quad H_a: M_d < 0$$

where M_d is the median.

Small-Sample Case ($n \leq 15$)

When sample size is small, a critical value against which to compare T can be found in Table A.14 to determine whether the null hypothesis should be rejected. The critical value is located by using n and α. Critical values are given in the table for $\alpha = .05, .025, .01$, and $.005$ for one-tailed tests and $\alpha = .10, .05, .02$, and $.01$ for two-tailed tests. If the observed value of T is less than or equal to the critical value of T, the decision is to reject the null hypothesis.

As an example, according to the Consumer Expenditure Survey conducted by the U.S. Bureau of Labor Statistics, the estimated average annual household expenditure for healthcare is about \$3,600. Suppose six families in Pittsburgh, Pennsylvania, are matched demographically with six families in Oakland, California, and their amounts of household spending on healthcare for last year are obtained. The data follow.

FAMILY PAIR	PITTSBURGH	OAKLAND
1	\$3,750	\$3,560
2	3,640	3,670
3	3,815	3,610
4	3,380	3,460
5	3,590	3,140
6	3,725	3,565

A healthcare analyst uses $\alpha = .05$ and the eight-step approach to test to determine whether there is a significant difference in annual household healthcare spending between these two cities.

Step 1 The following hypotheses are being tested.

$$H_0: M_d = 0$$
$$H_a: M_d \neq 0$$

Step 2 Because the sample size of pairs is six, the small-sample Wilcoxon matched-pairs signed ranks test is appropriate if the underlying distributions are assumed to be symmetrical.

Step 3 Alpha is .05.

Step 4 From Table A.14, if the observed value of T is less than or equal to 1, the decision is to reject the null hypothesis.

Step 5 The sample data were listed earlier.

Step 6

FAMILY PAIR	PITTSBURGH	OAKLAND	d	RANK
1	$3,750	$3,560	+190	+4
2	3,640	3,670	−30	−1
3	3,815	3,610	+205	+5
4	3,380	3,460	−80	−2
5	3,590	3,140	+450	+6
6	3,725	3,565	+160	+3

$$T = \text{minimum of } (T_+, T_-)$$
$$T_+ = 4 + 5 + 6 + 3 = 18$$
$$T_- = 1 + 2 = 3$$
$$T = \text{minimum of } (18, 3) = 3$$

Step 7 Because $T = 3$ is greater than critical $T = 1$, the decision is not to reject the null hypothesis.

Step 8 Not enough evidence is provided to declare that Pittsburgh and Oakland differ in annual household spending on healthcare. This information may be useful to healthcare providers and employers in the two cities and particularly to businesses that either operate in both cities or are planning to move from one to the other. Rates can be established on the notion that healthcare costs are about the same in both cities. In addition, employees considering transfers from one city to the other can expect their annual healthcare costs to remain about the same.

Large-Sample Case ($n > 15$)

For large samples, the T statistic is approximately normally distributed and a z score can be used as the test statistic. Formula 17.2 contains the necessary formulas to complete this procedure.

Wilcoxon Matched-Pairs Signed Rank Test

$$\mu_T = \frac{(n)(n+1)}{4}$$

$$\sigma_T = \sqrt{\frac{(n)(n+1)(2n+1)}{24}}$$

$$z = \frac{T - \mu_T}{\sigma_T}$$

(17.2)

where

n = number of pairs

T = total ranks for either + or − differences, whichever is less in magnitude

This technique can be applied to the airline industry, where an analyst might want to determine whether there is a difference in the cost per mile of airfares in the United States between 1997 and 2016 for various cities. The data in Table 17.3 represent the costs per mile of airline tickets for a sample of 17 cities for both 1997 and 2016.

Step 1   The analyst states the hypotheses as follows.

$$H_0: M_d = 0$$
$$H_a: M_d \neq 0$$

Step 2   The analyst applies a Wilcoxon matched-pairs signed rank test to the data to test the difference in cents per mile for the two periods of time. She assumes the underlying distributions are symmetrical.

Step 3   Use $\alpha = .05$.

Step 4   Because this test is two-tailed, $\alpha/2 = .025$ and the critical values are $z = \pm 1.96$. If the observed value of the test statistic is greater than 1.96 or less than −1.96, the null hypothesis is rejected.

Step 5   The sample data are given in Table 17.3.

Step 6   The analyst begins the process by computing a difference score, d. Which year's data are subtracted from the other does not matter as long as consistency in direction is maintained. For the data in Table 17.3, the analyst subtracted the 2016 figures from the 1997 figures. The sign of the difference is left on the difference score. Next, she ranks the differences without regard to sign, but the sign is left on the rank as an identifier. Note the tie for ranks 6 and 7; each is given a rank of 6.5, the average of the two ranks. The same applies to ranks 11 and 12.

After the analyst ranks all difference values regardless of sign, she sums the positive ranks (T_1) and the negative ranks (T_2). She then determines the T value from these two sums as the smallest T_1 or T_2.

TABLE 17.3   **Airline Ticket Costs for Various Cities**

CITY	1997	2016	d	RANK
1	20.3	22.8	−2.5	−8
2	19.5	12.7	+6.8	+17
3	18.6	14.1	+4.5	+13
4	20.9	16.1	+4.8	+15
5	19.9	25.2	−5.3	−16
6	18.6	20.2	−1.6	−4
7	19.6	14.9	+4.7	+14
8	23.2	21.3	+1.9	+6.5
9	21.8	18.7	+3.1	+10
10	20.3	20.9	−0.6	−1
11	19.2	22.6	−3.4	−11.5
12	19.5	16.9	+2.6	+9
13	18.7	20.6	−1.9	−6.5
14	17.7	18.5	−0.8	−2
15	21.6	23.4	−1.8	−5
16	22.4	21.3	+1.1	+3
17	20.8	17.4	+3.4	+11.5

$$T = \text{minimum of } (T_+, T_-)$$

$$T_+ = 17 + 13 + 15 + 14 + 6.5 + 10 + 9 + 3 + 11.5 = 99$$

$$T_- = 8 + 16 + 4 + 1 + 11.5 + 6.5 + 2 + 5 = 54$$

$$T = \text{minimum of } (99, 54) = 54$$

The T value is normally distributed for large sample sizes, with a mean and standard deviation of

$$\mu_T = \frac{(n)(n+1)}{4} = \frac{(17)(18)}{4} = 76.5$$

$$\sigma_T = \sqrt{\frac{(n)(n+1)(2n+1)}{24}} = \sqrt{\frac{(17)(18)(35)}{24}} = 21.1$$

The observed z value is

$$z = \frac{T - \mu_T}{\sigma_T} = \frac{54 - 76.5}{21.1} = -1.07$$

Step 7 The critical z value for this two-tailed test is $z_{.025} = \pm 1.96$. The observed $z = -1.07$, so the analyst fails to reject the null hypothesis. There is no significant difference in the cost of airline tickets between 1997 and 2016.

Step 8 Promoters in the airline industry can use this type of information (the fact that ticket prices have not increased significantly in 19 years) to sell their product as a good buy. In addition, industry managers could use it as an argument for raising prices.

DEMONSTRATION PROBLEM 17.3

During the 1980s and 1990s, U.S. businesses increasingly emphasized quality control. One of the arguments in favor of quality-control programs is that quality control can increase productivity. Suppose a company implemented a quality-control program and has been operating under it for two years. The company's president wants to determine whether worker productivity significantly increased since installation of the program. Company records contain the figures for items produced per worker during a sample of production runs two years ago. Productivity figures on the same workers are gathered now and compared to the previous figures. The following data represent items produced per hour. Using an eight-step approach, the company's statistical analyst uses the Wilcoxon matched-pairs signed rank test to determine whether there is a significant increase in per worker production for $\alpha = .01$.

WORKER	BEFORE	AFTER	WORKER	BEFORE	AFTER
1	5	11	11	2	6
2	4	9	12	5	10
3	9	9	13	4	9
4	6	8	14	5	7
5	3	5	15	8	9
6	8	7	16	7	6
7	7	9	17	9	10
8	10	9	18	5	8
9	3	7	19	4	5
10	7	9	20	3	6

Solution:

Step 1   The hypotheses are as follows.

$$H_0: M_d = 0$$
$$H_a: M_d < 0$$

Step 2   The analyst applies a Wilcoxon matched-pairs signed rank test to the data to test the difference in productivity from before to after. He assumes the underlying distributions are symmetrical.

Step 3   Use $\alpha = .01$.

Step 4   This test is one tailed. The critical value is $z = -2.33$. If the observed value of the test statistic is less than -2.33, the null hypothesis is rejected.

Step 5   The sample data are as already given.

Step 6   The analyst computes the difference values, and, because zero differences are to be eliminated, deletes worker 3 from the study. This reduces n from 20 to 19. He then ranks the differences regardless of sign. The differences that are the same (ties) receive the average rank for those values. For example, the differences for workers 4, 5, 7, 10, and 14 are the same. The ranks for these five are 7, 8, 9, 10, and 11, so each worker receives the rank of 9, the average of these five ranks.

WORKER	BEFORE	AFTER	d	RANK
1	5	11	−6	−19
2	4	9	−5	−17
3	9	9	0	delete
4	6	8	−2	−9
5	3	5	−2	−9
6	8	7	+1	+3.5
7	7	9	−2	−9
8	10	9	+1	+3.5
9	3	7	−4	−14.5
10	7	9	−2	−9
11	2	6	−4	−14.5
12	5	10	−5	−17
13	4	9	−5	−17
14	5	7	−2	−9
15	8	9	−1	−3.5
16	7	6	+1	+3.5
17	9	10	−1	−3.5
18	5	8	−3	−12.5
19	4	5	−1	−3.5
20	3	6	−3	−12.5

The analyst determines the values of T_+, T_-, and T to be

$$T_+ = 3.5 + 3.5 + 3.5 = 10.5$$
$$T_- = 19 + 17 + 9 + 9 + 9 + 14.5 + 9 + 14.5 + 17 + 17$$
$$+ 9 + 3.5 + 3.5 + 12.5 + 3.5 + 12.5 = 179.5$$
$$T = \text{minimum of } (10.5, 179.5) = 10.5$$

The mean and standard deviation of T are

$$\mu_T = \frac{(n)(n+1)}{4} = \frac{(19)(20)}{4} = 95$$
$$\sigma_T = \sqrt{\frac{(n)(n+1)(2n+1)}{24}} = \sqrt{\frac{(19)(20)(39)}{24}} = 24.8$$

The observed z value is

$$z = \frac{T - \mu_T}{\sigma_T} = \frac{10.5 - 95}{24.8} = -3.41$$

Step 7. The observed z value (-3.41) is in the rejection region, so the analyst rejects the null hypothesis. The productivity is significantly greater after the implementation of quality control at this company.

Step 8. Managers, the quality team, and any consultants can point to the figures as validation of the efficacy of the quality program. Such results could be used to justify further activity in the area of quality.

Figure 17.6 is Minitab output for Demonstration Problem 17.3. Minitab does not produce a z test statistic for the Wilcoxon matched-pairs signed rank test. Instead, it calculates a Wilcoxon statistic that is equivalent to T. A p-value of .000 is produced for this T value. The p-value of the observed $z = -3.41$ determined in Demonstration Problem 17.3 is .0003.

```
Wilcoxon Signed Rank Test: difference

Test of median = 0.000000 versus median < 0.000000

                    N for   Wilcoxon            Estimated
              N     Test    Statistic    P      Median
Difference    20    19      10.5         0.000  -2.000
```

FIGURE 17.6 Minitab Output for Demonstration Problem 17.3

17.3 Problems

17.13. Use the Wilcoxon matched-pairs signed rank test to determine whether there is a significant difference between the two groups of related data given. Use $\alpha = .10$. Assume the underlying distributions are symmetrical.

1	2	1	2
212	179	220	223
234	184	218	217
219	213	234	208
199	167	212	215
194	189	219	187
206	200	196	198
234	212	178	189
225	221	213	201

39	38
53	40
51	43
51	46
49	40
38	42
54	50
46	47
50	47
44	39
49	49
45	47

17.14. Use the Wilcoxon matched-pairs signed rank test and $\alpha = .05$ to analyze the before-and-after measurements given. Assume the underlying distributions are symmetrical.

BEFORE	AFTER
49	43
41	29
47	30

17.15. A corporation owns a chain of several hundred gasoline stations on the eastern seaboard. The marketing director wants to test a proposed marketing campaign by running ads on some local television stations and determining whether gasoline sales at a sample of the company's stations increase after the advertising. The following data represent gasoline sales for a day before and a day after the advertising campaign. Use the Wilcoxon matched-pairs signed rank test to determine whether sales increased significantly after the advertising campaign. Let $\alpha = .05$. Assume the underlying distributions are symmetrical.

STATION	BEFORE	AFTER
1	$10,500	$12,600
2	8,870	10,660
3	12,300	11,890
4	10,510	14,630
5	5,570	8,580
6	9,150	10,115
7	11,980	14,350
8	6,740	6,900
9	7,340	8,890
10	13,400	16,540
11	12,200	11,300
12	10,570	13,330
13	9,880	9,990
14	12,100	14,050
15	9,000	9,500
16	11,800	12,450
17	10,500	13,450

17.16. According to an NCR white paper, it can probably be concluded that most cashiers at high volume stores receive little or no training on how to properly scan items. What little cashier training that is done is typically focused on operating the point-of-sale terminal (register), while the scanner is overlooked. The common perception is that the scanner is intuitive—a cashier passes a product in front of the scanner, the scanner beeps, and the item is successfully scanned.

It turns out that scanning techniques can matter. First of all, as scanning became more prevalent, there was a rise in the number of cases of carpel tunnel syndrome (CTS) from the way in which scanned items were handled. NCR has developed a "power slide" technique which when cashiers receive training on it, can help reduce CTS cases and cut down the time required to scan each item thereby increasing the number of items scanned per hour.

In general, does having scanning training significantly increase the number of items scanned per hour? Suppose the following data are from an experiment in which a supermarket selected 14 of its best cashiers, gave them the NCR training, and measured their productivity both before and after the training. The data show the number of items checked per hour by each cashier both before and after the training. Use a Wilcoxon matched-pairs signed rank test and $\alpha = .05$ to test the difference. Assume the underlying distributions are symmetrical.

CASHIER	BEFORE	AFTER
1	426	473
2	387	446
3	410	421
4	506	510
5	411	465
6	398	409
7	427	414
8	449	459
9	407	502
10	438	439
11	418	456
12	482	499
13	512	517
14	402	437

17.17. American attitudes toward big business change over time and probably are cyclical. Suppose the following data represent a survey of 20 American adults taken in 1990 and again in 2016 in which each adult was asked to rate American big business overall on a scale from 1 to 100 in terms of positive opinion. A response of 1 indicates a low opinion and a response of 100 indicates a high opinion. Use a Wilcoxon matched-pairs signed rank test to determine whether the scores from 2016 are significantly higher than the scores from 1990. Use $\alpha = .10$. Assume the underlying distributions are symmetrical.

PERSON	1990	2016	PERSON	1990	2016
1	49	54	11	72	58
2	27	38	12	62	57
3	39	38	13	49	63
4	75	80	14	48	49
5	59	53	15	19	39
6	67	68	16	32	34
7	22	43	17	60	66
8	61	67	18	80	90
9	58	73	19	55	57
10	60	55	20	68	58

17.18. Suppose 16 people in various industries are contacted in 2015 and asked to rate business conditions on several factors. The ratings of each person are tallied into a "business optimism" score. The same people are contacted in 2016 and asked to do the same thing. The higher the score, the more optimistic the person is. Shown here are the 2015 and 2016 scores for the 16 people. Use a Wilcoxon matched-pairs signed rank test to determine whether people were less optimistic in 2016 than in 2015. Assume the underlying distributions are symmetrical and that alpha is .05.

INDUSTRY	APRIL 2015	APRIL 2016
1	63.1	57.4
2	67.1	66.4
3	65.5	61.8
4	68.0	65.3
5	66.6	63.5
6	65.7	66.4
7	69.2	64.9
8	67.0	65.2
9	65.2	65.1
10	60.7	62.2
11	63.4	60.3
12	59.2	57.4
13	62.9	58.2
14	69.4	65.3
15	67.3	67.2
16	66.8	64.1

17.4 Kruskal-Wallis Test

The *nonparametric alternative to the one-way analysis of variance* is the **Kruskal-Wallis test**, developed in 1952 by William H. Kruskal and W. Allen Wallis. Like the one-way analysis of variance, the Kruskal-Wallis test is used to determine whether $c \geq 3$ samples come from the same or different populations. Whereas the one-way ANOVA is based on the assumptions of normally distributed populations, independent groups, at least interval level data, and equal population variances, the Kruskal-Wallis test can be used to analyze ordinal data and is not based on any assumption about population shape. The Kruskal-Wallis test is based on the assumption that the c groups are independent and that individual items are selected randomly.

The hypotheses tested by the Kruskal-Wallis test follow.

H$_0$: The c populations are identical.

H$_a$: At least one of the c populations is different.

This test determines whether all of the groups come from the same or equal populations or whether at least one group comes from a different population.

The process of computing a Kruskal-Wallis K statistic begins with ranking the data in all the groups together, as though they were from one group. The smallest value is awarded a 1. As usual, for ties, each value is given the average rank for those tied values. Unlike one-way ANOVA, in which the raw data are analyzed, the Kruskal-Wallis test analyzes the ranks of the data.

Formula 17.3 is used to compute a Kruskal-Wallis K statistic.

Kruskal-Wallis Test

$$K = \frac{12}{n(n+1)}\left(\sum_{j=1}^{c}\frac{T_j^2}{n_j}\right) - 3(n+1) \tag{17.3}$$

where

c = number of groups
n = total number of items
T_j = total of ranks in a group
n_j = number of items in a group
$K \approx \chi^2$, with df = $c - 1$

The K value is approximately chi-square distributed, with $c - 1$ degrees of freedom as long as n_j is not less than 5 for any group.

Suppose a researcher wants to determine whether the number of physicians in an office produces significant differences in the number of office patients seen by each physician per day. She takes a random sample of physician-days from practices in which (1) there are only two partners, (2) there are three or more partners, or (3) the office is a health maintenance organization (HMO). Table 17.4 shows the data she obtained.

Three groups are targeted in this study, so $c = 3$, and $n = 18$ physician-days, with the numbers of patients ranked for these physicians. The researcher then sums the ranks within each column to obtain T_j, as shown in Table 17.5.

The Kruskal-Wallis K is

$$K = \frac{12}{18(18+1)}(1{,}897) - 3(18+1) = 9.56$$

The critical chi-square value is $\chi^2_{\alpha,df}$. If $\alpha = .05$ and df for $c - 1 = 3 - 1 = 2$, $\chi^2_{.05,2} = 5.9915$. This test is always one-tailed, and the rejection region is always in the right tail of the distribution. Because $K = 9.56$ is larger than the critical χ^2 value, the researcher rejects the

TABLE 17.4	Number of Office Patients per Doctor	
TWO PARTNERS	THREE OR MORE PARTNERS	HMO
13	24	26
15	16	22
20	19	31
18	22	27
23	25	28
	14	33
	17	

TABLE 17.5	Kruskal-Wallis Analysis of Physicians' Patients	
TWO PARTNERS	THREE OR MORE PARTNERS	HMO
1	12	14
3	4	9.5
8	7	17
6	9.5	15
11	13	16
	2	18
	5	

$T_1 = 29$ $T_2 = 52.5$ $T_3 = 89.5$

$n_1 = 5$ $n_2 = 7$ $n_3 = 6$ $n = 18$

$$\sum_{j=1}^{3} \frac{T_j^2}{n_j} = \frac{(29)^2}{5} + \frac{(52.5)^2}{7} + \frac{(89.5)^2}{6} = 1{,}897$$

null hypothesis. The number of patients seen in the office by a physician is not the same in these three sizes of offices. Examination of the values in each group reveals that physicians in two-partner offices see fewer patients per physician in the office, and HMO physicians see more patients per physician in the office.

Figure 17.7 is the Minitab computer output for this example. The statistic H printed in the output is equivalent to the K statistic calculated here (both K and H are 9.56).

```
Kruskal-Wallis Test on Patients

Group    N    Median   Ave Rank   Z
1        5    18.00    5.8        -1.82
2        7    19.00    7.5        -1.27
3        6    27.50    14.9        3.04
Overall  18            9.5

H = 9.56   DF = 2   P = 0.008
H = 9.57   DF = 2   P = 0.008 (adjusted for ties)
```

FIGURE 17.7 Minitab Output for the Physicians' Patients Example

DEMONSTRATION PROBLEM 17.4

Agribusiness researchers are interested in determining the conditions under which Christmas trees grow fastest. A random sample of equivalent-size seedlings is divided into four groups. The trees are all grown in the same field. One group is left to grow naturally, one group is given extra water, one group is given fertilizer spikes, and one group is given fertilizer spikes and extra water. At the end of one year, the seedlings are measured for growth (in height). These measurements are shown for each group. Use the Kruskal-Wallis test and the eight-step approach to determine whether there is a significant difference in the growth of trees in these groups. Use $\alpha = .01$.

GROUP 1 (NATIVE)	GROUP 2 (+WATER)	GROUP 3 (+FERTILIZER)	GROUP 4 (+WATER AND FERTILIZER)
8 in.	10 in.	11 in.	18 in.
5	12	14	20
7	11	10	16
11	9	16	15
9	13	17	14
6	12	12	22

Solution: Here, $n = 24$, and $n_j = 6$ in each group.

Step 1.   The hypotheses follow.

H_0: group 1 = group 2 = group 3 = group 4

H_a: At least one group is different.

Step 2.   The Kruskal-Wallis K is the appropriate test statistic.

Step 3.   Alpha is .01.

Step 4.   The degrees of freedom are $c - 1 = 4 - 1 = 3$. The critical value of chi-square is $\chi^2_{.01,3} = 11.3449$. If the observed value of K is greater than 11.3449, the decision is to reject the null hypothesis.

Step 5.   The data are as shown previously.

Step 6.   Ranking all group values yields the following.

1	2	3	4
4	7.5	10	22
1	13	16.5	23
3	10	7.5	19.5
10	5.5	19.5	18
5.5	15	21	16.5
2	13	13	24
$T_1 = 25.5$	$T_2 = 64.0$	$T_3 = 87.5$	$T_4 = 123.0$
$n_1 = 6$	$n_2 = 6$	$n_3 = 6$	$n_4 = 6$

$n = 24$

$$\sum_{j=1}^{c} \frac{T_j^2}{n_j} = \frac{(25.5)^2}{6} + \frac{(64)^2}{6} + \frac{(87.5)^2}{6} + \frac{(123)^2}{6} = 4{,}588.6$$

$$K = \frac{12}{24(24 + 1)}(4{,}588.6) - 3(24 + 1) = 16.77$$

Step 7.   The observed K value is 16.77 and the critical $\chi^2_{.01,3} = 11.3449$. Because the observed value is greater than the table value, the null hypothesis is rejected. There is a significant difference in the way the trees grow.

step 8.   From the increased heights in the original data, the trees with both water and fertilizer seem to be doing the best. However, these are sample data; without analyzing the pairs of samples with nonparametric multiple comparisons (not included in this text), it is difficult to conclude whether the water/fertilizer group is actually growing faster than the others. It appears that the trees under natural conditions are growing more slowly than the others. The following diagram shows the relationship of the observed K value and the critical chi-square value.

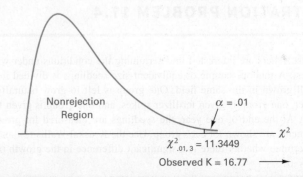

$\chi^2_{.01, 3} = 11.3449$

Observed K = 16.77

17.4 Problems

17.19. Use the Kruskal-Wallis test to determine whether groups 1 through 5 come from different populations. Let $\alpha = .01$.

1	2	3	4	5
157	165	219	286	197
188	197	257	243	215
175	204	243	259	235
174	214	231	250	217
201	183	217	279	240
203		203		233
				213

17.20. Use the Kruskal-Wallis test to determine whether there is a significant difference in the following groups. Use $\alpha = .05$.

Group 1	19	21	29	22	37	42
Group 2	30	38	35	24	29	
Group 3	39	32	41	44	30	27	33

17.21. Is there a difference in the amount of customers' initial deposits when they open savings accounts according to geographic region of the United States? To test this question, an analyst selects savings and loan offices of equal size from four regions of the United States. The offices selected are located in areas having similar economic and population characteristics. The analyst randomly selects adult customers who are opening their first savings account and obtains the following dollar amounts. Use the Kruskal-Wallis test to determine whether there is a significant difference between geographic regions. Use $\alpha = .05$.

REGION 1	REGION 2	REGION 3	REGION 4
$1,200	$225	$675	$1,075
450	950	500	1,050
110	100	1,100	750
800	350	310	180
375	275	660	330
200			680
			425

17.22. Does the asking price of a new car vary according to whether the dealership is in a small town, a city, or a suburban area? To test this question, a researcher randomly selects dealerships selling Buicks in the state of Illinois. The researcher goes to these dealerships posing as a prospective buyer and makes a serious inquiry as to the asking price of a new Buick Regal sedan (each having the same equipment). The following data represent the results of this sample. Is there a significant difference between prices according to the area in which the dealership is located? Use the Kruskal-Wallis test and $\alpha = .05$.

SMALL TOWN	CITY	SUBURB
$26,800	$27,300	$27,000
27,500	26,900	27,600
26,750	26,900	27,800
27,200	27,650	27,050
26,600	26,800	26,250
		27,550

17.23. A survey by the U.S. Travel Data Center showed that a higher percentage of Americans travel to the ocean/beach for vacation than to any other destination. Much further behind in the survey, and virtually tied for second place, were the mountains and small/rural towns. How long do people stay at vacation destinations? Does the length of stay differ according to location? Suppose the following data were taken from a survey of vacationers who were asked how many nights they stay at a destination when on vacation. Use a Kruskal-Wallis test to determine whether there is a significant difference in the duration of stay by type of vacation destination. Let $\alpha = .05$.

AMUSEMENT PARK	LAKE AREA	CITY	NATIONAL PARK
0	3	2	2
1	2	2	4
1	3	3	3
0	5	2	4
2	4	3	3
1	4	2	5
0	3	3	4
	5	3	4
	2	1	
		3	

17.24. Do workers on different shifts get different amounts of sleep per week? Some people believe that shift workers who regularly work the graveyard shift (12:00 A.M. to 8:00 A.M.) or swing shift (4:00 P.M. to 12:00 A.M.) are unable to get the same amount of sleep as day workers because of family schedules, noise, amount of daylight, and other factors. To test this theory, a researcher samples workers from day, swing, and graveyard shifts and asks each worker to keep a sleep journal for one week. The following data represent the number of hours of sleep per week per worker for the different shifts. Use the Kruskal-Wallis test to determine whether there is a significant difference in the number of hours of sleep per week for workers on these shifts. Use $\alpha = .05$.

DAY SHIFT	SWING SHIFT	GRAVEYARD SHIFT
52	45	41
57	48	46
53	44	39
56	51	49
55	48	42
50	54	35
51	49	52
	43	

Thinking Critically About Statistics in Business Today

Does an Iranian Auto Parts Manufacturer's Orientation Impact Innovation?

Two researchers, Ali Reza Maatoofi and Kayhan Tajeddini, studied Iranian auto parts manufacturers in an attempt to determine if there is any difference between companies whose strategic approach is more of a market orientation and companies whose strategic approach is more of an entrepreneurial orientation in the innovation of products. The researchers chose to study the auto parts industry because it is one of the most productive industries in Iran and it has always had governmental support.

Market-oriented companies pay close attention to their customers, study their rivals, and try to understand factors that may affect customer needs and preferences. Such companies learn to adjust to the environment and look for competitive advantages. One could say that market-oriented companies are somewhat reactive to customer needs. Entrepreneurial-oriented companies, on the other hand, focus more on risky products and tend to be more on the leading edge of new technological solutions. The approach of entrepreneurial-oriented companies is often exploratory and risky in nature. Some might argue that an entrepreneurial orientation might be more likely to lead to behavior that is congruent with an innovative product approach than that of a market orientation. The researchers set out to determine if that is true by studying 71 Iranian auto parts manufacturing firms. Based on a series of questions, they determined that 37 of these firms had more of a market orientation and 34 had more of an entrepreneurial orientation. They tested to determine if there was a significant difference between the two groups on five questions dealing with product innovation: (1) Is there a difference in the quality of products?

(2) Is there a difference in marketing synergy? (3) Is there a difference in the expertise in offering new products? (4) Is there a difference in the amount of management support? (5) Is there a difference in the intensity of the competitive environment?

Because they were using a 7-point Likert scale producing only ordinal-level data, they decided to use the Mann-Whitney U test to compare to two types of firms on each question. Somewhat surprisingly, they found no significant difference between market-oriented firms and entrepreneurial-oriented firms on four of the five questions. The one question that resulted in a significant difference was "management support for innovation," in which entrepreneurial-oriented firms scored significantly higher than market-oriented firms. There are many business research studies like this one where because of the level of data, researchers choose to use nonparametric statistics such as those presented in this chapter to study the data.

THINGS TO PONDER

1. Since the researchers failed to reject the null hypothesis of zero difference on four of the five questions, what might this say about a market-oriented culture and an entrepreneurial-oriented culture in terms of product innovation?

2. Consider two other industries different from auto manufacturing. Do you think the researchers might obtain different results from this study in either of those industries?

Source: Ali Reza Maatoofi and Kayhan Tajeddini. "Effect of Market Orientation and Entrepreneurial Orientation on Innovation, Evidence from Auto Parts Manufacturing in Iran," *Journal of Management Research*, Vol. 11, No. 1, April 2011, 20–30.

17.5 | Friedman Test

The Friedman test, developed by M. Friedman in 1937, is *a nonparametric alternative to the randomized block design* discussed in Chapter 11. The randomized block design has the same assumptions as other ANOVA procedures, including observations are drawn from normally distributed populations. When this assumption cannot be met or when the researcher has ranked data, the Friedman test provides a nonparametric alternative.

Three assumptions underlie the Friedman test.

1. The blocks are independent.
2. No interaction is present between blocks and treatments.
3. Observations within each block can be ranked.

The hypotheses being tested are as follows.

H_0: The treatment populations are equal.

H_a: At least one treatment population yields larger values than at least one other treatment population.

The first step in computing a Friedman test is to convert all raw data to ranks (unless the data are already ranked). However, unlike the Kruskal-Wallis test where all data are ranked together, the data in a Friedman test are ranked *within* each *block* from smallest (1) to largest (c). Each block contains c ranks, where c is the number of treatment levels. Using these ranks, the Friedman test will test to determine whether it is likely that the different treatment levels (columns) came from the same population. Formula 17.4 is used to calculate the test statistic, which is approximately chi-square distributed with df $= c - 1$ if $c > 4$, or when $c = 4$ and $b > 4$, or when $c = 3$ and $b > 9$.

Friedman Test

$$\chi_r^2 = \frac{12}{bc(c+1)} \sum_{j=1}^{c} R_j^2 - 3b(c+1) \qquad (17.4)$$

where

$\quad c$ = number of treatment levels (columns)
$\quad b$ = number of blocks (rows)
$\quad R_j$ = total of ranks for a particular treatment level (column)
$\quad j$ = particular treatment level (column)
$\quad \chi_r^2 \approx \chi^2$, with df $= c - 1$

As an example, suppose a manufacturing company assembles microcircuits that contain a plastic housing. Managers are concerned about an unacceptably high number of the products that sustained housing damage during shipment. The housing component is made by four different suppliers. Managers have decided to conduct a study of the plastic housing by randomly selecting five housings made by each of the four suppliers. To determine whether a supplier is consistent during the production week, one housing is selected for each day of the week. That is, for each supplier, a housing made on Monday is selected, one made on Tuesday is selected, and so on.

In analyzing the data, the treatment variable is supplier and the treatment levels are the four suppliers. The blocking effect is day of the week with each day representing a block level. The quality control team wants to determine whether there is any significant difference in the tensile strength of the plastic housing by supplier. The data are given here (in pounds per inch).

DAY	SUPPLIER 1	SUPPLIER 2	SUPPLIER 3	SUPPLIER 4
Monday	62	63	57	61
Tuesday	63	61	59	65
Wednesday	61	62	56	63
Thursday	62	60	57	64
Friday	64	63	58	66

Step 1   The hypotheses follow.

$\quad$ H$_0$: The supplier populations are equal.

$\quad$ H$_a$: At least one supplier population yields larger values than at least one other supplier population.

Step 2   The quality researchers do not feel they have enough evidence to conclude that the observations come from normally distributed populations. Because they are analyzing a randomized block design, the Friedman test is appropriate.

Step 3   Let $\alpha = .05$.

Step 4   For four treatment levels (suppliers), $c = 4$ and df $= 4 - 1 = 3$. The critical value is $\chi_{.05,3}^2 = 7.8147$. If the observed chi-square is greater than 7.8147, the decision is to reject the null hypothesis.

Step 5   The sample data are as given.

Step 6   The calculations begin by ranking the observations in each row (block) with 1 designating the rank of the smallest observation. The ranks are then summed for each column, producing R_j. The values of R_j are squared and then summed. Because the study is concerned with five days of the week, five blocking levels are used and $b = 5$. The value of R_j is computed as shown in the following table.

DAY	SUPPLIER 1	SUPPLIER 2	SUPPLIER 3	SUPPLIER 4
Monday	3	4	1	2
Tuesday	3	2	1	4
Wednesday	2	3	1	4
Thursday	3	2	1	4
Friday	3	2	1	4
R_j	14	13	5	18
R_j^2	196	169	25	324

$$\sum_{j=1}^{4} R_j^2 = (196 + 169 + 25 + 324) = 714$$

$$\chi_r^2 = \frac{12}{bc(c + 1)} \sum_{j=1}^{c} R_j^2 - 3b(c + 1) = \frac{12}{5(4)(4 + 1)}(714) - 3(5)(4 + 1) = 10.68$$

Step 7 Because the observed value of $\chi_r^2 = 10.68$ is greater than the critical value, $\chi_{.05,3}^2 = 7.8147$, the decision is to reject the null hypothesis.

Step 8 Statistically, there is a significant difference in the tensile strength of housings made by different suppliers. The sample data indicate that supplier 3 is producing housings with lower tensile strength than those made by other suppliers and that supplier 4 is producing housings with higher tensile strength. Further study by managers and a quality team may result in attempts to bring supplier 3 up to standard on tensile strength or perhaps cancellation of the contract.

Figure 17.8 displays the chi-square distribution for df = 3 along with the critical value, the observed value of the test statistic, and the rejection region. **Figure 17.9** is the Minitab output for the Friedman test. The computer output contains the value of χ_r^2 referred to as S along with the *p*-value of .014, which informs the researcher that the null hypothesis is rejected at an alpha of .05. Additional information is given about the medians and the column sum totals of ranks.

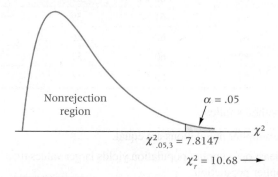

FIGURE 17.8 **Distribution for Tensile Strength Example**

```
Friedman Test: Tensile Strength Versus Supplier Blocked by Day

S = 10.68  DF = 3  P = 0.014

Supplier    N        Est Median      Sum of Ranks
1           5        62.125          14.0
2           5        61.375          13.0
3           5        56.875           5.0
4           5        64.125          18.0

Grand median = 61.125
```

FIGURE 17.9 **Minitab Output for the Tensile Strength Example**

DEMONSTRATION PROBLEM 17.5

A market research company wants to determine brand preference for refrigerators. Five companies contracted with the research company to have their products be included in the study. As part of the study, the research company randomly selects 10 potential refrigerator buyers and shows them one of each of the five brands. Each survey participant is then asked to rank the refrigerator brands from 1 to 5. The results of these rankings are given in the table. Use the Friedman test, $\alpha = .01$, and the eight-step approach to determine whether there are any significant differences between the rankings of these brands.

Solution:

Step 1. The hypotheses are as follows.

H$_0$: The brand populations are equal.

H$_a$: At least one brand population yields larger values than at least one other brand population.

Step 2. The market researchers collected ranked data that are ordinal in level. The Friedman test is the appropriate test.

Step 3. Let $\alpha = .01$.

Step 4. Because the study uses five treatment levels (brands), $c = 5$ and df $= 5 - 1 = 4$. The critical value is $\chi^2_{.01,4} = 13.2767$. If the observed chi-square is greater than 13.2767, the decision is to reject the null hypothesis.

Step 5. The sample data follow.

Step 6. The ranks are totaled for each column, squared, and then summed across the column totals. The results are shown in the table.

INDIVIDUAL	BRAND A	BRAND B	BRAND C	BRAND D	BRAND E
1	3	5	2	4	1
2	1	3	2	4	5
3	3	4	5	2	1
4	2	3	1	4	5
5	5	4	2	1	3
6	1	5	3	4	2
7	4	1	3	2	5
8	2	3	4	5	1
9	2	4	5	3	1
10	3	5	4	2	1
R_j	26	37	31	31	25
R_j^2	676	1,369	961	961	625

$$\Sigma R_j^2 = 4,592$$

The value of χ^2_r is

$$\chi^2_r = \frac{12}{bc(c+1)}\sum_{j=1}^{c} R_j^2 - 3b(c+1) = \frac{12}{10(5)(5+1)}(4,592) - 3(10)(5+1) = 3.68$$

Step 7. Because the observed value of $\chi^2_r = 3.68$ is not greater than the critical value, $\chi^2_{.01,4} = 13.2767$, the researchers fail to reject the null hypothesis.

Step 8. Potential refrigerator purchasers appear to have no significant brand preference. Marketing managers for the various companies might want to develop strategies for positively distinguishing their product from the others.

The chi-square distribution for four degrees of freedom, produced by Minitab, is shown with the observed test statistic and the critical value. In addition, Minitab output for the Friedman test is shown. Note that the p-value is .451, which underscores the decision not to reject the null hypothesis at $\alpha = .01$.

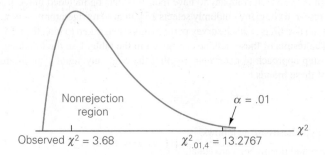

Nonrejection region

$\alpha = .01$

Observed $\chi^2 = 3.68$ $\chi^2_{.01,4} = 13.2767$

Minitab Friedman Output:

```
Friedman Test: Rank Versus Brand Blocked by Individual

S = 3.68   DF = 4   P = 0.451

Brand    N      Est Median     Sum of Ranks
1        10     2.300          26.0
2        10     4.000          37.0
3        10     3.000          31.0
4        10     3.000          31.0
5        10     1.700          25.0

Grand median = 2.800
```

17.5 Problems

17.25. Use the following data to test to determine whether there are any differences between treatment levels. Let $\alpha = .05$.

		TREATMENT			
		1	2	3	4	5
Block	1	200	214	212	215	208
	2	198	211	214	217	206
	3	207	206	213	216	207
	4	213	210	215	219	204
	5	211	209	210	221	205

		TREATMENT					
		1	2	3	4	5	6
	1	29	32	31	38	35	33
	2	33	35	30	42	34	31
	3	26	34	32	39	36	35
	4	30	33	35	41	37	32
Block	5	33	31	32	35	37	36
	6	31	34	33	37	36	35
	7	26	32	35	43	36	34
	8	32	29	31	38	37	35
	9	30	31	34	41	39	35

17.26. Use the Friedman test and $\alpha = .05$ to test the following data to determine whether there is a significant difference between treatment levels.

17.27. An experiment is undertaken to study the effects of four different medical treatments on the recovery time for a medical disorder. Six physicians are involved in the study. One patient with the disorder is sampled for each physician under each treatment, resulting in 24 patients in the study. Recovery time in days is the observed measurement. The data are given here. Use the Friedman test and $\alpha = .01$ to determine whether there is a significant difference in recovery times for the four different medical treatments.

		TREATMENT			
		1	2	3	4
	1	3	7	5	4
	2	4	5	6	3
Physician	3	3	6	5	4
	4	3	6	7	4
	5	2	6	7	3
	6	4	5	7	3

17.28. Does the configuration of the workweek have any impact on productivity? This question is raised by a researcher who wants to compare the traditional 5-day workweek with a 4-day workweek and a workweek with three 12-hour days and one 4-hour day. The researcher conducts the experiment in a factory making small electronic parts. He selects 10 workers who spend a month working under each type of workweek configuration. The researcher randomly selects one day from each of the 3 months (three workweek configurations) for each of the 10 workers. The observed measurement is the number of parts produced per day by each worker. Use the Friedman test to determine whether there is a difference in productivity by workweek configuration.

		WORKWEEK CONFIGURATION		
		5 DAYS	4 DAYS	3½ DAYS
	1	37	33	28
	2	44	38	36
	3	35	29	31
	4	41	40	36
Worker	5	38	39	35
	6	34	27	23
	7	43	38	39
	8	39	35	32
	9	41	38	37
	10	36	30	31

17.29. Shown here is Minitab output from a Friedman test. What is the size of the experimental design in terms of treatment levels and blocks? Discuss the outcome of the experiment in terms of any statistical conclusions.

```
Friedman Test: Observations Versus Treatment Blocked
by Block

S = 2.04    DF = 3    P = 0.564

                        Est        Sum of
Treatment    N       Median       Ranks
1            5        3.250        15.0
2            5        2.000        10.0
3            5        2.750        11.0
4            5        4.000        14.0

Grand median = 3.000
```

17.30. Shown here is Minitab output for a Friedman test. Discuss the experimental design and the outcome of the experiment.

```
Friedman Test: Observations Versus Treatment Blocked
by Block

S = 13.71    DF = 4    P = 0.009

                        Est        Sum of
Treatment    N       Median       Ranks
1            7       21.000        12.0
2            7       24.000        14.0
3            7       29.800        30.0
4            7       27.600        26.0
5            7       27.600        23.0

Grand median = 26.000
```

17.6 Spearman's Rank Correlation

In Chapter 12, the Pearson product-moment correlation coefficient, r, was presented and discussed as a technique to measure the amount or degree of association between two variables. The Pearson r requires at least interval level of measurement for the data. When only ordinal-level data or ranked data are available, **Spearman's rank correlation**, r_s, can be used to analyze the degree of association of two variables. Charles E. Spearman (1863–1945) developed this correlation coefficient.

The formula for calculating a Spearman's rank correlation is as follows:

Spearman's Rank Correlation

$$r_s = 1 - \frac{6 \sum d^2}{n(n^2 - 1)} \qquad (17.7)$$

where

n = number of pairs being correlated

d = the difference in the ranks of each pair

The Spearman's rank correlation formula is derived from the Pearson product-moment formula and utilizes the ranks of the n pairs instead of the raw data. The value of d is the difference in the ranks of each pair.

The process begins by the assignment of ranks within each group. The difference in ranks between each group (d) is calculated by subtracting the rank of a member of one group from the rank of its associated member of the other group. The differences (d) are then squared and summed. The number of pairs in the groups is represented by n.

The interpretation of r_s values is similar to the interpretation of r values. Positive correlations indicate that high values of one variable tend to be associated with high values of the other variable, and low values of one variable tend to be associated with low values of the other variable. Correlations near +1 indicate high positive correlations, and correlations near −1 indicate high negative correlations. Negative correlations indicate that high values of one variable tend to be associated with low values of the other variable, and vice versa. Correlations near zero indicate little or no association between variables.

Listed in Table 17.6 are the average prices in dollars per 100 pounds for choice spring lambs and choice heifers over a 10-year period. The data were published by the National Agricultural Statistics Service of the U.S. Department of Agriculture. Suppose we want to determine the strength of association of the prices between these two commodities by using Spearman's rank correlation.

The lamb prices are ranked and the heifer prices are ranked. The difference in ranks is computed for each year. The differences are squared and summed, producing $\Sigma d^2 = 108$. The number of pairs, n, is 10. The value of $r_s = 0.345$ indicates that there is a very modest positive correlation between lamb and heifer prices. The calculations of this Spearman's rank correlation are enumerated in Table 17.7.

TABLE 17.6	**Spring Lamb and Choice Heifer Prices over a 10-Year Period**	
YEAR	CHOICE SPRING LAMB PRICES ($/100 lbs.)	CHOICE HEIFER PRICES ($/100 lbs.)
1	77.91	65.46
2	82.00	64.18
3	89.20	65.66
4	74.37	59.23
5	66.42	65.68
6	80.10	69.55
7	69.78	67.81
8	72.09	67.39
9	92.14	82.06
10	96.31	84.40

TABLE 17.7	Calculations of Spearman's Rank Correlation for Lamb and Heifer Prices over a 10-Year Period			
YEAR	RANK: LAMB	RANK: HEIFER	d	d^2
1	5	3	2	4
2	7	2	5	25
3	8	4	4	16
4	4	1	3	9
5	1	5	−4	16
6	6	8	−2	4
7	2	7	−5	25
8	3	6	−3	9
9	9	9	0	0
10	10	10	0	0

$$\Sigma d^2 = 108$$

$$r_s = 1 - \frac{6\sum d^2}{n(n^2 - 1)} = 1 - \frac{6(108)}{10(10^2 - 1)} = 0.345$$

DEMONSTRATION PROBLEM 17.6

How strong is the correlation between crude oil prices and prices of gasoline at the pump? In an effort to estimate this association, an oil company analyst gathered the data shown over a period of several months. She lets crude oil prices be represented by the market value of a barrel of West Texas intermediate crude and gasoline prices be the estimated average price of regular unleaded gasoline in a certain city. She computes a Spearman's rank correlation for these data.

CRUDE OIL	GASOLINE
$14.60	$3.25
10.50	3.26
12.30	3.28
15.10	3.26
18.35	3.32
22.60	3.44
28.90	3.56
31.40	3.60
26.75	3.54

Solution: Here, $n = 9$. When the analyst ranks the values within each group and computes the values of d and d^2, she obtains the following.

CRUDE OIL	GASOLINE	d	d^2
3	1	+2	4
1	2.5	−1.5	2.25
2	4	−2	4
4	2.5	+1.5	2.25
5	5	0	0
6	6	0	0
8	8	0	0
9	9	0	0
7	7	0	0
			$\Sigma d^2 = 12.5$

$$r_s = 1 - \frac{6\Sigma d^2}{n(n^2 - 1)} = 1 - \frac{6(12.5)}{9(9^2 - 1)} = +.896$$

A high positive correlation is computed between the price of a barrel of West Texas intermediate crude and a gallon of regular unleaded gasoline.

17.6 Problems

17.31. Compute a Spearman's rank correlation for the following variables to determine the degree of association between the two variables.

x	y
23	201
41	259
37	234
29	240
25	231
17	209
33	229
41	246
40	248
28	227
19	200

17.32. The following data are the ranks for values of the two variables, x and y. Compute a Spearman's rank correlation to determine
the degree of relation between the two variables.

x	y	x	y
4	6	3	2
5	8	1	3
8	7	2	1
11	10	9	11
10	9	6	4
7	5		

17.33. Compute a Spearman's rank correlation for the following
data.

x	y	x	y
99	108	80	124
67	139	57	162
82	117	49	145
46	168	91	102

17.34. Over a period of a few months, is there a strong correlation
between the value of the U.S. dollar and the prime interest rate? The
following data represent a sample of these quantities over a period
of time. Compute a Spearman's rank correlation to determine the
strength of the relationship between prime interest rates and the value
of the dollar.

DOLLAR VALUE	PRIME RATE	DOLLAR VALUE	PRIME RATE
92	9.3	88	8.4
96	9.0	84	8.1
91	8.5	81	7.9
89	8.0	83	7.2
91	8.3		

17.35. Shown here are the percentages of consumer loans with
payments that are 30 days or more overdue for both bank credit
cards and home equity loans over a 14-year period, according to the
American Bankers Association. Compute a Spearman's rank correlation to determine the degree of association between these two
variables.

YEAR	BANK CREDIT CARD	HOME EQUITY LOAN
1	2.51%	2.07%
2	2.86	1.95
3	2.33	1.66
4	2.54	1.77
5	2.54	1.51
6	2.18	1.47
7	3.34	1.75
8	2.86	1.73
9	2.74	1.48
10	2.54	1.51
11	3.18	1.25
12	3.53	1.44
13	3.51	1.38
14	3.11	1.30

17.36. Shown here are the net tonnage figures for total pig iron and raw steel output in the United States as reported by the American Iron and Steel Institute over a 12-year period. Use these data to calculate a Spearman's rank correlation to determine the degree of association between production of pig iron and raw steel over this period. Was the association strong? Comment.

YEAR	TOTAL PIG IRON (net tons)	RAW STEEL (net tons)
1	43,952,000	81,606,000
2	48,410,000	89,151,000
3	55,745,000	99,924,000
4	55,873,000	97,943,000
5	54,750,000	98,906,000
6	48,637,000	87,896,000
7	52,224,000	92,949,000
8	53,082,000	97,877,000
9	54,426,000	100,579,000
10	56,097,000	104,930,000
11	54,485,000	105,309,478
12	54,679,000	108,561,182

17.37. Is there a correlation between the number of companies listed on the New York Stock Exchange in a given year and the number of equity issues on the American Stock Exchange? Shown here are the values for these two variables over an 11-year period. Compute a Spearman's rank correlation to determine the degree of association between these two variables.

YEAR	NUMBER OF COMPANIES ON NYSE	NUMBER OF EQUITY ISSUES ON AMEX
1	1774	1063
2	1885	1055
3	2088	943
4	2361	1005
5	2570	981
6	2675	936
7	2907	896
8	3047	893
9	3114	862
10	3025	769
11	2862	765

Decision Dilemma Solved

How Is the Doughnut Business?

The Dunkin' Donuts researchers' dilemma is that in each of the three studies presented, the assumptions underlying the use of parametric statistics are in question or have not been met. The distribution of the data is unknown, bringing into question the normal distribution assumption or the level of data is only ordinal. For each study, a nonparametric technique presented in this chapter could be appropriately used to analyze the data.

The differences in doughnut sizes according to machine can be analyzed using the Kruskal-Wallis test. The independent variable is machine with four levels of classification. The dependent variable is size of doughnut in centimeters. The Kruskal-Wallis test is not based on any assumption about population shape. The following Minitab output is from a Kruskal-Wallis test on the machine data presented in the Decision Dilemma.

```
Kruskal-Wallis Test: Diameter Versus Machine

Kruskal-Wallis Test on Diameter

Machine   N   Median   Ave Rank    Z
1         5   7.520    10.4      -0.60
2         6   7.415     3.5      -3.57
3         5   7.550    12.6       0.22
4         7   7.700    20.0       3.74
Overall  23            12.0

H = 19.48  DF = 3  P = 0.000
H = 19.51  DF = 3  P = 0.000 (adjusted
for ties)
```

Because the H statistic (Minitab's equivalent to the K statistic) has a p-value of .000, there is a significant difference in the diameter of the doughnut according to machine at $\alpha = .001$. An examination of median values reveals that machine 4 is producing the largest doughnuts and machine 2 the smallest.

How well did the advertising work? One way to address this question is to perform a before-and-after test of the number of doughnuts sold. The nonparametric alternative to the matched-pairs t test is the Wilcoxon matched-pairs signed rank test. The analysis for these data is:

BEFORE	AFTER	d	RANK
301	374	−73	−9
198	187	11	4
278	332	−54	−7
205	212	−7	−3
249	243	6	2
410	478	−68	−8
360	386	−26	−6
124	141	−17	−5
253	251	2	1
190	264	−74	−10

$$T_+ = 4 + 2 + 1 = 7$$
$$T_- = 9 + 7 + 3 + 8 + 6 + 5 + 10 = 48$$
$$\text{observed } T = \min(T_+, T_-) = 7$$
$$\text{critical } T \text{ for } .025 \text{ and } n = 10 \text{ is } 8$$

Using a two-sided test and $\alpha = .05$, the critical T value is 8. Because the observed T is 7, the decision is to reject the null hypothesis. There is a significant difference between the before and after number of donuts sold. An observation of the ranks and raw data reveals that a majority of the stores experienced an increase in sales after the advertising campaign.

Do bigger stores have greater sales? Because the data are given as ranks, it is appropriate to use Spearman's Rank Correlation to determine the extent of the correlation between these two variables. Shown below are the calculations of a Spearman's Rank correlation for this problem.

SALES	SIZE	d	d^2
6	7	−1	1
2	2	0	0
3	6	−3	9
7	5	2	4
5	4	1	1
1	1	0	0
4	3	1	1
		$\Sigma d^2 = 16$	

$$r_s = 1 - \frac{6\Sigma d^2}{n(n^2 - 1)} = 1 - \frac{6(16)}{7(49 - 1)} = .714$$

There is a relatively strong correlation (.714) between sales and size of store. It is not, however, a perfect correlation, which leaves room for other factors that may determine a store's sales such as location, attractiveness of store, population density, number of employees, management style, and others.

Ethical Considerations

The researcher should be aware of all assumptions underlying the usage of statistical techniques. Many parametric techniques have level-of-data requirements and assumptions about the distribution of the population or assumptions about the parameters. Inasmuch as these assumptions and requirements are not met, the researcher sets herself or himself up for misuse of statistical analysis. Spurious results can follow, and misguided conclusions can be reached. Nonparametric statistics can be used in many cases to avoid such pitfalls. In addition, some nonparametric statistics require at least ordinal-level data.

Summary

Nonparametric statistics are a group of techniques that can be used for statistical analysis when the data are less than interval in measurement and/or when assumptions about population parameters, such as shape of the distribution, cannot be met. Nonparametric tests offer several advantages. Sometimes the nonparametric test is the only technique available, with no parametric alternative. Nonparametric tests can be used to analyze nominal- or ordinal-level data. Computations from nonparametric tests are usually simpler than those used with parametric tests. Probability statements obtained from most nonparametric tests are exact probabilities. Nonparametric techniques also have some disadvantages. They are wasteful of data whenever a parametric technique can be used. Nonparametric tests are not as widely available as parametric tests. For large sample sizes, the calculations of nonparametric statistics can be tedious.

Many of the parametric techniques presented in this text have corresponding nonparametric techniques. The six nonparametric statistical techniques presented here are the runs test, the Mann-Whitney U test, the Wilcoxon matched-pairs signed rank test, the Kruskal-Wallis test, the Friedman test, and Spearman's rank correlation.

The runs test is a nonparametric test of randomness. It is used to determine whether the order of sequence of observations in a sample is random. A run is a succession of observations that have a particular characteristic. If data are truly random, neither a very large number of runs nor a very small number of runs is likely to be present.

The Mann-Whitney U test is a nonparametric version of the t test of the means from two independent samples. When the assumption of normally distributed data cannot be met and/or if the data are only ordinal in level of measurement, the Mann-Whitney U test can be used in place of the t test. The Mann-Whitney U test—like many nonparametric tests—works with the ranks of data rather than the raw data.

The Wilcoxon matched-pairs signed rank test is used as an alternative to the t test for related measures when assumptions cannot be met and/or if the data are ordinal in measurement. In contrast to the Mann-Whitney U test, the Wilcoxon test is used when the data are related in some way. The Wilcoxon test is used to analyze the data by ranks of the differences of the raw data.

The Kruskal-Wallis test is a nonparametric one-way analysis of variance technique. It is particularly useful when the assumptions underlying the F test of the parametric one-way ANOVA cannot be met. The Kruskal-Wallis test is usually used when the researcher wants to determine whether three or more groups or samples are from the same or equivalent populations. This test is based on the assumption that the sample items are selected randomly and that the groups are independent. The raw data are converted to ranks and the Kruskal-Wallis test is used to analyze the ranks with the equivalent of a chi-square statistic.

The Friedman test is a nonparametric alternative to the randomized block design. Friedman's test is computed by ranking the observations within each block and then summing the ranks for each treatment level. The resulting test statistic χ^2 is approximately chi-square distributed.

If two variables contain data that are ordinal in level of measurement, a Spearman's rank correlation can be used to determine the amount of relationship or association between the variables. Spearman's rank correlation coefficient is a nonparametric alternative to Pearson's product-moment correlation coefficient. Spearman's rank correlation coefficient is interpreted in a manner similar to the Pearson r.

Key Terms

Friedman test	nonparametric statistics	runs test	Wilcoxon matched-pairs signed
Kruskal-Wallis test	parametric statistics	Spearman's rank correlation	rank test
Mann-Whitney U test			

Formulas

Large-sample runs test

$$\mu_R = \frac{2n_1 n_2}{n_1 + n_2} + 1$$

$$\sigma_R = \sqrt{\frac{2n_1 n_2 (2n_1 n_2 - n_1 - n_2)}{(n_1 + n_2)^2 (n_1 + n_2 - 1)}}$$

$$z = \frac{R - \mu_R}{\sigma_R} = \frac{R - \left(\frac{2n_1 n_2}{n_1 + n_2} + 1\right)}{\sqrt{\frac{2n_1 n_2 (2n_1 n_2 - n_1 - n_2)}{(n_1 + n_2)^2 (n_1 + n_2 - 1)}}}$$

Mann-Whitney U test
   Small sample:

$$U_1 = n_1 n_2 + \frac{n_1 (n_1 + 1)}{2} - W_1$$

$$U_2 = n_1 n_2 + \frac{n_2 (n_2 + 1)}{2} - W_2$$

$$U' = n_1 \cdot n_2 - U$$

   Large sample:

$$\mu_U = \frac{n_1 \cdot n_2}{2}$$

$$\sigma_U = \sqrt{\frac{n_1 \cdot n_2 (n_1 + n_2 + 1)}{12}}$$

$$z = \frac{U - \mu_U}{\sigma_U}$$

Wilcoxon matched-pair signed rank test

$$\mu_T = \frac{(n)(n + 1)}{4}$$

$$\sigma_T = \sqrt{\frac{(n)(n + 1)(2n + 1)}{24}}$$

$$z = \frac{T - \mu_T}{\sigma_T}$$

Kruskal-Wallis test

$$K = \frac{12}{n(n + 1)} \left(\sum_{j=1}^{c} \frac{T_j^2}{n_j} \right) - 3(n - 1)$$

Friedman test

$$\chi_r^2 = \frac{12}{bc(c + 1)} \sum_{j=1}^{c} R_j^2 - 3b(c + 1)$$

Spearman's rank correlation

$$r_s = 1 - \frac{6\Sigma d^2}{n(n^2 - 1)}$$

Supplementary Problems

Calculating the Statistics

17.38. Use the runs test to determine whether the sample is random. Let alpha be .05.

```
1  1  1  1  2  2  2  2  2  2  2  2  1  1  1  1  2  2  2
2  2  2  2  2  1  2  1  2  2  2  1  1  1  1  1  2  2  2
```

17.39. Use the Mann-Whitney U test and $\alpha = .01$ to determine whether there is a significant difference between the populations represented by the two samples given here.

SAMPLE 1	SAMPLE 2
573	547
532	566
544	551
565	538
540	557
548	560
536	557
523	547

17.40. Use the Wilcoxon matched-pairs signed rank test to determine whether there is a significant difference between the related populations represented by the matched pairs given here. Assume $\alpha = .05$.

GROUP 1	GROUP 2
5.6	6.4
1.3	1.5
4.7	4.6
3.8	4.3
2.4	2.1
5.5	6.0
5.1	5.2
4.6	4.5
3.7	4.5

17.41. Use the Kruskal-Wallis test and $\alpha = .01$ to determine whether the four groups come from different populations.

GROUP 1	GROUP 2	GROUP 3	GROUP 4
6	4	3	1
11	13	7	4
8	6	7	5
10	8	5	6
13	12	10	9
7	9	8	6
10	8	5	7

17.42. Use the Friedman test to determine whether the treatment groups come from different populations. Let alpha be .05.

BLOCK	GROUP 1	GROUP 2	GROUP 3	GROUP 4
1	16	14	15	17
2	8	6	5	9
3	19	17	13	18
4	24	26	25	21
5	13	10	9	11
6	19	11	18	13
7	21	16	14	15

17.43. Compute a Spearman's rank correlation to determine the degree of association between the two variables.

VARIABLE 1	VARIABLE 2
101	87
129	89
133	84
147	79
156	70
179	64
183	67
190	71

Testing Your Understanding

17.44. Commercial fish raising is a growing industry in the United States. What makes fish raised commercially grow faster and larger? Suppose that a fish industry study is conducted over the three summer months in an effort to determine whether the amount of water allotted per fish makes any difference in the speed with which the fish grow. The following data represent the inches of growth of marked catfish in fish farms for different volumes of water per fish. Use $\alpha = .01$ to test whether there is a significant difference in fish growth by volume of allotted water.

1 GALLON PER FISH	5 GALLONS PER FISH	10 GALLONS PER FISH
1.1	2.9	3.1
1.4	2.5	2.4
1.7	2.6	3.0
1.3	2.2	2.3
1.9	2.1	2.9
1.4	2.0	1.9
2.1	2.7	

17.45. Manchester Partners International claims that 60% of the banking executives who lose their job stay in banking, whereas 40% leave banking. Suppose 40 people who have lost their job as a banking executive are contacted and are asked whether they are still in banking. The results follow. Test to determine whether this sample appears to be random on the basis of the sequence of those who have left banking and those who have not. Let L denote left banking and S denote stayed in banking. Let $\alpha = .05$.

S S L S L L S S S S S L S S L L L S S L
L L L S S L S S S S S S L L S L S S L S

17.46. Three machines produce the same part. Ten different machine operators work these machines. A quality team wants to determine whether the machines are producing parts that are significantly different from each other in weight. The team devises an experimental design in which a random part is selected from each of the 10 machine operators on each machine. The results follow.

Using alpha of .05, test to determine whether there is a difference in machines.

OPERATOR	MACHINE 1	MACHINE 2	MACHINE 3
1	231	229	234
2	233	232	231
3	229	233	230
4	232	235	231
5	235	228	232
6	234	237	231
7	236	233	230
8	230	229	227
9	228	230	229
10	237	238	234

17.47. In some firefighting organizations, you must serve as a firefighter for some period of time before you can become part of the emergency medical service (EMS) arm of the organization. Does that mean EMS workers are older, on average, than traditional firefighters? Use the data shown and $\alpha = .05$ to test whether EMS workers are significantly older than firefighters. Assume the two groups are independent and you do not want to use a t test to analyze the data.

FIREFIGHTERS	EMS WORKERS	FIREFIGHTERS	EMS WORKERS
23	27	32	39
37	29	24	33
28	30	21	30
25	33	27	28
41	28		27
36	36		30

17.48. Automobile dealers usually advertise in the yellow pages of the telephone book. Sometimes they have to pay to be listed in the white pages, and some dealerships opt to save money by omitting that listing, assuming most people will use the yellow pages to find the telephone number. A two-year study is conducted with 20 car dealerships where in one year the dealer is listed in the white pages and the other year it is not. Ten of the dealerships are listed in the white pages the first year and the other 10 are listed there in the second year in an attempt to control for economic cycles. The following data represent the numbers of units sold per year. Is there a significant difference between the number of units sold when the dealership is listed in the white pages and the number sold when it is not listed? Assume all companies are continuously listed in the yellow pages, that the t test is not appropriate, and that $\alpha = .01$.

DEALER	WITH LISTING	WITHOUT LISTING
1	1,180	1,209
2	874	902
3	1,071	862
4	668	503
5	889	974
6	724	675
7	880	821
8	482	567
9	796	602
10	1,207	1,097
11	968	962
12	1,027	1,045
13	1,158	896
14	670	708
15	849	642
16	559	327
17	449	483
18	992	978
19	1,046	973
20	852	841

17.49. Suppose you want to take a random sample of GMAT test scores to determine whether there is any significant difference between the GMAT scores for the test given in March and the scores for the test given in June. You gather the following data from a sample of persons who took each test. Use the Mann-Whitney U test to determine whether there is a significant difference in the two test results. Let $\alpha = .10$.

MARCH	JUNE
540	350
570	470
600	630
430	590
500	610
510	520
530	460
560	550
550	530
490	570

17.50. Does impulse buying really increase sales? A market researcher is curious to find out whether the location of packages of chewing gum in a grocery store really has anything to do with volume of gum sales. As a test, gum is moved to a different location in the store every Monday for four weeks (four locations). To control the experiment for type of gum, six different brands are moved around. Sales representatives keep track of how many packs of each type of gum are sold every Monday for the four weeks. The results follow. Test to determine whether there are any differences in the volume of gum sold at the various locations. Let $\alpha = .05$.

		LOCATION			
		1	2	3	4
	A	176	58	111	120
	B	156	62	98	117
Brand	C	203	89	117	105
	D	183	73	118	113
	E	147	46	101	114
	F	190	83	113	115

17.51. Does deodorant sell better in a box or without additional packaging? An experiment in a large store is designed in which, for one month, all deodorants are sold packaged in a box and, during a second month, all deodorants are removed from the box and sold without packaging. Is there a significant difference in the number of units of deodorant sold with and without the additional packaging? Let $\alpha = .05$.

DEODORANT	BOX	NO BOX
1	185	170
2	109	112
3	92	90
4	105	87
5	60	51
6	45	49
7	25	11
8	58	40
9	161	165
10	108	82
11	89	94
12	123	139
13	34	21
14	68	55
15	59	60
16	78	52

17.52. Some people drink coffee to relieve stress on the job. Is there a correlation between the number of cups of coffee consumed on the job and perceived job stress? Suppose the data shown represent the number of cups of coffee consumed per week and a stress rating for the job on a scale of 0 to 100 for nine managers in the same industry. Determine the correlation between these two variables, assuming you do not want to use the Pearson product-moment correlation coefficient.

CUPS OF COFFEE PER WEEK	JOB STRESS
25	80
41	85
16	35
0	45
11	30
28	50
34	65
18	40
5	20

17.53. A Gallup/Air Transport Association survey showed that in a recent year, 52% of all air trips were for pleasure/personal and 48% were for business. Suppose the organization randomly samples 30 air travelers and asks them to state the purpose of their trip. The results are shown here with B denoting business and P denoting personal. Test the sequence of these data to determine whether the data are random. Let $\alpha = .05$.

B P B P B B P B P P B P B P P
P B P B B P B P P B B P P B B

17.54. Does a statistics course improve a student's mathematics skills, as measured by a national test? Suppose a random sample of 13 students takes the same national mathematics examination just prior to enrolling in a statistics course and just after completing the course. Listed are the students' quantitative scores from both examinations. Use $\alpha = .01$ to determine whether the scores after the statistics course are significantly higher than the scores before.

STUDENT	BEFORE	AFTER
1	430	465
2	485	475
3	520	535
4	360	410
5	440	425
6	500	505
7	425	450
8	470	480
9	515	520
10	430	430
11	450	460
12	495	500
13	540	530

17.55. Should male managers wear a tie during the workday to command respect and demonstrate professionalism? Suppose a measurement scale has been developed that generates a management professionalism score. A random sample of managers in a high-tech industry is selected for the study, some of whom wear ties at work and others of whom do not. One subordinate is selected randomly from each manager's department and asked to complete the scale on their boss's professionalism. Analyze the data taken from these independent groups to determine whether the managers with ties received significantly higher professionalism scores. Let $\alpha = .05$.

WITH TIE	WITHOUT TIE
27	22
23	16
25	25
22	19
25	21
26	24
21	20
25	19
26	23
28	26
22	17

17.56. Many fast-food restaurants have soft drink dispensers with preset amounts, so that when the operator merely pushes a button for the desired drink the cup is automatically filled. This method apparently saves time and seems to increase worker productivity. To test this conclusion, a researcher randomly selects 18 workers from the fast-food industry, 9 from a restaurant with automatic soft drink dispensers and 9 from a comparable restaurant with manual soft drink dispensers. The samples are independent. During a comparable hour, the amount of sales rung up by the worker is recorded. Assume that $\alpha = .01$ and that a t test is not appropriate. Test whether workers with automatic dispensers are significantly more productive (higher sales per hour).

AUTOMATIC DISPENSER	MANUAL DISPENSER
$153	$105
128	118
143	129
110	114
152	125
168	117
144	106
137	92
118	126

17.57. A particular metal part can be produced at different temperatures. All other variables being equal, a company would like to determine whether the strength of the metal part is significantly different for different temperatures. Given are the strengths of random samples of parts produced under different temperatures. Use $\alpha = .01$ and a nonparametric technique to determine whether there is a significant difference in the strength of the part for different temperatures.

45°	55°	70°	85°
216	228	219	218
215	224	220	216
218	225	221	217
216	222	223	221
219	226	224	218
214	225		217

17.58. Is there a strong correlation between the number of miles driven by a salesperson and sales volume achieved? Data were gathered from nine salespeople who worked territories of similar size and potential. Determine the correlation coefficient for these data. Assume the data are ordinal in level of measurement.

SALES	MILES PER MONTH
$150,000	1,500
210,000	2,100
285,000	3,200
301,000	2,400
335,000	2,200
390,000	2,500
400,000	3,300
425,000	3,100
440,000	3,600

17.59. Workers in three different but comparable companies were asked to rate the use of quality-control techniques in their firms on a 50-point scale. A score of 50 represents nearly perfect implementation of quality control techniques and 0 represents no implementation. Workers are divided into three independent groups. One group worked in a company that had required all its workers to attend a 3-day seminar on quality control 1 year ago. A second group worked in a company in which each worker was part of a quality circle group that had been meeting at least once a month for a year. The third group of workers was employed by a company in which management had been actively involved in the quality-control process for more than a year. Use $\alpha = .10$ to determine whether there is a significant difference between the three groups, as measured by the ratings.

ATTENDED 3-DAY SEMINAR	QUALITY CIRCLES	MANAGEMENT INVOLVED
9	27	16
11	38	21
17	25	18
10	40	28
22	31	29
15	19	20
6	35	31

17.60. The scores given are husband-wife scores on a marketing measure. Use the Wilcoxon matched-pairs signed rank test to determine whether the wives' scores are significantly higher on the marketing measure than the husbands'. Assume that $\alpha = .01$.

HUSBANDS	WIVES
27	35
22	29
28	30
19	20
28	27
29	31
18	22
21	19
25	29
18	28
20	21
24	22
23	33
25	38
22	34
16	31
23	36
30	31

Interpreting the Output

17.61. Study the following Minitab output. What statistical test was run? What type of design was it? What was the result of the test?

```
Friedman Test: Observations Versus
Treatment Blocked by Block

S = 11.31   DF = 3   P = 0.010

                     Est      Sum of
Treatment   N     Median     Ranks
1          10     20.125     17.0
2          10     25.875     33.0
3          10     24.500     30.5
4          10     22.500     19.5

Grand median = 23.250
```

```
Mann-Whitney Test and CI

              N    Median
1st Group    16    37.000
2nd Group    16    46.500

Point estimate for η1 - η2 is -8.000
95.7 Percent CI for η1 - η2 is (-13.999,
-2.997)

W = 191.5
Test of η1 = η2 vs η1 ≠ η2 is significant
at 0.0067
```

17.62. Examine the following Minitab output. Discuss the statistical test, its intent, and its outcome.

17.64. Study the following Minitab output. What type of statistical test was done? What were the hypotheses, and what was the outcome? Discuss.

```
Runs Test

Runs above and below K = 1.4200

The observed number of runs = 28
The expected number of runs = 25.3600
21 Observations above K, 29 below
P-value = 0.439
```

17.63. Study the following Minitab output. What statistical test was being computed by Minitab? What are the results of this analysis?

```
Kruskal-Wallis Test on Observations

Machine   N    Median   Ave Rank    Z
1         5    35.00     14.8      0.82
2         6    25.50      4.2     -3.33
3         7    35.00     15.0      1.11
4         6    35.00     16.0      1.40
Overall  24              12.5

H = 11.21 DF = 3 P = 0.011
```

Analyzing the Databases

See **www.wiley.com/college/black**

1. Compute a Spearman's rank correlation between New Capital Expenditures and End-of-Year Inventories in the Manufacture database. Is the amount spent annually on New Capital Expenditures related to the End-of-Year Inventories? Are these two variables highly correlated? Explain.

2. Use a Kruskal-Wallis test to determine whether there is a significant difference between the four levels of Value of Industry Shipments on Number of Employees for the Manufacture database. Discuss the results.

3. Use a Mann-Whitney U test to determine whether there is a significant difference between hospitals that are general hospitals and those that are psychiatric (Service variable) on Personnel for the Hospital database. Discuss the results.

4. Use the Kruskal-Wallis test to determine if there is a significant difference in Annual Food Spending by Region in the Consumer Food database.

Case

Schwinn

In 1895, Ignaz Schwinn and his partner, Adolph Arnold, incorporated the Arnold, Schwinn & Company in Chicago to produce bicycles. In the early years with bicycle products such as the "Roadster," a single-speed bike that weighed 19 pounds, Schwinn products appealed to people of all ages as a means of transportation. By 1900, bicycles could go as fast as 60 miles per hour. Because of the advent of the auto in 1909, the use of bicycles as a means of transportation in the United States waned. In that same year, Schwinn developed

manufacturing advances that allowed bicycles to be made more cheaply and sturdily. These advances opened a new market to the company as they manufactured and sold bicycles for children for the first time. Meanwhile, Ignaz Schwinn bought out Arnold to become the sole owner of the company. Over the next 20 years, Schwinn bought out two motorcycle companies and developed mudguards as its major technological achievement. In the 1930s, Schwinn developed a series of quality, appearance, and technological breakthroughs including the balloon tire, which some say was the biggest innovation in mountain bike technology; the forewheel brake; the cantilever frame; and the spring fork. In 1946, built-in kickstands were added to their bikes. In the 1950s, Schwinn began an authorized dealer network and expanded its parts and accessory programs.

In the 1960s, Schwinn expanded into the fitness arena with in-home workout machines. In 1967, the company became the Schwinn Bicycle Company. The company introduced the airdyne stationary bike in the late 1970s. In 1993, the company filed for bankruptcy and in 1994, it was moved from Chicago to Boulder, Colorado, to be nearer the mountain bike scene. In the next several years, Schwinn's mountain bike products won accolades and awards. In 2001, Pacific Cycle, the United States' largest importer of quality bicycles, purchased Schwinn and united Schwinn bicycle lines with Pacific Cycle's other brands. Under new management in 2002, Schwinn bicycles began being featured, along with Pacific Cycle's other bikes, at mass retail outlets in the United States. In 2004, Dorel Industries, Inc., a global consumer products company located in Madison, Wisconsin, purchased Pacific Cycle and made it a division of Dorel. Schwinn bicycles, now a part of the Dorel empire, are still made with quality for dependability and performance, and they continue to lead the industry in innovation.

Discussion

1. What is the age of the target market for Schwinn bikes? One theory is that in locales where mountain bikes are more popular, the mean age of their customers is older than in locales where relatively little mountain biking is done. In an attempt to test this theory, a random sample of Colorado Springs customers is taken along with a random sample of customers in St. Louis. The ages for these customers are given here. The customer is defined as "the person for whom the bike is primarily purchased." The shape of the population distribution of bicycle customer ages is unknown. Analyze the data and discuss the implications for Schwinn manufacturing and sales.

COLORADO SPRINGS	ST. LOUIS
29	11
38	14
31	15
17	12
36	14
28	25
44	14
9	11
32	8
23	
35	

2. Suppose for a particular model of bike, the specified weight of a handle bar is 200 grams and Schwinn uses three different suppliers of handle bars. Suppose Schwinn conducts a quality-control study in which handle bars are randomly selected from each supplier and weighed. The results (in grams) are shown next. It is uncertain whether handle bar weight is normally distributed in the population. Analyze the data and discuss what the business implications are to Schwinn.

SUPPLIER 1	SUPPLIER 2	SUPPLIER 3
200.76	197.38	192.63
202.63	207.24	199.68
198.03	201.56	203.07
201.24	194.53	195.18
202.88	197.21	189.11
194.62	198.94	
203.58		
205.41		

3. Quality technicians at Schwinn's manufacturing plant examine their finished products for paint flaws. Paint inspections are done on a production run of 75 bicycles. The inspection data are coded and the data analyzed using Minitab. If a bicycle's paint job contained no flaws, a 0 is recorded; if it contained at least one flaw, the code used is a 1. Inspectors want to determine whether the flawed bikes occur in a random fashion or in a nonrandom pattern. Study the Minitab output. Determine whether the flaws occur randomly. Report on the proportion of flawed bikes and discuss the implications of these results to Schwinn's production management.

```
Runs Test: Paint Flaw

Runs above and below K = 0.2533

The observed number of runs = 29
The expected number of runs = 29.3733
19 observations above K, 56 below
P-value = 0.908
```

Source: Adapted from Schwinn, available at http://www.schwinnbike.com/heritage.

CHAPTER 18

Statistical Quality Control

LEARNING OBJECTIVES

This chapter presents basic concepts in quality control, with a particular emphasis on statistical quality control techniques, thereby enabling you to:

1. Explain the meaning of quality in business, compare the approaches to quality improvement by various quality gurus and movements, and compare different approaches to controlling the quality of a product, including benchmarking, just-in-time inventory systems, Six Sigma, lean manufacturing, reengineering, failure mode and effects analysis, poka-yoke, and quality circles.

2. Compare various tools that identify, categorize, and solve problems in the quality improvement process, including flowcharts, Pareto analysis, cause-and-effect diagrams, control charts, check sheets, histograms, and scatter charts.

3. Measure variation among manufactured items using various control charts, including $\bar{x}$ charts, R charts, p charts, and c charts.

Decision Dilemma

Italy's Piaggio Makes a Comeback

Piaggio, founded in Genoa, Italy, in 1884 by a 20-year-old young man named Rinaldo Piaggio, began as a luxury ship fitting company. Expanding on its services and products by the year 1900, the company was also producing rail carriages, luxury coaches, truck bodies, and trains. During the first World War, Piaggio began producing airplanes and sea-planes and then expanded capacity by purchasing a new plant in Pisa in 1917 and taking over a small plant in Pontedera (in Tuscany) in 1921, making the Pontedera plant the company's center for aeronautical production.

During World War II, the Pontedera plant was building state-of-the-art four-engine aircraft, but Allied planes destroyed the plant because of its military importance. With the Pontedera plant gone, the state of Italian roads a disaster, and the Italian economy in shambles, Enrico Piaggio (Rinaldo's son and now CEO) decided to focus the company's efforts on the personal mobility of the Italian people. Corradino D'Ascanio, Piaggio's ingenious aeronautical engineer who had designed, constructed, and flown the first modern helicopter, was commissioned to design a simple, sturdy, economical vehicle for people to get around in that was both comfortable and elegant. Drawing from his aeronautical background, D'Ascanio, who did not like motorcycles, developed a completely new vehicle that had a front fork, like an airplane, allowing for easy wheel changing, and was housed in a unibody steel chasis. It was not noisy or uncomfortable like a motorcycle, and the steel frame protected the rider from road dirt and debris.

Stephane Audras/REA//Redux Pictures

When Enrico Piaggio first saw the vehicle he said, "Sembra una vespa!" ("It looks like a wasp!"), and as a result, the vehicle became known as the Vespa.

By the end of 1949, 35,000 Vespas had been produced, and in 10 more years, over 1 million had been manufactured. Featured in such films as *Roman Holiday, The Talented Mr. Ripley,* and *Alfie,* the Vespa became popular around the world and known as a global symbol of Italy and Italian design. In 1959, Piaggio came under control of the powerful Agnelli family, owners of the carmaker Fiat SpA, and for the next two decades, the scooter maker flourished. However, during the latter half of the twentieth century, revolving-door management and millions of euros wasted on ill-conceived expansion plans left the company with crushing debt and vulnerable to competition from companies in the Pacific Rim. Losing money and market share, Piaggio was caught up in a downward spiral of increasing debt, bad quality, and inability to meet market demand. As the twenty-first century arrived, the company's status was looking bleak until the year 2003, when Italian industrialist Roberto Colaninno bought the company. Implementing a series of strategic moves and quality initiatives, Colaninno turned around the fortunes of Piaggio, now the fourth largest manufacturer of scooters and motorcycles in the world, producing more than 600,000 vehicles annually. In a recent year, Piaggio had a revenue of 1.2€ billion.

MANAGERIAL AND STATISTICAL QUESTIONS

1. Was the decline of Piaggio driven by poor quality? If so, how?
2. What quality initiatives did Colaninno implement at Piaggio that helped turn the company around?
3. Were company workers consulted about ways to improve the product and the process?

Sources: Piaggio Vespa Web site: http://www.vespausa.com/company/history.cfm; Gabriel Kahn, "Vespa's Builder Scoots Back to Profitability," *Wall Street Journal*, June 5, 2006, B1; Piaggio.com, 2016.

In the past three decades, institutions around the world have invested millions of dollars in improving quality, and in some cases, corporate cultures have been changed through the implementation of new quality philosophies. Much has been written and spoken about quality, and a great deal of research has been conducted on the effectiveness of various quality approaches. In order to study and explore the myriad of quality theories, approaches, tools, and concepts, it is important first to understand what quality is.

One major stumbling block to studying and implementing quality improvement methodologies is that quality means different things to different people. If you asked commuters whether their automobiles have quality, the response would vary according to each individual's perspective. One person's view is that a quality automobile goes 75,000 miles without needing any major repair work. Other people perceive automobile quality as comfortable seats and extra electronic gadgetry. These people look for "bells and whistles" along with form-fitting, cushy seats in a quality car. Still other automobile consumers define automobile quality as the presence of numerous safety features.

In this chapter, we examine various definitions of quality and discuss some of the main concepts of quality and quality control. We explore some techniques for analyzing processes. In addition, we learn how to construct and interpret control charts.

18.1 | Introduction to Quality Control

There are almost as many definitions of quality as there are people and products. However, one definition that captures the spirit of most quality efforts in the business world is that **quality** is *when a product delivers what is stipulated for it in its specifications.* From this point of view, quality is when the producer delivers what has been specified in the product description, as agreed upon by both buyer and seller. Philip B. Crosby, a well-known expert on quality, has said that "quality is conformance to requirements."[*] The product requirements must be met by the producer to ensure quality. This notion of quality is similar to the one based on specifications. Armand V. Feigenbaum, a well-known quality authority, says in his book *Total Quality Control* that "quality is a customer determination" as opposed to management's determination or a designer's determination.[†] He states that this determination is based on the customer's experience with the product or service and that it is always a moving target.

David A. Garvin, author of *Managing Quality,* claims that there are at least five types of quality: transcendent, product, user, manufacturing based, and value.[‡] **Transcendent quality** *implies that a product has an "innate excellence."* It has *"uncompromising standards and high achievement."* Garvin says that this definition offers little practical guidance to business people. **Product quality** *is measurable in the product.* Consumers perceive differences among products, *and quality products have more attributes.* For example, a personal computer with more memory has more quality. Tires with more tread have more quality.

[*]Philip B. Crosby, *Quality Without Tears.* New York: McGraw-Hill, 1984.
[†]Armand V. Feigenbaum, *Total Quality Control,* 3rd ed. New York: McGraw-Hill, 1991.
[‡]David A. Garvin, *Managing Quality.* New York: The Free Press, 1988.

User quality means that the *quality of a product is determined by the consumer* and is "in the eye of the beholder." One problem with user-based quality is that because there are widely varying individual preferences, there can be a plethora of views of quality for a given product or service. **Manufacturing-based quality** has to do with engineering and manufacturing practices. Once specifications are determined, *quality is measured by the manufacturer's ability to target the requirements consistently with little variability*. Most manufacturing-based definitions of quality have to do with "conformance to requirements." **Value quality** is defined in costs and prices. From a certain point of view, value quality is based on cost-benefit analysis; that is, by how much did the benefit of the good or service outweigh the cost? Did the customer get his or her money's worth?

What Is Quality Control?

How does a company know whether it is producing a quality product? One way is to practice quality control. **Quality control** (sometimes referred to as quality assurance) is *the collection of strategies, techniques, and actions taken by an organization to assure itself that it is producing a quality product.*

From this point of view, quality control begins with product planning and design, where attributes of the product or service are determined and specified, and continues through product production or service operation until feedback from the final consumer is looped backed through the institution for product improvement. It is implied that all departments, workers, processes, and suppliers are in some way responsible for producing a quality product or service.

Quality control can be undertaken in two distinct ways: after-process control and in-process control. **After-process quality control** involves *inspecting the attributes of a finished product to determine whether the product is acceptable, is in need of rework, or is to be rejected and scrapped.* The after-process quality-control method was the leading quality-control technique for U.S. manufacturers for several decades until the 1980s. The after-process method emphasizes weeding out defective products before they reach the consumer. The problem with this method is that it does not generate information that can correct in-process problems or raw materials problems nor does it generate much information about how to improve quality. Two main outcomes of the after-process methodology are (1) reporting the number of defects produced during a specific period of time and (2) screening defective products from consumers. Because U.S. companies dominated world markets in many areas for several decades during and after World War II, their managers had little interest in changing from the after-process method.

However, as Japan, other Asian nations, and Western European countries began to compete strongly with the United States in the world market in the late 1970s and 1980s, U.S. companies began to reexamine quality-control methods. As a result, many U.S. companies, following the example of Japanese and European manufacturers, developed quality-control programs based on in-process control. **In-process quality-control** *techniques measure product attributes at various intervals throughout the manufacturing process in an effort to pinpoint problem areas.* This information enables quality-control personnel in conjunction with production personnel to make corrections in operations as products are being made. This intervention in turn opens the door to opportunities for improving the process and the product.

Total Quality Management

W. Edwards Deming, who has been called the "father of the quality movement," advocated that the achievement of quality is an organic phenomenon that begins with top managers' commitment and extends all the way to suppliers on one side and consumers on the other. Deming believed that quality control is a long-term total company effort. The effort called for by Deming is **total quality management (TQM)**. Total quality management involves all members of the organization—from the CEO to the line worker—in improving quality. In addition, the goals and objectives of the organization come under the purview of quality control and can be measured in quality terms. Suppliers, raw materials, worker training, and opportunity for workers to make improvements all are part of total quality management. The antithesis of total quality management is when a company gives a quality-control department total responsibility for improving product quality.

Deming presented a cause-and-effect explanation of the impact of total quality management on a company. This idea has become known as the Deming chain reaction.* The chain reaction begins with improving quality. Improving quality will decrease costs because of less reworking, fewer mistakes, fewer delays and snags, and better use of machine time and materials. From the reduced costs comes an improvement in productivity because

$$\text{Productivity} = \frac{\text{Output}}{\text{Input}}$$

A reduction of costs generates more output for less input and, hence, increases productivity. As productivity improves, a company is more able to capture the market with better quality and lower prices. This capability enables a company to stay in business and provide more jobs. As a note of caution, while Deming advocated that improved quality results in a by-product of lower costs through efficiencies gained by streamlining and reducing waste, some managers have used it as an excuse to lay off workers in an effort to save money. It is likely that Deming would have argued that such cost-cutting actually reduces quality and productivity due to an increase in operational errors, errors of omission, and a lack of attention to detail by a reduced staff that is overworked, understaffed, and stressed.

Deming's 14 Points

Deming listed 14 points that, if followed, can lead to improved total quality management, and they are as follows[†]:

1. Create constancy of purpose for improvement of product and service.
2. Adopt the new philosophy.
3. Cease dependence on mass inspection.
4. End the practice of awarding business on price tag alone.
5. Improve constantly and forever the system of production and service.
6. Institute training.
7. Institute leadership.
8. Drive out fear.
9. Break down barriers between staff areas.
10. Eliminate slogans.
11. Eliminate numerical quotas.
12. Remove barriers to pride of workmanship.
13. Institute a vigorous program of education and retraining.
14. Take action to accomplish the transformation.

The first point indicates the need to seek constant improvement in process, innovation, design, and technique. The second point suggests that to truly make changes, a new, proactive point of view about quality must be taken; in other words, the viewpoint that poor quality is acceptable must be changed. The third point is a call for change from after-process inspection to in-process inspection. Deming pointed out that after-process inspection has nothing to do with improving the product or the service. The fourth point indicates that a company should be careful in awarding contracts to suppliers and vendors. Purchasers should look more for quality and reliability in a supplier than for just low price. Deming called for long-term supplier relationships in which the company and supplier agree on quality standards.

Point 5 conveys the message that quality is not a one-time activity. Management and labor should be constantly on the lookout for ways to improve the product. Institute training, the

---

*W. Edwards Deming, *Out of the Crisis*. Cambridge: Massachusetts Institute of Technology Center for Advanced Engineering Study, 1986.

[†]Mary Walton, *The Deming Management Method*. New York: Perigee Books, 1986.

sixth point, implies that training is an essential element in total quality management. Workers need to learn how to do their jobs correctly and learn techniques that will result in higher quality. Point 7, institute leadership, is a call for a new management based on showing, doing, and supporting rather than ordering and punishing. The eighth point results in establishing a "safe" work environment, where workers feel free to share ideas and make suggestions without the threat of punitive measures. Point 9, breaking down barriers, emphasizes reducing competition and conflicts between departments and groups. It is a call for more of a team approach—the notion that "we're all in this together."

Deming did not believe that slogans help affect quality products, as stated in point 10. Quality control is not a movement of slogans. Point 11 indicates that quotas do not help companies make quality products. In fact, pressure to make quotas can result in inefficiencies, errors, and lack of quality. Point 12 says that managers must find ways to make it easier for workers to produce quality products; faulty equipment and poor-quality supplies do not allow workers to take pride in what is produced. Point 13 calls for total reeducation and training within a company about new methods and how to do one's job more effectively. Point 14 implies that rhetoric is not the answer; a call for action is necessary in order to institute change and promote higher quality.

Quality Gurus

Some other important and well-known quality gurus include Joseph Juran, Philip Crosby, Armand Feigenbaum, Kaoru Ishikawa, and Genichi Taguchi. Joseph Juran, a contemporary of Deming, like Deming, assisted Japanese leaders in the 1950s in implementing quality concepts and tools so that they could produce products that would be attractive to world markets. Juran is particularly well known for his "Juran Trilogy," which included Quality Planning, Quality Control, and Quality Improvement. Philip Crosby, author of the popular book *Quality Is Free*, developed a zero-defects program to reduce defects in missile production in the United States in the late 1950s and early 1960s, and later established a Quality College. Crosby bases his approach to quality on four basic tenets that he refers to as "Absolutes": (1) Quality means conformance to requirements, (2) Defect prevention is the only acceptable approach, (3) Zero defects is the only performance standard, and (4) The cost of quality is the only measurement of quality. Armand Feigenbaum has been a worldwide leader in quality management for over a half century. Feigenbaum published his widely read text, *Total Quality Control*, in 1951 under the title *Quality Control: Principles, Practice, and Administration*. While W. Edwards Deming is often associated with total quality management, it was Feigenbaum who actually coined the term "total quality control." He originated the concept of "cost of quality" as a means of quantifying the benefits of a TQM approach, and he popularized the term "hidden factory," which describes the part of plant capacity wasted due to poor quality. Kaoru Ishikawa, a student of both Deming and Juran, is probably the best-known figure in the Japanese quality movement. He has been credited with originating the concept of "quality circle" and championed what is now seen as Japan's "company-wide" approach to quality. Ishikawa placed an emphasis on data measurement and using statistical techniques in improving quality. He is known for developing the "cause-and-effect" or "fishbone" diagram that is sometimes referred to as the Ishikawa diagram. Genichi Taguchi, an important figure in the Japanese quality movement, wrote a two-volume book on experimental designs that has been widely used in the quality-improvement efforts. In the 1970s, Taguchi developed the concept of the Quality Loss Function and refined a set of cost-saving quality-improvement techniques that later became known as Taguchi Methods.

Six Sigma

Currently, a popular approach to total quality management is Six Sigma. **Six Sigma** is a quality movement, a methodology, and a measurement. As a quality movement, Six Sigma is a major player throughout the world in both the manufacturing and service industries. As a methodology, it is used to evaluate the capability of a process to perform defect-free, where a defect is defined as anything that results in customer dissatisfaction. Six Sigma is customer focused and has the potential to achieve exponential quality improvement through the reduction of variation in system processes. Under the Six Sigma methodology, quality-improvement projects are carefully defined so that they can be successfully completed within a relatively short time frame. Financials are applied to each completed project so that management can estimate how much the project saves the institution. On each project, intense study is used to determine root cause. In the end, a metric known as a "sigma level" can be assigned to represent the level of quality that has been attained, and this is the measurement aspect of Six Sigma.

The Six Sigma approach to quality is said to have begun in 1987 with Bill Smith, a reliability engineer at Motorola.* However, Six Sigma took off as a significant quality movement in the mid-1990s when Jack Welch, CEO of General Electric, "went nuts about Six Sigma and launched it," calling it the most ambitious task the company had ever taken on.[†] "Six Sigma has taken the corporate world by storm and represents the thrusts of numerous efforts in manufacturing and service organizations to improve products, services, and processes."[‡] Six Sigma has been around for over 25 years and has shown a sustained impact on quality improvement within a variety of companies in many industries. Six Sigma is derived from a previous quality scheme in which a process was considered to be producing quality results if $\pm 3\sigma$ or 99.74% of the products or attributes were within specification. (Note: The standard normal distribution table, Table A.5, produces an area of .4987 for a z score of 3. Doubling that and converting to a percentage yields 99.74%, which is the portion of a normal distribution that falls within $\mu \pm 3\sigma$.) Six Sigma methodology requires that $\pm 6\sigma$ of the product be within specification. The goal of Six Sigma methodology is to have 99.99966% of the product or attributes be within specification, or no more than .00034% = .0000034 out of specification. This means that no more than 3.4 of the product or attributes per million can be defective. Essentially, it calls for the process to approach a defect-free status.

Why Six Sigma? Several reasons highlight the importance of adoption of a Six Sigma philosophy. First, in some industries the three sigma philosophy is simply unacceptable. For example, the three sigma goal of having 99.74% of the product or attribute be in specification in the prescription drug industry implies that it is acceptable to have .26% incorrectly filled prescriptions, or 2,600 out of every million prescriptions filled. In the airline industry, the three sigma goal implies that it is acceptable to have 2,600 unsatisfactory landings by commercial aircraft out of every million landings. In contrast, a Six Sigma approach would require that there be no more than 3.4 incorrectly filled prescriptions or 3.4 unsatisfactory landings per million, with a goal of approaching zero.

A second reason for adopting a Six Sigma approach is that it forces companies that adopt it to work much harder and more quickly to discover and reduce sources of variation in processes. It "raises the bar" of the quality goals of a firm, causing the company to place even more emphasis on continuous quality improvement. A third reason is that Six Sigma dedication to quality may be required to attain world-class status and be a top competitor in the international market.

Six Sigma contains a formalized problem-solving approach called the DMAIC process (*D*efine, *M*easure, *A*nalyze, *I*mprove, and *C*ontrol). At the beginning of each Six Sigma project, the project team carefully identifies the problem—not just the symptoms—at the Define stage. The scope of the project is limited so that it can be completed within four to six months. At the Measure stage, there is a heavy emphasis on metrics and measurement of current operating systems along with identifying variables and targeting data collection. During the Analyze stage, there is a focus on analyzing data and collecting information in an effort to determine what is occurring and uncovering root causes of problems. At the fourth stage, Improve, the project team generates ideas for solving problems and improving performance. Lastly, at the fifth stage, Control, there is a focus on putting into motion those tools, standards, etc., that are needed to maintain the new quality that has been achieved through the Six Sigma project.

Another important aspect of Six Sigma as a methodology and a quality movement is the strong focus on the customer that is often referred to as CTQ or Critical to Quality. Maintaining

---

*James R. Evans and William M. Lindsay, *The Management and Control of Quality*, 5th ed. Cincinnati: South-Western Publishing, 2002.

[†]Jack Welch, *Jack: Straight from the Gut*. New York: Warner Books, 2001, pp. 329–330.

[‡]James R. Evans and William M. Lindsay, *An Introduction to Six Sigma & Process Improvement*. Cincinnati: Thomson South-Western Publishing Company, 2005, p. 4.

a customer focus is vital to every stage of a Six Sigma project, keeping in mind that there are both internal and external customers. Six Sigma project team members work on things that are important to the customer and do not spend time on things that could be improved but are not important to the customer (not CTQ).

Under Six Sigma, most members of an organization are supposed to have at least some training in the methodology. Employees with minimal exposure to Six Sigma—perhaps only an introductory lecture—might be designated as "yellow belts" (named after the belt system in karate). Organizational members who have more extensive training and serve part-time on Six Sigma teams are designated as "green belts." Fully trained employees having over 150 hours of training in Six Sigma, usually including at least one Six Sigma project, are called "black belts." Black belts work full time within an organization, usually directing several Six Sigma projects simultaneously. Master black belts are "experts" in Six Sigma. They have advanced training in statistical techniques and other Six Sigma tools and methods, and they work in the organization developing teams, training black belts, and providing technical direction.

Design for Six Sigma

Companies using Six Sigma discovered that some processes, outcomes, and services, often designed before the Six Sigma era, contained so many flaws and problems that even the in-depth, root analysis of the Six Sigma methodology could not solve some quality issues, and thus a complete redesign was necessary. In fact, history has shown that most processes can only achieve about a 5.0 sigma status with quality improvement and to actually achieve 6.0 sigma status, organizations often need to *design* for 6.0 sigma; that is, because of constraints or limitations built in by its original design, there may be a ceiling on how much a process or operation can be improved. **Design for Six Sigma** (DFSS), an offshoot of Six Sigma, is a quality scheme that places an emphasis on designing the product or process right the first time, thereby allowing organizations the opportunity to reach even higher sigma levels through Six Sigma.

Lean Manufacturing

Lean manufacturing is a quality-management philosophy that focuses on the reduction of wastes and the elimination of unnecessary steps in an operation or process. Whereas the tenets of lean manufacturing have existed in successful manufacturing circles for over a century, the Toyota Production System is generally credited with developing the notion of lean manufacturing as it exists today. Lean manufacturing requires a disciplined attitude in seeking out and eliminating waste in all areas of business including supplier networks, customer relations, organization management, and design. Proponents of lean manufacturing claim it brings about an evaluation of the entire organization and restructures processes to reduce wasteful activities.

In particular, lean manufacturing focuses on seven wastes:

1. overproduction
2. waiting time
3. transportation
4. processing
5. inventory
6. motion
7. scrap

Overproduction can include making more than is needed or making it earlier than is needed. Waiting includes products waiting on the next production step or people waiting for work to do. Transportation waste can include moving products further than is minimally required, and inventory waste can include having more inventory than is minimally required at any point in the process, including end-product. Processing waste is doing more work than the customer values or needs, and motion waste is having people move around unnecessarily or wasting motion in performing their production or operation functions.*

Some advocates of lean manufacturing claim that even if a process or service is operating at a Six Sigma level, it does not necessarily follow that the process or service is lean. That is, the quality of the process or service can be quite high, but there can still be waste in the system. Some critics of Six Sigma say that just improving the quality does not necessarily reduce the time that it takes to perform the process. With this in mind, a newer approach to quality management has been developed by combining the investigative, variation-reduction aspects of Six Sigma with the emphasis on increased efficiency of lean manufacturing, resulting in what some refer to as Lean Six Sigma.

Some Important Quality Concepts

Of the several widely used techniques in quality control, six in particular warrant discussion: benchmarking, just-in-time inventory systems, reengineering, Failure Mode and Effects Analysis, poka-yoke, and quality circles/Six Sigma teams.

Benchmarking   One practice used by U.S. companies to improve quality is benchmarking. Benchmarking is *a method in which a company attempts to develop and establish total quality management from product to process by examining and emulating the "best practices" and techniques used in its industry.* The ultimate objective of benchmarking is to use a positive, proactive process to make changes that will affect superior performance. The process of benchmarking involves studying competitors and learning from the best in the industry.

One of the American pioneers in what is called "competitive benchmarking" was Xerox. Xerox was struggling to hold on to its market share against foreign competition. At one point, other companies could sell a machine for what it cost Xerox to make a machine. Xerox set out to find out why. The company instituted a benchmarking process in which the internal workings and features of competing machines were studied in depth. Xerox attempted to emulate and learn from the best of these features in developing its own products. In time, benchmarking was so successful within the company that top managers included benchmarking as a major corporate effort.[†]

Just-in-Time Inventory Systems   Another technique used to improve quality control is the just-in-time system for inventory, which focuses on raw materials, subparts, and suppliers. Ideally, a just-in-time inventory system means that *no extra raw materials or inventory of parts for production are stored.* Necessary supplies and parts needed for production arrive "just in time." The advantage of this system is that holding costs, personnel, and space needed to manage inventory are reduced. Even within the production process, as subparts are assembled and merged, the just-in-time philosophy can be applied to smooth the process and eliminate bottlenecks.

A production facility is unlikely to become 100% just-in-time. One of the residual effects of installing a just-in-time system throughout the production process is that, as the inventory "fat" is trimmed from the production process, the pressure on the system to produce often discloses problems previously undetected. For example, one subpart being made on two machines may not be produced in enough quantity to supply the next step. Installation of the just-in-time system shows that this station is a bottleneck. The company might choose to add another machine to produce more subparts, change the production schedule, or develop another strategy. As the bottleneck is loosened and the problem is corrected, other areas of weakness may emerge. Thus, the residual effect of a just-in-time inventory system can be the opportunity for production and operations managers to work their way methodically through a maze of previously unidentified problems that would not normally be recognized.

A just-in-time inventory system typically changes the relationship between supplier and producer. Most companies using this system have fewer suppliers than they did before installing

---

*Adapted from Wikipedia, the free encyclopedia, at: http://en.wikipedia.org/wiki/Lean_manufacturing.
[†]Robert C. Camp, *Benchmarking.* Milwaukee, WI: Quality Press, ASQC, 1989.

the system. The tendency is for manufacturers to give suppliers longer contracts under the just-in-time system. However, the suppliers are expected to produce raw materials and sub-parts to a specified quality and to deliver the goods as near to just in time as possible. Just-in-time suppliers may even build production or warehouse facilities next to the producer's. In the just-in-time system, the suppliers become part of total quality management.

Just-in-time (JIT) as a management philosophy has come to mean "eliminating manufacturing wastes by producing only the right amount and combination of parts at the right place at the right time;"* that is, JIT now generally signifies production with a minimum of waste.† The goal of JIT is to minimize "non–value-adding operations" and "non-moving inventory" in a production process or operation.‡ In this sense, some view JIT, also known as "lean production,"‡ as the forerunner of what is now referred to as "lean manufacturing." While some of the basic elements of JIT were used by Toyota in the 1950s, most historians give credit to Taiichi Ohno of Toyota for developing JIT in the 1970s, and Ohno is often referred to as the father of JIT.‡

Some of the basic elements that underscore the just-in-time philosophy include§:

1. Leveling the loads on work centers to smooth the flow of goods or services
2. Reducing or even eliminating setup times
3. Reducing lot sizes
4. Reducing lead times
5. Conducting preventive maintenance on machines and equipment to ensure that they work perfectly when needed
6. Having a flexible work force
7. Requiring supplier quality assurance and implement a zero-defects quality program
8. Improving, eliminating, or reducing anything that does not add value to the product
9. Striving for simplicity
10. Making each worker responsible for the quality of his or her output

By leveling loads at workstations throughout the process, bottlenecks are reduced or eliminated, and there is a greater chance that goods/services will flow smoothly through the process.

Reengineering   A more radical approach to improving quality is reengineering. Whereas total quality approaches like Deming's 14 points call for continuous improvement, reengineering is *the complete redesigning of the core business process in a company*. It involves innovation and is often a complete departure from the company's usual way of doing business.

Reengineering is not a fine-tuning of the present process nor is it mere downsizing of a company. Reengineering starts with a blank sheet of paper and an idea about where the company would like to be in the future. Without considering the present limitations or constraints of the company, the reengineering process works backward from where the company wants to be in the future and then attempts to determine what it would take to get there. From this information, the company cuts or adds, reshapes, or redesigns itself to achieve the new goal. In other words, the reengineering approach involves determining what the company would be like if it could start from scratch and then redesigning the process to make it work that way.

Reengineering affects almost every functional area of the company, including information systems, financial reporting systems, the manufacturing environment, suppliers, shipping, and maintenance. Reengineering is usually painful and difficult for a company. Companies that have been most successful in implementing reengineering are those that faced big shifts in the nature of competition and required major changes to stay in business.

Some recommendations to consider in implementing reengineering in a company are to (1) get the strategy straight first, (2) lead from the top, (3) create a sense of urgency,

---

*Quoted from the Web site for SEMICON FAREAST at http://www.semiconfareast.com/jit.htm.
†From http://www.ifm.eng.cam.ac.uk/dstools/process/jit.html.
‡http://www.semiconfareast.com/jit.htm.
§From http://www.ifm.eng.cam.ac.uk/dstools/process/jit.html and http://personal.ashland.edu/~rjacobs/m503jit.html.

(4) design from the outside in, (5) manage the firm's consultant, and (6) combine top-down and bottom-up initiatives. Getting the strategy straight is crucial because the strategy drives the changes. The company must determine what business it wants to be in and how to make money in it. The company's strategy determines its operations.

The focus of reengineering is outside the company; the process begins with the customer. Current operations may have some merit, but time is spent determining the need of the marketplace and how to meet that need.

A company need not necessarily reengineer its entire operation. A specific process, such as billing, production, distribution, etc., can be reengineered. For example, a mortgage loan company may completely rethink and restructure the process by which a loan applicant gets approved. In healthcare, a hospital might radically redesign its admissions procedure to significantly reduce admissions time and stress for both the patient and the admissions officer. An integral part of the reengineering effort is to question basic assumptions and traditions, rethink the way business has been done, and reinvent the process so that significant improvements can be made.

Failure Mode and Effects Analysis

Failure Mode and Effects Analysis, or FMEA, is a systematic way for identifying the effects of a potential product on process failure and includes methodology for eliminating or reducing the chance of a failure occurring.* It is used for analyzing potential reliability problems early in the development cycle where it is easier to take actions to overcome these issues, thereby enhancing reliability through design. A crucial step in the FMEA analysis is anticipating what might go wrong with a product, and while anticipating every failure mode is not possible, a development team should formulate an extensive list of potential failure modes when implementing a FMEA analysis. FMEA was developed in the 1960s in the aerospace industry and is now used extensively in the automotive industry. Because FMEA helps engineers identify potential product or process failures, they can minimize the likelihood of those failures, track and manage risks associated with the product or process, and ensure that failures that do occur will not injure or seriously impact the customer.[‡]

The first step in a FMEA analysis starts with the selection of the process or product to be reviewed and its function. Most FMEA projects involve processes or products that are candidates for a high risk of error. Initially, investigators determine which uses of the product or process fall inside the intended use and which fall outside, since product failure often leads to litigation.[†] Next, they assemble a team made up of people who understand or use the product or process regularly.[‡] Using a block diagram showing the major components and how they are related or a flowchart, the team searches to identify locations, types, and severities of failure modes. Such failure modes might include cracking, fatigue, corrosion, electrical short, spoilage, and others. After identifying failure modes, a criticality index or risk priority number is assigned to each. The Risk Priority Number, or RPN, is calculated by multiplying the Severity of the problem times the Probability that it will occur times the Detection rating. Severity has to do with the seriousness of the problem brought about by the failure. Occurrence is the frequency with which the failure happens. Detection is the likelihood that a failure can be discovered or noticed. In most FMEA systems, the scale for detection is reversed in the sense that a higher number means less detectable. For example, on a 1 to 10 scale, a 10 might be something like "highly unlikely to be detected" and a 1 might be something like "highly likely to be detected." Using the RPN, the failure mode items can be prioritized for action. The items with the highest scores receive the highest priorities and are acted on first. Such action could include inspections, testing, implementing quality control procedures, using different components or materials, limiting the operating range, redesigning the item, performing preventive maintenance, and including backup systems or redundancy.[†] After actions are taken, a FMEA reassessment is taken for possible RPN revision.

Most FMEA efforts include the use of an FMEA Worksheet or FMEA Data Collection and Analysis Form. Shown below is one such example.[‡]

---

*Pat Hammett, University of Michigan, "Failure Mode and Effects Analysis," PowerPoint presentation available at http://www.fmeainfocentre.com/.

[†]Kenneth Crow, DRM Associates, "Failure Modes and Effects Analysis (FMEA)." Document found at http://www.npd-solutions.com/fmea/html

[‡]Donald E. Lighter and Douglas C. Fair, *Quality Management in Health Care: Principles and Methods,* 2nd ed. Boston: Jones and Bartlett 2004, p. 85.

PROCESS:

Function/ Task	Failure Mode	Effect	Severity Score	Occurrence Score	Detection Score	RPN = S·O·D	Recommended Action	Target Date

Poka-Yoke Another common quality concept that can be used in continuous improvement is poka-yoke, which means "mistake proofing." Poka-yoke, pronounced POH-kah YOH-kay and developed by Japanese industrial engineer Shigeo Shingo in the early 1960s, uses devices, methods, or inspections in order to avoid machine error or simple human error. There are two main types of poka-yokes: (1) prevention-based poka-yokes and (2) detection-based poka-yokes. Prevention-based poka-yokes are mechanisms that sense that an error is about to occur and send some sort of signal of the occurrence or halt the process. Detection poka-yokes identify when a defect has occurred and stop the process so that the defect is not "built-in" to the product or service and sent downstream.

In contrast to Deming, who believed that poor quality is generally not the fault of the worker (but rather equipment, training, materials, etc.), Shingo believed that "the causes of defects lie in worker errors, and defects are the results of neglecting those errors. It follows that mistakes will not turn into defects if worker errors are discovered and eliminated beforehand."* As an example, suppose a worker is assembling a device that contains two push-buttons. A spring must be placed under each push-button in order for it to work. If either spring is not put in place, the associated push-button will not work, and an error has been committed. If the worker does an on-the-spot inspection by looking at the device or by testing it, then the cost of fixing the device (rework) is minimal, both in terms of the time to fix it and the time lost due to inspection. If, on the other hand, the error is not identified and the device goes on down the assembly line and is incorporated as a part into a product, the cost of rework, scrap, repair, or warranty claim can become quite high. A simple poka-yoke solution might be that the worker first counts two springs out of the supply bin and places them both in a small dish before each assembly. If the worker is not paying attention, is daydreaming, or is forgetful, he/she merely needs to look at the dish to see if there is a leftover spring before sending the device on to the next station. Some other examples of poka-yoke include machines with limit switches connected to warning lights that go on if an operator improperly positions a part on a machine, computer programs displaying warning messages if a file is being closed but has not been saved, plugs on the back of a computer tower that have different sizes and/or shapes along with color codes to prevent the connection of a plug into the wrong hole, electric hedge trimmers that force the user to hold down two "switches" before the trimmers will work to make it harder for users to accidentally cut themselves, and a plate, which is only supposed to be screwed down in one position (orientation), that has screw holes in nonsymmetrical positions so that the holes line up for mounting only if the plate is in the proper position.

Shingo believed that most mistakes can be prevented if people make the effort to identify when and where errors happen and take corrective actions. Simple poka-yoke mechanisms, such as a device, a switch, a guide pin, a procedure, or a visual inspection, can go a long way in preventing errors that result in defects and thereby reduce productivity.

Quality Circles and Six Sigma Teams In years past, the traditional business approach to decision making in the United States allowed managers to decide what was best for the company and act upon that decision. In the past three decades, the U.S. business culture underwent major changes as total quality management was adopted. One aspect of total quality management is team building. Team building occurs *when a group of employees are organized as an entity to undertake management tasks and perform other functions such as organizing, developing, and overseeing projects.*

---

*Shigeo Shingo, *Zero Quality Control: Source Inspection and the Poka-Yoke System*. University Park, IL: Productivity Press, 1986, p. 50.

Thinking Critically About Statistics in Business Today

Six Sigma Focus at GE

GE's focus on quality began late in the 1980s with a movement called Work-Out that reduced company bureaucracy, opened their culture to new ideas, and helped create a learning environment that eventually led to Six Sigma. In the mid-1990s, General Electric established a goal of attaining Six Sigma quality by the year 2000. By 1999, GE had already invested more than $1 billion in its quality effort. Today at General Electric, Six Sigma defines the way GE does business. It continues to strive for greater quality by following a Six Sigma philosophy. In its push for Six Sigma status, GE engaged more than 5,000 employees in Six Sigma methodology in more than 25,000 completed projects.

GE's Six Sigma approach is data driven and customer focused. All of its employees are trained in the techniques, strategy, and statistical tools of Six Sigma. The focus of Six Sigma at GE is on reducing process variation and increasing process capability. The benefits delivered by this process include reduced cycle times, accelerated product designs, consistent efforts to eliminate variation, and increased probabilities of meeting customer requirements. The adoption of Six Sigma resulted in a culture in which quality thinking is embedded at every level in every operation throughout the company.

Why has GE pursued a Six Sigma philosophy? GE discovered that its customers were demanding better quality, and its employees thought GE could be doing a better job. Its peer competitors such as Motorola, Texas Instruments, and Allied Signal had proven that following a disciplined, rigorous approach to quality significantly improved customer service and resulted in greater productivity. Internal process defects had been limiting GE's ability to achieve growth objectives. With increased globalization and information access, GE believes that its products and services continually change the way its customers do business, and the highly competitive worldwide marketplace leaves no room for error in designing, producing, and delivering products. Six Sigma provides the philosophy and approach needed to meet these goals.

The GE people point out the difference between three sigma and Six Sigma: With three sigma, there are 1.5 misspelled words per page in a book in a small library; with Six Sigma there is 1 misspelled word in all the books in a small library. In a post office with three sigma, there are 20,000 lost articles of mail per hour; with Six Sigma, there are only 7 per hour. GE also claims that Six Sigma can improve your golf score. If you played 100 rounds of golf per year, under a two sigma philosophy you would miss six putts per round. Under three sigma, you would miss one putt per round. Under Six Sigma, you would miss only one putt every 163 years!

Source: Adapted from General Electric, "Quality: GE's Evolution Towards Quality, What Is Six Sigma?" and "Achieving Quality for the Customer," available at http://www.ge.com/commitment/quality.htm; "Tip 'Six Sigma' Quality," accessed (formerly available) at http://trailers.ge.com/getip/news/june.html, and "What We Do," accessed (formerly available) at http://www.crd.ge.com/whatwedo/sixsigma.html; http://www.ge.com/company/worldwide_activities/index.html, 2011.

The result of team building is that more workers take over managerial responsibilities. Fewer lines of demarcation separate workers from managers and union from nonunion. Workers are invited to work on a par with managers to remove obstacles that prevent a company from delivering a quality product. The old "us and them" point of view is replaced by a cooperative relationship between managers and workers in reaching common goals under team building.

One particular type of team that was introduced to U.S. companies by the Japanese is the quality circle. A quality circle is *a small group of workers,* usually from the same department or work area, and their supervisor, *who meet regularly to consider quality issues.* The size of the group ranges from 4 to 15 members, and they meet as often as once a week.* The meetings are usually on company time and members of the circle are compensated. The supervisor may be the leader of the circle, but the members of the group determine the agenda and reach their own conclusions.

The Six Sigma approach to quality makes use of teams of various "belts" to work on Six Sigma projects. Such Six Sigma project teams are usually led by a black belt, who is a company employee, works full-time on Six Sigma projects, and has received extensive training in Six Sigma methodology. Virtually all Six Sigma team members possess at least a green belt and have at least some job-released time to work on the project. Somewhat in contrast to the traditional quality circle teams that come from a particular department or group, Six Sigma teams often include members from various functional groups in the organization, some of whom may come from different levels of the company. For example, it is not uncommon for hospital Six Sigma team membership to include physicians, nurses, pharmacists, technicians, administrators, and others in an attempt to uncover root causes, take targeted measurements, and brainstorm possible solutions.

The American Heritage Dictionary of the English Language, 3rd ed. Boston: Houghton Mifflin Company, 1992.

18.2 # Process Analysis

Much of what transpires in the business world involves processes. A **process** is *"a series of actions, changes, or functions that bring about a result."* Processes usually involve the manufacturing, production, assembling, or development of some output from given input. Generally, in a meaningful system, value is added to the input as part of the process. In the area of production, processes are often the main focus of decision makers. Production processes abound in the chemical, steel, automotive, appliance, computer, furniture, and clothing manufacture industries, as well as many others. Production layouts vary, but it is not difficult to picture an assembly line with its raw materials, parts, and supplies being processed into a finished product that becomes worth more than the sum of the parts and materials that went into it. However, processes are not limited to the area of production. Virtually all other areas of business involve processes. The processing of a check from the moment it is used for a purchase, through the financial institution, and back to the user is one example. The hiring of new employees by a human resources department involves a process that might begin with a job description and end with the training of a new employee. Many different processes occur within healthcare facilities. One process involves the flow of a patient from check-in at a hospital through an operation to recovery and release. Meanwhile, the dietary and foods department prepares food and delivers it to various points in the hospital as part of another process.

There are many tools that have been developed over the years to assist managers and workers in identifying, categorizing, and solving problems in the continuous quality-improvement process. Among these are the seven basic tools of quality developed by Kaoru Ishikawa in the 1960s.* Ishikawa believed that 95% of all quality-related problems could be solved using those basic tools,† which are sometimes referred to as the "seven old tools."‡ The seven basic tools are as follows:

1. Flowchart or process map
2. Pareto chart
3. Cause-and-effect diagram (Ishikawa or fishbone chart)
4. Control chart
5. Check sheet or checklist
6. Histogram
7. Scatter chart or scatter diagram

Flowcharts

One of the first activities that should take place in process analysis is the flowcharting of the process from beginning to end. A **flowchart** is *a schematic representation of all the activities and interactions that occur in a process.* It includes decision points, activities, input/output, start/stop, and a flowline. **Figure 18.1** displays some of the symbols used in flowcharting.

The parallelogram represents input into the process or output from the process. In the case of the dietary/foods department at the hospital, the input includes uncooked food, utensils, plates, containers, and liquids. The output is the prepared meal delivered to the patient's room. The processing symbol is a rectangle that represents an activity. For the dietary/foods department, that activity could include cooking carrots or loading food carts. The decision symbol, a diamond, is used at points in the process where decisions are made that can result in different pathways. In some hospitals, the dietary/foods department supports a hospital cafeteria as well as patient meals. At some point in the process, the decision must be made whether the food is destined for a patient room or the cafeteria. The cafeteria food may follow a general menu whereas patient food may have to be individualized for particular health conditions.

---

*Jason Paster, April 2, 2001. Internet source found at http://www.freequality.org/sites/www_freequality_org/Documents/knowledge/basicseventools.pdf.

†MPR Associates, Inc., Web site: http://www.devicelink.com/mddi/archive/98/04/012.html.

‡Nancy R. Tague. *The Quality Toolbox*, 2nd ed. Milwaukee, WI: ASQ Press, 2004, p. 15.

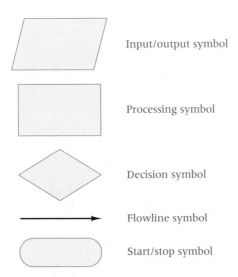

Input/output symbol

Processing symbol

Decision symbol

Flowline symbol

Start/stop symbol

Source: G. A. Silver and J. B. Silver, *Introduction to Systems Analysis*. Englewood Cliffs, N.J.: Prentice Hall, 1976, 142–147.

FIGURE 18.1   **Flowchart Symbols**

The arrow is the flowline symbol designating to the flowchart user the sequence of activities of the process. The flowline in the hospital food example would follow the pathway of the food from raw ingredients (vegetables, meat, flour, etc.) to the delivered product in patient rooms or in the cafeteria. The elongated oval represents the starting and stopping points in the process.

Particularly in nonmanufacturing settings, it is common that no one maps out the complete flow of sequential stages of various processes in a business. For example, one NASA subcontractor was responsible for processing the paperwork for change items on space projects. Change requests would begin at NASA and be sent to the subcontractor's building. The requests would be processed there and returned to NASA in about 14 days. Exactly what happened to the paperwork during the two-week period? As part of a quality effort, NASA asked the contractor to study the process. No one had taken a hard look at where the paperwork went, how long it sat on various people's desks, and how many different people handled it. The contractor soon became involved in process analysis.

As an example, suppose we want to flowchart the process of obtaining a home improvement loan of $10,000 from a bank. The process begins with the customer entering the bank. The flow takes the customer to a receptionist, who poses a decision dilemma. For what purpose has the customer come to the bank? Is it to get information, to cash a check, to deposit money, to buy a money order, to get a loan, or to invest money? Because we are charting the loan process, we follow the flowline to the loan department. The customer arrives in the loan department and is met by another receptionist who asks what type and size of loan the person needs. For small personal loans, the customer is given a form to submit for loan consideration, with no need to see a loan officer. The small personal loans are evaluated and the customer is given a response immediately. If the answer is yes, word of the decision is conveyed to a teller who cuts a check for the customer. For larger loans, such as the home improvement loan, the customer is given a form to fill out and is assigned to see a loan officer. The customer is interviewed by a loan officer, who then makes a decision. If the answer is yes, a contract is drawn up and signed. The customer is then sent to a teller who has the check for the loan. Figure 18.2 provides a possible flowchart for this scenario.

Pareto Analysis

Once the process has been mapped by such techniques as the flowchart, procedures for identifying bottlenecks and problem causes can begin. One technique for displaying process problems is Pareto analysis. **Pareto analysis** is *a quantitative tallying of the number and types of defects that occur with a product or service.* Analysts use this tally to produce *a vertical bar chart that displays the most common types of defects, ranked in order of occurrence from left to right.*

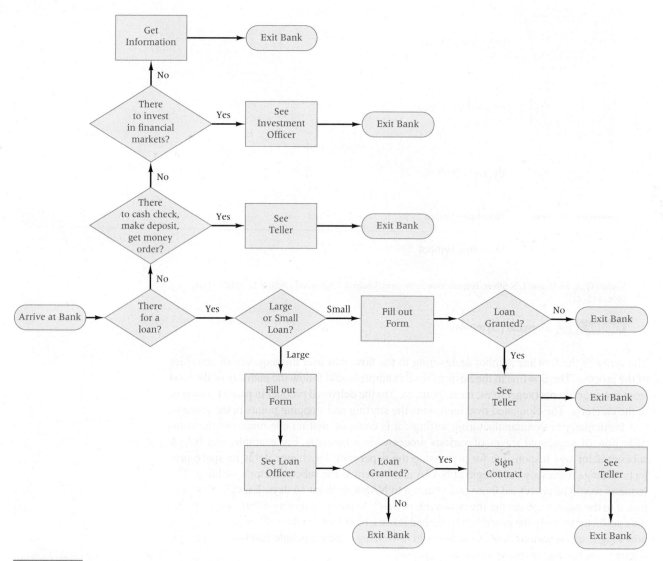

FIGURE 18.2 **Flowchart of Loan Process**

The bar chart is called a **Pareto chart**. Pareto charts are presented and explained in greater detail in Section 2.3 of Chapter 2. **Figure 18.3** contains a Minitab Pareto chart depicting various potential sources of medication error in a hospital. **Figure 18.4** redisplays Figure 2.10, which depicts the possible causes of electric motor problems.

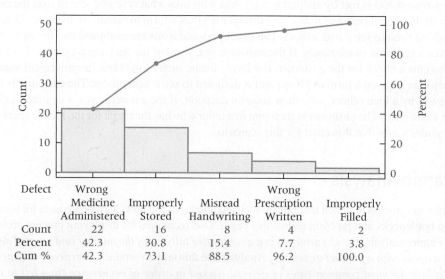

Defect	Wrong Medicine Administered	Improperly Stored	Misread Handwriting	Wrong Prescription Written	Improperly Filled
Count	22	16	8	4	2
Percent	42.3	30.8	15.4	7.7	3.8
Cum %	42.3	73.1	88.5	96.2	100.0

FIGURE 18.3 **Minitab Pareto Chart of Medication Errors in a Hospital**

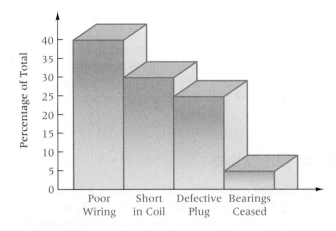

FIGURE 18.4   **Pareto Chart for Electric Motor Problems**

Cause-and-Effect (Fishbone) Diagrams

A tool for identifying problem causes is the **cause-and-effect diagram**, sometimes referred to as **fishbone**, or **Ishikawa**, **diagram**. This diagram was developed by Kaoru Ishikawa in the 1940s as a way to *display possible causes of a problem and the interrelationships among the causes*. The causes can be uncovered through brainstorming, investigating, surveying, observing, and other information-gathering techniques.

The name *fishbone diagram* comes from the shape of the diagram, which looks like a fish skeleton with the problem at the head of the fish and possible causes flaring out on both sides of the main "bone." Subcauses can be included along each "fishbone."

Suppose officials at the company producing the electric motor want to construct a fishbone diagram for the poor wiring problem shown as the major problem in Figure 18.4. Some of the possible causes of poor wiring might be raw materials, equipment, workers, or methods. Some possible raw material causes might be vendor problems (and their source of materials), transportation damage, or damage during storage (inventory). Possible causes of equipment failure might be out-of-date equipment, equipment that is out of adjustment, poor maintenance of equipment, or lack of effective tools. Poor wiring might also be the result of worker error, which can include lack of training or improper training, poor attitude, or excessive absenteeism that results in lack of consistency. Methods causes can include poor wiring schemes and inefficient plant layouts. **Figure 18.5** presents a Minitab fishbone diagram of this problem and its possible causes.

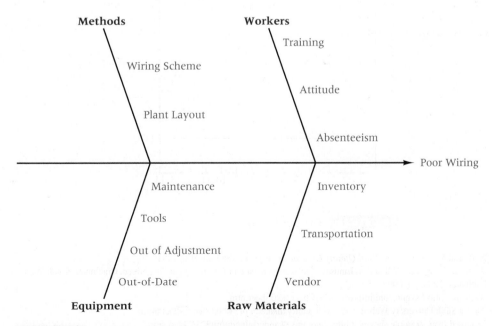

FIGURE 18.5   **Minitab Cause-and-Effect Diagram for Electric Motor Problems**

Control Charts

A fourth diagnostic technique is the control chart. According to Armand V. Feigenbaum, a renowned expert on control charts, a **control chart** is *a graphical method for evaluating whether a process is or is not in a "state of statistical control."* * Several kinds of control charts are used. **Figure 18.6** is an $\bar{x}$ control chart. In the next section, we will explore control charts in more detail.

Check Sheets or Checklists

Check sheets, sometimes called checklists, come in a variety of forms but usually display the frequency of outcomes for some quality-related event or activity under study or being observed by using some type of matrix in which an observer records in a category each outcome from the event or activity. Most check sheets are simple forms consisting of multiple categories and columns for recording tallies and are used for collecting data in a logical format and helping organize data by category. Some advantages of using check sheets are they are simple to use, they convert raw data into useful information, and the results may be interpreted on the form directly without additional processing.[†] Check sheets are especially useful in tracking problems and causes of problems and for providing hard evidence that supports fact rather than having to rely on opinion. They show how many times each particular item or value occurs, and their information is increasingly helpful as more data are collected. One of the side-effects of using check sheets is that the person using them becomes very aware of the data being captured and can often see patterns building.[‡]

In constructing a check sheet, there are several things to consider. First, decide what problem, activity, or event is being studied. Once the problem to study has been determined, it can be helpful to involve "process" workers in developing the check sheet categories. Once the problem has been identified and categories have been determined, the form can be designed. Check sheets should be user-friendly with all columns labeled clearly, and a format should be created that gives you the most information with the least effort.[§]

Shown below is an example of a check sheet that could be used to determine why patients in a hospital do not consume a meal within 1 hour of its delivery.[¶] Assume that a team of nurses, aides, dietary personnel, patients, and others was assembled to identify possible causes for this problem.

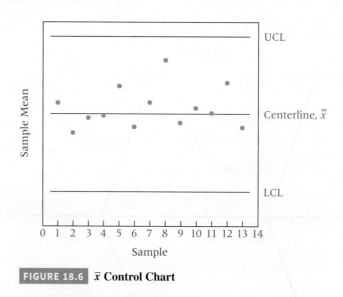

FIGURE 18.6 $\bar{x}$ **Control Chart**

*Armand V. Feigenbaum, *Total Quality Control.* New York, McGraw-Hill, 1991.
[†]James R. Evans and William M. Lindsay, *The Management and Control of Quality*, 5th ed. Cincinnati: South-Western Publishing, 2002, p. 609.
[‡]Web site: http://syque.com/improvement/Check%20Sheet.htm.
[§]De La Salle University Web site at http://quality.dlsu.edu.ph/tools/check_sheet.html.
[¶]Adapted from example shown at http://mot.vuse.vanderbilt.edu/mt322/Check.htm.

DATE: FLOOR: SHIFT: CHECKSHEET	MEALS NOT CONSUMED WITHIN 1 HOUR OF DELIVERY							
	MON	TUE	WED	THU	FRI	SAT	SUN	TOTAL
Menu Incorrect			1			1		2
Diet Order Changed	1			1			1	3
Wrong Order Delivered		1	1		1		1	4
Patient Asleep	11	111	1	11	111	11	111	16
Patient Out of Room	1111	1111	11	11	1	111	1	17
Doctor Making Rounds		1	111	11	1	1	1	9
Patient Not Hungry	1		11	1			1	5
Plate Warmer Broken	11	11	11	11			1	9
Nursing Unavailable	11	1	1111	111	11	1	1	14
TOTAL	12	12	16	13	8	8	10	79

From this check sheet it can be gleaned that the top three reasons for meals not being consumed within 1 hour of delivery are: patient asleep, patient out of the room, and nursing unavailable.

Histogram

Another important tool for quality improvement is the histogram. A histogram is used to depict a frequency distribution and was presented in Section 2.2 of Chapter 2 of this textbook. Most computer software packages, such as Excel, can produce a histogram from raw data. The histogram is a very useful tool in getting an initial overview of the data.

Scatter Chart or Scatter Diagram

Many times in the implementation of quality improvement techniques and in root-cause analysis, it is important to explore the relationship between two numerical variables. One graphical mechanism for examining the relationship between two variables is the scatter chart, sometimes referred to as a scatter diagram. A scatter chart is formally defined to be a two-dimensional graph plot of pairs of points from two numerical variables. Scatter charts are presented and discussed as scatter plots in Section 2.4 of Chapter 2 of this textbook. Often a scatter chart can aid the quality investigator in determining if there is a relationship between two variables; and if there is a relationship, what is the direction of the relationship. One note of caution about using the scatter chart as a tool is that even though there may appear to be a relationship between two variables, that does not mean that one variable causes the other variable to change or "drives" the other variable.

18.2 Problems

18.1. For each of the following scenarios, sketch the process with activities and decision points. Construct a flowchart by using the symbols depicted in Figure 18.1.

a. A customer enters the office of an insurance agent wanting to purchase auto insurance and leaves the office with a paid policy in hand.

b. A truckload of men's shirts enters a warehouse at the main distribution center for a men's retail clothing company that has four stores in that area. The shirts are on the racks inside the stores ready for sale.

c. A couple enters a restaurant to enjoy dinner out. An hour and a half later, they leave, satisfied, having paid their bill. Construct the flowchart from the restaurant's point of view.

18.2. An airline company uses a central telephone bank and a semi-automated telephone process to take reservations. It has been receiving an unusually high number of customer complaints about its reservation system. The company conducted a survey of customers, asking them whether they had encountered any of the following problems in making reservations: busy signal, disconnection, poor connection, too long a wait to talk to someone, could not get through to an agent, connected with the wrong person. Suppose a survey of 744 complaining customers resulted in the following frequency tally.

NUMBER OF COMPLAINTS	COMPLAINTS
184	Too long a wait
10	Transferred to the wrong person
85	Could not get through to an agent

37	Got disconnected
420	Busy signal
8	Poor connection

Construct a Pareto chart from this information to display the various problems encountered in making reservations.

18.3. A bank has just sent out a monthly reconciliation statement to a customer with an error in the person's monthly income. Brainstorm to determine some possible causes of this error. Try to think of some possible reasons for the causes. Construct a fishbone diagram to display your results.

18.3 | Control Charts

Control charts have been in existence for over 90 years. Walter A. Shewhart is credited with developing control charts at Bell Laboratories in the 1920s. Shewhart and others, including one of his understudies at Bell Laboratories, W. Edwards Deming, were able to apply control charts to industrial processes as a tool to assist in controlling variation. The use of control charts in the United States failed to gain momentum after World War II because the success of U.S. manufacturers in the world market reduced the apparent need for such a tool. As the Japanese and other international manufacturers became more competitive by using such tools, the control chart increased in popularity in the United States.

Control charts are easy to use and understand. Often it is the line workers who record and plot product measurements on the charts. In more automated settings, sensors record chart values and send them into an information system, which compiles the charts. Control charts are used mainly to monitor product variation. The charts enable operators, technicians, and managers to see when a process gets out of control, which in turn improves quality and increases productivity.

Variation

If no variations occurred between manufactured items, control charts would be pointless. However, variation occurs for virtually any product or service. Variation can occur among units within a lot and can occur between lots. Among the reasons for product variation are differences in raw materials, differences in workers, differences in machines, changes in the environment, and wear and tear of machinery. Small variations can be caused by unnoticeable events, such as a passing truck that creates vibrations or dust that affects machine operation. Variations need to be measured, recorded, and studied so that out-of-control conditions can be identified and corrections can be made in the process.

Types of Control Charts

The two general types of control charts are (1) control charts for measurements and (2) control charts for attribute compliance. In this section, we discuss two types of control charts for measurements, $\bar{x}$ charts and R charts. We also discuss two types of control charts for attribute compliance, p charts and c charts.

Each control chart has a **centerline**, an **upper control limit (UCL)**, and a **lower control limit (LCL)**. Data are recorded on the control chart, and the chart is examined for disturbing patterns or for data points that indicate a process is out of control. Once a process is determined to be out of control, measures can be taken to correct the problem causing the deviation.

$\bar{x}$ Chart

An $\bar{x}$ **chart** is *a graph of sample means computed for a series of small random samples over a period of time.* The means are average measurements of some product characteristic. For example, the measurement could be the volume of fluid in a bottle of rubbing alcohol, the thickness of a piece of sheet metal, or the size of a hole in a plastic part. These sample means are plotted on a graph that contains a centerline and upper and lower control limits (UCL and LCL).

$\bar{x}$ charts can be made from standards or without standards.* Companies sometimes have smoothed their process to the point where they have standard centerlines and control limits for a product. These standards are usually used when a company is producing products that have been made for some time and in situations where managers have little interest in monitoring the overall measure of central tendency for the product. In this text, we will study only situations in which no standard is given. It is fairly common to compute $\bar{x}$ charts without existing standards—especially if a company is producing a new product, is closely monitoring proposed standards, or expects a change in the process. Many firms want to monitor the standards, so they recompute the standards for each chart. In the no-standards situation, the standards (such as mean and standard deviation) are estimated by using the sample data.

The centerline for an $\bar{x}$ chart is the average of the sample means, $\bar{\bar{x}}$. The $\bar{x}$ chart has an upper control limit (UCL) that is three standard deviations of means above the centerline ($+3\sigma_{\bar{x}}$). The lower boundary of the $\bar{x}$ chart, called the lower control limit (LCL), is three standard deviations of means below the centerline ($-3\sigma_{\bar{x}}$). Recall the empirical rule presented in Chapter 3 stating that if data are normally distributed, approximately 99.7% of all values will be within three standard deviations of the mean. Because the shape of the sampling distribution of $\bar{x}$ is normal for large sample sizes regardless of the population shape, the empirical rule applies. However, because small samples are often used, an approximation of the three standard deviations of means is used to determine UCL and LCL. This approximation can be made using either sample ranges or sample standard deviations. For small sample sizes ($n \leq 15$ is acceptable, but $n \leq 10$ is preferred), a weighted value of the average range is a good approximation of the three-standard-deviation distance to the UCL and to the LCL. The range is easy to compute (difference of extreme values) and is particularly useful when a wide array of nontechnical workers is involved in control chart computations. When sample sizes are larger, a weighted average of the sample standard deviations ($\bar{s}$) is a good estimate of the three standard deviations of means. The drawback of using the sample standard deviation is that it must always be computed, whereas the sample range can often be determined at a glance. Most control charts are constructed with small sample sizes; therefore, the range is more widely used in constructing control charts.

Table A.15 contains the weights applied to the average sample range or the average sample standard deviation to compute upper and lower control limits. The value of A_2 is used for ranges and the value of A_3 is used for standard deviations. The following steps are used to produce an $\bar{x}$ chart:

1. Decide on the quality to be measured.
2. Determine a sample size.
3. Gather 20 to 30 samples.
4. Compute the sample average, $\bar{x}$, for each sample.
5. Compute the sample range, R, for each sample.
6. Determine the average sample mean for all samples, $\bar{\bar{x}}$, as

$$\bar{\bar{x}} = \frac{\Sigma\bar{x}}{k}$$

   where k is the number of samples.
7. Determine the average sample range for all samples, $\bar{R}$, as

$$\bar{R} = \frac{\Sigma R}{k}$$

---

*Armand V. Feigenbaum, *Total Quality Control*. New York: McGraw-Hill, 1991.

or determine the average sample standard deviation for all samples, $\bar{s}$, as

$$\bar{s} = \frac{\Sigma s}{k}$$

8. Using the size of the samples, n_i, determine the value of A_2 if using the range and A_3 if using standard deviations.

9. Construct the centerline, the upper control limit, and the lower control limit. For ranges:

$$\bar{\bar{x}} \text{ is the centerline}$$
$$\bar{\bar{x}} + A_2\bar{R} \text{ is the UCL}$$
$$\bar{\bar{x}} - A_2\bar{R} \text{ is the LCL}$$

For standard deviations:

$$\bar{\bar{x}} \text{ is the centerline}$$
$$\bar{\bar{x}} + A_3\bar{s} \text{ is the UCL}$$
$$\bar{\bar{x}} - A_2\bar{s} \text{ is the LCL}$$

DEMONSTRATION PROBLEM 18.1

A manufacturing facility produces bearings. The diameter specified for the bearings is 5 millimeters. Every 10 minutes, six bearings are sampled and their diameters are measured and recorded. Twenty of these samples of six bearings are gathered. Use the resulting data and construct an $\bar{x}$ chart.

SAMPLE 1	SAMPLE 2	SAMPLE 3	SAMPLE 4	SAMPLE 5
5.13	4.96	5.21	5.02	5.12
4.92	4.98	4.87	5.09	5.08
5.01	4.95	5.02	4.99	5.09
4.88	4.96	5.08	5.02	5.13
5.05	5.01	5.12	5.03	5.06
4.97	4.89	5.04	5.01	5.13

SAMPLE 6	SAMPLE 7	SAMPLE 8	SAMPLE 9	SAMPLE 10
4.98	4.99	4.96	4.96	5.03
5.02	5.00	5.01	5.00	4.99
4.97	5.00	5.02	4.91	4.96
4.99	5.02	5.05	4.87	5.14
4.98	5.01	5.04	4.96	5.11
4.99	5.01	5.02	5.01	5.04

SAMPLE 11	SAMPLE 12	SAMPLE 13	SAMPLE 14	SAMPLE 15
4.91	4.97	5.09	4.96	4.99
4.93	4.91	4.96	4.99	4.97
5.04	5.02	5.05	4.82	5.01
5.00	4.93	5.12	5.03	4.98
4.90	4.95	5.06	5.00	4.96
4.82	4.96	5.01	4.96	5.02

SAMPLE 16	SAMPLE 17	SAMPLE 18	SAMPLE 19	SAMPLE 20
5.01	5.05	4.96	4.90	5.04
5.04	4.97	4.93	4.85	5.03
5.09	5.04	4.97	5.02	4.97
5.07	5.03	5.01	5.01	4.99
5.12	5.09	4.98	4.88	5.05
5.13	5.01	4.92	4.86	5.06

Solution: Compute the value of $\bar{x}$ for each sample and average these values, obtaining $\bar{\bar{x}}$.

$$\bar{\bar{x}} = \frac{\bar{x}_1 + \bar{x}_2 + \bar{x}_3 + \cdots + \bar{x}_{20}}{20}$$

$$= \frac{4.9933 + 4.9583 + 5.0566 + \cdots + 5.0233}{20}$$

$$= \frac{100.043}{20} = 5.00215 \text{ (the centerline)}$$

Compute the values of R and average them, obtaining $\bar{R}$.

$$\bar{R} = \frac{R_1 + R_2 + R_3 + \cdots + R_{20}}{20}$$

$$= \frac{.25 + .12 + .34 + \cdots + .09}{20}$$

$$= \frac{2.72}{20} = .136$$

Determine the value of A_2 by using $n_i = 6$ (size of the sample) from Table A.15: $A_2 = .483$. The UCL is

$$\bar{\bar{x}} + A_2\bar{R} = 5.00215 + (.483)(.136) = 5.00215 + .06569 = 5.06784$$

The LCL is

$$\bar{\bar{x}} - A_2\bar{R} = 5.00215 - (.483)(.136) = 5.00215 - .06569 = 4.93646$$

Using the standard deviation instead of the range,

$$\bar{s} = \frac{\bar{s}_1 + \bar{s}_2 + \bar{s}_3 + \cdots + \bar{s}_{20}}{20}$$

$$= \frac{.0905 + .0397 + .1136 + \cdots + .0356}{20}$$

$$= .0494$$

Determine the value of A_3 by using $n_i = 6$ (sample size) from Table A.15:

$$A_3 = 1.287$$

The UCL is

$$\bar{\bar{x}} + A_3\bar{s} = 5.00215 + (1.287)(.0494) = 5.00215 + .06358 = 5.06573$$

The UCL is

$$\bar{\bar{x}} - A_3\bar{s} = 5.00215 - (1.287)(.0494) = 5.00215 - .06358 = 4.93857$$

The following graph depicts the $\bar{x}$ control chart using the range (rather than the standard deviation) as the measure of dispersion to compute LCL and UCL. Observe from the computations above that if the standard deviation is used instead of the range to compute LCL and UCL, because of the precision (or lack thereof) of this chart, there is little, if any, perceptible difference in LCL and UCL by the two methods.

Note that the sample means for samples 5 and 16 are above the UCL and the sample means for samples 11 and 19 are below the LCL. This result indicates that these four samples are out of control and alerts the production supervisor or worker to initiate further investigation of bearings produced during these periods. All other samples are within the control limits.

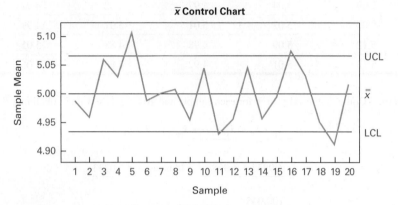

Shown next is the Minitab output for this problem. Note that the Minitab output is nearly identical to the control chart just shown.

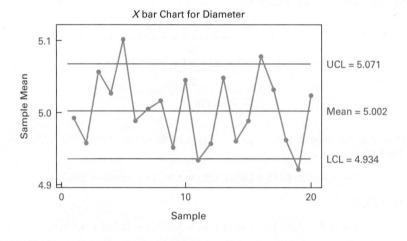

R Charts

R Charts   An *R* chart is a plot of the sample ranges and often is used in conjunction with an $\bar{x}$ chart. Whereas $\bar{x}$ charts are used to plot the central tendency values, $\bar{x}$, for each sample, *R* charts are used to plot the variation of each sample as measured by the sample range. The centerline of an *R* chart is the average range, $\bar{R}$. Lower control limits (LCLs) are determined by $D_3\bar{R}$ where D_3 is a weight applied to $\bar{R}$ reflecting sample size. The value of D_3 can be obtained from Table A.15. Upper control limits (UCLs) are determined by $D_4\bar{R}$ where D_4 is a value obtained from Table A.15, which also reflects sample size. The following steps lead to an *R* chart.

1. Decide on the quality to be measured.
2. Determine a sample size.
3. Gather 20 to 30 samples.
4. Compute the sample range, *R*, for each sample.
5. Determine the average sample range for all samples, $\bar{R}$, as

$$\bar{R} = \frac{\Sigma R}{k}$$

where *k* = the number of samples.
6. Using the size of the samples, n_i, find the values of D_3 and D_4 in Table A.15.

7. Construct the centerline and control limits.

$$\text{Centerline} = \bar{R}$$
$$\text{UCL} = D_4 \bar{R}$$
$$\text{LCL} = D_3 \bar{R}$$

DEMONSTRATION PROBLEM 18.2

Construct an R chart for the 20 samples of data in Demonstration Problem 18.1 on bearings.

Solution: Compute the sample ranges shown.

SAMPLE	RANGE
1	.25
2	.12
3	.34
4	.10
5	.07
6	.05
7	.03
8	.09
9	.14
10	.18
11	.22
12	.11
13	.16
14	.21
15	.06
16	.12
17	.12
18	.09
19	.17
20	.09

Compute $\bar{R}$:

$$\bar{R} = \frac{.25 + .12 + .34 + \cdots + .09}{20} = \frac{2.72}{20} = .136$$

For $n_i = 6$, $D_3 = 0$, and $D_4 = 2.004$ (from Table A.15):

$$\text{Centerline } \bar{R} = .136$$
$$\text{LCL} = D_3 \bar{R} = (0)(.136) = 0$$
$$\text{UCL} = D_4 \bar{R} = (2.004)(.136) = .2725$$

The resulting R chart for these data is shown next, followed by the Minitab output. Note that the range for sample 3 is out of control (beyond the UCL). The range of values in sample 3 appears to be unacceptable. Further investigation of the population from which this sample was drawn is warranted.

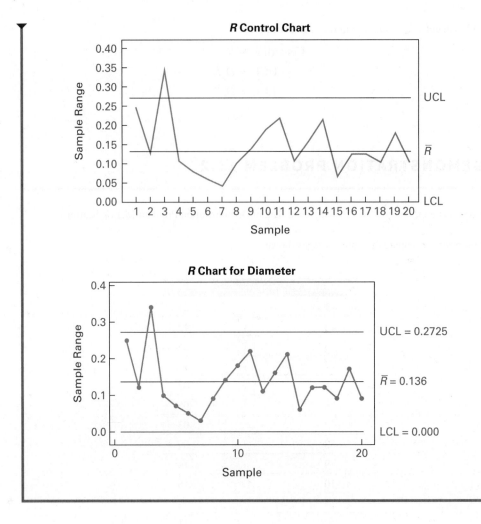

p Charts

When product attributes are measurable, $\bar{x}$ charts and R charts can be formulated from the data. Sometimes, however, product inspection yields no measurement—only a yes-or-no type of conclusion based on whether the item complies with the specifications. For this type of data, no measure is available from which to average or determine the range. However, attribute compliance can be depicted graphically by a *p* chart. A ***p* chart** *graphs the proportion of sample items in noncompliance for multiple samples.*

For example, suppose a company producing electric motors samples 40 motors three times a week for a month. For each group of 40 motors, it determines the proportion of the sample group that does not comply with the specifications. It then plots these sample proportions, $\hat{p}$, on a *p* chart to identify trends or samples with unacceptably high proportions of nonconformance. Other *p* chart applications include determining whether a gallon of paint has been manufactured with acceptable texture, a pane of glass contains cracks, or a tire has a defective tread.

Like the $\bar{x}$ chart and the R chart, a *p* chart contains a centerline. The centerline is the average of the sample proportions. Upper and lower control limits are computed from the average of the sample proportions plus or minus three standard deviations of proportions. The following are the steps for constructing a *p* chart:

1. Decide on the quality to be measured.
2. Determine a sample size.
3. Gather 20 to 30 samples.
4. Compute the sample proportion:

$$\hat{p} = \frac{n_{non}}{n}$$

where

n_{non} = the number of items in the sample in noncompliance
n = the number of items in the sample

5. Compute the average proportion:

$$p = \frac{\Sigma \hat{p}}{k}$$

where

$\hat{p} = \dfrac{n_{non}}{n}$ the sample proportion

k = the number of samples

6. Determine the centerline, UCL, and LCL, when $q = 1 - p$.

$$\text{Centerline} = p$$

$$\text{UCL} = p + 3\sqrt{\frac{p \cdot q}{n}}$$

$$\text{LCL} = p - 3\sqrt{\frac{p \cdot q}{n}}$$

DEMONSTRATION PROBLEM 18.3

A company produces bond paper and, at regular intervals, samples of 50 sheets of paper are inspected. Suppose 20 random samples of 50 sheets of paper each are taken during a certain period of time, with the following numbers of sheets in noncompliance per sample. Construct a p chart from these data.

SAMPLE	n	OUT OF COMPLIANCE
1	50	4
2	50	3
3	50	1
4	50	0
5	50	5
6	50	2
7	50	3
8	50	1
9	50	4
10	50	2
11	50	2
12	50	6
13	50	0
14	50	2
15	50	1
16	50	6
17	50	2
18	50	3
19	50	1
20	50	5

Solution: From the data, $n = 50$. The values of $\hat{p}$ follow.

SAMPLE	$\hat{p}$ (OUT OF COMPLIANCE)
1	4/50 = .08
2	3/50 = .06
3	1/50 = .02
4	0/50 = .00
5	5/50 = .10
6	2/50 = .04
7	3/50 = .06
8	1/50 = .02
9	4/50 = .08
10	2/50 = .04
11	2/50 = .04
12	6/50 = .12
13	0/50 = .00
14	2/50 = .04
15	1/50 = .02
16	6/50 = .12
17	2/50 = .04
18	3/50 = .06
19	1/50 = .02
20	5/50 = .10

The value of p is obtained by averaging these $\hat{p}$ values.

$$p = \frac{\hat{p}_1 + \hat{p}_2 + \hat{p}_3 + \cdots \hat{p}_{20}}{20}$$

$$= \frac{.08 + .06 + .02 + \cdots + .10}{20} = \frac{1.06}{20} = .053$$

The centerline is $p = .053$.

The UCL is

$$p + 3\sqrt{\frac{p \cdot q}{n}} = .053 + 3\sqrt{\frac{(.053)(.947)}{50}} = .053 + .095 = .148$$

The LCL is

$$p - 3\sqrt{\frac{p \cdot q}{n}} = .053 - 3\sqrt{\frac{(.053)(.947)}{50}} = .053 - .095 = -.042$$

To have −.042 item in noncompliance is impossible, so the lower control limit is 0.

Following is the p chart for this problem. Note that all 20 proportions are within the quality-control limits.

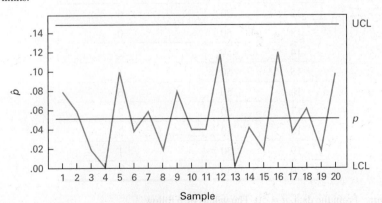

Shown next is the Minitab output for this p chart. Note that the computer output is essentially the same as the graph just shown.

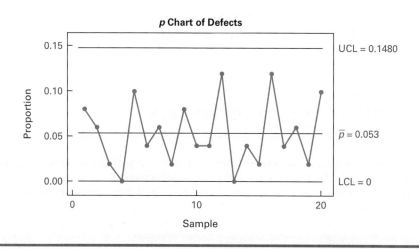

c Charts   The c chart is less widely used than the $\bar{x}$, the R, or the p chart. Like the p chart, the c chart attempts to formulate information about defective items. However, whereas the p chart is a control chart that displays the proportion of items in a sample that are out of compliance with specifications, a *c chart displays the number of nonconformances per item or unit.* Examples of nonconformances could be paint flaws, scratches, openings drilled too large or too small, or shorts in electric wires. The c chart allows for multiple nonconforming features per item or unit. For example, if an item is a radio, there can be scratches (multiple) in the paint, poor soldering, bad wiring, broken dials, burned-out light bulbs, and broken antennae. A unit need not be an item such as a computer chip. It can be a bolt of cloth, 4 feet of wire, or a 2×4 board. The requirement is that the unit remain consistent throughout the test or experiment.

In computing a c chart, a c value is determined for each item or unit by tallying the total nonconformances for the item or unit. The centerline is computed by averaging the c values for all items or units. Because in theory nonconformances per item or unit are rare, the Poisson distribution is used as the basis for the c chart. The long-run average for the Poisson distribution is λ, and the analogous long-run average for a c chart is $\bar{c}$ (the average of the c values for the items or units studied), which is used as the centerline value. Upper control limits (UCL) and lower control limits (LCL) are computed by adding or subtracting three standard deviations of the mean, $\bar{c}$, from the centerline value, $\bar{c}$. The standard deviation of a Poisson distribution is the square root of λ; likewise, the standard deviation of $\bar{c}$ is the square root of $\bar{c}$. The UCL is thus determined by $\bar{c} + 3\sqrt{\bar{c}}$ and the LCL is given by $\bar{c} - 3\sqrt{\bar{c}}$. The following steps are used for constructing a c chart.

1. Decide on nonconformances to be evaluated.
2. Determine the number of items of units to be studied. (This number should be at least 25.)
3. Gather items or units.
4. Determine the value of c for each item or unit by summing the number of nonconformances in the item or unit.
5. Calculate the value of $\bar{c}$.

$$\bar{c} = \frac{c_1 + c_2 + c_3 + \cdots + c_i}{i}$$

where

i = number of items
c_i = number of nonconformances per item

6. Determine the centerline, UCL, and LCL.

$$\text{Centerline} = \bar{c}$$
$$\text{UCL} = \bar{c} + 3\sqrt{\bar{c}}$$
$$\text{LCL} = \bar{c} - 3\sqrt{\bar{c}}$$

DEMONSTRATION PROBLEM 18.4

A manufacturer produces gauges to measure oil pressure. As part of the company's statistical process control, 25 gauges are randomly selected and tested for nonconformances. The results are shown here. Use these data to construct a c chart that displays the nonconformances per item.

ITEM NUMBER	NUMBER OF NONCONFORMANCES	ITEM NUMBER	NUMBER OF NONCONFORMANCES
1	2	14	2
2	0	15	1
3	3	16	4
4	1	17	0
5	2	18	2
6	5	19	3
7	3	20	2
8	2	21	1
9	0	22	3
10	0	23	2
11	4	24	0
12	3	25	3
13	2		

Solution: Determine the centerline, UCL, and LCL.

$$\text{Centerline} = \bar{c} = \frac{2 + 0 + 3 + \cdots + 3}{25} = \frac{50}{25} = 2.0$$

$$\text{UCL} = \bar{c} + 3\sqrt{\bar{c}} = 2.0 + 3\sqrt{2.0} = 2.0 + 4.2 = 6.2$$

$$\text{LCL} = \bar{c} - 3\sqrt{\bar{c}} = 2.0 - 3\sqrt{2.0} = 2.0 - 4.2 = -2.2$$

The lower control limit cannot be less than zero; thus, the LCL is 0. The graph of the control chart, followed by the Minitab c chart, is shown next. Note that none of the points are beyond the control limits and there is a healthy deviation of points both above and below the centerline. This chart indicates a process that is relatively in control, with an average of two nonconformances per item.

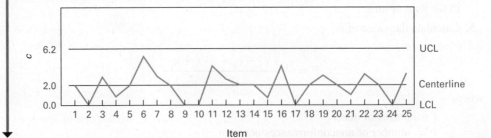

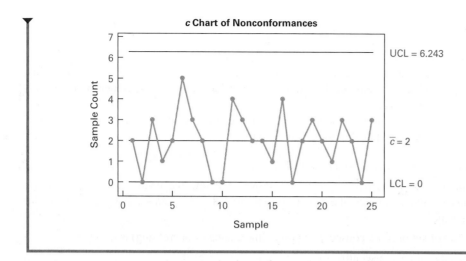

c Chart of Nonconformances

UCL = 6.243

$\bar{c} = 2$

LCL = 0

Interpreting Control Charts

How can control charts be used to monitor processes? When is a process out of control? An evaluation of the points plotted on a control chart examines several things. Obviously, one concern is points that are outside the control limits. Control chart outer limits (UCL and LCL) are established at three standard deviations above and below the centerline. The empirical rule discussed in Chapter 3 and the z table value for $z = 3$ indicate that approximately 99.7% of all values should be within three standard deviations of the mean of the statistic. Applying this rule to control charts suggests that fewer than .3% of all points should be beyond the upper and lower control limits by chance. Thus, one of the more elementary items a control chart observer looks for is points outside LCL and UCL. If the system is "in control," virtually no data points should be outside these limits. Workers responsible for process control should investigate samples in which sample members are outside the LCL and UCL. In the case of the c chart, items that are above the UCL line contain an inordinate number of nonconformances in relation to the average. The occurrence of points beyond the control limits call for further investigation.

Several other criteria can be used to determine whether a control chart is plotting a process that is out of control. In general, there *should* be random fluctuation above and below the centerline within the UCL and LCL. However, a process can be out of control if too many consecutive points are above or below the centerline. Eight or more consecutive points on one side of the centerline are considered too many. In addition, if 10 of 11 or 12 of 14 points are on the same side of the center, the process may be out of control.*

Another criterion for process control operators to look for is trends in the control charts. At any point in the process, is a trend emerging in the data? As a rule of thumb, if six or more points are increasing or are decreasing, the process may be out of control.† Such a trend can indicate that points will eventually deviate increasingly from the centerline (the gap between the centerline and the points will increase).

Another concern with control charts is an overabundance of points in the outer one-third of the region between the centerline and the outer limits (LCL and UCL). By a rationalization similar to that imposed on LCL and UCL, the empirical rule and the table of z values show that approximately 95% of all points should be within two standard deviations of the centerline. With this in mind, fewer than 5% of the points should be in the outer one-third of the region between the centerline and the outer control limits (because 95% should be within two-thirds of the region). A rule to follow is that if two out of three consecutive points are in the outer one-third of the chart, a control problem may be present. Likewise, because approximately 68% of all values should be within one standard deviation of the mean (empirical rule,

*James R. Evans and William M. Lindsay, *The Management and Control of Quality,* 4th ed. Cincinnati: South-Western College Publishing, 1999.
†Richard E. DeVor, Tsong-how Chang, and John W. Sutherland, *Statistical Quality Design and Control.* New York: Macmillan, 1992.

z table for $z = 1$), only 32% should be in the outer two-thirds of the control chart above and below the centerline. As a rule, if four out of five successive points are in the outer two-thirds of the control chart, the process should be investigated.*

Another consideration in evaluating control charts is the location of the centerline. With each successive batch of samples, it is important to observe whether the centerline is shifting away from specifications.

The following list provides a summary of the control chart abnormalities for which a statistical process controller should be concerned:

1. Points are above UCL and/or below LCL.
2. Eight or more consecutive points are above or below the centerline. Ten out of 11 points are above or below the centerline. Twelve out of 14 points are above or below the centerline.
3. A trend of six or more consecutive points (increasing or decreasing) is present.
4. Two out of three consecutive values are in the outer one-third.
5. Four out of five consecutive values are in the outer two-thirds.
6. The centerline shifts from chart to chart.

Figure 18.7 contains several control charts, each of which has one of these types of problems. The chart in (a) contains points above and below the outer control limits. The one in (b) has eight consecutive points on one side of the centerline. The chart in (c) has seven consecutive increasing points. In (d), at least two out of three consecutive points are in the outer one-third of the control chart. In (e), at least four out of five consecutive points are in the outer two-thirds of the chart.

In investigating control chart abnormalities, several possible causes may be found. Some of them are listed here.[†]

1. Changes in the physical environment
2. Worker fatigue
3. Worn tools

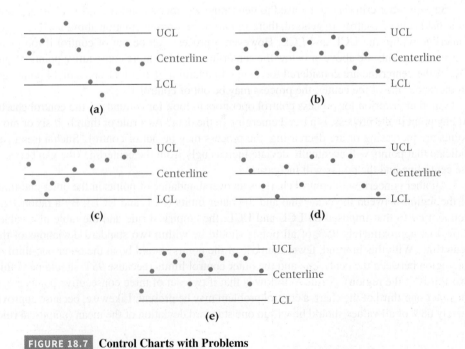

FIGURE 18.7 Control Charts with Problems

*DeVor, Chang, and Sutherland; Evans and Lindsay.
[†]Eugene L. Grant and Richard S. Leavenworth, *Statistical Quality Control*, 5th ed. New York: McGraw-Hill, 1980.

4. Changes in operators or machines

5. Maintenance

6. Changes in worker skills

7. Changes in materials

8. Process modification

The statistical process control person should realize that control chart abnormalities can arise because of measurement errors or incorrect calculation of control limits. Judgment should be exercised so as not to overcontrol the process by readjusting to every oddity that appears to be out of the ordinary on a control chart.

18.3 Problems

18.4. A food-processing company makes potato chips, pretzels, and cheese chips. Although its products are packaged and sold by weight, the company has been taking sample bags of cheese chips and counting the number of chips in each bag. Shown here is the number of chips per bag for five samples of seven bags of chips. Use these data to construct an $\overline{x}$ chart and an R chart. Discuss the results.

SAMPLE 1	SAMPLE 2	SAMPLE 3	SAMPLE 4	SAMPLE 5
25	22	30	32	25
23	21	23	26	23
29	24	22	27	29
31	25	26	28	27
26	23	28	25	27
28	26	27	25	26
27	29	21	31	24

18.5. A toy-manufacturing company has been given a large order for small plastic whistles that will be given away by a large fast-food hamburger chain with its kid's meal. Seven random samples of four whistles have been taken. The weight of each whistle has been ascertained in grams. The data are shown here. Use these data to construct an $\overline{x}$ chart and an R chart. What managerial decisions should be made on the basis of these findings?

SAMPLE 1	SAMPLE 2	SAMPLE 3	SAMPLE 4
4.1	3.6	4.0	4.6
5.2	4.3	4.8	4.8
3.9	3.9	5.1	4.7
5.0	4.6	5.3	4.7

SAMPLE 5	SAMPLE 6	SAMPLE 7
3.9	5.1	4.6
3.8	4.7	4.4
4.6	4.8	4.0
4.9	4.3	4.5

18.6. A machine operator at a pencil-manufacturing facility gathered 10 different random samples of 100 pencils. The operator's inspection was to determine whether the pencils were in compliance or out

of compliance with specifications. The results of this inspection are shown below. Use these data to construct a p chart. Comment on the results of this chart.

SAMPLE	SIZE	NUMBER OUT OF COMPLIANCE
1	100	2
2	100	7
3	100	4
4	100	3
5	100	3
6	100	5
7	100	2
8	100	0
9	100	1
10	100	6

18.7. A large manufacturer makes valves. Currently it is producing a particular valve for use in industrial engines. As a part of a quality-control effort, the company engineers randomly sample seven groups of 40 valves and inspect them to determine whether they are in or out of compliance. Results are shown here. Use the information to construct a p chart. Comment on the chart.

SAMPLE	SIZE	NUMBER OUT OF COMPLIANCE
1	40	1
2	40	0
3	40	1
4	40	3
5	40	2
6	40	5
7	40	2

18.8. A firm in the upper Midwest manufactures light bulbs. Before the bulbs are released for shipment, a sample of bulbs is selected for inspection. Inspectors look for nonconformances such as scratches, weak or broken filaments, incorrectly bored turns, insufficient outside contacts, and others. A sample of thirty-five 60-watt bulbs has just been inspected, and the results are shown here. Use these data to construct a c chart. Discuss the findings.

BULB NUMBER	NUMBER OF NONCON- FORMANCES	BULB NUMBER	NUMBER OF NONCON- FORMANCES
1	0	19	2
2	1	20	0
3	0	21	0
4	0	22	1
5	3	23	0
6	0	24	0
7	1	25	0
8	0	26	2
9	0	27	0
10	0	28	0
11	2	29	1
12	0	30	0
13	0	31	0
14	2	32	0
15	0	33	0
16	1	34	3
17	3	35	0
18	0		

7	2	20	0
8	0	21	0
9	1	22	1
10	3	23	4
11	1	24	0
12	4	25	2
13	2	26	1
14	1	27	1
15	0	28	3
16	1	29	0
17	3	30	1
18	1	31	2
19	2	32	0

18.10. Examine the three control charts shown. Discuss any and all control problems that may be apparent from these control charts.

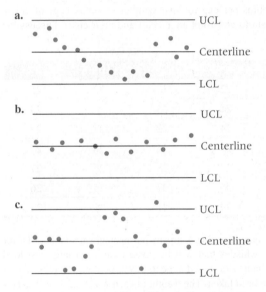

a.

b.

c.

18.11. Study each of the following Minitab control charts and determine whether any of them indicate problems in the processes. Comment on each chart.

18.9. A soft drink bottling company just ran a long line of 12-ounce soft drink cans filled with cola. A sample of 32 cans is selected by inspectors looking for nonconforming items. Among the things the inspectors look for are paint defects on the can, improper seal, incorrect volume, leaking contents, incorrect mixture of carbonation and syrup in the soft drink, and out-of-spec syrup mixture. The results of this inspection are given here. Construct a c chart from the data and comment on the results.

CAN NUMBER	NUMBER OF NONCON- FORMANCES	CAN NUMBER	NUMBER OF NONCON- FORMANCES
1	2	4	0
2	1	5	2
3	1	6	1

a.

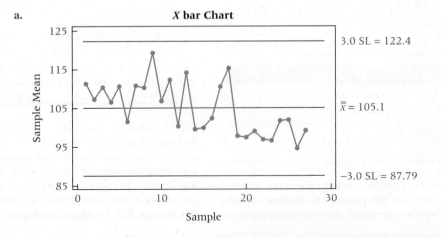

X **bar Chart**

b.

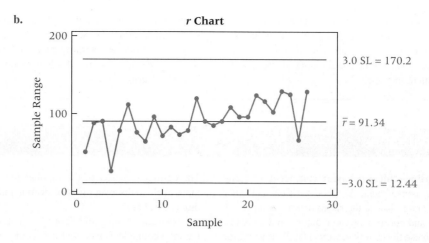

c.

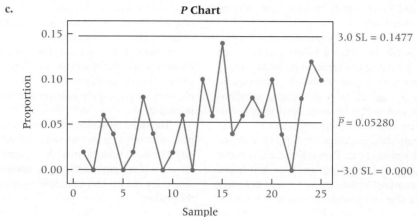

Decision Dilemma Solved

Italy's Piaggio Makes a Comeback

After many years in decline and after several attempts were made to recapture its luster, Piaggio was turned around under the ownership and leadership of Roberto Colaninno. How did he accomplish this?

In 2002, one year before Colaninno took over the company, Piaggio had lost 129 million euros and was 577 million euros in debt. Being optimistic and focusing on Piaggio's assets, Colaninno insisted that the company wasn't dying but that "it just needed to be treated better." After making an initial investment of 100 million euros through his holding company for a third of Piaggio and the mandate to run it, he began his run at improving the company. He quickly hired a chief executive, Rocco Sabelli, who led an effort to redesign the factory and its assembly lines. Previously, each of several assembly lines had been set up to produce only one particular scooter model, but because demands for the different models varied according to their popularity, some assembly lines would have significant downtime while others would be running continuously, unable to keep up with the demand of strong-selling models. Under Sabelli, each assembly line was redesigned, refitted, and retooled so that any of Piaggio's scooter models could be made on any line with little changeover time. This created increased capacity for the production of hot-selling models to meet demand and at the same time effected a leveling of both manufacturing and human resources in the plant. Given this was a radical departure from the way Piaggio had done business, one might say that Colaninno and Sabelli "reengineered" the company's manufacturing process. An even more dramatic example of reengineering had taken place following World War II when Piaggio transformed itself from an aeronautical production company to a scooter firm.

It has been a fairly common practice in Italian businesses for management to "keep its distance" from workers. Sabelli in his first days on the job announced to all workers, including assembly-line workers, that they were to let him know personally about any problems or delays in the production process. Giving workers such access to management shortened the lines of communication so as to quickly improve the product and the process. Such an approach may be viewed, at least in spirit, as not unlike the quality circles introduced by the Japanese.

In a move that surprised many, Colaninno did not fire a single worker, thereby gaining support of unions but also reinforcing a notion argued by Deming that poor quality is usually more about such things as tools, training, design, process efficiency, and supplies than it is about the worker. Colaninno based bonuses for both blue-collar workers and management on profit margins and customer satisfaction—a common quality approach in which company employees are empowered to become responsible for product quality as measured by customer satisfaction, units sold, product warrantee and repair claims, increased market share, and others. Colaninno also installed air conditioning in the factory, and productivity began to increase.

Company engineers were given deadlines for design projects in a manner similar to Six Sigma. As a result, the company recently rolled out two world firsts, including a gas–electric hybrid scooter and one with two wheels in front and one in the back for better road grip.

Ethical Considerations

Unethical or borderline-ethical behavior can occur in many areas of total quality management. At the top, CEOs and other high-level managers can profess to the world that the company is committed to quality and not truly promote quality in the organization. Managers who use the quality movement only as a tool for attention and leverage and do not actually intend to implement the process may be acting unethically.

Some of the specifics of quality control and statistical process control lend themselves to unethical behavior. Just-in-time systems can be used as an excuse to implement favoritism among suppliers. With the move to reduce the number of suppliers, contracting managers can be more selective in choosing suppliers. This practice can give contracting agents or purchasing agents more leverage in securing deals through unethical means.

Just-in-time systems often encourage the supplier to do the testing rather than the manufacturer. This self-evaluation opens opportunity for the falsification of records and tests. It is hoped that such behavior is uncovered by just-in-time systems that place pressure on suppliers to ship on-specification parts and materials.

The customer or user of the supplies in a just-in-time system is more likely to discover off-specification material than users in traditional systems.

Benchmarking could easily lend itself to violation of patent laws if a company is not careful. It could also encourage business espionage and unfair competitive practices. Benchmarking could create an atmosphere of continually seeking ways to "steal" competitive ideas and innovations.

Control charts present the same potential for unethical behavior as any sampling process. Those workers constructing the charts have opportunity to falsify data, selectively choose favorable items, or graphically misrepresent data to make a system look in control.

The implementation of a sound quality program in a company must be based on teamwork, mutual support, trust, and honesty. Unethical behavior in quality control can set the process back for years, if not permanently. The intent in the quality movement is to bring out the best in people so as to optimize the quality of the product.

Summary

Quality means many different things to different people. According to one definition, a quality product delivers to the customer those attributes that have been agreed upon by both buyer and seller. Leading quality experts such as Philip B. Crosby, Armand V. Feigenbaum, and David A. Garvin suggest various divergent views on the notion of quality.

Quality control is the collection of strategies, techniques, and actions an organization can use to ensure the production of a quality product. For decades, U.S. companies used after-process quality control, which essentially consisted of inspectors determining whether a product complied with its specifications. During the 1980s, U.S. companies joined Western European and Asian businesses in instituting in-process quality control, which enables the producer to determine weaknesses and flaws during the production process.

Total quality management occurs when all members of an organization—from the CEO to the line worker—are involved in improving quality. One of the main proponents of total quality management was W. Edwards Deming. Deming was known for his cause-and-effect explanation of total quality management in a company, which is sometimes referred to as the Deming chain reaction. In addition, Deming presented 14 points that can lead to improved total quality management. Some other well-known leaders in the quality movement are Joseph Juran, Philip Crosby, Armand Feigenbaum, Kaoru Ishikawa, and Genichi Taguchi.

In addition to total quality management, there are other major quality movements, including Six Sigma, Design for Six Sigma, and

lean manufacturing. Six Sigma, besides being a quality movement, is also a methodology and a measurement. A goal of Six Sigma is to have no more than 3.4 defects per million opportunities. It is essentially a philosophy of zero defects achieved through deep root analysis using a variety of statistical tools and methodologies in a team approach. Design for Six Sigma is a quality scheme that places an emphasis on designing a product or process right the first time so that higher sigma levels of quality are possible. Lean manufacturing is a quality-management philosophy that focuses on the reduction of wastes and the elimination of unnecessary steps in an operation or process.

Some important quality concepts include benchmarking, just-in-time inventory systems, reengineering, Failure Mode and Effects Analysis (FMEA), poka-yoke, quality circles, and Six Sigma teams. Benchmarking is a technique through which a company attempts to develop product and process excellence by examining and emulating the best practices and techniques used in the industry. Just-in-time inventory systems are inventory systems that focus on raw materials, subparts, and suppliers. Just-in-time is a philosophy of coordination and cooperation between supplier and manufacturer such that a part or raw material arrives just as it is needed. This approach saves on inventory and also serves as a catalyst for discovering bottlenecks and inefficiencies. Reengineering is a radical approach to total quality management in which the core business process is redesigned. Failure Mode and Effects Analysis is a systematic way for identifying the effects of potential product or process failure and includes methodology for eliminating or reducing the chance of failure. Poka-yoke means "mistake proofing," and it uses devices, methods, or inspections to avoid machine error or simple human error. Quality circles are small groups of workers who meet regularly to consider quality issues. Six Sigma teams, led by a black belt, attempt to uncover root causes of a quality problem or opportunity and through the DMAIC process seek to make significant improvement resulting in substantial savings to the company.

Ishikawa developed seven basic tools of quality that he believed could be used to solve most quality-related problems: flowchart, Pareto chart, cause-and-effect diagram, control chart, check sheet, histogram, and scatter chart. Flowcharts are schematic representations of all activities that occur in a process. Pareto analysis is a method of prioritizing types of defects that occur with a product. The result is usually a vertical bar chart that depicts the most common types of defects ranked in order of occurrence. The cause-and-effect (fishbone) diagram displays potential causes of quality problems. The diagram is shaped like a fish skeleton, with the head being the problem and the skeletal bones being the potential causes. A control chart is a graphic method of evaluating whether a process is or is not in a state of statistical control. Check sheets are simple forms consisting of multiple categories and columns for recording the frequency of outcomes for some quality-related event or activity under study so that data can be presented in a logical format. A histogram is a type of chart that is used to depict a frequency distribution. A scatter chart is a graphical mechanism for examining the relationship between two numerical variables.

Control charts are used to monitor product variation, thus enabling operators, technicians, and managers to see when a process gets out of control. The $\bar{x}$ chart and the R chart are two types of control charts for measurements. The $\bar{x}$ chart is a graph of sample means computed on a series of small random samples over time. The R chart is a plot of sample ranges. The $\bar{x}$ chart plots the measure of central tendency, whereas the R chart plots a measure of variability. The p chart and the c chart are two types of control charts for nonconformance. The p chart graphs the proportions of sample items that are in noncompliance. The c chart displays the number of nonconformances per item for a series of sampled items. All four types of control chart are plotted around a centerline and upper and lower control limits. The control limits are located three standard deviations from the centerline.

Key Terms

after-process quality control	fishbone diagram	Pareto analysis	scatter chart
benchmarking	flowchart	Pareto chart	Six Sigma
c chart	histogram	poka-yoke	team building
cause-and-effect diagram	in-process quality control	process	total quality management
centerline	Ishikawa diagram	product quality	(TQM)
check sheet	just-in-time inventory system	quality	transcendent quality
control chart	lean manufacturing	quality circle	upper control limit (UCL)
Design for Six Sigma	lower control limit (LCL)	quality control	user quality
Failure Mode and Effects	manufacturing quality	R chart	value quality
Analysis (FMEA)	p chart	reengineering	$\bar{x}$ chart

Formulas

$\bar{x}$ Charts

$$\text{Centerline: } \bar{\bar{x}} = \frac{\sum \bar{x}}{k}$$

$$\text{UCL: } \quad \bar{\bar{x}} + A_2\bar{R}$$
$$\text{UCL: } \quad \bar{\bar{x}} - A_2\bar{R}$$

or

$$\text{UCL: } \bar{\bar{x}} + A_3\bar{s}$$
$$\text{LCL: } \bar{\bar{x}} - A_3\bar{s}$$

R Charts

$$\text{Centerline: } \bar{R} = \frac{\sum R}{k}$$

$$\text{UCL: } \quad D_4\bar{R}$$
$$\text{LCL: } \quad D_3\bar{R}$$

p Charts

$$\text{Centerline: } p = \frac{\sum \hat{p}}{k}$$

$$\text{UCL: } \quad p + 3\sqrt{\frac{p \cdot q}{n}}$$

$$\text{LCL: } \quad p - 3\sqrt{\frac{p \cdot q}{n}}$$

c Charts

$$\text{Centerline: } \bar{c} = \frac{c_1 + c_2 + c_3 + \cdots + c_i}{i}$$

$$\text{UCL: } \quad \bar{c} + 3\sqrt{\bar{c}}$$
$$\text{LCL: } \quad \bar{c} - 3\sqrt{\bar{c}}$$

Supplementary Problems

Calculating the Statistics

18.12. Create a flowchart from the following sequence of activities: Begin. Flow to activity A. Flow to decision B. If Yes, flow to activity C. If No, flow to activity D. From C flow to activity E and to activity F. From F, flow to decision G. If Yes, flow to decision H. If No at G, stop. At H, if Yes, flow to activity I and on to activity J and then stop. If No at H, flow to activity J and stop. At D, flow to activity K, flow to L, and flow to decision M. If Yes at M, stop. If No at M, flow to activity N, then stop.

18.13. An examination of rejects shows at least 10 problems. A frequency tally of the problems follows. Construct a Pareto chart for these data.

PROBLEM	FREQUENCY
1	673
2	29
3	108
4	379
5	73
6	564
7	12
8	402
9	54
10	202

18.14. A brainstorm session on possible causes of a problem resulted in five possible causes: A, B, C, D, and E. Cause A has three possible subcauses, cause B has four, cause C has two, cause D has five, and cause E has three. Construct a fishbone diagram for this problem and its possible causes.

Testing Your Understanding

18.15. A bottled-water company has been randomly inspecting bottles of water to determine whether they are acceptable for delivery and sale. The inspectors are looking at water quality, bottle condition, and seal tightness. A series of 10 random samples of 50 bottles each is taken. Some bottles are rejected. Use the following information on the number of bottles from each batch that were rejected as being out of compliance to construct a p chart.

SAMPLE	N	NUMBER OUT OF COMPLIANCE
1	50	3
2	50	11
3	50	7
4	50	2
5	50	5
6	50	8
7	50	0
8	50	9
9	50	1
10	50	6

18.16. A fruit juice company sells a glass container filled with 24 ounces of cranapple juice. Inspectors are concerned about the consistency of volume of fill in these containers. Every two hours for three days of production, a sample of five containers is randomly selected and the volume of fill is measured. The results follow.

SAMPLE 1	SAMPLE 2	SAMPLE 3	SAMPLE 4
24.05	24.01	24.03	23.98
24.01	24.02	23.95	24.00
24.02	24.10	24.00	24.01
23.99	24.03	24.01	24.01
24.04	24.08	23.99	24.00

SAMPLE 5	SAMPLE 6	SAMPLE 7	SAMPLE 8
23.97	24.02	24.01	24.08
23.99	24.05	24.00	24.03
24.02	24.01	24.00	24.00
24.01	24.00	23.97	24.05
24.00	24.01	24.02	24.01

SAMPLE 9	SAMPLE 10	SAMPLE 11	SAMPLE 12
24.00	24.00	24.01	24.00
24.02	24.01	23.99	24.05
24.03	24.00	24.02	24.04
24.01	24.00	24.03	24.02
24.01	24.00	24.01	24.00

Use this information to construct $\bar{x}$ and R charts and comment on any samples that are out of compliance.

18.17. A metal-manufacturing company produces sheet metal. Statistical quality-control technicians randomly select sheets to be inspected for blemishes and size problems. The number of nonconformances per sheet is tallied. Shown here are the results of testing 36 sheets of metal. Use the data to construct a c chart. What is the center-line? What is the meaning of the centerline value?

SHEET NUMBER	NUMBER OF NONCON-FORMANCES	SHEET NUMBER	NUMBER OF NONCON-FORMANCES
1	4	11	2
2	2	12	0
3	1	13	5
4	1	14	4
5	3	15	1
6	0	16	2
7	4	17	1
8	5	18	0
9	2	19	1
10	1	20	3

21	4	29	5
22	0	30	3
23	2	31	1
24	3	32	2
25	0	33	0
26	0	34	4
27	4	35	2
28	2	36	3

18.18. A manufacturing company produces cylindrical tubes for engines that are specified to be 1.20 centimeters thick. As part of the company's statistical quality-control effort, random samples of four tubes are taken each hour. The tubes are measured to determine whether they are within thickness tolerances. Shown here are the thickness data in centimeters for nine samples of tubes. Use these data to develop an $\bar{x}$ chart and an R chart. Comment on whether or not the process appears to be in control at this point.

SAMPLE 1	SAMPLE 2	SAMPLE 3	SAMPLE 4	SAMPLE 5
1.22	1.20	1.21	1.16	1.24
1.19	1.20	1.18	1.17	1.20
1.20	1.22	1.17	1.20	1.21
1.23	1.20	1.20	1.16	1.18

SAMPLE 6	SAMPLE 7	SAMPLE 8	SAMPLE 9
1.19	1.24	1.17	1.22
1.21	1.17	1.23	1.17
1.21	1.18	1.22	1.16
1.20	1.19	1.16	1.19

18.19. A manufacturer produces digital watches. Every two hours a sample of six watches is selected randomly to be tested. Each watch is run for exactly 15 minutes and is timed by an accurate, precise timing device. Because of the variation among watches, they do not all run the same. Shown here are the data from eight different samples given in minutes. Use these data to construct $\bar{x}$ and R charts. Observe the results and comment on whether the process is in control.

SAMPLE 1	SAMPLE 2	SAMPLE 3	SAMPLE 4
15.01	15.03	14.96	15.00
14.99	14.96	14.97	15.01
14.99	15.01	14.96	14.97
15.00	15.02	14.99	15.01
14.98	14.97	15.01	14.99
14.99	15.01	14.98	14.96

SAMPLE 5	SAMPLE 6	SAMPLE 7	SAMPLE 8
15.02	15.02	15.03	14.96
15.03	15.01	15.04	14.99
14.99	14.97	15.03	15.02
15.01	15.00	15.00	15.01
15.02	15.01	15.01	14.98
15.01	14.99	14.99	15.02

18.20. A company produces outdoor home thermometers. For a variety of reasons, a thermometer can be tested and found to be out of compliance with company specifications. The company takes samples of thermometers on a regular basis and tests each one to determine whether it meets company standards. Shown here are data from 12 different random samples of 75 thermometers. Use these data to construct a p chart. Comment on the pattern of points in the chart.

SAMPLE	n	NUMBER OUT OF COMPLIANCE
1	75	9
2	75	3
3	75	0
4	75	2
5	75	7
6	75	14
7	75	11
8	75	8
9	75	5
10	75	4
11	75	0
12	75	7

18.21. A plastics company makes thousands of plastic bottles for another company that manufactures saline solution for users of soft contact lenses. The plastics company randomly inspects a sample of its bottles as part of its quality-control program. Inspectors look for blemishes on the bottle, size and thickness, ability to close, leaks, labeling problems, and so on. Shown here are the results of tests completed on 25 bottles. Use these data to construct a c chart. Observe the results and comment on the chart.

BOTTLE NUMBER	NUMBER OF NONCON- FORMANCES	BOTTLE NUMBER	NUMBER OF NONCON- FORMANCES
1	1	14	0
2	0	15	0
3	1	16	0
4	0	17	1
5	0	18	0
6	2	19	0
7	1	20	1
8	1	21	0
9	0	22	1
10	1	23	2
11	0	24	0
12	2	25	1
13	1		

18.22. A bathtub manufacturer closely inspects several tubs on every shift for nonconformances such as leaks, lack of symmetry, unstable base, drain malfunctions, and so on. The following list gives the number of nonconformances per tub for 40 tubs. Use these data to construct a c chart of nonconformances for bathtubs. Comment on the results of this chart.

TUB	NUMBER OF NONCON- FORMANCES	TUB	NUMBER OF NONCON- FORMANCES
1	3	21	2
2	2	22	5
3	3	23	1
4	1	24	3
5	4	25	4
6	2	26	3
7	2	27	2
8	1	28	0
9	4	29	1
10	2	30	0
11	3	31	2
12	0	32	1
13	3	33	2
14	2	34	1
15	2	35	1
16	1	36	1
17	0	37	3
18	4	38	0
19	3	39	1
20	2	40	4

18.23. A glass manufacturer produces hand mirrors. Each mirror is supposed to meet company standards for such things as glass thickness, ability to reflect, size of handle, quality of glass, color of handle, and so on. To control for these features, the company quality people randomly sample 40 mirrors every shift and determine how many of the mirrors are out of compliance on at least one feature. Shown here are the data for 15 such samples. Use the data to construct a p chart. Observe the results and comment on the control of the process as indicated by the chart.

SAMPLE	n	NUMBER OUT OF COMPLIANCE
1	40	2
2	40	0
3	40	6
4	40	3
5	40	1
6	40	1
7	40	5
8	40	0
9	40	4
10	40	3
11	40	2
12	40	2
13	40	6
14	40	1
15	40	0

Interpreting the Output

18.24. Study the Minitab chart on the fill of a product that is supposed to contain 12 ounces. Does the process appear to be out of control? Why or why not?

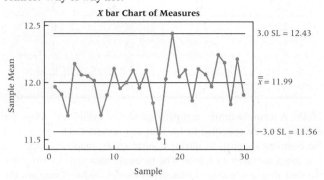

18.25. Study the Minitab R chart for the product and data used in Problem 18.24. Comment on the state of the production process for this item.

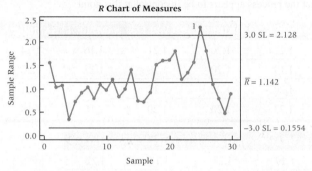

18.26. Study the Minitab p chart for a manufactured item. The chart represents the results of testing 30 items at a time for compliance. Sixty different samples were taken for this chart. Discuss the results and the implications for the production process.

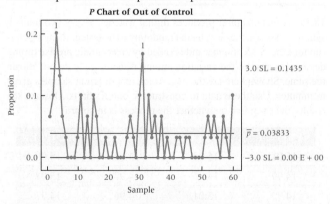

18.27. Study the Minitab c chart for nonconformances for a part produced in a manufacturing process. Comment on the results.

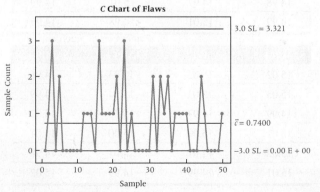

Analyzing the Databases

See **www.wiley.com/college/black and WileyPLUS**

1. A dairy company in the Manufacturing database tests its quart milk container fills for volume in four-container samples. Shown here are the results of 10 such samples and the volume measurements in quarts. Use the information to construct both an $\bar{x}$ and an R chart for the data. Discuss the results. What are the centerline, LCL, and UCL for each of these charts?

SAMPLE NUMBER	MEASUREMENTS			
1	.98	1.01	1.05	1.03
2	1.02	.94	.97	1.02
3	1.11	1.02	.93	1.01
4	.95	.98	1.02	.96
5	1.03	1.01	1.01	.95
6	1.04	.93	.91	.96
7	.94	1.12	1.10	1.03
8	1.03	.92	.98	1.03
9	1.01	1.01	.99	1.00
10	1.05	.96	1.00	1.04

2. A hospital in the Hospital database takes weekly samples of patient account statements for 12 weeks with each sample containing 40 accounts. Auditors analyze the account statements, looking for nonconforming statements. Shown here are the results of the 12 samples. Use these data to construct a p chart for proportion of nonconforming statements. What is the centerline? What are UCL and LCL? Comment on the control chart.

SAMPLE	NUMBER OF NONCONFORMING STATEMENTS
1	1
2	0
3	6
4	3
5	0
6	2
7	8
8	3
9	5
10	2
11	2
12	1

Case

Robotron-Elotherm

The Robotron-Elotherm company is known for its expertise in power electronics for welding, induction bonding, and process heating. Originally known as Robotron, the company manufactured bonding products for the automotive industry for more than two decades in the 1960s and 1970s. For several years, Robotron felt it produced and delivered a high-quality product because it rarely received complaints from customers. However, early in the 1980s General Motors gave Robotron an order for induction bonding machines to cure adhesive in auto door joints. Actually, the machines were shipped to a Michigan plant of Sanyo Manufacturing (a Japanese firm) that GM was using as a door builder.

Sanyo Manufacturing was unhappy with the quality of the machines sent by Robotron. Robotron president Leonard Brzozowski went to the Sanyo plant to investigate the situation in person and learned that the Japanese had a much higher quality standard than the usual American customers. Tolerances were much smaller and inspection was more demanding. Brzozowski said that he realized for the first time that the philosophy, engineering, management, and shop practices of Robotron did not qualify the company for world competition. Brzozowski said that this was the most embarrassing time of his professional career. What should Robotron do about this situation?

Brzozowski began by sending a group of hourly employees to the Sanyo plant. There they met the customer and heard firsthand the many complaints about their product. The workers could see the difference in quality between their machines and those of Sanyo. The plant visit was extremely effective. On the way home, the Robotron workers started discussing what they could do to improve quality.

The company took several steps to begin the process of quality improvement. It established new inspection procedures, bought more accurate inspection tools, changed internal control procedures, and developed baselines against which to measure progress. Teams were organized and sent out to customers six months after a purchase to determine customer satisfaction. A hotline was established for customers to call to report product dissatisfaction.

For one month, engineers assembled machinery in the shop under the direction of hourly employees. This exercise gave the engineers a new awareness of the importance of accurate, clear drawings; designing smaller, lighter-weight details; and minimizing the number of machined surfaces.

Robotron's effort paid off handsomely. Claims under warranty dropped 40% in three years, during which time orders rose at a compound annual rate of 13.5%. The company cut costs and streamlined procedures and processes. Sales increased and new markets opened.

In 1997, Robotron received ISO-9001 certification. Early in 1998, Robotron merged with ELOTHERM, a European company, so that Robotron could more easily enjoy a presence in the European market and at the same time provide ELOTHERM opportunities in North America. Robotron's bonding business expanded into induction heating systems, heat treating, tube welding, and electrical discharge machines. The company maintains a quality system that takes corrective action in response to customer complaints, employee suggestions, or supplier defects.

Discussion

1. As a part of quality improvement, it is highly likely that Robotron analyzed its manufacturing processes. Suppose that as Robotron improved quality, the company wanted to examine other processes including the flow of work orders from the time they are received until they are filled. Use the following verbal sketch of some of the activities that might take place in such a flow as a start, and add some of your own ideas as you draw a flowchart for the process of work orders.

Work order flow: Received at mailroom. Sent to order processing office. Examined by order-processing clerk who decides whether the item is a standard item or a custom item. If it is a standard item, the order is sent to the warehouse. If the item is available, the item is shipped and the order is sent to the billing department. If the item is not available, the order is sent to the plant where it is received by a manufacturing clerk. The clerk checks to determine whether such an item is being manufactured. If so, the order is sent to the end of the assembly line where it will be tagged with one such item. If not, the order is sent to the beginning of the assembly line and flows along the assembly line with the item as it is being made. In either case, when the part comes off the assembly line, the order is attached to the item and sent to shipping. The shipping clerk then ships the item and sends the order to billing. If the ordered item is a customized part, the order is sent straight from the order-processing clerk to manufacturing where it follows the same procedures as already described for standard items that have not been manufactured yet.

2. Virtually all quality manufacturers use some type of control chart to monitor performance. Suppose the Minitab control charts shown here are for two different parts produced by Robotron during a particular period. Part 173 is specified to weigh 183 grams. Part 248 contains an opening that is specified to be 35 millimeters in diameter. Study these charts and report to Robotron what you found. Is there any reason for concern? Is everything in control?

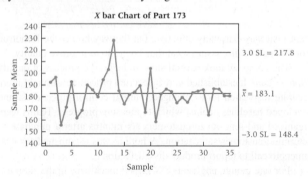

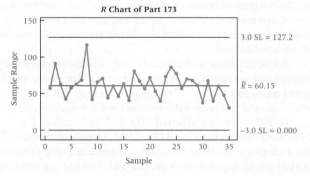

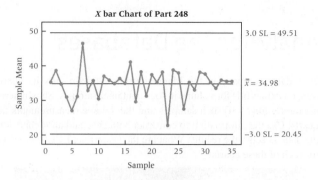

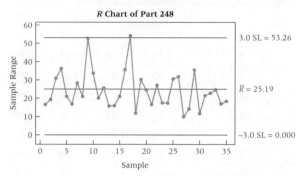

3. Suppose Robotron also keeps p charts on nonconformance. The Minitab chart shown here represents the proportion of nonconforming items for a given part over 100 samples. Study the chart and write a brief report to Robotron about what you learned from the chart. Think about overall performance, out-of-control samples, samples that have outstanding performance, and any general trends that you see.

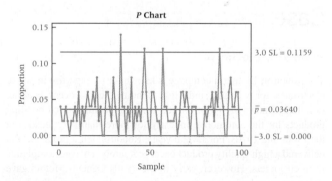

Source: Adapted from "ROBOTRON: Qualifying for Global Competition," *Real-World Lessons for America's Small Businesses: Insights from the Blue Chip Enterprise Initiative.* Published by *Nation's Business* magazine on behalf of Connecticut Mutual Life Insurance Company and the U.S. Chamber of Commerce in association with the Blue Chip Enterprise Initiative 1994. See also Robotron, available at http://www.robotron.com/aboutus/iso9001.html; http://www.robotron.com/products; http://www.robotron.com/aboutus/merger.html.

CHAPTER 19

Decision Analysis

LEARNING OBJECTIVES

This chapter describes how to use decision analysis to improve management decisions, thereby enabling you to:

1. Make decisions under certainty by constructing a decision table.

2. Make decisions under uncertainty using the maximax criterion, the maximin criterion, the Hurwicz criterion, and minimax regret.

3. Make decisions under risk by constructing decision trees, calculating expected monetary value and expected value of perfect information, and analyzing utility.

4. Revise probabilities in light of sample information by using Bayesian analysis and calculating the expected value of sample information.

Decision Dilemma

Decision Making at the CEO Level

CEOs face major challenges in today's business world. As the international marketplace evolves, competition increases in many cases. Technology is improving products and process. The political and economic climates both internationally and domestically shift constantly. In the midst of such dynamics, CEOs make decisions about investments, products, resources, suppliers, financing, and many other items. Decision making may be the most important function of management. Successful companies are usually built around successful decisions. Even CEOs of successful companies feel the need to constantly improve the company's position.

In 1994, Ford Motor Company posted a record profit of more than $4 billion with five of the 10 best-selling vehicles in the United States. Yet, CEO and chairman, Alex Trotman made the decision to merge the North American and European operations into one global unit. The decision was implemented with Ford 2000, a program to design "world cars," with common components that can be sold worldwide with minor style changes to suit local tastes.

In the same year, George Fisher, CEO of Eastman Kodak Company, reversed a decade of diversification for Kodak and led the company in a direction of digital and electronic imaging. He implemented this thrust by aligning digital and electronic imaging with traditional products that emphasize paper and film.

CEOs of smaller companies also make tough decisions. The most critical decision-making period for a CEO is likely to be during growth phases. A study of 142 CEOs from small, private companies attempted to ascertain the types of decisions undertaken by top managers. Most of the companies in the study had experienced healthy growth in revenues over the four-year period preceding the study. CEOs in this study suggested that decisions made during growth phases typically are in the areas of expansion, personnel, finances, operations, and planning and control systems. According to respondents in the study, many of these decisions carry system-wide implications for the company that make the decisions quite critical.

CEOs responded that during a growth phase, decisions need to be made about how to handle new business. How is capacity to be expanded? Does the company build, lease, expand its present facility, relocate, automate, and so on? Risk is inevitably involved in undertaking most of these decisions. Will customer demand continue? Will competitors also increase capacity? How long will the increased demand continue? What is the lost opportunity if the company fails to meet customer demands?

According to the study, another critical area of decision making is personnel. What is the long-term strategy of the company? Should significant layoffs be implemented in an effort to become "lean and mean"? Does the firm need to hire? How does management discover and attract talented managers? How can substandard personnel be released? In the area of production, how does management "level" personnel to match uneven product demand?

A third area of decision making that the study participants considered important was systems, business, and finance. How can the company make operations and procedures more efficient? How are cash flow problems handled? Under what conditions does the company obtain financial backing for capital development?

In the area of marketing, decisions need to be made about pricing, distribution, purchasing, and suppliers. Should the company market overseas? What about vertical integration? Should the company expand into new market segments or with new product lines?

The CEOs in the study enumerated decision choices that represent exciting and sometimes risky opportunities for growing firms. The success or failure of such decision makers often lies in their ability to identify and choose optimal decision pathways for the company.

MANAGERIAL AND STATISTICAL QUESTIONS

1. In any given area of decisions, what choices or options are available to the manager?

2. What occurrences in nature, the marketplace, or the business environment might affect the outcome or payoff for a given decision option?

3. What are some strategies that can be used to help the decision maker determine which option to choose?

4. If risk is involved, can probabilities of occurrence be assigned to various states of nature within each decision option?

5. What are the payoffs for various decision options?

6. Does the manager's propensity toward risk enter into the final decision and, if so, how?

The main focus of this text has been business decision making. In this chapter, we discuss another category of quantitative techniques for assisting managers in decision making. These techniques, generally referred to as decision analysis, are *particularly targeted at clarifying and enhancing the decision-making process* and can be used in such diverse situations as determining whether and when to drill oil wells, deciding whether and how to expand capacity, deciding whether to automate a facility, and determining what types of investments to make.

In decision analysis, decision-making scenarios are divided into the following three categories.

1. Decision making under certainty

2. Decision making under uncertainty

3. Decision making under risk

In this chapter, we discuss making decisions under each condition, as well as the concepts of utility and Bayesian statistics.

19.1 | The Decision Table and Decision Making Under Certainty

Many decision analysis problems can be viewed as having three variables: decision alternatives, states of nature, and payoffs.

Decision alternatives are *the various choices or options available to the decision maker in any given problem situation.* On most days, financial managers face the choices of whether to invest in blue chip stocks, bonds, commodities, certificates of deposit, money markets, annuities, and other investments. Construction decision makers must decide whether to concentrate on one building job today, spread out workers and equipment to several jobs, or not work today. In virtually every possible business scenario, decision alternatives are available. A good decision maker identifies many options and effectively evaluates them.

States of nature are *the occurrences of nature that can happen after a decision is made that can affect the outcome of the decision and over which the decision maker has little or no control.* These states of nature can be literally natural atmospheric and climatic conditions or they can be such things as the business climate, the political climate, the worker climate, or the condition of the marketplace, among many others. The financial investor faces such states of nature as the prime interest rate, the condition of the stock market, the international monetary exchange rate, and so on. A construction company is faced with such states of nature as the weather, wildcat strikes, equipment failure, absenteeism, and supplier inability to deliver on time. States of nature are usually difficult to predict but are important to identify in the decision-making process.

The payoffs of a decision analysis problem are *the benefits or rewards that result from selecting a particular decision alternative.* Payoffs are usually given in terms of dollars. In the financial investment industry, for example, the payoffs can be small, modest, or large, or the investment can result in a loss. Most business decisions involve taking some chances with personal or company money in one form or another. Because for-profit businesses are looking for a return on the dollars invested, the payoffs are extremely important for a successful manager. The trick is to determine which decision alternative to take in order to generate the greatest payoff. Suppose a CEO is examining various environmental decision alternatives. Positive payoffs could include increased market share, attracting and retaining quality employees, consumer appreciation, and governmental support. Negative payoffs might take the form of fines and penalties, lost market share, and lawsuit judgments.

Decision Table

The concepts of decision alternatives, states of nature, and payoffs can be examined jointly by using a **decision table**, or **payoff table**. Table 19.1 shows the structure of a decision table. On the left side of the table are the various decision alternatives, denoted by d_i. Along the top row are the states of nature, denoted by s_j. In the middle of the table are the various payoffs for each decision alternative under each state of nature, denoted by P_{ij}.

As an example of a decision table, consider the decision dilemma of the investor shown in Table 19.2. The investor is faced with the decision of where and how to invest $10,000 under several possible states of nature.

The investor is considering four decision alternatives.

1. Invest in the stock market
2. Invest in the bond market
3. Invest in government certificates of deposit (CDs)
4. Invest in a mixture of stocks and bonds

Because the payoffs are in the future, the investor is unlikely to know ahead of time what the state of nature will be for the economy. However, the table delineates three possible states of the economy.

1. A stagnant economy
2. A slow-growth economy
3. A rapid-growth economy

The matrix in Table 19.2 lists the payoffs for each possible investment decision under each possible state of the economy. Notice that the largest payoff comes with a stock investment under a rapid-growth economic scenario, with a payoff of $2,200 per year on an investment of $10,000. The lowest payoff occurs for a stock investment during stagnant economic times, with an annual loss of $500 on the $10,000 investment.

Decision Making Under Certainty

The most elementary of the decision-making scenarios is **decision making under certainty**. In making decisions under certainty, *the states of nature are known*. The decision maker needs merely to examine the payoffs under different decision alternatives and select the alternative with the largest payoff. In the preceding example involving the $10,000 investment, if it is known that the economy is going to be stagnant, the investor would select the decision alternative of CDs, yielding a payoff of $300. Indeed, each of the other three decision alternatives would result

TABLE 19.1 Decision Table

	s_1	s_2	s_3	...	s_n
d_1	$P_{1,1}$	$P_{1,2}$	$P_{1,3}$	...	$P_{1,n}$
d_2	$P_{2,1}$	$P_{2,2}$	$P_{2,3}$	...	$P_{2,n}$
d_3	$P_{3,1}$	$P_{3,2}$	$P_{3,3}$	...	$P_{3,n}$
d_m	P_{m1}	P_{m2}	P_{m3}	...	P_{mn}

State of Nature; Decision Alternative

where
s_j = state of nature
d_i = decision alternative
P_{ij} = payoff for decision i under state j

TABLE 19.2 Yearly Payoffs on an Investment of $10,000

Investment Decision Alternative	Stagnant	Slow Growth	Rapid Growth
Stocks	–$500	$700	$2,200
Bonds	–$100	$600	$900
CDs	$300	$500	$750
Mixture	–$200	$650	$1,300

in a loss under stagnant economic conditions. If it is known that the economy is going to have slow growth, the investor would choose stocks as an investment, resulting in a $700 payoff. If the economy is certain to have rapid growth, the decision maker should opt for stocks, resulting in a payoff of $2,200. Decision making under certainty is almost the trivial case.

19.2 | Decision Making Under Uncertainty

In making decisions under certainty, the decision maker knows for sure which state of nature will occur, and he or she bases the decision on the optimal payoff available under that state. **Decision making under uncertainty** occurs *when it is unknown which states of nature will occur and the probability of a state of nature occurring is also unknown.* Hence, the decision maker has virtually no information about which state of nature will occur, and he or she attempts to develop a strategy based on payoffs.

Several different approaches can be taken to making decisions under uncertainty. Each uses a different decision criterion, depending on the decision maker's outlook. Each of these approaches will be explained and demonstrated with a decision table. Included are the maximax criterion, maximin criterion, Hurwicz criterion, and minimax regret.

In section 19.1, we discussed the decision dilemma of the financial investor who wants to invest $10,000 and is faced with four decision alternatives and three states of nature. The data for this problem were given in Table 19.2. In decision making under certainty, we selected the optimal payoff under each state of the economy and then, on the basis of which state we were certain would occur, selected a decision alternative. Shown next are techniques to use when we are uncertain which state of nature will occur.

Maximax Criterion

The **maximax criterion** approach is an optimistic approach in which the decision maker bases action on a notion that the best things will happen. The decision maker *isolates the maximum payoff under each decision alternative and then selects the decision alternative that produces the highest of these maximum payoffs.* The name "maximax" means selecting the maximum overall payoff from the maximum payoffs of each decision alternative. Consider the $10,000 investment problem. The maximum payoff is $2,200 for stocks, $900 for bonds, $750 for CDs, and $1,300 for the mixture of investments. The maximax criterion approach requires that the decision maker select the maximum payoff of these four.

		State of the Economy			
		Stagnant	Slow Growth	Rapid Growth	Maximum
Investment Decision Alternative	Stocks	−$500	$700	$2,200	$2,200
	Bonds	−$100	$600	$900	$900
	CDs	$300	$500	$750	$750
	Mixture	−$200	$650	$1,300	$1,300

maximum of {$2,200, $900, $750, $1,300} = $2,200

Because the maximax criterion results in $2,200 as the optimal payoff, the decision alternative selected is the stock alternative, which is associated with the $2,200.

Maximin Criterion

The **maximin criterion** approach to decision making is a pessimistic approach. The assumption is that the worst will happen and attempts must be made to minimize the damage. The decision maker starts by examining the payoffs under each decision alternative and selects the worst, or minimum, payoff that can occur under that decision. Then the decision maker *selects the maximum or best payoff of those minimums selected under each decision alternative.* Thus, the decision maker has maximized the minimums. In the investment problem, the minimum payoffs are −$500 for stocks, −$100 for bonds, $300 for CDs, and −$200 for the mixture of investments. With the maximin criterion, the decision maker examines the minimum payoffs for each decision alternative given in the last column and selects the maximum of those values.

		State of the Economy			
		Stagnant	Slow Growth	Rapid Growth	Minimum
Investment	Stocks	−$500	$700	$2,200	−$500
Decision	Bonds	−$100	$600	$900	−$100
Alternative	CDs	$300	$500	$750	$300
	Mixture	−$200	$650	$1,300	−$200

maximum of $\{-\$500, -\$100, \$300, -\$200\} = \$300$

The decision is to invest in CDs because that investment alternative yields the highest, or maximum, payoff under the worst-case scenario.

Hurwicz Criterion

The Hurwicz criterion is an approach somewhere between the maximax and the maximin approaches. The **Hurwicz criterion** approach selects the maximum and the minimum payoff from each decision alternative. A value called alpha (not the same as the probability of a Type I error), which is between 0 and 1, is selected as a weight of optimism. The nearer alpha is to 1, the more optimistic is the decision maker. The use of alpha values near 0 implies a more pessimistic approach. The maximum payoff under each decision alternative is multiplied by alpha and the minimum payoff (pessimistic view) under each decision alternative is multiplied by $1 - \alpha$ (weight of pessimism). These weighted products are summed for each decision alternative, resulting in a weighted value for each decision alternative. The maximum weighted value is selected, and the corresponding decision alternative is chosen.

Following are the data for the investment example, along with the minimum and maximum values.

		State of the Economy				
		Stagnant	Slow Growth	Rapid Growth	Minimum	Maximum
Investment	Stocks	−$500	$700	$2,200	−$500	$2,200
Decision	Bonds	−$100	$600	$900	−$100	$900
Alternative	CDs	$300	$500	$750	$300	$750
	Mixture	−$200	$650	$1,300	−$200	$1,300

Suppose we are more optimistic than pessimistic and select $\alpha = .7$ for the weight of optimism. The calculations of weighted values for the decision alternative follow.

Stocks   ($2,200)(.7) + (−$500)(.3) = $1,390
Bonds   ($900)(.7) + (−$100)(.3) = $ 600
CDs   ($750)(.7) + ($300)(.3)   = $ 615
Mixture ($1,300)(.7) + (−$200)(.3) = $ 850

The Hurwicz criterion leads the decision maker to choose the maximum of these values, $1,390. The result under the Hurwicz criterion with $\alpha = .7$ is to choose stocks as the decision alternative. An advantage of the Hurwicz criterion is that it allows the decision maker the latitude to explore various weights of optimism. A decision maker's outlook might change from scenario to scenario and from day to day. In this case, if we had been fairly pessimistic and chosen an alpha of .2, we would have obtained the following weighted values.

Stocks   ($2,200)(.2) + (−$500)(.8) = $ 40
Bonds   ($900)(.2) + (−$100)(.8) = $100
CDs   ($750)(.2) + ($300)(.8)   = $390
Mixture ($1,300)(.2) + (−$200)(.8) = $100

Under this scenario, the decision maker would choose the CD option because it yields the highest weighted payoff ($390) with $\alpha = .2$.

Table 19.3 displays the payoffs obtained by using the Hurwicz criterion for various values of alpha for the investment example. The circled values are the optimum payoffs and represent the decision alternative selection for that value of alpha. Note that for $\alpha = .0$, .1, .2, and .3, the decision is to invest in CDs. For $\alpha = .4$ to 1.0, the decision is to invest in stocks.

Figure 19.1 shows graphically the weighted values for each decision alternative over the possible values of alpha. The thicker line segments represent the maximum of these under each value of alpha. Notice that the graph reinforces the choice of CDs for $\alpha = .0$, .1, .2, .3 and the choice of stocks for $\alpha = .4$ through 1.0.

TABLE 19.3   Decision Alternatives for Various Values of Alpha

		Stocks		Bonds		CDs		Mixture	
		Max.	Min.	Max.	Min.	Max.	Min.	Max.	Min.
α	$1 - \alpha$	2,200	−500	900	−100	750	300	1,300	−200
.0	1.0	−500		−100		300		−200	
.1	.9	−230		0		345		−50	
.2	.8	40		100		390		100	
.3	.7	310		200		435		250	
.4	.6	580		300		480		400	
.5	.5	850		400		525		550	
.6	.4	1,120		500		570		700	
.7	.3	1,390		600		615		850	
.8	.2	1,660		700		660		1,000	
.9	.1	1,930		800		705		1,150	
1.0	.0	2,200		900		750		1,300	

Note: Circled values indicate the choice for the given value of alpha.

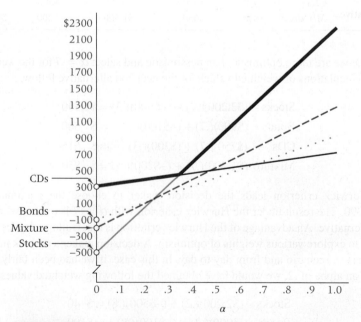

FIGURE 19.1   Graph of Hurwicz Criterion Selections for Various Values of Alpha

Between $\alpha = .3$ and $\alpha = .4$, there is a point at which the line for weighted payoffs for CDs intersects the line for weighted payoffs for stocks. By setting the alpha expression with maximum and minimum values of the CD investment equal to that of the stock investment, we can solve for the alpha value at which the intersection occurs. At this value of alpha, the weighted payoffs of the two investments under the Hurwicz criterion are equal, and the decision maker is indifferent as to which one he or she chooses.

$$\text{Stocks Weighted Payoff} = \text{CDs Weighted Payoff}$$
$$2{,}200(\alpha) + (-500)(1 - \alpha) = 750(\alpha) + (300)(1 - \alpha)$$
$$2{,}200\alpha - 500 + 500\alpha = 750\alpha + 300 - 300\alpha$$
$$2{,}250\alpha = 800$$
$$\alpha = .3555$$

At $\alpha = .3555$, both stocks and CDs yield the same payoff under the Hurwicz criterion. For values less than $\alpha = .3555$, CDs are the chosen investment. For $\alpha > .3555$, stocks are the chosen investment. Neither bonds nor the mixture produces the optimum payoff under the Hurwicz criterion for any value of alpha. Notice that in Figure 19.1 the dark line segments represent the optimum solutions. The lines for both bonds and the mixture are beneath these optimum line segments for the entire range of α. In another problem with different payoffs, the results might be different.

Minimax Regret

The strategy of **minimax regret** is based on lost opportunity. Lost opportunity occurs when a decision maker loses out on some payoff or portion of a payoff because he or she chose the wrong decision alternative. For example, if a decision maker selects decision alternative d_i which pays $200, and the selection of alternative d_j would have yielded $300, the opportunity loss is $100.

$$\$300 - \$200 = \$100$$

In analyzing decision-making situations under uncertainty, an analyst can transform a decision table (payoff table) into an **opportunity loss table**, which can be used to apply the minimax regret criterion. Repeated here is the $10,000 investment decision table.

		State of the Economy		
		Stagnant	Slow Growth	Rapid Growth
Investment	Stocks	−$500	$700	$2,200
Decision	Bonds	−$100	$600	$900
Alternative	CDs	$300	$500	$750
	Mixture	−$200	$650	$1,300

Suppose the state of the economy turns out to be stagnant. The optimal decision choice would be CDs, which pay off $300. Any other decision would lead to an opportunity loss. The opportunity loss for each decision alternative other than CDs can be calculated by subtracting the decision alternative payoff from $300.

Stocks $300 − (−$500) = $800
Bonds $300 − (−$100) = $400
CDs $300 − ($300) = $0
Mixture $300 − (−$200) = $500

The opportunity losses for the slow-growth state of the economy are calculated by subtracting each payoff from $700, because $700 is the maximum payoff that can be obtained from this state; any other payoff is an opportunity loss. These opportunity losses follow.

Stocks $700 − ($700) = $0
Bonds $700 − ($600) = $100
CDs $700 − ($500) = $200
Mixture $700 − ($650) = $50

TABLE 19.4 Opportunity Loss Table

		State of the Economy		
		Stagnant	*Slow Growth*	*Rapid Growth*
Investment Decision Alternative	*Stocks*	$800	$0	$0
	Bonds	$400	$100	$1,300
	CDs	$0	$200	$1,450
	Mixture	$500	$50	$900

The opportunity losses for a rapid-growth state of the economy are calculated similarly.

Stocks $2,200 − ($2,200) = $0

Bonds $2,200 − ($900)   = $1,300

CDs $2,200 − ($750)   = $1,450

Mixture $2,200 − ($1,300) = $900

Replacing payoffs in the decision table with opportunity losses produces the opportunity loss table, as shown in Table 19.4.

After the opportunity loss table is determined, the decision maker examines the lost opportunity, or regret, under each decision, and selects the maximum regret for consideration. For example, if the investor chooses stocks, the maximum regret or lost opportunity is $800. If the investor chooses bonds, the maximum regret is $1,300. If the investor chooses CDs, the maximum regret is $1,450. If the investor selects a mixture, the maximum regret is $900.

Thinking Critically About Statistics in Business Today

The RadioShack Corporation Makes Decisions

In the 1960s, Charles Tandy founded and built a tight vertically integrated manufacturing and retailing company, the Tandy Corporation. RadioShack, a retail unit of the Tandy Corporation, has been one of the company's mainstays. However, RadioShack, along with the Tandy Corporation, has seen many changes over the years both because of decisions management made and because of various states of nature that occurred.

In the early days, RadioShack was an outlet for Tandy products with a relatively narrow market niche. In the 1970s, the company made millions on the CB radio craze that hit the United States. In the early 1980s, Radio Shack did well with an inexpensive personal computer. By the mid-1980s, the stores were becoming neglected, with much of the retailing profits being poured back into such unsuccessful manufacturing experiments as low-priced laptop computers and videodisc players.

In 1993, Tandy decided to sell its computer-making operations and placed new emphasis on retailing by bringing in a new president for RadioShack. The subsequent series of decisions resulted in a significant positive turnaround for RadioShack. The company placed more emphasis on telephones and cut a deal with the Sprint Corporation to make Sprint its exclusive wireless provider. Sprint, in turn, provided millions of dollars to update RadioShack stores. In the year 2000, the Tandy Corporation became the RadioShack Corporation.

Since then, RadioShack Corporation sold off its Incredible Universe stores and its Computer City superstores. These moves left RadioShack with its 7,000 RadioShack stores as its main presence in the retail arena.

The fast-paced and ever-changing electronics industry presented many decision alternatives to RadioShack. In the early years, the corporation decided to sell mostly Tandy products in RadioShack stores. Then the corporation opened a variety of types and sizes of retail stores, only to sell most of them later. At one point, Tandy invested heavily in manufacturing new items at the expense of retail operations, then it sold its computer manufacturing operations and renewed its focus on retail. At some point, many retail chains had the decision alternatives of 1) carrying only national brands (other company's brands), 2) carrying only private brands (their own labels), or 3) carrying a mix of the two.

Some of the states of nature that occurred include the rise and fall of CB radios, the exponential growth in personal computers and wireless telephones, the development of the Internet as a market and as an outlet for goods and services, a strong U.S. economy, and a growing atmosphere of disgust by large electronics manufacturers with electronics superstores and their deeply discounted merchandise.

The payoffs from some of these decisions for the RadioShack Corporation have been substantial. Some decisions resulted in revenue losses, thereby generating still other decisions.

In February of 2015, RadioShack filed for Chapter 11 bankruptcy; and in April of 2015, General Wireless Inc., an affiliate of Standard General LP, announced that they were acquiring the inventory and leases of 1,743 RadioShack stores. In addition, over 1400 RadioShack stores will be co-branded with Sprint.

Source: Adapted from Evan Ramstad, "Inside RadioShack's Surprising Turnaround," *The Wall Street Journal*, 8 June 1999, p. B1. www.wsj.com/articles/radioshack-files-for-bankruptcy-1423175389; www.prnewswire.com/news-releases/radioshack-reaches. . .

In making a decision based on a minimax regret criterion, the decision maker examines the maximum regret under each decision alternative and selects the minimum of these. The result is the stocks option, which has the minimum regret of $800. An investor who wants to minimize the maximum regret under the various states of the economy will choose to invest in stocks under the minimax regret strategy.

DEMONSTRATION PROBLEM 19.1

A manufacturing company is faced with a capacity decision. Its present production facility is running at nearly maximum capacity. Management is considering the following three capacity decision alternatives.

1. No expansion
2. Add on to the present facility
3. Build a new facility

The managers believe that if a large increase occurs in demand for their product in the near future, they will need to build a new facility to compete and capitalize on more efficient technological and design advances. However, if demand does not increase, it might be more profitable to maintain the present facility and add no capacity. A third decision alternative is to add on to the present facility, which will suffice for a moderate increase in demand and will be cheaper than building an entirely new facility. A drawback of adding to the old facility is that if there is a large demand for the product, the company will be unable to capitalize on new technologies and efficiencies, which cannot be built into the old plant.

The following decision table shows the payoffs (in $ millions) for these three decision alternatives for four different possible states of demand for the company's product (less demand, same demand, moderate increase in demand, and large increase in demand). Use these data to determine which decision alternative would be selected by the maximax criterion and the maximin criterion. Use $\alpha = .4$ and the Hurwicz criterion to determine the decision alternative. Calculate an opportunity loss table and determine the decision alternative by using the minimax regret criterion.

		State of Demand			
		Less	No Change	Moderate Increase	Large Increase
Capacity Decision	No Expansion	−$3	$2	$3	$6
	Add On	−$40	−$28	$10	$20
	Build a New Facility	−$210	−$145	−$5	$55

Solution: The maximum and minimum payoffs under each decision alternative follow.

	Maximum	Minimum
No Expansion	$ 6	−$ 3
Add On	$20	−$ 40
Build a New Facility	$55	−$210

Using the maximax criterion, the decision makers select the maximum of the maximum payoffs under each decision alternative. This value is the maximum of {$6, $20, $55} = $55, or the selection of the decision alternative of building a new facility and maximizing the maximum payoff ($55).

Using the maximin criterion, the decision makers select the maximum of the minimum payoffs under each decision alternative. This value is the maximum of {−$3, −$40, −$210} = −$3. They select the decision alternative of no expansion and maximize the minimum payoff (−$3).

Following are the calculations for the Hurwicz criterion with $\alpha = .4$.

$$\text{No Expansion} \qquad \$6(.4) + (-\$3)(.6) \quad = \quad \$0.60$$
$$\text{Add On} \qquad \$20(.4) + (-\$40)(.6) \quad = \quad -\$16.00$$
$$\text{Build a New Facility} \quad \$55(.4) + (-\$210)(.6) = -\$104.00$$

Using the Hurwicz criterion, the decision makers would select no expansion as the maximum of these weighted values ($.60).

Following is the opportunity loss table for this capacity choice problem. Note that each opportunity loss is calculated by taking the maximum payoff under each state of nature and subtracting each of the other payoffs under that state from that maximum value.

		State of Demand			
		Less	No Change	Moderate Increase	Large Increase
	No Expansion	$0	$0	$7	$49
Capacity Decision	Add On	$37	$30	$0	$35
	Build a New Facility	$207	$147	$15	$0

Using the minimax regret criterion on this opportunity loss table, the decision makers first select the maximum regret under each decision alternative.

Decision Alternative	Maximum Regret
No Expansion	49
Add On	37
Build a New Facility	207

Next, the decision makers select the decision alternative with the minimum regret, which is to add on, with a regret of $37.

19.2 Problems

19.1. Use the decision table given here to complete parts (a) through (d).

		State of Nature		
		s_1	s_2	s_3
	d_1	250	175	−25
Decision Alternative	d_2	110	100	70
	d_3	390	140	−80

a. Use the maximax criterion to determine which decision alternative to select.

b. Use the maximin criterion to determine which decision alternative to select.

c. Use the Hurwicz criterion to determine which decision alternative to select. Let $\alpha = .3$ and then let $\alpha = .8$ and compare the results.

d. Compute an opportunity loss table from the data. Use this table and a minimax regret criterion to determine which decision alternative to select.

19.2. Use the decision table given here to complete parts (a) through (d)

		State of Nature			
		s_1	s_2	s_3	s_4
	d_1	50	70	120	110
	d_2	80	20	75	100
Decision Alternative	d_3	20	45	30	60
	d_4	100	85	−30	−20
	d_5	0	−10	65	80

a. Use the maximax criterion to determine which decision alternative to select.

b. Use the maximin criterion to determine which decision alternative to select.

c. Use the Hurwicz criterion to determine which decision alternative to select. Let $\alpha = .5$.

d. Compute an opportunity loss table from the data. Use this table and a minimax regret criterion to determine which decision alternative to select.

19.3. Election results can affect the payoff from certain types of investments. Suppose a brokerage firm is faced with the prospect of investing $20 million a few weeks before the national election for president of the United States. They feel that if a Republican is elected, certain types of investments will do quite well; but if a Democrat is elected, other types of investments will be more desirable. To complicate the situation, an independent candidate, if elected, is likely to cause investments to behave in a different manner. Following are the payoffs for different investments under different political scenarios. Use the data to reach a conclusion about which decision alternative to select. Use both the maximax and maximin criteria and compare the answers.

		Election Winner		
		Republican	Democrat	Independent
	A	60	15	−25
	B	10	25	30
Investment	C	−10	40	15
	D	20	25	5

19.4. The introduction of a new product into the marketplace is quite risky. The percentage of new product ideas that successfully make it into the marketplace is as low as 1%. Research and development costs must be recouped, along with marketing and production costs. However, if a new product is warmly received by customers, the payoffs can be great. Following is a payoff table (decision table) for the production of a new product under different states of the market. Notice that the decision alternatives are to not produce the product at all, produce a few units of the product, and produce many units of the product. The market may be not receptive to the product, somewhat receptive to the product, and very receptive to the product.

a. Use this matrix and the Hurwicz criterion to reach a decision. Let $\alpha = .6$.

b. Determine an opportunity loss table from this payoff table and use minimax regret to reach a decision.

		State of the Market		
		Not Receptive	Somewhat Receptive	Very Receptive
Production Alternative	Don't Produce	−50	−50	−50
	Produce Few	−200	300	400
	Produce Many	−600	100	1000

19.3

19.3 Decision Making Under Risk

In Section 19.1 we discussed making decisions in situations where it is certain which states of nature will occur. In section 19.2, we examined several strategies for making decisions when it is uncertain which state of nature will occur. In this section we examine decision making under risk. **Decision making under risk** occurs *when it is uncertain which states of nature will occur but the probability of each state of nature occurring has been determined.* Using these probabilities, we can develop some additional decision-making strategies.

In preceding sections, we discussed the dilemma of how best to invest $10,000. Four investment decision alternatives were identified and three states of the economy seemed possible (stagnant economy, slow-growth economy, and rapid-growth economy). Suppose we determine that there is a .25 probability of a stagnant economy, a .45 probability of a slow-growth economy, and a .30 probability of a rapid-growth economy. In a decision table, or payoff table, we place these probabilities next to each state of nature. Table 19.5 is a decision table for the investment example shown in Table 19.2 with the probabilities given in parentheses.

Decision Trees

Another way to depict the decision process is through the use of decision trees. **Decision trees** have a ☐ node to represent decision alternatives and a ◯ node to represent states of nature. If probabilities are available for states of nature, they are assigned to the line segment following the state-of-nature node symbol, ◯. Payoffs are displayed at the ends of the decision tree limbs. Figure 19.2 is a decision tree for the financial investment example given in Table 19.5.

TABLE 19.5 Decision Table with State of Nature Probabilities

		State of the Economy		
		Stagnant (.25)	Slow Growth (.45)	Rapid Growth (.30)
Investment Decision Alternative	Stocks	−$500	$700	$2,200
	Bonds	−$100	$600	$ 900
	CDs	$300	$500	$ 750
	Mixture	−$200	$650	$1,300

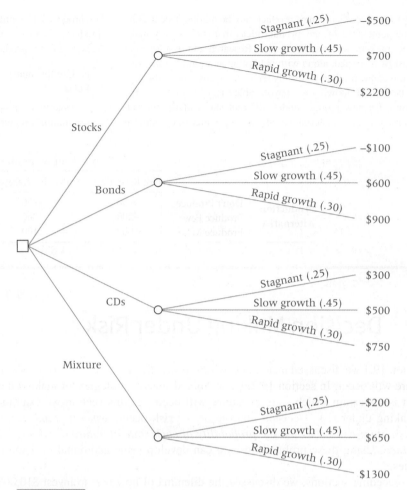

FIGURE 19.2   **Decision Tree for the Investment Example**

Expected Monetary Value (EMV)

One strategy that can be used in making decisions under risk is the **expected monetary value (EMV)** approach. A person who uses this approach is sometimes referred to as an **EMVer**. The expected monetary value of each decision alternative is calculated by multiplying the probability of each state of nature by the state's associated payoff and summing these products across the states of nature for each decision alternative, producing an expected monetary value for each decision alternative. The decision maker compares the expected monetary values for the decision alternatives and selects the alternative with the highest expected monetary value.

As an example, we can compute the expected monetary value for the $10,000 investment problem displayed in Table 19.5 and Figure 19.2 with the associated probabilities. We use the following calculations to find the expected monetary value for the decision alternative *Stocks*.

Expected Value for Stagnant Economy   = (.25)(−$500) = −$125
Expected Value for Slow-Growth Economy   = (.45)($700) = $315
Expected Value for Rapid-Growth Economy = (.30)($2,200) = $660

The expected monetary value of investing in stocks is

$$-\$125 + \$315 + \$660 = \$850$$

The calculations for determining the expected monetary value for the decision alternative *Bonds* follow.

Expected Value for Stagnant Economy $= (.25)(-\$100) = -\$25$
Expected Value for Slow-Growth Economy $= (.45)(\$600) = \$270$
Expected Value for Rapid-Growth Economy $= (.30)(\$900) = \$270$

The expected monetary value of investing in bonds is

$$-\$25 + \$270 + \$270 = \$515$$

The expected monetary value for the decision alternative *CDs* is found by the following calculations.

Expected Value for Stagnant Economy $= (.25)(\$300) = \$75$
Expected Value for Slow-Growth Economy $= (.45)(\$500) = \$225$
Expected Value for Rapid-Growth Economy $= (.30)(\$750) = \$225$

The expected monetary value of investing in CDs is

$$\$75 + \$225 + \$225 = \$525$$

The following calculations are used to find the expected monetary value for the decision alternative *Mixture*.

Expected Value for Stagnant Economy $= (.25)(-\$200) = -\$50$
Expected Value for Slow-Growth Economy $= (.45)(\$650) = \$292.50$
Expected Value for Rapid-Growth Economy $= (.30)(\$1,300) = \$390$

The expected monetary value of investing in a mixture is

$$-\$50 + \$292.50 + \$390 = \$632.50$$

A decision maker using expected monetary value as a strategy will choose the maximum of the expected monetary values computed for each decision alternative.

$$\text{Maximum of } \{\$850, \ \$515, \ \$525, \ \$632.5\} = \$850$$

The maximum of the expected monetary values is $850, which is produced from a stock investment. An EMVer chooses to invest in stocks on the basis of this information.

This process of expected monetary value can be depicted on decision trees like the one in Figure 19.2. Each payoff at the end of a branch of the tree is multiplied by the associated probability of that state of nature. The resulting products are summed across all states for a given decision choice, producing an expected monetary value for that decision alternative. These expected monetary values are displayed on the decision tree at the chance or state-of-nature nodes, ○.

The decision maker observes these expected monetary values. The optimal expected monetary value is the one selected and is displayed at the decision node in the tree, □. The decision alternative pathways leading to lesser, or nonoptimal, monetary values are marked with a double vertical line symbol, ‖, to denote rejected decision alternatives. **Figure 19.3** depicts the EMV analysis on the decision tree in Figure 19.2.

The strategy of expected monetary value is based on a long-run average. If a decision maker could "play this game" over and over with the probabilities and payoffs remaining the same, he or she could *expect* to earn an average of $850 in the long run by choosing to invest in stocks. The reality is that for any *one* occasion, the investor will earn payoffs of either −$500, $700, or $2,200 on a stock investment, depending on which state of the economy occurs. The investor will not earn $850 at any *one* time on this decision, but he or she could average a profit of $850 if the investment continued through time. With an investment of this size, the investor will potentially have the chance to make this decision several times. Suppose, on the other hand, an investor has to decide whether to spend $5 million to drill an oil well. Expected monetary values might not mean as much to the decision maker if he or she has only enough financial support to make this decision once.

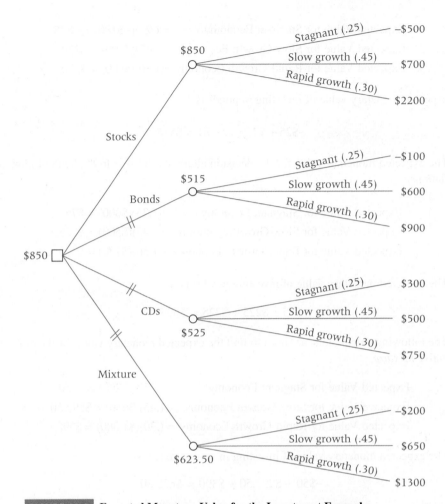

FIGURE 19.3 Expected Monetary Value for the Investment Example

DEMONSTRATION PROBLEM 19.2

Recall the capacity decision scenario presented in Demonstration Problem 19.1. Suppose probabilities have been determined for the states of demand such that there is a .10 probability that demand will be less, a .25 probability that there will be no change in demand, a .40 probability that there will be a moderate increase in demand, and a .25 probability that there will be a large increase in demand. Use the data presented in the problem, which are restated here, and the included probabilities to compute expected monetary values and reach a decision conclusion based on these findings.

		State of Demand		
		Less (.10)	No Change (.25)	Moderate Increase (.40)	Large Increase (.25)
Capacity Decision	No Expansion	−$3	$2	$3	$6
	Add On	−$40	−$28	$10	$20
	Build a New Facility	−$210	−$145	−$5	$55

Solution: The expected monetary value for no expansion is

$$(-\$3)(.10) + (\$2)(.25) + (\$3)(.40) + (\$6)(.25) = \$2.90$$

The expected monetary value for adding on is

$$(-\$40)(.10) + (-\$28)(.25) + (\$10)(.40) + (\$20)(.25) = -\$2.00$$

The expected monetary value for building a new facility is

$$(-\$210)(.10) + (-\$145)(.25) + (-\$5)(.40) + (\$55)(.25) = -\$45.50$$

The decision maker who uses the EMV criterion will select the no-expansion decision alternative because it results in the highest long-run average payoff, $2.90. It is possible that the decision maker will only have one chance to make this decision at this company. In such a case, the decision maker will not average $2.90 for selecting no expansion but rather will get a payoff of −$3.00, $2.00, $3.00, or $6.00, depending on which state of demand follows the decision.

This analysis can be shown through the use of a decision tree.

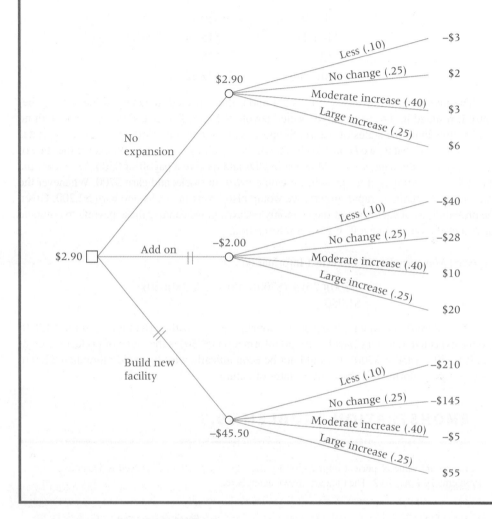

Expected Value of Perfect Information

What is the value of knowing which state of nature will occur and when? The answer to such a question can provide insight into how much it is worth to pay for market or business research. The **expected value of perfect information** is *the difference between the payoff that would occur if the decision maker knew which states of nature would occur and the expected monetary payoff from the best decision alternative when there is no information about the occurrence of the states of nature.*

Expected Value of Perfect Information

= Expected Monetary Payoff with Perfect Information
−Expected Monetary Value without Information

As an example, consider the $10,000 investment example with the probabilities of states of nature shown.

		State of the Economy		
		Stagnant (.25)	Slow Growth (.45)	Rapid Growth (.30)
Investment	Stocks	−$500	$700	$2,200
Decision	Bonds	−$100	$600	$900
Alternative	CDs	$300	$500	$750
	Mixture	−$200	$650	$1,300

The following expected monetary values were computed for this problem.

Stocks	$850
Bonds	515
CDs	525
Mixture	632.50

The investment of stocks was selected under the expected monetary value strategy because it resulted in the maximum expected payoff of $850. This decision was made with no information about the states of nature. Suppose we could obtain information about the states of the economy; that is, we *know* which state of the economy will occur. Whenever the state of the economy is stagnant, we would invest in CDs and receive a payoff of $300. Whenever the state of the economy is slow growth, we would invest in stocks and earn $700. Whenever the state of the economy is rapid growth, we would also invest in stocks and earn $2,200. Given the probabilities of each state of the economy occurring, we can use these payoffs to compute an expected monetary payoff of perfect information.

Expected Monetary Payoff of Perfect Information

$$= (\$300)(.25) + (\$700)(.45) + (\$2,200)(.30)$$
$$= \$1,050$$

The difference between this expected monetary payoff with perfect information ($1,050) and the expected monetary payoff with no information ($850) is the value of perfect information ($1,050 − $850 = $200). It would not be economically wise to spend more than $200 to obtain perfect information about these states of nature.

DEMONSTRATION PROBLEM 19.3

Compute the value of perfect information for the capacity problem discussed in Demonstration Problems 19.1 and 19.2. The data are shown again here.

		State of Demand			
		Less (.10)	No Change (.25)	Moderate Increase (.40)	Large Increase (.25)
	No Expansion	−$3	$2	$3	$6
Capacity Decision	Add On	−$40	−$28	$10	$20
	Build a New Facility	−$210	−$145	−$5	$55

Solution: The expected monetary value (payoff) under no information computed in Demonstration Problem 19.2 was $2.90 (recall that all figures are in $ millions). If the decision makers had perfect information, they would select no expansion for the state of less demand, no expansion for the state of no change, add on for the state of moderate increase, and build a new facility for the state of large increase. The expected payoff of perfect information is computed as

$$(-\$3)(.10) + (\$2)(.25) + (\$10)(.40) + (\$55)(.25) = \$17.95$$

The expected value of perfect information is

$$\$17.95 - \$2.90 = \$15.05$$

In this case, the decision makers might be willing to pay up to $15.05 ($ million) for perfect information.

Utility

As pointed out in the preceding section, expected monetary value decisions are based on long-run averages. Some situations do not lend themselves to expected monetary value analysis because these situations involve relatively large amounts of money and one-time decisions. Examples of these one-time decisions might be drilling an oil well, building a new production facility, merging with another company, ordering 100 new 737s, or buying a professional sports franchise. In analyzing the alternatives in such decisions, a concept known as utility can be helpful.

Utility is the degree of pleasure or displeasure a decision maker has in being involved in the outcome selection process given the risks and opportunities available. Suppose a person has the chance to enter a contest with a 50–50 chance of winning $100,000. If the person wins the contest, he or she wins $100,000. If the person loses, he or she receives $0. There is no cost to enter this contest. The expected payoff of this contest for the entrant is

$$(\$100,000)(.50) + (\$0)(.50) = \$50,000$$

In thinking about this contest, the contestant realizes that he or she will never get $50,000. The $50,000 is the long-run average payoff if the game is played over and over. Suppose contest administrators offer the contestant $30,000 not to play the game. Would the player take the money and drop out of the contest? Would a certain payoff of $30,000 outdraw a .50 chance at $100,000? The answer to this question depends, in part, on the person's financial situation and on his or her propensity to take risks. If the contestant is a multimillionaire, he or she might be willing to take big risks and even refuse $70,000 to drop out of the contest, because $70,000 does not significantly increase his or her worth. On the other hand, a person on welfare who is offered $20,000 not to play the contest might take the money because $20,000 is worth a great deal to him or her. In addition, two different people on welfare might have different risk-taking profiles. One might be a risk taker who, in spite of a need for money, is not willing to take less than $70,000 or $80,000 to pull out of a contest. The same could be said for the wealthy person.

Utility theory provides a mechanism for determining whether a person is a risk taker, a risk avoider, or an EMVer for a given decision situation. Consider the contest just described. A person receives $0 if he or she does not win the contest and $100,000 if he or she does win the contest. How much money would it take for a contestant to be indifferent between participating in the contest and dropping out? Suppose we examine three possible contestants, X, Y, and Z.

X is indifferent between receiving $20,000 and a .50 chance of winning the contest. For any amount more than $20,000, X will take the money and not play the game. As we stated before, a .50 chance of winning yields an expected payoff of $50,000. Suppose we increase the chance of winning to .80, so that the expected monetary payoff is $80,000. Now X is indifferent between receiving $50,000 and playing the game and will drop out of the game for any amount more than $50,000. In virtually all cases, X is willing to take less money than the expected payoff to quit the game. X is referred to as a **risk avoider**. Many of us are risk avoiders. For this reason, we pay insurance companies to cover our personal lives, our homes, our businesses, our cars, and so on, even when we know the odds are in the insurance companies' favor. We see the potential to lose at such games as unacceptable, so we bail out of the games for less than the expected payoff and pay out more than the expected cost to avoid the game.

Y, on the other hand, loves such contests. It would take about $70,000 to get Y not to play the game with a .50 chance of winning $100,000, even though the expected payoff is only $50,000. Suppose Y were told that there was only a .20 chance of winning the game. How much would it take for Y to become indifferent to playing? It might take $40,000 for Y to be indifferent, even though the expected payoff for a .20 chance is only $20,000. Y is a **risk taker** and enjoys playing risk-taking games. It always seems to take more than the expected payoff to get Y to drop out of the contest.

Z is an EMVer. Z is indifferent between receiving $50,000 and having a .50 chance of winning $100,000. To get Z out of the contest if there is only a .20 chance of winning, the contest directors would have to offer Z about $20,000 (the expected value). Likewise, if there were an .80 chance of winning, it would take about $80,000 to get Z to drop out of the contest. Z makes a decision by going with the long-run averages even in one-time decisions.

Figure 19.4 presents a graph with the likely shapes of the utility curves for X, Y, and Z. This graph is constructed for the game using the payoff range of $0 to $100,000; in-between values can be offered to the players in an effort to buy them out of the game. These units are displayed along what is normally the *x* axis. Along the *y* axis are the probabilities of winning the game, ranging from .0 to 1.0. A straight line through the middle of the values represents the EMV responses. If a person plays the game with a .50 chance of winning, he or she is indifferent to taking $50,000 not to play and playing. For .20, it is $20,000. For .80, it is $80,000.

Notice in the graph that where the chance of winning is .50, contestant X is willing to drop out of the game for $20,000. This point, ($20,000, .50), is above the EMV line. When the chance is .20, X will drop out for $5,000; for a chance of .80, X will drop out for $50,000. Both of these points, ($5,000, .20) and ($50,000, .80), are above the EMV line also.

Y, in contrast, requires $80,000 to be indifferent to a .50 chance of winning. Hence, the point ($80,000, .50) is below the EMV line. Contest officials will have to offer Y at least $40,000 for Y to become indifferent to a .20 chance of winning. This point, ($40,000, .20), also is below the EMV line.

X is a risk avoider and Y is a risk taker. Z is an EMVer. In the utility graph in Figure 19.4, the risk avoider's curve is above the EMV line and the risk taker's curve is below the line.

As discussed earlier in the chapter, in making decisions under uncertainty risk takers might be more prone to use the maximax criterion and risk avoiders might be more prone to

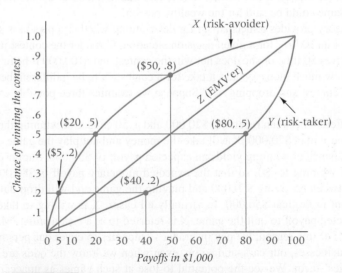

FIGURE 19.4 **Risk Curves for Game Players**

use the maximin criterion. The Hurwicz criterion allows the user to introduce his or her propensity toward risk into the analysis by using alpha.

Much information has been compiled and published about utility theory. The objective here is to give you a brief introduction to it through this example, thus enabling you to see that there are risk takers and risk avoiders along with EMVers. A more detailed treatment of this topic is beyond the scope of this text.

19.3 Problems

19.5. Use the following decision table to construct a decision tree.

State of Nature

		s_1	s_2	s_3	s_4	s_5
	d_1	50	20	15	5	1
Decision Alternative	d_2	75	50	20	−5	−20
	d_3	15	12	10	8	6

19.6. Suppose the probabilities of the states of nature occurring for Problem 19.5 are $s_1 = .15$, $s_2 = .25$, $s_3 = .30$, $s_4 = .10$, and $s_5 = .20$. Use these probabilities and expected monetary values to reach a conclusion about the decision alternatives in Problem 19.5.

19.7. How much is the expected monetary payoff with perfect information in Problem 19.5? From this answer and the decision reached in Problem 19.6, what is the value of perfect information?

19.8. Use the following decision table to complete parts (a) through (c).

State of Nature

		$s_1(.40)$	$s_2(.35)$	$s_3(.25)$
	d_1	150	250	500
	d_2	100	200	400
Decision Alternative	d_3	75	150	700
	d_4	125	450	650

a. Draw a decision tree to represent this payoff table.

b. Compute the expected monetary values for each decision and label the decision tree to indicate what the final decision would be.

c. Compute the expected payoff of perfect information. Compare this answer to the answer determined in part (b) and compute the value of perfect information.

19.9. A home buyer is completing application for a home mortgage. The buyer is given the option of "locking in" a mortgage loan interest rate or waiting 60 days until closing and locking in a rate on the day of closing. The buyer is not given the option of locking in at any time in between. If the buyer locks in at the time of application and interest rates go down, the loan will cost the buyer $150 per month more (−$150 payoff) than it would have if he or she had waited and locked in later. If the buyer locks in at the time of application and interest rates go up, the buyer has saved money by locking in at a lower rate. The amount saved under this condition is a payoff of +$200. If the buyer does not lock in at application and rates go up, he or she must pay more interest on the mortgage loan; the payoff is −$250. If the buyer does not lock in at application and rates go down, he or she

has reduced the interest amount and the payoff is +$175. If the rate does not change at all, there is a $0 payoff for locking in at the time of application and also a $0 payoff for not locking in at that time. There is a probability of .65 that the interest rates will rise by the end of the 60-day period, a .30 probability that they will fall, and a .05 probability that they will remain constant. Construct a decision table from this information.

Compute the expected monetary values from the table and reach a conclusion about the decision alternatives. Compute the value of perfect information.

19.10. A CEO faces a tough human resources decision. Because the company is currently operating in a budgetary crisis, the CEO will either lay off 1,000 people, lay off 5,000 people, or lay off no one. One of the problems for the CEO is that she cannot foretell what the business climate will be like in the coming months. If the CEO knew there would be a rapid rise in demand for the company's products, she might be inclined to hold off on layoffs and attempt to retain the workforce. If the business climate worsens, however, big layoffs seem to be the reasonable decision. Shown here are payoffs for each decision alternative under each state of the business climate. Included in the payoffs is the cost (loss of payoff) to the company when workers are laid off. The probability of each state occurring is given. Use the table and the information given to compute expected monetary values for each decision alternative and make a recommendation based on these findings. What is the most the CEO should be willing to pay for information about the occurrence of the various states of the business climate?

State of Business Climate

		Improved (.10)	About the Same (.40)	Worsened (.50)
Decision Alternative	No Layoffs	100	−300	−1700
	Lay Off 1000	−100	100	−700
	Lay Off 5000	−200	300	600

19.11. A person has a chance to invest $50,000 in a business venture. If the venture works, the investor will reap $200,000. If the venture fails, the investor will lose his money. It appears that there is about a .50 probability of the venture working. Using this information, answer the following questions.

a. What is the expected monetary value of this investment?

b. If this person decides not to undertake this venture, is he an EMVer, a risk avoider, or a risk taker? Why?

c. You would have to offer at least how much money to get a risk taker to quit pursuing this investment?

19.4 Revising Probabilities in Light of Sample Information

In Section 19.3 we discussed decision making under risk in which the probabilities of the states of nature were available and included in the analysis. Expected monetary values were computed on the basis of payoffs and probabilities. In this section we include the additional aspect of sample information in the decision analysis. If decision makers opt to purchase or in some other manner garner sample information, the probabilities of states of nature can be revised. The revisions can be incorporated into the decision-making process, resulting—one hopes—in a better decision.

In Chapter 4 we examined the use of Bayes' rule in the revision of probabilities, in which we started with a prior probability and revised it on the basis of some bit of information. Bayesian analysis can be applied to decision making under risk analysis to revise the prior probabilities of the states of nature, resulting in a clearer picture of the decision options. Usually the securing of additional information through sampling entails a cost. After the discussion of the revision of probabilities, we will examine the worth of sampling information. Perhaps the best way to explain the use of Bayes' rule in revising prior state-of-nature probabilities is by using an example.

Let us examine the revision of probabilities by using Bayes' rule with sampling information in the context of the $10,000 investment example discussed earlier in the chapter. Because the problem as previously stated is too complex to provide a clear example of this process, it is reduced here to simpler terms. The problem is still to determine how best to invest $10,000 for the next year. However, only two decision alternatives are available to the investor: bonds and stocks. Only two states of the investment climate can occur: no growth or rapid growth.

There is a .65 probability of no growth in the investment climate and a .35 probability of rapid growth. The payoffs are $500 for a bond investment in a no-growth state, $100 for a bond investment in a rapid-growth state, −$200 for a stock investment in a no-growth state, and a $1,100 payoff for a stock investment in a rapid-growth state. Table 19.6 presents the decision table (payoff table) for this problem.

Figure 19.5 shows a decision tree with the decision alternatives, the payoffs, the states of nature, the probabilities, and the expected monetary values of each decision alternative. The expected monetary value for the bonds decision alternative is

$$\text{EMV(bonds)} = \$500(.65) + \$100(.35) = \$360$$

The expected monetary value for the stocks decision alternative is

$$\text{EMV(stocks)} = -\$200(.65) + \$1,100(.35) = \$255$$

TABLE 19.6	Decision Table for the Investment Example	
	State of Nature	
	No Growth (.65)	Rapid Growth (.35)
Decision Alternative Bonds	$500	$ 100
Stocks	−$200	$1,100

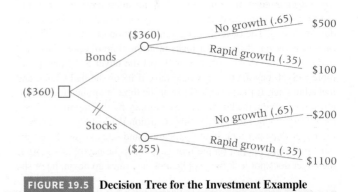

FIGURE 19.5 Decision Tree for the Investment Example

An EMVer would select the bonds decision alternative because the expected monetary value is $360, which is higher than that of the stocks alternative ($255).

Suppose the investor has a chance to obtain some information from an economic expert about the future state of the investment economy. This expert does not have a perfect record of forecasting, but she has predicted a no-growth economy about .80 of the time when such a state actually occurred. She has been slightly less successful in predicting rapid-growth economies, with a .70 probability of success. The following table shows her success and failure rates in forecasting these two states of the economy.

	Actual State of the Economy	
	No Growth (s_1)	Rapid Growth (s_2)
Forecaster predicts no growth (F_1)	.80	.30
Forecaster predicts rapid growth (F_2)	.20	.70

When the state of the economy is no growth, the forecaster will predict no growth .80 of the time, but she will predict rapid growth .20 of the time. When the state of the economy is rapid growth, she will predict rapid growth .70 of the time and no growth .30 of the time.

Using these conditional probabilities, we can revise prior probabilities of the states of the economy by using Bayes' rule, restated here from Chapter 4.

$$P(X_i \mid Y) = \frac{P(X_i) \cdot P(Y \mid X_i)}{P(X_1) \cdot P(Y \mid X_1) + P(X_2) \cdot P(Y \mid X_2) + \cdots + P(X_n) \cdot P(Y \mid X_n)}$$

Applying the formula to the problem, we obtain the revised probabilities shown in the following tables. Suppose the forecaster predicts no growth (F_1). The prior probabilities of the states of the economy are revised as shown in Table 19.7.

$P(F_1)$ is computed as follows.

$$P(F_1) = P(F_1 \cap s_1) + P(F_1 \cap s_2) = .520 + .105 = .625$$

The revised probabilities are computed as follows

$$P(s_1 \mid F_1) = \frac{P(F_1 \cap s_1)}{P(F_1)} = \frac{.520}{.625} = .832$$

$$P(s_2 \mid F_1) = \frac{P(F_1 \cap s_2)}{P(F_1)} = \frac{.105}{.625} = .168$$

The prior probabilities of the states of the economy are revised as shown in Table 19.8 for the case in which the forecaster predicts rapid growth (F_2).

TABLE 19.7 Revision Based on a Forecast of No Growth (F_1)

State of Economy	Prior Probabilities	Conditional Probabilities	Joint Probabilities	Revised Probabilities
No growth (s_1)	$P(s_1) = .65$	$P(F_1|s_1) = .80$	$P(F_1 \cap s_1) = .520$	$.520/.625 = .832$
Rapid growth (s_2)	$P(s_2) = .35$	$P(F_1|s_2) = .30$	$P(F_1 \cap s_2) = .105$	$.105/.625 = .168$
			$P(F_1) = .625$	

TABLE 19.8	Revision Based on a Forecast of Rapid Growth (F_2)			
State of Economy	Prior Probabilities	Conditional Probabilities	Joint Probabilities	Revised Probabilities
No growth (s_1)	$P(s_1) = .65$	$P(F_2\|s_1) = .20$	$P(F_2 \cap s_1) = .130$	$.130/.375 = .347$
Rapid growth (s_2)	$P(s_2) = .35$	$P(F_2\|s_2) = .70$	$P(F_2 \cap s_2) = .245$	$.245/.375 = .653$
			$P(F_2) = .375$	

These revised probabilities can be entered into a decision tree that depicts the option of buying information and getting a forecast, as shown in **Figure 19.6**. Notice that the first node is a decision node to buy the forecast. The next node is a state-of-nature node, where the forecaster will predict either a no-growth economy or a rapid-growth economy. It is a state of nature because the decision maker has no control over what the forecast will be. As a matter of fact, the decision maker has probably paid for this "independent" forecast. Once a forecast is made, the decision maker is faced with the decision alternatives of investing in bonds or investing in stocks. At the end of each investment alternative branch is a state of the economy of either no growth or rapid growth. The four revised probabilities calculated in Tables 19.7 and 19.8 are assigned to these states of economy. The payoffs remain the same. The probability of the forecaster predicting no growth comes from the sum of the joint probabilities in Table 19.7. This value of $P(F_1) = .625$ is assigned a position on the first set of states of nature (forecast). The probability of the forecaster predicting rapid growth comes from summing the joint probabilities in Table 19.8. This value of $P(F_2) = .375$ is also assigned a position on the first set of states of nature (forecasts).

The decision maker can make a choice from this decision tree after the expected monetary values are calculated.

In Figure 19.6, the payoffs are the same as in the decision table without information. However, the probabilities of no-growth and rapid-growth states have been revised. Multiplying the payoffs by these revised probabilities and summing them for each investment produces expected monetary values at the state-of-economy nodes. Moving back to the decision nodes

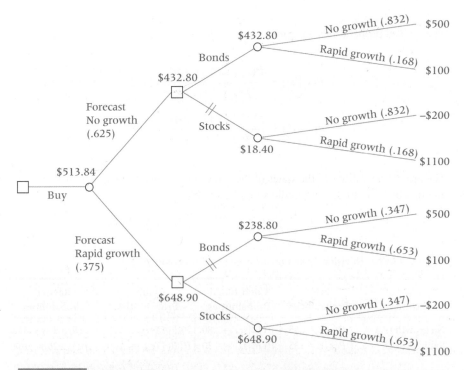

FIGURE 19.6 Decision Tree for the Investment Example after Revision of Probabilities

preceding these values, the investor has the opportunity to invest in either bonds or stocks. The investor examines the expected monetary values and selects the investment with the highest value. For the decision limb in which the forecaster predicted no growth, the investor selects the bonds investment, which yields an expected monetary value of $432.80 (as opposed to $18.40 from stocks). For the decision limb in which the forecaster predicted rapid growth, the investor selects the stocks investment, which yields an expected monetary value of $648.90 (as opposed to $238.80 for bonds).

The investor is thus faced with the opportunity to earn an expected monetary value of $432.80 if the forecaster predicts no growth or $648.90 if the forecaster predicts rapid growth. How often does the forecaster predict each of these states of the economy to happen? Using the sums of the joint probabilities from Tables 19.7 and 19.8, the decision maker gets the probabilities of each of these forecasts.

$$P(F_1) = .625 \,(\text{no growth})$$
$$P(F_2) = .375 \,(\text{rapid growth})$$

Entering these probabilities into the decision tree at the first probability node with the forecasts of the states of the economy and multiplying them by the expected monetary value of each state yields an overall expected monetary value of the opportunity.

$$\text{EMV for Opportunity} = \$432.80\,(.625) + \$648.90\,(.375) = \$513.84$$

Expected Value of Sample Information

The preceding calculations for the investment example show that the expected monetary value of the opportunity is $513.84 with sample information, but it is only $360 without sample information, as shown in Figure 19.5. Using the sample information appears to profit the decision maker.

$$\text{Apparent Profit of Using Sample Information} = \$513.84 - \$360 = \$153.84$$

How much did this sample information cost? If the sample information is not free, less than $153.84 is gained by using it. How much is it worth to use sample information? Obviously, the decision maker should not pay more than $153.84 for sample information because an expected $360 can be earned without the information. In general, the expected value of sample information is worth no more than *the difference between the expected monetary value with the information and the expected monetary value without the information.*

Expected Value of Sample Information

Expected Value of Sample Information
 	
     = Expected Monetary Value with Information
      − Expected Monetary Value without Information

Suppose the decision maker had to pay $100 for the forecaster's prediction. The expected monetary value of the decision with information shown in Figure 19.6 is reduced from $513.84 to $413.84, which is still superior to the $360 expected monetary value without sample information. Figure 19.7 is the decision tree for the investment information with the options of buying the information or not buying the information included. The tree is constructed by combining the decision trees from Figures 19.5 and 19.6 and including the cost of buying information ($100) and the expected monetary value with this purchased information ($413.84).

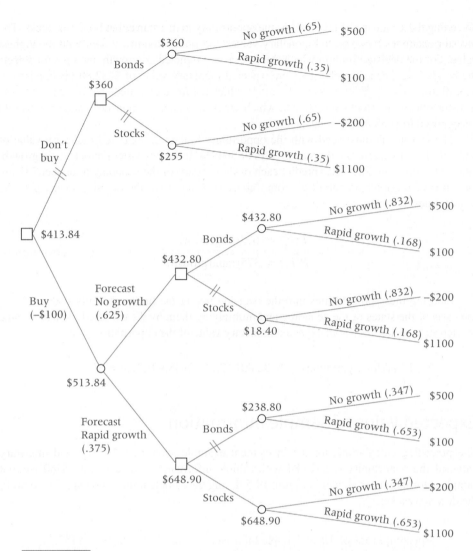

FIGURE 19.7 **Decision Tree for the Investment Example—All Options Included**

DEMONSTRATION PROBLEM 19.4

In Demonstration Problem 19.1, the decision makers were faced with the opportunity to increase capacity to meet a possible increase in product demand. Here we reduced the decision alternatives and states of nature and altered the payoffs and probabilities. Use the following decision table to create a decision tree that displays the decision alternatives, the payoffs, the probabilities, the states of demand, and the expected monetary payoffs. The decision makers can buy information about the states of demand for $5 (recall that amounts are in $ millions). Incorporate this fact into your decision. Calculate the expected value of sampling information for this problem.

The decision alternatives are: no expansion or build a new facility. The states of demand and prior probabilities are: less demand (.20), no change (.30), or large increase (.50).

		State of Demand		
		Less (.20)	No Change (.30)	Large Increase (.50)
Decision	No Expansion	−$ 3	$ 2	$ 6
Alternative	New Facility	−$50	−$20	$65

The state-of-demand forecaster has historically not been accurate 100% of the time. For example, when the demand was less, the forecaster correctly predicted it .75 of the time. When there was no change in demand, the forecaster correctly predicted it .80 of the time. Sixty-five percent of the time the forecaster correctly forecast large increases when large increases occurred. Shown next are the probabilities that the forecaster will predict a particular state of demand under the actual states of demand.

		State of Demand		
		Less	No Change	Large Increase
Forecast	Less	.75	.10	.05
	No Change	.20	.80	.30
	Large Increase	.05	.10	.65

Solution: The following figure is the decision tree for this problem when no sample information is purchased.

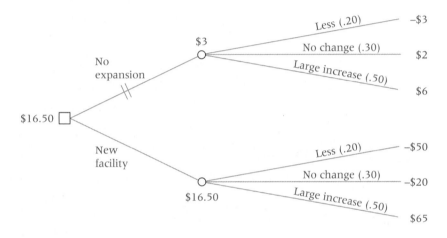

In light of sample information, the prior probabilities of the three states of demand can be revised. Shown here are the revisions for F_1 (forecast of less demand), F_2 (forecast of no change in demand), and F_3 (forecast of large increase in demand).

State of Demand	Prior Probability	Conditional Probability	Joint Probability	Revised Probability
For Forecast of Less Demand (F_1)				
Less (s_1)	.20	$P(F_1|s_1) = .75$	$P(F_1 \cap s_1) = .150$	$.150/.205 = .732$
No change (s_2)	.30	$P(F_1|s_2) = .10$	$P(F_1 \cap s_2) = .030$	$.030/.205 = .146$
Large increase (s_3)	.50	$P(F_1|s_3) = .05$	$P(F_1 \cap s_3) = .025$	$.025/.205 = .122$
			$P(F_1) = .205$	
For Forecast of No Change in Demand (F_2)				
Less (s_1)	.20	$P(F_2|s_1) = .20$	$P(F_2 \cap s_1) = .040$	$.040/.430 = .093$
No change (s_2)	.30	$P(F_2|s_2) = .80$	$P(F_2 \cap s_2) = .240$	$.240/.430 = .558$
Large increase (s_3)	.50	$P(F_2|s_3) = .30$	$P(F_2 \cap s_3) = .150$	$.150/.430 = .349$
			$P(F_2) = .430$	
For Forecast of Large Increase in Demand (F_3)				
Less (s_1)	.20	$P(F_3|s_1) = .05$	$P(F_3 \cap s_1) = .010$	$.010/.365 = .027$
No change (s_2)	.30	$P(F_3|s_2) = .10$	$P(F_3 \cap s_2) = .030$	$.030/.365 = .082$
Large increase (s_3)	.50	$P(F_3|s_3) = .65$	$P(F_3 \cap s_3) = .325$	$.325/.365 = .890$
			$P(F_3) = .365$	

From these revised probabilities and other information, the decision tree containing alternatives and states using sample information can be constructed. The following figure is the decision tree containing the sample information alternative *and* the portion of the tree for the alternative of no sampling information.

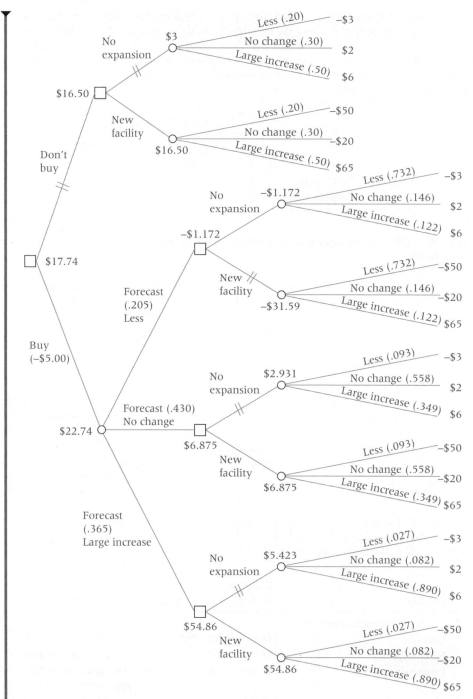

If the decision makers calculate the expected monetary value after buying the sample information, they will see that the value is $17.74. The final expected monetary value with sample information is calculated as follows.

$$\text{EMV at Buy Node: } -\$1.172(.205) + \$6.875(.430) + \$54.86(.365) = \$22.74$$

However, the sample information cost $5. Hence, the net expected monetary value at the buy node is

$$\$22.74 \text{ (EMV)} - \$5.00 \text{ (cost of information)} = \$17.74 \text{ (net expected monetary value)}$$

The worth of the sample information is

Expected Monetary Value of Sample Information

= Expected Monetary Value with Sample Information
 −Expected Monetary Value without Sample Information

= $22.74 − $16.50 = $6.24

19.4 Problems

19.12. Shown here is a decision table from a business situation. The decision maker has an opportunity to purchase sample information in the form of a forecast. With the sample information, the prior probabilities can be revised. Also shown are the probabilities of forecasts from the sample information for each state of nature. Use this information to answer parts (a) through (d).

	State of Nature	
	$s_1(.30)$	$s_2(.70)$
Alternative d_1	$350	−$100
d_2	−$200	$325

		State of Nature	
		s_1	s_2
Forecast	s_1	.90	.25
	s_2	.10	.75

a. Compute the expected monetary value of this decision without sample information.

b. Compute the expected monetary value of this decision with sample information.

c. Use a tree diagram to show the decision options in parts (a) and (b).

d. Calculate the value of the sample information.

19.13. a. A car rental agency faces the decision of buying a fleet of cars, all of which will be the same size. It can purchase a fleet of small cars, medium cars, or large cars. The smallest cars are the most fuel efficient and the largest cars are the greatest fuel users. One of the problems for the decision makers is that they do not know whether the price of fuel will increase or decrease in the near future. If the price increases, the small cars are likely to be most popular. If the price decreases, customers may demand the larger cars. Following is a decision table with these decision alternatives, the states of nature, the probabilities, and the payoffs. Use this information to determine the expected monetary value for this problem.

		State of Nature	
		Fuel Decrease (.60)	Fuel Increase (.40)
Decision Alternative	Small Cars	−$225	$425
	Medium Cars	$125	−$150
	Large Cars	$350	−$400

b. The decision makers have an opportunity to purchase a forecast of the world oil markets that has some validity in predicting gasoline prices. The following matrix gives the probabilities of these forecasts being correct for various states of nature. Use this information to revise the prior probabilities and recompute the expected monetary value on the basis of sample information. What is the expected value of sample information for this problem? Should the agency decide to buy the forecast?

		State of Nature	
		Fuel Decrease	Fuel Increase
Forecast	Fuel Decrease	.75	.15
	Fuel Increase	.25	.85

19.14. a. A small group of investors is considering planting a tree farm. Their choices are (1) don't plant trees, (2) plant a small number of trees, or (3) plant a large number of trees. The investors are concerned about the demand for trees. If demand for trees declines, planting a large tree farm would probably result in a loss. However, if a large increase in the demand for trees occurs, not planting a tree farm could mean a large loss in revenue opportunity. They determine that three states of demand are possible: (1) demand declines, (2) demand remains the same as it is, and (3) demand increases. Use the following decision table to compute an expected monetary value for this decision opportunity.

		State of Demand		
		Decline (.20)	Same (.30)	Increase (.50)
Decision Alternative	Don't Plant	$20	$0	−$40
	Small Tree Farm	−$90	$10	$175
	Large Tree Farm	−$600	−$150	$800

b. Industry experts who believe they can forecast what will happen in the tree industry contact the investors. The following matrix shows the probabilities with which it is believed these "experts" can foretell tree demand. Use these probabilities to revise the prior probabilities of the states of nature and recompute the expected value of sample information. How much is this sample information worth?

		State of Demand		
		Decrease	Same	Increase
Forecast	Decrease	.70	.02	.02
	Same	.25	.95	.08
	Increase	.05	.03	.90

19.15. a. Some oil speculators are interested in drilling an oil well. The rights to the land have been secured and they must decide whether to drill. The states of nature are that oil is present or that no oil is present. Their two decision alternatives are drill or don't drill. If they strike oil, the well will pay $1 million. If they have a dry hole, they will lose $100,000. If they don't drill, their payoffs are $0 when oil is present and $0 when it is not. The probability that oil is present is .11. Use this information to construct a decision table and compute an expected monetary value for this problem.

b. The speculators have an opportunity to buy a geological survey, which sometimes helps in determining whether oil is present in the ground. When the geologists say there is oil in the ground, there actually is oil .20 of the time. When there is oil in the ground, .80 of the time the geologists say there is no oil. When there is no oil in the ground, .90 of the time the geologists say there is no oil. When there is no oil in the ground, .10 of the time the geologists say there is oil. Use this information to revise the prior probabilities of oil being present in the ground and compute the expected monetary value based on sample information. What is the value of the sample information for this problem?

Decision Dilemma Solved

Decision Making at the CEO Level

The study of CEOs revealed that decision making takes place in many different areas of business. No matter what the decision concerns, it is critical for the CEO or manager to identify the decision alternatives. Sometimes decision alternatives are not obvious and can be identified only after considerable examination and brainstorming. Many different alternatives are available to decision makers in personnel, finance, operations, and so on. Alternatives can sometimes be obtained from worker suggestions and input. Others are identified through consultants or experts in particular fields. Occasionally, a creative and unobvious decision alternative is derived that proves to be the most successful choice.

Alex Trotman at Ford Motor, in a reorganization decision, chose the alternative of combining two operations into one unit. Other alternatives might have been to combine other operations into a unit (rather than the North American and European), create more units, or not reorganize at all. At Kodak, CEO George Fisher made the decision that the company would adopt digital and electronic imaging wholeheartedly. In addition, he determined that these new technologies would be interwoven with their paper and film products in such a manner as to be "seamless." Fisher had other alternatives available such as not entering the arena of digital and electronic imaging or entering it but keeping it separated from the paper and film operation.

CEOs need to identify as many states of nature that can occur under the decision alternatives as possible. What might happen to sales? Will product demand increase or decrease? What is the political climate for environmental or international monetary regulation? What will occur next in the business cycle? Will there be inflation? What will the competitors do? What new inventions or developments will occur? What is the investment climate? Identifying as many of these states as possible helps the decision maker examine decision alternatives in light of those states and calculate payoffs accordingly.

Many different states of nature may arise that will affect the outcome of CEO decisions. Ford Motor may find that the demand for a "world car" does not material, materializes so slowly that the company wastes their effort for many years, materializes as Trotman foresaw, or materializes even faster. The world economy might undergo a depression, a slowdown, a constant growth, or even an accelerated rate of growth. Political conditions in countries of the world might make an American "world car" unacceptable. The governments of the countries that would be markets for such a car might cause the countries to become more a part of the world economy, stay about the same, slowly withdraw from the world scene, or become isolated.

The decision maker should recognize whether he or she is a risk avoider or a risk taker. Does propensity toward risk vary by situation? Should it? How do the board of directors and stockholders view risk? Will the employees respond to risk taking or avoidance?

Successful CEOs may well incorporate risk taking, risk avoidance, and expected value decision making into their decisions. Perhaps the successful CEOs know when to take risks and when to pull back. Certainly, the decision by a successful company like Ford Motor, which had five of the top 10 vehicles at the time, to reorganize in an effort to make a "world car" is risk taking. Kodak's decision to embrace digital and electronic imaging and merge it with their paper and film operations is a risk-taking venture.

If successful, the payoffs from these CEO decisions could be great. The current success of Ford Motor may just scratch the surface if the company successfully sells their "world car" in the twenty-first century. On the other hand, the company could experience big losses or receive payoffs somewhere in between.

CEOs are not always able to visualize all decision alternatives. However, creative, inspired thinking along with the brainstorming of others and an extensive investigation of the facts and figures can successfully result in the identification of most of the possibilities. States of nature are unknown and harder to discern. However, awareness, insight, understanding, and knowledge of economies, markets, governments, and competitors can greatly aid a decision maker in considering possible states of nature that may impact the payoff of a decision along with the likelihood that such states of nature might occur. The payoffs for CEOs range from the loss of thousands of jobs including his/her own, loss of market share, and bankruptcy of the company, to worldwide growth, record stockholder dividends, and fame.

Ethical Considerations

Ethical considerations occasionally arise in decision analysis situations. The techniques presented in this chapter are for aiding the decision maker in selecting from among decision alternatives in light of payoffs and expected values. Payoffs do not always reflect all costs, including ethical considerations. The decision maker needs to decide whether to consider ethics in examining decision alternatives. What are some decision alternatives that raise ethical questions?

Some decision alternatives are environmentally damaging in the form of ground, air, or water pollution. Other choices endanger the health and safety of workers. In the area of human resources, some decision alternatives include eliminating jobs and laying off workers. Should the ethical issues involved in these decisions be factored into payoffs? For example, what effects would a layoff have on families and communities? Does a business have any moral obligation toward its workers and its community that should be taken into consideration in payoffs? Does a decision alternative involve producing a product that is detrimental to a customer or a customer's family? Some marketing decisions might involve the use of false or misleading advertising. Are distorted or misleading advertising attacks on competing brands unethical even when the apparent payoff is great?

States of nature are usually beyond the control of the decision maker; therefore, it seems unlikely that unethical behavior would be connected with a state of nature. However, obtaining sample or perfect information under which to make decisions about states of nature has the usual potential for unethical behavior in sampling.

In many cases, payoffs other than the dollar values assigned to a decision alternative should be considered. In using decision analysis with ethical behavior, the decision maker should attempt to factor into the payoffs the cost of pollution, safety features, human resource loss, and so on. Unethical behavior is likely to result in a reduction or loss of payoff.

Summary

Decision analysis is a branch of quantitative management in which mathematical and statistical approaches are used to assist decision makers in reaching judgments about alternative opportunities. Three types of decisions are (1) decisions made under certainty, (2) decisions made under uncertainty, and (3) decisions made with risk. Several aspects of the decision-making situation are decision alternatives, states of nature, and payoffs. Decision alternatives are the options open to decision makers from which they can choose. States of nature are situations or conditions that arise after the decision has been made over which the decision maker has no control. The payoffs are the gains or losses that the decision maker will reap from various decision alternatives. These three aspects (decision alternatives, states of nature, and payoffs) can be displayed in a decision table or payoff table.

Decision making under certainty is the easiest of the three types of decisions to make. In this case, the states of nature are known, and the decision maker merely selects the decision alternative that yields the highest payoff.

Decisions are made under uncertainty when the likelihoods of the states of nature occurring are unknown. Four approaches to making decisions under uncertainty are maximax criterion, maximin criterion, Hurwicz criterion, and minimax regret. The maximax criterion is an optimistic approach based on the notion that the best possible outcomes will occur. In this approach, the decision maker selects the maximum possible payoff under each decision alternative and then selects the maximum of these. Thus, the decision maker is selecting the maximum of the maximums.

The maximin criterion is a pessimistic approach. The assumption is that the worst case will happen under each decision alternative. The decision maker selects the minimum payoffs under each decision alternative and then picks the maximum of these as the best solution. Thus, the decision maker is selecting the best of the worst cases, or the maximum of the minimums.

The Hurwicz criterion is an attempt to give the decision maker an alternative to maximax and maximin that is somewhere between an optimistic and a pessimistic approach. With this approach, decision makers select a value called alpha between 0 and 1 to represent how optimistic they are. The maximum and minimum payoffs for each decision alternative are examined. The alpha weight is applied to the maximum payoff under each decision alternative and $1 - \alpha$ is applied to the minimum payoff. These two weighted values are combined for each decision alternative, and the maximum of these weighted values is selected.

Minimax regret is calculated by examining opportunity loss. An opportunity loss table is constructed by subtracting each payoff from the maximum payoff under each state of nature. This step produces a lost opportunity under each state. The maximum lost opportunity from each decision alternative is determined from the opportunity table. The minimum of these values is selected, and the corresponding decision alternative is chosen. In this way, the decision maker has reduced or minimized the regret, or lost opportunity.

In decision making with risk, the decision maker has some prior knowledge of the probability of each occurrence of each state of nature. With these probabilities, a weighted payoff referred to as expected monetary value (EMV) can be calculated for each decision alternative. A person who makes decisions based on these EMVs is called an EMVer. The expected monetary value is essentially the average payoff that would occur if the decision process were to be played out over a long period of time with the probabilities holding constant.

The expected value of perfect information can be determined by comparing the expected monetary value if the states of nature are known to the expected monetary value. The difference in the two is the expected value of perfect information.

Utility refers to a decision maker's propensity to take risks. People who avoid risks are called risk avoiders. People who are prone to take risks are referred to as risk takers. People who use EMV generally fall between these two categories. Utility curves can be sketched to ascertain or depict a decision maker's tendency toward risk.

By use of Bayes' theorem, the probabilities associated with the states of nature in decision making under risk can be revised when new information is obtained. This information can be helpful to the decision maker. However, it usually carries a cost for the decision maker. This cost can reduce the payoff of decision making with sample information. The expected monetary value with sample information can be compared to the expected monetary value without it to determine the value of sample information.

Key Terms

decision alternatives	decision table	expected value of sample	opportunity loss table
decision analysis	decision trees	information	payoffs
decision making under certainty	EMVer	Hurwicz criterion	payoff table
decision making under risk	expected monetary value (EMV)	maximax criterion	risk avoider
decision making under	expected value of perfect	maximin criterion	risk taker
uncertainty	information	minimax regret	states of nature

Formulas

Bayes' Rule

$$P(X_i \mid Y) = \frac{P(X_i) \cdot P(Y \mid X_i)}{P(X_1) \cdot P(Y \mid X_1) + P(X_2) \cdot P(Y \mid X_2) + \cdots + P(X_n) \cdot P(Y \mid X_n)}$$

Supplementary Problems

Calculating the Statistics

19.16. Use the following decision table to complete parts (a) through (d).

		State of Nature	
		s_1	s_2
	d_1	50	100
Decision Alternative	d_2	−75	200
	d_3	25	40
	d_4	75	10

a. Use the maximax criterion to determine which decision alternative to select.

b. Use the maximin criterion to determine which decision alternative to select.

c. Use the Hurwicz criterion to determine which decision alternative to select. Let $\alpha = .6$.

d. Compute an opportunity loss table from these data. Use this table and a minimax regret criterion to determine which decision alternative to select.

19.17. Use the following decision table to complete parts (a) through (c).

		State of Nature			
		$s_1(.30)$	$s_2(.25)$	$s_3(.20)$	$s_4(.25)$
Decision Alternative	d_1	400	250	300	100
	d_2	300	−100	600	200

a. Draw a decision tree to represent this decision table.

b. Compute the expected monetary values for each decision and label the decision tree to indicate what the final decision would be.

c. Compute the expected payoff of perfect information. Compare this answer to the answer determined in part (b) and compute the value of perfect information.

19.18. Shown here is a decision table. A forecast can be purchased by the decision maker. The forecaster is not correct 100% of the time. Also given is a table containing the probabilities of the forecast being correct under different states of nature. Use the first table to compute the expected monetary value of this decision without sample information. Use the second table to revise the prior probabilities of the various decision alternatives. From this and the first table, compute the expected monetary value with sample information. Construct a decision tree to represent the options, the payoffs, and the expected monetary values. Calculate the value of sample information.

		State of Nature	
		$s_1(.40)$	$s_2(.60)$
	d_1	$200	$150
Decision Alternative	d_2	−$75	$450
	d_3	$175	$125

		State of Nature	
		s_1	s_2
	s_1	.90	.30
Forecast	s_2	.10	.70

Testing Your Understanding

19.19. Managers of a manufacturing firm decided to add Christmas tree ornaments to their list of production items. However, they have not decided how many to produce because they are uncertain about the level of demand. Shown here is a decision table that has been constructed to help the managers in their decision situation. Use this table to answer parts (a) through (c).

		State of Demand		
		Small	Moderate	Large
Decision	Small Number	$200	$250	$300
Alternative	Modest Number	$100	$300	$600
(Produce)	Large Number	−$300	$400	$2,000

a. Use maximax and maximin criteria to evaluate the decision alternatives.

b. Construct an opportunity loss table and use minimax regret to select a decision alternative.

c. Compare the results of the maximax, maximin, and minimax regret criteria in selecting decision alternatives.

19.20. Some companies use production learning curves to set pricing strategies. They price their product lower than the initial cost of making the product; after some period of time, the learning curve takes effect and the product can be produced for less than its selling price. In this way, the company can penetrate new markets with aggressive pricing strategies and still make a long-term profit.

A company is considering using the learning curve to set its price on a new product. There is some uncertainty as to how soon, if at all, the production operation will learn to make the product more quickly and efficiently. If the learning curve does not drop enough or the initial price is too low, the company will be operating at a loss on this product. If the product is priced too high, the sales volume might be too low to justify production. Shown here is a decision table that contains as its states of nature several possible learning-curve scenarios. The decision alternatives are three different pricing strategies. Use this table and the Hurwicz criterion to make a decision about the pricing strategies with each given value of alpha.

		State of Nature		
		No Learning	Slow Learning	Fast Learning
Decision	Price Low	−$700	−$400	$1,200
Alternative	Price Medium	−$300	−$100	$550
	Price High	$100	$125	$150

a. $\alpha = .10$

b. $\alpha = .50$

c. $\alpha = .80$

d. Compare and discuss the decision choices in parts (a) through (c).

19.21. An entertainment company owns two amusement parks in the South. They are faced with the decision of whether to open the parks in the winter. If they choose to open the parks in the winter, they can leave the parks open during regular hours (as in the summer) or they can open only on the weekends. To some extent, the payoffs from opening the park hinge on the type of weather that occurs during the winter season. Following are the payoffs for various decision options about opening the park for two different weather scenarios: mild weather and severe weather. Use the information to construct a decision tree. Determine the expected monetary value and the value of perfect information.

		State of the Weather	
		Mild (.75)	Severe (.25)
Decision Alternative	Open Regular Hours	$2,000	−$2,500
	Open Weekends Only	$1,200	−$200
	Not Open at All	−$300	$100

19.22. A U.S. manufacturing company decided to consider producing a particular model of one of its products just for sale in Germany. Because of the German requirements, the product must be made specifically for German consumption and cannot be sold in the United States. Company officials believe the market for the product is highly price-sensitive. Because the product will be manufactured in the United States and exported to Germany, the biggest variable factor in being price competitive is the exchange rate between the two countries. If the dollar is strong, German consumers will have to pay more for the product in marks. If the dollar becomes weaker against the mark, Germans can buy more U.S. products for their money. The company officials are faced with decision alternatives of whether to produce the product. The states of the exchange rates are: dollar weaker, dollar stays the same, and dollar stronger. The probabilities of these states occurring are .35, .25, and .40, respectively. Some negative payoffs will result from not producing the product because of sunk development and market research costs and because of lost market opportunity. If the product is not produced, the payoffs are −$700 when the dollar gets weaker, −$200 when the dollar remains about the same, and $150 when the dollar gets stronger. If the product is produced, the payoffs are $1,800 when the dollar gets weaker, $400 when the exchange rates stay about the same, and −$1,600 when the dollar gets stronger.

Use this information to construct a decision tree and a decision table for this decision-making situation. Use the probabilities to compute the expected monetary values of the decision alternatives. On the basis of this information, which decision choice should the company make? Compute the expected monetary value of perfect information and the value of perfect information.

19.23. a. A small retailer began as a mom-and-pop operation selling crafts and consignment items. During the past two years, the store's volume grew significantly. The owners are trying to decide whether to purchase an automated checkout system. Their present manual system is slow. They are concerned about lost business due to inability to ring up sales quickly. The automated system would also offer some accounting and inventory advantages. The problem is that the automated system carries a large fixed cost, and the owners feel that sales volume would have to grow to justify the cost.

The following decision table contains the decision alternatives for this situation, the possible states of future sales, prior probabilities of those states occurring, and the payoffs. Use this information to compute the expected monetary payoffs for the alternatives.

		State of Sales		
		Reduction (.15)	Constant (.35)	Increase (.50)
Decision Alternative	Automate	−$40,000	−$15,000	$60,000
	Don't Automate	$5,000	$10,000	−$30,000

b. For a fee, the owners can purchase a sales forecast for the near future. The forecast is not always perfect. The probabilities of these forecasts being correct for particular states of sales are shown here. Use these probabilities to revise the prior state probabilities. Compute the expected monetary value on the basis of sample information. Determine the value of the sample information.

		State of Sales		
		Reduction	Constant	Increase
Forecast	Reduction	.60	.10	.05
	Constant	.30	.80	.25
	Increase	.10	.10	.70

19.24. a. A city is considering airport expansion. In particular, the mayor and city council are trying to decide whether to sell bonds to construct a new terminal. The problem is that at present demand for gates is not strong enough to warrant construction of a new terminal. However, a major airline is investigating several cities to determine which will become its new hub. If this city is selected, the new terminal will easily pay for itself. The decision to build the terminal must be made by the city before the airline will say whether the city has been chosen as its hub. Shown here is a decision table for this dilemma. Use this information to compute expected monetary values for the alternatives and reach a conclusion.

		State of Nature	
		City Chosen (.20)	City Not Chosen (.80)
Decision Alternative	Build Terminal	$12,000	−$8,000
	Don't Build Terminal	−$1,000	$2,000

b. An airline industry expert indicates that she will sell the city decision makers her best "guess" as to whether the city will be chosen as hub for the airline. The probabilities of her being right or wrong are given.

Use these probabilities to revise the prior probabilities of the city being chosen as the hub and then calculate the expected monetary value by using the sample information. Determine the value of the sample information for this problem.

		State of Nature	
		City Chosen	City Not Chosen
Forecast	City Chosen	.45	.40
	City Not Chosen	.55	.60

Analyzing the Databases

1. A carpet and rug manufacturer in the manufacturing database is faced with the decision of making expenditures in the form of machinery in anticipation of strong growth or not making the expenditures and losing market opportunity. Experts claim that there is about a 40% probability of having strong growth in the industry and a 60% probability of not having strong growth in the industry. If there is strong growth, the company will realize a payoff of $5,500,000 if the capital expenditure is made. Under strong growth, if the company does not make the capital expenditure, it will still realize a $750,000 payoff in new business, which it can handle with existing equipment. If there is not strong growth in the industry and the company has made the capital expenditure, the payoff will be −$2,000,000. If there is not strong growth and the capital expenditure has not been made, the company will receive a payoff of $500,000. Analyze this situation by using the decision analysis techniques presented in this chapter.

2. Suppose you are the CEO of a hospital in the hospital database. You are considering expansion of the physical facility. What are some decision alternatives to consider? What are some states of nature that can occur in this decision-making environment? How would you go about calculating the payoffs for such a decision?

3. Suppose you are the CEO of a company such as Procter & Gamble in the financial database. What are some decisions that you might make in which you would consider decision alternatives? Name three arenas in which you would be making substantial strategic decisions (e.g., marketing, finance, production, and human resources). Delineate at least three decision alternatives in each of these arenas. Examine and discuss at least two states of nature that could occur under these decision alternatives in each arena.

Case

Fletcher-Terry: On The Cutting Edge

The Fletcher-Terry Company of Farmington, Connecticut, is a worldwide leader in the development of glass-cutting tools and accessories for professional glaziers, glass manufacturers, glass artisans, and professional framers. The company can trace its roots back to 1868 when a young engineer, Samuel Monce, developed and patented a hardened steel tool that could effectively replace expensive diamonds as a cutting device. Using this invention as his centerpiece, Monce formed the Monce Company, which went on to become a leader in glass-cutting devices for several decades. Meanwhile, in 1894, Monce's nephew Fred Fletcher got a patent on a replaceable-wheel cutter. Ten years later he went into business with his father-in-law, Franklin Terry, forming the Fletcher-Terry Company. In 1935, the Fletcher-Terry Company bought the Monce Company, thereby combining the assets and knowledge of the two companies.

For the next four decades, Fletcher-Terry had much success making its traditional product lines of hand-held glass cutters and cutting wheels for the glass, glazing, and hardware markets. However, by the 1980s, Fletcher-Terry was facing a crisis. Its two largest customers, distributors of cutting devices, decided to introduce their own private-label cutters made overseas. By the end of 1982, Fletcher-Terry's sales of hand-held glass cutters were down 45%.

Fletcher-Terry responded by investing heavily in technology with the hope that automation would cut costs; however, the technology never worked. The company then decided to expand its line of offerings by creating private lines through imports, but the dollar weakened and any price advantage was lost. Eventually, Fletcher-Terry had to write off this line with a substantial loss.

Company managers realized that if they did not change the way they did business, the company would not survive. They began a significant strategic planning process in which they set objectives and redefined the mission of the company. Among the new objectives were to increase market share where the company was already strong, penetrate new markets with new products, provide technological expertise for product development, promote greater employee involvement and

growth, and achieve a sales growth rate twice that of the gross domestic product.

To accomplish these objectives, the company invested in plant and process improvements that reduced costs and improved quality. Markets were researched for both old and new products and marketing efforts were launched to reestablish the company's products as being "the first choice of professionals." A participatory management system was implemented that encouraged risk taking and creativity among employees.

Following these initiatives, sales growth totaled 82.5% from 1987 and 1993. Fletcher-Terry expanded its offerings with bevel mat cutters, new fastener tools, and a variety of hand tools essential to professional picture framers, and graduated from being a manufacturer of relatively simple hand tools to being a manufacturer of mechanically complex equipment and tools. Today, Fletcher-Terry maintains a leadership position in its industry through dedicated employees who are constantly exploring new ideas to help customers become more productive. Because of its continuous pursuit of quality, the company earned the Ford Q-101 Quality Supplier Award. In August of 2001, Fletcher-Terry introduced its FramerSolutions.com online business-to-business custom mat cutting service especially designed for professional picture framers. Fletcher-Terry holds over 90 patents, including the "original" glass cutting wheel, the first vertical glass cutting machine, and the "wide-track" all-carbide cutting wheel. The mission of Fletcher-Terry is to develop innovative tools and equipment for the markets they serve worldwide and make customer satisfaction their number one priority. Today, they have a distribution network to 60 countries worldwide.

Discussion

1. Fletcher-Terry managers have been involved in many decisions over the years. Of particular importance were the decisions made in the 1980s when the company was struggling to survive. Several states of nature took place in the late 1970s and 1980s over which managers had little or no control. Suppose the Fletcher-Terry management team wants to reflect on their decisions and the events that surrounded them, and they ask you to make a brief report summarizing the situation.

Delineate at least five decisions that Fletcher-Terry probably had to make during that troublesome time. Using your knowledge of the economic situation both in the United States and in the rest of the world in addition to information given in the case, present at least four states of nature during that time that had significant influence on the outcomes of the managers' decisions.

2. At one point, Fletcher-Terry decided to import its own private line of cutters. Suppose that before taking such action, the managers had the following information available. Construct a decision table and a decision tree by using this information. Explain any conclusions reached.

Suppose the decision for managers was to import or not import. If they imported, they had to worry about the purchasing value of the dollar overseas. If the value of the dollar went up, the company could profit $350,000. If the dollar maintained its present position, the company would still profit by $275,000. However, if the value of the dollar decreased, the company would be worse off with an additional loss of $555,000. One business economic source reported that there was a 25% chance that the dollar would increase in value overseas, a 35% chance that it would remain constant, and a 40% chance that it would lose value overseas. If the company decided not to import its own private label, it would have a $22,700 loss no matter what the value of the dollar was overseas. Explain the possible outcomes of this analysis to the management team in terms of EMV, risk aversion, and risk taking. Bring common sense into the process and give your recommendations on what the company should do given the analysis. Keep in mind the company's situation and the fact that it had not yet tried any solution. Explain to company officials the expected value of perfect information for this decision.

Source: Adapted from "Fletcher-Terry: On the Cutting Edge," Real-World Lessons for America's Small Businesses: Insights from the Blue Chip Enterprise Initiative. Published by *Nation's Business* magazine on behalf of Connecticut Mutual Life Insurance Company and the U.S. Chamber of Commerce in association with The Blue Chip Enterprise Initiative, 1994. www.fletcher-terry.com, 2016

Appendix A

Tables

TABLE A.1 Random Numbers

12651	61646	11769	75109	86996	97669	25757	32535	07122	76763
81769	74436	02630	72310	45049	18029	07469	42341	98173	79260
36737	98863	77240	76251	00654	64688	09343	70278	67331	98729
82861	54371	76610	94934	72748	44124	05610	53750	95938	01485
21325	15732	24127	37431	09723	63529	73977	95218	96074	42138
74146	47887	62463	23045	41490	07954	22597	60012	98866	90959
90759	64410	54179	66075	61051	75385	51378	08360	95946	95547
55683	98078	02238	91540	21219	17720	87817	41705	95785	12563
79686	17969	76061	83748	55920	83612	41540	86492	06447	60568
70333	00201	86201	69716	78185	62154	77930	67663	29529	75116
14042	53536	07779	04157	41172	36473	42123	43929	50533	33437
59911	08256	06596	48416	69770	68797	56080	14223	59199	30162
62368	62623	62742	14891	39247	52242	98832	69533	91174	57979
57529	97751	54976	48957	74599	08759	78494	52785	68526	64618
15469	90574	78033	66885	13936	42117	71831	22961	94225	31816
18625	23674	53850	32827	81647	80820	00420	63555	74489	80141
74626	68394	88562	70745	23701	45630	65891	58220	35442	60414
11119	16519	27384	90199	79210	76965	99546	30323	31664	22845
41101	17336	48951	53674	17880	45260	08575	49321	36191	17095
32123	91576	84221	78902	82010	30847	62329	63898	23268	74283
26091	68409	69704	82267	14751	13151	93115	01437	56945	89661
67680	79790	48462	59278	44185	29616	76531	19589	83139	28454
15184	19260	14073	07026	25264	08388	27182	22557	61501	67481
58010	45039	57181	10238	36874	28546	37444	80824	63981	39942
56425	53996	86245	32623	78858	08143	60377	42925	42815	11159
82630	84066	13592	60642	17904	99718	63432	88642	37858	25431
14927	40909	23900	48761	44860	92467	31742	87142	03607	32059
23740	22505	07489	85986	74420	21744	97711	36648	35620	97949
32990	97446	03711	63824	07953	85965	87089	11687	92414	67257
05310	24058	91946	78437	34365	82469	12430	84754	19354	72745
21839	39937	27534	88913	49055	19218	47712	67677	51889	70926
08833	42549	93981	94051	28382	83725	72643	64233	97252	17133
58336	11139	47479	00931	91560	95372	97642	33856	54825	55680
62032	91144	75478	47431	52726	30289	42411	91886	51818	78292
45171	30557	53116	04118	58301	24375	65609	85810	18620	49198
91611	62656	60128	35609	63698	78356	50682	22505	01692	36291
55472	63819	86314	49174	93582	73604	78614	78849	23096	72825
18573	09729	74091	53994	10970	86557	65661	41854	26037	53296
60866	02955	90288	82136	83644	94455	06560	78029	98768	71296
45043	55608	82767	60890	74646	79485	13619	98868	40857	19415
17831	09737	79473	75945	28394	79334	70577	38048	03607	06932
40137	03981	07585	18128	11178	32601	27994	05641	22600	86064
77776	31343	14576	97706	16039	47517	43300	59080	80392	63189
69605	44104	40103	95635	05635	81673	68657	09559	23510	95875
19916	52934	26499	09821	97331	80993	61299	36979	73599	35055
02606	58552	07678	56619	65325	30705	99582	53390	46357	13244
65183	73160	87131	35530	47946	09854	18080	02321	05809	04893
10740	98914	44916	11322	89717	88189	30143	52687	19420	60061
98642	89822	71691	51573	83666	61642	46683	33761	47542	23551
60139	25601	93663	25547	02654	94829	48672	28736	84994	13071

TABLE A.2 Binomial Probability Distribution

					$n = 1$				
				PROBABILITY					
x	.1	.2	.3	.4	.5	.6	.7	.8	.9
0	.900	.800	.700	.600	.500	.400	.300	.200	.100
1	.100	.200	.300	.400	.500	.600	.700	.800	.900

					$n = 2$				
				PROBABILITY					
x	.1	.2	.3	.4	.5	.6	.7	.8	.9
0	.810	.640	.490	.360	.250	.160	.090	.040	.010
1	.180	.320	.420	.480	.500	.480	.420	.320	.180
2	.010	.040	.090	.160	.250	.360	.490	.640	.810

					$n = 3$				
				PROBABILITY					
x	.1	.2	.3	.4	.5	.6	.7	.8	.9
0	.729	.512	.343	.216	.125	.064	.027	.008	.001
1	.243	.384	.441	.432	.375	.288	.189	.096	.027
2	.027	.096	.189	.288	.375	.432	.441	.384	.243
3	.001	.008	.027	.064	.125	.216	.343	.512	.729

					$n = 4$				
				PROBABILITY					
x	.1	.2	.3	.4	.5	.6	.7	.8	.9
0	.656	.410	.240	.130	.063	.026	.008	.002	.000
1	.292	.410	.412	.346	.250	.154	.076	.026	.004
2	.049	.154	.265	.346	.375	.346	.265	.154	.049
3	.004	.026	.076	.154	.250	.346	.412	.410	.292
4	.000	.002	.008	.026	.063	.130	.240	.410	.656

					$n = 5$				
				PROBABILITY					
x	.1	.2	.3	.4	.5	.6	.7	.8	.9
0	.590	.328	.168	.078	.031	.010	.002	.000	.000
1	.328	.410	.360	.259	.156	.077	.028	.006	.000
2	.073	.205	.309	.346	.313	.230	.132	.051	.008
3	.008	.051	.132	.230	.313	.346	.309	.205	.073
4	.000	.006	.028	.077	.156	.259	.360	.410	.328
5	.000	.000	.002	.010	.031	.078	.168	.328	.590

					$n = 6$				
				PROBABILITY					
x	.1	.2	.3	.4	.5	.6	.7	.8	.9
0	.531	.262	.118	.047	.016	.004	.001	.000	.000
1	.354	.393	.303	.187	.094	.037	.010	.002	.000
2	.098	.246	.324	.311	.234	.138	.060	.015	.001
3	.015	.082	.185	.276	.313	.276	.185	.082	.015
4	.001	.015	.060	.138	.234	.311	.324	.246	.098
5	.000	.002	.010	.037	.094	.187	.303	.393	.354
6	.000	.000	.001	.004	.016	.047	.118	.262	.531

				$n = 7$					
				PROBABILITY					
x	.1	.2	.3	.4	.5	.6	.7	.8	.9
0	.478	.210	.082	.028	.008	.002	.000	.000	.000
1	.372	.367	.247	.131	.055	.017	.004	.000	.000
2	.124	.275	.318	.261	.164	.077	.025	.004	.000
3	.023	.115	.227	.290	.273	.194	.097	.029	.003
4	.003	.029	.097	.194	.273	.290	.227	.115	.023
5	.000	.004	.025	.077	.164	.261	.318	.275	.124
6	.000	.000	.004	.017	.055	.131	.247	.367	.372
7	.000	.000	.000	.002	.008	.028	.082	.210	.478

				$n = 8$					
				PROBABILITY					
x	.1	.2	.3	.4	.5	.6	.7	.8	.9
0	.430	.168	.058	.017	.004	.001	.000	.000	.000
1	.383	.336	.198	.090	.031	.008	.001	.000	.000
2	.149	.294	.296	.209	.109	.041	.010	.001	.000
3	.033	.147	.254	.279	.219	.124	.047	.009	.000
4	.005	.046	.136	.232	.273	.232	.136	.046	.005
5	.000	.009	.047	.124	.219	.279	.254	.147	.033
6	.000	.001	.010	.041	.109	.209	.296	.294	.149
7	.000	.000	.001	.008	.031	.090	.198	.336	.383
8	.000	.000	.000	.001	.004	.017	.058	.168	.430

				$n = 9$					
				PROBABILITY					
x	.1	.2	.3	.4	.5	.6	.7	.8	.9
0	.387	.134	.040	.010	.002	.000	.000	.000	.000
1	.387	.302	.156	.060	.018	.004	.000	.000	.000
2	.172	.302	.267	.161	.070	.021	.004	.000	.000
3	.045	.176	.267	.251	.164	.074	.021	.003	.000
4	.007	.066	.172	.251	.246	.167	.074	.017	.001
5	.001	.017	.074	.167	.246	.251	.172	.066	.007
6	.000	.003	.021	.074	.164	.251	.267	.176	.045
7	.000	.000	.004	.021	.070	.161	.267	.302	.172
8	.000	.000	.000	.004	.018	.060	.156	.302	.387
9	.000	.000	.000	.000	.002	.010	.040	.134	.387

				$n = 10$					
				PROBABILITY					
x	.1	.2	.3	.4	.5	.6	.7	.8	.9
0	.349	.107	.028	.006	.001	.000	.000	.000	.000
1	.387	.268	.121	.040	.010	.002	.000	.000	.000
2	.194	.302	.233	.121	.044	.011	.001	.000	.000
3	.057	.201	.267	.215	.117	.042	.009	.001	.000
4	.011	.088	.200	.251	.205	.111	.037	.006	.000
5	.001	.026	.103	.201	.246	.201	.103	.026	.001
6	.000	.006	.037	.111	.205	.251	.200	.088	.011
7	.000	.001	.009	.042	.117	.215	.267	.201	.057
8	.000	.000	.001	.011	.044	.121	.233	.302	.194
9	.000	.000	.000	.002	.010	.040	.121	.268	.387
10	.000	.000	.000	.000	.001	.006	.028	.107	.349

(continued)

TABLE A.2 Binomial Probability Distribution (*continued*)

					$n = 11$				
				PROBABILITY					
x	.1	.2	.3	.4	.5	.6	.7	.8	.9
0	.314	.086	.020	.004	.000	.000	.000	.000	.000
1	.384	.236	.093	.027	.005	.001	.000	.000	.000
2	.213	.295	.200	.089	.027	.005	.001	.000	.000
3	.071	.221	.257	.177	.081	.023	.004	.000	.000
4	.016	.111	.220	.236	.161	.070	.017	.002	.000
5	.002	.039	.132	.221	.226	.147	.057	.010	.000
6	.000	.010	.057	.147	.226	.221	.132	.039	.002
7	.000	.002	.017	.070	.161	.236	.220	.111	.016
8	.000	.000	.004	.023	.081	.177	.257	.221	.071
9	.000	.000	.001	.005	.027	.089	.200	.295	.213
10	.000	.000	.000	.001	.005	.027	.093	.236	.384
11	.000	.000	.000	.000	.000	.004	.020	.086	.314

					$n = 12$				
				PROBABILITY					
x	.1	.2	.3	.4	.5	.6	.7	.8	.9
0	.282	.069	.014	.002	.000	.000	.000	.000	.000
1	.377	.206	.071	.017	.003	.000	.000	.000	.000
2	.230	.283	.168	.064	.016	.002	.000	.000	.000
3	.085	.236	.240	.142	.054	.012	.001	.000	.000
4	.021	.133	.231	.213	.121	.042	.008	.001	.000
5	.004	.053	.158	.227	.193	.101	.029	.003	.000
6	.000	.016	.079	.177	.226	.177	.079	.016	.000
7	.000	.003	.029	.101	.193	.227	.158	.053	.004
8	.000	.001	.008	.042	.121	.213	.231	.133	.021
9	.000	.000	.001	.012	.054	.142	.240	.236	.085
10	.000	.000	.000	.002	.016	.064	.168	.283	.230
11	.000	.000	.000	.000	.003	.017	.071	.206	.377
12	.000	.000	.000	.000	.000	.002	.014	.069	.282

					$n = 13$				
				PROBABILITY					
x	.1	.2	.3	.4	.5	.6	.7	.8	.9
0	.254	.055	.010	.001	.000	.000	.000	.000	.000
1	.367	.179	.054	.011	.002	.000	.000	.000	.000
2	.245	.268	.139	.045	.010	.001	.000	.000	.000
3	.100	.246	.218	.111	.035	.006	.001	.000	.000
4	.028	.154	.234	.184	.087	.024	.003	.000	.000
5	.006	.069	.180	.221	.157	.066	.014	.001	.000
6	.001	.023	.103	.197	.209	.131	.044	.006	.000
7	.000	.006	.044	.131	.209	.197	.103	.023	.001
8	.000	.001	.014	.066	.157	.221	.180	.069	.006
9	.000	.000	.003	.024	.087	.184	.234	.154	.028
10	.000	.000	.001	.006	.035	.111	.218	.246	.100
11	.000	.000	.000	.001	.010	.045	.139	.268	.245
12	.000	.000	.000	.000	.002	.011	.054	.179	.367
13	.000	.000	.000	.000	.000	.001	.010	.055	.254

				$n = 14$					
				PROBABILITY					
x	.1	.2	.3	.4	.5	.6	.7	.8	.9
0	.229	.044	.007	.001	.000	.000	.000	.000	.000
1	.356	.154	.041	.007	.001	.000	.000	.000	.000
2	.257	.250	.113	.032	.006	.001	.000	.000	.000
3	.114	.250	.194	.085	.022	.003	.000	.000	.000
4	.035	.172	.229	.155	.061	.014	.001	.000	.000
5	.008	.086	.196	.207	.122	.041	.007	.000	.000
6	.001	.032	.126	.207	.183	.092	.023	.002	.000
7	.000	.009	.062	.157	.209	.157	.062	.009	.000
8	.000	.002	.023	.092	.183	.207	.126	.032	.001
9	.000	.000	.007	.041	.122	.207	.196	.086	.008
10	.000	.000	.001	.014	.061	.155	.229	.172	.035
11	.000	.000	.000	.003	.022	.085	.194	.250	.114
12	.000	.000	.000	.001	.006	.032	.113	.250	.257
13	.000	.000	.000	.000	.001	.007	.041	.154	.356
14	.000	.000	.000	.000	.000	.001	.007	.044	.229

				$n = 15$					
				PROBABILITY					
x	.1	.2	.3	.4	.5	.6	.7	.8	.9
0	.206	.035	.005	.000	.000	.000	.000	.000	.000
1	.343	.132	.031	.005	.000	.000	.000	.000	.000
2	.267	.231	.092	.022	.003	.000	.000	.000	.000
3	.129	.250	.170	.063	.014	.002	.000	.000	.000
4	.043	.188	.219	.127	.042	.007	.001	.000	.000
5	.010	.103	.206	.186	.092	.024	.003	.000	.000
6	.002	.043	.147	.207	.153	.061	.012	.001	.000
7	.000	.014	.081	.177	.196	.118	.035	.003	.000
8	.000	.003	.035	.118	.196	.177	.081	.014	.000
9	.000	.001	.012	.061	.153	.207	.147	.043	.002
10	.000	.000	.003	.024	.092	.186	.206	.103	.010
11	.000	.000	.001	.007	.042	.127	.219	.188	.043
12	.000	.000	.000	.002	.014	.063	.170	.250	.129
13	.000	.000	.000	.000	.003	.022	.092	.231	.267
14	.000	.000	.000	.000	.000	.005	.031	.132	.343
15	.000	.000	.000	.000	.000	.000	.005	.035	.206

(*continued*)

TABLE A.2 Binomial Probability Distribution (*continued*)

n = 16

PROBABILITY

x	.1	.2	.3	.4	.5	.6	.7	.8	.9
0	.185	.028	.003	.000	.000	.000	.000	.000	.000
1	.329	.113	.023	.003	.000	.000	.000	.000	.000
2	.275	.211	.073	.015	.002	.000	.000	.000	.000
3	.142	.246	.146	.047	.009	.001	.000	.000	.000
4	.051	.200	.204	.101	.028	.004	.000	.000	.000
5	.014	.120	.210	.162	.067	.014	.001	.000	.000
6	.003	.055	.165	.198	.122	.039	.006	.000	.000
7	.000	.020	.101	.189	.175	.084	.019	.001	.000
8	.000	.006	.049	.142	.196	.142	.049	.006	.000
9	.000	.001	.019	.084	.175	.189	.101	.020	.000
10	.000	.000	.006	.039	.122	.198	.165	.055	.003
11	.000	.000	.001	.014	.067	.162	.210	.120	.014
12	.000	.000	.000	.004	.028	.101	.204	.200	.051
13	.000	.000	.000	.001	.009	.047	.146	.246	.142
14	.000	.000	.000	.000	.002	.015	.073	.211	.275
15	.000	.000	.000	.000	.000	.003	.023	.113	.329
16	.000	.000	.000	.000	.000	.000	.003	.028	.185

n = 17

PROBABILITY

x	.1	.2	.3	.4	.5	.6	.7	.8	.9
0	.167	.023	.002	.000	.000	.000	.000	.000	.000
1	.315	.096	.017	.002	.000	.000	.000	.000	.000
2	.280	.191	.058	.010	.001	.000	.000	.000	.000
3	.156	.239	.125	.034	.005	.000	.000	.000	.000
4	.060	.209	.187	.080	.018	.002	.000	.000	.000
5	.017	.136	.208	.138	.047	.008	.001	.000	.000
6	.004	.068	.178	.184	.094	.024	.003	.000	.000
7	.001	.027	.120	.193	.148	.057	.009	.000	.000
8	.000	.008	.064	.161	.185	.107	.028	.002	.000
9	.000	.002	.028	.107	.185	.161	.064	.008	.000
10	.000	.000	.009	.057	.148	.193	.120	.027	.001
11	.000	.000	.003	.024	.094	.184	.178	.068	.004
12	.000	.000	.001	.008	.047	.138	.208	.136	.017
13	.000	.000	.000	.002	.018	.080	.187	.209	.060
14	.000	.000	.000	.000	.005	.034	.125	.239	.156
15	.000	.000	.000	.000	.001	.010	.058	.191	.280
16	.000	.000	.000	.000	.000	.002	.017	.096	.315
17	.000	.000	.000	.000	.000	.000	.002	.023	.167

				$n = 18$					
				PROBABILITY					
x	.1	.2	.3	.4	.5	.6	.7	.8	.9
0	.150	.018	.002	.000	.000	.000	.000	.000	.000
1	.300	.081	.013	.001	.000	.000	.000	.000	.000
2	.284	.172	.046	.007	.001	.000	.000	.000	.000
3	.168	.230	.105	.025	.003	.000	.000	.000	.000
4	.070	.215	.168	.061	.012	.001	.000	.000	.000
5	.022	.151	.202	.115	.033	.004	.000	.000	.000
6	.005	.082	.187	.166	.071	.015	.001	.000	.000
7	.001	.035	.138	.189	.121	.037	.005	.000	.000
8	.000	.012	.081	.173	.167	.077	.015	.001	.000
9	.000	.003	.039	.128	.185	.128	.039	.003	.000
10	.000	.001	.015	.077	.167	.173	.081	.012	.000
11	.000	.000	.005	.037	.121	.189	.138	.035	.001
12	.000	.000	.001	.015	.071	.166	.187	.082	.005
13	.000	.000	.000	.004	.033	.115	.202	.151	.022
14	.000	.000	.000	.001	.012	.061	.168	.215	.070
15	.000	.000	.000	.000	.003	.025	.105	.230	.168
16	.000	.000	.000	.000	.001	.007	.046	.172	.284
17	.000	.000	.000	.000	.000	.001	.013	.081	.300
18	.000	.000	.000	.000	.000	.000	.002	.018	.150

				$n = 19$					
				PROBABILITY					
x	.1	.2	.3	.4	.5	.6	.7	.8	.9
0	.135	.014	.001	.000	.000	.000	.000	.000	.000
1	.285	.068	.009	.001	.000	.000	.000	.000	.000
2	.285	.154	.036	.005	.000	.000	.000	.000	.000
3	.180	.218	.087	.017	.002	.000	.000	.000	.000
4	.080	.218	.149	.047	.007	.001	.000	.000	.000
5	.027	.164	.192	.093	.022	.002	.000	.000	.000
6	.007	.095	.192	.145	.052	.008	.001	.000	.000
7	.001	.044	.153	.180	.096	.024	.002	.000	.000
8	.000	.017	.098	.180	.144	.053	.008	.000	.000
9	.000	.005	.051	.146	.176	.098	.022	.001	.000
10	.000	.001	.022	.098	.176	.146	.051	.005	.000
11	.000	.000	.008	.053	.144	.180	.098	.017	.000
12	.000	.000	.002	.024	.096	.180	.153	.044	.001
13	.000	.000	.001	.008	.052	.145	.192	.095	.007
14	.000	.000	.000	.002	.022	.093	.192	.164	.027
15	.000	.000	.000	.001	.007	.047	.149	.218	.080
16	.000	.000	.000	.000	.002	.017	.087	.218	.180
17	.000	.000	.000	.000	.000	.005	.036	.154	.285
18	.000	.000	.000	.000	.000	.001	.009	.068	.285
19	.000	.000	.000	.000	.000	.000	.001	.014	.135

(*continued*)

TABLE A.2   **Binomial Probability Distribution** (*continued*)

				n = 20					
				PROBABILITY					
x	.1	.2	.3	.4	.5	.6	.7	.8	.9
0	.122	.012	.001	.000	.000	.000	.000	.000	.000
1	.270	.058	.007	.000	.000	.000	.000	.000	.000
2	.285	.137	.028	.003	.000	.000	.000	.000	.000
3	.190	.205	.072	.012	.001	.000	.000	.000	.000
4	.090	.218	.130	.035	.005	.000	.000	.000	.000
5	.032	.175	.179	.075	.015	.001	.000	.000	.000
6	.009	.109	.192	.124	.037	.005	.000	.000	.000
7	.002	.055	.164	.166	.074	.015	.001	.000	.000
8	.000	.022	.114	.180	.120	.035	.004	.000	.000
9	.000	.007	.065	.160	.160	.071	.012	.000	.000
10	.000	.002	.031	.117	.176	.117	.031	.002	.000
11	.000	.000	.012	.071	.160	.160	.065	.007	.000
12	.000	.000	.004	.035	.120	.180	.114	.022	.000
13	.000	.000	.001	.015	.074	.166	.164	.055	.002
14	.000	.000	.000	.005	.037	.124	.192	.109	.009
15	.000	.000	.000	.001	.015	.075	.179	.175	.032
16	.000	.000	.000	.000	.005	.035	.130	.218	.090
17	.000	.000	.000	.000	.001	.012	.072	.205	.190
18	.000	.000	.000	.000	.000	.003	.028	.137	.285
19	.000	.000	.000	.000	.000	.000	.007	.058	.270
20	.000	.000	.000	.000	.000	.000	.001	.012	.122

				n = 25					
				PROBABILITY					
x	.1	.2	.3	.4	.5	.6	.7	.8	.9
0	.072	.004	.000	.000	.000	.000	.000	.000	.000
1	.199	.024	.001	.000	.000	.000	.000	.000	.000
2	.266	.071	.007	.000	.000	.000	.000	.000	.000
3	.226	.136	.024	.002	.000	.000	.000	.000	.000
4	.138	.187	.057	.007	.000	.000	.000	.000	.000
5	.065	.196	.103	.020	.002	.000	.000	.000	.000
6	.024	.163	.147	.044	.005	.000	.000	.000	.000
7	.007	.111	.171	.080	.014	.001	.000	.000	.000
8	.002	.062	.165	.120	.032	.003	.000	.000	.000
9	.000	.029	.134	.151	.061	.009	.000	.000	.000
10	.000	.012	.092	.161	.097	.021	.001	.000	.000
11	.000	.004	.054	.147	.133	.043	.004	.000	.000
12	.000	.001	.027	.114	.155	.076	.011	.000	.000
13	.000	.000	.011	.076	.155	.114	.027	.001	.000
14	.000	.000	.004	.043	.133	.147	.054	.004	.000
15	.000	.000	.001	.021	.097	.161	.092	.012	.000
16	.000	.000	.000	.009	.061	.151	.134	.029	.000
17	.000	.000	.000	.003	.032	.120	.165	.062	.002
18	.000	.000	.000	.001	.014	.080	.171	.111	.007
19	.000	.000	.000	.000	.005	.044	.147	.163	.024
20	.000	.000	.000	.000	.002	.020	.103	.196	.065
21	.000	.000	.000	.000	.000	.007	.057	.187	.138
22	.000	.000	.000	.000	.000	.002	.024	.136	.226
23	.000	.000	.000	.000	.000	.000	.007	.071	.266
24	.000	.000	.000	.000	.000	.000	.001	.024	.199
25	.000	.000	.000	.000	.000	.000	.000	.004	.072

TABLE A.3 Poisson Probabilities

x	λ									
	.005	.01	.02	.03	.04	.05	.06	.07	.08	.09
0	.9950	.9900	.9802	.9704	.9608	.9512	.9418	.9324	.9231	.9139
1	.0050	.0099	.0196	.0291	.0384	.0476	.0565	.0653	.0738	.0823
2	.0000	.0000	.0002	.0004	.0008	.0012	.0017	.0023	.0030	.0037
3	.0000	.0000	.0000	.0000	.0000	.0000	.0000	.0001	.0001	.0001

x	.1	.2	.3	.4	.5	.6	.7	.8	.9	1.0
0	.9048	.8187	.7408	.6703	.6065	.5488	.4966	.4493	.4066	.3679
1	.0905	.1637	.2222	.2681	.3033	.3293	.3476	.3595	.3659	.3679
2	.0045	.0164	.0333	.0536	.0758	.0988	.1217	.1438	.1647	.1839
3	.0002	.0011	.0033	.0072	.0126	.0198	.0284	.0383	.0494	.0613
4	.0000	.0001	.0003	.0007	.0016	.0030	.0050	.0077	.0111	.0153
5	.0000	.0000	.0000	.0001	.0002	.0004	.0007	.0012	.0020	.0031
6	.0000	.0000	.0000	.0000	.0000	.0000	.0001	.0002	.0003	.0005
7	.0000	.0000	.0000	.0000	.0000	.0000	.0000	.0000	.0000	.0001

x	1.1	1.2	1.3	1.4	1.5	1.6	1.7	1.8	1.9	2.0
0	.3329	.3012	.2725	.2466	.2231	.2019	.1827	.1653	.1496	.1353
1	.3662	.3614	.3543	.3452	.3347	.3230	.3106	.2975	.2842	.2707
2	.2014	.2169	.2303	.2417	.2510	.2584	.2640	.2678	.2700	.2707
3	.0738	.0867	.0998	.1128	.1255	.1378	.1496	.1607	.1710	.1804
4	.0203	.0260	.0324	.0395	.0471	.0551	.0636	.0723	.0812	.0902
5	.0045	.0062	.0084	.0111	.0141	.0176	.0216	.0260	.0309	.0361
6	.0008	.0012	.0018	.0026	.0035	.0047	.0061	.0078	.0098	.0120
7	.0001	.0002	.0003	.0005	.0008	.0011	.0015	.0020	.0027	.0034
8	.0000	.0000	.0001	.0001	.0001	.0002	.0003	.0005	.0006	.0009
9	.0000	.0000	.0000	.0000	.0000	.0000	.0001	.0001	.0001	.0002

x	2.1	2.2	2.3	2.4	2.5	2.6	2.7	2.8	2.9	3.0
0	.1225	.1108	.1003	.0907	.0821	.0743	.0672	.0608	.0550	.0498
1	.2572	.2438	.2306	.2177	.2052	.1931	.1815	.1703	.1596	.1494
2	.2700	.2681	.2652	.2613	.2565	.2510	.2450	.2384	.2314	.2240
3	.1890	.1966	.2033	.2090	.2138	.2176	.2205	.2225	.2237	.2240
4	.0992	.1082	.1169	.1254	.1336	.1414	.1488	.1557	.1622	.1680
5	.0417	.0476	.0538	.0602	.0668	.0735	.0804	.0872	.0940	.1008
6	.0146	.0174	.0206	.0241	.0278	.0319	.0362	.0407	.0455	.0504
7	.0044	.0055	.0068	.0083	.0099	.0118	.0139	.0163	.0188	.0216
8	.0011	.0015	.0019	.0025	.0031	.0038	.0047	.0057	.0068	.0081
9	.0003	.0004	.0005	.0007	.0009	.0011	.0014	.0018	.0022	.0027
10	.0001	.0001	.0001	.0002	.0002	.0003	.0004	.0005	.0006	.0008
11	.0000	.0000	.0000	.0000	.0000	.0001	.0001	.0001	.0002	.0002
12	.0000	.0000	.0000	.0000	.0000	.0000	.0000	.0000	.0000	.0001

(*continued*)

TABLE A.3 Poisson Probabilities (*continued*)

					λ					
x	3.1	3.2	3.3	3.4	3.5	3.6	3.7	3.8	3.9	4.0
0	.0450	.0408	.0369	.0334	.0302	.0273	.0247	.0224	.0202	.0183
1	.1397	.1304	.1217	.1135	.1057	.0984	.0915	.0850	.0789	.0733
2	.2165	.2087	.2008	.1929	.1850	.1771	.1692	.1615	.1539	.1465
3	.2237	.2226	.2209	.2186	.2158	.2125	.2087	.2046	.2001	.1954
4	.1733	.1781	.1823	.1858	.1888	.1912	.1931	.1944	.1951	.1954
5	.1075	.1140	.1203	.1264	.1322	.1377	.1429	.1477	.1522	.1563
6	.0555	.0608	.0662	.0716	.0771	.0826	.0881	.0936	.0989	.1042
7	.0246	.0278	.0312	.0348	.0385	.0425	.0466	.0508	.0551	.0595
8	.0095	.0111	.0129	.0148	.0169	.0191	.0215	.0241	.0269	.0298
9	.0033	.0040	.0047	.0056	.0066	.0076	.0089	.0102	.0116	.0132
10	.0010	.0013	.0016	.0019	.0023	.0028	.0033	.0039	.0045	.0053
11	.0003	.0004	.0005	.0006	.0007	.0009	.0011	.0013	.0016	.0019
12	.0001	.0001	.0001	.0002	.0002	.0003	.0003	.0004	.0005	.0006
13	.0000	.0000	.0000	.0000	.0001	.0001	.0001	.0001	.0002	.0002
14	.0000	.0000	.0000	.0000	.0000	.0000	.0000	.0000	.0000	.0001
x	4.1	4.2	4.3	4.4	4.5	4.6	4.7	4.8	4.9	5.0
0	.0166	.0150	.0136	.0123	.0111	.0101	.0091	.0082	.0074	.0067
1	.0679	.0630	.0583	.0540	.0500	.0462	.0427	.0395	.0365	.0337
2	.1393	.1323	.1254	.1188	.1125	.1063	.1005	.0948	.0894	.0842
3	.1904	.1852	.1798	.1743	.1687	.1631	.1574	.1517	.1460	.1404
4	.1951	.1944	.1933	.1917	.1898	.1875	.1849	.1820	.1789	.1755
5	.1600	.1633	.1662	.1687	.1708	.1725	.1738	.1747	.1753	.1755
6	.1093	.1143	.1191	.1237	.1281	.1323	.1362	.1398	.1432	.1462
7	.0640	.0686	.0732	.0778	.0824	.0869	.0914	.0959	.1002	.1044
8	.0328	.0360	.0393	.0428	.0463	.0500	.0537	.0575	.0614	.0653
9	.0150	.0168	.0188	.0209	.0232	.0255	.0281	.0307	.0334	.0363
10	.0061	.0071	.0081	.0092	.0104	.0118	.0132	.0147	.0164	.0181
11	.0023	.0027	.0032	.0037	.0043	.0049	.0056	.0064	.0073	.0082
12	.0008	.0009	.0011	.0013	.0016	.0019	.0022	.0026	.0030	.0034
13	.0002	.0003	.0004	.0005	.0006	.0007	.0008	.0009	.0011	.0013
14	.0001	.0001	.0001	.0001	.0002	.0002	.0003	.0003	.0004	.0005
15	.0000	.0000	.0000	.0000	.0001	.0001	.0001	.0001	.0001	.0002

					λ					
x	5.1	5.2	5.3	5.4	5.5	5.6	5.7	5.8	5.9	6.0
0	.0061	.0055	.0050	.0045	.0041	.0037	.0033	.0030	.0027	.0025
1	.0311	.0287	.0265	.0244	.0225	.0207	.0191	.0176	.0162	.0149
2	.0793	.0746	.0701	.0659	.0618	.0580	.0544	.0509	.0477	.0446
3	.1348	.1293	.1239	.1185	.1133	.1082	.1033	.0985	.0938	.0892
4	.1719	.1681	.1641	.1600	.1558	.1515	.1472	.1428	.1383	.1339
5	.1753	.1748	.1740	.1728	.1714	.1697	.1678	.1656	.1632	.1606
6	.1490	.1515	.1537	.1555	.1571	.1584	.1594	.1601	.1605	.1606
7	.1086	.1125	.1163	.1200	.1234	.1267	.1298	.1326	.1353	.1377
8	.0692	.0731	.0771	.0810	.0849	.0887	.0925	.0962	.0998	.1033
9	.0392	.0423	.0454	.0486	.0519	.0552	.0586	.0620	.0654	.0688
10	.0200	.0220	.0241	.0262	.0285	.0309	.0334	.0359	.0386	.0413
11	.0093	.0104	.0116	.0129	.0143	.0157	.0173	.0190	.0207	.0225
12	.0039	.0045	.0051	.0058	.0065	.0073	.0082	.0092	.0102	.0113
13	.0015	.0018	.0021	.0024	.0028	.0032	.0036	.0041	.0046	.0052
14	.0006	.0007	.0008	.0009	.0011	.0013	.0015	.0017	.0019	.0022
15	.0002	.0002	.0003	.0003	.0004	.0005	.0006	.0007	.0008	.0009
16	.0001	.0001	.0001	.0001	.0001	.0002	.0002	.0002	.0003	.0003
17	.0000	.0000	.0000	.0000	.0000	.0001	.0001	.0001	.0001	.0001

x	6.1	6.2	6.3	6.4	6.5	6.6	6.7	6.8	6.9	7.0
0	.0022	.0020	.0018	.0017	.0015	.0014	.0012	.0011	.0010	.0009
1	.0137	.0126	.0116	.0106	.0098	.0090	.0082	.0076	.0070	.0064
2	.0417	.0390	.0364	.0340	.0318	.0296	.0276	.0258	.0240	.0223
3	.0848	.0806	.0765	.0726	.0688	.0652	.0617	.0584	.0552	.0521
4	.1294	.1249	.1205	.1162	.1118	.1076	.1034	.0992	.0952	.0912
5	.1579	.1549	.1519	.1487	.1454	.1420	.1385	.1349	.1314	.1277
6	.1605	.1601	.1595	.1586	.1575	.1562	.1546	.1529	.1511	.1490
7	.1399	.1418	.1435	.1450	.1462	.1472	.1480	.1486	.1489	.1490
8	.1066	.1099	.1130	.1160	.1188	.1215	.1240	.1263	.1284	.1304
9	.0723	.0757	.0791	.0825	.0858	.0891	.0923	.0954	.0985	.1014
10	.0441	.0469	.0498	.0528	.0558	.0588	.0618	.0649	.0679	.0710
11	.0244	.0265	.0285	.0307	.0330	.0353	.0377	.0401	.0426	.0452
12	.0124	.0137	.0150	.0164	.0179	.0194	.0210	.0227	.0245	.0263
13	.0058	.0065	.0073	.0081	.0089	.0099	.0108	.0119	.0130	.0142
14	.0025	.0029	.0033	.0037	.0041	.0046	.0052	.0058	.0064	.0071
15	.0010	.0012	.0014	.0016	.0018	.0020	.0023	.0026	.0029	.0033
16	.0004	.0005	.0005	.0006	.0007	.0008	.0010	.0011	.0013	.0014
17	.0001	.0002	.0002	.0002	.0003	.0003	.0004	.0004	.0005	.0006
18	.0000	.0001	.0001	.0001	.0001	.0001	.0001	.0002	.0002	.0002
19	.0000	.0000	.0000	.0000	.0000	.0000	.0001	.0001	.0001	.0001

(*continued*)

TABLE A.3   **Poisson Probabilities** (*continued*)

x	7.1	7.2	7.3	7.4	7.5	7.6	7.7	7.8	7.9	8.0
0	.0008	.0007	.0007	.0006	.0006	.0005	.0005	.0004	.0004	.0003
1	.0059	.0054	.0049	.0045	.0041	.0038	.0035	.0032	.0029	.0027
2	.0208	.0194	.0180	.0167	.0156	.0145	.0134	.0125	.0116	.0107
3	.0492	.0464	.0438	.0413	.0389	.0366	.0345	.0324	.0305	.0286
4	.0874	.0836	.0799	.0764	.0729	.0696	.0663	.0632	.0602	.0573
5	.1241	.1204	.1167	.1130	.1094	.1057	.1021	.0986	.0951	.0916
6	.1468	.1445	.1420	.1394	.1367	.1339	.1311	.1282	.1252	.1221
7	.1489	.1486	.1481	.1474	.1465	.1454	.1442	.1428	.1413	.1396
8	.1321	.1337	.1351	.1363	.1373	.1381	.1388	.1392	.1395	.1396
9	.1042	.1070	.1096	.1121	.1144	.1167	.1187	.1207	.1224	.1241
10	.0740	.0770	.0800	.0829	.0858	.0887	.0914	.0941	.0967	.0993
11	.0478	.0504	.0531	.0558	.0585	.0613	.0640	.0667	.0695	.0722
12	.0283	.0303	.0323	.0344	.0366	.0388	.0411	.0434	.0457	.0481
13	.0154	.0168	.0181	.0196	.0211	.0227	.0243	.0260	.0278	.0296
14	.0078	.0086	.0095	.0104	.0113	.0123	.0134	.0145	.0157	.0169
15	.0037	.0041	.0046	.0051	.0057	.0062	.0069	.0075	.0083	.0090
16	.0016	.0019	.0021	.0024	.0026	.0030	.0033	.0037	.0041	.0045
17	.0007	.0008	.0009	.0010	.0012	.0013	.0015	.0017	.0019	.0021
18	.0003	.0003	.0004	.0004	.0005	.0006	.0006	.0007	.0008	.0009
19	.0001	.0001	.0001	.0002	.0002	.0002	.0003	.0003	.0003	.0004
20	.0000	.0000	.0001	.0001	.0001	.0001	.0001	.0001	.0001	.0002
21	.0000	.0000	.0000	.0000	.0000	.0000	.0000	.0000	.0001	.0001

x	8.1	8.2	8.3	8.4	8.5	8.6	8.7	8.8	8.9	9.0
0	.0003	.0003	.0002	.0002	.0002	.0002	.0002	.0002	.0001	.0001
1	.0025	.0023	.0021	.0019	.0017	.0016	.0014	.0013	.0012	.0011
2	.0100	.0092	.0086	.0079	.0074	.0068	.0063	.0058	.0054	.0050
3	.0269	.0252	.0237	.0222	.0208	.0195	.0183	.0171	.0160	.0150
4	.0544	.0517	.0491	.0466	.0443	.0420	.0398	.0377	.0357	.0337
5	.0882	.0849	.0816	.0784	.0752	.0722	.0692	.0663	.0635	.0607
6	.1191	.1160	.1128	.1097	.1066	.1034	.1003	.0972	.0941	.0911
7	.1378	.1358	.1338	.1317	.1294	.1271	.1247	.1222	.1197	.1171
8	.1395	.1392	.1388	.1382	.1375	.1366	.1356	.1344	.1332	.1318
9	.1256	.1269	.1280	.1290	.1299	.1306	.1311	.1315	.1317	.1318
10	.1017	.1040	.1063	.1084	.1104	.1123	.1140	.1157	.1172	.1186
11	.0749	.0776	.0802	.0828	.0853	.0878	.0902	.0925	.0948	.0970
12	.0505	.0530	.0555	.0579	.0604	.0629	.0654	.0679	.0703	.0728
13	.0315	.0334	.0354	.0374	.0395	.0416	.0438	.0459	.0481	.0504
14	.0182	.0196	.0210	.0225	.0240	.0256	.0272	.0289	.0306	.0324
15	.0098	.0107	.0116	.0126	.0136	.0147	.0158	.0169	.0182	.0194
16	.0050	.0055	.0060	.0066	.0072	.0079	.0086	.0093	.0101	.0109
17	.0024	.0026	.0029	.0033	.0036	.0040	.0044	.0048	.0053	.0058
18	.0011	.0012	.0014	.0015	.0017	.0019	.0021	.0024	.0026	.0029
19	.0005	.0005	.0006	.0007	.0008	.0009	.0010	.0011	.0012	.0014
20	.0002	.0002	.0002	.0003	.0003	.0004	.0004	.0005	.0005	.0006
21	.0001	.0001	.0001	.0001	.0001	.0002	.0002	.0002	.0002	.0003
22	.0000	.0000	.0000	.0000	.0001	.0001	.0001	.0001	.0001	.0001

x	9.1	9.2	9.3	9.4	9.5	9.6	9.7	9.8	9.9	10.0
0	.0001	.0001	.0001	.0001	.0001	.0001	.0001	.0001	.0001	.0000
1	.0010	.0009	.0009	.0008	.0007	.0007	.0006	.0005	.0005	.0005
2	.0046	.0043	.0040	.0037	.0034	.0031	.0029	.0027	.0025	.0023
3	.0140	.0131	.0123	.0115	.0107	.0100	.0093	.0087	.0081	.0076
4	.0319	.0302	.0285	.0269	.0254	.0240	.0226	.0213	.0201	.0189
5	.0581	.0555	.0530	.0506	.0483	.0460	.0439	.0418	.0398	.0378
6	.0881	.0851	.0822	.0793	.0764	.0736	.0709	.0682	.0656	.0631
7	.1145	.1118	.1091	.1064	.1037	.1010	.0982	.0955	.0928	.0901
8	.1302	.1286	.1269	.1251	.1232	.1212	.1191	.1170	.1148	.1126
9	.1317	.1315	.1311	.1306	.1300	.1293	.1284	.1274	.1263	.1251
10	.1198	.1210	.1219	.1228	.1235	.1241	.1245	.1249	.1250	.1251
11	.0991	.1012	.1031	.1049	.1067	.1083	.1098	.1112	.1125	.1137
12	.0752	.0776	.0799	.0822	.0844	.0866	.0888	.0908	.0928	.0948
13	.0526	.0549	.0572	.0594	.0617	.0640	.0662	.0685	.0707	.0729
14	.0342	.0361	.0380	.0399	.0419	.0439	.0459	.0479	.0500	.0521
15	.0208	.0221	.0235	.0250	.0265	.0281	.0297	.0313	.0330	.0347
16	.0118	.0127	.0137	.0147	.0157	.0168	.0180	.0192	.0204	.0217
17	.0063	.0069	.0075	.0081	.0088	.0095	.0103	.0111	.0119	.0128
18	.0032	.0035	.0039	.0042	.0046	.0051	.0055	.0060	.0065	.0071
19	.0015	.0017	.0019	.0021	.0023	.0026	.0028	.0031	.0034	.0037
20	.0007	.0008	.0009	.0010	.0011	.0012	.0014	.0015	.0017	.0019
21	.0003	.0003	.0004	.0004	.0005	.0006	.0006	.0007	.0008	.0009
22	.0001	.0001	.0002	.0002	.0002	.0002	.0003	.0003	.0004	.0004
23	.0000	.0001	.0001	.0001	.0001	.0001	.0001	.0001	.0002	.0002
24	.0000	.0000	.0000	.0000	.0000	.0000	.0000	.0001	.0001	.0001

TABLE A.4 The e^{-x} Table

x	e^{-x}	x	e^{-x}	x	e^{-x}	x	e^{-x}
0.0	1.0000	3.0	0.0498	6.0	0.00248	9.0	0.00012
0.1	0.9048	3.1	0.0450	6.1	0.00224	9.1	0.00011
0.2	0.8187	3.2	0.0408	6.2	0.00203	9.2	0.00010
0.3	0.7408	3.3	0.0369	6.3	0.00184	9.3	0.00009
0.4	0.6703	3.4	0.0334	6.4	0.00166	9.4	0.00008
0.5	0.6065	3.5	0.0302	6.5	0.00150	9.5	0.00007
0.6	0.5488	3.6	0.0273	6.6	0.00136	9.6	0.00007
0.7	0.4966	3.7	0.0247	6.7	0.00123	9.7	0.00006
0.8	0.4493	3.8	0.0224	6.8	0.00111	9.8	0.00006
0.9	0.4066	3.9	0.0202	6.9	0.00101	9.9	0.00005
1.0	0.3679	4.0	0.0183	7.0	0.00091	10.0	0.00005
1.1	0.3329	4.1	0.0166	7.1	0.00083		
1.2	0.3012	4.2	0.0150	7.2	0.00075		
1.3	0.2725	4.3	0.0136	7.3	0.00068		
1.4	0.2466	4.4	0.0123	7.4	0.00061		
1.5	0.2231	4.5	0.0111	7.5	0.00055		
1.6	0.2019	4.6	0.0101	7.6	0.00050		
1.7	0.1827	4.7	0.0091	7.7	0.00045		
1.8	0.1653	4.8	0.0082	7.8	0.00041		
1.9	0.1496	4.9	0.0074	7.9	0.00037		
2.0	0.1353	5.0	0.0067	8.0	0.00034		
2.1	0.1225	5.1	0.0061	8.1	0.00030		
2.2	0.1108	5.2	0.0055	8.2	0.00027		
2.3	0.1003	5.3	0.0050	8.3	0.00025		
2.4	0.0907	5.4	0.0045	8.4	0.00022		
2.5	0.0821	5.5	0.0041	8.5	0.00020		
2.6	0.0743	5.6	0.0037	8.6	0.00018		
2.7	0.0672	5.7	0.0033	8.7	0.00017		
2.8	0.0608	5.8	0.0030	8.8	0.00015		
2.9	0.0550	5.9	0.0027	8.9	0.00014		

TABLE A.5   Areas of the Standard Normal Distribution

The entries in this table are the probabilities that a standard normal random variable is between 0 and z (the shaded area).

z	0.00	0.01	0.02	0.03	0.04	0.05	0.06	0.07	0.08	0.09
0.0	.0000	.0040	.0080	.0120	.0160	.0199	.0239	.0279	.0319	.0359
0.1	.0398	.0438	.0478	.0517	.0557	.0596	.0636	.0675	.0714	.0753
0.2	.0793	.0832	.0871	.0910	.0948	.0987	.1026	.1064	.1103	.1141
0.3	.1179	.1217	.1255	.1293	.1331	.1368	.1406	.1443	.1480	.1517
0.4	.1554	.1591	.1628	.1664	.1700	.1736	.1772	.1808	.1844	.1879
0.5	.1915	.1950	.1985	.2019	.2054	.2088	.2123	.2157	.2190	.2224
0.6	.2257	.2291	.2324	.2357	.2389	.2422	.2454	.2486	.2517	.2549
0.7	.2580	.2611	.2642	.2673	.2704	.2734	.2764	.2794	.2823	.2852
0.8	.2881	.2910	.2939	.2967	.2995	.3023	.3051	.3078	.3106	.3133
0.9	.3159	.3186	.3212	.3238	.3264	.3289	.3315	.3340	.3365	.3389
1.0	.3413	.3438	.3461	.3485	.3508	.3531	.3554	.3577	.3599	.3621
1.1	.3643	.3665	.3686	.3708	.3729	.3749	.3770	.3790	.3810	.3830
1.2	.3849	.3869	.3888	.3907	.3925	.3944	.3962	.3980	.3997	.4015
1.3	.4032	.4049	.4066	.4082	.4099	.4115	.4131	.4147	.4162	.4177
1.4	.4192	.4207	.4222	.4236	.4251	.4265	.4279	.4292	.4306	.4319
1.5	.4332	.4345	.4357	.4370	.4382	.4394	.4406	.4418	.4429	.4441
1.6	.4452	.4463	.4474	.4484	.4495	.4505	.4515	.4525	.4535	.4545
1.7	.4554	.4564	.4573	.4582	.4591	.4599	.4608	.4616	.4625	.4633
1.8	.4641	.4649	.4656	.4664	.4671	.4678	.4686	.4693	.4699	.4706
1.9	.4713	.4719	.4726	.4732	.4738	.4744	.4750	.4756	.4761	.4767
2.0	.4772	.4778	.4783	.4788	.4793	.4798	.4803	.4808	.4812	.4817
2.1	.4821	.4826	.4830	.4834	.4838	.4842	.4846	.4850	.4854	.4857
2.2	.4861	.4864	.4868	.4871	.4875	.4878	.4881	.4884	.4887	.4890
2.3	.4893	.4896	.4898	.4901	.4904	.4906	.4909	.4911	.4913	.4916
2.4	.4918	.4920	.4922	.4925	.4927	.4929	.4931	.4932	.4934	.4936
2.5	.4938	.4940	.4941	.4943	.4945	.4946	.4948	.4949	.4951	.4952
2.6	.4953	.4955	.4956	.4957	.4959	.4960	.4961	.4962	.4963	.4964
2.7	.4965	.4966	.4967	.4968	.4969	.4970	.4971	.4972	.4973	.4974
2.8	.4974	.4975	.4976	.4977	.4977	.4978	.4979	.4979	.4980	.4981
2.9	.4981	.4982	.4982	.4983	.4984	.4984	.4985	.4985	.4986	.4986
3.0	.4987	.4987	.4987	.4988	.4988	.4989	.4989	.4989	.4990	.4990
3.1	.4990	.4991	.4991	.4991	.4992	.4992	.4992	.4992	.4993	.4993
3.2	.4993	.4993	.4994	.4994	.4994	.4994	.4994	.4995	.4995	.4995
3.3	.4995	.4995	.4995	.4996	.4996	.4996	.4996	.4996	.4996	.4997
3.4	.4997	.4997	.4997	.4997	.4997	.4997	.4997	.4997	.4997	.4998
3.5	.4998									
4.0	.49997									
4.5	.499997									
5.0	.4999997									
6.0	.499999999									

TABLE A.6 **Critical Values from the *t* Distribution**

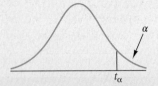

		Values of α for One-Tailed test and $\alpha/2$ for Two-Tailed Test				
df	$t_{.100}$	$t_{.050}$	$t_{.025}$	$t_{.010}$	$t_{.005}$	$t_{.001}$
1	3.078	6.314	12.706	31.821	63.656	318.289
2	1.886	2.920	4.303	6.965	9.925	22.328
3	1.638	2.353	3.182	4.541	5.841	10.214
4	1.533	2.132	2.776	3.747	4.604	7.173
5	1.476	2.015	2.571	3.365	4.032	5.894
6	1.440	1.943	2.447	3.143	3.707	5.208
7	1.415	1.895	2.365	2.998	3.499	4.785
8	1.397	1.860	2.306	2.896	3.355	4.501
9	1.383	1.833	2.262	2.821	3.250	4.297
10	1.372	1.812	2.228	2.764	3.169	4.144
11	1.363	1.796	2.201	2.718	3.106	4.025
12	1.356	1.782	2.179	2.681	3.055	3.930
13	1.350	1.771	2.160	2.650	3.012	3.852
14	1.345	1.761	2.145	2.624	2.977	3.787
15	1.341	1.753	2.131	2.602	2.947	3.733
16	1.337	1.746	2.120	2.583	2.921	3.686
17	1.333	1.740	2.110	2.567	2.898	3.646
18	1.330	1.734	2.101	2.552	2.878	3.610
19	1.328	1.729	2.093	2.539	2.861	3.579
20	1.325	1.725	2.086	2.528	2.845	3.552
21	1.323	1.721	2.080	2.518	2.831	3.527
22	1.321	1.717	2.074	2.508	2.819	3.505
23	1.319	1.714	2.069	2.500	2.807	3.485
24	1.318	1.711	2.064	2.492	2.797	3.467
25	1.316	1.708	2.060	2.485	2.787	3.450
26	1.315	1.706	2.056	2.479	2.779	3.435
27	1.314	1.703	2.052	2.473	2.771	3.421
28	1.313	1.701	2.048	2.467	2.763	3.408
29	1.311	1.699	2.045	2.462	2.756	3.396
30	1.310	1.697	2.042	2.457	2.750	3.385
40	1.303	1.684	2.021	2.423	2.704	3.307
50	1.299	1.676	2.009	2.403	2.678	3.261
60	1.296	1.671	2.000	2.390	2.660	3.232
70	1.294	1.667	1.994	2.381	2.648	3.211
80	1.292	1.664	1.990	2.374	2.639	3.195
90	1.291	1.662	1.987	2.368	2.632	3.183
100	1.290	1.660	1.984	2.364	2.626	3.174
150	1.287	1.655	1.976	2.351	2.609	3.145
200	1.286	1.653	1.972	2.345	2.601	3.131
∞	1.282	1.645	1.960	2.326	2.576	3.090

TABLE A.7   Percentage Points of the *F* Distribution

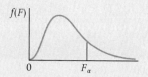

v_2 \ v_1	$\alpha = .10$ NUMERATOR DEGREES OF FREEDOM								
	1	**2**	**3**	**4**	**5**	**6**	**7**	**8**	**9**
1	39.86	49.50	53.59	55.83	57.24	58.20	58.91	59.44	59.86
2	8.53	9.00	9.16	9.24	9.29	9.33	9.35	9.37	9.38
3	5.54	5.46	5.39	5.34	5.31	5.28	5.27	5.25	5.24
4	4.54	4.32	4.19	4.11	4.05	4.01	3.98	3.95	3.94
5	4.06	3.78	3.62	3.52	3.45	3.40	3.37	3.34	3.32
6	3.78	3.46	3.29	3.18	3.11	3.05	3.01	2.98	2.96
7	3.59	3.26	3.07	2.96	2.88	2.83	2.78	2.75	2.72
8	3.46	3.11	2.92	2.81	2.73	2.67	2.62	2.59	2.56
9	3.36	3.01	2.81	2.69	2.61	2.55	2.51	2.47	2.44
10	3.29	2.92	2.73	2.61	2.52	2.46	2.41	2.38	2.35
11	3.23	2.86	2.66	2.54	2.45	2.39	2.34	2.30	2.27
12	3.18	2.81	2.61	2.48	2.39	2.33	2.28	2.24	2.21
13	3.14	2.76	2.56	2.43	2.35	2.28	2.23	2.20	2.16
14	3.10	2.73	2.52	2.39	2.31	2.24	2.19	2.15	2.12
15	3.07	2.70	2.49	2.36	2.27	2.21	2.16	2.12	2.09
16	3.05	2.67	2.46	2.33	2.24	2.18	2.13	2.09	2.06
17	3.03	2.64	2.44	2.31	2.22	2.15	2.10	2.06	2.03
18	3.01	2.62	2.42	2.29	2.20	2.13	2.08	2.04	2.00
19	2.99	2.61	2.40	2.27	2.18	2.11	2.06	2.02	1.98
20	2.97	2.59	2.38	2.25	2.16	2.09	2.04	2.00	1.96
21	2.96	2.57	2.36	2.23	2.14	2.08	2.02	1.98	1.95
22	2.95	2.56	2.35	2.22	2.13	2.06	2.01	1.97	1.93
23	2.94	2.55	2.34	2.21	2.11	2.05	1.99	1.95	1.92
24	2.93	2.54	2.33	2.19	2.10	2.04	1.98	1.94	1.91
25	2.92	2.53	2.32	2.18	2.09	2.02	1.97	1.93	1.89
26	2.91	2.52	2.31	2.17	2.08	2.01	1.96	1.92	1.88
27	2.90	2.51	2.30	2.17	2.07	2.00	1.95	1.91	1.87
28	2.89	2.50	2.29	2.16	2.06	2.00	1.94	1.90	1.87
29	2.89	2.50	2.28	2.15	2.06	1.99	1.93	1.89	1.86
30	2.88	2.49	2.28	2.14	2.05	1.98	1.93	1.88	1.85
40	2.84	2.44	2.23	2.09	2.00	1.93	1.87	1.83	1.79
60	2.79	2.39	2.18	2.04	1.95	1.87	1.82	1.77	1.74
120	2.75	2.35	2.13	1.99	1.90	1.82	1.77	1.72	1.68
∞	2.71	2.30	2.08	1.94	1.85	1.77	1.72	1.67	1.63

(continued)

TABLE A.7 Percentage Points of the *F* Distribution (*continued*)

				$\alpha = .10$						v_1	
			NUMERATOR DEGREES OF FREEDOM								
10	**12**	**15**	**20**	**24**	**30**	**40**	**60**	**120**	**∞**		v_2
60.19	60.71	61.22	61.74	62.00	62.26	62.53	62.79	63.06	63.33	1	
9.39	9.41	9.42	9.44	9.45	9.46	9.47	9.47	9.48	9.49	2	
5.23	5.22	5.20	5.18	5.18	5.17	5.16	5.15	5.14	5.13	3	
3.92	3.90	3.87	3.84	3.83	3.82	3.80	3.79	3.78	3.76	4	
3.30	3.27	3.24	3.21	3.19	3.17	3.16	3.14	3.12	3.10	5	
2.94	2.90	2.87	2.84	2.82	2.80	2.78	2.76	2.74	2.72	6	
2.70	2.67	2.63	2.59	2.58	2.56	2.54	2.51	2.49	2.47	7	
2.54	2.50	2.46	2.42	2.40	2.38	2.36	2.34	2.32	2.29	8	
2.42	2.38	2.34	2.30	2.28	2.25	2.23	2.21	2.18	2.16	9	
2.32	2.28	2.24	2.20	2.18	2.16	2.13	2.11	2.08	2.06	10	
2.25	2.21	2.17	2.12	2.10	2.08	2.05	2.03	2.00	1.97	11	
2.19	2.15	2.10	2.06	2.04	2.01	1.99	1.96	1.93	1.90	12	
2.14	2.10	2.05	2.01	1.98	1.96	1.93	1.90	1.88	1.85	13	
2.10	2.05	2.01	1.96	1.94	1.91	1.89	1.86	1.83	1.80	14	
2.06	2.02	1.97	1.92	1.90	1.87	1.85	1.82	1.79	1.76	15	
2.03	1.99	1.94	1.89	1.87	1.84	1.81	1.78	1.75	1.72	16	
2.00	1.96	1.91	1.86	1.84	1.81	1.78	1.75	1.72	1.69	17	
1.98	1.93	1.89	1.84	1.81	1.78	1.75	1.72	1.69	1.66	18	
1.96	1.91	1.86	1.81	1.79	1.76	1.73	1.70	1.67	1.63	19	
1.94	1.89	1.84	1.79	1.77	1.74	1.71	1.68	1.64	1.61	20	
1.92	1.87	1.83	1.78	1.75	1.72	1.69	1.66	1.62	1.59	21	
1.90	1.86	1.81	1.76	1.73	1.70	1.67	1.64	1.60	1.57	22	
1.89	1.84	1.80	1.74	1.72	1.69	1.66	1.62	1.59	1.55	23	
1.88	1.83	1.78	1.73	1.70	1.67	1.64	1.61	1.57	1.53	24	
1.87	1.82	1.77	1.72	1.69	1.66	1.63	1.59	1.56	1.52	25	
1.86	1.81	1.76	1.71	1.68	1.65	1.61	1.58	1.54	1.50	26	
1.85	1.80	1.75	1.70	1.67	1.64	1.60	1.57	1.53	1.49	27	
1.84	1.79	1.74	1.69	1.66	1.63	1.59	1.56	1.52	1.48	28	
1.83	1.78	1.73	1.68	1.65	1.62	1.58	1.55	1.51	1.47	29	
1.82	1.77	1.72	1.67	1.64	1.61	1.57	1.54	1.50	1.46	30	
1.76	1.71	1.66	1.61	1.57	1.54	1.51	1.47	1.42	1.38	40	
1.71	1.66	1.60	1.54	1.51	1.48	1.44	1.40	1.35	1.29	60	
1.65	1.60	1.55	1.48	1.45	1.41	1.37	1.32	1.26	1.19	120	
1.60	1.55	1.49	1.42	1.38	1.34	1.30	1.24	1.17	1.00	∞	

Denominator Degrees of Freedom

v_2	$\alpha = .05$ NUMERATOR DEGREES OF FREEDOM								
	1	2	3	4	5	6	7	8	9
1	161.45	199.50	215.71	224.58	230.16	233.99	236.77	238.88	240.54
2	18.51	19.00	19.16	19.25	19.30	19.33	19.35	19.37	19.38
3	10.13	9.55	9.28	9.12	9.01	8.94	8.89	8.85	8.81
4	7.71	6.94	6.59	6.39	6.26	6.16	6.09	6.04	6.00
5	6.61	5.79	5.41	5.19	5.05	4.95	4.88	4.82	4.77
6	5.99	5.14	4.76	4.53	4.39	4.28	4.21	4.15	4.10
7	5.59	4.74	4.35	4.12	3.97	3.87	3.79	3.73	3.68
8	5.32	4.46	4.07	3.84	3.69	3.58	3.50	3.44	3.39
9	5.12	4.26	3.86	3.63	3.48	3.37	3.29	3.23	3.18
10	4.96	4.10	3.71	3.48	3.33	3.22	3.14	3.07	3.02
11	4.84	3.98	3.59	3.36	3.20	3.09	3.01	2.95	2.90
12	4.75	3.89	3.49	3.26	3.11	3.00	2.91	2.85	2.80
13	4.67	3.81	3.41	3.18	3.03	2.92	2.83	2.77	2.71
14	4.60	3.74	3.34	3.11	2.96	2.85	2.76	2.70	2.65
15	4.54	3.68	3.29	3.06	2.90	2.79	2.71	2.64	2.59
16	4.49	3.63	3.24	3.01	2.85	2.74	2.66	2.59	2.54
17	4.45	3.59	3.20	2.96	2.81	2.70	2.61	2.55	2.49
18	4.41	3.55	3.16	2.93	2.77	2.66	2.58	2.51	2.46
19	4.38	3.52	3.13	2.90	2.74	2.63	2.54	2.48	2.42
20	4.35	3.49	3.10	2.87	2.71	2.60	2.51	2.45	2.39
21	4.32	3.47	3.07	2.84	2.68	2.57	2.49	2.42	2.37
22	4.30	3.44	3.05	2.82	2.66	2.55	2.46	2.40	2.34
23	4.28	3.42	3.03	2.80	2.64	2.53	2.44	2.37	2.32
24	4.26	3.40	3.01	2.78	2.62	2.51	2.42	2.36	2.30
25	4.24	3.39	2.99	2.76	2.60	2.49	2.40	2.34	2.28
26	4.23	3.37	2.98	2.74	2.59	2.47	2.39	2.32	2.27
27	4.21	3.35	2.96	2.73	2.57	2.46	2.37	2.31	2.25
28	4.20	3.34	2.95	2.71	2.56	2.45	2.36	2.29	2.24
29	4.18	3.33	2.93	2.70	2.55	2.43	2.35	2.28	2.22
30	4.17	3.32	2.92	2.69	2.53	2.42	2.33	2.27	2.21
40	4.08	3.23	2.84	2.61	2.45	2.34	2.25	2.18	2.12
60	4.00	3.15	2.76	2.53	2.37	2.25	2.17	2.10	2.04
120	3.92	3.07	2.68	2.45	2.29	2.18	2.09	2.02	1.96
∞	3.84	3.00	2.60	2.37	2.21	2.10	2.01	1.94	1.88

Denominator Degrees of Freedom

(*continued*)

TABLE A.7 Percentage Points of the *F* Distribution (*continued*)

					$\alpha = .05$					v_1	
				NUMERATOR DEGREES OF FREEDOM							
10	12	15	20	24	30	40	60	120	∞		v_2
241.88	243.90	245.90	248.00	249.10	250.10	251.10	252.20	253.30	254.30	1	
19.40	19.41	19.43	19.45	19.45	19.46	19.47	19.48	19.49	19.50	2	
8.79	8.74	8.70	8.66	8.64	8.62	8.59	8.57	8.55	8.53	3	
5.96	5.91	5.86	5.80	5.77	5.75	5.72	5.69	5.66	5.63	4	
4.74	4.68	4.62	4.56	4.53	4.50	4.46	4.43	4.40	4.36	5	
4.06	4.00	3.94	3.87	3.84	3.81	3.77	3.74	3.70	3.67	6	
3.64	3.57	3.51	3.44	3.41	3.38	3.34	3.30	3.27	3.23	7	
3.35	3.28	3.22	3.15	3.12	3.08	3.04	3.01	2.97	2.93	8	
3.14	3.07	3.01	2.94	2.90	2.86	2.83	2.79	2.75	2.71	9	
2.98	2.91	2.85	2.77	2.74	2.70	2.66	2.62	2.58	2.54	10	
2.85	2.79	2.72	2.65	2.61	2.57	2.53	2.49	2.45	2.40	11	
2.75	2.69	2.62	2.54	2.51	2.47	2.43	2.38	2.34	2.30	12	
2.67	2.60	2.53	2.46	2.42	2.38	2.34	2.30	2.25	2.21	13	
2.60	2.53	2.46	2.39	2.35	2.31	2.27	2.22	2.18	2.13	14	
2.54	2.48	2.40	2.33	2.29	2.25	2.20	2.16	2.11	2.07	15	
2.49	2.42	2.35	2.28	2.24	2.19	2.15	2.11	2.06	2.01	16	
2.45	2.38	2.31	2.23	2.19	2.15	2.10	2.06	2.01	1.96	17	
2.41	2.34	2.27	2.19	2.15	2.11	2.06	2.02	1.97	1.92	18	
2.38	2.31	2.23	2.16	2.11	2.07	2.03	1.98	1.93	1.88	19	
2.35	2.28	2.20	2.12	2.08	2.04	1.99	1.95	1.90	1.84	20	
2.32	2.25	2.18	2.10	2.05	2.01	1.96	1.92	1.87	1.81	21	
2.30	2.23	2.15	2.07	2.03	1.98	1.94	1.89	1.84	1.78	22	
2.27	2.20	2.13	2.05	2.01	1.96	1.91	1.86	1.81	1.76	23	
2.25	2.18	2.11	2.03	1.98	1.94	1.89	1.84	1.79	1.73	24	
2.24	2.16	2.09	2.01	1.96	1.92	1.87	1.82	1.77	1.71	25	
2.22	2.15	2.07	1.99	1.95	1.90	1.85	1.80	1.75	1.69	26	
2.20	2.13	2.06	1.97	1.93	1.88	1.84	1.79	1.73	1.67	27	
2.19	2.12	2.04	1.96	1.91	1.87	1.82	1.77	1.71	1.65	28	
2.18	2.10	2.03	1.94	1.90	1.85	1.81	1.75	1.70	1.64	29	
2.16	2.09	2.01	1.93	1.89	1.84	1.79	1.74	1.68	1.62	30	
2.08	2.00	1.92	1.84	1.79	1.74	1.69	1.64	1.58	1.51	40	
1.99	1.92	1.84	1.75	1.70	1.65	1.59	1.53	1.47	1.39	60	
1.91	1.83	1.75	1.66	1.61	1.55	1.50	1.43	1.35	1.25	120	
1.83	1.75	1.67	1.57	1.52	1.46	1.39	1.32	1.22	1.00	∞	

Denominator Degrees of Freedom

v_2 \\ v_1	$\alpha = .025$ NUMERATOR DEGREES OF FREEDOM								
	1	2	3	4	5	6	7	8	9
1	647.79	799.48	864.15	899.60	921.83	937.11	948.20	956.64	963.28
2	38.51	39.00	39.17	39.25	39.30	39.33	39.36	39.37	39.39
3	17.44	16.04	15.44	15.10	14.88	14.73	14.62	14.54	14.47
4	12.22	10.65	9.98	9.60	9.36	9.20	9.07	8.98	8.90
5	10.01	8.43	7.76	7.39	7.15	6.98	6.85	6.76	6.68
6	8.81	7.26	6.60	6.23	5.99	5.82	5.70	5.60	5.52
7	8.07	6.54	5.89	5.52	5.29	5.12	4.99	4.90	4.82
8	7.57	6.06	5.42	5.05	4.82	4.65	4.53	4.43	4.36
9	7.21	5.71	5.08	4.72	4.48	4.32	4.20	4.10	4.03
10	6.94	5.46	4.83	4.47	4.24	4.07	3.95	3.85	3.78
11	6.72	5.26	4.63	4.28	4.04	3.88	3.76	3.66	3.59
12	6.55	5.10	4.47	4.12	3.89	3.73	3.61	3.51	3.44
13	6.41	4.97	4.35	4.00	3.77	3.60	3.48	3.39	3.31
14	6.30	4.86	4.24	3.89	3.66	3.50	3.38	3.29	3.21
15	6.20	4.77	4.15	3.80	3.58	3.41	3.29	3.20	3.12
16	6.12	4.69	4.08	3.73	3.50	3.34	3.22	3.12	3.05
17	6.04	4.62	4.01	3.66	3.44	3.28	3.16	3.06	2.98
18	5.98	4.56	3.95	3.61	3.38	3.22	3.10	3.01	2.93
19	5.92	4.51	3.90	3.56	3.33	3.17	3.05	2.96	2.88
20	5.87	4.46	3.86	3.51	3.29	3.13	3.01	2.91	2.84
21	5.83	4.42	3.82	3.48	3.25	3.09	2.97	2.87	2.80
22	5.79	4.38	3.78	3.44	3.22	3.05	2.93	2.84	2.76
23	5.75	4.35	3.75	3.41	3.18	3.02	2.90	2.81	2.73
24	5.72	4.32	3.72	3.38	3.15	2.99	2.87	2.78	2.70
25	5.69	4.29	3.69	3.35	3.13	2.97	2.85	2.75	2.68
26	5.66	4.27	3.67	3.33	3.10	2.94	2.82	2.73	2.65
27	5.63	4.24	3.65	3.31	3.08	2.92	2.80	2.71	2.63
28	5.61	4.22	3.63	3.29	3.06	2.90	2.78	2.69	2.61
29	5.59	4.20	3.61	3.27	3.04	2.88	2.76	2.67	2.59
30	5.57	4.18	3.59	3.25	3.03	2.87	2.75	2.65	2.57
40	5.42	4.05	3.46	3.13	2.90	2.74	2.62	2.53	2.45
60	5.29	3.93	3.34	3.01	2.79	2.63	2.51	2.41	2.33
120	5.15	3.80	3.23	2.89	2.67	2.52	2.39	2.30	2.22
∞	5.02	3.69	3.12	2.79	2.57	2.41	2.29	2.19	2.11

(*continued*)

TABLE A.7 Percentage Points of the F Distribution (*continued*)

					$\alpha = .025$						v_1
			NUMERATOR DEGREES OF FREEDOM								
10	**12**	**15**	**20**	**24**	**30**	**40**	**60**	**120**	∞		v_2
968.63	976.72	984.87	993.08	997.27	1001.40	1005.60	1009.79	1014.04	1018.00	1	
39.40	39.41	39.43	39.45	39.46	39.46	39.47	39.48	39.49	39.50	2	
14.42	14.34	14.25	14.17	14.12	14.08	14.04	13.99	13.95	13.90	3	
8.84	8.75	8.66	8.56	8.51	8.46	8.41	8.36	8.31	8.26	4	
6.62	6.52	6.43	6.33	6.28	6.23	6.18	6.12	6.07	6.02	5	
5.46	5.37	5.27	5.17	5.12	5.07	5.01	4.96	4.90	4.85	6	
4.76	4.67	4.57	4.47	4.41	4.36	4.31	4.25	4.20	4.14	7	
4.30	4.20	4.10	4.00	3.95	3.89	3.84	3.78	3.73	3.67	8	
3.96	3.87	3.77	3.67	3.61	3.56	3.51	3.45	3.39	3.33	9	
3.72	3.62	3.52	3.42	3.37	3.31	3.26	3.20	3.14	3.08	10	
3.53	3.43	3.33	3.23	3.17	3.12	3.06	3.00	2.94	2.88	11	
3.37	3.28	3.18	3.07	3.02	2.96	2.91	2.85	2.79	2.72	12	
3.25	3.15	3.05	2.95	2.89	2.84	2.78	2.72	2.66	2.60	13	
3.15	3.05	2.95	2.84	2.79	2.73	2.67	2.61	2.55	2.49	14	
3.06	2.96	2.86	2.76	2.70	2.64	2.59	2.52	2.46	2.40	15	
2.99	2.89	2.79	2.68	2.63	2.57	2.51	2.45	2.38	2.32	16	
2.92	2.82	2.72	2.62	2.56	2.50	2.44	2.38	2.32	2.25	17	
2.87	2.77	2.67	2.56	2.50	2.44	2.38	2.32	2.26	2.19	18	
2.82	2.72	2.62	2.51	2.45	2.39	2.33	2.27	2.20	2.13	19	
2.77	2.68	2.57	2.46	2.41	2.35	2.29	2.22	2.16	2.09	20	
2.73	2.64	2.53	2.42	2.37	2.31	2.25	2.18	2.11	2.04	21	
2.70	2.60	2.50	2.39	2.33	2.27	2.21	2.14	2.08	2.00	22	
2.67	2.57	2.47	2.36	2.30	2.24	2.18	2.11	2.04	1.97	23	
2.64	2.54	2.44	2.33	2.27	2.21	2.15	2.08	2.01	1.94	24	
2.61	2.51	2.41	2.30	2.24	2.18	2.12	2.05	1.98	1.91	25	
2.59	2.49	2.39	2.28	2.22	2.16	2.09	2.03	1.95	1.88	26	
2.57	2.47	2.36	2.25	2.19	2.13	2.07	2.00	1.93	1.85	27	
2.55	2.45	2.34	2.23	2.17	2.11	2.05	1.98	1.91	1.83	28	
2.53	2.43	2.32	2.21	2.15	2.09	2.03	1.96	1.89	1.81	29	
2.51	2.41	2.31	2.20	2.14	2.07	2.01	1.94	1.87	1.79	30	
2.39	2.29	2.18	2.07	2.01	1.94	1.88	1.80	1.72	1.64	40	
2.27	2.17	2.06	1.94	1.88	1.82	1.74	1.67	1.58	1.48	60	
2.16	2.05	1.94	1.82	1.76	1.69	1.61	1.53	1.43	1.31	120	
2.05	1.94	1.83	1.71	1.64	1.57	1.48	1.39	1.27	1.00	∞	

Denominator Degrees of Freedom

v_2 \ v_1	$\alpha = .01$ NUMERATOR DEGREES OF FREEDOM								
	1	2	3	4	5	6	7	8	9
1	4052.18	4999.34	5403.53	5624.26	5763.96	5858.95	5928.33	5980.95	6022.40
2	98.50	99.00	99.16	99.25	99.30	99.33	99.36	99.38	99.39
3	34.12	30.82	29.46	28.71	28.24	27.91	27.67	27.49	27.34
4	21.20	18.00	16.69	15.98	15.52	15.21	14.98	14.80	14.66
5	16.26	13.27	12.06	11.39	10.97	10.67	10.46	10.29	10.16
6	13.75	10.92	9.78	9.15	8.75	8.47	8.26	8.10	7.98
7	12.25	9.55	8.45	7.85	7.46	7.19	6.99	6.84	6.72
8	11.26	8.65	7.59	7.01	6.63	6.37	6.18	6.03	5.91
9	10.56	8.02	6.99	6.42	6.06	5.80	5.61	5.47	5.35
10	10.04	7.56	6.55	5.99	5.64	5.39	5.20	5.06	4.94
11	9.65	7.21	6.22	5.67	5.32	5.07	4.89	4.74	4.63
12	9.33	6.93	5.95	5.41	5.06	4.82	4.64	4.50	4.39
13	9.07	6.70	5.74	5.21	4.86	4.62	4.44	4.30	4.19
14	8.86	6.51	5.56	5.04	4.69	4.46	4.28	4.14	4.03
15	8.68	6.36	5.42	4.89	4.56	4.32	4.14	4.00	3.89
16	8.53	6.23	5.29	4.77	4.44	4.20	4.03	3.89	3.78
17	8.40	6.11	5.19	4.67	4.34	4.10	3.93	3.79	3.68
18	8.29	6.01	5.09	4.58	4.25	4.01	3.84	3.71	3.60
19	8.18	5.93	5.01	4.50	4.17	3.94	3.77	3.63	3.52
20	8.10	5.85	4.94	4.43	4.10	3.87	3.70	3.56	3.46
21	8.02	5.78	4.87	4.37	4.04	3.81	3.64	3.51	3.40
22	7.95	5.72	4.82	4.31	3.99	3.76	3.59	3.45	3.35
23	7.88	5.66	4.76	4.26	3.94	3.71	3.54	3.41	3.30
24	7.82	5.61	4.72	4.22	3.90	3.67	3.50	3.36	3.26
25	7.77	5.57	4.68	4.18	3.85	3.63	3.46	3.32	3.22
26	7.72	5.53	4.64	4.14	3.82	3.59	3.42	3.29	3.18
27	7.68	5.49	4.60	4.11	3.78	3.56	3.39	3.26	3.15
28	7.64	5.45	4.57	4.07	3.75	3.53	3.36	3.23	3.12
29	7.60	5.42	4.54	4.04	3.73	3.50	3.33	3.20	3.09
30	7.56	5.39	4.51	4.02	3.70	3.47	3.30	3.17	3.07
40	7.31	5.18	4.31	3.83	3.51	3.29	3.12	2.99	2.89
60	7.08	4.98	4.13	3.65	3.34	3.12	2.95	2.82	2.72
120	6.85	4.79	3.95	3.48	3.17	2.96	2.79	2.66	2.56
∞	6.63	4.61	3.78	3.32	3.02	2.80	2.64	2.51	2.41

Denominator Degrees of Freedom

(*continued*)

TABLE A.7   **Percentage Points of the *F* Distribution** (*continued*)

$\alpha = .01$

v_1

NUMERATOR DEGREES OF FREEDOM

10	12	15	20	24	30	40	60	120	∞	v_2
6055.93	6106.68	6156.97	6208.66	6234.27	6260.35	6286.43	6312.97	6339.51	6366.00	1
99.40	99.42	99.43	99.45	99.46	99.47	99.48	99.48	99.49	99.50	2
27.23	27.05	26.87	26.69	26.60	26.50	26.41	26.32	26.22	26.13	3
14.55	14.37	14.20	14.02	13.93	13.84	13.75	13.65	13.56	13.46	4
10.05	9.89	9.72	9.55	9.47	9.38	9.29	9.20	9.11	9.02	5
7.87	7.72	7.56	7.40	7.31	7.23	7.14	7.06	6.97	6.88	6
6.62	6.47	6.31	6.16	6.07	5.99	5.91	5.82	5.74	5.65	7
5.81	5.67	5.52	5.36	5.28	5.20	5.12	5.03	4.95	4.86	8
5.26	5.11	4.96	4.81	4.73	4.65	4.57	4.48	4.40	4.31	9
4.85	4.71	4.56	4.41	4.33	4.25	4.17	4.08	4.00	3.91	10
4.54	4.40	4.25	4.10	4.02	3.94	3.86	3.78	3.69	3.60	11
4.30	4.16	4.01	3.86	3.78	3.70	3.62	3.54	3.45	3.36	12
4.10	3.96	3.82	3.66	3.59	3.51	3.43	3.34	3.25	3.17	13
3.94	3.80	3.66	3.51	3.43	3.35	3.27	3.18	3.09	3.00	14
3.80	3.67	3.52	3.37	3.29	3.21	3.13	3.05	2.96	2.87	15
3.69	3.55	3.41	3.26	3.18	3.10	3.02	2.93	2.84	2.75	16
3.59	3.46	3.31	3.16	3.08	3.00	2.92	2.83	2.75	2.65	17
3.51	3.37	3.23	3.08	3.00	2.92	2.84	2.75	2.66	2.57	18
3.43	3.30	3.15	3.00	2.92	2.84	2.76	2.67	2.58	2.49	19
3.37	3.23	3.09	2.94	2.86	2.78	2.69	2.61	2.52	2.42	20
3.31	3.17	3.03	2.88	2.80	2.72	2.64	2.55	2.46	2.36	21
3.26	3.12	2.98	2.83	2.75	2.67	2.58	2.50	2.40	2.31	22
3.21	3.07	2.93	2.78	2.70	2.62	2.54	2.45	2.35	2.26	23
3.17	3.03	2.89	2.74	2.66	2.58	2.49	2.40	2.31	2.21	24
3.13	2.99	2.85	2.70	2.62	2.54	2.45	2.36	2.27	2.17	25
3.09	2.96	2.81	2.66	2.58	2.50	2.42	2.33	2.23	2.13	26
3.06	2.93	2.78	2.63	2.55	2.47	2.38	2.29	2.20	2.10	27
3.03	2.90	2.75	2.60	2.52	2.44	2.35	2.26	2.17	2.06	28
3.00	2.87	2.73	2.57	2.49	2.41	2.33	2.23	2.14	2.03	29
2.98	2.84	2.70	2.55	2.47	2.39	2.30	2.21	2.11	2.01	30
2.80	2.66	2.52	2.37	2.29	2.20	2.11	2.02	1.92	1.80	40
2.63	2.50	2.35	2.20	2.12	2.03	1.94	1.84	1.73	1.60	60
2.47	2.34	2.19	2.03	1.95	1.86	1.76	1.66	1.53	1.38	120
2.32	2.18	2.04	1.88	1.79	1.70	1.59	1.47	1.32	1.00	∞

Denominator Degrees of Freedom

v_1					$\alpha = .005$				
					NUMERATOR DEGREES OF FREEDOM				
v_2	1	2	3	4	5	6	7	8	9
1	16212.46	19997.36	21614.13	22500.75	23055.82	23439.53	23715.20	23923.81	24091.45
2	198.50	199.01	199.16	199.24	199.30	199.33	199.36	199.38	199.39
3	55.55	49.80	47.47	46.20	45.39	44.84	44.43	44.13	43.88
4	31.33	26.28	24.26	23.15	22.46	21.98	21.62	21.35	21.14
5	22.78	18.31	16.53	15.56	14.94	14.51	14.20	13.96	13.77
6	18.63	14.54	12.92	12.03	11.46	11.07	10.79	10.57	10.39
7	16.24	12.40	10.88	10.05	9.52	9.16	8.89	8.68	8.51
8	14.69	11.04	9.60	8.81	8.30	7.95	7.69	7.50	7.34
9	13.61	10.11	8.72	7.96	7.47	7.13	6.88	6.69	6.54
10	12.83	9.43	8.08	7.34	6.87	6.54	6.30	6.12	5.97
11	12.23	8.91	7.60	6.88	6.42	6.10	5.86	5.68	5.54
12	11.75	8.51	7.23	6.52	6.07	5.76	5.52	5.35	5.20
13	11.37	8.19	6.93	6.23	5.79	5.48	5.25	5.08	4.94
14	11.06	7.92	6.68	6.00	5.56	5.26	5.03	4.86	4.72
15	10.80	7.70	6.48	5.80	5.37	5.07	4.85	4.67	4.54
16	10.58	7.51	6.30	5.64	5.21	4.91	4.69	4.52	4.38
17	10.38	7.35	6.16	5.50	5.07	4.78	4.56	4.39	4.25
18	10.22	7.21	6.03	5.37	4.96	4.66	4.44	4.28	4.14
19	10.07	7.09	5.92	5.27	4.85	4.56	4.34	4.18	4.04
20	9.94	6.99	5.82	5.17	4.76	4.47	4.26	4.09	3.96
21	9.83	6.89	5.73	5.09	4.68	4.39	4.18	4.01	3.88
22	9.73	6.81	5.65	5.02	4.61	4.32	4.11	3.94	3.81
23	9.63	6.73	5.58	4.95	4.54	4.26	4.05	3.88	3.75
24	9.55	6.66	5.52	4.89	4.49	4.20	3.99	3.83	3.69
25	9.48	6.60	5.46	4.84	4.43	4.15	3.94	3.78	3.64
26	9.41	6.54	5.41	4.79	4.38	4.10	3.89	3.73	3.60
27	9.34	6.49	5.36	4.74	4.34	4.06	3.85	3.69	3.56
28	9.28	6.44	5.32	4.70	4.30	4.02	3.81	3.65	3.52
29	9.23	6.40	5.28	4.66	4.26	3.98	3.77	3.61	3.48
30	9.18	6.35	5.24	4.62	4.23	3.95	3.74	3.58	3.45
40	8.83	6.07	4.98	4.37	3.99	3.71	3.51	3.35	3.22
60	8.49	5.79	4.73	4.14	3.76	3.49	3.29	3.13	3.01
120	8.18	5.54	4.50	3.92	3.55	3.28	3.09	2.93	2.81
∞	7.88	5.30	4.28	3.72	3.35	3.09	2.90	2.74	2.62

(*continued*)

TABLE A.7 Percentage Points of the *F* Distribution (*continued*)

α = .005 NUMERATOR DEGREES OF FREEDOM										v_2
10	12	15	20	24	30	40	60	120	∞	
24221.84	24426.73	24631.62	24836.51	24937.09	25041.40	25145.71	25253.74	25358.05	25465.00	1
199.39	199.42	199.43	199.45	199.45	199.48	199.48	199.48	199.49	199.50	2
43.68	43.39	43.08	42.78	42.62	42.47	42.31	42.15	41.99	41.83	3
20.97	20.70	20.44	20.17	20.03	19.89	19.75	19.61	19.47	19.32	4
13.62	13.38	13.15	12.90	12.78	12.66	12.53	12.40	12.27	12.14	5
10.25	10.03	9.81	9.59	9.47	9.36	9.24	9.12	9.00	8.88	6
8.38	8.18	7.97	7.75	7.64	7.53	7.42	7.31	7.19	7.08	7
7.21	7.01	6.81	6.61	6.50	6.40	6.29	6.18	6.06	5.95	8
6.42	6.23	6.03	5.83	5.73	5.62	5.52	5.41	5.30	5.19	9
5.85	5.66	5.47	5.27	5.17	5.07	4.97	4.86	4.75	4.64	10
5.42	5.24	5.05	4.86	4.76	4.65	4.55	4.45	4.34	4.23	11
5.09	4.91	4.72	4.53	4.43	4.33	4.23	4.12	4.01	3.90	12
4.82	4.64	4.46	4.27	4.17	4.07	3.97	3.87	3.76	3.65	13
4.60	4.43	4.25	4.06	3.96	3.86	3.76	3.66	3.55	3.44	14
4.42	4.25	4.07	3.88	3.79	3.69	3.59	3.48	3.37	3.26	15
4.27	4.10	3.92	3.73	3.64	3.54	3.44	3.33	3.22	3.11	16
4.14	3.97	3.79	3.61	3.51	3.41	3.31	3.21	3.10	2.98	17
4.03	3.86	3.68	3.50	3.40	3.30	3.20	3.10	2.99	2.87	18
3.93	3.76	3.59	3.40	3.31	3.21	3.11	3.00	2.89	2.78	19
3.85	3.68	3.50	3.32	3.22	3.12	3.02	2.92	2.81	2.69	20
3.77	3.60	3.43	3.24	3.15	3.05	2.95	2.84	2.73	2.61	21
3.70	3.54	3.36	3.18	3.08	2.98	2.88	2.77	2.66	2.55	22
3.64	3.47	3.30	3.12	3.02	2.92	2.82	2.71	2.60	2.48	23
3.59	3.42	3.25	3.06	2.97	2.87	2.77	2.66	2.55	2.43	24
3.54	3.37	3.20	3.01	2.92	2.82	2.72	2.61	2.50	2.38	25
3.49	3.33	3.15	2.97	2.87	2.77	2.67	2.56	2.45	2.33	26
3.45	3.28	3.11	2.93	2.83	2.73	2.63	2.52	2.41	2.29	27
3.41	3.25	3.07	2.89	2.79	2.69	2.59	2.48	2.37	2.25	28
3.38	3.21	3.04	2.86	2.76	2.66	2.56	2.45	2.33	2.21	29
3.34	3.18	3.01	2.82	2.73	2.63	2.52	2.42	2.30	2.18	30
3.12	2.95	2.78	2.60	2.50	2.40	2.30	2.18	2.06	1.93	40
2.90	2.74	2.57	2.39	2.29	2.19	2.08	1.96	1.83	1.69	60
2.71	2.54	2.37	2.19	2.09	1.98	1.87	1.75	1.61	1.43	120
2.52	2.36	2.19	2.00	1.90	1.79	1.67	1.53	1.36	1.00	∞

TABLE A.8 The Chi-Square Table

Values of χ^2 for Selected Probabilities

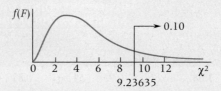

Example: df (Number of degrees of freedom) = 5, the tail above $\chi^2 = 9.23635$ represents 0.10 or 10% of area under the curve.

DEGREES OF FREEDOM	AREA IN UPPER TAIL									
	.995	.99	.975	.95	.9	.1	.05	.025	.01	.005
1	0.0000393	0.0001571	0.0009821	0.0039322	0.0157907	2.7055	3.8415	5.0239	6.6349	7.8794
2	0.010025	0.020100	0.050636	0.102586	0.210721	4.6052	5.9915	7.3778	9.2104	10.5965
3	0.07172	0.11483	0.21579	0.35185	0.58438	6.2514	7.8147	9.3484	11.3449	12.8381
4	0.20698	0.29711	0.48442	0.71072	1.06362	7.7794	9.4877	11.1433	13.2767	14.8602
5	0.41175	0.55430	0.83121	1.14548	1.61031	9.2363	11.0705	12.8325	15.0863	16.7496
6	0.67573	0.87208	1.23734	1.63538	2.20413	10.6446	12.5916	14.4494	16.8119	18.5475
7	0.98925	1.23903	1.68986	2.16735	2.83311	12.0170	14.0671	16.0128	18.4753	20.2777
8	1.34440	1.64651	2.17972	2.73263	3.48954	13.3616	15.5073	17.5345	20.0902	21.9549
9	1.73491	2.08789	2.70039	3.32512	4.16816	14.6837	16.9190	19.0228	21.6660	23.5893
10	2.15585	2.55820	3.24696	3.94030	4.86518	15.9872	18.3070	20.4832	23.2093	25.1881
11	2.60320	3.05350	3.81574	4.57481	5.57779	17.2750	19.6752	21.9200	24.7250	26.7569
12	3.07379	3.57055	4.40378	5.22603	6.30380	18.5493	21.0261	23.3367	26.2170	28.2997
13	3.56504	4.10690	5.00874	5.89186	7.04150	19.8119	22.3620	24.7356	27.6882	29.8193
14	4.07466	4.66042	5.62872	6.57063	7.78954	21.0641	23.6848	26.1189	29.1412	31.3194
15	4.60087	5.22936	6.26212	7.26093	8.54675	22.3071	24.9958	27.4884	30.5780	32.8015
16	5.14216	5.81220	6.90766	7.96164	9.31224	23.5418	26.2962	28.8453	31.9999	34.2671
17	5.69727	6.40774	7.56418	8.67175	10.08518	24.7690	27.5871	30.1910	33.4087	35.7184
18	6.26477	7.01490	8.23074	9.39045	10.86494	25.9894	28.8693	31.5264	34.8052	37.1564
19	6.84392	7.63270	8.90651	10.11701	11.65091	27.2036	30.1435	32.8523	36.1908	38.5821
20	7.43381	8.26037	9.59077	10.85080	12.44260	28.4120	31.4104	34.1696	37.5663	39.9969
21	8.03360	8.89717	10.28291	11.59132	13.23960	29.6151	32.6706	35.4789	38.9322	41.4009
22	8.64268	9.54249	10.98233	12.33801	14.04149	30.8133	33.9245	36.7807	40.2894	42.7957
23	9.26038	10.19569	11.68853	13.09051	14.84795	32.0069	35.1725	38.0756	41.6383	44.1814
24	9.88620	10.85635	12.40115	13.84842	15.65868	33.1962	36.4150	39.3641	42.9798	45.5584
25	10.51965	11.52395	13.11971	14.61140	16.47341	34.3816	37.6525	40.6465	44.3140	46.9280
26	11.16022	12.19818	13.84388	15.37916	17.29188	35.5632	38.8851	41.9231	45.6416	48.2898
27	11.80765	12.87847	14.57337	16.15139	18.11389	36.7412	40.1133	43.1945	46.9628	49.6450
28	12.46128	13.56467	15.30785	16.92788	18.93924	37.9159	41.3372	44.4608	48.2782	50.9936
29	13.12107	14.25641	16.04705	17.70838	19.76774	39.0875	42.5569	45.7223	49.5878	52.3355
30	13.78668	14.95346	16.79076	18.49267	20.59924	40.2560	43.7730	46.9792	50.8922	53.6719
40	20.70658	22.16420	24.43306	26.50930	29.05052	51.8050	55.7585	59.3417	63.6908	66.7660
50	27.99082	29.70673	32.35738	34.76424	37.68864	63.1671	67.5048	71.4202	76.1538	79.4898
60	35.53440	37.48480	40.48171	43.18797	46.45888	74.3970	79.0820	83.2977	88.3794	91.9518
70	43.27531	45.44170	48.75754	51.73926	55.32894	85.5270	90.5313	95.0231	100.4251	104.2148
80	51.17193	53.53998	57.15315	60.39146	64.27784	96.5782	101.8795	106.6285	112.3288	116.3209
90	59.19633	61.75402	65.64659	69.12602	73.29108	107.5650	113.1452	118.1359	124.1162	128.2987
100	67.32753	70.06500	74.22188	77.92944	82.35813	118.4980	124.3221	129.5613	135.8069	140.1697

TABLE A.9 Critical Values for the Durbin-Watson Test

Entries in the table give the critical values for a one-tailed Durbin-Watson test for autocorrelation. For a two-tailed test, the level of significance is doubled.

	SIGNIFICANT POINTS OF d_L AND d_U: $\alpha = .05$ NUMBER OF INDEPENDENT VARIABLES									
	1		2		3		4		5	
k										
n	d_L	d_U	d_L	d_U	d_L	d_U	d_L	d_U	d_L	d_U
15	1.08	1.36	0.95	1.54	0.82	1.75	0.69	1.97	0.56	2.21
16	1.10	1.37	0.98	1.54	0.86	1.73	0.74	1.93	0.62	2.15
17	1.13	1.38	1.02	1.54	0.90	1.71	0.78	1.90	0.67	2.10
18	1.16	1.39	1.05	1.53	0.93	1.69	0.82	1.87	0.71	2.06
19	1.18	1.40	1.08	1.53	0.97	1.68	0.86	1.85	0.75	2.02
20	1.20	1.41	1.10	1.54	1.00	1.68	0.90	1.83	0.79	1.99
21	1.22	1.42	1.13	1.54	1.03	1.67	0.93	1.81	0.83	1.96
22	1.24	1.43	1.15	1.54	1.05	1.66	0.96	1.80	0.86	1.94
23	1.26	1.44	1.17	1.54	1.08	1.66	0.99	1.79	0.90	1.92
24	1.27	1.45	1.19	1.55	1.10	1.66	1.01	1.78	0.93	1.90
25	1.29	1.45	1.21	1.55	1.12	1.66	1.04	1.77	0.95	1.89
26	1.30	1.46	1.22	1.55	1.14	1.65	1.06	1.76	0.98	1.88
27	1.32	1.47	1.24	1.56	1.16	1.65	1.08	1.76	1.01	1.86
28	1.33	1.48	1.26	1.56	1.18	1.65	1.10	1.75	1.03	1.85
29	1.34	1.48	1.27	1.56	1.20	1.65	1.12	1.74	1.05	1.84
30	1.35	1.49	1.28	1.57	1.21	1.65	1.14	1.74	1.07	1.83
31	1.36	1.50	1.30	1.57	1.23	1.65	1.16	1.74	1.09	1.83
32	1.37	1.50	1.31	1.57	1.24	1.65	1.18	1.73	1.11	1.82
33	1.38	1.51	1.32	1.58	1.26	1.65	1.19	1.73	1.13	1.81
34	1.39	1.51	1.33	1.58	1.27	1.65	1.21	1.73	1.15	1.81
35	1.40	1.52	1.34	1.58	1.28	1.65	1.22	1.73	1.16	1.80
36	1.41	1.52	1.35	1.59	1.29	1.65	1.24	1.73	1.18	1.80
37	1.42	1.53	1.36	1.59	1.31	1.66	1.25	1.72	1.19	1.80
38	1.43	1.54	1.37	1.59	1.32	1.66	1.26	1.72	1.21	1.79
39	1.43	1.54	1.38	1.60	1.33	1.66	1.27	1.72	1.22	1.79
40	1.44	1.54	1.39	1.60	1.34	1.66	1.29	1.72	1.23	1.79
45	1.48	1.57	1.43	1.62	1.38	1.67	1.34	1.72	1.29	1.78
50	1.50	1.59	1.46	1.63	1.42	1.67	1.38	1.72	1.34	1.77
55	1.53	1.60	1.49	1.64	1.45	1.68	1.41	1.72	1.38	1.77
60	1.55	1.62	1.51	1.65	1.48	1.69	1.44	1.73	1.41	1.77
65	1.57	1.63	1.54	1.66	1.50	1.70	1.47	1.73	1.44	1.77
70	1.58	1.64	1.55	1.67	1.52	1.70	1.49	1.74	1.46	1.77
75	1.60	1.65	1.57	1.68	1.54	1.71	1.51	1.74	1.49	1.77
80	1.61	1.66	1.59	1.69	1.56	1.72	1.53	1.74	1.51	1.77
85	1.62	1.67	1.60	1.70	1.57	1.72	1.55	1.75	1.52	1.77
90	1.63	1.68	1.61	1.70	1.59	1.73	1.57	1.75	1.54	1.78
95	1.64	1.69	1.62	1.71	1.60	1.73	1.58	1.75	1.56	1.78
100	1.65	1.69	1.63	1.72	1.61	1.74	1.59	1.76	1.57	1.78

This table is reprinted by permission of *Biometrika* trustees from J. Durbin and G. S. Watson, "Testing for Serial Correlation in Least Square Regression II," *Biometrika*, vol. 38, 1951, pp. 159–78.

<table>
<tr><td colspan="11" style="text-align:center">SIGNIFICANT POINTS OF d_L AND d_U: $\alpha = .01$
NUMBER OF INDEPENDENT VARIABLES</td></tr>
<tr><th>k</th><th colspan="2">1</th><th colspan="2">2</th><th colspan="2">3</th><th colspan="2">4</th><th colspan="2">5</th></tr>
<tr><th>n</th><th>d_L</th><th>d_U</th><th>d_L</th><th>d_U</th><th>d_L</th><th>d_U</th><th>d_L</th><th>d_U</th><th>d_L</th><th>d_U</th></tr>
<tr><td>15</td><td>0.81</td><td>1.07</td><td>0.70</td><td>1.25</td><td>0.59</td><td>1.46</td><td>0.49</td><td>1.70</td><td>0.39</td><td>1.96</td></tr>
<tr><td>16</td><td>0.84</td><td>1.09</td><td>0.74</td><td>1.25</td><td>0.63</td><td>1.44</td><td>0.53</td><td>1.66</td><td>0.44</td><td>1.90</td></tr>
<tr><td>17</td><td>0.87</td><td>1.10</td><td>0.77</td><td>1.25</td><td>0.67</td><td>1.43</td><td>0.57</td><td>1.63</td><td>0.48</td><td>1.85</td></tr>
<tr><td>18</td><td>0.90</td><td>1.12</td><td>0.80</td><td>1.26</td><td>0.71</td><td>1.42</td><td>0.61</td><td>1.60</td><td>0.52</td><td>1.80</td></tr>
<tr><td>19</td><td>0.93</td><td>1.13</td><td>0.83</td><td>1.26</td><td>0.74</td><td>1.41</td><td>0.65</td><td>1.58</td><td>0.56</td><td>1.77</td></tr>
<tr><td>20</td><td>0.95</td><td>1.15</td><td>0.86</td><td>1.27</td><td>0.77</td><td>1.41</td><td>0.68</td><td>1.57</td><td>0.60</td><td>1.74</td></tr>
<tr><td>21</td><td>0.97</td><td>1.16</td><td>0.89</td><td>1.27</td><td>0.80</td><td>1.41</td><td>0.72</td><td>1.55</td><td>0.63</td><td>1.71</td></tr>
<tr><td>22</td><td>1.00</td><td>1.17</td><td>0.91</td><td>1.28</td><td>0.83</td><td>1.40</td><td>0.75</td><td>1.54</td><td>0.66</td><td>1.69</td></tr>
<tr><td>23</td><td>1.02</td><td>1.19</td><td>0.94</td><td>1.29</td><td>0.86</td><td>1.40</td><td>0.77</td><td>1.53</td><td>0.70</td><td>1.67</td></tr>
<tr><td>24</td><td>1.04</td><td>1.20</td><td>0.96</td><td>1.30</td><td>0.88</td><td>1.41</td><td>0.80</td><td>1.53</td><td>0.72</td><td>1.66</td></tr>
<tr><td>25</td><td>1.05</td><td>1.21</td><td>0.98</td><td>1.30</td><td>0.90</td><td>1.41</td><td>0.83</td><td>1.52</td><td>0.75</td><td>1.65</td></tr>
<tr><td>26</td><td>1.07</td><td>1.22</td><td>1.00</td><td>1.31</td><td>0.93</td><td>1.41</td><td>0.85</td><td>1.52</td><td>0.78</td><td>1.64</td></tr>
<tr><td>27</td><td>1.09</td><td>1.23</td><td>1.02</td><td>1.32</td><td>0.95</td><td>1.41</td><td>0.88</td><td>1.51</td><td>0.81</td><td>1.63</td></tr>
<tr><td>28</td><td>1.10</td><td>1.24</td><td>1.04</td><td>1.32</td><td>0.97</td><td>1.41</td><td>0.90</td><td>1.51</td><td>0.83</td><td>1.62</td></tr>
<tr><td>29</td><td>1.12</td><td>1.25</td><td>1.05</td><td>1.33</td><td>0.99</td><td>1.42</td><td>0.92</td><td>1.51</td><td>0.85</td><td>1.61</td></tr>
<tr><td>30</td><td>1.13</td><td>1.26</td><td>1.07</td><td>1.34</td><td>1.01</td><td>1.42</td><td>0.94</td><td>1.51</td><td>0.88</td><td>1.61</td></tr>
<tr><td>31</td><td>1.15</td><td>1.27</td><td>1.08</td><td>1.34</td><td>1.02</td><td>1.42</td><td>0.96</td><td>1.51</td><td>0.90</td><td>1.60</td></tr>
<tr><td>32</td><td>1.16</td><td>1.28</td><td>1.10</td><td>1.35</td><td>1.04</td><td>1.43</td><td>0.98</td><td>1.51</td><td>0.92</td><td>1.60</td></tr>
<tr><td>33</td><td>1.17</td><td>1.29</td><td>1.11</td><td>1.36</td><td>1.05</td><td>1.43</td><td>1.00</td><td>1.51</td><td>0.94</td><td>1.59</td></tr>
<tr><td>34</td><td>1.18</td><td>1.30</td><td>1.13</td><td>1.36</td><td>1.07</td><td>1.43</td><td>1.01</td><td>1.51</td><td>0.95</td><td>1.59</td></tr>
<tr><td>35</td><td>1.19</td><td>1.31</td><td>1.14</td><td>1.37</td><td>1.08</td><td>1.44</td><td>1.03</td><td>1.51</td><td>0.97</td><td>1.59</td></tr>
<tr><td>36</td><td>1.21</td><td>1.32</td><td>1.15</td><td>1.38</td><td>1.10</td><td>1.44</td><td>1.04</td><td>1.51</td><td>0.99</td><td>1.59</td></tr>
<tr><td>37</td><td>1.22</td><td>1.32</td><td>1.16</td><td>1.38</td><td>1.11</td><td>1.45</td><td>1.06</td><td>1.51</td><td>1.00</td><td>1.59</td></tr>
<tr><td>38</td><td>1.23</td><td>1.33</td><td>1.18</td><td>1.39</td><td>1.12</td><td>1.45</td><td>1.07</td><td>1.52</td><td>1.02</td><td>1.58</td></tr>
<tr><td>39</td><td>1.24</td><td>1.34</td><td>1.19</td><td>1.39</td><td>1.14</td><td>1.45</td><td>1.09</td><td>1.52</td><td>1.03</td><td>1.58</td></tr>
<tr><td>40</td><td>1.25</td><td>1.34</td><td>1.20</td><td>1.40</td><td>1.15</td><td>1.46</td><td>1.10</td><td>1.52</td><td>1.05</td><td>1.58</td></tr>
<tr><td>45</td><td>1.29</td><td>1.38</td><td>1.24</td><td>1.42</td><td>1.20</td><td>1.48</td><td>1.16</td><td>1.53</td><td>1.11</td><td>1.58</td></tr>
<tr><td>50</td><td>1.32</td><td>1.40</td><td>1.28</td><td>1.45</td><td>1.24</td><td>1.49</td><td>1.20</td><td>1.54</td><td>1.16</td><td>1.59</td></tr>
<tr><td>55</td><td>1.36</td><td>1.43</td><td>1.32</td><td>1.47</td><td>1.28</td><td>1.51</td><td>1.25</td><td>1.55</td><td>1.21</td><td>1.59</td></tr>
<tr><td>60</td><td>1.38</td><td>1.45</td><td>1.35</td><td>1.48</td><td>1.32</td><td>1.52</td><td>1.28</td><td>1.56</td><td>1.25</td><td>1.60</td></tr>
<tr><td>65</td><td>1.41</td><td>1.47</td><td>1.38</td><td>1.50</td><td>1.35</td><td>1.53</td><td>1.31</td><td>1.57</td><td>1.28</td><td>1.61</td></tr>
<tr><td>70</td><td>1.43</td><td>1.49</td><td>1.40</td><td>1.52</td><td>1.37</td><td>1.55</td><td>1.34</td><td>1.58</td><td>1.31</td><td>1.61</td></tr>
<tr><td>75</td><td>1.45</td><td>1.50</td><td>1.42</td><td>1.53</td><td>1.39</td><td>1.56</td><td>1.37</td><td>1.59</td><td>1.34</td><td>1.62</td></tr>
<tr><td>80</td><td>1.47</td><td>1.52</td><td>1.44</td><td>1.54</td><td>1.42</td><td>1.57</td><td>1.39</td><td>1.60</td><td>1.36</td><td>1.62</td></tr>
<tr><td>85</td><td>1.48</td><td>1.53</td><td>1.46</td><td>1.55</td><td>1.43</td><td>1.58</td><td>1.41</td><td>1.60</td><td>1.39</td><td>1.63</td></tr>
<tr><td>90</td><td>1.50</td><td>1.54</td><td>1.47</td><td>1.56</td><td>1.45</td><td>1.59</td><td>1.43</td><td>1.61</td><td>1.41</td><td>1.64</td></tr>
<tr><td>95</td><td>1.51</td><td>1.55</td><td>1.49</td><td>1.57</td><td>1.47</td><td>1.60</td><td>1.45</td><td>1.62</td><td>1.42</td><td>1.64</td></tr>
<tr><td>100</td><td>1.52</td><td>1.56</td><td>1.50</td><td>1.58</td><td>1.48</td><td>1.60</td><td>1.46</td><td>1.63</td><td>1.44</td><td>1.65</td></tr>
</table>

TABLE A.10   **Critical Values of the Studentized Range (*q*) Distribution**

									$\alpha = .05$										
DEGREES OF								NUMBER OF POPULATIONS											
FREEDOM	2	3	4	5	6	7	8	9	10	11	12	13	14	15	16	17	18	19	20
1	18.0	27.0	32.8	37.1	40.4	43.1	45.4	47.4	49.1	50.6	52.0	53.2	54.3	55.4	56.3	57.2	58.0	58.8	59.6
2	6.08	8.33	9.80	10.9	11.7	12.4	13.0	13.5	14.0	14.4	14.7	15.1	15.4	15.7	15.9	16.1	16.4	16.6	16.8
3	4.50	5.91	6.82	7.50	8.04	8.48	8.85	9.18	9.46	9.72	9.95	10.2	10.3	10.5	10.7	10.8	11.0	11.1	11.2
4	3.93	5.04	5.76	6.29	6.71	7.05	7.35	7.60	7.83	8.03	8.21	8.37	8.52	8.66	8.79	8.91	9.03	9.13	9.23
5	3.64	4.60	5.22	5.67	6.03	6.33	6.58	6.80	6.99	7.17	7.32	7.47	7.60	7.72	7.83	7.93	8.03	8.12	8.21
6	3.46	4.34	4.90	5.30	5.63	5.90	6.12	6.32	6.49	6.65	6.79	6.92	7.03	7.14	7.24	7.34	7.43	7.51	7.59
7	3.34	4.16	4.68	5.06	5.36	5.61	5.82	6.00	6.16	6.30	6.43	6.55	6.66	6.76	6.85	6.94	7.02	7.10	7.17
8	3.26	4.04	4.53	4.89	5.17	5.40	5.60	5.77	5.92	6.05	6.18	6.29	6.39	6.48	6.57	6.65	6.73	6.80	6.87
9	3.20	3.95	4.41	4.76	5.02	5.24	5.43	5.59	5.74	5.87	5.98	6.09	6.19	6.28	6.36	6.44	6.51	6.58	6.64
10	3.15	3.88	4.33	4.65	4.91	5.12	5.30	5.46	5.60	5.72	5.83	5.93	6.03	6.11	6.19	6.27	6.34	6.40	6.47
11	3.11	3.82	4.26	4.57	4.82	5.03	5.20	5.35	5.49	5.61	5.71	5.81	5.90	5.98	6.06	6.13	6.20	6.27	6.33
12	3.08	3.77	4.20	4.51	4.75	4.95	5.12	5.27	5.39	5.51	5.61	5.71	5.80	5.88	5.95	6.02	6.09	6.15	6.21
13	3.06	3.73	4.15	4.45	4.69	4.88	5.05	5.19	5.32	5.43	5.53	5.63	5.71	5.79	5.86	5.93	5.99	6.05	6.11
14	3.03	3.70	4.11	4.41	4.64	4.83	4.99	5.13	5.25	5.36	5.46	5.55	5.64	5.71	5.79	5.85	5.91	5.97	6.03
15	3.01	3.67	4.08	4.37	4.59	4.78	4.94	5.08	5.20	5.31	5.40	5.49	5.57	5.65	5.72	5.78	5.85	5.90	5.96
16	3.00	3.65	4.05	4.33	4.56	4.74	4.90	5.03	5.15	5.26	5.35	5.44	5.52	5.59	5.66	5.73	5.79	5.84	5.90
17	2.98	3.63	4.02	4.30	4.52	4.70	4.86	4.99	5.11	5.21	5.31	5.39	5.47	5.54	5.61	5.67	5.73	5.79	5.84
18	2.97	3.61	4.00	4.28	4.49	4.67	4.82	4.96	5.07	5.17	5.27	5.35	5.43	5.50	5.57	5.63	5.69	5.74	5.79
19	2.96	3.59	3.98	4.25	4.47	4.65	4.79	4.92	5.04	5.14	5.23	5.31	5.39	5.46	5.53	5.59	5.65	5.70	5.75
20	2.95	3.58	3.96	4.23	4.45	4.62	4.77	4.90	5.01	5.11	5.20	5.28	5.36	5.43	5.49	5.55	5.61	5.66	5.71
24	2.92	3.53	3.90	4.17	4.37	4.54	4.68	4.81	4.92	5.01	5.10	5.18	5.25	5.32	5.38	5.44	5.49	5.55	5.59
30	2.89	3.49	3.85	4.10	4.30	4.46	4.60	4.72	4.82	4.92	5.00	5.08	5.15	5.21	5.27	5.33	5.38	5.43	5.47
40	2.86	3.44	3.79	4.04	4.23	4.39	4.52	4.63	4.73	4.82	4.90	4.98	5.04	5.11	5.16	5.22	5.27	5.31	5.36
60	2.83	3.40	3.74	3.98	4.16	4.31	4.44	4.55	4.65	4.73	4.81	4.88	4.94	5.00	5.06	5.11	5.15	5.20	5.24
120	2.80	3.36	3.68	3.92	4.10	4.24	4.36	4.47	4.56	4.64	4.71	4.78	4.84	4.90	4.95	5.00	5.04	5.09	5.13
∞	2.77	3.31	3.63	3.86	4.03	4.17	4.29	4.39	4.47	4.55	4.62	4.68	4.74	4.80	4.85	4.89	4.93	4.97	5.01

$\alpha = .01$																			
DEGREES OF																			

DEGREES OF FREEDOM	NUMBER OF POPULATIONS																		
	2	3	4	5	6	7	8	9	10	11	12	13	14	15	16	17	18	19	20
1	90.0	135.	164.	186.	202.	216.	227.	237.	246.	253.	260.	266.	272.	277.	282.	286.	290.	294.	298.
2	14.0	19.0	22.3	24.7	26.6	28.2	29.5	30.7	31.7	32.6	33.4	34.1	34.8	35.4	36.0	36.5	37.0	37.5	37.9
3	8.26	10.6	12.2	13.3	14.2	15.0	15.6	16.2	16.7	17.1	17.5	17.9	18.2	18.5	18.8	19.1	19.3	19.5	19.8
4	6.51	8.12	9.17	9.96	10.6	11.1	11.5	11.9	12.3	12.6	12.8	13.1	13.3	13.5	13.7	13.9	14.1	14.2	14.4
5	5.70	6.97	7.80	8.42	8.91	9.32	9.67	9.97	10.2	10.5	10.7	10.9	11.1	11.2	11.4	11.6	11.7	11.8	11.9
6	5.24	6.33	7.03	7.56	7.97	8.32	8.61	8.87	9.10	9.30	9.49	9.65	9.81	9.95	10.1	10.2	10.3	10.4	10.5
7	4.95	5.92	6.54	7.01	7.37	7.68	7.94	8.17	8.37	8.55	8.71	8.86	9.00	9.12	9.24	9.35	9.46	9.55	9.65
8	4.74	5.63	6.20	6.63	6.96	7.24	7.47	7.68	7.87	8.03	8.18	8.31	8.44	8.55	8.66	8.76	8.85	8.94	9.03
9	4.60	5.43	5.96	6.35	6.66	6.91	7.13	7.32	7.49	7.65	7.78	7.91	8.03	8.13	8.23	8.32	8.41	8.49	8.57
10	4.48	5.27	5.77	6.14	6.43	6.67	6.87	7.05	7.21	7.36	7.48	7.60	7.71	7.81	7.91	7.99	8.07	8.15	8.22
11	4.39	5.14	5.62	5.97	6.25	6.48	6.67	6.84	6.99	7.13	7.25	7.36	7.46	7.56	7.65	7.73	7.81	7.88	7.95
12	4.32	5.04	5.50	5.84	6.10	6.32	6.51	6.67	6.81	6.94	7.06	7.17	7.26	7.36	7.44	7.52	7.59	7.66	7.73
13	4.26	4.96	5.40	5.73	5.98	6.19	6.37	6.53	6.67	6.79	6.90	7.01	7.10	7.19	7.27	7.34	7.42	7.48	7.55
14	4.21	4.89	5.32	5.63	5.88	6.08	6.26	6.41	6.54	6.66	6.77	6.87	6.96	7.05	7.12	7.20	7.27	7.33	7.39
15	4.17	4.83	5.25	5.56	5.80	5.99	6.16	6.31	6.44	6.55	6.66	6.76	6.84	6.93	7.00	7.07	7.14	7.20	7.26
16	4.13	4.78	5.19	5.49	5.72	5.92	6.08	6.22	6.35	6.46	6.56	6.66	6.74	6.82	6.90	6.97	7.03	7.09	7.15
17	4.10	4.74	5.14	5.43	5.66	5.85	6.01	6.15	6.27	6.38	6.48	6.57	6.66	6.73	6.80	6.87	6.94	7.00	7.05
18	4.07	4.70	5.09	5.38	5.60	5.79	5.94	6.08	6.20	6.31	6.41	6.50	6.58	6.65	6.72	6.79	6.85	6.91	6.96
19	4.05	4.67	5.05	5.33	5.55	5.73	5.89	6.02	6.14	6.25	6.34	6.43	6.51	6.58	6.65	6.72	6.78	6.84	6.89
20	4.02	4.64	5.02	5.29	5.51	5.69	5.84	5.97	6.09	6.19	6.29	6.37	6.45	6.52	6.59	6.65	6.71	6.76	6.82
24	3.96	4.54	4.91	5.17	5.37	5.54	5.69	5.81	5.92	6.02	6.11	6.19	6.26	6.33	6.39	6.45	6.51	6.56	6.61
30	3.89	4.45	4.80	5.05	5.24	5.40	5.54	5.65	5.76	5.85	5.93	6.01	6.08	6.14	6.20	6.26	6.31	6.36	6.41
40	3.82	4.37	4.70	4.93	5.11	5.27	5.39	5.50	5.60	5.69	5.77	5.84	5.90	5.96	6.02	6.07	6.12	6.17	6.21
60	3.76	4.28	4.60	4.82	4.99	5.13	5.25	5.36	5.45	5.53	5.60	5.67	5.73	5.79	5.84	5.89	5.93	5.98	6.02
120	3.70	4.20	4.50	4.71	4.87	5.01	5.12	5.21	5.30	5.38	5.44	5.51	5.56	5.61	5.66	5.71	5.75	5.79	5.83
∞	3.64	4.12	4.40	4.60	4.76	4.88	4.99	5.08	5.16	5.23	5.29	5.35	5.40	5.45	5.49	5.54	5.57	5.61	5.65

TABLE A.11 Critical Values of R for the Runs Test: Lower Tail

n_1 \ n_2 ($\alpha = .025$)	2	3	4	5	6	7	8	9	10	11	12	13	14	15	16	17	18	19	20
2											2	2	2	2	2	2	2	2	2
3					2	2	2	2	2	2	2	2	2	3	3	3	3	3	3
4				2	2	2	3	3	3	3	3	3	3	3	4	4	4	4	4
5			2	2	3	3	3	3	3	4	4	4	4	4	4	4	5	5	5
6		2	2	3	3	3	3	4	4	4	4	5	5	5	5	5	5	6	6
7		2	2	3	3	3	4	4	5	5	5	5	5	6	6	6	6	6	6
8		2	3	3	3	4	4	5	5	5	6	6	6	6	6	7	7	7	7
9		2	3	3	4	4	5	5	5	6	6	6	7	7	7	7	8	8	8
10		2	3	3	4	5	5	5	6	6	7	7	7	7	8	8	8	8	9
11		2	3	4	4	5	5	6	6	7	7	7	8	8	8	9	9	9	9
12	2	2	3	4	4	5	6	6	7	7	7	8	8	8	9	9	9	10	10
13	2	2	3	4	5	5	6	6	7	7	8	8	9	9	9	10	10	10	10
14	2	2	3	4	5	5	6	7	7	8	8	9	9	9	10	10	10	11	11
15	2	3	3	4	5	6	6	7	7	8	8	9	9	10	10	11	11	11	12
16	2	3	4	4	5	6	6	7	8	8	9	9	10	10	11	11	11	12	12
17	2	3	4	4	5	6	7	7	8	9	9	10	10	11	11	11	12	12	13
18	2	3	4	5	5	6	7	8	8	9	9	10	10	11	11	12	12	13	13
19	2	3	4	5	6	6	7	8	8	9	10	10	11	11	12	12	13	13	13
20	2	3	4	5	6	6	7	8	9	9	10	10	11	12	12	13	13	13	14

Source: Adapted from F. S. Swed and C. Eisenhart, *Ann. Math. Statist.*, vol. 14, 1943, pp. 83–86.

TABLE A.12 Critical Values of R for the Runs Test: Upper Tail

n_1 \ n_2 ($\alpha = .025$)	2	3	4	5	6	7	8	9	10	11	12	13	14	15	16	17	18	19	20
2																			
3																			
4				9	9														
5			9	10	10	11	11												
6			9	10	11	12	12	13	13	13	13								
7				11	12	13	13	14	14	14	14	15	15	15					
8				11	12	13	14	14	15	15	16	16	16	16	17	17	17	17	17
9					13	14	14	15	16	16	16	17	17	18	18	18	18	18	18
10					13	14	15	16	16	17	17	18	18	18	19	19	19	20	20
11					13	14	15	16	17	17	18	19	19	19	20	20	20	21	21
12					13	14	16	16	17	18	19	19	20	20	21	21	21	22	22
13						15	16	17	18	19	19	20	20	21	21	22	22	23	23
14						15	16	17	18	19	20	20	21	22	22	23	23	23	24
15						15	16	18	18	19	20	21	22	22	23	23	24	24	25
16							17	18	19	20	21	21	22	23	23	24	25	25	25
17							17	18	19	20	21	22	23	23	24	25	25	26	26
18							17	18	19	20	21	22	23	24	25	25	26	26	27
19							17	18	20	21	22	23	23	24	25	26	26	27	27
20							17	18	20	21	22	23	24	25	25	26	27	27	28

TABLE A.13 *p*-Values for Mann-Whitney *U* Statistic Small Samples ($n_1 \leq n_2$)

$n_2 = 3$	U_0	n_1 1	2	3	
	0	.25	.10	.05	
	1	.50	.20	.10	
	2		.40	.20	
	3		.60	.35	
	4			.50	

$n_2 = 4$	U_0	n_1 1	2	3	4
	0	.2000	.0667	.0286	.0143
	1	.4000	.1333	.0571	.0286
	2	.6000	.2667	.1143	.0571
	3		.4000	.2000	.1000
	4		.6000	.3143	.1714
	5			.4286	.2429
	6			.5714	.3429
	7				.4429
	8				.5571

$n_2 = 5$	U_0	n_1 1	2	3	4	5
	0	.1667	.0476	.0179	.0079	.0040
	1	.3333	.0952	.0357	.0159	.0079
	2	.5000	.1905	.0714	.0317	.0159
	3		.2857	.1250	.0556	.0278
	4		.4286	.1964	.0952	.0476
	5		.5714	.2857	.1429	.0754
	6			.3929	.2063	.1111
	7			.5000	.2778	.1548
	8				.3651	.2103
	9				.4524	.2738
	10				.5476	.3452
	11					.4206
	12					.5000

Computed by M. Pagano, Dept. of Statistics, University of Florida. Reprinted by permission from William Mendenhall and James E. Reinmuth, *Statistics for Management and Economics*, 5th ed. Copyright © 1986 by PWS-KENT Publishers, Boston.

(continued)

TABLE A.13   *p*-Values for Mann-Whitney *U* Statistic Small Samples ($n_1 \leq n_2$) (*continued*)

$n_2 = 6$	U_0	1	2	3	4	5	6
				n_1			
	0	.1429	.0357	.0119	.0048	.0022	.0011
	1	.2857	.0714	.0238	.0095	.0043	.0022
	2	.4286	.1429	.0476	.0190	.0087	.0043
	3	.5714	.2143	.0833	.0333	.0152	.0076
	4		.3214	.1310	.0571	.0260	.0130
	5		.4286	.1905	.0857	.0411	.0206
	6		.5714	.2738	.1286	.0628	.0325
	7			.3571	.1762	.0887	.0465
	8			.4524	.2381	.1234	.0660
	9			.5476	.3048	.1645	.0898
	10				.3810	.2143	.1201
	11				.4571	.2684	.1548
	12				.5429	.3312	.1970
	13					.3961	.2424
	14					.4654	.2944
	15					.5346	.3496
	16						.4091
	17						.4686
	18						.5314

$n_2 = 7$	U_0	1	2	3	4	5	6	7
					n_1			
	0	.1250	.0278	.0083	.0030	.0013	.0006	.0003
	1	.2500	.0556	.0167	.0061	.0025	.0012	.0006
	2	.3750	.1111	.0333	.0121	.0051	.0023	.0012
	3	.5000	.1667	.0583	.0212	.0088	.0041	.0020
	4		.2500	.0917	.0364	.0152	.0070	.0035
	5		.3333	.1333	.0545	.0240	.0111	.0055
	6		.4444	.1917	.0818	.0366	.0175	.0087
	7		.5556	.2583	.1152	.0530	.0256	.0131
	8			.3333	.1576	.0745	.0367	.0189
	9			.4167	.2061	.1010	.0507	.0265
	10			.5000	.2636	.1338	.0688	.0364
	11				.3242	.1717	.0903	.0487
	12				.3939	.2159	.1171	.0641
	13				.4636	.2652	.1474	.0825
	14				.5364	.3194	.1830	.1043
	15					.3775	.2226	.1297
	16					.4381	.2669	.1588
	17					.5000	.3141	.1914
	18						.3654	.2279
	19						.4178	.2675
	20						.4726	.3100
	21						.5274	.3552
	22							.4024
	23							.4508
	24							.5000

$n_2 = 8$	U_0	1	2	3	4	5	6	7	8
	0	.1111	.0222	.0061	.0020	.0008	.0003	.0002	.0001
	1	.2222	.0444	.0121	.0040	.0016	.0007	.0003	.0002
	2	.3333	.0889	.0242	.0081	.0031	.0013	.0006	.0003
	3	.4444	.1333	.0424	.0141	.0054	.0023	.0011	.0005
	4	.5556	.2000	.0667	.0242	.0093	.0040	.0019	.0009
	5		.2667	.0970	.0364	.0148	.0063	.0030	.0015
	6		.3556	.1394	.0545	.0225	.0100	.0047	.0023
	7		.4444	.1879	.0768	.0326	.0147	.0070	.0035
	8		.5556	.2485	.1071	.0466	.0213	.0103	.0052
	9			.3152	.1414	.0637	.0296	.0145	.0074
	10			.3879	.1838	.0855	.0406	.0200	.0103
	11			.4606	.2303	.1111	.0539	.0270	.0141
	12			.5394	.2848	.1422	.0709	.0361	.0190
	13				.3414	.1772	.0906	.0469	.0249
	14				.4040	.2176	.1142	.0603	.0325
	15				.4667	.2618	.1412	.0760	.0415
	16				.5333	.3108	.1725	.0946	.0524
	17					.3621	.2068	.1159	.0652
	18					.4165	.2454	.1405	.0803
	19					.4716	.2864	.1678	.0974
	20					.5284	.3310	.1984	.1172
	21						.3773	.2317	.1393
	22						.4259	.2679	.1641
	23						.4749	.3063	.1911
	24						.5251	.3472	.2209
	25							.3894	.2527
	26							.4333	.2869
	27							.4775	.3227
	28							.5225	.3605
	29								.3992
	30								.4392
	31								.4796
	32								.5204

(continued)

TABLE A.13 *p*-Values for Mann-Whitney *U* Statistic Small Samples ($n_1 \leq n_2$) (*continued*)

$n_2 = 9$	U_0	1	2	3	4	5	6	7	8	9
	0	.1000	.0182	.0045	.0014	.0005	.0002	.0001	.0000	.0000
	1	.2000	.0364	.0091	.0028	.0010	.0004	.0002	.0001	.0000
	2	.3000	.0727	.0182	.0056	.0020	.0008	.0003	.0002	.0001
	3	.4000	.1091	.0318	.0098	.0035	.0014	.0006	.0003	.0001
	4	.5000	.1636	.0500	.0168	.0060	.0024	.0010	.0005	.0002
	5		.2182	.0727	.0252	.0095	.0038	.0017	.0008	.0004
	6		.2909	.1045	.0378	.0145	.0060	.0026	.0012	.0006
	7		.3636	.1409	.0531	.0210	.0088	.0039	.0019	.0009
	8		.4545	.1864	.0741	.0300	.0128	.0058	.0028	.0014
	9		.5455	.2409	.0993	.0415	.0180	.0082	.0039	.0020
	10			.3000	.1301	.0559	.0248	.0115	.0056	.0028
	11			.3636	.1650	.0734	.0332	.0156	.0076	.0039
	12			.4318	.2070	.0949	.0440	.0209	.0103	.0053
	13			.5000	.2517	.1199	.0567	.0274	.0137	.0071
	14				.3021	.1489	.0723	.0356	.0180	.0094
	15				.3552	.1818	.0905	.0454	.0232	.0122
	16				.4126	.2188	.1119	.0571	.0296	.0157
	17				.4699	.2592	.1361	.0708	.0372	.0200
	18				.5301	.3032	.1638	.0869	.0464	.0252
	19					.3497	.1942	.1052	.0570	.0313
	20					.3986	.2280	.1261	.0694	.0385
	21					.4491	.2643	.1496	.0836	.0470
	22					.5000	.3035	.1755	.0998	.0567
	23						.3445	.2039	.1179	.0680
	24						.3878	.2349	.1383	.0807
	25						.4320	.2680	.1606	.0951
	26						.4773	.3032	.1852	.1112
	27						.5227	.3403	.2117	.1290
	28							.3788	.2404	.1487
	29							.4185	.2707	.1701
	30							.4591	.3029	.1933
	31							.5000	.3365	.2181
	32								.3715	.2447
	33								.4074	.2729
	34								.4442	.3024
	35								.4813	.3332
	36								.5187	.3652
	37									.3981
	38									.4317
	39									.4657
	40									.5000

$n_2 = 10$	U_0	1	2	3	4	5	6	7	8	9	10
	0	.0909	.0152	.0035	.0010	.0003	.0001	.0001	.0000	.0000	.0000
	1	.1818	.0303	.0070	.0020	.0007	.0002	.0001	.0000	.0000	.0000
	2	.2727	.0606	.0140	.0040	.0013	.0005	.0002	.0001	.0000	.0000
	3	.3636	.0909	.0245	.0070	.0023	.0009	.0004	.0002	.0001	.0000
	4	.4545	.1364	.0385	.0120	.0040	.0015	.0006	.0003	.0001	.0001
	5	.5455	.1818	.0559	.0180	.0063	.0024	.0010	.0004	.0002	.0001
	6		.2424	.0804	.0270	.0097	.0037	.0015	.0007	.0003	.0002
	7		.3030	.1084	.0380	.0140	.0055	.0023	.0010	.0005	.0002
	8		.3788	.1434	.0529	.0200	.0080	.0034	.0015	.0007	.0004
	9		.4545	.1853	.0709	.0276	.0112	.0048	.0022	.0011	.0005
	10		.5455	.2343	.0939	.0376	.0156	.0068	.0031	.0015	.0008
	11			.2867	.1199	.0496	.0210	.0093	.0043	.0021	.0010
	12			.3462	.1518	.0646	.0280	.0125	.0058	.0028	.0014
	13			.4056	.1868	.0823	.0363	.0165	.0078	.0038	.0019
	14			.4685	.2268	.1032	.0467	.0215	.0103	.0051	.0026
	15			.5315	.2697	.1272	.0589	.0277	.0133	.0066	.0034
	16				.3177	.1548	.0736	.0351	.0171	.0086	.0045
	17				.3666	.1855	.0903	.0439	.0217	.0110	.0057
	18				.4196	.2198	.1099	.0544	.0273	.0140	.0073
	19				.4725	.2567	.1317	.0665	.0338	.0175	.0093
	20				.5275	.2970	.1566	.0806	.0416	.0217	.0116
	21					.3393	.1838	.0966	.0506	.0267	.0144
	22					.3839	.2139	.1148	.0610	.0326	.0177
	23					.4296	.2461	.1349	.0729	.0394	.0216
	24					.4765	.2811	.1574	.0864	.0474	.0262
	25					.5235	.3177	.1819	.1015	.0564	.0315
	26						.3564	.2087	.1185	.0667	.0376
	27						.3962	.2374	.1371	.0782	.0446
	28						.4374	.2681	.1577	.0912	.0526
	29						.4789	.3004	.1800	.1055	.0615
	30						.5211	.3345	.2041	.1214	.0716
	31							.3698	.2299	.1388	.0827
	32							.4063	.2574	.1577	.0952
	33							.4434	.2863	.1781	.1088
	34							.4811	.3167	.2001	.1237
	35							.5189	.3482	.2235	.1399
	36								.3809	.2483	.1575
	37								.4143	.2745	.1763
	38								.4484	.3019	.1965
	39								.4827	.3304	.2179
	40								.5173	.3598	.2406
	41									.3901	.2644
	42									.4211	.2894
	43									.4524	.3153
	44									.4841	.3421
	45									.5159	.3697
	46										.3980
	47										.4267
	48										.4559
	49										.4853
	50										.5147

TABLE A.14 Critical Values of T for the Wilcoxon Matched-Pairs Signed Rank Test (Small Samples)

1-SIDED	2-SIDED	$n = 5$	$n = 6$	$n = 7$	$n = 8$	$n = 9$	$n = 10$
$\alpha = .05$	$\alpha = .10$	1	2	4	6	8	11
$\alpha = .025$	$\alpha = .05$		1	2	4	6	8
$\alpha = .01$	$\alpha = .02$			0	2	3	5
$\alpha = .005$	$\alpha = .01$				0	2	3

1-SIDED	2-SIDED	$n = 11$	$n = 12$	$n = 13$	$n = 14$	$n = 15$	$n = 16$
$\alpha = .05$	$\alpha = .10$	14	17	21	26	30	36
$\alpha = .025$	$\alpha = .05$	11	14	17	21	25	30
$\alpha = .01$	$\alpha = .02$	7	10	13	16	20	24
$\alpha = .005$	$\alpha = .01$	5	7	10	13	16	19

1-SIDED	2-SIDED	$n = 17$	$n = 18$	$n = 19$	$n = 20$	$n = 21$	$n = 22$
$\alpha = .05$	$\alpha = .10$	41	47	54	60	68	75
$\alpha = .025$	$\alpha = .05$	35	40	46	52	59	66
$\alpha = .01$	$\alpha = .02$	28	33	38	43	49	56
$\alpha = .005$	$\alpha = .01$	23	28	32	37	43	49

1-SIDED	2-SIDED	$n = 23$	$n = 24$	$n = 25$	$n = 26$	$n = 27$	$n = 28$
$\alpha = .05$	$\alpha = .10$	83	92	101	110	120	130
$\alpha = .025$	$\alpha = .05$	73	81	90	98	107	117
$\alpha = .01$	$\alpha = .02$	62	69	77	85	93	102
$\alpha = .005$	$\alpha = .01$	55	61	68	76	84	92

1-SIDED	2-SIDED	$n = 29$	$n = 30$	$n = 31$	$n = 32$	$n = 33$	$n = 34$
$\alpha = .05$	$\alpha = .10$	141	152	163	175	188	201
$\alpha = .025$	$\alpha = .05$	127	137	148	159	171	183
$\alpha = .01$	$\alpha = .02$	111	120	130	141	151	162
$\alpha = .005$	$\alpha = .01$	100	109	118	128	138	149

1-SIDED	2-SIDED	$n = 35$	$n = 36$	$n = 37$	$n = 38$	$n = 39$	
$\alpha = .05$	$\alpha = .10$	214	228	242	256	271	
$\alpha = .025$	$\alpha = .05$	195	208	222	235	250	
$\alpha = .01$	$\alpha = .02$	174	186	198	211	224	
$\alpha = .005$	$\alpha = .01$	160	171	183	195	208	

1-SIDED	2-SIDED	$n = 40$	$n = 41$	$n = 42$	$n = 43$	$n = 44$	$n = 45$
$\alpha = .05$	$\alpha = .10$	287	303	319	336	353	371
$\alpha = .025$	$\alpha = .05$	264	279	295	311	327	344
$\alpha = .01$	$\alpha = .02$	238	252	267	281	297	313
$\alpha = .005$	$\alpha = .01$	221	234	248	262	277	292

1-SIDED	2-SIDED	$n = 46$	$n = 47$	$n = 48$	$n = 49$	$n = 50$	
$\alpha = .05$	$\alpha = .10$	389	408	427	446	466	
$\alpha = .025$	$\alpha = .05$	361	379	397	415	434	
$\alpha = .01$	$\alpha = .02$	329	345	362	380	398	
$\alpha = .005$	$\alpha = .01$	307	323	339	356	373	

From E. Wilcoxon and R. A. Wilcox, "Some Rapid Approximate Statistical Procedures," 1964. Reprinted by permission of Lederle Labs, a division of the American Cyanamid Co.

TABLE A.15 Factors for Control Charts

NUMBER OF ITEMS IN SAMPLE	AVERAGES			RANGES	
	FACTORS FOR CONTROL LIMITS		FACTORS FOR CENTRAL LINE	FACTORS FOR CONTROL LIMITS	
n	A_2	A_3	d_2	D_3	D_4
2	1.880	2.659	1.128	0	3.267
3	1.023	1.954	1.693	0	2.575
4	0.729	1.628	2.059	0	2.282
5	0.577	1.427	2.326	0	2.115
6	0.483	1.287	2.534	0	2.004
7	0.419	1.182	2.704	0.076	1.924
8	0.373	1.099	2.847	0.136	1.864
9	0.337	1.032	2.970	0.184	1.816
10	0.308	0.975	3.078	0.223	1.777
11	0.285	0.927	3.173	0.256	1.744
12	0.266	0.886	3.258	0.284	1.716
13	0.249	0.850	3.336	0.308	1.692
14	0.235	0.817	3.407	0.329	1.671
15	0.223	0.789	3.472	0.348	1.652

Adapted from American Society for Testing and Materials, *Manual on Quality Control of Materials*, 1951, Table B2, p.115. For a more detailed table and explanation, see Acheson J. Duncan, *Quality Control and Industrial Statistics*, 3d ed. Homewood, IL.: Richard D. Irwin, 1974, Table M, p.927.

TABLE A.16   Tree Diagram Taxonomy of Inferential Techniques

Hypothesis Tests (HT)

≥ 3-samples
- 1 Independent Variable — 11.2 One-Way ANOVA
- 1 Independent Variable + 1 Block Variable — 11.4 Randomized Block Design
- 2 Independent Variables — 11.5 Two-Way ANOVA

2-Samples
- Variances — 10.5 F HT for σ_1^2, σ_2^2
- Proportions — 10.4 z HT for $p_1 - p_1$
- Means
  - Dependent Samples — 10.3 t HT for D
  - Independent Samples
    - σ_1, σ_2 known — 10.1 z HT for $\mu_1 - \mu_2$
    - σ_1^2, σ_2^2 unknown — 10.2 t HT for $\mu_1 - \mu_2$

1-Sample
- Variances — 9.5 χ^2 HT for σ^2
- Proportions — 9.4 z HT for p
- Means
  - σ unknown — 9.3 t HT for μ
  - σ known — 9.2 z HT for μ

Confidence Intervals (CI) (Estimation)

2-Samples
- Proportions — 10.4 z CI for $p_1 - p_1$
- Means
  - Dependent Samples — 10.3 t CI for D
  - Independent Sample
    - σ_1, σ_2 known — 10.1 z CI for $\mu_1 - \mu_2$
    - σ_1^2, σ_2^2 unknown — 10.2 t CI for $\mu_1 - \mu_2$

1-Sample
- Variance — 8.4 χ^2 CI for σ^2
- Proportion — 8.3 z CI for p
- Mean
  - σ unknown — 8.2 t CI for μ
  - σ known — 8.1 z CI for μ

Appendix B

Answers to Selected Odd-Numbered Quantitative Problems

Chapter 1

1.7. a. ratio
b. ratio
c. ordinal
d. nominal
e. ratio
f. ratio
g. nominal
h. ratio

1.9. a. 900 electric contractors
b. 35 electric contractors
c. average score for 35 participants
d. average score for all 900 electric contractors

Chapter 2

2.3. 2.5 .0698 6
7.5 .0930 14
12.5 .1977 31
17.5 .2674 54
22.5 .2093 72
27.5 .1163 82
32.5 .0465 86

2.9. 21 2 8 8 9
22 0 1 2 4 6 6 7 9 9
23 0 0 4 5 8 8 9 9 9 9
24 0 0 3 6 9 9 9
25 0 3 4 5 5 7 7 8 9
26 0 1 1 2 3 3 5 6
27 0 1 3

2.29. 28 4 6 9
29 0 4 8
30 1 6 8 9
31 1 2 4 6 7 7
32 4 4 6
33 5

2.35. 22.5 .1509 8
27.5 .1132 14
32.5 .0943 19
37.5 .2264 31
42.5 .2830 46
47.5 .1321 53

2.39. a. 1 2, 3, 6, 7, 8, 8, 8, 9, 9
2 0, 3, 4, 5, 6, 7, 8
3 0, 1, 2, 2

Chapter 3

3.1. 4, 4
3.3. 41.7
3.5. 19, 27, 17, 25, 30
3.7. 31.77, 28, 21
3.9. 152.25, 182.8, 121.15, 158.75, 193.85, 398.6
3.11. a. 8
b. 2.041

c. 6.204
d. 2.491
e. 4
f. 0.69, −0.92, −0.11, 1.89, −1.32, −0.52, 0.29

3.13. a. 4.598
b. 4.598

3.15. 58 631.295, 242.139

3.17. a. .75
b. .84
c. .609
d. .902

3.19. a. 2.667
b. 11.060
c. 3.326
d. 5
e. −0.85
f. 37.65%

3.21. Between 113 and 137
Between 101 and 149
Between 89 and 161

3.23. 2.887

3.25. 95%, 2.5%, .15%, 16%

3.27. 4.64, 3.59, 1

3.29. 185.694, 13.627

3.31. a. 44.9
b. 39
c. 44.82
d. 187.2
e. 13.7

3.33. a. 38
b. 25
c. 32.857
d. 251
e. 15.843

3.35. skewed right

3.37. no outliers. negatively skewed

3.39. 2.5, 2, 2, 7, 1, 3, 2

3.41. 561.38, 202.7, 172.9, 419.25, 952.6, 172.0, 574.1, 3072.8, 402.1

3.43. a. 5.183, 4.0
b. 9.8, 2.5
c. 8.293, 2.88
d. −0.79, 0.04

3.45. a. 33.412, 32.5
b. 58.483, 7.647

3.47. 10.78%, 6.43%

3.49. a. 392 to 446, 365 to 473, 338 to 500
b. 79.7%
c. −0.704

3.51. skewed right

3.53. 21.93, 18.14

Chapter 4

4.1. 15, .60

4.3. {4, 8, 10, 14, 16, 18, 20, 22, 26, 28, 30}

4.5. 20, combinations, .60

4.7. 38,760

4.9. a. .7167
  b. .5000
  c. .65
  d. .5167

4.11. a. .69
  b. .42
  c. .96

4.13. a. .95
  b. .54
  c. .91
  d. .60

4.15. a. .2807
  b. .0526
  c. .0000
  d. .0000

4.17. a. .0122
  b. .0144

4.19. a. .3225
  b. .0475
  c. .1075
  d. .5225

4.21. a. .039
  b. .571
  c. .129

4.23. a. .2286
  b. .2297
  c. .3231
  d. .0000

4.25. not independent

4.27. a. .4054
  b. .3261
  c. .4074
  d. .32

4.29. a. .664
  b. .906
  c. .17
  d. .53
  e. .4087

4.31. .0538, .5161, .4301

4.33. .7941, .2059

4.35. a. .4211
  b. .6316
  c. .2105
  d. .1250
  e. .5263
  f. .0000
  g. .6667
  h. .0000
  i. not independent

4.37. a. .28
  b. .04
  c. .86
  d. .32

  e. .1739
  f. .66

4.39. a. .5410
  b. .7857
  c. .70
  d. .09
  e. .2143

4.41. a. .39
  b. .40
  c. .48
  d. not independent
  e. not mutually exclusive

4.43. a. .3483
  b. .5317
  c. .0817
  d. .226

4.45. a. .2625
  b. .74375
  c. .60
  d. .25625
  e. .0875

4.47. a. .20
  b. .6429
  c. .40
  d. .60
  e. .40
  f. .3333

4.49. a. .469
  b. .164
  c. .2360
  d. .1934
  e. .754

4.51. a. .2130
  b. .4370
  c. .2240
  d. .6086
  e. .3914
  f. .8662

4.53. a. .276
  b. .686
  c. .816
  d. .59
  e. .4023

Chapter 5

5.1. 2.666, 1.8364, 1.3552

5.3. 0.956, 1.1305

5.5. a. .0036
  b. .1147
  c. .3822
  d. .5838

5.7. a. 14, 2.05
  b. 24.5, 3.99
  c. 50, 5

5.11. a. .0815
  b. .0008
  c. .227

5.13. a. .585
  b. .009
  c. .013

5.15. a. .1032
b. .0000
c. .0352
d. .3480

5.17. a. .0538
b. .1539
c. .4142
d. .0672
e. .0244
f. .3702

5.19. a. 6.3, 2.51
b. 1.3, 1.14
c. 8.9, 2.98
d. 0.6, .775

5.21. 3.5
a. .0302
b. .1424
c. .0817
d. .42
e. .1009

5.23. a. .3012
b. .0988
c. .4628

5.25. a. .1106
b. .0028

5.27. a. .5091
b. .2937
c. .4167
d. .0014

5.29. a. .1022
b. .0144
c. .3814

5.31. a. .1333
b. .0238
c. .1143

5.33. .0474

5.35. a. .124
b. .849
c. .090
d. .000

5.37. a. .1607
b. .7626
c. .3504
d. .5429

5.39. a. .1108
b. .017
c. 5
d. .1797
e. .125
f. .0000
g. .056
h. 8, 8

5.41. a. .2644
b. .0694
c. .0029
d. .7521

5.43. a. 5
b. .0244

5.45. a. .0687
b. .020
c. .1032
d. 2.28

5.47. .174

5.49. a. .3012
b. .1203
c. .7065

5.51. a. .0002
b. .0595
c. .2330

5.53. a. .0907
b. .0358
c. .1517
d. .8781

5.55. a. .265
b. .0136
c. .0067

5.57. a. .3854
b. .7257
c. .1502

5.59. a. .0474
b. .1605
c. .9547

Chapter 6

6.1. a. 1/40
b. 220, 11.547
c. .25
d. .3750
e. .6250

6.3. 2.97, 0.098, .2941

6.5. 222.857, .0013, .2267, .0000, .1684

6.7. a. .8944
b. .0122
c. .2144

6.9. a. .1788
b. .0329
c. .1476

6.11. a. 188.25
b. 244.65
c. 163.81
d. 206.11

6.13. 454.55

6.15. 22.984

6.17. a. $P(x \leq 16.5 \mid \mu = 21 \text{ and } \sigma = 2.51)$
b. $P(10.5 \leq x \leq 20.5 \mid \mu = 12.5 \text{ and } \sigma = 2.5)$
c. $P(21.5 \leq x \leq 22.5 \mid \mu = 24 \text{ and } \sigma = 3.10)$
d. $P(x \geq 14.5 \mid \mu = 7.2 \text{ and } \sigma = 1.99)$

6.19. a. .1170, .120
b. .4090, .415
c. .1985, .196
d. fails test

6.21. .0495

6.23. a. .1271
b. .7226

c. .0119

d. .0787

6.27. a. .0012

b. .8700

c. .0011

d. .9918

6.29. a. .0000

b. .0000

c. .0872

d. .41 minutes

6.31. $\mu = 1052.6$

a. .5908

b. .1899

6.33. 15, 15, .1254

6.35. a. .1587

b. .0013

c. .6915

d. .9270

e. .0000

6.37. a. .0202

b. .9817

c. .1849

d. .4449

6.39. .0000

6.41. a. .0537

b. .0013

c. .1535

6.43. .5319, 41.5, .0213

6.45. a. .2643

b. .7013

c. .2651

d. .0013

6.47. a. .0188

b. .0735

c. .9957

d. .6524

6.49. a. .0025

b. .8944

c. .3482

6.51. a. .0655

b. .6502

c. .9993

6.53. $11428.57

6.55. a. .5488

b. .2592

c. 1.67 months

6.57. 1940, 2018.75, 2269

6.59. 4.01%, 0.66%

Chapter 7

7.7. 825

7.13. a. .0548

b. .7881

c. .0082

d. .8575

e. .1664

7.15. 11.11

7.17. a. .9772

b. .2385

c. .1469

d. .1230

7.19. .0075

7.21. a. .0681

b. .0239

c. .0000

d. 12.608

7.23. a. .1492

b. .9404

c. .6985

d. .1445

e. .0000

7.25. .26

7.27. a. .1977

b. .2843

c. .9881

7.29. a. .1020

b. .7568

c. .7019

7.31. 55, 45, 90, 25, 35

7.37. a. .3156

b. .00003

c. .1736

7.41. a. .0021

b. .9265

c. .0281

7.43. a. .0314

b. .2420

c. .2250

d. .1469

e. .0000

7.45. a. .8534

b. .0256

c. .0007

7.49. a. .6787

b. .0571

c. .0059

7.51. .9147

Chapter 8

8.1. a. $24.11 \le \mu \le 25.89$

b. $113.17 \le \mu \le 126.03$

c. $3.136 \le \mu \le 3.702$

d. $54.55 \le \mu \le 58.85$

8.3. $45.92 \le \mu \le 48.08$

8.5. 66, $62.75 \le \mu \le 69.25$

8.7. 5.3, $5.13 \le \mu \le 5.47$

8.9. $2.852 \le \mu \le 3.760$

8.11. $23.036 \le \mu \le 26.030$

8.13. $42.18 \le \mu \le 49.06$

8.15. $120.6 \le \mu \le 136.2$, 128.4

8.17. $15.631 \le \mu \le 16.545$, 16.088

8.19. $2.26886 \leq \mu \leq 2.45346$, 2.36116, $.0923$

8.21. $36.77 \leq \mu \leq 62.83$

8.23. $7.53 \leq \mu \leq 14.66$

8.25. a. $.386 \leq p \leq .634$
b. $.777 \leq p \leq .863$
c. $.456 \leq p \leq .504$
d. $.246 \leq p \leq .394$

8.27. $.38 \leq p \leq .56$
$.36 \leq p \leq .58$
$.33 \leq p \leq .61$

8.29. a. $.4287 \leq p \leq .5113$
b. $.2488 \leq p \leq .3112$

8.31. a. $.266$
b. $.247 \leq p \leq .285$

8.33. $.5935 \leq p \leq .6665$

8.35. a. $18.46 \leq \sigma^2 \leq 189.73$
b. $0.64 \leq \sigma^2 \leq 7.46$
c. $645.45 \leq \sigma^2 \leq 1923.10$
d. $12.61 \leq \sigma^2 \leq 31.89$

8.37. $9.71 \leq \sigma^2 \leq 46.03$, 18.49

8.39. $14{,}084{,}038.51 \leq \sigma^2 \leq 69{,}553{,}848.45$

8.41. a. 2522
b. 601
c. 268
d. $16{,}577$

8.43. 106

8.45. $1{,}083$

8.47. 97

8.49. 12.03, $11.78 \leq \mu \leq 12.28$, $11.72 \leq \mu \leq 12.34$, $11.58 \leq \mu \leq 12.48$

8.51. $29.133 \leq \sigma^2 \leq 148.235$, $25.911 \leq \sigma^2 \leq 182.529$

8.53. $9.19 \leq \mu \leq 12.34$

8.55. $2.307 \leq \sigma^2 \leq 15.374$

8.57. $36.231 \leq \mu \leq 38.281$

8.59. $.542 \leq p \leq .596$, $.569$

8.61. $5.892 \leq \mu \leq 7.542$

8.63. $.726 \leq p \leq .814$

8.65. $34.11 \leq \mu \leq 53.29$, $101.44 \leq \sigma^2 \leq 821.35$

8.67. $-0.20 \leq \mu \leq 5.16$, 2.48

8.69. 543

8.71. $.0026 \leq \sigma^2 \leq .0071$

8.73. $.213 \leq p \leq .247$

Chapter 9

9.1. a. Two-tailed
b. One-tailed
c. One-tailed
d. Two-tailed

9.3. a. $z = 2.77$, reject
b. $.0028$
c. 22.115, 27.885

9.5. a. $z = 1.59$, reject
b. $.0559$
c. 1212.04

9.7. $z = 1.87$, fail to reject

9.9. $z = 1.46$, fail to reject

9.11. $z = 2.98$, $.0014$, reject

9.13. $t = 0.56$, fail to reject

9.15. $t = 2.44$, reject

9.17. $t = 1.59$, fail to reject

9.19. $t = -3.31$, reject

9.21. $t = -2.02$, fail to reject

9.23. fail to reject

9.25. $z = -1.66$, fail to reject

9.27. $z = -1.89$, fail to reject

9.29. $z = 1.23$, fail to reject, $z = 1.34$, fail to reject

9.31. $z = -3.11$, reject

9.33. a. $\chi^2 = 22.4$, fail to reject
b. $\chi^2 = 42$, reject
c. $\chi^2 = 2.64$, fail to reject
d. $\chi^2 = 2.4$, reject

9.35. $\chi^2 = 21.7$, fail to reject

9.37. $\chi^2 = 17.34$, reject

9.39. a. $\beta = .8159$
b. $\beta = .7422$
c. $\beta = .5636$
d. $\beta = .3669$

9.41. a. $\beta = .3632$
b. $\beta = .0122$
c. $\beta = .0000$

9.43. $z = -0.48$, fail to reject, $.6293$, $.1492$, $.0000$

9.45. $t = -1.98$, reject

9.47. $\chi^2 = 32.675$, fail to reject

9.49. $z = 1.15$, fail to reject

9.51. $z = -3.72$, reject

9.53. $t = -5.70$, reject

9.55. $\chi^2 = 106.47$, reject

9.57. $t = -2.80$, reject

9.59. $z = 3.96$, reject

9.61. $t = 4.50$, reject

9.63. $\chi^2 = 45.866$, reject

Chapter 10

10.1. a. $z = -1.01$, fail to reject
b. -2.41
c. $.1562$

10.3. a. $z = 5.48$, reject
b. $4.04 \leq \mu_1 - \mu_2 \leq 10.02$

10.5. $-1.86 \leq \mu_1 - \mu_2 \leq -0.54$

10.7. $z = -2.32$, fail to reject

10.9. $z = 2.29$, reject

10.11. $t = -1.05$, fail to reject

10.13. $t = 4.64$, reject

10.15. a. $-10596.04 \leq \mu_1 - \mu_2 \leq -6203.96$
b. $t = -6.44$, reject

10.17. $t = 2.06$, reject

10.19. $t = 4.95$, reject, $2258.05 \leq \mu_1 - \mu_2 \leq 5541.64$

10.21. $t = 3.31$, reject

10.23. $26.29 \leq D \leq 54.83$

10.25. $-3415.6 \leq D \leq 6021.2$

10.27. $6.58 \leq D \leq 49.60$

10.29. $63.71 \leq D \leq 86.29$

10.31. a. $z = 0.75$, fail to reject
      b. $z = 4.83$, reject

10.33. $z = -3.35$, reject

10.35. $z = -0.94$, fail to reject

10.37. $z = 2.35$, reject

10.39. $F = 1.80$, fail to reject

10.41. $F = 0.81$, fail to reject

10.43. $F = 1.53$, fail to reject

10.45. $z = -2.38$, reject

10.47. $t = 0.85$, fail to reject

10.49. $t = -5.26$, reject

10.51. $z = -1.20$, fail to reject

10.53. $F = 1.24$, fail to reject

10.55. $-3.201 \leq D \leq 2.313$

10.57. $F = 1.31$, fail to reject

10.59. $t = 2.97$, reject

10.61. $z = 6.78$, reject

10.63. $3.553 \leq D \leq 5.447$

10.65. $t = 6.71$, reject

10.67. $.142 \leq p_1 - p_2 \leq .250$

10.69. $z = 8.86$, reject

10.71. $t = 4.52$, reject

Chapter 11

11.5. $F = 11.07$, reject

11.7. $F = 13.00$, reject

11.9. 4, 50, 54, 145.8945, 19.4436, $F = 7.50$, reject

11.11. $F = 10.10$, reject

11.13. $F = 11.76$, reject

11.15. 4 levels; sizes 18, 15, 21, and 11; $F = 2.84$, $p = .045$; means = 230.11, 238.17, 235.18, and 241.83.

11.17. HSD = 0.896, groups 3 & 6 significantly different

11.19. HSD = 1.586, groups 1 & 2 significantly different

11.21. HSD = 10.27, groups 1 & 3 significantly different

11.23. $HSD_{1,3} = .0381$, groups 1 & 3 significantly different

11.25. $HSD_{1,3} = 1.764$, $HSD_{2,3} = 1.620$, groups 1 & 3 and 2 & 3 significantly different

11.29. $F = 1.48$, fail to reject

11.31. $F = 3.90$, fail to reject

11.33. $F = 15.37$, reject

11.37. 2, 1, 4 row levels, 3 column levels, yes $df_{row} = 3$, $df_{col.} = 2$, $df_{int.} = 6$, $df_{error} = 12$, $df_{total} = 23$

11.39. $MS_{row} = 1.047$, $MS_{col.} = 1.281$, $MS_{int.} = 0.258$, $MS_{error} = 0.436$, $F_{row} = 2.40$, $F_{col.} = 2.94$, $F_{int.} = 0.59$, fail to reject any hypothesis

11.41. $F_{row} = 87.25$, reject; $F_{col.} = 63.67$, reject; $F_{int.} = 2.07$, fail to reject

11.43. $F_{row} = 34.31$, reject; $F_{col.} = 14.20$, reject; $F_{int.} = 3.32$, reject

11.45. no significant interaction or row effects; significant column effects.

11.47. $F = 8.82$, reject; HSD = 3.33 groups 1 & 2, 2 & 3, and 2 & 4 significantly different.

11.49. $df_{treat.} = 5$, $MS_{treat.} = 42.0$, $df_{error} = 36$, $MS_{error} = 18.194$, $F = 2.31$

11.51. 1 treatment variable, 3 levels; 1 blocking variable, 6 levels; $df_{treat.} = 2$, $df_{block} = 5$, $df_{error} = 10$

11.53. $F_{treat.} = 31.51$, reject; $F_{blocks} = 43.20$, reject; HSD = 8.757, no pairs significant

11.55. $F_{rows} = 38.21$, reject; $F_{col.} = 0.23$, fail to reject; $F_{inter} = 1.30$, fail to reject

11.57. $F = 7.38$, reject

11.59. $F = 0.46$, fail to reject

11.61. $F_{treat.} = 13.64$, reject

Chapter 12

12.1. -0.927

12.3. .744

12.5. 0.975, 0.985, 0.957

12.7. $\hat{y} = 144.414 - 0.898x$

12.9. $\hat{y} = 15.460 - 0.715x$

12.11. $\hat{y} = 622.65 - 82.89x$

12.13. $\hat{y} = 13.625 + 2.303x$, -1.1694, 3.9511, -1.3811, 2.7394, -4.1401

12.15. 18.6597, 37.5229, 51.8948, 62.6737, 86.0281, 118.3648, 122.8561; 6.3403, -8.5229, -5.8948, 7.3263, 1.9720, -6.3648, 5.1439

12.17. 4.0259, 11.1722, 9.7429, 12.6014, 10.4576; 0.9741, 0.8278, -0.7429, 2.3986, -3.4575

12.19. 4.7244, -0.9836, -0.3996, -6.7537, 2.7683, 0.6442; No apparent violations

12.21. The error terms appear to be non independent

12.23. Violation of the homoscedasticity assumption

12.25. SSE = 272.0, $s_e = 7.376$, 6 out of 7 and 7 out of 7

12.27. SSE = 19.8885, $s_e = 2.575$

12.29. $s_e = 4.391$

12.31. $\hat{y} = 118.257 - 0.1504x$, $s_e = 40.526$

12.33. $r^2 = .972$

12.35. $r^2 = .685$

12.37. $\hat{y} = -599.3674 + 19.2204x$, $s_e = 13.539$, $r^2 = .688$

12.39. $t = -13.18$, reject

12.41. $t = -2.56$, fail to reject

12.43. F is significant at $\alpha = .05$, $t = 2.874$, reject at $\alpha = .05$

12.45. $38.523 \leq y \leq 70.705$, $10.447 \leq y \leq 44.901$

12.47. $0.97 \leq E(y_{10}) \leq 15.65$

12.49. $\hat{y} = 145322.44 - 71.3929x$, $\hat{y}(2017) = 1322.96$

12.51. $r = -.94$

12.53. a. $\hat{y} = -11.335 + 0.355x$
      b. 7.48, 5.35, 3.22, 6.415, 9.225, 10.675, 4.64, 9.965, -2.48, -0.35, 3.78, -2.415, 0.745, 1.325, -1.64, 1.035
      c. SSE = 32.4649

d. $s_e = 2.3261$

e. $r^2 = .608$

f. $t = 3.05$, reject

12.55. a. $20.92 \le E(y_{60}) \le 26.8$

b. $20.994 \le y \le 37.688$

12.57. $r^2 = .826$

12.59. $\hat{y} = 3.77542 + 0.65208x$; $r^2 = .291$

12.61. $r = .8998$

12.63. $\hat{y} = -39.0071 + 66.36277x$, $r^2 = .906$, $s_e = 21.13$

12.65. $\hat{y} = 2.4995 + 0.00311235x$, $s_e = 0.789$, $r^2 = .0374$, $t = 0.558$, fail to reject

Chapter 13

13.1. $\hat{y} = 25.03 - 0.0497x_1 + 1.928x_2$, 28.586

13.3. $\hat{y} = 121.62 - 0.174x_1 + 6.02x_2 + 0.00026x_3 + 0.0041x_4$, 4

13.5. Per capita consumption = $-7,629.627 + 116.2549$ paper consumption $- 120.0904$ fish consumption $+ 45.73328$ gasoline consumption

13.7. 9, fail to reject null overall at $\alpha = .05$, only $t = 2.73$ for x_1, significant at $\alpha = .05$, $s_e = 3.503$, $R^2 = .408$, adj. $R^2 = .203$

13.9. Per capita consumption = $-7,629.627 + 116.2549$ paper consumption $- 120.0904$ fish consumption $+ 45.73328$ gasoline consumption; $F = 14.319$ with p-value = $.0023$; $t = 2.67$ with p-value = $.032$ for gasoline consumption. The p-values of the t statistics for the other two predictors are insignificant.

13.11. $\hat{y} = 3.981 + 0.07322x_1 - 0.03232x_2 - 0.003886x_3$, $F = 100.47$ significant at $\alpha = .001$, $t = 3.50$ for x_1 significant at $\alpha = .01$, $s_e = 0.2331$, $R^2 = .965$, adj. $R^2 = .955$

13.13. 3 predictors, 15 observations, $\hat{y} = 657.053 + 5.710x_1$ $-0.417x_2 - 3.471x_3$, $R^2 = .842$, adjusted $R^2 = .630$, $s_e = 109.43$, $F = 8.96$ with $p = .0027$, x_1 significant at $\alpha = .01$, x_3 significant at $\alpha = .05$

13.15. $s_e = 9.722$, $R^2 = .515$, adjusted $R^2 = .404$

13.17. $s_e = 6.544$, $R^2 = .005$, adjusted $R^2 = .000$

13.19. model with x_1, x_2: $s_e = 6.333$, $R^2 = .963$, adjusted $R^2 = .957$ model with x_1: $s_e = 6.124$, $R^2 = .963$, adjusted $R^2 = .960$

13.21. non normal distribution

13.23. 2, $\hat{y} = 203.3937 + 1.1151x_1 - 2.2115x_2$, $F = 24.55$, reject, $R^2 = .663$, adjusted $R^2 = .636$

13.25. $\hat{y} = 362 - 4.75x_1 - 13.9x_2 + 1.87x_3$; $F = 16.05$, reject; $s_e = 37.07$; $R^2 = .858$; adjusted $R^2 = .804$; x_1 only significant predictor

13.27. Employment = $71.03 + 0.4620$ Naval Vessels + 0.02082 Commercial

$F = 1.22$, fail to reject; $R^2 = .379$; adjusted $R^2 = .068$; no significant predictors

13.29. Corn = $-2718 + 6.26$ Soybeans $- 0.77$ Wheat; $F = 14.25$, reject; $s_e = 862.4$; $R^2 = .803$; adjusted $R^2 = .746$; Soybeans was a significant predictor

Chapter 14

14.1. Simple Model: $\hat{y} = -147.27 + 27.128x$, $F = 229.67$ with $p = .000$, $s_e = 27.27$, $R^2 = .97$, adjusted $R^2 = .966$ Quadratic Model: $\hat{y} = -22.01 + 3.385x_1 + 0.9373x_2$, $F = 578.76$ with $p = .000$, $s_e = 12.3$, $R^2 = .995$, adjusted $R^2 = .993$, for x_1: $t = 0.75$, for x_2: $t = 5.33$

14.3. Simple Model: $\hat{y} = -1456.6 + 71.017x$; $R^2 = .928$; adjusted $R^2 = .910$; $t = 7.17$; reject. Quadratic Model:

$\hat{y} = 1012 - 14.1x + 0.611x^2$; $R^2 = .947$; adjusted $R^2 = .911$; $t(x) = -0.17$, fail to reject; $t(x^2) = 1.03$, fail to reject

14.5. $\hat{y} = -28.61 - 2.68x_1 + 18.25x_2 - 0.2135x_1^2 - 1.533x_2^2 + 1.226$ x_1x_2; $F = 63.43$, reject; $s_e = 4.669$, $R^2 = .958$; adjusted $R^2 = .943$; no significant t ratios. Model with no interaction term: $R^2 = .957$

14.7. $\hat{y} = 13.619 - 0.01201x_1 + 2.988x_2$, $F = 8.43$ significant at $\alpha = .01$, $t = 3.88$ for x_2, (dummy variable) significant at $\alpha = .01$, $s_e = 1.245$, $R^2 = .652$, adj. $R^2 = .575$

14.9. x_1 and x_2 are significant predictors at $\alpha = .05$

14.11. Price = $7.066 - 0.0855$ Hours + 9.614 Probability + 10.507 French Quarter, $F = 6.80$ significant at $\alpha = .01$, $t = 3.97$ for French Quarter (dummy variable) significant at $\alpha = .01$, $s_e = 4.02$, $R^2 = .671$, adj. $R^2 = .573$

14.13. Step 1: x_2 entered, $t = -7.53$, $r^2 = .794$

Step 2: x_3 entered, $t_2 = -4.60$, $t_3 = 2.93$, $R^2 = .876$

14.15. 4 predictors, x_4 and x_5 are not in model.

14.17. Step 1: Dividends in the model, $t = 6.69$, $r^2 = .833$

Step 2: Net income and dividends in model, $t = 2.24$ and $t = 4.36$, $R^2 = .897$

14.19.

	y	x_1	x_2
x_1	$-.653$		
x_2	$-.891$	$.650$	
x_3	$.821$	$-.615$	$-.688$

14.21.

	Net Income	**Dividends**
Dividends	$.682$	
Underwriting	$.092$	$-.522$

14.23. $\hat{y} = -0.932546 - 0.0000323$ *Payroll*, Payroll expenditures is significant at $\alpha = .01$ and has a p-value of 0.008. Predicted value equals -3.516546. Prob. = $.0288$ of being a psychiatric hospital.

14.25. $\hat{y} = -3.07942 + 0.0544532$ *production workers*, Number of production workers is significant at $\alpha = .001$ and has a p-value of 0.000. Predicted value equals -1.445824. Prob. = $.19$ of being a large company.

14.27. $\hat{y} = 564 - 27.99x_1 - 6.155x_2 - 15.90x_3$, $R^2 = .809$, adjusted $R^2 = .738$, $s_e = 42.88$ $F = 11.32$ with $p = .003$, x_2 only significant predictor x_1 is a non-significant indicator variable

14.29. The procedure stopped at step 1 with only $\log x$ in the model, = $-13.20 + 11.64 \log x_1$, $R^2 = .9617$

14.31. The procedure went 2 steps, step 1: silver entered, $R^2 = .5244$, step 2: aluminum entered, $R^2 = .8204$, final model: gold = $-50.19 + 18.9$ silver + 3.59 aluminum

14.33. The procedure went 3 steps, step 1: food entered, $R^2 = .84$, step 2: fuel oil entered, $R^2 = .95$, step 3: shelter entered, $R^2 = .96$, final model: All = $-1.0615 + 0.474$ food + 0.269 fuel oil + 0.249 shelter

14.35. Grocery = $76.23 + 0.08592$ Housing + 0.16767 Utility + 0.0284 Transportation $- 0.0659$ Healthcare, $F = 2.29$ not significant; $s_e = 4.416$; $R^2 = .315$; Adjusted $R^2 = .177$; Utility only significant predictor.

14.39. Model: $\hat{y} = -3.94828 + 1.36988$ *Miles*. Number of miles is significant at $\alpha = .001$ with a p-value of 0.000. For 5 miles, prob. = $.948$. For 4 miles, prob. = $.822$. For 3 miles, prob. = $.54$. For 2 miles, prob. = $.23$. For 1 mile, prob. = $.07$.

Chapter 15

15.1. MAD = 1.367, MSE = 2.27

15.3. MAD = 3.583, MSE = 15.765

15.5. a. 44.75, 52.75, 61.50, 64.75, 70.50, 81
    b. 53.25, 56.375, 62.875, 67.25, 76.375, 89.125

15.7. $\alpha = .3$: 9.4, 9, 8.7, 8.8, 9.1, 9.7, 9.9, 9.8
    $\alpha = .7$: 9.4, 8.6, 8.1, 8.7, 9.5, 10.6, 10.4, 9.8

15.9. $\alpha = .2$: 332, 404.4, 427.1, 386.1, 350.7, 315, 325.2, 362.6, 423.5, 453, 477.4, 554.9
    $\alpha = .9$: 332, 657.8, 532, 253, 213.4, 176.1, 347, 495.5, 649.9, 578.9, 575.4, 836; $MAD_{\alpha=.2} = 190.8$; $MAD_{\alpha=.9} = 168.6$

15.11. Members = $192136 - 88.1$ year, $R^2 = 85.4\%$, $s_e = 315.452$

15.13. TC: 136.78, 132.90, 128.54, 126.43, 124.86, 122, 119.08, 116.76, 114.61, 112.70, 111.75, 111.36

SI: 93.30, 90.47, 92.67, 98.77, 111.09, 100.83, 113.52, 117.58, 112.36, 92.08, 99.69, 102.73

15.15. $D = 2.18$, fail to reject the null hypothesis—there is no significant autocorrelation

15.17. $D = 2.49$, no significant autocorrelation

15.19. 1 lag: Housing Starts = $35.5 + 0.887$ lag 1; $R^2 = 66.8\%$; $s_e = 65.67$

2 lags: Housing Starts = $182 + 0.49$ lag 2; $R^2 = 16.6\%$; $s_e = 104.12$

15.21. a. 100, 139.9, 144, 162.6, 200, 272.8, 310.7, 327.1, 356.6, 376.9, 388.8, 398.9, 415.2, 578.2
    b. 32.2, 45, 46.4, 52.3, 64.4, 87.8, 100, 105.3, 114.8, 121.3, 125.1, 128.4, 133.6, 186.1

15.23. 100, 103.2, 124.8

15.25. 121.6, 127.4, 131.4

15.27. a. Linear: $= 9.96 - 0.14\,x$, $R^2 = 90.9\%$,
    Quadratic: $= 10.4 - 0.252\,x + .00445\,x^2$, $R^2 = 94.4\%$
    b. MAD = .3385
    c. MAD $(\alpha = .3) = .4374$, MAD $(\alpha = .7) = .2596$
    d. $\alpha = .7$ did best
    e. 100.28, 101.51, 99.09, 99.12

15.29. 100, 104.8, 114.5, 115.5, 114.1

15.31. $MAD_{mov.avg.} = 534.71$, $MAD_{\alpha=.2} = 839.74$

15.33. Jan. 95.35, Feb. 99.69, March 106.75, April 103.99, May 100.99, June 106.96, July 94.53, Aug. 99.60, Sept. 104.16, Oct. 97.04, Nov. 95.75, Dec. 95.19

15.35. Laspeyres: 105.2, 111.0; Paasche: 105.1, 110.8

15.37. $MSE_{ma} = 129.3$; $MSE_{wma} = 84.4$

15.39. 98.07, 103.84, 97.04, 101.05

15.43. $D = 0.08$, reject

15.45. $D = 0.98$, reject

Chapter 16

16.1. $X^2 = 18.095$, reject.

16.3. $X^2 = 2.001$, fail to reject, $\lambda = 0.9$.

16.5. $X^2 = 198.48$, reject.

16.7. $X^2 = 2.45$, fail to reject

16.9. $X^2 = 9.346$, reject

16.11. $X^2 = 0.24$, fail to reject

16.13. $X^2 = 64.91$, reject

16.15. $X^2 = 72.34$, reject

16.17. $X^2 = 3.10$, fail to reject

16.19. $X^2 = 10.70$, reject

16.21. $X^2 = 90.36$, reject

16.23. $X^2 = 190.03$, reject

16.25. $X^2 = 54.63$, reject

Chapter 17

17.1. $R = 11$, fail to reject

17.3. p-value = .0264, reject

17.5. $R = 27$, $z = -1.08$, fail to reject

17.7. $U = 26.5$, p-value = .6454, fail to reject

17.9. $U = 11$, p-value = .0156, fail to reject

17.11. $z = -3.78$, reject

17.13. $z = -2.59$, reject

17.15. $z = -3.20$, reject

17.17. $z = -1.75$, reject

17.19. $K = 21.21$, reject

17.21. $K = 2.75$, fail to reject

17.23. $K = 18.99$, reject

17.25. $X^2 = 13.8$, reject

17.27. $X^2 = 14.8$, reject

17.29. 4, 5, $S = 2.04$, fail to reject

17.31. $r_s = .893$

17.33. $r_s = -.95$

17.35. $r_s = -.398$

17.37. $r_s = -.855$

17.39. $U = 20$, p-value = .2344, fail to reject

17.41. $K = 7.75$, fail to reject

17.43. $r_s = -.81$

17.45. $z = -0.40$, fail to reject

17.47. $z = 0.96$, fail to reject

17.49. $U = 45.5$, p-value = .739, fail to reject

17.51. $z = -1.91$, fail to reject

17.53. $R = 21$, fail to reject

17.55. $z = -2.43$, reject

17.57. $K = 17.21$, reject

17.59. $K = 11.96$, reject

Chapter 18

18.5. $\bar{\bar{x}} = 4.51$, UCL = 5.17, LCL = 3.85
    $\bar{R} = 0.90$, UCL = 2.05, LCL = 0

18.7. $p = .05$, UCL = .1534, LCL = .000

18.9. $\bar{c} = 1.34375$, UCL = 4.82136, LCL = .000

18.11. Chart 1: nine consecutive points below centerline, four out of five points in the outer 2/3 of the lower region

Chart 2: eight consecutive points above the centerline

Chart 3: in control

18.15. $p = .104$, LCL = 0.000, UCL = .234

18.17. $\bar{c} = 2.13889$, UCL = 6.52637, LCL = .0000

18.19. $\bar{\bar{x}} = 14.99854$, UCL = 15.02269, LCL = 14.97439
    $\bar{R} = .05$, UCL = .1002, LCL = .0000

18.21. $\bar{c} = 0.64$, UCL = 3.04, LCL = .0000

18.23. $p = 0.06$, LCL = 0.000, UCL = .1726

Chapter 19 (On Wiley Web Site)

19.1. a. 390
  b. 70
  c. 82, 296
  d. 140

19.3. 60, 10

19.7. 31.75, 6.50

19.9. Lock in = 85, 182.5, 97.5

19.11. a. 75,000
   b. Avoider
   c. >75,000

19.13. 244.275, 194.275

19.15. 21012.32, 12.32

19.17. b. 267.5, 235
   c. 352.5, 85

19.19. a. 2000, 200
   b. 500

19.21. 875,650

19.23. Reduction: .60, .2333, .1667
   Constant: .10, .6222, .2778
   Increase: .0375, .0875, .8750, 21425.55, 2675.55

Glossary

Adjusted R^2 A modified value of R^2 in which the degrees of freedom are taken into account, thereby allowing the researcher to determine whether the value of R^2 is inflated for a particular multiple regression model.

After-process quality control A type of quality control in which product attributes are measured by inspection after the manufacturing process is completed to determine whether the product is acceptable.

All possible regressions A multiple regression search procedure in which all possible multiple linear regression models are determined from the data using all variables.

Analysis of variance (ANOVA) A technique for statistically analyzing the data from a completely randomized design; uses the F test to determine whether there is a significant difference between two or more independent groups.

A posteriori After the experiment; pairwise comparisons made by the researcher after determining that there is a significant overall F value from ANOVA; also called post hoc.

A priori Determined before, or prior to, an experiment.

Arithmetic mean The average of a group of numbers.

Autocorrelation A problem that arises in regression analysis when the data occur over time and the error terms are correlated; also called serial correlation.

Autoregression A multiple regression forecasting technique in which the independent variables are time-lagged versions of the dependent variable.

Averaging models Forecasting models in which the forecast is the average of several preceding time periods.

Backward elimination A step-by-step multiple regression search procedure that begins with a full model containing all predictors. A search is made to determine if there are any nonsignificant independent variables in the model. If there are no nonsignificant predictors, then the backward process ends with the full model. If there are nonsignificant predictors, then the predictor with the smallest absolute value of t is eliminated and a new model is developed with the remaining variables. This procedure continues until only variables with significant t values remain in the model.

Bar chart or Bar graph A chart that contains two or more categories along one axis and a series of bars, one for each category, along the other axis. Usually the length of the bar represents the magnitude of the measure for each category. A bar graph is qualitative and may be either horizontal or vertical.

Bayes' rule An extension of the conditional law of probabilities discovered by Thomas Bayes that can be used to revise probabilities.

Benchmarking A quality control method in which a company attempts to develop and establish total quality management from product to process by examining and emulating the best practices and techniques used in their industry.

Bimodal Data sets that have two modes.

Binomial distribution Widely known discrete distribution in which there are only two possibilities on any one trial.

Blocking variable A variable that the researcher wants to control but is not the treatment variable of interest.

Bounds The error portion of the confidence interval that is added and/or subtracted from the point estimate to form the confidence interval.

Box-and-whisker plot A diagram that utilizes the upper and lower quartiles along with the median and the two most extreme values to depict a distribution graphically; sometimes called a box plot.

Categorical data Non-numerical data that are frequency counts of categories from one or more variables.

Cause-and-effect diagram A tool for displaying possible causes for a quality problem and the interrelationships among the causes; also called a fishbone diagram or an Ishikawa diagram.

c chart A quality control chart for attribute compliance that displays the number of nonconformances per item or unit.

Census A process of gathering data from the whole population for a given measurement of interest.

Centerline The middle horizontal line of a control chart, often determined either by a product or service specification or by computing an expected value from sample information.

Central limit theorem A theorem that states that regardless of the shape of a population, the distributions of sample means and proportions are normal if sample sizes are large.

Chebyshev's theorem A theorem stating that at least $1 - 1/k^2$ proportion of the values will fall within $\pm k$ standard deviations of the mean regardless of the shape of the population.

Check sheet Simple forms consisting of multiple categories and columns for recording tallies for displaying the frequency of outcomes for some quality-related event or activity.

Chi-square distribution A continuous distribution determined by the sum of the squares of k independent random variables.

Chi-square goodness-of-fit test A statistical test used to analyze probabilities of multinomial distribution trials along a single dimension; compares expected, or theoretical, frequencies of categories from a population distribution to the observed, or actual, frequencies from a distribution.

Chi-square test of independence A statistical test used to analyze the frequencies of two variables with multiple categories to determine whether the two variables are independent.

Classical method of assigning probabilities Probabilities assigned based on rules and laws.

Classifications The subcategories of the independent variable used by the researcher in the experimental design; also called levels.

Classification variable The independent variable of an experimental design that was present prior to the experiment and is not the result of the researcher's manipulations or control.

Class mark Another name for class midpoint; the midpoint of each class interval in grouped data.

Class midpoint For any given class interval of a frequency distribution, the value halfway across the class interval; the average of the two class endpoints.

Cluster (or area) sampling A type of random sampling in which the population is divided into nonoverlapping areas or clusters and elements are randomly sampled from the areas or clusters.

Coefficient of determination (r^2) The proportion of variability of the dependent variable accounted for or explained by the independent variable in a regression model.

Coefficient of multiple determination (R^2) The proportion of variation of the dependent variable accounted for by the independent variables in the regression model.

Coefficient of variation (CV) The ratio of the standard deviation to the mean, expressed as a percentage.

Collectively exhaustive events A list containing all possible elementary events for an experiment.

Column charts Vertical bar charts.

Combinations Used to determine the number of possible ways n things can happen from N total possibilities when sampling without replacement.

Complement of an event The complement of an event is all elementary events of an experiment that are not in the event being considered.

Complement of a union The only possible case other than the union of sets X and Y; the probability that neither X nor Y is in the outcome.

Completely randomized design An experimental design wherein there is one treatment or independent variable with two or more treatment levels and one dependent variable. This design is analyzed by analysis of variance.

Concomitant variables Variables that are not being controlled by the researcher in the experiment but can have an effect on the outcome of the treatment being studied; also called confounding variables.

Conditional probability The probability of the occurrence of one event given that another event has occurred.

Confidence interval A range of values within which the analyst can declare, with some confidence, the population parameter lies.

Confounding variables Variables that are not being controlled by the researcher in the experiment but can have an effect on the outcome of the treatment being studied; also called concomitant variables.

Contingency analysis Another name for the chi-square test of independence.

Contingency table A two-way table that contains the frequencies of responses to two questions; also called a raw values matrix.

Continuous distributions Distributions constructed from continuous random variables.

Continuous random variables Variables that take on values at every point over a given interval.

Control chart A quality control graph that contains an upper control limit, a lower control limit, and a centerline; used to evaluate whether a process is or is not in a state of statistical control.

Convenience sampling A nonrandom sampling technique in which items for the sample are selected for the convenience of the researcher.

Correction for continuity A correction made when a binomial distribution problem is approximated by the normal distribution because a discrete distribution problem is being approximated by a continuous distribution.

critical value method A method of testing hypotheses in which the sample statistic is compared to a critical value in order to reach a conclusion about rejecting or failing to reject the null hypothesis.

critical value The value that divides the non-rejection region from the rejection region.

Cross tabulation A process for producing a two-dimensional table that displays the frequency counts for two variables simultaneously.

Cross-tabulation table A process for producing a two-dimensional table that displays the frequency counts for two variables simultaneously.

Cumulative frequency A running total of frequencies through the classes of a frequency distribution.

Cycles Patterns of highs and lows through which data move over time periods usually of more than a year.

Cyclical effects The rise and fall of time-series data over periods longer than 1 year.

Data Recorded measurements.

Decision alternatives The various choices or options available to the decision maker in any given problem situation.

Decision analysis A category of quantitative business techniques particularly targeted at clarifying and enhancing the decision-making process.

Decision making under certainty A decision-making situation in which the states of nature are known.

Decision making under risk A decision-making situation in which it is uncertain which states of nature will occur but the probability of each state of nature occurring has been determined.

Decision making under uncertainty A decision-making situation in which the states of nature that may occur are unknown and the probability of a state of nature occurring is also unknown.

Decision table A matrix that displays the decision alternatives, the states of nature, and the payoffs for a particular decision-making problem; also called a payoff table.

Decision trees A flowchart-like depiction of the decision process that includes the various decision alternatives, the various states of nature, and the payoffs.

Decomposition Breaking down the effects of time-series data into the four component parts of trend, cyclical, seasonal, and irregular.

Degrees of freedom (df) A mathematical adjustment made to the size of the sample; used along with α to locate values in statistical tables.

Dependent samples Two or more samples selected in such a way as to be dependent or related; each item or person in one sample has a corresponding matched or related item in the other samples. Also called related samples.

Dependent variable In an experimental design, it is the response to the different levels of the independent variables. It is the measurement taken under the conditions of the experimental design that reflects the effects of the independent variable(s). In regression analysis, the variable that is being predicted.

Descriptive statistics Statistics that have been gathered on a group to describe or reach conclusions about that same group.

Deseasonalized data Time-series data in which the effects of seasonality have been removed.

Design for Six Sigma A quality scheme, an offshoot of Six Sigma, that places an emphasis on designing a product or process right the first time, thereby allowing organizations the opportunity to reach even higher sigma levels through Six Sigma.

Deterministic model Mathematical models that produce an "exact" output for a given input.

Deviation from the mean The difference between a number and the average of the set of numbers of which the number is a part.

Discrete distributions Distributions constructed from discrete random variables.

Discrete random variables Random variables in which the set of all possible values is at most a finite or a countably infinite number of possible values.

Disproportionate stratified random sampling A type of stratified random sampling in which the proportions of items selected from the strata for the final sample do not reflect the proportions of the strata in the population.

Dot plot A dot plot is a relatively simple statistical chart used to display continuous quantitative data where each data value is plotted along the horizontal axis and is represented on the chart by a dot.

Dummy variable Another name for a qualitative or indicator variable; usually coded as 0 or 1 and represents whether or not a given item or person possesses a certain characteristic.

Durbin-Watson test A statistical test for determining whether significant autocorrelation is present in a time-series regression model.

Elementary events Events that cannot be decomposed or broken down into other events.

Empirical rule A guideline that states the approximate percentage of values that fall within a given number of standard deviations of a mean of a set of data that are normally distributed.

EMVer A person who uses an expected monetary value (EMV) approach to making decisions under risk.

Error of an individual forecast The difference between the actual value and the forecast of that value.

Event An outcome of an experiment.

Expected monetary value (EMV) A value of a decision alternative computed by multiplying the probability of each state of nature by the state's associated payoff and summing these products across the states of nature.

Expected value of perfect information The difference between the expected monetary payoff that would occur if the decision maker knew which states of nature would occur and the payoff from the best decision alternative when there is no information about the occurrence of the states of nature.

Expected value of sample information The difference between the expected monetary value with information and the expected monetary value without information.

Experimental design A plan and a structure to test hypotheses in which the researcher either controls or manipulates one or more variables.

Experiment A process that produces outcomes.

Exponential distribution A continuous distribution closely related to the Poisson distribution that describes the times between random occurrences.

Exponential smoothing A forecasting technique in which a weighting system is used to determine the importance of previous time periods in the forecast.

Factorial design An experimental design in which two or more independent variables are studied simultaneously and every level of each treatment is studied under the conditions of every level of all other treatments. Also called a factorial experiment.

Factors Another name for the independent variables of an experimental design.

Failure Mode and Effects Analysis (FMEA) A systematic way for identifying the effects of potential product or process failure. It includes methodology for eliminating or reducing the chance of a failure occurring.

F distribution A distribution based on the ratio of two random variances; used in testing two variances and in analysis of variance.

Finite correction factor A statistical adjustment made to the z formula for sample means; adjusts for the fact that a population is finite and the size is known.

First-differences approach A method of transforming data in an attempt to reduce or remove autocorrelation from a time-series regression model; results in each data value being subtracted from each succeeding time period data value, producing a new, transformed value.

Fishbone diagram A display of possible causes of a quality problem and the interrelationships among the causes. The problem is diagrammed along the main line of the "fish" and possible causes are diagrammed as line segments angled off in such a way as to give the appearance of a fish skeleton. Also called an Ishikawa diagram or a cause-and-effect diagram.

Five-number summary The five numbers that determine a box-and-whisker plot. These are the median, the lower quartile, the upper quartile, the smallest value, and the largest value.

Flowchart A schematic representation of all the activities and interactions that occur in a process.

Forecasting The art or science of predicting the future.

Forecasting error A single measure of the overall error of a forecast for an entire set of data.

Forward selection A multiple regression search procedure that is essentially the same as stepwise regression analysis except that once a variable is entered into the process, it is never deleted.

Frame A list, map, directory, or some other source that is being used to represent the population in the process of sampling.

Frequency distribution A summary of data presented in the form of class intervals and frequencies.

Frequency polygon A graph constructed by plotting a dot for the frequencies at the class midpoints and connecting the dots.

Friedman test A nonparametric alternative to the randomized block design.

F value The ratio of two sample variances, used to reach statistical conclusions regarding the null hypothesis; in ANOVA, the ratio of the treatment variance to the error variance.

Grouped data Data that have been organized into a frequency distribution.

Heteroscedasticity The condition that occurs when the error variances produced by a regression model are not constant.

Histogram A type of vertical bar chart constructed by graphing line segments for the frequencies of classes across the class intervals and connecting each to the x axis to form a series of rectangles.

Homoscedasticity The condition that occurs when the error variances produced by a regression model are constant.

Hurwicz criterion An approach to decision making in which the maximum and minimum payoffs selected from each decision alternative are used with a weight, α, between 0 and 1 to determine the alternative with the maximum weighted average. The higher the value of α, the more optimistic is the decision maker.

Hypergeometric distribution A distribution of probabilities of the occurrence of x items in a sample of n when there are A of that same item in a population of N.

Hypothesis A tentative explanation of a principle operating in nature.

hypothesis testing A process of testing hypotheses about parameters by setting up null and alternative hypotheses, gathering sample data, computing statistics from the samples, and using statistical techniques to reach conclusions about the hypotheses.

Independent events Events such that the occurrence or nonoccurrence of one has no effect on the occurrence of the others.

Independent samples Two or more samples in which the selected items are related only by chance.

Independent variable In experimental designs, it is a variable that is controlled or manipulated in an experiment so as to determine the effect on a dependent variable or measurement. Independent variables are sometimes referred to as factors. In regression analysis, the predictor variable.

Index number A ratio, often expressed as a percentage, of a measure taken during one time frame to that same measure taken during another time frame, usually denoted as the base period.

Indicator variable Another name for a dummy or qualitative variable; usually coded as 0 or 1 and represents whether or not a given item or person possesses a certain characteristic.

Inferential statistics Statistics that have been gathered from a sample and used to reach conclusions about the population from which the sample was taken.

In-process quality control A quality control method in which product attributes are measured at various intervals throughout the manufacturing process.

Interaction When the effects of one treatment in an experimental design vary according to the levels of treatment of the other effect(s).

Interquartile range The range of values between the first and the third quartile.

Intersection The portion of the population that contains elements that lie in both groups of interest.

Interval estimate A range of values within which it is estimated with some confidence the population parameter lies.

Interval-level data Next to highest level of data. These data have all the properties of ordinal level data, but in addition, intervals between consecutive numbers have meaning.

Irregular fluctuations Unexplained or error variation within time-series data.

Ishikawa diagram A tool developed by Kaoru Ishikawa as a way to display possible causes of a quality problem and the interrelationships of the causes; also called a fishbone diagram or a cause-and-effect diagram.

Joint probability The probability of the intersection occurring, or the probability of two or more events happening at once.

Joint probability table A two-dimensional table that displays the marginal and intersection probabilities of a given problem.

Judgment sampling A nonrandom sampling technique in which items selected for the sample are chosen by the judgment of the researcher.

Just-in-time inventory system An inventory system in which little or no extra raw materials or parts for production are stored.

Kruskal-Wallis test The nonparametric alternative to one-way analysis of variance; used to test whether three or more samples come from the same or different populations.

Kurtosis The amount of peakedness of a distribution.

Lambda (λ) Denotes the long-run average of a Poisson distribution.

Laspeyres price index A type of weighted aggregate price index in which the quantity values used in the calculations are from the base year.

Lean manufacturing A quality-management philosophy that focuses on the reduction of wastes and the elimination of unnecessary steps in an operation or process.

Least squares analysis The process by which a regression model is developed based on calculus techniques that attempt to produce a minimum sum of the squared error values.

Leptokurtic Distributions that are high and thin.

Levels The subcategories of the independent variable used by the researcher in the experimental design; also called classifications.

level of significance The probability of committing a Type I error; also known as alpha.

Logistic regression A methodology often used to develop a regression-type model for predicting a dichotomous dependent variable. This method utilizes an "s-curve" type function to develop a math model from one or more variables, which can yield the probability of belonging to one group or the other.

Lower bound of the confidence interval The lower end of a confidence interval for means or proportions calculated by subtracting the margin of error from the point estimate.

Lower control limit (LCL) The bottom-end line of a control chart, usually situated approximately three standard deviations of the statistic below the centerline; data points below this line indicate quality control problems.

Mann-Whitney *U* test A nonparametric counterpart of the *t* test used to compare the means of two independent populations.

Manufacturing quality A view of quality in which the emphasis is on the manufacturer's ability to target consistently the requirements for the product with little variability.

Marginal probability A probability computed by dividing a subtotal of the population by the total of the population.

Margin of error of the interval The distance between the statistic (point estimate) computed to estimate a parameter and the parameter.

Matched-pairs test A *t* test to test the differences in two related or matched samples; sometimes called the *t* test for related measures or the correlated *t* test.

Maximax criterion An optimistic approach to decision making under uncertainty in which the decision alternative is chosen according to which alternative produces the maximum overall payoff of the maximum payoffs from each alternative.

Maximin criterion A pessimistic approach to decision making under uncertainty in which the decision alternative is chosen according to which alternative produces the maximum overall payoff among the minimum payoffs from each alternative.

Mean absolute deviation (MAD) The average of the absolute values of the deviations around the mean for a set of numbers.

Mean or expected value The long-run average of occurrences; also called the expected value.

Mean square error (MSE) The average of all squared errors of a forecast for a group of data.

Measurement When a standard process is used to assign numbers to particular attributes or characteristics of a variable.

Measures of central tendency One type of measure that is used to yield information about the center of a group of numbers.

Measures of shape Tools that can be used to describe the shape of a distribution of data.

Measures of variability Statistics that describe the spread or dispersion of a set of data.

Median The middle value in an ordered array of numbers.

Mesokurtic Distributions that are normal in shape—that is, not too high or too flat.

Metric data Interval and ratio level data; also called quantitative data.

Minimax regret A decision-making strategy in which the decision maker determines the lost opportunity for each decision alternative and selects the decision alternative with the minimum of lost opportunity or regret.

_mn_ counting rule A rule used in probability to count the number of ways two operations can occur if the first operation has *m* possibilities and the second operation has *n* possibilities.

Mode The most frequently occurring value in a set of data.

Moving average When an average of data from previous time periods is used to forecast the value for ensuing time periods and this average is modified at each new time period by including more recent values not in the previous average and dropping out values from the more distant time periods that were in the previous average. It is continually updated at each new time period.

Multicollinearity A problematic condition that occurs when two or more of the independent variables of a multiple regression model are highly correlated.

Multimodal Data sets that contain more than two modes.

Multiple comparisons Statistical techniques used to compare pairs of treatment means when the analysis of variance yields an overall significant difference in the treatment means.

Multiple regression Regression analysis with one dependent variable and two or more independent variables or at least one nonlinear independent variable.

Mutually exclusive events Events such that the occurrence of one precludes the occurrence of the other.

Naïve forecasting models Simple forecasting models in which it is assumed that the more recent time periods of data represent the best predictions or forecasts for future outcomes.

Nominal-level data The lowest level of data measurement; used only to classify or categorize.

Nonmetric data Nominal and ordinal level data; also called qualitative data.

Nonparametric statistics A class of statistical techniques that make few assumptions about the population and are particularly applicable to nominal and ordinal level data.

Nonrandom sampling Sampling in which not every unit of the population has the same probability of being selected into the sample.

Nonrandom sampling techniques Sampling techniques used to select elements from the population by any mechanism that does not involve a random selection process.

nonrejection region Any portion of a distribution that is not in the rejection region. If the observed statistic falls in this region, the decision is to fail to reject the null hypothesis.

Nonsampling errors All errors other than sampling errors.

Normal distribution A widely known and much-used continuous distribution that fits the measurements of many human characteristics and many machine-produced items.

null hypothesis The hypothesis that assumes the status quo—that the old theory, method, or standard is still true; the complement of the alternative hypothesis.

observed significance level Another name for the *p*-value method of testing hypotheses.

observed value A statistic computed from data gathered in an experiment that is used in the determination of whether or not to reject the null hypothesis.

Ogive A cumulative frequency polygon; plotted by graphing a dot at each class endpoint for the cumulative or decumulative frequency value and connecting the dots.

one-tailed test A statistical test wherein the researcher is interested only in testing one side of the distribution.

One-way analysis of variance The process used to analyze a completely randomized experimental design. This process involves computing a ratio of the variance between treatment levels of the independent variable to the error variance. This ratio is an F value, which is then used to determine whether there are any significant differences between the means of the treatment levels.

operating characteristic (OC) curve In hypothesis testing, a graph of Type II error probabilities for various possible values of an alternative hypotheses.

Opportunity loss table A decision table constructed by subtracting all payoffs for a given state of nature from the maximum payoff for that state of nature and doing this for all states of nature; displays the lost opportunities or regret that would occur for a given decision alternative if that particular state of nature occurred.

Ordinal-level data Next-higher level of data from nominal level data; can be used to order or rank items, objects, or people.

Outliers Data points that lie apart from the rest of the points.

Overregistration Occurs when a sampling frame contains additional units besides those of the target population.

Paasche price index A type of weighted aggregate price index in which the quantity values used in the calculations are from the year of interest.

Parameter A descriptive measure of the population.

Parametric statistics A class of statistical techniques that contain assumptions about the population and that are used only with interval and ratio level data.

Pareto analysis A quantitative tallying of the number and types of defects that occur with a product or service, often recorded in a Pareto chart.

Pareto chart A vertical bar chart in which the number and types of defects for a product or service are graphed in order of magnitude from greatest to least.

Partial regression coefficient The coefficient of an independent variable in a multiple regression model that represents the change that will occur in the value of the dependent variable from a one unit increase in the independent variable if all other variables are held constant.

Payoffs The benefits or rewards that result from selecting a particular decision alternative.

Payoff table A matrix that displays the decision alternatives, the states of nature, and the payoffs for a particular decision-making problem; also called a decision table.

p chart A quality control chart for attribute compliance that graphs the proportion of sample items in noncompliance with specifications for multiple samples.

Percentiles Measures of central tendency that divide a group of data into 100 parts.

Pie chart A circular depiction of data where the area of the whole pie represents 100% of the data being studied and slices represent a percentage breakdown of the sublevels.

Platykurtic Distributions that are flat and spread out.

Point estimate An estimate of a population parameter constructed from a statistic taken from a sample.

Poisson distribution A discrete distribution that is constructed from the probability of occurrence of rare events over an interval; focuses only on the number of discrete occurrences over some interval or continuum.

Poka-yoke Means "mistake proofing" and uses devices, methods, or inspections in order to avoid machine error or simple human error.

Population A collection of persons, objects, or items of interest.

Post hoc After the experiment; pairwise comparisons made by the researcher after determining that there is a significant overall F value from ANOVA; also called a posteriori.

power curve A graph that plots the power values against various values of the alternative hypothesis.

power The probability of rejecting a false null hypothesis.

Prediction interval A range of values used in regression analysis to estimate a single value of y for a given value of x.

Probabilistic model A model that includes an error term that allows for various values of output to occur for a given value of input.

Process A series of actions, changes, or functions that bring about a result.

Product quality A view of quality in which quality is measurable in the product based on the fact that there are perceived differences in products and quality products possess more attributes.

Proportionate stratified random sampling A type of stratified random sampling in which the proportions of the items selected for the sample from the strata reflect the proportions of the strata in the population.

p-value A method of testing hypotheses in which there is no preset level of α. The probability of getting a test statistic at least as extreme as the observed test statistic is computed under the assumption that the null hypothesis is true. This probability is called the p-value, and it is the smallest value of α for which the null hypothesis can be rejected.

Quadratic model A multiple regression model in which the predictors are a variable and the square of the variable.

Qualitative variable Another name for a dummy or indicator variable; represents whether or not a given item or person possesses a certain characteristic and is usually coded as 0 or 1.

Quality circle A small group of workers consisting of supervisors and six to 10 employees who meet frequently and regularly to consider quality issues in their department or area of the business.

Quality control The collection of strategies, techniques, and actions taken by an organization to ensure the production of quality products.

Quality When a product delivers what is stipulated in its specifications.

Quartiles Measures of central tendency that divide a group of data into four subgroups or parts.

Quota sampling A nonrandom sampling technique in which the population is stratified on some characteristic and then elements selected for the sample are chosen by nonrandom processes.

Randomized block design An experimental design in which there is one independent variable of interest and a second variable, known as a blocking variable, that is used to control for confounding or concomitant variables.

Random sampling Sampling in which every unit of the population has the same probability of being selected for the sample.

Random variable A variable that contains the outcomes of a chance experiment.

Range The difference between the largest and the smallest values in a set of numbers.

Ratio-level data Highest level of data measurement; contains the same properties as interval level data, with the additional property that zero has meaning and represents the absence of the phenomenon being measured.

R chart A plot of sample ranges used in quality control.

Rectangular distribution A relatively simple continuous distribution in which the same height is obtained over a range of values; also referred to as the uniform distribution.

Reengineering A radical approach to total quality management in which the core business processes of a company are redesigned.

Regression analysis The process of constructing a mathematical model or function that can be used to predict or determine one variable by any other variable.

rejection region If a computed statistic lies in this portion of a distribution, the null hypothesis will be rejected.

Related measures Another name for matched pairs or paired data in which measurements are taken from pairs of items or persons matched on some characteristic or from a before-and-after design and then separated into different samples.

Relative frequency The proportion of the total frequencies that fall into any given class interval in a frequency distribution.

Relative frequency of occurrence Assigning probability based on cumulated historical data.

Repeated measures design A randomized block design in which each block level is an individual item or person, and that person or item is measured across all treatments.

research hypothesis A statement of what the researcher believes will be the outcome of an experiment or a study.

Residual The difference between the actual y value and the y value predicted by the regression model; the error of the regression model in predicting each value of the dependent variable.

Residual plot A type of graph in which the residuals for a particular regression model are plotted along with their associated values of x.

Response plane A plane fit in a three-dimensional space and representing the response surface defined by a multiple regression model with two independent first-order variables.

Response surface The surface defined by a multiple regression model.

Response variable The dependent variable in a multiple regression model; the variable that the researcher is trying to predict.

Risk avoider A decision maker who avoids risk whenever possible and is willing to drop out of a game when given the chance even when the payoff is less than the expected monetary value.

Risk taker A decision maker who enjoys taking risk and will not drop out of a game unless the payoff is more than the expected monetary value.

Robust Describes a statistical technique that is relatively insensitive to minor violations in one or more of its underlying assumptions.

Runs test A nonparametric test of randomness used to determine whether the order or sequence of observations in a sample is random.

Sample A portion of the whole.

Sample proportion The quotient of the frequency at which a given characteristic occurs in a sample and the number of items in the sample.

Sample size estimation An estimate of the size of sample necessary to fulfill the requirements of a particular level of confidence and to be within a specified amount of error.

Sample space A complete roster or listing of all elementary events for an experiment.

Sampling error Error that occurs when the sample is not representative of the population.

Scatter plot A plot or graph of the pairs of data.

Search procedures Processes whereby more than one multiple regression model is developed for a given database, and the models are compared and sorted by different criteria, depending on the given procedure.

Seasonal effects Patterns of data behavior that occur in periods of time of less than 1 year, often measured by the month.

Serial correlation A problem that arises in regression analysis when the error terms of a regression model are correlated due to time-series data; also called autocorrelation.

Set notation The use of braces to group numbers that have some specified characteristic.

Simple average model A forecasting averaging model in which the forecast for the next time period is the average of values for a given number of previous time periods.

Simple average The arithmetic mean or average for the values of a given number of time periods of data.

Simple index number A number determined by computing the ratio of a quantity, price, or cost for a particular year of interest to the quantity price or cost of a base year, expressed as a percentage.

Simple random sampling The most elementary of the random sampling techniques; involves numbering each item in the population and using a list or roster of random numbers to select items for the sample.

Simple regression Bivariate, linear regression.

Skewness The lack of symmetry of a distribution of values.

Smoothing techniques Forecasting techniques that produce forecasts based on leveling out the irregular fluctuation effects in time-series data.

Snowball sampling A nonrandom sampling technique in which survey subjects who fit a desired profile are selected based on referral from other survey respondents who also fit the desired profile.

Spearman's rank correlation A measure of the correlation of two variables; used when only ordinal level or ranked data are available.

Standard deviation The square root of the variance.

Standard error of the estimate (s_e) A standard deviation of the error of a regression model.

Standard error of the mean The standard deviation of the distribution of sample means.

Standard error of the proportion The standard deviation of the distribution of sample proportions.

Standardized normal distribution z distribution; a distribution of z scores produced for values from a normal distribution with a mean of 0 and a standard deviation of 1.

States of nature The occurrences of nature that can happen after a decision has been made that can affect the outcome of the decision and over which the decision maker has little or no control.

Stationary Time-series data that contain no trend, cyclical, or seasonal effects.

Statistic A descriptive measure of a sample.

statistical hypothesis A formal hypothesis structure set up with a null and an alternative hypothesis to scientifically test research hypotheses.

Statistics A science dealing with the collection, analysis, interpretation, and presentation of numerical data.

Stem-and-leaf plot A plot of numbers constructed by separating each number into two groups, a stem and a leaf. The leftmost digits are the stems and the rightmost digits are the leaves.

Stepwise regression A step-by-step multiple regression search procedure that begins by developing a regression model with a single predictor variable and adds and deletes predictors one step at a time, examining the fit of the model at each step until there are no more significant predictors remaining outside the model.

Stratified random sampling A type of random sampling in which the population is divided into various nonoverlapping strata and then items are randomly selected into the sample from each stratum.

Subjective probability A probability assigned based on the intuition or reasoning of the person determining the probability.

substantive result Occurs when the outcome of a statistical study produces results that are important to the decision maker.

Sum of squares of error (SSE) The sum of the residuals squared for a regression model.

Sum of squares of x The sum of the squared deviations about the mean of a set of values.

Systematic sampling A random sampling technique in which every kth item or person is selected from the population.

t **distribution** A family of continuous probability distributions that describe the sample mean when the population standard deviation is unknown and the population is normally distributed.

Time-series data Data gathered on a given characteristic over a period of time at regular intervals.

Treatment variable The independent variable of an experimental design that the researcher either controls or modifies.

Trend Long-run general direction of a business climate over a period of several years.

Tukey-Kramer procedure A modification of the Tukey HSD multiple comparison procedure; used when there are unequal sample sizes.

Tukey's four-quadrant approach A graphical method using the four quadrants for determining which expressions of Tukey's ladder of transformations to use.

Tukey's HSD test In analysis of variance, a technique used for pairwise a posteriori multiple comparisons to determine if there are significant differences between the means of any pair of treatment levels in an experimental design.

Tukey's ladder of transformations A process used for determining ways to recode data in multiple regression analysis to achieve potential improvement in the predictability of the model.

t **value** The computed value of *t* used to reach statistical conclusions regarding the null hypothesis.

Two-stage sampling Cluster sampling done in two stages: A firstround of samples is taken and then a second round is taken from within the first samples.

two-tailed test A statistical test wherein the researcher is interested in testing both sides of the distribution.

Two-way analysis of variance The process used to statistically test the effects of variables in factorial designs with two independent variables.

Type I error An error committed by rejecting a true null hypothesis.

Type II error An error committed by failing to reject a false null hypothesis.

Underregistration When a sampling frame contains fewer units than the target population. That is, some units of the target population are not included in the sampling frame.

Ungrouped data Raw data, or data that have not been summarized in any way.

Uniform distribution A relatively simple continuous distribution in which the same height is obtained over a range of values; also called the rectangular distribution.

Union A new set of elements formed by combining the elements of two or more other sets.

Union probability The probability of one event occurring or the other event occurring or both occurring.

Unweighted aggregate price index number The ratio of the sum of the prices of a market basket of items for a particular year to the sum of the prices of those same items in a base year, expressed as a percentage.

Upper bound of the confidence interval The upper end of a confidence interval for means or proportions calculated by adding the margin of error from the point estimate.

Variable A characteristic of any entity being studied that is capable of taking on different values.

Variance The average of the squared deviations about the arithmetic mean for a set of numbers.

Variance inflation factor A statistic computed using the R^2 value of a regression model developed by predicting one independent variable of a regression analysis by other independent variables; used to determine whether there is multicollinearity among the variables.

Weighted aggregate price index numbers Price index numbers computed by multiplying quantity weights and item prices in determining the market basket worth for a given year.

Weighted moving average A moving average in which different weights are applied to the data values from different time periods.

Wilcoxon matched-pairs signed rank test A nonparametric alternative to the *t* test for two related or dependent samples.

z **distribution** A distribution of z scores; a normal distribution with a mean of 0 and a standard deviation of 1.

z **score** The number of standard deviations a value (x) is above or below the mean of a set of numbers when the data are normally distributed.